Sustainable Development: Asia-Pacific Perspectives

The Asia-Pacific region has been experiencing rapid development in the past 30 years, and issues relating to sustainable development will become increasingly important in the coming decades. This comprehensive overview presents sustainable development from the perspectives of Asia and the Pacific, with contributions from more than 70 leading international experts. The first part focuses on the theories and practices of sustainable development, including national and regional perspectives, as well as international policies and law concerning climate change. The second part highlights the challenges and opportunities of sustainable development and poverty reduction amid the changing ecological, social, cultural, economic, and political environment in this region. These include issues such as the importance of science for sustainable development and related areas, including sustainable energy, stratospheric ozone depletion, climate change, land-use change, biodiversity, and disaster risk reduction. The volume is an invaluable reference for all researchers and policy makers with an interest in sustainable development.

SUSTAINABLE DEVELOPMENT: ASIA-PACIFIC PERSPECTIVES

Edited by

PAK SUM LOW

CAMBRIDGE
UNIVERSITY PRESS

CAMBRIDGE
UNIVERSITY PRESS

University Printing House, Cambridge CB2 8BS, United Kingdom

One Liberty Plaza, 20th Floor, New York, NY 10006, USA

477 Williamstown Road, Port Melbourne, VIC 3207, Australia

314–321, 3rd Floor, Plot 3, Splendor Forum, Jasola District Centre,
New Delhi – 110025, India

103 Penang Road, #05–06/07, Visioncrest Commercial, Singapore 238467

Cambridge University Press is part of the University of Cambridge.

It furthers the University's mission by disseminating knowledge in the pursuit of
education, learning, and research at the highest international levels of excellence.

www.cambridge.org
Information on this title: www.cambridge.org/9780521897174
DOI: 10.1017/9780511977961

First published 2022

Printed in the United Kingdom by TJ Books Limited, Padstow Cornwall

A catalogue record for this publication is available from the British Library.

Library of Congress Cataloging-in-Publication Data
Names: Low, Pak Sum, editor.
Title: Sustainable development : Asia-Pacific perspectives / edited by Pak Sum Low,
National University of Malaysia and Bond University, Queensland.
Description: 1 Edition. | New York : Cambridge University Press, 2021. |
Includes bibliographical references and index.
Identifiers: LCCN 2020046974 (print) | LCCN 2020046975 (ebook) |
ISBN 9780521897174 (hardback) | ISBN 9780511977961 (ebook)
Subjects: LCSH: Sustainable development – Southeast Asia. | Climatic changes –
Southeast Asia. | Land use – Southeast Asia. | Biodiversity – Southeast Asia.
Classification: LCC HC441.E5 S867 2021 (print) | LCC HC441.E5 (ebook) |
DDC 338.95/07–dc23
LC record available at https://lccn.loc.gov/2020046974
LC ebook record available at https://lccn.loc.gov/2020046975

ISBN 978-0-521-89717-4 Hardback

Dedicated to Dr Mostafa Kamal Tolba

Contents

Notes on contributors

EDITOR

Dr Pak Sum Low, is an adjunct professor at the China-ASEAN College of Marine Sciences of Xiamen University Malaysia. He has previously worked as the Regional Adviser on Environment and Sustainable Development (2001–2007) at the United Nations Economic and Social Commission for Asia and the Pacific (UNESCAP); Programme Officer/Senior Programme Officer (1991–1999) at the United Nations Environment Programme (UNEP); Senior Research Associate (1988–1991), Climatic Research Unit, University of East Anglia, UK; and visiting researcher at the Institute of Applied Physical Chemistry (1987–1988) and the Institute for Atmospheric Chemistry (1986–1987), Nuclear Research Centre, Jülich, Germany. From 2009 to 2018, he was visiting professor/adjunct professor at Bond University, Australia. Dr Low was the inaugural Yayasan Sime Darby Chair in Climate Change at Universiti Kebangsaan Malaysia (2011–2013); a senior visiting professor at the UNEP International Ecosystems Management Partnership (IEMP), hosted by the Institute of Geographic Sciences and Natural Resources, Chinese Academy of Sciences, Beijing (2011–2012); and a visiting professor at the Institute of Desertification Studies, Beijing (2013, 2015). In addition, he was an international adviser (2010) for the Climate Change Adaptation Initiative project of the Mekong River Commission (MRC) in Vientiane, Lao PDR, as well as an international expert (2008) in the United Nations Development Programme (UNDP) – Vietnam, based at the Natural Disaster Mitigation Partnership Secretariat, Ministry of Agriculture and Rural Development, Hanoi, Vietnam. He was a member of the Expert Group on Technology Transfer of the United Nations Framework Convention on Climate Change (UNFCCC) (2010). He has served as a consultant for the UNFCCC secretariat (1999, 2000), United Nations Convention to Combat Desertification (UNCCD) secretariat (2000, 2008, 2009, 2011, 2015), and UNDP – Timor Leste (2008, 2009). Dr Low is a Fellow of the Academy of Sciences Malaysia; and the editor of *Climate Change and Africa* (Cambridge University Press, 2005).

CONTRIBUTORS OF FOREWORDS

Dr Mostafa Kamal Tolba, who passed away in March 2016, was the President of the International Centre for Environment and Development (ICED) (Geneva and Cairo) that he established in 1994. He was formerly Executive Director of the United Nations Environment Programme (UNEP) (1975–1992), and Professor of Microbiology at Cairo University. As the head of Egypt's delegation to the Stockholm Conference on the Human Environment in 1972, Dr Tolba was among the first to promote the view that there are no irreconcilable conflicts between the environment and development. He soon became internationally renowned as a champion of the global environment and continued to promote his philosophy of development without destruction. Under his leadership, UNEP became the core organization within the United Nations family, acting as a catalyst for governments, businesses, academic bodies, intergovernmental organizations, and non-governmental organizations to take meaningful action to protect the environment. Dr Tolba was known for his formidable negotiating skills and his expertise on the science of the environment. He also had an uncanny vision of emerging environmental problems. These attributes led him, as early as the 1970s, to concentrate on the issue of ozone layer depletion as an area that merited careful scientific monitoring. Because of his success in negotiating the Vienna Convention on the Protection of the Ozone Layer (1985) and its Montreal Protocol on Substances that Deplete the Ozone Layer (1987), he was credited with formulating the prototype model for dealing with global environmental issues and the effective transfer of technology and funds to developing countries. Dr Tolba held a BSc degree in botany and a PhD in plant pathology. He was the author of almost 100 papers (1950–1973) on plant diseases, anti-fungal substances, and the physiology of micro-organisms, and of more than 600 statements, books, and articles on the environment and sustainable development. He received honorary doctorates from universities around the world, including Moscow State University, the University of Guadalajara, Williams College, and Imperial College, London. He also received the following prizes in recognition of his work: the Sasakawa Environment Prize (1993), the Special Global Environment Leadership Award of the Global Environment Facility (2003), the Only One Earth Award of the René Dubos Centre, the Distinguished International Service Award of the Regents of the University of Minnesota, and the First Order Decoration of the Arab Republic of Egypt.

Sir Toke Tufukia Talagi passed away on 15 July 2020. He was the Premier of the Government of Niue from June 2008 to June 2020. He graduated with a Bachelor of Science (Agriculture Science) from Massey University, New Zealand, in 1975, after which he returned to Niue and started work as Livestock Officer. He was appointed Niue's Consul-General, in Auckland, when the office was first established in 1981, after which he returned to Niue and headed Niue's Economic Affairs Office as Director. Mr Talagi decided to practise what he preached in the early 1990s and resigned from government to set up a business in Niue. In 1999 he was elected as one of the Common Roll Members of the Niue Assembly. Re-elected in 2002, he was a member of Premier Young Vivian's Cabinet. In the latter capacity, he led the government's delegation to two international meetings: the World Summit on Sustainable Development, in September 2002 in Johannesburg, and the Mauritius 2005 (BPoA + 10) Meeting, in January 2005. As Minister for Education he attended many Pacific Islands Forum Education Ministers' meetings, as well as the University of the South Pacific Council meetings. Hon. Talagi was instrumental in spearheading the Taoga Niue, where at its first conference in October 2004, the Halavaka ke he Monuina Arrangement between the Government of Niue and the Government of NZ was signed. Hon. Talagi also contributed to non-government groups. He was former President of the Public Service Association, and an Alofi South Village council member. He was also founding patron of the Niue Weightlifting and Body Building Association, the past President of the Niue Rugby Union, and a senior member of the Alofi Ekalesia Church. In the 2017 New Year Honours, Hon. Talagi was appointed Knight Companion of the New Zealand Order of Merit (KNZM). In November 2019, Sir Talagi released an autobiography, *Niue Rising*.

Professor QIN Dahe Professor QIN Dahe, geographer, an Academician of the Chinese Academy of Sciences (CAS) and a member of The World Academy of Sciences (TWAS). He is currently the director of the Academic Committee of CAS, and the chairman of the Asian Geographical Society. Professor Qin has long been engaged in research on the cryosphere, climate change, and sustainable development. His studies of cryospheric changes and their effects and adaptation, as well as the functions and services of cryosphere, have contributed to building the theoretical framework of cryospheric science. Being the founder of the State Key Laboratory on Cryospheric Science and the Society on Cryospheric Science in China, he has led the compilation of

textbooks on the cryosphere. All this has contributed to the development of the field of cryospheric science. He has participated in or led many scientific expeditions to the Antarctic, Arctic, Qinghai-Tibetan plateau and Western China. He was a lead author of the Working Group I of the Third Assessment Report (2001) of the Intergovernmental Panel on Climate Change (IPCC), and co-chair of the Working Group I of the IPCC Fourth Assessment Report (2007) and the Fifth Assessment Report (2013). He was also involved in the leadership for the preparation of the assessment of climate and environment in China, and of extreme weather and climate events and disaster risk management in China, making significant contributions to deepening the understanding of climate change science. Professor Qin served as the Administrator of the China Meteorological Administration in 2000-2007. He was awarded the 2008 International Meteorological Organization Prize, the 2013 Volvo Environment Prize, and the 2014 Second Prize of National Natural Science Award.

Dr Sálvano Briceño retired from the United Nations on 30 April 2011. Following his retirement from the UN, he was elected Chair of the Science Committee of the Integrated Research on Disaster Risk programme of the International Council for Science (ICSU), also sponsored by the International Social Science Council (ISSC) and the UNISDR. His career has focused on the management of environmental and sustainable development programmes at the United Nations, the World Conservation Union (IUCN), and the Government of Venezuela. He was appointed Director and first head of the Secretariat of the International Strategy for Disaster Reduction (UNISDR, now UNDRR) in June 2001. Prior to joining UNISDR, Dr Briceño was Coordinator of the BIOTRADE and GHG Emissions Trading Initiatives of UNCTAD (1999–2001). Before that, he was Deputy Executive Secretary of the UN Convention to Combat Desertification (UNCCD) secretariat (1996–1999), following several years as the Coordinator of Intergovernmental and Institutional Support of the UN Framework Convention on Climate Change (UNFCCC). Earlier in his career, Dr Briceño was the first Coordinator of UNEP's Caribbean Environment Programme (1987–1991). He was the Executive Officer of IUCN's Commission on Education, where he focused on environmental education programmes and coordinated a worldwide network of experts (1985–1987). He started his public policy career at the Ministry of Environment and Renewable Natural Resources with the Government of Venezuela (1978–1983). Dr Briceño earned a Doctorate in Administrative Law (University of Paris II, Panthéon-Sorbonne) in 1975 and a master's in Public Administration, Harvard University in 1984. A Venezuelan and French national, his languages include Spanish, French, and English.

Dr Philip Michael (Mick) Kelly is a climate consultant with Tanelorn Associates, based in Whakapara, New Zealand. He is also a visiting fellow with the Climatic Research Unit at the University of East Anglia, from which he retired in 2007. On joining the newly formed Climatic Research Unit in 1972, Dr Kelly pursued an interdisciplinary research path, focusing on the causes of climatic change and the societal relevance of climate variability, particularly vulnerability to climate variability and trends. A member of the team that produced the definitive temperature record used in global warming detection studies, he has contributed to various international reviews of the global warming and nuclear winter issues. Concerned that all sectors of society have access to scientific information, Dr Kelly has appeared frequently on radio and television. He has acted as scientific consultant on a number of television documentaries, including *Can Polar Bears Tread Water?*, a winner of the prestigious Prix Italia award.

CONTRIBUTORS OF 'REMEMBERING DR MOSTAFA KAMAL TOLBA'

Ambassador Mikko Pyhälä graduated in Social Sciences from the University of Jyväskylä, writing theses on international development strategy, on transnational corporations, and on Guinea-Bissau. He was in the diplomatic service of Finland (1972–1990, 1995–2013). His posts included Venezuela (covering also Colombia), Peru, Pakistan, India, Italy, Mexico, and Czechoslovakia. Based at the Foreign Ministry in Helsinki, he also served as Environment Coordinator for FINNIDA (1988–1990), Ambassador for Asia and Oceania (2002–2006) with emphasis on Afghanistan and South Asia, and as Roving Ambassador to Venezuela and the Caribbean (2011–2013). He was with the United Nations Environment Programme (1991–1995) as Chief of Clearinghouse Unit, Chief of Global Environment Facility (GEF) Unit, and Secretary to the Scientific and Technical Advisory Panel (STAP) of the GEF. He played a significant role on behalf of Finland in the establishment of the Funding System for the Montreal Protocol on Substances that Deplete the Ozone Layer, and at UNEP in the establishment of the GEF. He has published books and reports on environment and development, and on political history. He has also written extensively on cinema, and ornithology, including the book *Birds of Islamabad* in 1998, and has uploaded more than 1,500 bird photographs from more than 40 countries on https://macaulaylibrary.org/catalog. He is a columnist to several newspapers in Finland. He received the Finlandia Award for best non-fiction book 1992 for *Amazonia* (co-authored with Dr Jukka Salo), and shared Peru's National Biodiversity Award 2002. In Peru, he helped to establish the Foundation Friends of the National History Museum, and he was conferred *Doctor honoris causa* by two universities, and Honorary Professor by three universities. His book *On Power and Resistance:*

Diplomacy with Empathy (2016) (in Finnish) is about wars and political murders he has observed, mostly in Asia, with emphasis on Vietnam, India, Sri Lanka, and Afghanistan. Another book, *Venezuela from Riches to Rags – Struggle for the Rule of Law* (2019) (also in Finnish) is about Venezuela. He is currently Chairman of the Governing Council for Ecofoundation – Sustainability Elders, in Finland.

Dr Sálvano Briceño (see previous).

Naigzy Gebremedhin served as the Dean of the Building College, Haile-Selassie University in Addis Ababa, Ethiopia, after graduating from the School of Architecture of the Massachusetts Institute of Technology (MIT) in 1964. He then established a private practice in architecture and urban planning, practising architecture and urban planning throughout Africa. But following the demise of Emperor Haile-Selassie, he left Ethiopia and moved to Nairobi, Kenya, to join the United Nations Environment Programme (UNEP), serving under Dr Mostafa Tolba as Chief of the Technology and Environment Branch. After mandatory retirement in 1994, Naigzy moved to Asmara, Eritrea, to establish and head the Eritrean Agency for the Environment. Between 1997 and 2005, he directed the effort to document and preserve Asmara's modernist architecture. That effort culminated in the enrolment of Asmara as a UNESCO World Heritage Site.

CONTRIBUTORS OF CHAPTERS

Professor Dilip R. Ahuja is the former Head of the Energy and Environment Policy Programme of the National Institute of Advanced Studies (NIAS) in Bengaluru, India. He was the Indian Space Research Organization (ISRO) Chair Professor of Science and Technology Policy at NIAS, and his research includes estimating global warming potentials and national contributions of greenhouse gases, energy savings from adjusting Indian Standard Time (IST), and emission factors from small-scale biomass burning. He has contributed to the Special Report of the Intergovernmental Panel on Climate Change (IPCC) on Methodological and Technological Issues in Technology Transfer (2000), Working Group III, as a lead author; Third Assessment Report (2001) as a review editor; and Fourth Assessment Report (2007) as a lead author of the IPCC, in Working Group III. He took his PhD in Biomedical Engineering from the University of Virginia at Charlottesville in 1978 and a Bachelor of Technology (BTech) in Electrical Engineering from the Indian Institute of Technology (IIT) Bombay in 1972.

Dr Bryant Allen did fieldwork on development on Mangaia, Cook Islands, for a master's degree from Massey University, New Zealand, in 1966, and in villages around Dreikikir, East

Sepik Province, Papua New Guinea (PNG), in 1971–1972 for a PhD at the Australian National University (ANU). His PhD research was on the adoption of cash crops and millenarian movements. He then studied shifting cultivation systems at Dreikikir, which he continues to the present day. From 1974 to 1981 he lectured at the University of PNG. In 1982, Dr Allen joined the Department of Human Geography at ANU. With Harold Brookfield, he co-edited a special edition of *Mountain Research and Development* on the impacts of ENSO-associated frosts and droughts on food supply in PNG. From 1990 to 1996, with co-researchers Mike Bourke, Robin Hide, and the late Geoff Humphries, he did fieldwork and created a database and GIS of all agriculture systems in PNG. These data were used to investigate rural poverty in PNG for the World Bank and child malnutrition with the PNG Institute of Medical Research. In 1997, with Mike Bourke, Michael Lowe, and PNG associates, Dr Allen organized field assessments of food and water supplies in response to an ENSO-related drought and frosts in PNG, which was used to organize relief distribution. He is Honorary Associate Professor at the Department of Pacific Affairs, Coral Bell School of Asia and the Pacific, the Australian National University, Canberra.

Dr Gopala Areendran is the Director of the Indira Gandhi Conservation Monitoring Centre (IGCMC) at WWF-India. He has more than 25 years of experience as a professional and leader in geospatial technology and has been the driving force of location-based data monitoring and analytics since 2001 at WWF-India. His work at WWF ranges from addressing conservation issues occurring in various landscapes, with a high focus on the tiger, elephant, and rhinoceros to overseeing several institutional GIS-based projects. He has led the core technical team within WWF-India to utilize current generation technology and has always been a partisan for applying GIS solutions to overcome challenges within the field of conservation. Being an integral part of the WWF network, he has participated in and overseen various international projects from understanding the impact of global forest fires, deforestation, and degradation to capacity-building programmes on GIS, and remote sensing for staff at WWF-Bhutan. Recently he has spearheaded WWF-India's geospatial and analytical contribution to UNDP's SECURE Himalaya project and is the current coordinator for the Green Skill Development Programme of Ministry of Environment, Forest, and Climate Change (MoEFCC) (Government of India), wherein he has been regularly conducting GIS-based skill development trainings for youth. Dr Areendran has an MS degree in Ecology from Pondicherry University and a PhD from the Wildlife the Institute of India. He has also worked with leading research centres like Salim Ali Centre for Ornithology and Natural History (SACON), Wildlife

Institute of India (WII) and Madras Environmental Society (MES), Chennai, and Institute of Remote Sensing, Anna University, Chennai. Dr Areendran has published several research papers and reports in peer-reviewed journals, and was involved in the publication of four books in the capacity of editor and co-author. As a pioneer of geospatial education, he has also supervised more than a hundred masters and research students.

Dr Bhishna Bajracharya has been Associate Professor of Urban Planning at the Faculty of Society and Design, Bond University, Australia, since 2008. He previously taught in the urban planning programme at the Queensland University of Technology (QUT) for more than 12 years. He also worked as a postdoctoral fellow at the Research School of Social Sciences, Australian National University. He practised as an architect while teaching at the architectural engineering programme in Tribhuvan University, Nepal, in the early 1980s. He completed his PhD in Geography and a master's degree in Urban Planning from the University of Hawaii, and a bachelor's degree in Architecture from the School of Planning and Architecture, Delhi University. Dr Bajracharya's research areas include master-planned communities, transit-oriented development, sustainable campuses, disaster management, and urban governance. He is an alumnus of the East-West Center, a Hawaii-based research organization with a strong focus on policy research in the Asia-Pacific region. He has served as the Chair of the University Sustainability Committee at Bond University. For his research profile, please see https://research.bond.edu.au/en/persons/bhishna-bajracharya

Dr Hans Juergen Boehmer is Full Professor of Biogeography at the University of the South Pacific (USP), with a broad background in applied ecology, including nature conservation, environmental planning, and policy advice. His research focuses on montane rainforests in the tropical Pacific islands, particularly on the complex interactions of natural vegetation dynamics, disturbance regimes, biological invasions, and climate change. He is editor of the international journal *Endangered Species Research* (ESR), co-coordinator of PABITRA (*Pacific-Asia Biodiversity Transect Network*), South Pacific coordinator of the IUFRO Taskforce *Monitoring Global Tree Mortality Patterns and Trends*, and Deputy Coordinator of the IUFRO Unit *Resource Data in the Tropics*. Professor Boehmer served as a member of the Pacific Island Development Forum *Agriculture and Forestry* committee in preparation for the 2015 Paris Climate Conference. He received several research grants for detailed studies on the regeneration of island rainforests after climate-induced decline, and the interactions of native tree population dynamics with invasive alien plant species. After joining USP in 2014, he designed a research project titled 'Structure and dynamics of Viti Levu's rainforests under impact of invasive alien ivory cane palm (*Pinanga coronata*)', funded by the Research Office of the University of the South Pacific (2016–2019). This inter- and trans-disciplinary project is currently the most complex study of alien plant invasions in the South Pacific region, and includes institutions from Fiji, Australia, New Zealand, France, and Germany.

Professor Janet F. Bornman is Director of the Future Legumes Research, Education, and Training Hub, at Murdoch University, Perth, Western Australia. Prior to that, she was the Founding Director of the International Institute of Agri-Food Security at Curtin University, Perth, where she established a cross-Faculty network with national and international outreach. She has held positions as Director of the International Global Change Centre, in Hamilton, New Zealand, and Research Director at the Danish Institute of Agricultural Sciences, in Denmark. She currently co-chairs the United Nations Environment Programme's Environmental Effects Assessment Panel. Professor Bornman's research is focused on effects of environmental constraints, in particular climate-change factors and UV radiation, from an integrative disciplinary perspective. Food security, sustainability, and climate risk issues are of particular interest, with respect to multi-functional plant crops that are both climate-tolerant and have potential health benefits. Professor Bornman is the recipient of numerous awards, including the Edna Roe Lecturer for accomplishments in the photosciences, the European Society for Photobiology (ESP) medal, the Ozone Layer Protection Award for '*Scientific expertise and leadership in protecting the ozone layer*', and the Finsen Medal in memory of Niels Finsen, Nobel laureate and celebrated pioneer in photobiology.

Dr R. Michael (Mike) Bourke is an agricultural scientist and geographer and is a specialist in Papua New Guinea (PNG) and Pacific Island agriculture. He is Honorary Associate Professor at the Australian National University and a self-employed consultant. He has been continuously involved in research, training, consulting, and development in PNG and other Pacific Island countries since 1970 and lived in PNG for 13 years. He is a fellow of the Australian Institute of Agriculture and was appointed in 2015 as an Officer of the Order of Logohu by Papua New Guinea for services to PNG agriculture. Mike has published extensively on PNG and Pacific Island agriculture and related topics, including articles on speleology in PNG. He edited and wrote much of the definitive book *Food and Agriculture in Papua New Guinea*. A recent book (with three colleagues) is *Assessing Village Food Needs Following a Natural Disaster in Papua New Guinea*. In 2020, he was very engaged with issues of COVID-19 and food security in PNG. He has conducted fieldwork in all 85 rural districts of PNG, as well as in parts of Vanuatu, Solomon Islands, and other Pacific Island countries. He has expertise in many aspects of rural livelihoods,

agricultural production, land use, and food security in PNG and other Pacific Island states.

Dr Sálvano Briceño (see previous)

Professor Peter Brimblecombe was born in Australia, but went to university in Auckland, New Zealand, where his PhD concerned the atmospheric chemistry of sulphur dioxide. His studies of long-term changes in urban air pollution and its effects on health and building damage are also an important activity; the historical aspects of subject resulted in a book, *The Big Smoke*. This encouraged an interest in the relationship between air pollution and architecture, literature, and even cinema. Peter has undertaken research on material damage by air pollutants in outdoor environments, but also within museum atmospheres, and has a continuing interest in the process of damage to cultural materials by air pollutants and climate. At present, his heritage research relates to climate change and insect damage to wooden buildings. He is currently a Distinguished Research Chair Professor at the Department of Marine Environment and Engineering, National Sun Yat-Sen University, Kaohsiung, Taiwan, though also an adjunct professor at the School of Energy and Environment at City University of Hong Kong (until 2020) and Emeritus Professor to the School of Environmental Sciences of the University of East Anglia in the UK.

Dr Gernot Brodnig has some 30 years of international experience in policy analysis, programme/project management and research in natural resources management, biodiversity conservation and climate change, with a focus on livelihood and governance issues. He currently works as a Senior Specialist for the World Bank in Washington, DC. Prior to this, he served as the Director for Social Sciences at IUCN, and as UNDP's Environment Adviser for Asia. Gernot holds a Doctorate in Law from the University of Vienna, as well as master's degrees in Geography (University of Cambridge) and Anthropology (University of Oxford). He spent five years as a research fellow at Harvard University, investigating environmental and social impacts of oil exploration, and has published on a number of natural resources management issues.

Dr Shoibal Chakravarty is a senior researcher at the Divecha Centre for Climate Change, Indian Institute of Science (IISc) in Bengaluru. He was formerly a fellow in the Climate Change Mitigation and Development Programme in the Centre for Environment and Development at the Ashoka Trust for Research in Ecology and the Environment (ATREE), Bengaluru, India. His research interests are in energy and climate policy, energy-economics modelling, and the study of equity in the context of energy and climate change. He was formerly a faculty member in the energy and environment policy programme at the National Institute of Advanced Studies (NIAS), Bengaluru, and was a Research Associate at the Princeton Environmental Institute, Princeton University, from 2006 to 2013. He received his PhD in Physics from Princeton University in 2005, and a Bachelor of Technology (BTech) in Engineering Physics from the Indian Institute of Technology (IIT) Bombay in 1998.

Dr Yi Chen is a Senior Research Fellow at the Käte Hamburger Centre for Apocalyptic and Post-Apocalyptic Studies at Heidelberg University, Germany. She was an Assistant Professor of Confucian Philosophy at Bond University, Gold Coast, Australia (2017–2020). As an Alexander-von-Humboldt research fellow at the Max Planck Institute for Empirical Aesthetics in Frankfurt am Main, Germany (2016–2017), she worked on 'deceptive simplicity' as an aesthetic principle. She has a PhD in Comparative Literature from the University of Toronto, Canada (2015); an MA in Classics from the University of Arizona, USA (2008); and a PhD in Philosophy from Fudan University, Shanghai, China (2001). Recent publications include 'A faceless subject: Exploring impersonal subjectivity through poems by Wang Wei, Paul Celan, and Wang Yipei' (2020), in Fechner, Matthias and Stahl, Henrieke (eds.), *Schwellenzeit – Gattungstransitionen – Grenzerfahrungen*. Berlin, Germany, Peter Lang, pp. 247–265; 'Phenomenological comparison: Pursuing Husserl's "time consciousness" in poems by Wang Wei, Paul Celan and Santoka Taneda' (*Comparative and Continental Philosophy* 9(3), 241–259, 2017), with Dr Boris Steipe. Her current research focuses on defining and leveraging the essence of Confucian philosophy to address the compelling issues of our time, including an aesthetically ethical approach to ecology and climate change, and a project to explore the relationship between Confucian philosophy, Japanese aesthetics, and organizational life.

Bernarditas de Castro-Muller, known simply by her first name to all her fellow negotiators, had negotiated the United Nations Framework Convention on Climate Change (UNFCCC) from its very inception. A career diplomat from the Philippines, she entered the negotiations as part of her responsibilities in the Philippine Mission to the United Nations in Geneva. She was then promptly involved in the negotiations leading to the United Nations Conference on Environment and Development (UNCED) in 1992, and followed all other negotiations leading to the three Rio Conventions: the UNFCCC, the Convention on Biological Diversity (CBD), and the United Nations Convention to Combat Desertification (UNCCD), as well as other Geneva-based multilateral environmental agreements (MEAs), and related agencies such as the Intergovernmental Panel on Climate Change (IPCC) and the Global Environment Facility (GEF). Bernarditas was a member of the Bureau of the Conferences of Parties (COP) of both the UNFCCC and the CBD, and served as one of the Vice-Presidents for Asia of the COP 7 Bureau of the UNCCD. Almost all throughout her involvement in these conventions, she was a lead negotiator for the Group of 77 (G77),

the group of developing countries, in particular on financial and technology issues. Bernarditas also convened the group that became the Like-Minded Group (LMG) in the negotiations prior to the adoption of the Cartagena Biosafety Protocol of the CBD. She was named Environmental Affairs Adviser to the Department of Foreign Affairs, the Philippines, after her retirement from active service. Her last foreign posting was as Chargé d'Affaires, *de missi*, of the Embassy of the Philippines, and Acting Permanent Representative to the UN Environment Programme and the UN Human Settlements Programme (UN-Habitat) in Nairobi, Kenya. At the end of COP 12 in Kenya in 2006, where she led the Philippine delegation, she left to return to the Home Office and retired from active service in 2007. She served as lead coordinator for the G77 and China in the ad hoc working group on long-term cooperative action of the Bali Action Plan process until COP 16 in Cancún, Mexico. Bernarditas likewise conducted training seminars and lectures on climate change negotiations in developing countries, mainly in Asia and in Central and Latin America. She was also a Special Adviser on Climate Change, South Centre, Geneva, Switzerland, and a Consultant, National Climate Change Commission of the Philippines, until she passed away in December 2018.

Dr Rosita Dellios is Associate Professor of International Relations at Bond University, Australia. She lectures and writes on the themes of Chinese philosophy and strategic culture, Indo-Pacific geopolitics, and the application of complexity theory and futures studies to global politics. She co-authored *The Politics and Philosophy of Chinese Power: The Timeless and the Timely* (Lexington Books, 2017) and *China's Quest for Global Order* (Lexington Books, 2013). Her other works may be found at https://research.bond.edu.au/en/persons/rosita-dellios

Michael J. Dyer is a young Australian currently working at the United Nations Development Programme as a GIS and project specialist in Apia, Samoa. He graduated from his Honours Year at the University of South Australia, publishing his thesis on the invasion history of *Pinanga coronata* in Fiji via correspondence from the University of the South Pacific, Fiji. For his Honours Year, Mr Dyer was the recipient of the Federal Government's Department of Foreign Affairs and Trade, New Colombo Plan Scholarship, Australia's most prestigious scholarship in the Asia-Pacific region. He graduated with a perfect grade point average and was the recipient of the University of South Australia Honours Medal, University of South Australia's Division for Information Technology, Engineering, and Environment, in addition to becoming an Australian Council of Environmental Deans and Directors Scholar.

Dr Stefan Erasmi gained his PhD in Geography in 2001 from the University of Göttingen, Germany. He has many years of experience in remote sensing-based monitoring of land-use and cover change. A focus of his work is on the spatio-temporal modelling of relations between land-use change, land degradation, and ecological indicators, such as biodiversity and climate. Since 2006, he has been employed as Assistant Professor at the Cartography, GIS, and Remote Sensing Department of the University of Göttingen, Germany.

FENG Qiya studied at Hebei Agricultural University from 2009 to 2013, majoring in agriculture economics and management, and obtained a bachelor's degree in management. During the years 2014–2017, she studied forestry and regional development at the Chinese Academy of Forestry, and obtained a master's degree in management. Since 2017, she has been studying for a PhD at the School of Agriculture and Rural Development, Renmin University of China, majoring in forestry economics and management under the supervision of Professor KE Shuifa. Her main research direction is the choice of farmers' behaviour and the development of China's green economy.

Dr R. James Ferguson is Director of the Centre for East-West Cultural and Economic Studies and Assistant Professor of International Relations in the Faculty of Society and Design, Bond University, Australia. He has been engaged in research, writing, teaching, and publication roles, and is a member of several international relations and strategic studies organizations. He is actively involved in research and teaching in International Relations, European and Eurasian Studies, the Indo-Pacific Region, and global governance processes. He has a background in history, cultural systems and Asian affairs. He has presented papers on these issues in Australia, Singapore, Malaysia, China, Japan, India, Austria, Serbia, Indonesia, and the UK. Recent books include *China's Eurasian Dilemmas: Roads and Risks for a Sustainable Global Power* (2018), and he co-authored *The Politics and Philosophy of Chinese Power: The Timeless and the Timely* (2017). He regularly visits Asia to assess new trends in regionalism and international relations. His current project is *Greening China's New Silk Roads: The Sustainable Governance of Belt and Road* (forthcoming).

Dr Stephen Galvin is Lecturer in Biogeography at the University of the South Pacific in Fiji. His research focuses on the use of dendrochronology as a means of understanding and contextualizing environmental change. In Fiji, he employs this methodology to investigate the ecological and economic impacts of invasive alien species on native forest stands, as well as the impact of climate change on productivity in tropical forests and coastal mangrove ecosystems. Dr Galvin has also examined the impacts of low-latitude and Icelandic volcanic eruptions on tree growth and weather patterns in Ireland, a study that was, globally, the first to successfully employ yew (*Taxus baccata*) as a source of high-resolution proxy data in this manner.

Dr Andrew N. Gillison is the Director of the Center for Biodiversity Management in Queensland, Australia. He has a long-term interest in improving methods of rapid natural resource appraisal that can be used to establish knowledge baselines for sustainable management. The aim is to build on science-based, low-cost, and user-friendly approaches that can be used by persons with relatively little training. Extensive experience as a botanist and plant ecologist in many of the world's tropical countries has facilitated the development of training modules in rapid survey and spatial modelling, one outcome of which is illustrated in Chapter 29. With more than 100 peer-reviewed publications, Dr Gillison has developed widely accepted methods of survey design by combining environmental, gradient-based (gradsect) sampling of plant vascular species with plant functional types, vegetation structure, and landscape-based physical variables (the VegClass method). Field data collected in the case study published in this book are contributing to a global database that is already being applied in bioregional planning worldwide.

Sunil Gopaul, a Guyanese scientist, completed his master's degree in Environmental Science at the University of the South Pacific. Prior to this, he was a forester with the Guyana Forestry Commission, specializing in forest monitoring and forest policy development. In 2016 Sunil, who also holds a BSc in Forestry from the University of Guyana, was awarded the Caribbean-Pacific Island Mobility Scheme scholarship by the European Union's Education, Audiovisual, and Culture Executive Agency to undertake postgraduate studies. His research interests focus on biological invasions in the South Pacific region, with specific emphasis on the fundamental changes to habitat conditions caused by invasive palms, particularly *Pinanga coronata*. At the University of the South Pacific, Sunil was awarded the 2017 Gold Medal and President's Prize for the Best Graduate in a Postgraduate Diploma. Sunil's work on the invasive *P. coronata* was presented to an audience of experts from academia and business at the Royal Society Te Apārangi in New Zealand and the Australian Academy of Science during the 2017 Falling Walls Lab. He currently serves as Environmental and Social Safeguards Coordinator for the Ministry of Housing and Water in Guyana, and Lecturer at the University of Guyana.

Dr Jamba Gyeltshen is a former faculty member of the Royal University of Bhutan at the College of Natural Resources, Lobesa, where he taught Agriculture. His knowledge of agriculture and its role in sustainable development comes from his farming background and involvement in agriculture education in Bhutan for more than 20 years. His insights on sustainable development challenges in the field of agriculture draw on his observations and experiences from his engagement in several research and consultancy services to determine the impact of agricultural development projects and national research and extension services in Bhutan. His core competency is crop pest and disease management, a skill founded on professional training and education. He has a bachelor's degree in Agriculture from India, a master's degree in Crop Protection from the University of Reading (UK), a Doctor of Plant Medicine (DPM) from the University of Florida, a PhD in Biological Sciences (spore survival of *Phytophthora cinnamomi*, a highly aggressive plant pathogen) from Murdoch University, Australia, and a master's degree in Business Administration (MBA) from Edith Cowan University, Australia.

Geon Christopher Hanson received his BSc in Natural Resource Management from the University of Belize in 2012, and his MSc in Environmental Science from the University of the South Pacific in Fiji in 2017. He received the Vice-Chancellor and President Gold Medal award for his outstanding academic performance during his time at the University of the South Pacific. Geon's main areas of research interest are conservation biology, plant population dynamics, and invasive plant species management. His recent research work is part of the 'Structure and dynamics of Viti Levu's rainforests under impact of invasive alien ivory cane palm (*Pinanga coronata*)' project.

Shababa Haque is a doctoral researcher in the Deptartment of Geography at Durham University, UK. She is trained as an environmentalist. She completed her master's degree in Environmental Technology from Imperial College, London. Ms Haque has since then worked in the field of climate change, focusing on climate mitigation and renewable energy in the context of Bangladesh. She has also worked on building climate resilience for disabled persons in Bangladesh, and from there on developed her interest in strengthening adaptation for those who are disproportionately vulnerable to climate change.

Dr Mikiko Hayashi received her BS and MS degrees in life science, primarily architectural environment, from Ochanomizu University, Japan. She was funded through the EPISCON project (European PhD in Science for Conservation), which supported the interdisciplinary character of this field of science, as a Marie Curie research fellow, from 2006 to 2009. She represented Japan (actually Asia) with 15 other selected fellows from all over the world. She received a PhD in conservation science from Bologna University, Italy, in 2009, with the PhD research undertaken at Alexandru Ioan Cuza University in Iasi, Romania, and Trees and Timber Institute (IVALSA) and Institute for the Conservation and Valorization of Cultural Heritage (ICVBC) at Consiglio Nazionale delle Ricerche (CNR) in Florence, Italy. She worked as a research assistant at the Tokyo National Research Institute for Cultural Properties (TNRICP) from 2009 to 2014, and as visiting researcher at the School of Energy and Environment at City University of Hong Kong from 2015 to 2018. She is currently an associate fellow at TNRICP and engaged in research for disaster risk mitigation for cultural heritage.

Professor Karen Hulme, LLB, LLM (Nottingham), PhD (Essex), joined the School of Law at the University of Essex, UK, in 2001. Her research is centred on the effectiveness of environmental protection in times of armed conflict, and her book *War Torn Environment: Interpreting the Legal Threshold* (2004), published by Martinus Nijhoff, won the Lieber Society's American Society of International Law prize for 2004. Professor Hulme has worked with the Essex Business and Human Rights Project (EBHR) on several reports and consultancies on the extractives industry, including legislation amendments and human rights impact monitoring, and, in particular, on issues of environmental law and environmental human rights. She is also the Chair of the IUCN's Specialist Group on Peace, Security, and Conflict. In 2009, she contributed, alongside the International Committee for the Red Cross, to the report for UNEP, *Protecting the Environment during Armed Conflict: An Inventory and Analysis of International Law*.

Dr Saleemul Huq has been the Director of the International Centre for Climate Change and Development (ICCCAD) since 2009. He is also a senior fellow at the International Institute for Environment and Development (IIED), where he is involved in building negotiating capacity and supporting the engagement of the Least Developed Countries (LDCs) in UNFCCC, including negotiator training workshops for LDCs, policy briefings, and support for the Adaptation Fund Board, as well as research into vulnerability and adaptation to climate change in the least developed countries. Dr Huq has published numerous articles in scientific and popular journals, was a lead author of the chapter on Adaptation and Sustainable Development in the Third Assessment Report of the Intergovernmental Panel on Climate Change (IPCC), and was one of the coordinating lead authors of 'Inter-relationships between adaptation and mitigation' in the IPCC's Fourth Assessment Report (2007).

Dr Luong Quang Huy holds a PhD in environmental sciences from the University of East Anglia, United Kingdom. He has researched vulnerability and adaptation to climate change for years, with a focus on developing countries in Southeast Asia. His research and policy advisory work for the Government of Vietnam covers greenhouse gas emission reduction, international negotiations, carbon markets, and sustainable development.

Dr KE Shuifa is Professor in the School of Agricultural Economics and Rural Development, Renmin University of China. He received his PhD from Beijing Forestry University and worked in this university for about 10 years. He did postdoctoral research at the Rural Development Institute of the Chinese Academy of Social Sciences. As a visiting scholar, he studied and undertook research work at the College of Environmental Science and Forestry, State University of New York. His research interests and expertise focus on the following areas: green economy and forestry development, and forestry policies and forest households' behaviour. He is a member of the Chinese Society for Sustainable Development. He has published more than 100 articles in academic journals.

Dr Philip Michael (Mick) Kelly (see previous)

Dr Gunnar Keppel is Associate Professor in Environmental Biology at the University of South Australia, Adelaide. He has a broad background in vegetation ecology, island biogeography, and conservation biology. Most of his recent work focuses on drivers of diversity patterns on islands and in climate change refugia. He has lived in Fiji for about 15 years, where he continues an active research programme.

Dr Safdar Ullah Khan is currently working as an economist (Investment Portfolio Officer) at the City of Gold Coast. He is also affiliated with Bond Business School, Bond University, Australia, where where he has been teaching Economics to undergraduate and postgraduate classes since 2009. He holds a PhD in Economics from Bond University, and an MPhil in Economics from Quaid-i-Azam University, Pakistan. Dr Khan served the State Bank of Pakistan (the central bank) from 2003 to 2009. He was selected from the International Monetary Fund, where he completed specialized courses, including 'Macroeconomic Modelling and Forecasting', 'Theory and Empirics of Growth', and 'Financial Programming'. He has also received prestigious awards in research, teaching, and organizational-level competences. Dr Khan specializes in applied and behavioural economics. His research interests include intersections of economics, law, finance, environment, demography, and sociology studies.

Dr Isara Khanjanasthiti is an Adjunct Teaching Fellow at the Faculty of Society and Design, Bond University, Australia. His research passions encompass a variety of areas in the built environment discipline, including smart cities, housing and placemaking. With a strong interest in urban planning for airports and their environs, Isara's PhD thesis investigated planning frameworks for economic development around Gold Coast Airport.

Professor Matthias Kowasch is a professor of geographical education at University College of Teacher Education Styria (Austria). He works on sustainability education, production/consumption patterns and the political ecology of mining

resources. After a joint PhD at the University of Heidelberg (Germany) and the University of Montpellier III (France) on the participation of indigenous people in the nickel sector in New Caledonia, he was a postdoc at the French Institute of Research for Development and taught at the universities of New Caledonia, Bremen, Berlin (Humboldt), Cologne, and Graz. He focuses on research in the Pacific Islands (especially New Caledonia), Austria, France, and Germany. His actual main focus is sustainability education in school geography.

Professor Craig Langston is Professor of Construction and Facilities Management at Bond University, Australia. He has a combination of industry and academic experience spanning more than 40 years. His research interests include measurement of sustainable development, adaptive reuse, life cycle costing, and productivity. Professor Langston has held four Australian Research Council Linkage Project grants, amounting to nearly AUD 1 million in external competitive funding. He was also the recipient of the Vice Chancellor's Quality Award (Research Excellence) at Bond University in 2010. He is an international author and has won a number of awards for his research, including the Queensland Award, the Australian Award, and Asia-Pacific Research Award in the project management discipline in 2016.

Marie-Isabell Lenz is a master's student at the United Nations University and the Rheinische Friedrich-Wilhelms University in Bonn, Germany, where she is enrolled in the Geography of Environmental Risks and Human Security programme. Ms Lenz has a background and research interest in Geography, Cultural Anthropology, Political Ecology, and Marine Conservation. She has worked and studied in Germany, Israel, and Fiji, alongside Professor Hans Juergen Boehmer, where she examined an invasive alien palm and its impact on native island biodiversity in the Colo-i-Suva Forest Reserve, on the island of Viti Levu. Her current research interests lie in the spatial planning, assessing, and implementing coastal and marine ecosystem-based disaster risk reduction and adaptation methods. She aims to assess socio-ecological vulnerabilities and risks, as well as incorporating indigenous and traditional knowledge, to support decision-making of viable climate change adaptation and risk reduction policies.

Sherri Lodhar is a graduate of the University of the West Indies, St Augustine, where she obtained both her BSc (2011) and MSc (2014) degrees. She is currently enrolled as a PhD student at the University of the South Pacific Laucala Campus, where her research focuses on the structure and dynamics of Colo-i-Suva rainforest of Viti Levu, Fiji, which is being impacted upon by a *Pinanga coronata* invasion. Biodiversity conservation has always been the primary focus of her interest. For her master's thesis, Ms Lodhar investigated the genetic structure and diversity of the endangered native orchid *Cyrtopodium parviflorum* Lindl., and for her undergraduate research, she assessed the impact of soil degradation on the vegetation of the Aripo Savannas in Trinidad and Tobago. Her present research will continue to feed her appetite for learning and her enthusiasm for conservation, while making valuable contributions to the field of science.

Zafar Manzoor has completed his MPhil in Applied Economics from Forman Christian College (A Chartered University), Lahore, Pakistan, with a *magna cum laude* certificate of higher distinction. Currently, he is a lecturer at Forman Christian College. In addition to teaching, he has also worked as a research fellow in the research grant project of PERI (Punjab Economic Research Institute) titled 'Study on crime, business activity, unemployment and economic growth in Punjab'. The results of the study revealed that crime adversely impacts economic growth, income per capita, and tourism in the province. Moreover, a rise in the rate of unemployment increases the incidents of crime in Punjab. He has worked on the Measurement of Pakistan's Informal Economy project. The outcome of the study suggested a positive significant effect of the tax burden on the demand for currency in Pakistan. Currently, he is working on the Higher Education Commission (HEC) thematic grant project titled 'Effectiveness of Criminal Justice System of Pakistan' as a Research Associate. He has wide-ranging research interests that include socio-economic issues related to institutions, governance, and climate change.

Naznin Nasir is a doctoral researcher in the Department of Geography at Durham University, UK. Her research focuses on the politics of climate change vulnerability and climate resilient development in Bangladesh. Ms Nasir previously worked as a Research Associate with the International Centre for Climate Change and Development (ICCCAD) at the Independent University and the Centre for Climate Change and Environmental Research at Brac University, Dhaka, Bangladesh. She received her master's in Environment and Sustainability from the University of Western Ontario, Canada. She did another master's in International Relations from the University of Dhaka, Bangladesh. She has also been working as a broadcast journalist for the past ten years.

Dr Nguyen Huu Ninh is Chairman of the Centre for Environment Research, Education and Development (CERED). He is Professor, Doctor Honoris Causa of the University of Pécs (Hungary), Doctor of Science Honoris Causa of the University of East Anglia (UK), and Honorary Member of Vietnam Business Council for Sustainable Development (VBCSD). He was a contributor to the Fourth Assessment Report (Working Group II) of the Intergovernmental Panel on Climate Change when it received the Nobel Peace Prize in 2007. He completed

his studies in Hungary, at the University of Szeged and the Hungarian Academy of Sciences from 1971 to 1986. He has conducted a series of projects on environment and development in Vietnam and the wider Southeast Asia over the course of 30 years, as well as consulting for several companies on climate-smart technologies. He was a lead and co-author of *Policy for Environmentally Sustainable Development: Perspectives from Vietnam* (World Scientific, 2014), *Flooding in Mekong River Delta, Vietnam* (UNDP Human Development Report, 2007), and *Living with Environmental Change: Social Vulnerability, Adaptation and Resilience in Vietnam* (Routledge, 2001).

Dr Natarika Wayuparb Nitiphon has worked as an official at the Ministry of Natural Resources and Environment, Royal Thai Government, for 25 years. She graduated with a PhD from Macquarie University, Australia, in 2005. Since 2004, Dr Nitiphon has been working on climate change at the Office of Natural Resources and Environmental Policy and Planning, Thailand's National Focal Point to the UNFCCC. Her main work stream includes several areas: technical support for climate change and GHG mitigation policy; Measurement, Reporting, and Verification (MRV) system for GHG mitigation towards the country's pledges; climate change capacity-building and training programmes; and corporate strategies and low-carbon innovation. Also, since 2004 at COP10 in Buenos Aires, Argentina, she has been a Thai delegate to the UNFCCC negotiations. Her focus in the negotiation process is climate change and GHG mitigation issues.

Professor David M. Ong is Research Professor of International and Environmental Law, Nottingham Trent University, UK, where he is the Director of the Marine Ecological Resilience and Geological Resources (MERGeR) Centre and Founding Director of the LLM Degree in Oil, Gas, and Mining (OGM) Law. His main research interests are in the international law of the sea, international environmental law, as well as international investment and development finance law. He published in major international law, international environmental law, and international economic law journals and yearbooks, such as the *American Journal of International Law* (1999); *European Journal of International Law* (2001); *Yearbook of International Environmental Law, 2006* (2008); *Irish Yearbook of International Law, 2006* (2008); *Nordic Journal of International Law* (2010 and 2016); and *Journal of International Economic Law* (2017). He has also co-edited four volumes of essays in these fields, namely 1) *The International Maritime Law Institute (IMLI) Treatise on Global Ocean Governance*, Vol. I: UN and Global Ocean Governance, co-edited with Dino Kritsiotis and David Attard, Director of IMLI, Oxford University Press (OUP) (2018); 2) *Global Project Finance, Human Rights and Sustainable Development*, co-edited with Sheldon Leader, Cambridge University Press (2011); 3) *Research Handbook on*

International Environmental Law, co-edited with Malgosia Fitzmaurice and Panos Merkouris, Edward Elgar Publishing (2010); and 4) *Law of the Sea: Progress and Prospects*, co-edited with Richard Barnes and David Freestone, OUP (2005). During 2017–2019, David worked on his fifth co-edited volume, provisionally titled *Beyond the Joint Development Agreement*, being a collection of papers delivered at two international workshops in 2017 (Kuala Lumpur, Malaysia) and 2018 (Nottingham, UK) on this topic. In 2019, David was appointed to the International Law Association (ILA) Study Group on Asian State Practice in the Domestic Implementation of International Law, as the principal Rapporteur for the 'Environment' section of the Study Group's report. More information on David's profile can be found at: https://www.ntu .ac.uk/staff-profiles/law/david-ong

Keith Openshaw, now retired, has had a varied career working with donor and international agencies, governments, NGOs, and private firms, in the fields of natural resources, economics, renewable energy, and the environment. He has lived in Africa and Asia for 17 years and worked in more than 50 countries. For five years, he was head of the forest economics section at the University of Dar es Salaam (Morogoro Campus), now Sokoine University. He was a staff member at FAO and the World Bank and was a Senior Fellow at the Beijer Institute, now the Stockholm Environmental Institute. He was a member of the ALGAS (Asia Least-cost Greenhouse Gas Abatement Strategy) project team, which documented GHG emissions for 11 Asian countries and proposed strategies for GHG mitigation. This was sponsored by UNDP/GEF and executed by the ADB. He has more than 180 publications, two books, and several book chapters and is a leading proponent of biomass energy.

Dr John Peet was born in the United Kingdom and has been living in Christchurch, New Zealand, for the last 50 years. John has a BSc in Chemical Technology and a PhD in Chemical Engineering, and has worked in the petroleum industry. He is a retired Senior Lecturer in Chemical and Process Engineering at the University of Canterbury, New Zealand, where his main focus over the last two decades was sustainable development. Dr Peet is the author of *Energy and the Ecological Economics of Sustainability* and numerous papers on systems, sustainability, and the ethical requirements of stakeholder involvement. Since retiring from the University of Canterbury, he is working closely with a number of local, national, and international non-government organizations on issues of sustainable development.

Dr Phan Toan is an economist at the Research Department of the Federal Reserve Bank of Richmond, Virginia, USA. He was an assistant professor at the University of North Carolina in Chapel Hill until 2017. He graduated with a PhD in Economics at Northwestern University in 2012. He is a native of Vietnam.

He has written research about the impacts of global warming on economic growth in the United States.

Dr Kanokwan Pibalsook was Environmentalist, Senior Professional Level, Office of International Cooperation on Natural Resources and Environment, Office of the Permanent Secretary, Ministry of Natural Resources and Environment, Thailand. She completed a master's degree in Environmental Social Sciences from Mahidol University, Thailand, in 1991, and a PhD in the Graduate School of the Environment (GSE), Macquarie University, Australia, in 2007, with the thesis titled 'An assessment of the application of Local Agenda 21 in Thailand for improving environmental policy and planning'. Sadly, Kanokwan passed away on 12 March 2016.

QIAO Dan is a postgraduate student at the School of Agriculture and Rural Development, Renmin University of China. She was a top student at Beijing Forestry University and holds a bachelor's degree in economics and management of forestry, a field of study that she continues under the supervision of Professor KE Shuifa.

Dr Mohammed Feisal Rahman is a Postdoctoral Research Associate in the Department of Geography at Durham University, UK. He was a former faculty member in the Department of Environmental Science at the Independent University, Bangladesh, based in Dhaka. An environmental engineer by training, he received his PhD from the University of Waterloo, Canada. He coordinated research activities at the International Centre for Climate Change and Development (ICCCAD). At ICCCAD, Dr Rahman was involved in several programmes, including Adaptation Technology, Urban Climate Change Resilience, and Capacity Development in Managing and Allocation of Natural Resources.

Dr Gulasekaran Rajaguru is Associate Professor of Economics in the Bond Business School, Bond University, Australia. He holds a PhD in Economics and MSocSci (Economics) from the National University of Singapore. He also has an MStat from the Indian Statistical Institute. He specializes in both theoretical and applied econometrics. His findings are published in both economics and econometrics journals, including *Journal of Forecasting*, *Econometrics*, *Economics Letters*, *Applied Economics*, *Economic Modelling*, *Empirical Economics*, *European Journal of Political Economy*, *Oxford Economic Papers*, *Economics Record*, *Japan and the World Economy*, *Journal of Asia Pacific Economy*, and *Journal of Economic Integration*. His research interests include irregular frequency modelling, high-frequency big data analytics, causal inferences with aggregated data, and panel data models.

Professor Dzulkifli (Dzul) Abdul Razak is the sixth Rector of the International Islamic University Malaysia. He is immediate

Past President of the International Association of Universities (IAU), based at UNESCO, Paris, after serving as the 14th President of IAU (2012–2016). He was also the Chairperson, Board of Directors, Universiti Sains Islam Malaysia, and has served as Honorary Professor at the University of Nottingham since 2014. As the fifth Vice-Chancellor/President of Universiti Sains Malaysia (USM) from 2000 to 2011, he convened and established the Penang Regional Centre of Expertise (RCE) on Education for Sustainable Development. Under his leadership, USM became Malaysia's first sustainability-led university based on the indigenous concept of *sejahtera*. In May 2017, he was awarded the prestigious 2017 Gilbert Medal in recognition of his long-term commitment to an integrated approach on sustainable (*sejahtera*) international development for Higher Education (HE) and his tireless work to support and develop the clearly public good dimensions of HE, according to the Universitas 21 (U21), a group of renowned research-intensive universities from 16 countries. Dzul is the first Asian and the seventh international academic to receive the Medal from U21. Of late, Dzul has been appointed Regional Coordinator of the Asia-Pacific Region in the International Research Project: Reorienting Education and Training Systems to Improve the Lives of Indigenous Youth, led by the UNESCO Chair at York University, Toronto, Canada. Dzul was awarded the 2017 Tokoh Akademik Negara (National Academic Laureate) and recipient of a number of Honorary Doctorate from various international universities. Dzul is a Fellow of the Academy of Sciences Malaysia, the World Academy of Art and Science (WAAS) and the World Academy of Islamic Management (WAIM). For almost 25 years he has written weekly Op-Ed columns for Malaysia's dailies, especially *The New Straits Times*.

Dr T. S. Gopi Rethinaraj is Professor and Programme Director of Energy Sciences at Atria University in Bengaluru. Before joining Atria University in January 2021, he was a visiting professor at the Divecha Centre for Climate Change, Indian Institute of Science (IISc) for two years. Earlier, he was an Associate Professor in the Energy and Environment Policy Programme of the National Institute of Advanced Studies (NIAS) in Bengaluru from June 2014 to September 2018, and a faculty member at the Lee Kuan Yew School of National University of Singapore from 2005 to 2014. He received his PhD in nuclear engineering from the University of Illinois at Urbana-Champaign in 2005, and was a research associate at the Program in Arms Control, Disarmament and International Security. He also worked as a science reporter for the *Indian Express* in Mumbai from 1995 to 1999, and received a master's degree in Physics from Bharathidasan University, India, in 1995. His research and teaching interests include energy policy, science and technology policy, and civilian and military uses of nuclear energy.

Professor Dietrich Schmidt-Vogt, Geographer and Fellow of the Alexander von Humboldt Foundation (AvH), is Honorary Professor at the Faculty of Environment and Natural Resources, Freiburg University, Germany, as well as Distinguished Adjunct Professor at the Asian Institute of Technology (AIT), Thailand, since 2015. From 2015 to 2017 he was also Director of the Mountain Societies Research Institute, University of Central Asia (UCA), in Bishkek, Kyrgyz Republic. Before joining UCA, he was stationed for six years in Kunming, China, as Head of the Research Programme at the World Agroforestry Centre (ICRAF) East and Central Asia Office and Professor at the Kunming Institute of Botany, Chinese Academy of Sciences. Prior affiliations were as Associate Professor with AIT from 2002 to 2009, and as Senior Lecturer with the South Asia Institute of Heidelberg University, Germany, from 1998 to 2002. Dietrich obtained his doctoral and postdoctoral degrees at Heidelberg University, Germany. He has more than 35 years of research experience in Asia, mainly in mountainous areas of the Eastern Himalayan and Mekong regions in South and Southeast Asia, but also in East Asia and Central Asia. His research interests include biodiversity conservation, land-use change, and sustainable mountain development. He is currently teaching courses and modules on Natural Resource Management, Land Use Change, and Integrated Land Use Systems at Freiburg University, Germany. He has experience also in capacity-building and curriculum development for academic institutions in Asia, such as the Royal University of Phnom Penh, Cambodia; Andalas University, Indonesia; National University of Laos; Hue University of Agriculture and Forestry, Vietnam; and Souphanouvong University, Laos.

Dr Rajeev L. Semwal holds a PhD in Botany and is an ecologist by training. As an ecologist, he has been making constant efforts to contribute towards developing science-based institutional support systems for conservation of forests and agroecosystems in the Himalayas. During his long research and professional career, he had an opportunity to work with WWF-India, LEAD-India, and subsequently also as the first coordinator of the Mountain Division at the Ministry of Environment, Forests, and Climate Change, Government of India. Till December 2020 he was working from School of Environmental Sciences, Jawaharlal Nehru University, India, for a Task Force under the National Mission for Sustaining the Himalayan Ecosystem. Dr Semwal has a large number of research papers to his credit and currently is an independent researcher.

Professor Amartya Sen is Thomas W. Lamont University Professor, and Professor of Economics and Philosophy at Harvard University, and was earlier the Master of Trinity College, Cambridge. He has served as President of the American

Economic Association, the Indian Economic Association, the International Economic Association, and the Econometric Society. He is an Honorary Fellow of All Souls College and of Nuffield College, Oxford, and also of Darwin College and St Edmund College in Cambridge. He was also Professor of Economics at Delhi University and at the London School of Economics. Dr Sen's numerous books have been translated into more than 40 languages, including *Collective Choice and Social Welfare* (1970, 2017), *On Economic Inequality* (1973, 1997), *Poverty and Famines* (1981), *On Ethics and Economics* (1987), *Inequality Reexamined* (1992), *Development as Freedom* (1999), *Rationality and Freedom* (2002), and *The Idea of Justice* (2009). His research has ranged over a vast number of fields in economics, philosophy, and decision theory. Among the awards he has received are the Bharat Ratna (the highest honour awarded by the President of India), Commandeur de la Legion d'Honneur (France), the National Humanities Medal (USA), Ordem do Merito Cientifico (Brazil), Honorary Companion of Honour (UK), Aztec Eagle (Mexico), Edinburgh Medal (UK), the George Marshall Award (USA), the Eisenhower Medal (USA), Peace Prize of the German Book Trade, and the Nobel Prize in Economics.

Dr Boris Steipe is Associate Professor in the Department of Biochemistry and the Department of Molecular Genetics, University of Toronto, Canada, and past Director of the University's Specialist Programme in Bioinformatics and Computational Biology. Previously research fellow at the Gene Center of the University of Munich, Germany (1995–2001), working on rational approaches to protein engineering; Habilitation in Biochemistry and appointment as Lecturer, Faculty of Chemistry and Pharmacy, Ludwig-Maximilians University of Munich (2000); Postdoctoral Fellow of the Department for Structural Biology at the Max Planck Institute for Biochemistry, Martinsried, Germany, with Professor Robert Huber (1990–1994); PhD (1990) and MD (1985) from the Faculty of Medicine, University of Munich. Recent publications include 'Phenomenological comparison: Pursuing Husserl's "time consciousness" in poems by Wang Wei, Paul Celan and Santoka Taneda' (*Comparative and Continental Philosophy*, **9**(3), 241-259, 2017), with Dr Yi Chen. Current research focuses on linguistic models for molecular self-organization and the philosophy of emergence in complex systems.

Professor Shabib Haider Syed holds a PhD in Economics from the Quaid-i-Azam University in Islamabad, Pakistan, and a postdoc from Bond University, Australia. He earned his MA (Economics) from Government College University (GCU) in Lahore, Pakistan. His PhD dissertation is in Applied Microeconomics. He has more than 26 years of

teaching and research experience in various national and international institutions. Currently, he is serving as a Professor and Dean in the Faculty of Economics and Management Sciences at Minhaj University, Lahore. He is a member of the Sustainable Development Policy Institute (SDPI), Islamabad, and WWF-Pakistan, and South Asian Network for Development and Environmental Economics (SANDEE). He has visited Australia, Thailand, Nepal, Bangladesh, and Sri Lanka for various training courses and presentations. He has supervised research in the areas of economic growth, finance, black economy, trade, energy, crime, terrorism, suicide, climate change, formal and informal institutions, and the environment. His work has been extensively published in credible international and national peer-reviewed journals. He has worked on various projects as an adviser or a consultant on subjects of national interest, such as crime, growth, and the environment. He was editor-in-chief of *Forman Journal of Economic Studies* from 2005 to 2019, and he serves as a peer reviewer and a member of the editorial board of various national and international peer-reviewed journals.

Dr Ros Taplin is Director of the MSc Environmental Management Programme, Centre for Development, Environment and Policy, SOAS, University of London. Her research interests include climate policy, low-carbon energy policy, sustainability indicators, environmental impacts of resource extraction, education for sustainability, and climate change art. Dr Taplin's former academic roles include Professor and Research Director, Australian Centre for Sustainable Mining Practices, University of New South Wales, Sydney; Professor and Head of the Department of Sustainability Science, Bond University; and Director of the Environmental Management Programme, Graduate School of the Environment, Macquarie University, Australia. Her qualifications include a PhD on environmental policy-making and a Doctor of Visual Arts on climate change art.

Dr Mostafa Kamal Tolba (see previous)

Karma Tshering is the Chief of Policy and Planning Division of the Ministry of Agriculture and Forests, Royal Government of Bhutan. He was previously the Head of Policy and Programming Services, National Environment Commission Secretariat. In January 2019, he was again nominated as the Alternate Board Member of the Green Climate Fund representing Least Developed Countries (LDC). Mr Tshering is the core negotiation team of LDC Finance and Technology in the UNFCCC. His main expertise is in the areas of mainstreaming environment, climate change, poverty, gender, and poverty concerns into policy and plans of both central and local governments. Other areas of his expertise are the field of negotiation, fund mobilization, planning, team building and coordination, project developments, monitoring, and evaluation, including networking. He also served as a member of the Technology Executive Committee under the UNFCCC from January 2015 to June 2017.

Dr TUN LWIN was a consultant and the founder of Myanmar Climate Change Watch (MCCW), a non-profit organization that provides information and education to the public about weather, climate, and natural disasters through social media, talks, radio, television, and more in Myanmar since 2009, until he passed away on 4 November 2019. Prior to this, Dr Tun Lwin served as a civil servant in the Department of Hydrology and Meteorology for more than 40 years, where he was awarded five medals during his service, until his retirement as the Director-General-cum-Adviser of the department. He completed his PhD in Physics from Yangon University, and his master's and bachelor's in meteorology from Florida State University, as well as a bachelor's in physics with Distinction from the Arts and Science University, Mandalay. His main fields of study were climate change vulnerability and adaptation assessment in Myanmar, natural disaster management, and monsoon climatology. Dr Tun Lwin was a member of the ASEAN Outstanding Scientists Group, a Chief Executive Council Member in National Committees on Climate Change Adaptation and Environmental Conservation and Disaster Management, and the lifetime World Wildlife Fund (WWF)-Myanmar Ambassador for Climate Change since 2017. He was also the Chairman and Technical Adviser for the Steering Committee of the Regional Integrated Multi-hazard Early Warning System (RIMES), the World Meteorological Organization (WMO) Focal Point for Public Information of Myanmar prior to his retirement. Dr Tun Lwin wrote six books, two of which were awarded the Best Science Literary Prize, the Thuta Swe Zone, and Tun Foundation Award. He was also the recipient of the *HERO Award* from 7Day Media Group in 2016, and the *Popular Public Figure Award: The People's Weatherman* by the Irrawaddy Media Group in 2017.

Swan Yee TUN LWIN is the lead Landscape Designer on the Alley Garden Projects, an urban revitalization project that transforms the many kilometres of back alleys in Yangon from wasteland to healthy recreational spaces together with the local community and governance, at Doh Eain, an urban heritage-led placemaking and capacity-building social enterprise based in Yangon, Myanmar. She is experienced in community engagement, asset-based research, and user design, in addition to creating designs for public spaces in the city. She graduated summa cum laude from Berkeley City College, concentrating on Natural Sciences, before completing her BA in Landscape Architecture with a focus on City and Regional Planning at the University of California, Berkeley. At UC Berkeley, she completed two Undergraduate Research Apprentice Programmes in 'Integrative Biology on Identification of Tropical Trees Using Drone Images and QGIS', and in 'Public Policy on Case Study of Natural Disaster Preparedness Policy in Myanmar with Field Work'. Her areas of interest are disaster risk management policies, urban transportation planning, monsoon climatology and climate change adaptation in urban design and planning, and incorporation of natural systems and elements within the city through public spaces for a more liveable and sustainable urban landscape.

Dr Sk Noim Uddin is a Senior Environmental Consultant with GHD Australia and is an Honorary Associate, with the Department of Geography and Planning of Macquarie University, Australia. He graduated with a PhD from Macquarie University in 2009. His research focuses on sustainable/low-carbon energy strategies, climate change policy, and greenhouse gas risk management. He serves as a lead author in WGIII of the IPCC Fifth Assessment Report.

Professor Jan C. van der Leun had his basic training in physics, with specializations in meteorology and biophysics. His research was directed primarily on influences of solar radiation on the human skin. He spent a year on similar research at Cornell University Medical College, New York, and became a professor of dermatology at Utrecht University, Netherlands. This background brought him into early contact, in 1971, with the problem of the depletion of the stratospheric ozone layer, and the effects of that danger. Later, that reality became the focus of investigations in his research group at Utrecht. After his retirement from the university in 1993, he continued these activities with an additional interest in interactions between stratospheric ozone depletion and climate change and the effects of these changes on living organisms. He did this work as a guest co-worker in a dynamic international company, Ecofys BV, that works for 'a sustainable energy supply for everyone', before he passed away in July 2016.

Dr Helena Varkkey is a Senior Lecturer at the Department of International and Strategic Studies, University of Malaya in Kuala Lumpur, Malaysia. She completed her doctorate at the Department of Government and International Relations, University of Sydney, Australia, in 2012. Dr Varkkey has been interested in sustainable development throughout her academic career. Her interest in the field has evolved to focus on transboundary pollution in Southeast Asia, particularly pertaining to the role of patronage in agribusiness, especially the oil palm industry, and its link to forest fires and haze in the region. Her findings were published as a book in 2016 as part of the

Routledge Malaysian Studies Series. Her writings have also appeared in many international academic journals, including *International Environmental Agreements*, *Wetlands*, and *Asia Pacific Viewpoint*. Her work was also featured in the 2014 *Routledge Handbook on Contemporary Malaysia*. She recently served as Chief Editor on a Local and Transboundary Haze Report sanctioned by the Academy of Sciences Malaysia. Dr Varkkey has been interviewed by various media for her views on haze, agribusiness, and ASEAN, including *The Wall Street Journal*, *The Economist*, *Financial Times*, Channel News Asia, *The Straits Times* (Singapore), and *The Star* (Malaysia). She continues to undertake research in sustainable development and haze issues. She maintains an academic blog at helenavarkkey.wordpress.com

WANG Baojin has been studying in Beijing for six years. She earned a bachelor's degree at the Economics and Management College of Beijing Forestry University and now is a master's student in Forestry Economics at Renmin University of China. At present, her main focus is forestry green economy and sustainable development. She worked as an intern in the State Forestry Administration and was responsible for collecting and analysing research data of the national collective forest areas. She participated in the surveys of farmers in Liaoning Province, Yunnan Province, Fujian Province, Guizhou Province, and others. She has a comprehensive understanding of the forestry management behaviour and development of farmers and rural areas in China.

Dr Dick Watling is Principal and Founder of Environmental Consultants Fiji, Ltd., Fiji's leading specialist environmental consultancy practice. In this capacity, his 35 years of consultancy experience encompasses a very broad range of environmental and conservation planning and management in Pacific Island Countries and South East Asia. Dr Watling read Zoology at Bristol University for his BSc and received his doctorate from the Department of Applied Ecology, University of Cambridge, UK. A resident of Fiji since childhood, Dr Watling is an internationally acknowledged authority on Fiji's environment, its birds, and terrestrial wildlife. In 2006, Dr Watling established the Fiji Nature Conservation Trust, which, through its working arm, NatureFiji-MareqetiViti, is Fiji's only membership-based biodiversity organization. He served as Managing Director until January 2013 and remains as the Executive Trustee. Currently, Dr Watling is retired and farms in the Sigatoka valley.

Professor Anoja Wickramasinghe is Emeritus Professor of Geography, University of Peradeniya, Sri Lanka. She has made significant contributions to the fields of energy, forestry, resource management, rural development, and poverty, and is also known as a policy and institutional analyst, gender activist, community mobilizer, and trainer. She has served as a consultant to several international and national agencies, including the United Nations Development Programme, FAO, International Fund for Agricultural Development (IFAD), World Bank, Millennium Challenge Cooperation and many others on gender and social inclusion, energy access and livelihood development, community forestry and biomass energy development, social and environmental safeguards, and land resource management. She has published several books, including an annotated bibliography on gender and energy in South Asia, funded by ENERGIA, and more than 100 research articles. She possesses extensive experience in undertaking collaborative projects and research in many countries in Asia and the West. She coordinated the Collaborative Regional Research Network in South Asia (CORRENSA), funded by the British Council, and, as the focal point for ENERGIA International Network, she leads the National Network on Gender, Energy, and Environment. Professor Wickramasinghe started her career as a geographer, with a BA Honours from the University of Peradeniya, Sri Lanka, and holds an MSc in Natural Resource Management and a PhD in Forest Ecology from the University of Sheffield, UK.

Dr Amirtharaj Christy Williams is the Country Director for WWF-Myanmar. He has more than 19 years of conservation leadership expertise with WWF in Asia. Since 2016, he has been leading the WWF-Myanmar Country Office to influence the conservation agenda of Myanmar as the country opens up. The work in Myanmar ranges from boots on the ground to protect wildlife from poaching to protecting the forests and freshwater by influencing investments in Myanmar via a green economy approach. Under his leadership, WWF-Myanmar has been able to build a programme of work on the ground despite the conflict by building relationships with key stakeholders including the CSOs, the government, and the Karen National Union (KNU), a political front of the armed ethnic group controlling significant parts of the forested landscape. Before this, he was the Programme Leader for Asian Rhino and Elephant Action Strategy (AREAS), a WWF conservation programme on elephants and rhinos that is being implemented in eight countries across Asia. He worked with WWF offices and its partners in implementing strategies to combat the illegal trade in wildlife, mitigating human-elephant conflict, and engaging in policy and advocacy work to address the impact of developmental infrastructure (e.g., roads, dams, oil drilling, human habitations, etc.) on elephant and rhino habitats. Christy is a large mammal biologist who did his PhD from the Wildlife Institute of India on 'Elephants and their habitats in Rajaji National Park'.

Peer reviewers

Professor Neil Adger, College of Life and Environmental Sciences, University of Exeter, UK.

Professor Emeritus Joseph A. Adler, Asian Studies and Religious Studies, Kenyon College, USA.

Professor Dilip Ahuja, National Institute of Advanced Studies, Bengaluru, India.

Dr Edvin Aldrian, Centre for Climate Change and Air Quality, Meteorological Climatological and Geophysical Agency, Indonesia.

Dr Patricia Alexander, former Regional Adviser on Gender, UNDP office, Colombo, Sri Lanka.

Professor A. T. M. Nurul Amin, Department of Economics and Social Sciences, Brac University, Bangladesh.

Dr Stephen O. Andersen, Institute for Governance and Sustainable Development, Washington, DC, USA.

Dr Lynne Armitage, Faculty of Society and Design, Bond University, Australia.

Dr Muhammad Salahuddin Ayyubi, Forman Christian College (a Chartered University), Lahore, Pakistan.

Dr Bhishna Bajracharya, Faculty of Society and Design, Bond University, Australia.

Dr Tariq Banuri, formerly of Division for Sustainable Development, UNDESA, New York, USA.

Dr Cihat Basocak, formerly of Information, Communication, and Space Technology Division, UNESCAP, Bangkok, Thailand.

Professor Jill Belsky, Department of Society and Conservation, College of Forestry and Conservation, University of Montana, USA.

Ranjit Bharvirkar, Principal and India Programme Director, The Regulatory Assistance, India Project, India.

Late Professor S. C. Bhattacharya, Indian Institute of Social Welfare and Business Management, Kolkata, India.

Professor Hans Juergen Boehmer, Faculty of Science, Technology, and Environment, University of the South Pacific, Fiji.

Dr Rizaldi Boer, Center for Climate Risk and Opportunity Management, IPB University, Bogor, Indonesia.

Dr Trevor H. Booth, formerly of Commonwealth Scientific and Industrial Research Organisation (CSIRO), Australia.

Dr Davina Boyd, College of Science, Health, Engineering, and Education, Murdoch University, Australia.

Professor G. Robert Brakenridge, Dartmouth Flood Observatory, Institute of Arctic and Alpine Research (INSTAAR), University of Colorado, USA.

Professor Peter Brimblecombe, Department of Marine Environment and Engineering, National Sun Yat-Sen University, Kaohsiung, Taiwan.

Dr Gernot Brodnig, World Bank, Washington, DC, USA.

Dr Prabhu Budhathoki, former Country Representative, IUCN Nepal Country Office, Kathmandu, Nepal.

Emeritus Professor Shelley Burgin, Faculty of Science and Health, University of Western Sydney, Australia.

Professor Emeritus Ian Burton, Department of Geography and Planning, University of Toronto, Canada.

Dr Melgabal Capistrano, formerly of Asian Disaster Preparedness Center, Thailand.

Dr Manab Chakraborty, Partners in Prosperity, New Delhi, India.

Dr CHEN Ying, Research Centre for Sustainable Development, Chinese Academy of Social Sciences, Beijing, China.

Professor Anthony S. F. Chiu, Center for Engineering and Sustainable Development Research, De La Salle University, Manila, Philippines.

Dr Pema Choejey, formerly of Ministry of Information and Communications, Bhutan.

Late CHOW Kok Kee, Sustainable Technology Resources Centre (STREC)., Ltd, Malaysia.

Late Dr Allen L. Clark, Professional Development Program, East-West Center, Honolulu, USA.

Dr David M. Clark, formerly of ICSU Panel on World Data Centers, NOAA/NGDC, Boulder, USA.

Late Dr Nowarat Coowanitwong, School of Environment, Resources, and Development (SERD), Asian Institute of Technology, Thailand.

Professor Alvin B. Culaba, Center for Engineering and Sustainable Development Research, De La Salle University, Manila, Philippines.

Asok Dasgupta, President, Independent Power Producers Association of India, New Delhi, India.

Late Bernarditas de Castro-Muller, former Special Adviser on Climate Change, South Centre, Geneva, Switzerland.

Dr Peter de Groot, Natural Resources Consultant, London, UK.

Dr Thanakvaro T. De Lopez, Cambodian Research Centre for Development, Phnom Penh, Cambodia.

Dr Uchita de Zoysa, Centre for Environment and Development (CED), Nugegoda, Sri Lanka.

Dr Claudio Delang, Department of Geography, Hong Kong Baptist University.

Dr Rosita Dellios, Faculty of Society and Design, Bond University, Australia.

Dr Pramod Deo, former Chairman, Central Electricity Regulatory Commission, Delhi, India.

Professor John C. Dernbach, Widener University, Harrisburg, USA.

Dr Subash Dhar, UNEP DTU Partnership, Technical University of Denmark (DTU), Denmark.

Dr Thea Dickinson, Department of Physical and Environmental Sciences, University of Toronto, Canada.

Dr Ramil Naufilievich Dissembayev, formerly of UNDP office, Astana, Kazakhstan.

Professor Kuntala Lahiri-Dutt, College of Asia and the Pacific, Australian National University, Australia.

Professor Paul Ekins, Policy Studies Institute, London, UK.

Mahboob Elahi, former Director-General of Environment, Government of Pakistan.

Dr Michael J. Ernst, formerly of UNDP/Bureau of Crisis Prevention and Recovery, Bangkok, Thailand.

Dr Sergio Feld, formerly of UNDP Regional Centre for Asia and the Pacific, Bangkok, Thailand.

Dr A. James Ferguson, Faculty of Society and Design, Bond University, Australia.

Dr Ian Fry, Ambassador for Climate Change and Environment, Ministry of Finance, Tuvalu.

Dr Hans-Martin Füssel, Potsdam Institute for Climate Impact Research, Germany.

Dr Andrew N. Gillison, Centre for Biodiversity Management, Yungaburra, Queensland, Australia.

Dr GOH Yong Kheng, Department of Mathematical and Actuarial Sciences, University of Tunku Abdul Rahman, Malaysia.

Dr Alan Grainger, School of Geography, University of Leeds, UK.

Dr Sujata Gupta, Asian Development Bank, Manila, Philippines.

Hans Guttman, Asian Disaster Preparedness Center, Thailand.

Dr Jamba Gyeltshen, formerly of College of Natural Resources, Royal University of Bhutan.

Dr Ian Hannam, Australian Centre for Agriculture and Law, University of New England, Australia.

Dr David A. Hastings, formerly of Information, Communication, and Space Technology Division, UNESCAP, Bangkok, Thailand.

Dr John E. Hay, Adjunct Professor, University of the South Pacific, Fiji; University of Auckland, New Zealand; and Griffith University, Australia.

Conrado Heruela, School of Renewable Energy and Smart Grid Technology, Naresuan University, Phitsanulok Province, Thailand.

Professor Emeritus Ryokichi Hirono, Seikei University, Tokyo, Japan.

Emeritus Professor Goen Ho, College of Science, Health, Engineering, and Education, Murdoch University, Australia.

Dr Gjalt Huppes, Institute for Environmental Sciences (CML), Leiden University, Netherlands.

Professor Muhammad Idrees, School of Economics, Quaid-i-Azam University, Islamabad, Pakistan.

Manjit Iqbal, former Legal Officer, UNEP Regional Office for Asia and the Pacific, Bangkok, Thailand.

Dr Aminul Islam, Senior Adviser for Programme Development, UNDP office, Dhaka, Bangladesh.

Dr Md Jakariya, Department of Environmental Science and Management, North South University, Dhaka, Bangladesh.

Dr M. L. Siripastr Jayanta, Department of Chemistry, Chulalongkorn University, Thailand.

Dr Terry Jeggle, formerly of United Nations International Strategy for Disaster Reduction, Geneva, Switzerland.

Sanny Ramos Jegillos, Disaster Risk Reduction, UNDP Regional Hub for Asia and the Pacific, Bangkok, Thailand.

Laurel Johnson, School of Earth and Environmental Sciences, University of Queensland, Australia.

Dr Anjeela D. Jokhan, Faculty of Science, Technology, and Environment, University of the South Pacific, Fiji.

Professor David Seth Jones, formerly of Faculty of Business, Economics, and Policy Studies, University of Brunei.

Professor Phil Jones, Climatic Research Unit, University of East Anglia, UK.

Dr Rezaul Karim, former Coordinator, Asia Unit, United Nations Convention to Combat Desertification secretariat, Bonn, Germany.

Dr Mick Kelly, Tanelorn Associates, Kamo, Whangarei, New Zealand.

Dr Ilan Kelman, Institute for Risk and Disaster Reduction and Institute for Global Health, University College London.

Dr Ohmar Khaing, formerly of Myanmar Food Security Working Group, Yangon, Myanmar.

Professor Mohammad Aslam Khan, formerly of University of Pershwar, Pakistan.

Dr Peter Noel King, Senior Policy Adviser, Institute of Global Environmental Strategies, Japan.

Dr Jeffery Kingwell, formerly of Space Technology Applications Section, UNESCAP, Bangkok, Thailand.

Dr Cody Knutson, National Drought Mitigation Center, University of Nebraska-Lincoln, USA.

Dr Lambert Kuijpers, A/gent B.V. Consultancy, 5911 BA Venlo, Netherlands.

Dr Raj Kumar, former Senior Economic Adviser, UNESCAP, Bangkok, Thailand.

Professor Emeritus Tai Joon Kwon, Graduate School of Environmental Studies, Seoul National University, Republic of Korea.

Professor Craig Langston, Faculty of Society and Design, Bond University, Australia.

Professor Felino P. Lansigan, University of the Philippines, Los Baños, Philippines.

Professor Mohd Talib Latif, Faculty of Science and Technology, Universiti Kebangsaan Malaysia.

Dr Paola Leardini, School of Architecture, University of Queensland, Australia.

Dr Louis Lebel, Unit for Social and Environmental Research, Chiang Mai University, Thailand.

Dr Helen Lee, National Assembly Research Service, Republic of Korea.

Dr Natchanun Leepipatpiboon, formerly of Department of Chemistry, Chulalongkorn University, Thailand.

Dr David Leifer, Faculty of Society and Design, Bond University, Australia.

LEONG Chow Peng, formerly of Malaysian Meteorological Department, Malaysia.

Late Dr Bo Lim, UNDP, New York, USA.

Dr LIM Teck Ghee, Centre for Public Policy Studies, Malaysia.

Dr Maxim Lobovikov, Forest Products Service, Food and Agriculture Organization of the United Nations, Rome, Italy.

Justin T. Locke, Rocky Mountain Institute, Washington DC, USA.

Dr Sarah K. Lowder, formerly of Environment and Development Division, UNESCAP, Bangkok, Thailand.

Dr LOY Hui Chieh, Department of Philosophy, National University of Singapore.

Dr Karl Mallon, Climate Risk Pty Ltd, Fairlight, NSW 2094, Australia.

Patti Moore, formerly of IUCN Regional Environmental Law Programme (Asia), Bangkok, Thailand.

Professor Lidia Morawska, School of Physical and Chemical Sciences, Queensland University of Technology, Australia.

Dr Amitava Mukherjee, formerly of Poverty and Development Division, UNESCAP, Bangkok, Thailand.

Dr Martin Mulenga, formerly of International Institute for Environment and Development (IIED), London, UK.

Dr Gulnara Musuralieva, Faculty of Medicine, Ala-Too International University, Bishkek, Kyrgyzstan.

Professor Vijay Naidu, School of Government, Development, and International Affairs, University of the South Pacific, Fiji.

Dr Sangmin Nam, Subregional Office for East and North-East Asia, UNESCAP, Incheon, Republic of Korea.

Dr Hisashi Ogawa, formerly of World Health Organization Western Pacific Regional Office, Manila, Philippines.

Dr ONG Chang Woei, Department of Chinese Studies, National University of Singapore.

Keith Openshaw, International Resources Group, USA (retired in 2004).

Dr Christine Padoch, New York Botanical Garden, USA.

Dr Jyoti Prasad Painuly, UNEP DTU Partnership, Technical University of Denmark (DTU), Denmark.

Professor Jyoti K. Parikh, Integrated Research and Action for Development, New Delhi, India.

Professor Jean Palutikof, National Climate Change Adaptation Research Facility, Griffith University, Australia.

Dr John Peet, Department of Chemical and Process Engineering, University of Canterbury, New Zealand.

Dr Renat Perelet, Institute for Systems Analysis, Russian Academy of Sciences, Moscow, Russian Federation.

Dr Rosa T. Perez, Manila Observatory; and Climate Change Commission, Philippines.

Dr Bill Physick, formerly of Commonwealth Scientific and Industrial Research Organisation (CSIRO) Marine and Atmospheric Research, Aspendale, Australia.

Dr Dorina Pojani, School of Earth and Environmental Sciences, University of Queensland, Australia.

Lene Poulsen, International Consultant on Land Management and Sustainable Development, Karl International Development, Denmark.

Dr Tauseef A. Quraishi, formerly of Institute of Environmental Engineering and Research, University of Engineering and Technology, Lahore, Pakistan.

Vivian Raksakulthai, Environment Consultant, Bangkok, Thailand.

Hitomi Rankine, Environment and Development Division, UNESCAP, Bangkok, Thailand.

Dr Kjeld Rasmussen, Department of Geography, University of Copenhagen, Denmark.

Professor Dzulkifli Abdul Razak, International Islamic University Malaysia.

Robert A. Reinstein, retired International Consultant, USA.

Patrick Richmond, Centre for Global Studies, University of Victoria, British Columbia, Canada.

Dr Marco Roncarati, Social Development Division, UNESCAP, Bangkok, Thailand.

Warren Rowe, Cities Research Institute, Griffith University, Australia.

Ina Rüdenauer, Öko-Institut e.V., Institute for Applied Ecology, Freiburg, Germany.

Dr Mohd Nor Salleh, Academy of Sciences Malaysia.

Dr Hiren Sarkar, formerly of Poverty and Development Division, UNESCAP, Bangkok, Thailand.

Professor Dr Cherla B. Sastry, C & R Associates Canada, Scarborough, Canada.

Dr E. Lisa F. Schipper, Environmental Change Institute, University of Oxford, UK.

Professor Dietrich Schmidt-Vogt, Faculty of Environment and Natural Resources, University of Freiburg, Germany.

Ali Tauqeer Sheikh, Leadership for Environment and Development (LEAD) Pakistan, Islamabad, Pakistan.

Professor Ralph E. H. Sims, Massey University, New Zealand.

Dr Russell Sinclair, School of Biological Sciences, Department of Ecology and Environmental Science, University of Adelaide, Australia.

Gurmit Singh, Centre for Environment, Technology, and Development, Malaysia.

Dr Vladimir Smakhtin, International Water Management Institute, Colombo, Sri Lanka.

Dr Anond Snidvongs, START Regional Center, Chulalongkorn University, Thailand.

Andréa Spear, former Regional Adviser for Trade and Investment Policy, UNESCAP, Bangkok, Thailand.

Dr Victor R. Squires, International Dryland Management Consultant, Adelaide, Australia.

Emeritus Professor Will Steffen, Fenner School of Environment and Society, Australian National University, Australia.

Professor Lindsay C. Stringer, Sustainability Research Institute, School of Earth and Environment, University of Leeds, UK.

Professor Shabib Haider Syed, Faculty of Economics and Management Sciences, Minhaj University, Lahore, Pakistan.

Professor Fredolin Tangang, Faculty of Science and Technology, Universiti Kebangsaan Malaysia.

Dr Ros Taplin, Centre for Development, Environment, and Policy, SOAS, University of London, UK.

Professor Alexandre Timoshenko, former Chief, Environmental Law Programme, Nairobi, UNEP.

Dr Charit Tingsabadh, Faculty of Economics, Chulalongkorn University, Thailand.

Dr John Todd, Eco-Energy Options, Tasmania, Australia.

Karma Tsering, Policy and Planning Division, Ministry of Agriculture and Forests, Bhutan.

Brandon Turner, United Nations Institute for Training and Research, Geneva, Switzerland.

Dr Akiko Ueda, formerly of UNDP office, Thimphu, Bhutan.

Dr Filemon A. Uriarte, Jr., National Academy of Science and Technology, Philippines.

Dr Rene van Berkel, United Nations Industrial Development Organization, Vienna, Austria.

Dr David Wadley, School of Earth and Environmental Sciences, University of Queensland, Australia.

Dr WANG Sen, Pacific Forestry Centre, Canadian Forest Service, Natural Resources Canada.

Dr Gullaya Wattayakorn, Department of Marine Science, Chulalongkorn University, Thailand.

Dr Jerome Weingart, Jerome Weingart and Associates, Consultancy Services for Sustainable Development, Arlington, USA.

Dr Tony Weir, Fenner School of Environment and Society, Australian National University, Australia (formerly of Pacific Centre for Environment and Sustainable Development, University of the South Pacific, Fiji).

Frederick Weston, Principal and Director, Policy, The Regulatory Assistance Project, USA.

Alastair Wilkinson, formerly of UNESCAP Pacific Office, Suva, Fiji.

Professor Stephen E. Williams, College of Science and Engineering, James Cook University, Australia.

Dr WU Liang, Institute of Geographic Science and Natural Resources Research, Chinese Academy of Sciences, Beijing, China.

Dr YAP Kioe Sheng, formerly of Poverty and Development Division, UNESCAP, Bangkok, Thailand.

Dr YAP Kok Seng, Academy of Sciences Malaysia.

Dr YE Qian, State Key Laboratory of Earth Surface Processes and Resource Ecology, Beijing Normal University, China.

Professor Bakhyt K. Yessekina, Green Academy, Scientific Research and Education Center, Astana, Kazakhstan.

Dr ZHAI Panmao, China Meteorological Administration, Beijing, China.

Professor ZHOU Jinxing, College of Soil and Water Conservation, Beijing Forestry University, China.

Editor's note

This book was first conceived during the Eminent Scientists Symposium on *Global Change and Sustainable Development* held on 24–25 March 2005 in Seoul, Republic of Korea. The symposium was a separate side event for the Fifth Ministerial Conference of Environment and Development (MCED-5) of the United Nations Economic and Social Commission for Asia and the Pacific (UNESCAP) that was held on 28–29 March 2005. I organized the symposium as the Regional Adviser on Environment and Sustainable Development of UNESCAP. Dr Mostafa Kamal Tolba, then at the age of 82, kindly travelled all the way from Geneva to chair the two-day symposium, which was attended by some 70 scientists from about 30 different countries, the majority from the Asia-Pacific region. It was a highly successful and memorable event.

The original idea was to publish the papers presented at the symposium. However, it took quite a few years for the draft book to be organized owing to a number of reasons, including my earlier than expected departure from UNESCAP at the end of 2007, which was followed by my work in Vietnam during the second half of 2008, and then Australia, Malaysia, and China. My frequent travels made the coordination of the draft book difficult, and it has taken much longer than anticipated.

Meanwhile, the issues related to global change and the progress in promoting sustainable development were rapidly advancing, including the adoption of the Sustainable Development Goals by the United Nations General Assembly in September 2015, to replace the Millennium Development Goals. Therefore, I decided to restructure the original draft of the book to include research on the most recent progress. Unfortunately, many former chapters in the draft book could not be updated. Only 17 chapters that have been updated remain in this volume, while 15 new chapters have been added. I wholeheartedly apologize to those authors whose chapters could not be included, as well as the authors who chose to spend time and effort to update their chapters, for the lengthy delay in getting this book published. It has been a long journey to reach this point.

This book presents 32 chapters contributed by more than 70 leading international experts on various aspects of sustainable development, from the perspectives of Asia and the Pacific. It contains two parts, each with 16 chapters.

Part I focuses on the theories and practices of sustainable development. It opens with the chapter by Amartya Sen, the Nobel Prize winner in Economics in 1998, titled *Asian identities*, which discusses the lasting impacts of diverse Asian traditions, beliefs, cultures, and civilizatons on the world. This is followed by the chapter by Mostafa Kamal Tolba, *On sustainable development* (Chapter 2), which traces the evolution of the concept of sustainable development from the publication of George Perkins Marsh's 1864 classic *Man and Nature*, and the chapter by John Peet on the scientific dilemma of sustainability (Chapter 3), in which he traverses some of the ground occupied by both the utility-based and metabolic models of economic activity, and shows that neither is of itself sufficient to address the entire spectrum of issues related to sustainable development. A chapter by Yi Chen and Boris Steipe (Chapter 4) discusses the respect and reward derived from the ecological aspects of the philosophy originating from the *Analects* of Confucius, who was an influential philosopher and teacher of ancient China more than 2,500 years ago. Rosita Dellios (Chapter 5) further discusses how the concept and practice of sustainable development can benefit humanity 'through an integration of traditions of thought culture' that 'entails cultivating the holistic approach found in Eastern philosophy and culture, while still valuing the analytical Western contribution', and this 'integrative or holistic model can work well for incorporating diverse approaches'. Two chapters, *Sustainable urbanism: Measuring long-term architectural merit* by Craig Langston (Chapter 6) and *Sustaining wooden architectural heritage* by Peter Brimblecombe and Mikiko Hayashi (Chapter 7), illustrate the practice of sustainability in architectural design, in modern urbanism, and in wooden architectural heritage, respectively.

Three national perspectives on the good practices of sustainable development are then presented. These are *Green development in China* (Chapter 8, by KE Shuifa, FENG Qiya, WANG Baojin, and QIAO Dan), *Bhutan's sustainable development initiatives in pursuit of Gross National Happiness* (Chapter 9, by

Jamba Gyeltshen), and *A different form of sustainable development in Thailand and Bhutan: Implementation of a sufficiency approach* (Chapter 10, by Ros Taplin, Sk Noim Uddin, Kanokwan Pibalsook, Karma Tshering, and Natarika Wayuparb Nitiphon). These examples illustrate the alternative approaches to sustainable development that value green development within the context of ecological civilization (China), Gross National Happiness (Bhutan), and Sufficiency Economy (Thailand) more than the ever-increasing economic growth in terms of Gross Domestic Product (GDP).

Bryant J. Allen and R. Michael Bourke highlight that the most important threats to the sustainability of food production and supply in Papua New Guinea (PNG) are high rates of population change, which threatens to bring about land degradation in shifting cultivation systems, an HIV/AIDS epidemic, and global climate change (Chapter 11). 'If global climate change increases rainfall, reduces diurnal temperature ranges or increases the frequency of El Niño-Southern Oscillation (ENSO) events, then food production will be adversely affected'. Dzulkifli Abdul Razak's chapter *Education for sustainable development: An overview of Asia-Pacific perspectives* (Chapter 12) emphasizes the importance of 'balancing' the spiritual and materialistic aspects of development, as observed within the diverse indigenous communities of the Asia-Pacific, such as in Japan, Indonesia, Malaysia, Thailand, and New Zealand, so as to further enhance, expand, and enrich the concept of sustainable development 'through real-life examples', and make it 'even more relevant and viable as a way of life'. I would even posit that it is more important to *integrate* rather than merely *balance* the delicate demands of various aspects (ecological, social, and economic) of sustainable development. The interests of each aspect should be thoroughly considered and then well integrated into the planning in the design and on the drawing board, rather than as an afterthought.

Bhishna Bajracharya and Isara Khanjanasthiti have developed a placemaking framework for social sustainability of master-planned communities (MPCs) and applied it to a case study from Australia (Chapter 13). It shows the importance of both physical design as well as the process of placemaking to build sustainable communities. The key concepts in placemaking include provision of places for social interaction, walkability, community governance, stakeholder engagement, legibility, safety, and sense of place. These ideas and the proposed framework are relevant for the sustainable development of MPCs in the Asia-Pacific region.

Anoja Wickramasinghe (Chapter 14) examines the interconnections between the large population, poverty, social inequity (including gender-based inequalities), and environmental degradation issues that threaten sustainable development in Asia. A new development paradigm, aided by supportive and guiding national policy instruments and commitments, is needed to address these issues, so as to enhance the benefits to vulnerable segments of the society and to geographically marginalized or deprived areas.

Two chapters present the international policies and international law related to climate change that have significant implications for sustainable development. Chapter 15, by Karen Hulme and David M. Ong, provides an overview in *The challenge of global climate change for international law*. The authors analyse the challenges that global climate change presented to certain basic concepts and principles of international law, such as the fundamental notion of statehood, and state responsibility and liability, as well as issues of sovereignty, human rights, and humanitarian intervention. Chapter 16, by Bernarditas de Castro-Muller, presents the perspectives of developing countries on *Sustainable development and climate change negotiations* that led to the adoption of the United Nations Framework Convention on Climate Change (UNFCCC) in 1992 and its Kyoto Protocol in 1997, and eventually the Paris Agreement in 2015. Bernarditas de Castro-Muller, a seasoned diplomat and a well-known negotiator, who unfortunately passed away in December 2018, had been a strong voice for defending developing countries' positions during negotiations on multilateral environmental agreements.

Part II highlights the challenges faced and the opportunities created by the implementation of sustainable development for poverty alleviation amid the changing ecological, social, cultural, economic, and political environment in the Asia-Pacific region. The topics discussed range from science, energy, gender equality and energy access, stratospheric ozone depletion, climate change, vulnerability, Sustainable Development Goals, land use, and biodiversity, to disaster risk reduction, all of which are relevant to achieving sustainable development.

Chapter 17, by Mostafa Kamal Tolba, discusses the important role of science, and emphasizes that policymaking should be based on the best available science, in addition to the consideration of many other social and economic factors. It is essential to maintain the ethics of scientific research, and the application of the precautionary principle should not be opposed to science-based regulation, but the two should be complementary. Chapter 18, by Helena Varkkey, discusses the transboundary haze issue in Southeast Asia originating largely from forest fires in Indonesia. The auhor observes that, in order to protect their tourism sectors during the haze events, national governments tend to under-represent the health risks of haze, both to citizens and tourists. In addition, ASEAN member states have yet to agree on a common regional air quality measurement system, with many continuing to use a system that under-represents health risks.

Three chapters assess energy and related issues. Chapter 19, by Keith Openshaw, examines energy consumption in general and biomass consumption in particular for all 69 countries in Asia and the Pacific (A-P). The author found that in 2015, the 20 low-income countries of South, Northeast, and Southeast Asia, containing 85% of the A-P population, consumed 57% of total primary energy and 97.5% of biomass energy. He argues that biomass is a promising fuel for sustainable development in Asia and the Pacific, and that the use of biomass for energy and other purposes could be increased substantially. Chapter 20, by Shoibal Chakravarty, T. S. Gopi Rethinaraj, and Dilip R. Ahuja, reviews the state of the coal-dominated electricity sector in India, examines the pathways to a more sustainable electricity sector, and analyses the challenges and benefits of increasing the share of renewables and nuclear power in India's electricity system. Chapter 21, by Anoja Wickramasinghe, assesses gender inequality and women's limited access to energy, which are barriers to maximizing development effectiveness in the South Asia Association for Regional Cooperation (SAARC) region, and suggests ways to overcome these barriers.

Chapter 22, by Jan C. van der Leun and Janet F. Bornman, discusses the interactions of the stratospheric ozone layer with the rapid climate change, especially from the viewpoint of the consequences for living organisms, and the involvement of living organisms in the interactions. Chapter 23, by R. James Ferguson, discusses the risks and prospects of the political challenge of linking the implementation of the Sustainable Development Goals (SDGs) (2015-2030) and the Paris Agreement (2015). The author points out that uneven implementation of these two agendas could slow down their progress 'if collective action on emission targets and related funding wavers'. A pluralist, multi-actor approach is needed to reassure developing countries of the benefits of sustaining emissions reduction alongside balanced implementation of the SDGs and continued use of resilient, 'low-emission' adaptation strategies. Chapter 24, by Nguyen Huu Ninh, Luong Quang Huy, Philip Michael Kelly, and Phan Toan, focuses on the social vulnerability to climate change in the nations of the Lower Mekong (Cambodia, Lao PDR, and Vietnam). Social vulnerability 'is a function of the social conditions and historical circumstances that put people at risk'. The authors highlight that 'poverty is the largest barrier to developing the capacity to cope and adapt effectively with change'. Chapter 25, by Shababa Haque, Naznin Nasir, M. Feisal Rahman, and Saleemul Huq, discusses the effects of climate change and the lack of funding mechanisms for implementing necessary actions as the main barriers for achieving the various targets of Sustainable Development Goals 2030 in Bangladesh, a low-lying country that is most vulnerable to sea-level rise and extreme climatic events. Consequently, it is important to implement national plans and policies that incorporate SDG targets as well as climate action with adequate national and international financial resources. Chapter 26, by Safdar Ullah Khan, Zafar Manzoor,

Gulasekaran Rajaguru, and Shabib Haider Syed, discusses sustainable development in Pakistan. The authors highlight Pakistan's vulnerabilities to a number of current environmental, social, economic, governance, and institutional issues, which are used as indicators directly and indirectly related to the achievement of the Sustainable Development Goals 2030. The findings reveal important insights into the interconnectedness of various indicators, which may be useful in guiding appropriate policy actions to successfully achieve the objectives of sustainable development in Pakistan.

Four chapters focus on land-use change and biodiversity. Chapter 27, by Gernot Brodnig, examines the challenges emerging from two distinct but related global threats: climate change and invasive alien species. It assesses the respective impacts of these drivers on ecosystems and biodiversity, and highlights the importance of adopting perspectives over a longer time and at larger spatial scales, as well as the need to look beyond the boundaries of conservation areas to address these challenges. Chapter 28, by Dietrich Schmidt-Vogt, provides an overview on the causes of land-use change and biodiversity losses in Monsoon Asia, and highlights that deforestation and forest degradation are considered to be the most detrimental processes of land-use and land-cover change that lead to biodiversity losses. Thus, it is important to create in the countries of Monsoon Asia, through education, awareness of the value of biodiversity, and to help generate the political will to promote and support land use that is compatible with the aims of biodiversity conservation. Chapter 29, by Andrew N. Gillison, Amirtharaj C. Williams, Gopala Areendran, and Rajeev L. Semwal, reports a low-cost, high-return, and readily transferable methodology that utilizes both ground-based and remotely sensed data to assess the linkages between land use and biodiversity that has been successfully used in a case study from the Eastern Himalayas. The low-cost methodology has wider implications for assessing the impact of global change on biodiversity. Chapter 30, by Marie-Isabell Lenz, Stephen Galvin, Gunnar Keppel, Sunil Gopaul, Matthias Kowasch, Michael J. Dyer, Dick Watling, Sherri Lodhar, Geon C. Hanson, Stefan Erasmi, and Hans Juergen Boehmer, highlights the problem of biological invasive alien species that threaten sustainability in a small island developing state in the tropical South Pacific. The authors illustrate this problem with two relatively recent biological invaders in Fiji – the ivory cane palm (*Pinanga coronata*) and the green iguana (*Iguana iguana*), and use these examples to examine the potential consequences of continuing inaction, despite awareness in relevant government departments, for native forest biodiversity and human livelihoods. They highlight the desperate need for on-the-ground action to control, eradicate, and prevent invasive alien species.

The final two chapters deal with disaster risk reduction and disaster risk management. Chapter 31, by Sálvano Briceño, reviews the approach to the response to the Indian Ocean tsunami that occurred on 26 December 2004, which, according to the UN Office for the Coordination of Humanitarian Affairs (OCHA), killed 230,000 people across a number of countries, with Indonesia, Thailand, Sri Lanka, India, and the Maldives sustaining massive damage. The author highlights the urgent need to improve preparedness and reduce risks from future disasters, including early warning and attempts to integrate disaster risk reduction into reconstruction. Chapter 32, by Tun Lwin and Swan Yee Tun Lwin, describes the tragic event of Cyclone Nargis that struck Myanmar on 2 May 2008 and left approximately 84,500 people dead and almost 54,000 people missing. Certainly, lessons can be learned from both tragic events in terms of developing more systematic disaster risk reduction strategies and capabilities for disaster-prone countries.

All the above chapters and the issues discussed in them have profound implications for the implementation of sustainable development in the region. I hope that the book will serve as a useful reference for all researchers and policy makers who have an interest in pursuing sustainable development under the continuing influence of global change within the context of Asia and the Pacific.

I would like to express my special appreciation and gratitude to the authors of this book. Without their persistent effort, patience, dedication, and great understanding, the completion of this book would have been impossible. I would also like to acknowledge the kind assistance provided by the peer reviewers, who voluntarily spent their time and effort to ensure the quality of each chapter that has been accepted for publication in this volume. Many authors also kindly served as peer reviewers.

I am most grateful for the forewords by Dr Mostafa Kamal Tolba, Sir Toke Tufukia Talagi, Dr Qin Dahe, Dr Sálvano Briceño, and Dr Mick Kelly.

This book is dedicated to my mentor, the late Dr Mostafa Kamal Tolba, former Executive Director of the United Nations Environment Programme (UNEP) (1975–1992), one of the great pioneers in promoting sustainable development throughout his career. Dr Tolba passed away on 28 March 2016 at the age of 93. I am most grateful to have contributions from three of Dr Tolba's former colleagues, Ambassador Mikko Pyhälä, Dr Sálvano Briceño, and Naigzy Gebremedhin, in the section *Remembering Dr Mostafa Kamal Tolba*. They have added their memories and perspectives to join the numerous international tributes that had already been written about Dr Tolba after his passing in 2016.

During the preparation and publication of this book, Dr Mostafa Kamal Tolba, Professor Jan van der Leun, Dr Kanokwan Pibalsook, Ms Bernarditas de Castro-Muller,

Dr Tun Lwin, and Sir Toke Tufukia Talagi unfortunately passed away. I deeply regret that they could not see the publication of this book, to which they made valuable contributions. I was most honoured to have had opportunities to work with Dr Tolba, Professor van der Leun, Ms de Castro-Muller, and Dr Tun Lwin. Dr Tolba was Executive Director of UNEP when I joined the Ozone Secretariat of UNEP as a scientist in 1991. Professor van der Leun co-chaired UNEP's Environmental Effects Assessment Panel (EEAP), established in 1988 under the Montreal Protocol on Substances that Deplete the Ozone Layer, when I assisted the Ozone Secretariat in serving the EEAP in 1991–1992. As a strong voice for developing countries, Ms de Castro-Muller's contribution in the negotiations of the United Nations Framework Convention on Climate Change (UNFCCC) were most significant. She and I were resource persons for a number of training courses in climate change negotiations, including those for Vietnam, Lao PDR, Timor-Leste, and Indonesia. I first met and worked with Dr Tun Lwin in 2005 when he was Director-General of the Department of Meteorology and Hydrology of Myanmar. I vividly recall how he desperately tried to provide early warning for the incoming Cyclone Nargis that struck the coastal areas of Myanmar on 2 May 2008. I met with Hon. Talagi on a few occasions, including my visits to Niue in 1997 and 2005. Hon. Talagi also participated in the Eminent Scientists Symposium that I organized in Seoul in 2005,

I wish to thank the book's sponsors: the Asia-Pacific Network (APN) for Global Change Research; China Meteorological Administration (CMA); United Nations Development Programme (UNDP) Regional Office for Asia and the Pacific; United Nations Disaster Risk Reduction (UNDRR) (formerly United Nations International Strategy for Disaster Reduction, UNISDR); and Tiempo.

After serving more than six years as the Regional Adviser on Environment and Sustainable Development at UNESCAP, I left in December 2007. In the later part of 2008, I spent five months in Hanoi, Vietnam, as an International Expert in the Natural Disaster Mitigation Partnership project located in the Ministry of Agriculture and Rural Development, a post funded by the UNDP-Vietnam. I returned to academia in January 2009, and became a visiting and adjunct professor at Bond University in Australia (2009–2018). I was appointed as the first Yayasan Sime Darby Chair in Climate Change, Universiti Kebangsaan Malaysia (National University of Malaysia) (2011–2013); Senior Visiting Scientist at the Institute of Geographic Sciences and Natural Resources, Chinese Academy of Sciences, Beijing (2011); and Visiting Scientist at the Institute of Desertification Studies, Beijing (2013, 2015). I was an International Adviser for the *Climate Change Adaptation Initiative* project, Mekong

River Commission Secretariat, Vientiane, Lao PDR (2010). I have also been a freelance consultant.

In August 2017, I was invited to participate in a project titled *Sustainable and Climate-Resilient Land Management in the Western Region, China*, funded by the Asian Development Bank and Global Environment Facility. Through this project, I had the honour of meeting many technical experts in various fields and visiting many demonstration sites in China (i.e., Inner Mongolia, Shaanxi, Gansu, Qinghai, and Sichuan), and I met many new colleagues and friends who warmly welcomed my participation in the project, which was completed in December 2018.

I would like to take this opportunity to express my sincere thanks to all the colleagues and friends whom I have met and worked with in the past 15 years. They have greatly enriched my professional and academic life. Special thanks and appreciation go to the following people: Dr John Todd, former Associate Professor of the University of Tasmania, Australia; Dr Mick Kelly, Tanelorn Associates, New Zealand; Dr Mohd Nor Salleh, Academy of Sciences Malaysia; Dr Rezaul Karim, former Coordinator, Asia Unit, United Nations Convention to Combat Desertification (UNCCD) secretariat, Bonn, Germany; Rae Kwon Chung and Siva Thampi, both former directors, Division of Environment and Sustainable Development, UNESCAP; the late Chow Kok Kee, former Director-General of the Malaysian Meteorological Department; Tan Meng Leng, former Director-General of the Department of Environment, Malaysia; Nguyen Ngoc Ly, Director, Centre for Environment and Community Research (CECR), Hanoi, Vietnam; Nguyen Mong Cuong, Director, Research Centre for Climate Change and Sustainable Development, Hanoi, Vietnam; Nguyen Khac Hieu, former Deputy Director-General, Department of Climate Change, Ministry of Natural Resources and Environment, Vietnam; Professor Ros Taplin, former Director, Environmental Management Programme, School of Sustainable Development, Bond University, Australia; the late Dr Allen Clark of the East-West Center, Hawaii, USA; Dr Qin Dahe, former Adminstrator,

China Meteorological Administration; Dr Jian Liu, former Director of the International Ecosystem Management Partnership (IEMP), Chinese Academy of Sciences; Professor Lu Qi, Director of the Institute of Desertification Studies, Beijing; Professor Fredolin Tangang and Professor Mohd Talib Latif, Faculty of Science and Technology, Universiti Kebangsaan Malaysia; Yang Youlin, former Regional Coordinator of the UNCCD secretariat for Asia, Bangkok, Thailand; Dr Ye Bing and Dr Meng Yongqing, Research Institute of Forestry Policy and Information, Chinese Academy of Forestry; Professor Li Junqing of Beijing Forestry University; Dr Victor R. Squires, International Dryland Management Consultant, Australia; Dr Michael H. Glantz, Director, The Consortium for Capacity Building, University of Colorado, USA; Dr Natchanun Leepipatpiboon, former Assistant Professor, Department of Chemistry, Chulalongkorn University, Thailand; Dr Tan Geok Chin, National Institute of Education, Singapore; Professor Peter Brimblecombe, Department of Marine Environment and Engineering, National Sun Yat-Sen University, Kaohsiung, Taiwan; my forner colleagues at Bond University, especially Dr Lynne Armitage, Dr Bhishna Bajracharya, Professor Shelley Burgin, Dr Rosita Dellios, Dr R. James Ferguson, Professor Craig Langston, Dr Daryl McPhee, and Dr Daniel O'Hare; and Kai Yin Low of University of Essex, UK, as well as Karma Thinley of Bhutan, for their persistent support and encouragement.

I must also express my gratitude to a number of people: Rick Whisenand and Ling Si Low for assisting in proofreading; Wang Chuyue for assisting in compiling the list of peer reviewers and acronyms and abbreviations of some chapters. Last but not least, I am grateful to Matt Lloyd, Senior Executive Editor of Cambridge University Press (CUP), for his great patience and understanding in overseeing the completion of this book over the past 10 years; to Sarah Lambert, Editorial Assistant; Esther Miguéliz Obanos, Senior Content Manager; Elle Ferns, Content Manager; and to Shalini Bisi, Administrative Assistant of CUP, for providing their efficient and effective assistance in getting this book published.

Foreword by Mostafa Kamal Tolba

Editor's note: This Foreword was written by Dr Mostafa Kamal Tolba when I was preparing an earlier version of the book that was not completed. It remains valid even though new chapters have been added in this version.

Our understanding of the concept of sustainable development is still evolving, even to this day. The concept itself was adopted universally at the Earth Summit in 1992 at Rio de Janeiro. However, the changing global conditions, be they economic, social, or environmental, are complicating the premises of sustainable development. This book gives insight into the impacts of various aspects of global change – such as stratospheric ozone depletion, climate change, biodiversity, and land-use change – on sustainable development. The book further includes another group of outstanding chapters on the relationships between environment and development, environment and economic development planning, and risk management. All these chapters are written by a host of very distinguished authorities, essentially from the Asia-Pacific region, which is endowed with a very rich group of talented scientists.

This is not the first time that Pak Sum Low has stuck his neck out to edit such a varied group of topics, knitting all of them into a fabric that brings forward the myriad complex issues of global change impact on sustainable development. The examples stressed in the book are from the Asia-Pacific region. However, the material in all of the chapters applies equally to the world at large.

The book is a solid piece of work that should constitute a basic reference source in the library of any person concerned with the issues of sustainable development: not only scientists, economists, and other social scientists but, more importantly, the decision makers.

Mostafa Kamal Tolba
International Centre for Environment and Development
Cairo, Egypt

Foreword by Toke Tufukia Talagi

Editor's note: Everyone who knew Sir Toke Tufukia Talagi was saddened to hear that he had passed away on 15 July 2020. He was the Premier of Niue, a small island state in the Pacific, from June 2008 to June 2020. As a strong voice advocating that developed countries ought to have a greater ambition for undertaking emissions reduction, as well as providing the necessary finance to help small island developing states with adaptation to climate change, he contributed this Foreword with great enthusiasm.

It has become an established fact that globalization in its many forms impacts the small Pacific states much more than the countries that created these globalized phenomena.

It is no different in terms of the global impacts of changes to our climate and the worldwide environmental changes that have taken place over the past few decades. The small island states in the Pacific have been the first to note and experience the rising sea levels, the erosion of their fragile islets, and the major impacts that the climate has had on their dwellings, ecosystems, agriculture, water and sanitation, and fragile economies. These adverse impacts have significant implications for sustainable development of the small island states.

The threat to their sovereignty is very real and poses international legal questions that are not as easily answered as some may think, by the supposed option of relocation to somewhere else. Aside from the legal status of the islands they would be vacating, it also raises questions as to the status the people would be granted in the places they may be relocated to. It is no wonder that they are resisting any pressure to relocate, seeking answers instead that will result in a global reduction in the factors that have caused the problem, as an initial response, and secondly compelling the world to look at practical solutions and adaptations.

It is the view of the small island states that even though there is now widespread acceptance of the fact of climate change and its causes, there is still not the same urgency of response, in comparison with the current economic, financial, and social crises in the world. The fact that the changes in climatic conditions will one day supersede all else seems ironic, and world leaders are urged to ensure that the changes needed to reduce the factors worsening climate changes are dealt with quickly and with alacrity.

Much of the work so far has been involved with measuring the levels of change and the impacts at local, regional, and international levels. The adaptation scientific studies conducted in the areas of production and changes required in the commercial and non-commercial fields are just starting to show some positive results. Many agree that this will offer opportunities for a new sector of the economic and commercial business fields. It would be a timely and appropriate measure to offer these changes in the economic and financial stimulus packages that are currently being mooted, thereby creating a win-win situation for everyone.

The adaptation measures needed to assist the small island states have been very slow and cumbersome. Funds have been allocated and pledged, but the process for approvals leaves a lot to be desired. The solutions have also not been as clearly defined as desired.

That action is urgent and widely needed must be realized and implementation targeted quickly to help the small island states now, not at some distant time in the future when all is too late.

After many years of international negotiations, the Paris Agreement was finally adopted in 2015. This Agreement aims to limit the increase in the global average temperature to 'well below 2°C' and even to 1.5°C above pre-industrial levels. However, even with the current 1.0°C increase, the Pacific small island states are already feeling the heat. Scientists have projected that the achievement of 2°C and 1.5°C targets will remain a great challenge. Therefore, more political will and decisive actions to ambitiously reduce the emissions of greenhouse gases are urgently needed.

However, we will never be able to make any real changes unless or until humanity's greed at all levels is managed so that we all realize, as our ancestors realized when they lived on these islands, that everything must be allowed to sustain itself and that our harvests must be managed to ensure long-term use and survival.

This is what humans must now learn if we are to survive the most important challenge in our time. This publication has helped with some of the answers and demonstrates that more needs to be done if we are all to make a significant difference.

To survive, we must mitigate and adapt. But to do so, we must also transcend our complacency and arrogance and put an end to our international political failure to make decisions in our time for the good of everyone.

Hon. Sir Toke Tufukia Talagi KNZM
Premier of Niue (June 2008–June 2020), and Chair of Pacific Island Forum 2009

Foreword by Qin Dahe

Over the past century, there have been major climate and environmental changes that can be attributed to global warming. The magnitude of these changes has gone beyond the range of natural variability and they are posing a major threat to sustainable development and the survival of humankind. Climate change is not only an environmental concern, but also a major development issue. It has become an imminent challenge encountered by all human beings in the world.

According to the latest findings of the IPCC Working Group I contribution to the Fifth Assessment Report (AR5), there has been a remarkable increase in global average surface temperature, continuous sea-level rise, and steady shrinkage of snow cover in most areas of the Northern Hemisphere, all indicating a trend of global warming. Over the past century (1880–2012), the mean global combined land and ocean surface temperature has increased by an average of 0.85 [0.65–1.06]°C. The average temperatures in the Northern Hemisphere during the second half of the 20th century were very likely higher than during any 50-year period in the last 500 years, and likely the highest in at least the past 1,300 years.

Climate change has had severe impacts on the climate and environment in the Asia-Pacific region, and it has brought challenges to the region's development. As indicated by the IPCC Working Group II contribution to the Fifth Assessment Report, major rivers and some large delta areas in Asia would most likely be under the threat of more severe consequences of climate change, for example, decrease of fresh water resources, increased risks of floods, reduction of agricultural productivity, increased hindrances due to higher dependency of economic development on natural resources and the environment, and increased exposure to diseases related to climate warming. A large number of developing countries are located along the circum-Pacific earthquake belt and within the Asian monsoon areas, yet they have relatively low capabilities for predicting and preventing disasters, such as earthquakes, typhoons, dust storms, floods, and droughts. For these reasons, proper responses to climate and environmental change are essential for achieving harmony between human beings and physical nature, and for sustainable development of humankind in this region.

In this book, more than 70 scientists and experts address the challenging issues related to sustainable development facing the Asia-Pacific region, including scientific and policy aspects, as well as challenges and good practices. I believe it will definitely improve our understanding and facilitate broader and deeper research studies in the future.

Qin Dahe
Academician, Chinese Academy of Sciences,
China Meteorological Administration, Beijing, China

Foreword by Sálvano Briceño

At a time when the frequency and severity of climate-related disasters herald the consequences of an increasingly warmer and urbanized planet, the need to see disaster risk reduction as a core development concern has never been so important for preventing needless death and destruction. There is an urgent need to bring disaster risk reduction and adaptation to climate change into mainstream policy and planning, and to strongly develop a culture of prevention. This is important for all countries but particularly for the developing countries in the Asia-Pacific region, as the developing world is predicted to bear the brunt of climate change-related catastrophe in the coming years, as well as the human cost of other disasters.

We are experiencing the effects of a building global crisis or tipping point. But with crisis comes opportunity for political and cultural change. The unprecedented devastation of the Indian Ocean tsunami that took place on Boxing Day 2004, and the Tohoku-Japan earthquake, tsunami, and nuclear radiation catastrophe of March 2011 shone a global political spotlight on the need for more sustainable and better-coordinated risk reduction (prevention, mitigation, and preparedness) strategies in the wake of disasters triggered by natural hazards that would carry on long after media attention faded.

Seizing on the political will to act, the second United Nations World Conference on Disaster Reduction (WCDR) held in Kobe, Hyogo, Japan in January 2005 adopted the *Hyogo Framework for Action 2005–2015: Building the Resilience of Nations and Communities to Disasters*, laying out a 10-year plan to make disaster risk reduction an essential component of development policies, plans, and programmes. In 2015, the third World Conference on Disaster Risk Reduction adopted the Sendai Framework for Disaster Risk Reduction 2015–2030, providing a 15-year plan to follow up on the Hyogo Framework, making disaster risk reduction an even higher priority in the international policy agenda and guiding work at regional, national, and local levels.

While the Indian Ocean and Japanese tsunamis were touched off by massive undersea earthquakes, climate-related catastrophes have held the world's attention over the following years.

Intensifying hurricane and typhoon seasons, floods, wildland fires, and drought meant that disaster risk reduction issues maintained their urgency. Stakeholders across the board in areas prone to natural hazards began to realize that they had to become more proactive in identifying, assessing, and reducing disaster risks.

The emerging focus on reducing risk rather than just getting prepared to respond to hazards offers a valuable opportunity for further positive change and substantive contributions to building various aspects of sustainable development. Disasters have the potential to be politically neutral, and to unify parties with conflicting priorities – even parties at war. This can create space for positive action in the most fraught of circumstances.

To fully take advantage of those openings and alliances, we must continue to strengthen linkages across the development agendas. The Hyogo Framework affirms that '[s]ustainable development, poverty reduction, good governance and disaster risk reduction are mutually supportive objectives'. For the rest of the development communities, disaster risk reduction's potential as a unifier can help create space for other closely related development issues.

Disasters resulting from vulnerability to natural hazards exert an enormous toll on development. In doing so, they pose a significant threat to prospects for achieving the Sustainable Development Goals and the goals outlined in the Sendai Framework for Disaster Risk Reduction, as well as those of the Paris Agreement on Climate Change and the New Urban Agenda.

The desired resilience of nations to disasters can be possible only when communities develop their capacities to reduce risk and vulnerability to natural hazards and the multiple risks that can derive from them.

The United Nations Office for Disaster Risk Reduction (UNDRR) (formerly United Nations International Strategy for Disaster Reduction (UNISDR)), which has the global mandate for coordinating disaster risk reduction in line with the Sendai Framework, attaches great importance to national, local, and community-based risk reduction initiatives. UNDRR has increased its efforts in strengthening the exchange of information, experience, and knowledge on risk reduction, now available on the PreventionWeb website.

I am pleased to welcome this publication, *Sustainable Development: Asia-Pacific Perspectives*, which should greatly contribute to increasing understanding and knowledge of individuals and organizations on the challenges of sustainable development requiring a risk reduction approach, with a long-term perspective and team-oriented efforts at all levels.

Sálvano Briceño
Former Director, UNISDR (2001–2011) and former Chair, Science Committee, IRDR programme of ICSU/ISSC/UNISDR <www.irdrinternational.org>

Foreword by Mick Kelly

Just as globalization has presented humanity with fresh challenges and opportunities, so global environmental change raises major questions about the sustainability of the development process. Indeed, given the tortuous progress of the climate negotiations, the global warming issue is also raising questions about the capacity of our politicians and political systems to guide us through these testing times. If we are to find sustainable ways forward, we must set aside the worn paradigms of the past and seek diverse perspectives, learning from as wide a range of experience as possible.

I am delighted, therefore, that the Tiempo Programme, with its commitment to global dialogue, has been able to support publication of this book. *Sustainable Development: Asia-Pacific Perspectives* provides a timely view from the Asia-Pacific region, thought-provoking and inspiring in its wealth of facts, ideas, and recommendations. While political progress may be frustratingly slow, it is clear from the examples given in the following pages that there are, regardless, people who are moving forward towards a more sustainable future.

Mick Kelly
Founding Editor, Tiempo

Environmental keystones: Remembering Dr Mostafa Kamal Tolba

MIKKO PYHÄLÄ

The decade from 1985 to 1995 was crucial in the formation of the most important institutions and conventions for the environmental governance of the globe. Also, for the first time, nations and governments became fully aware of the mortal danger of potential environmental collapse with the discovery of the 'ozone hole'. One could say that there was partial awareness of impending climate change and looming loss of biodiversity. Initially, short-term political expediency gave much importance to establishing national ministries of environment and funding them, as well as the United Nations Environment Programme (UNEP), but soon their high profile was diluted, and funding decreased, as did the authority of these ministries and of UNEP itself.

ENVIRONMENTAL GROUNDWORK

UNEP had been established in 1974 after the United Nations Conference on Human Environment, which was held in Stockholm in 1972. That conference had been inspired by Indira Gandhi, Prime Minister of India, and Pierre Trudeau, Prime Minister of Canada, and was chaired by Maurice Strong of Canada. There was much debate about whether UNEP should graduate into an environment agency, but arguments of 'environment as a cross-cutting issue' prevailed over counterarguments that an independent agency would have much more teeth. In the early years of the 21st century, after the approval of the Millennium Development Goals by the United Nations General Assembly in 2000, sustainable development was seen as the responsibility of all, and all tried to explain that what they were already doing was sustainable.

UNEP's role was somewhat overshadowed by the UN Commission for Sustainable Development, which was established in 1992, and national ministries of environment were scaled down by governments struggling with the economic straightjacket of unmanaged globalization. It was only in 2015, when environmental imperatives emerged upfront in an integrated manner, that the General Assembly adopted the Sustainable Development Goals, later enmeshed with Agenda 2030.

The adoption of the Vienna Convention for the Protection of the Ozone Layer in 1985 was the first time countries adopted a universally shared environmental obligation. That convention started to be implemented through the Montreal Protocol on Substances that Deplete the Ozone Layer (1987) and the London Agreement on the Financing of that Protocol (1990).

The Intergovernmental Panel on Climate Change (IPCC) was established in 1988 upon an initiative by UNEP and the World Meteorological Organization (WMO). It was only in its second assessment report in 1995 when developing countries' scientists came fully on board, thanks to financing from the Global Environment Facility (GEF), which had been created by UNEP, the World Bank, and UNDP in 1991, and which received its proper legal format only in 1994.

Environmental sustainability was brought on a par with social development, already suggested by Indira Gandhi in Stockholm, but largely based on the outstanding report *Our Common Future* of 1987 by the World Commission on Environment and Development chaired by Gro Harlem Brundtland, former Prime Minister of Norway. The most important vehicles of this were Agenda 21 and the Rio Declaration on Environment and Development, both of which emanated from the Rio de Janeiro Earth Summit of 1992, chaired by Maurice Strong with Dr Tolba at his side. Important global environmental conventions were signed – the United Nations Framework Convention on Climate Change and the Convention on Biological Diversity – and the Statement of Forest Principles was approved. Subsequently, the United Nations Convention to Combat Desertification was adopted in 1994.

DR TOLBA AS *PRIMUS MOTOR*

I limit myself in this note to my personal experience of working with Dr Tolba, whose life achievements are well covered in other contributions.

Dr Tolba in a way was the *primus motor* for the entire set of key global environmental conventions and for putting the environment on a par with economic and social development. He was skilful in bringing consensus behind closed doors with only the heads of delegations inside with him, for the final compromises. His great acumen was in recognizing scientific talent, and he excelled in formulating UNEP's messages on environmental priorities.

Perhaps the finest monument to Dr Tolba is the creation of the Vienna Convention and the Montreal Protocol system for the protection of the ozone layer, which has brought about the most tangible results of any environmental convention. Dr Tolba also had a decisive influence on the creation of the IPCC in 1988, which started working under the auspices of WMO, and which received the Nobel Peace Prize in 2007, jointly with Al Gore. Among Dr Tolba's significant achievements was the creation or facilitation of secretariats for the global environmental conventions, creation of a set of Regional Seas Conventions, launching the *Global 500*, the UN environmental prize, which received huge publicity, and the creation of a number of solid science-based global report series, as well as UNEP's environmental photography archives, open to all.

Dr Tolba had the stature and scientific knowledge to converse, particularly in Rio, with world leaders on a level footing, which some of his successors may not have managed to do as eloquently. However, being located in a developing country was a challenge that handicapped UNEP in the eyes of many key players in international environmental policies, and certainly played against UNEP's top expertise being easily recruited, or provided at key fora.

One fine example of Dr Tolba's wisdom in international environmental policies was that, when he no longer was the first actor, workable decisions among governments continued being made along lines which he had originally envisaged in climate, biodiversity, and desertification. In spite of trying very hard, Dr Tolba was not able to get sufficient obligations baked into these three conventions. Many of the ideas included in Agenda 2030, however, originated in Dr Tolba's speeches and writings.

Dr Tolba retired from his post in 1992. But he did not retire from the environment; on the contrary, he became quite active in giving direction to the UN Sustainable Development Commission as head of the Egyptian Delegation at its meetings.

DR TOLBA AND FINLAND

Finland established a Ministry of Environment in 1983, and it was clear that Finland wanted to work closely with UNEP. Finland and other Nordic countries were the largest providers of voluntary contributions to UNEP, and a lively dialogue flew in the axis of Helsinki-Nairobi as long as Dr Tolba was the head of UNEP.

In the creation of the Vienna Convention and the Montreal Protocol, Finland played a major role, as Dr Tolba had requested. When the First Meeting of the Parties to the Montreal Protocol was held in Helsinki in April 1989, it was decided to establish a Preparatory Committee for the Financial System for Phasing Out Ozone Depleting Substances. Finland's Ambassador Ilkka Ristimäki was elected as chair of that committee, and the committee finalized its work in one year, culminating in the London Conference in 1990, which adopted unanimously the final document, with an encouraging speech by Prime Minister Margaret Thatcher.

How was it possible to reach unanimity in only one year when harmonizing conflicting views and interests often had taken many years of negotiations? To begin with, at the Helsinki Meeting of the Montreal Protocol in April 1989, the Ministers of Environment of China (Wang Yuqing, Deputy Administrator of NEPA), Finland (Kaj Bärlund), India (Z. R. Ansari), and the Netherlands (Ed Nijpels) had decided to make an effort for a joint platform in preparing the financing system for the Montreal Protocol. That kind of a procedure in international negotiations has been a rare occurrence, at best.

Soon after the Helsinki Conference of the Parties, Finland convened a meeting in Geneva for representatives of the four countries, and a short text was agreed upon. Ambassador Ristimäki then started conversations in Nairobi with the clear-headed Ambassador of Mexico, Juan Antonio López Mateos, that country holding the presidency of the Group of 77, consisting of developing countries. With some nudging from China and India, 'G-77 and China' adopted the Geneva platform. After that, with the main guidelines already widely accepted, negotiations concentrated on the nuts and bolts of technical aspects and proceeded very well.

The last fence to cross was in London, when the World Bank was lobbying hard for the Global Environment Facility (which had not been formally established) to become the financial mechanism. With Ristimäki's careful navigation, the London Conference agreed on an intergovernmental Secretariat for the Financing Mechanism to be based in Montreal, the establishment of which was carried out by Finland. The Group of 77 would not have agreed to the GEF here because it did not exist yet. Being based in Nairobi, Ristimäki worked closely with Dr Tolba and got his enthusiastic support for this process. In London, India's representative was Minister Maneka Gandhi, and the Netherlands was represented by Minister Hans Alders.

Ristimäki was supported in this process by Ms Aira Kalela, a high-ranking official at the Ministry of the Environment, Professor Antti Kulmala from the Finnish Meteorological Institute (both of them were key negotiators), and myself from the Ministry for Foreign Affairs as spokesman for Finland in the Plenary. Our excellent, memorable counterparts included above all Madhava Sharma, Additional Secretary at the Ministry of Environment of India, who later became head of the Ozone Secretariat at UNEP, and the young lawyer-diplomat Ms Song Li at the Foreign Ministry of China, who later joined the United Nations and ended up in a high position at the World Bank. Naturally, we also became close personal friends.

WORKING WITH DR TOLBA

My personal relationship with Dr Tolba was truly enriching, and it was he who pushed for my recruitment as Chief, Clearing-house Unit, after he got to know me at the meeting of the Montreal Protocol in Helsinki. During a few consultancy weeks in 1990 in Nairobi, I learned that he wanted me to play a key role as UNEP's spearhead in the creation of the Global Environment Facility (GEF).

I started as a staff member on 1 January 1991, and already on the first working day, on 2 January, I was representing UNEP in New York in a working meeting between UNDP, the World Bank, and UNEP, to start planning the GEF operations. I was flanked by Dr Robert Watson, NASA's leading expert on strato-spheric ozone depletion, already then envisaged by Dr Tolba as the person who should lead the scientific advisory process to the GEF. I accompanied Dr Tolba to a meeting in early 1991 at the World Bank headquarters in Washington, DC, when he signed the founding declaration of the GEF with Barber Conable, President of IBRD, and Theodore Draper, Administrator of UNDP. While the GEF idea was precooked at the World Bank, Dr Tolba certainly defended environmentally sound parameters in preparation for that meeting, and at the meeting itself.

Dr Tolba was strong in giving detailed feedback on staff reports and initiatives, at least my own ones, but he may have overestimated the capacity of UNEP regular staff to contribute to the GEF. He himself was up to date with the most modern technological means and policies of communication, but had difficulty making UNEP as an organization do the same. Dr Tolba established a completely new GEF Unit, and I was to be its Chief, in addition to the work for which I had been recruited. Quickly I had to recruit staff for the GEF Unit, and had to rely much on (very) short-term consultants.

Dr Pak Sum Low was one key member of my team, and the two of us, with Dr Ramachandran from WMO, prepared the GEF funding document for developing country participation in the IPCC process. Our proposal was originally opposed by the World Bank, but support from UNDP and Dr Watson, who had become Chair of the Scientific and Technical Advisory Panel

(STAP) of the GEF, and Chair of IPCC, helped to get it approved. This financing made it possible for developing country scientists to fully take part in the IPCC process for the Second Assessment Report (1995). Without the full participation of developing country scientists, IPCC reports would have been lacking in political acceptance, and could also have been short on scientific support.

Dr Tolba gave me much independence, but when scientific issues started to cause friction with the institutional interests of other partners, it became customary for UNEP to have a senior staff member to accompany me (as an 'overcoat'), while I still was responsible for the statements and positions, with my own professional support staff.

An early success for Dr Tolba, UNEP and STAP were to influence the World Bank so that they stopped trying to leverage regular lending by the GEF add-ons, a practice which would not have been sustainable. Had Tolba remained at UNEP, this body might have had a stronger environmentally normative profile in the GEF, instead of being somewhat marginalized by the World Bank. However, the World Bank eventually 'greened' quite a bit, perhaps also thanks to their GEF experience, with its science-based priorities and portfolio reviews, and Dr Watson becoming Director of the Environment Department.

When Dr Tolba left UNEP in 1992, I truly was lost, feeling that I no longer had high-level support in defending the scientific integrity of the GEF process. Dr Tolba had always been quick to understand complex scientific, multidisciplinary issues, with his background as Under-Secretary of Higher Education in Egypt. It was a clever choice by Dr Tolba to promote Dr Robert Watson to head STAP of the GEF, which the United States readily accepted, and eventually Dr Watson was called by President Bill Clinton to become his Science and Technology Adviser and had to leave STAP. The Asian members in the first STAP were Dr Yingzhong Lu, a nuclear scientist from China; Dr Amulya J. K. Reddy, an energy expert from India; Dr Edgardo Gomez, a marine biologist from the Philippines; and Dr Michio Hashimoto, an environmental policy expert from Japan. It was a great privilege to work closely with Dr Tolba in setting up STAP in consultation with governments. Dr Tolba also assigned me to provide the Secretariat to STAP. I also helped to set up the second STAP for 1995–1996, Dr Emil Salim of Indonesia being the Asian member of the Search Committee. The confirmed Asian members of the second STAP were Professor Jyoti K. Parikh, an energy expert from India; Dr Mohd Nor Salleh, a forestry specialist from Malaysia; Professor Chirico Watanabe from Japan; and Professor Helen T. Yap, a marine biologist from the Philippines.

Remembering Dr Mostafa Kamal Tolba

SÁLVANO BRICEÑO

I first met Dr Tolba when I attended the 1978 UNEP Governing Council meeting in Nairobi, representing the Government of Venezuela. At my first international meeting, 29 years old, I was strongly impressed by his gentle and diplomatic manner coupled with shrewd and canny negotiating skills. Between 1978 and 1983, I met with him regularly at UNEP meetings and must admit, I kept learning from his selling capacities.

Little did I know that a few years later, in 1986, I was going to be hired by him to conduct, as its first Coordinator, the Caribbean Environment Programme, based in Kingston, Jamaica, my first UN job. In that capacity, our interaction, of course, evolved into a closer and more personal relationship. In our discussions in Nairobi, I was often accompanied by two other shrewd managers, Stjepan Keckes and Tony Brough, who usually smiled as I tried to convince Dr Tolba of something they knew he would probably not agree with. In perspective, I must recognize that whenever I was not able to convince him, at least I left having learned a lot from his arguments and reasoning.

During my tenure in the Caribbean, Dr Tolba helped me greatly in many ways, in particular in dealing with major countries, which usually were more concerned for their own national priorities and less inclined to accept the general interest that multilateral environmental negotiations represented for humankind, mainly due to their fear of having to foot the bill. Instead of accepting the will of the majority and then looking for more open or universal ways of sharing the cost, they tended to close the door too early, hindering a more positive outcome. Dr Tolba was one of the few international managers I knew who was able to convince them to go along and, in consequence, allow for a substantive investment in environmental projects around the world.

Dr Tolba belonged to a generation of international civil servants that not only effectively led international organizations and programmes but also managed to change international policy-making. It was the time of the Cold War, though, when the United Nations had a greater role to play.

Following many successes in facilitating international negotiations, and after 17 years at the helm of UNEP, Dr Tolba lost support from key governments, which preferred to shift negotiations, in particular on climate change, to the UN Secretariat, withdrawing from UNEP one of its major areas of involvement. Coupled with a few other divergences, it led to his decision to separate from UNEP, which I believe was a trying experience for him. He left, however, a solid and impressive legacy that still infuses UNEP's work, as well as the work of ministries of environment around the world.

Remembering Dr Mostafa Kamal Tolba

NAIGZY GEBREMEDHIN

An obituary in a leading international paper referred to Dr Tolba as 'The Green Giant'– an apt moniker. He was a gentle Green Giant, but one who demanded much from his staff members. I had the fortune to serve under him for 17 years at the headquarters of the United Nations Environment Programme (UNEP) in Nairobi, Kenya. In retrospect, it was an exciting time.

One of his favourite admonishments was to remind us all 'not to dig shallow wells'. I got the sense that he expected us to strive for depth and thoroughness in carrying out our assigned duties.

He read everything submitted to him with meticulous care: page after page coming back, marked with that ubiquitous red pen of his. He found time for everything and everyone. I remember once receiving a heavily edited draft statement I had submitted for his comments. In the corner of the draft he had entered the day and time he had read it … Sunday at 2:00 a.m. From then on, I simply gave up complaining about working long hours. If he, a much older person, with so much more responsibility, could stay up late working on a Sunday … why shouldn't I?

He expected programme officers to defend the format and substance of the programme for which they were responsible. These presentations took place periodically in front of the entire programme staff. Dr Tolba's questions were always thorough and relentless.

He directed his sharpest comments to the presumptuous: those who assumed that their Oxford or Cambridge accents imbued them with innate intellectual depth. In the end, whatever our individual accents were, we all buckled down and learned not to dig shallow wells. That life-long lesson continues to serve us well, years after Dr Tolba's tutorials at UNEP headquarters.

Dr Mostafa Kamal Tolba graduated from Cairo University in 1943, after which he earned his Doctor of Science degree from Imperial College. He taught at Cairo and Baghdad universities, and after serving in government in various capacities, including one as chairman of Egypt's Olympic Committee, led his country's delegation to the Stockholm World Environment conference in 1972. He joined UNEP as Deputy Executive Director, and later took over the leadership from Maurice Strong. He led UNEP for 17 years, retiring in 1992.

Dr Tolba had an amazing understanding of the environment. He was convinced that the environment was not a 'sector', like education, agriculture, population, or the welfare of children. As a 'cross-cutting' issue, it needed to be housed in an institution able to influence – subtly but effectively – the work of specialized UN agencies (like the World Health Organization or the Food and Agriculture Organization). In partial fulfilment of his conviction, he pioneered a complex and ambitious System-wide Medium-term Environment Programme, or SYMTEP. Programme officers worked hard with their respective partners in the specialized agencies, to define and implement SYMTEP. It was not an easy task, but clearly, it was the right thing to do.

He shunned the pressure to turn UNEP into a specialized agency because, he argued, it would lose its critical role to influence specialized agencies. The UNEP Dr Tolba envisioned was an intricate organization with an incredibly complex mandate. Only the genius of Dr Tolba could make it work effectively.

He worked brilliantly to build consensus. He pioneered, indeed, created 'environmental diplomacy', making it an effective tool for global environmental protection. Among his successes were the Vienna Convention for the Protection of the Ozone Layer (1985) and its Montreal Protocol on Substances that Deplete the Ozone Layer (1987); the Convention on Biological Diversity (1992); the Basel Convention on the Control of Transboundary Movements of Hazardous Wastes and their Disposal (1989); and almost ten conventions to protect regional seas, such as the Mediterranean and the Red Sea. He led teams that developed action plans to protect regional waters, such as the Zambezi Action Plan and the Chad Basin Action Plan. Without Dr Tolba's active participation, the United Nations Convention to Combat Desertification would not have been set in motion.

Codification is the final, possibly the most challenging stage in a continuum that identifies, analyses, organizes, and prioritizes environmental protection issues. Most efforts end up midway. Dr Tolba made sure that the organization he led for 17 years, UNEP, ran the full course. He was never one to dig a shallow well, after all.

I said he found time for everything and everyone. I would like to share one encounter that reminds me of this generous quality. It was during a difficult time in my life. I had lost my father and was unable to travel to Ethiopia to bury him because of the political turmoil underway at the time. I was walking along the corridor when I met Dr Tolba. He greeted me warmly and asked if I could walk with him to his car. As we walked he said something that I had never expected. He said that he had been thinking about me and was saddened by the fact that the rules of equitable geographic distribution (the euphemism for the 'quota' system) would make it difficult for him to recommend my promotion to the Director (D2) level. However, he had just received a note from Geneva to recommend a candidate for the position of Director of the United Nations Disaster Relief Organization (UNDRO). Dr Tolba said he would be sad to see me leave UNEP, but if I wanted it, he would recommend me. Here was a man with so many pressing responsibilities and yet he had my interest at heart. I was deeply touched. I went back to my room and 'communed' with my father in spirit, telling him not to worry about me because I was in good hands. True to his word, Dr Tolba sent in the recommendation. I never got the position, however … and it was just as well. I stayed in UNEP four years beyond Dr Tolba's retirement. And I never told the gentle Green Giant about my father. In some ways, I regret that.

The gentle Green Giant died on 28 March 2016. A Facebook admirer wrote, 'Even giants need to rest'. The world is fortunate: he inspired a generation of environmental practitioners to go beyond the first stages of the action continuum and proceed to the ultimate, decisive action: **Codification**. He was the scientist who became the father of environmental diplomacy.

Acronyms and abbreviations

AASHE	Association for the Advancement of Sustainability in Higher Education
AATHP	ASEAN Agreement on Transboundary Haze Pollution
ABC	Australian Broadcasting Corporation
ACA	Agency for Cultural Affairs
ACIAR	Australian Centre for International Agricultural Research
ADB	Asian Development Bank
ADC	Austrian Development Cooperation
Adh	Alcohol dehydrogenase
AERB	Atomic Energy Regulation Board
AfDB	African Development Bank
AF	Adaptation Fund
AHTEG-BDCC	Ad Hoc Technical Expert Group on Biological Diversity and Climate Change
AIIB	Asian Infrastructure Investment Bank
AILAC	Independent Association of Latin America and the Caribbean
AIT	Asian Institute of Technology
ALBA	Bolivarian Alliance for the Peoples of Our America
ALGAS	Asia Least-cost Greenhouse Gas Abatement Strategy
AMS	ASEAN Member States
ANU	Australian National University
ANZSEE	Australia-New Zealand Society for Ecological Economics
AOSIS	Alliance of Small Island States
A-P	Asia and the Pacific
APEC	Asia-Pacific Economic Cooperation
AR	Annual Report
AR5	Fifth Assessment Report
AREAS	Asian Rhino and Elephant Action Strategy
ARECOP	Asia Regional Cookstove Programme
ASEAN	Association of Southeast Asian Nations
asl	above sea level
ATREE	Ashoka Trust for Research in Ecology and the Environment
AusAID	Australian Agency for International Development
AvH	Alexander von Humboldt
BAF	Biosecurity Authority of Fiji
BASIC	Brazil, South Africa, India and China
BBC	British Broadcasting Corporation
BCCSAP	Bangladesh Climate Change Strategy and Action Plan
BCCRF	Bangladesh Climate Change Resilience Fund
BCCTF	Bangladesh Climate Change Trust Fund

BCE	Before the Common Era
BEE	Bureau of Energy Efficiency
BPBD	Badan Penanggulangan Bencana Daerah (Regional Disaster Management Agency)
BPoA	Barbados Programme of Action
BRI	Belt and Road Initiative
BTI	Bhutan Transparency Initiative
C40	Cities climate action network
C2ES	Center for Climate and Energy Solutions
CAIT	Climate Analysis Indicators Tool
CANSEE	Canadian Society for Ecological Economics
CARICOM	Caribbean Community
CAS	Complex Adaptive Systems
CAT	Climate Action Tracker
Cb	Cumulonimbus
CBD	Convention on Biological Diversity
CC	Climate Change
CCCCC	Caribbean Community Climate Change Centre
CCS	Carbon Capture and Storage
CDM	Clean Development Mechanism
CDP	Carbon Disclosure Project
CEA	Central Electricity Authority
CECR	Centre for Environment and Community Research
CEDAW	Convention on the Elimination of All Forms of Discrimination against Women
CEEST	Centre for Energy, Environment, Science and Technology (Tanzania)
CENWOR	Centre for Women Research
CEPF	Critical Ecosystem Partnership Fund
CER	Certified Emission Reduction
CERED	Centre for Environment Research, Education and Development
CFC	Chlorofluorocarbon
CIFOR	Centre for International Forestry Research
CIS	Colo-i-Suva forest reserve
CITES	Convention on International Trade in Endangered Species of Wild Fauna and Flora
CMA	China Meteorological Administration
CNR	Consiglio Nazionale delle Ricerche
COP	Conference of Parties
COP10	Tenth Session of the Conference of the Parties
CORRENSA	Collaborative Regional Research Network in South Asia
CoV	Coefficient of Variation
CPC	Communist Party of China
CRU	Climatic Research Unit
CSIRO	Commonwealth Scientific and Industrial Research Organisation
CSOs	Civil Society Organizations
DAC	Development Assistance Committee
DAL	Department of Agriculture and Livestock
dbh	diameter at breast height
DEQP	Department of Environment Quality Promotion
DFID	Department for International Development
DG	Director-General
DGPC	Druk Green Power Corporation
DIE	Direct Access Entity

DISCOM	Distribution Company
DMH	Department of Meteorology and Hydrology
DNV	Det Norske Veritas
DoE	Department of Environment
DoF	Department of Forests
DPRK	Democratic People's Republic of Korea
DPSEE	Driving Force, Pressure, State, Exposure and Effects
DPV	Discounted Present Value
EAs	Executing Agencies
EAEC	East Asian Economic Caucus
EBA	Endemic Bird Areas
EBRD	European Bank for Reconstruction and Development
EC	European Commission
ECLAC	Economic Commission for Latin America and the Caribbean
Ecodev	Ecology and Economic Development Company Limited
ECOSOC	United Nations Economic and Social Council
EEZ	Exclusive Economic Zone
EGTT	Expert Group on Technology Transfer
EHCA	Eastern Himalayas Conservation Alliance
EHS	Environmental, Health and Safety
EIA	Environmental Impact Assessment
ENERGIA	International Network on Gender and Sustainable Energy
ENSO	El Niño Southern Oscillation
EOS	Earth Observing System
EPI	Environmental Performance Index
ESD	Education for Sustainable Development
ESDIS	Earth Science Data and Information System
ESI	Environmental Sustainability Index
ESMAP	Energy Sector Management Assistance Programme
ESP	European Society for Photobiology
EU	European Union
ETM+	Enhanced Thematic Mapper Plus (Landsat 7)
FAO	Food and Agricultural Organization of the United Nations
FDI	Foreign Direct Investment
FINNIDA	Finnish International Development Agency
FREDA	Forest Resource Environment Development and Conservation Association (Myanmar)
FSU	Former Soviet Union
FS-UNEP	Frankfurt School-United Nations Environment Programme Centre
FYP	Five-Year Plan
G7	Group of Seven (advanced economies, without Russia)
G8	Group of Eight (industrialized nations, with Russia)
G20	Group of Twenty (leading economies)
G77	Group of developing nations (now with more than130 members)
GARP	Global Atmospheric Research Programme
GBCA	Green Building Council of Australia
GBRMPA	Great Barrier Reef Marine Park Authority
GCF	Green Climate Fund
GCP	Gross Cogenerated Power
GDI	Gender Development Index
GDP	Gross Domestic Product

GEF	Global Environment Facility
GEM	Global Earthquake Model
GFDRR	Global Facility for Disaster Reduction and Recovery
GHGs	Greenhouse gases
GII	Gender Inequality Index
GIS	Geographic Information System
GISP	Global Invasive Species Programme
GMO	Genetically Modified Organism
GNH	Gross National Happiness (Bhutan)
GNHC	Gross National Happiness Commission
GNI	Gross National Income
GNP	Gross National Product
GPS	Global Positioning System
GTZ	Deutsche Gesellschaft für Technische Zusammenarbeit GmbH (German Agency for Technical Cooperation)
GWP	Global Warming Potential
GOMA	Gallery of Modern Art
HCFC	Hydrochlorofluorocarbon
HDI	Human Development Index
HEC	Higher Education Commission
HESS	Pakistan Household Energy Strategy Study
HFCs	Hydrofluorocarbons
HI	High-Income
HIV/AIDS	Human Immunodeficiency Virus Infection and Acquired Immune Deficiency Syndrome
HLPF	High-Level Political Forum
HQ	Headquarters
IA	Implementing Agency
IAEA	International Atomic Energy Agency
IAP	Indoor Air Pollution
IAS	Invasive Alien Species
IASWG	Invasive Alien Species Working Group
IAU	International Association of Universities
ICA	Intelligence Community Assessment
ICCCAD	International Centre for Climate Change and Development
ICIMOD	International Centre for Integrated Mountain Development
ICJ	International Court of Justice
ICL	International Consortium on Landslides
ICRAF	International Centre for Research in Agroforestry (became World Agroforestry Centre in 2002)
ICSU	International Council for Science (formerly International Council for Scientific Unions)
ICVBC	Institute for the Conservation and Valorization of Cultural Heritage
IDB	Inter-American Development Bank
IDRL	International Disaster Response Laws, Rules and Principles programme
IEA	International Energy Agency
IEMP	International Ecosystems Management Partnership
IFAD	International Fund for Agricultural Development
IFC	International Finance Corporation
IFRC	International Federation of the Red Cross and Red Crescent Societies
IGCMC	Indira Gandhi Conservation Monitoring Centre
IGO	Intergovernmental Organization
IHDI	Inequality Adjusted Human Development Index
IIED	International Institute for Environment and Development

IIGCC	Institutional Investors Group on Climate Change
IISc	Indian Institute of Science
IISS	International Institute for Strategic Studies
IIT	Indian Institute of Technology
ILA	International Law Association
ILC	International Law Commission
ILO	International Labour Organization
IMF	International Monetary Fund
IMO	International Maritime Organization
INDC	Intended Nationally Determined Contribution
INSTAAR	Institute of Arctic and Alpine Research
IOC	Intergovernmental Oceanographic Commission
IPCC	Intergovernmental Panel on Climate Change
IRDR	Integrated Research on Disaster Risk
IRENA	International Renewable Energy Agency
IRRI	International Rice Research Institute
ISC	International Science Council
ISRO	Indian Space Research Organization
ISSC	International Social Science Council
IST	Indian Standard Time
IT	Information Technology
IUCN	International Union for Conservation of Nature
IUFRO	International Union of Forest Research Organizations
IVALSA	Istituto per la Valorizzazione del Legno e delle Specie Arboree (Italian) (Trees and Timber Institute)
IVL	Swedish Environmental Research Institute
IWRAW	International Women's Rights Action Watch
JICA	Japan International Cooperation Agency
JPoI	Johannesburg Plan of Implementation
JMA	Japan Meteorological Agency
KJMA	Koalisi Jambi Melawan Asap (Jambi Coalition Against Smoke)
KP	Kyoto Protocol
KPK	Khyber Pakhtunkhwa
LA21	Local Agenda 21
L&D	Loss and Damage
LANCE	Land, Atmosphere Near real-time Capability for Earth Observing System
LCC	Life Cycle Costing
LDCs	Least Developed Countries
LDCF	Least Developed Countries Fund
LEAD	Leadership for Environment and Development
LFP	Labour Force Participation
LFPR	Labour Force Participation Rate
LI	Low-Income
LIFE	Life International Foundation for Ecology
LMB	Lower Mekong Basin
LMDC	Like-Minded Developing Countries
LMP	Land Management Programme
LNG	Liquefied Natural Gas
LPG	Liquefied Petroleum Gas
MAB	Man and Biosphere Programme
MAIRS	Monsoon Asia Integrated Regional Study

MASP	Mapping Agriculture Systems Project
MCCW	Myanmar Climate Change Watch
mcwb	moisture content wet basis
MDG	Millennium Development Goal
MEA	Millennium Ecosystem Assessment
MEAs	Multilateral Environmental Agreements
MEE	Ministry of Ecology and Environment
MERGeR	Marine Ecological Resilience and Geological Resources
MI	Middle-Income
MIE	Multilateral Implementing Entities
MIGA	Multilateral Investor Guarantee Agency
MIT	Massachusetts Institute of Technology
MNRE	Ministry of New and Renewable Energy
MoA	Ministry of Agriculture
MoAF	Ministry of Agriculture and Forests
MODIS	Moderate Resolution Imaging Spectroradiometer
MoFA	Ministry of Foreign Affairs
MoEFCC	Ministry of Environment, Forest, and Climate Change
MoLHR	Ministry of Labour and Human Resources
MP	Member of Parliament
MPCs	Master-Planned Communities
MRC	Mekong River Commission
MRV	Measurement, Reporting and Verification
NAPCC	National Action Plan for Climate Change
NASA	National Aeronautics and Space Administration
NAZCA	Non-State Actor Zone for Climate Action
NBCA	National Biodiversity Conservation Areas
NBL	North Bank Landscape (Brahmaputra River)
NBSAP	National Biodiversity Strategy and Action Plan
NC	National Communication
NCEA	National Commission for Environmental Affairs
NDC	Nationally Determined Contribution
NEA	National Environment Agency
NEC	National Environment Commission
NESDB	National Economic and Social Development Board
NGO	Non-Governmental Organization
NIAS	National Institute of Advanced Studies
NIE	National Implementing Entity
NISAP	National Invasive Species Action Plan
NORAD	Norwegian Agency for Development Cooperation
NSB	National Statistics Bureau
NZ	New Zealand
OCHA	Office for the Coordination of Humanitarian Affairs
ODA	Official Development Assistance
ODS	Ozone Depleting Substances
OECD	Organization for Economic Cooperation and Development
OGM	Oil, Gas and Mining
4-P	Place, Programme, People and Perception
PABITRA	Pacific-Asia Biodiversity Transect Network
PCD	Pollution Control Department

PES	Payments for Ecosystem Services
PFC	Plant Functional Complexity
PFT	Plant Functional Type
pH	Hydrogen ion concentration
PHI	Poverty Headcount Index
PIC	Products of Incomplete Combustion
PIER	Pacific Island Ecosystems at Risk
PII	Pacific Invasive Initiative
PILN	Pacific Invasive Learning Network
PNG	Papua New Guinea
PNGRIS	Papua New Guinea Resource Information System
PPEW	Platform for the Promotion of Early Warning
PPP	Public-Private Partnership
PPPUS$	Purchasing Power Parity US$
PRC	People's Republic of China
PRISMSS	Pacific Regional Invasive Species Management Support Service
PRSP	Poverty Reduction Strategy Paper
PWHR	Pressurized Heavy Water Reactor
RAF	Resource Allocation Framework
R&D	Research and Development
RCE	Regional Centre of Expertise on Education for Sustainable Development
REDD	Reducing emissions from deforestation and forest degradation
REDD+	Reducing emissions from deforestation and forest degradation and the role of conservation, sustainable management of forests and enhancement of forest carbon stocks in developing countries
RGB	Royal Government of Bhutan
RIBA	Royal Institute of British Architects
RIMES	Regional Integrated Multi-Hazard Early Warning System (Thailand)
Rio+20	United Nations Conference on Sustainable Development
RPO	Renewable Purchase Obligation
RWEDP	Regional Wood Energy Development Programme
SAARC	South Asian Association for Regional Cooperation
SAGAR	Security and Growth for All in the Region
SAR	Special Administrative Region
SBI	Subsidiary Body for Implementation
SBSTA	Subsidiary Body on Scientific and Technological Advice
SCBD	Secretariat of the Convention on Biological Diversity
SCCF	Special Climate Change Fund
SC/DRR	Steering Committee for Disaster Risk Reduction
SCOPE	Scientific Committee on Problems of the Environment
SD	Sustainable Development
SDC	Swiss Agency for Development and Cooperation
SDG	Sustainable Development Goal
SDSN	Sustainable Development Solutions Network
SEADRIF	Southeast Asia Disaster Risk Insurance Facility
SEB	State Electricity Board
SEC	Securities and Exchange Commission
SEEPP	Social, Economic, Environmental, Physical and Political
SE4ALL	Sustainable Energy for All
SELF	Solar Electric Light Fund
SERD	School of Environment, Resources and Development

SFDRR	Sendai Framework for Disaster Relief Risk Reduction
SGESE	School of Geography, Earth Science and Environment
SIDA	Swedish International Development Cooperation Agency
SIDS	Small Island Developing States
SLCP	Sloping Land Conversion Programme
SLI	Sejahtera Leadership Initiative
SNR	Strict Nature Reserve
SOAS	School of Oriental and African Studies
SPC	Secretariat of the Pacific Community
SPICES	Spiritual, Physico-Psychological, Intellectual, Cognitive, Cultural, Ethical, Emotional, Ecological, Economic and Societal
SPREP	South Pacific Regional Environment Programme
SSTA	Sea Surface Temperature Anomalies
STAP	Scientific and Technical Advisory Panel
TCB	Tourism Council of Bhutan
TCG	Tripartite Core Group
TDRI	Thailand Development Research Institute
TEC	Tsunami Evaluation Coalition
THK	Tri Hita Karana
TM	Thematic Mapper (Landsat)
TGICA	Task Group on Data and Scenario Support for Impact and Climate Assessment
TNRICP	Tokyo National Research Institute for Cultural Properties
TWAS	The World Academy of Sciences
UCA	University of Central Asia
UEA	University of East Anglia
UK	United Kingdom
UN	United Nations
UNAIDS	Joint United Nations Programme on HIV/AIDS
UNCC	United Nations Compensation Commission
UNCCD	United Nations Convention to Combat Desertification
UNCED	United Nations Conference on Environment and Development
UNCLOS	United Nations Convention on the Law of the Sea
UNCSD	United Nations Commission on Sustainable Development
UNCTAD	United Nations Conference on Trade and Development
UNDESA	United Nations Department of Economic and Social Affairs
UNDP	United Nations Development Programme
UNDRR	United Nations Office for Disaster Risk Reduction
UNEP	United Nations Environment Programme
UNESCAP	United Nations Economic and Social Commission for Asia and the Pacific
UNESCO	United Nations Educational, Scientific and Cultural Organization
UNFCCC	United Nations Framework Convention on Climate Change
UNGA	United Nations General Assembly
UN-Habitat	United Nations Human Settlements Programme
UNHCHR	UN High Commissioner for Human Rights
UNICEF	United Nations Children's Fund
UNIDO	United Nations Industrial Development Organization
UNISDR	United Nations International Strategy for Disaster Reduction
UNODC	United Nations Office on Drugs and Crime
UNREDD	United Nations Reducing Emissions from Deforestation and Forest Degradation
UQ	University of Queensland

USA	United States of America
USD	United States Dollar
USGS-NPS	United States Geological Survey – National Park Service
USM	Universiti Sains Malaysia
USP	University of the South Pacific
UV	Ultraviolet
UV-B	UV radiation wavelengths 280–315 nm
VAR	Vector Autoregressive
VLCL	Varsity Lakes Community Limited
WAAS	World Academy of Art and Science
WAIM	World Academy of Islamic Management
WB	World Bank
WCDR	World Conference on Disaster Reduction
WCED	World Commission on Environment and Development
WCP	World Climate Programme
WCRP	World Climate Research Programme
WCDR	World Conference on Disaster Reduction
WCED	World Commission on Environment and Development
WCMC	World Conservation Monitoring Centre
WEDO	Women's Environment and Development Organization
WEF	World Economic Forum
WEN	Wood Energy News
WFP	World Food Programme
WHO	World Health Organization
WIM	Warsaw International Mechanism
WMO	World Meteorological Organization
WOCAN	Women Organizing for Change in Agriculture and Natural Resource Management
WRI	World Resources Institute
WRM	World Rainforest Moment
WSSD	World Summit on Sustainable Development
WTO	World Trade Organization
WTTC	World Travel and Tourism Council
WWAP	World Water Assessment Programme
WWF	World Wide Fund for Nature

SI prefixes

Prefix	Abbreviation	Factor
deca-	da	10
hecto-	h	10^2
kilo-	k	10^3
mega-	M	10^6
giga-	G	10^9
tera-	T	10^{12}
peta-	P	10^{15}
exa-	E	10^{18}
deci-	d	10^{-1}
centi-	c	10^{-2}
milli-	m	10^{-3}
micro-	μ	10^{-6}
nano-	n	10^{-9}
pico-	p	10^{-12}
femto-	f	10^{-15}
atto-	a	10^{-18}

Unit abbreviations

Linear measure

millimetre	mm
centimetre	cm
decimetre	dm
metre	m
kilometre	km

Square measure

square metre	m^2
kilometre	km^2
hectare	ha

Cubic measure

cubic centimetre	cm^3
cubic metre	m^3

Capacity measure

millilitre	ml
litre	l

Weight

milligram	mg
gram	g
kilogram	kg
gigagram	Gg
tonne	t
dry tonne	dt

Other units

pascal	Pa
joule	J
watt	W
kilowatt	kW
kilowatt of electricity	kWe
megawatt	MW
kilowatthour	kWh
terawatthour	TWh
second	s
year	yr

Chemical formulae

CH_4	methane
CO	carbon monoxide
CO_2	carbon dioxide
K	potassium
N	nitrogen
NO	nitrogen oxide
N_2O	nitrous oxide
NO_2	nitrogen dioxide
NO_x	nitrogen oxides
O_2	oxygen
O_3	ozone
OH	hydroxyl radical
P	phosphorus
Si	silicon

PART I

Sustainable Development: Theories and Practices

1 Asian identities

AMARTYA SEN

Department of Economics, Harvard University, Cambridge, MA, USA

Editor's note: This chapter was the keynote address of Professor Amartya Sen, who received a Lifetime Achievement Award on 28 March 2007 conferred by the United Nations Economic and Social Commission for Asia and the Pacific (UNESCAP) on its 60th anniversary. The editor is most grateful to Professor Sen for kindly giving his permission to use this address, fittingly, as the opening chapter of the book. The original speech, titled 'Asian immensities', is reproduced here, with only the addition of the keywords, which are provided by the editor to highlight the key elements of the chapter. Professor Sen changed the title to '*Asian identities*' before the publication of this chapter.

Keywords
Asian; identities; immensities; diverse beliefs; global civilization; diverse beliefs; education; religion; parliament; communication

It is marvellous that we are gathered here to celebrate the 60th anniversary of this wonderful organization, ESCAP, which is such a pre-eminent part of the United Nations system. I am also delighted to see that the rich history of ESCAP is being put together in a report that the Executive Secretary has appropriately commissioned (and which is already available in a pre-publication form), called 'The First Parliament of Asia', an apt name for an interactive process in Asia in which ESCAP has played such a leading role over the last six decades. I am very fortunate to be here and to be able to join in these anniversary celebrations.

As the subject of my talk I have chosen the expression 'Asian Immensities', which draws on a phrase made famous by W. B. Yeats, the poet: 'Asiatic vague immensities'. For various reasons the term 'Asiatic' is no longer much favoured: it somehow got, at least in the opinions of some, too mixed up with a racist description. And we Asians may not see ourselves as being engulfed in 'vagueness' in the way Yeats – and indeed many other Western observers – decided that we definitely were. But we can hardly dispute the immensities that are attributed to us. Asia is a huge part of the world, covering around 60% of the entire world population, and its immensities have been widely recognized for a very long time.

However, Asia's immensities are not confined only to its population size and geographical area but also encompass Asia's role in world history. Indeed, to take a clue from the report commissioned by the Executive Secretary, we have to look at the tradition in Asia of talking to each other, which is invoked in his choice of the word 'parliament' – a word that literally means a speech or a conversation. The celebration of that tradition is indeed very ancient in Asia, going back to the championing of that tradition by many

Asian authors, from Emperor Ashoka in the third century BC in India and Prince Shotoku in seventh-century Japan. Later on in this talk I must try to discuss why that tradition has been so momentous in the making of what we can call the world civilization, with rich contributions coming from Asia.

But first a bit of personal background. My own sense of belonging to Asia goes back a long time. While I am from India, my family is from Dhaka in Bangladesh, where I spent a large part of my childhood. When India and Bangladesh played each other in world cup cricket in the West Indies earlier this month, I was in the happy position of being able to celebrate something no matter which side won! I was also privileged in my early childhood to be in Mandalay in what was then called Burma (I still call it Burma, I must confess), and I have truly wonderful early memories of Mandalay as an immensely graceful city with an exquisite pagoda, among other objects of beauty, and of course very friendly people.

However, I also imbibed my Asianness from my school days in Santiniketan in India – a school that was started by Rabindranath Tagore, the visionary poet and writer. The school had an international orientation, but rather than looking only towards Europe – Britain in particular – which was quite common in British India, Tagore's school was particularly involved with Asia, with specific provisions for teaching about China, Japan, Korea, Indochina, Malaya, Java, Bali, and of course Thailand: I remember those classes well.

Tagore's enchantment with Asia received further support when he visited this country, Thailand. He came to the Vajiravudh College in this city to give a lecture and was received by my friend Anand Panyarachun's father, who was then heading Vajiravudh. Since our school curriculum reflected the influence of what Tagore learned in his travels in Asia, I see myself as a beneficiary – both direct and indirect – of long-standing Asian connections, which had a strong influence on my thinking from very early days in my life. So it is a very special privilege for me to be able to participate in the celebrations of the 60th anniversary of 'the first parliament of Asia'.

I mentioned earlier the fact that the immensities of Asia have received recognition in Europe for a very long time. However, I should also mention that those immensities have not always been admired and praised in the Western countries, and indeed sometimes they have appeared to Europeans to be rather terrible, with seriously damaging and corrupting influence on Europe. Now that 'Islamophobia' is quite common in parts of Europe, and many Europeans like to insist that the European Union should officially assert its uniquely 'Christian roots', it is worth recollecting that not that long ago, Nietzsche, the great German philosopher, asserted that we Asians were responsible for, yes, Christianity – and we did much damage to Europe through spreading it to gullible Europeans. Nietzsche argued that 'Christianity did everything possible to orientalize the Occident', and went into some eloquence in denouncing Asia and Christianity in the same breath: 'Christianity wants to destroy, shatter, stun, intoxicate; there is only one thing it does not want: *moderation*, and for this reason, it is in its deepest meaning barbaric, Asiatic, ignoble, un-Greek'.[1] Before signing up to the view that the essence of Europe lies in Christianity, perhaps Europeans should take some note of Nietzsche's diagnosis about the presence of Asian mischief there – and the views of others like Schopenhauer, another great European philosopher, who was convinced that given its contents, the New Testament 'must somehow be of Indian origin'!2

Confusion about Asia has occurred time and again in European thought, and there is a long tradition also of seeing a uniformity within Europe that may or may not actually exist. On our side though, in Asia, we are happy to take the blame, if any, for Christianity, and also for Islam, Buddhism, Hinduism, Confucianism, and Shintoism, and for many other systems of belief, including of course agnosticism and atheism, in which, too, Asia has an ancient history (Sanskrit, for example, has a much larger atheistic and materialistic literature than what exists in any other classical language in the world). Our immensity lies not just in our size, but also in our willingness to accept that we can have diverse beliefs and disparate life styles and can still cultivate constructive interactions with each other. Indeed, we have been doing so for thousands of years in history, coming down all the way to the present with ESCAP's role as a 'parliament of Asia', which we are celebrating today and which is a continuation of a very long tradition. If Asia has a strong claim to dignity, it lies not in our exclusivity or separatism, but in our acceptance of variety and the possibility of learning from each other.

On the occasion of the 60th anniversary of ESCAP, it is appropriate to ask why interactions across the borders of a country are so consequential and significant. This is a subject of great importance in the turbulent world in which we live. There are two ways of thinking of the history of civilization in the world. One way, which I shall call the 'fragmentary approach', segregates the beliefs and practices of different regions into self-contained entities and sees distinct civilizations as ships passing at night, without any communication with each other. The other, which I shall call the 'inclusive approach', pays full attention not just to the divisions between regions, but also to the interdependences involved, possibly varying over time, between the manifestations of civilization in different parts of the world.

We know, of course, that Western technological and cultural pursuits have recently had quite a profound impact on the rest of the world, but the ancestry of global ideas and innovations go back much longer than the interactions following the industrial revolution, which brought Europe into unique prominence. Indeed, Asia played a central part in the making of what we can now call the 'global civilization'. Asia's claim to civilization does not lie in its efforts to build some impenetrable uniqueness that could not be repeated anywhere other than in Asia. It lies rather in our efforts to develop knowledge and understanding from which the whole of humankind can benefit.

Partitioned and separatist comprehensions of world history have recently become increasingly popular in Europe and America, and this fragmentary approach has come much into prominence, especially in the threatening form of the so-called 'clash of civilizations'. The idea of some kind of a clash of civilizations has figured from time to time in the past, but it is only recently that the entire subject has been elevated to the position of being a central concern in many Western countries today. In this transformation, a major intellectual role has been played by the publication, in 1996, of Samuel Huntington's famous book, *The Clash of Civilizations and the Remaking of World Order*. And more recently, the dreadful events of 11 September 2001 have not only ushered in a period of awful conflicts and distrust in the world, but have also magnified the ongoing interest in the alarming thesis of an almost inescapable 'clash of civilizations'. Indeed, many influential commentators have been tempted to see a firm linkage between the profusion of atrocities that we see around us today and the civilizational divisions, primarily along religious lines. This is, in fact, a continuation of Nietzsche's denunciation of Asiatic mischief in Europe, even though Nietzsche himself placed Christianity as the central feature of that Asiatic abuse. That role is now given to Islam, through a similarly impoverished understanding of global civilization.

There is indeed a huge muddle in that thinking. Consider what is often called 'Western science'. Despite that regionalist

[1] Friedrich Nietzsche, *Human, All Too Human*, translated by Marion Faber and Stephen Lehmann (London, Penguin Books, 1994), p. 85.
[2] This occurs in *Parerga und Paralipomena*; see Wilhelm Halbfass, *India and Europe: An Essay in Understanding* (New York, State University of New York Press, 1988), p. 112.

nomenclature, what is identified as the content of Western science clearly draws on the innovations of ideas, reasoning, and technology that happened across the world – not just in the West. There is a chain of intellectual relations that link Western mathematics and science to a collection of distinctly non-Western works, for example Chinese, Iranian, Indian, and Arab innovations in mathematics. Even today, when a modern mathematician in, say, Princeton or Caltech invokes an 'algorithm' to solve a difficult computational problem, he/she helps to commemorate the contributions of the ninth-century Arab mathematician, Al-Khwarizmi, from whose name – Al-Khwarizmi – the term 'algorithm' is derived: the term 'algebra' comes from the title of his book, *Al Jabr wa-al-Muqabilah*. Al-Khwarizmi was an Asian and a Muslim, but that cannot be the most relevant description of him in the present context: the focus has to be on the mathematical contribution and leadership of Al-Khwarizmi. He was concerned not with spreading Islam or with engulfing Europe in 'Asiatic vague immensities', but with extending a more precise understanding of mathematics and science – at home and abroad.

The flowering of global science and technology since the European Enlightenment is not an exclusively West-led phenomenon; it was impacted by international interactions, many of which originated far away from Europe, quite often in Asia. Consider the development and use of printing, which Francis Bacon put among the advances that 'have changed the whole face and state of things throughout the world'. The technology of printing was, of course, a great contribution of East Asia, with Korea, Japan, and China competing with each other to get there first. The early printing technologists in ninth-century Asia were all Buddhist engineers, since Buddhism was very committed to spreading enlightenment and understanding to all, which is greatly helped by the use of printing.

In these efforts the national boundaries were persistently breached. Consider the first printed book in the world – or, to be exact, the first printed book that is actually dated. That book was the Chinese translation of a Sanskrit treatise from India on Buddhist philosophy, *Vajracchedika-prjnaparamita Sutra* (sometimes referred to as the *Diamond Sutra*), translated into Chinese from Sanskrit in the early fifth century: it was printed four centuries later in AD 868. The translator of the *Diamond Sutra*, Kumarajiva, was half-Indian and half-Turkish, lived in a part of eastern Turkistan called Kuch and travelled extensively in India, and then moved to China, and headed the newly established institute of foreign languages in Xian in the early fifth century: incidentally this was the first institute of this kind in the world – dedicated to foreign languages. The history of 'the first parliament of Asia', commissioned by Mr Kim Hak-Su, the Executive Secretary of ESCAP, can be, in a very general way, traced back to the time when the Koreans, the Chinese, and the Japanese were competing to be able to speak extensively to the world with speed and efficiency and when they were willing – and indeed eager – to publish books coming from countries other than their own. It is also worth noting that the book *Diamond Sutra*, printed in Chinese translation, carried a statement of purpose in the accompanying announcement of this first fruit of printing: 'Reverently made for *universal free distribution*'. What a huge vision this was, from AD 868, of which Asia and the whole world can claim to be proud inheritors!

The greatness of ideas went hand in hand with progress in high technology. Think of the nature of 'high technology' not right now – at the *end* of a millennium when the West is clearly dominant – but at the *beginning* of the millennium, around AD 1000. The high technology in the world of AD 1000 included paper and printing, the kite and the wheelbarrow, the crossbow and gunpowder, the clock and the iron chain suspension bridge, the magnetic compass, and the rotary fan. Each one of these cases of high technology of the world a millennium ago was very well established and extensively used in China, and was practically unknown in much of the rest of the world, including of course Europe and the West. But the knowledge of these technical innovations gradually moved from one country to another and became a part of global civilization.

What we now call 'Western science' draws not only on indigenous innovations (important as they were, through the Renaissance and European Enlightenment), but also on using the fruits of early progress in many non-Western parts of the world. Sometimes we can see some remnant marks of that global history in the nature of surviving words and language. I talked earlier about the Arab origins of the idea of algorithm; let me give another example, drawing from trigonometry. The ancient Indian mathematician Aryabhata had developed and made extensive use of the concept of 'sine' (central to trigonometry), in the fifth century. He called it *jya-ardha*, which literally means half-chord in Sanskrit. From there the term moved on in an interesting migratory way, as Howard Eves describes in his *An Introduction to the History of Mathematics* (1990, p. 237):

> Aryabhata called it *ardha-jya* ('half-chord') and *jya-ardha* ('chord-half'), and then abbreviated the term by simply using *jya* ('chord'). From *jya* the Arabs phonetically derived *jiba*, which, following Arabic practice of omitting vowels, was written as *jb*. Now *jiba*, aside from its technical significance, is a meaningless word in Arabic. Later writers who came across *jb* as an abbreviation for the meaningless word *jiba* substituted *jaib* instead, which contains the same letters, and is a good Arabic word meaning 'cove' or 'bay'. Still later, Gherardo of Cremona (ca. 1150), when he made his translations from the Arabic, replaced the Arabian *jaib* by its Latin equivalent, *sinus* [meaning a cove or a bay], from whence came our present word *sine*.

This is a part of the global history of world civilization, involving Indians, Arabs, and Italians, and it would be difficult to wipe all that out in the gross nomenclature of 'Western science' or 'Western mathematics'.

The fragmentary approach to civilizations is foundationally mistaken. The critically important interactions across borders, often involving Asian countries, are crucial not only in understanding Asia's role in world history, but also for an adequate understanding of the evolution of global civilization as a whole.

Before I end, I must say a few words on why the old tradition of talking to each other remains so important in the world today – no less so in Asia. The issue has relevance in global politics and in international diplomacy. The refusal of some powerful countries in the world to talk to others has substantially contributed, I would argue, to making the world more unstable and violent today. There is no substitute for talking – no serious alternative to the 'parliamentary' method – in making the world a peaceful place.

However, aside from its diplomatic and political relevance, the tradition of talking and interacting with each other has huge relevance for the making of social and economic policies, which is a primary concern of ESCAP. This applies to the whole world, but it remains critically important in Asia as well. Given the wide variations in achievements in different Asian countries, we have an enormous amount to learn from each other – from the respective successes and failures, in different fields, of different countries.

To a certain extent this has been happening quite strongly already, but the force and impact of this creative process can be further enhanced. The pace of economic progress has been much faster in Asia than elsewhere in the world over many decades now. Not surprisingly, countries have been learning from each other and correspondingly adjusting their respective economic policies. For example, in the economic changes made in India in recent decades, the experiences of countries like China and South Korea, and going further back, of Japan, have had quite a considerable effect. However, the process can be much further extended since there are still countries in this region that are struggling with their economic progress. Lessons of scrutinized experience can easily move across borders.

Aside from trade-related considerations, there have been major contributions of planned expansion of human capabilities – through education, healthcare, and so on – in raising the pace of economic expansion in one country after another in Asia. For example, an emphasis on education and skill formation has been a prime mover of change. Even at the time of the Meiji restoration in the middle of the 19th century, Japan already had a higher level of literacy than Europe, even though Japan had not yet had any industrialization or modern economic development, which Europe had experienced for nearly a century. That focus

on developing human capability was intensified in the early period of Japanese development, in the Meiji era (1868–1911). Education consumed a huge part of the budgets of the towns and villages, for Japan as a whole, and the results achieved were commensurate with that investment. By 1906, Japan was close enough to complete literacy. By 1913, though Japan was economically still quite underdeveloped, it had become one of the largest producers of books in the world – publishing more books than Britain and indeed more than twice as many as the United States.

To a great extent, the same priority can later on be seen all over East and Southeast Asia, though often this came rather more hesitantly and slowly. South Korea, Singapore, Thailand, China, and other countries have tended to follow this general approach with excellent results. The successes of the market economy in these economies, which have been widely praised (it is certainly an important part of a fuller story), have rested on the working of many other institutions along with the market. In India, school education had lagged and is only now catching up, but India's own economic expansion has been fed by its success in technical higher education, and the capability expansion resulting from this has been fruitfully used in information technology, pharmaceuticals, and other specialized sectors of modern production.

I do not have the time and the opportunity to try to list all the different ways in which Asians have learned from each other. But I must briefly mention some fields in which scope for further learning remains possible. This I do in the form of a sequence of questions: they are meant to be examples of useful inquiries – not in any way an exhaustive list.

– What can others learn from China's rapid progress in life expectancy in the pre-reform period through social intervention at a time when the country was still very poor? Are the comparable experiences of Sri Lanka and the state of Kerala in India driven by similar processes of imaginative social policy?
– What does Thailand's healthcare practice teach us about the possibility of an early health transition, including managing the prevention and control of epidemic diseases like AIDS?
– Is there something to learn from Singapore's success in building a constructive and peaceful multicultural society?
– What do we learn from religious coexistence in Indonesia, Malaysia, India, and Bangladesh in overcoming community-based confrontations?
– Are there lessons for others in India's and Japan's success with multiparty democracy?
– Can the sharing of the fruits of rapid economic growth be made less unequal in countries where they are very unequal

(for example China and also India), since there are other countries in which that is not the case?

- The long-standing blot in Asia's record in gender justice through higher female mortality rates compared with what could be expected on the basis of male mortality may have been reversed in many Asian countries, but can this terrible inheritance of Asia be made into a thing of the past in *all* Asian countries and regions?

- What should be done about natality differential against women in the form of sex-specific abortions, which is quite widespread in many countries such as South Korea, China, and even in the Northern and Western states in India (though not in the South and the East of India)? Why should 'son preference' be so strong even in countries in which women do so very well in many other ways, especially since that is not the case in other parts of Asia?

- Has Asia been doing enough in leading the world opinion on how to manage, and in particular not to mismanage, the global challenges that we face today, including those of terrorism, violence, and global injustice? Do we take an adequate interest in the problems of Africa, our sister continent, which has faced much worse adversities than we have? Asia's first parliament, which is a part of the global parliament of the United Nations, can also be a parliament in which the problems of the entire world receive serious notice.

I end my talk with these questions, which I believe deserve our attention. There are many questions to ask and many answers to seek. The relevance of these questions does not in any way diminish the value of what Asia has already achieved – over the recent years, over many centuries, and indeed over millennia. We have reason to be proud of what we Asians have been able to do for ourselves and for world civilization. But there is a lot to do still. The celebration of the past achievements of Asia's parliamentary inclinations as well as its vast immensities is also a good moment to think of the future. I would like to be able to say *the best is yet to come!* On that rather cheerful note, let me conclude this talk by thanking you all for listening.

2   On sustainable development

MOSTAFA KAMAL TOLBA[1]

International Centre for Environment and Development, Cairo, Egypt

Editor's note: This chapter was a speech given by the late Dr Mostafa Kamal Tolba at the conclusion of the Eminent Scientists Symposium organized by the United Nations Economic and Social Commission for Asia and the Pacific (UNESCAP), held on 24–25 March 2005 in Seoul, Republic of Korea. It has never been published before. The title, keywords, and sub-headings are added by the editor.

Keywords

Environment; development; nature; sustainable development; natural capital; Millennium Development Goals

2.1 INTRODUCTION

On sustainable development, I will cover three points:

1. The evolving perceptions on the relation between the environment and development: from Stockholm, through Rio and the Millennium Development Goals, to Johannesburg;
2. Challenges facing achieving sustainable societies; and
3. Formulating strategies for Sustainable Development.

2.2 ENVIRONMENT AND DEVELOPMENT

First the evolving perceptions.

The concept of sustainable development did not come up overnight. It is based on tenets expressed almost one and a half centuries ago. In his 1864 classic *Man and Nature*, George Perkins Marsh tells us, 'Man can control the environment for good as well as ill'; 'Wisdom lies in seeking to preserve the balance of nature'; and 'The present generation has an obligation, above all, to secure the welfare of future generations.' At the turn of the last century, Mohandas K. Gandhi, asked if he would like a free India to become like Great Britain, replied, 'Certainly not. If it took Britain half the resources of the globe to be what it is today, how many globes would India need?' More recently, Rachel Carson in 1962 with her book *Silent Spring*, which made the general American public aware of the dangers of pesticides, launched the modern popular environment movement.

At the beginning of the 1970s, the prestigious Club of Rome released *Limits to Growth*, warning that the planet's ability to sustain us, our industries, and our agriculture was being jeopardized and that what for a relatively small human population had seemed infinite was actually alarmingly finite. Later studies, including some by the club itself, would find the crisis somewhat overstated, but the report served to awaken scientists, policy makers, and the public to the dangers of environmental destruction.

Almost four decades ago, in Stockholm, in 1972 the governments of the world agreed on the urgent need to respond to the problem of environmental deterioration.

The Stockholm Conference clarified the link between development and the environment, and suggested an approach that would recognize the socio-economic factors behind many environmental problems and cure the effects by treating the causes. This was in contrast to the earlier technocratic approach, with its heavy emphasis on technology, itself directly descended from the Utopian dreams of the Industrial Revolution. Importantly, the conference redefined the aims of development, making a high quality of life, rather than endless acquisition of material possessions, the main criterion of success. In defining *environment* as the dynamic stock of physical and social resources available at any given time for the satisfaction of human needs, and *development* as a universal process aimed at increasing and maintaining human well-being, it became evident to the conference participants that environmental and development objectives are complementary.

Therefore, with the Stockholm Conference, a search began for a new, more rounded concept of development related to the limits of the natural resource base and in which environmental considerations play a central role, while still allowing opportunities for human activities. Clearly, earlier patterns of development were not sustainable. Current patterns of production and consumption, based on waste, extravagance, and planned obsolescence, would have to be replaced by those based on the conservation and reuse of resources.

Although this new kind of development has implications for both rich and poor countries and will lead to new directions for

---

[1] Former Executive Director of United Nations Environment Programme (UNEP) (1975–1992). Dr Tolba passed away in March 2016.

both growth and development, while incorporating the environmental dimension, it takes different forms in the industrialized and developing countries. The developing world, such as Asia, lacking the infrastructure and available resources to meet the needs and aspirations of its people, will continue to work towards material ends; meanwhile, the industrial world moves to value the non-physical areas of development that represent the highest levels of human achievements: the arts and humanities, education, and cultural pursuits.

In 1974, in the declaration adopted at the Cocoyoc Symposium on Patterns of Resource Use, Environment and Development Strategies, later adopted by the United Nation General Assembly, it was agreed that

1. economic and social factors were often the root cause of environmental degradation, as patterns of wealth, income distribution, and economic behaviour – both within and between countries – impeded development and led to inequities;
2. meeting the basic needs of the world's population was a primary goal, and the needs of the poorest, though urgent, must be met without jeopardizing the planet's carrying capacity;
3. different nations placed widely differing demands on the biosphere, with the rich pre-empting and wasting many cheap natural resources, whereas the poor were often left with no option except to destroy them;
4. developing countries must rely on their own judgment, rather than following in the footsteps of the industrialized world;
5. the principal means of achieving both environmental and developmental goals is to find alternative patterns of lifestyle and development; and
6. this generation must not jeopardize the well-being of future generations by squandering the planet's resources.

Concerns voiced at Stockholm and the subsequent international conferences have led to the evolution of the theory and practice now known as sustainable development. At its core is the requirement that current practices do not undermine future living standards: present economic systems must maintain or improve the resource and environmental base, so that future generations will be able to live as well as or better than the present one. Sustainable development does not require the preservation of the current stock of natural resources or any particular mix of human, physical, or natural assets, nor does it place artificial limits on economic growth, provided that such growth is both economically and environmentally sustainable. The parameters of sustainable development are broad, encompassing fiscal policy, international trade, industrial strategies, technology applications, labour rights, living conditions, natural resource conservation, and pollution reduction – in other words, all the components of development.

In 1987, the World Commission on Environment and Development chaired by Gro Harlem Brundtland elaborated the concept of sustainable development. In 1992, at the United Nations Conference on Environment and Development (the Earth Summit), held in Rio de Janeiro, the leaders of the world agreed that the protection of the environment and social and economic development were fundamental to sustainable development. To achieve such development, the global programme, titled Agenda 21, was adopted. A plan for the further implementation of Agenda 21 was adopted in 1997 at a United Nations Special Session of the General Assembly. Between Rio and Johannesburg, the world's nations have met in several major conferences under the auspices of the United Nations, including the International Conference on Financing for Development and the Doha Ministerial Conference on Trade. These conferences defined for the world a comprehensive vision for the future of humanity. The 20th century culminated with the United Nations Summit in 2000, which adopted the eight Millennium Development Goals:

1. Eradicate extreme poverty and hunger;
2. Achieve universal primary education;
3. Promote gender equality and empower women;
4. Reduce child mortality;
5. Improve maternal health;
6. Combat AIDS, malaria, and other diseases;
7. Ensure environmental sustainability;
8. Develop a global partnership for development.

At the Johannesburg Summit on Sustainable Development in 2002, leaders of the world at head of state and government level declared the following:

1. We, the representatives of the peoples of the world, assembled at the world Summit on Sustainable Development in Johannesburg, reaffirm our commitment to sustainable development; and
2. we commit ourselves to building a humane, equitable, and caring global society, cognizant of the need for human dignity for all.

They announced that they were determined to ensure that the rich diversity which is the world's collective strength will be used for constructive partnerships for change and for the achievement of the common goal of sustainable development. They agreed on the indivisibility of human dignity and to speedily increase access to such basic requirements as clean water, sanitation, adequate shelter, energy, healthcare, food security, and the protection of biodiversity. They reaffirmed their pledge to place focus on, and give priority attention to, the fight against the worldwide conditions that pose severe threats to the sustainable development of billions of people, which include the following: chronic hunger; malnutrition; foreign occupation; armed conflict; illicit drug problems; organized crime; corruption; natural disasters; illicit arms trafficking; trafficking in persons; terrorism; intolerance and incitement to racial, ethnic, religious, and other hatreds; xenophobia; and endemic, communicable, and chronic diseases. This reaffirming was a new confirmation and elaboration of the eight Millennium Development Goals. And the leaders in Johannesburg adopted a third plan of action and urged developed countries that have not done so to make concrete efforts to reach the internationally agreed levels of official development assistance to help implement the plan.

Have much of all these lofty declarations and ambitious plans been implemented? I very much doubt.

2.3 THE CHALLENGES FOR SUSTAINABLE SOCIETIES

And now I come to my second point: the challenges.

I am fully aware that there are serious challenges that face the world community in trying to put in place sustainable societies.

The first challenge is understanding the global systems.

Not in the next few generations will the global systems be so fully understood that they may be treated mechanically. Therefore, in prescribing solutions, a sense of humility is required. A spirit of not destroying what we are yet to comprehend, and a spirit of symbiotic partnership with all that matters on our planet, should guide our actions. Strategies for sustainable development must look to people, motivate them, and give them the tools to achieve their aspirations. To deal with the issues of environment as a component of sustainable development thus becomes a matter which transcends environmentalists. Consideration of environmental protection must be pursued within economic, social, and military activities. Conceptualization of such activities must start from a number of basic perceptions:

1. Life processes are interconnected in intricate ways.
2. Air, water, land, and life constitute an interlocking system; elements vital to all life move in cycles between the rocks, water, air, and living matter. Harsh experience has shown that, beyond certain limits, these cycles cannot be disturbed without causing irrevocable damage. A recognizing of these limits is at the heart of environment management and sustainable development. We must use nature but we must maintain the supportive cycles of the biosphere.
3. It is not only that the life processes are interconnected, but that the seamless web spun by today's trade, communications, and finances has also submerged the interconnections in the world's economic and political systems. These interconnections are increasingly placed in jeopardy by the conflicting demand for

resources and the growing divergence of need, interest, and power among countries at different stages of development. It is necessary, in the interest of all, to seek adjustment of these differences so that sustainable development of the poorer regions of the world receives first priority. Otherwise, population is less likely to be stabilized, and political tensions and pressures on resources will inevitably increase.

The second challenge is that poverty eradication, changing consumption and production patterns, and protecting and managing the natural resources base for economic and social development are overarching objectives of, and essential requirements for, sustainable development. But these goals are more easily said than done because of the same ills that governments themselves recognized at Johannesburg: particularly increasing hunger, foreign occupation, armed conflicts, corruption, and a very modest effort by the rich countries to help the poor ones. And we can add to this the dwindling political will for international cooperation.

The third challenge is the deep fault line that divides human society between the rich and the poor and the ever-increasing gap between the developed and developing worlds, which pose a major threat to global prosperity, security, and stability.

The fourth challenge lies in the fact that the global environment continues to suffer. Loss of biodiversity continues; fish stocks continue to be depleted; desertification claims more and more fertile land; and the adverse effects of climate changes are already evident. Natural disasters are more frequent and more devastating, and developing countries are more vulnerable. And finally, air, water, and marine pollution continue to rob millions of a decent life.

Globalization has added a new dimension to these challenges. It offers opportunities and challenges for sustainable development. Globalization and interdependence are offering new opportunities for trade, investment and capital flows, and advances in technology, including information technology, for the growth of the world economy, development, and the improvement of living standards around the world. At the same time, there remain serious financial crises, insecurity, poverty, exclusion, and inequality within and among societies. The developing countries face special difficulties in responding to those challenges and opportunities. Globalization should be fully inclusive and equitable, and there is a strong need for policies and measures at the national and international levels, formulated and implemented with the full and effective participation of developing countries to help them to respond effectively to globalization challenges and opportunities. This will require urgent action at all levels to

1. promote open, equitable, rules-based, predictable, and non-discriminatory multilateral trading and financial systems

that benefit all countries in the pursuit of sustainable development. It requires the implementation of the decision contained in the Doha Ministerial Declaration to place the needs and interests of developing countries at the heart of the work programme of the declaration;

2. enhance the capacities of developing countries to benefit from liberalized trade opportunities through international cooperation and measures aimed at improving productivity, commodity diversification and competitiveness, community-based entrepreneurial capacity, and transportation and communication infrastructure development;

3. promote corporate responsibility and accountability; and

4. assist developing countries in narrowing the digital divide, creating digital opportunities, and harnessing the potential of information and communication technologies for development through technology transfer and the provision of financial and technical support.

2.4 APPROPRIATE STRATEGIES FOR SUSTAINABLE DEVELOPMENT

My third and final point is the formulation of appropriate strategies for sustainable development. I believe that in formulating such strategies in a country or group of countries, including of course Asia, it is necessary

1. to evaluate the realistic options available to a country and groups of countries with different sociopolitical systems and at different stages of economic efficiency and technological advancement;

2. to disseminate information on environment and conservation problems and their place in the process of achieving sustainable development, so that decision-makers at all levels, and in different sectors, move from react and cure to anticipatory and preventive policies;

3. to make every effort to ensure public participation in the decision-making process and in the implementation of sustainable development strategies;

4. to work towards achieving a number of critical transitions: an energy transition to an era in which energy is produced and used at high efficiency without aggravating the environment; a demographic transition to a stable world population; and a resource transition to reliance on nature's income and not depletion of its 'capital'.

On these and many other issues we are all agreed. The main question now is how to translate conviction into commitment. I believe it is time to bite the bullet – to look seriously at international action that will penalize wasteful resource use and reward good planetary husbandry. Governments need to review budget priorities, to ensure that subsidies, project finance, energy, transportation, fiscal, and other policies work towards environmental protection, as well as economic expansion. New, revenue-generating mechanisms like green taxes, charges on so-called free goods like clean air and water, user's fees, pricing adjustments, concessionary loans, rebates, and fiscal incentives need to be introduced at the national and perhaps international level. Revenues generated should then be distributed – equitably – to the different sectors to get the global, across-the-board action we must have. Action must be predicated on a true costing of the economic value of a healthy environment.

Public opinion worldwide has reached the point where generating new revenues to safeguard the environment, and to give a new urgency to development, can be seriously contemplated. The environment is an issue all nations can agree on. It can be a healing force, something to bring us all together. People care deeply about the world their children will inherit. It is time to overcome inertia and act as though we care.

It is clear that countries must act together. It is clear that we need a global partnership. We may not share a common history, but we do share a common future. Nothing less than a new world order is therefore needed. The challenge is not merely to ease North and South, East and West tensions, but to erase such divisions altogether as we begin unified action.

Even if we faced no other environmental challenge than global warming, unprecedented international action on a global scale is urgently needed. We need to look no further than the 1988 Midwest drought in North America. Grain from the North American breadbasket finds its way to over 100 countries. A succession of such droughts catalysed by a rise in the earth's average temperature of between 1 and 3°C over the next 30 to 40 years would throw world food production, and thereby the world economy and security, into a grave crisis.

In the next 30 to 40 years, we may experience a greater climate change brought about by the build-up of greenhouse gases than the world has experienced over the previous 10,000 years. Biological productivity – already being undermined by unsustainable usage – will be diminished. Low-lying agricultural land could be inundated and small island nations condemned completely.

Scientists now believe we will have to reduce eventually CO_2-equivalent emissions by 60% if we are to meaningfully address climate change, and international cooperation must be complemented and reinforced with fundamental changes in national economic growth and, ultimately, in our daily lives.

2.5 CONCLUDING REMARKS

Difficult and idealistic as it may seem, we have no alternative other than to start thinking in longer time frames to stop thinking about immediate profit and convenience when there is no prospect that these can be sustained.

What is needed is a change in our perception of wealth. Natural resource endowments must be included in every nation's inventory of wealth. There can be no hope of preventing further environmental destruction unless we put a true value on the natural patrimony and end wasteful economic impatience.

Expanding the time horizons of economic practices riveted to quarterly results, monthly mortgage payments or trade figures, and yearly national income accounts is extremely difficult.

While the environment is embodied in all goods and services exchanged, the environment is not exchanged itself. It, therefore, eludes a market price and a market value. The upshot is that natural resources are treated as 'gifts' of nature rather than as productive assets. Economics has enormous difficulty placing value on anything outside of mercantile activities. As a scientist, I find it difficult to understand that so many economists confine value only to exchange, at the expense of non-market values like biological diversity or clean water, or ecological service.

While natural endowments like climate and port access were crucial to production specialization and comparative advantage in classical economic theory, resource scarcity or pollution-sink capacity was largely irrelevant in the scheme of the industrial revolution. Once a natural resource was depleted, a lake polluted or virgin forest exploited, new water sources were found, and new soils were cultivated. The environment was virtually ignored, because it seemed without limits. Resources were incorporated as a free good in production methods, pollution ignored as a market externality. 'Land' has been all but banished from economic priorities – particularly neo-classical economic models. Instead, economic development is viewed almost exclusively as a function of capital.

So while we treat industrial plant, machinery, and buildings as productive capital whose value depreciates over time, the natural wealth of nations is not so valued. Because we overestimate the natural regenerative capacity of soils, forests, freshwater, and fisheries, we dangerously undervalue them.

The challenge we face as a global community can be simply stated: we must pass on to future generations productive opportunities of equal or greater value than the existing capital portfolio. Easy to state, but immensely complex to achieve because, in essence, we are talking of the transfer of three types of capital:

First, critical natural capital, as for example, biogeochemical cycles and species diversity – that is, the vital processes that sustain the life support systems of the earth;

Second, natural resources – our forests, marine life, topsoil, and air;

Third, human resources – who use the technology, natural capital, and natural resources to produce wealth.

Achieving that goal boils down to breaking bad habits.

Two centuries ago, George Washington wrote in a letter to a friend, 'We ruin the lands that are already cleared and either cut down more wood of what we have or emigrate to the western country. A half, a third or even a fourth of the land we mangle which, well-wrought and properly dressed, would produce more than the whole under our system of management, yet such is the force of habit, that we cannot depart from it.' That force of habit is still with us. The challenge before us is to use our considerable skills and expertise to help break such habits before they break us.

And the father of capitalism, Adam Smith, did not suggest that private enterprise should work to the detriment of society as a whole. Quite the opposite, in his market system the profit of every individual reflected on the wider community. He would have been appalled by a system that knowingly undermined its own future. And had he been present to witness the extraordinary changes that have come about since his days, he would urge us to accept the principles of sustainable development.

3   Sustainability: A scientific dilemma

JOHN PEET

University of Canterbury, Christchurch, Aotearoa/New Zealand

Keywords

Sustainability; sustainable development; economics; growth; technology; production; resources; utility; energy; complexity; eco-efficiency

Abstract

Policy proposals on sustainability or sustainable development (SD) by mainstream economists, on the one hand, and mainstream scientists and engineers, on the other, are sufficiently different for it to be very difficult to find common ground. Approaches of these disciplines to the issue of continuous growth, for example of GDP, provide one obvious example.

In this chapter, the two approaches are shown to be derived from the utility-based and metabolic models of economic activity. These may be broadly described as representing, respectively, the weak and strong sustainability principles. In the opinion of the author, resolution of the apparent dilemma of choice between the two approaches is appropriately addressed not as an either/or dichotomy but as a both/and issue, reflecting an actualization hierarchy between the two models.

It is imperative that the scientific community contributes to identification of common ground and to policy developments in sustainability. Suggestions are made to assist in this process and move towards a holistic policy programme for SD in Aotearoa New Zealand.

(Note: While many aspects of the following discussion refer explicitly to Aotearoa/New Zealand, the overall argument is entirely general and relevant to most, if not all, countries.)

3.1 INTRODUCTION

For some decades, major differences between the political-economic and the scientific world views have been evident. These differences have been particularly pronounced in the context of environment and resource issues, the meaning of economic growth and the implications for development. It is not necessary to spend time on this here, but interested readers may care to follow up some of the issues as summarized in recent books and papers by Daly, in particular from the recent Canadian Society for Ecological Economic (CANSEE) conference (Daly, 2003), and in the author's book (Peet, 1992).

The most obvious result of these differences is that the two sides continue to 'talk past' each other in debate, while one (the political-economic) remains firmly in control of advice to government. As will be explained, neither approach is, of itself, sufficient to address the full scientific complexity of the issue of sustainable development (SD). It is therefore not surprising that, in practice, the debate is often seen as incoherent. A new synthesis is needed, which many people argue must be based on a biophysical systems world view, where both the political-economic and the scientific are in relationship. The nature of that relationship is summarized later. The outcome of such a synthesis is that it could aid the development of a coherent approach potentially able to resolve differences and enable building of real SD in New Zealand (NZ).

Following Daly (2002), one may ask the question: just what is it that is to be *sustained* in 'sustainable' development? There are two broad answers to this question:

- Firstly, *utility* should be sustained, so that the utility of future generations is no less than at present. Utility here refers to average per capita utility, or happiness. In practice, due to the difficulty of evaluating utility, surrogates such as consumption are used, normally expressed as dollars spent per capita on goods and services.

- Secondly, physical *throughput* should be sustained, so that the throughput of resources available to future generations is no less than at present. Throughput here means the total physical flow of low-entropy resources from nature's sources, through the economy and out to nature's sinks as high-entropy wastes. In current jargon, this relates to the principle that natural capital[1] must be kept intact.

---

[1] Natural capital is the capacity of the ecosystem to yield both a flow of natural resources and a flux of natural services. These include not only materials and energy but also the life-sustaining environment.

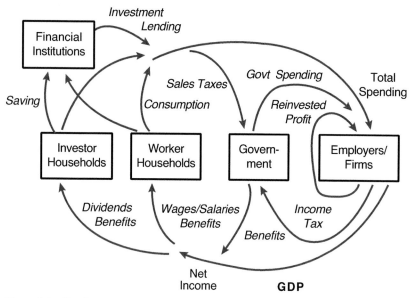

Figure 3.1. Circular monetary flow model of conventional macroeconomics.

These two concepts of sustainability are completely different and appear to be incompatible. It is argued that this is because they come from completely different world views, but they are actually related. Let us look at them more closely (Peet, 2002a; 2002c).

3.2 SOME CONVENTIONAL PARADIGMS OF SUSTAINABILITY

The circular flow diagram in Figure 3.1 characterizes the mainstream neoclassical (utility-based) macroeconomic model of the economic process, where goods and services made by employers/firms (producers) are sold to households (consumers), who in turn obtain money by selling their labour or capital (here, capital means human-made capital, not natural capital). Exchange relationships between capital and labour (the factors of production) that give rise to value added (related, implicitly, to utility gained by purchasers) are primary. Underlying physical production relations are largely ignored. A consequence is that *that to which value is added* (i.e., the physical resource being transformed by capital and labour into a consumer good or service) has no obvious part in the theory.[2]

Within this paradigm, according to Common (1996):

Economics conceptualizes the sustainability problem as that of maintaining a constant level of per capita aggregate consumption for ever.

[2] As Daly has pointed out, this is rather like asserting that a loaf of bread may be produced by means of the cook's labour and a kitchen, without any reference to flour, water, yeast, or fuel to heat the oven.

Common makes the point that, in economics, an individual's preferences can be represented by a well-behaved utility function and that an individual's behaviour can be understood in terms of the maximization of the utility function subject to constraints:

Utility = some function of consumption of a range of commodities, subject to expenditure on that consumption remaining within the individual's income.

i.e., Max $U_j (Q_{i\prime} .... Q_{im})$ subject to $\Sigma P_i Q_{ji} = Y_j$ $\qquad$ (3.1)

With Qji, as (the individual) j's consumption of the ith commodity, Pi as the price of the ith commodity, and Yj as j's income.

Under these circumstances, the standard representation of the production process of a firm is via what is known as a 'production function' of the general form

Output = some function of Capital and Labour inputs (usually expressed as prices):

$$Q_i = F_i (K_i, L_i) \qquad (3.2)$$

In the neoclassical approach, a primary purpose of the economy is to achieve (Pareto-efficient) optimal allocation of resources with its corresponding optimal set of prices. As Daly (2003, p. 4) points out, however, the economic problem is rather more complex:

*A good allocation of resources is **efficient** (Pareto optimal); a good distribution of income or wealth is **just** (a limited range of acceptable inequality); a good scale does not generate 'bads' faster than goods and is also ecologically **sustainable** (it could last a long time, although nothing is forever).*

The first item (allocation) is the main preoccupation of neoclassical economics and is achieved by means of the market mechanism. The second is often treated as an add-on, for the sake of social justice. The third is seldom included in discussions. All three are central concerns of ecological economics. These issues, especially the third, are discussed in more detail later.

The model of Figure 3.1 can be modified to show the essential part played by flows of raw resources from the environment, through the economy and out as pollution, as shown in Figure 3.2. Note that, although money flows in a circular pattern, resources enter at one place and end up somewhere else. In the process, a lot of high-quality energy (exergy, or low-entropy energy resources) is expended and disposal problems are generated. These comprise not only the obvious solid wastes but also CO_2 and toxins, as well as all other emissions to air, water, and soil.

The model therefore illustrates the throughput or 'metabolic' model of economic activity, in which the economy is 'fed' by raw resources from the environment and 'excretes' wastes back to that environment, resulting from public and private consumption, as well as firms by companies. Such a system is known in science as an 'open' or 'dissipative' system,

since it depends upon continuous flows of low-entropy resources in, and high-entropy wastes out, for survival.

In this perspective, value is added *to* the throughput flow of natural resources, *by* the transforming services of capital and labour (in the formal economy). A coherent model of SD should incorporate both, as well as acknowledge that while resources provide *that to which value is added*, and are therefore benefits, pollution and waste are inevitable consequences which involve costs. The latter are seldom charged to the transformation processes that create them. If this view were to be fully incorporated into an economic perspective, it would be possible to identify a level at which costs may exceed benefits, and hence the optimal (i.e., sustainable) scale of economic development, after which further growth in throughput involving resource depletion and/or pollution may be undesirable.

The model of Figure 3.2 can be seen as a basis for the application of mainstream neoclassical welfare economics, via its resource and environmental subsets. Again following Common (1996):

Resource economics recognizes that production does involve material inputs extracted from the environment, and modifies the

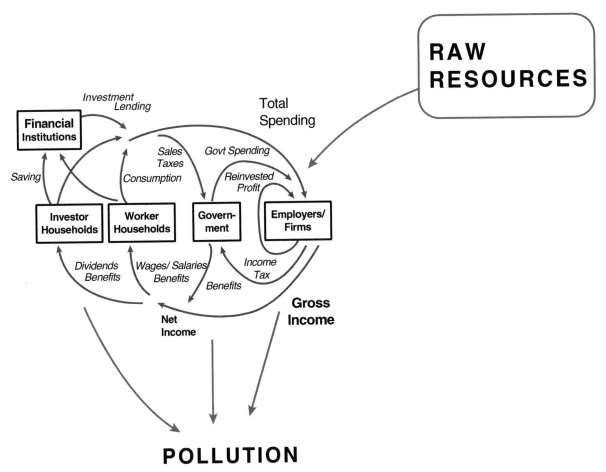

Figure 3.2. Resource requirements of economic activity.

standard production function along the lines *Output = some function of Capital, Labour, and the rate of Resource Extraction*:

$$Q_i = F_i(K_i, L_i, R_i) \qquad (3.3)$$

Environmental economics recognizes environmental insertions and wastes arising in production, and often uses a production function of the form

Output = some function of Capital, Labour, and the flow of Waste:

$$Q_i = F_i(K_i, L_i, W_i) \qquad (3.4)$$

This function is sometimes further modified along the lines

Output = some function of Capital, Labour, the flow of Waste and Ambient Pollution:

$$Q_i = F_i(K_i, L_i, W_i, A[\Sigma_i W_i]) \qquad (3.5)$$

Where ambient pollution A is a function of the flow of waste emissions across all firms.

There is a sense, therefore, in which from the neoclassical economic perspective the environment is simply a subsystem of the economy: a source of resources and a sink for wastes, with its primary purpose being that of enabling economic growth to continue, implicitly without limit. Figure 3.3 illustrates Daly's model of this perception (Daly, 1999, p. 12). Again, *that to which value is added* is absent, although the 'resource' and 'pollution' outcomes of its use are acknowledged, albeit via evaluation of prices that may be of questionable validity.

In political-economic practice, this model is usually taken as a 'given'. It has to be pointed out, however, that the model is inherently anti-ecological. The special and essential place of high-quality energy (exergy) in the biophysics of open systems is also completely absent, other than (implicitly) as just another (perhaps priced) source.

Common points out that a more meaningful approach would recognize the closed system (the total biosphere) within which economic activity occurs and would also acknowledge that if one believes output Equation (3.5), the waste flow has no material origin. Since in reality it is obviously impossible for economic activity to create matter, it has to be emphasized that the flow of waste is in fact a direct consequence of the material resource input. It is an obvious consequence that most waste problems are probably better and more easily dealt with via addressing the input of resources than by waste processing, but that is not at all obvious from the production functions listed previously. Resource and environmental economics are, from this viewpoint, two sides of the same coin.

The production function can be yet further modified from Equation (3.5) to give

Output = some function of Capital, Labour, the rate of Resource Extraction, the flow of Waste (itself a function of the rate of Resource Extraction), and Ambient Pollution (itself a function of the flow of Waste across all firms):

$$Q_i = F_i(K_i, L_i, R_i, W_i [R_i], A[\Sigma_i W_i]) \qquad (3.6)$$

3.3 SUBSTITUTABILITY OF FACTOR INPUTS

This line of argument should not be taken too far, of course. Bringing information together in the form of a production function implies that, if one wishes to obtain a given output, it is in theory possible to increase the input of one factor at the same time as decreasing another, via the near-universal assumption that the factors are substitutable, each with the other(s). Mathematically, it is quite possible for one factor to approach zero, provided another approaches infinity at the same time. The scientific absurdity, however, is absent both from the model and from its mathematics, implying a fundamental defect in the underlying world view.

Daly (2003, p. 8) points out that ecological economics sees natural and human-made capital as primarily complements, substitutable only over a very limited margin. Neoclassical economics regards them as overwhelmingly substitutes.

The conventional model (e.g., Equation (3.2)) involving only (human-made) capital and human labour is an example where substitution is indeed possible to a considerable extent, but the laws of conservation of energy and of matter cannot be so easily dealt with. In a physical production process, for example, the ability of high-quality input energy (exergy) to do 'work' is a clear exception, since there is an absolute minimum needed for any physical transformation, according to the second law of

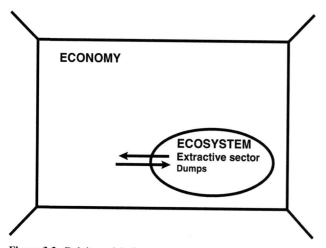

Figure 3.3. Daly's model of mainstream economics.

ECONOMY

ECOSYSTEM
Extractive sector
Dumps

thermodynamics. In other words, the energy input is at best only substitutable with other factors to the extent permitted by the laws of physics, and energy and matter are always conserved in real economic processes. None of these problems is adequately taken into account in conventional neoclassical economic models. It may be worth commenting that the author is also unaware of any evidence that non-physical (virtual) production has any useful meaning.

The neoclassical idea of factor substitutability, as described here, is central to what is termed 'weak sustainability' (see later).

3.4 POLITICS, THE PHYSICAL ECONOMY, AND GROWTH

As indicated earlier, unless the material(s) that comprise *that to which value is added* is included in the discussion about SD, an essential component is missing. This issue is worthy of further examination.

The NZ Government (2002) issued an SD report outlining its present approach in August 2002. In a press release accompanying its publication, announced shortly before she left for the World Summit on Sustainable Development (WSSD) meeting in Johannesburg, the Prime Minister made the following comments (emphasis added):

*[T]he government is committed to ensuring that New Zealand is at the forefront of international efforts to be economically, socially, and environmentally sustainable. The central issue is how we achieve **sustainable economic growth** in a manner which enables us to **improve the well-being of all our peoples without compromising the quality of the environment**.*

In that same report, the Minister for the Environment further commented on:

*[P]riorities ... such as **economic growth**, the implications of international population change for New Zealand, **decoupling of economic growth from environmental harm**, governance for sustainable development.*

The aims of this declared SD policy are entirely understandable, and recognition of the vision and principles is encouraging. The difficulty is that, while both vision and principles are enunciated, there is no explicit or implicit evidence as to whether they are in fact attainable – physically, technologically, economically, socially, or environmentally. The implicit assumption that economic growth equates to improved well-being is one area where major questions are being asked by ecological (and many other) economists (Daly, 2003, pp. 8–9). The further assumption that growth is always economic is another, where serious doubts exist as to the benefits of continuing growth in already-developed

nations (Daly, 2003, pp. 12–19) (such as NZ and Australia). Zovanyi (2004), in trenchant analyses of the NZ situation, has commented unfavourably on the labelling of what is nothing more than growth management (e.g., in Auckland) as 'sustainable'.

Economist Clive Hamilton commented recently (Hamilton, 2002):

We're often told and it's simple to believe, that we can have it all – economic growth and the environment if we do it cleverly. It's a convenient view for politicians and business people who say they're committed to sustainability. But there is certainly a conflict between economic growth and environmental protection.

3.5 TECHNOLOGY AND 'THAT TO WHICH VALUE IS ADDED'

The inescapability of a physical dimension of economic activity is well known to those from a scientific or technological background. However, this physical dimension is treated as of relatively minor importance by many economists and politicians, who continue to promote growth, albeit often claimed as 'decoupled' or 'eco-efficient'. But as affirmed by Daly (1994):

Quantities of goods and services have a physical dimension (mass and energy) and are therefore subject to physical laws of conservation and entropy. Economic value is certainly not reducible to physical laws, but neither is it exempt from them. Real GDP is a value index of quantitative change. The creation of a value index to measure aggregate quantitative change in output does not annihilate the physical dimensions of commodities, thereby allowing the economy to grow forever on a finite planet!!

To flesh out this general statement, consider the information on resource use and pollution from the main NZ economic sectors, selected for illustrative purposes from Patterson's data (obtained from 1997/98 input–output tables of the NZ economy, for the first time incorporating satellite accounts) (Patterson, 2003). The data in Table 3.1 give the total (direct plus indirect) energy (as PJ Oil Equivalent, first law-heating value), land ('000 ha), water discharges (million m^3), and biological oxygen demand (BOD) (tonnes) resource requirements or pollution emissions at the standard NZ SNA 24 sector breakdown. (Similar tables can be found for other countries. See, for example, recent special issues of the *Journal of Industrial Ecology*.)

From these data, it is evident that, although primary and manufacturing industries have heavy demands for resources and produce a great deal of pollution, the so-called service sectors, often held out as more benign alternatives for the future, also have substantial demands. This gives us some help in addressing the idea of 'decoupling of economic growth from environmental harm' as a recipe for sustainable economic growth.

Table 3.1. Total (direct and indirect) resources/pollutants of sectors of the NZ economy, 1997/98.

Sector	Energy (PJOE)	Land ('000 ha)	Water (million m³)	BOD5 (tonnes)
Agriculture	40	15,268	225	4,487
Fishing and hunting	8	21	5	25
Forestry	3	1,758	16	59
Mining and quarrying	8	78	1,368	52
Food, beverages, and tobacco	84	9,460	493	4,081
Textiles, clothing, and footwear	11	1,536	53	555
Wood and wood products	12	696	41	133
Pulp and paper products, printing and publishing	43	298	186	193
Petroleum chemicals, plastics, and rubber products	20	195	571	251
Non-metallic mineral products	10	43	180	68
Basic metal products	57	39	192	65
Fabricated metal products, machinery and equipment	30	221	118	370
Other manufacturing	2	14	30	20
Electricity, gas	3	69	326	89
Water distribution	2	112	20	228
Construction	37	492	275	649
Wholesale and retail trade	90	1,667	289	1,466
Transport and storage	50	169	62	462
Communication	6	75	31	233
Finance, Insurance, real estate, and bus services	27	264	126	1,057
Ownership of owner-occupied dwellings	3	83	21	118
Community, social, and personal services	30	674	1,072	24,160
Central government	10	215	64	766
Local government	2	97	9	61

Source: Patterson (2003).

To give a specific example, the government's policies for SD include promotion of ecotourism. It has to be pointed out, however, that air transport is normally used to bring tourists to our country, road transport takes them to their restaurants and hotels, and four-wheel drives (4WDs) and helicopters take many of them on scenic excursions. Patterson's data (not included here), for international tourism, in particular, show that as a sector it has very substantial demands, being one of the worst performing sectors when energy, land, BOD, and other water pollutants are included. It must be questioned whether there be much real benefit to the sustainability of the economy, if growth via 'ecotourism' is to be promoted heavily as one component of SD, with the inevitable consequence of increased numbers of jumbo jet flights.

Even if the entire economy were to move in the direction of industries such as finance and communication, there would still be substantial demands for energy and other resources. A further important point is that no matter how much industrial processes are improved, they are still subject to the laws of physics, which limit the extent to which high-quality energy resource inputs to economic processes can be reduced, especially the second law of thermodynamics. For that reason, *de*materialization of industrial production is not possible; *reduced* materialization is the best we can hope for.

3.6 TECHNOLOGY VERSUS CONTINUED ECONOMIC GROWTH – THE CENTRAL PROBLEM?

The following simple equation, due to Ehrlich and Ehrlich (1990), is a useful tool for quantifying some long-term aspects of economic growth and showing how long-term problems can often be the outcomes of apparent short-term successes:

Total Social Impact = Population × Affluence × Technology Impact (3.7)

or I = P × A × T

where Population (P) is expressed as a number; Affluence (A) as consumption of resources per person (R/P) (commonly GDP per capita); and Technology Impact as the per unit amount of resources used (I/R) (perhaps primary or fossil energy consumption per unit of GDP, which can be directly related to pollution emissions).

With today's values indexed to 1, the reference situation is as follows: I = 1 × 1 × 1 = 1

To illustrate use of this equation, assume that New Zealand proceeds along conventional lines of development, with 3% annual increase in GDP (as proposed by the main political parties) compounded over 50 years. Assuming no increase in population and no improvements in technology, the Social Impact 50 years hence will be around $(1 + 0.03)^{50}$ = 4.4 times current levels. If we want to keep the Total Social Impact constant at today's relative level under those conditions, then Technology Impact will have to improve (i.e. reduce) at the same 3% annual rate as Affluence is increasing, ending at a value of $(1 \div 4.4)$ = 23% of today's level.

The working of the IPAT equation over long periods of time is illustrated graphically in Figure 3.4, with each component of the equation presented separately. In this illustration, Population remains constant (for the sake of simplicity), Affluence grows exponentially at 3% per annum and Technology Impact is (arbitrarily) set to decrease annually, by 10% of the difference

between its previous value and an end-state value of 1/4, as suggested by the book *Factor 4* (von Weizsäcker *et al.*, 1997).

The result shows that while Total Social Impact I decreases significantly in the short term, over the long term it rises again, eventually exceeding the initial value and inexorably moving upwards. The reason the I curve has a U-shape is that the T variable stops declining, while the A variable continues to increase. For I to stay constant or decrease while A increases, T must continue to decline at least at the rate that A increases. Unless the central assumption of continuing growth in Affluence (e.g. exponential growth in GDP) is changed, growth in I is a mathematical inevitability (even though continued economic growth as we currently understand it is unlikely to be physically achievable anyway).

3.7 NOT BY TECHNOLOGY ALONE

Technologically, significant improvements in the direction of 'eco-efficiency' are indeed possible in the short term, but it is vital to make the point that these improvements are subject to severe limitations in the long term. This brings out a vital point that science and engineering can contribute to the discussion. It is, that **if continued growth in Affluence (e.g., in GDP)**

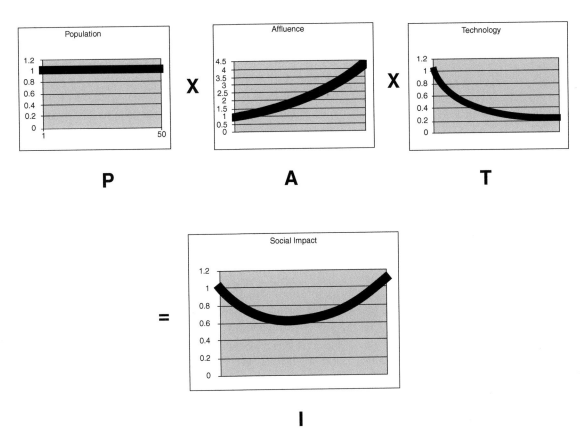

Figure 3.4. Illustration of the IPAT equation.

continues *'over a number of generations'* (as is explicit in the NZ Government's current SD policy), then the ability of technological improvements to reduce Technology Impact to an extent sufficient to stabilize Total Social Impact will be swamped.

Opportunities for substantial improvements in the efficiency with which resources are used to generate economic output are well established (Peet, 1992; von Weizsäcker *et al.*, 1997; Hawken et al., 1999); as a professional engineer, the writer is well acquainted with them! An important caveat coming from the aforementioned analysis is that these can only offer at best a breathing space if never-ending growth in economic output is the default expectation (Peet, 2002b). It is the idea that social 'well-being' (a desirable aim) somehow equates to continuing growth of GDP that is the central problem, not technology.

If we continue to see technological innovation as the answer to our perceived sustainability problems, we miss the fundamental point. The key to achieving sustainability is to address the idea of never-ending growth in consumption (GDP), not to hope that technology will provide the means to make more and more from less and less *in perpetuity*. Only within the theories of mainstream economics is it believed possible that unending growth in consumption of goods and services is both socially desirable and technologically possible, and then only because of a number of long-established fictions.

Opinions such as those expressed here are not new (Ehrlich *et al.*, 1999). Probably the most influential of the experts who have put forward related arguments are von Weizsäcker, Lovins, and Lovins (1997), in their book *Factor 4*:

They are right in saying that efficiency won't be enough. If exponential growth goes on at a rate of 5 per cent per annum, the entire Factor Four efficiency revolution would be eaten up within less than 30 years!

Similarly, in the follow-up book *Natural Capitalism*, by Hawken *et al.* (1999), the authors make the comment:

Eco-efficiency, an increasingly popular concept used by business to describe incremental improvements in materials use and environmental impact, is only one small part of a richer and more complex web of ideas and solutions. Without a fundamental rethinking of the structure and the reward system of commerce, narrowly focused eco-efficiency could be a disaster for the environment by overwhelming resource savings with even larger growth in the production of the wrong products, produced by the wrong processes, from the wrong materials, in the wrong place, at the wrong scale, and delivered using the wrong business models. With so many wrongs outweighing one right, more efficient production by itself could become not the servant but the enemy of a durable economy.

They go on in that book to describe four principles that are very valuable pointers to a way forward. Regrettably, these seldom get as much attention as eco-efficiency in the popular press, but need to be treated as equally, if not more, important, long term.

3.8 IMPROVED PARADIGMS

The neoclassical model of production and consumption linked by circular flows of exchange value can be modified by acknowledging the essential part played by the separate linear flows of material and energy (exergy) resources from the environment, through the economy, and out to 'pollution,' as shown in Figure 3.5. This can be seen as a thermophysical or engineer's model of economic activity (Peet, 2004).

Incorporation of the extra information gained from a material or energy analysis inevitably raises problems of commensurability of units, in that activities within the economy are conventionally represented in monetary units, whereas those in ecological and industrial systems are often better represented by material, energy, exergy, or entropy flows. There is no clear solution to this problem; multicriteria and multiobjective approaches are inevitable, in a context such as this, characterized by a high level of systemic complexity. Of one thing we can be sure, however; simply getting prices 'right' will never be more than part of a solution.

Again quoting Common (1996):

Ecology sees the problem [of sustainability] in terms of maintaining the resilience, or functional integrity, of ecosystems.

This definition is completely at variance with that of mainstream neoclassical economics, discussed earlier. It should not surprise one, therefore, that organizations such as, for example, the NZ Business Round Table, on the one hand, and Forest & Bird or Greenpeace, on the other, continue to talk 'past each other', in what often appears to be a 'dialogue of the deaf'.

Common goes on to make the comment:

The analysis of this problem shows that sustainability so conceived may require compromising consumer sovereignty. Human preferences may be such that economic activity is consistent with system integrity, but they may not be. If the latter is the case, correcting market failure is not sufficient for sustainability. In fact, we have rather little idea what the sustainability constraints are. We do not fully understand the implications, for human interests, of the interdependence of the systems.

In this quotation, Common clearly acknowledges that human activity (including the economic) is inherently constrained to obey the laws of Nature that govern the integrity of the system within which all our social and economic activities exist. The converse is not true!

Common then described **Ecological Economics** as:

An economics that takes what we think we know about our biophysical circumstances, and about human psychology, seriously – which

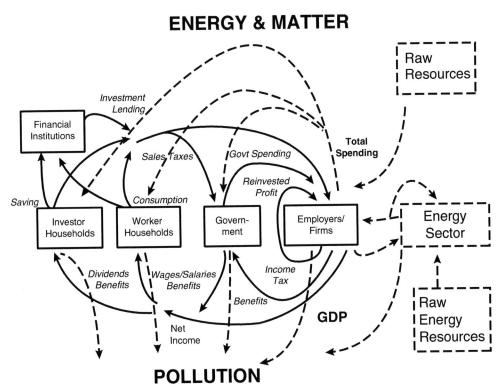

Figure 3.5. Thermophysical macroeconomic model.

standard neoclassical economics, including the sub-disciplines of environmental and resource economics, does not do. In fact, economics ignores the interdependence of the economic and ecological systems, and human psychology.

An approach that includes 'biophysical circumstances' is modelled in Figure 3.6, showing the thermophysical macroeconomic system of Figure 3.5 within, and at all times dependent upon, the 'super-system' ecological environment of Planet Earth (Peet, 2004).

This model also makes clear the necessity to define system boundaries with extreme care when examining issues such as SD. If the mainstream economic model (e.g., Figure 3.3) is used, everything of importance to the physical world (i.e., to full-system sustainability) is reduced to the level of an 'externality', when it is in reality central to the metabolism of the economy. This is because *that to which value is added* is largely invisible to the economic model – only the capital and labour spent on accessing resources from the environment and disposing of wastes are normally visible. If system boundaries are expanded, the dependence of economic systems on the import of net value from external natural systems becomes clearer. Since there is an upper bound upon this potential transfer, absolute scarcity exists and the question of optimum scale of the economy (and hence, the limits to economic growth) take centre stage.

3.9 WEAK AND STRONG SUSTAINABILITY

As Ekins *et al.* (2003) have pointed out, there are four different understandings of the meaning of sustainability, ranging from Very Weak, which assumes complete substitutability (including an implied equivalence in welfare terms between natural and human-made capital), to Very Strong, which assumes no substitutability, so that all natural capital must be conserved. Very Strong sustainability can actually be called 'absurdly strong' sustainability, since the author knows no ecological economist who holds to it.

This enables examination of the NZ Treasury position (NZ Treasury, 2002):

A 'strong' view of sustainability argues for conservation of natural resources based on the assumption that there will be little or no technological progress or substitution opportunities in the future.

The statement that strong sustainability implies 'little or no technological progress or substitution opportunities' shows that Treasury has used the absurdly strong sustainability meaning – presumably as a straw man in order to be able to dismiss it. But in doing so, Treasury has missed the point that ecological economists, are, in practice, committed to a much more moderate position, where substitutability of natural capital is seriously limited by environmental characteristics such as irreversibility,

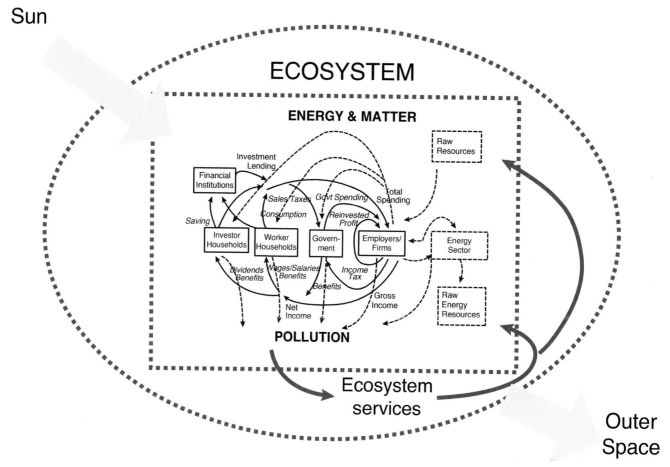

Figure 3.6. Biophysical model of the economy within Planet Earth.

indeterminacy, and the existence of 'critical' components of natural capital which are essential not only to human welfare, but also to the wider realm of the processes of life on Earth. Energy (in the particular sense of exergy) is a key example, in that the laws of thermodynamics unequivocally constrain the opportunities for substitution whenever physical processes are involved (as is always the case in economic production processes).

Ekins *et al.* (2003), as part of a powerful critique of weak sustainability (acknowledging strong sustainability as the preferred position), review the general situation admirably, while at the same time pointing to an improved methodology that incorporates the concept of Critical Natural Capital into a modified macroeconomic framework.

3.10 COMPLEX SYSTEMS

Human society is a complex system, in turn embedded in another – the natural environment. To ensure sustainability of the total system, the overall process must not only address each subsystem but also its contribution to the viability of the whole.

We can do this through generically examining the needs of systems, including human systems, a process which will inevitably include human valuations within social, cultural and institutional structures (see, for example, Peet and Bossel, 2000). It is suggested that SD means something like 'meeting human needs sustainably' (Peet and Peet, 2000).

At this point I would draw attention to Martinez-Alier *et al.*'s (1997) comment that '*[t]he economy is embedded in an institutional framework or context. The economy is also embedded in the social perceptions of the physical framework or context*'. Sociocultural perspectives are clearly no less important than the economic or physical, in this context. Given that point, it is essential to examine the social ethics that, implicitly or explicitly, guide us in our relationships with other people, other societies, other generations, and other species. They are at the base of our institutional structures.

Pursuit of a goal such as that of sustainability requires *responsible management of a complex system*, with the immediate qualification that *the complex system we are to manage is ourselves, individually and collectively*. In order to introduce management controls, however, we have to be very clear about both our goal (desired outcome) and the key criteria that will tell us whether we are making progress towards it. These criteria are generally known as *indicators*. The indicators, as well as the processes used to select them, will determine how we pursue our goal. These processes will ultimately depend, explicitly or implicitly, on our ethical position.

The choice of ethical framework has a major influence on our choice of those criteria (i.e., indicators) we intend to use to control our actions, in pursuit of responsible management of our own part of the whole complex socio-economic-environment system. It is also valid to assert a probable consequence, namely that what is not visible within our ethical horizon is of no interest to us. In other words, the ethical framework we adopt 'filters' what we see and what we do not see, and therefore constrains what we are prepared to use as control criteria. This explains, at least in part, why it is that those within the frameworks of the political-economic and the scientific world views appear unable to communicate with each other – they are unable to see and therefore understand, the other's position. This is a deeply unhelpful situation, and one that needs to be resolved as a matter of urgency.

One response – promoted here – is to point out that, as shown in Figure 3.6, the economic system exists within and is at all times subject to constraints imposed by the larger global ecosystem. Given the immense scale of human activity, on the global scale it can be suggested that they exist (for better or for worse) in a close relationship of interdependency. It is a fact that humanity as a whole is known to appropriate about as much of the planet's net photosynthetic production as is available for all other species combined. That alone confirms the importance of considering human activity at the same time as planetary ecosystem activity.

It is asserted that the ecosystem, the human social system, and the formal economy exist as parts of a hierarchy. Following Eisler (1987), there is a distinction between a *dominator* hierarchy (a power relationship) and an *actualization* hierarchy, which is a systemic descriptor of the way much of the world actually works. Currently, neoclassical economics is the tool of a dominator-type set of political theories (the neoliberal), based on encouragement of competition, conflict, and greed of individualistic humans who take centre stage in a society operating on utilitarian ethics.

The actualization hierarchy is the familiar one of systems within systems, for example, of molecules, cells, and organs of the body. Eisler (1987, p. 106) describes the actualization hierarchy as a progression towards a higher, more evolved, and more complex level of function. A dominator hierarchy, on the other hand, inhibits the actualization of higher functions, not only in the overall social system but also in individual humans.

The actualization hierarchy model also reflects the principles of strong sustainability, by acknowledging the dependence of all areas of society and the economy on the (higher) life-giving properties of the ecosystem of Planet Earth. From this viewpoint, the SD problem is reflected in three important economic problems – not one (allocation). Unless the associated economic problems of distribution (affecting the social domain and social justice) and scale (affecting the ecological domain and sustainability) are also included, the outcome cannot be regarded as comprehensive or coherent. Morality expressed in scientifically and socially informed ethics are the means whereby they can be brought together.

3.11 CONCLUSIONS

This chapter has traversed some of the ground occupied by both the utility-based and metabolic models of economic activity. It has been shown that neither is of itself sufficient to address the entire spectrum of issues that come under the heading of SD. How does one choose between them? In the author's opinion, one does not need to – both are necessary, albeit in different ways. The utility-based economic position, as described here, has relatively little of scientific importance to say about the natural world, but can contribute a lot to understanding many of the ways humans interact with each other. The science-based metabolic position, on the other hand, enables clear outer limits to be set on the extent of human interaction (e.g., throughput) with the natural world, but very little on how they should actually do it or how they should use the throughput flow.

As ecological economists, we should work to assist politicians and policy analysts to understand that these apparently incompatible models are in reality closely related, that both are important in their different ways and – perhaps most important of all – that they exist together as essential components of an actualization hierarchy. If that understanding can be achieved, it should be possible to move on from the current fractured and incoherent debate, where neither side appears able to find common ground, to one where each acknowledges the value of the other and where they jointly acknowledge, holistically, the complexity of the total system of humanity and all life within its global environment. If, instead of an either/or dichotomy, a both/and consensus can be reached, there is the potential to achieve coherent and creative policy development for sustainability in Aotearoa/New Zealand and in all other countries.

ACKNOWLEDGEMENTS

Assistance from Herman Daly and Murray Patterson in preparation of this chapter is gratefully acknowledged. Very helpful suggestions were also received from reviewers P. Ekins and G. Huppes.

An early version of this chapter was presented at the Australia-New Zealand Society for Ecological Economics (ANZSEE) Think Tank, *The Cutting Edge of Ecological Economics in Australasia*, 16 November 2003, University of Auckland, New Zealand.

REFERENCES

Common, M. (1996) What Is Ecological Economics? Land & Water Resources R&D Corporation Occasional Paper Series 09/96, Canberra.

Daly, H. E. (1994) Green delusions. *Ecological Economics*, **9**, 179–180.

Daly, H. (1999) *Ecological Economics and the Ecology of Economics: Essays in Criticism*, Cheltenham, United Kingdom, Edward Elgar Publishing.

Daly, H. (2002) Sustainable Development: Definitions, Principles, Policies. Invited Address, Washington, DC, World Bank, 30 April 2002.

Daly, H. (2003) *Ecological Economics: The Concept of Scale and Its Relation to Allocation, Distribution, and Uneconomic Growth.* Jasper, Alberta, Canada, Canadian Society for Ecological Economics Conference, 16–19 October.

Ehrlich, P. and Ehrlich, A. (1990) *The Population Explosion.* London, Hutchinson.

Ehrlich, P. R., Wolff, G., Daily, G. C., Hughes, J. B., Daily, S., Dalton, M. and Goulder, L. (1999) Knowledge and the environment. *Ecological Economics*, **30**(2), 267–284.

Eisler, R. (1987) *The Chalice and the Blade: Our History, Our Future.* New York, HarperCollins.

Ekins, P., Simon, S., Deutsch, L., Folke, C. and De Groot, R. (2003) A framework for the practical application of the concepts of critical natural capital and strong sustainability. *Ecological Economics*, **44**(2–3), 165–185.

Hamilton, C. (2002) Keynote address to the ECO Annual Conference, Environment and Conservation Organizations of NZ, Wellington, NZ, June 2002 (summarized in ECO newsletter ECOLINK, October 2002, p. 9).

Hawken, P., Lovins, A. and Lovins, L. H. (1999) *Natural Capitalism: Creating the Next Industrial Revolution.* Boston, New York, and London, Little, Brown & Company.

Martinez-Alier, J., Munda, G. and O'Neill, J. (1997) Some theories and methods in Ecological Economics: A tentative classification. Paper to ISEE Conference, Boston, MA, August 1997, p. 2.

NZ Government (2002) The Government's Approach to Sustainable Development, August 2002.

NZ Treasury (2002) Chapter Five: Growth and the Environment in its Briefing to the Incoming Government, 2002.

Patterson, M. (2003) Massey University, New Zealand, unpublished report to Landcare Research Ltd., with permission.

Peet, J. (1992) *Energy and the Ecological Economics of Sustainability.* Washington, DC, Island Press.

Peet, J. (2002a) Technology for Sustainability – A Noble Fallacy? ANZSEE 2002, Sydney, 2–4 December.

Peet, J. (2002b) Chemical Engineering & Sustainability: Is Green Processing Enough? Asia-Pacific Conference on Chemical Engineering (APCChE), Christchurch, New Zealand, September, paper # 235. Proceedings on CDROM.

Peet, J. (2002c) Sustainable development – Why is it so difficult? *Pacific Ecologist*, **4**, Summer 2002/2003, pp. 16–20.

Peet, J. (2004) Economic systems and energy, conceptual overview. In *Encyclopedia of Energy*, vol. II, pp. 103–115. Amsterdam, Elsevier Inc.

Peet, J. and Bossel, H. (2000) An ethics-based system approach to indicators of sustainable development. *International Journal of Sustainable Development*, **3**(3), 221–238.

Peet, K. and Peet, J. (2000) Poverties and Satisfiers: A Systems Look at Human Needs; Creating a New Democracy, Poverty, Prosperity, Progress. Devnet Conference, Wellington, NZ, 17–19 November.

von Weizsäcker, E., Lovins, A. B. and Lovins, L. H. (1997) *Factor 4: Doubling Wealth – Halving Resource Use.* The new Report to the Club of Rome, London. Earthscan, Australia, Allen & Unwin.

Zovanyi, G. (2004) A growth-management strategy for the Auckland region of New Zealand: pursuit of sustainability or mere growth accommodation? *International Journal of Sustainable Development*, **7**(2), 121–145.

4 Respect and reward: Ecology from the *Analects* of Confucius

YI CHEN[1,*] AND BORIS STEIPE[2]

[1]*Faculty of Society and Design, Bond University, Queensland 4229, Australia*
[2]*University of Toronto, Toronto, Canada*

Keywords:

Confucian philosophy; self-cultivation; propriety; respect; Confucius; Analects; ecology; climate change

Abstract

Today's ecological crises are scientifically well understood. Their dire consequences follow predictions with relentless accuracy. What is astounding is how little we can bring ourselves to do about them. Granted, powerful economic interests invest heavily in maintaining the status quo of consumption. But there is another side to this problem, a curious unwillingness, an inability to take personal responsibility. The reasons for this failure to respond are questions for philosophy.

The original sayings of Confucius are collected in a slim book, the *Analects*. Throughout, we find an emphasis on the nurture of ethical values that are derived from reciprocal forbearance, trustworthiness, and loyalty. In Confucian philosophy, the concept *Lǐ* 禮, generally translated as 'ritual propriety', expresses how a sincere respect for nature and society can manifest the self and how self-cultivation is a way to transform the private self into an open, transparent self that is in balance with the dynamics of one's environment. From this Confucian perspective, the self and its context, whether other individuals, society in general, 'nature', or the cosmos, exist in a constant, innate, gap-less encounter and dialogue, based upon meaningful differentiation rather than antagonistic struggle. The awareness of this immanent relationship is not based upon a set of imposed social rules, but an intuitive sensibility towards propriety, an 'enabling restraint', a procedure of propagation, derived from life's inner growth.

Grounded within an embodied self here and now, this attitude of sincere respect, independent of expectations of utility and reward, envisions behaviour in accordance with ecological needs and sustainable principles as an effortless response, fed by an aesthetic sensibility towards an environment that is constitutive of and cultivated within the self. Therefore, the key to ecological responsibility is an education through which we understand that responsible behaviour can be pursued because it is an expression of who we are as human beings, and for which economic gain, social status, and humanitarian responsibility are natural consequences. Such a personal yet not private response to our current challenges, day to day, and in every moment, is the ultimate win-win proposition.

4.1 INTRODUCTION: A QUESTION FOR PHILOSOPHY

When you sit in front of the panoramic window of the cafeteria of Tokyo's Nezu Museum and sip freshly made powdered green tea, the tea bowl in your hand, small as it is, nevertheless contains the entire green of the garden. In this tranquil moment, nature, you, and tea may become an original, inseparable, and harmonious unity.

Today's ecological crises – for example, pollution, climate change, mass extinctions – are scientifically well understood regarding their global scale[1] and the expected severity of outcomes (IPCC, 2014a). Their dire consequences follow predictions with relentless accuracy. We understand that the current challenges to ecology indeed constitute existential risks for humans and for humanity.[2] Therefore, rational actors should be

---

* Current address: Käte Hamburger Centre for Apocalyptic and Post-Apocalyptic Studies, Heidelberg University, Germany.

[1] Environmental impacts of humans on the planet are so profound (Waters *et al.,* 2016) that a proposal to label the 20th century as the beginning of a new geological epoch, the Anthropocene, is currently undergoing ratification by the International Union of Geological Sciences.

[2] Risk is loss multiplied by probability. If the result of an event is death or extinction, i.e., if we are considering loss of existential proportions, then even a small probability for the event to actually occur results in significant risk.

expected to pursue decisive, preventative action. Instead, policy makers are achieving too little, too late.[3]

A part of our inability to respond adequately to the challenges of climate change and others can be attributed to the targeted activities of influential lobby groups,[4] and powerful economic interests invested heavily in maintaining the status quo of consumption. However, macroeconomic effects derive from the actions of individuals, and while the process of decision-making rests on comparatively few actors in the private sector, politics, and law, these actors in turn are not isolated from the attitudes of consumers, voters, and their own social and professional networks. Policy makers are responsible to voters, company executives to shareholders, communities to their constituencies. It is a precondition of positive change that individuals take a stance in public discourse and hold their delegates and representatives responsible. This is, however, not the only way to make significant contributions: as the IPCC Fifth Assessment Report specifically states, 'Behaviour, lifestyle and culture have a considerable influence on energy use and associated emissions, with high mitigation potential in some sectors, in particular when complementing technological and structural change' (IPCC, 2014b, p. 20). Effective individual actions include having fewer children, living without a car, reducing intercontinental air travel, eating a plant-based diet, and purchasing renewable energy (Wynes and Nicholas, 2017). These are not trivial lifestyle choices, but they do emphasize that individual actions can indeed contribute significantly to mitigation – the role of the individual is not negligible.

In the face of the existential challenges of the Anthropocene, and given a perceived lack of options, it is becoming apparent that we are utilizing subconscious defence mechanisms, which lead to various forms of denial (Adams, 2016, pp. 129ff). The subsequent failure of individuals to respond broadly, across

cultures and societies, has been seen as a challenge for art as an alternative approach to understand factual information (Cape Farewell, 2018). As Cape Farewell's founder, David Buckland (2012) writes, 'Climate change proffers a unique cultural problem: it is a future truth' (p. 139). As such, its consequences are not tangible to our present society, and activists, artists, and scientists have collaborated in numerous projects to catalyse an intuitive awareness for such as yet intangible issues. Such intuitive awareness adds emotional and aesthetic dimensions to rational understanding and is thus expected to be a more effective way to change attitudes and behaviours. A recent study by Liselotte Roosen and colleagues (2018) reviews the effectiveness of Cape Farewell's and related activities and concludes that art indeed has benefits over other approaches to communicate climate-change issues. Art may show a way forward to help individuals understand 'what is'; the question 'what should be' is for philosophy.

In the following, we provide a philosophical exploration of the question how individuals could derive value from actions that are 'responsible' regarding the ecological crises sketched out above. We start from the text of the *Analects*, attributed to Confucius (551–479 BCE), to ask how the self is constituted in the everyday world and actualized in everyday activities, and we consider how sincere respect, encoded in rituals and rites, shapes the relationship between the self, others, and nature. We argue that there is an overlooked implication: such respect must be independent of an expectation of reward. And we outline that this reveals how utilitarian rewards to motivate individuals carry an inherent contradiction. This view on nurturing the self, derived from the *Analects* and based on a phenomenological understanding of the self-in-the-world, can act locally with global consequences and bring immediate benefits unconstrained by future truths.

4.2 ESSENTIAL CONFUCIANISM

Confucianism is one of the four great Asian philosophical traditions, along with Hinduism, Daoism, and Buddhism. Named after Confucius, it originated in ancient China some 2,600 years ago. The prevailing Western view of Confucianism is dominated by its supposed contrast to the Daoist and the Buddhist world view, in particular regarding the meaning of human life, how to manage human relations, and on the relationship between humans and nature.[5]

---

[3] Regarding 'doing too little', it is noteworthy that those countries that contribute most to global carbon emissions are also forecast to bear the highest country-level social cost of carbon (Ricke *et al.,* 2018), refuting arguments that activities in the developed world would disproportionally benefit other nations. As well, the magnitude of costs that are being downloaded to future generations has apparently been severely underestimated. Regarding 'acting too late', the IPCC report on the 1.5°C global warming milestone target contains a pessimistic outlook and a strongly worded warning (2018): *'Climate-related risks to health, livelihoods, food security, water supply, human security, and economic growth are projected to increase with global warming of 1.5°C and increase further with 2°C'* (p. 11). However, *'Pathways reflecting [the Paris accord] ambitions would not limit global warming to 1.5°C, even if supplemented by very challenging increases in the scale and ambition of emissions reductions after 2030'* (p. 24).

[4] For a poignant example, see the argumentation strategies against European Union action on climate change, authored by an influential industry lobby group, as detailed in a document leaked by the Greenpeace NGO (Greenpeace European Unit, 2018).

[5] The position of Confucianism on ecological and environmental ethics is discussed broadly in the literature and we can but provide a few recent results. A standard reference, albeit now 20 years old, is *Confucianism and Ecology* (Tucker and Berthrong, (eds.), 1998) in which a common thread is Neo-Confucian views on the relationship of humans and nature. Tracing environmental ethics to Neo-Confucian metaphysics provides a

A popular Asian artistic topos, however, is 'Three Vinegar Tasters', based on an apocryphal story about the three most accomplished intellectuals in China's Northern Sòng 北宋 dynasty: Sū Shì 蘇軾 (1037–1101), Huáng Tíngjiān 黃庭堅 (1045–1105), and the monk Fó Yìn 佛印 (1032–1098). The famed Chinese painter Lǐ Kěrǎn 李可染 painted the meeting as 'Three Sour-ness Painting' ('Sān Suān Tú' 《三酸圖》) (Lǐ, 1943), writing the following comment:

The monk at Golden Mountain Temple, Fó Yìn, was befriended with Huáng Tíngjiān and Sū Shì. One day, the two together visited the temple. Fó Yìn showed them a jar of freshly made 'peach flower vinegar'. After tasting the beautifully made vinegar, each of them showed a different expression of 'sour-ness'. Therefore, this painting is called 'Three Sour-ness Painting'.[6]

We may focus on the differences in experience from a Confucian, Buddhist, and Daoist perspective – but it is all the same vinegar.[7]

Like all great philosophies, including in particular Daoism and Buddhism, Confucianism has over millennia become a tradition of commentary as much as a platform for the words of its founders. But Confucianism served as state philosophy for a major part of Chinese history, and the ideas of Confucius and his disciples have been plied, interpreted from many vantage points, and adopted as a philosophical justification of authority by many different rulers and the commentators in their service. Indeed – and far removed from the founders' principles – Confucius' teachings are regarded today, especially in the West, as a philosophy that commands blind deference to received hierarchies. This is a profound misunderstanding. Yet, against the historical background, the actual position of Confucius and his disciples arguably might not be properly called 'Confucianism' at all.

Original sayings of Confucius are collected in a slim book, the *Analects*.[8] Throughout, we find an emphasis on the nurture of

ethical values that are derived from reciprocal forbearance, trustworthiness, and loyalty. These are the vehicles through which Confucianism is actualized: based on *Rén* 仁 (humanness), cultivated through *Lǐ* 禮 (propriety), and striving for *Hé* 和 (harmony).[9] The concise expressiveness of ancient Chinese lends itself well to excerption, and in the West, Confucius' *Analects* is often assumed to be aphoristic.

Take for example the 'Golden Rule': '*Do not impose on others what you would not wish for yourself*' (己所不欲，勿施於人) (*Analects* 12. 3. trans. Ni, 2017, p. 281), which is a first-order formulation of ethics that is common to virtually every philosophical tradition. Albeit hardly contentious, this and similar statements may have contributed to a perception of a doctrinal philosophy, a prescriptive, if not proscriptive world view.

As so often, even a cursory look at the actual source shows how the meaning of a quote changes, when seen in context. The *Analects* records a conversation between Zhòng Gōng 仲弓, the disciple, and the Master, on the question 'What is *Rén* 仁?'. Confucius responded: '*When you go out, behave as if you were going to greet a great guest; when you employ people, do it as if you were conducting a great sacrifice; do not impose on others what you would not wish for yourself. You will have no resentment either in the state or in the family*' (出門如見大賓，使民如承大祭。己所不欲，勿施於人。在邦無怨，在家無怨。*Analects* 12. 3[10]; trans. Ni, 2017, p. 281).

Herein lies a profound difference. Confucius did not command his disciple to behave in a certain way; he answered a philosophical question about the essence of *Rén* 仁 (humanness). Rather than teaching abstract moral principles, Confucius emphasized that *Rén* 仁 is a way of being humane. The specific examples of extending respect in encounters and in managing relationships manifest an *existential* aspect of the self, that is, *Rén* 仁, and this understanding of *Rén* 仁 happens to include the Golden Rule, which is however contextualized as one of many expressions of *Rén* 仁 through *Lǐ* 禮 (propriety).

Such humanness is the basis of Confucian philosophy and it is not rule-based, but expresses (the Confucian view on) human nature. Moreover, since every human is different, there is no

---

focus on 'reciprocity' in the most recent scholarship (Brasovan, 2017). For example, Zhou and Huang (2017) added 'aesthetic', 'moral', and 'social' dimensions to the previous metaphysical discussion on environmental issues but do not focus on 'respect' or 'reward'; Nuyen (2008) focuses on Confucian ethics as a philosophy of relationship, again with an emphasis on 'reciprocity'. Contributions to the current debates on ecological issues based on the *Analects* itself have not been adequately addressed in recent literature, with the exception perhaps of metaphysical questions raised by Tu Weiming in works cited elsewhere in this manuscript.

6   Translation by the authors; the original text is written on the painting itself (cf. Lǐ, 1943).

7   All three traditions have important contributions to make to environmental ethics, as does Hinduism. For a recent exposition of current approaches, such as 'comparative environmental philosophy', see Callicott and McRae (2014).

8   Numerous English translations are available; the most accessible online version is James Legge's translation available via Wikisource (https://

en.wikisource.org/wiki/Confucian_Analects). New, annotated translations in print include Ni (2017) and Chin (2014). Roger Ames and Henry Rosemont, Jr., offer a philosophical translation; see Ames and Rosemont (1999). A standard modern English translation can be found in Oxford World's Classics, translated by Raymond Dawson (Confucius, 2008).

9   For a more complete exposition of key Confucian concepts, we would need to add *Shù* 恕 (reciprocity), *Yì* 義 (righteousness), *Xìn* 信 (trustworthiness), and *Zhì* 智 (wisdom). These seven concepts were named the '*five plus two*' (*Rén, Yì, Lǐ, Zhì, Xìn, Shù, Hé*) by Alan Chan (Zēng Fán Rú 曾繁如), the 76th generation descendant of one the most respected Confucian disciples, Zēngzi 曾子 (or Zēng Diǎn 曾點) (cf. Chan and Chen, 2018).

10   For a positive formulation of the 'Golden Rule', see also *Analects* 6.28.

single doctrine that would be applicable to everyone and any time – such a doctrine would directly contradict *Rén* 仁. Therefore, while Confucianism does promote the Golden Rule, considering it a doctrine is based on a misreading of Confucius.

But if Confucian philosophy is not prescriptive, how can *Rén* 仁 be pursued? The Confucian approach is embodied in the Confucian concept *Lǐ* 禮.

4.3 THE CURIOUS NATURE AND ROLE OF RESPECT IN *LǏ* 禮

In Confucian philosophy, the concept *Lǐ* 禮, interpreted and translated as 'ritual', 'rites', 'etiquette', 'customs', 'ritual-propriety', 'observing ritual-propriety', or simply 'propriety', is, first of all, a concept that is devoted to shaping the integrity of mind and body through shaping day-to-day behaviour. *Lǐ* 禮 expresses respect and reverence for the context in which we exist, showing that both nature and society can manifest the self and, in turn, be cultivated through the self. *Lǐ* 禮 aims to foster a self that is fully aware, while situated within the complexity of social relations. Self-cultivation (*xiū shēn* 修身) in the Confucian tradition is a day-to-day, moment-by-moment process, regardless of the social and economic status of an individual. It is this 'self-cultivation' through *Lǐ* 禮 that transforms the private ego into an open, transparent, dialogical identity in a harmonious balance with the dynamics of the natural and social environment it experiences.

The directives that constitute the Confucian *Lǐ* 禮 are complex and detailed. Yet they express a common requirement: an attitude of respect, almost a spiritual awe towards every single entity, be it nature, human, or divine, that one encounters. *Lǐ* 禮 is the expression of this fundamental reverence, and staying true to this principle overrides all other considerations:

子曰：「麻冕，禮也；今也純，儉。吾從眾。拜下，禮也；今拜乎上，泰也。雖違眾，吾從下。」

The Master said, 'The use of a linen cap was prescribed by the rituals, but now a silk one is used instead. It is economical, and I follow the common practice. Bowing before ascending the hall was prescribed by the ritual, but now the practice is to bow only after ascending it. This is arrogant. I continue to bow below the hall, though it is contrary to the common practice'.

(*Analects* 9.3; trans. Ni, 2017, pp. 230–231)

In ancient China, linen was more precious than silk and this passage emphasizes that the actual rules of propriety must bend to the discerned principles for which they were formulated. The Confucian places the essence of *Lǐ* 禮 above widely accepted social norms. Blind acceptance of rules and unreflective conformity is in fact not proper. This has deep implications regarding the actualization of *Lǐ* 禮: it is not enough to

perform the ritual – it must be performed with an inner sense of meaning and with sincere respect. Obviously, respect can be nurtured but not commanded, and in exactly this sense *Lǐ* 禮 is not to be considered prescriptive; indeed, if it were, it would miss its point.

Lǐ 禮 is best understood as a *personal* yet *public* interpretation of a principle – 'personal' denotes its origin in self-reflective awareness, in an authentic exposure of the roots and motifs of day-to-day practice; 'public' characterizes its open and dialogical nature.[11] Confucius' explanation puts it clearly: an 'economical' choice might even enhance *Lǐ* 禮, whereas 'arrogance' is a defect of attitude and certainly not compatible.

This has profound implications for Confucian governance. The widely accepted *Lǐ* 禮, when genuinely practised, is expected to foster and nurture an awareness of the common good in a society, without the need to explicitly invoke that good as a reward. Such governance through *Lǐ* 禮 is considered to be much more natural and sustainable than an exertion of authority, enforced through punishment:

子曰：「道之以政，齊之以刑，民免而無恥；道之以德，齊之以禮，有恥且格。」

The Master said, 'Leading the common people with administrative regulations and keeping them in order with penal punishments, they will try to avoid troubles (mian 免) but will have no sense of shame (chi 恥). Leading them with virtue (de 德) and keeping them in order with ritual propriety, they will have a sense of shame and will constrain (ge 格) themselves'.

(*Analects* 2.3; trans. Ni, 2017, pp. 95–96)

Similar ideas appear throughout the *Analects*, for example when Confucius was asked by Jì Kāngzi 季康子, a member of the ruling family, whether it is right to kill the unrighteous, in order to be close to the righteous, Confucius replied, *'Sir, in governing, what is the need for killing? If you aspire to what is good, the common people will be good. The virtue of those in high stations (junzi 君子) is like the wind, and the virtue of common people (xiaoren 小人) is like the grass. The grass will surely bend when the wind blows across it'* (季康子問政於孔子曰：「如殺無道，以就有道，何如？」 孔子對曰：「子為政，焉用殺？子欲善，而民善矣。君子之德風，小人之德草。草上之風，必偃。」(*Analects* 12.19; trans. Ni, 2017, 293).

The Confucian idea of good governance is certainly not based upon indiscriminate love or naïve altruism. Confucians believe that human beings are not born equal, but with different

---

[11] The relationship between 'personal' and 'public' in the Confucian philosophy of 'self-cultivation' was highlighted in a recent keynote speech by Tu Weiming 杜維明, a widely acclaimed Confucian thinker and public intellectual, at the 24th World Congress of Philosophy held in Beijing, China, in August 2018 (Tu, 2018).

abilities, and the moral achievements of every one are different.[12] But beneath such a distinction is a premise that moral good is not only a constitutive part of being a human, a human universal, it is also beautiful and truly brings joy to each individual, in every moment. This is important; after all, what we consider to be ethical is more often than not a reflex of our aesthetics.

This aesthetic dimension of *Lǐ* 禮 is opened up by an immanent curiosity, which is often misinterpreted as external guidance and/or imposed regulation. One such instance can be found in a passage that is hardly questioned and rarely found ambiguous:

有子曰：「禮之用，和為貴。先王之道斯為美，小大由之。有所不行，知和而和，不以禮節之，亦不可行也。」

Master You said, 'Bringing harmony (he 和) is the most valuable practical function of ritual propriety. This is what makes the way of the former Kings beautiful, whether in things great or small. There are situations in which this will not work: if one tries to bring about harmony for harmony's sake without regulating it by ritual propriety, this is not going to work'.

(*Analects* 1.12; trans. Ni, 2017, p. 89)

The passage seems to be coherent with regarding *Lǐ* 禮 as external regulation, guidance, or prescription.[13] The crucial character, though, is *jié* 節, here translated as 'regulating'.

Etymologically, *jié* 節 denotes a 'node', in particular the nodes that segment the culm of the bamboo stalk, and that meaning survives in *zhú jié* 竹節, bamboo node. The anatomy of bamboo shows that the cells at the node are distorted, compressed by the growth of the shoots, and the fibres are significantly shorter than those of the flexible internodes, which gives the stalk stiffness, permits the culm to bend if necessary, and limits the extent of splitting when overstressed (Liese, 1998, p. 94). Interestingly, no matter how different the appearance of bamboo from species to species, the nodal area remains distinctively special. If we consider this original meaning of *jié* 節, the interpretation of the passage mentioned earlier changes, from an imposed *constraint* to an enabling *restraint*. The *node* structures but transmits; therefore, we translate *jié* 節 as *propagate* and the translation acquires a distinctly different tone: '*The use of* Lǐ 禮 *is for precious harmony. This way of former kings has beauty, and things small and large follow. Still they would not practice harmony through harmony: if not propagated through* Lǐ 禮, *harmony will not do.*'

When we interpret *jié* 節 as 'to propagate', we intend to reveal the etymological significance of the character, which has been forgotten in contemporary usage. The etymology provides a phenomenological footnote to the abstract meaning of 'restraint', as *jié* 節 is normally translated. Confucius himself never stopped inquiring and questioning the true meaning of *Lǐ* 禮, and he did not hesitate to say that he did not know much about it:

子入大廟，每事問。 或曰：「孰謂鄹人之子知禮乎？入大廟，每事問。」子聞之曰：「是禮也。」

When the Master entered the Grand Temple, he asked about everything. Someone said, 'Who says that the son of the man of Zou understands (zhi, 知) *the rituals? When he entered the Grand Temple, he asked about everything'. The Master heard the remark and said, 'It is itself a ritual'*

(*Analects* 3.15; trans. Ni, 2017, p. 122).

If we were to consider *Lǐ* 禮 to be an empty formula, then we might consider Confucius' questioning as a mere expression of courtesy. However, asking everything about even the most familiar matters allows meaning to grow from exchange. In this case, the *Lǐ* 禮 that Confucius performed in the Grand Temple illustrates that the true expert does not hesitate to question his expertise. Casting his questions as an expression of *Lǐ* 禮, the estrangement inherent in restraint propagates the inquiry. For Confucius, such learning is itself *Lǐ* 禮. Similarly, Confucius once claimed that he did not know about the *Dì* 禘 *rituals*: '*Someone asked the meaning of the* di *sacrifice. The Master said, "I do not know. Wouldn't one who understands it find the affairs under heaven* (tianxia 天下) *just as displaying them in this?" pointing to his palm*' (或問禘之說。 子曰：「不知也。知其說者之於天下也，其如示諸斯乎！」指其掌。(*Analects* 3.11; trans. Ni, 2017, p. 120)

Some may need doctrines and good examples to aspire to *Rén* 仁, but such growth is already enabled by the immanent propagation, or restraint, of *Lǐ* 禮. Since restraint in this sense is an attitude, not imposed behaviour, it cannot be enforced, nor does it need to be. Through properly, respectfully, and sincerely practising *Lǐ* 禮, adjusting one's own propriety in both self-cultivation as well as in governance, a common virtue, or social harmony (*Hé* 和), develops. In a phenomenological sense, this brings 'thickness' to the self; as in the examples of Confucius' own practice, *Lǐ* 禮 manifests the self as a phenomenon but does not constrain it.

We emphasize the dialectic of respect in this relationship: respect is attitude, not behaviour. However, proper behaviour can indeed foster an attitude of respect, which in turn becomes both an expression of the self and its constitution. Interestingly, this dialectic resonates, for example, with the familiar observation that the conscious behaviour of smiling can in fact improve well-being (Kraft and Pressman, 2012). In this way, a

---

[12] Note the profound difference in world view that underlies the notion of equality in a focus on equal rights, in the West, versus a focus on differentiated responsibilities in Confucianism.

[13] See, for example, previous translations such as Ames and Rosemont (1999, p. 74), Chin (2014, p. 9), and Leys (1997, p. 5).

Confucian path towards responsible, ecological behaviour turns on the notion of respect.

4.4 EXISTENTIAL CONFUCIANISM

The Confucian idea of a complex, situated self, rather than a one-dimensional private ego, is expressed in the Confucian philosophical term 'self-cultivation' (*xiū shēn* 修身), whose meaning is reflected in the Chinese character for the 'self': *shēn* 身, body. This body is both constituted and shaped as an integrated natural and cultural human-*becoming*, and the archetypical posture of this becoming is one of uprightness.[14] The body as an emerging, constitutive self grants a presence here and now; the dialectic of inward attitude and outward behaviour is a silent but immanent *encounter*. Note that we are not talking about the Cartesian mind-body dichotomy, but referring to the humanistic basis of the Confucian mode of self-cultivation, namely *Lǐ* 禮 (propriety).

Based on its etymology, the Chinese character *Lǐ* 禮 literally means 'sacrificial utensils'. Through adherence to *Lǐ* 禮, self-cultivation transforms the self into a phenomenon. Indeed, 'self' becomes a phenomenological *project* that situates the self both within and beyond society. To be authentic, such a dynamic process of self-cultivation cannot blindly follow *Lǐ* 禮 as a finite set of immutable norms. For those who properly adhere to *Lǐ* 禮, the practice is dynamic and comprehensive. This embodied expression of a transcendental objective is vividly illustrated through one of the core subjects of Confucian education: archery, *shè* 射, a martial art that originates from the closest point of the body, here and now, but nevertheless reaches the most remote, even seemingly invisible target.

Practising the Confucian *Lǐ* 禮, first of all, leads us back to 'real' activities in the 'real' world, a world that is referred to as 'the world of perception' by the French phenomenologist Maurice Merleau-Ponty (1908–1961), who reminds us of the very existence of *this* world thus:

The world of perception, or in other words the world which is revealed to us by our senses in everyday life, seems at first sight to be the one we know best of all. For we need neither to measure nor to calculate in order to gain access to this world and it would seem that we can fathom it simply by opening our eyes and getting on with our lives. Yet this is a delusion.

(Merleau-Ponty, 2008, p. 31)

Lǐ 禮 defends against this delusion, since it transforms everyday activities into performances, and this distancing makes

matters that we would otherwise take for granted, available to reflection, deeper insight, and restructuring. It provides the distance we need to examine the things that are closest to our self, so close that they would otherwise be invisible. This calls for examining the *Lǐ* 禮 of everydayness.

4.5 RITUAL IN THE KITCHEN

The existential view of Confucian philosophy integrates theory and practice or rather shows how they are one and the same. In the language of modern Continental Philosophy we can speak of phenomena and the dialectic of distancing to make the self as a phenomenon accessible to self-reflection. Intriguingly, this is the same approach that has been developed in Confucian *Lǐ* 禮 for a long time – moreover, with an emphasis to open up paths to self-improvement, not merely reflection. However, the *Analects* is not doctrine; it invites us to seek examples that resonate with us personally in our quest for *Lǐ* 禮. Confucius offers this concrete example:

食不厭精，膾不厭細。食饐而餲，魚餒而肉敗，不食。色惡，不食。臭惡，不食。失飪，不食。不時，不食。割不正，不食。不得其醬，不食。肉雖多，不使勝食氣。惟酒無量，不及亂。沽酒市脯不食。不撤薑食。不多食。祭於公，不宿肉。祭肉不出三日。出三日，不食之矣。食不語，寢不言。雖疏食菜羹，必祭，必齊如也。

He did not demand his rice to be superbly polished or his meat and fish to be finely minced. He did not eat rice that was spoiled, nor fish or meat that was rotten. He did not eat if the food was discolored, or it smelled bad. He did not eat anything that was improperly cooked or during periods other than regular mealtime. He did not eat meat if the animal was not properly slain, nor did he eat what was served without the right sauce. Though there might be plenty of meat, he would not eat more of it than rice. Only with alcohol did he set no limit, though not to the point of disorienting himself. Wine and dry meat purchased from the marketplace he would not eat. He would not remove ginger from his food, though he would not eat too much of it. During a court sacrifice, he would not keep the meat overnight (su rou 宿肉). Sacrificial meat could not be used three days after it was prepared. Beyond three days, he would not eat it. When eating, he would not converse (yu 語). When lying in bed, he would not talk (yan 言). Even when he had only coarse rice and vegetable soup, he would always (bi 必) offer them as sacrifice, and he always did so as if he were fasting.

(*Analects* 10.8–10.11; trans. Ni, 2017, pp. 251–254)

The English translation of this passage faces difficulties. For example, its beginning '*Shí bú yàn jīng, kuài bú yàn xì* 食不厭精，膾不厭細' has become a common Chinese idiom 'pursuing refinement in preparing rice, slicing meat in the thinnest way' which means pursuing the peak of refinement. Taken at face value this appears to contradict Confucius' overall attitude

---

[14] The original form of *shēn* 身 body, in the archaic Oracle Script style, highlights the curve of the body and that which supports it, the backbone.

of being content with a simple life: *'With coarse rice to eat, plain water to drink, and my bended arms for a pillow, joy can be found in the midst of these [...]'* (飯疏食飲水，曲肱而枕之，樂亦在其中矣)。(*Analects* 7.16; trans. Ni, 2017, p. 200). Moreover, the entire passage, as is usual in classical Chinese, was written without personal pronouns, thus equally valid translations, for example, of *shí bùyǔ* 食不語 express various registers of authority: 'Confucius never spoke when eating', 'One does not speak at a meal', or even 'Don't talk with your mouth full!'[15] But whatever the register, the essence is to demonstrate that the very same refinement of eating could be either vice or virtue – vice, if it fosters decadence; virtue, if it promotes reverent attention to detail. The difference does not derive from outward appearance but emerges from our innermost attitude. This is not cherry-picking – Confucian philosophy most certainly does not expound moral relativism – on the contrary: though the approaches are negotiable, the advancement of *Rén* 仁 is an absolute.

Focusing on the *Lǐ* 禮 of the kitchen in practice, every food item is given full consideration from both mind and body: sensational, emotional, and intellectual. Food is not merely consumed, but a source for appreciation and aesthetic enjoyment of what has been served; concern for the quality, the look, the smell, the taste, and the quantity of the food, and paying special attention to the right time, all contribute to the conscious ritual of eating.

Confucius intentionally positions eating alongside sacrificial rituals. This juxtaposition does not only transmit a sense of spiritual awe but, more importantly, transforms eating from an inconvenient interruption of more important affairs into a reverent way of life and meaningful activity of self-cultivation. Receiving food and returning respect realizes the metaphysical goal of 'Unity between Heaven and Human Beings' (*tiānrénhéyī* 天 人 合一), the highest achievement for a Confucian thinker.[16]

The proper balance between humans and nature, which is after all the quintessential concern of ecology, can be supported by this everydayness. The simple act of eating consciously can contribute to well-being, as has been recently reported in a large study on the psychological benefits of dietary regimes (Lassale *et al.,* 2018). The authors reported that 'healthy' dietary regimes – irrespective of their specifics – were correlated with a decreased risk for clinical depression. Intriguingly, this correlation was not apparent in regimes that aim to achieve a specific benefit for hypertension, although the dietary recommendations are virtually the same. A mechanical expectation of benefits might not only be misplaced, but might actually be counterproductive, and this has deep implications for a Confucian approach to ecology. Considering climate action to be an investment and demanding results as return, prompting action with the promise of reward would miss the point. Such is the trap of utilitarianism: in practice, universal utility remains elusive. But how else could we 'reward' respect?

4.6 RESPECT AND REWARD

In a frequently cited passage of the *Analects*, Confucius describes the meaning of sacrificial rituals through the state of mind in which they are performed: *'Sacrifice is as if [there is a] presence. Sacrifice to spirits is as if the spirits are present. The Master said: "Would I not [sincerely] participate in a sacrifice [it is] as if I would not sacrifice [at all]"'*[17] (祭如在，祭神如神在。子曰：「吾不與祭，如不祭。」) (*Analects* 3.12). In the expressive terseness of classical Chinese, the author's intent hinges on the understanding of two words: *'as if'* and *'participate'*. Regarding 'as if', Peimin Ni points out that a true sacrifice would channel spirituality and reverence, an attitude that would be appropriate for believers and atheists alike: 'This position does not focus on *believing* the existence or presence of the spirits as they are in themselves; instead, it guides one's mental disposition of their 'as-if-presence' in the practice' (Ni, 2017, p. 121). Regarding 'participate', we add *sincerely* to the translation, to emphasize the *Analects'* general attitude towards rituals that we have discussed at length above. In context, the passage emphasizes this: sacrifice means a sincere spiritual experience. This in turn means that it is inconceivable that such an attitude could involve an expectation of reciprocity, a benefit granted in return for the sacrifice. Indeed, 'as if the spirits are present' demands to be understood as a spontaneous expression of *unconditional* respect. This subtle but crucial point profoundly distinguishes the *Lǐ* 禮 of the *Analects* not only from traditional folk religion, but also from the state religion promoted by 'Confucianism'.[18] We contend that such 'respect, independent of

---

[15] In principle, we prefer the impersonal voice: 'Not speaking while eating' which retains the original ambiguity, attenuates the prescriptive implication, and thus makes it easier for the reader to relate the passage to the self, rather than to a deity, sage, or authority.

[16] Tu Weiming observed such unity as a common Confucian goal for the most distinguished Confucian thinkers in the 20th century from both mainland China, Taiwan, and Hong Kong and named this phenomenon the 'Ecological Turn in New Confucian Humanism' (Tu, 2004, p. 480). Tu's metaphysical approach to the relationship between mankind and nature, which is characteristic of the metaphysics of Neo-Confucianism, situates human beings within the cosmos, in an extension from the self to the family, to the state, to nature, and beyond, based upon an expanding network of reward in reciprocal relationships.

[17] Authors' translation. Peimin Ni translates, 'Sacrificing as if present. When sacrificing to the spirits, do it as if the spirits were present. The Master said, "If I did not participate in a sacrifice, it is no different from not having done the sacrifice"' (2017, p. 121).

[18] On the purpose of sacrificial rituals in the Confucian tradition, see, e.g., Ruin (2018).

reward' is more true to the attitudes promulgated in the *Analects* than the focus on reciprocity which is read into them up to today. And we further contend that this attitude provides an important alternative formulation of Confucian ethics and environmental ethics in general.

Let us illustrate this principle from a movie that is set in Japan, a society in which a high regard for mutual respect and harmony in relations pervades the social sphere and is ubiquitous in daily life. Famed director Hayao Miyazaki has made an inspiring movie that can be read as an ecological allegory from a Confucian perspective, with Shintoist overtones: *My Neighbour Totoro* (Miyazaki, 1988).[19]

The story is set in the *satoyama* (里山) landscapes of Saitama prefecture, near Tokyō. The *satoyamas* are the quintessential Japanese cultural landscapes, wherein small-scale sustainable farming centred around rice paddies integrates diverse crops, grassland plots, aquaculture, forest stands, and subsistence husbandry and has over millennia shaped nature and the inhabitants' attitudes towards nature. This agricultural model, based on harmony with nature and human beings, is indeed Confucian at its core – every activity, no matter whether it is planting, weeding, or harvesting, is taken care of with utmost respect and reverence. The year is approximately 1955, significantly at a time when Japan was regaining balance in its post-war reconstruction efforts, but before it had lost its ecological innocence in the environmental catastrophes of Minamata disease and Yokkaichi asthma (cf. Kagawa-Fox, 2010, p. 62) – some 20 years before the movie was made.

Two young girls move into an old farmhouse with their father and soon, in a narrative space between dream and reality, encounter Totoro, a large and benevolent spirit of the forest who lives in a hollow of a giant camphor tree. One dark night, waiting at a bus stop in the rain, the girl Satsuki offers her father's umbrella to Totoro, who has appeared waiting beside her. This offering is significant in that it initiates a relationship from a gesture of respect, and clearly without implied obligation. When Totoro leaves, he gives Satsuki a small package in return. These offerings of mutual respect and recognition establish harmony: the umbrella is given because it is proper to hand someone an umbrella in the rain. The package contains seeds and acorns. In Confucian terms, this exchange is an example of *Shù* 恕 (reciprocity).[20]

Satsuki and her little sister Mei plant the acorns – but at first they will not grow. Some days later in a moonlit night, the two girls join Totoro in a stalk-raising ritual and bring forth a gigantic towering tree from the seeds. While Totoro initiates the ritual, its success comes from the joint efforts between the two sisters and the spirits of nature. The movie's exchange of respect and harmony is not at all directed towards reward and compensation: if any benefits appear, they are joyfully accepted, but they are not to be expected.

This allegory perfectly illustrates how the Confucian principle of respect acts from the self and towards the self: expecting reward from a gesture of respect would void its sincerity, but mutual respect ensures reciprocal benefit. This is Confucian propriety, and it is an obvious model for environmental ethics (Kagawa-Fox, 2010), as it establishes a virtuous cycle of action and inner growth that does not depend on external validation. In this way, a principal problem of our culture of runaway consumption can be addressed: it appears unreasonable to expect the problems of unsustainable practices that are driven by consumer habits to be solved from a culture that expects (material) returns. In contrast, the prospects of establishing well-being through respectful, sustainable life choices appear far more promising. Confucian philosophy can contribute to the defining of creative, practical approaches to individual development and support a powerful win-win proposition.

---

[19] We follow Damian Cox and Michael P. Levine in asserting that film studies can be a valuable addition to the philosopher's toolbox. *'Philosophical problems [...] are ingredients of life. As such, and with varying degrees of success, they are often depicted and analysed in literature and film, as well as in art forms, such as music and painting that have less explicit narrative content, or perhaps no narrative content at all'* (2012, p. 18). Indeed, film is not just a domain for philosophical thinking; it can be a medium of philosophy in its own right. We further observe that whether a film is a critical or even commercial success is a salient fact by itself, since it reflects on the degree to which the work resonates with the general sentiment of a society. Therefore, we discuss *My Neighbour Totoro* since it not only illustrates the attitude of 'respect, independent of reward', but this attitude is essential to the storyline, which hinges on specific actions of the main protagonists that conform to the Confucian ideal we develop in this manuscript. Remarkably, the movie not only resonates with its original Japanese audience but has also become an enduring success in the Western world following its worldwide release.

[20] Note that 'reciprocity' in a Confucian sense is an exchange without expectation of reward, originating from the self. This concept cannot be exactly translated into English, where reciprocity implies 'reciprocation of cooperative or altruistic behaviour' (OED online, 2018). In the Confucian sense, however, we have sequential but independent unilateral actions, originating from sincere respect, and the reciprocal relationship only appears in the perspective of a third-person observer. *Shù* 恕, although regarded as a key concept in Confucian philosophy, is in fact mentioned only twice in the *Analects*. The first instance uses the term to express a sense of extending favours to others (*Analects* 4.15). The second instance is remarkable. To a disciple's request for one maxim that could direct his entire life, Confucius replies: *'Would that not be "reciprocity"? What [one] oneself does not wish, do not impose on others'* (「其恕乎、己所不欲、勿施於人。」) (*Analects* 15.24). The Golden Rule is expressed word by word as in *Analects* 12.3, discussed earlier, but here it defines the core of Confucian 'reciprocity' (*Shù* 恕); there it defines 'humanness' (*Rén* 仁). Since this establishes an equivalence of those two concepts, this further underscores that the English sense of the word 'reciprocity' is not an appropriate translation of the Confucian concept.

This does not come for free: *Lǐ* 禮 is not magic and there are no shortcuts. In *My Neighbour Totoro*, the acorns had to be planted and carefully tended before they grew. In the morning, the towering tree was no longer present. Nevertheless, as Satsuki and Mei dance around their little field in which their seeds have now actually sprouted, they can cheer: 'It was a dream, but it wasn't a dream' (Miyazaki, 1988, 1:00:55).

4.7 CODA: HARMONY

Respect in Confucian philosophy is a reward in and of itself. Social harmony and the harmony between humans and nature derive naturally from a life-long 'self-cultivation' (*xiūshēn* 修身). And indeed, this is the opening of the *Analects*:

子曰：「學而時習之，不亦說乎？有朋自遠方來，不亦樂乎？人不知而不慍，不亦君子乎？」

The Master said: "To learn (xue 學) *and to practice* (xi 習) *what is learned repeatedly* (shi 時)*, is it not pleasant? To have companions* (peng 朋) *coming from far distances, is it not delightful? To be untroubled when not recognized by others, is this not being an exemplary person* (junzi 君子)*?"*

(*Analects* 1.1; trans. Ni, 2017, p. 79)

Regarded as the quintessential Confucian agenda up to today,[21] 'learning for the self' sets the basic tone for Confucian philosophy – a philosophy for which learning is a lived and living foundation. Learning through proper timing and practice, learning to build and enjoy spiritual friendship, and learning to become the true self without aspiring to impress others – all these virtues converge.

To foster such learning, Confucius' renowned disciple Zēngzi 曾子 remarks, *'I daily examine myself on three counts — whether, in serving others, I have been not wholeheartedly devoted* (zhong 忠)*; whether, in interacting with friends, I have been not trustworthy* (xin 信)*; whether, having been given instruction, I have not practiced accordingly?'* (曾子曰：「吾日三省吾身：為人謀而不忠乎？與朋友交而不信乎？傳不習乎？」(*Analects* 1.4; trans. Ni, 2017, p. 82).

The negative emphasis of this passage may disguise the true enjoyment and the aesthetic value of this self-reflective mode of learning. Yet the apparent 'harshness' towards the self illustrates how restraint propagates self-cultivation, which underscores how *Lǐ* 禮 nurtures harmony from within and how harmony grows from the cultivated self.

Personal, individual decisions can indeed contribute to managing the existential risks of the Anthropocene. They may be associated with personal sacrifice. Why would we want to do this? Confucian philosophy gives the answer that such actions are 'proper', as they express respect for the world around us; through sincerely expressing respect, they become not merely something we do, but an expression of who we are. The *Analects* and the Confucians after it up to the present time affirm that respect is a constituting element of the self, balancing it with its relationships; we point out, in addition, that in order to extend *sincere* respect, that respect has to be independent of anticipated benefits. Apparently, it is so natural for us to focus on the beneficial returns of Confucian virtues – their reward – that the inherent contradiction between sincerity and expectation of reward is usually overlooked. But it is important to realize that being motivated by reward – however noble the outcome – makes the virtue itself contingent. Not only is this limitation unnecessary, it also perpetuates the root cause of our inability to respond adequately to the existential environmental challenges we face. If everyone's respect depends on the expectation of benefit, we are back at the irreconcilable tangle of conflicting objectives of utilitarianism, in which no agreement can be achieved on the 'best' approaches to a multi-polar, globally pluralistic world. As we extend respect for the sake of its own merit, rather than in anticipation of any benefit, we propagate our humanness. Once this objective is apparent, specific measures can facilitate it, and the insight we propose has actionable consequences with measurable outcomes. Educators have had success with activities that empower students through engagement; the ecological, community-based movement for restoring *satoyamas* is another example that comes to mind, and an increasing body of work in psychology is demonstrating that gratitude is correlated with reduced materialism. Indeed, interventions to increase gratitude in American adolescents have significantly decreased materialism and increased generosity (Chaplin *et al.*, 2018), and there are obvious parallels between this empirical evidence and our philosophical argument.

There is yet another crucial advantage to promoting respect through self-improvement: that is the question of the time horizon in which positive outcomes can be realized. The benefits of actions to prevent a global catastrophe may not become apparent in our lifetimes. In the best case, as a result of enormous effort, the environment does not degrade catastrophically – and the positive outcome may be no more than that the current status quo can be maintained. In contrast, the benefits of expending such efforts in a framework of sincere respect – perhaps codified in personal ritual – are manifest in every moment and with every act. They are not deferred; they do not depend on a large number of like-minded allies; they are immediate and personal.

---

[21] Tu Weiming's talk at the 24th World Congress of Philosophy held in Beijing, China, in August 2018 emphasizes 'learning for the sake of the self'. According to Tu, the Confucian Way of learning starts from a concrete self, here and now, situated within a societal network, formulated by various traits of the roles and relationships, yet able to navigate 'troubled waters' through learning and self-cultivation (Tu, 2018).

Buckland's dilemma that a 'future truth' seems unable to motivate current behaviour (2012) could yet be resolved.

We hope our thoughts will contribute a philosophical framework to creatively pursue the many specific activities that it implies and that those in turn can be expected to spark a virtuous cycle for individuals, for society, and for the world around us.

Back in Tōkyō's Nezu Museum, you finish your bowl of tea. The green of the surrounding garden is now within you, where it has always been in the first place.

ACKNOWLEDGEMENTS

The authors are deeply grateful to Joseph A. Adler, Kenyon College, Gambier, OH, USA; Loy Hui Chieh, National University of Singapore; Rosita Dellios, Bond University, Gold Coast, Australia; and an anonymous reviewer, for contributing their time and experience to provide valuable feedback and helpful suggestions.

REFERENCES

Adams, M. (2016) *Ecological Crisis, Sustainability and the Psychosocial Subject: Beyond Behaviour Change.* Studies in the Psychosocial series. Basingstoke, UK, Palgrave MacMillan.

Ames, R. and Rosemont Jr., H. (Trans.) (1999) *The Analects of Confucius: A Philosophical Translation.* New York, Random House.

Brasovan, N. S. (2017) *Neo-Confucian Ecological Humanism: An Interpretive Engagement with Wang Fuzhi (1619–1692).* Albany, State University of New York Press.

Buckland, D. (2012). Climate is culture. *Nature Climate Change*, **2**, 137–140.

Callicott, J. B. and McRae, J. (2014) *Environmental Philosophy in Asian Traditions of Thought.* Albany, State University of New York Press.

Cape Farewell (2018) Cape Farewell: The cultural response to climate change. https://capefarewell.com

Chan, A. and Chen, Y. (17 December 2018) Introduction to Confucian Principles in our Age. The Confucian Weekly Bulletin (Blog). https://confucianweeklybulletin.wordpress .com/2018/12/17/introduction-to-confucian-principles-in-our-age/

Chaplin, L. N., Roedder John, D., Rindfleisch, A. P. and Froh, J. J. (2018) The impact of gratitude on adolescent materialism and generosity. *The Journal of Positive Psychology*, **14**, 502–511.

Chin, A. (2014) *Confucius: The Analects.* New York, Penguin Classics.

Confucius (2008) *The Analects.* R. Dawson, trans. Oxford, Oxford University Press.

Cox, D. and Levine, M. P. (2012) *Thinking through Film: Doing Philosophy, Watching Movies.* Chichester, UK, Wiley-Blackwell.

Greenpeace European Unit (2018) Greenpeace comment on leaked EU industry climate change strategy. https://www.greenpeace .org/eu-unit/issues/climate-energy/1563/leaked-business-europe-climate-change-memo/

IPCC (2014a) Summary for policymakers. In C. B. Field, V. R. Barros, D. J. Dokken, K. J. Mach, M. D. Mastrandrea, T. E. Bilir, M. Chatterjee, K. L. Ebi, Y. O. Estrada, R. C. Genova, B. Girma, E. S. Kissel, A. N. Levy, S. MacCracken and P. R. Mastrandrea (eds.), *Climate Change 2014: Impacts, Adaptation, and Vulnerability. Part A: Global and Sectoral Aspects.* Contribution of Working Group II to the Fifth Assessment Report of the Intergovernmental Panel on Climate Change. Cambridge, Cambridge University Press. http://www .ipcc.ch/report/ar5/wg2/

(2014b) Summary for policymakers. In O. Edenhofer, R. Pichs-Madruga, Y. Sokona, E. Farahani, S. Kadner, K. Seyboth, A. Adler, I. Baum, S. Brunner, P. Eickemeier, B. Kriemann, J. Savolainen, S. Schlömer, C. von Stechow, T. Zwickel and J. C. Minx (eds.), *Climate Change 2014: Mitigation of Climate Change.* Contribution of Working Group III to the Fifth Assessment Report of the Intergovernmental Panel on Climate Change. Cambridge, Cambridge University Press. http://www.ipcc.ch/report/ar5/wg3/

(2018) Summary for Policymakers. In *Global Warming of 1.5°C.* An IPCC special report on the impacts of global warming of 1.5°C above pre-industrial levels and related global greenhouse gas emission pathways, in the context of strengthening the global response to the threat of climate change, sustainable development, and efforts to eradicate poverty. http://www.ipcc .ch/report/sr15/

Kagawa-Fox, M. (2010) Environmental ethics from the Japanese perspective. *Ethics, Place and Environment*, **13**(1), 57–73.

Kraft, T. L. and Pressman, S. D. (2012) Grin and bear it: The influence of manipulated facial expression on the stress response. *Psychological Science*, **23**(11), 1,372–1,378.

Lassale, C., Batty, G. D., Bhagdadli, A., Jacka, F., Sánchez-Villega, A., Kivimäki, M. and Akbaraly, T. (2018) Healthy dietary indices and risk of depressive outcomes: A systematic review and meta-analysis of observational studies. *Molecular Psychiatry*, **24**, 965–986.

Leys, S. (1997) *The Analects of Confucius.* New York, Norton Company.

Li, K. (1943) Three Sour-ness Painting (Sān Suān Tú 《三酸圖》). http://www.likeran.com/library/index/id/753/

Liese, W. (1998) *The Anatomy of Bamboo Culms.* Beijing, International Network for Bamboo and Rattan.

Miyazaki, H. (Director) and Tokuma, Y. (Producer) (1988) *My Neighbour Totoro* (となりのトトロ) (Video/DVD). Tokyo, Studio Ghibli.

Merleau-Ponty, M. (2008) *The World of Perception*. O. Davis, trans. New York, Routledge.

Ni, P. (2017) *Understanding the* Analects *of Confucius: A New Translation of* Lunyu *with Annotations*. Albany, State University of New York Press.

Nuyen, A. T. (2008) Ecological education: What resources are there in Confucian ethics? *Environmental Education Research*, **14**(2), 187–197.

OED Online (2018) *Reciprocity*. Oxford, Oxford University Press. http://www.oed.com/view/Entry/159546

Ricke, K., Drouet, L., Caldeira, K. and Tavoni, M. (2018) Country-level social cost of carbon. *Nature Climate Change*, **8**, 895–900.

Roosen, L. J., Klöckner, C. A. and Swim, J. K. (2018) Visual art as a way to communicate climate change: a psychological perspective on climate change-related art. *World Art*, **8**(1), 85–110. DOI:10.1080/21500894.2017.1375002.

Ruin, H. (2018) Death, sacrifice, and the problem of tradition in the Confucian Analects. *Comparative and Continental Philosophy*, **10**(2), 140–150. DOI:10.1080/17570638.2018.1488353.

Tu, W. (2004) The ecological turn in new Confucian humanism: Implications for China and the world. In Tu Weiming and M. E. Tucker (eds.), *Confucian Spirituality*, vol. 2, pp. 480–508. New York, Crossroad Publishing Company.

(2018) Spiritual humanism: Self, community, earth and heaven. In Proceedings of the XXIV World Congress of Philosophy, pp. 456–474. http://wcp2018.pku.edu.cn/yw/latestnews/82188.htm

Tucker, M. E. and Berthrong, J. (eds.) (1998) *Confucianism and Ecology*. Cambridge, MA, Harvard University Press.

Waters, C. N., Zalasiewicz, J., Summerhayes, C., Barnosky, A., Poirier, C., Gałuszka, A., Cearreta, A., Edgeworth, M., Ellis, E., Ellis, M., Jeandel, C., Leinfelder, R., McNeill, J., Richter, D., Steffen, W., Syvitski, J., Vidas, D., Wagreich, M., Williams, M., Zhisheng, A., Grinevald, J., Odada, E., Oreskes, N. and Wolfe, A. P. (2016) The Anthropocene is functionally and stratigraphically distinct from the Holocene. *Science*, **351** (6,269), 138–147.

Wynes, S. and Nicholas, K. A. (2017) The climate mitigation gap: Education and government recommendations miss the most effective individual actions. *Environmental Research Letters*, **12**, 074024.

Zhou, W. and Huang, G. (2017) Chinese ecological discourse: a Confucian-Daoist inquiry. *Journal of Multicultural Discourses*, **12**(3), 272–289.

5 Sustainable development from an East-West integrative perspective: Eastern culture meets Western complexity theory

ROSITA DELLIOS

Faculty of Society and Design, Bond University, Queensland 4229, Australia

Keywords

Sustainable development; complex adaptive systems; Daoism; yin-yang; Indian philosophy; mandala

Abstract

Sustainable development as a concept and a practice has much to gain through an integration of traditions of thought culture. This entails cultivating the holistic approach found in Eastern philosophy and culture, while still valuing the analytical Western contribution. The conceptual catalyst for this to occur is an emerging 'tradition' of thought: complexity theory. More specifically, complex adaptive systems, or CAS, represent a Western match to Eastern thinking. Therefore it is possible to have an integrative perspective, without having to privilege Western cultural perspectives on development, nor upturn them in favour of alternative models of development. The integrative or holistic model can work well for incorporating diverse approaches. This also appears to be Chinese President Xi Jinping's message when he conveys the Chinese approach to development in his 'common destiny' speeches. India's pluralistic traditions also sit well with the idea of 'the one and the many' and of the harmony of opposites.

5.1 INTRODUCTION

Sustainable development may be regarded as a preferred form of change that reflects a dynamic order. This resonates with the famous saying of the early Greek philosopher Heraclitus: You cannot step into the same river twice. His intellectual descendants in today's world, systems theorists, would explain that renewal of the waters of a river allows the river as a larger system to continue. Early Chinese philosophy, too, is premised on change: one polarity inherently gives rise to the other within a universal circle, as depicted by the *yin-yang* symbol. This circle exists by virtue of the dynamic parts. 'Going with the flow' is

the prescriptive message of Daoism (see Lau, 1963); stagnation, by contrast, is the fate of systems that seek only to preserve. If the very early philosophers of the East and West exhibit common cause in their notion of change, even if their arguments are often expressed differently, what does the modern West have to offer in advancing towards an integrative perspective on an issue of pressing global concern: sustainable development? One fruitful avenue of approach is the application of complex adaptive systems (CAS). It would not only encourage the incorporation of diverse approaches to sustainability – and hence greater 'resilience' through innovative combinations – but would also allow complexity to work itself out in cycles of renewal. This is why it is important to remind ourselves that sustainable development is predicated on change – and that change is a process that can be grasped both analytically through systems science and intuitively through Eastern (especially Chinese and Indian) philosophy.

5.2 WHAT IS A COMPLEX ADAPTIVE SYSTEM?

Complex adaptive system derives from systems theory – that is, systems that arise from the interaction of their parts. Systems can be distinguished from a collection of objects, such as a bag of sweets or seashells that are not connected to form a whole. Weather systems, social systems, and ecological systems, for example, are interconnected. By constantly adapting to the changing environment in a self-organizing way, they become known as complex systems. This is dynamic change that can be viewed as a spectrum of equilibrium-to-chaos. Modern science has traditionally concerned itself with equilibrium-to-equilibrium transitions, but this changed with chaos theory and the modelling via 'computer experiments' that came with it (Colchester, 2016). Out of chaos theory grew complexity theory (or complexity science), which gave rise to CAS as a field of study. One of CAS's key findings is that 'robust' (competitive) systems are not too static, as they desire innovation. But they are also careful not to fall apart – or go over the 'edge of chaos', a term referring to the transition phase between order and randomness. They want just enough innovation to thrive, but not so much as to be swamped by it. This makes them 'complex' (as distinct from 'complicated'). At this point it is worth noting that scientific understanding of 'sustainability' remains a work in progress, especially on 'how transitions to sustainability may occur, or can be actualized' (Peter and Swilling, 2014, p. 1,595). Complexity theory is regarded as a 'unifying principle' and an 'over-arching way of thinking' whose task is a practical one: 'to help better understand and support transitions to sustainability', but with the proviso that any such support needs to be 'plurifocal, multi-scale, multi-level and adaptive' (Peter and Swilling, 2014, p. 1,596).

This raises another feature of complexity: nested systems. Systems are embedded in larger complex sets and often contain smaller ones. The notion of sustainable development would need to take this into account, recognizing that the parts are not self-sufficient but interact within a larger context of relationships. This means that renewal at the lower scale may represent turbulence within its own horizon but stability for the larger system within which it is embedded. In other words, sustainable development may need to experience 'creative destruction' at sub-levels if the system as a whole is to adapt and evolve. Is this not a contradiction? How can a system be sustainable yet flirt with chaos and even destruction?

The answer may lie in shifting one's focus from 'sustainable' to 'development'. The idea of development – like change – is not a static one. Natural systems display a lifecycle of birth, growth, consolidation, decline, and death. Voinov and Farley (2006) made the point that '[i]f a system is sustained for too long, it borrows from the sustainability of a supersystem and rests upon lack of sustainability in subsystems. Therefore, by sustaining certain systems beyond their renewal cycle, we decrease the sustainability of larger, higher level systems' (p. 104). This implies that all the parts of a system need not be sustainable:

Fostering sustainability for too long at local and regional scales, and for lower level subsystems of the global human system and the global ecosystem may be detrimental to global sustainability. The function of the biosphere is more than a sum of functions of continents, countries and regions; local and regional goals and priorities may conflict with global ones and therefore we cannot envision the sustainable global design as a hierarchy of sustainable subsystems. (p. 110)

The message here is the same as that of the document which made sustainable development a defining slogan for the global era: *Our Common Future*. This report of the World Commission on Environment and Development (WCED, 1987) defined sustainable development as 'development that meets the needs of the present without compromising the ability of future generations to meet their own needs' and projected the whole planet as its unit of analysis. This returns us to the problem, well posed by Voinov and Farley (2006), of how 'we reconcile sustainability with systems dynamics in an ecological-economic system' (p. 111). The authors find the solution in subsystem sacrifice. Thus, 'if we are to build sustainable economies able to support a human population of 8bn–10bn, one inescapable conclusion is that we must destroy much of today's growth-driven economy and jettison many of the lifestyles it supports' (p. 111).

Still others, questioning the hierarchical assumptions in nested systems and the life-cycle analysis that comes with it, emphasize the fact that hierarchies change. In their examination of linked social, economic, environmental, physical, and political (SEEPP) systems, Peter and Swilling (2014) therefore advance the notion of heterarchy rather than hierarchy:

A heterarchy can be conceptualized as 'fishnet' or a flat hierarchy in which 'functions rise to authority' depending on context. As such, it is a more appropriate framework with which to 'track' the changing relationships and behaviours of complex systems. In a heterarchy, hierarchies can evolve. (p. 1,601)

Moreover, the sub-optimization of subsystems would require trade-offs that are 'acceptable to different sectors of society in actualizing sub-optimization' and that this would require these sectors to negotiate changes in the norms that could lead to such an outcome. Considering that *Our Common Future* was published in 1987 and the global level of analysis still remains a contested proposition, as evidenced by the climate change debates of more recent times, it is little wonder that a strategy towards sustainability will require 'integration, inclusion and coordination' among interest groups (Peter and Swilling, 2014, p. 1,607).

The interest groups that have made up the climate change debate are often more policy-oriented than concerned with climate science. In seeking justification for avoiding the implications of climate change, policymakers have afforded 'climate sceptics' the 'oxygen of publicity' – to borrow a famous turn of phrase from the United Kingdom's Thatcher government in the 1980s. While the then prime minister was referring to terrorists and calling on broadcasters to deny them an opportunity to gain publicity, 'climate sceptics' have been emboldened by an aversion by big business and politicians to reduce emissions – especially when the argument for change in behaviour and the way the socio-economic system operates concerns the unknowable future.

Indeed, the inherent nature of making projections for the long-term future is that there is no certainty, only degrees of likelihood. But when the likelihood approaches near certainty, can warnings be ignored? A prognosis that there is a certainty of more than 90% that global warming is caused by human activity represents a high degree of certainty for such a high-impact occurrence. It would call for concerted action. This assessment by the United Nations Intergovernmental Panel on Climate Change (IPCC) in 2007 was upgraded to 'extremely likely' (more than 95%) in the leadup to the 2015 Paris Agreement on Climate Change. A commitment was made by most countries to limit emissions so that global warming would not exceed 2°C, with a further attempt to keep it within 1.5°C above pre-industrial levels. While not technically binding, and funding promises to developing countries to assist in coping with emission cuts may prove inadequate, 'integration, inclusion and coordination' were instrumental in arriving at such a consensus. National conferences held prior to the Paris conference were accompanied by preparatory reports by the IPCC that involved the scientific community around the world. The inclusion of governments and organizations also advanced the cause of coordination with interest groups, so that the IPCC was able to provide advice that went beyond a superficial debate between climate change sceptics and supporters.

Nonlinearity is another feature of CAS. Rather than being determined by the principles of cause and effect, mathematical progression, or expecting the future to follow past trends, CAS are intersubjective. The parts mutually define themselves within their environment. While its nomenclature is modern, and systems terminology has become specialized, the phenomenon of CAS stretches as far back as one cares to search and may be discerned across many disciplines of endeavour. For example, the Western classical strategist Carl von Clausewitz was attuned to war's nonlinear nature (see Beyerchen, 1992). Therefore, the commanding 'genius' on the battlefield is the one who grasps the whole situation and can move decisively even in the face of uncertainty (Clausewitz, 1976, Book I, Ch. 3). This is an unexpected example of CAS applied to history and strategic studies. It is 'unexpected' because we are not trained to read Clausewitz's tome, *On War*, from this perspective. But in doing so, our experience is enriched by this novel configuration. As complexity theory would have it, new bridges of understanding have been formed. Before long, CAS is no longer an unexpected way of thinking about the world, but a way of opening up a bigger picture of possibilities. This is the quest that is also pursued in finding an integrative way of looking at sustainable development, not only from within the systems theory community and its offshoots but also across cultures – which themselves constitute complex systems.

5.3 THE HARMONY OF OPPOSITES

It is a truism that we not only believe what we see but also see what we believe. Alternative ways of thinking are therefore worth entertaining, not only because of their intrinsic worth but

also because, for many cultures, that which we call the alternative is in fact the mainstream. A clear example is holism versus reductionism. The first refers to interconnected thinking which is nonlinear, the latter to analytical thought. The first is typically Eastern, the second predominantly Western. Two Eastern cultures that display holistic thinking are the Chinese and Indian. They are also 'rising powers' that will be influential in shaping the discourse on sustainable development, as their cultural orientations become more globalized. China has already articulated a sustainable development ethos via its ecological civilization plans (see UNDP, 2013; Ferguson and Dellios, 2017, pp. 56–57) and Xi Jinping's efforts at 'inclusive development' (e.g., NDRC, 2015). Indian pluralism is well represented in the mandalic notion of interconnectedness. Because India has still to make the policy strides achieved by China, discussion here will focus mainly on China. The Indian mandala, however, serves as the unifying platform upon which different perspectives find 'common ground'. It is an uncommonly powerful metaphor that has much to offer the sustainable development dialogue.

Turning to China, perhaps the best-recognized systems symbol is that of the *yin-yang* (Figure 5.1). With its two mutually regarding hemispheres that form a whole, it has been adopted globally from health products to the martial arts to surf culture. Conceptually, *yin-yang* represents a theory of correlativity, even a 'dialectics' of harmonization. The complementary polarities of the *yin* (female) and *yang* (male) principles are seen in such pairings as waning-waxing, receptive-proactive, hidden-open, defensive-expansive. One gives rise to the other in a cycle of renewal. *Yin* and *yang* are forms of *qi* – a life energy which is both 'matter' and 'potentiality' – and give rise to the myriad phenomena (Zhang, 2002, pp. 45–46).

Reality, in Chinese ontology, contains its potential. Something exists, or has the potential to exist, in relation to something else. This is the *yin-yang* dialectic of mutual articulation. The pursuit of the *Dao* – the Way – entails harmonizing

Figure 5.1. *Yin-yang* symbol (*Source*: Wikimedia Commons).

with this process rather than controlling it. Thus, in CAS parlance, the trade-offs between different levels and agents within a system would indeed be inclusive rather than controlling, for the classical concept of harmony (*he*) is one in which diverse interests prevail in a dynamic balance. Harmony was understood as the 'unity of any nonidentical objects', as fulfilling 'living things', which in their diversity allowed for 'the possibility of new things arising' (Zhang, 2002, pp. 270–271). Translated into CAS, harmony is inclusive of discord but not overtaken by it. If discord does overtake the system, dynamic harmony loses its integrative quality and breaks up into chaos; alternatively, when it is stifled by uniformity, harmony ceases to exist – as it is not to be confused with 'assent' (see Zhang, 2002, p. 272; Neville, 1988).

Where the *yin-yang* symbol stands out as a Chinese mode of thought, the mandala has strong Indic associations. Sanskrit for 'circle', the mandala is a nested system of concentric forms that commonly depict Hindu and Buddhist cosmologies (Figure 5.2). It represents an inter-relational whole and carries Indian cultural concepts, including 'codependent origination'. This Buddhist idea teaches the interdependence of all phenomena. They are empty of their own existence, contingent, and pluralistic.

Beyond the spiritual, there was the political expression of mandala as a 'statal circle' that described the international politics of the Mauryan Empire (321–185 BCE). This was enshrined in the *Arthashastra* or *The Science of Polity* (Shamasastry, 1967), a third-century BCE Indian governance text, attributed to the Mauryan Chief Minister Kautilya. As a political structure, mandalas in pre-modern Southeast Asia, which was influenced

Figure 5.2. Mandala (*Source*: Wikimedia Commons).

by Indic culture, were regional complexes with shifting hierarchies of power. Use of the term 'mandala' can refer to a single entity with an internal structure of concentric circles comprising a dominant overlord and tribute-paying vassals, as well as to relations among a number of such entities in the region (Wolters, 1968, 1982). A single polity's structure was not rigid and often shifted from one centre to another, sometimes exhibiting polycentric characteristics (see Dellios and Ferguson, 2015). Even within a single centre, according to Gesick (1983), 'the secondary and tertiary centres preserved a great deal of their internal autonomy in exchange for acknowledging the centre's spiritual authority' (p. 3).

Political constructs in this traditional world order reflected a spiritual cosmology. In Buddhist thought, the centre, which represents perfected Buddhahood, can be either concentric or polycentric. Such an apparent paradox may be explained in terms of a dynamic relationship of codependent origination. Moreover, each sentient being harbours the potential for Buddhahood, thereby holding the centre within, just as 'the seeker is none other than the sought' (Sharma, 1995, p. 11), from the Hindu philosophical perspective. The mandala represents a cultural technology in which the world is seen 'in the round' – a unity for all its diversity.

In this respect it is interesting to note that the Sanskrit word for ocean, *sagar*, has been converted into an acronym. SAGAR stands for Security and Growth for All in the Region. It was used when Indian Prime Minister Narendra Modi visited Mauritius in 2015, saying, 'We seek a future for the Indian Ocean that lives up to the name of SAGAR – Security and Growth for All in the Region' (Bhaskar, 2017). Here may be found a Kautilyan application for modern Indian statecraft, using its own cultural vocabulary.

To India's inherent pluralism, so well depicted in the mandala's differentiation and interconnectedness as well as its oceanic metaphor, China adds mutuality, and together they contribute to a more adaptive international order, with an Eastern holistic outlook. At the start of this century, Beijing officially invoked the classical discourse of 'harmony' to give developing countries a stronger voice as part of the 'democratization' of international relations. When President Hu Jintao (China's leader from 2002 to 2012) articulated his country's 'harmonious world' foreign policy perspective at the United Nations in 2005, he addressed the need 'to preserve the diversity of civilizations in the spirit of equality and openness, make international relations more democratic and jointly build a harmonious world where all civilizations coexist and accommodate each other' (Xinhua, 2005; see also Dellios and Ferguson, 2013). The subsequent president's rendering of this message was captured in his 'common destiny' speeches. Two examples in 2015 are the Boao Forum, at which President Xi Jinping spoke of a 'Community of Common Destiny' in which 'we need to seek win-win cooperation and common development' (Xi, 2015a), and the 60th anniversary of the 1955 Asian-African Conference in Bandung. Apart from calling for an expansion of South-South cooperation, which was to be expected at such a conference, President Xi was even more inclusive. He saw the need for greater North-South cooperation: 'From the strategic perspective of building a community of common destiny for mankind, North-South relations are not merely an economic and development issue but one that bears on the whole picture of world peace and stability' (Xi, 2015b).

Here may be found the potential for an emerging SEEPP (social, economic, environmental, physical, and political) world system that enables sustainable development to take root. This requires both cultural and administrative channels. Without the cultural dimension of mutuality and inclusive harmony, it would be difficult to administer China's most ambitious project to date, the new silk roads. Collectively known as the Belt and Road Initiative (BRI), this endeavour seeks to transform the economies and connectivity of regions that adjoin China and beyond. The authoritative *Vision and Actions on Jointly Building Silk Road Economic Belt and 21st-Century Maritime Silk Road* (NDRC, 2015) states, 'We should promote ecological progress in conducting investment and trade, increase cooperation in conserving eco-environment, protecting biodiversity, and tackling climate change, and join hands to make the Silk Road an environment-friendly one.' One of the BRI's financing and investment bodies, the multilateral Asian Infrastructure Investment Bank (AIIB), which was initiated by China, is clear on this point. It seeks to meet 'the challenges of sustainable development in Asia' (AIIB, 2016, p. 1), and its Environmental and Social Framework document sets out detailed environmental and social requirements. These include the need for projects to demonstrate that they are environmentally and socially sound; are capable of addressing environmental and social risks and impacts; allow for public consultation and disclosure; address both short- and long-term development; and cooperate with development partners on environmental and social matters (AIIB, 2016, p. 2).

A successful BRI will need to become a set of evolving systems, incorporating SEEPP elements engaged by diverse international organizations, states, and private companies at different scales within major development corridors across Eurasia and South Asia. Although initially a Chinese-led mega-project, a developmentally successful BRI will need to evolve into a multilateral, multinational, and transnational complex system.

This is where President Xi Jinping's 'common destiny' message – reminiscent of WCED's *Our Common Future* in that we share in the fate of this planet and are co-creators of its well-being or otherwise – takes on an empirical presence. The BRI, in its transcontinental reach, is not only an expression of the world as one, but also a mandala of integration and differentiation. If China is a near-realized superpower, then its top leader is one step ahead in seeing the transition through. President Xi's accrual of power across the nation's policy-making apparatus has been advanced by the removal of constitutional constraints to the duration of his presidency. Perhaps more substantial than the penetration and perpetuation of Xi's rule is the elevation of his 'thought' in Chinese communist ideology. This lives beyond the grave and is enshrined in the party and state constitutions. 'Xi Jinping Thought on Socialism with Chinese Characteristics for a New Era' acts as a guide for the Chinese Communist Party in the 'new era' of China's global future. It adds to 'Mao Zedong Thought' and 'Deng Xiaoping Theory' in taking China to the next level of governance. Not surprisingly 'Xi Jinping Thought' includes three essential principles: *common human destiny* (discussed earlier); *new development ideas* that incorporate 'innovative, coordinated, green, open and shared development'; and *coexistence with nature* – 'We must establish and practise the philosophy that lucid waters and lush mountains are invaluable assets, uphold the basic national policy for energy conservation and environmental protection, treat the ecological environment as we treat life, ... and contribute to global ecological safety' (Xi Jinping quoted in *BBC Monitoring*, 2017).

5.4 CONCLUSION

With the return of Eastern civilizational thought in a contemporary context, a world system mandala may now be conceptualized as a diagram of relationships towards sustainable development. The mandala as a conceptual tool may be regarded as a high-context totality picture, which allows national development and future-oriented policies to be viewed 'in the round', incorporating the religious and spiritual alongside the material and scientific. The mandala is a dynamic process and accords with the Chinese view of change as the underlying principle of the universe, expressed through the alternating interaction of *yin* and *yang*. The traditional Western scientific view tends to concentrate on causal change – or that which we can attempt to control and seek to predict. The new science of complexity is more structured in scientific language than Daoist intuitive thinking but also less mechanistic than the Western model. It has more in common with the pre-Socratic philosopher of change, Heraclitus of Ephesus, who not only made the point that change in the subsystems (water) sustains the higher structure (the river), but also that the unity that manifests in diversity 'rests by changing' (see Guthrie, 1977, Ch. 7). This 'going with the flow', in Daoist terms, permits the paradox of resilience. Complex adaptive systems, in their nonlinear treatment of change, provide a bridge between East and West. Awareness of different scientific and cultural perspectives helps in identifying the future contours of sustainable development through an integrative perspective.

ACKNOWLEDGEMENTS

I would like to acknowledge Dr Dzulkifli Abdul Razak and Dr Salleh Mohd Nor as helpful and insightful reviewers of this chapter.

REFERENCES

AIIB (Asian Infrastructure Investment Bank) (2016) Environmental and social framework, February. https://www.aiib.org/en/policies-strategies/_download/environment-framework/20160226043633542.pdf

BBC Monitoring (2017) His own words: The 14 principles of 'Xi Jinping Thought'. from China Central TV-1, Beijing, in Mandarin Chinese, 18 October. https://monitoring.bbc.co.uk/product/c1dmwn4r

Beyerchen, A. (1992) Clausewitz, nonlinearity, and the unpredictability of war. *International Security*, **17**(3), 59–90.

Bhaskar, C. U. (2017). IORA Summit: India's maritime opportunity – Analysis. *Eurasia Review*, 18 March. http//www.eurasiareview.com/18032017-iora-summit-indias-maritime-opportunity-analysis/

Clausewitz, C. (1976) M. Howard and P. Paret (eds. and trans.), *On War*. Princeton, NJ, Princeton University Press.

Colchester, J. (2016) Edge of chaos. *Complexity Academy*, 24 August. http://complexityacademy.io/edge-of-chaos/

Dellios, R. and Ferguson, R. J. (2013) *China's Quest for Global Order: From Peaceful Rise to Harmonious World*. Lanham, MD, Lexington Books.

    (2015) Thinking through Srivijaya: Polycentric networks in traditional Southeast Asia. Paper presented at the Second Global South International Relations Conference – *Voices from Outside: Re-shaping International Relations Theory and Practice in an Era of Global Transformation*. Storrs, CN, International Studies Association (ISA). http://works.bepress.com/rosita_dellios/54/

Ferguson, R. J. and Dellios, R. (2017) *The Politics and Philosophy of Chinese Power: The Timeless and the Timely*. Lanham, MD, Lexington Books.

Gesick, L. (1983) Introduction. In L. Gesick (ed.), *Centres, Symbols, and Hierarchies: Essays on the Classical States of Southeast Asia*. Monograph No. 26. New Haven, CN, Yale University Southeast Asia Studies.

Guthrie, W. K. C. (1977) *History of Greek Philosophy*, 4th ed. Cambridge, Cambridge University Press.

Lau, D. C. (trans.) (1963) *Lao Tzu: Tao Te Ching*. Harmondsworth, UK, Penguin Books.

NDRC (National Development and Reform Commission, Ministry of Foreign Affairs, and Ministry of Commerce of the PRC, with State Council authorization) (2015) *Vision and Actions on Jointly Building Silk Road Economic Belt and 21st-Century Maritime Silk Road*, 1st ed. http://www.fmprc.gov.cn/mfa_eng/topics_665678/xjpcxbayzlt2015nnh/t1249618.shtml

Neville, R. C. (1988) Between chaos and totalization. In S. H. Liu and R. E. Allison (eds.), *Harmony and Strife: Contemporary Perspectives, East and West*. Hong Kong, Chinese University Press.

Peter, C. and Swilling, M. (2014) Linking complexity and sustainability theories: Implications for modelling sustainability transitions. *Sustainability*, **6**, 1,594–1,622.

Shamasastry, R. (trans.) (1967) *Kautilya's Arthasastra*, 8th ed. Mysore, India, Mysore Printing and Publishing House.

Sharma, A. (1995) Hinduism. In A. Sharma (ed.), *Our Religions*. San Francisco, CA, HarperCollins.

UNDP (2013) *National Human Development Report 2013: Sustainable and Liveable Cities: Towards Ecological Civilization*. With the Institute for Urban and Environmental Studies China. Beijing, China Translation and Publishing Company, August. http://www.cn.undp.org/content/dam/china/docs/Publications/UNDP-CH-HD-Publication-NHDR_2013_EN_final.pdf

Voinov, A. and Farley, J. (2006) Reconciling Sustainability, Systems Theory and Discounting. *Ecological Economics*, **63**, 104–113.

WCED (World Commission on Environment and Development) (1987) *Our Common Future*. Oxford and New York, Oxford University Press.

Wolters, O. W. (1968) Ayudhya and the rearward part of the world. *Journal of the Royal Asiatic Society*, **3** and **4**, 166–178.

    (1982) *History, Culture and Religion in Southeast Asian Perspectives*. Singapore, Institute of Southeast Asian Studies.

Xi, J. (2015a) Towards a community of common destiny and a new future for Asia. Boao Forum for Asia Annual Conference, 28 March, Boao, Hainan Province, China, China.org.cn. http://www.china.org.cn/business/2015–03/29/content_35185720.htm

    (2015b) Carry forward the Bandung spirit for win-win cooperation. Asian-African Summit, Jakarta, 22 April, *Theory China*. http://en.theorychina.org/xsqy_2477/201505/t20150511_322108.shtml

Xinhua (2005) President Hu makes four-point proposal for building harmonious world. *China View*, 16 September. http://news.xinhuanet.com/english/2005–09/16/content_3496789.htm

Zhang, D. (2002) E. Ryden (trans.), *Key Concepts in Chinese Philosophy*, 1st ed. Beijing, Foreign Languages Press.

6 Sustainable urbanism: Measuring long-term architectural merit[1]

CRAIG LANGSTON

Faculty of Society and Design, Bond University, Queensland 4229, Australia

Keywords

Sustainable development; architecture; built environment; durability; adaptability; sustainability; life cycle costing (LCC); 3 L Principle; long life; loose fit; low energy; discounted present value (DPV); obsolescence; physical life calculator; adaptSTAR; Green Star; good architecture; Australia

Abstract

Good architecture is something that we all seek, but which is difficult to define. Sir Alexander John Gordon, in his role as president of the Royal Institute of British Architects, defined 'good architecture' in 1972 as buildings that exhibit 'long life, loose fit and low energy'. These characteristics, nicknamed by Gordon as the 3 L Principle, are measurable. Furthermore, life cycle cost (LCC) provides a method for accessing the economic contribution or burden created by buildings to the society they aim to serve. Yet there is no research available to investigate the connection, if any, between 3 L and LCC. It might be hypothesized that buildings with a high 3 L index have a low LCC profile. If this is true, then LCC may be able to be used to assess 'good architecture'. This paper uses a case study methodology to assess the durability, adaptability, and sustainability of 22 projects that have won architectural design awards. The 3 L criteria can be measured and compared with average LCC per square metre using a long time horizon. The research is significant in that it tests a process to objectively assess what is commonly intangible and to determine if LCC is a suitable predictor of 'good architecture'.

[1] This chapter was presented at the 2nd International Conference on Sustainable Development held on 29–30 September 2014 in Rome, Italy. It has been updated and extended since first publication.

6.1 INTRODUCTION

Sir Alexander John Gordon (1917–1999) was a Welsh architect, born in Ayr (Scotland) and raised in Swansea and Cardiff. He had his own practice, Alex Gordon and Partners, and was a visiting professor at the Bartlett School of Architecture, University College London. He served as president of the Royal Institute of British Architects (RIBA) from 1971 to 1973. It was during this time he wrote a paper on the future shape of architecture, in which he argued that buildings should be designed for long life, loose fit, and low energy (Gordon, 1972). While his peers did not immediately embrace this idea, over time it became a mantra that potentially can define good architecture and its role in modern society.

The idea of building for permanence, yet incorporating flexibility to accommodate future change and minimizing the energy footprint throughout its physical life, is surely the ultimate holistic objective for the architecture profession (Murray, 2011). Today, these objectives may be summarized as durable, adaptable, and sustainable. Good architecture should reflect these properties and not merely be works of public art or a monument to their designers, technological prowess, or the financial wealth of their owner. Good architecture lies in the care with which buildings are designed to provide long-term benefits to the society they serve, and transcend the utilitarian and the fashionable in favour of performance and legacy.

The sustainable development movement arose more than a decade after Gordon coined the 3 L Principle and has continued to gain prominence, particularly in the developed world. Yet the focus has been on green building, with less consideration being given to durability and adaptability. Jacobs (1961) made the remark that the greenest buildings are the ones we already have. For this to be true, it implies that their original design must have considered issues of longevity and flexibility, else they would not have anything still to offer in the changing world within which we live. Good architecture must stand the test of time.

No one has ever demonstrated that long life, loose fit, and low energy are mutually exclusive. Nor has it been proven that beauty and performance are incompatible. On the contrary, our greatest buildings should possess all these fundamentals, as well as reflect the culture and achievements of their time. Good architecture should inspire, challenge norms, and encourage opinion. Are we able to recognize today what will be understood to be good architecture well into the future? How can we measure good architecture at the outset?

Sustainable development needs to embody Gordon's 3 L Principle and treat durability, adaptability, and sustainability as equally important. A zero-carbon building with a short lifespan and no consideration of alternative uses after its original function becomes obsolete is arguably only a minor contribution to modern society. While it might demonstrate technological advances and innovation, it is simply a prototype for ideas that demand integration into a broader and balanced design that should be more commonly practised.

Cost is usually an important factor in building procurement, and a high construction price may well preclude the pursuit of sustainability during design. Yet the costs of buildings can be many times greater when measured over their life, and there is an opportunity that good architecture can contribute to lower operational costs, even in cases where the initial cost is higher. The technique of life cycle costing (LCC) is able to express building costs over many years into a comparable figure today, enabling decisions concerning future value to be more objective. Good architecture cannot divorce itself from the financial implications of acquisition and maintenance, else it will be rendered ineffective in the practical realm.

The aim in this chapter is to explore a method for measuring good architecture in terms of durability, adaptability, and sustainability and to derive a combined rating. This outcome should be reflected in examples of good architecture that we see around us. Using an analysis of 22 recent award-winning buildings in Southeast Queensland, Australia, the relationship between good architecture and the 3 L Principle is tested. The LCC of projects (where cost data are available) can be modelled to demonstrate how their cost profile is influenced by time. Such outcomes are compared to average LCC performance to determine if they represent superior financial performance. The research is significant in that it tests a process to objectively assess what is commonly intangible and determine if LCC is a suitable predictor of 'good architecture'.

6.2 METHOD

The 22 case studies were distilled from a longer list of buildings in Southeast Queensland, recognized for a national, state, or regional award for architectural excellence in the last ten years, to focus on public commercial and institution buildings, thus excluding homes and special-purpose buildings or structures. Base data were gathered from online sources and used to inform subsequent investigations undertaken in the field.

Case Study No. 2, the (then) School of Sustainable Development (Bond University, Gold Coast), has been used herein to illustrate the process applied consistently across all case studies. It is significant because it was the only case study that had complete LCC information available in the public domain. This building is the first six-star Green Star educational building constructed in Australia and represents high sustainability performance in the context of the Green Star methodology (which is similar in concept to LEED, BREEAM, and other green rating tools). It won many awards for its design and innovation, including the RICS Sustainability Award in 2009. The building has an area of approximately 2,500 m^2 over three floors and is relatively small in comparison with other campus buildings. It was opened in October 2008 and now houses approximately 30 staff offices, together with a common area, teaching space, and laboratories (see Figure 6.1).

The case study's LCC was determined with the benefit of hindsight from at least three years of occupational data. Cost information was expressed in 2008 terms, when the building was finished, although inflation to the current date would have no impact on ratios. Designed performance was used unless actual performance to the contrary was available. Data were sourced from a combination of internal documents, public domain information, and expert opinion.

Expected improvements in worker productivity are often cited in relation to sustainable buildings and sometimes are factored into cash flows, as though they are tangible. This is not done in this case study for two reasons. First, there is considerable doubt over the longevity, let alone the legitimacy of productivity improvements in green buildings, despite their common inclusion as pseudo-income in order to help justify higher upfront costs. Second, productivity improvements were never discussed as a motivation for the construction of the building, and therefore it was considered inappropriate to include this criterion as part of the functional performance index, either.

Table 6.1 summarizes the LCC in terms of capital and operating costs and is presented in 2012 terms (Langston, 2013). It should be noted that more than a 30-year time horizon and using a 3% discount rate per annum, capital costs represent 80% of total discounted present value (DPV). This highlights two issues that apply in this case. First, the building was expensive to construct, owing mainly to its high innovation content. Second, the building has low operation costs thanks to natural ventilation, water harvesting, and 70% of its electricity generated from roof-mounted photovoltaic cells.

Figure 6.1. School of sustainable development, Bond University (Case Study No. 2).

Table 6.1. LCC profile for Case Study No.2.

LCC	Cost/m² (AUD)	DPV/m² (AUD)
Capital cost (year 0)	5,200	5,200
Operating cost (year 1–30)	2,100	1,336
Total cost	7,300	6,536

6.3 WHAT IS GOOD ARCHITECTURE?

The identification of good architecture is a combination of multiple criteria that equate to values individuals may not agree upon. Vitruvius (circa 80–15 BC) insisted that three fundamentals should be present: function, structure, and beauty. Others might argue the relationship of a building with its surroundings, cultural context, and society's expectations at the time is also important. Value for money might be added, based on cost-benefit evaluation that variously includes tangible and intangible components. Finally, Gordon's 3 L Principle provides another lens through which good architecture can be viewed. It sets a base performance level for architectural merit. As the famous architect Frank Gehry put it, 'Architecture should speak of its time and place, but yearn for timelessness' (see http://en.wikiquote.org/wiki/Frank_Gehry).

Of course, the question of what makes good architecture cannot be answered unequivocally. Nevertheless, just because a question has many answers does not mean that it should not be asked. In this chapter, good architecture is evaluated in the context of durability, adaptability, and sustainability. Each criterion is capable of objective measurement.

6.4 DURABILITY

The ISO-15686 series on service life planning for buildings and constructed assets is a useful resource on building durability. However, it is more applicable to building components and systems than entire buildings. The estimated service life of any component is calculated as its theoretical life multiplied by a series of factors that are each scored in the range 0.8 to 1.2 (1 = no impact). The factors comprise (a) quality of components, (b) design level, (c) work execution level, (d) indoor environment, (e) outdoor environment, (f) usage conditions, and (g) maintenance level. While a building is a sum of the parts, such parts can be replaced and hence renewed, leaving the basic structure to determine overall life expectancy. Other literature on service life discusses the effect of external and internal actions on building durability and principally identifies location, usage, and design as the main parameters.

Obsolescence is the inability to satisfy increasing requirements or expectations (Iselin and Lemer, 1993; Lemer, 1996; Pinder and Wilkinson, 2000). This is an area under considerable stress owing to changing social demand (Kintrea, 2007) and brings with it environmental consequences. Yet obsolescence does not mean defective performance. Douglas (2006) makes the further distinction between redundancy and obsolescence. The former means 'surplus to requirements', although this may be a consequence of obsolescence. Nutt *et al.* (1976) take the view that 'any factor that tends, over time, to reduce the ability or effectiveness of a building to meet the demands of its occupants, relative to other buildings in its class, will contribute towards the obsolescence of that building' (p. 6). A few researchers have included political changes to zoning, ascribed heritage classification, and other imposed regulatory control or change in stakeholder interest also as a form of obsolescence (e.g. Campbell, 1996; Gardner, 1993; Luther, 1988; Kincaid, 2000).

To assist in the forecast of physical life in years, Langston (2011) developed an Excel calculation template to model building age estimation. A series of simple questions gives insight into the longevity of a building according to three primary criteria: environmental context (location), occupational profile (usage), and structural integrity (design). Each category is equally weighted and comprises ten questions requiring simple yes/no answers. Where information is unknown, blank answers are ignored in the calculation. Three questions under each primary criterion are double weighted because of their relative importance. Figure 6.2 presents the physical life calculator (adapted from Langston, 2011).

PHYSICAL LIFE CALCULATOR

suggested forecast (years) =   **150**

Bond University School of Sustainable Development
Framed roof structure with concrete floors. Masonry walls to ground and first level. Opening windows for natural ventilation. Large covered courtyeard to north. Floor plate running east-west with offices off central corridor/atrium.   **y/n ?**

environmental context			
	Is the building located within 1 kilometre of the coast?		n
	Is the building site characterised by stable soil conditions?	#	y
	Does the building site have low rainfall (<500mm annual average)?		n
	Is the building constructed on a 'greenfield' site?		y
	Is the building exposed to potential flood or wash-away conditions?		n
	Is the building exposed to severe storm activity?		y
	Is the building exposed to earthquake damage?		n
	Is the building located in a bushfire zone?		n
	Is the building located in an area of civil unrest?	#	n
	Are animals or insects present that can damage the building fabric?	#	y

occupational profile			
	Is the building used mainly during normal working hours?		y
	Are industrial type activities undertaken within the building?	#	n
	Is the building open to the general public?		y
	Does the building comprise tenant occupancy?		n
	Is a building manager or caretaker usually present?	#	y
	Is the building intended as a long-term asset?	#	y
	Does the building support hazardous material storage or handling?		n
	Is the building occupation density greater than 1 person per 10 m²?		n
	Is the building protected by security surveillance?		y
	Is the building fully insured?		y

structural integrity			
	Is the building design typified by elements of massive construction?		n
	Is the main structure of the building significantly over designed?		n
	Is the building structure complex or unconventional?		n
	Are building components intended to be highly durable?	#	n
	Are there other structures immediately adjacent to the building?		n
	Is the building founded on solid rock?	#	n
	Was the workmanship standard for the project high?		n
	Is the roof susceptible to leaking in bad weather conditions?	#	y
	Is the building protected against accidental fire events?		y
	Is the building designed as a public monument or landmark?		y

Notes:
Questions indicated (#) are double weighted
Blank responses are ignored   100%   completed

Figure 6.2. Physical life calculator for Case Study No. 2.

Table 6.2. Durability star rating scheme.

Physical life (years)	Star rating
250 or above	★ ★ ★ ★ ★ ★
200–249	★ ★ ★ ★ ★
150–199	★ ★ ★ ★
100–149	★ ★ ★
75–99	★ ★
50–74	★
Below 50	

Some questions are worded so as to deliver a positive score, while some are negative and others neutral (positive or negative). The type of question is distributed evenly throughout the template. The calculation algorithm assumes a base of 100 years and then adds or deducts points (years) according to the responses to questions. It is similar in concept to the *Living to 100 Life Expectancy Calculator* (Living to 100, n.d.) that predicts human lifespan based on extensive medical and empirical data. But for buildings, some conservatism is applied to the estimate and the forecast is rounded down to one of the following outcomes: 25, 50, 75, 100, 150, 200, 250, or 300 years. The template is unsuitable for temporary structures or for iconic monuments, both of which require specialist judgment.

The construction of the calculator was informed from a broad survey of literature (unspecified), recent ISO-15686 standards, and personal experience. It was founded on an adaptive management principle (Gregory *et al.,* 2006; Linkov *et al.,* 2006) that purports to develop a model and then evaluate its robustness through subsequent field-testing and observation. While the results of this testing appear promising, definitive validation arguably can occur only by comparison of estimates with reality, where the latter is measured as the duration of the building before its collapse. But as this is rarely witnessed, certainly through natural causes, field-testing and observation are the best validation methods available to us.

For the purposes of this research, the results of the physical life calculator are translated to a star rating, as provided in Table 6.2.

6.5 ADAPTABILITY

For a wide range of reasons, buildings can become obsolete long before their physical life has come to an end. Investing in long-lived buildings may be suboptimal if their useful life falls well short of their physical life. It is wise to design future buildings for change by making them more flexible yet with sufficient structural integrity to support alternative functional use. The development of a design-rating scheme for adaptation potential enables building designers to understand the long-term impacts of their decisions prior to construction and thus enables optimization for adaptive reuse to occur from the outset. As adaptive reuse potential already embodies financial, social, and environmental criteria, the rating scheme would extend traditional operational considerations such as energy performance to include churn, retrofit, refurbishment, and renewal considerations.

Atkinson (1988) modelled the process of obsolescence and renewal (of housing stock) and developed a 'sinking stack' theory to explain the phenomenon. Comparing total building stock over time produces a rising profile in total stock (accumulating via new construction each year), stratified according to building age (older buildings are at lower layers in the profile strata). New stock is added annually to the top of the stack. It degenerates over time and gradually sinks towards the bottom of the stack as new buildings are created and older ones demolished. If little new construction is added, then the entire building stock will age, and greater resources will be required to maintain overall quality and amenity levels. Certain layers in the stack are likely to represent periods of poor quality construction, and these layers age more rapidly and absorb greater maintenance resources (Ness and Atkinson, 2001). Each layer in the stack reduces in height with the passage of time. Only the top layer grows because it represents the current rate of new construction. The net effect is a sinking of the stack, a phenomenon that occurs whether or not sufficient maintenance takes place.

Conejos (2013) developed *adaptSTAR* in an attempt to rate new building design for future 'adaptivity'. This rating is done normally when the project is in its design phase, although it can be applied in hindsight based on the latent conditions before a proposed intervention takes place. As such, it reflects the adaptability within a design concept that underpins the potential for change of functional use later in life.

The concept of the *adaptSTAR* design-rating scheme for adaptation potential was founded on the categories of obsolescence derived from the literature. These comprised physical, economic, functional, technological, social, legal, and political considerations (Conejos, 2013). Each category was broken down into sub-criteria that were also assembled from a review of the literature and from expert interviews with the design teams of eleven Australian award-winning adaptive reuse conversions in New South Wales and the Australian Capital Territory, as well as a pilot study involving the Melbourne General Post Office in Victoria. The sub-criteria were then rated by a sample of practising Australian architects experienced in adaptive reuse work in order to determine the relative importance of each sub-criterion, which then led to the weight of each respective obsolescence category being computed. The criterion weight is calculated from a five-point Likert scale (strongly disagree = 1, strongly agree = 5).

Table 6.3. Adaptability star rating scheme.

adaptSTAR score	Star rating
85 or above	★ ★ ★ ★ ★ ★
75–84	★ ★ ★ ★ ★
65–74	★ ★ ★ ★
55–64	★ ★ ★
45–54	★ ★
35–44	★
Below 35	

Table 6.4. Green Star weightings.

Environmental impact category	Weight (%)
Management	10
Indoor environment quality	20
Energy	25
Transport	10
Water	12
Materials	14
Land use and ecology	4
Emissions	5

Source: Yudelson (2010)

Table 6.5. Sustainability star rating scheme.

Green Star score	Star rating
75 or above	★ ★ ★ ★ ★ ★
60–74	★ ★ ★ ★ ★
45–59	★ ★ ★ ★
30–44	★ ★ ★
20–29	★ ★
10–19	★
Below 10	

The model can be applied using two approaches: either through a general ranking based on the main categories and their corresponding percentages or by using the detailed ranking based on the design criteria. The latter is recommended.

From this work it has been found that the seven obsolescence categories have reasonably equal weight. The coefficient of variation (CoV) of the seven criteria weights was just 8.32%. A scoring template was developed to enable new building design to be rated for future adaptation. This is illustrated in Figure 6.3 (adapted from Wilkinson *et al.,* 2014). In this case, the *adaptSTAR* score of 74.17 comprised 11.50% physical, 10.83% economic, 10.51% functional, 20.02% technological, 15.49% social, 15.55% legal, and 16.10% political criteria.

For the purposes of this research, the results of the *adaptSTAR* model are translated to a star rating, as provided in Table 6.3.

6.6 SUSTAINABILITY

In Australia, the Green Building Council of Australia (GBCA, 2010) operates Australia's only national voluntary comprehensive environmental rating system for buildings, known as Green Star. The GBCA established Green Star as a rating system for evaluating the environmental design of buildings in 2002 and it evaluates the green attributes of building projects in eight categories (plus bonus points for innovation). The GBCA promotes green building programmes, technologies, design practices, and operations. Rating tools are currently available or in development for most building market segments, including commercial offices, retail, schools, universities, multi-unit residential buildings, industrial facilities, and municipal buildings.

The goal of this rating system is to assess the current environmental potential (or sustainability) of buildings. It is a useful tool for property managers when identifying upgrade and retrofit priorities. The rating system also assists corporate sustainability and environmental reporting efforts. Every Green Star rating tool is organized into eight environmental impact categories and an innovation category. Credits are awarded within each of the categories, depending on a building's environmental performance and characteristics. Points are achieved when specified actions for each credit are successfully performed or demonstrated.

Table 6.4 outlines the categories and normal weightings within the Green Star building rating system, although weightings can differ according to building type and location.

An environmental weighting is applied to each category score, which balances the inherent weighting that occurs through the differing number of points available in each category. The weights reflect issues of environmental importance for each state or territory of Australia and thus differ by region. The weighted category score is calculated as follows:

Weighted category score (%) = Category score (%) × Weighting factor (%)/100

The sum of the weighted category scores, plus any innovation points, determines the project's rating. Only buildings that achieve a rating of four stars and above are certified by the GBCA. For the purposes of this research, the results of the Green Star checklist are translated to a star rating, as provided in Table 6.5.

SUSTAINABLE URBANISM

Bond University School of Sustainable Development

When nominating your opinion to EACH of the following statements, please assume that the latest adaptive reuse intervention has yet to occur. Your responses therefore relate to the latent conditions BEFORE such intervention. Please rate ALL statements using ONE opinion option and provide the key supporting REASON.

How do you judge the following statements for the above building/facility?	strongly disagree	disagree	neutral	agree	strongly agree	What is the key reason that influenced your opinion?	valid response ?
The building's foundations and frame have capacity for additional structural loads and potential vertical expansion.		■				Columns cannot be extended. Potential for light weight addition to roof.	✓
The building fabric is well constructed using durable materials, providing potential retention of existing exterior and interior finishes.			■			Concrete slabs and masonary walls. Timber showing aging and steel sheeting showing damage (dents).	✓
The building currently has a low maintenance profile with modest expected levels of component repair and replacement over its remaining lifespan.			■			Timber to exterior will require maintenance and possible replacement. Extensive painted surfaces internally	✓
The building is situated in a bustling metropolis comprising mixed use development and proximity to potential markets.			■			Low rise urban area.	✓
The building is located near transport facilities and provides convenience for vehicular and pedestrian mobility.			■			Bus service available. Otherwise car and pedestrian only.	✓
The building enjoys a site with favourable plot size, access, topography, area, aspect and surrounding views.			■			Satisfactory site. Views are internalised to courtyard.	✓
The building's interior layout exhibits strong versatility for future alternative arrangements without significant disruption or conversion cost.		■				A long thin floor plate with compartmentalised offices and teaching rooms.	✓
The building has significant components or systems that support disassembly and subsequent relocation or reuse.			■			Awarded green star credit for this aspect.	✓
The building has sufficient internal open space and/or atria that provides opportunity for spatial and structural transformations to be introduced.		■				Potential for external courtyard to be transformed but this would affect the passive features of the building.	✓
The building has large floor plates and floor-to-floor heights with minimal interruptions from the supporting structure.	■					Long thin floor plates with ceiling of approx. 3.5m ground and first floor.	✓
The building provides easy access to concealed ducts, service corridors and plant room space to ensure effective horizontal and vertical circulation of services.				■		Offices with grid ceilings.	✓
The building is designed in such a way that it maximizes its orientation with good potential for passive solar strategies.					■	Good access to daylighting and cross ventilation due to long east/west access.	✓
The building has appropriate fenestration and sun shading devices consistent with good thermal performance.					■	Passive solar strategies well considered.	✓
The building has an insulated external envelope capable of ensuring good thermal and acoustic performance for interior spaces.					■	Thermal mass and separation of spaces.	✓
The building is designed in ways that maximize daylight use and natural ventilation without significant mechanical intervention.					■	Good passive strategies.	✓
The building has low energy demand and is operating at or readily capable of achieving a 5-star Green Star® energy rating or equivalent.					■	Green Star credits received.	✓
The building supports efficient operational and maintenance practices including effective building management and control systems.					■	BMS and user controls installed.	✓
The building has developed strong intrinsic heritage values, cultural connections or positive public image over its life.					■	First 6 star Green Star for education. Building is used as an eduational tool.	✓
The building has high architectural merit including pleasing aesthetics and compatability with its surrounding streetscape.					■	Building sits well on the site and externally has pleasing aesthetics using a simple palette of materials.	✓
The building provides relevant amenities and facilities within its neighbourhood that can add value to the local community.					■	Living lab and courtyard facilities.	✓
The building displays a high standard of construction and finish consistent with current market expectations.				■		Fit-out and finishing is standard.	✓
The building complies with current standards for fire prevention and safety, emergency egress and disability provisions.					■	Recent building which complies with standards.	✓
The building offers an enhanced workplace environment that provides appropriate user comfort, indoor air quality and environmental health and safety.					■	Passive strategies provide daylighting, user control for thermal comfort and openable windows.	✓
The building's design is compatible with ecological sustainability objectives and helps minimize ongoing habitat disturbance.					■	Many environmental initiatives incorporated.	✓
The building displays a high level of community interest and political support for its future care and preservation.			■			It is an important building due to being first 6 star Green Star for education.	✓
The building's current or proposed future use conforms to existing masterplan, zoning and related urban planning specifications.					■	Education building on university campus.	✓

Figure 6.3. *adaptSTAR* scoring template for Case Study No. 2.

6.7 CASE STUDIES

A web search of buildings in Southeast Queensland that have been recognized for a national, state, or regional award for architectural excellence in the last ten years was conducted. The list was reduced to focus on public commercial and institution buildings, thereby excluding homes and special purpose buildings or structures. The case studies are summarized in Table 6.6.

It is proposed that award-winning buildings, as judged by experts from the architectural community, should demonstrate at least four stars in each of long life, loose fit, and low energy criteria. Anecdotal evidence suggests that three stars might be considered normal. While other criteria most certainly should apply, these three should be considered as essential qualifications. As argued in the literature, they should be given equal weight.

Each case study was evaluated objectively using the methods described earlier in this chapter. The raw scores were converted to a star rating. Where a Green Star rating exists, it was used, else a pseudo score was estimated. The 22 buildings and their performance results are shown in Figure 6.4. Independent validation of the models' results by a panel of seven architectural experts drawn from local industry found there was 62% overall agreement. Photographic evidence to support this validation process was compiled during physical site visits that took place during 2014.

It is worth noting that there were only rare instances of buildings (4.5% of dataset) scoring less than four stars in any of the measured criteria. That suggests that the judging process for architectural awards appears consistent with Gordon's 3 L Principle. The mean star rating across all 22 case studies was 5.09 stars for durability (CoV = 14.7%), 4.64 stars for adaptability (CoV = 14.2%), and 4.55 stars for sustainability (CoV = 21.2%). A CoV of less than 20% represents low variability within the dataset. The mean overall rating for the case studies was 4.76 stars.

Should the minimum standard for architectural award be specified at five stars, then 39.4% of the dataset criteria would not qualify. Only 5 out of 22 projects in fact met or exceeded this higher threshold in each criterion. None of the case studies sourced from Southeast Queensland over the last ten years scored six stars across the board.

Table 6.6. List of case studies.

ID	Project name	Location
1	Abedian School of Architecture	Bond University, Robina
2	School of Sustainable Development	Bond University, Robina
3	Ferry Road Market	107 Ferry Road, Southport
4	Global Change Institute	University of Queensland, St Lucia
5	UQ Advanced Engineering Building	University of Queensland, St Lucia
6	Queensland Brain Institute	University of Queensland, St Lucia
7	Sir Llew Edwards Building	University of Queensland, St Lucia
8	Translational Research Institute	37 Kent St, Woolloongabba
9	One One One Eagle Street	111 Eagle Street, Brisbane
10	Eco Sciences Precinct	41 Boggo Road, Dutton Park
11	The Cherrell Hirst Creative Learning Centre	70 Gregory Terrace, Brisbane
12	ABC Headquarters	South Bank, Brisbane
13	GOMA (Gallery of Modern Art)	Stanley Place, South Brisbane
14	AM60	60 Albert Street, Brisbane
15	Santos Place	32 Turbot Street, Brisbane
16	Queen Elizabeth II Courts of Law	415 George Street, Brisbane
17	State Library of Queensland	Stanley Place, South Brisbane
18	Lilley Centre	24 Gregory Terrace, Spring Hill
19	James Street Market	22 James Street, Fortitude Valley
20	Energex Newstead Riverpark	33 Breakfast Creek Road, Newstead
21	The Chancellery	University of Sunshine Coast
22	Ipswich Justice Precinct	43 Ellenborough Street, Ipswich

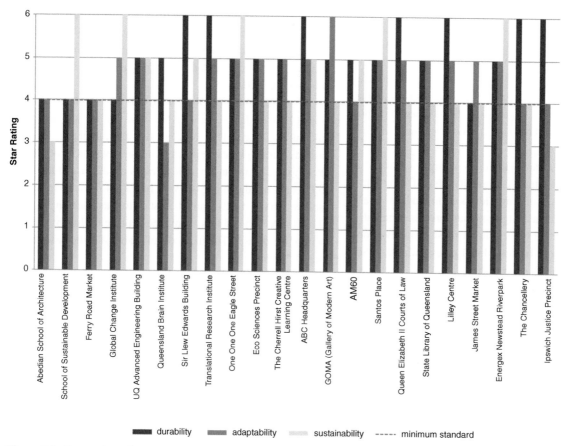

Figure 6.4. Case study performance summary.

6.8 LCC ANALYSIS

LCC is defined as the total costs of acquisition, ownership, and ultimate disposal over a building's existence. Comparing LCC per square metre requires both a common time horizon for the evaluation and use of discounting to bring all costs into present value terms. LCC has been around since the 1960s, although the technique has its roots in engineering economics and can be traced back around 150 years.

Nevertheless, LCC data are rarely available, either owing to no analysis being commissioned or for reasons of confidentiality. Only Case Study No. 2 had an available estimate of LCC. As summarized in Table 6.1 earlier, the comparative LCC for this case study in 2012 terms was AUD 6,536/m². Adjusted to 2016, this equates to AUD 6,928/m².

An earlier study based on 30 commercial buildings in Melbourne (Langston, 2006) found that the mean ratio of operating costs to capital costs equals 0.0361 per year. These buildings, which are examples of ordinary projects, had a mean capital cost of AUD 2,540/m² and a mean operating cost of AUD 4,175/m² over 30 years (in 2006 terms). Adjusted to 2016, this equates to an LCC (capital + operating cost) of AUD 8,399/m².

Case Study No. 2 has superior durability, adaptability, and sustainability performance to the Melbourne data and therefore suggests that good architecture may lead to lower LCC, albeit with potentially higher capital cost. Case Study No. 2 in fact had a capital cost of about double and an operating cost of about a third of the averaged Melbourne data. Clearly one case study is insufficient to define a generic relationship between the 3 L Principle and LCC, but it does suggest that higher upfront costs may be offset by recurrent costs that may represent good value over a building's life. Further investigation of this relationship is needed.

6.9 CONCLUSIONS

It can be concluded from this research that buildings that have recently been recognized for architectural excellence in Southeast Queensland portray the principles of long life, loose fit, and low energy and hence meet Gordon's 'test' for good architecture. His 3 L Principle is expected to be inversely proportional to the computed LCC per square metre of gross floor area. Buildings with high star ratings for long life, loose fit, and low energy, representing candidates for good architecture, should display a lower LCC profile when measured over a long time horizon (i.e., 30–100 years), although this requires further study.

The link between 3 L and LCC is suspected for three main reasons: (1) durability suggests lower maintenance and replacement costs due to reduced decay; (2) adaptability suggests lower rates of churn and refurbishment costs arising from functional obsolescence; and (3) sustainability suggests lower energy, water, and other inputs through a more responsive environmental design. What might also be found, as this research agenda continues to be pursued, is that good architecture leads to increased satisfaction, comfort, and productivity for building occupants. Overall, sustainable development is enhanced when buildings meet longer-term design performance thresholds, avoiding premature and at times unnecessary destruction well before their true use-by date has been reached.

Sustainable development ideologically demands that architects design buildings that reflect long life, loose fit, and low energy as a basic tenet. This research suggests that such a strategy does not conflict with objectives to deliver 'good architecture' and may well lead to lower LCC values that make good architecture also good value. None of these matters should be considered mutually exclusive.

ACKNOWLEDGEMENTS

The author would like to thank Dr Bhishna Bajracharya and Dr David Leifer for their review and constructive feedback regarding this chapter.

REFERENCES

Atkinson, B. (1988) Urban ideals and the mechanism of renewal. In proceedings of RAIA Conference, June, Sydney.

Campbell, J. (1996) Is your building a candidate for adaptive reuse? *Journal of Property Management*, **61**(1), 26–29.

Conejos, S. (2013) Designing for future building adaptive reuse. PhD thesis. Bond University, Gold Coast, Australia.

Douglas, J. (2006) *Building Adaptation* (2nd ed.). Oxford, Butterworth-Heinemann.

Gardner, R. (1993) The opportunities and challenges posed by refurbishment. In proceedings of the Building Science Forum of Australia, Sydney, pp. 1–13.

GBCA (2010) What is Green Star? https://new.gbca.org.au/rate/green-star/ (accessed 25 September 2020)

Gordon, A. (1972) Designing for survival: The President introduces his long life/loose fit/low energy study. *Royal Institute of British Architects Journal*, **79**(9), 374–376.

Gregory, R., Failing, L. and Higgins, P. (2006) Adaptive management and environmental decision making: A case study application to water use planning. *Ecological Economics*, **58**(2), 434–447.

Iselin, D. G. and Lemer, A. C. (eds.) (1993) *The Fourth Dimension in Building: Strategies for Minimizing Obsolescence*. Committee on Facility Design to Minimize Premature Obsolescence, Building Research Board. Washington, DC, National Academy Press.

Jacobs, J. (1961) *The Death and Life of Great American Cities*. New York, Random House.

Kincaid, D. (2000) Adaptability potentials for buildings and infrastructure in sustainable cities. *Facilities*, **18**(3/4), 155–161.

Kintrea, K. (2007) Housing aspirations and obsolescence: Understanding the relationship. *Journal of Housing and the Built Environment*, **22**, 321–338.

Langston, C. (2011) Estimating the useful life of buildings. In proceedings of the AUBEA2011 Conference, Gold Coast, Australia, April, pp. 418–432.

(2013) The role of coordinate-based decision-making in the evaluation of sustainable built environments. *Construction Management and Economics*, **31**(1), 62–77.

Langston, Y. L. (2006) Embodied energy modelling of individual buildings in Melbourne: The inherent energy-cost relationship. PhD thesis. Deakin University, Victoria, Australia.

Lemer, A. C. (1996) Infrastructure obsolescence and design service life. *Journal of Infrastructure Systems*, **2**(4), 153–161.

Linkov, I., Satterstrom, F. K., Kiker, G., Batchelor, C., Bridges, T. and Ferguson, E. (2006) From comparative risk assessment to multi-criteria decision analysis and adaptive management: Recent developments and applications. *Environment International*, **32**(8), 1,072–1,093.

Living to 100 (n.d.) Living to 100 Life Expectancy Calculator. http://livingto100.com

Luther, J. P. (1988) Site and situation: The context of adaptive reuse. In R. L. Austin (compiled), D. G. Woodcock, W. C. Steward and R. A. Forrester (eds.), *Adaptive Reuse: Issues and Case Studies in Building Preservation*, pp. 48–60. New York, Van Nostrand Reinhold.

Murray, G. (2011) Stirling Prize analysis: Long life, loose fit, low energy. e-Architect Newsletter article No. 125. http://www.e-architect.co.uk/articles/persistence-of-the-absurd (accessed 20 June 2014).

Ness, D. and Atkinson, B. (2001) Re-use/upgrading of existing building stock. *BDP Environment Design Guide*. Canberra, Building Design Professions.

Nutt, B., Walker, B., Holliday, S. and Sears, D. (1976) *Housing Obsolescence*. Farnborough, Hampshire, Saxon House.

Pinder, J. and Wilkinson, S. J. (2000) Measuring the gap: A user based study of building obsolescence in office property. The Cutting Edge 2000 Conference, September. London, RICS Research Foundation.

Wilkinson, S. J., Remøy, H. and Langston, C. (2014) *Sustainable Building Adaptation: Innovations in Decision-Making*. Oxford, Wiley Blackwell.

Yudelson, J. (2010) *Greening Existing Buildings*. New York, McGraw-Hill.

7 Sustaining wooden architectural heritage

PETER BRIMBLECOMBE[1] AND MIKIKO HAYASHI[2]

[1]*National Sun Yat-Sen University, Kaohsiung, Taiwan*
[2]*Tokyo National Research Institute for Cultural Properties, Japan*

Keywords

Fire; fungi; earthquakes; insects; preventive conservation; Shrines and Temples of Nikkō; tourism; Yingxian Pagoda

Abstract

Sustaining tangible heritage has long been seen as a key undertaking to maintain our sense of place and links with the past. This is well understood, yet at times the preservation of buildings and monuments in the face of environmental change has been neglected. Even the IPCC has paid scant attention to the impact of climate change on material heritage. Significant buildings and historic sites can be seen as a resource to promote tourism and attract funding, without a true awareness of the need to treat them as irreplaceable. This chapter looks at two important religious sites with notable wooden buildings, which are under threat from environmental change. Additionally, attack by insects or mould and the frequency of forest fires can be affected by a changing climate. Beyond this, shifts in the local environment can alter our experience of heritage ensembles. This requires improved scientific understanding and thoughtful approaches to long-term management.

7.1 INTRODUCTION

Asia and the Pacific are heir to some unique cultural heritage, yet their enormous richness can seem neglected. It may be that it is geographically remote or expressed in styles and materials which are unfamiliar to many practitioners, who have developed their conservation skills in the protection of more classical architectural forms. To mention some examples, we can find the coral megaliths and tombs of Tonga, the intricate almost Venetian-style city of Nan Madol on Pohnpei through to the palaces, temples, stupas of Japan, China, and Southeast Asia. These great works are often accompanied by more vernacular forms, such as the shophouses seen through so much of southern Asia, or the bridges, forts, and lighthouses. To these we must add more humble farming ensembles or acquired forms in terms of colonial buildings over recent centuries.

This magnificent inheritance is under threat from rapid economic development, tourism, natural disasters, and environmental change. Such pressures have generated new research on future threats and how guidelines for sustaining heritage may need to be reframed (e.g., Collette 2007; Markham *et al.,* 2016; Sabbioni *et al.,* 2010). Here we examine wooden heritage as a special example of Asia's unique contribution to human achievement. The traditional carpentry of Japan and China can be combined with the use of wood in the vernacular architecture of the Pacific. Of course, wood is well known as a tradition in architecture from all parts of the globe, but its expression in Asia has been very significant, with special characteristics such as size and architectural complexity. Its conservation in the region has also caused us to reframe the way heritage preservation is undertaken and has influenced thinking on authenticity, such as found in the *Nara Document on Authenticity* (Lemaire and Stovel, 1994). Additionally, some more recent studies have emerged concerning the sustainability of heritage in China (Xu *et al.,* 2015) and Japan (Sugio, 2015).

We consider Asian wooden heritage in terms of its sensitivity to contemporary change and make particular reference to management and environmental pressures at some religious sites in China and Japan. The future, under an altered climate, may impose novel threats from changes in temperature, rainfall, humidity, sea level, or various forms of biological attack. The preservation of this wooden heritage requires trained conservators and engagement with a broad group of stakeholders and focused scientific research.

We hope to give relevance to the sustainability issues faced by tangible heritage through examining some specific buildings and have chosen here to examine the 1,000-year-old wooden pagoda at Yingxian and the buildings of Nikkō (see Figure 7.1), as these are both very significant heritage ensembles. Although historically very significant, Shanxi Province has long seemed

Figure 7.1. Map showing the location of Yingxian in China's Shanxi Province and Nikkō in Japan.

rather remote. Here so much of China's remarkable Tang and Song Dynasty wooden heritage stands protected in the north, in or beyond the Hengshan and Wutai mountains. The great antiquity of this wooden heritage was neglected and as such was rediscovered by the eminent architectural historian Liang Sicheng and his wife Lin Hueyin in the 1930s (a colourful introduction to them and their work is found in Perrottet, 2017). Notable are the two early halls in the Wutai Mountains: (1) the main hall of Nanchan Monastery in the Wutai Mountains, Shanxi Province, the oldest extant wooden building in China, dating from the year 782 in the Tang Dynasty, and (2) the larger Foguang Temple of 857. Although these are truly remarkable buildings, here we will focus on the Song Dynasty pagoda at Yingxian, a small town in the north of Shanxi. The size and antiquity of the building has drawn recent comment as an example of wooden architecture, whose success and durability may be a model for wooden buildings today (Tollefson, 2017). Japan also has a long history of major wooden buildings, with such remarkable examples as the Ise Grand Shrine in Mie prefecture, with some 1,300 years of history. Here our attention will be directed to the shrines and temples of Nikkō, a major complex set within a forested landscape, where the natural landscape and built structures have coexisted for so long.

7.1.1 Yingxian (Sakyamuni) Pagoda

The Sakyamuni Pagoda of Fogong Temple at Yingxian in Northern China dates from 1056 and is a truly monumental wooden structure, some 70 m in height (Figure 7.2a). Locally it

is often referred to as *Yingxian muta* (Yingxian Pagoda). The building has a ground floor that houses an enormous Buddha, and four other floors contain groups of Buddhist figures. There are also four dark or hidden floors, which lack wooden lattice windows. Because of structural concerns, all but the ground floor with its massive statue of the Buddha Sakyamuni are closed to visitors. The smaller groups of statues on the upper floors of the pagoda are not readily accessible to visitors.

The pagoda was described by Tian Hui in the late Ming Dynasty, who presented the history of its repairs in *Zhongxiu Fogongsi ta zhi* (Steinhardt, 1994). The ancient structure has faced many threats – collapse from earthquakes and the impact of ever-present weathering processes, such that as damage accumulates it can cause critical threats. In 1961, the Wooden Pagoda of Yingxian County was among the first batch of sites given protection in a declaration by the Chinese State Council (WHC, 2013). The Ministry of Culture of the People's Republic of China is responsible for cultural policy and activities in the country, while the State Administration of Cultural Heritage, the administrative agency subordinate to the Ministry of Culture, is responsible for the development and management of museums, as well as protection of cultural relics of national importance.

7.1.2 The Shrines and Temples of Nikkō

More than a hundred important historic buildings make up the UNESCO World Heritage Site of Nikkō, north of Tokyo. Many of the buildings are additionally designated as National Treasures of Japan. The ensemble illustrates the application of the Edo architectural style to Shinto shrines and Buddhist temples (Figures 7.2c and 7.2d), although the site dates from the much earlier Nara period (710–794). The shrines and temples are set in a forested montane landscape that creates a striking visual effect, and making visits over the seasons each rather distinctive. The temples and their surroundings have long been a magnet for travellers and an inspiration for artists. The poets Sōgi (Carter, 1987) and Matsuo Basho made visits in 1468 and 1689, with Nikkō featuring in Basho's best-known work: *The Narrow Road to the Deep North* (Yuasa, 1966).

The shrines and temples at Nikkō were protected by the Shogunate until the Meiji Revolution. It conducted periodic restoration using craftsmen who resided in Nikkō. After the revolution, the buildings benefitted from a sort of benign neglect until the *shinbutsu bunri* was issued in 1871. National cultural properties were subjugated by rapid modernization as devastation seemed in progress. In 1879, the *Hokōkai* was established to promote restoration and conservation at Nikkō, this non-governmental group acting for 38 years. In 1897, the government promulgated a law for conservation of old shrines to ensure that fundamental repairs were done to rescue severely damaged buildings. In 1950, the

Figure 7.2. (a) Yingxian (Sakyamuni) Pagoda; (b) Floor 3 of Yingxian (Sakyamuni) Pagoda, where a group of four Buddhas face the cardinal directions. Note the four square posts (with railings and a doorway between) and also the two large round columns, which were architectural elements we monitored for temperature and water content; (c) Sanbutsudō in Rinnō-ji at Nikkō; (d) Taiyū-in Reibyō Nitemmon in Rinnō-ji at Nikkō. (Photo credits: (a), (b): Author PB; (c), (d): http://www.wikiwand.com/en/Shrines_and_Temples_of_Nikkō)

Nikkō Shrines and Temples Conservation Committee was formed as the forerunner to the present Association for the Preservation of the Nikkō World Heritage Site Shrines and Temples.

7.1.3 Methodological approach

This chapter is largely a review arising from a synthesis of available literature, along with discussions with heritage scientists and managers. However, it is supported by a number of observations and measurements from our research made during study visits to Yingxian Pagoda (June 2016, October 2016, June 2017, and January 2018), while observations from Nikkō come from earlier studies (e.g., Hayashi *et al.,* 2012), updated by more recent contacts with those working at the site.

The investigations in Yingxian have been limited to simple field measurements of temperature and water content, along with insect catches using flypapers as sticky traps. We were only able to set relatively few traps owing to the need for access during routine maintenance on the hidden floors of the pagoda. Five traps were recovered from the space between floors 1 and 2 after being exposed from June 2016 until October 2016, and 31 traps were recovered in January 2018 from a set exposed on various hidden floors in June 2017. The surface temperature of interior wood was measured with a simple digital thermometer. The temperature of the outdoor surface was captured with a hand-held thermal imaging camera (FLIR C2 FLIR Systems, Estonia). Water content was measured with a DM4A Doser Messtechnik Moisture meter calibrated at 5% and 30% with plastic standards (Doser Messtechnik PE05 and PE30).

We have used local climate data to model environmental pressure and climate projections to estimate the impact of climate change. The impact of a changing climate on insects at the sites has been predicted using a life-cycle model adapted from Watari *et al.* (2002) and fungal growth with the rather simpler Scheffer index. Future climate estimates for Shanxi Province used material from Dong *et al.* (2016). For Japan, we have taken projections from the Japanese Meteorological Agency (JMA, 2014), using the future seasonal anomalies these provide. The projections allowed us to estimate seasonal temperatures at Nikkō by adding these to current seasonal temperatures from online information (e.g. www.wunderground.com). We assumed that the insects caught at the site were distributed in a Poisson manner to calculate the standard deviation from the data, even though the presence of infestations means the Poisson distribution is often ineffective at explaining high catch rates (Brimblecombe and Querner, 2014).

7.2 NATURAL DISASTERS AND CLIMATE PRESSURES

Material heritage is exposed to a range of natural disasters, such as earthquakes, floods, storm, or fires. Building design and subsequent management have often attempted to lessen the extent of damage that arises from such events. Wooden heritage is especially vulnerable to changing risks from some natural disasters and climate pressures, so maintenance has a long history at both Yingxian and Nikkō. Although concerns about external threats to the Yingxian Pagoda were real, the Qing Dynasty stelae write of these in more mythological terms, such as attack by dragons, so protection was expressed more in terms of invocations than tangible responses. These inscriptions also record more practical, but generous donations for repair and restoration (e.g., Steinhardt, 1994).

7.2.1 Earthquakes

Major historical earthquakes have caused much damage to important buildings; Fengguo Temple at Yixian in Liaoning Province of northern China was severely damaged in 1290 by the Chihli earthquake of magnitude 6.8. The *Yingzhou zhi* suggests that the pagoda resisted seven earthquakes between 1056 and 1103 (e.g., Steinhardt, 1994). In Shanxi Province, the massive 1303 Hongdong earthquake (magnitude 8.0) caused extensive damage in Taiyuan and further south. Just two years later, the 6.5-magnitude earthquake of 3 May 1305 occurred just south of Datong and close to Yingxian (NOAA, 2018). In the south of Shanxi Province, 1695 saw a further magnitude 8.0 earthquake at Linfen, which caused the Great Cloud Temple and the Temple of Emperor Yao to collapse (CNIC, 2018), although its effects at Yingxian are not clear. Large earthquakes along the seismic belt of the Datong basin have not been especially common over the last millennium, but they still place Yingxian

Pagoda at continuing risk. However, there is a range of earthquake-resistant features evident in the architecture of ancient China. These include floating raft foundations, the *dougong* (a unique structural element of interlocking wooden brackets), and the mortise and tenon joints. All add protection against tremors and shocks, and more than fifty types of *dougong* were used in constructing the pagoda at Yingxian (Correia *et al.*, 2015). Despite the structural problems now evident in the pagoda, its resistance to damage had led to it being seen as a testament to the achievement of wooden construction in ancient China.

Japan, lying at the edge of the Pacific Plate, is especially prone to earthquakes (Table 7.1), and the record of significant earthquakes in Japan starts with accounts of events from the 5th century (Usami, 1979). The threat to buildings from earthquakes has long been recognized in the design of buildings in Japan, even during historic times, with lighter materials common. In the case of monumental structures, there were numerous attempts to create buildings that could resist shocks.

At Nikkō, earthquake damage was noted from the Edo or Tokugawa period (1603 to 1868), but these accounts list damage that in many cases seems superficial (see Brimblecombe and Hayashi, 2018). There was a large earthquake with aftershocks in 1683, and the damage was sufficient to require expensive restoration, such that the expenditure led to disagreements between the local Sendai fiefdom and the Tokugawa Shogunate. The dispute coincided with Matsuo Basho's travels northwards in early 1689, so it appears that the government in Tokyo (then Edo) hoped Basho could provide an update about restoration. Work was definitely underway when Basho and his companion Sora arrived at Nikkō (Sato, 1996). However, the great poet wrote relatively little about Nikkō in *The Narrow Road to the Deep North*, and there are hints that his thoughts would not be made public, leaving us with only the lines: 'To say more of the shrine would be to violate its holiness' (Yuasa, 1966).

The long experience with earthquakes has meant that buildings in Japan have been designed to respond to earth movements and minimize damage. The traditional five-storey Japanese pagoda consists of weakly linked floors held in vertical alignment by a central pole. Each floor is able to recover quickly from rocking. Buildings traditionally sat on large trays that allowed movement between the ground and the building (Okubo, 2016). The historical record of earthquake damage at Nikkō in Table 7.1 suggests that wooden buildings were resistant to earthquakes, and it was fixed structures such as *kasa-ishi* (coping stones) on fence tops that were affected, and more significantly a stone *hōtō* (i.e., a stupa, typically miniature, with a cylindrical body with a four-sided roof), stone *yarai* (fences), and stone stairs. The devastating earthquake of 2011 did not lead to structural damage at Nikkō, although some lacquer finishes were affected (Watanabe *et al.*, 2013, 2014).

Table 7.1. Earthquake damage at Nikkō.

Year	Damage recorded at Nikkō
1644	A little damage to a stone wall at Tōshōgu
1649	Damage to stone wall and stone *igaki*[a] at Tōshōgu
1650	Damage to Sōrintō and stone wall at Tōshōgu
1658	Minor damage in Nikkō
1683	June 17/18: Damage to *hōtō*[b] and *kasaishi* at Tōshōgu and Taiyu-in. October 20: Possible damage to buildings under restoration
1703 Genroku Earthquake	Little damage?
1707 Hōei Earthquake	Little damage?
1710	Nikkō shrines safe after main earthquake shock
1725	Damage to some 7–9 m length of a stone *yarai*, and three or four stone lanterns fell down
1735	Some minor damage to a stone wall at Tōshōgu
1746	Damage to stone *yarai*[c] and wall at Tōshōgu;
1755	Damage to stone *yarai*[c], wall, and stairs at Tōshōgu
1767	Fall of sculpture about 1.8 m
1827	Minor damage to Okusha, Sekisaku at Tōshōgu
1835	Collapse of stone wall
1888	Little damage recorded
1923 Kanto Earthquake	Little damage recorded
1931	Damage to stone wall
1949 Imaichi Earthquake	Little damage recorded
2011 Tōhoku Earthquake	Cosmetic damage

Source: Brimblecombe and Hayashi (2018)

Notes: (a) a fence usually with posts and rails; (b) a *hōtō* is typically a miniature stupa with a cylindrical body on stone foundations with a four-sided roof; (c) a *yarai* is a fence.

7.2.2 Floods and storms

The frequency of floods and storms will change in Northern China over the next century, with potential increases in these intense events (Ding *et al.*, 2016). At Yingxian, there are no major rivers, although surface flooding is possible, as in former times there were ponds in the vicinity. Nikkō, by contrast, has nearby rivers that flood in the steep valleys, with the Sacred Bridge (Shinkyō) especially vulnerable. Rivers are carefully managed, and in the reaches below Nikkō, their level is controlled at the gauging station, Ga (Observatory No. 303031283303130) on the Hitachitone River of the Tone Catchment.

Intense rainfall elevates flood risk, and there are general observations that typhoons over the northwest Pacific that cross land have increased over the past 37 years, with the proportion of storms of categories 4 and 5 doubling or even tripling (Mei *et al.*, 2016), but the future trends are difficult to assign with certainty. Nevertheless, there will likely be more heavy rainfall, with the frequency of daily falls exceeding 200 mm doubling (JMA, 2016). There have been a number of studies on the effects of future climate change on the upper Tone River basin,

which includes the Nikkō catchment (Fujihara *et al.*, 2006; Kim *et al.*, 2011a). Kim *et al.* (2011a) argue that changes in downstream river discharges may slightly decrease, or peak river flows could change a little, but the upper parts of the river at Nikkō will still be at risk of flooding.

7.2.3 Fire and forests

Fires, often caused by lightning strikes, are a particular risk for tall wooden buildings. Additionally, those in forested areas are potentially threatened by forest fires. These fires may increase because of future drier summers. The potential for increasing frequency is supported by various studies. In China, for example, Fire Weather Index values increase more for Scenario B2 (emphasis on local solutions to economic and environmental sustainability) than for Scenario A2 (a very heterogeneous world with an emphasis on family values and local traditions) during the 2050s and 2080s, with the potential burned areas rising by 10% and 18% for spring during the 2080s under Scenarios A2 and B2, respectively, and the fire season prolonged by 21 and 26 days under these scenarios (Tian *et al.*, 2011).

Given the sensitivity to lightning strikes, pagodas seem at great risk from fire. Although the pagoda at Yingxian has survived this threat, the Gojunoto Pagoda at Nikkō was destroyed by lightning-induced fire in 1815. It was rebuilt by Sakai Tadayuki in 1818. In 1961, there was a fire at Toshogu Honji-do (Yokota *et al.,* 2008). Official documents from the Disaster Management Agency of the Government of Japan (FDMA, 2015) reveal concern over damage to surrounding forests due to lightning strikes and the appropriate level of lightning protection. Okubo (2016) argued that historically fire suppression has been aided by the use of non-flammable materials such as clay-plaster, while in Japan, historic roof design has sometimes meant that they can rapidly be dismantled during fires. The Tokugawa government provided firemen (*Hachioji Sen-nin Doshin*) to protect the shrines and temples from 1652 to 1868, with the contribution they made commemorated on a memorial stone in the grounds of Rinnō-ji. If droughts become more common in future, the risk of fire can easily increase.

7.2.4 Climate

The IPCC has paid scant attention to the importance of climate change on material heritage. Although extreme events have a noticeable and catastrophic impact on wooden heritage, these may not be as important over time as the gradual weathering that occurs through the daily and seasonal cycles of weather and the ageing of materials so induced. Sometimes even gradual changes can lead to failure.

Typically, the changes arise from water relations in materials, so humidity and also temperature are important factors. Although increases in temperature, precipitation, or humidity may seem rather small (a few degrees or 10% or so), they can be amplified to have an impact on materials. In particular, phase changes, which occur at very exact values of temperature or relative humidity, can show dramatic alteration in frequency with small changes. The frequency of freeze-thaw cycles, which place enormous stress on stone, can be very sensitive to the average winter temperature (Grossi *et al.,* 2007). Salt weathering can be induced through stress exerted when brines crystallize in the pores of soft stone under dry conditions. The number of crystallization events is sensitive to relative humidity (Grossi *et al.,* 2011). While salts typically damage stone, wood can be subject to weathering pressures from salts (e.g., Oron *et al.,* 2016).

In addition, such amplification mechanisms can derive from a combination of meteorological parameters that act synergistically to enhance damage, so we might imagine a parameter of wet frosts related to the saturation of a porous surface by rainfall on a warm day, followed by a sub-zero day when the low temperatures freeze the water-laden pores and induce stresses that result in mechanical damage. Another combination could be rain and wind, when high winds drive the rain droplets deep inside porous materials or organic materials such as thatching. Alternatively, it should be recognized that damage accumulates from long exposure, for example, corrosion of metals from lengthy periods in a damp environment. These special types of weather can be considered part of heritage climatology (Brimblecombe, 2010, 2014).

The importance of meteorological factors in damaging heritage stimulated our measurements of the temperature and water content of wood as part of our work in the interior of Yingxian Pagoda in both summer and winter (2017 and 2018), along with thermal imaging of the outer skin of the pagoda. Figures 7.3a–c show thermal imaging at various times on a summer day and illustrate the way the outer surface changes. It is warmer on the eastern side in the morning and warmer on the western side in the afternoon. However, by the evening (21:00 hr), it attains a relatively even temperature of around 26°C. In winter, we see that the outer layer of the building has a much lower, but more even temperature distribution at about −15°C in the absence of sunshine (Figure 7.3d). The entrance hall in front is slightly warmer, as it is occupied. The winter sky is not as cold as the summer sky, probably because on the day the image was taken it was overcast and snowing lightly. The daily changes evident in summer are also observed inside, where the temperatures of interior wooden posts and columns (Figure 7.2b) are a degree or

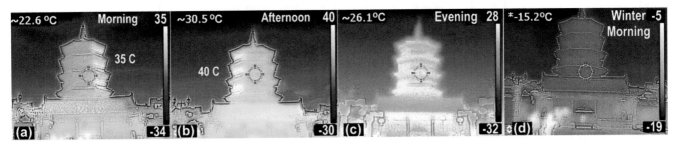

Figure 7.3. Thermal images of Yingxian Pagoda on (a) a summer morning, (b) summer afternoon, (c) early summer night, and (d) winter morning. The temperature scale is shown at the right of each image and the temperature of the centre spot is shown to the upper left of each image.

so higher in the late morning on the sunlit side (~24°C), compared with those in the north. Indoors in winter we find much lower temperatures. Although these are relatively evenly spread around the building, they can change dramatically from one day to the next. On successive days, the recorded wood temperatures could change by more than 10°C and were sometimes as low as −20°C. These large and rapid changes would have the potential to impose considerable stress on the wood if it had large amounts of moisture content, but fortunately the wood is dry.

The low water content of the wood in the inner circle of supporting columns of the pagoda has been measured on three occasions (October 2016, June 2017, and January 2018). The water content seems much lower than our expectations, based on the equilibrium moisture content estimated using the average temperature and relative humidity at the site. Figure 7.4a shows these expectations, where theoretical prediction would suggest an equilibrium moisture content of about 10.5%. However, measured moisture content is typically much lower than this, as evident in summer measurements on all the 125 posts spread across the four upper floors, with mean water content at 8.27±1.16%. In winter, the posts were 8.46±1.29%, while in summer the columns were 5.21±0.80% and in winter 5.6±0.72%. Despite the posts being slightly damper, the water content is still below expectations based on local climate. It is probable that the great age of the wooden supporting columns has allowed them to become very dry.

Each individual wooden piece seems to retain a characteristic water content that distinguishes it from its neighbours, as shown in Figures 7.4b–c. This is particularly evident in a single damp post (water content >12%) found on floor 2 of the pagoda. This was rather darker and possibly a newer piece of wood, which is satisfyingly closer to the expected equilibrium moisture content, although not yet quite as low as the expected 10.5%. The

comparative dryness of the columns is very clear from these plots. The difference between summer and winter, when there is slightly more water in the winter wood (more points in the white area), is significant via a paired t-test at <0.01 for both posts and columns. These measurements suggest wood that is stable with a low water content makes it resistant to any stresses that might be imposed by the extremely low winter temperatures and additionally resistant to attack by insect larvae.

7.3 BIOLOGICAL PRESSURE ON WOODEN HERITAGE

Various forms of damage result from attack by fungi, insects, and, sometimes, birds and small mammals or macrophytes growing on the building.

7.3.1 Fungal damage

The Scheffer index (Sch) can be used to estimate potential fungal damage to wood and is determined from the formula (Carll, 2009)

$$Sch = (1/16.7)\sum_{Jan}^{Dec}(D-3)(T-2)$$

where D is the number of wet days (defined at precipitation >0.25 mm) each month, and T is the average monthly temperature, where T is greater than 2; otherwise, the value is zero. It is not always easy to get a number for precipitation days >0.25 mm, as these are often absent from standard meteorological compilations. We have been able to approximate these for Yingxian using data from Datong for days with >0.1 mm. At Nikkō, it is most frequently available for >1.0 mm and so was modified using a fitting function described in Brimblecombe and Hayashi (2018).

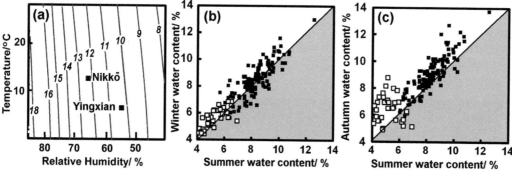

Figure 7.4. (a) The equilibrium moisture content of wood as a function of temperature and relative humidity shown as grid lines with italic numbers as percentage water content. (b) The water content of individual posts (black squares) and columns (open squares) in winter as a function of water content in summer. (c) The water content of individual posts (black squares) and columns (open squares) in autumn as a function of water content in summer. The grey triangular area denotes wooden elements where the water content is higher during the summer, while in the white triangular area it is lower during the summer.

The estimates from Datong would suggest that over the period 1971–2000, the Scheffer index was about 40. This is rather low compared with Nikkō; here the index is typically twice this value, hinting at the much greater risk of fungal attack on wood at the shrines and temples. The drier and colder climate of Yingxian lessens the risk, but in future a 4°C increase in temperature and a 25% increase in the number of wet days would make the Scheffer index about 65, a very substantial rise in the Scheffer index, but still smaller than present-day Nikkō. The index increases in Nikkō from 82 over the period 1961–1990 to almost 100 in the last years of the 21st century (2076–2095). This increase occurs despite a decline in the number of wet days, but the decreasing dampness is more than compensated by increases in the temperature (Brimblecombe and Hayashi, 2018). The suggestion of increasing fungal risk here is similar to results found in work from Korea, which suggests that, since 'Korean weather tends to turn into the weather of [a] subtropical region, the decay hazard of Korea seems to have high possibility to be gradually increased' (Kim *et al.*, 2011b).

Both at Yingxian and Nikkō, there is evidence of past damage through the activities of wood-boring insect larvae. In the case of Nikkō, recent years have seen damaging infestations, so wooden buildings seem at heightened risk. Insect development is sensitive to temperature and often humidity; daylight hours are also relevant at certain life-cycle stages. Climate change can alter insect distribution, and already some species are found to be moving northwards in Europe; for example, a bark beetle once found in the Canary Islands is now present in southwest England (Alexander, 2007). In the heritage environment, the changes have been seen as relevant to museums (Stengaard *et al.*, 2012) and historic properties (Brimblecombe and Lankester, 2013). However, an analysis of trapped insects in English Heritage properties suggests that climate may be just one of the factors. Habitat availability and food may also control insect abundance (Brimblecombe and Brimblecombe, 2015).

The sensitivity of insect life cycles to climate is easy to model. However, there is little information about temperature and relative humidity relevant to the development of anobiids such as those that damage the wood, as found at Nikkō. This has required us to treat a better-understood insect, so we have chosen the yellow-spotted longicorn beetle (*Psacothea hilaris hilaris*), which is common in Asia, where it damages fig and mulberry trees, although now also found in Italy in 2005 (Lupi *et al.*, 2013). The difficulty in controlling the longicorn beetle means that its life cycle is well parameterized, which allows its growth to be predicted in numerical simulations. The model of Watari *et al.* (2002) has been used here to establish the various stages in the life cycle of the beetle as a function of temperature and daylight. Details are available from their publication, but briefly the model determines the integrated temperatures required to allow transitions from one stage to the next. The model also allows for adults mating and laying eggs that undergo further development. The model can only be an indicator of sensitivity to climate, as different subspecies and varieties are found across Japan and China. However, using one particular subspecies enables us to see the comparative differences at the two sites.

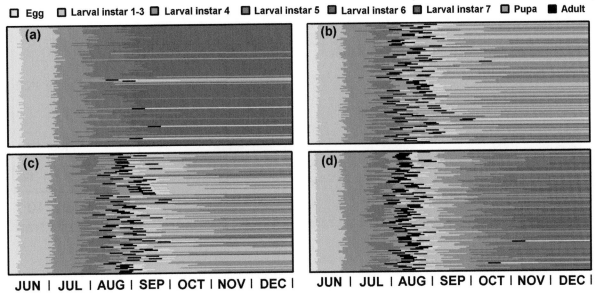

Figure 7.5. Modelled life cycle of *Psacothea hilaris* eggs oviposited 1st May for (a) contemporary Yingxian and (b) Yingxian at the end of the 21st century, and for (c) contemporary Nikkō and (d) Nikkō at the end of the 21st century.

We can see that at Yingxian there are profound changes that arise from an increase in temperature of almost 4°C. Currently, only 5% of the insects would be predicted to reach the adult stage without overwintering in diaphase. But at the end of the century, all surviving individuals would likely become adults over the summer. At Nikkō today, all would reach adulthood over the summer, and the model suggests that at the end of the century, a small number might go through two life cycles in a year.

Increasing warmth in the future will likely decrease the amount of time required for beetle eggs to hatch or adults to emerge. Such life-cycle stages are likely to occur earlier in the year as the century progresses, because of the increasing temperatures predicted for Nikkō; such changes are to be expected throughout much of Japan. Environmental controls on the life cycle of *Priobium* spp. are poorly known, so changes in the level of threat cannot be readily estimated.

At Yingxian, we have made observations of insects, although our visits of 2016, 2017, and 2018 did not reveal any active infestations, as indicated by the presence of frass. However, there were a number of live and dead insects in the building, for example, ladybirds and leaf beetles. These are not especially

harmful to wooden buildings but can cause aesthetic problems and attract birds. Occasionally, bags of natural insecticide (plant bark, etc.) have been set out on the upper non-public floors (Figure 7.6a).

We set out a limited number of traps in Yingxian Pagoda in the summer of 2016 and 2017 (Figure 7.6b). These caught only a few beetles (a leaf beetle is shown in Figure 7.6c). Although we were initially disappointed with the number of individual beetles, the catch rate (i.e., individuals/traps) was 0.40 ±0.28 (5 traps) and more recently 0.38±0.17 (13 traps) in the pagoda. This is not especially low and about the same magnitude as that found at the Rinnō-ji temple complex of Nikkō, where the 2010 collections reveal a catch rate of 0.86 (>14,000 traps), although if the two large infestations of *Sculptotheca hilleri* are removed, the catch rate reduces to about 0.45. At both sites, only a small fraction of the beetle species is likely to damage the wood.

At Nikkō, insect damage has been particularly severe in infestations at particular locations over the most recent decade. In 2008, this was evident in structural elements of the Sanbutsudō (in the large main hall: Hon-dō). The damage was caused by the presence of a rare anobiids in Japan, *Priobium cylindricum*, a form of death-watch beetle (Komine *et al.*,

Figure 7.6. Animal presence at Yingxian Pagoda: (a) bags of natural insecticide and dead ladybirds; (b) setting out the traps in the hidden floors 1–2; (c) leaf beetle caught in traps in autumn 2016; (d) starlings swarming around the pagoda in summer; (e) dead pigeon; (f) small mammal droppings on floor 5 in winter 2018; and (g) the number of feathers on traps set out on the hidden floors across the autumn of 2017, with the number of beetles trapped indicated as small icons. Note that hidden floors are numbered in terms of the floor above and below, while N and S refer to the north and south side of the pagoda. (Photo credits: Author PB)

2009). It led to surveys between 2009 and 2010 (Komine *et al.*, 2010; Hayashi *et al.*, 2011), with a large survey showing that the infestation in Sanbutsudō was dominated by *P. cylindricum*. At Taiyū-in Reibyō Nitemmon (belonging to Rinnō-ji), this large gate revealed the presence of anobiids, *Trichodesma japonicum*, and *Sculptotheca hilleri*, but *P. cylindricum* was absent (Hayashi *et al.*, 2012). Sanbutsudō was fumigated in 2013, an intervention which was largely successful, as revealed by a limited but well-structured survey carried out in 2016 (Komine *et al.*, 2017).

7.3.2 Birds and other biological interactions

Local people in Yingxian believe that the large flocks of birds (starlings) that swarm about the pagoda in the warmer months (Figure 7.6d) keep the insect numbers low. Bird droppings can cause chemical damage and staining to metals (Bernardi *et al.*, 2009), although at Yingxian this seems more to convey a lack of care, as they accumulate on the outer surfaces and inside, along with bird carcasses (Figure 7.6e). Droppings may also promote insect growth and enhance the abundance of flies; the latter were trapped at more than five times (i.e. 2.38±0.43) the rate for beetles. The flies may be a result of bird carcasses, along with bird and small animal droppings present in the upper levels of the pagoda. However, our insect traps also captured bird feathers in Yingxian Pagoda, which made it possible to explore this relationship between birds and insects. Nevertheless, as seen in Figure 7.6g, the relationship is not convincing. Rather, it appears that bird activity is quite evenly spread across the hidden floors, while insects were caught only on the hidden floor between floors 2 and 3 in sticky traps set in the last half of 2017.

Birds are not a special problem at Nikkō, although bats are sometimes found in the buildings. Small mammals such as weasels, civets, and raccoons can be a problem in some Japanese historical buildings, but they do not cause any particular problem at Nikkō. Deer, an integral part of ecosystems, are protected in Japan, which has increased their numbers so much that they cause damage to World Natural Heritage Sites, such as Shiretoko and Yakushima (Sugio, 2015).

7.4 ANTHROPOGENIC PRESSURES ON WOODEN HERITAGE

In addition to natural threats to heritage, a range of more anthropogenic pressures place heritage at risk or, in extreme cases, result in the complete destruction of the site. War, particularly, has the potential to cause grave damage to heritage. This may come about through defacement, inappropriate use, looting, severe damage through bombing or shelling, or wanton destruction, as in the case of dynamiting the Buddhas of Bamiyan (Afghanistan) in 2001. Both Yingxian Pagoda and Nikkō have not been greatly affected by wars, although Yiangxian Pagoda was damaged by cannon fire in the 1930s, which is often seen as a contributing factor to the deformation of the pagoda. At Nikkō, while a US B-29 Superfortress bomber also flew around the site on 10 March 1945, it did not drop bombs. There is a view that Liang Sicheng pressed the US military to avoid bombing Kyoto and Nara, which had so many important historic buildings. However, this has limited factual support, and hundreds of people were killed in Kyoto and Nara during air raids. Nevertheless, military planners are often worried about collateral damage to heritage and have made disastrous misjudgements, as in the Battle of Monte Cassino.

Urban change is incessant, so can readily encroach onto sites or interfere with the context. The Fogong Temple occupies some 5.1 ha, and once the visitor is inside the walls of the complex, it reveals an area nicely overlooked by the towering pagoda, although the setting can seem a little desolate. The town of Yingxian has grown (Yīngxiàn County increased from 279,483 in the 2000 census to 327,973 ten years later), with considerable development in the surrounding streets, yet these form an ensemble in keeping with the significance of the monument. In front of the pagoda, running east-west is a tidy street of interesting shops. An alternative approach to the building takes us through a Chinese gate and northwards along Liaodai Street (Figure 7.7), a route which provides a magnificent perspective of the pagoda defined by a long line of shops that are not overly modernized. However, in some adjacent streets of equally traditional architecture, building renovation has been more aggressive in such a way that completely glazed modern shopfronts and large illuminated signs conceal the original architectural intent. Despite this urban development, the setting has not been too greatly affected. The economy of the province has stagnated in recent years, and at the moment rural Shanxi remains relatively poor. Future changes could lead to a loss of the traditional charm if unconstrained, although currently there is a good local management plan in place.

Pressures deriving from urbanization and its impact on historic buildings can sometimes be restrained by adaptive reuse. This creates benefits in that it can reduce the need to destroy old buildings to make way for new, and there are considerable energy savings in reuse, though this may bring such significant changes in functionality that the original meaning becomes disguised. It is also possible that changing ownership can promote gentrification of suburbs that were industrial, or neighbourhoods which provided homes for poorer people. Such processes are now apparent in parts of China and can lead to dispossession, seeming part of the country's socialist legacy (Shin, 2016). An example of this is evident in Mayor Geng Yanbo's reconstruction

Figure 7.7. Perspective of the pagoda along Liaodai Street, Yingxian, in June 2016. (Photo credit: Author PB)

of a Ming Dynasty city centre in Datong, only 50 km to the north of Yingxian (GDN, 2014).

International tourism is still relatively limited at Yingxian, although the site is crowded with Chinese tourists in the summer. Pressures from tourism are enormous, even though one must concede that tourists are important for the economic well-being of a region. It can also enhance the recognition of important sites. Nevertheless, tourist pressures have the potential to damage both the local environment and way of life. Even where great effort has been made to retain historic character, tourists may not appreciate it. As an example, the ancient Shanxi town of Pingyao has expended much effort in preserving its character, yet tourists find it hard to appreciate. They can fail to 'understand the idea of a *historic hotel*, and would immediately ask to change to a bigger room, then leave after one night ... they wanted somewhere like a Hilton' (Perrottet, 2017).

Tourism in Japan and at Nikkō has a long history. The poet Sōgi made a visit in 1468, and Western tourism also started early, and there are a number of books from early travel writers (e.g., Bird, 1880). A rail connection (Tobu Railway) from Tokyo was developed by Nezu Kaichirō in the 1920s (Wakuda, 1996). Currently, there are typically some six million visitors to Nikkō each year, who go as much to enjoy the natural environment as the temples, with autumn popular for observing the leaves.

As a World Heritage Site, Nikkō has a well-developed conservation plan (ACA, 1998), which goes well beyond the site and includes the town and the surrounding National Park. The Nikkō Municipal Ordinance Concerning Townscape of 1985 covers many issues but seeks to ensure that areas where traditional buildings and other structures form a unit of the townscape are well-protected and that development is appropriate to the unique character of Nikkō. The plan invokes the need for the local government to financially support actions necessary for maintaining the townscape. There is a parallel Management Plan for Nikkō National Park, which also aims to protect built heritage within its bounds (ACA, 1998).

7.5 ENVIRONMENTAL CHANGE

Climate change is the best known of contemporary environmental changes and suggests a world where global temperature will increase as a result of greenhouse gas emissions. China has warmed by 0.5–0.8°C during the past 100 years (Luo *et al.*, 2016). Under the RCP 8.5 scenario, which assumes high population and high energy demand, temperatures will increase by more than 5.5°C at the end of the century (2071–2100). With relatively modest rates of emission growth, the northeast and north of northwest Shanxi will perhaps experience temperature rises of a degree or so less (Dong *et al.*, 2016). Observations show that during the past 50–100 years, precipitation across China varied on a cycle of 20–30 years, with no significant trend (Luo *et al.*, 2016). However, by the end of the century, there may be a 25% increase annually in precipitation in Shanxi (Dong *et al.*, 2016; Luo *et al.*, 2016). In 2015, temperatures in Japan are estimated at some 0.7°C above the 1981–2010 average. Rainfall records suggest a decrease in the annual number of wet days, but an increase in extremely wet days over the period 1901–2015 (JMA, 2016). The projected temperature increase in Japan is likely to be 4.2°C for the period 2071–2100 (under the A1B scenario), compared with that for 1971–2000. Summer precipitation will increase, with the annual average precipitation some 19% higher in the last 30 years of the 21st century. At Nikkō, annual mean temperature is projected to increase by about 3°C between 1980–1999 and 2076–2095. Summer mean relative humidity is projected to decrease, by about 4%, although in winter the mean humidity is likely to increase. The number of dry days each year, with less than 1 mm of rain, is likely to increase by 5–10 days (JMA, 2014).

Nikkō provides a natural setting for its shrines and temples, so the landscapes provide a context for the sites. In Japan, the changing seasons can be much celebrated, so viewing the cherry blossom is an important traditional custom (Hanami). However, in a changing climate, the cherry blossom may arrive some 30 days earlier than at present. The arrival of spring at Nikkō is celebrated with the Yayoi Festival or Gota Matsuri (Festival of Disputes), which occurs between April 13 and 17. Floats decorated with cherry blossom are prepared and the heads of local towns visit other towns to exchange ritual greetings. These ancient customs are followed faithfully, because any deviation is thought likely to cause trouble later in the year. The celebrations are affected by the early blooming dates of cherry blossoms in rural cities, so the floats must often be decorated with artificial flowers, a practice which will doubtlessly increase through the coming century.

A change in the way visitors use historic sites can be influenced by not only new social attitudes, but also the environment (Brimblecombe, 2016). It is possible that some visitors have avoided Shanxi Province in recent decades because it suffered from such serious air pollution problems. Air quality will likely improve in the future as its economic base shifts away from heavy and polluting industries, so a better environment could enhance its attraction in future. A warmer climate and milder winters might encourage a growth in tourist numbers in the early parts of the year, as currently the winter can be extremely cold at Yingxian Pagoda. In contrast, the summers might be rather uncomfortable, so the seasonal distribution of visitors could change, or they might seek to spend more time in air-conditioned interiors, and already there are exciting virtual tours that include the inaccessible upper floors in buildings near to the pagoda site. At Nikkō, viewing autumnal colours is also important and currently dominates the tourist calendar. However, the commencement of the autumnal tint to the Japanese maple has become progressively delayed, by more than 15 days over the last 50 years. This may affect the visitor season (Allen et al., 2013). Although winter visits are not so popular at Nikkō, elsewhere there are important traditions of viewing snow-covered landscapes, which may become less frequent, as snowfall will likely decline in a warmer world.

7.6 MANAGING WOODEN HERITAGE

Many see fire risk as the key concern in the protection of wooden buildings. Chinese buildings of wood or brick-wood structure have a low fire resistance. In historic districts, the courtyard architectural form increases the potential for fires to spread. Narrow historic streets with blind alleys often have high building density, making fires difficult to contain and limiting access by rescue equipment and fire engines (Xu et al., 2015). As an example, a fire broke out on Guangyi Street and Xianwen Alley of Lijiang Old Town in 2013 and lasted three hours, burning more than a hundred buildings. Xu et al. (2015) reviewed the causes of fires in Chinese historic buildings and identified these as predominantly arising from faulty electrical wiring (20%), but careless use of fire indoors (16%) and candles and incense (12%) were also important. Fires with environmental or natural causes were about 12%, with lightning strikes notable.

Fire protection and management requires a range of approaches. Where possible, non-historic elements should use resistant materials; in addition, fire suppression systems should be incorporated (consistent with the historic character) and fire-fighting equipment be made available, along with necessary drainage for water run-off (Marrion, 2016). At Nikkō, the dangers from fire were well-recognized historically, so the Tokugawa government funded firefighters from the mid-17th century.

At Yingxian Pagoda, wax burning and incense are no longer allowed within the Fogong Temple compound. Fire suppression equipment is readily seen throughout the property. Early in the 21st century, plans called for more than 20 firefighters and a fire engine to protect Yingxian's pagoda. The pagoda also gained a lightning rod, important because many fires in pagodas have been the result of lightning strikes, and there was a damaging strike in 2004 (Xinhua, 2004). At Nikkō, historic firefighters (Hachioji Sen-nindojin) mounted watch both night and day for some 200 years. From the Meiji period, the local fire brigade undertook this role and most notably are involved with Bunkazai Boka Day (Cultural Property Fire Prevention Day); at present an annual training runs at the shrines and temples.

Earthquakes have been a constant worry, despite the shock resistance afforded by wooden buildings. The courtyards found in traditional Chinese architecture can also make evacuation more difficult after severe earthquakes (Xu et al., 2015). Although Nikkō was little affected by the Tohoku earthquake of 2011, many other buildings and heritage sites suffered (Sugio, 2015). Disaster mitigation is key for reducing the risk from natural hazards to heritage sites. Therefore, disaster risk reduction plans are an increasing part of the management of cultural property.

There was a decision to undertake a large-scale fumigation with sulfuryl fluoride at Nikkō in the summer of 2013, in response to insect damage. This required a long debate about potential risks to workers and visitors. Such aggressive intervention appeared to be the only way to kill all *Priobium cylindricum* present (Harada *et al.,* 2014), but fortunately the treatment appears to have been successful.

Maintenance is clearly better than intervening after damage has occurred. It is likely that increased environmental pressures will make regular maintenance ever more important (Sabbioni *et al.,* 2010). In the case of wooden structures, there are traditions that seek to protect important buildings. In Japan, a major restoration is undertaken every century or so under the Shinto ideal of *shikinen sengu*, which sees the buildings within sanctuaries meticulously disassembled and rebuilt. At Ito, this occurs every 20 years, such that the traditions and craft skills are passed from one generation to the next. Traditional carpentry skills are still part of the Chinese approach, even though less rigorously applied than in Japan. Carpenters can still be seen working on historic buildings in Yingxian, using simple hand tools much as those of the distant past (Figure 7.8).

Transfer of scientific knowledge into policy remains problematic in the region, but it is a more general experience (Brimblecombe, 2018). Certainly, if we take the point that the changes experienced will be like those of the past, but simply more frequent or intense (Brimblecombe, 2018), management responses might be muted. Engaging with scientists and interpreting research output still proves a problem for many research managers, who may lack training in the sciences. Nevertheless, ecologists and architectural scientists are increasingly seen as part of heritage management, but experts on air pollution, climate change, or hydrology are less common. There are many good scientists in the region working on climate and environmental pressures, but the numbers contributing to heritage science are currently too small to address likely future problems (Brimblecombe and Hayashi, 2017). Sometimes the buildings under the greatest threat are not the most notable. In China, as elsewhere, there is a shortage of funds for lesser heritage items: '[S]tate-level protection are managed by dedicated persons. Heritage of low protection levels often lack maintenance funds' (Xu *et al.,* 2015).

7.7 CONCLUSION

The studies at Yingxian and Nikkō suggest that the building design has meant that they have tended to resist earthquakes. However, they remain vulnerable to fire and biological attack, particularly in damper climates, where considerations about the water content in the wood are important. Our environment is

Figure 7.8. Traditional skills, left to right: (a) using an adze to shape a column at Jingtu Monastery, Yingxian; (b) planing wood for a column at Jingtu Monastery, Yingxian; and (c) using mud to cement tiles to a roof near Yong'an Monastery, Hunyuan. (Photo credits: Author PB)

changing in ways which alter the threats to cultural heritage sites. Working in parallel, industrialization, urbanization, and social mobility add pressures to their preservation. The political contexts of these changes can make management a complex issue. Sustaining heritage seems inherently important to us, as historic neighbourhoods represent a framework to our lives, even though it may not always appear as important as the need for sustainable agricultural, forestry, or fisheries. Indeed, sustaining heritage is not just about maintaining a stock, but it must recognize the significance of individual important items to which we attribute great value.

Research on the impact of environmental change on heritage has often been done outside the Asia-Pacific region. The lack of research is likely driven by the relatively small numbers of scientists and other researchers who work in the heritage field in the region, but in the end it means that many studies lack specificity.

Protecting our tangible heritage requires approaches to management that are able to integrate the output of research into thoughtful policy. Although this is almost universally agreed to be sensible, policy makers and managers in the heritage field have often found it difficult to engage with the complexity of current research output, especially that which looks at potential impacts that lie far in the future. Managers are frequently preoccupied with pressing day-to-day problems. Organizations need to step back from immediate problems and perhaps formulate regional meetings or retreats that draw in wider groups, so those who manage heritage can share ideas of how best to confront change. The needs may be especially strong in the Asia-Pacific region, where research is less well-developed in the translation of research to practice.

This changing environmental pressure means that future conservation guidelines may need to be reframed. In the case of wooden buildings, this can be especially critical given the concomitant importance and sensitivity.

ACKNOWLEDGEMENTS

The authors would like to acknowledge the *DIMSum* initiative (3030327, 3030350, and 3030350) at City University of Hong Kong and funds from the Education Bureau's Pilot Mainland Experience Scheme, which have supported study trips to Shanxi to examine the environmental impacts on wooden buildings and, most notably, the investigation of wood-boring insects at the wooden pagoda of Yingxian County. We are also grateful to Shanxi Agricultural University for their generous support and hospitality, and the thoughtful comments from Professor Craig Langston and an anonymous reviewer.

REFERENCES

ACA (1998) Shrines and Temples of Nikkō. WHC Nomination Documentation, Agency for Cultural Affairs, Government of Japan. Submission to World Heritage Centre. http://whc.unesco.org/uploads/nominations/913.pdf

Alexander, K. N. A. (2007) *Atlantopsocus adustus* (Hagen) (Psoc.: Psocidae) new to Britain from East Cornwall. *Entomological Record*, **119**(76), 51.

Allen, J. M., Terres, M. A., Katsuki, T., Iwamoto, K., Kobori, H., Higuchi, H., Primack, R. B., Wilson, A. M., Gelfand, A. and Silander, J. A. (2013) Modeling daily flowering probabilities: expected impact of climate change on Japanese cherry phenology. *Global Change Biology*, **20**, 1,251–1,263.

Bernardi, E., Bowden, D. J., Brimblecombe, P., Kenneally, H. and Morselli, L. (2009). The effect of uric acid on outdoor copper and bronze. *Science of the Total Environment*, **407**, 2,383–2,389.

Bird, I. L. (1880) *Unbeaten Tracks in Japan*. London, John Murray.

Brimblecombe, P. (2010) Heritage climatology. In R.-A. Lefevre and C. Sabbioni (eds.), *Climate Change and Cultural Heritage*, pp. 57–54. Bari, Italy, Edipuglia.

(2014) Refining climate change threats to heritage. *Journal of the Institute of Conservation*, **3**, 85–93.

(2016) Visitor responses and climate change. In R.-A. Lefevre and C. Sabbioni (eds.), *Cultural Heritage from Pollution to Climate Change*, pp. 73–80. Bari, Italy, Edipuglia.

(2018) Policy relevance of small changes in climate with large impacts on heritage. In R.-A. Lefevre and C. Sabbioni (eds.), *Cultural Heritage Facing Climate Change*, pp. 25–32. Bari, Italy, Edipuglia.

Brimblecombe, P. and Brimblecombe, C. T. (2015) Trends in insect catch at historic properties. *Journal of Cultural Heritage*, **16**, 127–133.

Brimblecombe, P. and Hayashi, M. (2017) Perception of the relationship between climate change in Japan and traditional wooden heritage in Japan. In T. Dawson, C. Nimura, E. Lopez-Romero and M.-Y. Daire (eds.), *Public Archaeology and Climate Change*, pp. 288–302. Barnsley, UK, Oxbow.

(2018) Pressures from long term environmental change at the shrines and temples of Nikkō. *Heritage Science*, **6**(27).

Brimblecombe, P. and Lankester, P. (2013) Long-term changes in climate and insect damage in historic houses. *Studies in Conservation*, **58**(1), 13–22.

Brimblecombe, P. and Querner, P. (2014) Webbing clothes moth catch and the management of heritage environments. *International Biodeterioration and Biodegradation*, **96**, 50–57.

Carll, C. G. (2009) *Decay Hazard (Scheffer) Index Values Calculated from 1971–2000 Climate Normal Data*. Madison, WI, Department of Agriculture, FPL-GTR-179LESS.

Carter, S. D. (1987) Sōgi in the East Country. *Shirakawa Kikō*. *Monumenta Nipponica*, **42**, 167–209.

CNIC (2018) *Ruins of Earthquakes*. Computer Network Information Centre of Chinese Academy of Sciences. http://www.kepu.net.cn/english/quake/ruins/index.html

Collette, A. (2007) Climate change and world heritage: report on predicting and managing the impacts of climate change on world heritage and strategy to assist states parties to implement appropriate management responses. *World Heritage Report,* **22**.

Correia, M. R., Lourenco, P. B. and Varum, H. (2015) *Seismic Retrofitting: Learning from Vernacular Architecture*. London, Taylor and Francis Group.

Ding, Y., Mu, M., Zhang, J., Jiang, T., Zhang, T., Wang, C., Wu, L., Ye, B., Bao, M. and Zhang, S. (2016) Impacts of climate change on the environment, economy, and society of China. In D. Qin, Y. Ding and M. Mu (eds.), *Climate and Environmental Change in China: 1951–2012*, pp. 69–92. Heidelberg, Springer Environmental Science and Engineering.

Dong, W., Mu, M. and Gao, X. (2016) Projections of climate change and its impacts. In D. Qin, Y. Ding and M. Mu (eds.), *Climate and Environmental Change in China: 1951–2012*, pp. 93–106. Heidelberg, Springer Environmental Science and Engineering.

FDMA (2015) *Fire: White Paper*. Tokyo, Tokyo, Shobi, Fire and Disaster Management Agency of the Ministry of Internal Affairs and Communications.

Fujihara, Y., Ode, M., Kojiri, T., Tomosugi, K. and Irie, H. (2006) Effects of global warming on the water resources of the Tone River basin. *Proceedings of Hydraulic Engineering*, **50**, 367–372 (in Japanese).

GDN (Guardian News and Media) (2014) Fake it to make it. *Post Magazine.* http://www.scmp.com/magazines/post-magazine/article/1627359/fake-it-make-it

Grossi, C. M., Brimblecombe, P. and Harris, I. (2007) Predicting long term freeze-thaw risks on Europe built heritage and archaeological sites in a changing climate. *Science of the Total Environment*, **377**, 273–281.

Grossi, C. M., Brimblecombe, P., Menéndez, B., Benavente, D., Harris, I. and Déqué, M. (2011) Climatology of salt transitions and implications for stone weathering. *Science of the Total Environment*, **409**(2), 577–2,585.

Harada, M., Kigawa, R., Komine, Y. and Fujii, Y. (2014) Report on fumigation process conducted at Rin-noh-ji Temple. *Hozonkagaku*, **53**, 215–224 (in Japanese).

Hayashi, M., Kigawa, R., Harada, M., Komine, Y., Kawanobe, W. and Ishizaki, T. (2012) Analysis on distribution of beetles captured by adhesive traps in some historic wooden buildings in Nikkō. *Hozonkagaku*, **51**, 201–209 (in Japanese).

Hayashi, M., Komine, Y., Kigawa, R., Harada, M., Kawanobe, W. and Ishizaki, T. (2011) Methods and results of counting beetles captured by adhesive traps at historic buildings in Nikkō. *Hozonkagaku*, **50**, 123–132.

JMA (2014) *Global Warming Projection*, Vol. 8. Tokyo, Japan Meteorological Agency.

(2016) *Climate Change Monitoring Report 2015*. Tokyo, Japan Meteorological Agency.

Kim, S., Tachikawa, Y., Nakakita, E., Yorozu, K. and Shiiba, M. (2011a) Climate change impact on river flow of the Tone River basin, Japan. *Journal of Japan Society of Civil Engineers, Ser. B1 (Hydraulic Engineering)*, **67**, 185–190.

Kim, T. G., Ra, J. B., Kang, S. M. and Wang, J. (2011b) Determination of decay hazard index (Scheffer index) in Korea for exterior above-ground wood. *Journal of the Korean Wood Science and Technology*, **39**, 531–537.

Komine, Y., Harada, M., Nomura, M., Kigawa, R., Yamano, K., Fujii, Y., Fujiwara, Y. and Kawanobe, W. (2010) Survey of wood-boring anobiids at Rinnohji temple in Nikkō. *Science for Conservation*, **49**, 173–181 (in Japanese).

Komine, Y., Harada, M., Saito, A., Saito, Y., Kigawa, R. and Fujii, Y. (2017) Report on a new insect monitoring method in wooden historic buildings in Nikkō. *Science for Conservation*, **56**, 77–88 (in Japanese).

Komine, Y., Kigawa, R., Harada, M., Fujii, Y., Fujiwara, Y. and Kawanobe, W. (2009) Damage by a rare kind of anobiid, *Priobium cylindricum*, found during restoration work of Sanbutsu-do, Rinnohji temple in Nikkō. *Science for Conservation*, **48**, 207–213 (in Japanese).

Lemaire, R. and Stovel, H. (1994) *Nara Document on Authenticity*. Paris, International Council on Monuments and Sites. https://www.icomos.org/charters/nara-e.pdf

Luo, Y., Qin, D., Zhang, R., Wang, S. and Zhang, D. (2016) Climatic and environmental changes in China. In D. Qin, Y. Ding and M. Mu (eds.), *Climate and Environmental Change in China: 1951–2012*, pp. 29–46. Heidelberg, Springer Environmental Science and Engineering.

Lupi, D., Jucker, C. and Colombo, M. (2013) Distribution and biology of the yellow-spotted longicorn beetle *Psacothea hilaris hilaris* (Pascoe) in Italy. *EPPO Bulletin*, **43**, 316–322.

Markham, A., Osipova, E., Samuels, K. L. and Caldas, A. (2016) *World Heritage and Tourism in a Changing Climate*. Paris, UNESCO Publishing.

Marrion, C. E. (2016) More effectively addressing fire/disaster challenges to protect our cultural heritage. *Journal of Cultural Heritage*, **20**, 746–749.

Mei, W. and Xie, S. P. (2016) Intensification of landfalling typhoons over the northwest Pacific since the late 1970s. *Nature Geoscience*, **9**, 753–757.

NOAA (National Oceanic and Atmospheric Administration) (2018) *Significant Earthquake Database*. https://www.ngdc.noaa.gov/nndc/struts/form?t=101650&s=1&d=1

Okubo, T. (2016) Traditional wisdom for disaster mitigation in history of Japanese architectures and historic cities. *Journal of Cultural Heritage*, **20**, 715–724.

Oron, A., Liphschitz, N., Held, B. W., Galili, E., Klein, M., Linker, R. and Blanchette, R. A. (2016) Characterization of archaeological waterlogged wooden objects exposed on the hyper-saline Dead Sea shore. *Journal of Archaeological Science: Reports*, **9**, 73–86.

Perrottet, T. (2017) The couple who saved China's ancient architectural treasures before they were lost forever. *Smithsonian Magazine* (January). https://www.smithsonianmag.com/history/lovers-shanxi-saved-chinas-ancient-architectural-treasures-before-lost-forever-180961424

Sabbioni, C., Brimblecombe, P. and Cassar, M. (2010) *The Atlas of Climate Change Impact on European Cultural Heritage: Scientific Analysis and Management Strategies*. London, Anthem Press.

Sato, H. (1996) *Basho's Narrow Road: Spring and Autumn Passages*. Berkeley, CA, Stone Bridge Press.

Shin, H. B. (2016) Economic transition and speculative urbanisation in China: gentrification versus dispossession. *Urban Studies*, **53**, 471–489.

Steinhardt, N. S. (1994) Liao: An architectural tradition in the making. *Artibus Asiae*, **54**, 5–39.

Stengaard Hansen, L., Akerlund, M., Grontoft, T., Rhyl-Svendsen, M., Schmidt, A., Bergh, J. and Vagn Jensen, K. (2012) Future pest status of an insect pest in museums, *Attagenus smirnovi*: Distribution and food consumption in relation to climate change. *Journal of Cultural Heritage*, **13**, 22–27.

Sugio, K. (2015) Large-scale disasters on world heritage and cultural heritage in Japan: Significant impacts and sustainable management cases. *Landscape Research*, **40**, 748–758.

Tian, X.-R., Shu, L.-F., Zhao, F.-J., Wang, M.-Y. and McRae, D. J. (2011) Future impacts of climate change on forest fire danger in northeastern China. *Journal of Forestry Research*, **22**, 437–446.

Tollefson, J. (2017) The wooden skyscrapers that could help to cool the planet. *Nature*, **545**(7,654), 280–282.

Usami, T. (1979) Study of historical earthquakes in Japan. *Bulletin of the Earthquake Research Institute*, **54**, 399–439.

Wakuda, Y. (1996) Wartime railways transport policies. *Japan Railways and Transport Review*, **8**, 32–35.

Watanabe, T., Kato, K., Fukumoto, S. and Eto, K. (2013) Vibration characteristics of Nikkō-zan Rin-noji temple Hondo for the 2011 off the Pacific coast of Tohoku earthquake and its aftershocks. *Journal of Structural and Construction Engineering*, **78**, 521–528.

Watanabe, T., Kato, K. and Tateishi, H. (2014) Applicability of a dynamic analysis model for Nikkō-zan Rin-noji temple Hondo based on observed seismic records during the 2011 off the Pacific coast of Tohoku earthquake. *AIJ Journal of Technology and Design*, **20**, 533–538.

Watari, Y., Yamanaka, T., Asano, W. and Ishikawa, Y. (2002) Prediction of the life cycle of the west Japan type yellow-spotted longicorn beetle, *Psacothea hilaris* (Coleoptera: Cerambycidae) by numerical simulations. *Applied Entomology and Zoology*, **37**, 559–569.

WHC (World Heritage Centre) (2013) Wooden structures of Liao Dynasty – Wooden pagoda of Yingxian County Main Hall of Fengguo Monastery of Yixian County. *Tentative Lists*. Paris, UNESCO. http://whc.unesco.org/en/tentativelists/5803/

Xinhua (2004) Yingxian wooden pagoda to have fire fighters. Xinhua News Agency, 9 September. http://www.china.org.cn/english/culture/106572.htm

Xu, X., Heath, T., Xia, Q. and Zhang, Y. (2015) Disaster prevention and mitigation strategies for architecture heritage concentrated areas in China. *Archnet-IJAR*, **9**(1), 108–121.

Yokota, T., Sakamoto, S., Tachibana, H. and Ishii, K. (2008) Numerical analysis and auralization of the 'roaring dragon' phenomenon by the FDTD method. *Journal of Environmental Engineering*, **73**, 849–856.

Yuasa, N. (1966) *The Narrow Road to the Deep North*. London, Penguin Books.

8 Green development in China

KE SHUIFA, FENG QIYA, WANG BAOJIN, AND QIAO DAN

School of Agricultural Economics and Rural Development, Renmin University of China, China

Keywords

Green development; green economy; resource conservation; environmentally friendly; social harmony; historical course; China

Abstract

Green development has gradually become the trend in today's world. Because of the past development situation, China attaches great importance to green development in recent years. In this chapter, we first present China's green development model, which is based on the ecological environment and resource carrying capacity constraints, with green economy, resource conservation, environmental friendliness, and social harmony as the main contents, and green innovation is the basic approach to sustainable economic growth. The main objectives are maximization of resource utilization efficiency, optimization of environmental protection, and optimal allocation of social welfare. Then the course of green development in China is historically summarized. Furthermore, this research introduces a series of laws and regulations for promoting green development in the Chinese economic system, resources, and society. In addition, the chapter presents the current status of green development, the current range of issues and challenges it faces, and corresponding suggestions for countermeasures and suggestions proposed based on an evaluation index system under construction. Finally, a future action plan for green development in China is proposed.

8.1 INTRODUCTION

Economic development and scientific and technological progress have resulted in unprecedented progress in human understanding and the transformation of nature. However, the problems of global warming, environmental pollution, energy crises, and poverty are intensifying and posing a threat to the sustainable development of human society. Several noteworthy publications have drawn public attention to the environment and associated human issues. These works include *Silent Spring* (Carson, 1962), *The Limits to Growth* (Meadows, 1997), *Only One Earth* (Ward *et al.*, 1974), and *Our Common Future* (World Commission on Environment and Development, 1997). The United Nations Conference on Environment and Development (UNCED) held in Rio de Janeiro in 1992 led to the signing of five documents, including Agenda 21 (Environmental Protection and Integrated Management Committee, 2000) and the Rio Declaration on Environment and Development (United Nations Conference on Environment and Development, 1992), proposing sustainable growth as the official development path for all countries in the world and converting the theoretical discussions of sustainable growth into practical applications.

Since the beginning of the 21st century, this new concept of development for the international community has continuously evolved and improved, but its connotations have not changed much. The publication of *China's Human Development Report 2002: The Road to Green Development and the Mandatory Path* by the United Nations Development Programme marked the entry of the green development concept into various fields of China's economic construction and development (Zhao and Yang, 2011). As the second-largest economy and largest developing country in the world, China faces enormous difficulties and challenges in terms of economic development, environmental governance, energy integration, and social construction owing to its characteristic national conditions and complex reality. Faced with the grim reality of its economic development entering a 'new normal' level,[1] resource constraints becoming tighter, serious environmental pollution, and ecosystem degradation, China is paying serious attention to and actively exploring the green development path.

---

[1] The new normal: 'New' is 'different from the old'; 'normal' is the inherent state. The new normal is a different, relatively stable state. This is a trend and an irreversible state of development, which means that the Chinese economy has entered a new phase that is different from the period of high growth over the past three decades.

8.2 THE CONNOTATIONS AND COURSE OF CHINA'S GREEN DEVELOPMENT

8.2.1 The source of China's green development

The concept of China's green development comes primarily from three aspects. First, it can be traced back to ancient Chinese traditional culture, specifically to the splendid contribution of the 'one hundred contending schools of thought' that appeared during the Spring and Autumn Period (771–475 BCE) and the Warring States Period (475–221 BCE). These thoughts included Confucianism's 'harmony of human and nature' as an ecological ethic, its 'equal beings' concept, and Taoism's emphasis on the natural world. Second, it comes from the Marxist environmental philosophy, which includes the Marxist system of ecological theory, the natural substance cycle theory, and the concept of harmony between human beings and nature. Third, green development also arises from continuous development as well as constant innovation of sustainable development, which extends sustainable development to all aspects of the economy, resources, environment, and social life. As an important part of the 'five-in-one' national strategic layout[2] of ecological civilization, green development is the main approach to an ecological civilization.[3]

8.2.2 The connotations of China's green development

As can be seen in Figure 8.1, green development is a theory of growth that combines four developmental dimensions: the economic system, resource system, environmental system, and social system. It is based on the ecological environment's capacity[4] and resource carrying capacity[5] constraints. The main contents of green development are green economy, resource conservation, environment protection, and social harmony;

green innovation is the basic approach. The fundamental goals are sustainable development of the economy, maximal efficiency of resource utilization, optimal environmental protection, and optimal social welfare allocation. In other words, green development means that '[l]ucid waters and lush mountains are invaluable assets'.

Green development has four parts: economic development, resource conservation, environmental friendliness, and social harmony. Of these, resource conservation and environmental friendliness provide initial wealth and a proper external environment for 'green economic development', as they are the prerequisites for green and healthy economic development, since green economic development provides technical and capital support for resource conservation and environmental protection. In this chapter, social harmony means the smooth operation of the social system in a narrow sense. Environmental friendliness[6] is an external constraint on resource conservation. Only when environmental friendliness is achieved can resource conservation have practical significance. Resource conservation is also an important part of environmental friendliness. Green economic development also contributes to a harmonious society. On the other side, social harmony provides intellectual support and social security for green economic development. Environmental friendliness and resource saving are the prerequisites for a harmonious society.

It is widely believed that the green economy, recycling economy, or low-carbon economy is the main path to green development (Li, 2017). Pursuing a single economic growth model to realize socially sustainable development, green development is the coordination of economic development and environmental resources. The speed and scale of economic development must be kept within the scope of the ecological environment. In addition, green development emphasizes the rationality and continuity of development. It attaches great importance to economic development, while adjusting its economic structure to make it more reasonable. It also integrates environmental protection and resource conservation into all aspects of the economy, politics, culture, and social construction and pursues a win-win mode between development and the ecology.

To achieve green development, ecological environment protection is necessary. The economic system should focus on intensive rather than extensive development. The society should move from an unbalanced and underdeveloped economy to one of fairness and justice. It should adhere to humanistic thinking and share the fruits of development, while at the same time realizing that human development is the fundamental starting point and foothold of green development. The promotion of green

---

[2] The 'five-in-one' national strategic layout refers to economic construction, political construction, cultural construction, social construction, and ecological civilization construction.

[3] Ecological civilization: The purpose of this is harmonious symbiosis, a virtuous circle, and all-round development. Its development direction is personality civilization, ecological civilization, and industrial civilization. It emphasizes that we should do our own ecological construction, but more importantly, we should give environmental protection and resource conservation prominence over integration into all aspects of economic construction, political construction, cultural construction, and social construction.

[4] 'Eco-environment capacity' refers to the capacity to contain pollutants under conditions of maintaining ecosystem health and relative stability.

[5] 'Resource carrying capacity' refers to the maximum ability of our environment to provide basic survival and development for humans. When human activities are within a certain range, it can continuously satisfy people's needs through self-regulation and improvement. However, when it exceeds a certain limit, the entire system will collapse. This maximum is the carrying capacity of resources.

[6] 'Environmental friendliness' refers to the human activities that are conducive to the protection of the environment.

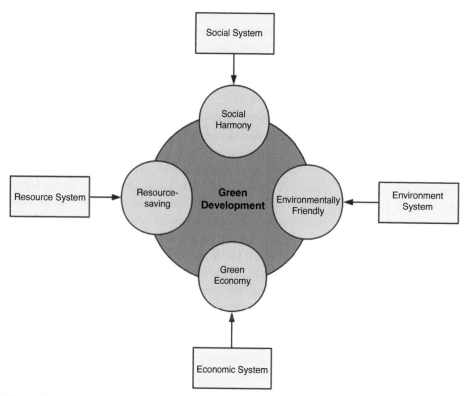

Figure 8.1. The connotations of green development.

development can effectively improve the quality of economic development, satisfy people's longing for a happy life, enable people to work and live in better natural and social harmony, and allow people to enjoy the beautiful environment based on green development and fair and equitable treatment of all green benefits, thus further improving general livelihood and the happiness index.

8.2.3 The course of China's green development

China's green development shows two main courses running through it. One is the sprouting of the theory of green development, involving its formation, progress, and innovation. The other is the gradual rise of the concept of green development as the state's political strategy for running the country.

(1) Formation and development of green development theory. Before the reform and opening-up period (1949–1977), less attention was paid to the concept and study of environmental protection. The main related study was on 'the relationship between geographical environment, population, and social development', made by Wang (1955). After the reform and opening-up period, several in-depth studies on the environment, resources, and development provided some significant results. These studies can be specifically divided into two periods. The first is the period of widespread concern about

green development (1978–2000). Studies made in this period pointed out that the increasing environmental pollution in China posed a serious threat to sustainable economic and social development, from the perspective of environmental science and economics. The representative works are 'China Environmental Protection Affairs (1981–1985)', published by China's Environmental Protection Bureau (1988), and 'China Development Report', published by Ma and Wang (1999). Studies in the second period covered the initial formation and progress of the green development theory (2000–present), mainly considering three aspects of green development. The first includes the theoretical sources (Zhang, 2014; Song, 2016; Shi, 2017; Wang and Yu, 2017), conception (Hu, 2005, 2012; Liu, 2010; Hu and Zhou, 2014), characteristics (Wu, 2015), significance (Wang, 2005; Chen, 2011; Zhang, 2013; Feng and Guan, 2017), and ways to achieve green development (Hu and Men, 2005; Hao and Zhao, 2011; Guo, 2013; Yan, 2016; Qin and Hu, 2017). The second includes the relationships between green development and laws and regulations (Yang, 2016a, 2016b), green development and fiscal and tax policies (Peng and Tian, 2016; Wang, 2017; Guan, 2017), green development and urbanization (Wang, 2014; Cai *et al.,* 2014), green development and science and technology innovation (Zhang, 2015; Huang, 2017), and green development and industry (Yue *et al.*, 2015; Zhang *et al.*, 2015; He and Wang, 2016), and other related indicators. The third consists of some indicator systems and methods for measuring the benefits of green development (Li and Pan, 2012; Zhao, 2013; Yang and Wen, 2017; You *et al.*, 2017; Huang and Li, 2017).

(2) Green development as the strategy of China. In 2007, the 17th Communist Party of China (CPC) Congress identified the Scientific Outlook on Development[7] as the guideline for green development. At the same time, the core of green development, ecological civilization, was written into the party constitution as one of the basic requirements for an all-round well-off society.[8] In 2011, China's 12th Five-Year Plan (FYP),[9] with a focus on green development and building a resource-saving and environment-friendly society, specifically stated as follows: 'In the face of increasingly constrained resources and the environment, we must enhance the sense of crisis, establish the concept of green and low-carbon development, focus on energy conservation and emission reduction, improve the incentive and restraint mechanisms, speed up the construction of an environmentally friendly mode of production and consumption, enhance the capacity of sustainable development, and enhance the level of ecological civilization.' In 2012, the 18th Congress of the Communist Party became a key turning point for the all-round promotion of green development when the concept of an ecological civilization was written into the country's development strategy at the national level. In the following years, green development rose to new heights in China. In 2016, the five development concepts of innovation, coordination, green, openness, and sharing as the 13th FYP Period of China were put forward in the 6th Plenary Session of the 18th Central Committee of the Communist Party of China. As the guiding ideology of economic and social development, the concept of green development became China's strategy for governing the country, together with the development of economics, politics, culture, and society. In the report of the 19th National Congress of the Communist Party of China in 2017, the idea of building a beautiful China[10] was related to green development. In 2018, in order to vigorously promote green development, the Central Government of China carried out institutional restructuring and reorganization, integrating the Ministry of Land and Resources, the State Oceanic Administration, and the National Bureau of Surveying and Mapping Geographical Information into the Department of Natural Resources; the Ministry of Environmental Protection was also renamed the Ministry of Ecology and Environment. The State Forestry Administration was expanded into the National Forest and Grassland Bureau. Nowadays, the practice of green development is carried out extensively and intensively in various regions, fields, and industries in China.

It is a long-term, arduous, and complicated task for China to build an ecological civilization and implement a green development strategy. The future of China's green development can be divided into three periods, as follows. The first period (2017–2020) is the primary stage of green development, which consists of solving numerous problems, such as the deepening economic reforms, growing ecological and environmental issues, tightening resource constraints, and frequent social conflict. The second period (2020–2035) is the mature stage of green development; this is a crucial period for China, when it plans to become a medium-sized developed country. This period will see the beginning of green development and the achievement of a stable, healthy, and rapidly developing economy. The third period (2035–2050) is the stage of consolidating and enhancing the achievements of green development, and the period of reaching the level of a modern developed country. This period (2035–2050) will see the building up of a prosperous, strong, democratic, civilized, beautiful, and modern socialist powerhouse sharing the fruits of green development.

---

[7] Scientific Outlook on Development: Adhering to the principle of 'putting people first, establishing a comprehensive, coordinated and sustainable development concept, and promoting the all-round economic, social and people-to-people development', Hu Jintao, then General Secretary of the CPC Central Committee, mentioned it in his speech of 28 July 2003. A methodology for promoting the reformation and development of various undertakings in accordance with the requirements of 'coordinating the urban and rural development, coordinating regional development, coordinating economic and social development, coordinating the harmonious development of man and nature, and coordinating domestic development and opening up to the outside world' was also a major strategy of the CPC's thought.

[8] The all-round well-off society: This aims to achieve a fundamental change in the mode of economic development and to build a world economic power; secondly, significant progress has been made in social construction and building a harmonious socialist society; thirdly, significant progress has been made in the building of political civilization and a socialist democratization; fourthly, enhancing cultural construction to prosperity and development of a strong socialist culture; fifthly, the construction of ecological civilization has entered a new phase and has built green China initially. Deng Xiaoping proposed in the blueprint of economic and social development of China in the late 1970s and early 1980s that the essence is to jointly develop the society and common prosperity.

[9] China's 12th Five-Year Plan: Short-term national planning texts formulated by China over a five-year period, starting in 2011 and ending in 2015 (Xinhua News Agency, 2011).

[10] 'Beautiful China' was proposed by the Communist Party of China, which aims to put ecological civilization construction in a prominent position; integrate it into all aspects of economic, political, cultural, and social construction and the whole process; ensure social fairness and justice; and realize the people's long-cherished vision for a better life.

8.3 GREEN DEVELOPMENT POLICIES, SYSTEMS, AND ACTIONS IN CHINA

8.3.1 Policy systems of green development in China

Since the reform and opening-up period, the environment in China and abroad has undergone profound changes. The Chinese government has formed a series of legal and policy systems to support green development. From the 'one horizontal and one vertical' perspective, the 'horizontal dimension' relates to China's green development in terms of its economy, resources, ecological environment, and social governance, while the 'vertical dimension' relates to the country's green development laws and policies framed by the constitution as the fundamental criteria, single-line laws, administrative regulations, local laws and regulations, administrative regulations, and policy documents.

Since the 1980s, the Chinese government has enacted numerous laws relating to green development in various fields. It has also built a full range of green development laws and regulations since the start of the new century (see Table 8.1).

Since China's 12th FYP in 2011 involves the concept of green development, the State Council and its subordinate ministries have successively formulated and promulgated a number of important policy documents relating to economic development, resource utilization, environmental protection, and social governance (see Table 8.2). In particular, the series of green policy systems, such as the Green Energy Policy, Green Manufacturing Policy, Green Logistics, Green Procurement Policy, Green Transportation Policy, Green Building Policy, Green Accounting Policy, Green Consumption Policy, and Green Energy Policy, have been strengthened.

8.3.2 China's institutional system for green development

With the gradual progress of the green development process, the Chinese government has established a more complete green development institutional system, which has played an increasingly important role in green development implementation. Generally, from the perspective of implementing green

Table 8.1. Main laws relating to green development in China.

Name of law	Course (apply, revise time)	Content
Forest Law	1985	Resource utilization
Prairie Law	1985	Resource utilization
Fishing Law	1986, 2000, 2004	Resource utilization
Mineral Resources Law	1986, 1996	Resource utilization
Compulsory Education Law	1986, 2006, 2015	Social harmony
Land Management Law	1987, 2004	Resource utilization
Wild Animal Conservation Law	1988, 2004, 2016	Environmental protection
Atmospheric Pollution Prevention Law	1988, 1995, 2000, 2016	Environmental protection
Environmental Protection Law	1989	Environmental protection
Soil and Water Conservation Law	1991, 2011	Environmental protection
Labour Law	1994	Social harmony
Food Safety Law	1995, 2009, 2015	Social harmony, Green economy
Electric Law	1996	Resource utilization
Coal Law	1996, 2011	Resource utilization
Solid Waste Pollution Control Law	1996, 2004, 2016	Environmental protection
Environmental Noise Prevention Law	1997	Environmental protection
Energy Saving Law	1997, 2007	Resource utilization
Ocean Environmental Protection Law	2000, 2013, 2016	Environmental protection
Population and Family Planning Law	2002, 2015	Social harmony
Cleaner Production Promotion Law	2003	Green economy
Radioactive Pollution Control Law	2003	Environmental protection
Renewable Energy Law	2005, 2010	Resource utilization
Employment Promotion Law	2008, 2015	Social harmony
Water Pollution Prevention Law	2008	Environmental protection
Circular Economy Promotion Law	2009	Green economy
Social Insurance Law	2010	Social harmony

Source: The authors, based on literature review

Table 8.2. China's policy documents relating to green development in 2011–2017.

Year	Policy document name	Contents of the file involving green development
2011	National Economic and Social Development, 12th FYP	Green development
	China Rural Poverty Alleviation and Development Programme (2011–2020)	Social harmony
2012	National Outline of Water Saving in Agriculture (2012–2020)	Resource utilization
2013	Opinions on Accelerating the Development of Energy-Saving and Environmental Protection Industry	Resource utilization, Environmental protection
	Livestock Scale Pollution Prevention and Control Regulations	Environmental protection
	Town Drainage and Sewage Treatment Ordinance	Environmental protection
2014	Guiding Opinions on Improving the Living Environment in Rural Areas	Social harmony, Environmental protection
	Air Pollution Prevention Action Plan	Environmental protection
2015	Opinions on Strengthening the Standardization of Energy Conservation	Resource utilization
	The 13th FYP for National Economic and Social Development	Green development
	Opinions of the CPC Central Committee and the State Council on Strengthening the Construction of Ecological Civilization	Green development
2016	Wetland Protection and Restoration System Programme	Environmental protection
	Several Opinions on Perfecting Support Policies and Promoting Farmers' Continuous Income Increase	Social harmony
	National Agricultural Modernization Planning (2016–2020)	Green development
	Guiding Opinions on Promoting Economic Growth by Adjusting the Structure of Petrochemical Industry	Resource utilization
	The 13th FYP for the Energy-saving Emission Reduction Comprehensive Programme of Work	Resource utilization
	Several Opinions on Further Promoting the Structural Reform of Agricultural Supply Side and Accelerating and Fostering New Motive Power for Agricultural and Rural Development	Green economy
	The 13th FYP for Poverty Alleviation	Social harmony
	The 13th FYP for Forestry	Resource utilization, Environmental protection
	National Groundwater Pollution Prevention and Control Plan (2011–2020)	Resource utilization, Environmental protection
	The 13th FYP for Eco-environmental Protection Planning	Environmental protection
	Opinions on Improving Compensation Mechanism for Ecological Protection	Environmental protection
2017	Opinions on the Implementation of Structural Reform to Promote Agricultural Supply Side	Green development
	People's Republic of China Environmental Protection Tax Law Enforcement Regulations	Environmental protection

Table 8.2 (cont.)

Year	Policy document name	Contents of the file involving green development
	Guiding Opinions on Institutional Mechanism for Innovative Rural Infrastructure Investment and Financing	Green economy
	Guiding Opinions on the Reform of the System of Compensated Use of All Natural Resources by All the People	Resource utilization
	Industrial Green Development Plan (2016–2020)	Green development
	Guiding Opinions on Promoting Green Consumption	Green development
	Opinions on Speeding up the Structural Reform on the Agricultural Supply Side and Developing the Economy of the Food Industry	Green economy
	Opinions on Supporting Social Forces to Provide Multi-level and Diversified Medical Services	Social harmony
	Notice on Promoting Financial Support to Agricultural Green Development	Green economy
	The 13th FYP for National Food Safety Planning	Social harmony
	Opinions on Innovating Institutional Mechanism to Promote Agricultural Green Development	Green development
	Opinions of the General Office of the State Council on Accelerating the Utilization of Livestock and Poultry Waste and Utilization of Resources	Resource utilization
	Ministry of Agriculture on the Implementation of Five Major Actions of Agricultural Green Development Notice	Green development

Source: The authors, based on literature review

development, there are two types of systems. The first type is the marketing system for promoting green development; this mainly includes (1) the resources and environmental property system, such as the right to use energy, the right to use water, the initial allocation system of carbon emission rights, the system of property rights of natural resources, the system of environmental property rights, the system of national rights and interests of mineral resources, the system of paid use of resources, the system of ecological value assessment, and the system of assets and liabilities of natural resources. The marketing system also includes (2) trading institution systems, such as the carbon emission rights trading system, the system of paid usage and trading of emission rights, the system of trading of water rights, the third-party environmental pollution control system, the carbon emission reporting of key units, the verification and certification and quota management system, and so on.

The second type of system is the government institutions for promoting green development, which includes the following. (1) The incentive institution: This includes the systems of ecological compensation, financial and taxation incentives,

assessment and evaluation incentives, and the green certification and government green procurement institution. (2) Restraint institution: This includes the systems of natural resource use control, most stringent environmental protection, most stringent water resources management, most stringent source protection, ecological restoration, the ecological red line, negative list of industry access for key eco-functional areas, total pollution control, intensive use of resources and conservation, extension of producer responsibility, and mandatory discharge of pollutants liability. (3) Government regulation: This includes the systems of natural resource management, provincial environmental protection agencies below the vertical monitoring and law enforcement, national parks, resource and environment carrying capacity monitoring and early warning mechanisms, land and space development permits, pollutant discharge permits, corporate environmental credit records and illegal polluting blacklist, and the emergency environment event reporting and information disclosure mechanism. (4) Accountability: This includes the systems of party and government co-responsibility, environmental damage liability accountability, audit system for outgoing leading cadres responsibility for natural resources assets and environmental protection, evaluation of environmental damage and compensation, environmental public interest litigation, and environmental law enforcement supervision (Li, 2016).

8.3.3 Green development of main actions

With the concept of green development deepening and rising to the level of national strategy, the Chinese government has formulated and implemented some green development initiatives in order to resolve the current grim situation.[11] This study elaborates the four aspects of promoting the development of green economy, realizing the intensive use of resources, promoting the protection of ecological resources, and building a harmonious society.

8.3.3.1 Promoting economic and green development

The Chinese government has vigorously developed its green economy by adjusting its industrial structure and promoting industrial technological progress. Its major actions include strictly controlling the additional production capacity of surplus industries; promoting the elimination of outdated and excessive capacity; developing modern eco-friendly, efficient, and safe modern agricultural technologies and further developing water-saving agriculture, recycling agriculture, organic agriculture, and modern forestry; formulating and implementing special treatment programmes for ten major water-consuming industries, such as chapter making and printing and dyeing; drastically reducing the emission intensity of pollutants; focusing on the ultra-low-emission retrofits of coal-fired power plants; implementing the comprehensive management of key industries such as electricity, steel, building materials, petrochemicals, and non-ferrous metals; carrying out synergistic control of multiple pollutants such as sulphur dioxide, nitrogen oxides, smoke, dust, and heavy metals; accelerating the research and demonstration of new energy vehicles and technology; promoting the industrialization of semiconductor lighting; promoting the complete set of garbage treatment technology and equipment to overcome the remediation of contaminated soil technology; deepening the comprehensive utilization of waste; promoting seawater desalination technology innovation; expanding the environmental service industry; and taking green building action, such as focusing on green food sources, green

storage, green factories, and green industrial parks, and building a green food industry system.

8.3.3.2 Achieving resource-intensive, efficient, and economical use

The Chinese government continues to promote the intensive use of resources by formulating relevant systems and implementing demonstration projects. The major actions include strictly implementing fishing and fishing-forbidden systems; exploring implementation of the offshore fishing quota management pilot; implementing the rare species rescue plan; improving the state-owned land, water, mineral, forest, and grassland resources, as well as the sea area island paid use system; expanding the rational crop rotation system subsidy pilot; expanding the scale of a new round of the Grain for Green programme; starting grassland disaster prevention and mitigation projects in pastoral areas; promoting new energy projects, such as rice husk power generation; implementing energy conservation and emission reduction projects, such as key air and water pollutant emission reduction projects; constructing a resource recycling industry demonstration base, an industrial waste comprehensive utilization industrial base, and workers' and peasants' complex circular economy demonstration areas; promoting circular links between production and living systems, building a green low-carbon cycle industrial system; implementing boiler and kilns renovation, electrical system energy saving, energy system optimization, waste heat and pressure utilization, and energy-saving alternative oil; building energy efficiency, green lighting, other energy-saving projects, energy-saving technology industry demonstration projects, energy-saving products, and projects for the benefit of citizens; contracting energy management promotion and energy-saving capacity-building projects; and construction of sponge cities.[12]

8.3.3.3 Promoting the protection of ecological environment

The Chinese government realizes the importance of protecting the ecological environment by strengthening the management and control of ecological space, promoting supply-side structural reform, preventing pollution from key industries, and strengthening green technologies. The major actions include guiding the gradual and orderly transfer of population and building national ecological safety barriers ('two barriers and three zones') (the

---

[11] The current grim situation in this article refers specifically to the severe situation in which economic development has entered tight resource constraints, severe environmental pollution, and degraded ecosystems.

[12] 'Sponge city' means that the city can be like a sponge and has good 'elasticity' in adapting to environmental changes and responding to natural disasters. When it rains, it can absorb, store, seep, and purify water. The water stored will be released and used when it is needed.

ecological safety barrier on the Tibetan Plateau, the ecological safety barrier on the Loess Plateau – Sichuan – Yunnan, the ecological safety barrier on the northeast forest belt, the anti-sand belt on the north ecological security barrier, and the ecological security barrier in the southern hills). It will integrate a number of national parks; develop forest cities, garden cities, and forest towns; protect forests, grasslands, and wetland systems; establish a biodiversity conservation network; control non-point source pollution; promote zero growth of the use of chemical fertilizers; build a batch of pest prevention and control and green prevention; control fusion demonstration bases; establish a traceability system for pesticide products; establish sewage treatment systems for farmer payment and comprehensive management of river basin pollution; improve the rural sewage treatment fee adjustment mechanism; implement land classification management, prevention, and control of soil pollution; implement circular economy key projects, such as comprehensive utilization of resources, waste recycling systems, 'urban mineral' demonstration bases, remanufacture industrialization, food waste recycling, industrial park recycling, resource recycling technology demonstration and promotion, and so on; achieve the national forecast of information sharing and networking release; reduce severe air pollution and improve the regional joint warning, control, and prevention; ask industrial enterprises to prepare annual sewage status reports; improve the industrial park sewage centralized treatment facilities and air pollution in key gasification areas; develop the key technologies of resource-saving recycling; establish municipal solid waste utilization of resources, recycling of renewable resources, and comprehensive utilization of industrial solid waste and other technology systems; focus on the atmosphere, water, soil, and other issues, the formation of source prevention, end of governance, and ecological environment restoration of complete sets of technologies; establish the ecological and environmental science and technology innovation theory system with scientific research as the guide; establish the eco-environmental technology research and development system with demonstration and application as support; establish environmental standards and systems with human health as the goal; establish the environmental protection industry cultivation system with competitiveness as the core; and establish the environmental protection technology management system based on service guarantees.

8.3.3.4 Building a harmonious society

Building a harmonious society is a complicated systematic proposal, which basically consists of several factors, such as education, healthcare, and residents' income level and quality. Therefore, the Chinese government's major initiatives include promoting the balanced development of compulsory education; creating a large number of social medical institutions with strong

service competitiveness; forming a number of influential health service industry cluster areas; improving the national health insurance system; comprehensively launching urban and rural residents' serious illness insurance, medical assistance for major and minor diseases, and emergency relief for diseases; building the capacity of food safety inspection (monitoring) projects; establishing a comprehensive food safety coordination mechanism and a clear office to promote a pesticide residues control project; promoting green consumption and large-scale development of green buildings; increasing the proportion of buses in urban built-up areas that cater to mobility; and promoting industrial poverty alleviation projects, such as agriculture and forestry breeding projects for poverty alleviation, training projects in poverty-stricken areas, asset-income poverty alleviation projects, rural road projects, rural power grid upgrading and upgrading projects, network communication poverty alleviation projects, rural community service system construction projects, rural industrial integration pilot projects, ecological construction poverty alleviation projects, land and environmental remediation projects, rural dilapidated building reconstruction projects, work-relief projects, public-health toilet construction, and so on.

8.4 CHINA'S GREEN DEVELOPMENT ASSESSMENT

8.4.1 China's green development evaluation index system

Based on the definition of green development (primarily as discussed in Section 8.2.2), the Annual Assessment Bulletin of Ecological Civilization Construction by the Ministry of Environmental Protection in 2016, and some research results (Huang, 2014; Wang, 2016), an indicator system for measuring China's green development is set out in this section. The system aims to measure the current green development situation in China in a more comprehensive and scientific manner from the perspectives of the four dimensions of the economy, resources, environment, and society (Development and Reform Commission, 2016), as shown in Table 8.3.

8.4.2 China's progress in green development

From the above index system, relevant statistical data, and policy planning, we find that, as of the end of 2015, China has taken a series of important steps to promote and implement green development. This study will elaborate on this from four aspects.

8.4.2.1 Economic green growth

During the years 2011–2015, China's green economy developed rapidly and achieved remarkable results. In 2015, the country's total economic output ranked the second in the world, with the

Table 8.3. China's green development evaluation index system.

Target level	System layer	Indicator layer
China's Green Development Evaluation System	(A) Green economy	1. Green energy-saving industry added value as a share of GDP (%) 2. Green products market share (energy efficient products market share) (%) 3. Research and experimental development expenditures as a share of GDP (%) 4. The proportion of the three major industrial structures 5. Green financial capital percentage (%)
	(B) Resource conservation	1. US$10,000 GDP coal consumption (t) 2. US$10,000 GDP sulphur dioxide emissions (t) 3. US$10,000 GDP water consumption (t) 4. US$10,000 GDP power consumption (kWh) 5. Coal's share of total energy consumption (%) 6. Cultivated land holdings (million hm²)
	(C) Environmentally friendly	1. Centralized sewage treatment rate (%) 2. Domestic garbage harmless treatment rate (%) 3. Chemical oxygen demand[13] (100 million t) 4. Prefecture level and above, city air quality excellent days ratio (%) 5. Coastal waters of good quality ratio (type one or two) (%) 6. Pesticide use per unit of cultivated land area (kg/hm²) 7. Forest coverage (%) 8. New afforestation area (ten thousand hm²) 9. National park construction (units) 10. Wetland and grassland holdings (million hm²)
	(D) Social harmony	1. Growth of new energy vehicle ownership (%) 2. Rural tap water penetration rate (%) 3. Rural sanitation toilet penetration rate (%) 4. Health literacy level[14] (%) 5. Characteristic town construction[15] (units) 6. Proportion of poor population with file legislation cards[16] (%) 7. Proportion of compulsory education[17] (%) 8. Number of general practitioners per 10,000 population[18]

Source: The authors, based on literature review

per capita gross domestic product (GDP) increasing to US$7,924; significant progress was made in economic restructuring; and the total output value of forestry was US$95.38 billion. The production and trade of forestry products continued to maintain a high growth rate of more than 7.5%. There was steady growth of agriculture and in the added value of the tertiary industry as a percentage of the GDP over the secondary industry; the annual growth rate of the added value of township

[13] Chemical oxygen demand: A chemical method is used to measure the amount of reductive substances that need to be oxidized in water samples.

[14] Health literacy level: The ability of individuals to acquire and understand health information and use it to maintain and promote their own health.

[15] Characteristic town construction: On the basis of the county's economy, using its own information economy, massive economy, landscape resources, historical and unique cultural advantages, high-end manufacturing, information technology, innovation, and entrepreneurship as the main features of the innovative economic model.

[16] Proportion of poor population with file legislation card: In accordance with the requirements of precision poverty alleviation, the number of the poor approved by the anti-poverty development and construction file system card information system was used.

[17] Compulsory education: This is also known as free education, and is based on China's constitution, and stipulates that both school-age children and adolescents must accept national education, which must be guaranteed by the state, society, and the family.

[18] Number of general practitioners per 10,000 population: This gives the number of doctors for every 10,000 citizens, covering all medical departments.

Table 8.4. Green growth in some indicators of the situations completed during the 12th FYP period.

Indicators	2010	2015	Growth rate (%)
Research and Experimental Development Expenditure (US$100 million)	1,134.06	2,275.17	100.62
Number of scientific and technological achievements registration (items)	42,108	55,284	31.29
High-tech industry in new product development expenditure (calibre and medium-sized industrial enterprises) (US$100 million)	161.68	413.39	155.69
Primary industry added value (%)	9.50	8.80	−7.37
Secondary industry added value (%)	46.40	40.90	−11.85
Tertiary industry added value (%)	44.10	50.20	13.83

Source: China Statistical Yearbook, 2011–2016

and village enterprises was 10%, and the average annual growth rate of land reclamation was 9%; the consumption rate of residents was continuously increasing; the urban-rural regional disparity tended to be narrow; the resident urbanization rate was 56.1%; and the level of infrastructure had risen overall. High-tech industries and the strategic emerging industries[19] accelerated the country's development. In addition, as compared with the end of 2010, some important indicators were showing a good trend (see Table 8.4).

Although the current green economy in China has made great achievements, it still faces many difficulties. For example, the top-level design of green development is effective, but the policy and legal system to promote green development is incomplete and imperfect. And the sustainability of policy implementation needs to be improved; the development of green financial innovation has been relatively slow. The authoritative norms and standards, and the relevant market supporting systems for green financial development, are not perfect and sometimes even lacking; they have not yet become a strong driving force for green development. Green technology innovation needs long-term accumulation, and it is difficult to produce qualitative change in a short time. Therefore, the Chinese government is building a green, low-carbon, and cyclically developing economic system in all aspects, vigorously developing a green financial industry, and promoting a market-oriented green technology innovation system for solving these difficulties.

8.4.2.2 Resource conservation and utilization

The efficiency of resource utilization in China improved in the period 2011–2015. As of 2015, the national energy consumption per 10,000 RMB of GDP dropped to 0.869 tons of standard coal

(calculated at 2005 prices), down 16%, from 1.034 tons of standard coal in 2010, and 32% below the 1.276 tons of standard coal in 2005; the energy conserved was 670 million tons of standard coal; the industrial boiler and furnace average operating efficiency increased by 5 and 2 percentage points, respectively; the motor system operating efficiency increased by 2 to 3 percentage points; the new waste heat pressure generating capacity was 20 million kilowatts; the existing residential building heating area for energy-saving transformation was 400 million m^2; the hot summer and cold winter area for energy-saving renovations in existing residential buildings was 50 million m^2; the public buildings energy-saving was 60 million m^2; a unit of industrial added value water consumption decreased 30%; the utilization of chemical fertilizers and pesticides significantly improved; the comprehensive utilization of crop straw was more than 80%; the popularization rate of biogas suitable for farmers reached more than 50%; the degradation of grasslands was effectively checked; the conservation of aquatic biological resources significantly increased; and aquatic species reached 150 billion. In addition, some important indicators were also better than the 2010 end figures (see Table 8.5).

However, China is in a period of new economic normality, facing a series of great difficulties in the transformation and upgrading of overcapacity, high energy consumption, and high pollution. The economic downturn and the pain of transition are inevitable. Therefore, we must strengthen industries that involve energy-saving, environmental protection, clean production, and clean energy; promote the revolution in energy production and consumption; build a clean, low-carbon, safe, and efficient energy system; implement national water-saving actions and reduce energy and material consumption, to achieve a cycle of production and living systems.

8.4.2.3 Ecological environment protection

During 2011–2015, green development showed great progress in the field of ecological environment protection. China's carbon intensity decreased by 21.8%, which was equivalent to a

---

[19] Strategic emerging industries are based on major technological breakthroughs and major development needs. They are major industries, which have a leading role in promoting overall and long-term economic and social development, intensive knowledge-based technologies, low consumption of material resources, great potential for growth, and comprehensive benefits.

Table 8.5. Some indicators of intensive use of resources completed during the 12th FYP period.

Indicators	2010	2015	Growth rate (%)
Water-saving irrigation area (thousand hm²)	27,313.90	31,060.40	13.72
The amount of cultivated land (million hm²)	121.20	121.20	0.00
Reuse of water resources (%)	77.39	80.00	3.30
US$10,000 coal consumption of GDP (t)	5.23	4.11	−21.43
US$10,000 oil consumption of GDP (t)	0.69	0.56	−18.18
Energy processing conversion efficiency (%)	72.52	73.72	1.65

Source: China Energy Statistical Yearbook, 2011–2016

Table 8.6. The ecological and environmental protection indicators completed during the 12th FYP period.

Indicators	2010	2015	Growth rate (%)
Sea area of seawater that does not meet the first type of seawater quality standards in the whole sea (km²)	177,720	154,610	−13.00
Sulphur dioxide emissions (10,000 t)	2,185.10	1,859.10	−14.92
Nature reserve areas (units)	2,588	2,740	5.87
New area for soil and water loss control this year (thousand hm²)	4,014.70	5,384.60	34.12
Wetland area (thousand hm²)	38,485.50	53,602.60	39.28
Sandy area (million hm²)	17,310.77	17,310.77	0.00
Total area of afforestation (10,000 hm²)	591.00	768.40	30.02
Natural forest protection forest management area (hm²)	104,857,371	114,267,121	8.97
Internationally important wetlands (units)	37	49	32.43
Sudden major environmental incidents (units)	420	334	-20.48
Total investment in environmental management (US$100 million)	1,222.25	1,414	15.69
Garbage disposal investment (US$100 million)	20.46	30.29	48.06
Ratio of the number of days with good air quality at prefecture-level and above cities (%)	–	76.70	–
Utilization rate of contaminated farmland (%)	–	70.60	–
Grassland vegetation coverage (%)	–	54	

Source: China Environmental Statistical Yearbook, 2011–2016

reduction in the emission of carbon dioxide by 2.34 billion t. The national chemical oxygen demand was controlled at 23.476 million t, down by 10% from the 2010 figures. The total ammonia nitrogen and nitrogen oxides emissions were controlled at 2.38 million t and 20.462 million t, respectively, down by 10% from the 2010 figures. The urban sewage treatment rate reached 85%. The rate of sewage treatment was 45.69 million m³ per day. The newly built sludge treatment and disposal scale was 5.18 million t (dry sludge) per year. The scale of newly built wastewater recycling facilities was 26.75 million m³ per day by building 100 demonstration bases for the comprehensive utilization of resources, 80 demonstration cities for recycling of waste products, 50 demonstration bases for 'city minerals', five remanufacturing industry clusters, and by utilizing kitchen waste in 100 cities, decontaminating treatment demonstration projects, and accelerating the improvement of vehicle fuel quality. The afforestation area in the country increased by 20%, to 30 million km², and forest tending area reached 39.68 million km². In addition, in comparison with the end of 2010, some important indicators had greatly improved (see Table 8.6).

Ecological protection is a duty that demands long-term adherence, and it is also a task that needs universal support. However, on the one hand, China's current system is still being perfected, and events that harm the ecological environment still occur from time to time. At the same time, it takes a long time for the ecological environment to self-repair, so China is still facing a severe environmental situation. What is more, the awareness of environmental protection and green awareness among Chinese citizens need to be further improved. It is difficult to change the lifestyle and consumption habits within a

Table 8.7. The 12th FYP period, harmonious society part of the indicators to complete the situation.

Indicators	2010	2015	Growth rate (%)
Number of beds per 10,000 medical institutions	35.80	51.12	42.30
Education funding (US$10,000)	31,409,308	58,010,521	84.69
Participate in the number of pensions (10 thousand)	25,707.30	35,361.20	37.55
Per capita parkland area (m²)	11.20	13.40	19.64
Sanitary toilet penetration rate (%)	67.40	78.40	16.32
Solar cooker (units)	1,617,233	2,325,927	43.82
Biogas production in rural areas (100 million m³)	139.60	153.90	10.24
Absolute poverty population (100 million)	0.6561	0.563	−11.50

Sources: China Environmental Statistical Yearbook, 2011–2016; China Statistical Yearbook, 2011–2016

short time. Therefore, the Chinese government has persisted in the pilot-amendment-enhanced policy formulation and implementation models to try to ensure the timeliness of the policy system. At the same time, it advocates a simple and moderate, green and low-carbon lifestyle; opposes extravagance and irrational consumption; and creates actions such as creating energy-saving organs, green families, green schools, green communities, and green travel, and so on to bring about a green and environmentally friendly social atmosphere.

8.4.2.4 The efforts to build a harmonious society

During the 2011–2015 period, China made major advances in various fields towards building a harmonious society. As of 2015, in terms of education, the country's compulsory education nationwide reached 93%, with the counties (cities and districts) achieving a basic balance of 65%. In healthcare, China has 3,883 sentinel hospitals for food-borne disease surveillance networks, which cover food contamination, with 2,656 monitoring points for food and harmful substances and 100 quality and safety risk assessment laboratories for agricultural products. The State Health and Family Planning Commission cleared 5,000 food standards, integrated 400 items, and issued 926 new national standards for food safety, with a total target of 14,000. In terms of residents' health, the Chinese life expectancy per capita reached 76.34 years, indicating an increase of 1.51 years as compared with 2010; the infant mortality rate dropped from 13.1‰ to 8.1‰; the mortality rate for children under five years dropped from 16.4‰ to 10.7‰; and the maternal mortality rate dropped from 30/100,000 to 20.1/100,000. The residents' main health indicators are generally better than the average of middle- and high-income countries. As regards reducing poverty and increasing incomes, the number of the poor fell to 56.3 million, and the added value of agriculture, forestry, animal husbandry, and fisheries increased by an average of 5%, and a total of 40 million agricultural labour workers transferred; the

average per capita net income of rural residents increased by more than 7%. In addition, some important indicators showed major improvements as compared with the end of 2010, as shown in Table 8.7.

As we all know, China is the country with the highest population in the world. At present, it is true that poverty is the biggest stumbling block on the road to building a well-off society. China has not yet achieved the goal of all people out of poverty in 2017. Even some of the people who rose out of poverty are likely to return to poverty again because of internal and external reasons. Therefore, China proposes a one-on-one assistance plan for every village. In this plan, civil servants selected from grassroots administrative organizations (usually at the township level) assist the villagers to reduce and eradicate poverty based on their actual situation and characteristics.

8.5 OUTLOOK

Although China has accomplished certain achievements in green development, it is still low, incomplete, and inadequate. China is the largest developing as well as the most populous country in the world, yet its basic national conditions have not changed. What is gratifying is that after almost 40 years of reform and opening up, China's GDP in 2017 exceeded US$12.7 trillion,[20] and the country shows confidence and capability of continuously and extensively implementing its green development strategy in all the dimensions of the economy, resources, environment, and society. According to the 13th FYP of the Chinese government (Xinhua News Agency, 2016) and the regulations and guidance on green development, the four

---

[20] The data are from the Statistical Communiqué of the People's Republic of China on National Economic and Social Development 2017, which was obtained through the conversion of the Sino-US exchange rate on the last day of 2017.

major goals of China's green development for the next five years will be as follows:

(1) In terms of promoting the green economy, aiming for reducing the high energy-consuming industries to achieve full coverage of energy consumption standards by 2020, more than 80% of the energy efficiency indicators will have already reached the international advanced level,[21] and the contribution rate of agricultural science and technology will rise from 56% to 60%, with the added value of the strategic emerging industries and service industries in GDP increased to 15% and 56%, respectively. The output value of the green and low-carbon industries, such as energy saving and environmental protection, new energy equipment, and new energy vehicles, exceeded US\$1.6 trillion, to become a pillar industry.

(2) In terms of effective utilization of resources, the amount of arable land was maintained at 124.33 million km^2; the grassland comprehensive vegetation coverage increased from 54% to 56%; the effective utilization coefficient of farmland irrigation water increased from 0.532 to 0.55; the utilization of major crops increased from 36.6% to 40%; the utilization rate of the main crops' chemical fertilizers increased from 35.2% to 40%; the plastic film recovery rate increased from 60% to 80%; the utilization rate of farming waste increased from 60% to 75%; and the energy consumption of the petrochemical industry, carbon dioxide emissions, and water consumption decreased by 8%, 10%, and 14%, respectively, over the period of the 12th FYP. The sewage in the built-up areas of the prefecture-level cities and above was basically fully collected and treated, and the sewage treatment rates in cities and counties reached 95% and about 85%, respectively; the food waste resource utilization rate reached 30%; and the non-fossil energy installed capacity reached 39%. The proportion of coal use for energy consumption fell below 58%.

(3) In terms of ecological environment protection, the area of wetlands nationwide will not be less than 53.33 million hm^2 by 2020, of which natural wetlands will account for not less than 46.67 million km^2 and the newly added wetlands will cover 0.2 million km^2; thus, the wetland protection rate should be raised to above 50%. The trend of increasing groundwater pollution has been contained, and the proportion of groundwater with poor quality[22] is maintained at about 15%. The natural

coastline of China (excluding the coastline of the island) has a preservation rate[23] of not less than 35%, with 1,000 km of rehabilitated coastline; in 10,000 hm^2 of forest area, the per unit area reached 95 m^3/hm^2, the forest vegetation carbon storage reached 9.5 billion t, and the construction of reserve forest was 14 million km^2; the urban per capita park green area reached 14.6 m^2, with the urban built-up area of 38.9% of green space.

(4) In terms of harmonious society construction, by 2020, the peasants' income will double from the 2010 level; the share of public transportation in major cities will reach 30%; the average fuel consumption of new passenger cars will drop to 5.0 L/100 km; and the national compulsory education consolidation rate will go up to 95%. The Standardized Production Demonstration Garden[24] (field) has been registered through the certification of 'three products and one product' (pollution-free agricultural products, green food, organic agricultural products, and agricultural products geographical indications) with an area of 3 million km^2 of organic agricultural products planting base and a green food planting base covering 12 million km^2. The basic medical and health system for both urban and rural residents has been established so that all people enjoy basic medical and health services and the population suffering absolute poverty is eliminated.

China's green development is complex, arduous, and dynamic. In the future, China's green development will shift from light green to deep green[25] and will transform itself into an independent innovative force by drawing from and assimilating and absorbing foreign advanced theories, technologies, and methodologies and actively promoting its own achievements in green development to radiate and bring along the neighbouring countries and gradually affect and benefit the world. China's green development will pay more attention to humanistic concerns, adhere to the fruits of development benefitting the broad masses of people, adhere to fairness and justice, and truly realize the harmonious coexistence of man and nature, to meet people's demand for all-round development. And China's future green development will firmly seize the opportunities of the Internet and big data, and expand and develop the potential of green development in time and space from the full range of all angles.[26]

---

[21] According to the *China Energy Statistics Yearbook*, taking alternating current power consumption for electrolytic aluminium as an example, China consumed 13,562kw·h/t in 2015, and the international advanced level was 12,900kw·h/t.

[22] According to *Groundwater Quality Standards of the People's Republic of China*, groundwater can be divided into five types. Among them, the fifth type of water is not suitable for drinking by humans or animals, based on human health, and it is also called water with extremely poor quality.

[23] 'Preservation rate' refers to the ratio of holding quantity to actual quantity.

[24] 'Standardized production demonstration parks' refers to production bases that use special rules as their criteria for production and provide demonstrations and driving roles.

[25] The phrase 'from light green to deep green' is used in this chapter to describe the process of green development from the primary development stage of a single field to the advanced development stage of various fields of the national economy.

[26] The phrase 'the full range of all angles' refers specifically to the various fields and stages of national economic development.

ACKNOWLEDGEMENTS

This work was supported by ADB-TA 8872-PRC, implemented by the Central Project Management Office of PRC-GEF Partnership on Land Degradation in Dryland Ecosystems (2nd Phase). We are particularly grateful to Professor Pak Sum Low for inviting and encouraging us to submit this chapter. We also wish to thank Dr Rosita Dellios, Dr Ian Hannam, Dr Mick Kelly, and Dr Wu Liang for their very constructive and useful reviews, which have greatly improved this chapter.

REFERENCES

Cai, N., Cong, Y. J. and Wu, J. W. (2014) Green development and new urbanization of China: a dual-dimensional analysis based on SBM-DDF model. *Journal of Beijing Normal University (Social Sciences)*, **5**, 130–139.

Carson, R. (1962) *Silent Spring*. Reviewed by G. S. Wu in *Science Press* edition (2007).

Chen, D. J. (2011) Green development: an inevitable choice for the transformation and upgrading of China's '12th Five-Year Plan'. *Inquiry into Economic Issues*, **8**, 153–158.

China's Environmental Protection Bureau (1988) *China Environmental Protection Affairs (1981–1985)*. China Environmental Science Press.

Development and Reform Commission (2016) Green Development Indicators System [EB / OL]. (2016–12–22) [2017–12–18]. http://www.gov.cn/xinwen/2016–12/22/content_5151575.htm

Department of Industrial Traffic Statistics, National Bureau of Statistics (2011) *China Energy Statistical Yearbook 2011*. Beijing, China Statistics Press.

(2012) *China Energy Statistical Yearbook 2012*. Beijing, China Statistics Press.

(2013) *China Energy Statistical Yearbook 2013*. Beijing, China Statistics Press.

(2014) *China Energy Statistical Yearbook 2014*. Beijing, China Statistics Press.

(2015) *China Energy Statistical Yearbook 2015*. Beijing, China Statistics Press.

(2016) *China Energy Statistical Yearbook 2016*. Beijing, China Statistics Press.

Environmental Protection and Integrated Management Committee (2000) *Agenda 21*. Beijing, Scientific and Technical Documentation Press.

Feng, L. J. and Guan, J. (2017) Historical investigation on the green development of the Communist Party of China. *Social Sciences in Yunnan*, **4**, 9–14, 185.

Guan, Y. F. (2017) China rural land transfer trust to promote agricultural green development. *Agricultural Economy*, **2**, 18–20.

Guo, B. (2013) Green economy: the realistic path of Chinese economy's switching from quantity to quality. *Journal of Hunan Finance and Economics University*, **29**, 5–12.

Hao, D. and Zhao, J. J. (2011) China green development road exploration. *Green Economy and Sustainable Development of Coastal Cities Proceedings of the Strategy Symposium*, **4**, 25–28.

He, J. and Wang, X. A. (2016) Analysis on the spatial-temporal characteristics of green development of Chinese industry. *Science and Technology Management Research*, **36**, 240–246.

Hu, A. G. (2005) China: Green development and green GDP (1970–2001). *Chinese Bulletin of National Natural Science Foundation of China*, **2**, 22–27.

Hu, A. G. (2012) *China: Innovation and Green Development*. Beijing, China Renmin University Press, 1–75.

Hu, A. G. and Men, H. H. (2005) green development and green rising: Discussion on China's development road. *Journal of the Party School of Tianjin Committee of the CPC*, **1**, 19–30.

Hu, A. G. and Zhou, S. J. (2014) Green development: Function definition, mechanism analysis and development strategy. *China Population, Resources and Environment*, **24**, 14–20.

Huang, J. (2017) Relationship between technological innovation and green development: road to green technology innovation with Chinese characteristics. *Journal of Xinjiang Normal University (Edition of Philosophy and Social Sciences)*, **38**, 33–41.

Huang, R. J. (2014) *Regional Green Development Efficiency and Green Total Factor Productivity in China: 2000–2010*. Jinan, Jinan University.

Huang, Y. and Li, L. (2017) A comprehensive assessment of green development and its spatial-temporal evolution in urban agglomerations of China. *Geographical Research*, **36**, 1, 309–1,322.

Li, C. F. (2017) *Research on Evaluation Index System of Ecological Civilization Construction in China*. Shenyang, Shenyang Normal University.

Li, X. X. and Pan, J. C. (2012) China green development index report summary. *Review of Economic Research*, **13**, 4–24.

Li, Z. J. (2016) Study on the approach and system guarantee of China's green development during the 13th five-year period. *Resource Recycling*, **9**, 24–27.

Liu, Y. H. (2010) Strategic thinking on some issues of green economy and green development [J]. *China Awards for Science and Technology*, **12**, 49–50.

Ma, H. and Wang, M. K. (1999) *China Development Report*. Beijing, China Development Press.

Meadows, D. L. (1997) *The Limits to Growth: A Report for the Club of Rome's Project on the Predicament of Mankind*. Chinese translation by B. H. Li. Changchun, Jilin People's Publishing Press.

Ministry of Environmental Protection of People's Republic of China (2016) Annual Assessment Results Communique of Ecological Civilization Building in 2016 [EB / OL]. (2016–10-11) [2018–1-18]. http://www.stats.gov.cn/tjsj/sjjd/201712/t20171226_1567038.html

National Bureau of Statistics of China (2011) *China Statistical Yearbook 2011*. Beijing, China Statistics Press.

(2012) *China Statistical Yearbook 2012*. Beijing, China Statistics Press.

(2013) *China Statistical Yearbook 2013*. Beijing, China Statistics Press.

(2014) *China Statistical Yearbook 2014*. Beijing, China Statistics Press.

(2015) *China Statistical Yearbook 2015*. Beijing, China Statistics Press.

(2016) *China Statistical Yearbook 2016*. Beijing, China Statistics Press.

National Bureau of Statistics and Ministry of Environmental Protection of China (2011) *China Environmental Statistical Yearbook 2011*. Beijing, China Statistics Press.

(2012) *China Environmental Statistical Yearbook 2012*. Beijing, China Statistics Press.

(2013) *China Environmental Statistical Yearbook 2013*. Beijing, China Statistics Press.

(2014) *China Environmental Statistical Yearbook 2014*. Beijing, China Statistics Press.

(2015) *China Environmental Statistical Yearbook 2015*. Beijing, China Statistics Press.

(2016) *China Environmental Statistical Yearbook 2016*. Beijing, China Statistics Press.

Peng, Z. J. and Tian, S. Y. (2016) Development 'Made in China 2025' and VAT reform. *Journal of Fujian Normal University (Philosophy and Social Sciences)*, **5**, 1–8, 168.

Qin, S. S. and Hu, N. (2017) Theoretical connotation and practice approach of China's green development concept. *Journal of Northeast University (Social Science)*, **19**(6), 631–636.

Shi, X. Y. (2017) Marx's ecological ethics and China's green development. *People's Tribune*, **23**, 98–99.

Song, R. H. (2016) *Research on the Concept of Green Development of the Communist Party of China*. Changchun, Changchun University of Science and Technology.

United Nations Conference on Environment and Development (1992) Rio Declaration on Environment and Development. *Environmental Protection*, **8**, 2–3.

Wang, A. X. (2016) *A Study of the Green Development Index and Its Influencing Factors of Regional Industry*. Chongqing, Chongqing Technology and Business University.

Wang, F. and Yu, S. Q. (2017) Green development: China's development of organic Marxist transcendence. *Journal of the Party School of Tianjin Committee of the CPC*, **19**, 32–37.

Wang, H. M. (2005) Green development: the only way to China's development. *Theory Horizon*, S1, 14–15.

Wang, Q. L. (2017) The impact of fiscal and tax policies on China's regional green development: empirical test based on spatial econometrics model. *China Soft Science*, **9**, 82–90.

Wang, Y. Q. (2014) The path selection of urban green development in China. *Journal of Hebei University of Economics and Business*, **35**, 51–53.

Wang, Z. D. (1955) *The Relationship between Geographical Environment, Population and Social Development*. Shanghai, New Knowledge Press.

Ward, B., Dubos, R. J. and Strong, M. F. (1974) *Only One Earth*. Beijing, Fuel Chemistry Press.

World Commission on Environment and Development (1997) *Our Common Future*. Chinese translation by Z. J. Wang. Changchun, Jilin People's Publishing Press.

Wu, Y. Y. (2015) *Research on Green Development under the Vision of 'Beautiful China'*. Southwest Petroleum University.

Xinhua News Agency (2011) Outline of the Twelfth National Economic and Social Development Plan [EB / OL]. (2011–03-16) [2017–12-18]. http://www.gov.cn/2011lh/content_1825838.htm

Xinhua News Agency (2016) Thirteenth Five-Year Plan for National Economic and Social Development [EB / OL]. (2016–03-17) [2017–12-18]. http://www.xinhuanet.com/politics/2016lh/2016–03/17/c_1118366322

Yan, Z. T. (2016) System construction to promote the green development of China's economy. *East China Economic Management*, **30**, 47–52.

Yang, J. J. (2016a) On the legal layout of China's green development. *Law Review*, **34**, 160–167.

Yang, J. J. (2016b) The transformation of contemporary China's development path and its propulsion: The legalization of the concept of green development. *Nanjing Journal of Social Sciences*, **10**, 88–95.

Yang, Z. J. and Wen, C. X. (2017) Evaluation on China's green development efficiency and regional disparity. *Economic Geography*, **37**, 10–18.

You, H. M., Fang, H., Zhai, Z. Y. and Fang, S. R. (2017) Study on green development efficiency of Chinese photovoltaic enterprises based on DEA and Tobit regression model. *Mathematics in Practice and Theory*, **47**, 63–71.

Yue, S. J., Zou, Y. L. and Hu, Y. Y. (2015) The impact of industrial agglomeration on the efficiency of urban green development in China. *Urban Problems*, **10**, 49–54.

Zhang, C. X., Wang, H. F., Zhang, S. R. and Duan, R.Y. (2015) Strategic study on green development of Chinese steel industry. *Iron and Steel*, **50**, 1–7.

Zhang, Y. J. (2013) Green development: the path choice of China's third generation modernization. *Journal of Luoyang Normal University*, **32**, 11–13.

Zhang, Y. Z. (2015) Qualification and efficiency innovation drive green development: an analysis of some important issues concerning China's mid- and long-term energy and power development. *State Grid*, **12**, 44–47.

Zhang, Z. Z. (2014) On the ethical implications of contemporary China's green development concept. *Study in Ethics*, **4**, 123–127.

Zhao, J. J. and Yang, T. F. (2011) The necessity and route to promote China's green development. *Urban*, **11**, 24–27.

Zhao, Z. (2013) Research on urban public expenditure efficiency based green development in China: An empirical analysis based on the four-stage DEA model and bootstrap-DEA model. *Journal of Yunnan University of Finance and Economics*, **29**, 31–40.

9 Bhutan's sustainable development initiatives and Gross National Happiness

JAMBA GYELTSHEN*

Edith Cowan University, Australia

Keywords

Bhutan; democratic constitutional monarchy; eastern Himalayas; landlocked; Gross National Happiness (GNH); good governance; hydropower; semi-subsistence farming; mountain ecosystem; Triple Gem; nature conservation; food security; self-reliance; sustainable development; middle path; rural-urban migration; glacial lake; extended family; biological corridor; five-year plan; unique identity; deities; pristine

Abstract

Bhutan has a short history of modernization, having embarked on planned development six decades ago. For centuries, it remained secluded from the outside world, partly because of its landlocked position, but mainly due to lack of modern transport and communication infrastructure. From such lowly beginnings, Bhutan has made a quantum leap into the 21st century. What triggered this rapid development, and how the country managed to follow a distinctive path of development, is what this chapter is about. The country's visionary kings initiated Bhutan's fast-paced development. In particular, the development journey was inspired by the philosophy of Gross National Happiness (GNH) enunciated by the Fourth King Jigme Singye Wangchuck, who believed in promoting happiness and well-being of the people as the main goal of development. The GNH-based development philosophy has shaped the country's development vision, strategies, goals, plans, and programmes. Unlike the GDP-based model of development, which measures progress in terms of material prosperity, the GNH model includes the dimensions of happiness and well-being. This chapter dwells on how the vision of GNH is pursued through different initiatives under the four areas of development: sustainable and equitable socio-economic development, environmental conservation, preservation and promotion of culture, and good governance. The chapter presents major challenges and enumerates relevant strategies to overcome those challenges in ways that are environmentally friendly, culturally acceptable, and financially sustainable.

9.1 INTRODUCTION

Bhutan is a small, landlocked country situated in the eastern Himalayas, sharing borders with China to the north and India to the south. It has an area of 38,394 sq km and an estimated population of 748,931 people (NSB, 2020). Bhutan has a distinctive culture and tradition with diverse ethno-linguistic groups speaking 19 languages (van Driem, 2004). Buddhism is the state religion but there is also a sizeable population who follow Hinduism. Bhutan embarked on a path of modernization only after 1960, ending a period of self-imposed isolation. Historically, Bhutan has maintained a neutral, sovereign, and independent status, having never been under any colonial rule.

Bhutan is an agrarian country and agriculture continues to be the predominant occupation, employing 58% of the population (MoLHR, 2015). With improved road and telecommunications networks, farmers today have better access to agriculture inputs and markets for their produce. There is a gradual shift from the traditional subsistence farming to a market-oriented, semi-subsistence farming.

Bhutan's socio-economic development is inspired and guided by the people-centred development philosophy of Gross National Happiness (GNH). The Gross Domestic Product (GDP) real growth rate over the period 2015–2017 averaged around 6.4% per annum (NSB, 2018) and poverty reduced from 12% in 2012 to 8.2% in 2017 (NSB, 2017b). In health and education, there was an appreciable reduction in mortality rates and a drastic increase in school enrolment. Life expectancy increased to 69 years, while general literacy reached 66% (NSB, 2017c).

Although economic growth has been impressive when compared to its lowly beginnings, the country faces challenges of increasing population, growing unemployment, rural-urban

---

*Formerly a faculty member of the College of Natural Resources, Royal University of Bhutan.

migration, and limited space for urbanization. Furthermore, Bhutan must contend with climate change impacts, including unpredictable weather patterns and rainfall, retreating glaciers, and glacial-lake outbursts.

The main objective of this chapter is to present Bhutan's sustainable development initiatives in pursuit of GNH. In trying to differentiate between the GNH model and the GDP model of development, this chapter largely reflects upon the GNH model of development, described by Ura *et al.* (2012) as being 'holistic, balanced, collective, sustainable, and equitable', and explains the process of how that GNH philosophy is translated into a development vision, strategies, and goals for implementation.

As a background, a brief review of Bhutan's history of planned development highlighting some salient features that characterize Bhutan's unique approach to sustainable development is presented. Subsequent sections deal with the four major identified areas of development (the four pillars of GNH). Each of these areas contains a brief mention of the implementation strategy and the status of achievement. The last section deals with the challenges facing the sustainable development initiative and outlines strategies to address those issues.

This chapter is based on insights and perspectives gained from various readings of documents cited at the end of the chapter. For further details, readers are encouraged to access the given links (URLs).

9.2 BHUTAN'S DEVELOPMENT HISTORY

Bhutan's baseline development status in 1960 was far from impressive, as it remained one of the world's most secluded countries, steeped in widespread illiteracy, infant mortality, food insecurity, and natural disasters (Ura and Kinga, 2004). However, thanks to the farsighted and dynamic leadership of the Wangchuck dynasty and collective sacrifices of the people, the country has made great strides in recent years, achieving human development progress comparable to the rest of South Asia (Ura and Kinga, 2004).

Bhutan's planned development began six decades ago with the launching of the first Five-Year Plan (FYP) in 1961. The focus of development during the first three FYPs (1961–1976) was on building basic infrastructure – mainly the road network – to pave the way for future development and establishing service facilities on health and education. Besides continuing to develop these basic service facilities, the subsequent plan periods, that is, the third (1971–1976), fourth (1976–1981), and fifth (1981–1986), focused on the development of hydropower, which supported the growth of service sectors and industries. The power plant was commissioned in 1986 (Units I & II) and 1988 (Units III & IV) (DGPC, 2017). However, all along, the nation advocated a development strategy that sought to strike the right balance between socio-economic development and environmental protection. The country's laws strictly regulated the use and exploitation of forests and allied natural resources.

For most people, contact with the outside world before 1960 was virtually non-existent as there was no modern transport or communications infrastructure; there was neither electricity nor postal services. Today, road networks connect almost every remote *gewog* centre (local administrative blocks). More than 92% of the households across the country have access to electricity; primary education enrolment stands at 94.7%, literacy rate at 66%, and life expectancy at 69 years (NSB, 2017c). According to the Bhutan Living Standard Survey Report 2017, more than 70% of the households across the country are connected to television (NSB, 2017c); and going by the number of subscribers, more than 97% of households have access to mobile phones, and 24% of households in urban areas have internet connections (NSB and ADB, 2013; NSB, 2017c). The Human Development Index (HDI) improved from 0.525 in 2010 to 0.584 in 2013, putting Bhutan in the Middle Human Development category of the UNDP (Bertelsmann Stiftung, 2016).

A dramatic change of this magnitude happening within a person's lifetime is testimonial to Bhutan's fast-paced development. Ura and Kinga (2004) suggest several reasons for this: good governance and dynamic leadership, political stability, a rich renewable natural resource base, lack of extreme poverty, long-term support from development partners, public service reforms, and a well-functioning administrative infrastructure. More recently, the concept of GNH, stressing the primacy of economic growth, cultural preservation, environmental conservation, and good governance, came to be the unifying force behind all policy formulation and has shaped the country's five-year planning cycles.

Out of the many factors contributing to Bhutan's development, leadership and development partners' goodwill support were instrumental. Good international relations have always played a crucial role in Bhutan's development efforts. Bhutan joined various regional and international organizations and established diplomatic relations with various states of the world. It joined the Colombo Plan in 1962, became a member of the Universal Postal Union in 1969, and became a member of the United Nations in 1971. Bhutan joined the United Nations Economic and Social Commission for Asia and the Pacific (ESCAP) in 1972, and the Non-Aligned Movement (NAM) in 1973, and has been a member of the South Asian Association for Regional Cooperation (SAARC) since its inception in 1985. The financial and technical assistance from the United Nations system and other friendly countries was supplemented by financial assistance from the World Bank and the Asian Development Bank. Bhutan has diplomatic relations with 54 countries and the

European Union (MoFA, 2021). As global partnership is indispensable for achieving sustainable development, this has been a move in the right direction.

Within a short span of time, the country has been able to pursue its policy of social and economic transformation and raise the standard of living and quality of life of its people. Bhutan has been able to achieve what for many others took much longer. As of 2020, Bhutan is in its third year of the 12th FYP (2018–2023).

9.3 GROSS NATIONAL HAPPINESS DEVELOPMENT PARADIGM

Bhutan's sustainable development initiatives for GNH fully draw upon the concept of GNH. This section dwells on the conceptual framework of GNH and provides a logical frame of reference for deriving the country's vision, strategies, and goals for development. It also provides accounts of how the GNH index was developed to measure the progress of development and how it provides more than what the conventional GDP-based model offers.

9.3.1 The concept of GNH

Gross National Happiness as a development paradigm was first espoused in the 1970s by His Majesty the Fourth King Jigme Singye Wangchuck, who believed that GNH is more important than gross national product (RGoB, 2005). Today, Bhutan's sustainable development initiatives continue to be guided by that philosophy, which is rooted in the belief that material wealth does not bring true and lasting happiness, just as a growing personal income does not always lead to a proportionate increase in happiness (Thinley, 1999). Unlike conventional GDP-based measures of economic development, GNH is based on a set of values that promote collective happiness. As most succinctly stated by His Majesty the Fifth King Jigme Khesar Namgyel Wangchuck, GNH is 'Development with Values' (Ura *et al.,* 2012a).

9.3.2 Vision and strategies derived from GNH

Bhutan's development vision is derived from the GNH-based development paradigm, which lays emphasis on development that is holistic, balanced, inclusive, equitable, and sustainable (Ura *et al.,* 2012b). The country's vision document, *Bhutan 2020: A Vision for Peace, Prosperity and Happiness* (NSB, 2017c), provides a 20-year development perspective for Bhutan, using the year 2000 as the base year. The document continues to provide inspiration and remains relevant to this day, as it was when it was first published in 1999 (GNHC, 2017). The document reflects on the six guiding principles to be considered when pursuing GNH-based development. The guiding principles include identity, unity and harmony, stability, self-reliance, sustainability, and flexibility (Planning Commission, 1999). Similarly, it identifies the main areas of development: human development, culture and heritage, balanced and equitable development, governance, and environmental conservation.

The vision document envisages Bhutan as a respected and active member of the international community, responsible for the promotion of peace and stability in the region, without overlooking the even more important necessity of maintaining independence, sovereignty, and security as a nation state to pursue development goals (Planning Commission, 1999). It also underlines the need to have a well-developed government and legal institutions that support a system of governance that promotes transparency, efficiency, and accountability. In order to generate domestic revenue to finance development programmes, development of sustainable hydropower is identified as one of the three avenues of economic development, the other two being agriculture and industrial development (NEC, 1998). The agriculture sector considered increases in exports of high-value and low-volume produce. Through provision of equitable access to and delivery of quality social services, such as standard healthcare and education, it envisages an enhanced quality of life and living standard for the people. In terms of the natural environment, Bhutan is committed to maintaining at least 60% forest cover for all time in future and conserve its rich biodiversity.

9.3.3 Components of GNH framework and GNH index

If the GNH-based development framework is to be operationalized, it needs to be translated into a form that is measurable so that development could be guided, progress monitored, and resources gainfully allocated. To this end, four key areas of development (also known as the four pillars of GNH) were divided into nine dimensions or domains of development with 33 different indicators to measure progress (Ura *et al.,* 2012b). The nine domains are psychological well-being, health, education, cultural diversity and resilience, time use, good governance, community vitality, living standard, and ecological diversity and resilience. According to Ura *et al.* (2012b), living standard, health, and education are traditional dimensions of public policy, while ecological diversity and good governance are areas that are becoming more common across many countries. What is distinctive and innovative about GNH indices is the prominence of psychological well-being, time use, community vitality, and cultural diversity (Ura *et al.,* 2012b).

9.3.4 Development planning process for GNH

Conventional wisdom on sustainable development recognizes the importance of simultaneous and balanced development in the four dimensions: social, economic, ecological, and political (SDSN, 2013). Development is believed to be socially unsustainable if it fails to promote harmony and justice, just as development is economically unsustainable if it fails to contribute to greater self-reliance and to sustainable improvements in standards of living and the quality of life (Planning Commission, 1999). Sustainability is an essential component of GNH-based development goals.

Bhutan's approach to sustainable development is best understood by examining the process of how the four pillars of GNH and the nine domains are operationalized through an instituted system whereby the development objectives are translated into strategies and programmes for implementation through the planned development programmes (GNHC, 2017).

Starting from the first FYP in 1961, Bhutan followed a five-year socio-economic development planning cycle. The FYPs articulate the socio-economic development priorities and programmes to be implemented over the plan period. The planning process has gone through progressive changes in the recent plan periods in a bid to be more inclusive and participatory. What is most conspicuous is the extensive consultations with all relevant stakeholders, including individuals, government agencies, local governments, private sector, civil society organizations, and political parties. In addition to the consultations, the Gross National Happiness Commission Secretariat reviews various documents and reports to take stock of the development progress and to identify critical issues and challenges. Some of the documents that are generally referred to include the royal addresses, vision document, mid-term review reports, strategy documents, international documents such as the 2030 Agenda for Sustainable Development, and survey reports (GNHC, 2017).

The GNHC prepares a detailed Guideline for Preparation of the Five-Year Plan. The guideline outlines the strategic planning framework including the objective, the National Key Result Areas (NKRAs) with associated Key Performance Indicators (KPI); preliminary fiscal projections and the resource allocation framework; division of responsibility framework between central and local governments; and a guide to formulation of central agency and local government key result areas and plans/programmes (GNHC, 2017).

9.4 SUSTAINABLE AND EQUITABLE SOCIO-ECONOMIC DEVELOPMENT

Bhutan's sustainable socio-economic development initiative generally focuses on maximizing people's happiness through improvement in the standard of living. The objective is pursued through reduction in population growth, improving access to education and health services, and pursuing economic development in areas with comparative advantages, such as hydropower, horticulture, cottage and small industries, and tourism. Strengthening the private sector and further developing infrastructure to improve transport, communications, and information technology are other important areas that contribute to the same goal.

Bhutan has made steady progress in many areas of socio-economic development. Through education and family planning, the population growth rate was reduced to 1.3% (GNHC, 2017). Life expectancy at birth rose from 55 years in 1993 to 69 in 2017 (NSB, 2017c). Youth literacy in 2017 was 97%, while general literacy reached 66% (NSB, 2017a). Poverty decreased from 12% in 2012 to 8.2% in 2017 (NSB, 2017b).

Welfare outcomes of its people have been improving as well. The GNH survey carried out in 2015 reported that overall, 91.2% of Bhutanese are identified as happy (GNHC, 2017). According to the country report of the International Monetary Fund (IMF, 2016), Bhutan has made significant economic progress in recent years, and the GDP per capita more than doubled during 2004–2014, rising from $1,108 (IMF, 2016) to $2,879 (NSB, 2017b). In the aftermath of the rupee shortage episode of 2012–2013, GDP growth slowed to below 4% in fiscal year (FY) 2012/13 and FY2013/14 but was estimated to have picked up to 5.2% in FY2014/15 and was projected to reach 6.49% in FY2015/16 (IMF, 2016; NSB, 2016).

9.4.1 Opportunities for future development

9.4.1.1 Generation of sustainable energy

As economic growth depends on a reliable supply of energy, the demand for energy will always increase as countries engage in developmental activities. In this regard, Bhutan could use hydropower to support its development programmes. Through run-of-the-river technologies, the fast-flowing rivers can be harnessed to produce enough power to export to countries in the region with energy deficits. The idea of commissioning the SAARC Grid to facilitate energy distribution in the South Asian region would be an opportunity for Bhutan (Choden and Penjore, 2004).

The rivers of Bhutan are either snow-fed or dependent on well-distributed rainfall on a well-conserved terrain. Out of the estimated potential hydropower generation capacity of 30,000 MW, of which 23,760 MW is technically feasible, about 1,500 MW has been tapped (Planning Commission, 1999; GNHC, 2017).

Although hydropower is a clean source of energy, initial investments to tap this natural resource can be extremely high. Moreover, the cost of protecting and conserving the watersheds is often not obvious. Hydropower generation can be sustained only through better management of watersheds. Deforestation and poor management of watersheds upstream would affect temporal and spatial distribution of the water resource, not only resulting in seasonal water shortages for drinking and irrigation, but also causing great fluctuations of flow for hydropower (MoA, 2002a). If natural vegetation is lost, there would be rampant soil erosion, landslides, flash floods, and increased sedimentation, causing the same problem of poor water flow and suboptimal generation of hydropower. Sustainable energy development, therefore, incurs huge investments in watershed management. The main strategy to manage watersheds in Bhutan to a large extent is accomplished through implementation of planned programmes and strict enforcement of Forest and Nature Conservation Rules.

9.4.1.2 Tourism

Bhutan is regarded as one of the most exclusive travel destinations in the world and enjoys a reputation for authenticity, remoteness, and a well-protected cultural heritage and natural environment (TCB, 2016). It is a vibrant industry with a high potential for growth and expansion. However, Bhutan has taken a more cautious approach in opening the floodgates of tourism, to avoid being overwhelmed by a huge influx of visitors. It has adhered to the policy of 'High Value, Low Impact' tourism and aspires to let it grow sustainably in a way that is environmentally and ecologically friendly, socially and culturally acceptable, and economically viable (TCB, 2016). As of 2016, 54,600 dollar-paying tourists visited the country (NSB, 2017a).

9.4.2 Strategies for enhancing food security

The income and living standard of many Bhutanese people, particularly in rural areas, are low, but abject poverty and hunger are non-existent (MoAF, 2012). This can be attributed to a culture of extended families, a strong sense of communal feeling, and the influence of Buddhist values of compassion for the poor and the downtrodden. This is not to say that there is no poverty. According to Bhutan's Poverty Analysis Report (PAR) of 2007, 23.2% of the population were below the national poverty line fixed at Nu. 1097 (~US$23) per person per month (NSB, 2007). There was a special thrust during the 10th FYP (2008–2013) and 11th FYP (2013–2018) to alleviate poverty, as a result of which, poverty went down to 12% in 2012 and then to 8% in 2017 (NSB and ADB, 2013; NSB, 2017a). Certain sections of the rural population who live on marginal and unproductive land are vulnerable and are likely to face seasonal food shortages. Occasional disruptions with the food supply line could happen even to the urban population, who are very dependent on imported food items. When the heavy monsoon wreaks havoc, causing landslides, roadblocks, and flash floods that destroy farmland, bridges, and dwellings, there can be temporary

upheavals. Such occasional disruptions only accentuate the importance of ensuring food security. With a considerable improvement in road networks within the country, such disruptions would be minimal in future and the food security situation in the country would improve. There have always been concerted efforts to achieve self-reliance in food production, the country's main aim and goal. It is the mandate of the Ministry of Agriculture and Forests to formulate policies and develop strategies to enhance food security.

Bhutan's diverse agro-ecological conditions provide clear regional and seasonal comparative advantages for food production, and Bhutan needs to take advantage of this opportunity. The agriculture sector's policies in the 10th FYP (2008–2013) were guided by the 'Triple Gem Concept', which placed emphasis on enhancing production, promoting accessibility to markets, and improving marketing. Production is to be primarily enhanced using good agricultural practices (GAP) and appropriate technology. Accessibility was to be promoted through the extensive development of farm roads in rural areas, thereby also ensuring better access to markets and other economic and social services. Marketing was to be improved and strengthened through various mechanisms, including development of linkages for domestic and external markets, boosting value addition, ensuring quality standards, and promoting exportable organic and high-value low-volume produce (GNHC, 2008). The agriculture development policy objectives in the 11th FYP (2013–2018) fundamentally remained the same as in the previous plan, with the focus on improving food and nutrition security, enhancing rural livelihood to overcome poverty, and sustainably managing and utilizing natural resources (MoAF, 2012).

9.5 ENVIRONMENTAL AND NATURE CONSERVATION

Environmental protection and nature conservation find a special place in Bhutan's development policies, as the country is cognizant of the potentially adverse impacts of increased population and economic activity on a fragile mountain environment. It has even more of a stake in sustainable development, as watershed protection is crucial for sustainable generation of hydropower, which fuels economic growth. The need to protect the environment is therefore a constitutional mandate requiring the maintenance of 60% forest cover for all time. Today, Bhutan has about 70.5% of its area under forest cover (NSB, 2017a). Incidentally, protection of the environment is a respected Buddhist value; many places are associated with local deities, divinities, and spirits and thus remain protected because of their spiritual interest. The commitment towards conservation is evident from the steps taken long before the global community woke up to the disturbing facts of global climate change and deteriorating environmental health. Bhutan's planned efforts in environmental conservation date back to 1952, when the Department of Forests was created to be the main custodian of Bhutan's pristine forests (MoA, 2006). The first national park was created in 1962, and today, the country has at least 26% of its forest designated as protected areas to preserve the country's astonishing biodiversity. As the protected areas are scattered across the country, another 9% is maintained as biological corridors, which are narrow stretches of natural areas, joining the otherwise discrete protected areas. The so-called biological corridors serve as free passageway for the wildlife to move from one protected area to the other.

The Wildlife Conservation Division (WCD) of the Ministry of Agriculture and Forests, which is the focal agency for management of the protected areas, has a well-defined vision and strategy for nature conservation. Much wildlife, including animal and bird species, is protected by law. Hunting and fishing on a government-reserved area are prohibited (DoF, 1995). A commitment to maintain at least 60% forest cover for all time is featured in the 1974 Forest Policy.

The Forest and Nature Conservation Rules of Bhutan 2006 govern the use of forest resources (MoA, 2006). The rules are based on the provisions of the Forest and Nature Conservation Act of Bhutan 1995, which is the revised version of the Forest Act of 1969. Commercial exploitation of forest resources is strictly regulated by law, while slash-and-burn (shifting) cultivation has been discouraged since the Forest Act of 1969 came into force (Upadhyay, 1995). Forest utilization is well regulated, perhaps highly so in some areas, but rural communities have access to subsidized timber for house construction and other household needs.

A government-approved comprehensive management plan is a prerequisite for any timber harvesting practice (MoA, 2006). It is mandatory for projects to have carried out an environmental impact assessment and obtain environmental clearances before embarking on a development project. Apart from the government-reserved forests, which are well protected and centrally controlled, there are social and community forestry programmes that solicit people's participation in management. All these are geared towards reducing pressure on government-reserved forests and improving the livelihood of people and local communities.

To conserve the country's rich biodiversity of more than 5,500 species of vascular plants, 770 species of avifauna, and more than 165 species of mammals, with many species endemic to Bhutan, the National Biodiversity Centre (NBC) was established in 1998 (MoA, 2002b). The centre's comprehensive 'Biodiversity Action Plan for Bhutan 2002' elaborates on the various strategies and future development plans. The conservation policy of Bhutan has received international acclaim: Bhutan was declared then as one of the world's ten biodiversity 'hotspots', and in 2005, His Majesty the Fourth King Jigme Singye Wangchuck and the people of Bhutan received the United Nations Environment Programme's Champion of the Earth Award for the Asia-Pacific region.

The National Environment Commission (NEC), the highest decision-making body on environment, was established as a regulatory authority to develop legislation, policies, and strategies on environment and environmental conservation. The National Environment Protection Act 2007 is the main legislation, from which all mandates, roles, and responsibilities are drawn. Since 1992, various policy documents and guidelines have been produced. The Environment Assessment Act 2000, with environmental assessment guidelines covering mining, roads, industries, hydropower, transmission lines, forestry sectors, tourism, and urban development, is a good example. Several Environmental Codes of Best Practices were developed to support the guidelines (NEC, 2004). These guidelines were intended to guide project proponents through the process of acquiring an environmental clearance, a legal requirement.

Environmental standards have been set for water, air, and noise. To maintain air quality, emission tests are conducted for motor vehicles. Burning wood for cooking and heating may decrease as the electricity grid spreads throughout the country. Rice cookers and water boilers, two of the most-used appliances in a Bhutanese kitchen, are on the rise. Similarly, use of electric heaters and cooking ovens is picking up, and in 2014 there was a move by the government to import electric cars for the same reason.

Bhutan is a carbon-neutral country and, as the forests sequester three times more carbon dioxide than what the entire country emits, it is in fact a carbon-negative country (MoAF, 2012).

To protect the river systems from pollution, sewerage systems are improved in urban centres and effluents treated; despite such measures, municipal waste management continues to be a big challenge, as urban centres are increasingly overcrowded.

9.6 PRESERVATION OF CULTURE

Culture is the most ambitious guiding principle for sustainable development, as it must contend with the continuous exposure to forces of global cultural diffusion. Ura and Kinga (2004) believe that 'the diffusion of transnational culture can set in motion forces of silent dissolution of local languages, knowledge, beliefs, customs, skills, trades and institutions, and even species of crops and plants' (p. 13).

While the older generation may possess a good understanding of Bhutan's cultural values and appreciate their role in development, the new generation may not have the same understanding and appreciation. This generation gap is likely to challenge our efforts in enhancing cultural distinctiveness. In some ways, it is a sail against the wind. Arguably, however, culture can be cultivated and revived using values and institutions as anchors against the sea of change (Ura and Kinga, 2004). Bhutan recognizes the need to promote awareness, appreciate, and preserve its rich cultural heritage, vital to Bhutan's unique identity. Culture contributes to the fulfilment of spiritual and emotional needs while counteracting the negative impacts of modernization. More crucially, a distinctive national identity has a bigger role in maintaining sovereignty and independence as a nation state (Planning Commission, 1999).

The goal of preserving cultural heritage is pursued through protection and promotion of languages, arts, crafts, literature, religion, religious artefacts, monuments, sports, and other traditions (Planning Commission, 1999). A fully fledged department was created to implement the national policies on promotional activities. These include educating the cultural custodians, providing access to important historical and architectural sites, and promoting the national language, traditional arts, crafts, and cultural etiquettes. The monastic bodies and other religious institutions receive state support. Activities potentially detrimental to Bhutan's cultural heritage are being restrained through legal acts.

In the recent years, there have been efforts towards digitizing Dzongkha, the national language. The Dzongkha Development Commission was established solely with a mandate to promote the national language. Today, the media has done an impressive service in promoting the language through its regular telecasts of national news and reports, important national events, parliamentary proceedings, and entertainment shows. The Bhutanese film industry is yet another instrumental agent of change.

9.7 GOVERNANCE

Bhutan continues to promote and enhance good governance by emphasizing efficiency, transparency, and accountability. The transition from an absolute monarchy to a democratic constitutional monarchy was a step towards building a sustainable system of governance. The political system of Bhutan has evolved over time, together with its tradition and culture. It first developed from a fragmented and disoriented regional rule by local chieftains, lords, and clans into a dual system of governance instituted in 1616 by a spiritual leader, Zhabdrung Ngawang Namgyel (Ura and Kinga, 2004). However, a landmark change occurred in 1907, when the people unanimously instituted Gongsar Ugyen Wangchuck as the first hereditary King of Bhutan. He united the country and brought an end to a century of strife and instability. Since then, successive monarchs, who gradually introduced the elements of a democratic system of governance, ruled the country. The Third King Jigme Dorji

Wangchuck instituted the National Assembly (*Tshogdu*) in 1953 and the Royal Advisory Council (*Lodroe Tshogde*) in 1963. The Fourth King Jigme Singye Wangchuck further continued the process of democratization. The King established the *Dzongkhag Yargay Tshogdu* (District Development Assembly) in 1981 and *Gewog Yargay Tshogchung* (County Development Assembly) in 1991. In a significant move towards decentralization, he shocked the nation by devolving the power of the King to the cabinet ministers in 1998. The King, thereafter, began to serve as the head of the state, while the prime minister runs the government. In November 2001, the King ordered a committee chaired by the Chief Justice of Bhutan to draft the constitution of Bhutan. In 2006, he stepped down in favour of the then Crown Prince Jigme Khesar Namgyel Wangchuck, who was formally crowned as the Fifth King on 6 November 2008. The devolving of the executive power and the establishment of a democratic constitutional monarchy heralded a new era in the political history of Bhutan. The constitution was launched in 2008 and a parliamentary democracy was thus introduced. The progression from hereditary monarchy to that of a parliamentary democracy culminated in the country's first democratic elections in 2008. The government comprises the legislature, judiciary, and the executive branches. The ruling political party, the opposition, and the National Council form the legislative body.

9.8 CHALLENGES AND CONSTRAINTS

9.8.1 Sustainable food production

Although poverty to the extent of hunger and starvation is absent, Bhutan still deals with poverty alleviation. There was a decrease in poverty from 23.2% in 2003 to 12% in 2012, and then to 8.2% in 2017 (NSB and ADB, 2013; NSB, 2016; NSB, 2017b). Sustainable food production is a challenge in Bhutan because of the geo-topographical conditions. Land for arable agriculture is limited, as only 2.9% of the total area is suitable for arable agriculture (MoAF, 2012). Steep slopes, rugged terrain, and fragmented land holdings are not conducive to large-scale and mechanized agriculture. Another major challenge for sustainable food production is the crop damage by wild animals. About 26% of the agricultural land is fallowed for this and various other reasons, including lack of irrigation water, shortage of farm labour, natural calamities, and availability of better non-farm employment options (MoAF, 2012). Where farming is carried out close by the forests, crops are constantly ravaged by wild pigs, monkeys, bears, deer, porcupines, and elephants. Livestock is also frequently lost to tigers, leopards, wild dogs, and bears. If such problems continue, national food security and food self-sufficiency will be hard to achieve. There are rampant criticisms about the stringent wildlife and nature conservation rules, overzealously implemented by those who do not understand the difficulties faced by farmers. These issues are constantly discussed at the national level, and some compensation schemes have been introduced in the past.

The government's development efforts were on the creation of enabling conditions to make farming a profitable economic activity. If farming is to progress from a subsistence stage to a commercial venture, support in creating marketing infrastructure to sell farm produce is critical. Towards this end, the 9th FYP (2003–2008) and 10th FYP (2008–2013) invested considerably in farm roads to create access to markets for procuring agriculture inputs and for selling farm produce. This was also aimed at encouraging participation of the private sector and foreign direct investment (FDI) in certain potential agriculture commodities (MoAF, 2012). The government also considered extending rural credit facilities to help farmers invest in profitable ventures.

9.8.2 Soil fertility management constraints

Globally, mountain ecosystems are increasingly recognized as important water reservoirs. Besides being one of the largest repositories of biological diversity, mountains support 10% of the world population, possessing diverse cultures and heritage, and are popular destinations for recreation and tourism (Jayalakshmi, 2002). But ecologically, they are one of the most fragile ecosystems in the world, which was a warning of the United Nations Conference on Environment and Development in 1992, in Rio de Janeiro. The conference adopted Agenda 21: Mountain Agenda (Managing Fragile Ecosystems: Sustainable Mountain Development). Besides being geologically unstable, landslides, flash floods, and soil erosion are rampant. Soil erosion is the main cause of decline in soil fertility in the mountain farming system, and the cost of replenishing the nutrients is high. With the government's thrust on organic agriculture, the use of chemical fertilizers is questionable from the standpoint of organic agriculture. Under the prevailing circumstances, there is a dilemma. The use of some quantity of fertilizer on cash crops like potatoes is unavoidable, because farmyard manure will never be sufficient for such crops grown over a relatively large area, and occasionally far from homesteads.

The Ministry of Agriculture has been seriously advocating measures to combat land degradation problems. Relocating farmlands and land-swapping provisions have been considered in the past. Land management campaigns and soil fertility management training have been organized by the agriculture sector to address soil fertility issues.

9.8.3 Balancing conservation and economic activity

The Bhutanese farming system integrates crops, livestock, and forestry. Farmers depend on the forest for fuel wood, fodder, timber, and leaf litter. Free grazing of livestock in the adjoining forests is a common practice, although it is being increasingly regulated. With the increase in population, there is mounting pressure on surrounding natural resources. This is where government intervenes and exercises control over forest utilization by enforcing the Forest and Nature Conservation Rules of Bhutan 2006 (MoA, 2006). The country's strict and uncompromising stand on forest conservation, and its management of biodiversity in accordance with international standards, often sparks policy debates. The existing rules are viewed as unaccommodating, and some rural development workers wonder whether conservation should override the priority of food production for sustenance. Striking the right balance between conservation and economic activity is a topic that is under frequent debate at the national level.

9.8.4 Balanced and equitable development

Over the years, migration of people from rural areas to urban centres became an issue of national concern. The estimated percentage of the population residing in urban areas was about 26% in 2007, which increased to 31% in 2012 and to 34% in 2017 (NSB 2007, 2013, 2017b). Difficult living conditions in the rural areas, as opposed to the 'attractive' urban life, were generally believed to be the cause of rural-urban migration. A policy of balanced development with a multi-pronged approach, including an urbanization strategy, was considered the way to mitigate the problem. Potential locations across the country were surveyed to be developed as urban centres. Many development activities, such as establishment of roads, schools, agriculture, and health centres, were initiated. This strategy, in conjunction with other development programmes, such as rural electrification, water supply, and credit schemes, contributed towards enhancing the standard of living and the quality of life of the rural community. Young people who left school were enrolled for training programmes on agriculture farm businesses. Similar efforts were made in making agriculture farming more profitable to attract the rural youth who perceived farming as no more than a subsistence activity, indicative of backwardness. The training was provided at the Rural Development Training Centre (RDTC) established in Zhemgang in 2004.

9.9 CONCLUSION

Within the last six decades, Bhutan has achieved much in all spheres of socio-economic development. This rapid progress can be rightfully attributed to the farsighted vision, wisdom, and leadership of Bhutan's monarchy. Under their esteemed leadership, Bhutan has been able to enjoy the status of a sovereign state with a stable and peaceful government that has been able to define its own path of development based on cultural ethos. While preserving its unique culture and traditions, the country has been able to adopt innovative changes towards the goal of peace, prosperity, and happiness. Within a single generation, people's lives have changed from a near-medieval period to the 21st century – a quantum leap by any standard. Bhutan has been able to accommodate this rapid change and yet maintain its unique cultural and national identity. For the future, Bhutan's economic development will depend in good part on revenues generated from hydropower. A reliable flow of water for sustainable hydropower generation may be ensured by sustained protection and conservation of the watersheds. Therefore, environmental protection has become the nation's priority in terms of sustainability. Being part of the global community, Bhutan recognizes the importance of global partnership and remains a willing advocate to many global commitments to save the Earth and sustain future developments. As a late joiner in the modern development process, Bhutan has been able to draw on the experiences of other countries and thus avoid costly mistakes. The country remains committed to maintaining the biological productivity and diversity of the pristine natural heritage, which is undeniably an asset of global significance worth protecting and preserving for the present and future generations.

ACKNOWLEDGEMENTS

The author would like to thank Professor A. T. M. Nurul Amin of the Asian Institute of Technology; Ms Andrea Spear, former Regional Adviser of UNESCAP on Trade Policy; and Dr Thanakvaro De Lopez, Mr Karma Tsering, and Dr Pema Choejey for their well-considered suggestions for improving the chapter. Special thanks also to Dr Pak Sum Low for encouraging me to write this chapter.

REFERENCES

Bertelsmann Stiftung (2016) BTI 2016: Bhutan Country Report. Gütersloh, Bertelsmann Stiftung. https://www.bti-project.org/content/en/downloads/reports/country_report_2016_BTN.pdf

Choden, T. and Penjore, D. (2004) *Economic and Political Relations between Bhutan and Neighbouring Countries.* Thimphu, Centre for Bhutan Studies.

DGPC (Druk Green Power Corporation, Ltd.) (2017) Chukha Hydropower Plant. https://www.drukgreen.bt/chp/

DoF (Department of Forests) (1995) *Forest and Nature Conservation Act 1995.* Thimphu, Department of Forests, Ministry of Agriculture, Royal Government of Bhutan.

(GNHC) Gross National Happiness Commission (2008) Draft Tenth Five-Year Plan [2008–2013] Vol. I: Main Document. GNH Commission, Royal Government of Bhutan.

(2017). Guidelines for Preparation of the 12th Five-Year Plan. https://www.gnhc.gov.bt/en/wp-content/uploads/2017/05/Finalized-Guideline.pdf

IMF (International Monetary Fund) (2016) Bhutan: 2016 Article IV Consultation. IMF Country Report No. 16/206. International Monetary Fund, Washington, D.C. www.imf.org/external/pubs/cat/longres.aspx?sk=44036.0

Jayalakshmi, C. P. (2002) International Year of the Mountains 2002 – Putting Mountains on the Global Agenda: UN Declares 2002 as the Year of Mountains. ICIMOD Newsletter No. 39. International Centre for Integrated Mountain Development, Kathmandu, Nepal. https://lib.icimod.org/record/26630

MoA (Ministry of Agriculture) (2002a) *Renewable Natural Resources Sector Ninth Plan (2002–2007): Path to Gross National Happiness – The Next Five Miles.* Thimphu, Ministry of Agriculture, Royal Government of Bhutan.

(2002b) *Biodiversity Action Plan for Bhutan 2002.* Thimphu, Ministry of Agriculture, Royal Government of Bhutan.

(2006) *Forest and Nature Conservation Rules of Bhutan 2006.* Thimphu, Department of Forests, Ministry of Agriculture, Royal Government of Bhutan.

MoAF (Ministry of Agriculture and Forests) (2012) RNR Sector: 11th Five-Year Plan 2013–2018. Ministry of Agriculture and Forests, Thimphu.

MoFA (Ministry of Foreign Affairs) (2021). Bilateral Relations. https://www.mfa.gov.bt/?page_id=8824

MoLHR (Ministry of Labour and Human Resources) (2015) Labour Force Survey Report 2015. Labour Market Information and Research Division, Department of Employment, Ministry of Labour and Human Resources, Thimphu.

NEC (National Environment Commission) (1998) *The Middle Path. National Environment Strategy for Bhutan.* National Environment Commission, Thimphu, Royal Government of Bhutan.

(2004) Environmental Discharge Standard. National Environment Commission, Royal Government of Bhutan, Thimphu. http://www.nec.gov.bt

NSB (National Statistics Bureau) (2007) Poverty Analysis Report 2007. National Statistics Bureau, Royal Government of Bhutan. http://www.nsb.gov.bt/publication/files/pub4kf7409pu.pdf

(2013) Poverty Analysis Report 2012. http://www.nsb.gov.bt/publication/files/pub6pg3078cg.pdf

(2016) Statistical Yearbook of Bhutan 2016. http://www.nsb.gov.bt/publication/publications.php?id=3

(2017a) Statistical Yearbook of Bhutan 2017. http://www.nsb.gov.bt/publication/publications.php?id=3

(2017b) Bhutan Poverty Analysis Report 2017. http://www.nsb.gov.bt/publication/files/2017_PAR_Report.pdf

(2017c) Bhutan Living Standards Survey Report 2017. http://www.nsb.gov.bt/publication/files/pub2yo10667rb.pdf

(2018) Bhutan at a Glance 2018. http://www.nsb.gov.bt/publication/files/pub3kw5078sm.pdf

(2020) Statistical Yearbook of Bhutan 2020. https://www.nsb.gov.bt/publications/statistical-yearbook/

NSB and ADB (Asian Development Bank) (2013) Bhutan Living Standard Survey Report2012. A joint publication by National Statistics Bureau and Asian Development Bank. https://www.adb.org/sites/default/files/publication/30221/bhutan-living-standards-survey-2012.pdf

Planning Commission (1999) *Bhutan 2020: A Vision for Peace, Prosperity and Happiness.* Planning Commission Secretariat, Royal Government of Bhutan.

RGoB (Royal Government of Bhutan) (2005) *Bhutan National Human Development Report 2005: The Challenge of Youth Employment.* Thimphu, Royal Government of Bhutan.

SDSN (Sustainable Development Solutions Network) (2013) An action agenda for sustainable development: Report for the UN secretary general. https://unstats.un.org/unsd/broader progress/pdf/130613-SDSN-An-Action-Agenda-for-Sustainable-Development-FINAL.pdf

TCB (Tourism Council of Bhutan) (2016) Policy. Tourism Council of Bhutan. http://www.tourism.gov.bt/tourism-policy/tourism-policy

Thinley, Jigmi Y. (1999) Values and development: 'Gross National Happiness'. In S. Kinga, K. Galay, P. Rapten and A. Pain (eds.), *Gross National Happiness: Discussion Papers*, 2013 (pp. 12–23), Thimphu, Bhutan, Centre for Bhutan Studies.

Upadhyay, K. P. (1995) Shifting cultivation in Bhutan: a gradual approach to modifying land use patterns. A case study from Pema Gatshel district, Bhutan. Community Forestry Case Study Series 11. Food and Agriculture Organization of the United Nations. http://www.fao.org/3/V8380E/V8380E00.htm

Ura, K., Alkire, S., Zangmo, T. and Wangdi, K. (2012a) *A Short Guide to Gross National Happiness Index.* Thimphu, Centre for Bhutan Studies.

Ura, K., Alkire, S., Zangmo, T. and Wangdi, K. (2012b) *An Extensive Analysis of GNH Index.* Thimphu, Centre for Bhutan Studies.

Ura, K. and Kinga, S. (2004) *Bhutan–Sustainable development through good governance. A case study from reducing poverty, sustaining growth.* http://documents.worldbank.org/curated/en/880451468743944567/pdf/308210BHU0Governance-01see0also0307591.pdf

van Driem, G. (2004) Bhutan's Endangered Languages Documentation Programme under the Dzongkha Development Authority: The Three Rare Gems. Paper presented at the First International Seminar on Bhutan, Studies, Thimphu.

10   A different form of sustainable development in Thailand and Bhutan: Implementation of a sufficiency approach

ROS TAPLIN[1], SK NOIM UDDIN[2], KANOKWAN PIBALSOOK[3], KARMA TSHERING[4], AND NATARIKA WAYUPARB NITIPHON[5]

[1]Centre for Development, Environment and Policy, Department of Development Studies, SOAS University of London, United Kingdom
[2]Department of Geography and Planning, Macquarie University, Sydney, Australia; and Climate Policy and Markets Advisory International, Uppsala, Sweden
[3]Ministry of Natural Resources and Environment, Bangkok, Thailand
[4]Policy and Programming Services, National Environment Commission Secretariat, Royal Government of Bhutan, Thimphu, Bhutan
[5]Thailand Greenhouse Gas Management Organization (TGO), Bangkok, Thailand

Keywords

Sufficiency Economy; Gross National Happiness; the Middle Path; the Middle Way; Thailand; Bhutan; sustainable development; sustainability; environment; development; Local Agenda 21; LA 21; energy

Abstract

The pressures of economic development on society and environment in Asia have resulted in national sustainability policy responses in two countries, Thailand and Bhutan, that derive from a traditional Buddhist approach but which have been modernized in the light of the contemporary global challenges that these Asian nations face. Referred to as *Sufficiency Economy* in Thailand and *Gross National Happiness* in Bhutan, these responses have been adopted because of the pressures of development and associated environmental and social costs. The Sufficiency Economy and Gross National Happiness approaches have been shaped to assist in the formulation and implementation of ethically sound policies to protect the environment, society, and individuals – in line with traditional Buddhist spiritual, ethical, and cultural teachings. This chapter examines examples of how Sufficiency Economy and Gross National Happiness have been realized. Aspects of Thailand's process of implementing Sufficiency Economy and Bhutan's adoption of Gross National Happiness are discussed via two empirical case examples: Local Agenda 21/Local Action 21 projects in Thailand in 2000–2003, and the implementation of energy and environmental policy projects in Bhutan. It is concluded that the furtherance of these contemporary sustainability approaches sourced from Buddhist principles is very important for the future of these nations.

10.1 INTRODUCTION

After the 1992 Rio Conference, both developing and developed nations grappled with how best to implement the Agenda 21 action plan and incorporate sustainable development principles into their institutions of government. This chapter looks at a sustainability approach adopted by Thailand and Bhutan, unique to these countries, which has strong cultural and spiritual links with the Buddhist tradition.

Before examining these nations' particular experiences with sustainable development, the best-practice prescriptions of developed country experts on sustainable development are delineated so as to provide context for the strategies adopted in Bhutan and Thailand. There are challenges in governance for sustainable development for all nations, and Thailand's and Bhutan's adoptions of alternative approaches to sustainability are very worthwhile experiences to explore.

10.2 THE CHALLENGES OF GOVERNANCE FOR SUSTAINABILITY

Policy directed towards sustainability outcomes has been a significant focus of United Nations (UN) agencies and national governments for three decades. Both developed and developing nations have formulated approaches to sustainable development over a spectrum of enacting domestic law to providing policy guidance. Nevertheless, the terms 'sustainability' and 'sustainable development', since the release of the Brundtland Report in 1987 (WCED, 1987), have been highly disputed terms in their definition. In the view of Dryzek (2005), 'There is still no consensus on the exact meaning of sustainability; but sustainability is the axis around which discussion occurs' (p. 14).

Going further than definitions, aspects of sustainability that have become the standards of best practice are the following:

- Adoption of the precautionary principle;
- Staying within source and sink constraints;
- Maintenance of natural capital at or near current levels;
- Adoption of the 'polluter pays' principle; and
- Maintenance of inter-generational and intra-generational equity.

These standards have been implemented and policy formulated at the UN Convention level and at the national decision-making level in many countries. Nevertheless, many nations are not seriously attempting to keep resource use within source and sink constraints or to maintain their natural capital. This reflects the relationship between sustainable development and economic development goals and the priority that sustainability is given.

O'Riordan and Voisey (1998) observe that sustainability implementation ranges from 'very weak', where there is tokenistic policy integration, to 'very strong' where comprehensive shifts in economic, environmental, cultural governance approaches and thinking have been implemented. Because of the variations in implementation of sustainable development, many challenges have been made that the concept is too vague (e.g., Young, 1992). A more optimistic interpretation is that learning about sustainability is a necessary and important part of a transition towards sustainability. As Tilbury (2004) emphasizes, the 'vagueness of the term is the point', as the lack of precise definition facilitates different stakeholders with different values and beliefs coming together. She points out that the definition of the term has been negotiated at the UN level since Rio and that education has become seen as a crucial part of the process of moving towards sustainability. Sterling (2001) also advocates that there must be 'shifts from mechanistic to ecological thinking' via *education for sustainability* (p. 53). Education for sustainability focuses on critical thinking, challenging false consciousness, and assisting values clarification, power relationships, and participatory learning activities, and it emphasizes quality of life and futures thinking using action research as a means for change (Tilbury, 2004).

Milbrath (1989), in his book *Envisioning a Sustainable Society: Learning Our Way Out*, stressed that learning is the path to a sustainable society:

> We must learn how to become conscious of our ways of knowing ... As we do so, we will come to recognize the key role that society plays in knowledge development, in development of beliefs about how the world works, and in value clarification (or obfuscation). Recognizing that our beliefs and values are culturally derived frees us to reexamine them to see if they can be revised to serve us better (p. 85).

This is why approaches adopted by Thailand and Bhutan to sustainability are of significance because of the differences in the beliefs and values from which their policies are developed in comparison to those of developed nations.

10.2.1 Governance framework

A governance framework for sustainability is fundamental to transition to a sustainable society. However, governance is still predominantly centred in the dominant social paradigm rather than the new environmental paradigm in Western nations (Milbrath, 1989; Sterling, 2001). In response to this, Milbrath (1989) proposed overlaying a *learning governance structure* on existing traditional governmental structures, with the potential of strengthening governments in the move towards a sustainable society. He recommended that a learning governance structure should have four basic components: an education and information system; a systemic and futures thinking capacity; an intervention capability for stakeholders; and a long-range sustainability impact assessment capacity for policy initiatives (Milbrath, 1989). Milbrath urged the advantages of a learning governance structure:

> First, if government can better anticipate the future, it has a better chance of creatively dealing with such problems as climate change, overpopulation, resource shortages, species extinction and ecosystem damage ... Second, government could better undertake the new functions that are being assigned to it: encouraging social learning, facilitating quality of life, and helping society to become sustainable. Third, the learning structure could improve the processes and outcomes of government by helping to avoid mistakes or to avoid governmental aid to special interests at the expense of the general welfare. (pp. 301–302)

Bossel (1998) advises that sustainability, subsidiarity, self-organization, and sufficiency (Four Ss) are needed for sustainable governance. Subsidiarity, the concept that political power should ideally be exercised by the smallest possible unit and at the most grassroots level of government, was identified in Chapter 28 of Agenda 21, the 'Local authorities' initiatives in support of Agenda 21', referred to as Local Agenda 21 (LA 21) or Local Action 21.

LA 21 was the practical implementation of Agenda 21 at the local level. At the 2012 UN Conference on Sustainable Development, Rio+20, commitment was reaffirmed to LA 21, and likewise at the 2015 UN Sustainable Development Summit in New York.

The remainder of this chapter focuses on approaches adopted by Thailand and Bhutan on sustainable development, including case examples, which have focused on sufficiency, in particular, but also on subsidiarity and self-organization. First, however, the following section looks at the Buddhist spiritual tradition and its relation to environmental protection and sustainability. Then, in the sections that follow, some LA 21 projects in Thailand 2000–2003 and energy sustainability projects in Bhutan are overviewed to look for evidence of implementation of sufficiency approaches in policy implementation.

10.3 BUDDHIST ECONOMICS AND SUSTAINABILITY

Many major spiritual traditions concur that over-exploitation and degradation of nature for human profit are unjust and immoral, and provide ethical guidelines for the preservation of nature, which followers of those religions are expected to respect (Schumacher, 1973; Dwivedi, 1996). Buddhist doctrine, in particular, views humankind as an integral part of nature, with the consequence that when nature is polluted, people also suffer. Sponsel and Natadecha-Sponsel (1993) argue that '[e]nvironmental ethics are inherent in Buddhism' (p. 80).

One of the first Western economists to advocate the merits of the Buddhist approach to economic development was the late E. F. Schumacher in his book *Small Is Beautiful: Economics as if People Mattered* (Schumacher, 1973). Schumacher, who learned about the Buddhist approach to nature in Myanmar, reiterated that *right livelihood* is one of the requirements of the Buddha's Noble Eightfold Path, one of the basic foundations of Buddhist practice. Right livelihood focuses on well-being via four human necessities: food, clothing, shelter, and medicine. Schumacher reflected:

> The keynote of Buddhist Economics, therefore, is simplicity and non-violence. From an economist's point of view, the marvel of the Buddhist way of life is the utter rationality of its pattern – amazingly small means leading to extraordinarily satisfactory results ... While the materialist is mainly interested in goods, the Buddhist is mainly interested in liberation. But Buddhism is 'The Middle Way' and therefore in no way antagonistic to physical well-being. It is not wealth that stands in the way of liberation but the attachment to wealth, not the enjoyment of pleasurable things but the craving for them. (pp. 52–53)

Using local resources to provide for local needs is seen to be the desirable economic approach from a Buddhist perspective (Schumacher, 1973). All citizens should have a minimum standard of living in regard to the four necessities of food, clothing, shelter, and medicine (Rigg, 2003). The concept of the Middle Way highlights the differences between mainstream Western and Buddhist lifestyle concepts. Western economics encourages maximizing consumption, with standard of living being related to per capita annual consumption, but the Middle Way focuses on moderate and contented consumption for well-being. The Middle Way thus is the fundamental principle guiding Buddhist interactions between humans and the environment (Sponsel and Natadecha-Sponsel, 1993).

In the twentieth century, the cultures and environments of countries such as Thailand, Japan, India, and Sri Lanka, which have many Buddhist citizens, were impacted by Western materialism, which came hand in hand with development of their economies. These nations' natural environments were degraded and in some cases, in part even destroyed in pursuit of economic growth, even though such actions were against religious teachings and cultural norms (Dwivedi, 1996). Sponsel and Natadecha-Sponsel's (1993) writing in the early 1990s suggested that 'modernization has undermined adherence to Buddhism in nations like Thailand' (p. 80). However, over the last two decades Thailand and Bhutan have attempted to promote sustainable development and reaffirm their cultural heritage by adopting two particular approaches to development, Sufficiency Economy and Gross National Happiness, respectively, which arguably have strong links with Buddhist traditions.

10.4 THAILAND'S SUFFICIENCY ECONOMY PATH

Thailand shares borders with Myanmar, Laos, Cambodia, and Malaysia and had a population of 66.18 million in 2017 (National Statistical Office, 2018). It is one of the 'tiger economies' of Asia but has had a history of democratic instability over decades, and since 2000, evidenced by a military coup in 2006 (Ockey, 2007), a political crisis resulting in a 'judicial coup' in 2008 (McCargo, 2014), violent protests against the ruling government in 2010 (Thabchumpon and McCargo, 2011), and another military coup in 2014 (Sopranzetti, 2016). Issues with regard to Thailand's governance, military, and monarchy linkages, administration, decentralization, and economy have been examined by many researchers (see, e.g., Pasuk and Baker, 2002; Bowornwathana, 2002; McCargo, 2004, 2014; Sopranzetti, 2016). The monarchy in particular has exerted considerable influence in contemporary Thailand as well as traditionally (Klausner, 2002; Hewison, 2002). Suwannathat-Pian (2002) has said about the influence of King Bhumibol Adulyadej:

> [T]he Royal version of constitutional monarchy which King Bhumibol himself has partly resurrected from the traditional concept of Thai Kingship, and mainly recreated and readjusted to suit the requirements of his time, derives its authority not from the written constitution but from His Majesty's personal close bond with his subjects. (p. 68)

Following the financial crisis in Asia during late 1997 and 1998, King Bhumibol Adulyadej decreed that the philosophy of Sufficiency Economy or the Middle Path should be a guiding principle of national development and management for Thailand (Chaipattana Foundation, 2000; Office of the National Economic and Social Development Board, 2002). This was not the introduction of a new philosophy, as it had been previously propounded in a royal speech in 1974 (Sachayansrisakul, 2009). However, in 1998, the then Thai Government took up this concept as a major strategic policy approach. Therefore, Sufficiency Economy was introduced in the Ninth National Economic and Social Development Plan (2002–2006) and continued as the guiding philosophy of the 10th Economic and Social Development Plan (2007–2011). According to the Thai Government, the Sufficiency Economy approach was first introduced in national planning in order to (1) overcome the Thai economic crisis that occurred from unexpected rapid globalization and (2) achieve sustainable development (Office of the National Economic and Social Development Board, 2002). The meaning of Sufficiency Economy, according to the then Thai government, was described as follows:

> A philosophy that stresses the middle path as the overriding principle for appropriate conduct and way of life by the populace at all levels. It applies to conduct and way of life at individual, family, and community levels. At the nation level, the philosophy is consistent with a balanced development strategy that would reduce the vulnerability of the nation to inevitable shocks and excesses that may arise as a result of globalization. (Office of the National Economic and Social Development Board, 2002, p. 1)

Sufficiency Economy was not only in accord with royal edicts but was incorporated in the 1997 revision of the Thai Constitution. The 1997 Constitution supported enhancement of the autonomous economic position of Thai citizens and has been commended by human rights groups (IWRAW, 1997). Section 9 of the Constitution indicated that 'the King is a Buddhist and upholder of religions', while Section 78 gave significance to the power of local communities:

> The State shall decentralize powers to localities for the purpose of independence and self-determination of local affairs, develop local economics, public utilities and facilities systems and information infrastructure in the locality thoroughly and equally throughout the country as well as develop into a large-sized local government organization a province ready for such purpose, having regard to the will of the people in that province. (Office of the Council of State, 1997)

King Bhumibol Adulyadej emphasized in 1998 that a self-sufficient economy reflects Dharma-Buddhist teaching with regard to moderation, equilibrium, and balance (the Middle Way). He emphasized that this teaching is essential to lead Thai people to live productively, peacefully, and happily. The King also explained his meaning of self-sufficiency:

> Whatever we produce, we have enough for our own use. We do not have to borrow from other people. We can rely on ourselves, like what people say, we can stand on our own legs. But self-sufficiency carries a broader meaning. It means having enough and being satisfied with the situation ... If any country values this idea – the idea of doing just to have enough which means being satisfied at a moderate level, being honest and not being greedy, its people will be happy. (Chaipattana Foundation and TDRI, 1999)

Interestingly, in response to arguments that his ideas are not congruent with mainstream economic theory, the King has reflected that his philosophy could probably be applied to only a quarter of each person's way of life (Rigg, 2003).

The Royal Thai Government firmly supports the application of the Sufficiency Economy Philosophy and encourages people and organizations at all levels – the public sector, private sector,

and communities alike – to apply it to their practice as a vehicle towards sustainable development (Vichitranuja *et al.*, 2018).

Sufficiency economy was promoted by Thailand at the UN World Summit on Sustainable Development in Johannesburg in September 2002 as the Thai response to sustainable development. Princess Chulabhorn Mahidol, who led the Thai delegation, stated:

> Our current Ninth Economic and Social Development Plan for the period 2002 to 2006 has been guided by the philosophy of 'sufficiency economy' first propounded in Thailand by His Majesty King Bhumibol. The main principle of this approach to development is the adherence to a middle path in all aspects of social interaction at individual, family and community levels. This philosophy encourages people to achieve a sustainable way of life in harmony with existing domestic resources and local knowledge and wisdom. People are thus at the centre of development. (Government of Thailand, 2002, p. 2)

The Sufficiency Economy approach has continued as a philosophy of governance in Thailand, notwithstanding changes in government. In 2016, the Government of Thailand's Ministry of Foreign Affairs published *A Practical Approach toward Sustainable Development: Thailand's Sufficiency Economy Philosophy* (Government of Thailand, 2016). Section 10.4.1 discusses aspects of how LA 21 sustainability policy-making was implemented in Thailand in 2000–2003.

10.4.1 The experience of LA 21 in Thailand

LA 21 became a key mechanism internationally for implementation of sustainability at the local level. The case of LA 21 implementation in Thailand has been selected here to reflect on how the Sufficiency Economy approach had an impact in Thailand in early LA 21 implementation. Pibalsook *et al.* (2003) and Pibalsook (2007) have discussed this implementation experience with LA 21 in Thailand in the period 2000–2003. Aspects of their findings are recapped here.

National planning and development, and associated social and environmental planning, are formulated and implemented in Thailand for five-year periods (OECD, 2002). Under the laws on decentralization enacted in 1997, citizens had the right to participate in the development of project proposals and planning processes at the local level for submission to the Thai Budget Bureau, a part of the national administration that determines all projects and budgets for local and provincial authorities (OECD, 2001). As a major obstacle to effective environmental management of natural resources in Thailand was seen to be poor implementation of policies at the local level, the Thai environmental administration was reorganized to support the decentralization concept. It was believed that the primary problem with environmental policy-making in Thailand had been lack of public participation and access during all stages of the policy process (Daniere and Takahashi, 2002).

Despite Thailand's constitution of 1997 mandating citizens' rights for participation and promotion of the enhancement of effective participation, the Thai Government faced three major problems in promoting public participation. First, Thai citizens had little experience in participating in public policy and local politics as a result of the previously centralized and top-down approach of the Thai political and administrative system and therefore did not know how to become involved. Second, bureaucrats and local authorities demonstrated difficulty in giving up their power of previous decades and were not used to being questioned by citizens. Third, Thai citizens needed assistance on how to become involved in public policy and decision-making (Klein, 2003). Accordingly, LA 21 was seen as an appropriate mechanism to solve the problems of the many weaknesses or limitations in local development planning and environmental management.

10.4.1.1 Thai-European cooperation

A survey by the International Council for Local Environmental Initiatives (2002) identified that some 21 LA 21 programmes had been implemented in Thailand by 2002. Through the authors' investigation and development of an inventory (via the interviewing of officials from ministries and national, provincial, and local levels of government and non-governmental organization (NGO) representatives), a total of 84 municipalities were identified in May 2011 that had committed to undertaking an LA 21 programme or project in Thailand. Leknoi (2017) reported that by 2017:

> [O]nly 188 (2.39%) of the 7,852 local governments in 53 provinces have implemented LA 21 to some extent …. Thus, the effort to bring LA 21 into practice … was relatively slow, and so far has failed to encourage the other 7,667 local governments to embrace the principle (p. 84).

Different municipal areas in Thailand adopted differing approaches to LA 21. In general, early approaches adopted were influenced by European models and experiences through cooperation with Germany, Denmark, and Sweden. Early LA 21 programmes initiated via Thai-Swedish cooperation are discussed further below.

10.4.1.2 Thai-Swedish LA 21 cooperation

By 2000, the Thai Department of Environmental Quality Promotion (DEQP) had decided to implement several LA 21 projects with Swedish assistance that would involve developing local action plans focusing on community participation (Department of Environmental Quality Promotion, n.d.). These LA 21 projects could be initiated as the 1997 Thai constitution supported human rights and citizens' participation in decision-making.

Cooperation between the Thai DEQP and Swedish agencies (the Swedish International Development Cooperation Agency (SIDA), LIFE Academy/LIFE Partners, and the Swedish Environmental Research Institute (IVL)) resulted in three pilot LA 21 projects: in Trang and Nakorn Ratchasima provinces (2000–2002) and Lamphun Province (2002–2003). The objectives of these LA 21 projects were to:

- raise awareness and encourage people to participate in environmental protection in order to embrace the sustainable development concept; and
- enhance the capacity and efficiency of local leaders in environmental management, including the preparation of guidelines for achieving sustainable environmental development at the local level. (Department of Environmental Quality Promotion, 2002a, 2002b)

The intention in the longer term was to disseminate the LA 21 guidelines that would be developed, as examples from which other Thai municipalities would learn.

In order to learn about the LA 21 experience, study tours to investigate best practice in Sweden were organized for Thai senior town hall and municipality officials, including the mayors of the municipalities. A study tour was undertaken in 2000 by Nakhon Ratchasima municipality and another was held in 2003 for Lamphun municipality. Also, Swedish experts visited and promoted LA 21 activities in Nakhon Ratchasima municipality in July 2000. A Thai-Swedish LA 21 Working Model was developed and the central tasks were to formulate a five-year master plan for sustainable development with stakeholders and citizens and to develop an action plan detailing how the municipalities were to meet the targets set in the five-year plans. The seven steps in the LA 21 working model were as follows:

- Organization (setting up an LA 21 secretariat);
- Commitments for sustainable development;
- Analysis and review of issues (review needs and problems);
- Formulating visions, policies, and strategies;
- Action planning;
- Implementation;
- Monitoring and evaluation (LIFE Partners, 2002).

LA 21 did not conform in any way to traditional Thai planning procedures. Traditionally, planning was hierarchical with policy and strategic planning statements formulated by political and administrative leaders in a top-down manner. Accordingly, support from stakeholders was seen as a most important step for those initiating Thai LA 21 programmes. Working with stakeholders in sharing knowledge and assessing current environment problems, future needs, and possible plans were the key features of the LA 21 programme's *bottom-up* approach. The analysis and review of issues (the third step in the working model) was the main task associated with this bottom-up approach. The local authority was required to provide a State of the Environment report and guidelines for sustainable development to stakeholders for use as fundamental background material.

The following were the best practices, 'learning by doing' guidelines for LA 21, that were introduced to the stakeholders in Thai LA 21 areas to facilitate local sustainable development:

- *Waste is not always waste* – This guideline was based on the concept that the 'eco-cycles' in society can be closed by reusing and recycling materials and products; waste banks and composting via effective micro-organisms (small- and larger-scale projects) were promoted in communities and schools;
- *Water is life* – Citizen learning that the most valuable resource of water must not be contaminated was facilitated;
- *Clean air* – As air pollutants come from combustion of fossil fuels, solar energy and bicycle use for personal transportation were promoted;
- *Greening the city* – Tree planting along roads was promoted;
- *Healthy food* – Learning about organic methods of agriculture was introduced and promoted as an environmentally friendly practice at community meetings and in schools. (LIFE Partners, 2002)

From the former Thai government's perspective, the LA 21 programmes in Trang, Nakhon Ratchasima, and Lamphun municipality implemented via the Thai-Swedish LA 21 Working Model were successful in getting stakeholders and citizens at the local level to participate in the policy and planning process. At the national government level, there was also a perception that there was greater success with LA 21 implementation in the smaller municipalities of Trang and Lamphun (Pibalsook, 2007). Tonami and Mori (2007) have evaluated the implementation of these LA 21 projects and have concluded that 'the goals of the subsidiarity principle and public participation at the local level were not fully achieved', the reason supposedly being that mayors and municipality offices drove the projects, so expansion of further new projects in the municipalities did not occur. The perspective of Tonami and Mori has validity, but it should be noted that it is also common for LA 21 projects in developed nations to be initiated and driven by local government authorities.

Overall, it is doubtful if the degree of success with LA 21 implementation that was achieved in the three municipalities in 2001–2003 could have been realized without the then Thai government's adoption of Sufficiency Economy and the 1997

changes to the Thai constitution with regard to the rights of citizens to participate in decision-making. Leknoi (2017) found the following:

> There are three critical success factors that affect the likely success of LA 21 implementation in Thailand; namely (1) the number of private groups in the working group …; (2) the implementation budget allocated …; and (3) the level of multilateral participation … The estimate of the three factors … is given … with a predictability of 60.7%. (p. 99).

10.5 BHUTAN'S GROSS NATIONAL HAPPINESS APPROACH

Another example of the implementation of sustainable development via a sufficiency approach is found in Bhutan. Bhutan is a tiny, mountainous, landlocked South Asian country of 38,394 km² in the eastern Himalayas, with the Tibetan autonomous region of China to its north and India to the west, south, and east (RGB, 2017c). Its natural environments are relatively untouched, with 71% of the nation's land area under forest cover (RGB, 2017a, 2017b). One of the ten global biodiversity hotspots is contained within Bhutan's borders and it was the recipient of a debt-for-nature swap for forest land in the late 1990s (NEC, 1997). The population of Bhutan totals less than one million people – 735,553 as per the Population and Housing Census 2017 (RGB, 2018) – and the nation became a two-party parliamentary democracy after elections in March 2008 (Bothe, 2015). Modernization of Bhutan's economy was initiated more than 50 years ago, although the agricultural sector still predominates as the main source of livelihood, with many rural and remote communities in Bhutan dependent on subsistence farming. In 2016, the agricultural, livestock, and forestry sectors contributed 16.5% of gross domestic product (GDP) (RGB, 2017c), and the industrial and service sectors contributed 45% and 37.5% of GDP, respectively (WB, 2017). The country's chief source of outside revenue is hydroelectricity, harnessing the power from its swift flowing rivers via run-of-the-river plants.

In the early 1960s, after centuries of being isolated from the rest of the world, Bhutan's then King Jigme Dorji Wangchuck opened his country and initiated the path towards modernization (Giri, 2004). Bhutan's socio-economic development, which started in 1961, is based on a five-year-plan period. This five-year plan provides the framework to formulate all developmental activities, including allocation of resources to all central government agencies and local governments. The nation continued as a monarchy and gradually started preparation towards democracy through a decentralization process initiated by the wise and farsighted His Majesty the Fourth King Jigme Singye Wangchuck, by establishing the Dzongkhag Tshodue (District

Assembly) in 1982 and Geog Tshochung (Block Assembly) in 1992. The country has completed more than five decades of planned development, moving from a non-monetized traditional economy based on agriculture to a wage-based exchange economy since 1961 (UNEP, 2001; Frame, 2005).

The *Maximization of Gross National Happiness*, Bhutan's unique approach to development, was first promulgated by His Majesty the Fourth King in the early 1970s, when His Majesty proclaimed that Gross National Happiness was more important than GDP (RGB, 1999). Keeping this wise guidance and historic declaration, the Gross National Happiness Index and a policy screening tool to review and evaluate all new policies were developed (CBS, 2017). His Majesty the Fourth King further outlined:

> a specific Bhutanese path to development in pursuit of values that were consonant with Bhutan's culture, institutions and spiritual values, rather than values that were defined by factors external to Bhutanese society and culture. This reflection was the genesis of the concept of Gross National Happiness. (Ura and Galay, 2004, p. vii)

Gross National Happiness is used as a measure of national development as an alternative to the standard economic measure of gross national product.

Gross National Happiness is considered a 'Buddhist concept' but is also seen as being '"refracted" – in other systems of thought as well' (Ura and Galay, 2004, p. viii). At a conference organized by the Centre for Bhutan Studies in 2004, where the theoretical underpinnings of Gross National Happiness were discussed:

> [T]here were those who emphasized Buddhism as the underlying foundation of Gross National Happiness and those who considered Gross National Happiness to be consonant with Buddhism and inspired by, but not necessarily synonymous with, it. (Ura and Galay, 2004, p. x)

Gross National Happiness is also referred to as the 'Middle Path of development' and has parallels to Thailand's adoption of a Sufficiency Economy or Middle Way. The Bhutanese approach to development is via balancing economic forces, environmental preservation, and reduction of dependence on finite global resources, cultural and spiritual values, and good governance. Differences between the concepts of wealth and prosperity of the nation and its citizens are thus emphasized.

Bhutan 2020: A Vision for Peace, Prosperity and Happiness, released in 1999, provided long-term visions for the nation's development (RGB, 1999). Five areas were identified as the main pillars of development, or sustainable development, for the nation:

- Human development;
- Balanced and equitable economic growth and development;
- Preservation and promotion of cultural heritage;
- Preservation and sustainable use of the environment; and
- Good governance (RGB, 1999).

Former King Jigme Singye Wangchuck (Fourth King) said in 2000, '[A]s we modernize it is inevitable that some of our traditions will be affected. What we are trying to do is blend development with our traditions, to preserve our culture and identity as Bhutanese' (Gregson, 2000). Gross National Happiness is a multifaceted approach to sustainable development that aims to balance economic forces, environmental preservation, cultural and spiritual values, and good governance, maintaining harmony, minimizing dependence on global finite resources, and maximizing happiness.

In particular, the Ninth Five-Year Plan (2002–2007) developed in a time of unprecedented historical changes in Bhutan, gave special attention to the country's long-term development vision of Gross National Happiness with the following goals:

- Improvement of quality of life and income, especially for the poor;
- Ensuring good governance; promotion of private sector growth and employment generation;
- Preserving and promoting cultural heritage and environmental conservation; and
- Achievement of rapid economic growth and transformation of the economy.

It also placed emphasis on subsidiarity and self-organization, with decentralization of planning and policy-making, and incorporated procedures for communities, together with their elected leaders, to prepare their own plans (RGB, 2002).

Citizens were asked in Bhutan's 2005 national census about their own degree of individual happiness; remarkably, 45.1% of respondents said they were 'very happy', 51.6% reported being 'happy', and only 3.3% were 'not very happy' (RGB, 2006).

In July 2006, Jigme Thinley, then Minister for Home and Cultural Affairs, and subsequently Bhutan's first elected Prime Minister, for 2008–2013, reflected on Bhutan's experience with Gross National Happiness at that time:

> GNH does question the dominant materialistic ethic that growth is good. Excessive production, excessive consumption leads to excessive waste and what we would like to achieve is to raise the level of consciousness that human well-being is what can be achieved if one is able to balance material and spiritual growth … What Gross National Happiness does, it embraces this idea of sustainable development. One thing that we must not be mistaken [about] is to have this impression that Bhutan has found happiness. No, we are concerned about unemployment. Yes, we are concerned about environmental degradation. In fact, in some parts of our country survival is a daily struggle … We could have been far more prosperous than we are, but at every stage of our

development we have been concerned about: Are we really growing in a proper way, in a good way, in a sensible way, in a responsible way and in a sustainable and equitable way? (Lustig, 2006)

The 10th Five-Year Plan (2008–2013) also focused on achievement of Gross National Happiness and emphasized a primary objective of poverty reduction, together with a core strategy of vitalizing industry via national spatial planning, synergizing integrated rural-urban development for poverty alleviation, expanding strategic infrastructure, investing in human capital, and fostering an enabling environment through governance. The 11th Five-Year Plan (2013–2018; RGB, 2013) and the 12th Five-Year Plan (RGB, 2017d) have been developed based on National Key Result Areas and Sector Key Result Areas to enhance implementation of the Gross National Happiness principle more effectively.

10.5.1 Energy and environment in Bhutan

Since Bhutan first commenced modernization of its economy, the nation has interacted with other countries with regard to trade and development. Energy, in particular, has been a source of income for Bhutan, as well as being central to improvement of the livelihoods and domestic situation of the Bhutanese people. The result has been that Bhutan, as in the case of other nations, has been subjected to environmental impacts associated with energy generation and use. Uddin *et al.* (2007) have looked at Bhutan's energy and environmental approaches to development. Aspects of this research are overviewed further below.

Bhutan has abundant renewable sources in the form of water and forest resources. Notwithstanding this, both fossil fuel and renewable resources, in the form of fuelwood, imported petroleum products, and hydropower, are used in Bhutan for energy. The Power System Master Plan gives an estimate of Bhutan's overall hydropower potential as 30,000 MW, with production capacity of about 120,000 GWh; however, the hydropower capacity in 2017 was only 1,488 MW – this capacity will increase significantly with completion of the Punatsangchhu I, Punatsangchhu II, and Mangdechhu hydropower projects (RGB and JICA, 2017). Other renewable resources used in Bhutan, albeit on a small scale, include micro/mini hydropower (<1 MW), solar photovoltaics (PV), biogas, and wind power (Uddin, 2001). In particular, rural and isolated areas of the nation where there is no electricity grid have started to benefit from electricity generated from renewable resources, and 100% rural electrification is planned for Bhutan by 2020 (RGB, 2002; ADC, 2005). In 2003, 99.5% of the nation's electricity was hydroelectric-based; total electricity demand was 664 GWh (105 MW) (Tshering and Tamang, 2004) and total electricity demand

grew to 990 GWh in 2007/2008 (Lhendup *et al.*, 2010). Per capita electricity consumption in Bhutan grew by 50% from 610 kWh in 1997–1998 (Tshering and Tamang, 2004) to 1,141 kWh in 2005–2006 (Lhendup, 2008). Bhutan had a total installed hydropower plant capacity of 1,497 MW in 2009, and projects are underway to install 11,576 MW in 2009–2020 (Lhendup *et al.*, 2010).

In relation to the readily accessible hydropower for electricity, and forest resources, Bhutan has experienced environmental impacts. Pressures on local fuelwood availability and impacts of hydroelectric development have occurred (UNEP, 2001).

About 75% of total electricity generated from hydropower schemes in Bhutan is sold to India, and this is Bhutan's major contributor to national revenue. Hydropower exported to India contributed around 45% of government revenues in 2000–2001 (Kezang and Whalley, 2004), and electricity exports contributed 12% of GDP in 2006 (Lhendup, 2008). Further development of the energy sector is seen by the RGB to be essential, and Bhutan's development plans have focused strongly on energy. In the Ninth Five-Year Plan, development strategies relevant to the energy sector included the following: (1) creation of an enabling environment for energy sector development – especially goals for new hydropower schemes; (2) rural electrification; (3) strengthening of institutional capacity; (4) automation of generation, transmission, and distribution of electricity; (5) determination of tariff systems; (6) preparation of an Energy and Water Resources Master Plan; and (7) further construction of the electricity transmission grid network (RGB, 2002). Energy conservation and efficiency projects were also included in the plan. The Tenth Five-Year Plan had goals to provide electricity to all by 2013, increase GDP contribution of the energy sector to more than 15%, enhance the revenue contribution from hydropower to 36% of national revenue, and expand hydropower to 1,602 MW by 2013.

The Gross National Happiness Commission (GNHC) coordinates Bhutan's sustainable development, while the National Environment Commission coordinates, oversees, and monitors environmental activities (NEC, 2005a). The NEC monitors the environmental impact issues associated with the nation's various development activities and oversees compliance (NEC, 2005a). The long-term objectives of the NEC include formulation and implementation of policies, plans, and actions for the sustainability of Bhutan's natural resources, including addressing climate change, water, and waste. The NEC Secretariat also oversees Bhutan's obligations to numerous regional and global environmental conventions and treaties (NEC, 2005a). To ensure an effective environmental conservation programme, Bhutan has initiated a unique environmental trust fund, the Bhutan Trust Fund for Environment Conservation (BTFEC). The BTFEC was established in 1991 as a sustainable, domestic funding source for Bhutan's environmental programmes (Namgyal, 2001).

Bhutan's current environmental strategies focus on the conservation of natural resources, including forest and water resources, and the protection of wildlife and their habitats. The National Environment Strategy (NEC, 1998) provides guidance on the nation's major environmental policies. It includes policy on hydropower schemes, given their importance to Bhutan (NEC, 2005b). The National Environment Protection Act 2007 provides an effective system to conserve and protect the environment (RGB, 2007), while the Environment Assessment Act 2000 and its regulations require sectors, including the hydropower sector, to conduct their works as per the Act and Regulations (NEC, 2004). Additionally, forestry legislation and policies, including the 1991 Forest Policy of Bhutan (RGB, 1991), have been framed to ensure that forest resources are used according to sustainability principles.

Bhutan's strong commitment to protect the environment and to follow the Middle Path of development has resulted in the implementation of several sustainable energy demonstration projects, including the following:

- The Improved Community Cooking Stoves Project – An Alternative to Mitigate Fuel Wood Pressure in Trashigang, and the Biomass Fuel Efficiency Project funded under the Global Environment Facility (GEF) Small Grants Programme (SGP) (Norbu and Giri, 2004);
- A solar energy project initiated in 2003 by the Solar Electric Light Fund (SELF) with support from the RGB, the Bhutanese Royal Society for the Protection of Nature, Tshungmed Solar, Inc., the Bhutan Development Finance Corporation, and the Bhutan Trust Fund (SELF, 2003);
- The Promoting Sustainable Rural Biomass Energy project was initiated by the GEF in 2009 and will be implemented by the Department of Energy, Royal Government of Bhutan. This project aims to remove barriers to sustainable utilization of available biomass resources in the country and application of biomass energy technologies that will support economic and social development in country's rural sector, in order to reduce greenhouse gas emissions;
- The e7 Micro-Hydropower Project – Bhutan has hosted one of the earlier small-scale Clean Development Mechanism (CDM) projects under the Kyoto Protocol in a remote area of the country. This 70-kW, small-scale hydro project has been in operation generating electricity since 2005 (Ikoma and Tshering, 2005; Dwivedi, 2005);
- The Dagachhu hydropower plant – a 114-MW-capacity hydropower plant under CDM – has been in operation since 2015 generating 500 GWh of electricity per annum at a plant load factor of 50% and thus is expected to reduce 498,998 tCO_2/

year during its first seven years of operation (DNV, 2010; Dagachhu Hydro Power Corporation Limited, 2018).

To date, Bhutan has been attempting to carefully monitor development and use of its natural assets and to prevent environmental impacts – via the NEC's work discussed earlier – together with monitoring via State of the Environment reporting (see, for example, NEC, 2005a, 2005b, 2016, 2017). However, one step that has not been taken to date is formulation and implementation of a comprehensive national sustainable energy strategy. This would be in accord with the Gross National Happiness approach and would assist in planning, financing, and facilitation of further sustainable energy development.

Bhutan made a commitment to remain carbon neutral at UNFCCC COP10 in Copenhagen for all time to come and to maintain forest cover of 60% in perpetuity, as per the Constitution of Bhutan. This further endorses Bhutan's assigning importance to Gross National Happiness over GDP (NEC, 2016).

10.6 DISCUSSION

On O'Riordan and Voisey's (1998) continuum of sustainable development from very soft to very strong, Thailand's experience to date has been at the soft end, but the constitutional, strategic, and administrative framework, established after the 1997 crash under the auspices of Sufficiency Economy and still in use, is nonetheless an example of considerable interest. Significant sustainability steps were taken in decentralization of decision-making to the local level and encouragement of community participation. Bhutan is currently at the stronger end of O'Riordan and Voisey's (1998) continuum. It is a tiny nation but its example is powerful for other developing nations whose culture and environments have been threatened by development that is not sustainable.

Comparison of these countries' experiences with Milbrath's (1989) learning governance framework shows that aspects of his recommendations (sustainability education and information systems, futures thinking capability, stakeholder involvement, and long-range impact assessment of all policies) were taken up in Thailand and with regard to Local Agenda 21, and in Bhutan with energy and environmental decision-making. Also, Bossel's (1998) Four Ss (sustainability, subsidiarity, self-organization, and sufficiency) arguably have been seriously addressed in Bhutan and Thailand.

Bhutanese uncertainties that may influence its future direction are as follows: first, the country's governance as a fledgling democracy, with political transition from a monarchy having occurred only in 2008; and second, the effect of communications – satellite TV and Internet – on values. It is hard to predict Bhutan's actual future with regard to sustainability, but the nation is seriously implementing policies based on Gross National Happiness and the Middle Way.

In contrast, Thailand is far more developed economically than Bhutan. However, it continues to suffer from political instability. Democracy, accountability, and transparency remain yet to be achieved for the nation.

10.7 CONCLUSIONS

Thailand and Bhutan have forward-looking sustainable development policy approaches. This can be seen in their adoption of Sufficiency Economy and Gross National Happiness, respectively, and in their addressing of sustainable development in government planning and procedures. They are striving to balance sustainability with the pursuit of affluence and increasing standards of living.

Arguably, the key difference between developed nations' implementation of sustainable development and that of the experience of Bhutan and Thailand, discussed in this chapter, is that sufficiency is not addressed as seriously in the developed world. At the level of the individual, having 'too much', with regard to wealth, assets, or consumption, is not a matter that is generally seen as a problem. Sufficiency is an important principle that developed nations are neglecting, and yet it is a principle that all nations need to adopt to move towards sustainability.

Furtherance of sustainability will be a significant political challenge for Thailand and Bhutan over the next few decades, as it will be for all nations. Thailand has difficult governance issues to resolve. It is hoped that their resolution may be driven by the philosophy of Sufficiency Economy to provide a basis for a stable democracy and future sustainable development. As Sachayansrisakul (2009) has commented:

> [I]f Thailand seriously implemented this economic philosophy, the … problems of instability, poverty, and socioeconomic conflicts would be alleviated and the well-being of the Thai people as a whole would be improved. (p. 1)

Also, the continuing advancement of the Gross National Happiness approach in Bhutan may have its successes and disappointments, but the experiences of this tiny nation are well-worth watching.

ACKNOWLEDGEMENTS

The four reviewers of this chapter, Dr Charit Tingsabadh (Chulalongkorn University, Thailand), Dr Jamba Gyeltshen (Royal University of Bhutan), and two anonymous reviewers, are thanked with much appreciation for their helpful suggestions. Dr Anna Lyth, University of Tasmania, is gratefully acknowledged for her advice on environmental planning and Local Agenda 21 implementation. Our appreciation is also extended to Honorary Associate Professor Xiaojiang Yu, University of Sydney, for his contributions with regard to sustainable energy policy. The authors also wish to thank Dr David Annandale, Murdoch University, and Anders Arvidson, Stockholm Environment Institute, for their kind assistance in provision of information with regard to Bhutan. Additionally, the authors acknowledge the useful information given by representatives of Thailand's Ministry of Foreign Affairs, Ministry of Interior, Ministry of Natural Resources and Environment (Office of Natural Resources and Environment Policy and Planning; Department of Environmental Quality Promotion; Provincial Office for Natural Resources and Environment; and Regional Environmental Office), Office of the National Economic and Social Development Board, Lamphun and Nakhon Ratchasima town halls and municipalities, and the Thailand Environment Institute, an NGO.

REFERENCES

ADC (2005) *Bhutan Subprogram Energy 2005–2007: Support of Rural Energy, Hydropower Generation and Capacity Building.* Vienna, Austrian Development Cooperation.

Bossel, H. (1998) *Earth at a Crossroads: Paths to a Sustainable Future.* Cambridge, Cambridge University Press.

Bothe, W. (2015) In the name of king, country, and people on the Westminster model and Bhutan's constitutional transition. *Democratization,* **22**(7), 1,338–1,361.

Bowornwathana, B. (2002) Governance reform in Thailand: Questionable assumptions, uncertain outcomes. *Governance,* **13**(3), 393–408.

CBS (Centre for Bhutan Studies) (2017) *Happiness, Transforming the Development Landscape.* Thimphu.

Chaipattana Foundation and TDRI (Thailand Development Research Institute) (1999) From crisis to sustainable development. *TDRI Quarterly Review,* **14**(1), 10–20.

Chaipattana Foundation (2000) Sufficiency Economy. *Chaipattana Foundation Journal,* December. https://www.chaipat.or.th/publication/journal/cpf-journal-1.html?start=60 (accessed 18 September 2020)

Dagachhu Hydro Power Corporation Limited (2018) *UNFCCC Monitoring Report 2017.* Bhutan, Dagachhu Hydropower Project. https://cdm.unfccc.int/filestorage/J/W/B/JWBXG80RK1L9C5FHD3Y4A6EZ2POM7Q/MR.pdf?t=N298cWd1cHNsfDCE--YuEham7BD5_iIy6ngB (accessed 18 September 2020)

Daniere, A. and Takahashi, M. L. (2002) *Rethinking Environmental Management in the Pacific Rim: Exploring Local Participation in Bangkok, Thailand.* Burlington, VT, Ashgate Publishing.

Department of Environmental Quality Promotion (n.d.) *A Guideline to Sustainable Development.* Bangkok.

(2002a) *Korat Municipality towards Sustainable Development: Local Agenda 21 in Thailand*. Final Report of the Thai-Swedish Cooperation Programme on Local Agenda 21. Bangkok.

(2002b) *Trang Municipality towards Sustainable Development: Local Agenda 21 in Thailand*. Final Report of the Thai-Swedish Cooperation Programme on Local Agenda 21. Bangkok.

DNV (Det Norske Veritas) (2010) Validation report Dagachhu Hydropower project in Bhutan. Report No. 2006–0614. http:// cdm.unfccc.int/Projects/DB/DNV-CUK1247228633.76/view (accessed 24 September 2018)

Dryzek, J. (2005) *The Politics of the Earth: Environmental Discourses* (2nd ed). Oxford, Oxford University Press.

Dwivedi, P. O. (1996) Satyagraha for conservation: Awakening the spirit of Hinduism. In S. R. Gottlieb (ed.), *This Sacred Earth: Religion, Nature, Environment*, pp. 151–163. New York, Routledge.

e7 (2005) *e7 Bhutan Micro Hydropower CDM Project*. Project Design Document, e7 Fund for Sustainable Energy Development, UNFCCC Secretariat. http://cdm.unfccc.int/Projects/DB/ JACO1113389887.76/view (accessed 24 September 2018)

Frame, B. (2005) Bhutan: A review of its approach to sustainable development. *Development in Practice*, **15**(2), 216–221.

Giri, S. (2004) *The Vital Link: Monpas and Their Forests*. Thimphu, The Centre for Bhutan Studies. https://dorjipenjore.files .wordpress.com/2015/09/the-vital-linkc2a0-monpas-and-their-forests.pdf (accessed 13 January 2019)

Government of Thailand (2002) *Speech of Princess Chulabhorn Mahidol*. Johannesburg, World Summit on Sustainable Development.

(2016) *A Practical Approach toward Sustainable Development: Thailand's Sufficiency Economy Philosophy*. Bangkok, Ministry of Foreign Affairs. https://data.opendevelopment mekong.net/en/dataset/a-practical-approach-toward-sustainable-development-thailand-s-sufficiency-economy-philosophy/ resource/d566301e-1f2a-4344–8837-68d7e6d27112?inner_ span=True (accessed 13 January 2019)

Gregson, J. (2000) Interview of King Jigme Wangchuck. In *Kingdoms Beyond the Clouds: Journeys in Search of the Himalayan Kings*. London, Macmillan.

Hewison, K. (2002) Responding to economic crisis: Thailand's localism. In D. McCargo (ed.), *Reforming Thai Politics*. pp. 143–162. Copenhagen, Nordic Institute of Asian Studies.

Ikoma, M. and Tshering, K. (2005) *Lessons from e7 Bhutan Micro Hydro Power CDM Project*. In *e7 Open Forum at COP11/ MOP1*, Montreal.

International Council for Local Environmental Initiatives (2002) *Second Local Agenda 21 Survey, Background Paper No. 15*, submitted to Commission on Sustainable Development, UN Department of Economic and Social Affairs, New York. https://divinefreedomradio.files.wordpress.com/2013/10/ sustainabledevelopment2nd-prepsession.pdf (accessed 24 September 2018)

IWRAW (International Women's Rights Action Watch) (1997) *Country Report: Thailand*. http://hrlibrary.umn.edu/iwraw/ publications/countries/thailand.htm (accessed 13 January 2019)

Kezang, K. and Whalley, J. (2004) Telecommunications in the land of the thunder dragon: recent developments in Bhutan. *Telecommunications Policy*, **28**(11), 785–800.

Kingdom of Bhutan and JICA (Japan International Cooperation Agency) (2019) Project on Power System Master Plan 2040: Final Report. https://openjicareport.jica.go.jp/pdf/12326856_ 01.pdf (accessed 18 September 2020)

Klausner, J. W. (2002) *Thai Culture in Transition*. Bangkok, Amarin Printing and Publishing.

Klein, R. J. (2003) Public participation and hearings in the new Thai political context. In J. K. Haller and P. Siroros (eds.), *Legal Foundations for Public Consultation in Government Decision-Making*, pp. 113–129. Bangkok, Executive Public Administration Foundation, Thammasat University.

Leknoi, U. (2017) Analysis of the critical success factors that affect the implementation of Local Agenda 21 in Thailand. *Journal of International Buddhist Studies*, **8**(1), 82–98.

Lhendup, T. (2008) Rural electrification in Bhutan and a methodology for evaluation of distributed generation system as an alternative option for rural electrification. *Energy for Sustainable Development*, **12**(3), 13–24.

Lhendup, T., Lhundup, S. and Wangchuk, T. (2010) Domestic energy consumption patterns in urban Bhutan. *Energy for Sustainable Development*, **14**, 134–142.

LIFE Partners (2002) *A Guide for Local Agenda 21 in Thailand*. Stockholm, LIFE Partners Sweden.

Lustig, R. (Presenter) (22 June 2006) Bhutan's Policy of Happiness. *Assignment* (radio programme), 22 minutes (Guest speaker: Jigme Thinley). London, BBC World Service. https://www .bbc.co.uk/programmes/p03ghvrv (accessed 17 December 2018)

McCargo, D. (2004) Buddhism, democracy and identity in Thailand. *Democratization*, **11**(4), 155–170.

(2014) Competing notions of judicialization in Thailand. *Contemporary Southeast Asia: A Journal of International and Strategic Affairs*, **36**(3), 417–441.

Milbrath, L. (1989) *Envisioning a Sustainable Society: Learning Our Way Out*. Albany, NY, SUNY Press.

Namgyal, T. S. (2001) Sustaining conservation finance: Future directions for the Bhutan Trust Fund for Environmental Conservation. *The Journal of Bhutan Studies*, **3**(1), 48–82.

National Statistical Office (2018) Population Survey and Housing. Bangkok, Government of Thailand. http://statbbi .nso.go.th/staticreport/page/sector/en/01.aspx (accessed 24 September 2018)

NEC (1997) *Biodiversity Action Plan for Bhutan*. Thimphu, National Environment Commission, Royal Government of Bhutan.

(1998) *National Environment Strategy*. Thimphu, National Environment Commission, Royal Government of Bhutan.

(2004) *Application for Environmental Clearance: Guidelines for Hydropower*. Thimphu, National Environment Commission, Royal Government of Bhutan.

(2005a) *Brief State of the Environment*. Thimphu, National Environment Commission, Royal Government of Bhutan.

(2005b) *A Brief Report on Bhutan's State of Environment for Fiscal Year 2004–2005*. Thimphu, National Environment Commission, Royal Government of Bhutan.

(2016) *Bhutan State of Environment 2016*. Thimphu, National Environment Commission, Royal Government of Bhutan.

(2017) *Bhutan State of Environment at Glance*. Thimphu, National Environment Commission, Royal Government of Bhutan.

Norbu, U. P. and Giri, S. (2004) Working with rural communities to conserve wood energy: a case study from Bhutan. In S. Chamsuk, K. Rijal and M. Takada (eds.), *Energy for Sustainable Development in Asia and the Pacific Region*, pp. 23–31. New York, United Nations Development Programme.

Ockey, J. (2007) Thailand's 'professional soldiers' and coup-making: the coup of 2006. *Crossroads: An Interdisciplinary Journal of Southeast Asian Studies*, 19(1), 95–127.

OECD (2001) *The DAC Guidelines for Sustainable Development*. Organization for Economic Cooperation and Development. http://www.oecd.org/dataoecd/34/10/2669958.pdf (accessed 24 September 2018)

(2002) *Sustainable Development Strategies: A Resource Book*. New York, Earthscan Publications.

Office of the Council of State (Government of Thailand) (1997) *Constitution of Thailand*. Bangkok.

Office of the National Economic and Social Development Board (2002) *The Ninth National Economic and Social Development Plan (2002–2006)*. Bangkok, Kurusapa Press.

O'Riordan, T. and Voisey, H. (1998) *The Transition to Sustainability: The Politics of Agenda 21 in Europe*. London, Earthscan.

Pasuk, P. and Baker, C. J. (2002) *Thailand, Economy and Politics*. Oxford, Oxford University Press.

Pibalsook, K. (2007) *An Assessment of the Application of Local Agenda 21 in Thailand for Improving Environmental Policy and Planning*. PhD thesis. Sydney, Graduate School of the Environment, Macquarie University.

Pibalsook, K., Taplin, R. and Lyth, A. (2003) Assessing Local Agenda 21 Policy and Planning in Thailand. *Ecopolitics XV International Conference: Environmental Governance: Transforming Regions and Localities*, 12–14 November, Sydney, Graduate School of the Environment, Macquarie University.

RGB (Royal Government of Bhutan) (1991) *Forest Policy of Bhutan*. Thimphu, Ministry of Agriculture.

(1999) *Bhutan 2020: A Vision for Peace, Prosperity and Happiness*. Thimphu, Planning Commission.

(2002) *Ninth Five-Year Plan 2002–2007*. Thimphu, Planning Commission.

(2006) *Results of Population and Housing Census of Bhutan 2005*. Thimphu, Office of the Census Commissioner. http://www.nsb.gov.bt/publication/files/pub6ri44cs.pdf (accessed 17 December 2018)

(2007) *National Environmental Protection Act*. Thimphu, Government of Bhutan.

(2013) *11th Five-Year Plan 2013–2018*. https://www.gnhc.gov.bt/12rtm/wp-content/uploads/2013/10/Eleventh-Five-Year-Plan-Volume-I-Final.pdf [accessed 24 September 2018]

(2017a) *Forest Facts and Figures, 2017*. Thimphu, Department of Forests and Park Services, Ministry of Agriculture and Forests.

(2017b) *National Forestry Inventory*, Vol. 1. Thimphu, Department of Forests and Park Services, Ministry of Agriculture and Forests.

(2017c) *Statistical Year Book of Bhutan 2017*. Thimphu, National Statistical Bureau.

(2017d) *12th Five-Year Plan Guideline*. https://www.gnhc.gov.bt/en/wp-content/uploads/2017/05/gnh.pdf (accessed 24 September 2018)

(2018) *2017 Population and Housing Census of Bhutan*. Thimphu, National Statistical Bureau.

Rigg, J. (2003) *Southeast Asia: The Human Landscape of Modernization and Development*. London, Routledge.

Sachayansrisakul, N. (2009) Sufficiency Economy: A reasonable approach for Thailand's future. *NIDA Development Journal*, 49(2), 1–22.

Schumacher, E. F. (1973) *Small Is Beautiful: A Study of Economics as if People Mattered*. London, Abacus (1974 edition).

SELF (Solar Electric Light Fund) (2003) *A Solar Energy Project in Bhutan*. Washington, DC.

Sopranzetti, C. (2016) Thailand's relapse: The implications of the May 2014 coup. *The Journal of Asian Studies*, 75(2), 299–316.

Sponsel, L. E. and Natadecha-Sponsel, P. (1993) The potential contribution of Buddhism in developing an environmental ethic for the conservation of biodiversity. In L. S. Hamilton and H. F. Takeuchi (eds.), *Ethics, Religion, and Biodiversity: Relations Between Conservation and Cultural Values*, pp. 75–97. Cambridge, White Horse Press.

Suwannathat-Pian, K. (2002) The monarchy and constitutional change since 1972. In D. McCargo (ed.), *Reforming Thai Politics*, pp. 57–72. Copenhagen, Nordic Institute of Asian Studies.

Sterling, S. (2001) *Sustainable Education: Re-Visioning Learning and Change*. Foxhole, Devon, UK, Green Books.

Thabchumpon, N. and McCargo, D. (2011) Urbanized villagers in the 2010 Thai Redshirt Protests. *Asian Survey*, 51(6), 993–1,018.

Tilbury, D. (2004) *Action Research for Change Towards Sustainability: Change in Curricula and Graduate Skills Workshop Notes*. Sydney, Graduate School of the Environment, Macquarie University.

Tonami, A. and Mori, A. (2007) Sustainable development in Thailand: Lessons from implementing Local Agenda 21 in three cities. *Journal of Environment and Development*, **16**(3), 269–289.

Tshering, S. and Tamang, B. (2004) Hydropower – Key to sustainable, socio-economic development of Bhutan. In *United Nations Symposium on Hydropower and Sustainable Development*, Beijing, UNDESA, 27–29 October. http://www.academia .edu/36260182/Hydropower_-Key_to_sustainable_socio-economic_development_of_Bhutan (accessed 13 January 2019)

Uddin, S . N. (2001) Renewable energy in South Asia. *Asian Energy News*, Special Issue. Bangkok, Asian Institute of Technology.

Uddin, S. N, Taplin, R. and Yu, X. (2007) Energy, environment and development in Bhutan. *Renewable and Sustainable Energy Reviews*, **11**(9), 2083–2103.

UNEP (United Nations Environment Programme) (2001) State of the Environment Bhutan 2001. UNEP Regional and Resource Centre for Asia and the Pacific, Bangkok. http://www.sacep .org/pdf/Reports-Technical/2001-State-of-Environment-Report-Bhutan.pdf (accessed 24 September 2018)

Ura, K. and Galay, K. (2004) Preface. In K. Ura and K. Galay (eds.), *Gross National Happiness and Development: Proceedings of the First International Conference on Operationalization of Gross National Happiness*. Thimphu, Centre for Bhutan Studies. http:// www.grossnationalhappiness.com/gnh-and-development/ (accessed 24 September 2018)

Vichitranuja, N., Stotlar, D., Samahito, S., Noikasem, S. and Nitiphon, N. (2018) State-owned golf course management model: Case study of Suanson Pradipat applying Sufficiency Economy Philosophy towards sustainable development. *National Defence Studies Institute Journal*, **9**(3). https://www .tci-thaijo.org/index.php/ndsijournal/index

WB (World Bank) (2017) *Bhutan at a Glance*. Washington, DC, 12 October. http://www.worldbank.org/en/country/bhutan/ overview (accessed 24 September 2018)

WCED (World Commission on Environment and Development) (1987) *Our Common Future*. Oxford, Oxford University Press.

Young, J. (1992) *Post Environmentalism*. London, Belhaven.

11 The sustainability of food production in Papua New Guinea

BRYANT J. ALLEN AND R. MICHAEL BOURKE

College of Asia and the Pacific, Australian National University, Canberra, Australia

Keywords

Papua New Guinea; food production systems; imported food; global climate change; HIV/AIDS; population growth; ENSO; shifting cultivation; land degradation; cash incomes; governance

Abstract

More than 80% of the people of Papua New Guinea (PNG) live in rural areas and produce most of the calories they consume. The rest comes from imported food, mainly rice and wheat. An estimated 83% of all food energy consumed in PNG in 2006 was derived from locally grown food. Rapid population change, an HIV/AIDS epidemic, and global climate change are the main threats to the sustainable production of this food into the future. Rapid population change threatens to bring about land degradation in shifting cultivation systems; also, HIV/AIDS will slow population growth but will selectively remove working-age people from the population, while the outcomes of global warming are less certain. Global warming is apparent in rises in temperatures and some observable changes in plant distributions. If global climate change increases the frequency of El Niño-Southern Oscillation (ENSO) events, then food production will be adversely affected. On the other hand, global warming may have some positive effects. Governance in PNG is poor, so rural people will have to face the outcomes of these three threats largely using their own resources of resilience, innovativeness, and hard work.

11.1 INTRODUCTION

This chapter is concerned with the sustainability of the production of food in Papua New Guinea (PNG), food that is critical to both the well-being of the majority of PNG's people and the national economy. The three major threats to the sustainability of food production in PNG are rapid population growth, an HIV/AIDS epidemic, and global climate change. First PNG's

food production systems and the environmental factors that influence them are described. The main features of population growth, the HIV epidemic, and climate change are then described. The possible impacts of these changes on sustainable food production are discussed. Finally, the capacity of the PNG state to respond to these challenges to food production is assessed.

11.1.1 Papua New Guinea: history

During the last years of the nineteenth century, colonial powers divided the large island of New Guinea into three parts (Moore, 2003). By 1884, the western half had become part of the Dutch East Indies and now comprises two provinces of Indonesia known as Papua and Papua Barat; northeast New Guinea and the Bismarck Archipelago became a German colony with an administrative headquarters in Rabaul; and the south-east mainland became a British colony until 1906, when it became the Australian Territory of Papua, administered from Port Moresby. In 1914, Australia invaded the German colony and in 1921 was given New Guinea to administer as a League of Nations Mandate. Until 1942, when Japanese forces occupied most of New Guinea, New Guinea and Papua were administered separately as a mandated territory and a colony, respectively, by Australia. In 1942, they were placed under a single Australian military command with a headquarters in Port Moresby. After the war, Papua and New Guinea were administered by Australia as a single territory until self-government in 1973 and independence in 1975, when it became Papua New Guinea (Figure 11.1).

In both the German and the British colonies, early attempts to clear lowland rainforest to grow field crops failed after a few years because of pests, diseases, and rapid loss of soil fertility. The most important commercial agricultural activity became the production of copra from existing village plantings and newly established plantations, located on high-quality land, near good harbours. Labour was brought to the plantations under indenture systems from areas of poorer-quality land. After the Pacific War, coffee, cocoa, and oil palm were rapidly adopted by villagers as

Figure 11.1. Papua New Guinea: locations.

cash crops, such that today villagers produce most of the coffee and cocoa exported. All of the colonial administrations recognized the concept of 'customary' land tenure, in which the people of PNG occupy their land under 'custom', so that today more than 95% of the total land area remains in the legal control of customary land-owning groups.

In 1966, the first complete PNG census counted 2.15 million inhabitants. By 1990 there were 3.76 million. The most recent census in 2011 counted 7.1 million people, 87% of whom lived in rural areas. In 2017, only Burundi had a greater proportion of people living in rural areas than PNG (World Bank, 2018).

It is somewhat ironic that agriculture probably began in PNG as a result of global warming. Archaeological evidence suggests that around 10,000 years ago, global warming coincided with the beginnings of agriculture in PNG (Denham *et al.*, 2004). *Colocasia* taro starch has been identified on stone tools that are thought to be 10,000 years old. There is evidence in the pollen record of secondary growth species of forest clearing taking place at least 7,000 years ago. From 7,000 years ago, the evidence for agriculture is stronger: bananas were being cultivated and archaeological features suggest tilling and localized

drainage. Between 4,000 and 2,500 years ago, extensive swamp drainage was being carried out in a number of locations. Clearly, PNG food production systems are very old and have been developed and sustained by people who have proven themselves to be energetic, innovative, and resilient. This chapter concludes that they are going to need all these qualities to meet the present-day challenges of global warming.

11.1.2 The PNG economy

PNG has a dual economy. The monetary sector depends heavily on the export of minerals (mostly gold and copper), oil, and LNG, which brings in 72% of foreign earnings, and agricultural products (mainly palm oil, coffee, and cocoa), which makes up around 25% of foreign earnings. Arguably, however, the most important part of the PNG economy is the non-monetary food production sector, which provides 80% of the food energy consumed in PNG (Gibson, 2001). The balance is imported, mostly as rice and wheat, but fish, meat, fats, and oils are also imported. Urban people obtain half their food energy from imported food, while rural people rely on imported food for only 16% of their food energy.

The proportion of food energy gained from locally grown food has almost certainly increased in the past decade, because imports of rice and wheat are static and per person consumption is falling. A decline in the value of the PNG currency against foreign currencies from around 1997 has caused the price of imported food to increase substantially.

Bourke and Vlassak (2004) estimated that 4.5 million tonnes of energy (staple) foods are grown in PNG each year, which is a little more than one tonne per rural person per year. Although most of this agricultural production was consumed by its producers, in monetary terms it was worth around US$870 million in 2004. A small proportion of this food is marketed in large urban centres and across the country in markets of all sizes. Fresh food sales provide monetary incomes for a greater number of rural people than any other rural activity. However, many of the people who produce this food also produce the majority of the coffee and cocoa exported from PNG, and in doing so they blur the boundaries between the monetary and the non-monetary sectors of the economy.

11.2 AGRICULTURAL ENVIRONMENTS

PNG is a mountainous country; 52% of the total land area is classified as mountains and hills and 48% of the population live on mountains or hills (McAlpine and Quigley, n.d.). Less than 1% of the total land area is classed as 'very high quality land' and almost 60% as 'low' or 'very low'-quality land (Hanson *et al.*, 2001). Poor-quality land is higher, steeper, has higher rainfall, floods more often, is cloudier, and has less fertile soils than better-quality land. Altitude is the main influence on temperatures (Table 11.1). Temperature is also influenced by latitude, or distance from the equator; the further away from the equator, the greater the range in temperatures during the year.

The ideal annual rainfall for many tropical crops is 1,500 mm to 3,000 mm. Most of the rural people of PNG live in places where annual rainfall is in the range of 1,800–3,500 mm. Population densities are lower in wetter areas because localities where the annual rainfall is more than 4,000 mm tend to be too wet and have too much cloud cover for good agricultural production. In many parts of PNG, most rain falls between January and April, and the least rain falls between May and August. In some parts of the country this pattern is reversed, and in other parts, rain is received all year round and has no seasonal pattern. There are no parts of PNG that are dry all year round. From time to time, however, PNG experiences periods of uncharacteristically low rainfall that are associated with the El Niño-Southern Oscillation (ENSO) phenomenon. These events can seriously disrupt food production. The most recent such events occurred in 1997–1998 and in 2015–2016.

Soil water has an important influence on agricultural systems. Where rainfall is high and regular, soils are usually saturated and must be drained for agricultural use. Where seasonal soil water deficits occur, a number of techniques are used to overcome the lack of soil water. The most common technique is to plant a mix of different crop species. Irrigation in PNG has never been common and is now practised in only one location.

PNG is a very cloudy country; between 2 p.m. and 4 p.m. from December to February and from June to August, the skies over most of the country are up to 63% cloud covered (5 oktas). Mountain areas have consistently heavier cloud cover. In areas of seasonal rainfall, cloud cover is greatest during the wetter season. The highlands have lower sunshine than other parts of the country, ranging from four hours per day to six hours per day, but most places in PNG are likely to receive some sunshine every day.

Table 11.1. Altitude classes, associated maximum and minimum temperatures, area of land in use and population, Papua New Guinea, 2018.

Altitude Class (m asl)	Maximum temperature (°C)	Minimum temperature (°C)	Land in use (km²)	%	Estimated 2018 rural population[1]	%
0–600	32–30	23–19	73,531	63	3,463,382	51
600–1,200	30–27	19–16	16,766	14	462,209	7
1,200–1,800	27–23	16–12	18,844	16	1,919,284	28
1,800–2,400	23–19	12–9	7,126	6	770,990	11
2,400–2,800	19–16	9–7	1,591	1	156,609	2
>2,800	<16	<7	0	0	0	0
			117,858	100	6,772,474	100

Source: Bellamy and McAlpine (1995)

Note 1: Population estimate extrapolated from PNG National Census 2000. The 2011 National Census was the latest and was declared a 'failure' (see elsewhere in the text).

Agricultural environments can be assessed by examining constraints critical to food production. Here we use three constraints to growing sweet potato, the most common source of food: altitude (as a surrogate for temperature), soil-water deficit, and flooding. When all possible combinations of these constraints are combined, 15 environments are identified, one of which is a very high-altitude environment that is presently uninhabited and not used for agriculture.

More than half of all rural PNGeans live in lowlands environments (below 600 m). A further 28% of the rural population live in highlands environments (1,200–1,800 m) and 13% in high-altitude environments (1,800–2,800 m), leaving only 7% in intermediate-altitude environments (600–1,200 m). Of those who live in lowland environments, around 70% favour environments which do not flood and which do not have a strong soil-water deficit. Across the country, flooding is associated with very low population densities. In highland environments, population densities are higher where there is a moderate soil-water deficit and no flooding.

11.3 FOOD PRODUCTION SYSTEMS AND CROPS

PNG food production systems use only human labour and almost no external inputs. All food is produced from systems that use fallowing of land to maintain soil fertility, the main differentiating factor between systems being the intensity with which land is used. Land-use intensities range from very low extensive forest fallow systems to higher intensity, almost permanent cultivation, using frequent short cycle grass fallows within a much longer tall grass and scrub fallow cycle.

Two different estimates are available of the most important sources of food in PNG. The first is the 1996 PNG Household Income and Expenditure Survey, which collected information on all food consumed by 1,200 households in 73 rural and 47 urban census units (Gibson, 2001) (Table 11.2). The second is the Mapping Agricultural Systems in PNG project (Allen et al., 1995) (Table 11.3), which used field observations in all districts in PNG between 1990 and 1996, to estimate the relative importance of food plants growing in village gardens. Both surveys found the most important food crop species were sweet potato, banana, Colocasia taro, Xanthosoma taro, yam, cassava, sago, potato, and coconuts.

In order to assess the possible impacts of global climate change on food production, it is necessary to examine the most important ecological features of the main food plants.

Sweet potato (Ipomoea batatas) was introduced, probably from Indonesia around AD 1700, and was widely adopted in the highlands. It displaced taro as the most important food in the highlands and by 1940 was providing an estimated 40% of food energy from locally grown staple foods. It now provides around 65% of food energy. Sweet potato production depends on the numbers and size of tubers: the number of tubers produced is determined between four and twelve weeks after planting in what is known as the 'tuberization' phase of the plant's development; tuber weight is determined between 20 and 35 weeks after planting during what is known as the 'rapid tuber bulking' phase. Tuberization is depressed by saturated soil-water conditions and tuber bulking by soil-water deficits (Lowe and Wilson, 1974; Wilson, 1982). At higher altitudes, frost is an additional occasional constraint to sweet potato production.

Table 11.2. Proportion of the population consuming particular foods (National Household Survey, 1996).

Food	Rural (%)	Urban (%)	PNG (%)
Greens	74.3	78.9	75.0
Sweet potato	65.0	33.6	60.2
Rice (imported)	25.8	87.4	35.1
Banana	33.6	38.7	34.3
Coconut	28.4	34.2	29.2
Colocasia taro and Xanthosoma taro	23.9	9.6	21.7
Sago	13.3	18.9	14.2
Legumes	12.7	7.8	12.0
Yam	12.5	4.8	11.3
Fresh fish, shellfish	7.1	28.2	10.3
Cassava	6.9	4.3	6.5

Source: Gibson (2001)

Note: The survey was conducted in 1996 and it has not been repeated for the whole country.

Table 11.3. Estimated rural population in 2018, producing a particular crop as their most important staple food.

Crop	Estimated 2018 rural population	Percentage of rural population
Sweet potato	4,415,653	65.2
Sago	778,835	11.5
Mixed staples	568,888	8.4
Banana	474,073	7.0
Colocasia taro	338,624	5.0
D. esculenta yam	135,449	2.0
Xanthosoma taro	27,090	0.4
Cassava	20,317	0.3
Coconut	6,772	0.1
Swamp taro	6,772	0.1
	6,772,474	100.0

Source: Bourke and Allen (2009)

Note: Proportions of rural population remain the same in the estimated 2018 rural population data.

Of the other root crops, yam (*Dioscorea* spp) species are grown by 60% of the rural population and the lesser yam (*D. esculenta*) is a staple or sub-staple for 13% of rural villagers. It is grown up to 1,550 m, but most production occurs in the lowlands (Bourke, 2010). Taro (*Colocasia esculenta*) is grown by 95% of rural villagers, but it is now a staple food for only 6% of the rural population, although a further 25% grow it as a sub-staple. Taro is grown from sea level to an altitude of 2,400 m, over a wide range of annual rainfall (1,500 mm to more than 7,000 mm). In the past, taro was the sole staple food in wetter and less seasonal environments. Production has declined since 1940, however, partly because of taro blight (*Phytophthora colocasiae*), which caused a sudden and severe loss of production in some lowland areas after 1940, and partly because of declining soil fertility associated with more intensive land use, virus infections, and taro betel damage. Chinese taro (*Xanthosoma sagittifolia*) is a staple or sub-staple food for 22% of the rural population and grows from sea level to 2,000 m altitude. It is a more important crop in intermediate-altitude locations and intermediate-to-highland locations (500–1,500 m altitude) and in places where rainfall is higher and not seasonal. Chinese taro was introduced into PNG in the late nineteenth century. It increased in importance from 1940 until the 1980s, when a root disease, possibly caused by a fungus (*Pythium* sp), affected production. Cassava (*Manihot esculenta*) is grown by more than half the rural population but is a staple food for only one percent of rural people. Cassava grows from sea level up to 1,800 m but is an important food only in the lowlands. Cassava was introduced into PNG in the nineteenth century but became

more widely grown after 1950. Production is expanding rapidly, with a threefold increase in its relative importance as a food between 1960 and 2000.

Two other sources of food are important. Bananas (*Musa* cvs) are grown from sea level to an altitude of 2,150 m and are a staple food for at least seven percent of rural people. Sago (*Metroxylon sagu*) is produced from cultivated and natural stands of a tall palm in large swamps, or from numerous small stands of between 10 and 20 palms in poorly drained upland sites, up to 1,100 m above sea level. The palm is harvested only once, at maturity, at 12–15 years from planting, when it is cut down and the starch extracted. Sago is almost completely carbohydrate but is a very efficient way of producing energy; sago producers can achieve food energy returns of twenty-three times the energy expended in production (Ulijaszek and Poraituk, 1993).

11.4 THREATS TO SUSTAINABLE FOOD PRODUCTION

A number of threats exist to the sustainability of this food production. The most important is a population doubling time of thirty years that will put pressure on land resources and will increase the possibility of land degradation in particular places. An epidemic of HIV/AIDS will selectively remove working-age people from the PNG population, reducing the supply of labour, which in most PNG food production systems is a greater constraint to food production than land. The less well-defined influences of global climate change may bring about complex and difficult-to-predict changes to PNG food production systems. In this section, present threats are described, and the possible threats from global warming are described in the following section.

11.4.1 Population growth

Determining population growth rates in PNG is somewhat problematic. In the absence of the registration of almost all births and deaths in PNG, estimates of population growth rates must be calculated from censuses. However, if censuses are flawed for any reason, estimates of growth will also be inaccurate. After the 2000 census, the National Statistical Office estimated the annual rate of population growth between 1980 and 2000 to be 2.7% per year. No further breakdown by age, sex, or geographical location was available. Population projections by Booth *et al.* (2006) predicted the rate of increase of the PNG population will decline from 2.29% per year in 2009 to between 2.07% and 1.49% per year by 2029 and that the total PNG population will grow to between 8.9 million and 9.8 million by 2029. These predictions did not take the HIV epidemic into account (see Section 11.4.5).

These figures are close to those predicted by just averaging the between-census population growth rates from 1966 and 2000. The total counted population of PNG has been increasing at between 2.2% and 2.6% per year with an average rate of growth over this period of about 2.5% per year. At this rate of increase, the total population doubles around every 30 years. If the 2000 population continues to increase at 2.5% per year, it will reach around 10 million by 2030, close to the 9.8 million in 2029 predicted by Booth et al. (2006).

The most striking thing about population density in PNG is that around 72% of the total land area is *not* occupied, even though some of this land is used for hunting and collecting wild foods. A further 34% of the total land area is occupied at population densities below 30 persons per km². Only four percent of the total land area is occupied at densities higher than 30 persons per km². The highest population densities occur in the highlands, in the inland East Sepik, on the Gazelle Peninsula in East New Britain, and on many small offshore islands in a number of provinces.

In general, higher population densities are associated with higher land-use intensities, and both are associated with better-quality land (Allen, 2001), but some exceptions occur. Three provinces in particular have areas of poorer-quality land occupied at higher population densities. In the Southern Highlands, Enga and Simbu, there are population densities of over 80 persons per km² on 'low to very low'-quality land. In the Southern Highlands and Enga, almost 310,000 people are involved. In the Eastern Highlands, 115,000 people cultivate 'low to very low'-quality land at population densities of over 70 persons per km². In Enga and Simbu and the Western Highlands, a further 172,000 people occupy 'moderate'-quality land at densities of over 115 persons per km².

Child malnutrition is chronic in these areas, and the birth weights of infants are significantly lower than in nearby areas. The primary cause of the malnutrition has been identified as lower sweet potato yields on poorer environments, with moderate population densities (Allen, 2002). When women in the poorer environments were compared with those in the better environments, both were found to expend about the same amount of energy in food production activities, but in the poorer environments, significantly less sweet potato was produced per woman and a number of women there were expending more energy in their daily work (planting, weeding, caring for children, caring for pigs, collecting firewood, and so on) than they were obtaining from the consumption of the sweet potato that they produced (Yamauchi and Ohtsuka, 2002).

Very high population densities alone are of concern, even in the absence of other significant environmental constraints. A distinction must be made, however, between the environments of the highlands and lowlands. Highland rainfall is generally better distributed in the sense that it occurs relatively evenly all year round, and falls are less intense and lack the erosive power of lowland downpours. Temperatures are lower in the highlands than the lowlands. As a result, in simple terms, 'everything' in the highlands happens more slowly than in the lowlands, including soil degradation. Lowland land degradation can occur at lower population densities and at lower land-use intensities than are needed to cause the same amount of damage in the highlands. Importantly, however, the highest population densities in PNG, over 300 persons per km² in some places, occur on small islands. The population living in these lowland, high population-density areas is around 372,000. About 100,000 live on the islands and atolls; they are isolated by the ocean, have very limited resources, and are often overlooked in a national overview of problems.

A rapidly growing population and a finite amount of land from which to produce food raise a number of questions about the relationships between population and food production. The most reliable source of information about the area of land in use in PNG is the Papua New Guinea Resource Information System (PNGRIS) (Bellamy and McAlpine, 1995). Other easily accessible sources of information on the area of land in use in PNG contain errors and should be used with caution (e.g., the statistics on the FAO web pages).

PNGRIS divides the total land area of 459,854 km² into the 'land in use' and 'unused land'. 'Land in use' is divided into 'cultivated land' and 'uncultivated land'. 'Cultivated land' includes land currently planted in food and cash crops *and* land that is in fallow. Fallow land is discussed in Section 11.4.2, but much fallow land is covered in secondary forest at various stages of development and appears to observers not familiar with PNG agriculture to be not in use. However, the inclusion of fallow land as 'land in use' is justified, because it is land that is an integral part of a rotational cultivation system.

11.4.2 Land degradation

All PNG food systems use fallowing of some sort or another to maintain soil fertility. Even continuous cultivation systems switch cultivation onto fallowed land after 60 or so years of cultivation in one place; the fallow land is used for pig grazing and is fenced off from the cultivated land. A 'fallow' is a period when land is not planted to crops and so is usually not weeded or otherwise interfered with, although fallows are important sources of firewood, small feral animals, fruits and nuts, and medicinal plants. During a fallow, usually unplanted 'natural' vegetation grows spontaneously and covers the previously planted land (particular trees known to improve soil fertility are planted in fallows in some places). On newly fallowed land, this fallow vegetation comprises weeds that over time give way to woody shrubs and eventually to trees. Because these natural fallow plant communities follow, or succeed, one another, they are called 'fallow vegetation successions'. Larger fallow shrubs and trees draw up minerals from deeper in the soil profile and a thick layer of leaf litter accumulates on the soil surface, which decomposes to form humus and so increases soil organic matter. The shrub and tree canopy protect the soil surface from the direct effects of heavy rainfall and high temperatures. Finally, the pests and diseases that had lived on the crops and reduced their productivity are significantly reduced in number, because the crops they depended upon have gone from the site.

The importance of fallows in terms of sustaining food production over the long term is related to the amount of organic material produced by the fallow vegetation. The quantity of leaves, stalks (trunks and branches), and roots that make up fallow vegetation is known as the fallow biomass. Grasses and weeds have less biomass than shrubs, and shrubs have less biomass than trees. As the fallow stages proceed and plants of earlier successions die and are replaced by those of the next stage, they decompose and add minerals and humus to the soil. The successional stage reached by a fallow is therefore more important than the chronological time that it lasts, and PNG villagers monitor the successional stages of a fallow and do not keep track of how long the land has been in fallow. The rate at which successions proceed depends upon rainfall, temperature, and soil conditions. For a system to be sustainable, the successions must reach a stage where the fallow vegetation is able to draw minerals from deep in the soil profile and deposit them into the upper soil horizons as leaf litter. The soil surface must be protected from the tropical elements for sufficient time to allow a build-up of humus, and, most importantly, the quantity of biomass in the fallow vegetation must have reached a point where it can provide enough minerals to the soil, through its decomposition, to allow food plants to produce satisfactorily. Furthermore, if fallow successions are allowed to proceed to the point where the forest returns to its original biomass and soil organic carbon status, although there is a small net release of other greenhouse gases during the cropping cycle, the net CO_2 balance in a shifting cultivation system is near zero. Forest clearing for permanent agriculture, on the other hand, can cause large losses of CO_2 from the soil and vegetation and may lead to changes in evapo-transpiration, run-off, and local climate (Tinker et al., 1996).

About 95% of PNG agricultural systems use a 'long' fallow, where the fallow lasts for many years, where the time the land is planted to crops is much shorter than the time the land is fallowed, and the fallow successions proceed to a tall secondary forest stage. Around 38% of food production systems use fallows that last more than 15 years; 42% use fallows from five to 15 years long; and 20% use fallows of less than 5 years. But about 5% of systems also use 'short' fallows, where the fallow lasts less than six months before land is again planted to crops and where the time land is cultivated is longer than the time it is fallowed.

If additional food for a rapidly growing population is to be produced from about the same area of land, either the productivity of the food plants must be increased (e.g., by selecting higher producing crop varieties or species), or the land must be used more intensively; that is, either the length of fallows must be shortened or the number of times the land is planted before a fallow must be increased.

But if the fallows become shorter, the time available for the fallow successions to proceed to a satisfactory stage will be lessened. At some point, the fallows will become too short to bring the soil fertility back to the point it was at before cultivation began. Similarly, if the number of times land is planted before a fallow is increased, a greater quantity of the soil minerals will be removed by the food crops; the soil will be exposed to rainfall and sunshine for longer; and the number of weeds, pests, and diseases will increase, which will reduce the productivity of plants. Soil exhaustion trials carried out at a lowland agricultural experiment station using continuous plantings of sweet potato (without a fallow) showed a decline in yields from around 25 tonnes/ha to 3 tonnes/ha over eight years (Bourke, 1977). A study of highland sweet potato gardens showed declines in yields from 8 tonnes/ha to 2 tonnes/ha on weathered volcanic ash soils, and 18 tonnes/ha to 10 tonnes/ha over 120 years on drained peat soils (Wood, 1984). Some speculation exists over whether the declines in yields are caused more by a loss of soil chemical elements or by a build-up of pests and diseases. PNG food producers do not use inorganic fertilizers to maintain soil fertility, nor do they use chemicals to kill pests or reduce diseases.

An analysis of PNGRIS shows that in 1975, an area of 117,858 km^2 (25% of the total land area) was 'cultivated'; that is, it was currently planted in crops or was in fallow. In 1996, the 1975 land-use map was updated using satellite imagery, and the area of 'cultivated land' was found to have increased by about 11% between 1975 and 1996, significantly less than the rate of increase of the population. In the absence of evidence of widespread increases in malnutrition and rural poverty, it must be assumed that the production of food increased by at least 66% during these 20 years, while the area cultivated increased only by 11%. Land use was intensified, raising the threat of land degradation. The challenge of maintaining soil fertility under conditions of falling crop yields has been met by planting nitrogen fixing trees in fallows, hand tillage of soils, the construction of small, medium, and large mounds, long and square beds, and green manuring. These techniques are discussed further in Section 11.6.1.

PNG is a mountainous country with high rainfall, where much agriculture takes place on steep slopes, conditions that would seemingly favour high levels of erosion, but the more spectacular evidence of erosion caused by agriculture on slopes is not often seen. A number of field experiments and intensive studies in the 1980s showed that the main reasons for lower than expected levels of soil erosion are moderately fertile, loamy to clayey soils with high levels of organic matter, as well as good structure and fast-growing, prolific vegetation (Humphreys, 1998). Bare soil on slopes up to 30° were found to erode at rates of up to 50 tonnes/ha/year, but with 50% ground cover, soil loss rates fell to less than 10 tonnes/ha/year. The use of long fallows and short cultivation times does not expose the soils to the elements for long periods, and experiments suggest that agriculture results in soil losses of around 2.7 tonnes/ha/year, a low figure by international standards.

11.4.3 High rainfall, drought, and frost

A significant influence on PNG food production is the Walker Circulation (Nicholls, 1974), the equatorial circulation of air across the Pacific and Indian oceans (Renguang and Kirtman, 2004). For much of the time, the western Pacific Ocean is warmer than the eastern Pacific, and air rises over PNG, moves east at high altitudes and descends over the eastern Pacific. At or near the surface, air moves from east to west across the Pacific. Under these conditions, warm, moist air rises over PNG and forms large cumulonimbus cells up to 15 km high. Cloud cover and rainfall are high. From time to time, however, in association with an El Niño-Southern Oscillation (ENSO) event, the Pacific Walker Circulation slows and even reverses. Under these conditions, adiabatically dried air descends over PNG. As a result, many parts of PNG experience low rainfall and a reduction in the usually high level of cloud cover. The lack of cloud cover allows heat absorbed from the sun during the day to radiate into the night sky; at 1,800 m above sea level and sometimes lower, air temperatures at ground level can fall to below freezing. The above ground parts of most PNG staple food plants are severely damaged by air temperatures below freezing. The severity of the impact of frost on food production from sweet potato, in which the underground tubers are eaten, depends upon the time since the crop was planted, but a number of frosts spaced some weeks apart can completely disrupt the food supply for some months. Another outcome of a period without rain is widespread wild fires in what is 'normally' a humid tropical environment.

The major ENSO event in 1997–1998 caused a drought over much of the country and a series of frosts in the highlands and stopped most food production for up to six months in many parts of PNG (Allen, 2000; Bourke, 2000). In many places where sago is the staple food, a lack of water made sago manufacturing impossible, and where it was possible to manufacture sago, people complained that sago palms had become woody and lacked starch. Wild fires occurred in many places and burned for months. The fires burned large areas of grass and forest fallows, destroyed houses, and in a few case killed people. They also burned deeply into unoccupied forested mountains.

The most recent major ENSO event, in 2015–2016, also caused drought over much of PNG and a series of frosts at very high-altitude locations (above 2,200 m). This resulted in very widespread shortages of drinking water, closure of many schools, and food shortages for a significant proportion of the rural population. These impacts continued in parts of the country until late 2016, with food scarce at many very high-altitude locations, as well as in the inland Western Province, in the Saruwaget Mountains on the Huon Peninsula, and on atolls and other small islands in Milne Bay Province.

Less severe, but significant, food shortages also occurred in 1972 and 1982 (Allen *et al.*, 1989). ENSO events can disrupt food production about once every 15–20 years, but disruptions on the scale of 1997 and 2015 are less common, with comparable events over the past century in 1914 and 1941.

It is common for episodes of very high rainfall to occur on either side of an ENSO event. In continuous production sweet potato systems in the highlands, the influence of this rainfall pattern on the growth of sweet potato and the way in which rural people respond can result in two food shortages, the second more severe than the first and occurring up to two years after the first spell of heavy rainfall. The tuberization of sweet potato is determined about six weeks after planting. If the plant is waterlogged at this time, it produces very few tubers six to eight months later. If it does not receive enough water when the tubers are developing around five to six months after planting, the tubers do not develop properly. Women respond to sweet potato supply that is less than adequate by planting larger areas. They respond to over-supply by planting smaller areas. Planting and harvesting are continuous, so the outcomes of the plant's reaction to soil-water fluctuations and the peoples' reactions to the sweet potato supply which results, sometimes combine to produce significant fluctuations in supply, a phenomenon that is similar to the hog-cycle or the cobweb model in economics (Bourke, 1988). The time between the initiating wet period and the second food shortage means the real cause of the food shortage is not recognized. People who earn cash from coffee or fresh food sales can buffer these fluctuations in food supply by buying imported rice. The failure of sweet potato production in the highlands is felt as far away as the Port Moresby fresh food markets, where sweet potato price rises as the highland supply fails.

11.4.4 Pests and diseases

Plant diseases have previously seriously disrupted food production in PNG and have the potential to do so again. In 1941, *Phytophthora* (taro blight) appeared in Bougainville where taro was the staple food. Village food production and the functioning of the colonial administration were then disrupted by the Japanese occupation, as taro production failed and an unknown number of people starved to death (Packard, 1975). The long-term outcome on Bougainville was a switch in crops from taro to sweet potato. Sweet potato remains the staple food there and in other lowland locations, where taro production declined sharply as a result of taro blight. What is probably a *Pythium* root rot in Chinese taro appeared in the 1980s, coffee rust in coffee in 1986, potato late blight in the Western Highlands in 2003, and cocoa pod borer in cocoa in 2005. The two latter cases may have been the result of quarantine rules being ignored.

Elsewhere in the world, serious diseases of bananas and sugarcane exist. West of the border with Indonesian Papua, in very similar food production systems to those of PNG highlands, pigs are infected with the pork tapeworm *Taenia solium*, and the movement of this parasite into the heavily populated PNG highlands would create severe human health problems (Gajdusek, 1978). Cocoa pod borer appeared in two places in PNG in 2005, and coffee berry borer is damaging coffee crops in the PNG highlands. Both pests have the potential to seriously reduce the cash incomes of villagers and so reduce their capacity to purchase imported food with which to even out fluctuations in food supply. Although at present there appears to be no severe diseases of sweet potato anywhere in the world, the reliance on sweet potato as a food in PNG, particularly in the highlands, increases PNG's vulnerability to the appearance of a serious pest or disease of sweet potato.

11.4.5 HIV/AIDS

PNG is the site of an epidemic of HIV/AIDS. A 2006 modelling of the epidemic in PNG (Kaldor *et al.,* 2006) found that unless sexual behaviour changed quickly, by 2025 the prevalence of HIV would reach five percent of the total population and 11% of the population aged from 15 to 49 years. But a recent report estimated only 0.5% of the total population was HIV positive in 2012, approximately 25,000 people. This report also found a possible slowing of the rate of new infections, which was thought to be less than 1,000 new cases per year down from 3,500 new cases per year in 2001 (UNAIDS, 2013).

In 2006 it was predicted that the present high rates of population increase would be reduced by HIV-related deaths but that population growth rates would not become negative. All age groups in the population are predicted to increase by less than they would have in the absence of the epidemic, but the greatest

reductions will occur in those aged between 15 and 49 years. About one-third of the expected deaths in this age group will be women, which will reduce the reproductive capacity of the population and also may be associated with a reduction in fertility as women chose not to have children or to have fewer children (Kaldor *et al.,* 2006). Women contribute importantly to the labour of food production.

The experience of HIV/AIDS in rural East Africa suggests that the loss of persons in the 25–45-year age group from rural communities will have a significant effect on food and cash crop production, and on the well-being of children (Barnett and Blaikie, 1992; Barnett and Whiteside, 2002). HIV/AIDS will possibly have the greatest impact in places that already have a chronic shortage of food (energy and protein), an existing labour shortage (e.g. from migration), and an inability to substitute less labour-demanding crops for present staple crops. But Barnett and Blaikie (1992) argue that the impact of HIV/AIDS is determined more by the ability of individuals, households, and governments to cope, than by the magnitude of the epidemic itself. The PNG epidemic appears to be concentrated in urban areas among commercial sex workers who have been the target of antiretroviral therapies.

11.5 GLOBAL CLIMATE CHANGE

The above descriptions of the main threats to the sustainability of PNG's food production are based on present-day environmental parameters. But global climate is changing and PNG's environmental parameters will also change (Pachauri and Reisinger, 2007; IPCC, 2013). This section describes the changes that have been observed in PNG to the present time.

11.5.1 Changes in temperature

Studies of temperature change in PNG have found that temperatures have increased during the 20th century, with most of the increase occurring from about the mid-1970s. An important finding from the perspective of plant growth and food production is that the rate of temperature increase has been greater for minimum than for maximum temperatures.

An analysis of temperature change from nine coastal locations shows that minimum, mean, and maximum air temperatures have increased by an average of 0.2°C per decade (Figure 11.2). Temperatures tend to be lowest in El Niño years and higher in La Niña years. The more limited long-term temperature data runs available for highland stations show similar trends to the lowland stations. For example, at Aiyura in the Eastern Highlands Province, maximum temperature has increased by 0.75°C (0.3°C per decade) over 25 years to 2001 (although the daily minimum did not increase over this period).

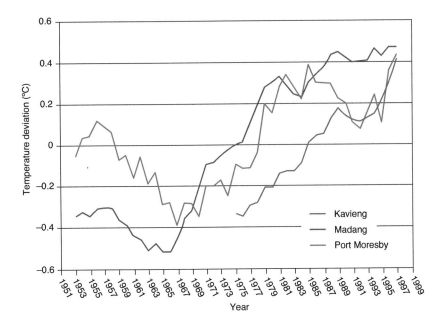

Figure 11.2. Temperature deviations from the long-term average, Port Moresby, Madang, and Kavieng. *Source:* Bourke *et al.* (2002). The most recent data are not available.

Another indication that temperatures are increasing in the highlands comes from observations on the upper and lower altitudinal limits of crops. For example, until around 1980, although coconuts grew up to 1,700–1,800 m altitude, they did not bear nuts. By late 2008, coconuts were bearing very small nuts at up to 1,580 m altitude in at least three highland valleys, which suggests that temperatures there have increased by about 1.0°C over 30 years, which is consistent with the changes in maximum temperature recorded at Aiyura and in other equatorial tropical highlands.

Highland villagers also report that crops have been bearing at higher altitudes since around the mid-1990s. They have observed that coconuts, betel nut, mango, and breadfruit are now bearing where the trees previously grew but did not bear. Similar changes have been documented at a village at about 1,900 m altitude on the Huon Peninsula, where villagers say that from around 1980 it became possible to grow *Pandanus conoideus* and another cultivated palm at higher altitudes, and that a bird species was being seen at higher altitudes than previously (Kocher Schmid, 1991).

11.5.2 Changes in rainfall

Less evidence exists for changes in rainfall. The majority of rural rainfall recording stations in PNG ceased recording around 1980. An analysis of monthly rainfall patterns at Goroka in Eastern Highlands Province from 1946 to 2002 found that there had been a shift to longer, but less pronounced, rainy seasons. Throughout PNG, however, villagers say that seasonal rainfall patterns have changed or are less predictable. They generally do not report an overall increase or decrease in rainfall, but because rainfall is already high at most locations it is unlikely they would notice an increase unless it was significant.

11.5.3 Sea-level rise

There is much anecdotal evidence for rises in sea level in PNG. In Bougainville Province, people on small islands state that the sea is eroding the coastline and that these changes commenced some 30–40 years ago. In the Mortlock Islands, people are concerned about the invasion of sea water into the freshwater lens beneath the pits in which the staple swamp taro is grown (Bourke and Betitis, 2003). Other reports of encroachment by the sea in recent years come from the Carteret Islands (Connell, 2016), Murik Lakes in East Sepik Province (Lipset, 2014), on the Wewak waterfront, some small islands in Manus Province, and along the coast in Gulf and Western provinces.

11.6 SUSTAINABLE FOOD PRODUCTION

This section describes how people are responding at present to the main threats to food production, in an attempt to assess how they may respond in the future.

11.6.1 Population growth and land degradation

A strong awareness exists among villagers that fallows must be long enough to allow soil fertility to be sustained, but if the pressure to produce food for a growing population becomes too great and fallows are shortened to the point where yields suffer, a variety of agricultural practices are available that can slow the decline of soil fertility.

One of the simplest practices is the planting of particular tree species in gardens and fallows in order to speed up the establishment of a tree fallow and to enhance the recovery of soil fertility. The most common tree planted into fallows in PNG is *Casuarina ologidon* (yar in Pidgin), but *Parasponia rigida, Schleinitiza novo-guineensis*, and *Albizia* spp are also used. These are all species that are known to fix atmospheric nitrogen. However, examples of true alley cropping do not yet exist in PNG. The physical movement of soil down slope as wash or by slumping is slowed by the construction of barriers across the slope and in some places by benching. True terracing does not occur. Another important practice is soil tillage and the formation of mounds and beds. Grassland soils are tilled by digging with sticks or spades. Circular mounds and rectangular beds are constructed to improve drainage, to increase the depth of topsoil and to allow the application of green manure to the soil, a practice known in PNG as 'composting'.

Green manuring is not used everywhere in PNG. It is presently restricted to areas between 600 m and 2,800 m in altitude, on slopes of less than 15° and is most common where rainfall is between 2,200 mm and 3,000 mm. The soils on which it is most often practised are derived from volcanic ash. Volcanic ash soils are well-structured and friable but have low levels of available phosphate and potassium and low cation exchange capacity. Green manuring is almost exclusively associated with sweet potato production. Agronomic trials suggest that green manuring increases the availability of potassium to the sweet potato plants, increases top growth in sweet potato, reduces the incident of fungal black rot in tubers, and increases soil temperature by up to 6°C, which reduces the time to harvest (because time to maturity is temperature-dependent in sweet potato). It has been suggested that green manuring protects sweet potato from frosts at high altitudes, but this is unlikely. Villagers agree that green manuring increases crop yields, reduces the time to harvest, and reduces the incidence of rot, and these probably are the greatest benefits of the practice.

11.6.2 ENSO-induced food shortages

The most common response of people to the severe food shortages induced by ENSO is to eat alternative foods not normally eaten. These include cassava, coconuts, mango, ferns, wild figs and fig leaves, sea almonds, and *Gnetum gnemon* nuts. When these foods are also depleted, so-called famine foods are eaten, including banana roots, wild yams, immature pawpaw, *Pueraria* roots, and a variety of green leaves. Migration is a traditional response of people at higher altitudes to frosts. People are also forced to move to larger rivers to be nearer to drinking water when local sources dry up.

However, the most important determinant of village responses to the 1997–1998 and 2015–2016 droughts was the amount of money they had available to them to buy imported food, mainly rice. The money came from savings, the sale of crops, wage employment, or small business activities. During 1997, rice imports into PNG increased over the predicted sales by 66,000 tonnes. Of this extra rice, the PNG government purchased 5,500 tonnes; the Australian government purchased 2,700 tonnes; the Japanese government donated 8,000 tonnes; and 50,000 tonnes was sold through commercial outlets. This implies that more than 75% of the additional rice imported during 1997 was purchased by villagers from savings or earnings. People bought the additional food for themselves and for relatives who did not have the means to buy it. People living in towns working for wages and salaries also purchased food and sent it to rural-dwelling relatives.

The importance of family and social networks as the most important means of responding to a complete failure of food supply was first encountered in 1972, during a similar but less severe ENSO event. In 1972, when Australian colonial administrators encountered frost for the first time, they assumed correctly that people would migrate, but they thought, incorrectly, that the migrants would encounter resistance at their destinations and that fighting and social unrest would be widespread. They therefore tried to prevent people from moving by feeding them in their home areas (Waddell, 1975). A study of one group of high-altitude dwellers showed that they maintained a network of social relations with people in a number of locations, including those living at lower altitudes where frosts can be expected to be less severe. These people participated in exchange activities and marriages that provided the means to access dispersed garden land and places of refuge and held an 'ideology of descent-group solidarity' that encouraged them to assist fellow group members, including inviting them to come to a distant host if they did not have one of their own (Wohlt, 1989).

11.7 FOOD PRODUCTION AND GLOBAL CLIMATE CHANGE

Many questions remain unanswered about the impact of global climate change in PNG, but the outcomes are unlikely to be simple. The influence of global climate change on PNG food production will be the outcome of complex interactions of climate, plants, and humans. At the level of climate-plant interactions, for example, will higher levels of carbon dioxide in the atmosphere increase photosynthetic activity and decrease evaporation and transpiration in plants, resulting in higher crop production worldwide, and if so, how will this affect PNG food plants (Bourke *et al.*, 2002; Inape and Humphrey, 2001; McGregor *et al.*, 2016)? At the level of climate-plant disease, for example, will an increase in temperature increase the severity of coffee rust in the highlands? But if highlands rainfall and humidity are reduced, will the incidence of coffee rust decline? If rainfall and temperature increase, will the severity of rust increase? Will villagers adopt improved rust control techniques or rust-resistant coffee varieties and so reduce the impact of rust?

In this section, we have restricted our speculation to two main areas, temperature and rainfall changes, and have raised a number of other broader possible implications of global climate change for PNG.

11.7.1 Food production and temperature

Because of the direct relationship between altitude and temperature in PNG, if global temperatures increase, it is likely that many crops will be able to be grown at marginally higher altitudes, so the areas where they can be grown will expand. However, the lower altitudinal limit of some crops, such as potato, Arabica coffee, and *Pandanus jiulianettii* (a *pandan* grown at high altitudes, which yields a nut), will also increase, reducing the area in which these crops can be grown.

Tuber formation in sweet potato is significantly reduced at temperatures above 34°C. Maximum temperatures in the lowlands are now around 32°C, so an increase of 2.0–4.5°C over 100 years could reduce sweet potato production in lowland locations, perhaps within one or two generations. It is likely that overall temperature increases will marginally reduce productivity in the lowlands and in the main highland valleys, but will marginally increase productivity at locations above 2,000 m.

Diurnal temperature ranges also have an important influence on productivity. In PNG, the diurnal temperature range is greater in the highlands than in the lowlands and is one reason why crop yields are higher in the highlands. If, as reported by the Intergovernmental Panel on Climate Change (IPCC) for most of the rest of the planet, the PNG diurnal temperature range has also decreased over the period 1950–2004, it will have tended to reduce crop yields to an unknown extent.

Increases in temperature may also change the incidence of some plant diseases, especially those influenced by rainfall and humidity. Taro blight is less severe in PNG at a few hundred metres above sea level than at sea level and is rarely found above an altitude of 1,300 m (Bourke, 2010). The fungus is sensitive to temperature, and a small rise in temperature could mean that the fungus will reduce taro yield at higher altitudes than now. Similarly, coffee rust is present in the main highland valleys at 1,600–1,800 m where it does little damage, but is a more serious problem at lower altitudes, below about 1,200 m. A rise in temperature is likely to increase the altitude at which coffee rust has a severe impact on coffee production (Brown *et al.*, 1995).

Although the probable influence of global climate change on ENSO events remains speculative (Collins, 2000), if ENSO events become more frequent, as predicted by some global change models, one outcome would be more frosts at high-altitude locations, so more disruptions to food production there, a greater frequency of droughts, possibly of the magnitude of 1941 and 1997, with the resultant food shortages, fires in fallows, and drinking water problems. More episodes of ENSO-induced high rainfall will result in the disruptions to sweet potato production associated with them.

11.7.2 Food production and rainfall

The IPCC predicts higher rainfall in the South Pacific, including PNG, under global warming. Rainfall patterns in PNG are complex, so it is likely that any changes in rainfall patterns will also be complex and hence difficult to predict. With a few exceptions, however, most places in PNG already receive high annual rainfalls. While in the lower-rainfall areas, an increase in rainfall and reduced seasonality of distribution could be beneficial for agriculture, for most of PNG, an increase in total rainfall and a less seasonal distribution would have a negative impact on agriculture. The most vulnerable locations are those where rainfall is already more than 3,500 mm per year. Increased rainfall may also increase the rate of fallow recovery and hence shorten the time for fallows to produce the biomass required to replace soil fertility lost during cultivation. For example, fallow species are very similar in lowland East Sepik and Madang provinces, but in East Sepik, where annual rainfall is presently around 1,800 mm, the fallow successions include a three-year cane grass stage, which is missing in Madang, where present rainfall is 3,000 mm, and fallow successions go straight to a softwood tree stage.

If ENSO events become more frequent, regional droughts across PNG could also become more frequent, as well as the number of episodes of very high rainfall associated with ENSO events. Both situations would cause serious disruptions to food production. Increased rainfall would be associated with increased cloudiness and less bright sunshine, which would probably reduce crop productivity, especially where cloud cover is already high. More episodes of high-intensity rainfall could increase soil erosion and slumping. An increased frequency of wild fires could have a significant impact on fallow regeneration; fires destroy the biomass of mature fallows and set the fallow 'clock' back to zero again. Fires in unoccupied mountainous areas also extend existing grasslands at the expense of forest, reducing the capacity of the forests to absorb CO_2.

11.7.3 Food production and sea level rise

Rising sea levels are having a minor negative impact on food production on some atolls, and it is likely that a further rise in sea levels will cause problems for villagers living on very small islands and in other low-lying estuarine locations, such as in the Gulf of Papua and the Fly River estuary, where higher salinity water may kill sago. In the Pacific, global change concerns have been focused on small island states such as Tuvalu, with a population of 12,000, or Kiribati with 108,000. However, there are at least 100,000 people in PNG living on around 140 small islands less than 10 km² in area and with population densities greater than 100 persons/km². These people also face the as yet unknown consequences of rising sea levels as a result of global warming.

Caution is advisable in attributing all shoreline changes or atoll food production problems to sea level rise. The cause of higher sea levels on the Duke of York Islands is geo-tectonic activity; land at nearby Rabaul is rising out of the sea for the same reason. In the Carteret Islands, where international print and television media have stridently blamed sea level rise for chronic food shortages (the Carteret islanders have been called the 'world's first climate change refugees'), food production problems are caused by very a high population density, very short fallows, and shortage of land for food gardens, and only partly by sea level rise (Bourke and Betitis, 2003; Connell, 2016).

11.7.4 Other implications of global climate change for PNG food supply

Global climate change has a number of other possible implications in PNG. In particular, what are the impacts on the insect vectors of malaria and dengue fever, the production of the most important foods imported into PNG, and changes in the world economy that will impact on the PNG economy?

Malaria kills mainly children in PNG, but it affects the ability of people to work in the production of food. Malaria is endemic in the PNG lowlands, but prior to colonial contact was epidemic only in the lower altitude parts of the highlands. Highland malaria epidemics worsened after colonization allowed greater personal movement between the highlands and lowlands. Highland malaria epidemics are associated with ENSO events, which are also linked to dysentery and typhoid epidemics. For example, during the 1997–1998 ENSO event, malaria and dysentery killed an estimated seven percent of the population in northern Gulf Province (Lemonnier, 2001), and a typhoid epidemic killed at least 75 people at Lake Kopiago in the Southern Highlands Provinces (Robinson, 2001). Other unreported deaths almost certainly occurred. ENSO events aside, increases in temperature will almost certainly expand the area in which the malaria vector can exist and so increase the possibility that malaria will become endemic over a wider area (Mueller et al., 2003; Mueller et al., 2005).

Rice and wheat are the most important foods imported into PNG. Since 1990, rice imports have averaged 152,000 tonnes

per year, excluding the exceptionally high 208,000 tonnes imported during the 1997 food shortages caused by the drought and frosts of that year. Wheat imports have averaged 117,000 tonnes per year since 1990. Until 2002, almost all rice imported into PNG came from Australia and comprised 24% of Australian rice exports. When a drought in Australia between 2002 and 2005 greatly reduced rice production, rice imported into PNG came from Vietnam, the United States, China, Egypt, India, and Thailand, as well as Australia. By 2006, the Australian rice industry had recovered and most imports were again from Australia, the preferred source because of the high quality of the Australian product and the predictability of shipping arrangements. Future production shortfalls in Australia, which result from environmental restrictions on the availability of irrigation water from rivers may make rice exports from Australia less reliable. A lack of direct shipping routes from Southeast Asia to PNG makes the supply of Asian-grown rice more expensive than Australian-grown rice.

Other changes in the world economy that may result from global climate change go beyond the focus of this chapter, but briefly, they include reductions in availability of fossil fuels; a greater demand for bio-fuels from oil crops, such as oil palm and coconut; increased demand for hydro-electricity (which is potentially abundant in PNG) for industrial uses; and carbon trading that recognizes the large area of primary and secondary forest in PNG that can absorb CO_2, all of which will present economic opportunities that could be beneficial for PNG.

11.8 ADEQUACY OF PNG'S RESPONSE

PNG can do almost nothing to divert the progress of global climate change. With no heavy industry, very few motor vehicles per head of population and almost no electrification, PNG's main contribution to atmospheric greenhouses gases come from LNG wells, pipelines, and processing plants, the annual burning of fallow vegetation as part of shifting cultivation cycles, and a number of large swamps. On the other hand, PNG's large areas of forest make it a net greenhouse gas sink. So what we are concerned with here is how well the challenges presented by population growth, HIV/AIDs, and global climate change can be responded to within PNG. The capacity of the PNG state to respond is discussed first and then the response of households is examined.

11.8.1 The PNG state

Two aspects of PNG governance restrict its capacity to respond to the challenges global climate change. Firstly, an extremely complex and poorly understood law (known as the Organic Law) governs the relationships between national, provincial, district, and local level governments, such that even the most hardworking and honest administrator has difficulty promoting change. Secondly, the frequent appointment of unqualified and incompetent political supporters, close family members, and friends to many governing bodies cripples these bodies and creates conditions where good policy development and effective administration is not possible. In 2016, PNG was ranked 139 out of 168 nations on a corruption perceptions index (Transparency International, 2016).

The stated aim of the 1995 Organic Law reforms was to improve the delivery of services to rural areas by decentralizing them to district and local level governments. An unintended outcome has been a dislocation of administration and service delivery at all levels of government. A review of the decentralization process found widespread confusion over administrative and financial accountability, responsibility for service delivery, the transfer and funding of functions, the separation of capital and recurrent expenditure, and taxation powers (Whimp, 2005). A review of the PNG economy in 2015 found a 20% fall in revenue caused by a fall in world oil and gas prices. Reductions in expenditure had occurred: 37% in health, 36% in infrastructure, and 30% in education. The combined budget deficits for the three years 2012–2015 of 24% of GDP were the largest for a three-year period in PNG's history (Flanagan, 2016). As a result, health, education, agricultural extension, and infrastructure maintenance programmes are chronically underfunded.

Policies about food production for domestic consumption are also fraught. A 2004 review by the Asian Development Bank of the PNG Department of Agriculture and Livestock (DAL), responsible for food production policies, found that it was without clear sector roles, did not have the capacity to plan or develop policy, was 'uncoordinated', 'unsure of budget allocations', was 'poorly served by national and provincial financial information systems', and was unable to develop or implement national plans (ADB, 2004). This situation has not improved. A senior economist described the government's treatment of agriculture as 'scandalous', with reputable institutions being 'undermined or left to deteriorate with inadequate financial support, poor management and oversight' (Barker, 2013).

PNG's present lack of capacity to monitor population growth deserves attention. It is not possible at present to examine population change below the level of the province for the three censuses carried out between 1980 and 2000, because changes have been made to the census collection units in an attempt to align them with electorates. The 2010 national census was postponed to 2011 and, although described by the Prime Minister as a 'failure' (*The National*, 2012), produced final figures in 2013. At the Local Level Government Area level, increases and decreases in population between 2000 and 2011 are inexplicable and the census is widely believed to be unusable (Allen, 2014).

It has to be concluded that at the present time, the PNG state is not well-prepared to cope with rapid population growth or an HIV epidemic, *let alone* global climate change, and that the severity of the impacts of these challenges may well be made worse by poor governance.

11.8.2 The people

On the other hand, the rural people of PNG have shown themselves to be hardworking, innovative, productive, and resilient to hardship. PNG agricultural systems have a striking history of adaptation and change: new crops have been skilfully integrated into farming systems, including cash crops, without disrupting ongoing food production; the means of maintaining soil fertility by tilling, mounding, and green manuring have been independently invented in PNG; and people have a deep knowledge of fallow plant communities and food crop species. Three cases that have involved the loss of a significant part of the labour force, brought by labour migration (Boyd, 1981; Morauta, 1984) and *kuru* (a human prion disease) (Alpers, 1992), have demonstrated that PNG households have a considerable capacity to resist, adapt to, and to cope with threats to their livelihood (Allen, 1997). In these cases, households coped by men taking on women's roles in food production and child care and vice versa, by changing to less labour-demanding crops, by cultivating grasslands instead of forests, and by abandoning the most labour-demanding agricultural practices. While food production declined, it remained at a level adequate for the maintenance of human nutrition.

We hope that the rural people of PNG will be able to again meet the challenges that are confronting them, while we fear that the magnitude of some of the coming changes may be too much for even the most resilient of people. Unless a significant change occurs quickly in the governance of PNG, rural people will have to face these challenges largely on their own. Almost all state-sponsored extension services have already failed. With the exception of long-suffering school teachers and health workers, who continue to provide minimal services under very difficult circumstances, only Christian missions and international NGOs remain active in rural areas.

Perhaps most worrying is the state's lack of capacity to know what is happening in rural areas, which means that the struggles of rural people to meet these challenges will go unobserved. Barnett and Blaikie (1992) concluded a study of rural Uganda with the argument that instead of 'more sophistication in the techniques of prediction … it may be more useful to develop cheap, robust methods of monitoring the impact'. They were writing about an HIV/AIDS epidemic, but their remarks could be applied to all of the challenges facing the rural people of PNG. While we have attempted a certain amount of prediction in this chapter, much more important than prediction is the ability to know what is happening in rural areas of PNG as population change, HIV/AIDS, and global warming begin to have an impact on food production.

SUMMARY

More than 80% of the people of PNG live in rural areas and produce most of the calories they consume. The balance of food consumed in PNG is imported and is mainly rice and wheat. An estimated 83% of all food energy consumed in PNG in 2006 was derived from locally grown food (Bourke and Vlassak, 2004).

The most important threats to the sustainability of food production and supply in PNG are high rates of population change, an HIV/AIDS epidemic and global climate change.

Rapid population change threatens to bring about land degradation in shifting cultivation systems through the need to feed more people by shortening fallow times and lengthening cropping cycles, which on poorer-quality soils will result in losses of soil fertility and consequent declines in food crop yields. HIV/AIDS will slow population growth, but not reverse it. Importantly, it will selectively remove working-age people from the population, which will also reduce the capacity to grow food, in a country where labour, not land, has been the most important constraint on agriculture. The outcomes of global warming are less certain. Global warming is apparent in rises in temperatures and some observable changes in plant distributions. If global climate change increases rainfall, reduces diurnal temperature ranges, or increases the frequency of El Niño-Southern Oscillation (ENSO) events, then food production will be adversely affected. On the other hand, global warming may have some positive effects in allowing the production of some crops at higher altitudes.

Governance in PNG is poor, the provision of services to rural areas has declined, and government has lost the capacity to know what is happening in many rural areas. This means that rural people will have to face the impacts of these future threats with little help from outside, using their own resources of resilience, innovativeness, and hard work. High levels of agriculture skills, the local invention of techniques to manage soil fertility, and a history of highly successful adaptations to the introduction of new food and cash crops over the previous 100 years suggest they have the qualities needed to meet the coming challenges.

ACKNOWLEDGEMENTS

Much of the information presented in this chapter is derived from two research projects: the Papua New Guinea Resource Information System (PNGRIS) by the CSIRO Division of Water and Land Resources, and the Mapping Agriculture Systems Project (MASP) by the Land Management Programme (LMP), Department of Human Geography, College of Asia and the Pacific, Australian National University. Both projects were partially funded by the then Australian Agency for International Development (AusAID), now the Department of Foreign Affairs and Trade (DFAT). Both projects were conducted in close collaboration with the PNG Department of Agriculture and Livestock. The CSIRO project was led by the late John McAlpine, and the DAL contribution by the late Balthasar Wayi. The LMP was instigated and led by Emeritus Professor Harold Brookfield. The late Geoff Humphreys and Robin Hide were members of the MASP team. Thousands of rural villagers in PNG gave freely of their time and immense knowledge over many years. Two anonymous referees offered comments on a first draft of the paper. The assistance of these individuals and organizations is gratefully acknowledged.

REFERENCES

ADB (Asian Development Bank) (2004) Preparing the agriculture and rural development project, Papua New Guinea: Agricultural markets, marketing and rural enterprise development. ADB TA4055-PNG. Asian Development Bank.https://www.adb.org/projects/documents/preparing-agriculture-and-rural-development-project-tcr

Allen, B. J. (1997) HIV/AIDS in rural Melanesia and South-East Asia: Divination or description. In G. Linge and D. Porter (eds.), *No Place for Borders: The HIV/AIDS Epidemic and Development in Asia and the Pacific*, pp. 114–123. St Leonards, NSW, Allen and Unwin.

(2000) The 1997–98 Papua New Guinea drought: Perceptions of disaster. In R. H. Grove and J. Chappell (eds.), *El Niño – History and Crisis: Studies from the Asia-Pacific Region*, pp. 109–122. Cambridge, White Horse Press.

(2001) Boserup and Brookfield and the association between population density and agricultural intensity in Papua New Guinea. Special issue on agricultural transformation and intensification. *Asia Pacific Viewpoint Special Issue*, **42**(2/3), 237–254.

(2002) Birthweight and environment at Tari. *Papua New Guinea Medical Journal*, **45**(1–2), 88–98.

(2014). Papua New Guinea National Census 2011: Rates of population change in local level government areas. *State, Society and Governance in Melanesia Program In-Brief*, 2014/44. https://openresearch-repository.anu.edu.au/handle/1885/143353

Allen, B. J., Brookfield, H. and Byron, Y. (1989) Frost and drought in the highlands of Papua New Guinea: A special collection of papers. *Mountain Research and Development*, **9**(3), 199–334.

Allen, B. J., Bourke, R. M. and Hide, R. L. (1995) The sustainability of Papua New Guinea agricultural systems: The conceptual background. *Global Environmental Change*, **5**(4), 297–312.

Alpers, M. P. (1992) Kuru. In M. P. Alpers and R. Attenborough (eds.), *Human Biology in Papua New Guinea: The Small Cosmos*. Research Monographs on Human Population Biology, pp. 313–334. Oxford, Clarendon Press.

Barker, P. (2013) Opinion: Give Papua New Guinea agriculture the break it needs. *Business Advantage PNG*, 22 May. https://www.businessadvantagepng.com/opinion-give-papua-new-guinea-agriculture-the-break-it-needs-2/

Barnett, T. and Blaikie, P. (1992) *AIDS in Africa: Its Present and Future Impacts*. New York, Guilford Press.

Barnett, T. and Whiteside, A. (2002) *AIDS in the Twenty-First Century: Disease and Globalization*. New York, Palgrave Macmillan.

Bellamy, J. A. and McAlpine, J. R. (1995) *Papua New Guinea Inventory of Natural Resources, Population Distribution and Land Use Handbook*. Second edition. PNGRIS Publication No. 6. Canberra, Australian Agency for International Development.

Booth, H., Zhang, G., Rao, M., Taomia, F. and Duncan, R. (2006) Population pressures in Papua New Guinea, the Pacific Island economies, and Timor Leste. *Working Papers in Demography*, 102. https://demography.cass.anu.edu.au/sites/default/files/sod/publications/working-papers/102.pdf

Bourke, R. M. (1977) Sweet potato (*Ipomoea batatas*) fertiliser trials on the Gazelle Peninsula of New Britain: 1954–1976. *Papua New Guinea Agricultural Journal*, **28**(2–4), 73–95.

— (1988) *Taim hangre*: Variation in subsistence food supply in the Papua New Guinea highlands. PhD thesis. Australian National University, Canberra.

— (2000) Impact of the 1997 drought and frosts in Papua New Guinea. In R. H. Grove and J. Chappell (eds.), *El Niño – History and Crisis: Studies from the Asia-Pacific Region*, pp. 149–170. Cambridge, White Horse Press.

— (2010) Altitudinal limits of 230 economic crop species in Papua New Guinea. In S. G. Haberle, J. Stevenson and M. Prebble (eds.), *Altered Ecologies: Fire, Climate and Human Influence on Terrestrial Landscapes. Terra Australia, 32*, pp. 473–512. Canberra, ANU E-Press, Australian National University. http://epress.anu.edu.au/wp-content/uploads/2011/02/ch271.pdf

Bourke, R. M. and Allen, B. J. (2009) Staple food crops. In R. M. Bourke and T. Harwood (eds.), *Food and Agriculture in Papua New Guinea*, pp. 194–200. Canberra, ANU Press.

Bourke, R. M. and Betitis, T. (2003) Sustainability of agriculture in Bougainville Province, Papua New Guinea. Land Management Group, Department of Human Geography, Research School of Pacific and Asian Studies, Australian National University, Canberra.

Bourke, R. M., Humphreys, G. S. and Hart, M. (2002) Warming in Papua New Guinea: Some implications for food productivity. Unpublished paper. Department of Human Geography, Research School of Pacific and Asian Studies, Australian National University, Canberra.

Bourke, R. M. and Vlassak, V. (2004) *Estimates of Food Crop Production in Papua New Guinea*. Canberra, Australian National University.

Boyd, D. J. (1981) Village agriculture and labor migration: Interrelated production activities among the Ilakia Awa of Papua New Guinea. *American Ethnologist*, **8**(1), 74–93.

Brown, J. S., Kenny, M. K., Whan, J. H. and Merriman, P. R. (1995) The effect of temperature on the development of epidemics of coffee leaf rust in Papua New Guinea. *Crop Protection*, **14**(8), 671–676.

Collins, M. (2000) Understanding uncertainties in the response of ENSO to greenhouse warming. *Geophysical Research Letters*, **27**(21), 3,509–3,512.

Connell, J. (2016) Last days in the Carteret Islands? Climate change, livelihoods and migration on coral atolls. *Asia Pacific Viewpoint*, **57**(1), 3–15. https://onlinelibrary-wiley-com.virtual.anu.edu.au/doi/10.1111/apv.12118

Denham, T., Haberle, S. and Lentfer, C. (2004) New evidence and revised interpretations of early agriculture in Highland New Guinea. *Antiquity*, **78**(302), 839–857.

Flanagan, P. (2016) PNG's frightening final budget outcome. *DevPolicy Blog*, Development Policy Centre, Crawford School of Public Policy, College of Asia and the Pacific, Australian National University, 4 April. https://devpolicy.org/pngs-frightening-final-budget-outcome-20160404/

Gajdusek, D. C. (1978) Introduction of *Taeniasolium* into west New Guinea with a note on an epidemic of burns from cysticercus epilepsy in the Ekari people of the Wissel Lakes area. *Papua New Guinea Medical Journal*, **21**(4), 329–342.

Gibson, J. (2001) The economic and nutritional importance of household food production in PNG. In R. M. Bourke, M. G. Allen and J. G. Salisbury (eds.), *Food Security for Papua New Guinea*. Proceedings of the Papua New Guinea Food and Nutrition 2000 Conference. *ACIAR Proceedings* 99, pp. 37–44. Canberra, Australian Centre for International Agricultural Research.

Hanson, L. W., Allen, B. J., Bourke, R. M. and McCarthy, T. J. (2001) *Papua New Guinea Rural Development Handbook*. Canberra, Australian National University.

Humphreys, G. S. (1998) A review of some important soil studies in Papua New Guinea. *Papua New Guinea Journal of Agriculture, Forestry and Fisheries*, **41**(1), 1–19.

Inape, K. and Humphrey, B. (2001) Potential impact of global climatic change on smallholder farmers in PNG. In R. M. Bourke, M. G. Allen and J. G. Salisbury (eds.), *Food Security for Papua New Guinea*. Proceedings of the Papua New Guinea Food and Nutrition 2000 Conference. ACIAR Proceedings 99, pp. 73–78. Canberra, Australian Centre for International Agricultural Research.

IPCC (2013) Chapter 2 Observations: Atmosphere and surface. In T. F. Stocker, D. Qin, G.-K. Plattner, M. Tignor, S. K. Allen, J. Boschung, A. Nauels, Y. Xia, V. Bex and P. M. Midgley (eds.), *Climate Change 2013: The Physical Science Basis. Contribution of Working Group I to the Fifth Assessment Report of the Intergovernmental Panel on Climate Change*, pp. 159–254. Cambridge and New York, Cambridge University Press.

Kaldor, J., Worth, H., Henderson, K., Law, M., McKay, J., Warner, B. and Razali, K. (2006) Impacts of HIV/AIDS 2005–2025 in Papua New Guinea, Indonesia and East Timor: Final Report of the HIV Epidemiological Modelling and Impact Study. AusAID, Canberra.

Kocher Schmid, C. (1991) *Of People and Plants: A Botanical Ethnography of Nokopo Village, Madang and Morobe Provinces, Papua New Guinea*. Basler Beiträgezur Ethnologie, Band 33. Ethnologisches Seminar der Universität und Museum für Völkerkunde, Switzerland, Basel.

Lemonnier, P. (2001) Drought, famine and epidemic among the Ankave-Anga of Gulf Province in 1997–98. In R. M. Bourke, M. G. Allen and J. G. Salisbury (eds.), *Food Security for Papua New Guinea*. Proceedings of the Papua New Guinea Food and Nutrition 2000 Conference. *ACIAR Proceedings 99*, pp. 164–167. Canberra, Australian Centre for International Agricultural Research.

Lipset, D. (2014) Place in the Anthropocene: A mangrove lagoon in Papua New Guinea in the time of rising sea-levels. *Journal of Ethnographic Theory*, **4**(3), 215–243.

Lowe, S. B. and Wilson, L. A. (1974) Comparative analysis of tuber development in six sweet potato (*Ipomoea batatas* (L) Lam.) cultivars 1. Tuber initiation, tuber growth and partition of assimilate. *Annals of Botany*, **38**, 307–317.

McAlpine, J. and Quigley, J. (n.d.) *Natural Resources, Land Use and Population Distribution of Papua New Guinea: Summary Statistics from PNGRIS*. PNGRIS Report No. 7. Australian Agency for International Development, Canberra.

McGregor, A., Taylor, M., Bourke, R. M. and Lebot, V. (2016) Vulnerability of export commodities to climate change. In M. Taylor, A. McGregor and B. Dawson (eds.), *Vulnerability of Pacific Island Agriculture and Forestry to Climate Change*, pp. 161–238. Noumea, New Caledonia, Pacific Community.

Moore, C. (2003) *New Guinea: Crossing Boundaries and History*. Honolulu, University of Hawai'i Press.

Morauta, L. (1984) *Left Behind in the Village: Economic and Social Conditions in an Area of High Outmigration*. IASER Monograph 25. Port Moresby, Institute of Applied Social and Economic Research.

Mueller, I., Bockarie, M., Alpers, M. and Smith, T. (2003) The epidemiology of malaria in Papua New Guinea. *Trends in Parasitology*, **19**(6), 253–259.

Mueller, I., Namuigi, P., Kundi, J., Ivivi, R., Tandrapah, T., Bjorge, S. and Reeder, J. C. (2005) Epidemic malaria in the highlands of Papua New Guinea. *American Journal of Tropical Medicine and Hygiene*, **72**(5), 554–560.

Nicholls, N. (1974) *The Walker Circulation and Papua New Guinea Rainfall*. Technical Report No. 6. Canberra, Department of Science, Bureau of Meteorology.

Pachauri, R. K. and Reisinger, A. (eds.) (2007) *Climate Change 2007: Report of the Intergovernmental Panel on Climate Change*. Geneva, Switzerland, Intergovernmental Panel on Climate Change.

Packard, J. C. (1975) *The Bougainville Taro Blight*. Pacific Islands Studies Program Miscellaneous Work Papers. Honolulu, University of Hawaii.

Renguang, W. and Kirtman, B. P. (2004) Understanding the impacts of the Indian Ocean on ENSO variability in a coupled GCM. *Journal of Climate*, **17**(20), 4,019–4,031.

Robinson, R. (2001) Subsistence at Lake Kopiago, Southern Highlands Province, during and following the 1997–1998 drought. In R. M. Bourke, M. G. Allen and J. G. Salisbury (eds.), *Food Security for Papua New Guinea. Proceedings of the Papua New Guinea Food and Nutrition 2000 Conference. ACIAR Proceedings 99*, pp. 190–200. Canberra, Australian Centre for International Agricultural Research.

The National (2012) Census, a 10-year debacle. 19 February 2012. https://www.thenational.com.pg/census-a-10-year-debacle/

Tinker, P. B., Ingram, J. S. I. and Struwe, S. (1996) Effects of slash-and-burn agriculture and deforestation on climate change. *Agriculture, Ecosystems & Environment*, **58**(1), 13–22.

Transparency International (2016) Papua New Guinea. https://www.transparency.org/country/#PNG

Ulijaszek, S. J. and Poraituk, S. P. (1993) Making sago in Papua New Guinea: is it worth the effort? In C. L. Hladik, A. Hladik, O. F. Linares, H. Pagezy, A. Semple and M. Hadley (eds.), *Tropical Forests, People and Food: Biocultural Interactions and Applications to Development*, pp. 271–279. Paris and Pearl River, NY, UNESCO and Parthenon Publishing Group.

UNAIDS (2013) Global Report: UNAIDS Report on the Global AIDS Epidemic. New York, Joint United Nations Programme on HIV/AIDS (UNAIDS). https://www.unaids.org/en/resources/documents/2013/20130923_UNAIDS_Global_Report_2013

Waddell, E. W. (1975) How the Enga cope with frost: responses to climatic perturbations in the Central Highlands of New Guinea. *Human Ecology*, **3**(4), 249–272.

Whimp, K. (2005) Comments on problems with the Organic Law on provincial governments and local-level governments. Unpublished paper. PNG Economic and Fiscal Commission, Port Moresby.

Wilson, K. (1982) Tuberisation in sweet potato (*Ipomoea batatas* (L) Lam.). In R. L. Villareal and T. D. Griggs (eds.), *Sweet Potato. Proceedings of the First International Symposium*, pp. 79–94. Tainan, Taiwan, Asian Vegetable Research and Development Centre.

Wohlt, P. (1989) Migration at Yumbisa, 1972–75. *Mountain Research and Development*, **9**(3), 224–234.

Wood, A. W. (1984) Land for tomorrow: subsistence agriculture, soil fertility and ecosystem stability in the New Guinea highlands. PhD thesis, University of Papua New Guinea, Port Moresby.

World Bank (2018) Rural population (% of total population). https://data.worldbank.org/indicator/SP.RUR.TOTL.ZS

Yamauchi, T. and Ohtsuka, R. (2002) Nutritional adaptation of women in contrasting agricultural environments in Tari, Papua New Guinea. *Papua New Guinea Medical Journal*, **45**(1–2), 99–105.

12 Education for sustainable development: An overview of Asia-Pacific perspectives

DZULKIFLI ABDUL RAZAK

International Islamic University Malaysia (IIUM)

Keywords

Education for sustainable development (ESD); indigenous knowledge and wisdom; spirituality; balance and harmony; guardianship; interconnectedness; sense of higher purpose; Japan; Indonesia; Malaysia; Thailand; New Zealand; East; West

Abstract

In the 30 years since the introduction of sustainable development and its acceptance as a concept in education, much can be gained from its successful implementation across the world. It is largely driven by the Brundtland Report of 1987, when the term 'sustainable development' (SD) was coined. While much has been achieved since then, there are, however, still a number of gaps, conceptually and in practice, when viewed from the perspectives of indigenous knowledge and wisdom, especially the non-Western-centric worldviews. This can be well observed within the diverse indigenous communities of the Asia-Pacific, such as in Japan, Indonesia, Malaysia, Thailand, and New Zealand. Overall, each provides a unique input to the understanding of SD as a concept and its practice beyond what is conventionally framed by the Brundtland Report. By taking due consideration of the various indigenous perspectives, the vista of SD could be further enhanced and expanded, at the same time enriching the concept through real-life examples, making SD even more relevant and viable as a way of life. Instead of regarding these as divergent views, it is more instructive to integrate them into what has been constructed thus far to generate a more holistic and balanced framework with a higher sense of purpose, as spelt out by the overarching goals of the United Nations Sustainable Development Goals, namely dignity, justice, and partnership, apart from the usual 3Ps of planet, people, and prosperity.

12.1 INTRODUCTION

The Brundtland Report, released in October 1987, has managed to bring to light the term 'sustainable development' (SD), or 'sustainability', as one of the most-used catchphrases in the last few decades. Known also as the World Commission on Environment and Development (WCED), it made SD a major topic of discussions at various levels and from several perspectives and viewpoints. However, not everyone agrees with the concept, which is generally understood as 'the development that meets the needs of the present generations without compromising the ability of the future generations to meet their own needs' (WCED, 1987).

Notwithstanding this, SD resonates well with the report expressed by the United Nations General Assembly (1987), which highlighted 'the accelerating deterioration of the human environment and natural resources and the consequences of that deterioration for economic and social development'. The report was an important document that helped to rally countries to work and pursue SD together on a common platform. In 1988, the Centre for Our Common Future was established in place of the commission. The main aim of the organization is to create a united international community with shared sustainability goals by identifying sustainability problems worldwide, raising awareness about them, and suggesting the implementation of solutions. This was to be achieved by rethinking the concepts of economic development as the new idea of SD – as it was called in the Brundtland Report (Council of Foreign Relations, 2013).

The commission's mandate was three-fold, namely '[1] re-examine the critical issues of environment and development and to formulate innovative, concrete, and realistic action proposals to deal with them; [2] strengthen international cooperation on environment and development and assess and propose new forms of cooperation that can break out of existing patterns and influence policies and events in the direction of needed change;

125

and [3] raise the level of understanding and commitment to action on the part of individuals, voluntary organizations, businesses, institutes, and governments' (WCED, 1987, p. 347).

Despite these goals, however, the discussion and articulation of SD from indigenous and faith-based points of views are still wanting. It is noted that '[t]he Commission focused its attention on the areas of population, food security, the loss of species and genetic resources, energy, industry, and human settlements – realizing that all of these are connected and cannot be treated in isolation one from another' (WCED, 1987, p. 27), with hardly any reference to other non-physical aspects like issues of culture and values based on indigenous knowledge and wisdom, as practised in the Asia-Pacific region, for example. It is important to bear this in mind, as some 60% of the seven billion people in the world are inhabitants of this geographical region.

It is imperative, therefore, to attempt to bridge this gap so that SD can be better understood and implemented on a more comprehensive basis through education for sustainable development (ESD). More importantly, each indigenous belief or piece of knowledge and its practices may have somewhat similar or even broader concepts and wisdom relative to what has been conventionally defined, as above. This is because most indigenous beliefs and practices, especially the major ones, have been in existence for centuries and are present in multiple situations – nationally, geographically, and socioculturally. The fact that they have long been an important part of local cultures provides them with several advantages that can be further explored to enhance the contemporary, if limited, meaning of SD.

To quote Diamond (2012) in the monumental book, *The World until Yesterday*, '"Modern" conditions have prevailed, even just locally, for only a tiny fraction of humanity history, all human societies have been traditional for far longer than any society has been modern' (p. 7). 'Traditional societies in effect represent thousands of natural experiments in how to construct a human society. They have come up with thousands of solutions to human problems' (p. 9).

'My own outlook on life has been transformed and enriched by my years among one set of traditional societies,' according to Diamond (2012, p. 466).

12.2 INDIGENOUS CULTURE, KNOWLEDGE, AND WISDOM IN SD

The chapter aims to highlight and illustrate relevant cases so as to demonstrate the need to embrace the aspects of indigenous culture, knowledge, and wisdom in making SD even more participatory, involving the larger spectrum of the population, who are often marginalized. For instance, one of the two basic ideas of SD is the concept of 'needs', which, especially in relation to basic necessities of the extreme poor, deserves to be given

highest priority. The second basic idea is the recognition of the constraints imposed on the environment in meeting the needs – both present and future – with reference to the state of technology and socio-economic organization. The limitations of environmental biocapacity to cope with economic growth, as well as the 'continuous economic growth' model of development, are two clear examples where the indigenous aspects are of significance. Unless this is appreciated, the key elements of SD and related concepts are not well supported, if at all, when we perceive them from the various indigenous perspectives, and not only those limited to the Asia-Pacific region. In other words, the spread of SD through other translational approaches remains affected, especially when it relates to the intergenerational aspect that is essential for SD vis-à-vis the quality of life; also, its close association with an ecology (planet), the life of which depends on the balancing of the economic (prosperity) and the sociocultural (people) dimensions, must be borne in mind.

The Brundtland Report attempts to 'reunify' the idea that 'ecology' is an integral part of the human existence (psyche and action), united with 'development', which is not just external to our human existence (e.g. in terms of economic and political aspects) but also internal (emotionally and spiritually). For this reason, cultural and religious aspects are excellent entry points, where SD can form learning platforms in different sociocultural contexts. By making SD more culturally relevant, sensitive, and appropriate, it could further enrich and enhance the practical use and implementation of SD, thus making the concept more acceptable and inclusive throughout the world. Here is where Asia-Pacific perspectives and approaches, in particular, and others more generally, can play a significant role in advancing work on SD. Given what has been achieved so far, by opening other vistas that have not been visited or articulated thus far, beyond the conventional views and interpretations, it can be turned into part of the transformative learning process.

According to the Association for the Advancement of Sustainability in Higher Education (AASHE, 2011), in the presentation 'Grounding sustainability in faith-based mission and identity', '[a]t its core, … [i]t is about our human stewardship of God's creation and our responsibility to those who come after us.' For example, to respond 'to the Church's call for faithful climate action – and to explicitly and consistently ground this sustainability work in Catholic mission and identity – a group of Catholic individuals, organizations, and higher education institutions has worked with AASHE to publish "Sustainability and Catholic higher education: A toolkit for mission integration"' (DiLeo, 2011). In similar ways, the Asia-Pacific region relates to even wider traditions of Buddhism, Hinduism, and Islam, to name just three, which are equally vocal in advocating respect for nature and all living things since immemorial, as explained in Section 12.3.

Gardner (2002) recognized the following situation:

To further the engagement of environmentalism and spirit, religious people and institutions would do well to consider applying their strong assets to the pursuit of sustainability. Environmentalists, meanwhile, would gain by opening to the rich spiritual dimensions of environmentalism, recognizing that they need to do more to appeal to the public on an emotional/spiritual level.

Gardner also stated that '[m]utual misperceptions and divergent worldviews are at the root of most issues that separate them' (p. 6), which have historically kept the environmental and religious groups apart. The author acknowledged that 'concern over the checkered history of religious involvement in societal affairs, and divergent perspectives on the role of women, the nature of truth, and the moral status of humanity in the natural order have posed obstacles to cooperation. But none of these differences need prevent collaboration on the many areas of interest common to the two groups'. By appealing to the 'emotional/spiritual level … a new ethics encompassing humans, the divine, but nature as well, can be developed to establish a just and sustainable civilization' (p. 7).

This is in line with the United Nations' rich history, which carries with it a host of values related to human dignity and rights, equity, and care for the environment and SD. It comes with valuing biodiversity and conservation along with human diversity, inclusivity, and participation. The goal is to create a locally relevant and culturally appropriate value component to ESD that is informed by the principles and values inherent in SD and humanity. This point was clarified as early as 1999, when the World Culture Report (UNESCO, 1999) in its preface reported the following:

Culture shapes the way we see the world. It therefore has the capacity to bring about the change of attitudes needed to ensure peace and sustainable development which, we know, form the only possible way forward for life on planet Earth. Today, that goal is still a long way off. A global crisis faces humanity at the dawn of the 21st century, marked by increasing poverty in our asymmetrical world, environmental degradation and short-sightedness in policy-making. Culture is a crucial key to solving this crisis. (p. 4)

As is often the case, this view is inclusive of faith-based traditions as a way of life in harmony with nature in a sustainable way. Osborne (2008, p. 16) suggested that we must be able and willing to resolve the intellectual and emotional resistance to the ideas of a civilization that are different from the current ideas.

The important issues that have been dealt with include the following: (a) integrating the non-physical/spiritual elements of sustainability in education; (b) strengthening coordination and collaboration in enriching the concept of SD beyond the conventional; (c) closing the information and knowledge gaps through indigenous, faith-based approaches; and (d) developing a greater latitude for sustainability by incorporating the different concepts and approaches in creating a sustainable balance, focusing on the actions of persons, especially leaders. As a parting thought, the challenges and responsibilities ahead of us require us to be bold enough to do what it takes to change the course for SD in prompting the next civilizational transformation towards a more comprehensive, sustainable, and balanced civilization.

At this juncture, the perspectives of indigenous knowledge and wisdom inter alia faiths and traditional beliefs should be fully taken into account so as to further enrich the idea of sustainable development. For example, Brundtland argues that 'environment' is where we live and 'development' is what we all do in attempting to improve our lot within that abode and that '[t]he two are inseparable' (WCED, 1987, p. xi). This is very akin to the indigenous and faith-based worldviews, where both environment and development are two sides of the same coin. It goes beyond any geographical location as normally understood; rather, it embraces humanity globally, across all divides and barriers, towards an equitable and sustainable society.

The common goal is to achieve a peaceful, fair, and just global community framed on ethical and moral principles in tandem with the aspirations of the United Nations Sustainable Development Goals (SDGs), from 2016 to 2030, those being dignity, justice, and partnership, as well as the 3Ps of sustainable development – people, planet, and prosperity.

Overall, the WCED calls for institutional reform, that is, balancing the terms of trade in the international economy to 'produce an international economic system geared to growth and the elimination of world poverty' (WCED 1987, p. 18), and changing the nature of institutions and laws to reflect the interconnectedness of environmental and economic problems (WCED, 1987, pp. 17–21).

In this chapter, we will also focus on the various Asia-Pacific indigenous cultural traditions in the approach and framework that promote the values and thinking to make SD relevant and alive. This will be followed by an exploration into the breadth and depth of various perspectives, with emphasis on the region, aimed at demonstrating the following:

• The deeper cultural relevance and context of understanding of SD in the region;
• The similarities and compatibilities of SD to the basic indigenous concepts and wisdoms;
• The broader and humanizing dimensions that indigenous and cultural traditions have to offer in strengthening the global discourse on SD;
• The underlying universality of SD values that embraces indigenous-based models.

It is worthwhile to note, in conjunction with the end of the United Nations Decades of Education for Sustainable Development in Aichi-Nagoya on 8 November 2014, that Traditional (Indigenous) Knowledge and Biodiversity was one of the themes discussed at the ninth Global Regional Centres of Expertise (RCE) Conference, which was held on 4–7 November 2014 in Okayama, Japan. It focused on engaging with and feeding into the international sustainability policy processes, and how various multiple-stakeholder processes have helped create links with different international policies. Earlier, in March, the International Association of Universities (IAU, 2014) issued a statement following the IAU 2014 International Conference on Blending Higher Education and Traditional Knowledge for Sustainable Development, held in Iquitos, Peru. In particular, it reaffirmed the need for community engagement to anchor SD in local tradition, language, and culture, and to better blend traditional knowledge in higher education.

12.3 FROM CONCEPT TO PRACTICE: SELECTED COUNTRY EXAMPLES

Civilization is the ultimate object of society, when a society shows features that are advanced in not only the externalities – structures and forms – but also the internalities, in terms of cultural values and virtues. It implies an achievement of quality of well-being that is both sustainable as well as balanced. In the Asia-Pacific region, indigenous cultures and lifestyles that illustrate this are very well-documented. In this section we will briefly review the case in four different Asian countries of various mixes – Japan, Indonesia (Bali in particular), Malaysia, and Thailand – and the case of the Maori for the Pacific. Some common salient points are highlighted as per the Asia-Pacific perspectives vis-à-vis those outside the region, especially the perspective of the West.

Japan, a pioneer of education for sustainable development (ESD) and a major proponent of SD globally, is culturally rich and still relevant in the context of ESD, despite being technologically advanced. Japanese cultural understanding is often linked to the natural and social environment in ways that induce peaceful and harmonious relationships with people and their way of life. At times this is described as a form of 'uniqueness', in an attempt to explain how Japanese cultural concepts embrace philosophical thoughts that are able to blend Buddhism, Shintoism, and Taoism together, as well as ancestor worship. More importantly, it brings with it values and attitudes that are unfamiliar to the conventional, Western-centric ESD. Take 'gratitude' for instance, a cultural theme that permeates Japanese society as a whole as 'a method of rigorous self-reflection based on the philosophy that humans are fundamentally in debt since all existence implies mutual dependency' (Whelan, 2004). It underscores a 'worldview that considers all things to be interconnected' – even the deceased. For example, Whelan wrote about the expression of gratitude towards laboratory animals that had been 'sacrificed' for the benefit of science in a 'memorial services' conducted twice a year in a pharmaceutical university in Tokyo:

That afternoon, under the shade of a huge tree on campus, all the laboratory employees turned up in their white lab coats. Although no 'religious' official was present, a master of ceremonies made a short speech and then read from a white scroll that listed the kinds and precise numbers of animals that had been killed: guinea pigs 400, monkeys 22, mice 700, and so on. University staff members from other departments also attended the service and stood quietly with hands folded and heads bowed. The altar erected for the ceremony overflowed with offerings. A university administrator stood nearby with a bag of bananas and oranges and passed them out to participants who formed a long queue to the altar where each one placed the fruit, and offered incense and a little prayer. The entire service took no more than forty-five minutes out of the usual working day.

Yet this is just the tip of the iceberg, because there are others, such as 'a memorial service for (broken) sewing needles', which were kept for an annual event and placed onto 'a soft bed of fresh tofu on the altar' (Whelan, 2004), as witnessed at a Buddhist temple. Other inanimate objects ranging from 'old combs', to 'stubby calligraphy brushes' were never too small to be remembered with a type of gratitude that 'affirms not only the complex webs of human relations, but also those with the environment', relations that make up the indivisible world of animate beings and the inanimate, the past and the present.

This no doubt illustrates one 'unique' perspective that expands the depth of ESD in enhancing relationships and interconnectedness beyond what is conventionally understood and practised. Exercises involving breathing and meditation are further practices deemed to deepen and enhance human connections, creating harmony by placing attention on wholesome emotions. Therefore, embedded in the Japanese cultural instinct is attention more about the 'way' rather than the 'work', when undertaking physical (external) tasks or exercises. In other words, the Japanese are equally (if not more) concerned with 'being' as well as with 'doing', by focusing on the inner, spiritual aspect in order to experience the natural world's balance and harmony, beyond the needs of the materialistic ego (Dürckheim, 1974).

This sense of balance and harmony is equally relevant, as Japanese culture values group consciousness and solidarity more than individuals and personal ideas, leading to greater sustainability based on collaboration and loyalty at various levels rooted in traditions (Davis and Ikeno, 2002).

A research poster presented at Okayama (Mushakoji, 2017) utilizing 'local and traditional knowledge' as ESD resources attempted to develop 'global human resources who [*sic*] have the sensibility to respect both domestic and foreign traditional knowledge as wisdom for coexisting with nature, and to respect the people who live with such traditional knowledge'. In this way, it reckoned that by developing a method for rediscovering traditional knowledge from ancient calendars (such as the lunisolar calendars), educational programmes for understanding the traditional cultures of other countries and locales could be facilitated. The idea is to propose a system for human resource development and the development of society based on sustainability; the ongoing activities are evidence that there is a genuine effort to integrate ESD with Asia-Pacific perspectives, in this case, Japan (RCE, 2018).

The same can be said of other countries in the region, which are culturally different from Japan, as in the case of Indonesia. Yet the values and attitudes adopted in tandem with ESD are not too far off from those in Japan. In the rice-growing areas in the island of Bali, Indonesia, where Hindu influences (blended with some Buddhist practices) are prominent, the *Tri Hita Karana* (THK) philosophy takes precedence. It translates literally as 'three reasons for well-being', encompassing the forging of harmony with God, among fellow humans, and with nature or the environment. Uniquely a Balinese spiritual belief and experience, it encourages peaceful coexistence and compassion by maintaining sustainability and balance between these three aspects. All rituals are centred on maintaining the balance, since the inception of THK some 900 years ago. It has been credited as being responsible for the island's prosperity as a whole, its relatively stable record of development, environmental practices, and the overall quality of life for its residents (Krishna, 2008). A former president of Indonesia, Susilo Bambang Yudhoyono, even invoked it in his address to the International Conference on Sustainable Development during APEC 2013, which was held in Bali (PHRI Bali, 2013). As practised in their way of life, the blend between the cultural values posed by the THK philosophy and Hindu religion is so blurred that even the Balinese themselves find it difficult to distinguish between the two. According to UNESCO (World Heritage Convention, 2012), the 'fusion' is the result of cultural exchange between Bali and India over the past 2,000 years. They are interconnected in a balanced and harmonious way between the material and spiritual, the past and the future, and the macrocosm and microcosm, as demonstrated through the *subak* (irrigation) system (Surata, 2013). The system, which was awarded World Heritage Cultural Landscape status by UNESCO in 2012, dates back to the ninth century and encompasses a cooperative water management system of canals and weirs as part of the pristine cultural landscape, with temples as the focus. Ingrained therein is a democratic and egalitarian farming system that subscribes to sustainability practices, thus enabling the Balinese to become the most prolific rice growers in the archipelago without much use of artificial (chemical) pesticides and fertilizer. It is said that the authenticity of the terraced landscapes, forests, water management structures, temples, and shrines collectively convey 'Outstanding Universal Value' in such a way that it is reflected by the *subak* system (World Heritage Convention, 2012).

Beyond this, like the Japanese cultural wisdom, THK also has its version of 'gratitude', which must be offered periodically to the world of the living and non-living, the seen and unseen. For example, there is a day of grateful offerings to plants (paddy, coconut trees); domestic animals (cows, pigs); shadow-play puppets and musical instruments (masks and costumes); also tools and weapons like daggers – all to be recognized for the 'help' extended in making life more pleasant, prosperous, and sustainably balanced, as prescribed by the THK philosophy. Not a day passes without a ceremony taking place, although there are periods when some activities are prohibited with the aim of maintaining the natural balance and harmony. It is a firm reminder to act conscientiously when it comes to ensuring strong interconnectedness in the world at all levels, and with nature in particular.

In similar ways, the principle of THK advocates mutual communal activity, generally known as *gotong-royong*, which is also practised elsewhere in Indonesia (Koentjaraningrat, 2009). It is a collaborative endeavour among the village members, which in the case of Bali includes maintaining the *subak*. At the same time, it acts as sociocultural glue, connecting and bringing the communities even closer to functionally serve, among others, as a platform for conflict resolution, inclusive ritual and religious activities, and sharing of resources apart from water, to include rice and finances, as well. In turn, it further enhances sustainability based on balanced and harmonious relationships through the concept and practice of *gotong-royong* as a sustainable community platform.

Gotong-royong is also prevalent in neighbouring Malaysia, which shares much of Bali's THK philosophy, with a slight adjustment. Better known as *sejahtera* (in the Malay language), it has an added fourth dimension, namely forging harmony between each human and his or her inner self – apart from God, fellow humans, and nature. The four dimensions in this worldview focus 'inwards' (spiritually) as their primary thrust, which is regarded as vital for the purposes of maintaining a harmonious balance within the larger societal framework. This is done by (micro-)balancing each element that makes up *sejahtera*, summed up by the acronym SPICES (Dzulkifli, 2017a; Dzulkifli *et al.*, 2018, p. 212), namely the spiritual, physico-psychological, intellectual, cognitive, cultural, ethical, emotional, ecological, economic, and societal dimensions. It is rooted in the Islamic spiritual belief and experiences within the Asia-Pacific region, more specifically the cultural framework of the Malay Archipelago (*Nusantara*).

Sejahtera is not easily rendered into other languages because of its comprehensive and multi-layered meanings and nuances. It underscores the realization that indigenous knowledge and wisdom have their own uniqueness, strength, and relevance for the local community, influencing people over the years. It spans the macrocosmic and microcosmic nexus. Where it is the former that relates humans to the external environment – nature, fellow beings, and other species – the latter is microcosmic because it embraces the 'self' and the inner (esoteric) dimensions, including spiritual consciousness. Taken as two concepts in one, the status of *sejahtera* as a balanced lifestyle is summarized by SPICES. Not only must each aspect be in a (micro-)balance with itself, but each must be in balance with all the rest to achieve an overall state of well-being that is lasting (sustainable) over generations.

The last point is pertinent because it implies that *sejahtera* as a sustainability concept is not new, relative to the well-acknowledged Brundtland Report. Like THK, *sejahtera* is an ancient concept in many indigenous traditions that has been overtaken and lost in the drive towards modern (unsustainable) development. Its etymology can be traced back to a Sanskrit origin, with possible derivations that include *sadhya* (celestial being), *sudatra* (granting gifts), and *sucitra* (distinguished). Although the meanings of these Sanskrit words only narrowly imply the meaning of *sejahtera*, their root is a reflection of local indigenous influences that shape the meaning from the local cultural (sustainable) perspectives (Dzulkifli *et al.*, 2018, pp. 212–213). It draws away from the idea that development is purely a physical venture and need no longer to focus on building collaborative relationships or interconnectedness between humans, the community, the environment, or indeed the 'creator' to build an enduring lifestyle. In so doing, it reinstates the fine state of balance that is severely offset by a hefty price tag for future generations. In short, the embodiment of *sejahtera* goes beyond the conventional 3Ps of planet, people, and prosperity. Although each aspect can be individually targeted and developed, for example, *sejahtera ekonomi* (economic well-being), it is only when expanded into the socio-ecological dimension within the SPICES framework that all the elements are harmoniously blended and nurtured, turning it into a holistic endpoint for a sustainable future.

Without a doubt, 'relationship' (or coexistence) is an important concept in making *sejahtera* work in a balanced way, if we fully appreciate the in-depth meaning of 'relationship' and take the cultural context and nuances into account (Dzulkifli, 2020). Collaborative relationship in particular embraces compassion, empathy, and the uncompromising spirit of oneness, transcending differences and bitterness, bringing about the much-needed

close relationship, coexistence, and interdependency. Seyyed Hossein Nasr, the well-known Muslim thinker, in contrast, describes the 'near total disequilibrium between modern man and nature', as if we are seeking 'to offer a challenge to nature rather than to cooperate with it' (Nasr, 1968, p. 20). Similarly, within the context of SD, we need the traits of cooperation and relationship to aid the millions who are under urgent threats from global warming and climate change. The unprecedented occurrences of crisis after crisis cannot be handled effectively without nurturing the relationship that binds people via a set of common values and ethics. In reality, the world is highly complex, dynamic, and interdependent; therefore, isolated, compartmentalized, and conventionally linear approaches are most likely to fail because they are disconnected (Khalid and O'Brien, 1992) and thus unsustainable. Instead, constructive relationships and networks are essential to enable people to have an unselfish self-reliance and to be steadfast in mitigating and preventing potential crises, which are happening at an ever-increasing rate and severity. Having people nurture deeper relationships early in life is part of arriving at the deeper, spiritual meaning of *sejahtera* that must be cherished, protected, and lived in the metaphysical sense (Dzulkifli, 2017b).

In Malaysia, a *Sejahtera* Leadership Initiative (SLI) has evolved to address the issues of ESD from a leadership standpoint. It highlights a human-centric dimension of leadership focused on balance and trusteeship, in addition to justice, as a continuum of leadership evolution into the twenty-first century. SLI is a citizens' initiative that enshrines more than one decade of aspirations and efforts to hold up to the community and institutions in Malaysia and elsewhere. The initiative is an attempt to help redress 'the emerging promise of a Malaysian development balances … whilst giving space for religious, spiritual and cultural practices' (Sahabat Alam Malaysia, n.d., p. 195).

To the north of Malaysia, Thailand offers yet another classic example based on its philosophy of 'Sufficiency Economy' (SDG Partnerships Platform, n.d.), the term for a local development approach attributed to the late King Bhumibol Adulyadej (Office of the Royal Development Projects Board, 2012). Sufficiency Economy is therefore officially promoted by the Government of Thailand, involving more than 23,000 villages that have adopted and implemented the philosophy, including ESD. It too has three aspects, namely reasonableness, moderation, and prudence (the need for self-immunity against internal and external change), with two essential underlying conditions, that is, knowledge and virtue as guidelines (Chaipattana Foundation, 2017).

According to U-tantada *et al.* (2016), reasonableness refers to thoughtful consideration; moderation, the middle way between hunger and luxury; and prudence or self-immunity signifies the alleviation and prevention of economic, social, and environmental risks. While knowledge focuses on the wisdom and insight of the know-how, skills, and acquired effort within the self or an organization, virtue refers to the ability to show humanity to all living species.

The concept promotes 'balanced physical and mental development; the true essence of the human being is the combination of body and mind, increasing the balance of both the physical comfort and mental happiness' (U-tantada *et al.*, 2016, p. 2). While it 'does not mean that one must constantly be frugal' (Chaipattana Foundation, 2017), provided that it is within one's capacity, it does caution that most people often spend beyond their means. And this can threaten stability. The king said in his 1998 birthday speech, 'Sufficiency means to lead a reasonably comfortable life, without excess, or overindulgence in luxury, but enough. Some things may seem to be extravagant, but if it brings happiness, it is permissible as long as it is within the means of the individual' (Chaipattana Foundation, 2017).

It proposes the idea of limited production in order to protect the environment and conserve scarce resources in a sustainable way. It puts sustainability at the core by taking local values/virtues into consideration. This philosophy is therefore considered a means of strengthening the moral fibre of the nation, so that everyone, particularly public officials, academics, and business people at all levels, adheres first and foremost to the principles of honesty and integrity. In this way, life based on patience, perseverance, diligence, wisdom, and prudence is indispensable in creating balance and in coping appropriately with critical challenges arising from extensive and rapid socio-economic, environmental, and cultural changes in the world (NESDB, 2011).

In practical terms, at the individual and family level, it means living a simple and sustainable life, living within one's means, and refraining from taking advantage of other people. At the community level, however, it involves joining together to participate in decision-making, developing mutually beneficial knowledge, and applying technology where appropriate, with an emphasis on partnership and collaboration. It favours the natural principle wherein one employs natural resources readily available in each locality. At the national level, it postulates a holistic approach with an emphasis upon appropriateness, competitive advantage, low risk, and avoiding over-investment. It involves keeping abreast with what is happening elsewhere in the world, hedging investments, and reducing imports and over-dependence on other countries (Partnerships for the SDGs, n.d.).

Interestingly enough, the principles of sufficiency economy have much in common with Buddhist economics, the term coined and promoted in *Small Is Beautiful* by Schumacher (1973), a book translated by King Bhumibol into Thai (National Identity Office, 2000). (An official biography of King Bhumibol says he 'used part of the material in the book … for a Thai discourse on Buddhist Economics'.) Overall, it shares fundamental

common principles and objectives with SDGs, seeking to eradicate poverty and reduce inequality as a means to achieve sustainable development and create a mindset that seeks balance among the three dimensions of SD. It therefore could support and complement the successful implementation and realization of the 2030 Agenda on Sustainable Development (Ministry of Foreign Affairs of Thailand, 2017).

As for the Pacific, the Maori worldview has many similarities to the views already discussed. The Maori people are the early navigators to the land they called *Aotearea*, translated as the 'Land of the long white cloud', now known as New Zealand. The Maori culture and tradition remain an integral part of its indigenous history (Dzulkifli, 2017c). Foremost is the belief that the human is an integral part of the finely tuned natural ecosystem that must be preserved. The Maori 'staked the coastal seas and inland waters to delineate the family, food-gathering boundaries', and unlike those whose survival depended on the land, they have no farmable animals and few crops (Durie, 2017, p. 4). Their law is based on spiritual beliefs connecting tribal members to their past and future, to each other, and to the natural world. This is clearly another example of an indigenous concept that has its origins in ancient times, like the origins of other Asian perspectives. The Maori, the wildlife, the land, and the waters are all related by descent from primordial ancestors. Indeed, the living and the dead share the land and waters and hold them for the generations to come (Durie, 2017, p. 6). To determine their own status, their place in the world, and their relationship to other Maori throughout the country, they are 'judged' by the length and breadth of their genealogies. In fact, the land, mountains, rivers, and streams each have their own life force, called *mauri*. They descend from ancestors and thus are treated as 'living beings', and that allows the Maori to identify themselves according to the ancestral mountains and rivers of their customary villages (Durie, 2017, p. 7).

In this regard, the Maori are unique in that the institution of ancestral genealogy comes into play in thematic symbols like the tree developing from seed to fruit, which the real (natural) world represents. Each thing has its own rooted foundations in the 'cosmic tree', and the Maori perceive the universe as a 'cosmic process' that is unified and bound together by spirit (Marsden, 2003, p. 31). As an integral part of the cosmic process, man is both human and divine, while the spirit is ubiquitous, sustaining all things by its *mauri*. As such, the Maori approach to life is holistic, with no sharp division between culture, society, and their institutions. In other words, from a Maori perspective, everything is connected: not just land, sea, and air, but relationships between people and relationships between people and the environment as parts of this larger whole. Maori look at resource issues and sustainability in a holistic way, never separating the sea from the land and the land from the air. They see all things being connected when dealing with issues of environment or land. It is important to understand how crucial the spiritual aspects of relationships are in order to discover the in-depth meaning in a Maori context. The relationships are further suggested in the three basic building blocks involving the sustainability of communities (which is dependent on the strength of the land and in turn depends on soil and water and air), the sustainability of families, and that of people, all premised on relationships termed as *aroha* (love) and *wairua* (spirit or natural instinct).

Given that the Maori people are more dependent on the coastal seas and inland waters than on the land, they have a deep sense of respect for water bodies, the rivers, streams, springs, lakes, wetlands, and groundwater as ancestral entities and address them as living organisms. This ushers in a novel view of sustainability, as water bodies are deemed to have a life force of their own, along with a distinct personality and authority (Durie, 2017, p. 9). As in THK, the water too is provided by the gods for human survival, as drinking water, for growing food supplies, or a means of transport, and even has medical value, especially for those who are sick through spiritual imbalance or contamination. The strength and health of most water bodies are of utmost importance and may be measured by the abundance of wildlife and 'water demons' which inhabit it. Their absence or reduction in numbers is a serious omen for the tribe. Framed in the context of sustainability, observations in nature are critical for survival and are closely monitored (Durie, 2017, p. 10). For instance, practices like washing and bathing are conducted in separate streams, where practical, or in a discrete part of the river, or by carrying the water away from the river's edge. Contaminating the water bodies is not just wrong but deemed a spiritual offence. Even boiled water used for cooking is regarded as 'dead water' and thus not discharged into living water. Such profound views on safeguarding the sanctity of water and its sources go far deeper than the current understanding of SD.

This is especially true when water is also deemed significant in spiritual healing and invocation or giving thanks, generally termed as *karakia*. This gesture of 'gratitude' is offered in practically all situations to achieve well-being and wellness, including before surgery, reaffirming the same basic principles and beliefs, as expressed in this 'song' (Edwards, 2002):

> *Greeting to the Creator, the supreme power*
> *Io Matua-nui, God, you created the universe*
> *and the splendours you put in place to enhance*
> *the world you gave to this earthly kingdom,*
> *Nature in its glory, so we all may live.*
> *You planned everything so well.*
> *We greet also your descendants, the Sky Father and Earth Mother,*
> *Ranginui the heavens, Papatuanuku the planet.*
> *They become the perfect balance, the parents of the gods,*
> *the spiritual caretakers of the planet.* (p. 121)

12.4 ENRICHING ESD WITH ASIA-PACIFIC PERSPECTIVES

The Asia-Pacific perspectives detailed above are novel, rich inputs to the picture of sustainable development and ESD. They further illustrate that the close links between culture and indigenous or faith-based knowledge about sustainability are imperative in the region. Essentially, they take off from the pristine idea of SD that took root many centuries before it was introduced to the broader world in 1987. Major recurring themes include spirituality, guardianship in the context of responsibility and accountability, ethics and values, holistic worldviews and interconnectedness, balance and harmony between micro- and macrocosm, and a sense of higher purpose. The main concepts of each are contrasted below with the respective non-Asia-Pacific (largely Western-centric) counterpoints:

- Spirituality is often seen as an integral part of the holistic cultural landscape, especially in relation to nature. In this way, it widens the current understanding of ESD and our perspective on sustainability. The spiritual dimension also lifts other related values, such as ethics and morality, that act as a spiritual compass, creating a higher sense of purpose in a transcendental way connecting humans, as well as other created beings (as part of nature), and the Divine.
- Spirituality, however, is seldom fully grasped outside the region, in particular in the Global North, leaving a wide gap in understanding between the two. Even when there is acceptance of simple spirituality by people in the North or West, the deeper notion of spirituality and its interconnectedness with the Divine in a transcendental way is not fully acknowledged, if not denied. Consequently, the meanings, approaches, and final aspirations towards ESD promoted by the two worldviews may be divergent, arriving at very different impacts.
- Guardianship in the context of responsibility and accountability is similar to the concept of stewardship or vicegerency. It conveys the idea that humans are no more than caretakers of Mother Earth and the planetary system. They have no 'ownership' over the environment, and they have no right to overexploit nature as they please. In contrast, they are duty-bound to conserve and preserve the natural world and its resources as much as possible, notably the non-renewable and finite ones. These resources are regarded as 'gifts' from heaven (i.e., nature) and therefore considered sacred, not to be squandered at the dictate of one's selfish interests. Humans are accorded the responsibility of carrying out their sacred roles in an accountable manner.

Generally, this is in contrast with the Western view of being human, which is to rule over nature and the world, leading to the state of crisis that we are in today. Central to this is the misuse of natural resources for individual or commercial interest at the expense of the majority. There are no apparent limits or constraints on what humans can do under the pretext that they 'own' natural resources, which are then compartmentalized for the narrow purposes of economic benefit, with little regard for the ecological and sociocultural consequences.

- Ethics and moral values are the supporting elements in the realm of spirituality. In many ways, they cut across various religions and creeds to form a common platform for spirituality. Values like compassion, justice, and dignity seldom vary and hence add new vistas in the articulation of ESD in creating partnership with various cultures in achieving global sustainability.

- The counterpoint is that, instead of spiritual values being supported by ethics and morality, the foundation for human behaviour is material or economic value, which becomes the benchmark for all other values. When nature is assigned price tags, based on institutionalized or individualized, self-centred considerations, those involved may claim to honour some deviant form of ethics and morality, but it is completely removed from the holistic worldview.

- Holistic worldviews and interconnectedness characterize the overall orientation of the traditional Asia-Pacific perspectives towards ESD, where all things are interconnected – the animate and inanimate worlds, the material/secular and spiritual – in shaping a sustainable future. The overarching culture is based on 'cooperation' rather than 'competition' driven by domination, as reflected by the pyramidal/hierarchical structure (with humans at the top). For the former, happiness and security are regarded as wealth, not possessions or money, as in the latter case.

- It is obvious that the overall prevailing worldview is quite the opposite of the Asia-Pacific perspectives; that is, life is not unified but instead is partitioned into the secular and spiritual. At the same time, interconnectedness is lost as institutions and knowledge become disconnected from the greater world. In fact, spirituality is marginalized and isolated, as the scientific (reductionist) method takes a dominant stance, threatening the balance and harmony between the micro- and macrocosm.

- The balance and harmony between the small and the large suggest that, if we view the world on a grand scale, humans are in fact a microcosmic representation of the outer macrocosm. Both must be in a finely balanced state in order to bring about harmonious relationships between all the elements, as the world evolves towards a sustainable system. It is about the balance between what is 'in here' (internals) and 'out there' (externals).

- As 'mechanical materialism' spreads through the Western-centric cultural landscape, more of society becomes restrictively reductionist, with the introduction of each new technological advance. Problems arise, however, when the natural world proves too complex for mechanical, linear, and hierarchical approaches. 'Complex life cannot be governed through the imposition of policy-directives', which means that it needs to evolve 'through local adaptation' (Chandler, 2014, p. 40). Life and nature, in their diversity and infinite complexity, present a clear contrast against the unbalanced relationship between the internal and the external, as discussed earlier. But when the mechanical outlook presides as the all-knowing master of Mother Earth, we see the triumph of imbalance and the unsustainable.

- Achieving the sense of a higher purpose is perhaps the overarching aspiration of the Asia-Pacific perspectives, on the path towards sustainability, and it should be a goal in education for sustainable development. It is a point of departure, marking the overall difference from the conventional understanding. It is not limited to just the material and the secular; rather it is the convergence of the two, together with spiritual and transcendental values. Chopra (2012) explains this in terms of the three levels of awareness: contracted, expanded, and pure awareness, each a step closer to the true self.

- In the final analysis, the higher goal of human endeavours is to achieve the micro- and macrocosmic balance and harmony aligned to the holistic worldviews, while maintaining the innate interconnectedness throughout. This may not make sense to those who are unable to accept the notion of spirituality as expressed intrinsically in the microcosm. The resulting apparent disconnect thus leads to the prevailing compartmentalization, or silos, based on the differences in worldviews as governed by the various institutional ethics, dictated by short-term situations, rather than coming from a common platform. As a result, much of ESD also appears culturally unbalanced, with Western-centric views prominent.

Notwithstanding the above, the Asia-Pacific views have often been ridiculed when other considerations and dimensions are included in discussions, especially views pertaining to the realm of spirituality and other intangible aspects. Yet these are the very distinctive elements for which the Asia-Pacific perspectives are known; they depart from the current understanding, which lacks the spiritual aspects and all their implications. A recent article, 'A new theory based on quantum physics says there's life after death' (Power of Ideas, 2017), points to an emerging perspective that could change the current entrenched situation. Then it may be possible for the Asia-Pacific perspectives to become part of the mainstream (once again, as argued by Krishna, 2008; Diamond, 2012) in the quest for a sustainable future.

12.5 THE CHALLENGE FORWARD

In his classic work *The Meeting of East and West*, Northrop (1979) recounted the impact of Eastern thought on the culture of the United States and Western Europe, which was seen in the spread of Buddhism, meditation, martial arts, yoga, oriental art, and hundreds of other Asian imports. Northrop recognized then that 'the full significance of Eastern culture, its distinctive features, and its potential for influencing the rest of the world' (back cover) had been noted even earlier, in his writing during the 1940s and 1950s. The author suggested that the synthesis of cultures (via the arts) resonated with the idea and effort to create interconnectedness and holistic approaches. This synthesis is increasingly being accepted, and the field of ESD is no exception (Dzulkifli *et al.*, 2018, p. 218).

As Northrop (1964) further noted, Eastern thought in general deals with the world as an 'undifferentiated aesthetic continuum' (pp. 67–71), perceived qualitatively. That is, at a level deeper than everyday utility, reality is all connected and unified, not separated into distinct objects. Northrop contrasted Western thought as abstract, with a mathematical or formal conception of reality, along with an atomistic conception of reality as composed of fundamentally separate objects. Concepts occur in the West 'by postulation', while in the East 'by intuition' (Northrop, 1979, chap. 2). In spite of these differences, the East and West can learn from each other to avoid future conflict and to flourish together, as stipulated in the United Nations SD Goal 16: Promote just, peaceful, and inclusive societies; as well as Goal 17: Partnerships for the goals. The first goal is dedicated to sustainable development, the provision of access to justice for all, and building effective, accountable institutions at all levels, while Goal 17 recognizes that the world today is more interconnected than ever before. Improving access to technology and knowledge is an important way to share ideas and foster innovation, but not the only one, or the most desirable, if the non-physical (intangible) dimensions are left by the wayside. The aim is to enhance North-South and South-South cooperation by supporting national plans to achieve as many of the targets as possible, but not limited only to those conventionally recognized, if the Asia-Pacific (indigenous) perspectives are to be taken into consideration. This is imperative, as strengthening global solidarity is one of the SDGs that make up the 2030 Agenda for Sustainable Development. An integrated holistic approach is crucial for progress across the multiple goals. That said, the effort will require coherent policies, an enabling environment for sustainable development at all levels and by all actors, and a reinvigorated Global Partnership for Sustainable Development.

Watts (1991) made the following observations:

The harsh divisions of spirit and nature, mind and body, subject and object, controller and controlled are seen more and more to be awkward conventions of language. These are misleading and clumsy terms for describing a world in which all events seem to be mutually interdependent – an immense complexity of subtly balanced relationships which, like an endless knot, has no loose end from which it can be untangled and put in supposed order …

We have less and less use for words which denote stuffs, entities, and substances, for mind and matter have together disappeared into *process*. Things have become events, and we think of them in terms of pattern, configuration, or structure, no longer finding any meaning in the question, 'Of what stuff is this pattern made?' But the important point is that a world of interdependent relationships, where things are intelligible only in terms of each other, is a seamless unity. (p. 4)

Watts further argued that in such a world it is 'impossible to consider man apart from nature, as an exiled spirit which controls this world by having its roots in another' (p. 4). And ultimately, '[c]ontrary to its avowed philosophy of living for the future, its perspective is really no longer than the day after tomorrow, for it exploits the resources of the earth and the energies of radioactivity with only the most fragmentary knowledge of the complex relationships so disturbed' (p. 5).

As suggested by Dürckheim (1974, p. 6), it looks as though human nature in the West is in danger of being overshadowed by materialist, reductionist forces to such an extent that the innermost self is imperilled. Western mentality is characterized by an exaggerated impulse to be independent of Nature and exist in a material civilization that thinks it can dispose of Nature, as it strives towards extreme objectivity – what is termed as 'the Western form disease' (Watts, 1991, p. 10).

Consonant with the above observations, as far back as the fourteenth century, scholar-thinker Ibn Khaldun (1958) observed that civilizations with high levels of culture, wealth, and refined practices are also highly self-indulgent. Over a period of time, they become devoid of qualities like 'social (tribal) cohesion' or 'group feelings/consciousness', which Ibn Khaldun collectively termed *'asabiyya*, borrowed from pre-Islamic Arab culture, signifying loyalty, unity, and solidarity, and founded on 'sustenance' (Ibn Khaldun, 1958, pp. 297ff). The author considers *'asabiyya'* as the engine of development for attainment of a supposedly great and humane civilization, but which later regresses, leading ultimately to its own destruction. Ibn Khaldun alludes to social injustice as one factor that breeds unsustainable practices and eventually destroys a civilization (Enan, 2007, p. 94).

Ibn Khaldun is better recognized for introducing an innovative new discipline, *ilm al-'umran* (science of culture) (Mahdi, 2006), which interconnects human civilization (*al-'umran al-bashari*) and social phenomena in order to provide a more comprehensive worldview of the total human experience. This could be seen as a basis for sustainability, as *al-'umran*, derived from its Arabic root, means 'to build up, to cultivate' a humane civilization, and therefore is used to designate any settlement or population that transcends the level of individual barbarity (Ibn Khaldun, 1958, pp. 267–269). It deals with the larger social dimensions of human life: the interplay of various factors, including climatic and environmental extremes (Oliver, 2005, p. 333). Above all, Ibn Khaldun believed in the dynamic nature of civilization as a continuum. A major 'Khaldunian' concept involves cycles of rise ('conquest') and fall ('collapse') of civilizations, inter alia 'sustainability' and the converse, respectively (Oliver, 2005, pp. 272–273).

It is tempting to interpret the former as the cycles of sustainability, while the latter is the converse since, according to Ibn Khaldun, the decline is set off by the loss of a common set of unified traditional beliefs and interdependence among diverse inhabitants. This loss of interconnectedness is one important sign of ensuing unsustainability, from the perspective of Asia-Pacific cultures. It lessens cohesiveness in a diverse ecosystem – economic, social, and environment – at the peak of a civilization. Consequently, the decline continues as unsustainable practices set in, while contending groups with systems they consider more 'sustainable' emerge to take its place, resulting in a new civilization or dynasty. The Khaldunian cycle is thus repeated. Every cycle is disrupted when there is a triumph of imbalance – yet the emerging rivals rarely if ever prove to be more sustainable or balanced over the long term. Learning how to break or slow this cycle of failure should be one objective of a spiritually and morally balanced ESD programme.

One such disruption was well-articulated by the Prince of Wales *et al.* (2010) when they wrote the following:

Essentially it is the spiritual dimension to our existence that has been dangerously neglected during the modern era – the dimension which is related to our intuitive feelings about things. The increasing tendency in mainstream Western thinking to ignore this spiritual dimension comes from a combination of the growth in cynicism during the latter half of the twentieth century and the wholesale dismissal of the big philosophical questions about our existence. (p. 9)

If we simply concentrate on fixing the outward problems without paying attention to this central, inner problem, then the deeper problem remains, and we will carry on casting around in the wilderness for the right path without a proper sense of where we took the wrong turning. (p. 6)

The authors called this a 'crisis of perception' (p. 5) – the way we see the world is ultimately at fault. The basis of this idea can be traced back to the teachings of spirituality in the context of maintaining 'balance', which is akin to the concept of SD as described by the commission (WCED, 1987, p. 18), which also claims that the root cause of unsustainable growth is that the common meaning of growth has been narrowed down to utilitarian and material gain, leading to an imbalanced phenomenon globally, focused mainly on economic rationality.

12.6 SUSTAINABLE LEADERSHIP

Leadership is an important component in advancing sustainability. The SLI in Malaysia, as indicated earlier, is one such effort to address the issues of ESD taking on other intangible dimensions as a continuum of leadership evolution into the twenty-first century. Pruzan (2011) in his essay 'Spirituality as the context for leadership' argued that many of the modern concepts of leadership were developed in a period characterized in the main by economic growth and increasing standards of living among the nations of the West. A perspective of spirituality-based leadership is by no means comparable to the conceptual scheme based on utilitarianism and economic rationality. The same could be said about SD in its leadership role for ESD. In the West, the approach is focused more on leadership related to 'concepts, processes and the roles that had not until recently been central to the traditional themes of management' (p. 4). This modern approach seeks to contribute to a humanistic, democratic, and sustainable frame of reference for the profession of management, encompassing economic, environmental, social, and ethical responsibility and viability (p. 15).

In contrast, the Eastern approach to leadership is not rooted in new concepts and catchwords, but in fundamental perspectives regarding the purpose and potentials of human life and on the qualities and competencies of leaders (taking into account values, virtues, and integrity), rather than just on methods and processes. The dichotomy is rather obvious and it is clear that there is much that each can learn from the other, but the West can learn even more from the Asia-Pacific perspectives, whose fundamental notions of spirituality and of humans 'as a spiritual being' are a vital context for purposeful activity, including SD (Pruzan, 2011, p. 15). Leadership is important to bear in mind, in light of the current assertions that much of the global unsustainable activities are anthropogenic in origin, namely the person, be they formal leader or otherwise. The vastness of 'spirituality' can comfortably accommodate the deeper concept of SD at both the microcosmic and macrocosmic levels (as further explained here), since balance in a holistic and harmonic way is also applicable to the 3Ps of SD, where the ecological (planet) component is interchangeably connected with the economic (prosperity) system in ensuring equitable distribution socioculturally (people), thus allowing all the components to converge in a harmonious state. That is, the whole depends on its parts, as much as the parts rely on the whole in balancing sustainability (Dzulkifli, 2016). Such interdependency is not an unfamiliar notion in the Asia-Pacific region, as explicated above. It conveys the 'interconnectedness' of a world endowed with various resources, often referred to as the 'gifts' of God, implying that humans have been granted the wisdom, if they will use it, to observe the natural balance that is inherent to Mother Earth, and this duty even extends to other planetary ecosystems we may explore, which must be duly maintained.

As we are reminded by Suzuki (2011), the renowned environmentalist, our brash exuberance over our incredible inventiveness and productivity has made us forget where we belong: 'If we are to balance and direct our remarkable technological muscle power, we need to regain some ancient virtues: the humility to acknowledge how much we have yet to learn the respect that will allow us to protect and restore nature, and the love that can lift our eyes to distant horizons, far beyond the next election, paycheque or stock dividend'. Suzuki (1999) emphasized that recognizing and accepting these limitations with humility is 'the birth of wisdom and the beginning of hope' that we will finally rediscover our place in the natural order (pp. 207–208).

12.7 CONCLUSION

In many ways, this chapter has expounded on the claim that sustainable development is not a new concept that suddenly entered the mainstream with the Brundtland Report in 1987 and then was gradually sidelined as development took a different, unbalanced trajectory, leading to unsustainable development. In this chapter, the focus has been on the issues of physical/spiritual (tangible/intangible) aspects that go beyond the conventional framework of the 3Ps of SD or that of the Brundtland Report per se. In the final analysis, the roots of SD are found in the indigenous practices in most pristine societies, predating the anthropogenic turning point when humans became the major source of an imbalanced and 'unsustainable' world. Despite the imminent dangers, that ancient local knowledge, the cultural practices, indigenous intellectual traditions, stories, histories, and languages are denigrated or regarded as 'used' visions to be discarded and supplanted by the 'new' and 'modern'.

What is taking place in shaping the modern, unsustainable lifestyle is the loss of the very essence of human spiritual values, which have the power to turn the tide. Unless this void is re-energized through appropriate nurturing, the disconnect will continue to exist, and widen, leading to more cycles of rising and collapsing, as envisaged by Ibn Khaldun. To untangle the present predicament, we must be willing to learn from the past and one another, as noted above.

To conclude, it is useful to recall the UNESCO Universal Convention on Cultural Diversity (UNESCO, 2001) as another multilateral policy instrument which recognizes the significance of cultural knowledge 'as a source of intangible and material wealth' (p. 13), particularly in indigenous communities. With respect to SD, it emphasizes that '[c]ultural diversity widens the range of options open to everyone; it is one of the roots of development, understood not simply in terms of economic growth, but also a means to achieve a more satisfactory intellectual, emotional, *moral* and *spiritual existence*' (emphasis added) (Article 3). In this chapter, specific references pointing towards the Asia-Pacific perspectives are cited to illustrate just that.

ACKNOWLEDGEMENTS

The author wishes to acknowledge the assistance of Dr Tan Geok Chin Ivy, Associate Professor, Humanities and Social Studies Education, National Institute of Education, Singapore, and Johan Dzulkifli, Lisbon School of Economics and Management, University of Lisbon, Portugal, for some of the engagement and discussion in developing the materials for the chapter; and an anonymous reviewer, for the constructive and useful comments on and assessment of the paper.

REFERENCES

AASHE (Association for the Advancement of Sustainability in Higher Education) (2011) DiLeo, D. and Kalkbrenner, L. D. (2016) Grounding sustainability in faith-based mission and identity. https://slideplayer.com/slide/4250425/

Chaipattana Foundation (2017) Philosophy of Sufficiency Economy. http://www.chaipat.or.th/eng/concepts-theories/sufficiency-economy-new-theory.html

Chandler, D. (2014) *Resilience*. London, Routledge.

Chopra, D. (2012) *Self Power*. Sydney, Ridder.

Council of Foreign Relations (2013) Rethinking the meaning of development. Blog post by Terra Lawson-Remer, 12 August 2013. https://www.cfr.org/blog/rethinking-meaning-development

Davis, R. and Ikeno, O. (2002) *The Japanese Mind: Understanding Contemporary Japanese Culture*. Tokyo, Tuttle Publishing.

Diamond, J. (2012) *The World until Yesterday: What Can We Learn from Traditional Societies?* Melbourne, Viking.

DiLeo, D. R. (2011) Sustainability and Catholic higher education: A toolkit for mission integration. *Conversations on Jesuit Higher Education*, **41**, Article 29, 48–49. https://epublications.marquette.edu/conversations/vol41/iss1/29

Dürckheim, K. (1974) *The Japanese Cult of Tranquillity*. York Beach, ME, Samuel Weiser, Inc.

Durie, E. T. (2017) *Indigenous Law and Responsible Water Governance*. Kuala Lumpur, Malaysia, TunSuffian Foundation.

Dzulkifli, Abdul Razak (2016) *Leadership and Islam*. Putrajaya, Malaysia, Razak School of Government.

(2017a) 'Sejahtera' thrives in Bali. *The Sun Daily*, 17 October 2017. http://www.thesundaily.my/news/2017/10/17/sejahtera-thrives-bali

(2017b) *Nurturing a Balanced Person: The Leadership Challenge.* Nilai, Malaysia, Penerbit Universiti Sains Islam Malaysia (Islamic Science University) (USIM) and Institut Terjemahan and Buku Malaysia (Malaysian Institute of Translation and Books) (ITBM).

(2017c) The wonders of Aotearoa. *The Sun Daily*, 11 April 2017. http://www.thesundaily.my/news/2017/04/11/wonders-aotearoa

(2020) *Essay on Sejahtera: Concept, Principle and Practice.* Gombak, Malaysia, IIUM Press.

Dzulkifli, Abdul Razak, Khaw, Nasha Roziadi, Baharom, Zulkifly, Mutalib, Mahazan Abdul and Salleh, Hood Mohd (2018) Decolonising the paradigm of sustainable development through the traditional concept of Sejahtera. In Z. Fadeeva, L. Galkute and K. B. Chhokar (eds.), *Academia and Communities: Engaging for Change*, pp. 210–219. Innovation in Local and Global Learning Systems for Sustainability series. Tokyo, Japan, United Nations University, Institute for the Advanced Study of Sustainability (UNU-IAS).

Edwards, M. (2002) *Mihipeka: Call of an Elder/Karanga a te Kuia.* Wellington, NZ, Steele Roberts.

Enan, M. A. (2007) *Ibn Khaldun: His Life and Works.* Kuala Lumpur, Malaysia, The Other Press.

Gardner, G. (2002) Invoking the spirit: religion and spirituality in the quest for a sustainable world. Worldwatch Paper #164, December 2002. http://www.worldwatch.org/system/files/EWP164.pdf

Ibn Khaldun, M. A. R. (1958) Rosenthal, F. (Tr.). *The Muqaddimah*, 6: 7 (para. 38–39). https://asadullahali.files.wordpress.com/2012/10/ibn_khaldun-al_muqaddimah.pdf https://www.scribd.com/document/413581090/Ibn-Khaldun

International Association of Universities (2014) International Conference on Blending Higher Education and Traditional Knowledge for Sustainable Development. https://iau-aiu.net/IMG/pdf/policy-statement_hesd_declaration_iquitos_2014-en-2.pdf

Khalid, F. and O'Brien, J. (1992) *Islam and Ecology.* London, Cassell Publishers.

Koentjaraningrat (2009) *Gotong-royong.* Singapore, Equinox Publishing.

Krishna, A. (2008) *Tri Hita Karana: Ancient Balinese Wisdom for Neo Humans.* Jakarta, Indonesia, Anand Ashram Foundation.

Mahdi, M. (2006) *Ibn Khaldun's Philosophical History.* Kuala Lumpur, Malaysia, The Other Press.

Marsden, M. (2003) *The Woven Universe.* Otaki, New Zealand, Estate of Rev. Maori Marsden.

Ministry of Foreign Affairs of Thailand (2017) *Sufficiency Economy Philosophy: Thailand's Path towards Sustainable Development Goals. A special publication for the Ministry of Foreign Affairs of Thailand*, 2nd edition. http://www.mfa.go.th/dvifa/contents/files/articles-20170626–142701-203959.pdf.

Mushakoji, K. (2017) The bioregion/watershed based ESD practice and dialogue. First RCE Thematic Conference: Towards Achieving the SDGs, 5–7 December 2017, Okayama, Japan.

Nasr, S. H. (1968) *The Encounter of Man and Nature: The Spiritual Crisis of Modern Man.* London, Allen and Unwin.

National Identity Office (2000) *King Bhumibol: Strength of the Land.* Bangkok, Thailand, Secretariat of the Prime Minister.

NESDB (National Economic and Social Development Board) (2011) *Sufficiency Economy: Implications and Applications.* https://www.nesdc.go.th/ewt_w3c/ewt_dl_link.php?nid=2621

Northrop, F. S. C. (1964) The undifferentiated aesthetic continuum. *Philosophy East and West*, **14**(1), 67–71.

(1979) *The Meeting of East and West: An Inquiry Concerning World Understanding.* New York, USA, Ox Bow Press.

Office of the Royal Development Projects Board (ORDPB) (2012) *The Philosophy of Sufficiency Economy: The Greatest Gift from the King.* Bangkok, Thailand, ORDPB.

Oliver, J. E. (ed.) (2005) *The Encyclopedia of World Climatology.* New York, USA, Springer Publishing.

Osborne, R. (2008) *Civilization: A New History of the Western World.* New York, USA, Pegasus Books.

PHRI Bali (2013) Tri Hita Karana International Conference on Sustainable Development: Special Focus on Tourism. http://www.phribali.or.id/news/tri-hita-karana-international-conference-on-sustainable-development-special-focus-on-tourism.htm

Power of Ideas (2017) A new theory based on quantum physics suggests that life after death is not the end. http://www.positivethingsonly.com/theory-based-quantum-physics/

Prince of Wales, Juniper, T. and Skelly, I. (2010) *Harmony: A New Way of Looking at Our World.* London, Harper Perennial.

Pruzan, P. (2011) Spirituality as the context for leadership. In L. Zsolnai (ed.), *Spirituality and Ethics in Management*, pp. 3–21. London, Springer.

RCE (2018) *Good Practices for ESD: Case Reports from Japanese RCEs.* Japan, Regional Centre of Expertise on Education for Sustainable Development (RCE). http://www.rcenetwork.org/portal/sites/default/files/GoodPracticesforESD%2020181203.pdf

Sahabat Alam Malaysia (n.d.) *Malaysian Environment in Crisis.* Penang, Malaysia, Sahabat Alam Malaysia.

Schumacher, E. F. (1973) *Small Is Beautiful: A Study of Economics As If People Mattered.* London, Blond and Briggs.

SDG Partnerships Platform (n.d.) Sufficiency Economy Philosophy https://sustainabledevelopment.un.org/partnership/?p=2126

Surata, S. P. K. (2013) *Lanskap Budaya Subak.* Denpasar, Indonesia, Universitas Mahasaraswati Press.

Suzuki, D. (1999) *The Sacred Balance: Recovering Our Place in Nature.* Vancouver, Canada, Greystone Books.

(2011) Returning to the sacred balanced. Science Matters. https://commonground.ca/returning-to-the-sacred-balance/

UNESCO (1999) *World Culture Report.* Paris, UNESCO. Preface. http://www.unesco.org/education/tlsf/mods/theme_c/mod10.html

(2001) *Universal Convention on Cultural Diversity.* Paris, UNESCO. http://portal.unesco.org/en/ev.php-URL_ID=13179&URL_DO=DO_TOPIC&URL_SECTION=201.html

United Nations General Assembly 4/187 report (1987). *Report of the World Commission on Environment and Development.* http://www.un.org/documents/ga/res/42/ares42-187.htm

U-tantada, S., Mujtaba, B. G., Yolles, M. and Shoosanu, A. (2016) Sufficiency economy and sustainability. https://www.researchgate.net/publication/311677101_SUFFICIENCY_ECONOMY_AND_SUSTAINABILITY

Watts, A. (1991) *Nature, Man and Woman.* New York, USA, Vintage Books.

WCED (World Commission on Environment and Development) (1987) *Report of the World Commission on Environment and Development: Our Common Future.* http://www.un-documents.net/wced-ocf.htm

Whelan, C. (2004) Gratitude: A Japanese lesson. Kyoto International Cultural Association. http://kicainc.jp/english/contest/essay2004-3.html

World Culture Report (1998) *Culture, Creativity and Markets.* Preface. https://unesdoc.unesco.org/ark:/48223/pf0000112074

World Heritage Convention (2012) Cultural landscape of Bali Province: The *subak* system as a manifestation of the Tri Hita Karana philosophy. https://whc.unesco.org/en/decisions/4797

13 A placemaking framework for the social sustainability of master-planned communities: A case study from Australia

BHISHNA BAJRACHARYA AND ISARA KHANJANASTHITI

Faculty of Society and Design, Bond University, Queensland 4229, Australia

Keywords

Placemaking; social sustainability; community building; sense of place; master-planned communities; sustainable communities; Varsity Lakes; Gold Coast

Abstract

Placemaking creates environments which are more active, memorable, and meaningful for people. It can provide several benefits, such as a high quality of life, a strong sense of community, and the creation of distinctive places. There is, however, a paucity of theoretical literature on placemaking in master-planned communities (MPCs). Therefore, this chapter develops a 4-P framework for placemaking in MPCs with the four important factors of Place, Programme, People, and Perception. It then applies the framework to a case study of Varsity Lakes, an MPC on the Gold Coast of Australia. It analyses the placemaking performance of the MPC in terms of social sustainability using the four factors and draws implications from the study. The chapter shows the importance of physical design as well as the process of placemaking to build sustainable communities. Some of the key ideas for placemaking include provision of places for social interaction, walkability, community governance, stakeholder engagement, legibility, safety, and sense of place. These ideas and the proposed framework could be relevant for the sustainable development of MPCs in the Asia-Pacific region.

13.1 INTRODUCTION

Placemaking, as an urban design approach, is focused on facilitating community development and creating distinctive and vibrant places. To achieve these outcomes, it seeks to create active physical environments, encourage social interaction, and establish and reinforce local identity. Placemaking is related to the concept of place, which denotes a meaningful and valued environment for people.

Master-planned communities (MPCs), unlike conventional housing estates, are large-scale integrated housing developments with diverse facilities and land uses. Placemaking can provide several benefits to MPCs. It can make MPCs more socially sustainable through a strong sense of community and the creation of distinctive and vibrant places.

While there is extensive literature on placemaking, there have been limited investigations into placemaking in the context of MPCs. This chapter seeks to address this literature gap by developing a theoretical framework for placemaking in MPCs and applying the framework to Varsity Lakes, an MPC on the Gold Coast of Australia. It tests the framework and analyses the extent to which placemaking is achieved in Varsity Lakes. Lastly, the chapter concludes with key lessons from the case study, which could be applicable for placemaking and social sustainability of other MPCs in the Asia-Pacific region.

13.2 METHODOLOGY

To develop the framework, the chapter first conducts a review of the literature to identify key principles for successful placemaking in MPCs. The subsequent case study analysis, is primarily based on field observation of Varsity Lakes and findings from a community feedback survey of local residents and workers initiated and collected in March 2015 by degenhartSHEDD (2015), an architecture firm based in Varsity Lakes. The survey questionnaire contains 36 questions, which focus on various lifestyle factors such as parks, neighbourhood design elements, street maintenance, local amenities, transport, and events. The survey solicited responses from a total of 36 respondents, 89% of whom live or work in the MPC. In terms of the age profile of survey respondents, 14% were in the 20–34 years age group, 36% in the 35–48 years age group, 22% in the 49–59 years age group, and 28% in the 60 years or older age group. The case study discussion is also supplemented by a literature review on concepts of social sustainability.

13.3 PLACEMAKING IN MASTER-PLANNED COMMUNITIES

13.3.1 What are master-planned communities?

No universal definition currently exists for MPCs, and literature in different fields often contains varying definitions of such communities (McGuirk and Dowling, 2007). An MPC can be broadly defined as a large-scale, private-sector-driven, integrated housing development on a greenfield or brownfield site. Furthermore, it typically comprises a mix of housing options, shops, lifestyle amenities, and local employment opportunities (Cheshire *et al.*, 2010; Gwyther, 2005; McGuirk and Dowling, 2007; Minnery and Bajracharya, 1999; Schmitz and Bookout, 1998).

McGuirk and Dowling (2007) classify master-planned estates according to the level of intervention and support from developers in terms of establishing and strengthening a sense of community. Conventional planned estates are normally subject to restrictive covenants for the design and layout of dwellings and landscapes in line with the developer's overall vision for the estates. Lifestyle estates are similar to conventional planned estates but often contain additional amenities, such as a golf course and forest tracks, and are therefore subject to a higher level of developer intervention than conventional planned estates. In contrast to these estates, MPCs contain the highest intensity of developer intervention in creating positive social and physical outcomes through such instruments as lifestyle amenities, a formal governance structure or body, and a developer-funded social coordinator(s) (McGuirk and Dowling, 2007).

MPCs can be proprietary or gated communities in which communal infrastructure is accessible only to residents (Goodman and Douglas, 2008). Such developments are commonly securitized by hard edges and/or clear closure through signage or architectural features (Atkinson *et al.*, 2005). A range of community facilities, such as sports grounds, exercise amenities, walking tracks, and parks, are often provided. These facilities are a major selling feature, which attracts residents to live in MPCs due to the higher quality of life they promote.

Each MPC is often developed to promote a certain image and appeal to a clientele (Moudon and Wiseman, 1990). Schmitz and Bookout (1998) discuss emerging ideas and concepts of how MPCs are planned and designed. Some of them include increased community interest in environmentally sustainable development, safer communities, and integration of education and healthcare infrastructure.

13.3.2 What is placemaking?

Extensive literature on placemaking exists, which can provide a useful basis for developing a framework for placemaking in MPCs. Most of the existing placemaking literature, however, is not directly in the context of MPCs, but is instead related to general urban communities from an urban design perspective (Bajracharya *et al.*, 2006). Buchanan (1988) proposes that urban design is essentially about placemaking, where places are not just spaces, but rather result from an amalgamation of events and activities that provide meaning to such places. Similarly, Carmona *et al.* (2003) assert that urban design is a process of making places which are better for people than conventional places that would normally be created without urban design considerations.

According to the Project for Public Spaces (2018), a key organization in the field, placemaking is 'a collaborative process by which we can shape our public realm in order to maximize shared value … [and strengthen] the connection between people and the places they share'. Similarly, Placemaking Chicago (2008) defines placemaking as 'a people-centred approach to the planning, design and management of public spaces'. Placemaking is related to the creation of built environments that convey a distinct sense of place while meeting both the psychological and physiological needs of people (Fleming, 2007; Nasar, 1998). Meanwhile, Schneekloth and Shibley (1995) define placemaking as the way people transform the places in which they live. They propose that placemaking is concerned with not only the relationship of people to places but also fostering relationships between people through places. Implicit in their definition, placemaking is closely related to social sustainability, with a focus on strengthening social relationships.

13.3.3 Placemaking in master-planned communities

MPCs often have a strong emphasis on placemaking for nurturing local community and social interaction (McGuirk and Dowling, 2007; Bajracharya *et al.*, 2006). However, according to Cheshire *et al.* (2010), the design of these developments is typically reflective of the overall vision of the ideal lifestyle perceived for their targeted consumer group by the developers, thus allowing for minimal input from these end users. Consequently, MPCs are often identical or similar in terms of their spatial, architectural, and land-use attributes. As a result, they commonly lack a unique place identity, which is one of the key attributes of successful placemaking (Cheshire *et al.*, 2010).

Placemaking can lead to local economic benefits for MPCs. According to Wardner (2011), one of the common features of recent MPCs is the provision of employment centres where residents are able to live and work locally. To attract local employment in MPCs, successful placemaking outcomes, such as community interactions and place image, can act as pull factors for firms which are considering locating their offices in an MPC (Elgar and Miller, 2009; Wardner, 2012).

13.3.4 Place, placelessness, and sense of place

Before discussing placemaking principles, it is important first to define and distinguish the following key terms: place, placelessness, and sense of place. The concept of place in the literature is primarily related to 'the emotional, psychological, and physical experience of an environment' (Clifton, 2013, p. 5). As an environment where associations and meanings are clustered and organized (Lynch, 1960), place is linked to sense of belonging and place attachment (Carmona et al., 2003). Places are different from physical or social spaces, since the former are created only when the latter 'are well-loved, well-used, and evoke meaningful associations for their users' (Marshall, 2016, p. 193). Importantly, places provide people with rootedness and a sense of belonging to a territory or group, which are essential mental qualities for people (Carmona et al., 2003).

In contrast to place, 'placelessness' is a term conceptualized and defined by Relph (1973, pp. 182–183) as 'a weakening of the identity of place to the point where they not only look alike but feel alike and offer the same bland possibilities for experience'. It is related to the disappearance of distinctive places due to various modernization forces, such as mass culture, mass communication, technological innovations, and standardized and impersonal planning (Liu and Freestone, 2016; Relph, 1976). Spaces that are considered to be placeless not only lack human scale, but also are exchangeable, formless, impermanent, and unstable (Liu and Freestone, 2016).

In the urban design literature, there is a wide use of such terminologies as 'place identity', 'genius loci', and 'sense of place' (e.g., Jiven and Larkham; 2003; Lynch, 1960; Menin, 2003; Norberg-Schulz, 1980). Place identity provides a place with individuality or distinction from other places, so that it can be recognized as a unique, separate entity (Lynch, 1960). Genius loci, meanwhile, is used by Norberg-Schulz (1980) to represent the sense of place with which people associate specific locations. As the sum of all physical and symbolic values in the natural and built environments, genius loci refers to the unique 'spirit of place' or the distinctive atmosphere of a place (Vogler and Vittori, 2006, p. 2). On the other hand, Jiven and Larkham (2003) propose that sense of place is a result of experiences of people using the place, rather than an outcome of deliberate placemaking by urban designers. Therefore, placemaking initiatives alone do not create a sense of place – the people that use the place collectively create it. Therefore, creating a place is simultaneously a material construct as well as a construct of mind, which highlights the need to consider both the physical and mental perceptions of a place (Menin, 2003). Placemaking creates places which are vibrant, memorable, and meaningful to people.

13.3.5 Placemaking elements

The chapter now identifies a range of elements that contribute to successful placemaking. Montgomery (1998) develops a framework for placemaking comprising three key elements that make each place distinctive: activity, form, and image. 'Activity' refers to the level of human interactions and activities in the area, which can be influenced by such factors as street life, café culture, active frontages, events and local traditions, and local businesses' opening hours. Second, 'form' refers to various physical elements, including scale and intensity of development, permeability, landmarks, public realm, and the ratio of buildings to space. Lastly, 'image' is related to how the place is perceived by the users through such attributes as symbolism and memory, imageability, legibility, and sensory experiences.

Watson and Bentley (2007), through an investigation of how urban design affects place identity through a series of international case studies, conceptualize four key elements for identity establishment. They include empowerment, rootedness, inclusiveness, and co-dwelling with nature. Project for Public Spaces (2016) specifies four key attributes as ideal placemaking outcomes: comfort and image, uses and activities which attract people, sociable environments, and, lastly, access and linkages.

Knox (2005) criticizes new MPCs in the United States for their lack of character, which is essential to a sense of place, and their lack of social cohesion, identity, and vitality. To overcome these issues, he highlights the importance of developing 'third places' (where home is the first place and the workplace is the second place (Oldenburg, 1999)). Third places, as the 'loci of routine activities and sociocultural transactions', provide opportunities for casual encounters as well as settings for sustained conversations and interactions (Knox, 2005, p. 8). Examples of third places include sidewalk cafés, pubs, post offices, pharmacies, and corner stores.

To establish and maintain an area's character, Schmitz and Bookout (1998) suggest the use of active edges, such as parklands and other natural features, instead of conventional hard edges such as boundary concrete walls. Other design attributes recommended by Schmitz and Bookout include less prominent garages, narrow lots, and building design features such as windows, front porches, and ornamental elements. Lang (2016), meanwhile, suggests that a sense of place can be established over time through the personalization of places that people use. Personalization, driven by residents or other stakeholders on their behalf, can occur in several ways, such as changes to street signage and building facades and using windows to display a variety of objects and information. In addition, artwork can be incorporated throughout the public realm to illustrate local artistic skills or memorialize key historical events in the community, thus reinforcing the neighbourhood's sense of place (Marshall, 2016; Walljasper and Project for Public Spaces, 2014).

Town centres, also referred to as public squares, urban squares, plazas, piazzas, courtyards, or gardens, play an important role in activating public life, thus contributing to the creation of image and character for urban areas (Marshall, 2016). Successful town centres comprise an appropriate mix of green and grey spaces, maximize the sensory experiences of their users, and are heavily used and loved by the public (Marshall, 2016). A variety of park activities should also be introduced to encourage interaction between people and activate the use of public spaces in town centres (Walljasper and Project for Public Spaces, 2014). Bohl (2002) analyses several MPCs in terms of the design, marketing, management, and performance of their town centres. He argues that MPCs face dual challenges of creating and maintaining both a sense of community and a sense of place. Furthermore, he proposes that town centres in MPCs play a major role as a literal and symbolic centre of the community and a place where local communities are assimilated.

Walkability, which 'can enhance the experience of visitors to a place, making it more memorable and attractive', is proposed by Clifton (2013, p. 9) as a key component of placemaking. Although the exact definition of walkability varies, it generally refers to an environment that is conducive to pedestrian activity (Clifton, 2013). Some of the key attributes of a walkable environment include connected sidewalks, street network connectivity, the absence of heavy and high-speed traffic, perceived and actual safety for walking, and street trees for maximizing pedestrian comfort through shade (Lo, 2009). In addition to creating a safe environment for pedestrians, it is also equally important to improve the general level of safety in a neighbourhood. Doing so can encourage interaction between people in the community, thereby contributing to the creation of a strong sense of community (Walljasper and Project for Public Spaces, 2014). Bohl (2002, p. 3) argues that placemaking through proper design of mixed land uses and the pedestrian environment can be 'a marketable development putting communities on a map and establishing a strong sense of place identity for [MPCs]'.

The contemporary way of thinking about placemaking projects and their underlying governance structures is moving towards a place-led approach. This process 'relies not on community input, but on a unified focus on place outcomes built on community engagement' (Project for Public Spaces, 2016, p. 20). In this regard, group activities that involve local stakeholders in the planning and management of their public spaces can lead to strong social capital and shared values. Such shared management approaches can range from an informal network of local communities and businesses to more formal governance structures (City of Onkaparinga, 2014). In this regard, social coordinators commonly funded by MPC developers can be involved in engaging with local stakeholders. Furthermore, opportunities for social interaction and strengthening community pride should be promoted through a variety of multicultural events (Walljasper and Project for Public Spaces, 2014).

Twohig (2016) explores case studies of successful placemaking at different scales and in a variety of settings around the world. For any scale of development, he suggests that building a place brand is an important placemaking strategy. In this regard, developers should move beyond the conventional 'brand identity', which can be established through such elements as signage and logos, towards 'brand image' for their development projects. Brand image represents 'the collective opinion of a development's customer base about the developer's company, property or place' (Twohig, 2016, p. 73). In the context of MPCs, early community engagement through events, which reflect the developer's vision and its MPC, prior to commencing the MPC's development, can help build a positive brand image among the public.

13.3.6 Framework of placemaking in master-planned communities

Based on the literature review findings above, the following four factors are critical for placemaking in MPCs:

- Place – physical form, structure, and layout of MPCs;
- Programme – governance structure and other formal arrangements for strategic placemaking;
- People – social elements that can contribute to a sense of community in MPCs;
- Perception – how MPCs are perceived by outsiders, visitors, and residents.

Based on the four themes above, an original 4-P framework for placemaking in MPCs has been developed. The framework, which integrates both the principles of placemaking and the context of MPCs, is outlined in Figure 13.1, along with the various elements under each factor.

Table 13.1 provides a brief description of the different elements articulated by the framework.

13.3.7 Links between placemaking and social sustainability in master-planned communities

There is growing literature on the diverse concepts of social sustainability and links between placemaking and social sustainability (Putnam, 2000; Bohl, 2002; WACOSS, 2002; Hurley, 2011; Woodcraft et al., 2012; Totikidis et al., 2005). Social sustainability is about creating communities which are diverse, equitable, connected, democratic, and with good quality

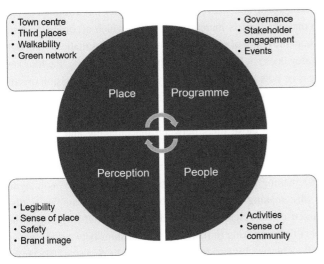

Figure 13.1. 4-P framework for placemaking in master-planned communities.

of life (WACOSS, 2002). Related to the idea of social sustainability is the concept of social capital by Putnam (2000), which emphasizes the importance of social networks for facilitating cooperation within the community for mutual benefits. These social networks and shared experiences can result in goodwill, trust, and reciprocity among community members. Another related concept is community governance, which implies the capacity of the community to actively engage in the process of community building by themselves. It is about community-level decision-making, with the broader aims of addressing community needs and building community capacity and well-being (Bowles and Gintis, 2002; Totikidis *et al.*, 2005).

Social sustainability has many important dimensions, and different authors have highlighted its various aspects. First, it is about creating places that support well-being and a strong sense of community (Palich and Edmonds, 2013). Second, it is about ensuring sustenance of diverse social relations between community members (Palich and Edmonds, 2013). Third, it involves active engagement with the people living in these places. Fourth, it means creating quality public spaces through collaborative planning (Bohl, 2002). Fifth, it implies building communities with strong perception of safety and positive image of the place (Cheshire *et al.*, 2010). Last of all, it is about equitable access to services and facilities and sustainability of the

Table 13.1. Placemaking elements and their description.

Element	Description of elements
Place	
Town centre	The existence of a quality town centre, which activates public life and enhances the MPC's image
Third places	The provision of both indoor and outdoor settings for community interaction in the MPC
Walkability	The extent to which the MPC is conducive to walking, which can be enhanced by such factors as connected sidewalks, street trees, and vehicular traffic calming measures
Green network	The availability of natural features, which function as active edges and positively reinforce the MPC's image
Programme	
Governance	The extent to which the developer promotes placemaking in the MPC through such governance arrangements as social coordinators and community events
Stakeholder engagement	The involvement of local stakeholders in the planning and management of public spaces and placemaking initiatives in the MPC
Events	The frequency and variety of events provided in the MPC, which can promote a strong sense of community
People	
Activities	The level of human activities in the MPC's public realm, which can be enhanced by such factors as active street frontages, local café culture, and long opening hours of local businesses
Sense of community	The local sense of community, which can be established and strengthened by social networking opportunities in the MPC
Perception	
Legibility	The ease of wayfinding in the MPC, which can be influenced by such factors as clear signage and street layout
Sense of place	The extent to which the MPC fosters a sense of place through its physical design features such as public artwork, personalized built environment, and landmarks
Safety	The perceived and actual level of safety in the public realm in day and night times
Brand image	The brand image of the MPC, which is related to the collective opinion about the developer and its development projects

community in terms of community stability and social networks (Dempsey *et al.*, 2009).

Dempsey *et al.* (2009) identify two types of factors contributing to social sustainability (as identified by various authors): non-physical factors and predominantly physical factors. According to the authors, non-physical factors include sense of community, social capital, quality of life and well-being, safety, social inclusion, participation, and democracy. The predominantly physical factors include an attractive public realm, accessibility to green spaces and services, and a walkable neighbourhood.

Social sustainability is about both the process of engagement and the social outcomes of place design (Palich and Edmonds, 2013). Designing social sustainability should include four building blocks: provision of amenities and social infrastructure, promotion of social and cultural life, giving voice and influence to the community, and planning for spaces to grow in the future (Woodcraft *et al.*, 2012). While the past focus on placemaking was on the 'design' of places, there should be increased focus on the 'making' of places, which includes building and nurturing the community, increasing focus on process (programming), and new collaboration between public and private sectors (Silberberg *et al.*, 2013). These ideas provide a more holistic perspective on building social sustainability in communities and link well with the placemaking framework.

Hurley (2011) identifies two objectives relating to what he calls socio-economic sustainability in MPCs. The first objective is increasing quality of life, which he suggests includes community development and provision of safe urban environments. The second objective is increasing equality, which according to him, covers provision of affordable housing and consultation. Although Hurley does not link these objectives to placemaking, the four key ideas he puts forward (community development, provision of safe urban environments, provision of affordable housing, and consultation) are indeed relevant for social sustainability.

There are close links between placemaking and social sustainability, as place is an important context in which many social interactions take place in a community. Much of the placemaking literature suggests social sustainability as integral to placemaking objectives and outcomes. For example, as discussed earlier, Schneekloth and Shibley (1995) highlight the role of placemaking in fostering relationships between people as well as places. Likewise, Project for Public Spaces (2018) talks about placemaking as a collaborative process to share the public realm and maximize shared value. Lang (2016) suggests developing a sense of place over time through personalization of places by community members themselves. Based on the previous review of literature on placemaking as well as social sustainability (Project for Public Spaces, 2018; Lang, 2016; Palich and Edmonds, 2013; Woodcraft *et al.*, 2012; Putnam, 2000; Hurley, 2011; Dempsey *et al.*, 2009; Silberberg *et al.*, 2013; Cheshire *et al.*, 2010), the links between the two ideas have been summarized in Table 13.2.

After developing the placemaking framework and reviewing links between placemaking and social sustainability, the next section provides a brief overview of the Varsity Lakes MPC.

Table 13.2. Placemaking factors and their links to social sustainability.

Placemaking factors	Links to social sustainability
Place	• Connection between people and the place they share (Project for Public Spaces, 2018) • Creating places which support well-being and strong sense of community (Palich and Edmonds, 2013) • Provision of amenities and social infrastructure (Woodcraft *et al.*, 2012) • Housing diversity (Hurley, 2011)
Programme	• Community governance (Totikidis *et al.*, 2005) • Equitable access to services/facilities and sustainability of community (Dempsey *et al.*, 2009) • Collaborative process to share public realm and maximize shared value (Project for Public Spaces, 2018) • Building and nurturing the community (Silberberg *et al.*, 2013) • Collaboration between public and private sectors (Silberberg *et al.*, 2013)
People	• Social relations between community members (Palich and Edmonds, 2013). • Social capital (Putnam, 2000) • Promotion of social and cultural life (Woodcraft *et al.*, 2012) • Strengthening connections between people and places (Project for Public Spaces, 2018) • Fostering relationships between people as well as places (Schneekloth and Shibley, 1995)
Perception	• Sense of place over time through personalization of places (Lang, 2016) • Strong perception of safety (Cheshire *et al.*, 210) • Provision of safe urban environments (Hurley, 2011)

13.4 OVERVIEW OF VARSITY LAKES

Situated approximately 80 kilometres south of Brisbane on the Gold Coast, Varsity Lakes is an MPC located seven kilometres from the beaches on an urban site adjoined by Bond University, Robina Woods Golf Course, and several existing canal residential estates. With construction commencing in 1999 and completed in 2013 by Lendlease,[1] Varsity Lakes covers a total area of 343 hectares (Lendlease, 2013). It is a popular residential community for 'empty nesters', professional couples, and mature families due to its high-quality built form and access to local facilities and employment.

Varsity Lakes comprises a variety of land uses, including residential precincts, educational hubs, and several commercial, mixed-use, and industrial areas providing local employment opportunities. Furthermore, a number of recreational amenities are provided in the MPC, including the 80-hectare Lake Orr, 56 hectares of open spaces, and 20 kilometres of cycling and walking tracks. Developed with the vision to accommodate 4,500 jobs, Varsity Lakes has a total of 12 different precincts, which are referred to as 'villages' by Lendlease (2013).

The residential villages immediately adjoining the town centre and overlooking the lake contain medium-density residential complexes and mixed-use development. The other residential villages provide more traditional low-density residential development. Dwellings in Varsity Lakes consist primarily of detached homes with rendered brick and tile roof.

The 2016 census indicates that Varsity Lakes[2] has about 15,000 people living in the area, with 46% male and 54% female population. The average number of people per household is 2.6, with a median weekly household income of A$1,363. The top three occupations of the people living in the area are professionals (20.3%), technician and trade workers (14.1%), and sales workers (13.5%). There is a diversity of house type in the area, with about 45.9% living in separate houses, followed by 36.9% in semidetached houses and 17.2% in flats and apartments. While 51.3% houses are owned, 46.2% are rented and the remaining 2.5% are of other types (Australian Bureau of Statistics, 2017).

The chapter now applies the previously developed framework to evaluate the case study of Varsity Lakes in terms of its placemaking performance and social sustainability. The discussion from Sections 13.5 to 13.8 is organized according to the different themes articulated by the 4-P framework: Place, Programme, People, and Perception.

13.5 PLACE FACTOR

The Place factor is associated with the extent to which several built environment aspects of an MPC – which include its form, structure, and layout – promote placemaking.

13.5.1 Town centre

The town centre, located in the northern area of the MPC and adjoining Lake Orr, comprises a mixture of residential, retail, educational, and commercial uses. As per Lendlease's vision for the MPC, the town centre also includes technology parks, which provide specialized infrastructure and facilities for high-tech businesses. It encompasses three precincts, namely Varsity Central, Market Square, and Bermuda Point. The Varsity Central precinct contains an office park, mixed-use development, and educational facilities. Two schools are located there, including a senior campus of Varsity College state school and a Goodstart kindergarten. Meanwhile, Market Square, which adjoins the southern end of the university and backs onto the lake, comprises a variety of shopping, dining, and entertainment facilities. There are also SOHO (Small Office/Home Office) dwellings in and around Market Square, which can be used as offices, homes, or both. Such dwellings can encourage work-life balance and accommodate work-from-home professionals and small businesses. Furthermore, several of the ground-floor retail shops in Market Square are located below residential apartments. On the other hand, to the east of the university campus lies Bermuda Point, a waterfront business precinct with a focus on mixed-use commercial and high-tech commercial activities.

Market Square plays a major role in promoting placemaking in Varsity Lakes. As an interface between Bond University, commercial spaces, residential precincts, and schools, it is the place where the public gathers most frequently in Varsity Lakes. It comprises several key public spaces that are regularly utilized by locals and visitors alike. Central Park is a large park located adjacent to Varsity College and regularly used by the school and public for sporting activities and events. Figure 13.2 shows the Market Square town centre area of Varsity Lakes.

Warren Rowe, the former Director of Planning and Environment at the City of Gold Coast,[3] makes the following observations about the history of the development of Varsity Lakes and the importance of Market Square in placemaking:

The original history/background of this area is also relevant here. Delfin, the initial developer of Varsity Lakes, established the first main building in the Market Square as an initial contribution to the

---

[1] Varsity Lakes was developed by Delfin, an Australian development company which later became a part of Lendlease, a global company.
[2] The statistics shown here pertain to the suburb of Varsity Lakes. The Varsity Lakes MPC constitutes the majority of the suburb.

[3] The City of Gold Coast is the local government agency responsible for the governance of the Gold Coast.

Figure 13.2. Market Square as a major public realm in Varsity Lakes.

creation of community. It included the developer's sales office and a café. The building was designed with a clock tower to provide a visual point of reference for the new community. The café soon became a focus for the new community and the adjoining car park was used for various community events. The café became a licensed restaurant with the license being granted to Delfin. It is assumed that early residents would have a very positive view about this area which formed an early and important piece of community infrastructure creating initial social capital. (Warren Rowe, personal communication, 26 May 2018)

Market Square also contains lakeside terraces, which are frequently used for informal community interactions during the day time. In addition, a network of boardwalks provided around Lake Orr not only serves as a popular walking, running, and cycling track for residents but also encourages social interactions (Bajracharya *et al.*, 2014). Figure 13.3 shows the terraces and the boardwalk.

13.5.2 Third places

Market Square provides a variety of venues which actively function as 'third places' both day and night. For instance, a local bar and restaurant is a popular spot for corporate functions, business meetings, and live music. Meanwhile, a boutique café is frequented for informal gatherings. Several other cafés and restaurants are also located in the area. Many of these businesses provide seats and tables on the streets, which increase the vibrancy of the place.

In addition to restaurants and cafés, several shops, such as printing stores, groceries, pharmacies, and florists, are established in Market Square and raise the likelihood of social interactions between shopkeepers and customers as well as among customers. The wide local streets in Market Square also serve as effective third places for social interaction, given that the precinct is frequented by residents, students, and workers alike. Bond University, meanwhile, provides a variety of settings for community interactions and events, including libraries, a sports centre, event venues, and an amphitheatre. However, there is a scarcity of third places in the MPC outside the Market Square and Bond University precincts.

13.5.3 Walkability

The developer has designated three roads in the MPC, namely University Drive, Varsity Parade, and Christine Avenue, as the 'main access roads' (Lendlease, 2013, p. 27). While footpaths along these roads are shaded by trees and contain sufficient lighting at night, other walkways in Varsity Lakes generally lack adequate shade and lighting, thus limiting walking attractiveness throughout the community. Some of the major roads in the area are wide and could well do with some traffic calming measures to enhance walkability. As of October 2020, a study indicated that the entire suburb of Varsity Lakes achieves a Walk Score of 53 out of 100. It indicates that Varsity Lakes is 'Somewhat Walkable' and the 18th most-walkable suburb out of the 81 suburbs on the Gold Coast (Walk Score, 2020). Given the

Figure 13.3. Terraces and boardwalks in Market Square, Varsity Lakes.

reasons outlined above, the overall level of walkability in the MPC is evidently low. As such, walking is a relatively less utilized transport mode than driving among local residents and workers. In this regard, only 42% of the community feedback survey respondents said that they engage in walking often or very often when travelling in the MPC, in comparison to a figure of 94% for driving (degenhartSHEDD, 2015).

While the entire Varsity Lakes contains a variety of land uses, the MPC's predominant land use is residential, which is mostly not within walking distance to other uses such as schools, shops, and offices. The only major mixed-use area in Varsity Lakes is Market Square. However, given its location on the northern end of the MPC, the town centre is not within viable walking distance from most residential villages. This is particularly the case for residents living in one of the villages on the southern end of the MPC. Consequently, most of the residents are forced to rely on their car to travel to the town centre. Furthermore, Lake Orr reduces pedestrian connectivity between the different precincts in the MPC. Bermuda Point can only be accessed via a pedestrian bridge adjoining the eastern end of Bond University. As such, pedestrian connectivity to Bermuda Point is limited in the MPC.

13.5.4 Green network

As part of the MPC development, the developer created Varsity Lakes Conservation Park, a 20-hectare wetlands reserve that

naturally improves the quality of stormwater and provides a wildlife habitat (Australasian Leisure Management, 2010). Lake Orr is the major natural feature and selling point of the MPC. The community feedback survey indicates that 79% of respondents perceive access to the lake as an important, very important, or critical neighbourhood design element (degenhartSHEDD, 2015). Therefore, Lake Orr is a major natural asset of Varsity Lakes that is highly valued locally. In addition, Lake Orr Catchment Reserve, another wetlands reserve, borders the MPC on the western end. These natural assets not only improve the amenity for adjoining residents but also provide walking tracks for recreational activities.

From the perspective of local residents and workers, having adequate access to a park network is a significant neighbourhood design element. In this regard, more than 88% of the community feedback survey respondents indicate the feature as an important, very important, or critical neighbourhood design feature (degenhartSHEDD, 2015). Throughout Varsity Lakes, a network of small-scale open spaces, which are incorporated with artwork, are provided as 'interesting places for play and reflection' to enhance the 'perception of the community' (Lendlease, 2013, p. 29). The inclusion of artwork into these open spaces also promotes a sense of place for local communities. Each home in Varsity Lakes is in proximity to the open space network, thereby providing residents with equitable access to open spaces. The community feedback survey findings illustrate active utilization of local parks by residents, since

77% of respondents indicated that they use the parks occasionally, often, or very often. Furthermore, the majority of the survey respondents indicate a high level of satisfaction with the parks. In this regard, approximately two-thirds of the respondents indicate they are moderately or extremely satisfied with the quality, style, size, maintenance, and safety attributes of the parks. More than 91% of the respondents also rated the park network in the MPC favourably or very favourably. However, approximately half of the respondents seemed displeased with the park's facilities, with their responses being neither satisfied nor dissatisfied, moderately dissatisfied, or extremely dissatisfied with the facilities (degenhartSHEDD, 2015).

13.6 PROGRAMME FACTOR

13.6.1 Governance

Varsity Lakes Community Limited (VLCL) is the main body responsible for community governance and management in Varsity Lakes. As a local, not-for-profit organization established by Lendlease in 2006, VLCL aims to promote 'community prosperity' in Varsity Lakes (Sports House, 2018a). With representatives from local stakeholder groups, VLCL is responsible for engaging residents in events and a variety of sport and recreational activities. In the early stage of the development of Varsity Lakes, the developer invested in several programmes and events to establish and enhance the sense of community in the MPC.

After VLCL was founded, the responsibility for managing these programmes and events was passed on to the organization, marking the transition from private to community governance for community building in the MPC. VLCL represents one of the first models on the Gold Coast through which an MPC developer establishes an ongoing mechanism for sustained community building before it leaves the scene (Bajracharya and Khan, 2010). Furthermore, a full-time sport and recreational officer has been employed by VLCL to coordinate local sport clubs and assist them in applying for external grants (Bajracharya et al., 2014). Nevertheless, the community feedback survey suggests that there is only limited awareness of VLCL among community members, since 70% of the respondents indicated they are not aware of the organization.

In 2011, Sports House was developed as a 'state-of-the-art community, sports and recreational facility' (Sports House, 2018b). It contains storage facilities for sport clubs, indoor recreation space for fitness and recreation activities, commercial spaces, and corporate meeting venues. Managed by VLCL, Sports House functions as an important facility for the promotion of sport activities and sense of community, as discussed further in this chapter. Figure 13.4 illustrates the Sports House building.

13.6.2 Stakeholder engagement

VLCL plays an important role in engaging the local community in the planning and management of public spaces and

Figure 13.4. The Sports House building.

placemaking initiatives such as various events and programmes. VLCL, through its website, engages local stakeholders by providing information on local events, businesses, and sport clubs. Several partnerships among local stakeholders have led to the advancement of community prosperity in Varsity Lakes. Firstly, Sports House was developed through a partnership between the City of Gold Coast and Lendlease. The site for Sports House was purchased by the council for a sum of A$1.5 million, which was then invested by Lendlease in the development of the facility. Secondly, a partnership between Bendigo Bank, Adelaide Bank, and the local community has led to the creation of the Varsity Lakes Community Bank. At least 80% of its profits are invested in local events and sponsorships (Bajracharya *et al.*, 2014). These partnerships between public, private, and community sectors are an important part of placemaking in Varsity Lakes.

13.6.3 Events

Several events are regularly organized throughout Varsity Lakes by local sport clubs, VLCL, or other local stakeholders. While several events are run by private operators on a user-pays basis, other higher-priced ones have been subsidized by VLCL and sponsors such as Lendlease and local businesses (Lendlease, 2013). These events, which range from sport activities and informative seminars to networking events, are electronically advertised via three platforms, namely the Sports House website, the VLCL website, and the City of Gold Coast website. While the Sports House and VLCL websites provide up-to-date information on upcoming community or sport events in Varsity Lakes, the council website lists all events throughout the city, which can be filtered according to event category and location. Furthermore, VLCL has a Varsity Lakes Events Facebook site, which regularly advertises local events in the MPC. While the Sports House website focuses primarily on sport and health events, the VLCL and Varsity Lakes Events sites provide information on other types of events.

Several event venues exist throughout Varsity Lakes. Central Park is frequently used for such events as Gold Coast Pet Expo, Christmas carols, and Movies in the Park. Lake Orr, meanwhile, is regularly used by local sports clubs for water-based sports activities, including dragon boating, kayaking, rowing, and sailing (Lendlease, 2013).

According to the community feedback survey, approximately three-quarters of the respondents indicate that they attend events in the MPC (degenhartSHEDD, 2015). As such, the survey illustrates active participation of community members in locally organized events as a positive Programme aspect of placemaking.

13.7 PEOPLE FACTOR

The chapter now discusses case study findings under the People factor, which focuses on social elements that contribute to placemaking through establishing and enhancing a sense of community in MPCs.

13.7.1 Activities

There is a range of public activities in the MPC around Market Square, owing to its hub design and variety of functions, services, facilities, and businesses. In addition, the regular use of parks and Lake Orr for public events and sports activities further enhances the area's general level of activity.

Local businesses throughout the town centre generally close by 5 p.m. However, most restaurants, all of which are located in the Market Square precinct of the town centre, operate until 8:30 p.m., with a few restaurants remaining operational until 11 p.m. Varsity Lakes is also home to several award-winning cafés, which are often fully occupied by residents, workers, and university students alike. Therefore, while the streets throughout the town centre are activated with pedestrians and restaurant or café patrons throughout the daytime, only certain sections of Market Square remain active in the evenings. Outside the town centre, there is little public activity and interactions because of the lack of third places, shops, and walkability, which have been discussed previously.

13.7.2 Sense of community

VLCL functions as 'the hub of community life by producing and disseminating a community newsletter, hosting events and supporting local charities (Lendlease, 2013, p. 123). Furthermore, VLCL manages Varsity Lakes Online, a community intranet for residents, which was initially launched and managed by Lendlease in 2005. The website, as a source of local news and information, allows residents to participate in online discussions or create their own club page. The content on the site is kept up to date by journalism students from Bond University (Lendlease, 2013), thus demonstrating further evidence of partnerships being employed to promote placemaking in the MPC.

As outlined previously, the Varsity Lakes Events, Sports House and VLCL websites provide information on local sport clubs and businesses, restaurants, and cafés. As such, they play a pivotal role in establishing and enhancing the sense of community by connecting residents with these local clubs and businesses. Additionally, several locally organized events in Varsity Lakes seek to create and reinforce the sense of community in the MPC through networking between local stakeholders. For instance, the Varsity Social Business Forums are held regularly to connect local businesses and residents in an informal, relaxed setting. Such events are expected to spread information, initiate actions, connect local people and, ultimately, make 'local culture … grow and thrive' (VLCL, 2017).

More than 12,000 people participate in various sport and recreation activities annually in Varsity Lakes. Meanwhile, Lake Orr is utilized by approximately 8,000 people for sport activities (Lendlease, 2013). The community feedback survey findings illustrate that more than 96% of the respondents know other residents in their immediate neighbourhood casually, quite well, or extremely well. Furthermore, more than 70% of the respondents indicate that the sense of community in MPC is moderately strong, quite strong, or extremely strong (degenhartSHEDD, 2015). The survey findings and the active participation of local stakeholders in both organising and attending events indicate a strong sense of community in Varsity Lakes.

13.8 PERCEPTION FACTOR

The chapter next investigates placemaking in Varsity Lakes under the Perception factor, which is linked to how MPCs are perceived by the public.

13.8.1 Legibility

In Market Square, legibility is relatively high, owing to two reasons. Firstly, the town centre is clearly defined through a large, highly visible Market Square signage and a clock tower, both of which function as the centre's major landmarks. Secondly, the extensive use of business or address signage on building facades significantly enhances legibility throughout the town centre. Outside Market Square, however, the general level of legibility is relatively low.

13.8.2 Sense of place

As per the developer's vision, each residential precinct has a specific focus based on either its proximity to the lake, town centre, or golf course, or its access to vistas of nearby hinterland and coastal areas. To achieve a specific design vision for each village, design covenants for dwellings were implemented by the developer. Furthermore, the developer intended to expand the traditional models of predominantly detached housing in MPCs (Lendlease, 2013). As a result, a variety of housing forms is achieved throughout Varsity Lakes, particularly in and around the town centre area, as shown in Figure 13.5.

Figure 13.5. Housing diversity in Varsity Lakes.

Figure 13.5 demonstrates not only the high variety of housing options throughout Varsity Lakes but also the diversity in built form and appearance, which enhances the MPC's streetscapes and overall sense of place (Lendlease, 2013). Diversity is achieved throughout Varsity Lakes through mixing traditional suburban development with a vibrant, integrated mixed-use hub around Varsity Central and Market Square, which combines several facilities, services, and activities. Such diversity in built form and activities further promotes a sense of place in Varsity Lakes.

The urban design of Market Square has been carefully implemented to 'create a "village" atmosphere' within the town centre (Lendlease, 2013). Basement car parks are utilized to keep the town centre compact. The town centre is also predominantly composed of two- and three-storey buildings, which are strategically aligned with their respective street to 'create a sense of vibrancy' (Lendlease, 2013).

The installation of three-piece sculpture of spinning fishes on the top of poles in Lake Orr by the developer creates visual interest and enhances the area's sense of place. The fish sculpture moves with the prevailing wind around the lake, making it a dynamic sculpture. There are other examples of promoting public art in Varsity Lakes through such events as Varsity Street Fest encompassing street art programs. Likewise, there is a growing level of space personalization by local community members. This is done through several measures such as incorporating a diverse array of plantings in their front gardens, the use of a variety of colours in their building facades, and a range of activities on balconies, all of which contribute to creating distinctive places. The use of public art and personalization of spaces are both important aspects of placemaking. Given the reasons outlined above, the MPC, particularly the Market Square town centre, evidently promotes a strong sense of place.

13.8.3 Safety

All respondents of the community feedback survey indicate safety as an important, very important, or critical neighbourhood design element (degenhartSHEDD, 2015). In this regard, safety is one of the most valued components among all design elements for residents and workers in the MPC.

Several streets in Market Square are directly adjoined by businesses, restaurants, or cafés. Furthermore, as previously mentioned, several restaurants and cafés contain seats and tables on their respective streets. As such, the town centre area contains a high level of perceived safety owing to the passive surveillance from eyes on the street. Due to the evening operation of restaurants, the Market Square precinct's natural surveillance remains relatively high at night. Outside the town centre, however, there is limited surveillance as the predominant land use is residential, which is dominated by fences and gates.[4] In addition, some areas lack adequate street lighting, which significantly reduces both perceived and actual safety in the evening. Consequently, safety incidents have been higher outside the Market Square precinct compared to inside the precinct. From October 2019 to October 2020, a total of 629 offences were recorded throughout the MPC by the Queensland Police Service (2020). Only 15% of the offences were in the Market Square area. Thus, although the level of safety is relatively high in Market Square, there is scope for improvement outside the town centre.

13.8.4 Brand image

The developer of Varsity Lakes is Lendlease, which is a major multinational development company with long years of experience in creating large-scale residential communities. With a vision to create communities 'with an emphasis on environmental and social impacts', Lendlease is well known for delivering MPCs which are 'much more than places to live' (Lendlease, 2018). To this end, the developer emphasizes creating a strong sense of community and a high quality of life to form enriched communities with positive legacies for residents. Varsity Lakes reflects this vision through its extensive provision of natural and lifestyle amenities, such as parks and Lake Orr and its surrounding network of boardwalk. Similarly, several of Lendlease's MPCs in Queensland focus on creating a nature-based lifestyle through environmental features such as lakes and parks. Furthermore, the developer has displayed intent to create the imagination of lakeside living among its customer base through its estate names such as Elliott Springs, Springfield Lakes, and Varsity Lakes. The developer's establishment of VLCL and Sports House also highlights its commitment to create and sustain a sense of community through governance arrangements.

Given the reasons outlined above, the MPC evidently demonstrates a strong level of brand image, which positively contributes to the MPC's placemaking performance under the Perception factor.

13.9 ANALYSIS OF PLACEMAKING IN VARSITY LAKES IN TERMS OF SOCIAL SUSTAINABILITY

This chapter has presented findings on placemaking in Varsity Lakes based on the 4-P framework. Based on these findings, this section of the chapter briefly identifies the placemaking performance of the MPC using the Place, Programme, People, and Perception factors for social sustainability. The key findings have

---

[4] Throughout Varsity Lakes, there are several apartment complexes which are gated communities with limited access to the public.

Table 13.3. Links between placemaking factors and social sustainability in Varsity Lakes.

Placemaking factors	Social sustainability of Varsity Lakes
Place	• Third places, such as Market Square and parks, encourage community activities and interactions • Mixed-use developments such as SOHOs can minimize travel and encourage work-life balance • Green networks of open spaces and Lake Orr are major natural assets highly valued by local residents
Programme	• VLCL plays a major role in community governance • Sports House is an important initiative for the promotion of sports activities and sense of community • Partnership between the city council, the developer, and VLCL to set up the community hub of Sports House • Organization of various community events by VLCL and other local stakeholders in areas which are regularly attended by local residents and workers
People	• Provision of community intranet for information, online discussion, linking local businesses with residents, enhancing networking and promoting sense of community • Active participation by residents in various sport and recreational activities, indicating a strong sense of community
Perception	• Diversity of housing and built forms enhances streetscapes and overall sense of place • Village atmosphere of Market Square creates a sense of vibrancy and place • Public art and personalization of spaces by residents contributes to sense of place • Perception of safety around Market Square with passive surveillance due to adjoining businesses, cafés and restaurants, and mixed uses • Positive brand image of Varsity Lakes

been summarized in Table 13.3. The notion of social sustainability has also been implicitly covered in the previous section.

As shown in the table, there are many areas where the placemaking elements in Varsity Lakes have contributed to the social sustainability. They include the Market Square town centre, green spaces, mixed-use developments as physical spaces for social interaction (under Place factors), the role of VLCL and Sports House in community building (under Programme factors), active participation by people in various sports and recreational activities (People factor), and brand image of the development and diverse built forms creating a distinctive sense of place (Perception factor). There are also potential areas of improvement (such as walkability and lack of safety outside Market Square), which can further enhance the social sustainability of the MPC.

Table 13.3 shows the importance of both the physical design (such as the provision of Market Square, green open spaces, and walkability), as well as the process of placemaking (such as community governance, stakeholder engagement, and organization of events) to build sustainable communities.

13.10 CONCLUSION

Although there is currently extensive debate on placemaking in the literature, limited literature exists on placemaking in the context of MPCs. To address this gap, this chapter has developed a conceptual 4-P framework, which comprises four critical factors for promoting placemaking in MPC: Place, Programme, People, and Perception. The framework has been applied to a case study of Varsity Lakes to identify its performance in terms of placemaking and social sustainability.

Key lessons have emerged from the analysis of placemaking in Varsity Lakes using the 4-P framework. From the Place factor perspective, placemaking initiatives should be implemented beyond the boundary of the town centre of an MPC. The majority of placemaking success in Varsity Lakes across the Place, People, and Perception factors is centred around the Market Square town centre. This is primarily due to the good urban design and the concentration of activities, people, restaurants, and businesses in the town centre. The majority of land use in Varsity Lakes is residential, with Market Square as the dominant mixed-use precinct of the MPC. From the perspective of the Programme factor, the establishment of VLCL as a non-profit community manager illustrates an innovative method through which developers can ensure that ongoing community building efforts are in place once they leave the scene. From the People perspective, the active engagement of community members in diverse sports and recreational activities are very crucial for building a strong sense of community. Through the Perception factor, public art can and should be used to create distinctive places. In Varsity Lakes, public art displayed throughout parks and Lake Orr plays a major role in creating and sustaining the MPC's sense of place. All these initiatives could enhance placemaking and the social sustainability of the community.

This chapter contributes to theory building on placemaking in MPCs with the development of the 4-P framework, drawing ideas from the literature on placemaking, social sustainability, and MPCs. The 4-P framework integrates all important aspects of Place (town centre and other third places, walkability, and green network), Programme (governance, engagement, and events), People (activities and sense of community), and Perception (legibility, safety, sense of place, and brand image) into one framework, which can contribute to social sustainability in MPCs. The chapter also highlights how a public-private partnership between the city council, the developer, and the local community has helped establish community infrastructure, such as Sports House in Varsity Lakes. Likewise, the chapter demonstrates the importance of both the physical design of public spaces and the process of collaborative engagement in placemaking.

With rapid urbanization in the Asia-Pacific region, MPCs are being developed to accommodate the growing housing demand across many cities in the region. The ideas of placemaking and social sustainability discussed in the chapter could be important considerations for new MPCs in the region. The framework developed in the chapter could be tested in other MPCs to examine the relevance of the 4-P factors, taking into consideration the local contexts for social sustainability.

ACKNOWLEDGEMENTS

We would like to express our gratitude to Amy Degenhart from degenhartSHEDD for sharing the Varsity Lakes community feedback survey findings with us for this study. We appreciate the valuable feedback by David Wadley, Warren Rowe, Laurel Johnson, and an anonymous reviewer, as well as the support provided by the editor Pak Sum Low. We would also like to acknowledge the funding support for this research from the Faculty of Society and Design, Bond University.

REFERENCES

Atkinson, R., Blandy, S., Flint, J. and Lister, D. (2005) Gated cities of today? Barricaded residential development in England. *Town Planning Review*, **76**(4), 401–422.

Australian Bureau of Statistics (2017) 2016 Census QuickStats: Varsity Lakes. https://bit.ly/3d9wUcw

Australasian Leisure Management (2010) Varsity Lakes hands over last environmental areas. September. https://bit.ly/3jHOpTO

Bajracharya, B. and Khan, S. (2010) Evolving governance model for community building: Collaborative partnerships in master planned communities. *Urban Policy and Research*, **28**(4), 471–485.

Bajracharya, B., Morris, G. and Cook, V. (2006) Evaluating placemaking strategies in masterplanned communities. Paper presented at the 47th annual conference of American Collegiate Schools of Planning, 9–12 November, Fort Worth, TX.

Bajracharya, B., Too, L. and Khanjanasthiti, I. (2014) Supporting active and healthy living in master-planned communities: A case study. *Australian Planner*, **51**(4), 349–361.

Bohl, C. (2002) *Place Making: Developing Town Centers, Main Streets, and Urban Villages*. Washington, DC, Urban Land Institute.

Bowles, S. and Gintis, H. (2002) Social capital and community governance. *The Economic Journal*, **112**(483), F419–F436.

Buchanan, P. (1988) What city? A plea for place in the public realm. *Architectural Review*, **184**(1,101), 31–41.

Carmona, M., Heath, T., Oc, T. and Tiesdell, S. (2003) *Public Places – Urban Spaces: The Dimensions of Urban Design*. Burlington, MA, Elsevier.

Cheshire, L., Walters, P. and Wickes, R. (2010) Privatisation, security and community: how master planned estates are changing suburban Australia. *Urban Policy and Research*, **28**(4), 359–373.

City of Onkaparinga (2014) Placemaking strategy 2014–19. https://bit.ly/3iFJZLS

Clifton, M. B. (2013) Placemaking and walkability in Austin's Capitol Complex. MPR and MSc thesis submitted to the University of Texas, Austin, TX.

degenhartSHEDD (2015) Varsity Lakes Community Feedback Survey. Unpublished survey findings collected in Gold Coast, Australia by degenhartSHEDD.

Dempsey, N., Bramley, G., Power, S. and Brown, C. (2009) The social dimension of sustainable development: defining urban social sustainability. *Sustainable Development*, **19**(5), 289–300. Published online on Wiley InterScience.

Elgar, I. and Miller, E. (2009) How office firms conduct their location search process?: an analysis of a survey from the greater Toronto area. *International Regional Science Review*, **33**(1), 60–85.

Fleming, R. K. (2007) *The Art of Placemaking: Interpreting Community through Public Art and Urban Design*. London, Merrell Publishers.

Goodman, R. and Douglas, K. (2008) Privatised communities: the use of owner's corporations in master planned estates in Melbourne. *Australian Geographer*, **39**(4), 521–536.

Gwyther, G. (2005) Paradise planned: community formation and the master planned estate. *Urban Policy and Research*, **23**(1), 57–72.

Hurley, J. (2011) Sustainability and master planned estates: From principles to practice. PhD thesis. Royal Melbourne Institute of Technology, Melbourne, Australia.

Jiven, G. and Larkham, P. (2003) Sense of place, authenticity and character: a commentary. *Journal of Urban Design*, **8**(1), 67–81.

Knox, P. (2005) Creating ordinary places: slow cities in a fast world. *Journal of Urban Design*, **10**(1), 1–11.

Lang, J. (2016) An urban designer's perspective: paradigms, places and people. In R. Freestone and E. Liu (eds.), *Place and Placelessness Revisited*, pp. 37–48. New York, NY, Routledge.

Lendlease (2013) The history of Varsity Lakes: An inspired community. Lendlease.

Lendlease (2018) Lendlease communities. https://bit.ly/34woEQ9

Liu, E. and Freestone, R. (2016) Revisiting placelessness. In R. Freestone and E. Liu (eds.), *Place and Placelessness Revisited*, pp. 1–9. New York, NY, Routledge.

Lo, R. H. (2009) Walkability: What is it? *Journal of Urbanism: International Research on Placemaking and Urban Sustainability*, **2**(2), 145–166.

Lynch, K. (1960) *The Image of the City*. Boston, MA, MIT Press.

McGuirk, P. and Dowling, R. (2007) Understanding master-planned estates in Australian cities: a framework for research. *Urban Policy and Research*, **25**(1), 21–38.

Marshall, N. (2016) Urban squares: A place for social life. In R. Freestone and E. Liu (eds.), *Place and Placelessness Revisited*, pp. 186–203. New York, NY, Routledge.

Menin, S. (2003) *Constructing Place: Mind and Matter*. New York, NY, Routledge.

Minnery, J. and Bajracharya, B. (1999) Visions, planning processes and outcomes of master planned communities in South East Queensland. *Australian Planner*, **36**(1), 33–41.

Montgomery, J. (1998) Making a city: urbanity, vitality and urban design. *Journal of Urban Design*, **3**(1), 93–116.

Moudon, A. and Wiseman, B. (1990) *Masterplanned Communities: Shaping Exurbs in the 1990s*. Proceedings of conference held by the Urban Design Programme, College of Architecture and Urban Planning, 20–21 October 1989, Seattle, WA.

Nasar, J. (1998) *The Evaluative Image of the City*. Thousand Oaks, CA, Sage Publications.

Norberg-Schulz, C. (1980) *Genius Loci: Towards a Phenomenology of Architecture*. New York, NY, Rizzoli.

Oldenburg, R. (1999) *The Great Good Place: Cafes, Coffee Shops, Bookstores, Bars, Hair Salons, and Other Hangouts at the Heart of a Community*. New York, NY, Marlowe and Company.

Palich, N. and Edmonds, A. (2013) Social sustainability: creating places and participatory processes that perform well for people. *Environment Design Guide*, **78** (October 2013), 1–13.

Placemaking Chicago (2008) What is placemaking? https://bit.ly/3jEnGI3

Project for Public Spaces (2016) Placemaking: What if we built our cities around places? https://bit.ly/2SCeLed

Project for Public Spaces (2018) What is placemaking? https://bit.ly/33BlTOg

Putnam, R. (2000) *Bowling Alone: The Collapse and Revival of American Community*. New York, NY, Simon and Schuster.

Queensland Police Service (2020) QLD Police Service – Online Crime Map. https://bit.ly/3d8BIiy

Relph, E. (1973) The phenomenon of place: An investigation of the experience and identity of places. PhD thesis submitted to the University of Toronto, Toronto, Ontario.

Relph, E. (1976) *Place and Placelessness*. London, Pion.

Schmitz, A. and Bookout, L. (1998) *Trends and Innovations in Master-planned Communities*. Washington DC, Urban Land Institute.

Schneekloth, L. and Shibley, R. (1995) *Placemaking: The Art and Practice of Building Communities*. New York, NY, Wiley.

Silberberg, S., Lorah, K., Disbrow, R. and Muessig, A. (2013) *Places in the Making: How Placemaking Builds Places and Communities*. Boston, MA, Massachusetts Institute of Technology.

Sports House (2018a) VLCL: Connecting Varsity. https://bit.ly/3dbibhl

Sports House (2018b) Welcome to Sports House at Varsity Lakes. https://bit.ly/3iFPNVG

Totikidis, V., Armstrong, A. and Francis, R. (2005) The concept of community governance: a preliminary review. Refereed paper presented at the GovNet Conference, 28–30 November, Monash University, Melbourne, Australia. https://bit.ly/2SBY4Q8

Twohig, D. (2014) *Living in Wonderland: Urban Development and Placemaking*. Petersfield, Hampshire, UK, Harriman House.

VLCL (2017) The Varsity Social Business Forum. https://bit.ly/3iEMhev

Vogler, A. and Vittori, A. (2006) Genius loci in the space-age. The first Infra-Free Life Symposium, 11–15 December, Istanbul, Turkey.

WACOSS (Western Australian Council of Social Service) (2002) WACOSS Housing and Sustainable Communities Indicators Project. https://bit.ly/36MDuF3

Walk Score. (2018) Living in Varsity Lakes, Gold Coast. https://bit.ly/30YI67l

Walljasper, J. and Project for Public Spaces (2014) *The Great Neighborhood Book: A Do-it-Yourself Guide to Placemaking*. New York, Project for Public Spaces.

Wardner, P. (2011) Master planned community employment centres: The 'wall flower' of business locations. The State of Australian Cities National Conference, 29 November to 2 December, Melbourne. https://bit.ly/3npH79J

Wardner, P. (2012) Understanding the role of 'sense of place' in office location decisions. The 18th Annual Pacific-Rim Real Estate Society Conference, 15–18 January, Adelaide, Australia. https://bit.ly/36HpWdG

Watson, G. B. and Bentley, I. (2007) *Identity by Design*. Burlington, MA, Elsevier.

Woodcraft, S., Bacon, N., Caistor-Arendar, L. and Hackett, T. (2012) Design for social sustainability: A framework for creating thriving new communities. https://bit.ly/3lpBmHo http://www.social-life.co/media/files/DESIGN_FOR_SOCIAL_SUSTAINABILITY_3.pdf

14 Poverty, inequity, and environmental degradation: The key issues confronting the environment and sustainable development in Asia[1]

ANOJA WICKRAMASINGHE[2]

Department of Geography, University of Peradeniya, Sri Lanka

Keywords

Poverty; gender; inequity; inequality; environmental degradation; mal-development; sustainable development

Abstract

Asia and the Pacific are blessed with diverse development options and areas rich in natural resources and biodiversity. Its large population, poverty, social inequity, and environmental degradation, however, challenge its development. This chapter, referring to secondary data, examines the sustainable development issues in the poverty-inequity-environment nexus and reveals that the social development so far has not led to a significant transformation, especially in eradicating poverty and inequity, or in mitigating environmental degradation. Three interconnected paradigms – poverty, inequity, and environmental degradation – threaten sustainability because of the continued deprivation of the poor and women of their right to use the local environment and a lack of equal opportunities to access services. The declining quality of the primary source of livelihood, particularly the land, and their lack of assets and low capacity to enter into the development process fall heavily on the poor. The evidence is drawn by referring to various aspects, such as health, malnutrition, employment, and income to strengthen the debate on equity and equal opportunities. In order to reverse the trend, the analysis presented here suggests that a shift in the development paradigm is needed for enhancing the benefits to vulnerable segments of the society and to geographically marginalized or deprived areas. To materialize this, governance for new partnerships and reciprocal relations are needed. The three issues confronting society – poverty, inequality, and environmental degradation – require constant local action aided by supporting and guiding national policy instruments and commitments. Analytical frameworks are presented for diagnosis and to form the basis for discussion. In this respect, the social inclusion process has to make some progress in promoting local authority and proper form of control and ownership for building a sustainable relationship between the environment and the communities, with strong cascading effects.

14.1 INTRODUCTION

Poverty, inequity, and environmental degradation are the main issues impeding the economic growth and inclusive development in Asia, implying that states have to navigate multiple dimensions and issues in their efforts to ensure sustainable development. Irrespective of the pathways adopted by the individual states, the situation that persists in many countries in Asia is not encouraging in this triple-facet paradigm. The state agencies have failed to address drivers of disparities by providing acceptable and adequate solutions guaranteeing human needs and equal opportunities. Historical landmarks disclose that in 1987, with the initiative of the World Commission on Environment and Development, the term 'sustainable development' entered the development jargon and the political agenda, and it has had some transitional effects on the pathway to development. Agenda 21 and the Rio Declaration on Environment and Development (1992) are testimony to the subsequent initiatives for collective action for change. The principles of sustainable development intended to have direct environmental, social, and economic consequences in all these countries in the region. The reciprocal linkages between the environment and development have been accepted as a key entry point primarily since the Stockholm Conference held in 1972, in which the world nations paid attention to 'limits to growth'. The Agenda 21, the Rio Declaration on Environment and Development, the World Summits on Sustainable Development and the United Nations Millennium Development Goals (2006a) (MDGs), and many

---

[1] The initial analysis carried out in this chapter was presented at the Eminent Scientists Symposium on 24–25 March 2005 in Seoul, Republic of Korea. However, the data and the analysis have been updated before publication.

[2] Emeritus Professor of Geography, University of Peradeniya, Sri Lanka, since 2008.

others recognize that strong reciprocal relationships are crucial in making global changes. The most recently stated Global Goals for Sustainable Development placed a wide spectrum of emerging or unresolved issues the global community has to pay attention to.

Considering the three mutually reinforcing pillars supporting sustainable development – the social, economic, and the environmental – during the past, steps have been taken at the Ministerial Conferences on Environment and Development in Asia and the Pacific organized by United Nations Economic and Social Commission for Asia and the Pacific (UNESCAP), the 21st Session of the Conference of the Parties (COP 21) to the United Nations Framework Convention on Climate Change (UNFCCC) held in in Paris in December 2015, and many others. For instance, the Intergovernmental Panel on Climate Change (IPCC) has concluded that climate change will severely affect food production, water availability and access, livelihoods, and other dimensions of life. IPCC figures show that rising temperatures and unreliable rainfall will make it harder for farmers to grow staple crops like rice, wheat, and maize, reducing the yields (IPCC, 2018). The World Bank (2015a), in a call for ending poverty and hunger by 2030, insisted on more climate-smart agriculture, improving nutritional outcomes, and strengthening value chains and improving market access. At national levels, several measures have been adopted by updating environmental laws and policies, capacity-building, introducing national conservation strategies, and preparing national agenda to facilitate the adoption of Agenda 21 and Sustainable Development Goals. Countries in the region have introduced policies for environmental conservation and multi-stakeholder participation, pursuing activities for preventing and mitigating environmental degradation and climate change.

While recognizing the development options associated with the ecological diversity within the region, as well as in individual countries, the major anthropogenic causes of environmental stress have also been taken into account. On the one hand, the Asian and Pacific region is very rich in terrestrial, coastal, and marine resources, as well as inherent biophysical and cultural diversity. On the other hand, the sustainable development of the region is threatened by the constant resource destruction and land degradation. For instance, deforestation, which contributes to soil erosion, land degradation, loss of biodiversity, and ecosystem services (Scholes *et al.,* 2018), is a critical issue in many developing countries. The global forest area continues to decline, from 16 million hectares per year in the 1990s to an estimated 13 million hectares per year between 2000 and 2010 (FAO, 2011), mostly in developing countries (FAO, 2011), though the pace of loss has slowed in recent years (FAO, 2016, 2018). Around 40% of the extreme rural poor (or some 250 million people) live in forest and savannah areas (FAO, 2018). UNCCD (2019) reports

that around two billion hectares of land is now degraded because of various drivers, including deforestation, over-exploitation of natural resources, and unsustainable land management. The impacts on the rural people, particularly the poor, caused by the loss of productive land are significant. The well-being of at least 3.2 billion people is negatively affected by land degradation (Scholes *et al.,* 2018). Consequently, combating land degradation by avoiding, reducing, and reversing land degradation (through restoring degraded land) is an urgent priority to protect the biodiversity and ecosystem services and improve the well-being of the vulnerable people who rely on productive land for subsistence and livelihoods (Scholes *et al.,* 2018). However, the increasing population pressure on land and its resources has contributed to resource depletion and environmental degradation. Under these circumstances, deepening poverty, health deterioration, malnutrition, higher morbidity, inequity, and the social, economic, and spatial gaps challenge conservation initiatives. Seeking solutions through development has become more complex than ever. Countries in the region have realized that it is urgent to promote local action for change, to achieve their goals regarding the environment and development, from the Millennium Development Goals in 2015 to the Sustainable Development Goals in 2030.

Several perspectives have expanded the analysis of sustainable development, providing important pointers to enable all the countries in the region to identify areas with gaps and challenges. For instance, the *2016 Human Development Report: Human Development for Everyone* (UNDP, 2016) indicated the challenges to be dealt with. Based on 15 indicators, countries are placed on a dashboard of sustainable development. A mix of level and change indicators related to renewable energy consumption, carbon dioxide emissions, change in forest area, and freshwater withdrawals are used to examine environmental sustainability. Adjusted net savings, external debt stock, natural resources depletion, diversity in economy, and government spending on research and development are used to reveal economic sustainability. Social sustainability looks into the changes in income and gender inequality, multidimensional poverty, and the projected old-age dependency ratio. The assessment of these three components indicates the performance of the respective country relative to others, while reflecting the poorly performing areas. According to human development progress as shown by the Human Development Index (HDI), in 2015 Sri Lanka showed a value of 0.766, which was above the average of 0.746 for the countries in the high human development and well above the average of 0.621 noted for the countries in South Asia. However, when the HDI value is discounted for inequality, Sri Lanka's HDI falls to 0.678, losing 11.6% because of inequality. India and Pakistan, also because of inequality, lost 27.2% and 30.9%, respectively.

Three issues confronting society – poverty, inequality, and environmental degradation – require constant local action with supporting and guiding national policy instruments and commitments. An overview of the existing situation shows that the cascade effects driven by the local context lead to environmental degradation (Figure 14.1). This profile is crucial for enhancing the understanding of the context, where multiple causes of poverty and inequality are interlocked. In many countries, inequality and poverty are featured with social, economic, and environmental deprivation and imbalances (UNEP, 2012). Inefficiency in the use of resources causes widespread environmental degradation (UNEP, 2016). The challenge in the process of development is to address the issues of deprivations that are interlocked in the triple-facet nexus, where all three facets – poverty, inequity, and environmental degradation – abound (see Figure 14.2). In Asia, the development policies and the institutional and regulatory frameworks have been confronted by crucial issues of poverty, inequity, and environmental degradation. The importance of a mutually benefiting, reciprocal approach needs recognition in order to address the imbalance between development and the environment. The interventions on environment and development are to be facilitated using locally acceptable, practical experience of the communities.

In many instances, the poor are pressured by all three facets. Referring to community-based innovations with greater reciprocal and scaling-up effects, this chapter also tries to draw attention to the need for sharing 'good practices' and 'good governance'

for eliminating poverty and inequality, while redressing environmental degradation.

14.2 POVERTY AND DEVELOPMENT CHALLENGES

The state of the environment in the region reveals that poverty is often concentrated in environmentally fragile ecological zones, where communities live on degraded and exhausted resources, and this often contributes to furthering different kinds of environmental degradation. Poverty has been examined by using various analytical approaches that challenge the lack of development: gender equality, gender and energy poverty, Sustainable Development for All initiatives, MDGs, climate change, health, and many others. What has been suggested throughout is the importance and the potentiality of equality and equity principles for lifting people out of poverty. The environmental changes caused by climate change, the water scarcity and land degradation caused by human activities are among the most powerful and least understood challenges for sustainable development (UNDP, 2004). Features in the poverty-environment nexus reveal that, while degraded resources precipitate a downward spiral threatening the livelihood of the poverty-stricken populations, poverty makes the poor over-exploit the resources in their day-to-day living.

Looking back at the Millennium Declaration, one is struck by the extent to which multiple issues of development have been

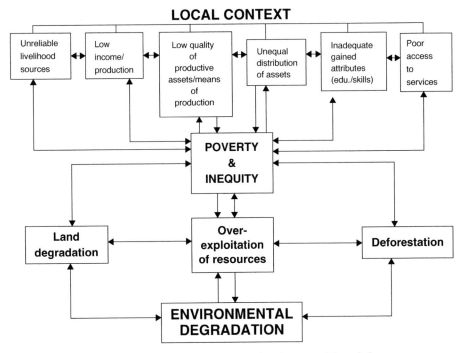

Figure 14.1. Cascading effects of the local contexts and environmental degradation.

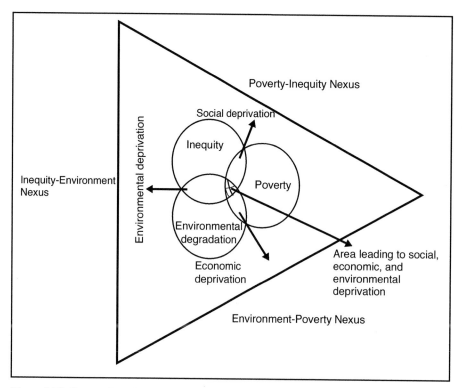

Figure 14.2. Poverty-inequity-environment nexus confronting the environment and development in Asia.

incorporated as a matter of urgency concerning developing countries. Available information shows that, in spite of the progress made during the past, outstanding disparities exist between sub-regions (see Table 14.1) between South Asia and East Asia and the Pacific (UNDP 2016).

Geographically, South Asia is marked by a heavy concentration of population, with 1.8 billion people in 2015 (UNDP, 2016). The Multidimensional Poverty Index (MPI) shows that out of 1.5 billion people living in multidimensional poverty in developing countries, 53.9% are in South Asia (UNDP, 2016). In 2015, in South Asia nearly 27.7% of the population were living on less than one dollar a day. On the basis of per capita daily income (US$1 a day), past estimations revealed that close to 900 million people, or nearly 75% of the world's poor, lived in Asia and the Pacific region (UNESCAP, 2006). Recent estimations suggest that South Asia has the highest concentration of the poor, accounting for more than half a billion, with 450 million in India alone (UNDP, 2016). According to the UNDP (2018) estimation for India, nearly 364 million people are in poverty and around 21% of its population live on less than US$1.90 a day. The percentage of poor people shown in the poverty headcount of the countries is in the range of 1.88, which is for Maldives, and 56.10 reported for Afghanistan. The population in multidimensional poverty varies between 0.07%, which is reported in the Maldives, and 25% in Afghanistan. The

estimation also suggests that South Asia is marked with a high percentage of working poor (with PPP$3.10 a day), at 52.5%, with the highest rate, 89.8%, reported in Afghanistan and the lowest, at 10.9%, reported in Bhutan. Differences exist in many other aspects, especially in the employed-to-population ratio, which is 52.2%, with 54.55% labour force participation (LFP), 47.3% in agriculture, and 30.9% in services. However, the population falling into the category of the poor has declined from 50% to around 33% between the 1970s and 2000.

The spatial disparity in the region is outstanding, and, as reflected by various development indicators, South Asia lags behind East Asia and the Pacific region. The implications of high geographical concentration of the poor in South Asia increase the gravity of environmental degradation and the increasing demand for the resources, land, and water in particular. The persisting imbalances between social and economic development, especially the distribution of productive assets, are an indication of the mismatch of its population and the slow rate of economic options. The composite indices on human development given in Table 14.2 reveal the gaps, which demand more focused efforts to reduce the barriers pertaining to inequalities in order to march faster on the global scale.

A marked disparity in the income distribution among the poorest, the richest, and the intermediate sectors has also been revealed in all these countries in South Asia. Early estimations of

Table 14.1. Demographic, poverty, and economic indicators for Asia and the Pacific for 2015.

	South Asia	East Asia and the Pacific
Population (million) 2015	1,823.0	2,041.6
Urban population (%)	34.8	52.9
Human Development Index (HDI)	0.62	0.72
GDI	0.822	0.956
Inequality in education	39.5%	12.8%
Inequality in income	18.3%	27.4%
Inequality adjusted HDI	0.449	0.581
Gross National Income per capita (PPP$)	5,799	12,125
Working poor (PPP$ 3.10 a day)	52.5	20.7
Depth of food deficit (kilocalories per person per day)	115	79

Source: UNDP (2016)

Table 14.2. Achievements and status of human development and the gaps in five countries in South Asia for 2017.

Country	HDI (rank)	GDI Value	GDI Rank	IHDI (% loss)	GNI per capita (PPP$)	Life expectancy (years)	Expected years of schooling	Mean years of schooling
Sri Lanka	0.770 (76)	0.354	80	13.8	11,326	75.5	13.9	10.9
Bangladesh	0.608 (136)	0.542	134	24.1	3,677	72.8	11.4	5.8
India	0.640 (130)	0.524	127	26.8	6,353	68.8	12.3	6.4
Nepal	0.574 (149)	0.480	118	25.6	2,471	70.6	12.2	4.9
Pakistan	0.562 (150)	0.541	133	31.0	5,311	66.6	8.6	5.2
Maldives	0.717 (101)	0.343	76	23.4	13,587	77.6	12.6	6.3

HDI = Human Development Index; GDI = Gender Development Index; IHDI = Inequality Adjusted HDI; GNI = Gross National Income per capita (PPP$ for 2011)
Source: UNDP (2018)

the United Nations (2006) showed that income distribution disparity in the countries in Asia, with the richest 20% of the population having 28.5–54.6% of the income and the poorest 20% with less than one-tenth of the total income, is a barrier to development. Recent reports suggest that a wider disparity exists in the Gross National Income (GNI) per capita; UNDP (2018) reports PPP$6,473 for South Asia and PPP$15,295 for the world. In South Asia, the lowest of PPP$2,471 is recorded for Nepal and the highest of PPP$13,587 for Maldives (Table 14.2). Estimated GNI for women and men in the South Asia region shows a wider gender gap with PPP$2,694 for women and PPP$10,035 for men. The GNI for women is in the range of PPP$541 to PPP$7,064 and the lowest is reported from Afghanistan and the highest is from Maldives. The GNI for men is in the range of PPP$2,738 to PPP$18,505, and the lowest is reported from Nepal, while the highest is reported from Maldives (UNDP, 2018). Trends in poverty, spatial, and sectoral disparities within these countries make this phenomenon more complex and demand crucial strategic measures for resolving them. It is important to note that income

has a strong bearing on the sources of livelihood, especially the regularity and the reliability.

UNESCAP (2017) in its volume on *Gender, the Environment and Sustainable Development in Asia and the Pacific* provides a comprehensive examination of gender in the spheres of food security, agriculture, energy, water, fisheries, and forestry. It shows that lives of a significant portion of the population in the region are inextricably tied to the use of the environment for daily support and livelihood. In South Asia 42.2% of the employed are in agriculture and 34.6% are in services. The dimensions of poverty and drivers of inequalities are interconnected, so context-specific assessments are needed to disclose the ground realities. However, the gender inequality scores of the respective countries and poverty situation reflected in terms of poverty headcount reflect the persistent inequities manipulated by gender ideology and social and gender-exclusive development processes.

The internal disparities of the individual countries show that geographically backward areas have not been able to reduce the spatial concentration of poverty. Sri Lanka itself demonstrates that internal disparities impact on national-level achievements. It has made remarkable achievements in human development, with the highest life expectancy of 75 years, and the lowest infant mortality rate of 17 per 1,000 by the year 2015; it has almost parity in literacy rate of around 92%, and 14 years of expected schooling and 10.9 years of mean schooling in 2015. The regions with disparities are rather backward in getting access to services, entitlements, and opportunities, indicating the need to work out specific menus for filling the gaps while celebrating the achievements. In this regard, two pathways – one with a focus on poverty reduction and the other on gender mainstreaming – have been introduced. Many countries have adopted consultative process and gender mainstreaming for ensuring inclusivity.

These circumstances have led the countries to focus clearly on improving the quality of life as a means for intergenerational sustainability. Despite the persistent gaps in their scores, the countries in the region made different degrees of progress in regard to human development (see Table 14.3). For example, all the countries have improved the basic human development as reflected in HDI values, raising their positions on the HDI ladder. In 2015 for instance, with an HDI of 0.766, Sri Lanka reached above the average of 0.621 shown for the countries in South Asia, and above 0.746, for the countries in high human development. However, the inequality-based losses have reversed the gained positions, placing the countries in lower ranks. The values discounted for inequality point out the need for introducing target-oriented strategic measures for addressing the issue of creating equal space for women and the marginalized sectors and areas.

Poverty is a phenomenon with a strong bearing on spatial contextualities, so the disparity is quite significant in almost all aspects of poverty. It is influenced by the unequal income distribution, sources of livelihood, and access to and control over resources, including land, as well as demographics and resource ecology. In agrarian areas, it has a direct association with land use and the environment, including the following:

- The distribution of land, especially the productive agricultural land, where efficient and equitable utilization by the poor, including women, is hampered by lack of land ownership, resources, technology, services, and employment;
- The exploitation of fragile and marginal lands, where opportunities for increasing agricultural productivity or economic diversification are limited;
- The increasing pressure on the coastal areas and their resources, where restrictive use of marine resources is conditioned by natural or manipulated systems;
- The unequal distribution, availability, and access to services where the poor are concentrated into marginalized areas and in urban areas to slums and squatter settlements.

These situations tend to explain the geographical concentration by which greater concentration of poverty and marginalization could be explained in relation to the local context. It is important to note that, although the proportion of the population living in poverty varies, the contextual grounds are often associated with the unequal distribution of assets, access to services and employment, low income, and unreliable sources of livelihood.

14.3 INEQUITY AND INEQUALITY

Inequity is directly connected with inequality and it is one of the areas taken into consideration by the international community. Within the framework of sustainable development, goal

Table 14.3. Gender development indices and the inequalities relative to the countries in South Asia for 2017.

Country	GDI	HDI		Life expectancy		Expected years of schooling		Mean years of schooling		GNI	
		F	M	F	M	F	M	F	M	F	M
Bhutan	0.893	0.576	0.645	70.9	70.3	12.4	12.2	2.1	4.2	6,002	9,889
Bangladesh	0.881	0.567	0.644	74.6	71.2	11.7	11.3	5.2	6.7	2,041	5,285
India	0.841	0.575	0.683	70.4	67.3	12.9	11.9	4.8	8.2	2,722	9,729
Nepal	0.925	0.552	0.598	72.2	69.0	12.6	11.8	3.6	6.4	2,219	2,738
Pakistan	0.750	0.465	0.620	67.7	65.6	7.8	9.3	3.8	6.5	1,642	8,786
Sri Lanka	0.935	0.738	0.789	78.8	72.1	14.1	13.6	10.3	11.4	6,462	16,582
Maldives	0.919	0.679	0.739	78.8	76.7	12.7	12.6	6.2	6.4	7,064	18,501

Source: UNDP (2018)

HDI = Human Development Index; GDI = Gender Development Index; GNI = Gross National Income per capita (PPP$ for 2011)

number 10 has been introduced, focusing on reducing inequality within and among countries. Its targets refer to the multiple dimensions of inequalities, enabling each country to work out its own strategies for prioritizing the issues based on the local context. Critical areas include reducing inequalities in income and the contextually induced conditions driven by gender, and the spatial imbalances in the distribution of services, assets, and opportunities. Inequality in getting access to services, resources, and assets is a cause of mal-development and is also a result of inefficiencies and ineffectiveness that impede the potential to ensure better quality of life for all. In many countries, the areas indicating poor performance suggest that the individual countries have failed to address the barriers that perpetuate marginalization of some segments of the population who deserve multiple opportunities and options on the basis of their citizenship rights. This also refers to the inequalities that exist among countries in their representation, as well as in migration and development assistance.

The numerous targets of goal 10 were introduced in order to achieve and sustain income growth of the bottom 40% of the population at a target higher than the national average by 2030; empowerment and promotion of social, economic, and political inclusion for all; equal opportunities and reducing inequalities of outcome; fiscal, wage, and social protection; representation and voices for developing countries in decision-making; and safe and regular migration and mobility – all of the above are quite descriptive in defining development directions. Provisions made through Sustainable Development Goal 5, on gender equality, are in the centre of development debates and are directly connected with this goal. South Asia lags behind other regions because of the gravity of repercussions experienced in relation to the exclusion of women in mainstream development, gender disparities in getting access to assets and ownership, deprivations and marginalization, low achievements, stereotyped divisions in the labour market, discrimination, and violence. The evidence reveals that income inequality has risen substantially; for instance, on average, women in their labour market earn 24% less than men globally, and it is less by nearly 30% in Sri Lanka. These tendencies reveal the need for furthering the goals of poverty alleviation and reducing inequality in a sustainable development agenda.

The issue of inequity is seen in the hierarchy of livelihood, where poor and rural women occupy the bottom strata, struggling for family subsistence. Despite the efforts made by the global nations, especially since 1976, the configuration remains the same across the region, demanding targets oriented towards development inclusive of women, to reduce poverty and inequality. The geographical context of the region as a whole and the countries in particular stimulate in-depth analysis, referring to internal conditions marked with critical and specific

areas. These include 'feminization of poverty', 'globalization of female labour for economic growth', 'domestication of women', and 'feminization of domestic energy', which are connected with the well-being of the respective families. These demonstrate the gender-specific nature of the issues that are often treated as women's issues rather than development issues. How can we change cultural preferences and socialized differences or the socially ascribed attributes in favour of sustainable development? This is a question that needs to be fully addressed in furthering the implementation of sustainable development. The issues related to the disproportionate distribution of poverty between men and women; different impacts of the scarcity of biomass for providing common energy services (cooking); and the occupation of migratory space by women for securing employment opportunities to alleviate poverty, among other issues, have been covered in the past (Wickramasinghe, 2002, 2003a, 2003b, and 2004a). The conditions protracting the feminization of poverty include women's engagement as unpaid family workers in productive work, the low wages earned by women, and the relatively small share of income they earn. Female labour is largely concentrated in the informal economy and is connected with their lack of endowment to production, the predominance of home-based work, greater dependence on marginal and unreliable livelihoods, and their dependence on free subsidies.

The gender-based inequalities in South Asia are quite significant, according to the Gender Inequality Indices (GII). The average GII for South Asia is rather low and is 0.575 in 2017, and the HDI for men and women shows a 16.3% gap (UNDP, 2018). From the perspective of justice and fairness, the countries in the region require structured and focused development agendas. The development agencies such as ADB include gender equity as one of the five drivers of change towards inclusive growth (ADB, 2018). The overall situation suggests some impressive progress in life expectancy, years of schooling, and expected years of schooling but the variations contribute to regional disparities. For instance, Pakistan reports the lowest of 8.6 expected years of schooling, while the highest of 13.9 is in Sri Lanka. Life expectancy of the population in these countries also varies, and the lowest of 64 years is recorded in Afghanistan and 77.6 in Maldives. Development indicators reveal significant gaps in the values for females and males, indicating the need for introducing specific interventions for improving the lives of women, especially for increasing income per capita (Table 14.3). These have a strong ideological footing in several countries, most seriously in Bangladesh, India, Nepal, and Pakistan. The inequality between female and male achievement is a loss in human development (UNDP, 2016), and this situation challenges the sustainable development in the region, especially the 2030 agenda for sustainable development.

The gender inequality in economic activity has continued over the years, creating gaps, disparities, and imbalances, revealing the detrimental results of exclusion reiterated during the past. The past records, despite some marginal trends, show a substantial gap in the activity rate of women and men and their labour force participation. The figures pertaining to women have been consistently lower than those for men, owing to the lower involvement of women in paid and formal employment. Past records show very marginal changes in this area and in 1997, for example, the female economic activity rate was around 29.1% in South Asia, which was 10% less than the reported figure for all developing countries. For Sri Lanka, it was 30.5%; India 29%; Pakistan 20.8%; Nepal 37.9%; Bhutan 38.8%; and Bangladesh 44.4%. By 2004, the female economic activity rate in South Asia had increased to 47.7%, while the male economic activity rate rose to 66%. The figure for East Asia and the Pacific was comparatively high, with 65.4% female economic activity rate in 2004, and around 79% male economic activity rate. In 2004, the female activity rate for Sri Lanka had increased to 35%, and for men, the rate was 45%. In Bangladesh, the situation has been comparatively better, reporting 52.9% female activity and 61% for male activity rate. Nepal had also made progress with a 49.7% female activity rate and around 63% for the male activity rate. In 2006, the lowest figure for South Asia was in Pakistan, reporting 32% female activity rate, in comparison with 38% for male (UNDP, 2006b). This situation has seriously affected the women's earned income, forcing them to earn less than their male counterparts. In Sri Lanka,

for example, women secured only about 42% of men's earned income, and it was 31% in India, 29% in Pakistan, 46% in Bangladesh, and 50% in Nepal. Gender gaps and disparities are seen in all the aspects, especially in the distribution of Gross National Income (GNI), gender disparity in labour force participation, the percentage share of females and males in the labour force, and also their sectoral distribution (Table 14.4). Except in Nepal, in all other countries the gender gap in GNI is rather wide. GNI for women is extremely low. The country profiles for Bangladesh and Pakistan reveal that the percentage of persons in poverty is greater than the percentage of women in the labour force, while in Bhutan, Maldives, Nepal, and Sri Lanka it is less (Figure 14.3). It is important to note that an increase in the labour force participation of women is required to increase the GNI for women.

The working age population is another important measure; the percentage of the population above 15 years old that is employed in the respective countries is low, implying that available human capital is not fully accommodated into the productive domain (Table 14.4). The situation in Nepal is relatively better, with more than 80% of the population more than 15 years of age being employed, but the trends captured in other countries in recent estimations confirm that achievements made through interventions for empowering women have not made a serious transition. In 2015, Pakistan recorded a wider gap, driven by the lowest rate of women's labour force participation, with 24.3%, compared to 82.2% recorded for men. The gap in this domain remains wide in India, while Nepal, which is

Table 14.4. Features of labour force participation, by gender in 2017.

Country	% employed*	LFPR*	LFP in agriculture **	LFP in services**	GNI per capita (2011 PPP$)**	LFPR: Female**	LFPR: Male **
Maldives	59.9	68.0	7.5	67.7	F – 7,064 M – 18,505	42.9	82.1
India	59.9	53.7	42.7	33.5	F – 2,722 M – 9,729	27.2	78.8
Bangladesh	59.4	62.2	39.1	39.9	F – 2,014 M – 5,285	33.0	79.8
Pakistan	51.0	53.9	42.0	34.3	F – 1,642 M – 8,786	24.9	82.7
Nepal	80.5	83.0	71.7	20.2	F – 2,219 M – 2,738	82.7	85.9
Sri Lanka	49.3	51.8	26.7	50.5	F – 2,462 M – 16,581	27.9	79.1

Source: *UNDP (2016)
        **UNDP (2018)

LFPR = Labour Force Participation Rate; GNI = Gross National Income per capita (PPP$ for 2011); F = Female; M = Male

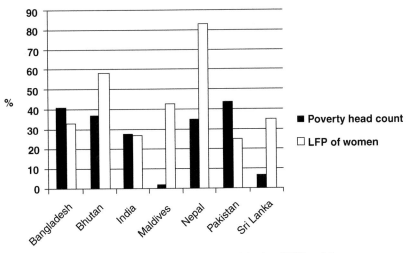

Figure 14.3. Disparity in women's labour force participation (LFP) and the poverty headcount of selected countries in South Asia.

marked with relatively low gross income per capita, shows a relatively narrow gap, with a figure of 79.7% labour force participation for women and 86.8% recorded for men.

The spatial distribution of disparities within countries demonstrates situations to be captured through deep-dive assessments. Sri Lanka, as an example, displays a spatial pattern in both consumption (poverty, income, or expenditure) and Headcount Index, and in selected variables pertaining to poverty. In-depth analysis places this phenomenon over an extended contextual profile, including social, economic, and environmental conditions of the administrative districts, where synergy between poverty and inequality could be established. The income inequalities represented by income quintiles in Sri Lanka reveal that an excessively wide gap exists between the income received by the poorest 20% and the richest 20%. The poorest 20% have received only 5%, while the richest 20% received 51% of the total household income (Table 14.5). It is also important to note that the disparity in the distribution of the economically active

Table 14.5. Household income, distribution pattern, and the principal source of cooking fuel, by administrative districts of Sri Lanka in 2016.

District	% share of income received by the poorest 20% of the Hhs	% share of income received by the richest 20% of Hhs	PHI %	Median monthly Hh income	Mean monthly Hh income	% of Hhs using fuelwood as the principal type of cooking fuel	Economically active population, by gender	
							M	F
Colombo	5.4	52.3	0.9	70,000	104,581	20.0	66	34
Gampaha	5.8	48.7	2.0	53,123	72,834	46.8	67	33
Alutara	5.3	49.6	2.9	49,106	69,171	60.2	74	36
Kandy	5.0	47.2	5.5	41,858	55,194	69.9	64	36
Matale	5.7	47.9	3.9	42,579	56,075	84.7	60	40
Nuwa-Eliya	5.6	46.7	6.3	35,488	46,517	75.5	56	44
Galle	5.6	49.3	2.9	45,333	63,093	71.1	64	36
Matara	5.8	45.5	4.4	42,146	54,019	76.0	62	38
Hambantota	5.4	49.1	1.2	42,539	59,932	84.4	66	34
Jaffna	4.2	48.7	7.7	35,500	47,731	78.9	74	26
Mannar	5.0	47.4	1.0	35,150	45,608	72.9	77	23
Vavunia	5.7	46.9	2.0	44,043	58,625	71.4	63	37
Mullaitivu	4.3	46.5	12.7	25,526	31,868	90.9	56	34
Kilinochchi	4.2	41.4	18.2	27,050	31,576	86.0	71	29

Table 14.5. (cont.)

District	% share of income received by the poorest 20% of the Hhs	% share of income received by the richest 20% of Hhs	PHI %	Median monthly Hh income	Mean monthly Hh income	% of Hhs using fuelwood as the principal type of cooking fuel	Economically active population, by gender	
							M	F
Batticaloa	5.0	50.7	11.3	28,297	40,356	67.2	71	29
Ampara	5.7	44.8	2.6	34,486	43,821	66.9	75	25
Trincomalle	5.0	46.9	10.0	37,000	46,137	74.8	75	25
Kurunegala	4.5	50.9	2.9	42,287	59,661	87.1	60	40
Puttalam	4.6	52.6	2.1	40,890	61,981	74.4	66	34
Anuradhapura	4.6	51.5	3.8	41,629	58,326	84.3	58	42
Polonnaruwa	5.0	51.5	2.2	44,180	64,525	90.0	67	33
Badulla	4.1	50.7	6.8	36,870	53,236	87.4	60	40
Moneragala	4.8	47.7	5.8	35,838	48,842	94.0	64	36
Ratnapura	5.6	47.0	6.5	35,183	46,977	85.7	61	39
Kegalle	5.5	47.1	7.1	39,779	51,865	85.3	59	41

Source: Department of Census and Statistics (2016)
PHI = Poverty Headcount Index; Hh = Household

population is quite significant, having higher rates of female participation in agriculturally predominant districts.

Women's share of earned income has been consistently low across the districts and it varies in the range of 20% to 38%. It is marginally higher in Nuwara-Eliya, with 38%, where women formally work for wages in tea plantations. It is difficult to draw concrete conclusions in regard to household energy consumption; because the expansion of access to electricity has reached almost 100%, a wide disparity is found in regard to the use of fuelwood as a source of cooking fuel. While recognizing the development implications of electricity access, which has been recognized as a crucial input to development (DFID, 2002), it is also crucial to consider the configurations induced in relation to the behavioural changes and energy decision-making where local renewable energy-based options are available. However, the potential of energy services to contribute towards eradicating poverty and for enhancing women's share of earned income should be considered as a development priority, rather than simply concentrating on the positive side effects of having clean energy for domestic lighting alone. Similar arguments could be extended to examining economic opportunities for women. A full recognition of the women's contributions to informal economies, subsistence farming in particular, and the newly emerging income generation in industry is required in order to make a drastic change in the national picture of women's share of the earned income (Wickramasinghe, 2002). A large majority of the employment available in the informal sector for women is low paid, and the wage gap is high, around 20–30% less than the

amounts received by men in the market. The data pertaining to various dimensions suggest that the goal of reducing inequality has not fully materialized over the years.

The spatial nexus can guide local development investments and the community-based multiple solutions. For instance, the quartile ranking of 17 districts of Sri Lanka on five indicators suggests that the situations are specific to the local contexts marked with ideologies of women's labour, women in paid work or in employment, and in farming. The configurations are sculpted by women's work in casual or informal employment for income. Turning back to the broader goal of eradicating extreme poverty and hunger, to help the proportion of people living on less than a dollar a day, as stated in the Millennium Development Goals, the rationale for adopting a strategic framework for decentralized interventions can be explained. Inequity and deprivation are the most serious issues pertaining to development and services in rural situations, more than in urban conditions. However, there is no clear matching between the labour force participation of men and household income, where the LFP rate for men is reported more than 70%, except in Kilinochchi district, and the same was found in regard to women's labour force participation and household income. The findings suggest that higher rates of LFP alone do not address the issues interwoven in multidimensional poverty, inequity, and inequalities. It is quite clear that the people in rural areas are far more likely than people in urban areas to be multidimensionally poor. According to the available information, 64% of the rural population and 25% of the urban population are multidimensionally poor. These disparities are driven by the disparities in the distribution of services, resources, access to, and ownership of productive assets, as well as the economic options.

14.4 EQUITY, LOCAL CONTEXT, AND THE ENVIRONMENT

Equity and equal opportunities receive a high priority from the perspectives of economic growth and development, particularly in regard to human development and local environments. Three of the 17 Sustainable Development Goals are dedicated to environmental sustainability and include resource depletion and climate change, highlighting the importance of integrating environmental sustainability in development. Why equity and equality matter for safeguarding the environment and what is the value of inclusive development in achieving sustainable development are important to analyse. As in the case of poverty, issues of equity are presented from various perspectives, including rights to resources and the local environment. The distribution of assets, employment, and earned income are crucial areas of concern for the countries in the region. The distribution of assets, such as land – the source of livelihood of rural farmers – is highly skewed; 80% of the farms in South Asia have an average area of 0.6 hectares.

The challenge here is how to 'ensure a better quality of life for all, now and in the future, in a just and equitable manner, while living within the limits of supporting systems' (Agyeman et al., 2003). Equity is a matter pertaining to social inclusion and respect, reciprocity and cohesiveness, ownership and public partnership, and democracy and the citizen's rights. Concentrating on the uneven distribution of nuclear risks, Blowers (2003) explained the social, political, and environmental dimensions of equity. Accordingly, sustainable development is not only an environmental problem, but also a social and political issue. Environmental inequality has a social context, and mitigation of risk and pollution is a moral issue. The United Nations (2000), in the report on *The State of the Environment in Asia and the Pacific*, clearly stated that the interaction of poverty and environmental degradation sets off a downward spiral of ecological deterioration that threatens the physical security, the economic well-being, and the health of many of the region's poorest people. Efficient use of resources is crucial for safeguarding the environment, especially for addressing the issues of environmental degradation (UNEP, 2016). When we consider the situation in the Asia region, multiple and detrimental implications of development imbalance make us realize the seriousness of the issues of inequity in resource distribution and the necessity for certain changes in the development paradigm. Poverty, inequity, and environmental degradation provide not only the contextual grounds but also the justification for having

practical measures and mechanisms for making such changes. The evidence from Asia and many other parts of the world reveals that during the recent past, issues of equity have been considered key issues affecting development. Spatial and social inequity is a result of wider resource options reaped by a small section of society rather than by the deserving groups, including the poor, the resourceless, women, indigenous people, and minorities. Transitional effects of development interventions reflect their ability to deal with persistent challenges associated with this. Poverty in rural areas, where difficulties with access to services remain an impediment to economic advancement, provides a good example. In the same manner, poverty, inequity, and lack of income-earning opportunities and investable assets with reasonable returns strengthen the debate on equity and equal opportunities for women in the process of development.

There are striking differences in social and economic development, and such contexts provide common ground to concentrate seriously on equity, justice, and equal opportunities. These three key terms are linked with one another and support the idea of providing favourable conditions for enabling the present and future generations to lead a healthy life. The extent to which positive achievements are made following the principles of equity in the process of environment and development in the region is a question still to be solved. The arguments in favour of equity, justice, and equal opportunities are driven by several facts:

- The constant environmental degradation that disproportionately threatens the livelihood of millions of the poor relying on the land and its resources;
- The disproportionate distribution of the over-exploitation of resources and environmental degradation and consumption patterns, including consequences such as global warming and climatic change;
- The long-lasting effects of unequal opportunities in access to assets and services;
- The effects of environmental disasters experienced by the people living in geographically remote and vulnerable areas and those in socially disadvantaged conditions, especially women and the poor. For instance, during Rio+20, the United Nations Conference on Sustainable Development committed to focusing on gender and environment;
- The widening gap between the rich and the poor and the domination of development decisions and management by socially and economically advanced people.

Past trends show that a substantial proportion of the population lives in rural areas, without access to services, and relies on land and its resources for livelihood. In South Asia, 48.3% of the population have access to sanitation services, while 88.4% of the population, with marked variations between 63.0% and 97.9%

among countries, have access to improved drinking water (UNDP, 2018). It is envisaged that the competition for resources, especially for land and water, is causing increasing stress because of high population densities, growing demand, and climate change (World Bank 2015a). Food security challenges the development process seriously, and ADB (2013) pointed out that more than 60% of undernourished or chronically hungry people of the world live in the Asia-Pacific region with a heavy concentration in South Asia. UNESCAP (2017), referring to data on the share of food expenditure in South Asia countries, has shown that expenditure on food purchases is in the range of 49%, which is reported from Afghanistan, and 75% reported from Pakistan.

A greater emphasis has been repeatedly placed on policy challenges and environmental degradation. The analysis of the environmental trends reveals that deterioration of the environmental conditions in the Asia-Pacific region is continuing. Pollution, deforestation, and land degradation on local, national, and global conditions have direct and trans-boundary effects (United Nations, 2000). Reviewing the available data, UNESCAP (2017) revealed an upward trend in the forest cover in India and Bhutan, while Bangladesh, Sri Lanka, Nepal, and Pakistan reported a decrease in the area under forest. The cross-boundary effects of deforestation, forest fires, pollution, and the declining biodiversity urge us to concentrate seriously on collective action and shared responsibility, while considering intergenerational equity. The declining quality of the environment presents a gloomy outlook on its capacity for meeting the needs of future generations. The same decline points to the possibilities of facing deepening health risks, resource scarcity, and food, energy, and nutritional insecurity, from which socially and environmentally handicapped sectors will suffer seriously.

It is also important to note that resource depletion, deforestation, and land degradation, which result from human activity, affect the population disproportionately. The deepening water scarcity and the shortage of biomass fuel for domestic cooking incur multiple implications, especially on women's health, nutrition, and sanitation. The ADB (2018) explained that social issues unravel the implications of the issue of energy poverty and underscore the need to attend to both supply- and demand-side energy generation and distribution. The outstanding speciality pertaining to energy in Asia is the dependence on renewable sources. The UNDP (2016) reported that in 2012, in South Asia 32.5% of the total energy consumption was renewable energy. It was 90% in Bhutan, 84.7% in Nepal, 60.9% in Sri Lanka, 45.5% in Pakistan, 39% in India, and 38.3% in Bangladesh. Biomass is the most widely used source of cooking energy in these countries. The studies carried out in these countries confirmed that women's labour and time are over-exploited by the need for them to secure water and fuel for household consumption (see UNESCAP, 2017; Wickramasinghe, 2004a, 2004b, and 2004c). Geographically, the

impact of the social and spatial differences is serious in the poverty-stricken, disadvantaged areas and among certain social sectors. The urban-rural differences in the access to energy services and the involvement in decision-making, as well as social and economic stratification, income, and health and nutritional status, create disparities in the environmental stresses.

In South Asia, issues involving equity have occupied the broader societal, economic, and environmental domains over generations, contributing to the structuring of social hierarchies, wealth clustering, and stratification. The unfair outcomes distribute the consequences disproportionately between men and women and recreate stereotyped division of responsibilities and roles. The inequity in the distribution of employment, paid employment in particular, assets, and the labour market continue to strengthen gender-based inequalities. One of the strongest pieces of evidence for the prevalence of inequity, unequal opportunities, and social disparity is found in the difference between the male and female shares in the labour force, particularly their sectoral distribution. The female labour is largely concentrated in less-well-paid sectors like agriculture (Table 14.5). This situation reveals a significant difference between men and women in the distribution of earned income and their subjection to poverty. This also leads to rural-urban gaps in earned income and gaps in the distribution of property, assets, and wealth. The inequalities continue to maintain impoverishment across space and communities. One of the best proofs of inequity and unequal opportunities is found in the difference between the male and female share in income distribution and opportunities in development sectors. It is revealed that most of the countries in South Asia performed poorly in achieving the commitments and objectives of RIO+20, MDGs, Beijing+20,[3] and Convention to Eliminate Discrimination Against Women (CEDAW). Gender inequality stands as a barrier to development in Asia, so it is acknowledged that means and strategies to bridge the gaps are crucial. For instance, the long-term strategic framework of the ADB recognizes that gender equality and women's empowerment are important for achieving economic growth, reducing poverty, and supporting social inclusive development, so promoting gender equity is recognized as one of the five drivers of change (ADB, 2018). A vast number of agencies and organizations have opened up differential entry points that are of multiple importance to all the countries in Asia.

This overview suggests that the provision of equal opportunities has not yet materialized; instead, women have been confined to the domain of household work or unpaid work. When service

---

[3] Beijing+20 indicates the process to assess implementation by governments and other stakeholders of the Beijing Declaration and Platform for Action adopted at the 4th World Conference on Women held in Beijing in 1995.

sector employment is greater, as in Maldives and Sri Lanka, the number of women in paid employment expands, and they become visible as service providers rather than producers in the economy or as a work force in labour-intensive work in service-related sectors. In spite of some progress, the injustice continues because the existing models of operations have failed to evolve away from the conventionally inculcated systems.

14.5 ENVIRONMENTAL DEGRADATION

Attention given to the environment pillar of sustainable development has increased over the years, with the deepening effects of degradation of the atmosphere, soil, and the biosphere in particular. The implications of degradation are experienced seriously by the land-based economies and the communities across the region. As a result, the focus has moved beyond discussing the ecological and conservation implications of the degradation, to include the decline of biodiversity and encouraging more gender and social inclusive approaches to conservation. The discussion on the challenges of biodiversity has looked into the implications for agro-biodiversity, as well as gender (UNESCAP, 2017). The experience-based lessons put forward the need to secure access to diversity of plants, ecosystems, and forests for greater protection and conservation through communities. It has also recognized that the region is seriously affected by sudden natural disasters related to extreme weather events like flooding and intensified and unpredictable storms, as well as prolonged droughts, heat stresses, and periodic depletion of water resources normally available for irrigation and other purposes. For example the Women's Environment and Development Organization (WEDO) (2013) stressed that forest initiatives recognize and incorporate the social value of the forest and deliver social, environmental, and climate co-benefits that contribute to a healthy, sustainable, and just world. Issues of poverty, gender, and equity have moved to the forefront of the development paths in the region because these have deepened and magnified the disparities, especially the inequalities between women and men and their vulnerability to changing climate and the disparity in their resilience and ability to cope with the trends. The Global Alliance for Clean Cookstoves (2013) looked into the repercussions, risks, and drudgery experienced by women in collecting fuelwood for cooking.

Various types of initiatives have been made by the global communities and the states for reducing environmental degradation. Such efforts have made a progressive change in regard to the understanding of the global trends, and locally appropriate strategic measures to address changes have been introduced. Climate change mitigation through forest conservation has become an advancing initiative focused on 'Reducing Emissions from Deforestation and Forest Degradation' and

enhancing forest carbon stocks (REDD+). Many states are making a concerted effort to maximize the benefits of REDD+ while reducing the risks of conservation-related action on the livelihoods of forest-based and forest-resource-dependent communities. A series of studies have been carried out in several countries by Women Organizing for Change in Agriculture and Natural Resource Management (WOCAN), as part of the UN-REDD and identified entry points for women inclusion in REDD initiatives for reducing deforestation and forest degradation (UN-REDD, WOCAN, and USAID, 2013). The case studies show that deforestation affects women and men differently, and women are equipped with local practices applicable to sustainable management of environment and the resources. Efforts are also being made to introduce social safeguard policies for risk minimization (WEDO, 2013).

Several analytical frameworks, such as the Driving force, Pressure, State, Exposure and the Effect (DPSEE) Framework (WHO, 2003), have been introduced to look into environment and health covering DPSEE (Figure 14.4). This encouraged individual nations to look into the total cycle, including driving forces, pressure, state, impacts, and the responses. The regional overviews suggest that environmental degradation takes place under various anthropogenic pressures, with detrimental effects

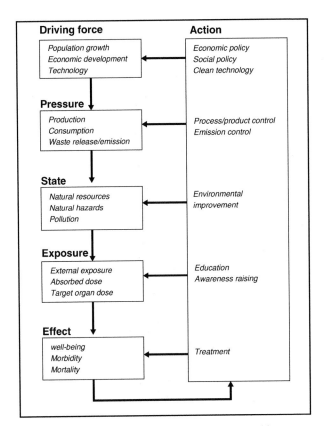

Figure 14.4. The DPSEE framework of the World Health Organization (*Source*: WHO, 2003).

on production of goods and services, on the integrity of a life support system and functional linkage, and on quality of natural resources. The meaning of degradation has been interpreted in various ways and explained at various scales, from global to local; through various lenses, such as poverty, gender, justice, and others; purely in terms of adverse consequences related to resources, water, energy, health, agriculture, biodiversity, and so forth; in connection with increasing events of droughts, floods, landslides, and the like; and in relation overall to climate change. Irrespective of the variations, the changes have serious effects on the sustainability of the living world, including people's livelihood, biological resources, and the production and service functions. The impacts of environmental degradation on food production, food insecurity, and water availability are being placed in the forefront by those who rely on local land-based resources for their living. A local, national, and international policy intervention, which requires coalitions and partnerships, has become crucial to maintaining quality and eradicating the root causes of degradation.

Within the context of Asia, the intensity of climate-related changes has increased, affecting the land and local-resource-based livelihood systems, especially of the poor, women, and the marginalized sectors. This has increased the demand for public investments for environmental resource restoration and rehabilitation. Depending on the interest in dismantling the adverse dimensions, many perspectives – covering ecology, health, deforestation, gender, food and nutrition, green economy, and many others – have been entertained, exploring the root causes of environmental degradation and its consequences. Ecological and livelihood insecurity have induced food insecurity, malnutrition, deprivation, and stagnation of poverty in rural areas. The life support system, including land, water, forests, and biodiversity, is threatened by the nature of agricultural change experienced in South Asia (Mahbub Ul Haq Human Development Centre, 2002). Degradation means low income, food insecurity, and lack of capacity for investing in restoration and rehabilitation for the rural farmers who depend upon small plots of land. The interrelationship between the environment and poverty, food and nutrition, health, resources, production, and threats to ecosystem functions (including climatic changes) can be established, which would improve efforts to synthesize knowledge and address the causes and effects (see Table 14.6). Each of these consists of a wide range of issues, contextual conditions, and their results. Poverty, for instance, has a bearing on health, resources, production, and more, while poverty itself leads to degradation and creates disproportionate consequences.

The possible contribution of the environment to sustainable development has been constructed from the perspectives of

Table 14.6. Areas of concern and the issues leading to environmental degradation.

Areas of concern	Consequences
Poverty	• Lack of assets
	• Social stratification
	• Inequity
	• Disempowerment
	• Unequal access to services and resources
	• Inefficiency
	• High external dependency
	• Vulnerability
Food and nutrition	• Hunger and starvation
	• Malnutrition
	• Reduced efficiency
	• Scarcity of biomass for cooking and food processing
Health	• Vulnerability
	• Disease, infections
	• Reduced well-being
	• High morbidity rates
	• Exhaustion
	• Low labour efficiency
	• Low life expectancy
Resources	• Water scarcity
	• Pollution
	• Biomass scarcity
	• Scarcity of forest resources/services
	• Soil degradation
	• Declining biodiversity
Production	• Low output from land
	• Livelihood insecurity
	• High chemical input
	• Increased cost of production
	• Reduced income
	• Reduced employment opportunities
	• Labour migration
Threats and climate change	• Pollution
	• Desertification
	• Drought events
	• Landslides
	• Floods
	• Siltation/sedimentation
	• Fragmentation of natural habitats

Source: Community-based assessments carried out by the author during 2009 to 2011 while engaged in a project on Biodiversity Conservation and Buffer Zone Development in the Knuckles forest in Sri Lanka (see Wickramasinghe (2015) for research details).

poverty and the environment (World Bank, 2002), the environment and health (WHO, 2003), climate change and food system (World Bank, 2015b), and gender equality (UNESCAP, 2017). These demonstrate the central importance of the environment for sustainable development for the present and future generations. Along these lines, strategies and actions are being introduced from global to local levels. For instance, the MDG targets for reducing by half the proportion of people without sustainable access to drinking water secured the urgent attention of the state agencies in the region. The provision of improved water and sanitation services for an additional 164 million people has been recognized as a challenge. It has required additional services for 445,000 people each day in Asia up to the year 2015. Estimated figures reveal that around 668 million people (that is, around 18% of the population in Asia and the Pacific) lack access to safe drinking water, and 1,888 million, which is about 52% of the population, lack adequate sanitation. While we advocate pro-poor policies in the water-related service sector, urgent attention must be drawn to the problem of deepening water scarcity resulting from climatic changes and the detrimental use of land and increased contamination of traditional sources of water used by the rural people. Depletion and degradation of wood fuel supply sources, degradation of forests and reduced agro-biodiversity, alienation of poor people from their resource bases, and soil degradation due to poor management and exhaustive use are grave threats to sustainable development.

Often the link between poverty and environmental degradation has been explained in relation to a vicious circle, focusing on interconnected features (see UNESCAP, 2006). On the one hand, poverty, increasing population, and pressure on resources for subsistence lead to resource over-exploitation and unsustainable use. On the other hand, the degraded conditions directly and indirectly affect the poor who live in marginal areas and depend on the land for subsistence; those who do not have alternative means of livelihood are the victims of degradation. The existing situation shows that land scarcity experienced by the population impedes the development prospects, and a high density of population, which is around 90 persons per square kilometre, creates environmental and resource stresses. Population density is 186 persons in South Asia and three persons in the South Pacific. The availability of arable land in the region also varies; it is 39% in South Asia and 9% in North and Southeast Asia. These circumstances lead to the conclusion that land and its capacity are crucial factors directly affecting spatial variations pertaining to livelihood security of the people, which in turn is needed to safeguard the environment. The depletion of natural resources and biodiversity, atmospheric pollution, drying up of aquifers, pollution, and increasing production of waste

are of multiple implications. While the interventions contributed to furthering economic growth, the poor are directly and indirectly affected by environmental degradation, increasing their vulnerability to degradation and rising detrimental effects of degradation on health, hunger, and malnutrition across the region.

14.6 HEALTH AND WELL-BEING FOR ALL

Health and well-being are fundamental to human progress and they are essential for achieving sustainable development and reducing the development gaps that have emerged over the years. Why poverty, inequality, and environmental degradation matter for sustainable development and what we want to achieve are often answered from political and development perspectives. There is no simple answer acceptable to all, but concerns expressed by the people refer seriously to health and well-being. For example the World Water Assessment Programme (WWAP) (2015) shows that exposure of people and assets to hydro-meteorological hazards has been growing. In 2013, more than 17,000 people died from water-related disasters in the region, accounting for more than 90% of all such deaths globally. The poverty-health and environment nexus is extremely complex in terms of interaction and is specific to the contextual conditions. In this context, concerns also involve the right to drinking water and improved sanitation, which is a prerequisite for realizing other human rights, such as the right to life and dignity and to adequate food, health, and well-being (WWAP, 2016). Disease-prone conditions, pollution, resource scarcity, and human occupations in hazardous conditions seriously contribute to this phenomenon, especially in degraded areas. The public health challenges, such as malaria and dengue, as well as diseases connected with poor hygiene and sanitation, undermine development. As in the case of all previously discussed domains, the multiple dimensions pertaining to health and well-being entertain a wide range of analysis. From the perspectives of environment and development, environmental health has been widely reviewed using various lenses: gender, energy, health, food security, nutrition, and disease, as well as morbidity, life expectancy, and similar issues. Poor health implies low labour productivity, output, and exhaustion of human energy, leading to less output per labour unit. There are multiple analytical approaches and frameworks, such as the gender mainstreaming (UNDP, 2007), which has been used widely during the last few decades, and several others with the potential to deal with the growing development concerns.

In this regard, the DPSEE framework suggested by WHO (2003) is applicable to deal with environmental health. It builds connections between driving forces, pressure, state, exposure with health effects, emphasizing action at each level (Figure 14.4). This framework is useful for strategic planning that can address environmental health issues. This framework suggests that various types of action, including treatment, and also the preventive measures such as education, environmental improvement, pollution control, and policy, among others, are needed in response to driving forces. Looking at the condition of Asia and the Pacific, particularly South Asia with its high population, poverty, and poor living conditions, it is important to realize the need for dealing with contextual conditions. The actions can prevent proximal to distal exposure, that is, from home and community to the ambient environment, and the remedial measures by which environmental health can be sought are crucial for change. Social achievements in Asia and the Pacific make it clear that preventive environmental improvements have not been very effective, owing to poor public partnerships, weaknesses in institutional mechanisms, and the unsatisfactory living conditions of the poor. People who live in poor conditions and disaster-prone environments are more vulnerable to environmental health problems than other people.

During the recent past, various types of strategic solutions have been introduced to address the issue of cooking fuel, focusing on biomass degradation, health, and technology. Almost all the countries in South Asia have attempted to address the problems associated with the use of biomass as a source of cooking fuel and rudimentary cooking practices, which proved to have serious health repercussions and environmental impacts. The household energy procuring behaviour and strategies of the poor are influenced by gender and connected with multiple sources, some of which may not be in favourable conditions. This phenomenon is linked with depletion of productive resources, as well. The dependence of Asian households on poor-quality biomass and low calorific materials like residues, animal dung, and leaf biomass has increased over the years. When such materials are burnt inside, the smoke and the particulates released during burning lead to pollution, affecting the health of the people indoors. Despite the interventions made on cooking fuels by many nations, around 2 billion people depend on solid fuels in cooking (ADB, 2015), and IEA (2015) estimated that around 276 million of them live in Southeast Asia. The dependence on biomass for cooking is extremely high in the rural areas, and WHO (2016) showed that more than 80% of rural households use mainly biomass, while it is only 25% among urban households. Inefficient and rudimentary cooking practices kill nearly 4 million people every year (Global Alliance for Clean Cookstoves, 2013; WHO, 2016, 2018), and millions more suffer from health problems. This situation points out the seriousness of the equality and inequity issues pertaining to energy access, availability, affordability, and safety and safeguards that affect development. It is also widely recognized that the use of degraded agricultural land for production is exhaustive, raises the cost of production, and provides inadequate, low returns to farm households. The health implications of degradation have been bundled with crop failures, depletion of ground water, lack of safe drinking water, scarcity of biomass fuel for cooking, and reduced food diversity in the family diet. In order to mitigate the environmental repercussions while rehabilitating the degraded conditions, an inclusive approach integrating the triple goals of development is needed. Unless the poor and the marginalized sectors become capable and economically and socially empowered, they will continue to be the victims of environmental health problems and disastrous events, such as landslides, droughts, and floods, to mention only a few. The climate change-related matters, including the disasters highlighted during the recent past, make clear the gravity of the social impacts that magnify the gender- and poverty-based disparities. One serious concern here is to deal with social, economic, and environmental contexts, using a framework suitable not only for analysis but also for planning and implementation. From the perspectives of development, the South Asian region should pay attention to the promotion of preventive measures.

14.7 RECIPROCAL CONNECTIONS AND CHANGE

Reciprocity exists at various scales and levels in all spheres pertaining to social, economic, and environment development. It can be materialized for integration and inclusion as a key instrument for resolving the persisting challenges of poverty, imbalances, inequity, and environmental degradation. The reciprocal relationships between the environment and development are central to making changes at different levels, especially within and between regions and countries. The human initiatives that take place within spatial, political, social, economic, and ecological systems provide conditions for strengthening reciprocal linkages for inclusive development. In this regard, the policy linkages, political linkages between hierarchical levels, institutional linkages, and social linkages have become crucial, especially because of the need for working collectively and with great responsibility to deal with the issues of environmental and resource degradation. It is necessary to ensure a balanced flow of capital to ensure spatial linkages through various processes and activities.

Reciprocal linkages can be seen as generations-long social practices in Asia. Sharing responsibilities, common goods and services, employing knowledge, experience and understanding, capacity-building, and integration take place through this lateral process. Conventional reciprocal exchange of labour is practised as a means of sharing local human capital for smoothing gaps. The underlying principles can be used to instate linkages between local and global regions that are defined in terms of biophysical zones, or in relation to economy-industrial and non-industrial sectors, or in terms of achievements-development and developing regions. In the region, these linkages are in multiple forms and can be described in relation to environment, resources, capital investments, welfare delivery, trade, technology, and many more. Locally, within a nation state or in the region, the reciprocal linkages have become essential for social, political, economic, and environmental achievements.

The spatial linkages in development are essential because in many countries, disparities or differences, both natural and manipulated, need to be reduced for environmental sustainability. Providing opportunities for the backward sectors and regions necessitates the commitment of the advanced and resource-rich areas. As has been discussed by van den Bergh (2002) in his work on integrated modelling, the spatial dimensions of sustainable development provide grounding for strong relationships. Climatic change tends to reveal the global impact of local activities and the local effects of global trends, both qualitatively and quantitatively. Locally, the cross-boundary effects of policies pertaining to resource conservation are another example drawing our attention to such linkages. Locally, for instance, the declaring of Strict Nature Reserves (SNRs), Man and Biosphere Reserves (MABs), and protected areas, where the systems have been part of the local livelihood of indigenous people over generations, leads to questioning of the spatial, socio-economic, and cultural aspects of reciprocal relationships, in the paradigm of environment and development. Pollution control and the management of watersheds and forest landscapes are also examples that demonstrate spatial linkages through social and institutional mechanisms.

Several globally supported initiatives, such as the United Nations Reducing Emissions from Deforestation and Forest Degradation (UN-REDD), United Nations Framework Convention on Climate Change (UNFCCC), Convention on Biological Diversity (CBD), and United Nations Convention to Combat Desertification (UNCCD), have been facilitated through local policies. These are guided by the principles of equity and are expected to contribute to poverty reduction and sustainable management of the environment. The policy instruments are state-led commitments that are to be designed appropriately to address the issues of demoralization, marginalization, disempowerment, and impoverishment. The linkage effects extend beyond the places of origin or the project-specific areas, creating detrimental effects locally. For instance, in the management of protected areas, the isolation of protected areas from local communities, and their culture and traditions, has severely impeded efforts to bridge conservation, development, and technology with local knowledge. This implies that the cascade effects of global and project-specific initiatives or human intervention on the environment ought to be examined at the same strength at local levels. Therefore, the sustainability of the environment needs to be promoted from the grassroots, where the scaling-up effects would become significant over a longer period.

14.8 LOCAL COMMITMENT AND FUTURE DIRECTIONS

The effectiveness of development should be seen in poverty alleviation, equity, and environmental management. This demands that institutional structures and mechanisms place social capital in the centre, dismantling the three issues interlocked in the most stressful nexus: poverty-inequity-environment, as shown in Figure 14.2. The reversal of degradation becomes possible through a strong local commitment, through which the strong process of scaling up and cascading would take place. The main reason is that it internalizes the environment and development through reciprocity, local capacity, and equal opportunities. The second reason is that strong social capital is an instrument facilitating scaling up vertically while spreading out laterally. Prerequisites in this direction are numerous, but the most crucial one is institutional building with an accommodative policy framework.

In promoting local action for change, one could draw attention to scaling up the community-based approaches that have been successful. One approach seen in many places is the community initiatives in resource conservation to meet the basic needs of local communities. Two success cases from Sri Lanka could be mentioned in this regard, though a full account is not given here. The first is the community water supply initiative in Wanaraniya, where a women's organization has organized the water resource management for providing clean water for household use. The second is the Akkaraseeya Community Water Project introduced under the Upper Mahaweli Watershed Management Project, where forest regeneration and conservation have been undertaken as a strategic measure to maintain the water sources for community use. In both cases, the common concern over collective involvement and control over resources has been strengthened and guided by the need for maintaining the water supply. The experiences in these two cases include (1) shared responsibility of environmental management, especially the catchment management, including reforestation and enrichment integrated into day-to-day living of the people; (2) equity and equality assured by providing access to water by all and the benefits of water supply; (3) inclusion of water-related issues pertaining to health, sanitation, gender, and seasonal droughts addressing poverty; and (4) the organization of a local social capital engaged in sustainable management.

Community-based forestry conservation strategies in many countries, including India, Nepal, and Sri Lanka, where tangible and non-tangible values have been built into indigenous conservation strategies, also represent collective and shared responsibility over the environment and development. Asia, notable for its local resource-based livelihood systems, has a long-standing culture rich with conservation concerns. Cultural landscapes that are spread across the region are testimony to the local, scaled-up, innovative measures. One living example is the home gardens that contribute to the well-being, food and energy security, biodiversity, and so forth of individual family units, with cascading effects generated through a process of establishing mosaics of forest landscapes.

The significant lessons learned from these projects include the following:

1. Necessity-based priorities that internalize the interventions for promoting collective action;
2. Promotion of a feeling of authority, control, and ownership by reinstating entitlement to resources;
3. Building social capital to promote reciprocity and collective responsibility over local resources/environment;
4. Building local capacity for intra- and inter-generational sustainability;
5. Social inclusion, providing equal opportunities on the basis of community – in relation to the occupation of village eco-systems and resource sharing;
6. Gender inclusion as a strategy and a means to eradicate inequalities.

These examples reveal that, in the first place, water was the priority concern or common ground which enabled the community to mobilize. Mitigation of forest denudation through community initiatives for effective conservation of soil, water, and plants was important in the second; and home-based resource conservation with cross-boundary effects in mosaics of home gardens for promoting biodiversity for food security and poverty alleviation was very significant in the third case. The key elements in all three cases are the sharing of equity, network, responsibility, and ownership, which are central in making transitional effects.

What is lacking is the effort to integrate these into policy and institutional mechanisms to promote integrated action for sustainable development and coordination and linkage in this process. Institutional coordination is the way to integrate development and the environment and to facilitate action. Success cases offer isolated experiences in communicating policy recommendations for state agencies on how to mobilize local communities effectively, so as to have scaling-up effects of local action towards regional and global change.

14.9 CONCLUSION

The process of sustainable development in Asia and the Pacific region is disturbed by inequality, affecting the outcomes of sustainable development. In this situation, regional achievements that depend upon the progress made by the individual states have been hindered. The Asia-Pacific region has to deal with more than half of the world's population, and the largest concentration of the world's poor. Therefore, the process of contributing towards sustainable development should begin with addressing three crucial challenges pertaining to gender, inequality, and poverty. During this process, the richness of the biodiversity, the unique ecosystems, and strong cultural characteristics could be integrated into a strategically promoted development process. Under these circumstances, measures to design development options while addressing the unmet needs, secluded areas, and social sectors are essential.

In this chapter, an attempt has been made to discuss the key persisting and interrelated issues confronting the environment and development in the region. Many countries have worked backwards with negative consequences, working from the symptoms and indicators towards the contextual conditions. Yet pro-poor strategies have not made substantial upward movement in eradicating poverty and inequity or in securing environmental stability for livelihood and health security. Policies on social development have made progress in the areas pertaining to well-being. But this implies that two of the three pillars in sustainable development – the environmental and the economic – have not been strengthened in an integrated manner; as a result, social development made by using external deliveries has not been able to address the crucial issues of poverty, inequity, gender, and exclusion. Therefore, the arguments forwarded in this work make it clear that poverty, inequity, unequal opportunities, and environmental degradation are the waves of destruction paralysing sustainable development.

In these circumstances, it is recommended to promote the following:

• National policies to make a new paradigm responsive to local contexts are needed, thus strengthening the three pillars of sustainable development. An integrated policy framework with an inclusive approach is needed to deal with the destructive waves, such as poverty and inequity, by which many areas and social sectors – the poor and women in particular – can be included and addressed. Environmental degradation, by which health and livelihoods or the resource base have been weakened, is a key area to be given priority attention;
• The process of development should be structured from local contextual grounds, with local agendas and targets to promote local authority, control, and ownership over development. The development decision-making must include voices and concerns, and in this regard the urgent task is to promote institutional mechanisms with new stewardships to articulate local development, enabling the wider society to have more

responsibility and a decent standard of living. This requires much more than democracy or involvement of people in decision-making, but new partnerships. Provision of equal opportunities and eradication of many forms of poverty, exclusion, and inequity can enhance recognition, respect, competence, reciprocity, and a sense of equity, which are central to making progress;

• Facilitate reciprocal relationships between the environment and development while involving poor rural communities through partnership-building, while mitigating disadvantages. This is central for building in intergenerational sustainability and reciprocal relationships. A locally promoted and facilitated development process, decentralization of operational mechanisms, and local capacity-building are needed to change the contextual conditions;

• These circumstances suggest the need for gender-inclusive and social-inclusive instruments, strategic measures, institutional mechanisms, and services to promote knowledgeable, capable, and committed public or local communities. In this regard, building social capital is a prerequisite for managing local development, using all possible instruments, particularly education, training, awareness raising, financing, information technology, networking, dialogue, and idea exchange, among others;

• Appropriate analytical approaches are to be applied by the countries to improve understanding and enhance diagnosis to form integrated strategic formulas for the eradication of spatially concentrated social and economic imbalances that exist within countries and across the region.

ACKNOWLEDGEMENTS

This chapter is based on materials collected in preparation of regional and national profiles on gender, poverty, and energy, funded by ENERGIA, the International Network on Gender and Sustainable Energy. The comments received from Ms Patricia Alexander and Dr Pak Sum Low are gratefully appreciated.

REFERENCES

Agyeman, J., Bullard, R. D. and Evans, B. (2003) Joined-up thinking: bringing together sustainability, environmental justice and equity. In J. Agyeman *et al.* (eds.), *Just Sustainabilities: Development in an Unequal World* (Introduction), pp. 1–16. London, Earthscan Publications Ltd.

Asian Development Bank (2013) *Key Indicators for Asia and the Pacific 2013*. Manila, ADB.

(2018) *Gender Equality: Bridging the Gap*. Manila, Asian Development Bank.

(2015) *Sustainable Energy for All: Tracking Progress in Asia and the Pacific: A Summary Report*. Manila, ADB.

Blowers, A. (2003) Inequality and community and the challenge to modernization: evidence from the nuclear oases. In J. Agyeman, R. D. Bullard and B. Evans (eds.), *Just Sustainabilities: Development in an Unequal World* (Chapter 3), pp. 64–80. London, Earthscan Publications Ltd.

Department of Census and Statistics (2016) *Poverty Indicators: Household Income and Expenditure Survey*. Colombo, Sri Lanka.

DFID (2002) *Energy for the Poor, Underpinning the Millennium Development Goals*. United Kingdom, Department for International Development.

FAO (2011) State of the World's Forests 2011. Food and Agriculture Organization of the United Nations, Rome. http://www.fao.org/3/i2000e/i2000e00.htm

(2016) State of the World's Forests 2016. Food and Agriculture Organization of the United Nations, Rome. http://www.fao.org/publications/sofo/2016/en/

(2018) State of the World's Forests 2018: Forest pathways to sustainable development. Food and Agriculture Organization of the United Nations. Rome. https://www.fao.org/state-of-forests/2018/en

Global Alliance for Clean Cookstoves (2013) *Scaling Adoption of Clean Cookstoves through Women's Empowerment: A Resource Guide*. Washington, DC, Global Alliance for Clean Cookstoves.

International Energy Agency (IEA) (2015). Southeast Asia Outlook 2015. World Energy Outlook Special Report. Paris.

IPCC (2018) Global Warming of 1.5°C Report. https://www.ipcc.ch/sr15/

Mahbub ul Haq Human Development Centre (2002) *Human Development in South Asia 2001*. Karachi, Oxford University Press.

Scholes, R. J., Montanarella, L., Brainich, A., Barger, N., ten Brink, B., Cantele, M., Eramus, B., Fisher, J., Gardner, T., Holland, T. G., Kohler, F., Kotiaho, J. S., Von Maltitz, G., Nangendo, G., Pandit, R., Parrotta, J., Potts, M. D., Prince, S., Sankaran, M. and Willemen, L. (eds.) (2018) IPBES (2018): *Summary for Policymakers of the Assessment Report on Land Degradation and Restoration of the Intergovernmental Science-Policy Platform on Biodiversity and Ecosystem Services*. Bonn, Germany, Intergovernmental Science-Policy Platform on Biodiversity and Ecosystem Services.

UNCCD (2019) *Land in Numbers 2019. Risks and Opportunities*. Bonn, Germany, United Nations Convention to Combat Desertification. http://catalogue.unccd.int/1202-Land%20in%20numbers_2%20new-web.pdf

UNDP (2004) *Energy for Sustainable Development in Asia and the Pacific Region: Challenges and Lessons from UNDP Projects*. New York, United Nations Development Programme.

(2004) *Human Development Report*. New York, United Nations Development Programme.

(2006a) *The Millennium Development Goals Report*. New York, United Nations.

(2006b) *Human Development Report*. New York, United Nations Development Programme.

(2007) Gender mainstreaming: A key driver of development in environment and energy, Training Manual. New York, UNDP.

(2016) *Human Development Report*. New York, United Nations Development Programme.

(2018) *Human Development Report*. New York, United Nations Development Programme.

UNEP (2012) *Global Environment Outlook 5*. Nairobi, United Nations Environment Programme.

(2016) *Global Environmental Outlook 6*. Nairobi, United Nations Environment Programme.

UNESCAP (2006) *Economic and Social Survey of Asia and the Pacific*. New York, United Nations.

(2017) *Gender, the Environment and Sustainable Development in Asia and the Pacific*. Bangkok, Thailand, UNESCAP.

United Nations (2000) *The State of the Environment in Asia and the Pacific*. New York.

UN-REDD, WOCAN, and USAID (2013) Women's inclusion in REDD+ in Sri Lanka: Lessons from good practices in forest, agriculture and other natural resource management. Bangkok, WOCAN.

van den Bergh, J. C. J. M. (2002) Integrated modelling and evaluation of spatial and dynamic-evolutionary processes in environment-economy system. In H. Abaza and A. Baranzini (eds.), *Implementing Sustainable Development: Integrated Assessment and Participatory Decision-making Processes*, pp. 203–234. United Nations Environment Programme. Cheltenham, UK, Edward Elgar Publishing Limited.

WHO (2003) *Making a Difference: Indicators to Improve Children's Environmental Health*. Geneva, World Health Organization.

(2016) Burning opportunity: Clean household energy for health, sustainable development and well-being of women. Geneva, World Health Organization.

(2018) Household air pollution and health. Key facts. 8 May 2018. Geneva, World Health Organization. https://www.who.int/newsroom/fact-sheets/detail/household-air-pollution-and-health

Wickramasinghe, A. (2002) Global action for women towards sustainable and equitable development. National Report for the World Summit on Sustainable Development – Rio+10 (Chapter 24). Ministry of Environment and Natural Resources, Sri Lanka.

(2003a) Women and environmental justice in South Asia. In J. Agyeman *et al.* (eds.), *Just Sustainabilities: Development in an Unequal World* (Chapter 11), pp. 229–251. London, Earthscan Publications.

(2003b) Gender and health issues in the biomass energy cycle: impediments to sustainable development. *Energy for Sustainable Development*, the Journal of the International Energy Initiative (IEI), **7**(3), 51–61.

(2004a) Biomass energy and rural development: Livelihood sustainability in Asia. Paper presented at the World Renewable Energy Congress (WREC-VIII), August 29–September 3, Denver, CO, USA.

(2004b) Gender and health threats related to energy: Issues of women's rights to energy resources and services. Paper presented at the World Renewable Energy Congress (WREC-VIII), August 29–September 3, Denver, CO, USA.

(2004c) Implications of biomass energy system for women in Sri Lanka. *Glow*, **3**, 18–25. Asia Regional Cookstove Programme.

(2015) Forest dependence for enhancing social responsibility over forest management and buffer zone development. *The Sri Lanka Forester*, **36** & **37**, 1–25. Forestry Department, Sri Lanka.

Women's Environment and Development Organization (2013) From research to action, leaf by leaf: Getting gender right in the REDD+ Social and Environmental Standards. New York. https://wedo.org/wedo-launches-from-research-to-action-leaf-by-leaf-getting-gender-right-in-redd-ses/

World Bank (2002) Linking poverty reduction and environmental management: Policy challenges and opportunities. Washington, DC.

(2015a) Ending poverty and hunger by 2030: An agenda for the global food system. Washington, DC.

(2015b) Future of food: Shaping a climate-smart global system. Washington, DC. https://www.worldbank.org/en/topic/agriculture

WWAP (World Water Assessment Programme) (2015) United Nations World Water Development Report 2015: Water for a sustainable world. Paris, United Nations Educational, Scientific and Cultural Organization.

(2016) The United Nations World Water Development Report 2016: Water and jobs. Paris, United Nations Educational, Scientific and Cultural Organization.

15 The challenge of global climate change for international law: An overview

KAREN HULME AND DAVID M. ONG[*]

University of Essex & Nottingham Trent University, United Kingdom

Keywords

Biological diversity; climate change; common but differentiated treatment/responsibility; dispute settlement; ecological security; human rights; humanitarian intervention; international law; investment risk; Law of the Sea; sea-level rise; statehood; sovereignty; use of force

Abstract

Global climate change presents an unprecedented challenge for all academic disciplines. Here we analyse the challenge presented to certain basic concepts and principles of international law. While new legal regimes have been created and others adapted to respond to the threats posed by climate change, many foundational aspects of international law remain unchanged in the face of very significant problems. The first problematic area is that of the fundamental notion of statehood, as well as issues of sovereignty. And what of the impact of climate change on human rights and humanitarian intervention, as well as on notions of State responsibility and liability? The Asia-Pacific region is already feeling the impacts of frequent intense weather events (whether one sees these as climate change impacts or not) and has the highest figures for the number of displaced persons by region for natural disasters. Thus, where possible, this chapter will draw from examples in the Asia-Pacific region.

15.1 INTRODUCTION

Global climate change, whether in the short, medium, or long term, presents an undeniable challenge for all knowledge disciplines, whether in the natural or social sciences and humanities fields. In this contribution, we will examine the challenges that

the phenomenon of climate change presents to certain basic concepts and principles of international law. These include basic notions of international law such as statehood itself, State sovereignty, international law-making and implementation, as well as State responsibility and liability. Apart from assessing the impact of climate change on these fundamental notions of international law, the specific implications will also be raised of large-scale environmental change on such important fields of international law as international human rights law, international environmental law, international dispute settlement, international investment law, and the use of military force. Examples from the Asia-Pacific setting will be used to highlight the challenges that global environmental change represents for international law. Many of these questions are not new, but it is perhaps surprising that they still remain unanswered or unaddressed, particularly as they involve fundamental issues within international law.

15.2 GLOBAL CLIMATE CHANGE AND ITS IMPLICATIONS FOR INTERNATIONAL LAW

Before we begin our foray into the implications of global climate change for the very discipline and subject matter of international law, it is incumbent upon us to lay out a general understanding of the phenomenon that we are rendering our analysis from, namely human-induced environmental change, which is affecting the core or fundamental elements of the global climatic system – as recognized in the 1992 United Nations Framework Convention on Climate Change (UNFCCC), the 1997 Kyoto Protocol, and the 2015 Paris Agreement (hereinafter, collectively known as the Climate Change Convention regime). Essentially, this requires an explication of two interlinked concepts: first, the phenomenon of global climate change itself, and secondly, the fact that such global climate change is a function of certain significant factors, both natural and human. A further aspect of the phenomenon that will be touched on here is the impact and implications of such change within the Asia-Pacific region.

[*] Professor at the School of Law, University of Essex, United Kingdom, and Research Professor in International and Environmental Law, Nottingham Law School, Nottingham Trent University, United Kingdom, respectively.

In the fourth and fifth Assessment Reports of the Intergovernmental Panel on Climate Change (IPCC), there is clear recognition and evidence of 'substantially more impacts in recent decades now attributed to climate change' on a global scale (IPCC, 2014a). According to the report,

A large fraction of species faces increased extinction risk due to climate change during and beyond the 21st century ... Most plant species cannot naturally shift their geographical ranges sufficiently fast to keep up with current and high projected rates of climate change in most landscapes ... Coral reefs and polar ecosystems are highly vulnerable. Coastal systems and low-lying areas are at risk from sea level rise, which will continue for centuries even if the global mean temperature is stabilized ... Climate change is projected to undermine food security ... global marine species redistribution and marine biodiversity reduction in sensitive regions will challenge the sustained provision of fisheries productivity and other ecosystem services ... [as well as] wheat, rice and maize in tropical and temperate regions ... [and] is projected to reduce renewable surface water and groundwater resources in most dry subtropical regions, intensifying competition for water among sectors.

Thus, we are starting to discern the truly epic scale of climate change and, consequently, the potentially equally dramatic implications for the international law discipline.

Within the legal context, it is also important to note the now well-accepted view of the human contribution to climate change. Regardless, destructive climatic events are occurring on a more frequent scale and with increasing intensity and are causing greater human and environmental suffering; thus, the law needs to adapt and respond. Consequently, the implications of climate change are being felt across a range of related international policy and legal dimensions. As far back as 2008, a joint report by the European Union's High Representative and the European Commission on Climate Change and International Security, for example, began by stating unequivocally that '[t]he risks provided by climate change are real and its impacts are already taking place' (Solana, 2008). The IPCC's Fourth Assessment Report was also equally unambiguous in its statements on this point in 2007, notably that '[t]he understanding of anthropogenic warming and cooling influences on climate has improved since the TAR [Third Assessment Report, 2001], leading to *very high confidence* that the global average net effect of human activities since 1750 has been one of warming' (emphasis added) (IPCC, 2007a). And about future risks, the Fifth Assessment Report states that '[c]limate change will amplify existing risks and create new risks for natural and human systems. Risks are unevenly distributed and are generally greater for disadvantaged people and communities in countries at all levels of development' (IPCC, 2014a).

More specifically, on the legal front, as of September 2020, 189 countries have ratified the 2015 Paris Agreement, which is aimed at 'enhancing the implementation of the Convention' and recognizes the need 'to strengthen the global response to the threat of climate change, in the context of sustainable development and efforts to eradicate poverty' (Article 1). The key commitments to achieving this objective are set out in Article 1 and include holding the increase in the global average temperature to 'well below 2°C' and 'pursuing efforts' to limit temperature rise to 1.5°C, increasing adaptability to climate change and fostering climate resilience – including by making finance flows consistent with a pathway towards low greenhouse gas emissions and climate-resilient development. Pivotal to the agreement was the acceptance of a universal obligation of nationally appropriate mitigation actions, including emissions reductions, the levels of which are determined nationally. Such nationally determined contributions, however, are non-binding. Thus, while the agreement was reached on the basis of consensus, it came at the cost of legally binding reduction commitments.

The projected scale and mode of impacts from global environmental change are outlined by other contributions in this volume, but arguably the truest test of the flexibility and thus value of international law will be determined by the way this legal discipline faces up to the challenges raised by two issues in particular: These are, first, the human and environmental effects of climate change impacting upon established social, economic, and cultural norms, and second, the loss of territory – especially the complete loss of territory in the case of so-called disappearing or submerging states (those small island and low-lying states that will be inundated by sea-level rises) (Hampson, 2005). The IPCC noted in 2007 that '[c]limate change puts the long-term sustainability of societies in atoll countries at risk. The potential abandonment of sovereign atoll countries can be used as one benchmark of the "dangerous" change that the UNFCCC seeks to avoid' (IPCC, 2007b). As summed up by the Tuvaluan Governor-General as far back as 2002, 'We want the islands of Tuvalu and our nation to remain permanently and not be submerged as a result of greed and uncontrolled consumption of industrialized countries. We want our children to grow up the way we grew up in our own islands and in our own culture' (Puapua, 2002). In this respect, a 2007 World Bank study on the consequences of projected sea-level rise due to climatic change for 84 developing countries suggested that 'hundreds of millions of people in the developing world are likely to be displaced by sea-level rise within this century; and accompanying economic and ecological damage will be severe for many. At the country level, results are extremely skewed, with severe impacts limited to a relatively small number of countries' (Dasgupta *et al.*, 2007). For those countries that will be the worst affected, however, suggested to be Vietnam, Egypt, and the Bahamas, the study predicted that the consequences of sea-level rise would be 'potentially catastrophic'. Significantly, for the focus of the present volume, this World Bank study noted that East Asia and the Middle East/North African regions will exhibit the greatest relative impacts. Finally, the World Bank study concluded by noting that at that point in time, there was little evidence that the international community had seriously considered the implications of sea-level rise for population location and infrastructure planning in developing countries (Dasgupta *et al.*, 2007), although clearly this situation has changed, but actions are arguably still far too limited.

Section 15.3 will focus on the pivotal notion of statehood in international law and will pose the fundamental question of whether the current concept of statehood can survive global climate change unscathed. Subsequent sections then probe the questions raised by climate change in other fields and concepts of international law, for example, how the international community needs to revisit fundamental notions of responsibility and liability, and perceptions of rights and decision-making, when addressing the phenomena of climate change.

15.3 PARADISE LOST: CAN 'STATEHOOD' SURVIVE CLIMATE CHANGE?

The notion of 'statehood' is fundamental to the functioning of the modern international legal system and affords an entity the most complete sense of international legal personality. The paradigmatic concept of a 'State' within international law is of a sovereign nation State with a defined land territory that is afforded all the inherent rights and duties, privileges, and immunities of such statehood (Schwarzenberger, 1976). But what makes such an entity a 'State' in the first place? And consequently, what impact does the partial, or indeed complete, loss of its terrestrial aspect due to sea-level rise have on this fundamental notion of a State under international law? An examination of these questions requires a prior discussion of the legal concept of the 'State' itself within the international legal system, especially in terms of its acquisition of international legal personality.

15.3.1 What is a 'State'? Challenging fundamental notions of 'statehood'

The starting point for defining the notion of a 'State' is the fourfold criteria of 'statehood' established in the 1933 Montevideo Convention on the Rights and Duties of States, namely (1) a permanent population, (2) a defined territory, (3) government, and (4) capacity to enter into relations with other States (Crawford, 2006). Many would also add the fifth criterion of recognition. While these criteria are generally applied at the point at which an entity wishes to be designated as a State, the problems posed to the notion of statehood by global climate

change are very different and include the question of continuation of statehood despite the loss of a fundamental criterion – that of territory.

For those States that lose only a portion of their territory to the sea, for example Bangladesh, these States are not going to lose their statehood. Despite the inevitable population movement within their territory (or in the case of island States, from one island to another), the population will still be sufficiently permanent for the purposes of criterion (1) mentioned earlier, and the territory will undoubtedly still be sufficiently defined for criterion (2) (though we will return to questions of maritime boundaries later). The issue is, of course, more pertinent for those States that will lose all of their land territory, the so-called submerging States phenomenon. Many low-lying island and atoll States, of which there is a large number in the Asia-Pacific region, face the prospect within decades of being submerged by rising sea levels. Do any precedents exist for statehood where the State has no territorial base? If not, will States such as Kiribati, the Maldives, and Tuvalu lose their statehood when they lose their last habitable island territory? Upon inundation, will these States lose all international personality or will international law adapt to accommodate the notion of a 'landless State'?

At the core of the criteria for 'statehood' is the notion of independence; that independence, however, appears to be entwined with a claim to territory. As was stipulated by Judge Huber in the 1928 Island of Palmas Arbitration, 'Sovereignty in the relations between States signifies independence. Independence in regard to a *portion of the globe* is the right to exercise therein, to the exclusion of any other State, the functions of a State' (emphasis added). And later in the same case, 'Territorial sovereignty ... involves the exclusive right to display the activities of a State'. Further comments from US Ambassador Jessup, arguing on behalf of Israel's admittance to the United Nations in 1949 despite not possessing precisely defined borders, stipulate that '[t]he reason for the rule that one of the necessary attributes of a State is that it shall possess territory is that one cannot contemplate a State as a kind of disembodied spirit ... There must be some portion of the earth's surface which its people inhabit and over which its Government exercises authority' (Crawford, 2006). Yet many of these questions seem to concern the original acquisition of title to territory. While there is no requirement of permanency for the territorial element in the Montevideo criteria (unlike for the population), is this nevertheless required by implication, so that once a State loses any one of the four criteria it simply ceases to exist?

15.3.1.1 Landless 'States'?

International law does not require a minimum size of land territory for statehood. The territory of the State of Nauru is only

21 km², Tuvalu 26 km², San Marino 61 km², and Monaco 2 km² (Crawford, 2006). Smaller still is the territory of the Vatican City, and its 'Government' the Holy See, which stands at a mere 0.4 km² and is recognized to be a 'State', albeit not universally agreed, by the 1929 Treaty between the Holy See and Italy establishing the Vatican State. While the Vatican City has a defined territory, albeit a minuscule one, it does not have a fixed population, but this peculiarity has not prevented the international community from recognizing the entity as a State. Undoubtedly, many authors view the Vatican City as being recognized as a State on 'special grounds' (Crawford, 2006). More specifically, however, the Holy See, comprising the Pope, the College of Cardinals, and central departments that govern the Church, appears at certain times to have had a degree of international personality separate from a territorial base (Crawford, 2006). The example of the Holy See is a peculiar one and appears to be unique. A different approach is taken to the Sovereign Military Order of St. John of Jerusalem, of Rhodes, and of Malta, an ancient religious order which lost its sovereignty over the territory of Rhodes and Malta in the eighteenth century. Unlike the Holy See/Vatican City, the order is not recognized as a State, but merely an entity having limited functional international personality (Crawford, 2006).

Despite a very particular situation with the Vatican City/Holy See, the notion of statehood appears to be relatively uniform in the requirement of a territorial base at the point of acquisition of that title. The pertinent question is whether international law is suitably flexible to allow a State to continue in being once a central criterion is missing.

15.3.1.2 Analogous precedents?

Are submerging States analogous to 'failed' or 'extinct' States? This section will analyse these potentially analogous legal situations to see if there is any scope for similar treatment to be afforded to submerging states, and if so, what restraints or benefits such similar treatment might entail.

Key to the analogy with the 'failed' State phenomenon is that once an entity is recognized as fulfilling the criteria for statehood, that designation is not lost during the period of 'failure' (Thürer, 1999). On its face, such a designation hardly appears to be a helpful or favourable label for submerging States and seems to be based on the absence of any effective government, such as was the situation in Somalia for many years. This is, at least, evidence that statehood can endure without one of the essential criteria. In essence, while the 'failed' State continues in name it has temporarily lost the practical ability to exercise the legal capacity of statehood. Although the submerging States may face similar civil violence as occurred in Somalia, it may only be too temporary before the other criteria are also lost.

Whether States would be willing to stretch the concept of 'failed' States to incorporate the submerging States phenomenon is highly questionable, and, besides, such a designation does not appear to be particularly appropriate or helpful.

A second analogy with submerging States may lie with the notion of 'extinct States' (Oppenheim, 1905), but does this simply refer to a past designation; is an extinct State, therefore, still a State? And on what basis can a State be viewed as 'extinct'? According to Oppenheim, 'A State ceases to be an international person when it ceases to exist' (Oppenheim, 1905). More common scenarios of extinction of States concern voluntary mergers between States and the breaking up of a State into several smaller States. In these cases, the territory will have been physically and legally brought under the domain of another, possibly new entity. In his treatise on international law, Oppenheim goes on to suggest, 'Theoretically such extinction of international persons is possible through emigration or the perishing of the whole population of a State', which cases he believed would 'hardly ever occur in fact' (Oppenheim, 1905). Similar to this view of the necessity of a population base, is a 'useable' territory also then an essential aspect of statehood? Thus, the notion of continuing statehood for submerged States raises a multitude of questions, not least because it is possible that all four of the Montevideo criteria of statehood could be absent. With the loss of territory, questions will be raised with respect to the destination of its population. If the population are dispersed throughout many countries would they still be viewed as that State's 'permanent population'? Once the government loses its territorial and popular basis, there might be problems with the third criterion of 'government', and, of course, with no government and people how can a State demonstrate the 'capacity to enter into relations with other States' (the fourth criterion for statehood)?

A third possibility following on from the notion of a displaced government makes an analogy with the wartime phenomenon of 'government-in-exile'. The notion of a government continuing in office and temporarily holding the sovereignty of the dispossessed State has arisen through the aspect of recognition by other States in the international community. Such recognition has specifically attached to governments-in-exile, where the territory and population of that State have been invaded or occupied, usually with the recognizing States viewing the invasion/occupation as illegal. Consequently, belligerent occupation does not affect the continuity of the State; this is so since acquisition of title to territory by conquest is no longer valid. This rule was contained within the 1970 Declaration on Principles of International Law concerning Friendly Relations and Co-operation among States in accordance with the Charter of the United Nations, adopted by consensus in the General Assembly in 1970 (Res.2625 (XXV) of 24 October 1970). An obvious example of a government-in-exile was seen in the recognition of the Kuwaiti government-in-exile following the 1990 Iraqi invasion and occupation (SC Res.661, 6 August 1990, SC Res.662, 9 August 1990). Similar to a government-in-exile, the governments of submerged States will be displaced from their land, and possibly their people, and if allowed to continue in being they could be housed in a foreign country. The analogy is possibly the closest so far, but does the rightful claim to a dispossessed land inherent in the concept of 'government-in-exile' actually require the existence of that land? If so, the concept would again need stretching to accommodate the phenomenon of submerging States.

15.3.1.3 Continuation of statehood by the building of a permanent structure?

When the last vestige of land is subsumed by the sea, might the 'State' retain its claim to international personality by the artificial continuation of a territorial base? In a ground-breaking series of research studies, Soons suggested that it may be possible to continue island status by building a permanent structure on the territory, which remains at all times above sea level (Soons, 1990). Soons made this suggestion, however, not under the notion of statehood but under the rules governing the various maritime zones open to claim by coastal States, notably within the 1982 United Nations Convention on the Law of the Sea (UNCLOS).

The 1982 Convention draws a distinction between 'islands', surrounding which States can claim the same extensive maritime zones as their mainland territory, and 'rocks', for which they cannot (Freestone, 1991). Thus, while islands afford the same designated width of territorial sea, contiguous zone, exclusive economic zone (EEZ), and continental shelf, 'rocks' only afford a 12-nautical mile territorial sea. According to the legal definition of 'rocks', these are landmasses which 'cannot sustain human habitation or economic life of their own' (Article 121(3), 1982 UNCLOS). This position of having a landmass which is unable to sustain human habitation or economic life of its own would appear similar to that in which submerged States will find themselves. Hence, according to the definition within the 1982 UNCLOS, what was once an 'island' may regress to being a mere 'rock'. Even this notion, however, may be undermined by the assumption within Article 121(1) of the 1982 UNCLOS that such a 'rock' remains above water at high tide, a criterion which some of the island/atoll nations may not be able to fulfil. An even worst-case scenario may ensue should the now-submerged island State be downgraded further to merely a 'low-tide elevation', which is defined in Article 13(1) of UNCLOS as 'a naturally formed area of land which is surrounded by and above water at low tide but submerged at high tide'. Under Article 13(2), where such low-tide elevations are

not within the 12-nautical mile territorial sea of another island or mainland territory, which is itself presumably above sea level, it is unable to possess a territorial sea of its own (as can a 'rock'). Thus, with either of these new designations, as a 'rock' or a 'low-tide elevation', the question that arises is whether international law would automatically erase that State's maritime jurisdiction zones from the map.

Just as states might artificially expand the terrain of islands by shipping in rocks and sand, in order to build a runway for an airport or to create an artificial beach or resort, there is an argument that submerging States could build up their landmass in order to prevent the downgraded designation from island to rock. Soons suggested that submerging States take such an approach and build artificial structures on their landmass, such as lighthouses (Soons, 1990). But this argument might have limited effect: if these were viewed as 'artificial islands' under Article 60(8) of UNCLOS, these 'artificial islands' would 'not possess the status of islands'. The question, therefore, is whether an 'island' that has become a 'rock' or 'low-tide elevation' due to rising sea levels, and which is then built up to remain above sea level at high tide, can still be designated as an 'island' and, consequently, whether the maritime zones attached to that 'island' status also continue, or whether such a built-up 'island' has in fact become an 'artificial island' under international law and, therefore, unable to claim such maritime zones.

The primary question remains that of whether the State itself continues to exist in international law – this question raises more fundamental issues of what it is that the international community wishes to be fulfilled by the notion of a 'State' under international law. Similarly, the question of whether the United Nations (UN) would continue to recognize the entity as a State and so afford it a seat and participatory rights at the UN is raised. Whether the entity would continue to be allowed to ratify international law treaties and agreements is highly questionable, especially since it may not be able to enforce compliance by its own people, who may be spread around the globe. International law is governed by States and what States choose to recognize. As a result, if the international community agrees that submerged States should continue to have an international personality (including UN representation), this can be achieved. If recognition were to be afforded on an ad hoc basis, this may not be wholly satisfactory and could lead to disparity in recognition and, subsequently, treatment. Recognition of continuation could, however, be achieved by treaty or agreement which could establish relevant criteria and stipulate the rights and obligations of such an entity and its people. Under this latter method, of course, the international community could create a new entity rather than simply looking to the notion of statehood, with any or all of the benefits of international personality. The ultimate question would be, what is to be gained by the continuation in existence of a 'State' that has no territory?

15.3.1.4 Continuation of statehood *ex situ* by agreement or treaty

Of greater importance than the issue of losing territory is the effect on the population of losing their home and community. Negotiations have been underway for some time now between some Asia-Pacific nations to secure destinations for the populations of submerging States, largely to no avail. In the meantime, New Zealand has agreed to annual immigration (Pacific Category visas) by ballot of 75 persons from each of Tuvalu and Kiribati, and 250 persons from Fiji and Tonga, but these numbers are within the existing regional immigration policies established by New Zealand. While there is no agreement yet between New Zealand and Tuvalu for the acceptance of the Tuvaluan population when Tuvalu becomes uninhabitable, there has been some recent suggestion that a specific category of 'climate change refugee' status be created (Cole, 2018). Once persons are selected by the visa ballot, the requirements are principally that the primary applicant can secure an offer of an ongoing job that meets a minimum income level and is able to speak reasonable English. The applicant and family members must also be in good health and be of good character. In addition, while such regional immigration biases are clearly very beneficial in this case to these particular island nation States, such means are not perfect and they are certainly not a long-term or comprehensive solution. In a 2016 report the World Bank suggested that a more structured migration programme from submerging States would prevent forced migration in future generations by the populations of Tuvalu and Kiribati and would bring many economic benefits to Australia and New Zealand (Curtain *et al.,* 2016). The report suggested a new model of an Australia-New Zealand Atoll (open) Access Agreement.

There are a number of options available to negotiators of such agreements, including the moving of the submerging State's entire population onto the territory of another State. This would clearly be the best possible option for the submerging State, as it would mean that its community would remain together. If this could be achieved, possibly by the submerging State purchasing territory, could the State continue to enjoy its statehood and sovereignty? Again, would existing international law allow for such continuation of an entity which has a new territory but the same population? Or would a new State be created? This latter option might not raise too many problems since it would still be a State, albeit with a significant difference in terms of its newly defined territory, under the Montevideo statehood criterion (2) mentioned earlier. An alternative solution would be for the international community to purchase territory for the submerging State. Such possibilities do not appear to have been contemplated by the existing Climate Change Convention regime, but the Conferences of Parties (COPs) to the UNFCCC could certainly be used as a forum for the elaboration of a procedural mechanism for the allocation of resources for submerging States. It does not appear to be on the agenda at present but it remains one possibility. Other possibilities could include a separate, free-standing UN mechanism or inter-governmental organization to handle relocation packages and possibly even reparation and resettlement claims.

Much of the notion of statehood in the scenarios mentioned earlier would, however, require a transaction that ensured the full purchase and transfer of title to the territory. If this full transfer of rights were not available, the entity may again fail to qualify as a State owing to the fourth Montevideo statehood criterion (mentioned earlier) of 'capacity to enter into relations with other States', but some sui generis personality may still be recognized (Freestone, 1991). If the transfer of territorial sovereignty under such an agreement or treaty, therefore, was not complete, this would leave the new entity with something less than statehood. Without fulfilling the traditional criteria for statehood, the new entity might simply be an autonomous or semi-autonomous province of another State. Clearly, this would remain a valuable option for submerging States, since at least they could guarantee that their population remained in community but would require very detailed agreements concerning such issues as citizenship, property rights, and, ultimately, foreign policy. Such agreements might also need to designate jurisdiction over maritime zones and rights for the new State to the living and non-living resources of the oceans. The fact that maritime zones can extend for up to 200 nautical miles from the coastline (for the EEZ) and 350 nautical miles, or even further for the continental shelf, means that it is unlikely that such important issues would be left to the Law of the Sea regime alone to resolve (UNCLOS Articles 57 and 76(5)) (Di Leva and Morita, 2008).

A further option that could fall within existing international law would be for a submerging State to merge with another, non-submerging state. Under this approach the submerged State's sovereignty and statehood would be subsumed within the new State, either completely subsumed so that the non-submerging State did not change its name, or partially subsumed in the sense that the 'new' State was renamed to reflect the conjoining of the two. This might be a particularly interesting proposition were any submerging States in close proximity to other States, so that if they joined as one, the landmass of the submerging State could influence the drawing of the maritime boundaries. In this way, the non-submerging State would indeed benefit from an agreement to receive its submerging neighbour.

But such benefits may be relatively short-lived, once the territory submerges and the designation of rock/low-tide elevation again needs to be made.

15.3.2 Legal obligations and rights of states: A simple ending?

Entities can be the bearer of rights and duties under international law without needing to be States. Insurgent groups within States, for example, are often the bearer of duties and rights under international humanitarian law, and individuals can claim rights under international human rights treaties. As 'States', though, the submerging States will have a number of obligations, particularly towards their own populations, before the date of inundation by the sea. What these legal obligations entail, therefore, as well as whether and when they 'end' are important questions for the populations of submerging States. At the level of inter-State obligations and duties, what rights and benefits can a submerging State assume from its fellow States? What State obligations and rights exist *inter se*?

The position is clearer for those States for whom an increase in incidents and impacts will occur, such as Bangladesh, who will have the right to seek emergency aid and assistance from other States, the UN, and other organizations to alleviate the impact. The position is less clear for submerging States, particularly at the point of submersion. Until the point of submersion, such States should continue to be treated as any other State dealing with the impacts of global climate change, in the sense of emergency aid and the implementation of mitigation measures, particularly under the Climate Change Convention regime. Furthermore, while still at the point of 'submerging', are any duties owed the State by the international community?

Some authors have suggested that a general duty has evolved, outside of the Climate Change Convention regime, for States to cooperate in the *planning* of responses to climate change (Freestone, 1991). Yet, even if it exists as a universal rule, it is clearly a vague one. There appears to be no concrete obligation on States to cooperate and put these mechanisms and action plans into effect now, before the actual need arises. Aside from the more specific treaty mechanisms under the Climate Change Convention regime, the Security Council could, of course, designate a situation to be a threat to international peace and security (reflected in such scenarios by the fleeing of persons) and so able to mandate State action. Once a breach of the peace is established, the Security Council can mandate enforcement action under chapter VII of the 1945 United Nations Charter. But what kind of international action can in fact be enjoined upon UN Member States in respect of other Member States that are gradually disappearing below the waves? Consequently, if there is no legal duty on States to save their brethren from

inundation by the sea, when that point is reached and the island is no longer habitable, what then?

What becomes of treaty obligations undertaken by States that disappear? What about its debts? Conversely, what about its revenue? The case of Tuvalu should be noted for its very lucrative internet hosting sites (.tv), which may be lost were Tuvalu to lose its statehood. The general rule of international law is that treaty obligations must be performed or the State violates the treaty (the notion of *pacta sunt servanda*). Situations of warfare and internal civil conflict can allow a State to displace many of its treaty obligations for a period, but for submerged States the obligations might be completely frustrated by events. While international law certainly allows for this contingency, there are some obligations that it views as too fundamental to allow to simply lapse, notably human rights obligations (section 15.6).

As noted earlier, international law affords States with a coastline certain maritime zones. These maritime zones, such as exclusive economic/fisheries zones (EEZs or EFZs) and continental shelves, can be very lucrative in terms of fishery resources, as well as non-living resource exploitation (particularly where fossil fuels are discovered). What happens to these maritime zones if the State ceases to exist? At the point of submersion there would appear to be no land territory to which a maritime zone could attach (as discussed earlier). And so again it is the case that at the heart of the international concept of maritime zones is the notion of a territorial base. This is not to suggest that the people/entity could not fish the high seas, of course, but the sovereign rights to resource exploitation within the EEZs/EFZs and continental shelves belonging exclusively to that State would appear to be lost on submersion. Is there any possibility of continuation of the maritime zones despite the loss of the land territory of a State?

Under the provisions of the 1982 UNCLOS (Articles 5–7) governing the drawing of maritime zones, these zones are measured from baselines which run along the State's low-tide points. As these baseline points move inwards, it would appear reasonable that the maritime zones follow suit. The 1982 UNCLOS, however, specifically recognizes, as an exceptional situation, cases where baselines will move landwards due to flooding of a low-lying delta. In these cases, UNCLOS allows such States, for example Bangladesh, to maintain its seaward baselines until officially changed under the mechanism provided in the 1982 UNCLOS. Thus, Article 7(2) stipulates, 'Where because of the presence of a delta and other natural conditions the coastline is highly unstable, the appropriate points may be selected along the furthest seaward extent of the low-water line and, notwithstanding subsequent regression of the low-water line, the straight baselines shall remain effective until changed by the coastal State in accordance with this Convention'. This rule appears to be of little value, however, to submerging States.

Some authors have suggested, therefore, that a submerging State should, similarly, be able to 'fix' the baselines of its maritime zones at a particular point in time, say the year 2000 for want of a better date (Paskal, 2008). The question is why? What would this baseline-setting achieve? One of the purposes suggested, for essentially freezing in time a State's baselines, is so that these maritime zones could continue to be recognized as belonging to that State on the submersion of the territory. With fixed maritime zones despite the State having disappeared territorially, it is further suggested, the population or government could then sell the resource rights to secure a better deal for re-homing its population (Paskal, 2008). This is an interesting argument, but could international law accommodate such transactions? The simple answer for now appears to be in the negative, but it may be a development worth pursuing. Furthermore, there is nothing in the meantime to prevent submerging States 'selling' the resources within their maritime zones such as the EEZ or continental shelf as a bargaining tool, subject of course to their own subsistence needs. The question has already been raised of the potential purchase or allocation of land for submerging States under private State-to-State deals or treaties or, indeed, under the aegis of an international organization. If a submerging State were afforded a piece of land in this way, very important questions of maritime zones and rights would need to be included in the deal.

15.4 COMMON BUT DIFFERENTIATED RESPONSIBILITIES: A CHALLENGE TO 'SOVEREIGN EQUALITY' UNDER INTERNATIONAL LAW?

Aside from the clear challenges to statehood itself and the sovereignty of a State within its territorial jurisdiction (with both these notions losing their sense of permanence and becoming distinctly shaky in the wake of large-scale environmental change that threatens the very physical existence of the State itself), another fundamental notion of international law that has become qualified within the international environmental law field is arguably that of 'sovereign equality'. The traditional notion of sovereign equality under international law stipulates that any State that fulfils the accepted legal criteria for statehood and is recognized as such by the international community of States, for example, by its acceptance into the membership of a pre-eminent inter-State organization such as the United Nations, is then able to rely on this status as being formally equal to that of any other State, notwithstanding the often clear disparity in their actual standing in world affairs. Accordingly, Article 2(1) of the UN Charter stipulates, 'The Organization is based on the principle of the sovereign equality of all its Members'. Viewed in this way, it is clear that the notion of 'sovereign equality'

between States under international law is little different from that of the principle of 'equality before the law', which is observed within most domestic or municipal legal systems. Yet in both these legal systems there are exceptions.

Within international law (Cullet, 1999) – and in particular, international environmental law – this notion of 'sovereign equality' has arguably been subject to modification, owing to the acceptance of the notion of differential treatment between States as per their obligations within global environmental agreements (Cullet, 1999; Rajamani, 2006). The notion of differential commitments of States appears to have developed as a general recognition of the notion of equity in international environmental law – in that there is an inequality in resources and contributions to environmental degradation, as well as the financial and technological capacity for environmental damage mitigation. The principle was included in the non-binding, 1992 Rio Declaration on Environment and Development, such that '[i]n view of the different contributions to global environmental degradation, States have common but differentiated responsibilities. The developed countries acknowledge the responsibility that they bear in the international pursuit to sustainable development in view of the pressures their societies place on the global environment and of the technologies and financial resources they command' (Principle 7). The concept has also been viewed as a consequence of the recognition by the international community that, in certain environmental matters, there is a need for all States to cooperate: the notion of the common concern of mankind (Brunnée, 2007). The Climate Change Convention regime, adopted at the same time in Rio as the 1992 Declaration, recognized both concepts within the Preamble of the 1992 instrument:

> Acknowledging that change in the Earth's climate and its adverse effects are a *common concern* of humankind … Acknowledging that the global nature of climate change calls for the widest possible cooperation by all countries and their participation in an effective and appropriate international response, in accordance with their *common but differentiated responsibilities* and respective capabilities and their social and economic conditions (emphasis added).

Rajamani suggests that the notion of differential commitments exists in other legal disciplines, too, such as human rights law, the law of the sea, and international economic law (Rajamani, 2006). Certainly, in the Climate Change Convention regime, the original adoption of the concept was acceptable to most developed States and encouraged developing States to ratify the treaty (see Article 4). Of course, quoting the escalating carbon emissions of China and India, in particular, for which they, as developing States, had no emission reduction commitments under the 1997 Kyoto Protocol, the United States consistently refused to ratify to concrete emissions reductions that did not insist on universal obligations. Such negotiations were finally secured in the 2015 Paris Agreement, only for Trump's US administration to pull out of the deal in May 2017, referencing the deal's potentially negative impact on the US economy. Thus, while the notion of common but differentiated responsibility (CBDR) was originally a necessity to encourage developing States to attend the negotiations, over time the position of omitting the largest carbon emitters of the developing countries, such as China and India, from reduction obligations became untenable.

Returning to the issue of 'differentiated responsibility', what exactly is it within the regimes outlined that is differentiated? Is it merely the responsibility for environmental harm or is it the obligations to remedy or mitigate future harm? Under the Climate Change Convention regime, there has been differentiation in a number of ways, including the commitments (in terms of timelines for reductions and the degree of reductions) and in the provision of technical and financial assistance to developing countries. Indeed, the Convention regime originally made developing country implementation of their commitments contingent upon the provision of such assistance (see Article 4(7)). Mushkat, however, is concerned to observe that there is still arguably more that is 'common' in the treatment of States under international law than that which is 'differentiated' between them (Mushkat, 2004). Moreover, she also notes that the 'differentiated' elements of the relationship between developing countries and their international environmental obligations usually relate more to the implementation of these obligations, rather than their relative normative 'density' as such between developed and developing States. This accords with French's earlier analysis of the evolution of the 'common but differentiated responsibilities' principle within the Rio Declaration, where he notes that developed States were concerned to transform this principle into a basis for forward-looking, differential obligations between developed and developing States, rather than for a backward-looking basis of responsibility for environmental degradation already caused by developed States' activities, as initially advocated by developing countries (French, 2000).

What has such asymmetric treatment between States as to how they perform their environmental treaty obligations meant for international law itself? Many would observe that differential treatment has existed throughout history and so its further development is no surprise. Indeed, Stone suggests that the concept is probably no more than a restatement of the notion of the polluter-pays principle and, as a consequence, adds nothing new to international law (Stone, 2004). It can certainly be argued, however, that it is one significant 'effect' of climate change within international law – that such environmental change has in turn caused international law to adapt its approach and its way of working. This will also be witnessed in other dimensions, such as human rights and such notions as transnational obligations. In addition, of course, the concept does appear to have allowed a mechanism by which to bring together the many and diverse State groupings involved in the climate change arena. On the other hand, the response by the United States, in particular, denotes discomfort in the international community regarding the notion of such stark differential commitments. In pushing for the alleviation of the commitments of poorer countries, based on developmental needs and lack of resources, there has also been a focusing of the blame on the developed countries, a push for developed States to make recompense for their wrongs (Stone, 2004). At which point, we turn to the notion of State liability for global climate change.

15.5 STATE RESPONSIBILITY AND LIABILITY: NO ROLE TO PLAY?

The issue of State responsibility and consequent State-based liability has proven to be a non-starter in relation to climate change. Over the last two decades, any action to raise the issue of compensation or liability in terms of State responsibility for climate change impacts has failed. The possible reasons for this failure are manifold and some of these may seem obvious even to a non-legal observer. How can one go about assigning State responsibility, let alone liability, for any damaging effects of global climate change with any legal precision, given the immense time-distance scales that we need to grapple with in response to this phenomenon? The fact that both the international law on State responsibility and international dispute settlement mechanisms are traditionally predicated upon bilateral claims between States as to alleged breaches of international obligations entailing State responsibility has caused much difficulty when it comes to assigning responsibility and thus possible liability for alleged environmental damage. This is especially the case when such environmental damage is caused to the so-called areas of global commons, such as the high seas, the global atmosphere, and even Antarctica.

Within international environmental law, the so-called golden rule providing for State responsibility for transboundary environmental harm was initially enunciated in Principle 21 of the 1972 Stockholm Declaration on the Human Environment, adopted at the conclusion of the eponymous conference, and states as follows:

> States have, in accordance with the Charter of the United Nations and the principles of international law, the sovereign right to exploit their own natural resources pursuant to their own environmental policies, and the responsibility to ensure that activities within their jurisdiction or control do not cause damage to the environment of other States or of areas beyond the limits of national jurisdiction.

This principle was later reiterated with slight modifications in Principle 2 of the 1992 Rio Declaration on Environment and Development.

Significantly, the scope of the notion of harm from activities across international borders incorporates transboundary damage to the 'environment'. This paves the way for international recognition and acceptance by States of an extension of the 'golden' or primary rule to damage inflicted upon the 'natural' or wildlife/ecosystem aspects of the 'environment' (Ong, 2008b). On the other hand, the belated recognition of the possibility of damage to the 'natural' aspects of the 'environment' from human activities does not render the consequent task of valuing such damage any easier to undertake. Shaw's comment on the relative success of efforts to expand the concept of transboundary harm in this respect is both succinct and quite apt: 'The type of harm that is relevant clearly now extends beyond damage to property, but problems do remain with regard to general environmental injury that cannot be defined in material form' (Shaw, 2003, p. 767). Nevertheless, environmental law and economics are progressing well in arriving at a legally viable definition of 'pure' environmental or ecological damage and how this can be valued in strict monetary terms. In this respect, the work of the United Nations Compensation Commission (UNCC), established in the aftermath of the 1991 Gulf War, has made significant contributions to the definition and valuation of damage to natural resources and the environment, including the costs of monitoring and assessing such environmental damage (Elias, 2004). This 'golden' or primary rule was also expansive in terms of its geographical scope, covering 'areas beyond national jurisdiction'. Part XII of the 1982 UN Convention on the Law of the Sea (UNCLOS) on the Protection and Preservation of the Marine Environment contains yet another, even more extensive formulation of this rule, enunciated in Article 194(2) of the above instrument, as follows: 'States shall take all measures necessary to ensure that activities under their jurisdiction or control are so conducted as not to cause damage by pollution to other States and their environment, and that *pollution arising from incidents or activities under their jurisdiction or control does not spread beyond the areas where they exercise sovereign rights in accordance with this Convention*' (emphasis added).

The legal implications of these conceptual innovations are significant for the progressive development of the international environmental law field, but serious questions still linger. For example, even if it were to be accepted that this rule has now been expanded in both its scope and definition to include transboundary *environmental* damage, it can still only be expected to apply to international incidents of a strictly *transboundary* nature. As such, this rule would not necessarily extend to cover diffuse sources of pollution into regional or global commons areas, such as transboundary lakes or river systems, or high seas areas, for example. Nor would the conceptual extension of such a rule per se cover situations of regional or global environmental degradation composed of dispersed indications of environmental damage such as that encountered when considering the causes and effects of global climate change, for example, where a handful of mainly Western, industrialized States historically and contemporaneously contribute to a disproportionately significant increase in greenhouse gases in the earth's atmosphere, while the negative effects of greenhouse gases built-up in the atmosphere in respect of global mean temperature rises, sea-level rise, and extreme weather conditions are disproportionately felt by other, small island States. Shaw neatly encapsulates this last difficulty in respect of the application of the classical State responsibility approach when he notes,

> The need to demonstrate that particular damage has been caused to one state by the actions of another state means that this model can only with difficulty be applied to more than a small proportion of environmental problems. In many cases it is simply impossible to prove that particular damage has been caused by one particular source, while the bilateral focus cannot really come to terms with the fact that the protection of the environment of the earth is truly a global problem requiring a global or pan-state response and one that cannot be successfully tackled in such an arbitrary and piecemeal fashion. Accordingly, the approach to dealing with environmental matters has shifted from the bilateral state responsibility paradigm to establishment and strengthening of international co-operation (Shaw, 2003, p. 771).

As a result, one of the greatest obstacles in the climate change debate is that of responsibility and liability for the resulting harm (Verheyen, 2005). In the Preamble to the 1992 Framework Climate Change Convention, developed country parties recognize their historical as well as current global emissions as being the largest contributions, and that developing countries may need to increase their emissions to meet their social and development needs. Yet this recognition does not easily lead to attribution of harm to the biggest contributor States.

Litigation has instead occurred with much more success in many domestic forums, resulting in the strengthening of the responsibilities of domestic institutions under national law instruments. For example, one of the earliest developments was seen in the United States in 2007, where the Supreme Court ruled that the Environmental Protection Agency did have authority to issue regulations aimed at reducing global climate change (Massachusetts *et al.* v. Environmental Protection Agency *et al.* (No. 05–1120) 415 F. 3d 50, 2 April 2007). The number of climate cases is increasing, with more than 654 cases filed in the United States in climate-related matters by 2017 (UNEP, 2017), making the United States one of the most active locations for climate-related cases. In another early development, climate change litigation in Australian courts appears to have resulted there in the strengthening of environmental governance by the requirement of impact assessments to consider future climate change impacts (Walker v. Minister of Planning, 2007; Gippsland Coastal Board v. South Gippsland Shire Council (No. 2), 2008; Northcape Properties Pty Ltd v. District Council of Yorke Peninsula, 2008). Indeed, today Australia boasts the second largest number of cases litigated after the United States, and its Asia-Pacific neighbour, New Zealand, has seen 16 cases, with India and Pakistan having two each, and Micronesia and the Philippines both having one each (UNEP, 2017). According to the 2017 report *The Status of Climate Change Litigation: A Global Review*, published by UNEP, climate change cases have been filed in 24 countries. The report documented the range of legal bases upon which citizens and non-governmental organizations (NGOs) have tried to hold domestic governments to account for climate-related commitments (UNEP, 2017). Possibly the most famous case in recent times has been the 2015 Urgenda case in the Dutch courts, in which the State was told that it was not doing enough to meet its international and European Union climate change commitments (Urgenda Foundation v. Kingdom of the Netherlands, 2015). And in a recent report by the NGO the Climate Justice Programme, it is likely that '[c]limate litigation will dwarf all other litigation in terms of both the number of plaintiffs and the timeframe over which it can happen' (Boom *et al.*, 2016).

More elementary to the legal debate regarding liability and responsibility is the question of what is served by recourse to the law to solve such problems as climate change. Clearly, laws best serve the public good by preventing harm. This reasoning certainly forms one aspect of the Climate Change Convention regime, despite the Convention's acceptance that change is inevitable. The Convention regime, at Article 4, follows the approach favoured in decades of environmental law treaties of prevention, notably in terms of mitigation and adaptation obligations. But is this sufficient? And what becomes of the central environmental principle (recognized in the Rio Declaration at Principle 16), known as the 'polluter-pays principle'? There is certainly still evidence from the developing country perspective that, despite the addition of new mechanisms such as the Green Climate Fund and the Mechanisms for Loss and Damage established at the Cancun round of talks in 2010, they are not receiving sufficient funding and technology resources under the Convention regime to meet their adaptation and mitigation needs.

The lack of sufficient financial, technical, and technology transfer from industrialized countries to developing countries to enable them to improve their endogenous capacity to adopt carbon-friendly socio-economic development pathways has for a long time forestalled attempts by the industrialized nations to get developing countries to accept concrete greenhouse gas emissions reduction targets. This impasse has in turn arguably negated the possibility of notions of State responsibility and liability for greenhouse gas emissions in breach of the Climate Change Convention regime targets being universally applied throughout the international community. International law itself is relatively clear regarding State responsibility; Article 1(1) of the 2001 International Law Commission Articles on Responsibility of States for Internationally Wrongful Acts stipulates, 'Every internationally wrongful act of a State entails the international responsibility of that State'. Thus, the international responsibility of a State can only arise from an act (or omission) that violates a settled rule of international law, which is directly applicable to that State. For such international responsibility to occur within the Climate Change Convention regime, the State concerned must have formally accepted its treaty obligations and yet contrived to act in breach of these. Here, it is important to reiterate that countries that were not included within Annex I to the Convention were not required to meet any specific greenhouse gas emissions targets under the UNFCCC and Kyoto Protocol, despite being formal parties to one or both of those instruments. This position has now changed with the move to non-binding *nationally determined contributions*. Thus, in the absence of such specific and binding emission targets, states are unlikely to incur international responsibility for failing to curb their greenhouse gas emissions despite being under a general treaty obligation (i.e., the UNFCCC) to do so.

Beyond a specific breach of the Climate Change Convention regime, States are also subject to the universal notion of international responsibility for transboundary harm, enunciated, for example, in the Trail Smelter Arbitration case (1939–1941) between the United States and Canada. As noted earlier, this obligation has now arguably been expanded to cover transboundary *environmental* harm in the universally accepted Principle 21 of the 1972 Stockholm Declaration on the Human Environment, and reaffirmed as Principle 2 of the 1992 Rio Declaration on Environment and Development. Principle 21/2 of the Stockholm/Rio Declarations recognizes two pivotal and linked issues, of particular relevance to the climate change debate, notably (1) international responsibility for transboundary *environmental* harm, including damage to areas beyond national jurisdiction, but also (2) the sovereign right of States to exploit natural resources within their territory and associated maritime jurisdiction zones, such as the territorial sea, EEZ, and continental shelf.

More problematic for the success of any claim for climate change damage under the customary international rules of State responsibility for transboundary environmental harm are the five legal questions in need of answers for any such claim.

These are as follows: (1) What constitutes significant 'environmental damage' in the climate change scenarios? (2) What is the standard of care required for such claims – fault-based liability, strict or absolute? (3) Is the State responsible for non-State actors and activities? One of the main contributors of carbon emissions, for example, are individual people performing lawful activities such as driving cars and heating their homes. (4) What reparation would be available for such environmental damage and how would it be quantified? And finally (5) how to prove causation of harm to any specific State? It is in proving a direct causal link between the harm caused on Tuvalu and Bangladesh and the emissions of the United States, for example, which may offer the greatest challenge to such State-to-State claims for compensatory actions. Such difficulties have plagued the concept of international responsibility for environmental harm for decades, especially where the effects of the emissions/pollution are cumulative, or one source is a natural pollutant. Time is also a factor, in that proving the causal link is made more problematic since the effects of the emissions have not manifested for many years, making it harder to prove the actual source of harm. Furthermore, there are always legal difficulties in attributing blame for lawful activities that were not envisaged as causing harm at the point carried out. This argument may be useful in providing sufficient latitude for a successful argument based on post-1992 emissions (or whatever was judged to be the date from when the harmful effects of greenhouse gases emissions were known). Is this an adequate conclusion for the law, or does the concept of State responsibility need to be re-examined in circumstances involving the damaging effects of climate change?

Consequently, to date, there have been few attempts to construct the legal bases and pathways for asserting the responsibility of any specific State for alleged climate change-induced damage due to the actions, or more likely, the omissions of that State in respect of its international obligations to prevent, mitigate, and/or reduce greenhouse gas emissions that apparently cause such climate change-induced damage. Even in cases where the causal link has been more easily demonstrated, such as the radiation damage caused across Europe following the 1987 explosion at the Ukrainian Chernobyl reactor, States have remained reluctant to establish a litigation precedent. As regards harm for climate change, it was widely reported in 2002 that Tuvalu planned to file a claim at the International Court of Justice against the United States and Australia based on their failure to reduce their carbon emissions. In the event, no claim was filed because of a change of government in Tuvalu, but it is questionable, however, whether the case would have been found admissible. Jurisdiction at the court is based on State consent to that jurisdiction and it is unlikely to have been found, particularly for the claim against the United States, which withdrew its

standing recognition of the court's jurisdiction in 1986. Thus, jurisdiction is a further hurdle for potential litigants to pursue a legal claim for State responsibility and liability. Apart from the difficulties of imputing State responsibility in the international sphere, scientific risk analysis studies conducted within individual domestic jurisdictions suggest that it is possible that human activities are contributing what is known as a 'fractional attributable risk' to the damaging effects of extreme weather events, which, if isolated, can in turn form the basis for a legal claim for compensation (Allen, 2003; Allen and Lord, 2004). In this context, commentators note that English law has taken a flexible approach to questions of causation, citing a House of Lords case (Fairchild v. Glenhaven, 2002) which suggested that the 'material increase in risk' might be an appropriate test (Allen and Lord, 2004).

Litigation has been attempted in other domains, for example, under the human rights treaty monitoring bodies. This avenue of litigation has potential at both the regional and international levels but is again dependent upon the specific provision of the regimes – whether court proceedings are available such as in the case of the European Convention on Human Rights or an individual petition to an international monitoring body. A petition was filed against the United States on behalf of the Inuit of Alaska and Canada before the Inter-American Commission on Human Rights over a decade ago in 2005 but was held to be inadmissible. Would such a case succeed today? Among the claimed violations were the right to life, physical integrity and security, right to enjoy personal property as well as the inviolability of their home, right to enjoy the benefits of their culture, right to their own means of subsistence, and rights to residence and movement. The Inuit claim could be observed to suggest a novel and growing impetus for regional attribution of climate change fault. Other international/regional legal avenues include making a claim under the 'right to a healthy environment' provision found in some regional human rights instruments (such as Article 24, 1981, African Charter on Human and Peoples' Rights; Article 11, 1988, Additional Protocol to the American Convention on Human Rights in the Area of Economic, Social and Cultural Rights; Article 38, 2005, Revised Arab Charter on Human Rights), but again difficulties of attribution and proof remain. Does human rights law, more broadly, offer any answers?

15.6 HUMAN RIGHTS CHALLENGES IN A CLIMATE-CHANGED WORLD

The consequences of a changing climate are clearly anticipated to be unevenly distributed around the globe, but it is expected that those countries already facing severe environmental conditions will be among those hardest hit. As the world is witnessing already, the impacts of climate change will not involve simple one-off disasters that most policy and planning models are based upon, but continuous and multifaceted events. Change will occur – and in some places is already occurring, on an unprecedented scale and timeframe – and it is these two elements combined which will place a continuous strain on the coping mechanisms of States. In addition, the current stage of development rights assumes a relatively stable starting point (including a stable environment), which will steadily improve as the State develops. This situation can no longer be assumed due to the phenomenon of climate change. Those most affected, in both developing and developed States, are likely to be the poorest sections of the community. For example, already suffering from the lowest living standards in Asia, the plight of the Burmese (Myanmar) population was made worse still by the effects of the natural disaster in 2008 when struck by Cyclone Nargis (Miliband and Kouchner, 2008). The spread of disease, as well as the loss of livelihoods, food and water sources, and culture, are just some of the potential effects of global environmental change which will impact essential human rights. What, accordingly, are the legal obligations under human rights law of States to their own population in these circumstances? And what, if any, legal obligations are owed under human rights law by States to the populations of other States?

International human rights law has developed to a relatively advanced stage, but divergences remain between so-called first-generation rights (civil and political rights under the 1966 International Covenant on Civil and Political Rights) and other generations of rights (notably second-generation economic, social, and cultural rights under the 1966 *International Covenant on Economic, Social and Cultural Rights* and the third-generation right to development under the 1986 *Declaration on the Right to Development*). Human rights organizations were relative latecomers to the potential problems that climate change will pose and are arguably still trying to play catch-up. The loudest voice in forcing a discussion of the human rights consequences of global climate change has been the Maldives, which drew attention to the plight of submerging States (ICHRP, 2008; AHREOC, 2008). Notable advances included the adoption of the soft-law declaration by the Small Island Developing States which met in Malé (the Malé Declaration on the Human Dimension of Global Climate Change of 14 November 2007), which precipitated the adoption of Resolution 7/23 (28 March 2008) by the Human Rights Council (A/HRC/7/L.11/Add.1), entitled Human Rights and Climate Change, in which the council requested a study by the UN High Commissioner for Human Rights on the impact of climate change on human rights. In the High Commissioner's Report of 2009, the Commissioner noted, 'States are obliged to take measures towards the full realization of economic, social

and cultural rights ... and that as climate change will place an additional burden on the resources available to States, economic and social rights are likely to suffer' (UNHCHR, 2009). Finally, in March 2012 the Human Rights Council created the three-year post of independent expert (now special rapporteur) on 'the issue of human rights obligations *related to* the enjoyment of a safe, clean, healthy and sustainable environment'. The dialogue created by subsequent resolutions (especially Resolution 18/22 of 2011) has undoubtedly aided in the increasingly global recognition of the need for human rights to be infused into discussions regarding climate change solutions.

Important questions, of course, remain unanswered in this area of the law. Submerging States will clearly owe human rights obligations to their own populations, but when will such obligations cease and how are they to be fulfilled in the meantime? This issue will also, of course, be one of concern to those States that will not be totally inundated by rising sea levels but which will nevertheless experience encroaching seas, and the consequent impact on its populations' human rights. What, for example, becomes of an individual's right to life when the State is completely submerged? Must the State find an alternative 'home' for its population or is it up to them as individuals? On the other hand, can a State force its population to move before the point of inundation to comply with its human rights obligations? What happens to the property rights of the people? Can they receive compensation for their property loss from their government or, indeed, from other States under international law? When property is inundated by the sea, is it still owned by the individual? And to what effect is it still owned if it is unusable? Surely property that was once land and is subsequently sea will simply fall into the realm of coastline belonging to the State and not owned by individuals. Does the State need to pay compensation to persons who lose their property in this way? Do States have an obligation to protect their own population by adopting climate change adaptation or mitigation strategies?

In the case of Budayeva and Others v. Russia (2008) App. Nos. 15339/02, 21166/02, 20058/02, 11673/02, and 15343/02, 20 March 2008, heard at the European Court of Human Rights, the court gave a glimpse of how it might handle future incidences of climate change impacts, such as floods and mudslides. Ultimately, the court appeared to be at pains to limit the liabilities of the State under Article 2 (the right to life) in such cases of natural disasters. The case involved several deaths and injuries caused by a mudslide, attributable to State failure to repair a dam. Although a frequently recurring natural disaster in this Russia town, and despite advance warning from the Russian Agency tasked with monitoring the river and dam, the State issued no emergency warning. Thus, recognizing the severity of the incident and the applicability of Article 2 to 'any activity, whether public or not', the court's focus was clearly on an expansive reading of the right to life, to extend beyond the sphere hitherto established of industrial risks or dangerous activities. Albeit, ultimately, in cases of natural disasters, the court held that only *foreseeable and clearly identifiable* impacts on the right to life would be contemplated as fulfilling the Article 2 requirements. In 2012, however, the court had another chance to rule on naturally occurring flooding and the right to life in the case of Kolyadenko and Others v. Russia (2012) App. Nos. 17423/05, 20534/05, 20678/05, 23263/05, 24283/05, and 35673/05, 28 February 2012, ECHR. Here, while again the court found a violation of the right to life, on this occasion no deaths had actually occurred. Here the court emphasized that the flooding was preventable and created severe risks to life.

Most of the questions, however, do not have answers at present. The situation for non-submerging States is likely to be clearer but will still be affected by the declaration of a 'state of emergency', which generally allows a State to derogate from observance of most, but not all, human rights. It is also lamentable that many states that will be affected by the 'submerging States' phenomenon have not ratified the main two international human rights covenants.

A more interesting question might be whether other States have human rights obligations with respect to the populations of such States. What obligations, therefore, do States have to the people in other States – especially, but not limited to, those in submerging States? Developments have been made within the notion of transnational or extraterritorial human rights (Coomans and Kamminga, 2004; Skogly, 2006), based specifically on the obligations undertaken by States in the area of economic, social, and cultural rights. Accordingly, Article 2(1) of the 1966 International Covenant of Economic, Social and Cultural Rights stipulates, 'Each State Party to the present Covenant undertakes to take steps, individually and *through international assistance and co-operation*, especially economic and technical, to the maximum of its available resources, with a view to achieving progressively the full realization of the rights recognized in the present Covenant by all appropriate means, including particularly the adoption of legislative measures' (emphasis added) (CESCR, 1991). Similar to the concept in international environmental law, therefore, human rights dialogue is moving, albeit slowly, towards recognition that certain human rights obligations do not stop at the border.

Much work has been done in this area by the UN special rapporteurs, especially those concerned with the rights to health and food. Two decades ago, the Special Rapporteur Paul Hunt, regarding the right to the highest attainable standard of health (CESCR, 2000), wrote of the potential detrimental impact on the right to health of climate change, particularly with regard to the most economically and socially vulnerable in society (Hunt, 2007). In his 2007 Report to the General Assembly, the

Rapporteur noted, 'Despite the[se] disturbing trends, the international community has not yet confronted the health threats posed by global warming. The failure of the international community to take the health impact of global warming seriously will endanger the lives of millions of people across the world' (Hunt, 2007). The obligation might clearly entail a duty on States to cooperate with other States to achieve higher human rights standards for the population of the latter. Yet more specifically, could transnational human rights obligations stretch to prohibit a State's policies if those policies had a direct impact on the enjoyment of human rights of people in other countries? For example, in cutting government aid or imposing sanctions, trade tariffs, or prohibiting certain activities, could a State be found in violation of the human rights of persons in other countries, say with regard to the right to health? How about if the link between the government policy and the human rights impact abroad was only indirect, such as in educating its population to reduce their carbon footprint or to buy energy-efficient products, this indirectly causes a loss of revenue from tourism or trade for African countries, with knock-on impacts on health and education choices within that country? Clearly, much work is to be done in the area of human rights and climate change, particularly with regard to the notion of a right to development; it would appear that climate change poses fundamental questions for such a 'right'. Linked to the idea of dimensions of obligations, and intrinsic to the environmental law notion of sustainable development, is the concept of intergenerational equity: a concept which enshrines the idea that future generations must also form part of the equation when deciding on action today. While the concept is firmly established in international environmental law, it has yet to form a solid basis in human rights law. This situation may need to change, however, if the international community is to put in place policies and strategies today to alleviate the consequences of a climate-changed world tomorrow.

Serious concerns have been raised within the human rights community that mitigation and adaptation strategies are being developed without consideration of the potential impacts of those strategies on human rights. For example, the submerging States phenomenon will cause huge numbers of people to flee their homes and homeland, and it has been very clearly established for many years that the 1951 Geneva Convention Regarding the Status of Refugees does not recognize the concept of an 'environmental refugee'. Furthermore, proposals for an international quota scheme do not necessarily take into account fundamental rights, such as non-discrimination and cultural rights. Indeed, while the New Zealand immigration agreements with its small island neighbours are a positive development, the immigration rules applied to such migrants do raise human rights issues of discrimination. As mentioned, the immigration requirements between New Zealand and the island nations of Kiribati, Tuvalu, Tonga, or Fiji stipulate that applicants must possess citizenship status for Kiribati, Tuvalu, Tonga, or Fiji; are aged between 18 and 45; have an acceptable offer of employment in New Zealand; have a minimum level of skills in English language; have a minimum income requirement if the applicant has a dependant; exhibit certain health and character requirements; and have no history of unlawful entry into New Zealand since 1 July 2002. It has been pointed out that these 'normal' immigration requirements effectively rule out anyone more than 45 and who may be unemployable due to disability or education. Consequently, it is clear that human rights will need to be balanced *inter se*, but also against competing interests of security and pragmatism, yet still there seems to be little debate about who will make these hard decisions and on what basis. While the communities of submerging States might prefer to remain together and to keep their cultural distinctiveness and way of life, how is this to be fulfilled? And given that the option may be between (1) keeping the whole community together but with a different way of life and (2) splitting the community with some retaining that way of life and others not, who will make the final decision? These are fundamental questions which need to be answered within the policymaking process; at least, such communities need to know that the human rights dialogue is informing the policymakers and, subsequently, the options made available to them.

15.7 INTERNATIONAL LAW OBLIGATIONS TO PROTECT BIOLOGICAL DIVERSITY FROM THE DAMAGING EFFECTS OF CLIMATE CHANGE

A further significant impact that climate change has on States' international obligations relates to wildlife protection, whether in the form of species, habitats, or ecosystems. The 2008 and 2011 versions of the Garnaut Climate Change Review, reporting on the potential effects on the Australian economy of climate change, recognize that impacts on species and biodiversity will be uneven; some will be able to cope with a warmer or wetter climate or saltier water, for example, but others will become extinct (Garnaut, 2008 and 2011). Of particular concern to the Australian government has been the impact on the Great Barrier Reef, which shows signs of significant coral bleaching (Garnaut, 2008 and 2011; IPCC, 2007b; Hughes and Kerry, 2017). Similar damage is also occurring off the coast of several South Pacific small island States, including Tuvalu, where bleaching is a threat to the sustainability of the entire social ecosystem.

Within the global context, such legal provision for wildlife protection is encapsulated within the framework of the 1992 Convention on Biological Diversity (CBD). The Biodiversity Convention again recognizes that 'the conservation of biological diversity is a common concern of humankind', as well as '[r]eaffirming that States have sovereign rights over their own biological resources' (Preamble). The Convention's objectives are stated as 'the conservation of biological diversity, the sustainable use of its components and the fair and equitable sharing of the benefits arising out of the utilization of genetic resources' (Article 1). Consequently, the Biodiversity Convention aims to maintain as far as possible the biological diversity – or species and intra-species variability – of the earth's ecosystems (Article 2). Despite beginning their treaty lives together during the 1992 Earth Summit at Rio, there was arguably insufficient recognition at the time of the possibility that the greatest threat to global biological diversity is in fact from climate change. Accordingly, it is now recognized that conservation responses to threats imposed by climate change must have two components – 'one adapting conservation strategies to deal with dynamic biodiversity; and two, constraining greenhouse gas levels within bounds that keep biological changes manageable' (Hannah *et al.*, 2005).

The history of wildlife species protection under international law has seen many developments, from the earliest notions of protection of harvestable species in order to maintain a viable population for future exploitation, to the application of the sustainable conservation/wise use concept and finally, the preservation of species to avoid extinction. Various methods of species protection have also been adopted along the way, including quotas on takings, international trade restrictions on endangered wildlife species, and ultimately, through the device of conservation sites and/or 'protected areas', the protection of wildlife habitats and ecosystems. In this respect, it is possible to trace a clear trend from individual species protection, notably through international trade controls introduced by the 1973 Convention on International Trade in Endangered Species (CITES) to natural wildlife habitat and ecosystem protection via the prioritization of in situ conservation, as provided by Article 8 of the 1992 Biodiversity Convention. And yet, despite the relative comprehensiveness of the modern international laws for wildlife protection, the threats imposed by global climate change to the continuing biological diversity of the planet are so fundamental as to render even the 'protected area' concept almost nugatory.

The Asia-Pacific region is especially rich in biological diversity and, as a consequence of climate change, along with inter alia deforestation and extensive logging, this rich biodiversity is now very vulnerable. As the full impacts of impending global environmental change are experienced, how will wildlife habitats fare in the face of the predictable scramble for new, alternative, and safer human habitation? Moreover, what is to happen to native species of submerging States? There is a clear need for the re-homing of the wildlife of submerging island States, which is arguably similar to the need for the island State's people to be evacuated and re-homed prior to the inundation of these submerging States. The magnitude of the climate change threats faced by wildlife species on submerging island States and elsewhere around the globe has required both the 1992 Climate Change and Biodiversity Convention regimes to undertake in-depth collaboration on a coordinated and concerted set of responses to this unprecedented challenge. This joined-up approach is most apparent in the Strategic Plan for Biodiversity 2011–2020 and the Aichi Biodiversity Targets adopted at the COP 10 in 2010, which have a focus on the contribution of biodiversity in building resilience and restoration of ecosystems in order to contribute to climate change mitigation and adaptation (Target 15).

15.8 THE IMPLICATIONS OF CLIMATE CHANGE FOR INTERNATIONAL DEVELOPMENT FINANCE AND INVESTMENT DECISION-MAKING PROCESSES

Up to this point, we have been concerned with the implications of climate change for international law, in particular in terms of its impact on various aspects of State sovereignty and statehood itself. This focus on statehood in itself highlights the paradigmatic nature of the State within international law and international relations generally. It is increasingly clear, however, that the challenges of addressing both the causes and effects of climate change require the participation of all international actors. Increasingly included within this grouping are private, transnational actors – especially in the form of business entities – whose activities increasingly drive human economic endeavour across the globe. Already there is evidence that domestic climate change regulation is becoming a common feature within developed States (UK Climate Change Act, 2008), but what about the practice of the business entities themselves? For example, what are the implications of increasingly predictable long-term climate change on investment risk-modelling calculations and thus on foreign investment decision-making processes, especially when globalization has placed so much of the financial decision-making powers on this issue within the hands of essentially private, transnational actors, such as investment banks, asset management funds, venture capital, pension funds, etc.? In so far as international law has arguably facilitated and protected such private and public investment when they are made across national boundaries, it (international law) now has to take into account the rise of social and environmental awareness, leading to a growing consensus that business cannot carry on as before, without adequate risk assessment of both environmental and other concerns, such as human rights, for example.

While international law is showing signs of accepting the need for (private, foreign, or transboundary) investor responsibilities, as opposed to the protection of their rights, significant systemic and substantive obstacles still remain (ILA, 2008). Chief among these are as follows: (1) jurisdictional difficulties arising from the fact that the 'home' country of the investor will not be able to regulate the investor's activities abroad in an effective way, especially within the territorial jurisdiction of the 'host' State receiving the foreign investment concerned; and (2) the sovereign autonomy of the 'host' State within which the (foreign) investor is operating may result in lower social and environmental standards being applied, despite the 'host' State's international obligations in this regard, because the 'host' State is keen to 'recruit and retain' foreign investors within this State for economic development reasons. The resulting 'race to the bottom' scenarios that occur are now well-known and even predictable in some cases but still proving difficult to counteract. Major international financial institutions such as the World Bank have become more pro-active in this regard, for example, by integrating specific climate change management risk concerns into their lending projects (World Bank, 2006). A further aspect of these policies is the development of environmental, health, and safety (EHS) guidelines and standards for assessing the environmental and social impacts of infrastructure projects that international financial institutions such as the World Bank are funding or for which they are providing credit or loan guarantees. These initiatives from the World Bank Group (including the International Finance Corporation (IFC) and the Multilateral Investor Guarantee Agency (MIGA)) have been followed by their counterparts within the private, commercial bank lending sector, most notably through the Equator Principles, to which a growing number of such banks are paying heed in their risk assessment lending criteria for major infrastructure development projects, such as oil and gas exploration, processing, and pipelines (Ong, 2008a). Both these *public* international development finance institutional initiatives, in the form of Performance Standards and EHS Guidelines, as well as those their *private* counterparts, namely the Equator Principles, have now gone through several iterations (Ong, 2010, 2016).

This trend towards the promulgation and application of environmental and social standards for major infrastructure development projects financed by these public and private institutions has now been accepted and implemented even by newly established regional development banks in the Asia-Pacific region. For example, the Asian Infrastructure Investment Bank (AIIB) moved quickly from its inception on Christmas Day, 2015, and operationalization in January 2016, through to the establishment of its Environmental and Social Framework in February 2016, as well as its Risk Assessment Framework in November 2016

(Ong, 2017), followed by its Directive on Environmental and Social Policy, in December 2017 (AIIB, 2019). Moreover, the AIIB Environmental and Social Framework explicitly supports the three aims of the 2015 Paris Agreement to strengthen the global response to the threat of climate change, comprising mitigation, adaptation, and the redirection of financial flows. To this end, the bank supports its client (States) in their evaluation of both the potential climate change impacts of proposed infrastructure development projects, as well as the implications of climate change itself on the proposed projects. The bank also plans to prioritize investments promoting greenhouse gas emission-neutral and climate resilient infrastructure, including actions for reducing emissions, climate-proofing, and promotion of renewable energy (AIIB, 2016).

In this context, the actions of other private, transnational actors have also been both innovative and potentially quite far-reaching in their implications for the functioning of the global capital movement system. For example, it has been noted that the Institutional Investors Group on Climate Change published ground-breaking research in 2007 showing that incorporating climate change risk was essential for effective investment strategies (IIGCC, 2007). Nor has this group of (mainly UK-based) investors been acting alone in its efforts. Similar research and advice was produced by the Investor Group on Climate Change for superannuation (pension) fund trustees in the Asia-Pacific region, specifically, Australia and New Zealand, culminating in an IGCC policy brief setting outlong-term climate change strategies for sustainable investment by institutional investors, such as superannuation or pension funds (IGCC, 2019). On the other side of the Pacific Ocean, a similar coalition of investors has called on the US Senate to enact strong (US) federal legislation to curb greenhouse gas emissions and for the US Securities and Exchange Commission (SEC) to provide guidance on corporate climate risk disclosure. According to this coalition of investors, these actions are necessary to reduce uncertainty – the bane of any investor – with strong and decisive action from government necessary to 'open the floodgates on large-scale clean technology investments, enabling investors and businesses to lead rather than lag on climate change solutions' (INCR, 2008). Even by 2008, it was reported that no pension fund had yet grasped the nettle of the implications of the international consensus on climate change in particular, in terms of the unprecedented shift in investment capital required by such funds and other holders of long-term assets (Green New Deal Group, 2008). Indeed, the advice mentioned earlier for Australian and New Zealand superannuation fund trustees was prepared on the presumption that it was crucial for them to take actions to address climate risk because it was unlikely that other key actors in the

investment community would make early or significant moves towards integrating climate change factors into investment decision-making in the absence of explicit client (i.e., fund trustees) demand and leadership. More recently, the Washington, DC-based US-SIF, the Forum for Sustainable and Responsible Investment, has provided a brochure, *Investing to Curb Climate Change: A Guide for the Individual Investor* (US-SIF, 2013). More generally, in October 2015, the US Department of Labour rescinded its 2008 bulletin on Economically Targeted Investments, which had discouraged fiduciaries for private sector retirement plans from considering environmental and social factors in their investments, and was a major departure from its 1994 guidance that had essentially stated the opposite (Global Sustainable Investment Review, 2016, p. 14). However it remains to be seen what impact the financial policies of the Trump administration will continue to have in this area.

Reflecting and building on the initiatives mentioned earlier from both the public (World Bank group, etc.) and private (Equator Banks, etc.) financial institutions, the UN Conference on Sustainable Development (also known as Rio+20 Summit)[1] focused heavily on key socio-economic development themes, such as (a) a green economy in the context of sustainable development and poverty eradication, and (b) the institutional framework for sustainable development (UN General Assembly Resolution 64/236, at para.20(a)). On the green economy, four major strands can be discerned in the United Nations system. The first was a pioneering contribution from the Economic and Social Commission for Asia and the Pacific (ESCAP), which resulted in the adoption of a green growth strategy in 2005. This strategy included four tracks: sustainable consumption and production; greening business and markets; sustainable infrastructure; and green tax and budget reform. Two additional tracks were included later, namely investment in natural capital, and eco-efficiency indicators (UN Secretary-General Report to 1stPrepCom, 2010, at para.46). The synthesis report on 'best practices and lessons learned' from the second PrepCom meeting states that, when supported by a conducive policy framework, public and private investments provide mechanisms for the reconfiguration of businesses, infrastructure, and institutions towards greater energy and resource efficiency, and lower pollution and waste intensity, through adoption of sustainable consumption and production processes. It goes on to suggest that such reconfiguration should lead to more green jobs and lower the energy and materials intensities of production, waste and pollution, and greenhouse gas emissions (Synthesis Report on Best Practices and Lessons (2011) at para.70). The synthesis

---

[1] UN Conference on Sustainable Development home website accessible at http://www.uncsd2012.org/rio20/index.html.

report also listed 'areas where there is need for further analysis and discussion', which include, inter alia, the following:

- Scaling up investments in green infrastructure, green energy, and other sectors: what are the options for mobilizing international investment?
- Institutions and policies to support a green economy: how can government capacities to design and implement fiscal incentives, regulation and legislation, sustainable procurement, and policies to support green industries as new growth drivers be strengthened? (Synthesis Report (2011) at para.119)

15.9 THE IMPLICATIONS OF GLOBAL CLIMATE CHANGE FOR INTERNATIONAL DISPUTE SETTLEMENT: THE EMERGENCE OF ENVIRONMENTAL TREATY COMPLIANCE REGIMES

Yet another result of the impact of the climate change phenomenon for basic international law concepts relates to the eschewing of traditional, international dispute settlement mechanisms based on the presumption of bilaterally oriented disputes, in favour of more collectively oriented international compliance mechanisms.

Through the establishment of such international compliance mechanisms, international environmental law has arguably pursued an alternative pathway towards ensuring adherence to its treaty obligations, by securing the cooperation of errant States to first accept and then act upon their non-compliant behaviour, in respect of their specific (environmental) treaty obligations. The emergence of these international compliance mechanisms at least implicitly highlights the shortcomings of international dispute settlement as a whole and the dispute settlement mechanisms established by the multilateral environmental agreements (MEAs) in particular. As Churchill and Ulfstein note in this context, allegations of non-compliance with environmental treaty obligations 'could in theory be resolved through traditional forms of dispute settlement. MEAs, however, offer fairly limited possibilities for binding dispute settlement' (Churchill and Ulfstein, 2000, p. 644). Fitzmaurice and Redgwell make the same point, noting that '[m]any recent environmental agreements also incorporate traditional dispute settlement mechanisms, though rarely with provision for compulsory third party dispute settlement' (Fitzmaurice and Redgwell, 2000, pp. 43–44). Thus, Churchill and Ulfstein observe that '[r]ather than place much emphasis on traditional dispute settlement procedures, some MEAs establish specific bodies to determine and deal with cases of non-compliance with substantive commitments' (Churchill and Ulfstein, 2000). Fitzmaurice and Redgwell again caution against the easily

arrived-at conclusion arising from these progressive developments in non-compliance procedures, to the effect that the availability of traditional dispute settlement mechanisms does not assist in the prevention of environmental harm, as these are usually only engaged in after the damage has occurred as a result of the alleged non-compliance and, hence, breach of environmental treaty obligation. While the preventive effect of traditional dispute settlement mechanisms should not be doubted, it is nevertheless the case that these mechanisms must be both compulsory in procedure and binding in result to be capable of exerting the maximum preventive effects on States parties contemplating the non-compliance of their environmental treaty obligations (Fitzmaurice and Redgwell, 2000).

A further legal difficulty relates to the constraining effect on the capability of traditional international dispute settlement mechanisms, especially those of a judicial character, to resolve disputes arising over the alleged non-compliance or breaches of environmental treaty obligations. This legal problem relates to the nature of environmental treaty obligations, specifically their non-reciprocal yet arguably *erga omnes partes* nature (denoting obligations owed to all parties to a particular regime). As Fitzmaurice and Redgwell note, 'Obligations *erga omnes partes* are of particular relevance in the environmental context' (Fitzmaurice and Redgwell, 2000), where all States parties to a particular environmental treaty regime have a common interest in its implementation but at the same time will not necessarily be able to make a claim against a non-compliant State party, as 'injured' States under international law, despite the recent broadening of this concept within Article 42 of the International Law Commission's (ILC) Articles on State Responsibility, which provides, inter alia, that '[a] State is entitled as an injured State to invoke the responsibility of another State if the obligation breached is owed to: (a) That State individually; or (b) A group of States including that State, or the international community as a whole'.

The first of these treaty-based non-compliance procedures was established pursuant to Article VIII of the 1987 Montreal Protocol on Substances that Deplete the Ozone Layer to the 1985 Vienna Convention for the Protection of the Ozone Layer. More recently, these non-compliance mechanisms have arisen in the context of, inter alia, the 1997 Kyoto Protocol to the 1992 UNFCCC, and the 1989 Basel Convention on Transboundary Movement of Hazardous and Other Wastes. By far the most interesting of these environmental treaty compliance mechanisms so far adopted must be the mechanism agreed by the State parties to the 1998 Aarhus Convention on Environmental Information, Participation in Environmental Decision-Making and Access to Justice (Koester, 2007), which will be elaborated upon in Section 15.9. That these non-compliance mechanisms are clearly formulated as alternatives rather than replacements for the traditional means of international law enforcement by recourse to peaceful dispute settlement is a fact that can easily be discerned by the continuing presence of such dispute settlement provisions within these treaties.

It is possible, therefore, to envisage the various modes of peaceful international dispute settlement as different points along a single continuum or spectrum. This spectrum ranges from bilateral negotiations at one end of the scale, through to the introduction of various third-party roles within the dispute settlement process. At this intermediate stage of the international dispute settlement continuum or spectrum, the use of third parties ranges from use of the good offices of the UN Secretary-General, through other types of third-party mediation, and moving on towards more judicially oriented, independent third-party dispute settlement procedures, using various types of international (judicial) arbitration, ultimately ending with recourse to the International Court of Justice (ICJ). Treaty compliance regimes occupy a suitable point on this scale within the section of the continuum or spectrum devoted to the introduction of a third-party, judicial-type role in dispute settlement. Within this section of the dispute settlement continuum or spectrum, treaty compliance regimes would be placed somewhere before, or prior to, the formal arbitration or judicial dispute settlement procedures (Ong, 2008b). As Fitzmaurice and Elias note presciently in this respect, the established environmental treaty compliance mechanisms 'allow for the resolution of these problems without recourse to international adjudication' (Fitzmaurice and Elias, 2005, p. 292). Churchill and Ulfstein offer additional reasons for the utilization of these non-compliance procedures:

> The advantages of using the noncompliance [sic] mechanisms rather than traditional dispute settlement procedures are twofold. First, because questions of compliance with MEA commitments are multilateral in character and usually affect all parties equally rather than any particular party or parties specifically, they should preferably be addressed in a multilateral context, rather than in a bilateral dispute settlement procedure. Second, non-compliance procedures may promote the resolution of compliance problems in a co-operative, rather than adversarial manner (Churchill and Ulfstein, 2000, pp. 644–645).

Indeed, with the exception of the Kyoto Protocol, which established enforcement as well as facilitative branches in the Compliance Committee, these environmental treaty compliance mechanisms do not include provisions for exerting sanctions against the non-compliant States. In other words, they are designed to play mainly facilitative, rather than enforcement, roles in ensuring compliance with specific environmental treaty obligations. For example, all these compliance regimes adopt, as an alternative to the traditional confrontational style of

international judicial dispute settlement, the possibility for a 'confessional'-type procedure whereby a State party that is aware of the very real possibility it will not be able to comply with its international obligations under the specific environmental treaty regime is able to present itself before the appropriately established compliance committee/commission in order for its case to be considered by the committee, with a view to assisting the errant State party to achieve compliance using similarly appropriate cooperative methods, rather than relying upon possible economic or other types of international sanctions, as would usually be the case (Ong, 2008b).

When set against the backdrop of internationally recognized and well-established dispute settlement procedures traditionally utilized by States, it is possible to suggest that these environmental treaty compliance mechanisms have 'cherry picked' only the non-confrontational aspects of such established international dispute settlement procedures or mechanisms. Thus, it would appear at first glance that international environmental law has once again developed innovative means to ensure compliance with substantive rules and standards provided within the individual environmental treaty regimes. So far, so good. Taking a step back, however, to view the broader picture and consider how far the resulting practice from these individual non-compliance mechanisms may be able to inform the general development of international environmental law in terms of arriving at an optimum standard for State compliance to adopted environmental rules and standards, we are again confronted by the fragmented nature of individual treaty regimes, which does not bode well for the development of a general rule or standard on compliance that could be applied either to non-party States to a particular environmental treaty or when addressing new (or remaining) areas of environmental threats that are yet to be subject to a separate treaty instrument dealing specifically with this new (or remaining) threat (Ong, 2008b).

A comparison of the various environmental compliance mechanisms provides further evidence of the regime-specific nature of these compliance mechanisms, in that there is no possibility of innovative best practice within one of these regimes being held to apply to any other treaty compliance regimes, let alone to non-party States as a matter of general or customary international law. A good example of this legal disability afflicting the potential application of international environmental law to all States, and not merely those States that are not parties to the individual environmental treaty regimes, is in respect of the innovative extension of the right to complain against a State party's alleged non-compliance to the Compliance Committee established under Article 15 of the Aarhus Convention to individual members of the public and even environmental and/or human rights non-governmental organizations without their necessarily having to prove a direct interest in the environmental information requested. Moreover, any person complaining need not be a citizen of the State party concerned, nor in the case of an NGO complaint, need it be based in the State party concerned. This clearly progressive right, however, cannot be invoked outside the confines of the immediate (Aarhus) regime, nor can it be implied within any other environmental protection or human rights treaty regime. Still less can it be said to be an enforceable right under general or customary international law (Ong, 2008b). As von Moltke notes in relation to the 1998 Aarhus Convention, this agreement 'represents a first step towards developing universally applicable rules – although they do not apply to (other) international agreements but rather are binding countries that are party to the Convention only' (von Moltke, 2005, p. 196).

15.10 INTERNATIONAL LAW CONCEPTS OF USE OF FORCE AND ARMED CONFLICT: NEED FOR REAPPRAISAL IN LIGHT OF CLIMATE CHANGE IMPACTS?

Since it is evident that the people hardest hit by the impacts of climate change will generally be those least able to adapt and react, such impacts will, therefore, lead to greater stresses on resources already at a critical stage. A consequence of this is likely to be conflict (Moon, 2007). This consequence is made more likely because of the potential magnitude of the population movements fleeing flooding and starvation (Stern, 2006). Millions of people on the move across borders and even continents could spark hundreds of conflicts. Asia alone has 11 mega-deltas, with an area greater than 10,000 km², which are vulnerable to sea-level rises, in addition to the fastest-receding glaciers in the world (located in the Himalayas) (IPCC, 2007b). The Asia region frequently experiences the greatest number of internally displaced persons from natural disasters. According to the Internal Displacement Monitoring Centre statistics for 2019, weather-related hazards around the globe triggered almost 25 million new displacements, a figure which towers above the 8.6 million new displacements triggered by violence and conflict during that year (IMDC, 2019). Monsoon floods, storms, and cyclones were the main causes of displacement, with India, the Philippines, Bangladesh, and China, accounting for the highest numbers of people displaced in 2019, totalling over 17 million displaced (IMDC, 2019).

The report continues that in 2019 more than 10 million of those new displacements occurred as a result of flooding (IMDC, 2019). Consequently, areas within the region could be further vulnerable to urban unrest and conflict, both within States (civil or internal armed conflict) and between States (international armed conflict). With a projected increase in resource-scarcity conflicts, therefore, are the current laws governing the use of armed force and armed conflict sufficient?

States do not have a right to use force in international law to secure for their population much-needed food or water resources or to compel reception onto a foreign State's territory of their population. Indeed, the law governing the use of force, actually its near absolute prohibition, is one of the most fundamental rules in international law and is universally binding. The prohibition recognizes few situations of necessity or exception in the use of force, the main ones being in case of self-defence against a military attack and Security Council-authorized action. Furthermore, and probably of more relevance, is the Security Council's power to authorize peacekeeping forces. As conflicts and violence increase in particular regions, it is likely that the Security Council will be called upon to establish peacekeeping or peace-enforcing forces to protect civilian populations or to keep warring factions apart. Indeed, with the possible scale of conflict caused by climate change impacts, it is questionable whether the current mechanisms for the staffing and financing of peacekeeping missions are sufficient. One thing is for sure: the totality of the missions authorized by the Security Council demonstrates an increasing willingness on its part to intervene in the domestic affairs of States for humanitarian purposes (Lowe et al., 2008). Would the Security Council, therefore, authorize force to secure humanitarian assistance or aid to a population suffering the devastating impacts of climate change?

Were a State to risk the survival of its people by refusing emergency relief, is a forceful intervention by outside States an option? A stark example was the delay in allowing the delivery of aid caused by the military junta in Burma (Myanmar) in 2008, following the devastating impact of Cyclone Nargis (Selth, 2008). These actions may have been less objectionable if Burma had been in a strong position to undertake the necessary relief activities itself, but this was not the situation. Consequently, questions were raised regarding a forceful humanitarian approach. The then British Foreign Secretary David Miliband stated in Parliament that the United Kingdom supported the 'use of *any and all* United Nations action that will help the people of Burma' (emphasis added) (Miliband, 2008). This is a clear reference to the viability of the option of using military force to secure aid in circumstances of a humanitarian emergency, albeit one caused by a natural disaster (Brown, 2008). What the Secretary of State was referring to was the 2005 Responsibility to Protect doctrine, as endorsed by the UN General Assembly (A/60/L.1, 20 September 2005). The so-called R2P doctrine allows for Security Council-authorized military actions and was adopted on the premise of protecting populations from genocide, war crimes, crimes against humanity, and ethnic cleansing. Its first real outing was the authorization of force in Libya in 2011 (UN Security Council Resolution 1973 (2011)). Expanding the remit to cover natural disasters, even where the government is blocking aid, may, therefore, not easily fit into the original conceptual framework of the R2P. Consequently, following the rejection in Security Council debates (primarily due to the objections of China and Russia) of French Foreign Minister Kouchner's suggested use of the doctrine to impose the delivery of aid on the Burmese government, its remit may remain unchanged.

What may be more flexible, however, is the controversial notion of humanitarian intervention. Seized upon by NATO forces, the concept of humanitarian intervention exists, if it exists at all, outside the UN Charter system. Although trumpeted by Britain and to a lesser extent the United States, particularly after NATO's routing of Serbian forces from Kosovo in 1999, the concept has gained few State supporters and courts a large measure of controversy. While the United Kingdom has suggested a number of requirements for a lawful forceful intervention, these have not received widespread support and again suggest intervention only in limited exceptions on the basis of averting an immediate and overwhelming humanitarian catastrophe (Gray, 2002). On the few occasions on which this legal justification has been suggested, notably the interventions in Kosovo 1999 and Iraq 1991–1992 (Operation Provide Comfort), the situations involved more direct human rights violations in the form of persecution, not a natural disaster. The main reason for the controversial nature of the humanitarian intervention doctrine is its potential for abuse. The doctrine is generally deemed too open for abuse by States wanting to impose their own power on others – often on the tenuous basis of promoting human rights or democracy. To expand the doctrine further, therefore, by allowing force to be used to protect a State's population from natural disaster, or to ensure delivery of aid, would generally be an unwelcome development in the law.

Finally, with the global security implications of climate change remaining largely unknown (IPCC, 2007b), how will the current laws of armed conflict address the new challenges posed? Will new rules need to be developed for such resource-scarcity conflicts? In this context, the EU's former High Representative for Common Foreign and Security Policy, Javier Solana, noted, 'Climate change is best viewed as a threat multiplier which exacerbates existing trends, tensions and instability. The core challenge is that climate change threatens to overburden States and regions that are already fragile and conflict prone. It is important to recognize that the risks are not just of a humanitarian nature; they also include political and security risks' (Solana, 2008). This is one area of law that may not require a great deal of adaptation to cope with the impacts of climate change. The laws of armed conflict are neutral as to the cause of conflict and apply universal rules of humanitarian protection for people as well as

rules that protect the wartime environment (Hulme, 2004). The ultimate tragedy, of course, would be the destruction in war of the very thing that caused the conflict in the first place, the scarce natural resources. To conclude this section, therefore, an area that could benefit from greater international attention is that of conflict-prevention strategies and dispute-settlement processes. Bodies dealing with such issues will, no doubt, be of imperative need in the coming years.

15.11 CONCLUSIONS

There is no doubt that global climate change has already had a profound effect on international law, particularly in relation to negotiated agreements (such as the CBDR concept), trade and investment disputes, and the protection of wildlife, but it will also have more profound future impacts. Areas of international law that have not altered in decades or even centuries will be tested over the next few years, as States disappear into the ocean, and others face a tumultuous future of extreme climatic events. The very notion of statehood may need revisiting, as might the notions of sovereignty and State responsibility, as events unfold and the international community reacts. One aspect that is in particular need of urgent attention is the potential effect on the observance of human rights, not only for those facing the disappearance of their homeland but also those who are forced to cross State borders in search of food, water, and shelter. It is no exaggeration to suggest that global climate change is probably the most devastating and multifaceted phenomenon to face the international community since at least the Second World War. International law is relatively flexible, albeit often slow-moving; it does have the flexibility and tools to deal with global climate change but it will need the will of the international community, namely States, to do this.

Moreover, the exercise of this collective will of the international community will need to take the form of concerted action at several levels of political interaction: the global, regional, sub-regional, national, and even sub-national. At the global level, such concerted international cooperative action has arguably already begun to take place, both within the Climate Change Convention negotiations and within well-established international organizations and institutions, such as the World Bank (World Bank, 2008). In the Asia-Pacific context, it remains to be seen whether the regional trade and economic development organizations such as the East Asian Economic Caucus (EAEC) and sub-regional institutions such as the Association of Southeast Asian Nations (ASEAN) can mobilize themselves in the same way as the Economic and Social Commission for Asia and the Pacific (ESCAP) did in advance of the Rio+20 Summit.

ACKNOWLEDGEMENTS

The authors would like to express their gratitude to Professor Dr Alexandre Timoshenko and Professor John C. Dernbach for their incisive and helpful comments on an earlier version of this paper. All remaining errors and omissions are the responsibility of the authors alone.

REFERENCES

AHREOC (2008) *Human Rights and Climate Change*, Background Paper. Sydney, Australian Human Rights and Equal Opportunity Commission. https://humanrights.gov.au/our-work/commission-general/publications/human-rights-climate-change-2008 (1 October 2020)

AIIB, Environmental and Social Framework, February 2016, amended 2019, para.16. https://www.aiib.org/en/policies-strategies/_download/environment-framework/Final-ESF-Mar-14-2019-Final-P.pdf

Allen, M. (2003) Liability for climate change: will it ever be possible to sue anyone for damaging the climate? *Nature*, **421**, 27 February, 891–892.

Allen, M. R., and Lord, R. (2004) The blame game: who will pay for the damaging consequences of climate change? *Nature*, **432**, 551–552.

Asian Infrastructure Investment Bank (AIIB) (2017) Directive on Environmental and Social Policy, adopted on 4 December 2017, amended 2019. https://www.aiib.org/en/about-aiib/who-we-are/role-of-law/.content/index/_download/Directive-on-Environmental-and-Social-Policy.pdf

Boom, K., Richards, J. A. and Leonard, S. (2016) Climate justice: The international momentum towards climate litigation. https://www.boell.de/en/2016/11/15/climate-justice-international-momentum-towards-climate-litigation

Brown, A. (2008) *Reinventing Humanitarian Intervention: Two Cheers for the Responsibility to Protect?* House of Commons Research Paper, 08/55, 17 June. https://commonslibrary.parliament.uk/research-briefings/rp08-55/

Brunnée, J. (2007) Common areas, common heritage, and common concern. In D. Bodansky, J. Brunnée and E. Hey (eds.), *The Oxford Handbook of International Environmental Law*. Oxford, Oxford University Press.

CESCR (Covenant of Economic, Social and Cultural Rights) (1991) *The Nature of States Parties Obligations* (Art. 2, par.1). 14 December 1990. General Comment 3, E/1991/23.
    (2000) *The Right to the Highest Attainable Standard of Health*. 11 August. E/C.12/2000/4, General Comment 14.

Churchill, R. R. and Ulfstein, G. (2000) Autonomous institutional arrangements in multilateral environmental agreements: A little-noticed phenomenon in international law. *American Journal of International Law*, **94**(4), 623–659.

Climate Change Act (2008) Chapter 27, United Kingdom.

Cole, L. (2018) Changing climate: New refugee visa? *Geographical*, January 2018. http://geographical.co.uk/people/the-refugee-crisis/item/2539-changing-climate

Coomans, F. and Kamminga, M. T. (eds.) (2004) *Extraterritorial Application of Human Rights Treaties*. Antwerp/Oxford, Intersentia.

Crawford, J. (2006) *The Creation of States in International Law*, (2nd ed). Oxford, Oxford University Press.

Cullet, P. (1999) Differential treatment under international law: towards a new paradigm of inter-state relations. *European Journal of International Law*, **10**, 549–582.

Curtain, R., Dornan, M., Doyle, J. and Howes, S. (2016) *Pacific Possible: Labour Mobility: The Ten Billion Dollar Prize*. World Bank. http://pubdocs.worldbank.org/en/555421468204932199/pdf/labour-mobility-pacific-possible.pdf

Dasgupta, S., Laplante, B., Meisner, C., Wheeler, D. and Yan, J. (2007) The impact of sea level rise on developing countries: a comparative analysis. World Bank Policy Research Working Paper 4136, February. https://openknowledge.worldbank.org/bitstream/handle/10986/7174/wps4136.pdf?sequence=1&isAllowed=y

Di Leva, C. and Morita, S. (2008) *Climate Change and Maritime Boundaries: Should States Adapt to Submerged Boundaries?* World Bank, Law and Development Working Paper Series, No. 5. http://documents1.worldbank.org/curated/en/461271468138869143/pdf/449020NWP0Box311number5010JULY02008.pdf

Elias, O. (2004) The UN compensation commission and liability for the costs of monitoring and assessment of environmental damage. In M. Fitzmaurice and D. Sarooshi (eds.), *Issues of State Responsibility before International Judicial Institutions: The Clifford Chance Lectures*, pp. 219–236. Oxford, Hart.

Fitzmaurice, M. and Elias, O. (2005) The Kyoto Protocol compliance regime and the law of treaties. In *Contemporary Issues in the Law of Treaties*, pp. 289–313. Utrecht, Netherlands, Eleven International Publishing.

Fitzmaurice, M. A. and Redgwell, C. (2000) Environmental non-compliance procedures and international law. *Netherlands Yearbook of International Law*, **XXXI**, 35–65.

Freestone, D. (1991) International law and sea level rise. In R. Churchill and D. Freestone (eds.), *International Law and Global Climate Change*. London, Graham and Trotman/Martinus Nijhoff.

French, D. (2000) Developing states and international environmental law: the importance of differentiated responsibilities. *International & Comparative Law Quarterly*, **49**, 35–60.

Garnaut, R. (2008) Garnaut Climate Change Review, Draft Report 2008. http://library.bsl.org.au/jspui/bitstream/1/1002/1/Garnaut%20Climate%20Change%20Review%20-%20Final%20Report2008.pdf

(2011) The Garnaut Review 2011: Australia in the global response to climate change. http://www.garnautreview.org.au/update-2011/garnaut-review-2011/garnaut-review-2011.pdf

Global Sustainable Investment Review (2016) Global Sustainable Investment Alliance. http://www.gsi-alliance.org/wp-content/uploads/2017/03/GSIR_Review2016.F.pdf

Gray, C. (2002) From unity to polarization: international law and the use of force against Iraq. *EJIL*, **13**, 1–24.

Green New Deal Group (2008) *A Green New Deal*. New Economics Foundation. https://neweconomics.org/uploads/files/8f737ea195fe56db2f_xbm6ihwb1.pdf

Hampson, F. J. (2005) The human rights situation of indigenous peoples in States and other territories threatened with extinction for environmental reasons. Sub-Commission on the Promotion and Protection of Human Rights. E/CN.4/Sub.2/2005/28, 16 June. https://documents-dds-ny.un.org/doc/UNDOC/GEN/G05/144/71/PDF/G0514471.pdf?OpenElement

Hannah, L., Lovejoy, T. E. and Schneider, S. H. (2005) Biodiversity and climate change in context. In T. E. Lovejoy and L. Hannah (eds.), *Climate Change and Biodiversity*. New Haven and London, Yale University Press.

Hulme, K. (2004) *War Torn Environment: Interpreting the Legal Threshold*. Leiden, Netherlands, Martinus Nijhoff.

Hughes, T. and Kerry, J. (2017) Two-thirds of Great Barrier Reef hit by back-to-back mass coral bleaching. Coral Reef Studies Centre, 10 April. https://www.coralcoe.org.au/media-releases/two-thirds-of-great-barrier-reef-hit-by-back-to-back-mass-coral-bleaching

Hunt, P. (2007) *Report of the Special Rapporteur on the Right of Everyone to the Enjoyment of the Highest Attainable Standard of Physical and Mental Health*. 8 August, A/62/214. https://documents-dds-ny.un.org/doc/UNDOC/GEN/N07/453/79/PDF/N0745379.pdf?OpenElement

ICHRP (2008) *Climate Change and Human Rights: A Rough Guide*. International Council on Human Rights Policy. https://www.ohchr.org/documents/issues/climatechange/submissions/136_report.pdf

IDMC (Internal Displacement Monitoring Centre) (2019) Global Report on Internal Displacement. https://www.internal-displacement.org/sites/default/files/publications/documents/2019%20IDMC%20Annual%20Report.pdf

IIGCC (2007) Investor Statement on Climate Change Report 2007. Institutional Investors Group on Climate Change. https://www.iigcc.org/download/investor-statement-on-climate-change-report-2007/?wpdmdl=1691&refresh=5f760d5baf5441601572187

IGCC (2019) Delivering an Investable Long-Term Emissions Strategy. http://www.igcc.rg.au/

ILA (2008) International Law on Foreign Investment Committee, Final Report. International Law Association Rio de Janeiro Conference. https://www.ila-hq.org/index.php/committees

INCR (Investor Network on Climate Risk) (2008) Investor Letter to Congress, reported in Citywire, Funds Insider, 'Investor group calls on US Senate to tackle climate change', by Richard Harris, 22 May, 2008. https://citywire.co.uk/funds-insider/news/investor-group-calls-on-us-senate-to-tackle-climate-change/a303727 https://www.internal-displacement.org/sites/default/files/publications/documents/2019%20IDMC%20Annual%20Report.pdf

IPCC (2007a) *Climate Change 2007: The Physical Science Basis. Contribution of Working Group I to the Fourth Assessment Report of the Intergovernmental Panel on Climate Change*. Cambridge, Cambridge University Press.

(2007b) *Climate Change 2007: Impacts, Adaptation and Vulnerability*. Contribution of Working Group II to the Fourth Assessment Report of the IPCC. Cambridge University Press.

(2014a) *Climate Change 2014: Synthesis Report*. Contribution of Working Groups I, II and III to the Fifth Assessment Report of the Intergovernmental Panel on Climate Change. Core Writing Team, R. K. Pachauri and L. A. Meyer (eds.). Geneva, Switzerland, IPCC.

Koester, V. (2007) The convention on access to information, public participation in decision-making and access to justice in environmental matters (Aarhus Convention). Chapter 8. In G. Ulfstein, T. Marauhn and A. Zimmermann (eds.), *Making Treaties Work: Human Rights, Environment and Arms Control*, pp. 179–217. Cambridge, Cambridge University Press.

Lowe, V., Roberts, A., Walsh, J. and Zaum, D. (eds.) (2008) *The United Nations Security Council and War: The Evolution of Thought and Practice since 1945*. Oxford University Press.

Miliband, D. (2008) HC Deb, 13 May, c1195. https://hansard.parliament.uk/Commons/2008-05-13/debates/08051353000010/ForeignAndCommonwealthOffice

Miliband, D. and Kouchner, B. (2008) Emergency aid must come before politics. *The Times*, 9 May, p. 19.

Moon, B. K. (2007) A climate culprit in Darfur. *The Washington Post*, 16 June.

Mushkat, R. (2004) *International Environmental Law and Asian Values: Legal Norms and Cultural Influences*. Vancouver and Toronto, University of British Columbia Press.

Ong, D. M. (2008a) The contribution of state-multinational corporation 'transnational' investment agreements to international environmental law. *Yearbook of International Environmental Law 2006*. Oxford, Oxford University Press, Vol. 17, pp. 168–212.

(2008b) International environmental law's 'customary' dilemma: Betwixt general principles and treaty rules. *Irish Yearbook of International Law 2006*. Oxford, Hart Publishing, Vol. 1, pp. 3–60.

(2010) From 'international' to 'transnational' environmental law? A legal assessment of the contribution of the 'equator principles' to international environmental law. *Nordic Journal of International Law*, **79**(1), 35–74.

(2016) Public accountability for private international financing of natural resource development projects. *Nordic Journal of International Law*, **85**(3), 201–233.

(2017) The Asian infrastructure investment bank: Bringing 'Asian values' to global economic governance. *Journal of International Economic Law*, **20**(3), 535–560.

Oppenheim, L. (1905) *International Law: A Treatise*. Vol. I.

Paskal, C. (2008) Unpublished paper. Humans and habitats: Rethinking rights in an age of climate change. London, 26 April.

Puapua, T. (2002) Tuvalu Statement. 57th Session of the UN General Assembly. http://www.un.org/webcast/ga/57/statements/020914tuvaluE.htm (1 October 2020). Cited in Friends of the Earth (FOE), *A Citizen's Guide to Climate Refugees*. https://www.safecom.org.au/foe-climate-guide.htm

Rajamani, L. (2006) *Differential Treatment in International Environmental Law*. Oxford, Oxford University Press.

Schwarzenberger, G. (1976) *A Manual of International Law*, (6th ed.). London, Professional Books.

Selth, A. (2008) Even paranoids have enemies: Cyclone Nargis and Myanmar's fears of invasion. *Contemporary Southeast Asia*, **30**(3), 379–402.

Shaw, M. (2003) *International Law*, (5th ed.). Cambridge, Cambridge University Press.

Skogly, S. (2006) *Beyond National Borders: States' Human Rights Obligations in International Cooperation*. Antwerp/Oxford, Intersentia.

Solana, J. (2008) Joint Report: Climate change and international security. S113/08. Issued on 14 March. https://www.consilium.europa.eu/uedocs/cms_data/docs/pressdata/en/reports/99387.pdf

Soons, A. H. A. (1990) The effects of sea level rise on maritime limits and boundaries. *Netherlands International Law Review*, **37**, 207–232.

Stern, N. (2006) *The Economics of Climate Change: The Stern Review*. Cambridge, Cambridge University Press.

Stone, C. (2004) Common but differentiated responsibilities in international law. *AJIL*, **98**, 276–301.

Synthesis report on best practices and lessons learned on the objective and themes of the United Nations Conference on Sustainable Development, A/CONF.216/PC/8, 21 January 2011. Prepared for UNGA, Preparatory Committee for the United Nations Conference on Sustainable Development, Second session, 7 and 8 March 2011.

Thürer, D. (1999) The 'failed state' and international law. *IRRC*, **836**, 731–761.

Ulfstein, G., Marauhn, T. and Zimmermann, A. (eds.) (2007) *Making Treaties Work: Human Rights, Environment and Arms Control*. Cambridge, Cambridge University Press.

UNHCHR (2009) Report of the Office of the United Nations High Commissioner for Human Rights on the Relationship Between Climate Change and Human Rights, A/HRC/10/61, 15 January. https://www.ohchr.org/Documents/Press/AnalyticalStudy.pdf

UN General Assembly Resolution 64/236: Implementation of Agenda 21, the Programme for the Further Implementation of Agenda 21 and the outcomes of the World Summit on Sustainable Development A/RES/64/236 (31 March 2010). https://undocs.org/en/A/RES/64/236

UN Secretary-General Report to 1st Preparatory Committee for Rio+20 Summit (April2010) A/CONF.216/PC/2. https://undocs.org/en/A/CONF.216/PC/2

UN Security Council Resolution 1973 (2011) Libya, S/RES/1973 (2011).

UNEP (United Nations Environment Programme) (2017) *The Status of Climate Change Litigation: A Global Review*. Nairobi, UNON, Publishing Services Section.

Urgenda Foundation v. Kingdom of the Netherlands (2015) HAZA C/09/00456689.

US-SIF (2013) *Investing to Curb Climate Change: A Guide for the Individual Investor*. US Sustainable Investment Foundation, The Forum for Sustainable and Responsible Investment, http://www.ussif.org/files/Publications/SRI_Climate_Guide.pdf

Verheyen, R. (2005) *Climate Change Damage and International Law: Prevention Duties and State Responsibility*. Leiden, Netherlands, Martinus Nijhoff.

von Moltke, K. (2005) Clustering international environmental agreements as an alternative to a world environment organization. In F. Biermann and S. Bauer (eds.), *A World Environment Organization: Solution or Threat for Effective International Environmental Governance?* pp. 175–204. Aldershot, UK, Ashgate.

World Bank (2006) *Managing Climate Risk: Integrating Adaptation into World Bank Group Operations*. World Bank Group, Global Environmental Facility Programme, Working Paper No. 37462. https://www.preventionweb.net/files/2597_374620Managing0Climate0Risk01PUBLIC1.pdf

(2008) Towards a strategic framework on climate change and development for the World Bank Group: Concept and issues paper, consultation draft, 27 March. https://www.devcommittee.org/sites/dc/files/download/Documentation/DC2008-0002%28E%29ClimateChange.pdf

16 Sustainable development and climate change negotiations: Perspectives of developing countries

BERNARDITAS DE CASTRO-MULLER

Former Environmental Affairs Adviser, Department of Foreign Affairs, Philippines; Former Special Adviser on Climate Change, South Centre, Geneva, Switzerland; Former Consultant, National Climate Change Commission of the Philippines

Editor's note: While I was in the process of sending this chapter to the publisher, I was shocked and profoundly saddened by the passing of Bernarditas on 14 December 2018. I am most grateful for Bernarditas's important contribution to this book. I deeply regret that she was unable to see the publication of her chapter.

Keywords

United Nations Framework Convention on Climate Change (UNFCCC); Kyoto Protocol (KP); sustainable development; multilateral environmental agreements (MEAs); principle of common but differentiated responsibilities; G77 and China; impacts; vulnerability; adaptation; mitigation; clean development mechanism (CDM); negotiations; national communications; financial mechanism; Berlin Mandate; Agreed full cost; Technology Development and Transfer Board; Multilateral Technology Acquisition Fund; Adaptation Fund

Abstract

This chapter provides a reading of the United Nations Framework Convention on Climate Change (UNFCCC) from the perspectives of developing countries, as a basis for the positions taken by developing countries in the UNFCCC negotiations. It focuses on what is referred to as developing country issues in the UNFCCC: adaptation, the financial mechanism, transfer of technology, capacity-building, and non-Annex I[1] national communications, as well as the approach guiding the positions taken by developing countries in negotiating these issues. It also provides recommendations for breaking the impasse and moving forward on many of these issues.

This chapter demonstrates the balance of commitments under the UNFCCC, based on the principle of common but differentiated responsibilities that is embodied in each and every provision of the UNFCCC. It shows that the Convention promotes sustainable development, the pursuit of which is the biggest contribution of developing countries in addressing climate change and its adverse effects, through the integration of climate change considerations in social and economic development policies.

This chapter also points to the contributions of developing countries in the Kyoto Protocol (KP) to dispel the *false* perception that developing countries *do not have commitments under the Kyoto Protocol*. While contributing to a protocol that is primarily aimed at rendering adequate the commitments *on limitations of emissions* of developed countries in the Convention, developing countries also underline the importance of the need for adaptation.

In all this, the chapter maintains that the UNFCCC is a convention that addresses climate change and its adverse effects through sustainable development, which renders it of vital importance to developing countries.

Much has transpired in climate change negotiations affecting all of the issues presented in this chapter. These developments are summarized in the final section to capture the substantive alterations that have occurred since the chapter was first written. Developments on specific issues are added to the sections dealing with these issues.

16.1 INTRODUCTION

As the international debate heats up on global warming, it has become clearer that a better understanding is needed of the commitments that developing countries have undertaken under the United Nations Framework Convention on Climate Change (UNFCCC) (United Nations, 1992) and its Kyoto Protocol (United Nations, 1998).[2] Contrary to the general perception,

---

[1] Annexes to the Convention are based on the levels of responsibilities for historical emissions that have caused the concentrations of GHGs in the atmosphere since the Industrial Revolution. Non-Annex I countries are mainly developing countries that have little or no responsibility for historical emissions. Some non-Annex I countries, such as Mexico and the Republic of Korea, left the Group of 77 developing countries when they became members of the Organization of Economic Cooperation and Development (OECD), but still remain non-Annex I countries under the Convention. Others, like Chile, chose to remain in the G77 after having joined the OECD, accepted by the G77 on an exceptional basis.

[2] The texts of the Convention and its Kyoto Protocol, as well as the COP or COP/MOP decisions, can be accessed at the Secretariat's website: http://www.unfccc.int. UNFCCC documents are published by the United Nations Office in Geneva.

developing country Parties have undertaken legally binding obligations under the Convention, and likewise, within the terms of the Berlin Mandate, have contributed to the Kyoto Protocol. They have *also* undertaken these long-term commitments because they are most vulnerable to the adverse effects of climate change, while having contributed the least to it.

At the same time, the Convention affirms the 'legitimate priority needs of developing countries for the achievement of sustained economic growth and the eradication of poverty' (Preamble, paragraph 21 of the UNFCCC) and recognizes that in order to pursue sustainable development, 'their energy consumption will need to grow taking into account the possibilities for achieving greater energy efficiency' (Preamble, paragraph 22).

This chapter tries to clarify the driving principles behind positions taken by developing countries in the negotiations both in the Convention and the Kyoto Protocol. It does not go into the scientific bases for climate change that guide these positions, which are taken fully into account in the negotiations. Among the many issues under negotiation, this chapter will deal with what is collectively referred to as developing country issues: adaptation, *the provision of* financial resources, transfer of technology, national communications, and capacity-building. All these issues are interlinked, and these links are based on the balance of *common but differentiated* responsibilities of the Parties to the Convention and its Kyoto Protocol.

It must be recognized, however, that negotiations are ongoing on many of these issues. This chapter does not attempt to capture all of these developments, but mainly deals with basic considerations and common positions taken by developing country Parties in these negotiations. The wide diversity of circumstances of the 132 countries that make up the Group of 77 (G77, UN negotiating group of developing countries) also means that there is a range of different and constantly evolving positions within them. The Group's unity in their diversity has been their strength in climate change negotiations. Time and again, despite predictions of splits within the Group, they have been able to arrive at common positions, after admittedly very difficult negotiations between them. While positions evolve and change, however, the basic understanding of the Convention that developing countries share allows them to achieve this unity.

Articles referred to in this chapter are those of the UNFCCC, unless specified as being those of the Kyoto Protocol. The views expressed in this chapter are the author's alone, as her own reading of the UNFCCC and its Kyoto Protocol evolved through years of negotiations within the G77, and as lead negotiator for the G77 and China. The author was also the G77 lead coordinator and negotiator for the ad hoc working group on Long-term Cooperative Action (AWG-LCA), and for financial issues under the ad hoc working group on the Durban Platform (ADP), which led to the Paris Agreement of 2015.

The chapter is not meant to represent official positions of the G77 in general or any developing country in particular.

16.2 THE PRINCIPLE OF COMMON BUT DIFFERENTIATED RESPONSIBILITIES

The overarching principle on which the UNFCCC and its Kyoto Protocol are based is the principle of common but differentiated responsibilities. *This principle reflects Principle 7 of the Rio Declaration on Environment and Development of 1992.* The Preamble of the Convention best articulates this principle. It states in its first paragraph that the Parties acknowledge 'that change in the Earth's climate and its adverse effects are a common concern of mankind'.

It is, however, the third paragraph of the Preamble that best guides the approach of developing countries in the Convention and the Protocol:

<u>Noting</u> that the largest share of historical and current global emissions of greenhouse gases has originated in developed countries, that per capita emissions in developing countries are still relatively low and that the share of global emissions originating in developing countries will grow to meet their social and development needs.

Since the entry into force of the UNFCCC on 21 March 1994, this paragraph remains valid. The reference to per capita emissions is crucial to an understanding of developing countries' positions. It is not merely a matter of numbers, however, but the nature of these emissions. In developing countries, emissions are mainly 'survival emissions',[3] necessary for attaining basic humane living conditions for the large majority of their populations, and not what can be deemed 'luxury emissions', meant to sustain high standard lifestyles.

The Preamble also amply demonstrates that the UNFCCC is about sustainable development. This is the principal obligation of developing countries under the Convention and their biggest contribution to climate change: the pursuit of sustainable development, that is, social and economic development that fully integrates environmental management, including climate change, considerations.

---

[3] The terms 'survival emissions' and 'luxury emissions' were first enunciated in the UNFCCC negotiations by the late Professor Zhong Shukong, Ambassador of the People's Republic of China. It is also the title of the book by Professor Mark J. Mwandosya, *Survival Emissions: A Perspective from the South on Global Climate Change Negotiations*, published in 1996 by DUP, Ltd., Dar-es-Salaam, University of Tanzania and the Centre for Energy, Environment, Science and Technology (CEEST), Dar-es-Salaam, Tanzania. Professor Mwandosya chaired the Group of 77 during the final sessions of the Kyoto Protocol negotiations. This book is 'must' reading for all those who wish to understand how the G77 and China conducted their negotiations for the Kyoto Protocol and why they took their positions in these negotiations.

Developing countries under the Convention have undertaken the commitment to pursue development that is socially just and respectful of human rights and one that takes fully into account the need to ensure the integrity of the environment. Given the difficult choices of policies that the pursuit of sustainable development means for developing countries, and taken within the context of what is known as globalization, it is clear that this is not an easy task. Any given decision in favour of sustainable development could mean livelihoods for developing countries, and not merely slight percentage changes in profit margins, as it would be for others.

However, because developed countries achieved their development in a manner that, among other things, did not take into account the environment, they have the corresponding obligation to 'take the lead in combating climate change and the adverse effects thereof' (Article 3.1 of the UNFCCC). Under the Convention, developed countries also have commitments to provide financial resources, including those for the transfer of technology, to developing countries. 'Taking the lead' implies that somebody follows this lead, and developing countries have consistently *shown their determination* to contribute their share to the achievement of the objective of the Convention, consistent with the principle of common but differentiated responsibilities.

This principle also provides the basis of the balance of differentiated responsibilities that is reflected in all the articles of the Convention. As the chapter will demonstrate, this balance of commitments is reflected in each and every article of the Convention.

16.3 ADAPTATION AND SUSTAINABLE DEVELOPMENT

The objective of the Convention (Article 2) not only refers to the ultimate objective, which is the 'stabilization of greenhouse gas concentrations in the atmosphere at a level that would prevent dangerous anthropogenic interference with the climate system', but also sets the parameters for such stabilization. Article 2, in its second sentence, states that the time frame for the achievement of such a level should be sufficient 'to allow ecosystems to adapt naturally to climate change' and allows for sustainable development, 'to ensure that food production is not threatened and to enable economic development to proceed in a sustainable manner'. The ultimate objective of the Convention is best pursued through mitigation, on the condition that adaptation is likewise equally pursued, in a manner that ensures food security *and* sustainable development.

Developing countries have consistently underlined the need for adaptation, in the face of growing scientific evidence that recognizes that climate change is taking place and that

developing countries are the least able to cope with its adverse effects. Just as consistently, developed countries choose to focus on mitigation to be undertaken by all Parties, starting with the most economically progressive among them.

Generally, in negotiations, the common understanding is that addressing climate change refers to mitigation, and addressing the adverse effects of climate change refers to adaptation measures, unless these are further specified. And while, under the principle of common but differentiated responsibilities, *Annex I countries have the legal obligation to address climate change through mitigation through* limitation of emissions *(Article 4.2), all Parties (including developing country Parties) have the obligation to employ technology that would* reduce, prevent and control emissions *(Article 4.1 c). Moreover, this commitment is directly linked to the commitment of 'developed country Parties and other developed Parties included in Annex II' to provide financial resources, including for the 'transfer of technology' needed by developing country Parties to implement this commitment (Article 4.3).* In addition, developing country Parties are principally concerned with addressing the adverse effects of climate change through adaptation.

However, many developing countries have limited capacities for mitigation, owing to their level of economic development. Moreover, many of them have resources that render them as sinks rather than sources of emissions. In many cases, these very same countries are those that are particularly vulnerable to the adverse effects of climate change.

The Convention in its Preamble recognizes conditions under which countries are 'particularly vulnerable to the adverse effects of climate change'. These countries are 'low-lying and other small island countries, countries with low-lying coastal, arid and semi-arid areas or areas liable to floods, drought and desertification, and developing countries with fragile mountainous ecosystems'.

Article 4.8 also lists the specific conditions of developing countries with special needs and concerns arising from adverse effects of climate change and/or the impacts of the implementation of response measures. Articles 4.8 and 4.9, on the specific needs and special situations of least-developed countries, make up a very important and contentious issue for negotiations under the Convention. The contention mainly arises from the different considerations that are to be given to developing country Parties vulnerable to the adverse effects of climate change and those that are adversely affected by impacts of the implementation of response measures.

There is one very important word that appears only once in the Convention, in the heading (or '*chapeau*') of Article 4.8, and that word is 'insurance'. As more and more countries, including developed countries, are affected by extreme weather events causing tragic loss of lives and great damage of property, the insurance industry has intensified its moves to take more seriously into account the adverse effects of climate change. They too have to adapt their policies in the face of increasing manifestations of adverse impacts of climate change.

Under Article 3, this balance of differentiated responsibilities is also reflected. Adaptation is given priority for developing countries (Article 3.2), while mitigation, as a measure under the precautionary principle, is a principle for all Parties, both developing and developed countries (Article 3.3). These, together with the right to promote sustainable development and 'a supportive and open international economic system that would lead to sustainable economic growth and development', make up the basic principles of the Convention.

For too long in the implementation of the Convention, however, the need for adaptation has been put aside, with financial resources available for developing countries mainly allotted to mitigation activities, serving the primary obligations of developed country Parties. The policies, programme priorities, and eligibility criteria for the various stages of adaptation adopted at the First Session of the Conference of the Parties (COP 1) in 1995 remain largely unfulfilled. The five-year work programme on adaptation, finally adopted at the Twelfth Session of the Conference of the Parties (COP 12) in 2006 at the last stages of the meeting, still confined itself largely to vulnerability assessments and capacity-building for adaptation. In order to reflect more faithfully what the work programme is all about, and in deference to the Presidency of Kenya, who made adaptation its priority issue, it was renamed the 'Nairobi Work Programme on Impacts, Vulnerability and Adaptation to Climate Change'.

The second part of the Fourth Assessment Report of the Intergovernmental Panel on Climate Change (IPCC) repeats the strong recommendations for the need for adaptation already underlined in the Second and Third Assessment Reports. This time, however, the rapidity of change has caught even some scientists by surprise, adding the question of how fast and how much climate change will occur to the uncertainties that still have to be addressed in the science of climate change. Once again, the ones to suffer the most damage, because they are least able to cope and are most vulnerable, are the developing countries.

16.4 ADAPTATION AND MITIGATION CAN BE MUTUALLY SUPPORTIVE

While all Parties to the Convention are undertaking obligations for both mitigation and adaptation, it is important to underline that Annex I countries in the Convention *have the legal commitment to undertake mitigation*, that is, to take 'the lead in modifying longer-term trends in anthropogenic emissions', which would include reduction of emissions, but also implies the

necessary changes in production and consumption lifestyles. This was one of the underlying considerations in the setting up of targets for Annex I countries under the Kyoto Protocol.

In the implementation of the Convention, and in particular in the provision of financial resources for implementation through the Global Environment Facility (GEF), emphasis has been placed mainly on mitigation activities. Increasingly, however, the need for adaptation is being felt. As more experience is acquired in addressing the adverse effects of climate change, it is likewise becoming evident that adaptation activities could contribute to mitigation, as well. This is the case, for example, for reforestation/afforestation activities and protection of watersheds, or sustainable land management for the generation and promotion of renewable sources of energy. Both mitigation and adaptation activities are, moreover, fully supportive of sustainable development.

16.5 NATIONAL COMMUNICATIONS

The commitments of all Parties to the UNFCCC are, again, subject to the principle of common but differentiated responsibilities (heading or *chapeau* of Article 4).

Foremost among these commitments is the submission of national communications, the contents of which are outlined in Article 12. In its first paragraph, the contents of the national communications of 'each Party' are listed. This sub-article is strictly followed in the preparation of decisions containing guidelines for national communications of non-Annex I Parties. These decisions are, in turn, the bases for the provision of 'agreed full costs' of the preparations of non-Annex I communications. 'Agreed full costs' is understood by developing countries as subject to transparent negotiations between the GEF, as an operating entity of the financial mechanism of the Convention, and the developing country concerned, for the financing of national communications.

It is important to underline that there are separate and specific obligations for Annex I countries for inclusion in their national communications. These include 'a detailed description of the policies and measures' adopted to implement its commitments under the Convention, in its Articles 4.2 (a) and (b), the review of which led to the Berlin Mandate and the Kyoto Protocol. Moreover, *developed country Parties and other developed Parties included in Annex II* are also required to 'incorporate details of measures taken' in accordance with their obligations for the provision of financial resources, for meeting the costs of adaptation, and for transfer of technology (Article 12.3).

The implementation of these obligations by *each developed country Party and each other Party included in Annex I* is to be considered in order to carry out the reviews by the Conference of the Parties through the Subsidiary Body for Implementation

(SBI), as provided for in Article 10.2 (b). For *each Party*, the SBI shall 'assess the overall aggregated effect of the steps taken by the Parties in the light of the latest scientific assessments concerning climate change' (Article 10.2 a).

This is mentioned here in detail because one of the main issues of contention in the discussions of non-Annex I communications is the insistence of developed countries for these communications also to be subject to review by the SBI. Not only is any such review contrary to the provisions of the Convention, it is also unnecessary in the light of the contents of non-Annex I communications. National inventories of emissions of developing countries are subject to methodologies agreed upon by Parties (Article 7.2 d), and the rest is a general description of steps to implement the Convention, which are easily verifiable, and information to be given voluntarily, likewise easy to identify (Article 7.2 e). Any country may ask for such a review, should it see fit to do so.

It is important to note that a Party may also designate any given information as confidential, based on criteria established by the Conference of the Parties (Article 12.9). This information 'shall be aggregated by the secretariat before being made available to any of the bodies involved in the communication', including for the review of this information.

On the other hand, contents of Annex I communications are subject to review, which are in fact regular reviews to be conducted by the COP (Article 4.2 d) and related to the review required under Article 9 of the Kyoto Protocol, now currently the subject of ongoing discussions under the Protocol. Such reviews are to be conducted by the Conference of the Parties of the UNFCCC, which, as 'the supreme body' of the Convention, 'shall keep under regular review the implementation of the Convention and any other related legal instruments' as mandated under Article 7.2 (a).

The current discussions on Article 9 of the Kyoto Protocol have therefore expanded the scope of the reviews and have shifted from the original purpose of the reviews under the Convention, which is to review the adequacy of the commitments under Articles 4.2 (a) and (b) of the Convention, to the need to involve developing countries' commitments. This development is not irrelevant to the insistence of Annex I countries to review non-Annex I national communications, as well.

This being said, an assessment of the commitments of all Parties by the Conference of the Parties of the UNFCCC is provided for in Article 7.2 (a) of the Convention. This article provides for the periodic examination of the 'obligations of the Parties and the institutional arrangements under the Convention, in the light of the objective of the Convention, the experience gained in its implementation and the evolution of scientific and technological knowledge'. Given the publication of the IPCC Fourth Assessment Report in 2007, it would be timely to conduct this periodic examination at the next COP.

It must be noted that Article 9 of the Kyoto Protocol stipulates that reviews of the Protocol 'shall be coordinated with pertinent reviews under the Convention, in particular those required by Article 4, paragraph 2 (d), and Article 7, paragraph 2 (a) of the Convention'. This particular provision states that 'the Conference of the Parties, as the supreme body' of the Convention, 'shall keep under regular review the implementation of the Convention and any related legal instruments', which would include the Kyoto Protocol.

The current discussions, conducted by the Conference of the Parties, serving as the Meeting of the Parties (COP/MOP) of the Kyoto Protocol, should in effect be conducted by the COP of the Convention and cover not only 'obligations of the Parties', but also the 'institutional arrangements under the Convention'. The contents of national communications would be included in these discussions.

16.6 THE FINANCIAL MECHANISM

Negotiations on financial issues are among the most contentious in the Convention. Much depends on a common understanding between all Parties of the definition of the financial mechanism of the Convention. Once again, the principle of common but differentiated responsibilities governs the understanding of developing countries of the financial mechanism under the Convention. For developing countries, the financial mechanism of the Convention is the channel through which legally binding commitments for the provision of financial resources, including those for the transfer of technology, are implemented. This obligation cannot therefore be subject to the usual donor conditionalities applied to the provision of resources for development assistance, and especially for loans. Developing countries under the Convention are not aid-recipient countries, as financial resources are accorded to them for the implementation of the Convention, as part of obligations under the Convention.

Article 11 defines 'the mechanism for the provision of financial resources on a grant and concessional basis, including for the transfer of technology' in the Convention. The operation of the mechanism shall be entrusted to one or more international entities. Furthermore, it was specified that the mechanism 'shall have an equitable and balanced representation of all Parties within a transparent system of governance'.

As part of the interim arrangements for the entry into force of the Convention, the operation of the financial mechanism was entrusted to the GEF, subject to the condition that it 'should be appropriately restructured and its membership made universal' to enable it to fulfil its designated role for the Convention. Developed country Parties may also provide, and developing country Parties may avail themselves of, resources through bilateral, regional, and other multilateral channels (Article

11.5). *These channels have been considered by the COP as being outside of the framework of the financial mechanism of the Convention (Decision 11/CP.1, paragraph 2 a).*

From the outset, therefore, the intention of the Convention was not to confine the operations of the financial mechanism to one entity alone, but to all entities able to meet the requirements of the mechanism. There has also been a constant debate in the negotiations on financial issues under the Convention as to whether or not the restructured GEF fulfils the requirements of the mechanism, given the ministerial role played by the GEF Assembly, which meets only once every four years, and the two-tiered voting system in the GEF Council. For these reasons, and in order to provide for other operational entities to meet the huge financial resources necessary for the implementation of the Convention, the reference to the GEF has always been as an operating entity of the financial mechanism of the Convention.

The Convention also provides that developed country Parties shall provide 'new and additional' resources to developing country Parties to meet their obligations. The understanding reached at the United Nations Conference on Environment and Development (UNCED) of 1992 was that new and additional resources are those that are over and above Official Development Assistance (ODA), in addition to being provided on a grant and concessional basis. For ODA, a target of 0.7% of the developed countries' Gross National Product (GNP) has been set. Here once more, it is clear for developing countries that financing provided through the GEF cannot be subject to any donor requirements.

The Convention, however, allows for the provision by developed country Parties of financial resources through bilateral, regional, and other multilateral channels, within the financial mechanism (Article 11.5). Moreover, there are also developing countries that are contributors to the GEF, not as a legally binding obligation, but as a voluntary move to help attain the objective of the Convention.

The financial mechanism 'shall function under the guidance of, and be accountable to the Conference of the Parties, which shall decide on its policies, programme priorities and eligibility criteria related to this Convention' (Article 11.1). Guidance is provided through decisions of the COP, and the GEF regularly reports on its activities related to the UNFCCC at every COP session. A review and evaluation of the GEF is provided for in the Memorandum of Understanding between the UNFCCC COP and the GEF Council. This review takes into account the conformity of the activities of the GEF with the guidance of the COP, as well as evaluating its effectiveness in terms of the modalities provided for in the Convention (Article 11.3).

Long years of negotiations on the financial mechanism and the GEF have shown that large gaps exist between what is provided for in the Convention and the actual operations of the

GEF at national level. The role of the Implementing Agencies (IAs) of the GEF has been identified early in the negotiations as being part of the problem. The three IAs are the World Bank, the United Nations Environment Programme (UNEP), and the United Nations Development Programme (UNDP). There are also seven Executing Agencies (EAs) under expanded opportunities: International Fund for Agricultural Development (IFAD), UN Food and Agriculture Organization (FAO), UN Industrial Development Organization (UNIDO), African Development Bank (AfDB), Asian Development Bank (ADB), European Bank for Reconstruction and Development (EBRD), and Inter-American Development Bank (IDB). It is important to recognize that GEF presence at the national level is felt only through its IAs and EAs.

These IAs and EAs have generally little understanding or even knowledge of the Convention and COP decisions that are supposed to guide the activities they undertake for the GEF. COP decisions have called upon the GEF to inform the IAs and EAs of this guidance. As these agencies undertake activities mainly using donor funds, they generally apply similar conditions to GEF-funded projects that they are called upon to implement, thereby acting contrary to the decisions adopted by the COP.

The Memorandum of Understanding between the GEF Council and the UNFCCC COP, adopted through decision 12/CP.2 in 1996 (paragraph 6), stipulates that the GEF include in its reports details of implementation of its projects by the IAs and EAs and for this purpose requests the GEF to inform the implementing/executing agencies of its requirements for disclosure of information. This has not been fully complied with. In fact, the terms of reference of the GEF Evaluation Unit, even now, do not include any requirement for information on how IAs and EAs implement GEF-financed projects.

As early as the interim period of the GEF as an operating entity of the financial mechanism of the Convention, problems have arisen on the handling of GEF-financed projects by implementing/executing agencies. In its Decision 2/CP.4 (1998), operative paragraph 4, therefore, the COP requested the 'GEF to ensure that its implementing/executing agencies are made aware of Convention provisions and decisions adopted by the COP in the performance of their GEF obligations and are encouraged, as a first priority, whenever possible, to use national experts/consultants in all aspects of project development and implementation'.

That these very same problems are still encountered by developing countries at the national level clearly demonstrates that there is a need for the GEF to set up a mechanism to ensure that decisions of the COP are taken into account, not only by the GEF itself, but in particular by its IAs and EAs, in order to operationalize the MOU and relevant COP decisions. This could be made part of its enabling activities, through capacity-building, and by requiring an evaluation as well of the performance of IAs and EAs in its monitoring functions. The GEF could likewise provide detailed guidelines harmonizing the implementation of GEF-funded projects by all implementing/executing agencies.

Another big difficulty is the representation of countries in the GEF Council. Many Annex I countries are represented by their finance or development assistance officials, who either do not know or do not take into account COP guidance when dealing with matters related to financing climate change projects. Developing countries' representatives, rotating in their constituencies, are often not much better informed and consider their projects in the same manner as ODA-funded projects.

In September 2005, unilateral policy decisions were taken by the GEF Council, in particular the Resource Allocation Framework (RAF), which pre-allocates resources to developing countries on the basis of donor requirements. The COP was not consulted in the adoption of this policy that is not even consistent with the provisions under the Convention on the provision of financial resources. In its initial implementation period, beginning in June 2006, the RAF is applicable only to the climate change and biodiversity windows of the GEF. Modalities for this implementation are still evolving, in particular since the fourth replenishment of the resources in the GEF is considered lower, in real terms, than the third replenishment. This has resulted in confusion among GEF Operational Focal Points on the status of their project proposals or on the modalities to be followed under the RAF. It must be recognized, however, that the GEF Secretariat is making the necessary efforts to address these problems.

At the level of the Convention, therefore, a '*dialogue des sourds*', or a dialogue of deaf people, often takes place as developing countries speak of their difficulties at national-level implementation, filtered through IAs and EAs, which developed country Parties cannot fully comprehend, largely due to these gaps.

Developing countries, as a result, have tried to set up other funds that at the outset were to be operated by entities other than the GEF. When they were first brought forward in the negotiations, in 2000, this was the case for the Special Climate Change Fund (SCCF) and the Least Developed Countries Fund (LDCF). In the end, however, developing countries were forced to accept that there is no viable choice for the operation of the financial mechanism for these funds other than the GEF. To assuage developing countries, projects under these funds are not to be subject to the RAF. Still, little financing has come through these funds, and such conditions as co-financing are imposed on the use of these funds. The decision on the SCCF has the dubious distinction of having taken almost four years to negotiate.

The best solution to these difficulties would be a transparent dialogue between developed and developing country Parties and concrete action taken to address their causes. A common understanding should be reached on the role of the financial mechanism of the Convention. This understanding should be shared with all implementing/executing agencies. An institutionalized mechanism should be put in place by the GEF to ensure that decisions of the COP are taken into account not only in project decisions by the GEF but likewise in project implementation by its implementing/executing agencies.

The financial resources needed to address climate change and its adverse impacts are great. These needs are urgent. Effective global cooperation requires that all countries consider all possibilities for financing under the Convention. Distorted practices through which, because of requirements for co-financing, GEF funds are to be accessed only if tied to other funding sources, such as loans, should be eliminated. Innovative financing schemes, including national or regional environmental funds, should be explored. Only through a frank, transparent, and open dialogue within the Convention could all these be accomplished, focused on achieving the objective of the Convention, consistent with COP decisions, and devoid of any need to put all resources for climate change under one entity alone.

The establishment of the Green Climate Fund (GCF) by the COP and its designation as an operating entity of the financial mechanism was an important development in strengthening the provision of financial resources, including for the transfer of technology and capacity-building under the Convention. Both the GCF and the GEF as operating entities of the financial mechanism serve the Paris Agreement. The GCF was able to implement its initial resource mobilization by 2014 and started to fund projects by COP 21 in Paris. Problems still abound in its functioning but are slowly being addressed. Developing country Parties under the Convention place their hopes on the GCF for financing their enhanced actions under the Paris Agreement of 2015.

16.7 TRANSFER OF TECHNOLOGY

Transfer of technology was already one of the most contentious issues under discussion during the UNCED preparatory meetings and remains so for the Convention. Reams of paper and endless hours of discussions have been spent on the subject, with few visible results. The language of Article 4.5 of the Convention reflects the difficulties related to the subject of technology transfer. It states that developed country Parties 'shall take all practicable steps to promote, facilitate and finance, as appropriate, the transfer of, or access to, environmentally sound technologies and know-how to other Parties, particularly developing country Parties, to enable them to implement the provisions of the Convention'. The translation of this language into decisions of the COP has become an art of its own.

Developed countries maintain that since technology is mainly in the hands of the private sector, governments that undertake the legally binding obligation under the Convention are not in a position to 'transfer' this technology. Market mechanisms, therefore, must be used to allow any transfer of technology. Developing countries, on the other hand, point out that, since governments have undertaken the commitments, they have the obligation to 'promote, facilitate and finance, as appropriate' this transfer. The UNFCCC or COP decisions are not necessary for market mechanisms to function. Developing countries also pointed to publicly held technologies that are, at least partly, government-funded and therefore owned, that could be transferred, but the notion met extreme reluctance from developed countries.

Perhaps the most important decision taken by the COP on technology transfer was at its first session in 1995, when it was agreed that a review of the implementation of commitments on transfer of technology shall be made at every COP session, as a separate agenda item under 'matters relating to commitments' (Decision 13/CP.1, paragraph 4 a). It ensured that technology transfer negotiations are not taken out of the agenda for any COP. Its importance became evident in the light of recent attempts to 'consolidate' decisions or 'retire' them as no longer useful for the Convention.

COP decisions cover the setting up of a consultative process for the identification of technologies, 'enabling environments' for access to technology, reports of the secretariat, adopting the technology transfer framework and listings of priorities, as well as numerous workshops at national, subregional, regional, and multilateral levels.

After a series of difficult negotiations, the Expert Group on Technology Transfer (EGTT) was set up through Decision 4/CP.7 in 2001. The EGTT, after five years of work, published its findings and concluded that, while the EGTT has promoted an 'understanding of transfer of technology at a conceptual level', there is now a need to move to a 'more practical and results-oriented level by providing actions on specific sectors and programmes' (UNFCCC Secretariat, 2007a).

A companion brochure (UNFCCC Secretariat 2007b) on the results of workshops on '[i]nnovative options for financing the development and transfer of technologies' also provided only 'theoretical considerations' that still 'need to be matched by action on the ground'.

Frustrated by years of inaction, and the lack of effective transfer of technology, the G77 and China tabled a decision at the COP 12 in 2006, calling for the establishment of a Technology Development and Transfer Board, and a Multilateral Technology Acquisition Fund, to be handled by another entity operating the financial mechanism of the Convention. The ideas were new, innovative, and forward-looking – so much so that it was almost a foregone conclusion that no decision would be taken at that COP, and indeed the discussions were postponed for the 2007 subsidiary bodies' meetings and the COP session later that year.

Innovative as the ideas are, they remain consistent with the Convention provisions and are in fact also reflected in Chapter 34 of Agenda 21, adopted at the UNCED in 2002. They become particularly important in the light of the IPCC Fourth Assessment Report, which underlines the essential role of technology both for mitigation and adaptation to climate change. These ideas, given the chance, could represent a breakthrough in the bogged-down negotiations on technology transfer in the Convention.

Another, perhaps more feasible way forward is something that is also found in Agenda 21, and that is cooperative development of technology. Technology developed in cooperation between developed and developing countries would have a double benefit of addressing the problem of ownership as well as ensuring the adaptability of the technology thus developed to the user's conditions. Countless technology transfer workshops have demonstrated the need for technology to be adapted to local conditions for them to be effective. What better way to ensure adaptability of technology than to develop it in accordance with local conditions?

The Convention also refers to the 'development and enhancement of endogenous capacities and technologies of developing country Parties'. This would be particularly useful for adaptation technologies, since these technologies and capacities are available in local communities. Moreover, as mentioned earlier, mitigation and adaptation technologies can be mutually supportive.

Finally, after almost two decades of negotiations on this issue, a decision was adopted at COP 21 in Paris in 2015 (Decision13/CP.21) on the Linkages between the Technology Mechanism and the Financial Mechanism of the Convention, which 'invites the Board of the Green Climate Fund, in line with paragraph 38 of the Governing Instrument of the Green Climate Fund, to consider ways to provide support, pursuant to the modalities of the Green Climate Fund, for facilitating access to environmentally-sound technologies in developing country Parties, and for undertaking collaborative research and development for enabling developing country Parties to enhance their mitigation and adaptation action' (paragraph 10).

The very same language was also adopted in Decision 7/CP.21, paragraph 22, on the guidance provided by the COP to the GCF.

Once again, political will is necessary for the effective implementation of commitments for *facilitating access to and financing transfer of technology to developing country Parties*.

16.8 CAPACITY-BUILDING

Developing countries took the first step in consolidating capacity-building activities for the implementation of the Convention by tabling a decision that was adopted in 1999 (Decision 10/CP.5). Faced with a multitude of capacity-building activities undertaken by various institutions serving the needs of the institutions or of donor countries, developing countries decided to provide guidelines for these activities and to ensure that these effectively serve their interests in the Convention. The decision was accompanied by a listing of capacity-building needs emanating from the developing countries themselves.

The decision ensured that these activities would be driven by the needs of the developing countries, that these would be conducted with the use of local expertise and assisted by institutions and national centres of excellence. It also required that the national focal points or national authorities in charge of climate change would be part of any capacity-building activity conducted in the country itself.

Subsequent decisions on capacity-building built upon this initial framework, including decisions for the Kyoto Protocol. Developing countries are determined to drive the process of building their own capacities, a process that serves their own needs, while making use of locally available resources whenever possible. Here, too, the COP needs to move from holding workshops into concrete action, recognizing that capacity-building is a continuing process.

A separate article on capacity-building, Article 11, is found in the Paris Agreement of 2015, in the face of the insistence of developing country Parties that capacity-building is essential for them to be able to enhance both mitigation and adaptation actions required by the agreement. A Paris Committee on Capacity-Building was also established at COP 21. However, what is conspicuously lacking is the support to be provided to capacity-building, other than a weak reference to it in Article 11.3 of the Paris Agreement, which states that '*developed country Parties should enhance support for capacity-building actions in developing country Parties*'.

Article 11.5 of the Paris Agreement also provides that '*capacity-building activities shall be enhanced through appropriate institutional arrangements to support the implementation of this Agreement*'.

What is necessary is to operationalize the provision in the Governing Instrument of the Green Climate Fund that 'the Board shall also ensure adequate resources for capacity-building and technology development and transfer' (paragraph 38).

16.9 DEVELOPING COUNTRIES AND THE KYOTO PROTOCOL

Contrary to what is generally believed, developing countries have obligations under the Kyoto Protocol. These are contained in Articles 10, 11, and in particular in Article 12 of the Protocol.

The Berlin Mandate, the basis for the negotiations of the Kyoto Protocol, was adopted at the first COP session in 1995. Parties of the Convention, in conducting the first review of the commitments of developed countries under the Convention, found them to be inadequate and thus decided to start the process leading to the adoption of the Kyoto Protocol in 1997.

The Kyoto Protocol, as mandated, therefore implements those articles of the Convention that relate exclusively to developed countries' commitments. Its complete title establishes this relation: The Kyoto Protocol to the United Nations Framework Convention on Climate Change. The guiding principle of the Protocol is the same as that of the Convention: the principle of common but differentiated responsibilities.

The Berlin Mandate specifies that the process 'will not introduce any new commitments for Parties not included in Annex I, but reaffirm existing commitments in Article 4.1 and continue to advance the implementation of these commitments to achieve sustainable development'. Article 10 of the Protocol was negotiated to conform to this mandated provision.

Each sub-paragraph of Article 10 of the Protocol refers to specific sub-articles in Article 4.1 of the Convention that could contribute to mitigation activities. Article 11 refers to the financing of these activities through the GEF, as an operating entity of the financial mechanism of the Convention. There is no financial mechanism under the Protocol, as it refers to developed countries' commitments. So far, Articles 10 and 11 have remained largely forgotten. It is important to note, however, that the implementation of Article 10 of the Protocol would enhance the developing countries' capacities to undertake mitigation activities. It would also allow this information to be included in their national communications (Article 10, paragraphs b (ii) and f). Article 12 defines the clean development mechanism (CDM) of the Protocol. It was originally conceived as a compliance fund and was tabled by the G77 and China as the Clean Development Fund. In the course of the negotiations, in recognition of political realities, it was turned into a mechanism '*to assist Parties not included in Annex I in achieving sustainable development and in contributing to the ultimate objective of the Convention, and to assist Annex I Parties in achieving compliance with their quantified emission limitation and reduction commitments*'.

Certified emission reduction units accruing from CDM project activities may be used by Annex I Parties to contribute to compliance with part of their targets. The long negotiations that ensued on the use of the CDM established the parameters that would ensure that the CDM did not effectively establish 'emission rights' for Annex I countries. These safeguards should ensure that the CDM would generate environmental benefits and not merely allow Annex I countries to transfer their mitigation obligations to non-Annex I countries.

One must recognize that every CDM project activity in effect mitigates emissions of developing countries, at the same time that the same number of reduction units can be added to the assigned amounts of emissions of Annex I countries, allowing the latter a certain 'flexibility' in achieving their targets.

Recognizing that developing countries have different mitigation capabilities and that these countries are, in many cases, those that are particularly vulnerable to the adverse effects of climate change, the decision also includes a provision ensuring *'that a share of the proceeds from certified project activities is used to … assist developing countries Parties that are particularly vulnerable to the adverse effects of climate change to meet the costs of adaptation'* (Article 12.8). An Adaptation Fund was subsequently established by the COP to render this article operational.

The Adaptation Fund is the way through which developing countries share the benefits to be derived from CDM projects with other developing countries that are least capable of mitigation, but which are the most vulnerable to the adverse effects of climate change. The share of the proceeds from CDM projects is not a tax on the projects, which would mean an additional cost to the projects. Rather, this share is taken from the monetized CERs, part of which is used as well to cover administrative expenses.

Developing countries, therefore, are the major contributors to the Adaptation Fund. The Fund would be open to voluntary contributions from Annex I Parties, but it must be ensured that this would not again be one of those funds that would be subject to donor conditionalities.

It is in this light that developing countries negotiated the decision on the management of the Adaptation Fund. Given their previous experience with funding under the Convention, and the provisions of Article 12, developing countries wanted to ensure that the Adaptation Fund would be subject to the Parties' authority, and not merely 'guidance' alone, which is subject to interpretation. Developing countries also ensured that they would have a majority in the management of the Fund and that projects to be funded were truly country-driven. In particular, projects under this Fund should go to concrete adaptation projects and not merely be confined to vulnerability assessments and capacity-building activities for adaptation.

Much remains to be done, however, to operationalize the Fund and to choose an entity to manage the Fund that would meet all the requirements of the decision. In order to ensure the

generation of sufficient funds, and predictability of funding, ways must be found to control the price of Certified Emission Reduction Units (CERs). There must be agreement on the monetization of CERs, on the use of the funds, and what consists of 'concrete adaptation projects'. Agreement should also be reached on the policies, programme priorities, and eligibility criteria for the use of the resources to be generated under the Fund.

These are among those issues to be resolved among developing countries themselves. It should be done on the same basis of sharing as that which guided the inclusion of Article 12.8 in the Protocol. There is need for urgent action, however, and an early operationalization of the Fund.

Since this chapter was first written, and in 2016, as Parties prepare for the 22nd session of the Conference of the Parties, the Adaptation Fund under the Kyoto Protocol has been fully operationalized and has been highly successful in its operations, especially in the implementation of its direct access modality. The main problem facing the Adaptation Fund is the drastic reduction of resources of its main financing channel, the monetization of CERs, because of the plunge in the prices in the carbon market following the financial crisis, mainly in developed countries. Moreover, there remains the uncertain future of the Kyoto Protocol, whose second commitment period, adopted through amendments at the 18th session of the Conference of the Parties in Doha, Qatar, in 2012, has not yet entered into force.[4]

Given this situation, decision 1/CP.21 provided that the Adaptation Fund may serve the Paris Agreement and has laid out the process through which this could be done. The developing countries have been insisting on keeping the integrity of the Adaptation Fund, in the light of the increasing need for adaptation due to the increase in number and intensity of extreme weather events.

16.10 THE BALI ROAD MAP

UNFCCC negotiations have gained unprecedented international prominence since 2007, at the 13th Conference of the Parties in Bali, Indonesia. The Intergovernmental Panel on Climate Change (IPCC) and former US Vice-President Al Gore were both awarded the Nobel Peace Prize for their work on bringing climate change to the forefront of public recognition of the challenge of climate change. The IPCC Fourth Assessment Report (AR4) acknowledged that there is unequivocal evidence of

---

[4] Editor's note: As of 28 October 2020, 147 Parties have deposited their instrument of acceptance of the Doha Amendment. A total of 144 instruments of acceptance are required for the entry into force of the amendment. Therefore the threshold for entry into force of the Doha Amendment has been met. Please see https://unfccc.int/process/the-kyoto-protocol/the-doha-amendment.

human interference in climate, causing rapid and extensive changes affecting all aspects of life in this planet. Al Gore, through a hugely acclaimed documentary, raised widespread public awareness of the global challenge of climate change. Expectations were raised that assertive global action would at last be taken at the only legal international arena for addressing climate change, the UNFCCC and its Kyoto Protocol.

The Bali Road Map put on track two negotiating processes. The first, the ad hoc working group on further commitment for Annex I Parties to the Kyoto Protocol (AWG-KP), started two years earlier in 2005, to pursue the legal mandate to start negotiations on subsequent commitment periods for quantified emission limitation and reduction commitments under the Kyoto Protocol, upon the end of the first commitment period in 2012. The process meandered fruitlessly for two years in the face of the reluctance of developed countries to put on the table specific numbers for the second commitment period, claiming the need to gain experience and more knowledge from the first commitment period beginning in 2008. The overriding but unspoken reason was the flat refusal of the United States to ratify the Kyoto Protocol, putting the developed countries that are Parties to the Protocol at a seemingly grave economic disadvantage.

The second, the Bali Action Plan (BAP), launched a process through an ad hoc working group for long-term cooperative action (AWG-LCA) for the 'full, effective and sustained implementation of the Convention'. The BAP contained only one new element, but a crucial one for developing countries, and that is a paragraph that linked mitigation actions of developing countries to the effort of the developed countries to undertake a second commitment period. It also contained a reference to 'comparability of efforts' for developed countries that are Parties to the KP and the only one that is not, the United States.

Through two years of negotiations, the developing countries sought to keep a firewall between the two tracks, whereas the developed countries, in particular the United States, saw the opportunity of finally reaching their objective since the negotiations for the Convention in 1991, that of obliging developing countries to undertake mitigation actions and sharing what was seen to be an increasingly economically difficult burden of *limiting* greenhouse gas emissions, in particular that of fossil fuels. When the new administration took over the United States in 2008, expectations were high that they would engage actively in the global effort to address climate change. They did, only to proclaim that they would never ratify the KP, that they would only undertake voluntary mitigation action, and that now was the time for the developing countries, beginning with the more economically advanced among them, to take on deep mitigation actions. The efforts of the United States, immediately joined by the developed countries, were focused on making this happen in Copenhagen the next year.

Expectations reached stratospheric heights for Copenhagen in 2009, stimulated by a series of worldwide high-profile events, through the United Nations, through all international economic conferences, and through 'vulnerable countries' 'circles of commitment', all involving developing countries. At the negotiating tables, the AWG-KP continued to mark time, at one point forcing the African Group to stage a walk-out in frustration to force developed countries to engage productively in the negotiations. What were they waiting for? Despite repeated denials by the Danish Presidency, a separate document, negotiated entirely by a small group of countries, was produced at a dramatic final plenary. The entirely inclusive, non-transparent, undemocratic, and closed process that produced the Copenhagen Accord was rejected by the COP, and the document was 'taken note of', and denied any legal standing in the negotiations. It was then claimed that the multilateral process failed, while in fact Copenhagen failed precisely because of the travesty of the intergovernmental process.

16.11 THE CANCUN AGREEMENTS

The road to Cancun in 2010 was marked by intense efforts by developed countries, led by the United States, to get developing countries to endorse, support, or associate with the Copenhagen Accord. At the negotiating table, the developed countries inserted language verbatim from the Accord, and a climate change fund was proposed by the United States, with elements taken entirely from the Copenhagen Accord. In the course of the year, negotiations were marked by the consistent efforts of developed countries to get the developing countries to agree to essential elements of the Copenhagen Accord, all of which fundamentally altered the principles of the Convention, in particular the principles of equity and common but differentiated responsibilities.

The Cancun Agreements, as it was named by the Presidency, Mexico, marked a substantive shift of the balance of the common but differentiated responsibilities in the Convention, in effect placing new obligations on developing countries without any assurance of the implementation of commitments of developed countries related to financing, technology, and capacity-building. The decision dismantled the key to the balance of common but differentiated responsibilities, that of Article 4.7 of the Convention.

The final text of the Cancun Agreements reflects mainly the options of developed countries in the negotiations and put aside options of developing countries. Much of the text distorts or is inconsistent with the principles and provisions of the Convention. Finally, the Cancun Agreements also paved the way to the merger of the two tracks, those of the AWG-LCA and the AWG-KP, called for by developed countries to be contained in a new, legally binding agreement.

New obligations were placed on developing countries on all fronts, but in particular on mitigation, with financing contingent upon pledges of mitigation actions and for these actions to be subject to either measurement, verification, and reporting if provided with support, or to international consultation and analysis, if financed through domestic sources. Such obligations for reporting and verification in effect render a mitigation action into a mitigation commitment.

An Adaptation Framework was adopted, consisting of prescriptions for adaptation action at national levels, without any clear links to the financial mechanism. An Adaptation Committee, proposed by developing countries, would still have to be further defined in terms of its composition, modalities, and procedures.

The same goes for a Technology Mechanism, consisting of a Technology Executive Committee (TEC) that replaced the Expert Group on Technology Transfer, and a still-to-be-defined Climate Technology Centre and Network (CTCN). Here again, the decision only specified 'potential links' between the Technology Mechanism and the financial mechanism. Moreover, the Technology Executive Committee's decisions would be mainly recommendatory in nature. Further work will focus on the CTCN, to be established outside of the Convention, with functions mainly related to facilitating transfers through partnerships and exchange of information. Neither one addresses the need for concrete action in technology development and transfer, including through financing, that would allow developing countries to undertake mitigation and adaptation actions.

The Green Climate Fund was also established at Cancun, mainly along the lines of the US proposal as contained in the Copenhagen Accord, without many of the elements of the G77 and China proposal made two years earlier. A Transitional Committee to design the new fund was set up, to make recommendations to render the Fund operational to the 17th session of the COP to be held in Durban, South Africa, at the end of 2011. The work of the Transitional Committee would be critical to shape a fund that would address all the problems with financing faced by the developing countries as described in this chapter. But here also, the developed countries, led by the United States, were intent on legitimizing the failed delivery systems of financing as in the past, through the usual financing channels, with additional conditions related to mitigation actions by developing countries. The biggest issues to be addressed remain those of governance and predictable sources of financing.

The past few years that took the Convention from Bali to Cancun have witnessed catastrophic climate-related events that wrought untold damage and loss of lives, settlements, and food crops in developing countries, but also in developed countries. Many developing countries are taking mitigation and adaptation

actions, as a matter of necessity and survival, using their own resources. Despite all these difficulties, developing countries should continue to engage at the international level. Climate change is a global problem that needs global solutions. All countries must face their responsibilities, as the Convention says, 'for the benefit of present and future generations'.

16.12 THE DURBAN PLATFORM

Still unsatisfied with the Cancun Agreements, developed country Parties, in particular the Umbrella Group of countries led by the United States, pressed for the adoption of the Durban Platform in 2011.

The process to adopt this decision was highly innovative in many ways and consisted of deviations from normal multilateral, intergovernmental processes. A supposedly transparent consultation process, the 'indaba', adopted from a South African practice, actually left many of the Parties out of a limited table of consultations. No negotiations took place, but only 'consultations', something that would be replicated in Paris in 2015.

The final decision on the Durban Platform was adopted in a nearly empty plenary hall, two days after the official closure of the session. It was the first time that a document was adopted that was not seen by the plenary, no text having been made available to them. A 'huddle' took place among a few countries with onlookers craning their necks to see and to hear what was going on in order to determine what outcome would be decided as a result of the Durban Platform process. The text agreed was so unclear that it remained wide open to interpretation all throughout the process. Were we looking at a legal outcome, or an outcome with legal effect, whatever that meant, and what would be the meaning of all these?

A decision was then gavelled through, and many were unsure of what it was that was decided. Many heads of delegations, mainly of developing countries, knew of what happened only later when they had returned to their countries. The official text came out even later. Were we not dealing with such a grave and serious global problem, it would have been a perfect scenario for a farcical comedy.

Inevitably, the next sessions were devoted to understanding what was agreed. What seemed clear was that the Bali Road Map and the work of the AWG-KP and AWG-LCA would have to be agreed before the ad hoc working group on the Durban Platform (ADP) could start working. Many developing country Parties thought that the 'deal' was that we adopt the amendments to the Kyoto Protocol and have an agreed outcome in the AWG-LCA before we could tackle work on the ADP.

One very important decision was the launching of the Green Climate Fund, again under the caveat that the Governing Instrument, which met with objections in the final plenary, was not to be opened in Durban. A suggestion of the Presidency to conduct 'consultations' on it was strenuously objected to by the G77, and intensive negotiations then took place which sought to remedy many of the gaps in the Governing Instrument. In particular, the main contention was on whether the GCF was under the Convention (the position of developing country Parties) or was an independent fund that would be much like all the other existing multilateral financing institutions. What did it really mean for the GCF to be designated as an operating entity of the financial mechanism of the Convention? These problems still underlie much of what is going on in the Board of the GCF currently, five years after it was launched, but are slowly being resolved as developing countries strengthen their presence on the board.

In 2012, in Doha, Qatar, the amendments to the Kyoto Protocol were adopted at a tense, final plenary that drew out contention among the developed country Parties of the Kyoto Protocol. Even before this, Japan, which lent the name of one of its most historic cities to the Protocol, announced that they would not honour any agreement reached in Doha. Shortly thereafter, Canada withdrew from the KP, and other members of the Umbrella Group declared that they were not ready to go into a second commitment period.

In 2016, the KP amendments still have not entered into force. Therefore, one of the main elements of the 'deal' to undertake the Durban process remains unfulfilled.

16.13 THE DURBAN PLATFORM PROCESS AND THE PARIS AGREEMENT

Developing countries continued to call for an 'open, transparent and inclusive' process all throughout the negotiations under the Durban Platform. To no avail. Trust and confidence in the process had been so eroded that, despite all attempts, and up to the very end, suspicions were rife on the manipulation of the process by the co-chairs of the ADP.

The situation was such that there was no common understanding among Parties as to what would be the process followed in Paris by the French Presidency of COP 21, nor the nature of the outcome in Paris.

A strong new negotiating group of developing countries within the G77, the 'Like-Minded Developing Countries' (LMDC), emerged towards the end of the Bali Action Plan process. It proved to be instrumental in strengthening the positions of developing countries in the UNFCCC. Members of the LMDC became subject to pressure from developed country Parties to the very end, but the group remained cohesive.

The year 2015 also revealed the extent and benefits of the unity of developing countries. A strong G77 chairmanship was crucial to the success of Paris for developing countries, and

South Africa lived up to the challenge. The full strength of the LMDC within the G77 was felt throughout the year and, together with a cohesive African Group, contributed to the unity of the Group.

The G77 and China remained united and strongly defended their positions on adaptation, loss and damage, and all means of implementation, in particular on finance, as well as on all elements of the mitigation and transparency sections.

A series of 'consultations' replaced negotiations during the Paris COP. No real negotiations took place in Paris on what was to become the Paris Agreement. The only negotiations took place under the COP and the CMP. When the draft text was finally taken over by the Presidency, they held limited sessions of 'indabas', which amounted to no more than restatements of positions from groups.

Groupings arose that sought to divide developing countries, but it was too late in the process. The developing countries held on, in particular the LMDC. A last-minute objection from the United States on the use of the word 'shall', considered legally binding, was admitted without question as a 'technical glitch' by a subservient secretariat.

The Paris Agreement was again adopted by acclamation, as in Cancun. However, this time, the raised flag of Nicaragua to object to the Agreement was completely ignored. Media, ever favourable to developed countries, hailed a success. Responsible voices from developed and developing countries warned that this would not be enough to save the planet, but were not heard.

16.14 THE PARIS AGREEMENT

The Paris Agreement (United Nations, 2015) is designed to enable a number of developed country Parties, in particular the United States, to adopt it without the necessity of going through parliamentary or congressional ratification processes. It, therefore, does not go beyond existing obligations for developed country Parties and especially does not imply any new financial obligations for them.

The Agreement, however, gives rise to new obligations for developing country Parties on all climate actions, in particular on limitation of emissions. Adaptation, loss and damage associated with adverse effects of climate change, and capacity-building are given special attention at the insistence of developing countries, but all links of these activities to the financial mechanism are practically non-existent under the Paris Agreement. These have to be strengthened in the period leading to the entry into force of the Agreement, and negotiations are continuing on these issues.

Of particular importance for finance, technology, and adaptation is the delinking of all climate change actions in the Agreement from Articles 4.3, 4.4, and 4.5 of the Convention, which refer in particular to obligations of 'developed country Parties and other developed Parties included in Annex II'. The Agreement no longer refers to the Annexes of the Convention, based on a scientific assessment of responsibilities for historical emissions, but instead only refers to 'developing country Parties' and 'developed country Parties', for which there is no internationally agreed definition. This leaves wide open the determination as to which Parties are developing or developed to their 'national circumstances' and thus also in relation to the subsequent differentiated obligations.

Obligations of developed country Parties and Annex II Parties were watered down from their direct provision to mobilization, and included references to resources from 'other Parties', albeit on a voluntary basis. It remains unclear how financial resources would be scaled up to meet the needs of developing country Parties for the enhancement of their climate actions in order to attain the purpose of the Agreement.

A bottom-up, voluntary, 'nationally-determined' approach of 'contributions' by each Party to the Convention characterizes the Paris Agreement. The term 'intended nationally-determined contributions' (INDCs) was agreed in a 'huddle' to capture the essence of common but differentiated responsibilities that many developed country Parties to the Convention preferred to do away with under the Agreement. As such, there is no common understanding on the content and scope of these INDCs. Because these are nationally determined, each Party could decide on the nature of their INDCs. Under the Agreement, these intended contributions are no longer 'intended' and become commitments. Under a transparency framework still to be determined, these commitments are then reviewed. For developing countries, therefore, these NDCs in effect constitute new obligations.

At the same time, there remains no clarity as to the predictability, accessibility, and scaling-up of financial resources to be provided to developing country Parties by developed country Parties, no reference to facilitated access to technology, much less the financing technology transfer or the financing channels for adaptation financing, and it becomes a mere talk shop for capacity-building. While there is Article 8 in the Agreement, which defines cooperation on loss and damage associated with adverse effects due to climate change, it was specified in the decision to give effect to the agreement that this Article 'does not involve or provide a basis for liability and compensation'.

Further action is necessary in the period leading up to the entry into force of the Agreement to strengthen provisions for predictable, accessible, and scaled-up financial resources that would allow enhanced climate actions of developing countries. A process must be put in place to translate INDCs into quantified needs for financial resources and technology, as well as capacity-building. This must then become the basis for any

identification of goals for scaled-up resources. A strong country-driven approach in financing would be necessary, based on needs identified by developing countries themselves so as to allow them to enhance their actions.

The Paris Agreement was built on a mountain of unfulfilled obligations. At this time, the pledges to the Agreement still would not be enough to achieve the purpose of the Agreement. Developing countries alone cannot bridge the huge gigatonne gap that exists for us to hold 'the increase in the global average temperature to well below 2°C above pre-industrial levels and pursuing efforts to limit the temperature increase to 1.5°C above pre-industrial levels'. It must likewise be recognized that a 'global average temperature' translates to much more when taken at regional levels, in particular in developing country regions.

At the very least, the Doha amendments to the Kyoto Protocol must enter into force. Studies have shown that developing countries are pledging to do more than their 'fair share' of limitation of emissions, given their small or negligible contribution to the problem of climate change. At the same time, even the strictest limitations of emissions right now would still mean that extreme weather events and adverse effects of climate change would continue to increase. Adaptation remains absolutely crucial. There is no meaningful mitigation action unless there is meaningful adaptation action.

Most of all, a shift to renewable sources of energy must be accompanied by significant changes in consumption patterns, in particular in the developed world. We must not confine ourselves to looking for fixes for our addiction, but must find a cure for the addiction itself.

16.15 CONCLUSION

Developing countries are fully concerned by climate change and, as demonstrated in this chapter, are actively taking the necessary measures to address climate change and its adverse effects, in pursuit of sustainable development.

As stated in the first principle of the Convention, all Parties 'should protect the climate system for the benefit of present and future generations of humankind, on the basis of equity and in accordance with their common but differentiated responsibilities and respective capabilities'.

The key to the balance of commitments under the Convention is best expressed in Article 4.7 of the Convention that guides all developing countries' positions:

The extent to which developing country Parties will effectively implement their commitments under the Convention will depend on the effective implementation by developed country Parties of their commitments ... related to financial resources and transfer of technology and will take fully into account that economic and social *development and poverty eradication are the first and overriding priorities of the developing country Parties.*

The rest is political will.

Given the rapid evolution of climate change and its adverse impacts, the private sector has taken the lead in forcing governments to take the necessary measures to implement this obligation. Where the government has instituted changes, the private sector has generally complied. Where a regulatory framework is deemed necessary, the private sector has encouraged governments to act. What this implies is that political will is essential in addressing climate change and its adverse effects. There remains a huge gap between what is grandiosely announced as intentions in high-level summit conferences and what is happening at negotiating levels in the Convention. Until this announced political will is translated into concrete action in the UNFCCC, there can be no meaningful global cooperation to address climate change and its adverse effects.

AN UPDATE

Much has changed since this chapter was first written, not the least of which is the increasing number of extreme weather events worldwide, along with the deepening realization among all countries and peoples of the world that action should be taken NOW and that these actions must be taken by peoples themselves. Foremost among these actions are changes in consumption patterns, the most difficult to do but the most effective response to climate change. Food production and food consumption in particular have gained ground globally, in ways in which we produce and consume energy, and the shift of attention from economic gains to environmental and social benefits of responding to climate change. For a very long time, it was thought that poverty causes environmental degradation, but now we know that it is wealth, and the pursuit of more wealth that, from the beginning, has caused climate change.

ACKNOWLEDGEMENTS

I wish to acknowledge my great debt of gratitude to the late Professor Zhong Shukong of China, prime mover in the Group of 77 and one of the architects of the UNFCCC and its Kyoto Protocol, for his friendship and for providing invaluable guidance throughout almost a decade of climate change negotiations.

I also wish to express my gratitude to all friends and colleagues, members of the Group of 77, too numerous to mention individually, for teaching me how to listen and to understand their concerns, as well as contributing their insights, for almost 17 years in the UNFCCC. Much of what I have written is taken from a number of position papers, statements, and draft decisions that I have authored in collaboration with members of the Group, since the Philippines chaired the Group of 77 in 1995.

My gratitude also goes to Dr Pak Sum Low for his encouragement and kind persistence, without which I would not have had the courage to put down in one chapter the essence of all that has been guiding me through these years of negotiations. I wish to acknowledge the valuable comments of the reviewers of this chapter, in particular Ian Fry and Robert Reinstein, for assisting me in making the Convention better understood outside of the negotiating process.

REFERENCES

Mwandosya, M. J. (1996) *Survival Emissions: A Perspective from the South on Global Climate Change Negotiations.* DUP, Ltd., Centre for Energy, Environment, Science, and Technology (Dar es Salaam), Tanzania.

UNFCCC Secretariat (2007a) EGTT: Five years of work. Brochure published on 25 May by the UNFCCC Secretariat, Bonn, Germany. https://unfccc.int/resource/docs/publications/egtt_eng.pdf

(2007b) Innovative options for financing the development and transfer of technologies. Brochure published on 25 May by the UNFCCC Secretariat, Bonn, Germany. https://unfccc.int/resource/docs/publications/innovation_eng.pdf

United Nations (1992) United Nations Framework Convention on Climate Change. http://unfccc.int/resource/docs/convkp/conveng.pdf

(1998) Kyoto Protocol to the United Nations Framework Convention on Climate Change. http://unfccc.int/resource/docs/convkp/kpeng.pdf

(2015) Paris Agreement. http://unfccc.int/files/essential_background/convention/application/pdf/english_paris_agreement.pdf

PART II

Sustainable Development: Challenges and Opportunities

17 Scientific responses in an era of global change

MOSTAFA KAMAL TOLBA[1]

International Centre for Environment and Development, Cairo, Egypt

'Science should be on tap, not on top': Winston Churchill

Editor's note: This chapter is based on the Chairman's Address at the Eminent Scientists Symposium, held on 24–25 March 2005 in Seoul, Republic of Korea. It has never been published before. The keywords and the sub-headings are added by the editor.

Keywords

Global change; globalization; terrorism; Western model; post-normal science; scientific research ethics; ecosystem assessment; environment; sustainable development; eco-efficiency; precautionary principle; scientific research; indicators; Millennium Ecosystem Assessment; ecosystem change; ecosystem services

17.1 INTRODUCTION

The phenomenon of globalization has been spurred by geopolitical upheavals, including the collapse of the Soviet Union, the obvious presence on the global stage of a single superpower, the appearance of strong economic groupings, and the current activities against what is termed *terrorism*, as well as technical progress, particularly in the field of information and communication technologies and genetic engineering. Spurred by all this, the phenomenon of globalization has accelerated with the free movement of capital and goods, the general adoption of the Western model, the decreased power of governments in relation to that of multinational corporations and even of non-government organizations (NGOs). The World Trade Organization (WTO) is now taking decisions affecting the global environment and that of individual countries, sometimes even ignoring existing multilateral environmental agreements. There are also rising social and economic expectations and changing consumer preferences everywhere. The paradigm of sustainable development, with its social, economic, and environmental components, has been formally adopted worldwide. It is generally agreed that, despite the vagueness of the concept, sustainable management and use of natural resources and sustainable patterns of production and consumption are the only ways to meet the needs of present and future generations. A central concept in this respect is eco-efficiency, which aims to make increases in production of goods and services use proportionally less natural resources and generate less environmental damage. To strive towards this goal implies the integration of environmental and economic decision-making and the inclusion of an environmental dimension in all sectoral policies (agriculture, industry, energy, transport, tourism, and the like).

17.2 POST-NORMAL SCIENCE AND THE PRECAUTIONARY PRINCIPLE

In the past, scientific responses dealt mainly with correcting the impacts of development activities on human health and on the environment. Then came action on pressures, such as emission reductions of air and water pollutants. In future, the emphasis should be put on action at the driving force level. This can be done either by R&D that would lead to modifying the processes and products that provide a certain service or to managing demand for this same service, or more likely both. Scientific research directed towards policies should aim at optimizing the responses, which should not only identify the issues, but also contribute to determining the most effective options to deal with them. Once a policy is implemented, its effectiveness should be checked. And this also requires research.

Another consideration governing scientific responses in the current era is that of complexity and uncertainty. Major issues relating to natural systems (such as climate) are complex in themselves and fraught with uncertainty. This is compounded by the need for modifications of human behaviour in order to implement solutions. All this requires new ways to achieve effective interaction between scientists, whether they be in the natural or social sciences, and all other stakeholders, hence the development of post-normal science, that is, science which takes account of the uncertainty of quantitative data and the biases of scientists themselves. Another point that needs to be

[1] Former Executive Director of United Nations Environment Programme (UNEP) (1975–1992). Dr Tolba passed away in March 2016.

stressed is that the implementation of the precautionary principle, which is now widely accepted, should not be opposed to science-based regulation, but the two should be complementary. This is all the more important since scientific risk analysis is unavoidably and inextricably intertwined with subjective framing assumptions, values, and trade-offs.

17.3 INDICATORS

Policy-related research is under strong pressure to provide 'magic numbers' (as few as possible) to facilitate the tasks of political and administrative decision makers, hence the current high popularity of indicators. While these can undoubtedly be useful tools, much care must be exercised in selecting them and in clarifying their limits. Indicators are useless if the data on which they are based are lacking or unreliable, hence the need for continuing time series of good quality data. Such data concern environmental, as well as economic and social parameters.

It is now broadly recognized that it is in a holistic, integrated manner that global environmental issues must be tackled, taking account of linkages between these issues, including climate change, loss of biodiversity, stratospheric ozone depletion, freshwater degradation, land degradation and desertification, deforestation and unsustainable use of forests, marine environment, and persistent organic pollutants. Not only that but also between these environmental issues and basic human needs: food, shelter, health, and clean water.

Against this background, science should of course continue to concentrate on basic research into the functioning of the life support systems of the planet, and how these are affected by human activities. It should also detect and tackle emerging issues.

17.4 LARGE SCIENTIFIC RESEARCH PROGRAMMES

Early on, scientists foresaw several of the large-scale environmental issues that have subsequently developed, such as acidification, stratospheric ozone depletion, and the impact on the climate of the release of carbon dioxide into the atmosphere from coal combustion. But these warnings went initially unheeded. In the late 1960s, the international scientific community as a whole, represented, inter alia, by the International Council for Scientific Unions (ICSU) and its Scientific Committee on Problems of the Environment (SCOPE), became deeply concerned with the new environmental threats. SCOPE identified and assessed the main environmental problems of the time and made recommendations, which provided an important input to the 1972 United Nations Conference on the Human Environment. By the end of that decade of the seventies, international scientific bodies planned and coordinated several large research programmes, such as WMO's Global Atmospheric Research Programme and World Climate Research Programme, UNESCO's Man and Biosphere, and ICSU's International Geosphere-Biosphere Programme, and others. These programmes were meant to acquire additional knowledge necessary to respond effectively to global environmental threats. The programmes provided a framework for defining and funding research priorities at the national, supranational, and international levels. Assessments of research findings paved the way for signing various international conventions (e.g. the Vienna Convention for the Protection of the Ozone Layer (1985), the United Nations Framework Convention on Climate Change (1992), the Convention on Biological Diversity (1992), and the United Nations Convention to Combat Desertification (1994)). It was soon realized that human factors were all important if successful solutions were to be found and implemented, hence the rise of research programmes like the International Human Dimension Programme.

17.5 THE MILLENNIUM ECOSYSTEM ASSESSMENT

Science also played a most important role in providing the basis for the development of technologies aimed at monitoring the environment and at curing environmental damage, or better yet, at preventing it through better industrial processes and cleaner production. Results of monitoring effects were assessed by various quarters. One of the latest significant efforts in this respect is the Millennium Ecosystem Assessment launched in 2001. Its results will be made public in a number of press conferences around the world. Its objective was to assess the consequences of ecosystem change for human well-being and to establish the scientific basis for actions needed to enhance the conservation and sustainable use of ecosystems and their contribution to human well-being.

There are four main findings of this assessment:

First. Over the past 50 years, humans have changed ecosystems more rapidly and extensively than in any comparable period of time in human history, largely to meet rapidly growing demands for food, freshwater, timber, fibre, and fuel. This has resulted in a largely irreversible loss in the diversity of life on Earth.

Second. The changes that have been made to ecosystems have contributed to substantial net gains in human well-being and economic development, but these gains have been achieved at growing costs in the form of degradation of many ecosystem services, and exacerbation of poverty for various groups of people. The assessment declares that such degradation will substantially diminish the benefits that future generations will obtain from ecosystems.

The *third* finding is that the degradation of ecosystem services could grow significantly worse during the first half of this century and is a barrier to achieving the Millennium Development Goals.

And the *fourth* is that the challenge of reversing the degradation of ecosystems while meeting increasing demands for their services can be achieved under some scenarios involving significant policy and institutional changes, but these changes are large and not currently under way.

17.6 PRIORITY AREAS FOR SCIENTIFIC RESEARCH IN ENVIRONMENTAL FIELDS

Environmental issues are now generally classified into three groups: science-driven issues, issues with unknown probability, and policy-driven issues.

Among the science-driven issues, those already well recognized are (1) sustainable management of natural resources; (2) socio-economic drivers of environmental change (population, globalization, changing production and consumption patterns, transport, tourism, and urbanization); (3) assessing the interactions among global mega-issues, such as population, environment, and development; and (4) intensification of environmental stressors, such as exposure to human-made chemicals or disruption of biogeochemical cycles.

Issues with low or unknown probability but unacceptable consequences include natural disasters, genetically modified organisms (GMOs), the rapid evolutionary nature of microbes and other pests, and the collapse of ecosystems.

Policy-driven issues include, inter alia, environmental impacts of proposed strategies and policies, and the implementation issues, such as how to implement the precautionary principle.

Experts defined a large number of research needs related to these environmental issues. Methodological needs came up pre-eminently, as could be expected, considering the complexity of most issues and the necessity to combine quantitative natural science data with qualitative social science data.

Specific priorities identified as requiring urgent research programmes included the following:

1. Comprehensive environmental and health research in the tropical regions;
2. Ecosystem restructuring in response to global change;
3. More work on biogeochemical cycling, especially the decoupling of the carbon and nutrient cycles and the effects of the global nitrogen overload;
4. The effects of multiple stresses on ecological and social systems;
5. Perturbations of the hydrological cycle;
6. Environmental implications of GMOs;
7. Mechanisms of carbon dioxide sequestering in nature and through technology;
8. Issues related to chemicals covering disposal of persistent substances, reduction of residues in food, and risk assessment;
9. Improvement of water management systems and efficient water use;
10. Efficient energy systems;
11. Disposal of nuclear waste; and finally,
12. Economic issues such as natural resource and ecological accounting and the valuation of ecological services.

17.7 SCIENTIFIC RESEARCH ETHICS

An issue that is very much discussed nowadays, and which is applicable to all fields of science, is the need for high ethical standards, in terms of scientific integrity and quality control, knowledge sharing, communication with the public, and education of the younger generation. This is of significant importance, considering the need to establish relations of trust among all stakeholders to achieve progress towards the goal of sustainable development.

17.8 SURPRISES

The last point that needs to be emphasized in this context is that surprises cannot be excluded. Despite progress in modelling and forecasting, scientists must always be ready to move fast when the unexpected happens.

In 1972, at Stockholm, we were not concerned about stratospheric ozone depletion, climate change, or loss of biodiversity. In a short 15 years, we all became involved in these unexpected issues.

At the top of this chapter I quoted an old statement by a famous British politician, Winston Churchill: 'Science should be on tap, not on top'. He meant that policy-making should be based on the best available science, but many other social and economic factors have to be taken into account.

18 Government communication on transboundary haze: The nexus between public health and tourism

HELENA VARKKEY

Department of International and Strategic Studies, University of Malaya

Keywords

Transboundary haze; forest fires; Indonesia; Malaysia; Singapore; tourism; public health; government responses; international media; sensationalism; air quality indices; excess deaths; ASEAN

Abstract

Haze has been a serious transboundary problem in Southeast Asia for decades. Originating largely from fires in Indonesia, the smoke travels across borders, affecting up to six Southeast Asian states almost annually. Haze contains fine particles which irritate the eyes and penetrate the lungs. As a result, scores of Indonesians, Malaysians, and Singaporeans suffer from respiratory, dermatological, and ophthalmological problems. These health risks, together with reduced visibility, have also caused tourist numbers to drop dramatically. This chapter observes that governments worked hard to protect and maintain their tourism sectors in the face of the haze. The main tactic used was to underrepresent the health risks of haze, both to citizens and tourists. As a result, regional governments largely failed to recognize the haze as a serious public health issue. At the national level, states often under-report health effects in the attempt to keep tourism levels stable. At the regional level, member states have yet to agree on a common ASEAN-wide regional air quality measurement system, with many continuing to use a system that tends to underrepresent health risks. At the international level, affected states have been quick to debunk research that indicates higher levels of mortality. As a result, citizens lack the awareness and sense of urgency to make wise health and well-being decisions during haze episodes. Sustainable development involves economic growth balanced with social development and environmental sustainability. However, the case of the haze shows that Southeast Asian states still find it challenging to balance these elements in the spirit of sustainable development.

18.1 HAZE IN SOUTHEAST ASIA

One of the most severe environmental issues afflicting the Southeast Asian region in the recent decades is air pollution. The region suffers from various types of air pollution, including those that are urban, industrial, and agricultural in origin. However, by far the most serious and recursive type of air pollution in the region is what is known as transboundary haze. Haze is defined as 'sufficient smoke, dust, moisture, and vapour suspended in air to impair visibility', and it is classified as transboundary when 'its density and extent is so great at the source that it remains at measurable levels after crossing into another country's airspace' (ASEAN Secretariat, 2008).

The Southeast Asian region experiences transboundary haze on an almost annual basis. The causes of haze are both natural and anthropogenic, and regional weather patterns influence the extent to which the smoke travels across Southeast Asia. Haze originates from peat and forest fires, primarily from Indonesia and to a lesser extent Malaysia. Forest fires have been a part of the landscape and ecology of Southeast Asia, particularly in Indonesia, since the 19th century (Eaton and Radojevic, 2001). While these fires have been naturally occurring during the dry seasons (around August to October) for generations, they have grown in severity and intensity over the years owing to anthropogenic activities (Mayer, 2006). Nowadays, many of these fires are linked to accidental (as a result of the drying out of land during clearing) or deliberate (as a quick, cheap, and easy way to clear land for planting) behaviour of commercial plantations, especially palm oil and pulp and paper plantations (Varkkey, 2016a).

The 'Great Fire of Borneo' in 1982, the worst fires the region had seen at that time, destroyed 3.6 million hectares of forestland. However, the haze events of 1997–1998 massively surpassed the scale of the 1982 fires, burning an estimated 10 million hectares around Indonesia, destroying forests and bushland, including conservation areas and national parks (Dauvergne, 1998). The region experienced serious transboundary haze episodes again in 2005, 2006, 2009, 2013, 2015, and most recently in 2019.

The El Niño-Southern Oscillation (ENSO) is what primarily determines the extent to which this smoke haze travels across the region. ENSO describes the fluctuations in temperature between the ocean and atmosphere in the east-central Equatorial Pacific. During severe El Niño years, drier conditions and stronger winds create conditions ripe for fires and push the resultant smoke far across the region. At its worst, the haze can travel to reach six Southeast Asian nations: Indonesia, Malaysia, Singapore, Thailand, Brunei, and the Philippines (Mayer, 2006). Due to their proximity to the source of most of the fires, Indonesia, Singapore, and Malaysia are hit hardest and most regularly by transboundary haze.

The negative effects of the regional transboundary haze are manifold. The particles in the air cast a greyish pall over the atmosphere, drastically reducing visibility. This also blocks a significant amount of sunlight from reaching the ground, which affects plant health and agricultural production by reducing the rate of photosynthesis. During bad episodes, affected governments may declare emergencies in worst-hit areas, closing schools for extended periods, and restricting outdoor activities. Indonesians living closest to the fires suffer the brunt of the haze pollution, in the form of severe health effects and direct monetary losses and damage to crops and property as a result of out-of-control fires. The haze episode in 2015 was estimated by the World Bank to have cost Indonesia alone US\$16 billion in economic losses (about 2% of their gross domestic product (GDP)) (World Bank Group, 2016). This eclipses even China's huge cost of particulate pollution, which resulted in economic losses of about 1.1% of its GDP (Lu *et al.,* 2016, 2017; Xia *et al.,* 2016). In Singapore, the 2013 haze was estimated to have resulted in around US\$50 million in losses to retailers, hotels, tourism, and the economy overall (Quah and Tan, 2015), while Malaysian forecasts of the 2015 haze put loss estimates higher than in 1997.

18.1.1 Effects on health

It is undeniable that some of the most concerning effects of transboundary haze are those related to human health. In general, air pollution is increasing the risk of strokes, lung cancer, heart disease, and other serious health problems in populations all around the world. Historically, the notorious London Fog incident of 1952 was found to have caused 4,000 premature deaths (Saliluddin, 2015) and showed a notable reduction in human health and well-being for extended periods after the fog cleared (Nazeer and Furuoka, 2017). Outdoor air pollution causes at least 22% of the global burden of death and disease from ischaemic health disease (Amul, 2013). Cognizant of this, the United Nations Environment Programme (UNEP) recently adopted a resolution on air quality, noting that 'poor air quality

is a growing challenge in the context of sustainable development, in particular relating to health in cities and urban areas' (Lode *et al.,* 2016).

The minute particles that make up the smoke haze in Southeast Asia can be as small as 2.5μ or less (identified as particulate matter or PM2.5). These particles can easily penetrate lung tissue of those exposed to the haze, settle deep in the lungs, and interfere with lung function after long exposure (Amul, 2013). This can cause a variety of respiratory, dermatological, and ophthalmological problems, and even deaths. The World Health Organization (WHO) in fact warned in 2012 that exposure to these minute 2.5μ particles can trigger a chronic symptomless heart disease called atherosclerosis, adverse birth outcomes, and childhood respiratory diseases. The reduced attractiveness of physical outdoor activity due to uninviting outside conditions also reduces the ability of people, especially those with existing respiratory infections or cardiovascular conditions, to maintain a healthy lifestyle (Amul, 2013).

During the severe 1997 haze period, about 18 million Malaysians were exposed to haze, or 83.2% (Mohd Shahwahid and Othman, 1999). In Indonesia, 47.6 million Indonesians were exposed to the haze (Ruitenbeek, 1999), while in Singapore it can be assumed that almost the whole population was exposed, considering the tiny size of the island and its proximity to the fire-prone areas of Sumatra. There were more than 1.8 million cases of bronchial asthma, bronchitis, and acute respiratory infections among people exposed to haze in Indonesia. Even more sadly, haze was said to have caused more than 15,600 'missing children' (related to miscarriages and pregnancy complications) across Indonesia during the five-month period of high exposure in 1997 (Othman *et al.,* 2014). Singapore showed an increase of 30% outpatient attendance in hospital for haze-related admissions, with similar increases of hospitalization in Malaysia, especially for chronic obstructive pulmonary disease and asthma (WHO, 2007). The elderly above 65 years was the group of people which suffered the most, health-wise (Nazeer and Furuoka, 2017), followed by very young children.

Related to this are the economic losses incurred because of the loss of man-hours and workdays due to sickness, as well as additional spending on hospital visits and medication. It was estimated that in 1997, the estimated health costs of the haze across the region was approximately US\$164 million (Tacconi, 2003). In Malaysia, the cost of illness (including hospitalization costs, out-patient treatment, and self-medication, and productivity loss from illness) was US\$8 million or an equivalent of 2.6% total damage cost (Mohd Shahwahid and Othman, 1999). For Singapore, this was estimated as US\$6 to US\$19 million, or 6% to 17% of the total economic losses incurred as a result of haze (Hon, 1999). As a result of being closest to the fires and smoke,

Indonesia suffered the most health-related economic losses from haze during this time. Health costs amounted to US$924 million or about 84% of total haze impacts (Ruitenbeek, 1999).

18.1.2 Effects on tourism

Another concerning effect of haze is its impact on tourism in the region. All three of the worst-hit countries, Indonesia, Malaysia, and Singapore, are among the most famous tourism destinations in the region. The three countries consistently list in the top ten most-visited destinations by international tourist arrivals in the Asia-Pacific, with Malaysia ranked 3rd, Singapore 9th, and Indonesia 10th in the World Tourism Barometer 2016. All three countries are highly dependent on tourism revenue for a significant portion of their GDP. According to the World Travel and Tourism Council (WTTC) (2015), tourism generated US$49 billion for Malaysia in 2014, which translates to 6% direct impact on GDP, and 15% indirect impact. Tourism in Malaysia in turn employs 724,000 people directly and another 1 million people indirectly. In Singapore, tourism generated US$66 billion in 2014, amounting to 8% direct and 18% indirect impact on GDP, and employed 300,000 people directly and indirectly. Tourism in Indonesia generated US$80 billion, contributing 4% directly and 9% indirectly to its GDP and employing 3.3 million directly and 6.5 million indirectly.

Holidaymakers tend to pay attention to the aesthetics, weather, and environment of their destinations (Hon, 1999). Malaysia, Indonesia, and Singapore are indeed famous among tourists for their sites of natural beauty and majestic skylines. However, the haze not only threatens the aesthetic beauty of these countries by casting a grey shroud over the scenery, which reduces visibility of the beauty of the surrounding natural environment or cityscape, it also affects the weather by blocking out some of the sunlight. On top of this, tourists are also concerned about how the haze would affect their health. Nobody would want to visit places where breathing is dangerous to health and sightseeing is impossible (Leiper and Hing, 1998). The reduced visibility also affects vital transportation systems which tourists depend on, including causing airport shutdowns, cancelled and delayed flights and ships, and accidents, too. For example, the 1997 haze was blamed for the fatal crash of a Silk Air passenger liner in Sumatra (Leiper and Hing, 1998) and a Garuda Indonesia airplane, and a bus crash in Medan, Indonesia, in 2002, which killed five passengers, was also linked to low visibility due to haze (Varkkey, 2016a). Therefore, it is not surprising that tourism numbers to this heavily tourist-dependent region typically fall during the haze months, with airlines, travel agencies, and bus companies seeing their revenues and profits predictably plummet during each haze season.

During the well-documented 1997 period, it was found that several tour group operators from Hong Kong, Britain, and Japan delayed or cancelled their tours to Malaysia because of haze. Compared with the same period in 1996 (when there were 457,273 non-ASEAN visitors), non-ASEAN tourist arrivals in Malaysia from 1 August to 31 October 1997, during the peak of the haze, was only 320,091. This translated to an income reduction of US$127.4 million, compared with the 1996 period. Even after the haze dispersed in November 1997, states like Sarawak saw a reduced inbound volume of up to 70%, with national numbers falling to less than 30% of previous years. Related to tourism earning as well were the flight cancellations (1,800 domestic and international flights, or US$2.6 million sales losses) and airport closures (US$179,693 profits foregone) due to low visibility. All in all, tourism- and airline-related losses accounted for about 40% of total losses to Malaysia during this haze period (Mohd Shahwahid and Othman, 1999).

Indonesia in turn lost an estimate of between 187,000 and 281,000 visitors during the three-month haze period, which translates to economic losses of about US$46.9 to US$70.3 million. In all, 1,108 flights were cancelled during this period, which cost US$7.54 million to the Indonesian airline industry. Foregone costs due to airport closures were estimated at US$10 million. Tourism and airline losses totalled about 8% of total haze losses to Indonesia that year (Ruitenbeek, 1999). In 1997, Singapore recorded a drop in tourist arrivals for the first time since 1983. Arrivals for the whole year fell 1.3%, with arrivals falling 14.4% during the hazy fourth quarter. Furthermore, major airlines operating out of Singapore reported a significant number of flight cancellations due to haze, with Singapore Airlines reporting the cancellation of 14,000 bookings. The loss in revenue for Singapore's tourism industry during the 1997 haze was calculated to be around US$58.4 million (about 75% to 80% of total losses for Singapore). This does not include losses to the related airline industry (cancelled flights and foregone costs), which took up almost 10% of losses. For Singapore, the tourism industry and its related sectors suffered the worst economically from haze (Hon, 1999).

18.2 BETWEEN PUBLIC HEALTH AND TOURISM

The nexus between public health and tourism in the context of the haze is an interesting subject for analysis in terms of government responses to serious environmental issues. Here is a situation in which the health and well-being of large numbers of local populations are put at risk. However, at the same time, over-stressing the health risks of the haze would adversely affect the willingness of foreign tourists to visit the affected countries. As seen earlier, the countries involved are significantly dependent on tourism as a major foreign exchange earner and source of GDP, so any threat to the continuity of this sector cannot be taken lightly.

Shocks like human crises (diseases, wars, financial crises, or terrorism), disasters (natural disasters, climate change, or pandemics), or structural changes (new political loyalties, demographic changes, ethnic uprisings, scarcity, or environmentalism) can all negatively influence tourism flows to a country. The way a government manages these events and responds to them will affect the rate of recovery of the tourism industry after the shock. For example, if governments withdraw the support for tourism promotion and development during the event, the impact of the shock can be quickly exacerbated. However, if governments steadily assist the industry, the impacts may be minimized (Prideaux *et al.*, 2003). Throughout the haze years, it can be observed that the governments of Malaysia, Indonesia, and Singapore worked hard to assist the tourism industry to reduce the negative impacts of haze on tourism in these countries.

While this would seem honourable, this chapter raises the concern that this has been done at the expense of under-representing the health risks posed by transboundary haze, both to the countries' own citizens and to tourists. As a result, regional governments fail to recognize the haze as a serious public health issue. At the national level, member states often under-report health effects in an attempt to keep tourism levels stable. At the regional level, member states have yet to agree on a common ASEAN-wide regional air quality measurement system.[1] At the international level, member states have been quick to debunk research that indicates higher levels of mortality during haze.

18.2.1 Responding to international media

In general, the international media can have a significant role in publicizing environmental issues and hence bring them onto the political agenda at the national, regional, or international level. They can be useful in translating research-based findings into popular formats. However, sometimes, they can fall prey to sensationalism and exaggeration (Murdiyarso *et al.*, 2004). The recurring haze episodes in Southeast Asia repeatedly focused the world's attention on the region over an environmental issue, beginning as early as in 1972. Both local and international news

media covered the incidents as they occurred with increasing frequency, and the governments of Malaysia, Singapore, and Indonesia were constantly faced with the twin challenges of managing the practicalities of the crisis internally while also managing external perceptions of the crisis fuelled by international media coverage.

Sensationalism was rife among the foreign media that covered the transboundary haze. The image portrayed was that all of Southeast Asia was collapsing from fires, political instability, and chaos. Understandably, Southeast Asian governments responded defensively. All were keen to maintain their countries' good image and avoid discouraging tourism (Forsyth, 2014). Indonesia focused on trying to convince international markets that haze did not affect particularly popular tourist destinations like Bali (Murdiyarso *et al.*, 2004). *The Straits Times* of Singapore reported that a British news team had asked a tourist to pose for photographs wearing a gas mask beside a swimming pool, which it declared to be 'comical if it were not so damaging in its inaccuracy and dishonesty' (Forsyth, 2014). The Malaysian Information Ministry warned television stations not to blow the haze problem out of proportion or they would have their licenses revoked (McLellan, 2001). Malaysian ministers also criticized the international press for continuing to raise the issue (Eaton, 2001).

Among the tactics used by Southeast Asian governments to strengthen these arguments and defend its tourism industries was the tactic of downplaying and denying that haze posed any serious health risks to their citizens or, by extension, tourists that might venture there. For example, in Singapore, the Pollution Control Department (PCD) spokespersons maintained that there was no need for public alarm over the haze, as it was not radioactive or photochemical (did not contain any chemicals that would react in sunlight, which can be very dangerous to health) and did not increase pollution levels in Singapore. The PCD declared that it was not hazardous to be outdoors. The Singaporean Ministry for the Environment maintained that eye irritation and a slight odour in the air were nothing to be concerned about (Varkkey, 2016a). Even during the worst haze episode in the region in 1997, the then minister maintained that most Singaporeans would be able to cope with the haze without any equipment like purifiers or filters (Singapore Hansard, 1998). Similarly in Malaysia, the Minister of Science, Technology, and the Environment frequently declared that haze particles were not hazardous to health, as they were not active and non-toxic. Even after the Health Ministry acknowledged the increase of haze-related diseases, public health advisories frequently advised the public to merely 'not breathe too vigorously' while outdoors (Varkkey, 2016a).

Southeast Asian governments also pushed back against foreign media by controlling domestic news media content to show

---

[1] There are actually numerous ASEAN agreements on haze mitigation and related issues (e.g., Policy Framework for Environmental Cooperation in ASEAN, Environmental Objectives and Strategies in ASEAN, Environmental Programmes and Activities in ASEAN, Ministerial Declaration on the Environment, ASEAN Environmental Programmes, ASEAN Strategic Plan of Action on the Environment, Hanoi Plan of Action, ASEAN Cooperative Plan on Transboundary Pollution, ASEAN Regional Haze Plan, ASEAN Haze Monitoring System (HMS), and the ASEAN Plan of Action for Energy Cooperation). However, most have not been effective or even implemented. I have discussed this in depth elsewhere; please see Varkkey (2013).

a less sensationalist picture of haze (Murdiyarso *et al.*, 2004). As the Asian practice of journalism is traditionally infused with an intense sense of national loyalty, with the mainstream press commonly acting as the governments' ally (Massey, 2000), this was relatively easy to do. For example, at the early stages of the haze, local press carried statements by the Malaysian Ministry of Culture and Tourism insisting that the haze was (contrary to international reports) not affecting tourist arrivals to the country (Varkkey, 2016a). The Malaysian press was also careful not to use more serious-sounding expressions to describe haze, like 'smog'[2] or 'air pollution' (McLellan, 2001).

In 1997, the government also barred academic researchers from talking to the media on haze. Najib Razak, Malaysia's former Prime Minister and Minister of Education at the time, was quoted in Malaysia's *New Straits Times* saying that

> if we make statements that the haze here is bad and it has long-term effects on health, citizens and foreign visitors will have doubts about Malaysia … [W]e cannot have statement after statement which can be picked up by the foreign media that could create a very distorted picture that can affect the country … [W]e do not want tourists to cancel bookings and visitors to spread stories about Malaysia (McLellan, 2001).

However, the international damage was done, and despite the best efforts of the regional governments, tourist numbers were clearly dropping in all major regional destinations. Regional governments immediately blamed this drop on outdated coverage of haze by foreign media (Varkkey, 2016a), based on distortions of local media reports. The Malaysian government in particular engaged in a campaign of coordinated denial particularly targeting the British, American, and Australian media for alleged misrepresentation of haze in 1997 and 2000 (McLellan, 2001). In fact, the Malaysian Information Ministry lobbied this matter so avidly that it managed to get an apology and compensation (in the form of airtime promoting Malaysia) from the American network CNN for its supposedly 'less-than-fair' reports on the haze (Varkkey, 2016a).

18.2.2 Regional air quality indices

As a result of this defensiveness in the face of international media, the region's general public ended up unsure and in the dark about what effect the haze was really having on their health (Eaton, 2001). Public concerns and outcry led to affected governments eventually publicizing ambient air quality indices as a way

to evaluate the harmfulness of air on human health (Chooi and Yong, 2016). These indices identify individual pollutants and the concentrations at which they become harmful to public health and the environment (Saliluddin, 2015). Each country used their own preferred index: Air Pollution Index (API) in Malaysia, Pollutant Standards Index (PSI) in Singapore, and Indeks Standar Pencemar Udara (ISPU) in Indonesia. All three indices follow a roughly standard system of reporting air quality; for example, a value of 81–100 PSI (Singapore) is moderate, 101–200 unhealthy, 201–300 very unhealthy, 301–400 hazardous, and above 400 very hazardous (Jones, 2014). Action on the ground was meant to be guided by this rating. For example, in Malaysia, when API levels reached more than 300, school and working hours would be reduced; if readings continued more than 400 for 24 hours, a state of emergency was recommended; and at levels more than 500, towns should be evacuated (even though this figure was breached before in Sarawak, evacuation has never occurred owing to logistical challenges) (Eaton, 2001).

All three countries have set up air quality measurement stations at strategic urban and rural locations. These monitoring stations measure the presence of several gases like carbon monoxide, sulphur dioxide, and nitrogen dioxide, together with fine particles in the atmosphere (Saliluddin, 2015). Calculating the concentration of these gases and particles results in a numerical value which indicates the healthiness of the air. This value is then made available to the public at set intervals through several government-mandated channels (usually government agency websites and government-owned television stations). However, some governments remain uneasy about openly announcing that the air was 'unhealthy'. For example, in June 1999, the Malaysian Cabinet used the Official Secrets Act 1972 (allowing them to mark any document 'secret' for an unspecified period) to withhold the dissemination of daily API updates to the public, as it 'did not want irresponsible parties to take advantage of the situation and exaggerate conditions' (Article 19 and CIJ, 2007). The API figures were declassified only in 2005. Therefore, for six years, the Malaysian public did not have any reliable way to judge if they were safe breathing the outdoor air.

At first, all three countries measured only fine particles of PM10 (10μ, please see explanation in Section 18.1.1). However, scientists have raised concerns that PM10 measurements do not accurately reflect air quality, especially during haze periods. If PM10 is used to determine the API, although the visibility is bad, a moderate air quality reading can still be obtained (Chooi and Yong, 2016). The WHO had in fact already warned that the health effects of PM2.5 are more adverse than PM10 (Caballero-Anthony and Tian, 2015), as finer PM2.5 particles enter cells passively, while larger particles can be filtered out by microphages. Temporal exposure to high concentrations of PM2.5 increases the risk of myocardial infarction after a few hours in high-risk populations, and

---

[2] Governments generally denied that the haze could be classified as 'industrial smog' or 'photochemical smog' (see previous section), but the chemical reactions between these particulates with existing urban pollution in big cities like Kuala Lumpur is a continuing cause for concern for scientists (e.g. a group of atmospheric scientists at LESTARI, Universiti Kebangsaan Malaysia, are avidly researching this (Latif *et al.*, 2018)), as it would make the haze much more dangerous to health.

PM2.5 was found to have a direct correlation with the upper respiratory tract infections during haze periods. PM2.5 has also been found to have effects on all-cause, cardiopulmonary, and lung cancer mortality (Chooi and Yong, 2016). For this reason, PM2.5 is the more critical pollutant that should be measured (Caballero-Anthony and Tian, 2015; Chooi and Yong, 2016).

Singapore started to include PM2.5 in their air quality measurements instead of PM10 in 2014. However, Indonesia's ISPU is still using PM10 as their fine particle measurement, while Malaysia only officially adopted PM2.5 measurements during the recent 2019 haze episode. This has resulted in huge differences between air quality readings in Singapore based on PM2.5 and those in nearby cities in Malaysia and Indonesia based on PM10 (Chooi and Yong, 2016), where ratings are usually much lower than those in Singapore. This has resulted in huge differences between air quality readings in Singapore and those in nearby cities in Malaysia and Indonesia (Chooi and Yong, 2016), where ratings are usually much lower than those in Singapore.

The matter was raised in Malaysia recently in 2015 by an opposition member of parliament (MP), Wong Chen, after he returned from a visit to Singapore and observed the stark differences in air quality ratings (Varkkey and O'Reilly, 2019). Malaysia's Deputy Minister of Natural Resources and the Environment absurdly responded that 'for Malaysia, our API is more sensitive to health effects while Singapore's is more targeted towards outside activities, so if their API reading is 120 or 150, they would possibly tell their people not to participate in outdoor activities, but ours is pegged to health, that is why we use the international protocol' (Wong Chen, 2015b). The Department of Environment (DOE) further said that readings could be moderate but visibility poor because API readings represented an average. These responses were pooh-poohed by Chen, insisting that both PM10 and PM2.5 are health measures, with PM2.5 being the far superior measure (Wong Chen, 2015b).

Actually, the DOE was quoted in a newspaper report in 2012 saying that Malaysia should be ready to shift over to PM2.5 reporting in 2016 (Wong Chen, 2015a). However, up to now, this shift has not yet occurred. There are currently 12 air monitoring facilities that can measure PM2.5 in Malaysia, up from five in 2012, but the government claims this is still not enough to shift over to PM2.5 reporting (Varkkey and O'Reilly, 2019). Chen pointed out that this rate of implementation does not demonstrate any form of urgency on the part of the government to improve its haze reporting (Wong Chen, 2015b). He reasoned that Malaysia was still insisting on using PM10 to produce lower readings and create a more positive but illusory picture of the nation's air quality, and that the government had failed to take into account the greater health dangers posed by the smaller particles of PM2.5. He states that the public has the right to be 'fully informed of the air quality, so that they can choose to mitigate their own risks while pursuing outdoor activities. The act of white washing the haze will not with any certainty, improve economic or tourist numbers but it will, with certainty, exact a heavy healthcare and human cost on the uninformed public' (Wong Chen, 2015a).

The standardization of air quality reporting is in fact mandated in the 2002 ASEAN Agreement on Transboundary Haze Pollution (AATHP) (Amul, 2013), which all ASEAN countries, including the three discussed, have fully ratified. However, to this date, there has been no urgency from either the governments or the ASEAN organization to agree upon a region-wide standardized air quality monitoring index based on PM2.5 which can be used to keep the general Southeast Asian public informed. Governments have also been in no rush to implement more accessible means of communicating air pollution indices to the public, for example, the electronic quotation boards installed at street level in Korea (Ku Yusof et al., 2017).

18.2.3 Haze and premature deaths

Most recently, in 2016, a highly publicized study by scholars from Cambridge, Columbia, and Harvard universities (Koplitz et al., 2016, p. 1) estimated that the serious regional haze in 2015 resulted in 100,300 excess deaths across Indonesia, Malaysia, and Singapore. This was estimated to be more than double the excess deaths caused by the 2006 event. Breaking this figure down by country, the researchers estimated that excess deaths in Indonesia were 91,600, Malaysia 6,500, and Singapore 2,200. The study used the CEOS-Chem chemical transport model to estimate population-weighted smoke exposure, which enabled the researchers to measure consequent morbidity and premature mortality due to severe haze (Koplitz et al., 2016). By studying how the chemical compounds in the smoke change as they move through space and time before they reach people, the concentration of PM2.5 that people are breathing can be estimated, and from this, health impacts can be deduced. The American study was picked up by various international media outlets, as an example of the media translating research-based findings into popular formats (Murdiyarso et al., 2004).

The news reports generated a lot of interest, especially from the Southeast Asian public, and prompted swift responses from regional governments. Even though tourist populations were beyond the scope of this study, nevertheless the implications of these findings on tourism in the region were clearly a major concern among governments. All three countries responded in the same way: denial.[3] For example, the Indonesian Health Ministry said that the figure far exceeded the country's own official death

---

[3] Please refer to newspaper articles in the region dated around 19 and 20 September 2016, especially in *The Straits Times* (Singapore), *Jakarta Post* (Indonesia), and *The Star*, *Malay Mail*, and *The Sun* (Malaysia) for government responses to the study.

records as a result of haze (according to cause of death listed in death certificates), which was a mere 19 deaths. Indonesia's Jambi Health Department also continued to deny the increasing number of smoke victims, especially among toddlers (Arfan, 2016). These countries largely ignore the explanation given by the scholars that their figures do not just account for deaths from acute smoke inhalation, but also increases in strokes, heart attacks, and other illnesses that can be brought on by excessive exposure to PM2.5 particles. While there are indeed limitations to the validity of the researchers' figures,[4] these findings paint a more accurate picture of mortality than the somewhat simplistic (e.g., haze listed as cause of death) parameters used by these countries.

Independent voices in these countries, however, echoed the study's conclusions.[5] Mr Yuyun Indradi, a Greenpeace Indonesia forest campaigner, in turn said that the figures were 'alarming but not surprising'.

The stark differences between the tone of response from government officials and independent voices ring loud and clear. While there is always room for critique in academia, the blatant denial displayed by all three country officials only serves to further legitimize concerns like those of the Malaysian MP Wong Chen, who argues that the authorities are trying to create a 'positive but illusory' picture to bolster tourism numbers in the face of bad air quality, despite the public health risks at stake. Furthermore, the quickness of these governments to reject Koplitz et al.'s (2016) findings overlooks the fact that the paper also makes an excellent proposal to mitigate further deaths: the model framework introduced in the study enables countries to rapidly identify those areas where land-use management to reduce or avoid fires would yield the greatest benefit to regional health. While it may be impossible for governments to stop all fires, governments could use this framework to potentially pinpoint priority areas to focus their fire prevention and suppression efforts that would save the largest number of lives (Koplitz et al., 2016). However, there has thus far been no indication that any of the governments involved are taking this into consideration.

18.3 HAZE AS A NON-PUBLIC HEALTH ISSUE

The three cases detailed earlier can all be seen as tactical approaches by regional governments to prevent transboundary haze from negatively affecting their respective tourism industries. While tourism is very important in all three countries and any risk to this keystone industry should indeed be mitigated, this comes at the dire expense of public health.

In addition to this, governments have also largely ignored opposition and civil society demands to treat the haze as more of a public health issue. The Malaysian opposition has long berated the government for having given consistently 'belated' and 'lackadaisical' responses about the haze and its impact on the health and safety of millions of Malaysians. The opposition pointed out examples like the DOE website being down during a particularly hazy morning, the lack of hourly updates[6] of API figures, and the lack of freely available N95 (able to filter out at least 95% of airborne particles larger than 0.3μ – including PM2.5) face masks, coupled with rising prices of masks that were on sale, despite their being controlled items (Teo, 2013). In the Indonesian province of Jambi, demands by the civil society group Jambi Coalition Against Smoke (KJMA) for N95 masks and equipment to treat victims of smoke during the 2015 haze resulted in the government providing only cotton and other monthly medical equipment. Evacuation houses that were promised to Jambi did not reach the villagers closest to the fires, ironically, because they were too close to the fires and thus unreachable by authorities. Indonesian civil society groups also regularly complained that the central government was slow in implementing treatment and evacuation of smoke casualties, as well as being slow in declaring 'national disaster status' in badly hit areas, which would technically enable bodies like the Regional Disaster Management Agency (BPBD) to act more quickly in response to fires and haze (Arfan, 2016).

The decades of 'white washing' and downplaying of the health risks of haze have resulted in a regional public that has had to make decisions for their health based on incomplete and inconclusive information. Indeed, a recent survey done by De Pretto et al. (2015) found that many respondents in Malaysia lacked even basic awareness of the haze. The researchers hypothesized that this was due to the stifling of news and public discussion by the Malaysian media during the 1997 to 2005 period (when the OSA was in force on API figures). As a result, it was found that the Southeast Asian public experienced only mild psychological stress over the haze, not (as would be expected in the face of such a dire environmental crisis) amounting to acute stress reaction syndrome (Ho et al., 2014). Hence, this has resulted in the 'out of sight, out of mind'

---

[4] For example, the impact of PM2.5 exposure is typically estimated on the basis of exposure to particulate matter in European or US cities (Laden et al., 2000), while other types of particulates, that is, haze, may have lower (or indeed higher) toxicity. See also reservations raised by one of the study's authors in Section 18.3.1 on Singapore.

[5] Please refer to newspaper articles in the region dated around 19 September and 20 September 2016, especially in The Straits Times (Singapore), Jakarta Post (Indonesia) and The Star, Malay Mail, and The Sun (Malaysia) for responses from independent voices (like doctors, academicians, and NGOs) to government reactions to the study.

[6] Note that PM2.5 impacts are generally on a 24-hour basis, so the request for hourly updates may be difficult, considering current technological limitations, though Singapore has already shifted to hourly updates (as mentioned in Section 18.3.1). However, the accuracy of this extrapolation from 24 hours to hourly should be examined further for usefulness and accuracy.

attitude among the regional population, where they generally only care about the haze during a haze episode (Tay, 2010) and even then do not take it as seriously as they should, especially in terms of taking care of their health and well-being.

Governments can indeed play an important role in reducing psychological stress among the public in the event of such crises (Ho *et al.*, 2014), and indeed this can be important to avoid public panic. However, by underplaying the serious health risks of this particular crisis, government responses can be seen to be counterproductive: a heightened amount of psychological stress is needed to ensure that the public takes the necessary precautions to protect themselves against the health risks that they face. Reduced psychological stress would lead to a lackadaisical response by the public, which would lead to unnecessary dangerous exposure to health risks and higher incidences of illness and deaths. This indeed does seem to have happened, as detailed in the recent controversial American study (Koplitz *et al.*, 2016).

It can be concluded that the attempts by the governments affected by haze in Southeast Asia to moderate the effects of haze on tourism have ultimately resulted in haze being treated (initially by the government and as a result by the public, as well) as a non-public health issue. While this may not be such a problem among the upper- and middle-class society members, who can likely educate themselves independently on the health risks of haze, afford medical treatment, and perhaps even leave the country for greener pastures on the worst days, the consequences of treating the haze as a non-public health issue are likely highest and most severe among at-risk, poorer populations in these countries, because of their pre-existing susceptibility to ill health.

18.3.1 A Singaporean shift?

There have been some recent positive shifts towards acknowledging haze as a serious public health issue; however, this has largely been confined to one country: Singapore. Much of this was fuelled by the civil society outcry spearheaded by Singaporean environmental and health NGOs. Singaporean groups like People's Movement to Stop Haze (PMHaze), Haze Elimination Action Team (HEAT), and multinational groups like the Fire Free Village Programme actively used publicly available data on websites such as the World Resources Institute's Global Forest Watch (http://fires.globalforestwatch.org/home) to call for boycotts of products linked to unsustainable plantation practices and urge greater accountability in Indonesia and Singapore related to their plantation and forestry practices.

This heightened public concern and outcry has been influential in mobilizing better government responses towards the haze problem. Through 2013–2016, this led to intense negative diplomacy between Singapore and Indonesia, with President Yudhoyono even giving a public apology. Singapore also brought into force its own Transboundary Haze Pollution Act in 2014, which provides extraterritorial jurisdiction to legally hold accountable any entity that causes haze in Singapore (Letchumanan, 2015; Tan, 2015; Tan and Bassano, 2014). On the ground, as discussed earlier, Singapore has been the first Southeast Asian country to move to PM2.5 measurements for their PSI, which more accurately reflects atmospheric health risks. Singapore also provides hourly, PM2.5-based PSI updates to its citizens, available on their www.haze.gov.sg portal (NEA, 2018). Furthermore, Singapore has been significantly improving their crisis response systems during haze events. For example, during the recent 2015 haze episode, the Singapore National Environment Agency (NEA) was especially efficient in advising the public to engage in protective measures to protect their health, such as wearing N95 masks, limiting outdoor activities, and seeking medical assistance if they are feeling unwell. A Haze Subsidy Scheme is also activated when the PSI is consistently in the higher range, to make it affordable for those with haze-related conditions to seek treatment (Ministry of Health, 2015). The Ministry of Health also provides health advisories for the general public recommending specific protective measures, depending on their health conditions and levels of haze pollution.

Indeed, Singapore's mitigation actions as well as Singapore's relatively more developed status have enabled Singapore's citizens to avert the worst effects of the haze. One of the authors of the premature deaths study, Joel Schwartz, did acknowledge in response to Singapore's argument that the study 'did not take into consideration the mitigating measures taken' by Singapore, that 'in Singapore, if you close all the windows and turn on the air conditioning you get some protection, which may have happened' (Salvo, 2017). Hence, even though the study estimated that there would have been 2,200 premature deaths related to the 2015 episode in Singapore, the fact that most Singaporean citizens are able to have the luxury of sealed, air-conditioned homes, as well as awareness of and access to the government's mitigation efforts, would have enabled Singapore to avert most of these premature deaths.

In contrast, it is important to note that, as Schwartz explains, in most of the affected areas in Indonesia and the more rural areas of Malaysia, 'particles penetrate indoors, and housing ... is very well ventilated, so I don't think there is any avertive behaviour that people there could have taken that would have been effective' to avert premature deaths (Salvo, 2017). Because of the limited avertive behaviours that can be taken by most Indonesian and Malaysian citizens, coupled with the 'white washing' of the government on the health risks of the haze, which has trickled down to a situation of complacency among the public, the estimated premature deaths as reported by the American study could be a much closer depiction of reality.

I have argued elsewhere (Varkkey, 2016b) that this possible shift in Singapore's treatment of the haze problem towards being considered a serious health issue may be because Singapore is becoming increasingly cognizant of the importance of protecting its most previous resource: its citizens. In contrast with neighbouring Malaysia and Indonesia, which are rich not only in population but also in other forms of natural resources, Singapore's people are its wealth. Being much smaller than its neighbours, any haze event would cover Singapore almost entirely, affecting not only part of its citizens, as in Indonesia and Malaysia, but practically all of them. Related health effects of the haze, like the loss of man-hours and increased medical spending, would thus have a much larger knock-on effect on Singapore in comparison with other countries. Therefore, for Singapore in particular, there is a higher potential for public health to be given priority in its national interest considerations.

18.4 CONCLUSION

Sustainable development involves economic growth balanced against social development and environmental sustainability. However, this chapter has argued that, in general, states in the Southeast Asian region still find it challenging to balance the important elements of the economy, environment, and society in the true spirit of holistic sustainable development. Perhaps this is not very surprising – Southeast Asian countries are historically known to prioritize economic growth above all else. This can be evidenced by ASEAN's founding documents, which states that the organization was founded with the focus of promoting economic cooperation and prosperity among its members, with the ultimate goal of accelerating economic growth in the region (ASEAN Secretariat, 1976; Smith, 2004). As a result, environmental and social objectives are often overlooked in the pursuance of these economic goals (Campbell, 2005). This mentality has somewhat trickled down to the population: De Pretto's (2015) survey found that about 35% were willing to accept that haze events are 'a fair price to pay for economic development'.

As a result, for most of the history of the haze and in most affected countries, the economy, that is, the tourism sector, was clearly given priority over the society, that is, public health. This in turn results in a lackadaisical approach towards addressing the root environmental causes of haze – as long as the risk to the economy can be adequately mitigated. The region consequently continues to suffer from haze on an almost annual basis. Indeed, regional governments are not shy to quickly and harshly respond to any voices that threaten the continued prosperity of the tourism sector in the face of the haze. Ironically, the main response tactic used is one that underplays the health risks of haze, in the hopes that visitors will not be perturbed. However, governments have failed to consider the bigger picture on how this would affect public health in the long run.

As a result, we have today a Southeast Asian public who lack the awareness and urgency to make wise health and well-being decisions in the face of haze, which results in increased health costs and mortality region-wide. This is not impossible to overcome, as discussed in the previous section on Singapore's positive shift. Malaysia and Indonesia should take pointers from their island neighbour to mainstream the issue in the public arena and government thinking, via education, national policy reform, training of officials, websites, and civil society action.

ACKNOWLEDGEMENTS

I would like to thank the Association for Asian Studies for awarding me a travel grant to present and discuss an early version of this chapter at the AAS Conference in Washington, DC, in March 2018, as part of a Rising Voices in Southeast Asian Studies Panel chaired by Dr Michele Thompson, Professor at Southern Connecticut State University. Dr Mitch Aso, Associate Professor at SUNY, provided useful feedback on the chapter during the conference, for which I am grateful. I am also thankful for the thoughtful and detailed feedback provided by Professor Peter Brimblecombe, Chair Professor of Environmental Chemistry, School of Energy and Environment, City University of Hong Kong, and Dr R. James Ferguson, Faculty of Society and Design, Bond University, Australia, as reviewers on this chapter. Special thanks to Dr Pak Sum Low for inviting me to be part of this important collection.

REFERENCES

Amul, G. (2013) Haze and air pollution: the potential health crisis. *RSIS Commentary*, **122**, 1–3.

Arfan, A. (2016) Managing the impact of smoke haze disaster: response of civil society groups towards Jambi provincial government performance. *Jurnal Bina Praja*, **8**, 59–68.

Article 19 and CIJ (2007) *A Haze of Secrecy: Access to Environmental Information in Malaysia*. London, Article 19 and Centre for Independent Journalism.

ASEAN Secretariat (1976) *Treaty of Amity and Cooperation in Southeast Asia*. Jakarta, ASEAN.

ASEAN Secretariat (2008) Information on Fire and Haze. *HazeOnline*. Retrieved from http://haze.asean.org/about-us/information-on-fire-and-haze/ on 1 August 2009.

Caballero-Anthony, M. and Tian, G. (2015) ASEAN's haze shroud: grave threat to human security. *RSIS Commentary*, **207**, 1–3.

Campbell, L. B. (2005) The political economy of environmental regionalism in Asia. In T. J. Pempel (ed.), *Remapping East Asia: The Construction of a Region*. Ithaca, Cornell University Press, pp. 216–235.

Chooi, Y. H. and Yong, E. L. (2016) The influence of PM2.5 and PM10 on Air Pollution Index. *Environmental Engineering, Hydraulics and Hydrology*, **3**, 1–12.

Dauvergne, P. (1998) The political economy of Indonesia's 1997 forest fires. *Australian Journal of International Affairs*, **52**, 13–17.

De Pretto, L., Acreman, S., Ashfold, M. J., Mohankumar, S. K. and Campos-Arceiz, A. (2015) The link between knowledge, attitudes, and practises in relation to atmospheric haze pollution in Peninsular Malaysia. *PLoS One*, **10**, 1–18.

Eaton, P. (2001) Policy implications and government responses to the fires and haze of 1997 and 1998. In M. Radojevic and P. Eaton (eds.), *Forest Fires and Regional Haze in Southeast Asia*. New York, Nova Science Publishers.

Eaton, P. and Radojevic, R. (2001) *Forest Fires and Regional Haze in Southeast Asia*. New York, Nova Science Publishers.

Forsyth, T. (2014) Public concerns about transboundary haze: a comparison of Indonesia, Singapore and Malaysia. *Global Environmental Change*, **25**, 76–86.

Ho, R. C., Zhang, M. W., Ho, C. S., Pan, F., Lu, Y. and Sharma, V. K. (2014) Impact of 2013 South Asian haze crisis: study of physical and psychological symptoms and perceived dangerousness of pollution level. *BMC Psychiatry*, **14**, 1–8.

Hon, P. M. L. (1999) Singapore. In D. Glover and T. Jessup (eds.), *Indonesia's Fires and Haze: The Cost of Catastrophe*. Singapore Institute of Southeast Asian Studies, pp. 51–85.

Jones, W. (2014) Human security & ASEAN transboundary haze: an idea that never came. *Journal of Alternative Perspectives in the Social Sciences*, **5**, 603–623.

Koplitz, S., Mickley, L., Marlier, M., Buonocore, J., Kim, P., Liu, T., Sulprizio, M., DeFries, R., Jacob, D., Schwartz, J., Pongsiri, M. and Myers, S. (2016) Public health impacts of the severe haze in Equatorial Asia in September–October 2015: demonstration of a new framework for informing fire management strategies to reduce downwind smoke exposure. *Environmental Research Letters*, **11**, 1–10.

Ku Yusof, K. M. K., Azid, A., Samsudin, M. S. and Jamalani, M. A. (2017) An overview of transboundary haze studies: the underlying causes and regional disputes on Southeast Asia region. *Malaysian Journal of Fundamental and Applied Sciences*, **13**, 747–753.

Laden, F., Neas, L. M., Dockery, D. W. and Shchwartz, J. (2000) Association of fine particulate matter from different sources with daily mortality in six U.S. cities. *Environmental Health Perspectives*, **108**, 941–947.

Latif, M. T., Othman, M., Idris, N., Juneng, L., Abdullah, A. M., Hamzah, W. P., Khan, M. F., Sulaiman, N. M. N., Jewaratnam, J., Aghamohammadi, N., Sahani, M., Chung, J. X., Ahamad, F., Amil, N., Darus, M., Varkkey, H., Tangang, F. and Jaafar, A. B. (2018) Impact of regional haze towards air quality in Malaysia: a review. *Atmospheric Environment*, **177**, 28–44.

Leiper, N. and Hing, N. (1998) Trends in Asia-Pacific tourism in 1997–98: from optimism to uncertainty. *International Journal of Contemporary Hospitality Management*, **10**, 245–251.

Letchumanan, R. (2015) Singapore's Transboundary Haze Pollution Act: silver bullet or silver lining? *RSIS Commentary*, **21**, 1–3.

Lode, B., Schönberger, P. and Toussaint, P. (2016) Clean air for all by 2030? Air quality in the 2030 Agenda and in international law. *Review of European, Comparative & International Environmental Law*, **25**, 27–38.

Lu, X., Lin, C., Li, Y., Yao, T., Fung, J. C. H. and Lau, A. K. H. (2017) Assessment of health burden caused by particulate matter in Southern China using high-resolution satellite observation. *Environment International*, **98**, 160–170.

Lu, X., Yao, T., Fung, J. C. H. and Lin, C. (2016) Estimation of health and economic costs of air pollution over the Pearl River Delta region in China. *The Science of the Total Environment*, **566–577**, 134–143.

Massey, B. (2000) How three Southeast-Asian newspapers framed the 'haze' of 1997–98. *Asian Journal of Communication*, **1**, 72–94.

Mayer, J. (2006) Transboundary perspectives on managing Indonesia's fires. *The Journal of Environment & Development*, **15**, 202–233.

McLellan, J. (2001) From denial to debate – And back again! Malaysian press coverage of the air pollution and 'haze' episodes, July 1997–July 1999. In P. Eaton and M. Radojevic (eds.), *Forest Fires and Haze in Southeast Asia*. New York, Nova Science Publishers, pp. 253–262.

Ministry of Health (2015) Haze Subsidy Scheme. *HealthHub*. Retrieved from https://www.healthhub.sg/a-z/costs-and-financing/21/haze-subsidy-scheme on 30 December 2018.

Mohd Shahwahid, H. O. and Othman, J. (1999) Malaysia. In D. Glover and T. Jessup (eds.), *Indonesia's Fires and Haze: The Cost of Catastrophe*. Singapore, Institute of Southeast Asian Studies, pp. 22–50.

Murdiyarso, D., Lebel, L., Gintings, A., Tampubolon, S., Heil, A. and Wasson, M. (2004) Policy responses to complex environmental problems: Insights from a science–policy activity on transboundary haze from vegetation fires in Southeast Asia. *Agriculture, Ecosystems and Environment*, **104**, 47–56.

Nazeer, N. and Furuoka, F. (2017) Overview of ASEAN environment, transboundary haze pollution agreement and public health. *International Journal of Asia Pacific Studies*, **13**, 73–94.

NEA (2018) Historical PSI readings. *Resources*. Retrieved from https://www.haze.gov.sg/resources/historical-readings on 3 January 2019.

Othman, J., Sahani, M., Mahmud, M. and Ahmad, M. (2014) Transboundary smoke haze pollution in Malaysia: inpatient health impacts and economic valuation. *Environmental Pollution*, **189**, 194–201.

Prideaux, B., Laws, E. and Faulkner, B. (2003) Events in Indonesia: Exploring the limits to formal tourism trends forecasting methods in complex crisis situations. *Tourism Management*, **24**, 475–487.

Quah, E. and Tan, T. S. (2015) When the haze doesn't go away – Opinion Piece. Singapore, *The Straits Times*, 22 September.

Ruitenbeek, J. (1999) Indonesia. In D. Glover and T. Jessup (eds.), *Indonesia's Fires and Haze: The Cost of Catastrophe*. Singapore, Institute of Southeast Asian Studies, pp. 86–129.

Saliluddin, S. (2015) Trans-boundary haze: The annual exo-'dust'. *International Journal of Public Health and Clinical Sciences*, **2**, 1–9.

Salvo, A. (2017) *Local Pollution Drives Global Pollution: Emissions Feedback via Residential Electricity Usage* (under review).

Singapore Hansard (1998) ASEAN Environment Ministers' Meeting (Progress towards addressing problems of fires and haze pollution. *Parliament No. 9, Session No. 1.* https://sprs.parl.gov.sg/search/report?sittingdate=20–04-1998.

Smith, A. L. (2004) ASEAN's Ninth Summit: solidifying regional cohesion, advancing external linkages. *Contemporary Southeast Asia*, **26**, 416.

Tacconi, L. (2003) Fires in Indonesia: causes, costs, and policy implications. *CIFOR Occasional Papers*, **38**, 1–34.

Tan, A. K. J. (2015) The 'haze' crisis in Southeast Asia: assessing Singapore's Transboundary Haze Pollution Act. *SSRN Electronic Journal*, **2**, 1–44.

Tan, D. and Bassano, M. (2014) *Dissecting the Transboundary Haze Pollution Bill of Singapore*. Unpublished paper, Columbia School of International and Public Affairs, New York, pp. 1–20.

Tay, S. (2010) Hardest path is only way forward – Opinion Piece. Singapore, *Wild Singapore News*, 29 October.

Teo, N. C. (2013) Haze: A matter of national emergency! – Opinion Piece. Kuala Lumpur, *The Rocket*, 25 June.

Varkkey, H. (2013) Regional cooperation, patronage, and the ASEAN agreement on transboundary haze pollution. *International Environmental Agreements: Politics, Law and Economics*, **14**, 65–81.

Varkkey, H. (2016a) *The Haze Problem in Southeast Asia: Palm Oil and Patronage*. London, Routledge.

Varkkey, H. (2016b) Transboundary haze and human security in Southeast Asia: national and regional perspectives. *Georgetown Journal of Asian Studies*, **3**, 42–49.

Varkkey, H. and O'Reilly, P. (2019) Socio-political responses towards transboundary haze: The oil palm in Malaysia's discourse. In S. Kukreja (ed.), *Southeast Asia and Environmental Sustainability in Context*, Maryland, Lexington Books.

WHO (2007) *A Safer Future: Global Public Health Security in the 21st Century*. Geneva, World Health Organization.

Wong Chen (2015a) Malaysia must use global standards to measure haze – Opinion Piece. Kuala Lumpur, *Malay Mail*, 27 September.

Wong Chen (2015b) Both PM2.5 and PM10 are health measures and PM2.5 is a far superior measure. *Press Statements*. Retrieved from http://www.wongchen.com/2015/10/press-statement-both-pm2-5-and-pm10-are-health-measures-and-p2-5-is-a-far-superior-measure/ on 28 December 2018.

World Bank Group (2016) *The Cost of Fire: An Economic Analysis of Indonesia's 2015 Fire Crisis*. Jakarta, World Bank.

WTTC (2015) *Benchmarking Travel and Tourism: How Does Travel and Tourism Compare to Other Sectors?* London, World Travel and Tourism Council.

Xia, Y., Guan, D., Jiang, X., Peng, L., Schroeder, H. and Zhang, Q. (2016). Assessment of socioeconomic costs to China's air pollution. *Atmospheric Environment*, **139**, 147–156.

19 Biomass energy prospects: A promising fuel for sustainable development in Asia and the Pacific

KEITH OPENSHAW

Retired forest and energy economist

Keywords

Asia and the Pacific; biomass energy; employment generation; energy efficiency; greenhouse gas mitigation; global warming; climate change; poverty alleviation; sustainable development

Abstract

Energy consumption in general and biomass consumption in particular was examined for all 69 countries in Asia and the Pacific (Asia-Pacific: A-P) based on 2000 and 2015 data. In 2015, the 20 low-income countries of South, Northeast, and Southeast Asia, containing 85% of the A-P population, consumed 57% of total primary energy and 97.5% of biomass energy. Most biomass energy is still used in the unprocessed form by households, the service sector, and industry, but more and more solid, liquid, and gaseous fuels are being manufactured to substitute for fossil fuels, especially motor ethanol and biodiesel. Biomass is also used to generate heat and/or electricity. In many A-P countries, biomass is an important traded fuel, valued at US\$42 billion in 2015, and gives full-time employment to an estimated 27 million each year. It is and will remain the dominant renewable energy in Asia and the Pacific. The supply and demand of biomass was examined, and for wood, the sustainable supply is more than three times the annual demand, with crop residues and dung many times more than demand. The use of biomass for energy and other purposes could be increased substantially. While biomass fuels are saving an estimated 685 million t of carbon emissions each year, at present, excluding China (and India), there is a net emission of greenhouse gases (GHG) from forests and forest soils of at least 615 million tC/yr due to agricultural clearing. This could and should be reversed. If China is included, then there is a net saving. All 69 A-P countries have signed the Paris Agreement (United Nations, 2015), which pledges to limit the global average temperature increase to well below 2°C above pre-industrial levels. Various strategies are proposed to maintain if not increase the share of biomass in the energy mix and to ensure there is a net sequestration of GHG in plants and soils under perennial crops. These initiatives are opportunities to alleviate poverty for millions by ensuring that rural people play a full part in sustainable economic and social development based on indigenous and renewable resources.

19.1 INTRODUCTION

It is generally true that, as per-capita income rises and people move away from subsistence agriculture, people undergo lifestyle changes and use more and more convenient, versatile, and time-saving energy forms, especially natural gas, petroleum products, and electricity. However, the supplies of fossil fuels have finite time horizons, ranging from an estimated 50 years for crude oil to about 200 years for coal (IEA, 2015). Most importantly, these fuels produce greenhouse gases (GHG), especially carbon dioxide (CO_2), the principal contributor to global warming that induces climate change.

The scientific, technical, technological, and policy issues related to global warming and climate change, including the impacts of climate change, have been well-documented by the assessment reports of the Intergovernmental Panel on Climate Change (IPCC) (IPCC, 2013, 2014a, 2014b, 2018). Based on the IPCC assessments, the international community has adopted the 1992 United Nations Framework Convention on Climate Change (UNFCCC) and its 1977 Kyoto Protocol, and the Paris Agreement in 2016 (see https://unfccc.int/). In particular, the Paris Agreement aims to limit 'the increase in global average temperature to well below 2°C above pre-industrial levels' while pursuing efforts to limit it further to 1.5°C (United Nations, 2015). However, to achieve this 'well below 2°C' goal provides great challenges to the Parties of the UNFCCC (IPCC, 2013, 2018; Climate Action Tracker, 2018). Concerted action has to be taken to (1) temper fossil fuel burning, (2) substantially increase energy efficiency measures, (3) greatly expand the use of renewable energy, and (4) accelerate carbon capture and storage (IPCC, 2014b).

The principal causes of the accumulation of atmospheric GHG are emissions from fossil fuel burning and land-use changes, as well as methane production and emissions from plants, animals, and fossil fuels. It is difficult both economically and practically to reduce the consumption of fossil fuels in the short run (IEA, 2014).

Unlike fossil fuels, biomass fuels are more or less GHG benign if they are from a sustainable supply. This is because the annual sequestration of CO_2 by plants is at least equal to the release of CO_2 from burning biomass.

Therefore, while the use of fossil fuels may be cheap and convenient in financial terms, in economic and environmental terms, not only are they expensive, but also their continued and expanded use could lead to calamitous consequences for many people in the Asia-Pacific (A-P) region (and the world), especially the poor.

This chapter examines the current use of (renewable) biomass energy in the A-P region and suggests ways not only to expand its use, but also as a substitute for fossil fuels, while acting as an increased store of atmospheric carbon, thus providing alternative and sustainable sources of carbon-based energy to meet some of the future energy demands.

19.2 ASIA-PACIFIC REGION

The A-P region covers 69 countries, as listed in the various tables (UN Country Classification, 2014.), excluding some very small island states,[1] with a combined land area of nearly 40 million km². It ranges from Turkey in the east (27° E) to French Polynesia in the west (135° W). It has two countries with more than a billion people – China and India – and some very small islands, such as Niue with 2,000 people and Nauru and Tuvalu with 11,000 people each. There is a variety of countries, from the rich gulf oil states, which consume practically no biomass energy, to countries like Cambodia and Nepal that are very dependent on biomass for their energy requirements. Some countries, namely Bangladesh and the Maldives, have population densities of more than 1,000 people per km², yet others, such as Australia, Kazakhstan, Mongolia, and Turkmenistan, have fewer than 10 people per km².

[1] Appropriate data for all the 69 countries and two Special Administrative Regions (SAR) (Hong Kong, Macau) and one Province (Taiwan) of China were collected and used to generate the various tables in this chapter. The small island states include Wallis and Futuna; Tokelau, Santa Cruz Island, now part of the Solomon Islands; Line Islands, some of which are US territories and others part of Kiribati; and Rarotonga, now part of the Cook Islands. All these islands have extensive forest areas. All these islands have a combined area of 133,000 ha and a population of 35,000 people.

Both 2000 and 2015 data collected from various sources are presented. Where appropriate, estimates were made by the author. The estimated population in 2000 was 3,746 million, whereas in 2015 it is estimated to be 4,433 million, an increase of 687 million (Population Pyramid, 2015), ranging from a decrease of 16% in Georgia to an increase of 280% in Qatar. Naturally, energy consumption will have increased to account for population and wealth increase. Energy consumption for low-income countries in Asia increased by about 150% between 2000 and 2015 according to the International Energy Agency (IEA, 2002, 2010, 2015), but population increased by only 18%. This rise in energy consumption was driven especially by increased demand in China (280%) and to a lesser extent in India (50%). Also, China's rural population decreased by 22%, a principal driver of biomass energy demand, whereas in India, it increased by 18% (based on author's analysis of individual country data).

Table 19.1 summarizes some basic statistics for the five groups of countries for the years 2000 and 2015. It is noted that the rural population increased by only 1% over the 15-year period, whereas total population increased by 18%. Likewise, biomass energy increased by only 8.5%, whereas total energy demand increased by more than 100%, principally from fossil fuel consumption; this could have very adverse climatic effects.

19.3 ENERGY CONSUMPTION IN ASIA AND THE PACIFIC

As is to be expected, the consumption and type of energy vary enormously in the region, mainly as a result of income differences, but also because of climate. In cold regions and in the cool season, energy is required for heating purposes, and likewise, to reduce the temperature during the hot season. Also, fuel is used to produce more convenient and versatile forms of energy: converting wood to charcoal, and extracting methane from dung and so forth. Table 19.2 gives basic information about groups of low-income countries for 2000 and 2015.

In 2000, the Northeast and South Asia groups of countries have large populations, accounting for 43% of the world's total (6,127 million). The per-capita GDP is relatively low, with the exception of Brunei, a small oil-rich state, with a per-capita GDP of US$24,630. The 2000 population density in South Asia is high – 332 per km² – whereas in the other groups of countries it ranges from 111 to 127 per km². Also, these groups of countries have a large rural population percentage, many still in a semi-subsistence mode, hence the relatively large consumption of biomass energy (7.15 GJ per-capita on average) and the modest consumption of fossil fuels of the total energy consumption (16.90 GJ per-capita). China is in the process of reforestation, whereas in the 'insular' countries, deforestation is occurring

Table 19.1. Asia-Pacific countries: Some basic statistics for 2000 and 2015.

Region	Population (million)		Rural population (million) (%)		Per-capita GDP/PPP (US$)		Land area (million hectare)		Forest area (million hectare) (%)		Total energy use EJ (10^{18} J)		Biomass energy EJ (% total)	
	2000	2015	2000	2015	2000	2015	2000	2015	2000	2015	2000	2015	2000	2015
LI group	3,183.83	3,743.33	2,132.17(67)	2,132.22 (57)	685	9,300	1,952.12	1,952.12	494.30 (25)	518.70 (27)	76.63	195.09	22.79 (29.7)	24.65 (12.6)
MI group	177.00	224.96	62.37 (35)	63.42 (28)	1,990	16,080	311.09	311.09	20.87 (7)	23.84 (8)	10.24	18.53	0.14 (1.4)	0.16 (0.9)
HI group	268.68	310.35	50.37 (19)	35.37 (11)	24,090	43,410	1,108.19	1,108.19	174.89 (16)	170.70 (15)	46.58	61.93	0.30 (6.4)	0.34 (0.5)
FSU	108.56	143.43	68.23 (63)	89.35 (62)	620	7,790	528.73	528.73	17.84 (3)	17.90 (3)	4.84	8.64	0.19 (4.0)	0.27 (3.1)
Pacific Is.	7.86	10.53	6.08 (77)	6.08 (77)	2,085	5,160	52.25	52.25	37.79 (72)	37.75 (72)	0.34	0.54	0.20 (58.8)	0.23 (42.6)
Total or average*	3,745.93	4,432.60	2,319.22 (62)	2,326.44 (52)	2,425	11,970	3,952.38	3,952.38	745.69 (19)	768.89 (19)	138.63	284.73	23.62 (17.0)	25.65 (9.0)
Difference between 2015/2000	686.67		45.22		9,545		Same		23..20		146.10		2.03	

Note: The countries in the various groups are given in Tables 19.2 to 19.6. These were taken from data of individual countries.

Hong Kong, Macau, and Taiwan are part of China, but they are included in the high-income (HI) group.

Income levels: GDP values in US$: LI (low-income) group. <1,000; MI (middle-income) group <2,000, and HI (high-income) group >10,000 (based on author's assessment).

Income levels: GDP values in US$: For 2000, LI (low-income) group <2,000; MI (middle-income) group 2,000–10,000, and HI (high-income) group >10,000; for 2015, LI <10,000. MI 10,000–20,000, and HI >20,000 (based on author's assessment).

The purchasing parity power (PPP/GDP) was in 2000 and 2015 values for their respective years.

* GDP in the 'Total' row is the average value. The purchasing parity power (PPP/GDP) was in 2000 and 2015 values for their respective years. Forest area excludes woodlands.

Sources: FAO, 2001a, 2003, 2010a, 2010b; IEA, 2002, 2015; Population Pyramid, 2015; World Bank, 2000, 2003a, 2004, 2015a

Table 19.2. Asia low-income (LI) countries: Some basic statistics for 2000 and 2015.

Region	Population (million)		Rural population (million) (%)		Per-capita GDP/PPP (US$)		Land area (million hectare)		Forest area (million hectare) (%)		Fossil fuels and hydroelectric GJ/capita		Biomass energy GJ/capita (% total)	
	2000	2015	2000	2015	2000	2015	2000	2015	2000	2015	2000	2015	2000	2015
NE Asia LI	1,295.21	1,404.18	818 (65)	640 (46)	840	13,850	1,106.22	1,106.22	195.65 (18)	225.90 (20)	20.47	87.61	5.18 (20)	4.13 (5)
S Asia LI	1,366.37	1,711.33	988 (73)	1,156 (68)	460	5,320	411.88	411.88	75.68 (18)	82.05 (20)	11.78	16.01	7.52 (39)	7.45 (32)
SE Asia Cont.	208.16	237.69	153 (74)	150 (63)	840	8,540	188.16	188.16	91.79 (49)	88.43 (47)	20.56	31.17	14.70 (42)	12.00 (28)
SE Asia Insular	314.07	390.13	173 (55)	186 (48)	910	10,820	245.86	245.86	129.28 (53)	122.32 (50)	22.15	32.09	8.73 (28)	8.59 (21)
Total or average*	3,183.83	3,743.33	2,132 (67)	2,132 (57)	685	9,300	1,952.12	Same	492.40 (25)	518.70 (27)	16.90	45.43	7.15 (30)	6.59 (13)
Difference between 2015/2000	559.50		0		8,615		Same		26.30		28.53		−0.56	

Note: NE Asia Low-Income: China, DPR Korea, Mongolia. *South Asia Low-Income*: Bangladesh, Bhutan, India, Maldives, Nepal, Pakistan, Sri Lanka. *SE Asia Continental*: Cambodia, Laos, Myanmar, Thailand, Vietnam. *SE Asia Insular*: Brunei, Timor Leste, Indonesia, Malaysia, Philippines.
The purchasing parity power (PPP/GDP) was in 2000 and 2015 values for their respective years. Forest area excludes woodlands.
*The GDP, fossil fuel, and biomass fuel in the 'Total' row are average values, which were weighted according to population, energy, forest area, and tree volume.
Sources: FAO, 2001a, 2003, 2010a, 2010b, 2015; IEA, 2002, 2015; Population Pyramid, 2015; UN, 2002, 2005; World Bank, 2000, 2003a, 2004, 2015; various other documents

because of agricultural clearing. Also, some tropical forests are being replaced by oil palm. The forest area excludes woodlands and trees outside the forest.

The population of these groups of countries has increased by 560 million (17.5%) over the 15-year period, with the greatest increase in South Asia – 119 million (25%); it also has the smallest increase in per-capita GDP and a large rural population (Table 19.2). For these groups of countries, the rural population has declined from 67% to 57%, with China showing the largest decline from 64% to 46%, equal to 179 million people. The average per-capita GDP has increased over 13 times from 2000 to 2015, with China having the largest increase – nearly 17 times. The forest areas in NE Asia and South Asia have increased, but those in SE Asia have declined because of agricultural clearing. It should be noted that the forest area in DPR Korea declined by 1.9 million ha (27%) in the 15-year period, again mainly owing to agricultural clearing. It is in such countries as DPRK that great efforts have to be made to reforest and to increase the growing stock of trees in existing forest areas.

Table 19.3 examines the middle-income countries of the Mediterranean and the Gulf States for 2000 and 2015. In 2000, the Mediterranean and Gulf States middle-income countries had a combined population of 177 million with a growth rate of more than 2%. The overall population density of people per km² was 569, with 35% in rural areas. This group of countries has a low forest cover – on average about 7% – and low per-capita biomass energy consumption. However, from personal experience working in Jordan and Turkey on environmental/energy projects, the author believes that there is a considerable under-recording of biomass energy use.

In the gulf oil-producing countries of Iran and Iraq, fossil fuel consumption is relatively high. In both countries, petroleum products are subsidized; this leads to excessive use of these fuels and poor energy efficiency, and it curtails the use of biomass energy.

Between 2000 and 2015, the population of the Asian middle-income countries increased by 48 million, or 27%, whereas the rural population barely increased (1.05 million). Per-capita income increased eight times, with the largest increase in Iraq (15 times), followed by Iran (11 times). On average, in Mediterranean countries, the forest area increased by an average of 14%. As is to be expected, per-capita biomass energy consumption decreased by 0.06 GJ between 2000 and 2015, whereas per-capita fossil fuel consumption increased by 43%. The aim of these countries should be to increase the stock of woody biomass and use more biomass for energy purposes.

Table 19.4 examines the high-income group in the Asia-Pacific region. In 2000, in the N Asia high-income group, one set (Hong Kong, Macau, and Singapore) had a relatively small population (less than 10.3 million) and a small percentage of rural people. The other set containing Japan, the Republic of Korea, and Taiwan, had combined populations of more than 194 million for a group total of 205.44 million, but with a relatively small rural population of 40 million (21%). This latter set has considerable forest areas – 33 million ha, 66% of the land area. All the high-income groups, except the Pacific high-income group, have a low per-capita consumption of biomass energy.

One problem with biomass energy statistics is that little of its production and consumption is recorded. Consumption surveys have to be undertaken to obtain an estimate of biomass used by households, industry (formal and informal), and the service sector. In Australia and New Zealand, it was found that wood was used extensively for household heating purposes in the winter, especially in rural areas, and the many wood-using industries use waste wood, and the sugar industry uses bagasse as a boiler fuel.

In 2015, the population of the high-income group was 310 million, an increase of nearly 42 million (16%), compared with 2000. There is a considerable surplus of biomass in many of these countries, and together with solar, wind, water, and geothermal, much more could be done to expand renewable energy use, as well as increasing the tree stock.

Another set of countries with fairly low incomes and relatively dry climates is Afghanistan, Yemen, and the eight former Soviet Union (FSU) countries. In 2000, Afghanistan and Yemen had large rural populations with few natural resources. Many of the areas are desert and/or barren, hence the relatively low rural population density of 32 per km². Pastoral agriculture is the principal rural pursuit, although in parts of Afghanistan, poppy growing is common, and in Yemen the tree *Catha edulis* is cultivated, from which *miraa* (*qat* or Somali tea) is extracted from the leaves. The forest cover in these two countries is very low, although there are areas of shrub and bushland, not counted as forests.

In 2000, like Afghanistan and Yemen, the FSU countries had high rural population percentages and low per-capita incomes. However, for these countries as a group, the consumption of fossil fuels is relatively high; this is because there are fossil fuel deposits in many of these countries. Over the last decade, oil and gas deposits in/around the Caspian Sea have been exploited by Azerbaijan, Kazakhstan, and Turkmenistan. Only Armenia and Georgia have scarce oil deposits.

The consumption of biomass energy is low, but data are unavailable for all the countries except Armenia, Kazakhstan, and Kyrgyzstan. In these countries, official biomass energy consumption is underestimated. For example, in Kazakhstan the official figure in 2015 was 0.1 GJ/capita, whereas it is nearer 0.5 GJ/capita. Likewise, in Georgia biomass energy consumption in 2015 was about 5.0 GJ/capita. Georgia has the largest forest area (47%) and Tajikistan has the smallest (0.2%). The average

Table 19.3. Asia middle-income (MI) countries: Some basic statistics for 2000 and 2015.

Region	Population (million)		Rural population (million) (%)		Per-capita GDP/ PPP (US$)		Land area (million hectare)		Forest area (million hectare) (%)		Fossil fuels and hydroelectric GJ/capita		Biomass energy GJ/capita (% total)	
	2000	2015	2000	2015	2000	2015	2000	2015	2000	2015	2000	2015	2000	2015
Med MI	87.58	109.43	31.12 (36)	30.77 (28)	2,540	15,540	104.80	104.80	10.72 (10)	12.32 (12)	43.03	58.09	1.15 (2.6)	1.03 (1.7)
Gulf MI	89.42	115.53	31.25 (35)	32.65 (28)	1,450	16,590	206.29	206.29	10.15 (4)	11.52 (5)	70.82	103.97	0.41 (0.6)	0.42 (0.4)
Total or average*	177.00	224.96	62.37 (35)	63.42 (28)	1,990	16,080	311.09	311.09	20.87 (7)	23.84 (8)	57.07	81.65	0.78 (1.3)	0.72 (0.9)
Difference between 2015/2000	47.96		1.05		14,090		Same		2.97		24.58		−0.06	

Note: Mediterranean Middle-Income (*Med MI*): Jordan, Palestine National Authority, Syria, Turkey. *Gulf States Middle-Income (MI*): Iran, Iraq.
The purchasing parity power (PPP/GDP) was in 2000 and 2015 values for their respective years. Forest area excludes woodlands.
* The GDP, fossil fuel, and biomass fuel in the 'Total' row are average values, which were weighted according to population, energy, forest area, and tree volume.
Sources: FAO, 2001a, 2003, 2010a, 2010b, 2015; Population Pyramid, 2015; UN, 2002, 2005; World Bank, 2000, 2003a, 2004, 2015a; various other documents

Table 19.4. Asia-Pacific high-income (HI) group: Some basic statistics for 2000 and 2015.

Region	Population (million)		Rural population (%)		Per-capita GDP/ PPP (US$)		Land area (million hectare)		Forest area (million hectare) (%)		Fossil fuels and hydroelectric GJ/capita		Biomass energy GJ/capita (% total)	
	2000	2015	2000	2015	2000	2015	2000	2015	2000	2015	2000	2015	2000	2015
N Asia HI	205.44	213.82	40.32 (20)	23.31 (11)	27,170	40,660	49.97	49.97	33.32 (67)	33.18 (67)	153.59	172.28	0.13 (0.08)	0.11 (0.06)
Pacific HI	23.18	28.76	3.10 (13)	3.35 (12)	19,380	44,260	796.83	796.83	139.82 (18)	135.74 (17)	228.90	228.26	11.39 (4.74)	10.57 (4.76)
Gulf HI	29.87	52.70	5.66 (19)	8.01 (15)	10,700	58,750	257.29	257.29	1.30 (0.5)	1.31 (0.5)	280.41	314.12	0.13 (0.05)	0.11 (0.04)
Med HI	10.19	15.07	1.29 (13)	0.70 (5)	11,950	27,140	4.10	4.10	0.45 (11)	0.47 (11)	102.55	102.55	0.49 (0.48)	0.56 (0.56)
Total or average*	268.68	310.35	50.37 (19)	35.37 (11)	24,090	43,410	1,108.19	1,108.19	174.89 (16)	170.70 (15)	172.25	197.55	1.12 (0.64)	1.10 (0.56)
Difference between 2015/2000	41.67		−15.00		19,320		Same		−4.19		25.30		−0.02	

Note: *N Asia*: Japan, Republic of Korea, and Singapore, as well as Hong Kong, Macau, and Taiwan, which are part of China. *Pacific HI*: Australia, New Caledonia, New Zealand. *Gulf HI*: Bahrain, Kuwait, Oman, Qatar, United Arab Emirates, Saudi Arabia. *Mediterranean HI*: Cyprus, Israel, Lebanon. Hydro plus nuclear and geothermal electricity where applicable.

The purchasing parity power (PPP/GDP) was in 2000 and 2015 values for their respective years. Forest area excludes woodlands.

*The GDP, fossil fuel, and biomass fuel in the 'Total' row are average values, which were weighted according to population, energy, forest area, and tree volume.

Sources: FAO, 2001a, 2003, 2010a, 2010b, 2015; IEA, 2015; Population Pyramid, 2015; UN, 2002, 2005; World Bank, 2000, 2003a, 2004, 2015a; various other documents

forest cover is 4% for the FSU group, but in many countries, there is shrubland and bushland, and these are a source of fuel and poles. According to the Global Forest Resource Assessment (FAO, 2015), Afghanistan had 29.47 million ha of woodland – 45% of land area.

In 2015, the population of Afghanistan and Yemen had increased to 59 million, nearly 22 million more than 2000 (Table 19.5). The rural population was still high at 58%. The per-capita income was estimated to be US$2,780, more than five times of that in 2000. Total energy consumption doubled between 2000 and 2015, with the estimated biomass energy consumption increasing by 58%. The present conflict in Yemen has increased the dependency on biomass energy.

A similar picture emerges for the former Soviet Union countries. Between 2000 and 2015, the population of the FSU countries increased by 13 million, and the rural population was still high at 58%. The estimated biomass energy consumption in the period 2000 to 2015 increased by a modest 7.3 PJ. It is certain that the stored carbon in woody biomass and forest soils could be increased with funding from various sources.

In 2000, the 'large island' states in the Pacific had relatively low GDPs (Table 19.6). It ranged from US$1,830 in Fiji to US$630 in the Solomon Islands. They have large rural populations (82%) and considerable forest cover (73%). Therefore, the estimated average biomass energy consumption is greater than the fossil fuel consumption. On the other hand, the 'small island' states have medium-sized forest areas; they are small, with a relatively large GDP, and the population has easy access to markets. Therefore, fossil fuel consumption is high and the estimated biomass energy consumption low. Many small islands are low-lying atolls, and with increases in sea level, several could be submerged or swamped at high tides (Haq, 1994). For this reason, they are very concerned about global warming and its negative effects.

Compared with 2000, in 2015, the population in the large island countries increased by 38%, whereas that in the small island states increased by only 8%. The rural population in both groups increased by more than 2 million; between 2000 and 2015, average GDP increased nearly fourfold in large island countries, but only doubled in small island states. In the large island countries, per-capita biomass energy decreased by 15%, whereas in small island states it increased by 218 TJ (Table 19.6).

19.4 PRESENT ROLE OF BIOMASS ENERGY

The principal consumers of biomass energy are rural households, followed by urban households, then (mainly) rural formal and informal industries, and finally the service sector, both public and private. Fuelwood – including bamboo and rattan from stems, branches, and twigs, plus woody shrubs and brush – is the most commonly used form of biomass; unprocessed crop residues and coconut/palm oil fronds are used in season or when wood is in short supply, and in some areas of some countries, mainly in South Asia, dung is used. Dead wood and other forms of dry biomass are preferred, but semi-dry and 'green' biomass is used when dry wood is unavailable. When these fuels are at a premium, even plant roots, leaves, and grass are burnt.

Unprocessed and semi-processed biomass is used for cooking, par-boiling rice, preparing animal food (pig and poultry), and for water and space heating by households, restaurants, food shops, canteens (armed forces, hospitals, and schools). Sometimes, smoke from the fire is used as an insect repellent and to preserve grain; wood fires are even used to provide some light.

Biomass is an important formal and informal industrial fuel, especially in rural areas. For many industries, biomass is the cheapest and most readily available fuel. For some industries, such as rubber curing, sugar production, and wood processing, the biomass energy supply is available on site, being a waste in the production process, whereas for other industries, fuelwood may be grown specifically as a boiler fuel for tea drying and tobacco curing in barns. Many industries buy their biomass fuel, and this provides gainful employment for rural people. Some biomass is processed, the most frequent form being charcoal. It is a more manageable fuel than fuelwood and has about twice the energy value of wood per unit weight. Principally, it is used for cooking and roasting. In addition, it has industrial uses for iron smelting and it is used by blacksmiths.

Several liquid fuels are made from biomass, the commonest being (motor) ethanol, followed by bio-diesel (from plant oils) and methanol (wood alcohol). It is also possible to make petrol by applying temperature and pressure to biomass (e.g., the Fischer Tropsch reaction), but production is relatively expensive.

Biogas is produced anaerobically from biomass, usually dung. It contains about 60% methane and, therefore, has similar properties to natural gas. Producer gas is another gaseous fuel from biomass made through an exothermic reaction when biomass is heated to high temperatures. (When coal is the feedstock, the gas is called 'town gas' and coke is the by-product.) The main volatiles in producer gas are carbon monoxide and methane. In order to control the temperature during the manufacture of producer gas, specific quantities of water may be added. The water splits into hydrogen and oxygen and is called water gas. The combined gases have a higher energy value than producer gas alone and can be used in stationary/mobile engines and used for drying and other purposes. China uses producer gas enriched with water gas (ScienceDirect, 2019).

Biomass is practically GHG-neutral, unlike coal and other fossil fuels. If biomass is burnt inefficiently it gives off products

Table 19.5. Afghanistan, Yemen, and former Soviet Union (FSU) low-income countries: Some basic statistics for 2000 and 2015.

Region	Population (million)		Rural population (million) (%)		Per-capita GDP/ PPP (US$)		Land area (million hectare)		Forest area (million hectare) (%)		Fossil fuels and hydroelectric GJ/capita		Biomass energy GJ/capita (% total)	
	2000	2015	2000	2015	2000	2015	2000	2015	2000	2015	2000	2015	2000	2015
Af./Yemen LI	37.50	59.36	28.73 (77)	41.78 (70)	510	2,780	118.09	118.09	1.90 (2)	1.90 (2)	9.99	13.77	3.08 (23.54)	3.08 (18.27)
FSU LI	71.06	84.07	39.50 (56)	47.57 (57)	680	11,320	410.64	410.64	15.94 (4)	16.00 (4)	71.06	89.85	1.11 (1.82)	1.03 (1.13)
Total or average*	108.56	143.43	68.23 (63)	89.35 (62)	620	7,790	528.73	528.73	17.84 (3)	17.90 (3)	42.79	58.36	1.79 (4.02)	1.88 (3.11)
Difference between 2015/2000	34.87		21.12		7,170		Same		0.06		15.57		−0.09	

Note: Af. = Afghanistan; Yemen. Former Soviet Union (FSU) Low-Income (LI) Countries: Armenia, Azerbaijan, Georgia, Kazakhstan, Kyrgyzstan, Tajikistan, Turkmenistan, Uzbekistan. Forest areas exclude woodlands.

The purchasing parity power (PPP/GDP) was in 2000 and 2015 values for their respective years. Forest area excludes woodlands.

*The GDP, fossil fuel, and biomass fuel in the 'Total' row are average values, which were weighted according to population, energy, forest area, and tree volume.

Sources: FAO, 2001a, 2003, 2010a, 2010b, 2015; IEA, 2015; Population Pyramid, 2015; UN, 2002, 2005; World Bank, 2000, 2003a, 2004, 2015a; various other documents

Table 19.6. Pacific large and small island countries: Some basic statistics for 2000 and 2015.

Region	Population (million)		Rural population (%)		Per-capita GDP/ PPP (US$)		Land area (million hectare)		Forest area (million hectare) (%)		Fossil fuels and hydroelectric GJ/capita		Biomass energy GJ/capita (% total)	
	2000	2015	2000	2015	2000	2015	2000	2015	2000	2015	2000	2015	2000	2015
Pacific Large	6.77	9.35	5.57 (82)	7.69 (82)	910	3,420	51.14	51.14	37.29 (73)	37.20 (73)	5.68	14.42	29.00 (84)	24.70 (63)
Pacific Small	1.09	1.18	0.51 (47)	0.55 (47)	9,425	18,980	1.11	1.11	0.50 (45)	0.55 (50)	97.36	147.63	2.00 (2)	2.00 (2)
Total or average*	7.86	10.53	6.08 (80)	8.24 (77)	2,085	5,130	52.25	52.25	37.79 (72)	37.75 (72)	18.36	29.29	25.28 (58)	22.09 (43)
Difference between 2015/2000	2.67		2.16		3,045		Same		−0.04		10.93		−3.19	

Note: Pacific – Large Islands: Fiji, Solomon Islands, Papua New Guinea, Vanuatu. *Pacific – Small Islands*: American Samoa, Cook Islands, French Polynesia, Guam, Kiribati, Marshall Islands, Micronesia, Nauru, Niue, North Mariana Islands, Palau, Samoa, Tonga, Tuvalu.
The purchasing parity power (PPP/GDP) was in 2000 and 2015 values for their respective years. Forest area excludes woodlands.
*The GDP, fossil fuel, and biomass fuel in the 'Total' row are average values, which were weighted according to population, energy, forest area, and tree volume.
Sources: FAO, 2001a, 2003, 2010a, 2010b, 2015; Population Pyramid, 2015; UN, 2002, 2005; World Bank, 2000, 2003a, 2004, 2015a; various other documents

of incomplete combustion (PIC), including GHGs such as carbon monoxide (CO), methane (CH_4), and oxides of nitrogen (NOx), plus particulates; these latter can cause pollution, resulting in adverse health effects, especially for cooks in poorly ventilated kitchens; this is especially so when 'green' biomass is burnt. But these effects can be and are mitigated by adopting certain simple practices, such as drying fuel, ensuring adequate ventilation, and using filters, chimneys, and more efficient burning methods, equipment, and end-use devices. Also, charcoal causes very little indoor air pollution (IAP), especially if the stove is lit outside, before taking it into the kitchen, and a sizeable fraction of households cook outside at least part of the year (up to 30–40%). Unfortunately, most energy planners regard biomass, especially unprocessed biomass, as a non-sustainable fuel to be replaced as quickly as possible with (modern and 'efficient')[2] fossil fuels and electricity. It is regarded as a 'backward' (traditional) non-commercial energy form, which causes deforestation, and places an undue burden on the people who collect and use these fuels. The underlying message is 'ban biomass energy from the kitchen' (World Bank, 1992). However, people are reluctant to purchase fuel when it can be collected, and electricity is rarely used for cooking by the poor. While the deaths from IAP are unacceptable, steps can be taken to drastically reduce this number – this is discussed later.

19.5 TRADE IN BIOMASS ENERGY

Despite being classified as non-commercial – another misleading term – biomass is a significant traded fuel and, in some countries, the most important 'commercial' fuel. Employment is generated, especially rural employment, in biomass growing and management, production, transport, and trade. The growing and tending of biomass creates the fewest jobs, but it has a large multiplier effect on employment. For every job in the growing of wood, many more jobs are created in production, transport, and trade, the majority of which are rural, so the trade in biomass energy is a stimulus to rural employment based on an indigenous renewable resource. Even today, the Indian sub-continent relies on traded biomass; this is documented in the Annual Reports of the Indian Ministry of New and Renewable Energy (MNRE, 2009–10, 2010–11, 2016–17, 2017–18).

If it is considered that all the biomass energy is used for cooking and the substitute fuel is kerosene, then in 2000, taking end-use efficiency into consideration, the substitute cost of traded biomass would be about US$45 billion at a price of US$0.45 per litre[3] (World Bank, 2015b), and for all biomass energy the kerosene substitute cost would be US$127 billion.[4] This illustrates the importance of biomass energy. Also, many countries subsidize fossil fuels, especially kerosene and liquid petroleum gas (LPG). Therefore, biomass energy is saving the governments the subsidized portion of these fuels.

19.6 ESTIMATED BIOMASS ENERGY CONSUMPTION IN THE A-P REGION

In 2000, the total estimated consumption of biomass energy in Asia and the Pacific was 23,620 PJ, equivalent to 1.5 billion tonnes (t) of air-dry wood, with an estimated 35% traded (8,356 PJ) worth US$22.6 billion with an average price of US$42/t (Table 19.7). This provided 'full-time' employment to an estimated 24.3 million people in the region. The low-income countries in NE, South, and SE Asia account for 96.5% of consumption.

However, for some people, biomass production and trading are not a full-time occupation but are a seasonal or part-time activity, so more than 32 million people could benefit from the growing, production, transport, and trade in biomass energy. Many of the jobs are in rural areas, indicating its importance as a means to earn income. It is an easy industry to enter or leave, for very little cash and equipment are required, except for transportation, but vehicles and boats can be hired.

Compared with 2000, the population of the Asia and Pacific region in 2015 had increased by 18%, whereas biomass energy consumption increased only 8.6% to 25,634 PJ or 1,654 million t (Table 19.7). However, traded biomass in 2015 was estimated to be 669 million t valued at US$42 billion, an increase of 82% compared to 2000 and a 12% increase in estimated employment to more than 27.2 million 'full-time' jobs, providing much more part-time employment.

From personal observation, it was noted that many women plant and tend trees, collect fuelwood, residues, and dung, and trade in these products. But, in some countries, producers,

---

[2] This is deliberate misinformation. There is no such thing as efficient energy. It is the way that energy is used and the device in which it is used that determines its efficiency. Again, to term fossil fuels as modern energy and recently produced biomass as traditional (or old) energy engenders in the readers' mind a bias against biomass. All energy forms have their costs and benefits, including social/environmental costs and benefits; evaluating their full economic, social, and environmental costs is essential.

[3] This is the average world pump price for diesel, which includes taxes and subsidies. Diesel is similar to kerosene. An estimated 100 billion litres are required to substitute for the biomass energy.

[4] It is assumed that kerosene is the cheapest substitute fossil fuel. The efficiency of the stove is 35% and its energy value is 36 MJ/l. The efficiency of a wood stove is 15% and wood's energy value is 15.5 MJ/kg (air-dry 15% moisture content wet basis (mcwb)). In 2015, the unsubsidized price of kerosene was US$1.17/l (US$1,400/t) and that for the wood equivalent was US$63/t. Taking efficiency and energy value differences into consideration, the equivalent price of kerosene was US$260/t.

Table 19.7. Asia and the Pacific 2000 and 2015: Estimated biomass energy consumption (total and traded), its value and estimated employment in traded biomass fuels by various groups in the region.

Region	Population (million)		Area (million hectare)		Biomass energy PJ (GJ/capita)		Wood equivalent (air-dry) (million tonne)				Traded value (million US$)		Estimated employment (000 person yr)	
							Total		Traded					
	2000	2015	2000	2015	2000	2015	2000	2015	2000	2015	2000	2015	2000	2015
Asia LI	3,183.83	3,743.33	1,952.12	1,952.12	22,782 (7.16)	24,632 (6.58)	1,469.81	1,589.16	514.43	635.66	20,577	38,140	23,410	26,060
Asia MI	177.00	224.96	311.09	311.09	138 (0.78)	161 (0.72)	8.90	10.39	3.56	4.68	267	515	150	180
A-P HI	268.68	310.35	1,108.19	1,108.19	300 (1.12)	342 (1.10)	19.35	22.06	11.61	14.56	1,161	2,184	370	440
FSU LI	108.56	143.43	528.73	528.73	193 (1.78)	267 (1.86)	12.45	17.23	4.98	7.75	374	853	200	300
P Islands	7.86	10.53	52.25	52.25	199 (25.32)	232 (22.03)	12.84	14.97	4.49	5.99	180	359	200	250
Total	3,745.93	4,432.60	3,952.38	3,952.38	23,612 (6.30)	25,634 (5.78)	1,523.35	1,653.81	539.07	668.64	22,559	42,051	24,330	27,230
Difference between 2015/2000	686.67		Same		2,022		130.46		129.57		19,492		2,900	

Note: The energy value of wood is 15.5 GJ/t (15% moisture content wet basis). The estimated percentage of traded biomass was 60% for Asia high-income group, 40% for Asia middle-income countries, and the FSU, and 35% for the remaining countries. The assumed value of traded biomass was US$100/t for high-income group, US$75/t for Asia middle-income countries and the FSU, and US$40/t for the remaining countries. The estimated employment per 100 t of traded biomass energy was 4.55 for Asia LI and the Pacific Islands, 4.10 for the Asia MI and FSU, and 3.20 for A-P HI.

Sources: Archer 1993; Dougherty, 1993; Ouerghi, 1993; Openshaw, 2010; author's calculation

transporters, and traders are harassed or penalized. Licences may be required to cut trees even on private land, and permits may be required to transport and trade in biomass energy. Vehicles may be stopped by police in order to solicit bribes. Fees may be charged for passing from one province to the next and taxes levied on the fuel. On the other hand, in many countries, fossil fuels and electricity are subsidized, which means that biomass energy may be at a competitive disadvantage. However, given the correct incentives, biomass trade could be expanded in an effective way to assist with poverty alleviation.

19.7 EXISTING STOCK AND SUSTAINABLE SUPPLY OF BIOMASS

All biomass is renewable, but it is sustainable only if no more than its annual production (growth) is used. Of course, annual crops have little if any accumulation of stock. Food and residues can be stored over a short period of time. Some crops, such as sugar cane, have a life cycle of up to 18 months before the cane is harvested. While food is the principal product of annual crops, other products are harvested, such as cotton, jute, hops, tobacco, etc. All these crops have residues which can be burnt. But many residues have other competing uses, such as animal bedding and feed, building material, fertilizer and soil conditioner, paper making, and so forth. However, it is not possible to use more than the yearly production of annual crops, and therefore, this kind of biomass is sustainable.

The supply of residues is seasonal, being abundant after harvest, so its use as an energy source is mainly seasonal. But excrement is produced daily by all animals and it is available throughout the year. Cattle dung is used extensively as a fuel in regions of some countries, especially in South Asia. Like plant biomass, dung has other uses, especially as a fertilizer, but it is used in buildings as a binder. If excrement accumulates, then anaerobic breakdown can occur, with methane as a principal product. This is a useful form of energy, but is also a potent greenhouse gas if vented to the atmosphere. Capturing and using methane (biogas) or burning the dung directly may prevent most of the methane emissions.

Both residues and dung are less-desirable fuels than wood because these fuels contain a smaller amount of energy per unit weight at the same moisture content. Residues tend to burn more quickly than wood, so the fire needs greater attention. Wood is a perennial crop and the store of biomass in trees is usually many times more than its annual growth. Therefore, in the short term, it is possible to use more wood than the annual growth. If this continues, then eventually, all the tree capital will be eliminated. For this reason, wood is conditionally renewable, provided that, on average, only an amount up to the annual growth is used each year.

19.7.1 Estimated stock and yield of woody biomass

In the countries where biomass energy is used extensively, namely in the low-income countries of Asia and the large island countries of the Pacific, there is an overall surplus of residues and dung and usually of woody biomass; in some countries there is a large surplus. But even in such countries there may be local shortages, especially near large population concentrations. Yet many inventories of woody biomass significantly underestimate both stock and yield. Traditionally, forest inventories are confined to natural forests, woodlands, and plantations and sometimes only state-owned ones. Generally, just (live) stem wood is measured in trees over a specific diameter at breast height (dbh), and sometimes only the stem wood of 'industrial' trees is measured.[5] Stem wood may represent less than 40% of total biomass stock and yield. In an inventory in Benin, 37% of the mass was stem wood more than 15 cm dbh; 22% was branch wood, 4% small trees and shrubs, 8% dead wood, and 30% roots. Excluding roots, stem wood more than 15 cm dbh was just more than 50% of the above-ground woody biomass (Openshaw, 2000b).

Of the low-income countries of Asia, China has the greatest forest area (163 million ha), but Malaysia and Indonesia have the biggest percentage of forest (59% and 58%, respectively) and the largest growing stock within the forest. However, the Cook Islands (92%) and the Solomon Isles (89%) have the greatest percentage of forest cover. The author determined the forest cover for all countries in Asia and the Pacific, except some small island states, as well as the land use by region. For Asia and the Pacific as a whole, forests cover 19% of the land area, arable agriculture 16%, and pasture 41%. Dry areas have large pasture lands and deserts, whereas wetter regions have large forest, arable, and permanent agricultural crops. Table 19.8 gives a summary of land use in various regions for 2000 and 2015.

In tropical and semi-tropical areas, there is little inventory data on woody growing stock and yield, and the most information is confined to forests and plantations. Only in a few countries have comprehensive measurements been taken of forest and non-forest trees, for example, in Benin (Openshaw, 2000b), Kenya (Openshaw, 1983), Pakistan (Archer, 1993), and Malawi (Openshaw, 1977). Assessments were made in the Philippines (Soussan, 1991) and Bangladesh (Openshaw, 2004), based on small samples and dated inventories. Some sample plots have been measured in many countries, especially in plantations, and

---

[5] Industrial trees are generally classified as species that can be used for transmission poles, sawnwood, veneer, plywood, board products, paper, and regenerated fibres. For sawlogs and veneer logs, the minimum diameter at breast height may be 60 cm. Excluded are fuelwood, charcoal wood, small poles, and posts.

Table 19.8. Asia and the Pacific 2000 and 2015: Estimated land use by broad sector and region.

Region	Total land area (million hectare)		Forest and plantation (million hectare)		Woodland (million hectare)		Agriculture (million hectare)				Other land uses (million hectare)	
							Arable		Pasture			
	2000	2015	2000	2015	2000	2015	2000	2015	2000	2015	2000	2015
Asia LI	1,952.12	1,952.12	492.30	518.70	161.58	168.44	422.40	427.72	557.39	540.68	318.45	296.58
Asia MI	311.09	311.09	20.87	23.84	16.37	14.11	52.81	53.24	74.00	57.18	147.04	162.72
A-P HI	1,108.19	1,108.19	174.89	170.70	255.27	255.20	60.85	59.72	514.13	516.31	103.05	106.26
FSU LI	528.73	528.73	17.84	17.90	46.09	48.39	43.77	44.63	308.40	306.22	112.63	111.59
P Islands	52.25	52.25	37.81	37.77	4.88	4.82	1.46	1.67	0.46	0.47	7.64	7.52
Total	3,952.38	3,952.38	743.71	768.91	484.19	490.96	581.29	586.98	1,454.38	1,420.86	688.81	684.67
Difference between 2015/2000	Same		25.20		6.77		5.69		−33.52		−4.14	

Note: Other land uses include rangelands, wasteland, semi-deserts, deserts, scrub and bush, alpine areas, infrastructure, urban, small water bodies, wetlands, and rocky outcrops. In some cases, the areas of the broad land uses added to more than the total land area. This could be because, for example, shifting cultivation was counted as both forest and agriculture, or, as in the case of Australia, pasture and woodlands were double-counted. The totals of the different land uses were adjusted so as to ensure that they did not exceed the total land area of each country.
Source: Calculated by the author

volume tables/management tables by species have been produced, for example, in Australia, Japan, and New Zealand, but much work has to be done to obtain more reliable information on stock and yield of woody biomass on all land-use types. Without reliable information, meaningful planning and forecasting may be impossible.

In the Asia-Pacific region as a whole, the forest, woodland, and arable agricultural areas increased between 2000 and 2015, whereas the pasture lands and other lands decreased. The increase in forest land in Asia low-income countries was mainly due to increases in China and to a lesser extent in India, Vietnam, Laos, and the Philippines, plus small increases in several other countries, although some of the forest areas in these countries could have been degraded.

There were decreases in forest areas, notably in Indonesia, Myanmar, Laos, Cambodia, and DPR Korea, and small decreases in several other countries. However, the decrease in the forest area in Indonesia was partially offset by an increase in the woodland area, though this may be a case of re-classification; the woodland areas also increased in China and Vietnam. Therefore, it is important not only to keep good records of changes in forest and woodland areas, but also to monitor their stock and yield. Again, the forest and woodland areas give only a partial picture of woody biomass, for there are many trees outside the 'forest' on all land-use types and they are an important supply source, especially for fuelwood.

Regarding the other groups of countries, there were minor changes in forest and woodland areas except in Australia, which

lost 4 million ha of forest, and Uzbekistan, which lost 1 million ha of woodlands, in the period 2000 to 2015. However, Turkey gained 1.5 million ha of forest, but lost 0.5 million ha of woodlands.

The forest area increased by more than 25 million hectares, mainly due to increases in China and India, although in two regions it declined. Woodland also increased, as did agriculture. The largest decline was in pasture land with a smaller decline in other land-use area (Table 19.8). Arable areas increased significantly in SE Asia's continental and insular countries in the period 2000 to 2015, mainly because of forest clearing. Pastoral/other land-use areas decreased by 37.6 million ha, whereas wooded and agricultural areas increased by nearly the same amount (FAO, 2001c, 2010c, 2014, 2015). Some of the changes in forest and woodland areas may be because of reclassification rather than actual changes.

19.7.2 Lack of inventory data

The forest growing stock in Table 19.9 was estimated from information in FAO's *State of the World's Forests 2001* (FAO, 2001a) and the Global forest resource assessment (FAO, 2015). There was inconsistency in the values given for wood volume in forests and wood biomass in forests, and considerable underestimates seem to have been made, especially of standing volume. An earlier FAO report (FAO, 1993) gave estimates of area and above-ground woody biomass for 1990 in tropical countries.

Table 19.9. Asia and the Pacific 2000 and 2015: Estimated stock and yield of woody biomass.

million tonne dry wood

Region	Total Stock (yield) 2000	Total Stock (yield) 2015	Forest and plantation Stock (yield) 2000	Forest and plantation Stock (yield) 2015	Woodland Stock (yield) 2000	Woodland Stock (yield) 2015	Agriculture Arable Stock (yield) 2000	Agriculture Arable Stock (yield) 2015	Agriculture Pasture Stock (yield) 2000	Agriculture Pasture Stock (yield) 2015	Other land uses Stock (yield) 2000	Other land uses Stock (yield) 2015
Asia LI	45,976 (2,298.80)	51,267 (2,563.35)	38,780 (1,939.00)	43,880 (2,194.00)	2,072 (103.60)	2,334 (116.70)	2,125 (106.25)	2,141 (107.05)	2,791 (139.55)	2,708 (135.40)	208 (10.40)	204 (10.20)
Asia MI	2,088 (104.40)	2,349 (117.45)	1,344 (67.20)	1,672 (83.60)	66 (3.30)	76 (3.80)	264 (13.20)	267 (13.35)	370 (18.50)	286 (14.30)	44 (2.20)	48 (2.40)
A-P HI	20,782 (1,039.10)	21,482 (1,074.10)	14,563 (728.15)	15,305 (765.25)	3,852 (192.60)	3,857 (192.85)	289 (14.45)	285 (14.25)	2,054 (102.70)	2,016 (100.80)	24 (1.20)	19 (0.95)
FSU LI	2,979 (148.95)	2,950 (147.50)	1,017 (50.85)	982 (49.10)	289 (14.45)	300 (15.00)	200 (10.00)	206 (10.30)	1,445 (72.25)	1,434 (71.70)	28 (1.40)	28 (1.40)
P Islands	4,822 (241.10)	4,807 (240.35)	4,660 (233.00)	4,644 (232.20)	145 (7.25)	144 (7.20)	7 (0.35)	9 (0.45)	3 (0.15)	3 (0.15)	7 (0.35)	7 (0.35)
Total	76,647 (3,832.35)	82,855 (4,142.75)	60,364 (3,018.20)	66,483 (3,324.15)	6,424 (321.20)	6,711 (335.55)	2,885 (144.25)	2,908 (145.40)	6,663 (333.15)	6,447 (322.35)	311 (15.55)	306 (15.30)
Percentage	100	100	78.7	80.2	8.4	8.1	3.8	3.5	8.7	7.8	0.4	0.4
Difference between 2015/2000	6,208 (310.40)		6,119 (305.95)		287 (14.35)		23 (1.15)		−216 (−10.80)		−5 (−0.25)	

Note: The estimates of stock and yield in dry weight are based on an FAO publication in 2015, which gives details of above-ground biomass volume and stock for 2000 and 2015, including inventories undertaken in Benin, Pakistan, and the Philippines and assessments made in Bangladesh, China, Laos, Thailand, and Vietnam. The FAO publication contains several inconsistencies, such as the weight being less than the volume or the weight being much more than the volume. For many woodland areas, no stock was given, so estimates were made. It also differs significantly from a 1990 FAO report. From the results of the Benin inventory, the ratio between stem volume and above-ground weight should be about 1:1.33; also, stem volume is about half the above-ground volume of all trees and shrubs. Therefore, the FAO figures were adjusted. For arable and pastoral areas, the average stock of woody biomass is taken as 5 dry t/ha; this is based on various inventories of trees outside the forest. The stock on other lands varies from 1 t ha to 0.1 t ha, depending on the country land type, as judged by the author. The yield is taken as 5% of the stock. This includes dead wood, which was not included in the FAO figures, and small shrubs.

Sources: Archer, 1993; FAO, 1993, 2001a, 2001b, 2001c, 2003, 2010a, 2010b, 2010c, 2014, 2015; Openshaw, 1983, 2004, 2000b; RWEDP, 1986–1997; RWEDP, 1991–2001; Soussan, 1991; UK Forestry Commission, 1971; various tropical volume tables; author's estimates

For South Asia, the above-ground biomass in 2000 in tonnes per ha was only 77% of that in 1990. In continental SE Asia, the 2000 figure was 26% of 1990, and in insular SE Asia, the 2000 figure was 73% of 1990.[6] Over the years, there has been a decline in the forest stock, but sustainable supply is still larger than demand. The 2018 State of the World's Forests reiterates that wood energy is still a very important fuel in SE Asia (FAO, 2018).

19.7.3 Non-forest woody biomass

Trees outside the 'forest' are an important source of wood for fuel, poles, and sometimes timber. In the 1991 inventory in Pakistan, 52% of the woody stock was on farmland, 8% was in semi-arid and arid areas, and only 40% was in forests. What is more, 66% of the annual growth was from farm trees, 10% from trees in dry lands, and only 24% from forest trees. In 2000, the forest area of Pakistan was about 4 million ha and shrinking due to population pressure. The (irrigated) farmland area is an estimated 24 million, with the rest classified as rangelands (49 million ha). It is these two latter areas where most of the fuelwood comes from (FAO 2009). This is what was projected in 1991. And the information is still relevant today. In Bangladesh, 51% of the growing stock and 61% of the yield was from trees, bamboo, and shrubs outside the natural forest and plantations (Openshaw, 2004). And in the Philippines, 85% of wood energy came from outside the forest (Soussan, 1991). Therefore, neglecting small-diameter wood, dead wood, and trees outside the forest can lead to significantly underestimated biomass stock and yield. The author has worked in all these three countries (and many more within Asia on energy/forestry projects) and can verify the importance of such data.

Estimations of non-forest trees, bamboo, shrubs, and bushes for all the countries were made by land-use type. The land areas (Table 19.8) were used to estimate 'non-forest' tree stock, which is shown in Table 19.9, together with the estimates for forest and woodland trees.

In 2000, the estimated total stock of woody biomass was more than 76.6 billion t (dry), and this gives an annual yield of more than 3.8 billion t. Detailed information of the stock of woody biomass on all land-use types by country was collected and estimates were made of annual (sustainable) yield. By 2015, the estimated stock on all land-use types was more than 87.7 billion t, giving an annual yield of more than 4.1 billion t.

There has been an overall increase in stocks and yields in the Asia lower-income groups, principally because of increases in China, India, and Indonesia. There were reductions in Myanmar, Nepal, Cambodia, and Laos, but overall, between 2000 and 2015 the estimated sustainable yield has slightly increased (8%). Therefore, the consumption of wood energy and other wood products has not led to deforestation, although some degradation may have occurred in certain areas. Also, there were several incidences of illegal felling, when public property was diverted to private pockets. Some Thai teak (*Tectona grandis*) originated in Myanmar; sal (*Shorea robusta*) was cut illegally in Nepal, and so on. In most countries in the A-P region, cases of illegal felling have been reported, but it has not led to widespread deforestation. This has been and is caused by land-use changes, principally to agriculture expansion. Nature abhors a vacuum. If an area is felled and left, there will be regrowth, but usually not in the same composition mix. This information about sustainable yield, together with estimates of crop residue and dung production, will be used to see if supply is sufficient to meet demand for biomass energy and other wood products.

19.8 SUSTAINABLE SUPPLY AND DEMAND FOR BIOMASS ENERGY AND OTHER WOOD PRODUCTS

As is detailed in Table 19.7, the estimated demand for wood energy in 2000 for all Asia and the Pacific countries, as well as Hong Kong, Macao, and Taiwan, was nearly 1.04 billion t (air dry) or 0.9 billion t dry. Crop residues and dung supplied an estimated 0.38 billion t (wood equivalent). The total yield from all trees is 3.8 billion t or about four times the demand. But there are demands for other forest products, such as industrial wood and poles. This brought the total annual demand for woody biomass to 1.11 billion t in 2000 (Table 19.10), but sustainable supply is still more than three times annual demand. However, some forests and grasslands should be set aside for biosphere reserves, watershed protection, and similar purposes. If up to 20% of forest areas were reserved as conservation areas, this would reduce the available sustainable supply by about 0.6 billion t (Table 19.9), but annual yield would still be about 2.9 times annual demand, and in the low-income Asian countries to about two times demand.

There are ample supplies of crop residues and dung (Table 19.10) but greater efforts should be made to use both sources of biomass more efficiently, especially to reduce the amount of methane vented to the atmosphere. Countries and individuals should be encouraged to plant more trees both inside and outside the forest – generally, deforestation cannot be blamed on the use of wood products. Agricultural land clearing is the main

---

[6] The figures in tonnes per ha for S Asia, SE continental Asia, and SE insular Asia for 1990 are 100, 187, and 213, respectively. For 2000, they are 77, 49, and 156, respectively. Between 1990 and 2000, S Asia lost 2,162,000 ha of natural forests and gained 14,895,000 ha of plantations; SE continental Asia gained 1,257,000 ha of forests and 4,399,000 ha of plantations; and SE insular Asia lost 8,136,000 ha of forest and gained 3,221,000 ha of plantations (FAO, 1993).

Table 19.10. 2000 and 2015: Sustainable supply and demand for biomass energy and other wood products.

Region	Sustainable supply						Demand										
							million tonne dry wood equivalent										
	Wood		Crop residues		Dung		Total		Biomass energy		Of which wood		Other wood products		Total wood products	
	2000	2015	2000	2015	2000	2015	2000	2015	2000	2015	2000	2015	2000	2015	2000	2015
Asia LI	2,298.80	2,563.35	1,068.20	1,513.60	211.50	259.40	3,578.50	4,336.35	1,218.29	1,317.18	845.92	954.36	154.71	280.42	1,000.63	1,234.78
Asia MI	104.40	117.45	58.60	85.70	12.70	15.70	175.70	218.85	7.38	8.62	6.63	7.75	9.70	15.06	16.33	22.81
A-P HI	1,039.10	1,074.10	70.93	68.20	40.13	43.55	1,150.16	1,185.85	16.82	18.30	15.88	17.32	54.98	74.19	70.86	91.51
FSU LI	148.95	147.50	33.40	51.70	7.90	22.20	190.25	221.40	10.37	14.32	8.86	12.69	2.33	3.80	11.19	16.49
P Islands	241.10	240.35	1.38	1.14	0.32	0.33	242.80	241.82	10.63	12.43	10.09	11.81	2.82	3.54	12.91	15.35
Total	3,832.35	4,142.75	1,232.51	1,720.34	272.55	341.18	5,337.41	6,204.27	1,263.49	1,370.85	887.38	1,003.93	224.54	377.01	1,111.92	1,380.94
Percentage	71.8	66.7	23.1	27.8	5.1	5.5	100	100	100	100	70.2	73.2				
Difference between 2015/2000	310.40		487.83		68.63		866.86		107.36		116.55		152.47		269.02	

Note: Crop residues include only an estimate for grain crop residues, whereas bagasse, cotton stalks, and tobacco stems are also used for energy purposes, which means that crop residues are underestimated. An average multiplying factor of 1.4 t of residues per t of grain was applied to the FAO grain statistics by country for 2000 and 2013 (taken as 2015). Similarly, for the dung assessment, only bovines were counted, so again it is an underestimate. Ovines, pigs, poultry, and others are not included. An average annual figure of 425 kg of dry dung production per cow is assumed. It is assumed that 0.85 t dry wood = 1 t air-dry wood.

Sources: FAO, 2014. Annual agricultural production statistics; Openshaw, 1997; other sources in various tables; author's estimates

cause; increasing agricultural productivity and tempering population increase should be given priority.

In 2015, both the sustainable supply of biomass and the demand for biomass energy, especially wood, increased to 4.1 billion t (Table 19.10). Total woody biomass demand from indigenous resources (including exports) is an estimated 1.4 billion t (dry), of which 1.0 billion t is for energy. Crop residues and dung supplied about 0.37 billon t (wood equivalent). Again, assuming that 20% of forest land is set aside for conservation and the like, the sustainable supply is about 3.3 billion t or 2.3 times demand.

19.8.1 Reliable local inventory data

Of course, there are actual or latent shortages of wood in some regions of most countries; this expresses itself in the 'excessive' use of residues and dung. Wood is the most desirable biomass fuel, especially for household use, but if it is difficult to collect or is relatively expensive to purchase, then residues and dung are used (as well as fossil fuels). As stated earlier, the 2000 demand for residues was estimated to be about 264 million t and that for dung 113 million t in wood equivalent terms, of which about 97% is consumed in the low-income Asian countries. In 2015, residues and dung accounted for about 0.37 billion t of energy supply. The sustainable supply of both residues and dung is several times the demand for fuel, but there are other uses such as for animal feed, as fertilizer/soil improver and for construction purposes.

While there is a surplus of biomass energy in most countries, there are local shortages. This is why accurate information of supply and demand is essential. Then in areas of shortages, steps can be taken to increase supply, and in surplus areas existing markets can be expanded or new ones sought. And of course, demand mitigation, through energy efficiency measures, should be vigorously pursued in all situations. Where smoke and other products of incomplete combustion are health and environmental hazards, then steps should be taken to reduce them to a minimum so as to eliminate their adverse effects.

For 2000, the total estimated demand for primary energy in Asia and the Pacific regions was 138.63 EJ (10^{18} J), of which 115.00 EJ is fossil fuels and hydroelectricity (83%) and 23.63 EJ is biomass (17%) (Tables 19.1 and 19.10). Only the low-income countries of Asia and the island countries of the Pacific have significant shares of biomass energy – 30% and 59%, respectively – but the island countries account for only 0.2% of total energy demand in the A-P region. With 85% of the population, the low-income countries accounted for 55% (76.63 EJ) of total primary energy demand and 96.5% (22.80 EJ) of biomass energy demand. By 2015, the primary energy demand in the Asia-Pacific region had more than doubled to 284 EJ, but that of

biomass energy had only increased by 2 EJ, compared with 2000 (Tables 19.1 and 19.10). Therefore, its share had fallen to 9% of energy demand (25.63 EJ). For the Asian low-income group, the total energy demand is an estimated 194.6 EJ, of which China's share was 128.3 EJ (IEA, 2015). Economic growth, especially in China, accounted for the bulk of the energy increase. While the demand for fossil fuel increased the most, the demand for biomass fuels increased by only 8%, with drops especially in China and Thailand.

Is this trend inevitable as wealth increases and demand for more convenient fuels decreases? This will now be discussed, especially in the endeavour to reduce global warming, principally caused by the burning of fossil fuels.

19.9 FUTURE POTENTIAL OF BIOMASS ENERGY

At present, households are the main users of biomass energy, although industry and the service sector consume between 10% and 20% of demand. Usually the fuel is unprocessed (fuelwood and crop residues) or semi-processed (agricultural processing waste, wood industry waste, and dung). Charcoal is the principal processed biomass, although biogas may be used by rural farming families, mainly in South Asia and China. Where petroleum products are relatively expensive, motor ethanol is substituted in part for petrol (gasoline). It is produced in China, India, Pakistan, the Philippines, and Thailand. Generally, since 2014/15, biodiesel made from plant oils is on the market and there are factories in China, India, Indonesia, Malaysia, and the Philippines.

Unprocessed and processed biomass is used by industry to raise heat, produce steam, generate electricity, and supply heat to factories, offices, and houses in areas with low winter temperature. Sugar factories use bagasse as their principal energy source, and likewise pulp and paper mills use black liquor. Again, biomass energy is used by the service sector for food processing. There are several 5–50 MW power or combined heat/power plants in operation or planned. For example, in India by 2018, the installed capacity for biomass power, cogeneration, and gasification was 8,414 MW, with an estimated potential of 35,000 MW, of which 7,000 MW is from bagasse and 18,000 MW from agricultural and forest residues (MNRE, Annual Reports 2009–10, 2010–11, 2016–17, 2017–18). In the Inner Mongolia Autonomous Region of China, two biomass heat and power plants were planned, namely a 24 MW plant using 200,000 t of crop residues and a 12 MW plant using 110,000 t of wood per year (ESMAP, 2005). These two plants will displace about 130,000 t of standard coal (30 MJ/kg) per year and save about 100,000 t of carbon emissions annually. In the low-income countries of Asia, which contain 84% of the A-P population, biomass energy accounted for 9% of primary energy demand in 2015. Therefore, there are many existing and potential uses of biomass energy: it could play a prominent role in the renewable energy mix to help temper global warming.

Between 2000 and 2015, the population in Asia and the Pacific grew by an estimated 687 million. Of this increase, 560 million are in the low-income Asian countries, countries that already are the largest consumers of biomass energy. In these countries, per-capita income increased 13.5 times, so there is much more disposable income available. At the household level, there was a gradual shift from unprocessed biomass to more convenient forms of energy such as charcoal, biogas, LPG, natural gas, and kerosene. Over the same time period (and beyond), there was a considerable increase in motorized transport and liquid fuels. By 2030, most houses should be electrified, so electricity demand will expand, driven by population growth and the increase in wealth. This means that there is considerable potential for all forms of biomass energy.

The World Bank and the UN project that the population will stabilize at about 11.5 billion around 2100 and the Asia-Pacific share will be about 6.9 billion. This increase in population and wealth will put pressure on the natural resources, and if they are not managed judiciously, there could be serious environmental damage, on top of which, climate change will exacerbate the situation. Also, tempering population increase should be given priority as part of efforts to improve rural income, access, and facilities. China and Thailand are examples where this has happened: from 2000 to 2015 their population only increased at an average of 0.5% per year (Population Pyramid, 2015).

19.9.1 Encourage tree planting, forest management and improved agricultural methods

Increased use of (traded) biomass could assist in several ways. It should encourage the planting of trees, especially on farmland and on marginal lands. Many trees fix nitrogen and they could improve soil fertility and provide browsing material for farm animals, especially when other fodder is at a premium. Usually, such trees can be grown on short rotations of one to five years and need replanting after only about five to ten rotations because they coppice. These trees produce small-diameter wood suitable for fuel, poles, and paper production. Excluding deserts and the like, there are up to 250 million ha of abandoned farmland, wasteland, scrub, and bush in the 'low-income' countries of Asia. There is a variety of species that grow in low rainfall areas and it still may be profitable to grow suitable plants in these areas, particularly trees, especially if they provide more than one product, such as fodder, wood, plant oil, medicine, honey nuts, and so forth. Biomass cover may provide protection against wind and soil erosion and improve the local micro-climate, such as vetiver grass (*Chrysopogon zizanioides*).

Existing forests and woodlands will be better protected if the local people have user rights; they should then manage these wooded areas and reap monetary rewards from the various goods and services they provide, while at the same time maintaining, if not improving them.

To slow down and hopefully reverse deforestation, agricultural productivity has to keep pace with population increase and the increased demand for more animal proteins. Already Asia, through the 'green revolution', has increased grain productivity substantially, especially rice. However, wasteful use of water has caused salination on some irrigated lands, rendering these areas unproductive for arable agriculture. Also, there are increasing shortages of water for household and industrial uses. Therefore, there have to be improved irrigation methods that will provide the crops with sufficient water for growth. Increased production of animal proteins will lead to more excrement. If this is managed properly, methane could be extracted from it for energy use, while the slurry, a better fertilizer than the original waste, could be returned to the soil.

Saline soils and other marginal lands could be brought back into productivity by planting appropriate and usually woody biomass species. Many of these species fix nitrogen and provide pods that could be used for animal feed. Other species, like *Jatropha curcas*, give plant oils used for biodiesel or soap making (Openshaw, 2000a). Work is being done on breeding jatropha and planting it in marginal areas (Shetty, 2005). This could prevent forests being cleared for palm oil.

19.9.2 Making biomass fuels more competitive by improving efficiency and reducing PIC

The increased use of biomass (and other renewables) by A-P countries could displace some fossil fuels, thus reducing CO_2 emissions and promoting the goals of sustainable development. Also, a net increase of woody biomass will mean more sequestration of atmospheric carbon dioxide in the wood and the soils beneath the trees, thus tempering global warming.

One problem of burning biomass (and coal) on an open fire in a confined, poorly ventilated kitchen, especially if the biomass is not dry, is pollution from smoke and other products of incomplete combustion (PIC).[7] This affects the health of the cook and small children who may be with their mother in the kitchen. Improved cookstoves, especially those with chimneys when the cooking is done indoors, lose some versatility, but cooking efficiency is increased and indoor air pollution is considerably

---

[7] This does not apply to charcoal stoves, except at the combustion phase, when PICs are produced, especially carbon monoxide. The cook is aware of this and generally lights the stove outdoors before bringing it into the kitchen. While charcoal stoves are usually more efficient than wood stoves, their efficiency could be improved considerably.

reduced. There have been many improved cookstove pro-grammes throughout Asia and the rest of the world. One such book is *Cleaner Hearths, Better Homes: Improved Stoves for India and the Developing World* (Barnes *et al.*, 2012). Improved stove programmes work best when people pay the market price for stoves, have locally produced parts, and are relatively inex-pensive. However, success also occurs when improved stoves are part of a package to enhance village life. This may include initiatives in health, sanitation, clean water, better-ventilated kitchens, and enhanced kitchen and stove practices. Even if the cooks use existing cooking methods, they should be educated about keeping young children away from smoke and having well-ventilated areas. More than 2 billion people may cook with biomass (and coal) in the A-P region. Increasing stove effi-ciency could reduce the demand for household energy and make this energy available for expanded use in the industrial/service sectors.

19.9.3 Energy pricing policy

Improved stoves may slow down the switch to more convenient fossil fuels, namely kerosene, natural gas, and LPG. However, if fossil fuels are subsidized, as is the case with kerosene in India and Iran, natural gas in Bangladesh and Thailand, and LPG and kerosene in Indonesia, then it may be more difficult for traded biomass to compete with these fuels. There should be a level playing field regarding fuel pricing, and if governments are con-cerned about global warming and climate change, a carbon tax could be imposed on fossil fuels!

19.9.4 Expanded role for biogas

Biogas contains about 60% methane. It is extracted from dung and other forms of biomass through anaerobic digestion; it is used for cooking, heating, lighting, and electricity generation. It has been used by rural households in China, DPRK, India, and Nepal for more than 50 years. China has an estimated 25 mil-lion and India more than 4 million digesters (Ren 21, 2010). The traditional digester is made of metal or concrete and the cost can range from US$150 to US$250. Cheaper sausage-like plastic digesters have been developed in Vietnam and these use domestic animal and human wastes and some vegetation. Their cost is about US$40, making them considerably cheaper than the fixed or mobile dome-type digesters (Bui Zuan An *et al.*, 1997). Digesters have advantages: they prevent methane vent-ing, kill most pathogens in animal excreta, stop river and stream pollution, provide an excellent fertilizer, and give a more con-venient cooking fuel. This could free up woody biomass for other uses. From a global warming perspective, digesters should be encouraged, as methane is 25 times more potent as a GHG than CO_2 when vented (IPCC, 2007).

19.9.5 Biomass for small-scale electrical generation and rural industries

Small electrical generators are one solution for supplying elec-tricity to isolated rural communities when grid connections are too expensive. Wind, water (micro-hydro), and solar systems are at the forefront to meet these needs, especially in developed countries, but unprocessed or processed biomass could play an important role by providing boiler fuel for electrical generation. There are many examples. The author has seen a producer gas engine supplying power to an Indian village. One important use was to irrigate mulberry trees. The leaves were used to feed silk worms, and the wood fed the boiler to make the producer gas (Ravindranath *et al.*, 2004). This article describes a small wood-fired generator that provides electricity to isolated villages in India. The villagers were planting trees to fuel the generator and collecting wood from farms, roadsides, woodlots, and commu-nal forests. The provision of electricity has led to an improve-ment in the quality of life, an increase in small cottage industries, and more wealth. Biomass feedstock has an advan-tage over wind and solar systems, in that 24 hours per day, pro-duction of electricity is guaranteed.

Many studies have been undertaken in agricultural process-ing, brick and tile making, and other uses. There should be a clearing house to gather all the information and make it avail-able to the industries and energy departments throughout the region. This also applies to the service sector. The former Regional Wood Energy Development Programme (RWEDP), implemented by the FAO Regional Office for Asia and the Pacific in Bangkok, collected and published in Wood Energy News, and other outlets, information on industries using bio-mass fuel for many countries in Asia (RWEDP, 1986–1997b; 1991–2001). Such initiatives need to be revived if countries are serious about pursuing sustainable development.

19.9.6 Biofuel potential from photosynthesis and bio-mass availability

In the first half of 2019, the price of crude oil ranges from US$56 to US$68 per barrel. However, it reached US$100+ in 2011–2012, so there is renewed interest in providing alternative and renewable fuels for stationary and mobile engines. Sugar from cane is the most cost-effective feedstock for motor ethanol production. In 2009, the estimated production of motor ethanol was as follows: China 2.1 billion litres, Thailand 1.65 billion litres, and India 350 million litres (Ren 21, 2010). For 2015, China's production was 2.8 billion litres and Thailand's 1.2 bil-lion litres (Ren 21, 2018).

Biodiesel made from plant oils such as palm, coconut, and jatropha is being manufactured in several countries of S and SE Asia. In 2009, the estimated production of biodiesel was between 1,750 and 2,000 billion litres (Ren 21, 2010). In 2015 the production was as follows: Indonesia 1.7 billion litres, Malaysia 0.7 billion litres, and China 0.35 billion litres (Ren 21, 2018). There is concern that in Malaysia and Indonesia, tropical forests are being cleared to plant palms. Better land-use planning is required to ensure that this is minimized, if not halted. Breeding is underway to increase the yields of palms and jatropha to offset the need for more forest land.

Plants provide a constant source of carbohydrates and other substances that keep all animals (and plants) alive (the carbon cycle) (Hall and Rao, 1994). The potentially available carbon from plants is about five to seven times the amount of carbon burnt in fossil fuels. At present only about 5–7.5% of this potential is used. But there is considerable scope to use much more biomass for all energy purposes than is done today. This is why biomass could and should play an important role in providing sustainable carbon-based fuels to meet a major part of the renewable energy mix.

19.10 THE CONTRIBUTION OF BIOMASS TO GHG MITIGATION AND ENVIRONMENTAL PROTECTION

Biomass is a convenient store of the sun's energy that can be used if and when required. With annual plants, this store of energy is short-term. In grasslands and perennial woody biomass, there is not only a long-term store of carbon in the plants, but also in the soils beneath these plants. A mature tropical forest with a nominal rotation age of about 100 years[8] can store between 200 and 300 t of carbon per ha in above- and below-ground biomass, whereas in grasslands, the store may only be about 1.6 t of C per ha in the grass woody biomass. The mature tropical forest will yield about 2.25 to 3.0 t C per year of above-ground woody biomass, plus 1.0 to 1.5 t C in the leaves and other parts, and the grasslands will yield about 0.75 to 1.25 t C/yr in the above-ground biomass. Short-rotation tree species on a seven-year rotation, with an equal representation of all age classes, may store on average between 10 and 40 t/ha of C in the biomass depending on rainfall (500 to 1,500 mm/yr). Each year, this tree crop will yield between 5 and 20 air-dry t/ha of above-ground wood containing between 2.1 to 8.4 t of carbon. Through tree breeding, it is possible to have an annual

above-ground yield of between 18 and 23 t C (42–54 t air-dry wood) with an average carbon store on a seven-year rotation of 95 to 120 t C/ha (rainfall 1,250–1,500 mm/yr).

With perennial crops, there is more of a build-up of soil carbon than with annual crops (Lal et al., 1995). In a mature, fully stocked tropical forest, the organic carbon[9] stored in acrisol soils may be about 220 t/ha, in secondary forests about 165 t/ha, in grassland about 160 t/ha, and in cropland 110 t/ha (Bouwman, 1990, Table 4.4, p. 72). In glaysol soils, the store of organic carbon in primary forests and grasslands is given as 350 t/ha, and 260 t/ha in secondary forests, whereas in croplands it is 200 t/ha (Bouwman, 1990). Consistently throughout the various soil types, there is the most organic soil carbon in primary forests, whereas secondary forests and grasslands have less, with the least in croplands. This gradual build-up of soil carbon is mainly due to undisturbed soils.

Table 19.9 gives an estimate of above-ground stock (including dead wood) and annual yield of woody biomass by broad land-use types for 2000 and 2015. The average above-ground stock in forests and plantations was about 86.6 t/ha of dry wood. Assuming that about one-third of the woody biomass is below ground, then on average there will be about 130 t/ha of dry wood per ha. This is equivalent to about 65 t C per ha (67 t C/ha in low-income Asian countries). This figure is far lower than anticipated, especially with countries such as Indonesia, Laos, Malaysia, and Myanmar having considerable areas of undisturbed or partially disturbed tropical forests, and with about 25% of the forest area in Asia being plantations (FAO, 2015). Therefore, the figure of forest stock given in Table 19.9 should be taken as a minimum. This emphasizes the urgent need to undertake inventories, especially in forests, but trees outside the forests must not be neglected. Even if the average stock of carbon in above-and below-ground woody biomass in forests is increased by 50% to about 100 t C/ha, it still may be an underestimate, but whichever number is nearer the truth, it appears that many forests, woodlands, and plantations are under-stocked as a result of over-cutting and poor management. With proper incentives and good governance, the average stocking in forests, woodlands, and plantations could be increased considerably. Again, with appropriate tree species, the stocking volume and yield would also increase.

In 2015, assuming the stocking figures in Table 19.9 for Asia and the Pacific, the total above- and below-ground woody biomass on all land-use types (with one-third of woody biomass below ground) was a minimum of 124 billion t dry wood,

---

[8] It is assumed that the annual rainfall will be between 1,200 and 1,500 mm for tropical forests. In a fully stocked, mature tropical forest, the average age of the trees with a nominal rotation of 100 years will be about 75 years and not 50 years, because there is a preponderance of older trees, whereas in plantations, the average age will be about half the rotation age. If there is an equal representation of all age classes in a tropical forest on a 100-year rotation, the average store of above- and below-ground carbon would be between 150 and 200 t C/ha with about the same annual yield.

[9] In some soils, there is inorganic carbon in the form of limestone (calcium carbonate). Lime is also added to acidic soils to increase the pH. Acid soils inhibit the uptake by plants of phosphorus and other minerals, so adding lime enables their uptake.

equivalent to 61.6 billion t C. To this must be added the store of carbon in grasslands; this is estimated to be about 2.2 billion t in the grass, assuming a store of 1.6 t C/ha, for a total of 64 billion t of organic carbon. In addition, there may be an extra 58 billion t of organic carbon stored in forest soils, 20 billion t C in woodlands and 50 billion t C under grasslands[10] for a total of 128 t C in soils (Lal *et al.,* 1995). In this way, trees and grasslands have sequestered at least 192 billion t of atmospheric carbon, of which about 70% is in woody biomass and forest soils. The actual figure may be 250 to 290 billion t C.

There is considerable scope for sequestering much more CO_2 in woody biomass, through improved management of existing forests, woodlands, and plantations; reclaiming marginal lands; increasing farm tree planting, and other measures. However, some countries in Asia and the Pacific are losing forests, mainly to arable agriculture, but also to plantations (oil palm, coconut), and urbanization. On average, between 1991 and 2000, Asia lost 346,000 ha of forests, and the Pacific area lost 365,000 each year (FAO, 2001a). In terms of GHG emissions, the minimum annual loss of woody biomass and soil carbon from 711,000 ha could be 93 million t of wood, equivalent to 46 million t C and 35 million t of organic soil carbon, for a total of 81 million t of C, and it may be in the region of 120 million t. Of course, where agricultural plantations such as palm oil replace tropical forests, there will be a gradual recapture of carbon in the palms and the soils, but not to the extent that previously existed. And with the conversion to arable agriculture, the store of organic carbon is mainly lost. Therefore, up to the year 2000, rather than forests sequestering atmospheric carbon in Asia and the Pacific, they were net emitters of GHG because they were being cleared faster than tree planting and plantations could take their place.

Since 2000, there has been a net increase in forests and woodlands in the A-P region, mainly due to increases in China and India, but there were decreases in Indonesia, Myanmar, and other countries. There has been an increase of nearly 44.5 million ha of forests in nine of the 20 countries in the Asia lower-income group; some of this increase may be due to reclassification of woodland, for three countries lost a total of about 4 million ha of woodlands. China had the largest increase of more than 31 million ha of forest and 6 million ha of woodlands, with India being the next country, with an increase of nearly 5.3 million ha, although there was a decrease in woodland areas. The overall increase in these nine countries in forests and woodland between 2000 and 2015 was an estimated 48.6 million ha. This is a very positive step.

However, eleven of the countries in the Asia low-income group lost more than 20 million ha, between 2000 and 2015,

with Indonesia losing an estimated 8.4 million ha. But according to FAO statistics (FAO 2015), there was a gain of more than 4 million ha of woodlands between 2000 and 2015, so the net loss was nearly 4.3 million ha. On the other hand, Myanmar lost an estimated 5.8 million ha of forest and 1.6 million ha of woodland, for an overall loss of 7.4 million ha.

All these 11 countries need to reverse these losses if they are serious about reducing global warming and the emissions of carbon dioxide resulting from clearing forests and woodlands. This could and should be reversed. There should be proper land-use planning, so that forests are not cleared without undertaking a full cost/benefit analysis. There is a lack of proper management in many forest areas. Governments own the bulk of forests but have little control over them. Local people use the forests but have little legal jurisdiction. There has to be a concordat between government and people affording much more control to people in exchange for their proper management, use, and boundary retention.

If areas are to be reserved as national parks, watersheds, wetlands, or conservation areas, then the people in these areas should be compensated accordingly. If forests are of international and regional importance, then their upkeep should be the world's responsibility, especially the richer nations.

Apart from protecting the forest estates and improving their stocking, other measures should be taken by governments. Agricultural productivity has to increase faster than population increase, and land resettlement policies should be re-examined. Alternatives to palm oil, such as jatropha, should be promoted; these could be planted on marginal/abandoned agricultural lands. There should be efforts to improve village life through improved water and sanitation; better healthcare and family planning; increased education, especially for girls; improved stoves and kitchen practices; access to electricity and other measures. All the initiatives mentioned earlier should be coordinated so as to ensure that assets are not destroyed but used sustainably.

The use of biomass energy in Asia and the Pacific is saving GHG emissions. The estimated demand for biomass energy in 2015 was 1.37 billion t of wood equivalent, containing about 685 million t of carbon. Only about 25% of the potentially available woody biomass is used today, and much less of the potentially available residues and dung. Much more wood, residues, and dung could be used. This would increase the store of carbon in biomass and soils, while at the same time providing renewable energy in place of fossil fuels, thus tempering the increase of GHG.

Global warming and climate change adversely affect flora and fauna. The human population cannot isolate itself from these effects. If food crops are negatively affected, such as rice flowers not producing grain, then millions may be affected. If

---

[10] It is assumed that the additional store of soil carbon per ha is 75 t in forests, 40 t in woodlands, and 35 t in grasslands.

governments, businesses, organizations, and individuals do not act quickly, the consequences for subsequent generations may be catastrophic. The Paris Climate Accord agreed in 2015 is a necessary and vital step. A recent report (Crowther, 2019) has proposed a worldwide planting of 1.2 trillion (10^{12}) trees on 1.7 billion (10^9) hectares to cancel out decades of CO_2 emissions. Much of this abandoned land would be in the A-P region.

19.11 DISCUSSION AND CONCLUSIONS

In some circles, biomass is dismissed as a subsistence fuel to be substituted as quickly as possible. It is seen as a fuel that causes indoor air pollution, endangering the health of the cook and young children in the vicinity of the stove. Its use is regarded as a burden on the women and girls who mainly collect the fuel and it is credited with causing deforestation. However, in 2015, for Asia and the Pacific as a whole, the annual growth of woody biomass was about 2.75 times demand, and for the low-income countries of Asia, annual growth is about two times demand (Table 19.9). It is not the use of wood that causes deforestation, but land-use changes, principally converting land to arable agriculture. Granted that in some forests there is over-cutting, chiefly for sawlogs and there may be shortages of wood around population concentrations, but much more wood could and should be used, without making inroads into the tree stock.

Indoor air pollution does cause premature deaths, but this pollution could and should be drastically reduced through improved stoves and kitchen practices, chimneys, better ventilation, and keeping young children in well-ventilated areas. These initiatives have to go hand in hand with improving the quality of life in villages. Of course, having energy at the flick of a switch and the turn of a knob should be the goal for all households, but in Asia and the Pacific, there are more than 2 billion people (350 million households) cooking with biomass (and coal). It will be many decades before all these households have more convenient (and less polluting) cooking fuel. And it is possible that much of this fuel could come from renewable resources, including biomass.

Regarding the shortages of woody biomass near to the house, this could be overcome by increasing the planting of trees on farms, along paths and in woodlots. There are many short-rotation nitrogen-fixing trees that improve the fertility of arable land and/or provide protein-rich browse for farm animals. There are also salt-tolerant trees and grasses that could be used to reclaim abandoned farm land. And abandoned shrimp farms could revert to mangrove areas, which would be a breeding ground for many fish and crustacean species. Therefore, such tree planting initiatives could help in the effort to increase agricultural productivity and perhaps provide surplus food and wood that can be traded.

Biomass is an important traded household and service sector fuel and a fuel of choice for many rural industries. In 2015, the estimated value of traded biomass in Asia and the Pacific was US$42 billion, and this provided about 27 million full-time jobs, many of them in rural areas. If substitution to fossil fuel is encouraged, then some of the people employed in biomass energy would have to find alternative occupations, which for many would be reverting back to subsistence arable/pastoral agriculture or a move to urban areas. Most likely this would lead to increased clearing of forests and woodlands, thus exacerbating deforestation and increasing GHG not only from deforestation but also from increased consumption of fossil fuels. This is a lose-lose strategy! Rural people would have fewer employment opportunities with more environmental degradation.

On the other hand, a win-win situation could arise if subsidies were removed from fossil fuels and barriers eliminated from biomass energy production, transport, and trade. With a level playing field, growers would be encouraged to plant and manage more trees and preserve forests for all the goods and services they provide, including fuel. More rural employment would be created, and then people would be in a better position to afford electricity, preferably made from renewable energy, including biomass. Hundreds of millions of people are at risk from the effects of global warming in Asia and the Pacific region. If governments are serious about the consequences of global warming (as they pledged in the Paris Climate Accord in December 2015), then they should earnestly think about imposing/increasing a carbon tax on fossil fuels, investing in energy efficiency measures and encouraging the production of all kinds of renewable energy.

In many countries, information on the stock and yield of biomass is lacking, especially at the local level and particularly for wood. In order to plan for sustainable biomass use, it is essential to have good local data both in the field and at the factories where processed residues are available. Such information would indicate where biomass use can be expanded and where interventions are required. Such interventions include increased agricultural and silvicultural productivity, increased tree planting, better management, fuel substitution, and improved energy efficiency.

The use of biomass energy is saving a considerable amount of GHG emissions. In 2000, in Asia and the Pacific, biomass energy accounted for an estimated 17% of total primary energy – 23.6 exaJoules (EJ) (10^{18} J) out of 138.6 EJ (Table 19.1). In 2015, there was an explosion in fossil fuel use, especially coal, so the biomass energy share had fallen to 9% of total primary energy (25.6 EJ out of 284.7 EJ) (Table 19.1). In the low-income Asian countries, containing 84% of the A-P region's population, biomass accounted for 13% (24.6 EJ) of total primary energy consumption in 2015, an increase of 1.9 EJ in comparison with 2000, despite the massive use of coal in China and India. Now both of these countries have pledged to considerably reduce emissions intensity by 2030 through increased use of renewable energy, improved energy efficiency, and the creation of additional carbon sinks.

True sustainable development cannot occur with the use of finite energy resources, especially if these energy resources are causing global warming and environmental degradation. By promoting biomass use, biomass stock could increase, rather than decrease as at present in several countries, thus improving carbon sequestration in woody biomass and the soils beneath the trees.

Much greater efforts are required to improve biomass productivity, both agricultural and silvicultural. These include species choice, breeding/cloning, better management, improved and appropriate tools and equipment, and much more. Energy efficiency gains are easier to achieve when existing intermediate and end-use efficiencies are low. Generally, this is the case for biomass fuels. Research, development, training, and commercialization are required for stoves, industrial and service equipment, charcoal production, liquid and gaseous fuels, and power/heat production. There has to be appropriate land-use and user rights policies, which guarantee access to and use of natural resources by local people in return for guardianship of common and government-owned lands. Training should be provided in agroforestry, forest management, sustainable use of goods and services, and other fields. This will require demonstrations, good extension services, monitoring and evaluation, and supervision.

Many of the former Soviet Union countries, as well as China and Mongolia, have vast areas of grasslands, but many are in poor shape, but they could and should be improved. Experiments are being carried out in Kazakhstan, and if successful, they could be expanded to other areas within Kazakhstan and countries in the region (World Bank, 2003b). Similar dryland reclamation efforts are ongoing in Egypt, Jordan, and Iran. These initiatives will sequester carbon and provide gainful employment to local people and nomads. Inner Mongolia is also examining the use of manure for biogas production for its large dairy herd industries. At present, the manure is a waste product.

There are international, national, and private programmes that could promote biomass sequestration and use and assist with the planting of a trillion trees (Crowther, 2019). These include the Paris Agreement 2015; the UN Framework Convention on Climate Change (UNFCCC); the Global Environment Facility (GEF); the Clean Development Mechanism (CDM); the Carbon Fund; REDD+ (Reducing Emissions from Deforestation and Forest Degradation, and the role of conservation, sustainable management of forests, and enhancement of forest carbon stocks); the United Nations Economic and Social Commission for Asia and the Pacific (UNESCAP); the Global Alliance for Clean Cookstoves; various multilateral and bilateral initiatives, especially from wealthy nations in the region; NGOs, both local and international; and international and private donors. International donors may include the Asian Development Bank (ADB), the Food and Agricultural Organization (FAO) of the United Nations, UNDP, and the World Bank. Also, there should be information exchange between and within countries and organizations in the region.

Energy planners and governments have to be convinced that biomass is not merely a fuel of the past, but an infinite energy source in the present and future. It will be around after all the fossil fuels have been exhausted, provided it is managed judiciously. It is a versatile fuel that people know how to grow, tend, and use. It is a rural activity that can assist with poverty alleviation. Without continual and concerted investments in people and products from renewable resources, the world will not achieve sustainable development. Developing countries, especially those in Asia and the Pacific, already use considerable quantities of renewable biomass energy. They could expand its use and show industrialized nations the path to energy and environmental sustainability – and a way of keeping the increase in global average temperature well below 2°C.

ACKNOWLEDGEMENTS

The author would like to thank Dr Peter de Groot, and Dr John J. Todd and the editor for their reviews of this article and helpful comments. Any errors and mistakes are my sole responsibility.

REFERENCES

Archer, G. (1993) *Biomass Resource Assessment. Pakistan Household Energy Strategy Study (HESS)*. Washington, DC, UNDP/WB.

Barnes, D. F., Kumar, P. and Openshaw, K. (2012) *Cleaner Hearths, Better Homes: New Stoves for India and the Developing World*. New Delhi, Oxford University Press and World Bank.

Bouwman, A. F. (ed.) (1990) *Soils and the Greenhouse Effect: The Present Status and Future Trends Concerning the Effect of Soils and Their Cover on the Fluxes of Greenhouse Gas*. New York, John Wiley and Son.

Bui Xuan An, Preston, T. R. and Dolberg, F. (1997) The introduction of low-cost polyethylene tube biodigesters on small-scale farms in Vietnam. *Livestock Research for Rural Development* 9(2). https://www.lrrd.cipav.org.co

Crowther, T. (2019) A trillion trees. https://www.crowtherlab.com/trillion-trees-plantahead/

Dougherty, W. W. (1993) *Firewood Markets in Pakistan: Supply, Distribution and Profitability.* Washington, DC, HESS. UNDP/WB.

ESMAP (2005) *Aide Memoire. Scoping Study for Biomass Energy Development in Xing'an Meng, Inner Mongolia.* Washington, DC, World Bank.

FAO (1993) Forest resource assessment 1990: *Tropical Countries. Forest Paper 112.* Rome, FAO.

(2001a) *State of the World's Forests 2001.* Rome, FAO.

(2001b) *Annual (agricultural) Production.* Vol. 55. Rome, FAO.

(2001c) *Agricultural Statistics.* Rome, FAO.

(2003) *Wood Energy Information Analysis in Asia.* Bangkok, Thailand, FAO Regional Office for Asia and the Pacific.

(2010a) *State of the World's Forests 2010.* Rome, FAO.

(2010b) What woodfuels can do to mitigate climate change. FAO Forestry Paper, No. 162.

(2010c) Global forest resource assessment 2010. Main report. FAO Forestry Paper, No. 163.

(2014) *Annual Agricultural Production 2000–2014. FAOSTAT 2014.* Rome, FAO.

(2015) Global forest resource assessment: Desk reference. FAO, Rome.

(2018) *State of the World's Forests 2018. Forest Pathways to Sustainable Development.* http://www.fao.org/state-of-forests/en/

Hall, D. O. and Rao, K. K. (1994) *Photosynthesis* (5th ed.). Cambridge, UK, Cambridge University Press.

Haq, B. U. (1994) *Sea Level Rise and Coastal Subsidence: Rates and Threats. ENVLW Technical Note No. 1.* Washington, DC, World Bank.

IEA (2002) *International Energy Agency: World Energy Statistics.* Paris, France, IEA.

(2010) *World Energy Statistics.* Paris, France, IEA.

(2014) *World Energy Statistics.* Paris, France, IEA.

(2015) *World Energy Outlook 2015.* Paris, France, IEA.

IPCC (Intergovernmental Panel on Climate Change) (2007) *Climate Change 2007: The Physical Science Basis.* Working Group I Contribution to the Fourth Assessment Report of the Intergovernmental Panel on Climate Change.

(2013) *Climate Change 2013: The Physical Science Basis.* Working Group I Contribution to the Fifth Assessment Report of the Intergovernmental Panel on Climate Change. https://www.ipcc.ch/site/assets/uploads/2018/02/WG1AR5_all_final.pdf

(2014a) *Climate Change 2014: Impacts, Adaptation, and Vulnerability.* Working Group II Contribution to the Fifth Assessment Report of the Intergovernmental Panel on Climate Change. https://www.ipcc.ch/report/ar5/wg2/

(2014b) *Climate Change 2014: Mitigation of Climate Change.* Working Group III Contribution to the Fifth Assessment Report of the Intergovernmental Panel on Climate Change. https://www.ipcc.ch/report/ar5/wg3/, https://www.ipcc.ch/site/assets/uploads/2018/02/ipcc_wg3_ar5_full.pdf

(2018) *Special Report on Global Warming.* Geneva, Switzerland, IPCC Secretariat. https://www.ipcc.ch/sr15/

Lal, R., Kimble, J., Levine, E. and Stewart, B. A. (eds.) (1995) *Soil Management and Greenhouse Effect.* London, CRC Lewis Publishers.

MNRE (Ministry of New and Renewable Energy). Annual Reports (2009–10, 2010–11, 2016–17, 2017–18). New Delhi, India.

Openshaw, K. (1983) *An Inventory of Biomass in Kenya.* Stockholm, Beijer Institute (Swedish Academy of Sciences).

(1997) *Malawi: Biomass Energy Strategy Study.* Washington, DC, and IRG, Washington, DC, World Bank.

(2000a) A review of *Jatropha curcas:* An oil plant of unfulfilled promise. *Biomass and Bioenergy,* **19**, 1–15.

(2000b) Government of Benin/WB and GEF. A baseline survey of organic carbon in woody biomass and soils on different land-use types in the project areas. Benin: PGFTR Project. World Bank, Washington, DC.

(2004) *Bangladesh: Biomass Energy Supply (draft report).* UNDP/WB ESMAP. Washington, DC, World Bank.

(2010) Employment generation by biomass energy and its contribution to poverty alleviation in Malawi and other developing countries. *Biomass and Bioenergy Journal,* **34**(3), 365–378.

Ouerghi, A. (1993) *Household Energy Demand: Consumption Patterns.* Washington, DC, HESS. UNDP/WB.

Population Pyramid (2015) Population Pyramids of the World from 1950 to 2100. https://www.populationpyramid.net/

Ravindranath, N. H., Somashekar, H. I., Dasappa, S. and Jayasheela Reddy, C. N. (2004) Sustainable biomass power for rural India: Case study of biomass gasifier for village electrification. *Current Science,* **87**(7), 932–941. https://www.jstor.org/stable/24109397?seq=1#page_scan_tab_contents

Ren 21 (2010) Renewable global status report 2009. Ren 21 Secretariat, Paris, France.

(2018) Renewable global status report 2018. Ren 21 Secretariat, Paris, France.

RWEDP (Regional Wood Energy Development Programme) reports 1986–1997. Bangkok, Thailand, FAO Regional Office for Asia and the Pacific.

(1986) Wood energy systems for rural and other industries – Sri Lanka. GCP/RAS/111/Net. Field document 4.

(1988) Wood based energy systems in rural industries and village applications – Nepal Field document 11.

(1990a) Trees and fuelwood from non-forest lands: A methodology for assessment – India Field document 23.

(1990b) Wood energy systems for rural industries and village application. Regional expert consultation. GCP/RAS/131/Net. April 1990.

(1990c) Rural energy appraisal. Workshop report. GCP/RAS/131/Net. July 1990.

(1990d) Social forestry in integrated rural development and planning – Sri Lanka. GCP/RAS/131/Net. Field document 24.

(1991) Wood fuel flows. Rapid rural appraisal in four Asian countries. GCP/RAS/131/Net. Field document 26.

(1993) Patterns of commercial woodfuel supply, distribution and use in the city and province of Cebu, Philippines. Field document 42.

(1997a) Review of wood energy data in RWEDP member countries. Field Document 47.

(1997b) Regional study on wood energy today and tomorrow in Asia. Field Document 50.

RWEDP (1991–2001) *Wood Energy News*. Three volumes per year. Bangkok, Thailand, FAO Regional Office for Asia and the Pacific.

ScienceDirect (2019) Producer gas – An overview. https://www.sciencedirect.com/topics/engineering/producer-gas

Shetty, S. (2005) Essential crop/plant management for biofuels. Proceedings of the workshop 'Alternative fuels and energy choices 2005', Kuala Lumpur, Malaysia, 7–8 December. Universal Network Intelligence Training PTE, Ltd., Singapore.

Soussan, J. (1991) *Philippines Household Energy Strategy: Fuelwood Supply and Demand*. UNDP/WB ESMAP. Washington, DC, World Bank.

UK Forestry Commission (1971) Forest management tables (metric). Forestry Commission Booklet No. 34. Her Majesty's Stationery Office, London. https://www.forestresearch.gov.uk/documents/6443/FCBK034.pdf

United Nations (2002) *Energy Statistics Yearbook 2001*. United Nations Department of Economic and Social Affairs. New York, United Nations.

(2005) *Energy Statistics Yearbook 2004*. United Nations Department of Economic and Social Affairs. New York, United Nations.

(2014) *UN Country Classification*. New York, United Nations.

(2015) Paris Agreement. https://unfccc.int/site/default/files/english_paris_agreement.pdf

World Bank (1992) World Development Report: Development and the environment.

(2000) *World Development Report 2004*. Washington, DC, World Bank.

(2003a) *World Development Report 2003*. Washington, DC, World Bank.

(2003b) *Kazakhstan: Drylands Management Pilot Project*. Washington, DC.

(2004) *World Development Report 2000*. Washington, DC, World Bank.

(2015a) World Bank open data. GDP country figures. https://datacatalog.worldbank.org/

(2015b) World Bank. The pump price for diesel fuel in US$/litre. https://datacatalog.worldbank.org/pump-price-diesel-fuel-us-liter-0

20 Pathways to a more sustainable electricity sector in India

SHOIBAL CHAKRAVARTY[1], T. S. GOPI RETHINARAJ[2], AND DILIP R. AHUJA[3]

[1]Indian Institute of Science, Bangalore, India
[2]Atria University, Bangalore, India
[3]Independent researcher, Bangalore, India

Keywords

India; electricity; energy; climate change; energy access; coal; Intended Nationally Determined Contributions (INDC); e-vehicles; renewable energy; nuclear policy; carbon capture and storage (CCS)

Abstract

India is the third-largest emitter of greenhouse gases in the world, and its coal-dominated electricity sector contributes approximately half of these. In addition, air pollution from burning coal is a serious challenge for public health. India also has approximately 200 million people without access to electricity and therefore has low per capita electricity consumption. These are unflattering realities when India is also expected to be among the fastest-growing economies in the world for the next few decades.

At the Paris summit in 2015, India committed to increasing the share of non-fossil electric generation capacity to 40% by 2030. The recent decline in the cost of solar photovoltaic systems and wind generation, and strong policy support for renewables-based distributed generation and micro-grids, make this target achievable. While the role of nuclear power in meeting this goal is uncertain, India's re-entry in global nuclear trade and commerce following the 2008 civilian nuclear agreement with the United States and negotiation of a partial safeguards agreement with the International Atomic Energy Agency (IAEA) have revived interest in a major expansion programme. Reducing coal's share in the Indian electricity sector, expanding electrification of transport, and improving efficiency can reduce India's urban air pollution problems. At the same time, improving access and quality of service are key components of the United Nations' Sustainable Development Goals (SDG). In this chapter, we analyse the challenges and benefits of increasing the share of renewables and nuclear power in India's electricity system.

20.1 INTRODUCTION

In the Sustainable Development Goals (SDGs) adopted by the United Nations for the period 2015–2030, which replace the Millennium Development Goals, energy was explicitly included. The seventh SDG exhorts all countries to 'ensure access to affordable, reliable, sustainable and modern energy for all'. The provision of modern energy services is essential for the attainment of several other SDGs, which seek to achieve or ensure food security, good healthcare, quality education, availability of water and sanitation, productive employment, sustainable industrialization, and resilient infrastructure. Every country aspires, at least outwardly, to make progress in these sectors that will lead to development and economic growth.

Supporting growth in agriculture, industry, manufacturing, services, and commerce entails a significant increase in overall energy consumption. Although an increase in energy efficiency is observed to reduce the energy intensity of economies in most countries over time, these declines have thus far been unable to offset the increases in energy use due to growth in population and incomes. Moreover, energy efficiency improvements do not obviate demand for more energy in countries that are in early stages of economic development. Whenever economic growth exceeds population growth, the increased per capita incomes lead to increased consumption of energy for personal mobility and other services provided by electricity. The increased consumption of energy is not without consequences. Energy derived from conventional sources causes adverse impacts at all spatial scales – local, regional, and global – and at all temporal scales – immediate, intermediate, and long term. The impact that is increasingly worrisome is caused by carbon emissions leading to anthropogenic global warming and the deleterious effects as a result of a changing climate.

As an emerging economy with unmet aspirations of a majority of its people, the importance of energy security for India's economic development cannot be overstressed. India's energy sector is, however, at a crossroads and suffers from a fragmented and

257

uncoordinated development. For more than six decades, between 1951 and 2014, only the Planning Commission of India's federal government had a mandate to adopt an integrated view of the country's energy sector, even though the states controlled electricity transmission and distribution and a significant share of production. In 1997, the ninth plan articulated issues facing India in the energy sector: 'The key issues facing India which have energy implications are rising population, need for economic growth, access to adequate commercial energy supplies and the financial resources needed to achieve this, rational pricing regime, improvements in energy efficiency of both the energy supply and consumption, technological up-gradation, a matching R&D base and environmental protection' (PC, IX, 1997, En. p. 7/11). These concerns remain just as valid today. From time to time, the Planning Commission also articulated policy goals. In the tenth plan, it identified these to be 'economic efficiency, energy security, access, and the environment'. It also described the thrust of the reforms as 'to deregulate the prices of commercial energy resources (which until recently were entirely administered), increase competition and reduce subsidies' (PC, X, 2002, p. 766).

There have been major changes in India's energy market. Prior to independence, most of the energy consumed in the country was from non-commercial sources, while today most (more than 80%) is from commercially traded fuels. Before 1947, almost all electricity was generated by the private sector. After 1947, electricity generation became almost an exclusive activity of the public sector. India is again moving to a mixed situation where generation has again been opened to the private sector. In addition, in retail sales of energy the country has moved gradually from entirely administered prices to largely market-based pricing.

The growth in total primary and secondary energy consumption during the past seven decades is nothing short of remarkable, and the Indian energy sector has made impressive strides since 1947. However, the list of persisting problems is also long. India has around 200 million people without access to electricity and other modern fuels. Even for those who have access, the poor quality of electricity and its unreliability impose huge distributed uncounted costs on the economy in the form of captive generators, uninterrupted power systems, voltage stabilizers, burnt-out appliances, and other problems. The issue of displacement of people due to energy projects and their insensitive resettlement and rehabilitation continues to be a major obstacle for expansion plans. The financial unsustainability of the business model of the utilities has been worrisome for decades now. Air pollution from burning coal is a serious challenge for public health. These are unflattering realities when India is also expected to be among the fastest-growing economies in the world for the next few decades. Serious observers of

India's energy scene often find it perplexing. A recent international report opined, 'Clarity of vision for the energy sector is difficult to achieve in India, not least because of the country's federal structure and complex institutional arrangements' (IEA, 2015, p. 40).

In addition, as the third-largest emitter of greenhouse gases, India wants to decarbonize its coal-dominated electricity sector, which contributes approximately half of the total greenhouse gas emissions. At the Paris summit in 2015, India committed to increasing the share of non-fossil electric generation capacity to 40% by 2030. The recent decline in the cost of solar photovoltaic systems and wind generation, and strong policy support for renewables-based distributed generation and micro-grids, make these targets achievable. While the role of nuclear power in meeting this goal is uncertain, India's re-entry in global nuclear trade and commerce following the 2008 civilian nuclear agreement with the United States and negotiation of a partial safeguards agreement with the International Atomic Energy Agency (IAEA) have revived interest in a major expansion programme. We attempt in this chapter to bring some clarity to the transformation underway to more sustainability in the electricity sector and specifically examine the challenges and benefits of increasing the share of renewables and nuclear power.

20.2 STATE OF THE ELECTRICITY SECTOR

The Indian electricity sector has grown from a small and modest base of about 4 gigawatts (GW) in 1947 to the world's third-largest generator of electricity in 2017. It currently has 340 GW of generation capacity, producing 1300 terawatt hours (TWh) annually (CEA, 2018b, 2018c). The expansion in electricity generation up to 1980 came mostly from large hydroelectric projects and coal power plants. In 1980, coal power plants and hydroelectric plants had a roughly equal share in the country's electricity generation. An ambitious nuclear power programme was also launched soon after independence, with commercial generation starting in 1969 with a turnkey project built by General Electric. Despite a long history of R&D in nuclear technologies and commercial nuclear electricity generation, its contribution to overall electricity generation has remained marginal. Since 1980, there has been a significant expansion of coal power plants, and coal has been the dominant player in India's electricity sector, contributing more than 70% of generation. Most major rivers of peninsular India have been dammed and a strong environmental movement has slowed further expansion of hydroelectric power, which contributed approximately 10% of total generation in 2017 and is likely to see a reduced relative role in future. Renewable electricity generation from wind and solar plays a significant role now and is expected to expand significantly in the future.

The State Electricity Boards (SEBs) were given the responsibility of expanding electricity generation and distribution from 1947 and were vertically integrated state-owned and state-managed entities. The Central Electricity Authority (CEA) was set up in 1948 to advise the state and central governments on policy issues pertaining to the electricity sector. The SEBs and other public sector entities, like the National Thermal Power Corporation, and electricity equipment manufacturing firms, like Bharat Heavy Electricals, Ltd., played a significant role in expanding the electricity grid, generation, and access till the 1980s. A deterioration of the performance of the SEBs in the 1980s, primarily a result of poor technology, administration, and increased political interference, led to attempts to reform the sector and unbundle and privatize the vertically integrated SEBs.

The last couple of decades have seen a significant increase in coal power plants and renewable power plants, along with a massive expansion of the transmission and distribution networks. The liberalization of the Indian economy in 1991, incremental reforms in the electricity sector culminating in the landmark Electricity Act of 2003 (CEA, 2003), and subsequent and continuing reforms were the key enablers in the rapid expansion of the electricity sector. These reforms led to the privatization and unbundling of the SEBs to autonomous state-owned corporations. The impact of these reforms has been significant in the electricity sector, especially in electricity generation. Electricity generation was completely de-licensed (allowing any company to bid to be a generator), and special incentives were provided to renewable sources. Prayas (2017) provides an excellent discussion of the past and present state of India's electricity sector.

State-led growth during the period from 1980 to 2002 saw a sevenfold increase in coal-powered generation from 55.7 GWh to 371 GWh and a fourfold increase in coal capacity from 16 GW to 62 GW (see Tables 20.1 and 20.2). This period also saw a significant increase in power plant efficiency and plant load factors. Competitive bidding for new generation, better availability of capital and debt, and the significant entry of the private sector since the Electricity Act of 2003 have increased the pace of new coal power plants. The twelfth five-year plan (2012–2017) saw approximately 80 GW of new coal generation, which was the fastest expansion ever. This rapid expansion also led to a temporary shortage of coal, as domestic mining could not keep pace with the growth. At the same time, there is a significant overcapacity in coal generation. Only 130–140 GW of the approximately 195 GW of coal power plants are generating power at any given time. Another 50 GW of coal power plants are in various stages of construction. The CEA projects that no new coal plants will be required till 2022, and 50 GW of new capacity would be required by 2027 (CEA, 2018a, 2018b) (Tables 20.1 and 20.2).

Table 20.1. Generation-wise breakdown of India's electricity sector (Central Electricity Authority).

Financial year^	Generation (terawatt hours)								
	Hydro	Coal/ Lignite	Gas/ Diesel	Nuclear	Solar	Wind	Other#	Renewables	Total
31.12.1947	2.2	1.7	0.1	0.0				0.0	4.1
31.12.1950	2.5	2.6	0.2	0.0				0.0	5.1
31.03.1956 (End of 1st Plan)	4.3	5.4	0.2	0.0				0.0	9.7
31.03.1961 (End of 2nd Plan)	7.8	9.1	0.4	0.0				0.0	16.9
31.03.1966 (End of 3rd Plan)	15.2	17.8	0.4	0.0				0.0	33.0
31.03.1969 (End of 3 Annual Plans)	20.7	26.7	0.3	0.0				0.0	47.4
31.03.1974 (End of 4th Plan)	29.0	34.9	0.5	2.4				0.0	66.7
31.03.1979 (End of 5th Plan)	47.2	52.0	0.6	2.8				0.0	102.5
31.03.1980 (End of Annual Plan)	45.5	55.7	0.6	2.9				0.0	104.6
31.03.1985 (End of 6th Plan)	53.9	97.0	1.9	4.1				0.0	156.9
31.03.1990 (End of 7th Plan)	62.1	172.6	6.0	4.6				0.0	245.4
31.03.1992 (End of 2 Annual Plans)	72.8	197.2	11.5	5.5				0.0	287.0
31.03.1997 (End of 8th Plan)	68.9	289.4	27.7	9.1				0.9	395.9
31.03.2002 (End of 9th Plan)	73.6	370.9	51.4	19.5				2.1	517.4
31.03.2007 (End of 10th Plan)	113.5	461.8	66.7	18.8				9.9	670.7
31.03.2012 (End of 11th Plan)	130.5	612.5	95.9	32.3				51.2	922.5
31.03.2013 (Ist yr of 12th Plan)	113.7	691.3	69.1	32.9				57.4	964.5
31.03.2014 (IInd yr of 12th Plan)	134.8	745.5	46.5	34.2				65.5	1,026.6
31.03.2015 (IIIrd yr of 12th Plan)	129.2	835.3	42.7	36.1				61.8	1,116.9

Table 20.1. (cont.)

Financial year^	Generation (terawatt hours)								
	Hydro	Coal/ Lignite	Gas/ Diesel	Nuclear	Solar	Wind	Other#	Renewables	Total
31.03.2016 (IVth yr of 12th Plan)@	121.4	896.3	47.5	37.4	7.5	33.0	25.0	65.8	1,168.4
31.03.2017 (End of 12th Plan)	122.3	944.9	49.4	37.7	13.5	46.0	22.1	81.9	1,241.7
31.03.2018	126.1	985.9	50.4	38.1	25.6	51.9	23.5	100.9	1,306.5
31.03.2022*	*155.7*	*1,071.8*	*82.6*	*62.6*	*162.0*	*112.0*	*52.0*	*327.0*	*1,699.8*
31.03.2027*	*268.9*	*1,238.9*	*86.2*	*110.7*	*243.0*	*188.0*	*87.0*	*518.0*	*2,222.6*

^ The financial year in India is 1 April to 31 March.

Other: Other renewables (biomass, small hydro, and waste heat)

@ Breakdown of renewables generation into different sources is available from 2016 onwards.

* Projections from the National Electricity Plan (January 2018)

Table 20.2. Capacity-wise breakdown of India's electricity sector (Central Electricity Authority).

Financial year^	Capacity (GW)								
	Hydro	Coal/ Lignite	Gas/ Diesel	Nuclear	Solar	Wind	Other#	Renewables	Total
31.12.1947	0.5	0.8	0.1	0				0	1.4
31.12.1950	0.6	1.0	0.1	0				0	1.7
31.03.1956 (End of 1st Plan)	1.1	1.6	0.2	0				0	2.9
31.03.1961 (End of 2nd Plan)	1.9	2.4	0.3	0				0	4.7
31.03.1966 (End of 3rd Plan)	4.1	4.4	0.5	0				0	9.0
31.03.1969 (End of 3 Annual Plans)	5.9	6.6	0.4	0				0	13.0
31.03.1974 (End of 4th Plan)	7.0	8.7	0.4	0.6				0	16.7
31.03.1979 (End of 5th Plan)	10.8	14.9	0.4	0.6				0	26.7
31.03.1980 (End of Annual Plan)	11.4	16.0	0.5	0.6				0	28.4
31.03.1985 (End of 6th Plan)	14.5	26.3	0.7	1.1				0	42.6
31.03.1990 (End of 7th Plan)	18.3	41.2	2.5	1.6				0	63.6
31.03.1992 (End of 2 Annual Plans)	19.2	44.8	3.3	1.8				0	69.1
31.03.1997 (End of 8th Plan)	21.7	54.2	6.9	2.2				0.9	85.8
31.03.2002 (End of 9th Plan)	26.3	62.1	12.3	2.7				1.6	105.0
31.03.2007 (End of 10th Plan)	34.7	71.1	14.9	3.9				7.8	132.3
31.03.2012 (End of 11th Plan)@	39.0	112.0	19.6	4.8	0.9	16.9	6.7	24.5	199.9
31.03.2013 (Ist yr of 12th Plan)	39.5	130.2	21.3	4.8	1.7	18.5	7.4	27.5	223.3
31.03.2014 (IInd yr of 12th Plan)	40.5	145.3	23.0	4.8	2.6	21.0	11.3	35.0	248.6
31.03.2015 (IIIrd yr of 12th Plan)	41.3	164.6	24.3	5.8	3.7	23.4	11.9	39.0	274.9
31.03.2016 (IVth yr of 12th Plan)	42.8	185.2	25.5	5.8	6.8	26.8	12.4	45.9	305.2
31.03.2017 (End of 12th Plan)	44.5	192.2	26.1	6.8	12.3	32.3	12.7	57.2	326.8
31.03.2018	45.3	197.2	25.7	6.8	19.6	33.0	13.0	65.5	340.5
31.03.2022*	*51.3*	*217.3*	*25.7*	*10.1*	*100.0*	*60.0*	*15.0*	*175.0*	*479.4*
31.03.2027*	*63.3*	*238.2*	*25.7*	*16.9*	*150.0*	*100.0*	*25.0*	*275.0*	*619.1*

^ The financial year in India is 1 April to 31 March.

Other: Other renewables (biomass, small hydro, and waste heat)

@ Breakdown of renewables capacity into different sources is available from 2012 onwards.

* Projections from the National Electricity Plan (January 2018)

The period 1980–2012 also saw a substantial increase in gas-based generation from almost zero to about 96 GWh and a capacity of about 20 GW. Gas generation has since then decreased to 50 GWh per year in 2017–2018, as domestic sources of gas have not delivered, and power from imported LNG is too expensive. Gas-based power is not expected to play a major role in the near future. Despite a significant investment in R&D and unflagging government support for more than seven decades, nuclear power plays a limited role in India's energy mix, with a generating capacity of 6.2 GW and generated just about 3% (35 GWh) of India's electricity in 2018 (PRIS, 2018). Nuclear power could play a major role in a low-carbon future of the Indian electricity sector and is considered in detail in Section 20.4.

Transmission and distribution (T&D) losses across India are among the highest in the world and were reported to be 20.7% for the year 2016–2017, with some marginal improvement over the past six years (CEA, 2018e). These figures do not include theft and other unmetered commercial consumption. Theft of power and free or heavily subsidized power to farmers or poor residential customers are both a part of the client-patron nature of Indian politics. The electricity distribution companies (or DISCOMs), though nominally independent public utilities, are often under strong political control. Reducing these technical and commercial losses will require a combination of political will and significant investment in the distribution grid, especially in planning and maintenance.

The DISCOMs are susceptible to political interference, and the health of the electricity sector as a whole is unlikely to improve unless distribution reform is completed. The cost of power to industrial and commercial customers is higher in India than in most developed and developing countries, as these subsidize the agricultural (primarily for groundwater pumping) and residential sectors. This business model is under severe pressure, as renewable power and rooftop solar power are below grid parity for high-paying customers.

While the growth of the electricity sector has been impressive, it also hides a number of important issues. For instance, coal power is a major source of pollution in India and it has been estimated that coal plants contributed to approximately 110,000 deaths in 2015 (GBD MAPS, 2018). New stringent emission norms promulgated in 2015 are yet to be implemented. An increase in the share of renewables will significantly reduce emissions from the electricity sector. Another issue is the lack of universal access to electricity and unreliability of the power supply to those who have access. While all of India's approximately 600,000 villages have recently been connected to the electricity grid, about 40 million households still do not have an electricity connection (Bhaskar, 2018b) (see Figure 20.1). Most rural areas and many small urban areas also suffer from unreliable power and frequent power cuts. In this context, renewable sources can add to the power supplied by the grid, and distributed renewables such as rooftop solar PV can significantly increase access and reliability of power.

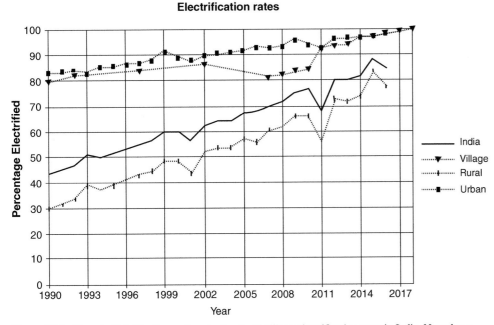

Figure 20.1. Household (all India, rural, and urban) and village electrification rates in India. Note that a village is considered electrified if 10% of households and public areas are electrified (*Source*: CEA (2018a, 2018b)).

20.3 RENEWABLES IN INDIA'S ELECTRICITY SECTOR

Renewable energy is one of the major beneficiaries of the liberalization of the Indian economy in 1991 and the opening up of electricity generation to private companies in 1992. India was one of the first countries in the world to set up a separate Ministry of Non-Conventional Energy Sources (now the Ministry of New and Renewable Energy, or MNRE) in 1992. Initial growth in renewables, primarily in the wind sector, was due to a feed-in tariff and generous tax incentives in the form of accelerated depreciation benefits. It was the 2003 Electricity Act that provided the real incentive in the form of Renewable Purchase Obligations (RPO) for distribution companies, which were to be mandated and regulated by the State Electricity Regulatory Commission. A subsequent policy push for renewables came from the National Action for Plan for Climate Change (NAPCC) 2008, which laid out policies for renewable energy (MOEFCC, 2008).

The National Solar Mission was announced in 2010 to promote solar photovoltaic (PV) and solar thermal technologies by deploying 2 GW per year, with a target of 20 GW by 2022 (MNRE, 2010). In 2015, this target was enhanced to 100 GW of solar capacity alone and 175 GW of renewable capacity by 2022 (PMO, 2015). A competitive reverse auction-based bidding policy, along with significant reduction in manufacturing costs in solar PV, led to a reduction in price by 80% between 2011 and 2017. Generation from solar PV has increased from a negligible number in 2010 to approximately 25 GWh in 2018 (CEA, 2018d).

Wind power is India's first and commercially mature renewable energy source and generated 52 GWh in 2018 (CEA, 2018d). Wind deployments grew steadily at about 2 GW per year during 2003–2015 in response to feed-in tariffs and generous depreciation-based tax incentives and various generation incentives. Wind power transitioned to reverse auction-based pricing in 2017 and has led to a significant reduction in tariffs.

At the UNFCCC Conference of Parties in Paris in December 2015, India put forward in its Intended Nationally Determined Contribution two ambitious targets that concerned energy and the electricity sector (UNFCCC, 2015):

1. To reduce the emissions intensity of its GDP by 33 to 35% by 2030 from the 2005 level;
2. To achieve about 40% cumulative electric power installed capacity from non-fossil fuel-based energy resources by 2030, with the help of transfer of technology and low-cost international finance, including from the Green Climate Fund.

The success of these goals depends on the role that renewables can play in the future of the Indian energy system, especially in the electricity sector. The 2008 National Action Plan for Climate Change and the 2010 National Solar Mission envisioned a major role for renewables in India's energy future. This was reiterated in 2015 when the present government enhanced the goals to achieve 175 GW of renewables capacity by 2022, including 100 GW of solar and 60 GW of wind.

India has gained significantly from the global trend of cost reduction in renewable technologies, especially solar PV and wind. Significant improvements, such as better project management, lower cost of capital, and a reverse auction-based price discovery mechanism, have ensured that India has among the least-expensive renewable energy tariffs in the world. The lowest price from the recent auctions is ₹2.44 (US$0.038) per kWh for both wind and utility scale solar PV (Bhaskar, 2018c). This price is likely to stay around ₹2.50 per kWh for a few years and go below ₹2.00 per kWh in the near future (IRENA, 2018). These costs are 60% cheaper than electricity produced by coal plants in India. More importantly, renewables can generate electricity at a price that is cheaper than the running cost of coal power plants, which are typically 500–600 km away from coal mines.

Renewables such as solar and wind have significant advantages over conventional sources of power. Renewables capacity can be added in less time and in smaller project sizes, making them financially attractive. During the period 2017–2018, capacity addition of renewables exceeded that of new coal projects. This trend is likely to continue, as wind and solar are the least expensive sources of new electricity capacity in India (Figure 20.2). Another impact has been the lower utilization of existing coal power plants, a consequence of the RPO as well as the lower cost of electricity from renewables. The Southern Regional Grid, which serves the renewables-rich South Indian states, saw an absolute decline in electricity generated from coal in 2017–2018, while the share of renewables increased from 9.7% to 15.9% in the period 2015–2016 to 2017–2018 (CEA, 2018c, 2018d). Because of the growth in the renewable energy sector, the share of coal is projected to go down to 55.7% by 2027, while the share of non-fossil electricity generation is projected to be 40.4%. Solar, wind, and biomass are projected to contribute 23.3% of total generation in 2027. Therefore, electricity from renewables could increase by a factor of five in the next 10 years (CEA, 2018a) (Table 20.1).

Renewable power with storage, such as solar thermal and wind or solar PV with battery storage, could be cost-competitive with coal by 2025–2030. Solar thermal power plants with a power tower and molten salt storage technology saw a steep decline in costs in 2017 (Kraemer, 2017). Bids for plants projected to start production in 2020–2022 have reached 5–7 US cents (₹ 3.3–4.7) per kWh. The cost in 2025–2030 in India could be as low as ₹ 4–6, after accounting for further price

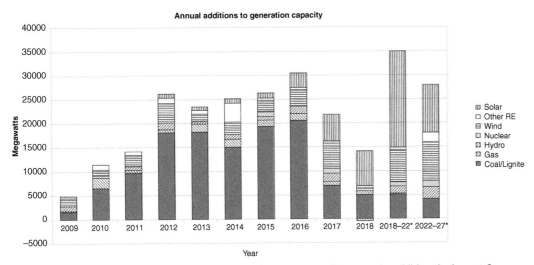

Figure 20.2. New capacity added in the past ten years. Average expected net capacity additions in the next five-year plan years (2018–2022 and 2022–2027) are also shown. Note that more renewables than coal will be deployed in the foreseeable future (*Source*: CEA (2018a, 2018b)).

declines, India's high cost of capital, and India's lower irradiance. This would put solar thermal plants as a base-load generating option in direct competition with coal. On the other hand, lithium battery technologies (in combination with solar PV or wind) could serve peaking load at 10–12 US cents (₹ 6–8) per kWh in less than ten years if cost declines continue at the current rate (Kittner *et al.*, 2017).

The discussion has thus far been limited to utility-scale renewable plants. Distributed renewables, especially rooftop solar PV, have yet to take off in India. Currently, about 2 GW, or about 10%, of India's solar PV consists of rooftop plants (BTI, 2018). Rooftop solar PV has reached grid parity for commercial, industrial, and large residential consumers in most states of India. A lack of clarity in policies regarding the business model of rooftop solar, as well as opposition from some DISCOMs fearing the loss of high-paying customers, is handicapping growth at present (SRPC, 2016). With the right policy support, grid-connected rooftop solar PV, solar-powered irrigation pump-sets, and hybrid solar with storage or diesel backup could become a substantial component of the Indian electricity infrastructure.

The most important challenge in the next decade will be the integration and management of variable and intermittent power from renewables (GIZ, 2017). This would require significant transmission infrastructure in order to connect renewables, as well as to provide a large balancing area to spatially average the variance. Coal, gas, and nuclear power plants will have to run more flexibly, and this will require new grid and operation codes and more training, as well as investments in boilers and other equipment. Monitoring and forecasting of renewable generation and load at time scales varying from five minutes to days will help planning and deployment of conventional power plants. Grid-scale storage in the form of pumped hydro, grid-scale batteries, and solar thermal storage can significantly increase the penetration of renewables. Smart grid infrastructure and demand-response technologies and programmes can provide load flexibility to further enhance the share of renewables. Air-conditioning and heating, which are among the fastest-growing loads in large cities, are well-suited for demand-response programmes. A final source of system flexibility and reliability is likely to be grid-connected solar PV pump-sets, which could operate both as distributed generation as well as flexible loads. This potential is significant, as agricultural loads account for 18% of total demand.

Significant investments have already been made in the transmission network of the Indian grid, and additional investments are underway. The Power Grid Corporation of India, Ltd., the state-owned transmission utility, operates a national high-voltage transmission grid that has an inter-regional power transfer capacity of 72 GW that is projected to expand to 91 GW by 2022 (CEA, 2016). State-level transmission and distribution utilities also have to invest significantly in strengthening the transmission and distribution networks. The state-owned grid operator, Power System Operation Company (POSOCO), is in the process of setting up eleven Regional Energy Management Centres (REMC) at the national, regional, and state level (in renewable-rich states) to forecast renewable generation using weather models and other statistical techniques (POSOCO, 2017). A study by POSOCO, the National Renewable Energy Laboratory (NREL), USA, and the Lawrence Berkeley National Laboratory (LBNL), USA, suggests that the integration of the proposed renewable expansion plans till 2022 can be achieved and will lead to lower coal consumption growth and reduced emissions (NREL, 2017).

The growth of large hydropower has slowed down significantly owing to various environmental restrictions and public resistance over the loss of land and livelihoods they entail. Most of India's technically feasible hydropower sites are located in the ecologically fragile and earthquake-prone regions of Western Ghats and Himalayan foothills in the north-eastern parts of the country. Moreover, the available large hydropower sites are in remote mountainous regions and are likely to be very expensive, in comparison with coal or renewables. Given these technical constraints and India's strong environmental and social justice movements, it is very unlikely that large hydropower will expand significantly from its current installed capacity.

Renewables, hydropower, and nuclear power generate 20% of India's electricity, with 42% of the total installed capacity. Non-hydro renewables like solar PV and wind are the fastest-growing segment of the Indian electricity sector. The installed renewable generation capacity in March 2018 comprised 19.6 GW solar, 33 GW wind, 49.8 GW hydro (including large hydro), and 8.5 GW of biomass. The potential resources are significantly higher with onshore wind at 302 GW at 100 m hub height (MNRE, 2018), solar at 800 GW, hydro power at 120 GW, and biomass at 30 GW (IRENA, 2017). Offshore wind potential is expected to be large but no official estimates exist. The current offshore policy envisages about 5 GW of offshore wind by 2032 near the coasts of Gujarat and Tamil Nadu (FOWIND, 2017). Current market conditions and policy support offer bright prospects for expansion of electricity generation from renewable sources and will therefore significantly contribute to the decarbonization of India's electricity sector.

20.4 INDIA'S NUCLEAR POWER DEVELOPMENT

The potential role of nuclear power in decarbonizing India's electricity sector cannot be discounted, despite the several challenges it faces. The nature of impediments for expanding nuclear power varies across countries, but Indian governments during the past seven decades have generally been favourable to nuclear energy development, owing to its perceived importance for the nuclear weapons programme.

Even though India launched an ambitious research and development programme with international assistance for commercial nuclear power production soon after 1947, the 1974 'peaceful' nuclear test abruptly cut off international technology assistance and nuclear fuel supplies and slowed the growth of nuclear power for nearly three decades. In contrast to the international response to the 1974 nuclear test, the negative impact of the 1998 military nuclear tests was short-lived thanks to

India's enhanced economic status and changed geopolitical realities. These helped India in 2005 to sign the civilian nuclear deal with the United States, which formally ended India's isolation and led to its accommodation in the international nuclear trade system after approval by the Nuclear Suppliers Group cartel and the IAEA in 2008. Following this rapprochement and removal of restrictions to nuclear fuel and technology imports, the Department of Atomic Energy (DAE) announced major expansion plans to increase nuclear electricity-generation capacity to 63 GW by the year 2032 (Banerjee, 2010).

For many years, the biggest constraint for India's nuclear power programme was domestic uranium availability and technology sanctions after its refusal to sign the Nuclear Nonproliferation Treaty (NPT). Since 1969, when the first commercial power reactor at Tarapur (a US-supplied turnkey project) was connected to the grid, nuclear power has played only a marginal role (at no point in time exceeding a few percent of total generation) in meeting India's electricity demand. Although India overcame the technological barriers through the, albeit slow and relatively inefficient, indigenization of reactor design and fuel cycle technologies, uranium supply was still a problem.

The domestic uranium resource handicap was recognized even during the pre-sanctions era by Homi Bhabha, the founder and architect of India's nuclear programme (Bhabha and Prasad, 1958). India therefore adopted, and still subscribes to, an expensive and technologically daunting 'three stage' closed nuclear fuel cycle programme. This option envisages developing a suite of advanced reactor and fuel-cycle technologies to use the vast domestic thorium resources, which could theoretically free India from domestic uranium resource constraints and support a large nuclear power programme far into the future.

But this strategy entails complex nuclear fuel reprocessing and recycling technologies yet to be demonstrated on a large scale in India. Through the 1960s, India's policy was in sync with the rest of the world when global uranium resources were perceived to be inadequate to support major expansion, and nuclear power growth was projected to grow exponentially. The international isolation and technology sanctions era following the 1974 test only helped reinforce India's rhetoric and belief in the virtues of a closed nuclear fuel cycle policy and breeder reactor development but is now out of sync with the priorities of the global nuclear industry and economic realities.

Even the formal end of nuclear sanctions in 2008 and flexibility for uranium and reactor imports from international vendors have not prompted any rethink on the desirability of the complex indigenous reactor development, chasing the goal of thorium utilization. The economic case for plutonium-based breeder and thorium reactors pursued by India also appears weak. The usual claim of breeder reactor proponents is that they will greatly extend the fissionable energy of mined uranium by a factor of 50 or more, since the current type of commercial reactors operating worldwide uses only a small fraction (not more than 2%) of uranium. This argument is valid if nuclear utilities are willing to put some price on or pay an insurance premium for fuel supply security. Or the price of freshly mined uranium has to reach a point when the resource case for breeder reactors makes economic sense. The current annual requirement of uranium for fuelling the world's civilian nuclear fleet is about 56,600 tU (tonne of uranium metal) (NEA and IAEA, 2016). Even after factoring in the various future growth projections made by the IAEA, currently identified uranium resources are adequate (5.7 million tU in the less than US$130/kgU category) through the middle of this century. Additional resources from expansion of uranium exploration, a large resource base of unconventional uranium resources, and uranium extraction from seawater all seem to suggest that the case for breeder reactors may not hold up through the end of this century.

India may still continue to plough a lonely furrow, but technical and economic realities suggest that breeder reactors are unlikely to play any significant role in the country's electricity generation before 2050. Large nuclear capacity additions until then are possible through reactor imports and domestic builds of heavy water reactors. Imported light water reactors (LWRs), which come in sizes ranging from 1 GW to 1.6 GW, were long recognized as the key to quick capacity additions owing to the size limitations of the indigenously designed and built pressurized heavy water reactors (PHWRs) – most of which are 0.2 GW units. Only recently India has started building 0.7 GW PHWRs. The 22 operating commercial reactors have a combined capacity of just about 6.2 GW and produced 35 TWh of electricity in 2017, which is 3.2% of the total electricity generation (PRIS, 2018). Six reactors are under construction with a combined capacity of 4.4 GW; 19 reactors with a combined capacity of 17.2 GW are being planned; and another 57 reactors with a combined capacity of 65 GW have been proposed (WNA, 2018a). The Department of Atomic Energy (DAE) projects that 25% of total electricity produced by 2050 will come from nuclear sources.

However, two major developments have slowed the pace of reactor constructions and prevented a fuller exploitation of India's normalization of nuclear trade relations with the rest of the world in 2008. The Civil Liability for Nuclear Damage Act passed in 2010 as a compromise to secure broader political support for the civilian nuclear deal with the United States assigns vendors some liability for damages in the event of a major nuclear accident. Even though some provisions of this law (especially the right to recourse against suppliers) are at variance with international norms that channel all liability claims through utilities, it was passed in the parliament after a divisive political debate. The law has also proved to be a major impediment for reactor imports because of the wariness of international nuclear vendors to do business with India and the cost implications of complying with the new liability regime. India also ratified the Convention on Supplementary Compensation for Nuclear Damages (CSC) in 2016 to assuage international nuclear vendors. But this ratification is problematic because Section 17(b) of India's nuclear liability law is at odds with Article 10 of the annex to CSC (Sengupta, 2016). The upshot of all these complications is an escalation of nuclear construction costs.

For instance, the capital cost of the third and fourth reactor units in Kudankulam, Tamil Nadu, where India is setting up a multiple reactor park with Russian assistance, has more than doubled to ₹ 397 billion, in comparison with the first and second units (₹ 173 billion) that were connected to the grid in 2013 and 2016, respectively (MAE, 2014). Reactor imports from the United States and France can be significantly more expensive than Russian reactors, for which costs are reasonably known. There is no clarity yet regarding when or if the actual commercial deal with these two countries to build reactors in India will be finalized, and the liability law is clearly the albatross. The American and French reactors that India plans to import are newer designs (EPR1600 and AP1000) that have suffered construction delays and cost overruns elsewhere, because of technical and regulatory reasons. Toshiba-Westinghouse, the nuclear division of Westinghouse Electric, went bankrupt in 2017 after suffering cost overruns in the Georgia and South Carolina projects in the United States. The future of the Kovvada project in Andhra Pradesh, where the company planned to build six reactors (1.2 GW each), will be known only after a resolution of the financial troubles that prompted the company to file a bankruptcy petition in 2017 (LiveMint, 2017). The French are in any case not keen to sign on to anything until their concerns regarding some of the provisions in the liability law are fully addressed by India (Private communication, 2012). India's interest in importing reactors from these countries seems to be driven by larger geopolitical considerations than hard-nosed economic assessments. The promise of reactor imports was originally an implicit quid pro quo for countries (especially the United States and France) that did the 'heavy lifting' to end the nuclear sanctions regime faced by India. While prospects of large reactor imports from foreign vendors remain uncertain, the Indian government approved in 2017 building 10 large PHWRs of indigenous design (700 MW each) at a cost of more than ₹ 700 billion (US$10.5 billion) (PMO, 2017). This initiative was announced as part of India's 'low-carbon growth strategy' and commitment to 'sustainable development, energy self-sufficiency and bolsters global efforts to combat climate change'.

Even though capital costs of nuclear plants are higher than most other options, the tariffs on nuclear electricity are comparable to conventional base load-power generating units from coal stations located in the region. The reported nuclear power tariffs in India for the period 2014–2015 range from a low of ₹ 0.94 per kWh for the oldest plant to ₹ 3.88 per kWh for the newest plant, and they average ₹ 2.78 per kWh (DAE, 2015). These numbers can be compared to the power tariffs from pithead coal plants (₹ 1.63 to 3.47 per kWh), non-pithead coal plants (₹ 3.6 to 5.29 per kWh), natural gas plants using fuel at administered prices (₹ 4.3 to 5.79 per kWh), natural gas plants using fuel at market prices (₹ 5.9 to 6.57 per kWh), LNG plants (₹ 10.4 to 12.73 per kWh), and naphtha plants (₹ 7.9 to 15 per kWh) reported during the same period. Even though tariffs reported earlier for nuclear power plants appear competitive, the tariff for the third and fourth Russian reactors under construction in Kudankulam is ₹ 6.3 per kWh, and the estimated tariffs for the proposed American and French reactors range from ₹ 9 per kWh to ₹ 12 per kWh (Mohan, 2016). These numbers show that current and future nuclear power tariffs will be much higher in comparison with electricity generated from solar and wind plants discussed in Section 20.3.

The second major development to have slowed India's nuclear power growth is the social impact of the 2011 Fukushima nuclear accident. Public resistance and mobilization against nuclear power plants in India were earlier muted or non-existent or sporadic. The Fukushima accident prompted mass protests in Jaitapur in Maharashtra (the proposed site for French reactors) and Kudankulam, where the first of the two Russian-built reactors were nearing completion. While opposition to the Jaitapur project was based partly on reported seismic activity in the region and concerns about the impact of plant operation on fruit orchards (the region produces the famed alphonso mangoes) and agriculture, there were also fears about access and disruption to fishing grounds when the entire nuclear complex is completed. The public protests in Kudankulam were most intensive and sustained because of the government's heavy-handed approach to dealing with the dissenters initially. Although the government appointed an independent expert panel to assess the safety of the Kudankulam project to address public concerns about reactor safety, the composition of that independent panel and limitations affected its credibility (Srinivasan and Rethinaraj, 2013). India's Atomic Energy Regulatory Board (AERB) should have occupied the space as a truly independent watchdog guarding public safety and interests. But the AERB has long been seen as a pliant entity because of various structural deficiencies and anomalies. It is not sufficient that the regulator is independent, but must also be perceived so by the public. Although the government promised soon after the Fukushima accident to convert AERB's independence from de facto to de jure status, the work to create the new statutory entity (the Nuclear Safety Regulatory Authority) has

been delayed because of protracted parliamentary processes and a lower priority for its completion.

Public resistance to nuclear power traditionally revolved around concerns relating to reactor safety, environmental impacts during routine operation and accident situations, and nuclear waste management. The Fukushima accident has highlighted the importance of reactor siting and regulatory independence. Although the existing and proposed nuclear sites in India lie in stable seismic zones and have not historically experienced earthquakes greater than magnitude 6 (Wolfram, 2018), the threat of flooding triggered by an intense monsoon or distant tsunamis exists in coastal locations. Another issue that does not receive adequate attention is whether it is even possible to identify and acquire enough sites to support a large expansion programme. Expansion of nuclear capacity beyond 20 GW may not be even desirable owing to siting constraints and waste management difficulties in a country with high population density and a scarcity of remote sites (Private communication, 2006). India will have to face the challenge of widespread public resistance that a large expansion programme entails. Even though newer reactors designed by international vendors claim very low reactor core meltdown probabilities, in the range of 10^{-6} to 10^{-7} per reactor year, the difficulty would lie in communicating this to the public. Even if those goals can be achieved, a pure engineering analysis cannot guarantee public acceptance of nuclear power. And public opinion, even if based on misinformation, matters in a democratic country like India for the future growth of nuclear power.

Globally, nuclear power's share of electricity generation has reduced to about 11% (WNA, 2018b) from a high of about 17% during the 1990s. With the growth of renewable energy globally, nuclear power's share is expected to slip to single digits in the near term. Prohibitive costs and concerns about India's nuclear liability law have made many international vendors wary of building nuclear plants.

20.5 EQUITY, EFFICIENCY, AND SUSTAINABILITY

Sustainable access to energy sources like electricity is one of the preconditions for economic growth that can address climate change, equity, and energy poverty. India has made considerable progress in improving access to electricity in the 70 years since 1947. The number of villages (not rural households) electrified has increased from 3,061 in 1950 to 597,464 (100%) in April 2018 (Bhaskar, 2018a). A village is considered electrified if public offices and at least 10% of the household are connected. The per capita electricity consumption is approximately 950 kWh per year, less than one-third the global average. About 40 million, predominantly rural, households (approximately 200 million people), or 15% of the country, do not have access to electricity. The central government's Saubhagya scheme (Saubhagya, 2017) promises to electrify all households by December 2018. While the pace sounds ambitious, past electrification rates suggest that 100% household electrification will likely happen by 2025.

A more significant concern has been the quality, reliability, and affordability of service. CEEW (2015) surveyed the most energy-deprived North Indian states found that nearly 60% of the rural households had just 0 to 4 hours of electricity, even though village electrification rates were above 90%. For households with some access to electricity, reliability and affordability (even at low levels of consumption) were an issue. The electricity distribution companies subsidize poor residential customers and charge industrial, commercial, and richer residential customers extra to cover the cost of subsidy. Improving the quality and affordability of service requires this business model to be replaced with a direct-benefit transfer model, where the subsidy is transferred directly to the consumer and the finances of the distributor are not affected. This transition to a more affordable and sustainable electricity sector will take a few years, as a national identity system is being rolled out for such schemes.

Less than 5% have more than 20 hours of electricity per day. The reliability and hours of supply of power in India are likely to improve significantly in the next few years, as the country has a surplus in coal generation capacity and plans to add a significant amount of inexpensive renewables. Solar PV and small hydro-based micro-grids can supplement the grid in remote regions.

Indoor air pollution, primarily from cooking using biomass and lighting from kerosene lamps, is a major cause of mortality among women and children. Cheap and reliable electricity would make a significant difference to indoor air pollution if induction cook stoves were promoted, following the example of Ecuador (Martinez *et al.*, 2017).

The establishment of the Bureau of Energy Efficiency (BEE) in 2002 as a result of the Energy Efficiency Act 2001 has made energy efficiency a part of the strategies for a sustainable electricity sector. BEE has introduced a successful appliance standards and labelling programme and an energy conservation building code. BEE is also running pilot projects in demand-side management from the agricultural and residential sectors. The Perform Achieve and Trade (PAT) Scheme, a component of the National Mission for Enhanced Energy Efficiency under NAPCC, is a regulatory mechanism to reduce energy consumption in select industries and create a market for energy savings certificates (ESCerts). PAT has already saved the country approximately 100 TWh since 2012 (BEE, 2017). The Energy Efficiency Services Limited, a government of India–owned company, is implementing the world's largest energy efficiency programme. It has distributed about 300 million LED bulbs and reduced the evening peak demand by about 8 GW, while bringing down the cost of an LED bulb by a factor of 10. The programme has been expanded to other appliances like fans and air conditioners, as well as smart meters, LED street lights, and irrigation pumps (EESL, 2018).

India has 14 of the 20 most-polluted cities in the world. Electric mobility and electric vehicles can contribute to significantly lowering the dangerously high pollution levels. There is already a plan to introduce metro rail transit in cities with a population of at least one million. New Delhi has one of the largest metro systems in the world, and a number of other large Indian cities are building and expanding their metro network. India also has about half a million electric vehicles on the road, consisting of electric two-wheelers, e-rickshaws, and a small number of cars and buses. A clear policy regarding electric vehicles is currently lacking, but automobile manufacturers and start-ups have already made plans to release electric two- and four-wheel vehicles in the market in the next couple of years (Sen and Murali, 2018). The Society of Indian Automobile Manufacturers has released a whitepaper recommending a roadmap, which states that all new public transport and 40% of new private vehicles should be electric by 2030 (SIAM, 2018). These recommendations are likely to be part of an electric vehicle action plan to be released later in 2018.

20.6 CONCLUDING REMARKS

We have attempted in this chapter to bring some clarity to the transformation underway towards more sustainability in the Indian electricity sector by focusing mainly on the renewable and nuclear sectors. In this section, we conclude with a recapitulation of some of the accomplishments of the sector that make the glass half-full, along with some of the remaining challenges that make the glass half-empty.

Among what makes the glass half-full is the phenomenal increase in primary and secondary energy consumption since 1947. India is not only the third-largest electricity-generating country but also the third largest in terms of deployment of new renewable sources of electricity such as solar and wind. However, the continuing lack of access to electricity and modern fuels for millions of people must be one of the factors that make the glass half-empty. The inadequate appreciation of the retarding effects that insufficient, unreliable electricity supply of poor quality imposes on the economy and the debilitating effects of pollution from the energy sector are of grave concern. Another issue is the displacement of people due to energy projects and their insensitive resettlement and rehabilitation, aside from their deleterious effects on biodiversity. Finally, given the size of the sector, both the quantity and quality of R&D and innovation in the energy sector continue to be inadequate.

The nuclear industry too has its share of achievements and shortcomings. Despite being subjected to technology-denial regimes for decades, many complex power plants have been built and have operated safely without major accidents. But, as discussed in Section 20.4, nuclear establishment also has its share of troubles. The indigenous three-stage closed-cycle nuclear programme, which may have appeared attractive in the past but not anymore, continues to be on the DAE's wish-list. The department also continues to view public opposition to nuclear power as misinformed and misguided and believes that it can be managed with an effective public relations campaign.

Thanks to the steep drop in the prices of renewables, facilitated often by the reverse-bidding auctions, India's transition to sustainable energy systems has been accelerated. Chakravarty and Ahuja (2016) have discussed policy and regulatory conditions that would catalyse the transformation from the currently rigid electricity sector to a more flexible and responsive sector. Improved financial sustainability of the business model of DISCOMs and the availability of long-term financing with lower interest rates will make the transition both faster and a lot easier.

Given their relatively benign nature and the more modest scales, renewables have thus far avoided the kind of public opposition large hydro, coal-fired, and nuclear power plants have witnessed. However, when the cumulative impact of renewables grows larger and begins to encroach upon areas with spectacular landscapes and heritage value over time, they will also invite and encounter public opposition. Increasing the share of distributed and decentralized renewables will minimize such opposition. Current market conditions and policy support in India offer bright prospects for the expansion of electricity generation from renewables. This in turn will contribute to the decarbonization of India's electricity sector.

The extension of the electricity grid to every village, and to every house in a few years, will finally enable every Indian to access a clean, modern source of energy. The successful implementation of a direct benefit transfer for poor consumers, as well as administrative and technological improvement of the distribution companies, is required to sustain the universal access of electricity.

India is very likely to meet and exceed the Paris Agreement's Intended Nationally Determined Contributions (INDC) goals, as expansion of renewable power is the most economical option going forward. India will require significant energy storage capacity by 2030; this is likely to be met by storage in grid-scale lithium batteries and thermal storage in solar thermal plants. Successfully managing the integration and storage challenges of high renewable penetration will be key to a transition to a sustainable electricity sector.

ACKNOWLEDGEMENTS

We thank Asok Dasgupta and an anonymous referee for comments and suggestions on a previous draft.

REFERENCES

Banerjee, S. (2010) Towards a sustainable nuclear energy future. 35th Annual Symposium of the World Nuclear Association, 15–17 September, London. https://www.hcilondon.in/indiadigest/Issue320/pdf/6.pdf

BEE (Bureau of Energy Efficiency) (2017) *Annual Report 2016–2017.* https://beeindia.gov.in/content/annual-report

Bhabha, H. J. and Prasad, N. B. (1958) A study of the contribution of atomic energy to a power programme in India. Proceedings of the Second United Nations International Conference on the Peaceful Uses of Atomic Energy, Geneva, pp. 89–101.

Bhaskar, U. (2018a) After power in all villages, next step is all households. Thursday, 3 May. https://www.livemint.com/Politics/cmw5WuVGTrDRexEqiet7uL/After-power-in-all-villages-next-step-is-all-households.html

(2018b) Electricity reached all Indian villages on Saturday. Saturday, 28 April 2018. https://www.livemint.com/Industry/ORuZWrj6czTef21a2dIHGK/Electricity-reached-all-Indian-villages-on-Saturday.html

(2018c) Wind power tariffs stay near record low of Rs 2.44/unit in SECI auction. 15 February. https://www.livemint.com/Industry/w1YII5apaYDLhM4jW5LaAO/Firms-bid-Rs244-per-unit-in-Indias-wind-power-auction.html

BTI (Bridge to India) (2018) India Solar Compass 2017 Q4. http://www.bridgetoindia.com/wp-content/uploads/2018/03/BRIDGE-TO-INDIA-Solar-Compass-Executive-Summary.pdf

CEA (Central Electricity Authority) (2003) The Electricity Act, 2003. http://www.cercind.gov.in/Act-with-amendment.pdf

(2016) Report (Part A) on Advance National Transmission Plan for 2021–22. http://www.cea.nic.in/reports/others/ps/pspa2/ptp.pdf

(2018a) National Electricity Plan (Volume I), Generation. January. http://www.cea.nic.in/reports/committee/nep/nep_jan_2018.pdf

(2018b) Growth of the Electricity Sector in India from 1947–2017. http://www.cea.nic.in/reports/others/planning/pdm/growth_2017.pdf

(2018c) Monthly Executive Summary 2018. March. http://www.cea.nic.in/reports/monthly/executivesummary/2018/exe_summary-03.pdf

(2018d) Renewable Energy Generation Report. http://www.cea.nic.in/reports/monthly/renewable/2018/renewable-03.pdf

(2018e) Monthly Executive Summary 2018. July. http://www.cea.nic.in/reports/monthly/executivesummary/2018/exe_summary-07.pdf

CEEW (Council on Energy, Environment and Water) (2015) Access to clean cooking energy and electricity: Survey of States. http://ceew.in/pdf/CEEW-ACCESS-Report-29Sep15.pdf

Chakravarty, S. and Ahuja, D. R. (2016) Bridging the gap between intentions and contributions requires determined effort. *Invited Guest Editorial in Current Science*, 110(4), 475–476.

DAE (Department of Atomic Energy) (2015) Government of India. http://www.dae.nic.in/writereaddata/parl/winter2015/rsus487.pdf

EESL (Energy Efficiency Services Limited) (2018) https://eeslindia.org

FOWIND (Facilitating Offshore Wind in India Consortium) (2017) From zero to five GW: Offshore wind outlook for Gujarat and Tamil Nadu (2018–2032). http://gwec.net/wp-content/uploads/2017/12/FOWIND_2017_Final_Outlook_2032.pdf

GBD MAPS (Global Burden of Disease Major Air Pollution Sources Working Group) (2018) *Burden of Disease Attributable to Major Air Pollution Sources in India*. Health Effects Institute. https://www.healtheffects.org/publication/gbd-air-pollution-india

GIZ (GIZ Indo-German Energy Programme) (2017) *Green Energy Corridors – Large-Scale Integration of Renewable Energy: Summary of findings and key recommendations*. https://www.energyforum.in/fileadmin/user_upload/india/media_elements/publications/20190909_GEC_report/GIZ_Summary_Report.pdf

IEA (International Energy Agency) (2015) *India Energy Outlook*. OECD/IEA, Paris.

IRENA (International Renewable Energy Agency) (2017) Renewable energy prospects for India: A working paper based on Remap, 2017. http://www.irena.org/publications/2017/May/Renewable-Energy-Prospects-for-India

(2018) Renewable power generation costs in 2017. http://www.irena.org/publications/2018/Jan/Renewable-power-generation-costs-in-2017

Kittner, N., Lill, F. and Kammen, D. M. (2017) Energy storage deployment and innovation for the clean energy transition. *Nature Energy*, **2**, article no. 17125, July. http://dx.doi.org/10.1038/nenergy.2017.125

Kraemer, S. (2017) Solar thermal power prices have dropped an astonishing 50% in six months. SolarPACES, October. http://www.solarpaces.org/solar-thermal-energy-prices-drop-half/

LiveMint (2017) Westinghouse: Bankruptcy in US won't impact India nuclear power project. 27 October. https://www.livemint.com/Companies/nSIQTsQq5cSMb5omo8BQFN/Westinghouse-Bankruptcy-in-US-wont-impact-India-nuclear-po.html

MAE (Ministry of Atomic Energy) (2014) Unstarred Question No. 1655 in the Lok Sabha, answered on 3 December 2014 by the Minister of Atomic Energy, Government of India. http://164.100.47.194/Loksabha/Questions/QResult15.aspx?qref=7804&lsno=16

Martinez, J., Marti-Herrero, J., Villacis, S., Riofrio, A. J. and Vaca, D. (2017) Analysis of energy, CO_2 emissions and economy of the technological migration for clean cooking in Ecuador. *Energy Policy*, **107**, 182–187.

MNRE (Ministry of New and Renewable Energy) (2010) Jawaharlal Nehru National Solar Mission. https://mnre.gov.in/file-manager/UserFiles/mission_document_JNNSM.pdf

(2018) *Annual Report, 2017–18*. https://mnre.gov.in/file-manager/annual-report/2017–2018/EN/index.html

MOEFCC (Ministry of Environment, Forest and Climate Change) (2008) India's National Action Plan on Climate Change (NAPCC). http://www.moef.nic.in/ccd-napcc

Mohan, A. (2016) The future of nuclear energy in India. ORF Occasional Paper #98. Observer Research Foundation. August. https://www.orfonline.org/wp-content/uploads/2016/08/OccasionalPaper_98_NuclearEnergy.pdf

NEA and IAEA (Nuclear Energy Agency and the International Atomic Energy Agency) (2016) Uranium 2016: Resources, Production and Demand. https://www.oecd-nea.org/jcms/pl_15004#:~:text=It%20offers%20updated%20information%20on,uranium%20supply%20and%20demand%20issues.

NREL (National Renewable Energy Laboratory, USA) (2017) Power System Operation Corporation Limited (India) and Lawrence Berkeley National Laboratory (USA). *Greening the Grid: Pathways to Integrate 175 Gigawatts of Renewable Energy into India's Electric Grid*, Vol. I and Vol. II. https://www.nrel.gov/analysis/india-renewable-integration-study.html

PC (Planning Commission, Government of India) Five Year Plans I through XII (1951, 1956, 1961, 1969, 1974, 1980, 1985, 1997, 2002, 2007, 2012) (chapters dealing with energy). New Delhi. https://niti.gov.in/planningcommission.gov.in/docs/plans/planrel/index.php

PMO (Prime Minister's Office) (2015) Revision of cumulative targets under National Solar Mission from 20,000 MW by 2021–22 to 1,00,000 MW. https://www.pmindia.gov.in/en/news_updates/revision-of-cumulative-targets-under-national-solar-mission-from-20000-mw-by-2021-22-to-100000-mw/

(2017) Cabinet approves construction of 10 units of India's indigenous Pressurized Heavy Water Reactors (PHWR). 17 May. https://www.pmindia.gov.in/en/news_updates/cabinet-approves-construction-of-10-units-of-indias-indigenous-pressurized-heavy-water-reactors-phwr/#:~:text=In%20a%20significant%20decision%20to,Heavy%20Water%20Reactors%20(PHWR).

POSOCO (Power System Corporation) (2017) Corporate Plan 2017–18. https://posoco.in/wp-content/uploads/2017/05/Corporate-Plan-2017–18.pdf

Prayas (Prayas Energy Group) (2017) Many sparks but little light: The rhetoric and practice of electricity sector reforms in India. http://www.prayaspune.org/peg/publications/item/332-many-sparks-but-little-light-the-rhetoric-and-practice-of-electricity-sector-reforms-in-india.html

PRIS (Power Reactor Information System) (2018) India: Power reactor information system. International Atomic Energy Agency. https://www.iaea.org/pris/CountryStatistics/CountryDetails.aspx?current=IN

Private communication (2006) Private conversation of the second author with A. Gopalakrishnan, former Chairman of India's Atomic Energy Regulatory Board (AERB), in January in Singapore.

(2012) Private conversation of the second author with Rémy Autebert, Senior Executive Vice President (Asia), AREVA, on 2 September in Singapore.

Saubhagya (Pradhan Mantri Sahaj Bijli Har Ghar Yojana – 'Saubhagya') (2017) http://saubhagya.gov.in/

Sen, S. and Murali, A. (2018) The story of India's flip-flops on its electric vehicle policy – and how it will hurt. *The Factor Daily*, 19 March. https://factordaily.com/india-u-turn-on-electric-vehicles-policy/

Sengupta, A. (2016) India's nuclear liability regime is still up in the air. https://thewire.in/diplomacy/indias-nuclear-liability-regime-is-still-up-in-the-air

SIAM (Society of Indian Automobile Manufacturers) (2018) Adopting pure electric vehicles: Key policy enablers. December 2017. http://www.siam.in/uploads/filemanager/114SIAMWhitePaperonElectricVehicles.pdf

Srinivasan, T. N. and Rethinaraj, T. S. Gopi (2013) Fukushima and thereafter: reassessment of risks of nuclear power. *Energy Policy*. **52**, 726–736. January.

SRPC (Solar Rooftop Policy Coalition) (2016) Unleashing private investment in rooftop solar in India. http://shaktifoundation.in/report/solar-rooftop-policy-coalition/

UNFCCC (United Nations Framework Convention on Climate Change) (2015) India's Intended Nationally Determined Contribution. http://www4.unfccc.int/ndcregistry/PublishedDocuments/India%20First/INDIA%20INDC%20TO%20UNFCCC.pdf

WNA (World Nuclear Association) (2018a) Nuclear power in India. http://www.world-nuclear.org/information-library/country-profiles/countries-g-n/india.aspx

(2018b) Nuclear power in the world today. http://www.world-nuclear.org/information-library/current-and-future-generation/nuclear-power-in-the-world-today.aspx

Wolfram, S. (2018) Mathematica 11.3 returns a geographical plot with locations of historically recorded seismic activities for a given country using a free-form input. https://www.wolframalpha.com/input/?source=frontpage-immediate-access&i=earthquakes+in+india+greater+than+6+last+30+years

21 Gender equality and energy access: Barriers to maximizing development effectiveness in the SAARC region

ANOJA WICKRAMASINGHE

Emeritus Professor of Geography, University of Peradeniya, Peradeniya, Sri Lanka

Keywords

South Asia; SAARC region; energy access; gender inequality; indicators; inequality index; challenges

Abstract

Gender inequality is revealed by using measurable indices assessing gender disparities within countries and across regions, while tracing the gaps and the effectiveness of the past development processes. The key dimensions, such as economic participation, education, health, and politics, that are often incorporated when introducing measures to redress gender inequality do not reflect the effects of energy access or the implications of lack of energy access in realizing the effectiveness of development. The situation of the countries in the South Asian Association for Regional Cooperation (SAARC) region reveals that the development effectiveness is highly skewed, with greater achievements in welfare service-related areas that are not manifested in women's economic and political participation or decision-making. Drawing evidence from energy access-related data available in secondary sources and using the field research data gathered in Sri Lanka, the researcher carried out an assessment highlighting the nexus between gender equality and energy access. The discussion presented in this paper reveals that countries in the SAARC region have made progress through various interventions, particularly health, education, and employment generation. However, the effectiveness of the interventions in changing the local situation pertaining to gender equality is low or has been rather slow. This is partly owing to the fact that the policies in the countries in the SAARC region are less responsive to gender equality, women's participation and representation, and engagement in policy advocacy. How to begin a more effective process is a question that may be asked by energy experts looking for answers from gender experts or women activists. Findings indicate the necessity for creating a conducive environment with a gender-inclusive energy policy and improving the readiness of women and the sectors affected by imbalances, by means of building social capital and accountability systems. Findings point out failures in expanding energy access as a locomotive to reach the most deserving sectors of society, the women, and some countries have not been able to fully realize the full effectiveness of development.

21.1 INTRODUCTION

Countries in the South Asian Association for Regional Cooperation (SAARC) region are marked with highly diverse geographical and ecological conditions, cultural diversity, and a wide range of biophysical features, varying from islands to landlocked and to widely spread subcontinents like India. Gender-differentiated data suggest that countries are faced with significant differences in the status of women, such as gender inequality, stratification, unequal access to energy services, deprivation and marginalization, and disparities in resource access and entitlements. The diversity and inequalities offer opportunities to unpack the development process and to follow responsive pathways to accelerate the development process. South Asia, in this respect, forces the development practitioners to work through the distinguishing characteristics of local resource-based work done by men and women for improving social and environmental conditions in order to sustain their economies. While energy access facilitates and accelerates development factoring services, gender equality is a principle to be followed for realizing the outcomes. The Global Gender Gap Index (World Economic Forum, 2016) suggests that out of the eight global regions, South Asia is the second-lowest region and is marked with substantial variations between the countries (Table 21.1). The higher the score, the better the outcome, and substantial trends have been revealed during one decade, between 2006 and 2016. During this period, India and Bangladesh saw increases in their scores and in their overall ranking, but Sri Lanka, which had peaked in terms of global

Table 21.1. Gender equality gaps in South Asia.

Country	Overall score	Overall rank	Regional rank
Bangladesh	0.698	72	1
India	0.683	87	2
Sri Lanka	0.673	100	3
Nepal	0.661	110	4
Maldives	0.650	115	5
Bhutan	0.642	121	6
Pakistan	0.556	143	7

Source: World Economic Forum (2016)

ranking in 2006 at the 13th position (out of 130 countries), fell to 100th position in 2016. The rationale for this drastic drawback is driven by the gaps in women's labour force participation, estimated earned income, and wage inequality. This 90% reversal in Sri Lanka shows that the services expanded through the state agency for improving educational attainments, health, and life expectancy have not been adequate for reducing gender inequality.

The features found in South Asia involving women's access to energy are similar to those revealed in the Asia-Pacific region. The global picture shows that 73% of the world population depending on solid fuels for cooking is in the Asia-Pacific region. Past records show that, out of a total population of 3,109 million relying on solid fuels in the Asia-Pacific region, 801 million are in India alone. According to IEA (2017), 834 million people in India are without access to clean fuel for cooking. In five countries in the region – India, Bangladesh, Nepal, Pakistan, and Sri Lanka – 1,044 million people depend on solid fuel for cooking.

The most obvious features are the higher extent of energy deprivation, featuring low per capita consumption, poor access to electricity and modern sources by the rural population, predominance of subsistence and welfare uses, greater dependence on informal sources, and a substantial share of the population lacking access to modern cooking energy sources. These features make the region a hotspot on the global map, which in turn leads to the establishment of regional collaboration and indicates that women have to bear triple burdens in collecting, portaging, and combusting energy. The excessive burdens that are faced by women are connected with the rural settings and subsistence living, geographically deprived conditions, and gender-specific inequalities, including lack of mobility and assets.

The status of access to modern sources of fuels for cooking is far worse than access to electricity for lighting. This is mainly because it is not treated as a business of the state agency. Past trends show that, though the South Asia region accounts for only 43% of the population in Asia and the Pacific, in 2007,

nearly 82% of the population had no access to electricity. The gravity of this situation becomes more visible owing to the fact that, even where electricity is available, the per capita consumption is rather low. Energy deprivation is quite a significant feature, reflected in the low per capita electricity consumption and the 605 million people living without electricity. The per capita electricity consumption is 144 kWh in Bangladesh, 542 in India, 338 in Nepal, and 417 in Sri Lanka. A huge gap is seen when compared with the global figure of 3,240 kWh, and 1,271 estimated for the Asia-Pacific region. The lowest per capita household electricity consumption levels, which have been reported in Bangladesh and Nepal, indicate the energy poverty context and the differential implications on women. The greater share contributed by biomass to energy illustrates, in turn, not only their dependence on traditional sources but also the continuing use of biomass, which is secured nearly free of financial cost.

Inequalities differentiated and disclosed through empirical research demand a transitional move, enabling those who have gained from education and health services to acquire sufficient skills, assets, resources, services, investments, and technologies to engage in economic development. Such requirements are needed to address the issues of poverty and inequality, providing a menu for dissolving the barriers to development effectiveness. Development implications of energy access are revealed from various perspectives, including poverty, gender inequality, and many others. Guruswamy (2016), referring to the World Bank, stressed that access to beneficial energy to meet the basic human needs (cooking, heating, water, sanitation, illumination, transportation, and mechanical power) is crucial, and around one-third of the global population, nearly 2.8 billion, is 'energy poor'. The geographical distribution of the energy poor includes more than 95% in Sub-Saharan Africa and developing Asia, predominantly in rural areas. Poverty and the rural context deepen the inquiry, as women account for more than 74% of the poor who are in rural areas and in land-based or non-remunerative informal occupations. Women's vulnerability has heightened over the years, because of environmental changes like increased intensity of natural calamities, as well as the unequal distribution of resources and options contributing to the intensification of poverty, labour exploitation, and low entrepreneurial skills among women.

The *World Development Report* (World Bank, 2012) analysed the multiple dimensions of gender equality and the issues and conditions relating to it. It made clear that gender equality is a core development objective in its own right. Greater gender equality can enhance productivity, improve development outcomes for the next generation, and make institutions more representative. Moreover, the Asia-Pacific Human Development Report *Power, Voice and Rights: Turning*

Point for Gender Equality in Asia and the Pacific (UNDP, 2010a) advocated a comprehensive analysis of the situation based on fairness in freedoms and choices focusing on human development. Gender equality entails equipping both genders with equal access to capabilities, so they have the freedom to choose opportunities that improve their lives. Unless barriers to equal participation are resolved on the principles of equality and women's access to energy, especially for increasing productive use, development effectiveness cannot be achieved in South Asia. The evidence-based concerns raised in this paper include the following:

(1) Gender inequality reduces opportunities for women to reap the benefits of development on equal terms and getting equal access to energy and the services;

(2) Social and human development efforts, especially health and education, are not manifested in gender empowerment and equality in energy access and applications;

(3) Access to clean energy and other services helps reduce gender gaps and empowers women, enhancing their contribution through effective application of energy in productive activities;

(4) Women make a difference in energy behaviour and efficient management of energy when equal opportunities are provided to manage household energy;

(5) Energy is a means for enhancing income, creating employment, labour efficiency, and productivity, while reducing the drudgery related to labour-intensive work.

21.2 THE OVERALL PICTURE

Energy access and gender inequality independently and interactively measure development, while indicating unjust conditions, deprivation, marginalization, and the gaps in the sectors and total development. Gender equality and energy access suffer from over-empathized theoretical discussions and less effective development strategies. To what extent and in what ways can sustainable energy access for all become a pathway to gender equality, and how can gender equality contribute to sustainable energy for all? Linkages between these two paradigms have been established to work through interrelated parameters. Several landmarks can be traced since 1992, with the initiative of the United Nations Conference on Environment and Development, the 'Earth Summit', and the United Nations 'Fourth World Conference on Women', which took place in 1995. As a follow-up to these meetings, the chapter on 'Global Action for Women towards Sustainable Development' in Agenda 21 reiterated the need for an agenda committed to women's equity and sustainable development. Efforts are also being made in international circles to set aside energy targets in relation to the United Nations Millennium Development Goals (MDGs) established at the 'Millennium Summit'.

The basic arguments regarding energy access have been taken up in discussion forums over decades, but even in countries like Sri Lanka, where access to electricity has reached more than 96% of the population, the gender gaps in production, resource endowments, skills, and assets remain persistent. The UNDP in 2001 stated that without access to modern forms of energy for lighting, cooking, heating, and cooling, refrigeration, pumping, transportation, and productive purposes, people must spend much of their time and physical energy on basic subsistence activities, and the failure to address gender disparities, marginalization, and discriminatory practices in many regions has contributed to entrenched conditions of poverty for women. The World Bank policy research report *Engendering Development through Gender Equality in Rights, Resources and Voice* (World Bank, 2011) with analysis showed that gender inequalities undermine the effectiveness of development policies. The basic thesis on gender recognizes the existence of socially manipulated differences between men and women in every aspect of their lives. Less well understood are the conditions that have emerged because of disparities in acquired services, access to means of production, and modern energy technologies and endowments. This means that the energy challenges pertaining to sustainable development expand beyond the perspectives of providing energy services, such as lighting, heating, cooking, motive power, mechanical power, transport, and telecommunication, which have been discussed by the United Nations (2005). It stressed that access to modern fuels is particularly important for women and girls, since they are often the most affected by inadequate energy services. The meaning of this situation is vital for the countries in the South Asia region because gender gaps in most aspects, especially in production, income, and economic assets, remain wide, indicating that women have not secured equal treatment or equal opportunities.

Past experiences show that women in most countries continue to have limited opportunities, earn less, and exercise poor command over resources and services. Matching gender equality perspectives with energy has established a strong conceptual backing. It has challenged the gender experts by advocating the concept as a cross-cutting societal parameter that is engaged in expanding energy access and services for factoring development. Similarly, the energy sector and the technical experts are being challenged to deal with gender, placing it in a broader human development context. The absence of specific reference to gender in energy policy suggests that policies are assumed to affect or contribute to men and women equally. However, the limitations of this assumption are evident from differential intensity of energy applications by men and women, outcomes, and the transitional effects.

21.3 DRIVERS DEMANDING TRANSFORMATION IN SOUTH ASIA

South Asia has faced decades of constant poverty, gender inequality, unequal distribution of assets, access to services and opportunities, exclusions, and vulnerabilities to external risks. The primary concern over increasing energy access and gender equality is driven by the failure of policies to reach a vast majority of the population or to reach the development targets. South Asia is a region with one-fifth of the global population, more than 1.4 billion people. South Asia is characterized by socially induced and economically structured inequalities. The urgent need for transformative action is driven by several forces:

(1) Global initiatives such as Sustainable Energy for All (SE4ALL) and the rather low development achievements made during the past;
(2) The local context of energy and inequalities in access and applications;
(3) Commitments made by state agencies for reducing persistent gender inequalities that prevent women from reaping equal opportunities to act and to benefit from development;
(4) The potentialities for realizing the effectiveness of development through gender inclusion;
(5) The gender inequalities and the exclusions manipulated through energy access.

Most of the countries in the region, including India, Pakistan, Bangladesh, Sri Lanka, Maldives, and Bhutan, are under pressure from the increasing demand for energy by the population, and they are committed to achieving Millennium Development targets and carrying out the initiatives of SE4ALL. Countries in the region recognize that an efficient supply of energy services is a means of addressing poverty, inequalities, deprivation, mechanization, and economic growth. There are considerable variations in energy access, consumption, and the level of development (see

Table 21.2). The Human Development Index (HDI) suggests that countries in the region should either follow a fast track to move up the ladder or respond to the areas blocking the development process. Even the countries like Maldives and Sri Lanka, which are in the forefront with 100% electricity access, have not made a progressive change in their positions on HDI values.

Energy access in the context of SAARC countries is a fundamental input to the service sectors, such as education, health, and communication, and for developing economic and productivity for men and women who have responsibilities over their own households, communities, and the local economies and the environment. The huge population and density in South Asia demand equal participation of men and women in development in order to eliminate the ideological barriers, conventional practices, and the societal norms. The existing situation is partly a result of the past development paths that were not focused on addressing gender inequalities. The Human Development Index (HDI), which is a standard measure of development, reveals that more needs to be done to improve the situation in these countries. This involves expanding people's choices so that they can develop their full potential and lead productive and creative lives according to their capabilities and interests (UNDP, 2010b). It has also been recognized that HDI alone has limited application as a gender advocacy tool, so gender-differentiated data are being used in planning interventions.

In this context, gender inequality has been postulated in many aspects of life, varying from reproduction to production, economic activity, employment and occupations, political decision-making, and control over assets. The Gender Inequality Index, the measure used to make a global comparison, is a pointer for designing targeted policy measures, and it also reflects the limitations or the limited effectiveness of the development measures to address inequalities. The Gender Inequality Index and the development indicators trace the disparities between countries and the status reached by individual countries (see Table 21.3).

Table 21.2. Energy-related indicators of selected countries and development.

Country	Electrification rate (%)	Population without access to clean cooking (%)	Population without access to clean cooking (millions)	Production-consumption ratio	Population without access to electricity (millions)	Energy supply per capita (giga-joules): 2017	HDI 2015*
Bangladesh	75	83	133	0.76	41	11	0.58
India	82	64	834	0.69	239	27	0.62
Nepal	77	70	20	0.40	7	19	0.56
Pakistan	74	50	95	0.66	51	17	0.56
Sri Lanka	100	83	17	0.17	0	20	0.77

Sources: IEA (2017); *UNDP (2016)

Table 21.3. Indicators of outcome of development and human development in South Asia.

Country	HDI value 2015	HD rank	Life expectancy: 2015	Mean yrs schooling: 2015	Yrs of schooling: 2015	% with access to water	% with access to sanitation
Bangladesh	0.579	137	72	5.2	10.2	80	53
India	0.624	131	68	6.3	11.7	88	31
Nepal	0.558	144	70	4.1	12.2	88	31
Sri Lanka	0.766	72	75	10.9	14	90	91
Bhutan	0.607	132	69.9	3.1	12.5		
Pakistan	0.550	148	66.4	5.1	8.1		
Afghanistan	0.479	169	60.7	3.6	10.1		
Maldives	0.701	105	77	6.2	12.7		
South Asia	0.621		68.7	6.2	11.3		

Source: UNDP (2016)

The HDI indicates the disparities between countries and the gaps in development achievements. All these indicators have a bearing on energy access. Implications of energy for providing access to water and sanitation, as well as for schooling, affect men and women and boys and girls differently. Access to such services would create an environment enabling women to have more time to engage in productive options to change their own positions and the gender relations within and outside households. Field lessons suggest that women save an average of more than five hours per day by having access to water and sanitation. Such services are the means to reduce time spent on welfare-related domestic chores and labour-intensive work, which in turn is used as capital for production. The spill-over effects of women having access to supplies include the reduced drudgery of repetitive attendance to water and sanitation chores. Research also suggests that an increased enrolment of girls in schools enhances their ability to handle and engage in productive work. The demand for child labour used for fetching water and fuelwood impedes opportunities for children to enjoy childhood and engage in education and extracurricular activities. The division of energy-related tasks impacts badly on women because they bear responsibility for collecting more than 80% of the energy used by the households.

The present situation shows that benefits have spread disproportionately, and have not been very effective in terms of changing the lives of the poor and women.

21.4 INEQUALITY AND DEVELOPMENT CHALLENGES

Access to energy, electricity in particular, has multiple implications for development, especially on the psychological and physical well-being of the people; it also improves convenience and enhances production. Past experience suggests that equality perspectives of energy access are at the core of improving access to electricity and reducing the number of people relying on the traditional use of biomass for cooking. Electricity access and clean cooking fuel expands development choices of the people, while creating a favourable environment, especially for those who have not benefited from other interventions. Drawing attention to energy access for different needs, Trace (2016) identified the complexities and the issues pertaining to 'over-crowding' and 'under-counting' in measuring and defining energy access. Energy access, according to IEA (2017), is a key factor in economic, social, and human development, owing to the fact that an estimated two billion people lack access to modern energy. Having access to modern energy has been defined as a household having reliable and affordable access to clean cooking facilities, a first connection to electricity, and then an increasing level of electricity consumption to reach the regional average (IEA, 2011). An important challenge in South Asia in particular is the inequality in energy access that is seen between those with the best access to multiple sources and those with the worst access to poor sources with minimum potential. Several factors affect the situation, such as the right of the people to have modern sources of energy, the affordability of the sources, and the responsibility of the states and the global community to ensure that all persons have the opportunity to consume at least a minimum level satisfying their requirements. The situation in SAARC countries illustrates that matters pertaining to access are much more complex than a simply defined universal access, because the social stratifications and differentiations pertaining to gender ideologies are quite serious. Universal access to energy, with the effects of socially established inequalities, becomes unrealistic. This has been proved even within a household, which functions as a social organization with energy use, and the needs differ between men and women largely in relation to differences in their status and capacities for making decisions on energy.

Household-based work allocation patterns in Asia are the pointers demanding policy solutions to issues of deprivation. Household time allocation is marked with a greater engagement of women, who spend more than 12 hours a day attending to reproductive and productive activities. Lessons disclosed through research suggest that gaps between men and women can be attributed to the differences in education, income, employment, property ownership, use of electricity and appliances, and access to technology. In other words, gender gaps locate the entry points for energy interventions that reduce gender equality and that can make development more effective. In rural areas in particular, the access to electricity and energy services affect the economic advancement of women more seriously than men. Services like education, transport, communication, and health are driven by gender-neutral policies that are being formed without responding to the need for creating specific options for women who are in non-remunerative work in the domestic sphere. Examples drawn through participatory analysis revealed that biomass dependence allows women to make decisions over food preparation simply because more than 82% of the fuelwood for domestic use is gathered by them. The negative implication of this situation is their relatively low contribution to the labour force and economic activity (see Figure 21.1). The importance of women's earned income and labour force participation for the households and the economy, and its effect on society, the economy, and environmental sustainability, is recognized. These can be materialized by providing access to energy, technology, training, and productive applications.

The existing situation (Figure 21.1) points out the areas which require gender responsive solutions that would create enabling opportunities in defining innovations with decentralized development options/solutions for strengthening women's productive roles. Women often spend 8 to 10 hours a day in collecting firewood and cooking. A study carried out in Sri Lanka suggests that women get up earlier and have to be awake for 16 hours or more, often working for more than 13 hours a day (Masse and Samaranayaka, 2002). If options are made available to women to use their time for productive work or in economic activity, that can contribute to economic empowerment of women, their families, and the communities. Indeed, for such a transformation to become an effective reality requires many ingredients. For development effectiveness, investing in building capacity, endowments, technology, and service extension is crucial for reducing the time pressure arising from exclusively heavy engagement in unpaid reproductive tasks by women, and for addressing such issues as poverty, inequality, and low mobility.

21.5 MANIFESTED INEQUALITIES

The measures of inequalities that have entered the development paradigm during the recent past reflect the outcomes of the interventions made through the state machinery, and how such outcomes are manifested in economic participation of women in particular. In this regard, a comprehensive insight with analysis has been documented by UN Women (2015) in *Progress of the World's Women: Transforming Economies and Transforming Rights*. There have been significant achievements in some areas, especially in education and health, but changes have been less effective in arresting the persistent gender gaps, leaving women

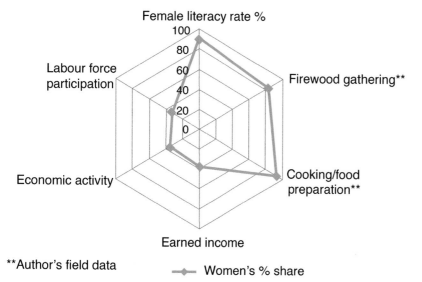

**Author's field data

Figure 21.1. Female percentage share reflected in selected variables.
Sources: National census and statistics of Sri Lanka and author's field research

Table 21.4. Gender inequalities reflected by some variables in selected countries in the region.

Inequality Index	Sri Lanka	Maldives	India	Bhutan	Bangladesh	Nepal	Pakistan
Gender Inequality Index	0.386	0.312	0.530	0.477	0.52	0.497	0.546
(rank)	(87)	(64)	(125)	(110)	(119)	(115)	(130)
Inequality in Life Expectancy Index %	8.3	8.1	25.0	22.2	20.1	27.8	29.9
Inequality in Education Index %	14.6	41.2	42.1	13.3	37.8	44.0	45.2
Inequality in Income Index %	19.6	23.2	16.1	25.1	28.3	18.3	11.0
Inequality in Life Expectancy (years)	M 71.7 F 78.4	M 76 F 78	M 66.9 F9.9	M 69.6 F 70.1	M 70.7 F 73.3	M 68.6 F 71.5	M 65.4 F 67.4
Labour Force Participation rate	M 76 F 30	M 79 F 57	M 79 F 27	M 73 F 59	M 81 F 43	M 87 F 80	M 82 F 24
Mean years of schooling above age 25 years	M 11.4 F 10.3	M 6.3 F 6.2	M 8.2 F 4.8	4.2 2.1	M 5.6 F 5.0	M 5.0 F 3.2	M 6.5 F 3.7
Gross National Income per capita (US$)	M 15,869 F 6,017	M 13,591 F 7155	M 8,897 F 2,184	M 8,308 F 5,657	M 4,285 F 2,379	M 2,718 F 1,979	M 8,376 F 1,498

Source: UNDP (2016), *Human Development Report*
*UN Women (2015)

unable to grasp equal opportunities to engage in decision-making and economic development. From the perspectives of equality and sustainable development, there is a crucial need to reduce the multiple dimensions of gender inequalities in all the countries in South Asia (see Table 21.4). The basic premise behind this momentum is connected with the women's enhanced capacity for making development more effective and their enhanced options and opportunities. The overall picture suggests, however, that the progress made by these countries has been inadequate for securing better scores and escalating their ranking. Gender inequality means that Sri Lanka, for example, ranks below the Maldives, in spite of relatively less inequality in education and higher mean years of schooling by girls. The Gender Inequality Index shows the disparity between the countries with relatively better scores – Maldives with 0.312 and Pakistan with 0.546, placing these countries well apart. The same grounds suggest the potential for reducing the gaps through regional cooperation.

The contextual conditions strongly indicate the necessity for women to have promising economic opportunities, so that they are able to engage in income generation while increasing their labour force participation. Increased access to adequate and suitable energy sources is crucial for realizing economic opportunities and also for increasing labour efficiency while eliminating exposure to an unhealthy environment. The lower the access to electricity and energy technologies, the greater the difficulties that women face and the less output they derive from their time

and investments. The average household energy consumption of many countries in the region is below the estimated universal energy demand of 250 kWh per household, which is used by the IEA (2010). In 2017, a wide disparity in the energy supply per capita was recorded, with the highest, 82 gigajoules, recorded in Bhutan and the lowest, only 5, in Afghanistan. The household energy demand and consumption in Sri Lanka revealed that this is a highly variable phenomenon influenced by the household income and dependence on modern utensils and appliances (Wickramasinghe, 2005). Women's dependence on men's income and decisions to purchase items like irons, kettles, rice cookers, and liquidizers impede the application of energy for convenience and for saving labour. As income earners, the men enjoy the liberty to decide what they want to purchase, often giving priority to leisure items, such as a television, battery charger, or radio, and so forth.

The countries in the region are specific in the patterns of their biomass-dominated energy utilization. Women, because of their household management responsibility, make conscious efforts to provide substitutes as a way to reduce energy expenditure, and they adopt conservation measures, including improved cookstoves and energy-saving light bulbs. Despite the variations between countries, around 58–80% of the population are in rural areas, with electricity access in the range of 60–100%, and dependence on biomass in the range of 42–88%. The issues pertaining to inequality in energy access are country-specific, affecting them differently or at different scales. Energy access has become a right of the people, many of whom are being deprived geographically, socially, or economically of their proper capacities and their right to the benefits of health, education, and transport and communication services.

Energy has the potential to widen opportunities for the people, particularly for the disadvantaged sectors of the society – the poor and women. These have to be fully materialized, empowering them to make their own choices. Concerns that are reflected in national policies are driven more by global initiatives, including the Beijing Platform for Action for Women, Principle 20 of the Rio Declaration, Chapter 24 of the UN Resolution, Agenda 21 and many others, rather than merely a felt commitment. In recent years, the vital roles played by women in households, communities, and national economies have called for a gender-responsive and women-inclusive approach to development. The UN Millennium Development Declaration, in addition to its targets in Goal 3, which focus on promotion of gender equality and empowerment of women, has made a progressive drive by recognizing the gender perspective as a key to promoting sustainable development. The local commitments towards gender equality and participation have been initiated by ratifying various global conventions of this nature. Nevertheless, as discussed in the *World Development Report* (World Bank, 2012), women have less technical and reading skills and experience in hardware than men have. Gender-based barriers to technology access mean that they must go through the drudgery that they have had to bear over many generations. The ADB, based on the experience gained in several countries in South Asia, recognizes and advocates the Gender Equality and Social Inclusion (GESI) framework for addressing inequality issues from the level of policy to project cycle (ADB, 2018).

21.6 GENDER INEQUALITY AND COOKING ENERGY

Estimations made during the recent past revealed that worldwide, 2.9 million people rely on traditional biomass for cooking and heating, and an estimated 70% of them are women, whose access to resources and decision-making is limited (World Bank, 2015). Women's primary responsibility for biomass procurement, portaging, and management is a serious barrier to development, owing to the inequalities in the division of tasks, energy resource management, land ownership, and energy decision-making. In South Asia the energy application picture is more blurred and it is sculpted by several key features pertaining to the share of biomass fuel, multiple production source dependence, free gathering for domestic consumption, wider application for cooking, and a greater share of energy provided by women. In reality, women carry fuelwood from various sources over long distances, either on their head or tightened on

their back, and engage in combustion for cooking using rudimentary devices. For responding to cooking energy, two requirements are needed. The first is the integration of biomass into the mainstream energy and development policy; the second is the inclusion of key stakeholders, particularly women, in the energy policy process. In the matter of energy deprivation, which refers to the lack of access to electricity and modern fuels for cooking or clean cooking solutions, a wide range of issues are to be tackled. The key issues deal with the bulk of residential end users, women, who bear serious burdens. The issues pertaining to the exclusion of gender from biomass development interventions and the lack of options provided for the population without modern fuels for cooking are intertwined.

The household energy consumption in most of the countries in South Asia is dominated by biomass because a higher percentage of the population uses rudimentary sources for cooking. The solid fuel consumption is quite common, and around 89% of the population in Bangladesh – followed by Afghanistan and Nepal each with 80%, Sri Lanka 74%, India 64% and Pakistan 58% – relies on solid fuels. It is relatively high in rural areas when compared with the urban areas, and the data suggest that except in Maldives it varies between 56 and 95%. Bangladesh and Afghanistan reported the highest, with more than 95% of the population using solid fuels (Table 21.5). This situation suggests that cooking energy is not being put in the focus in the effort of providing universal access to modern energy carriers. South Asia is a biomass-based hotspot marked with rudimentary cooking systems, gender inequalities, and poor adoption capacity to use alternatives or supplementary clean energy sources, as well as highly variable energy consumption. If LPG is to be seen as a cleaner source of cooking fuel, more groundwork is to be done to make women capable of transforming to such commercial sources.

In conjunction with international initiatives, the access to modern energy sources, electricity in particular, has been

Table 21.5. Percentage of population using biomass fuels in South Asia countries in 2013.

Country	Rural	Urban	Total
Afghanistan	>95	28	80
Bangladesh	>95	59	89
Bhutan	56	<5	36
India	81	26	64
Maldives	9	<5	<5
Nepal	91	29	80
Pakistan	84	14	58
Sri Lanka	83	34	74

Source: WHO (2016)

factored into the national energy development agendas of these countries. A general overview shows that the households rely on multiple sources for multiple applications and make internal decisions or adjustments in their demand, depending on accessibility, availability, and affordability. While the household sector furnishes the configurations in the energy consumption profile, the solid-fuel-based cooking energy dominates the total energy profile. The data given in Table 21.5 reveal that, except in the Maldives, the situation with regard to cooking energy is rather similar in the countries in South Asia, indicating women's greater dependence on local sources and resources. This illustrates the needs for expanding the services, focusing on the basic energy needs of the households and by responding to the concerns of those bearing responsibility. Cooking and lighting, as essential service requirements of the households, take a greater share of biomass, including wood, dung, and electricity. The most widely required services, including cooking and heating, are satisfied by using biomass procured mostly by women with a minimum cost to a family, but placing rather heavy burdens and pressure on women, who are engaged in procuring and combusting. The unequal distribution of responsibilities, together with stereotyped division of energy-related tasks, have a negative impact on women, seriously deteriorating their health, undervaluing their labour, and depriving them of time needed for investing in self, skill development, and productive work.

Modern energy sources for cooking or clean combustion technologies are less affordable and accessible for women. Two perspectives – gender and health – stress the need for clean cooking solutions that would eliminate repercussions connected with biomass combustion in cooking. The injustice of depending on rudimentary cooking practices that consume much of women's time and energy in the biomass energy chain extends to women's poverty, low income, domesticity, health deterioration, fewer opportunities to engage in remunerative employment, and many other serious issues (Wickramasinghe, 2011). Providing solutions that would avoid the conditions forcing women to become over-burdened with the existing energy situation should be a priority for the countries in the region. This is essential for increasing the economic efficiency of women's labour and productivity, thereby improving the development outcomes.

Gender inequality in this domain is shaped by the unorganized nature of widely used energy sources, resources, and ownership, carriers, management, and the disparities in institutionalized service delivery, as well as the policies. For instance, women in the countries depending on fossil fuel-based sources are seriously deprived of chances, because of their lack of income, to secure enough energy to meet their needs. In the case of renewable sources like biomass, their rights to the resources are conditioned by their ownership rights to the sources or the ways through which they get access to sources. The principles of equality work differently or are adjusted according to personal capacities. Two critical barriers – low income and lack of property ownership – are preventing women from getting access to sources. Access is manipulated by the income distribution in regard to commercial energy, while the property distribution manipulates access to suitable biomass. Both these domains make it clear that access to energy is controlled by many other conditions, such as income, endowments, resource ownership, and employment.

21.7 GENDER ROLES AND DIFFERENTIATIONS

There are well-marked differences in the roles played by men and women in reproductive and productive domains, bringing about several development implications. Women are more in the informal, subsistence, and welfare-related work domains, while men are more in production and management. These socially fixed expectations are being used to place advanced technologies and energy-based mechanical operations in the hands of men. The same cultural expectations have shaped the gender-specific differentiations in fuelwood production and the supply chain. Women take the lead in providing biomass for subsistence, while men take the commercial opportunities to harvest fuelwood and supply it to the market.

These differences are perpetrated also in the financial and technical capacities, scale of production, volumetric harvesting, procuring solid materials (either by self-collection or contracting), and portaging either on their head or in vehicles. Often, the supplying of fuelwood for cash or profit is a business handled by men, and the supplying of fuelwood for household cooking and family food preparations is handled by women. Inequalities are also connected with the technology, and women are often clustered into the labour-intensive domain of the supply and production chain, while men handle machinery, transportation, harvesting, and business. As for residential energy use, the small-scale, home-based applications for enterprises are handled by women.

Similar differentiations are seen in relation to the scale of modernization, technologies, and enterprises. In these, women are in small-scale operations and men are in the technologically advanced areas. These differences and ideologies are reinforced in the formal energy sector, with men occupying leading decision-making positions involving improved technologies and investments, while women occupy the technologically and financially deprived areas of energy (FAO, 1999). The injustice here is the fact that biomass contributes a large share of energy to the energy mix, and women's labour makes a major contribution to the total energy sector. Under these circumstances, gender inclusion has become a must in energy development, through which unjust situations are expected to be corrected and potential contributions to the energy sector are to be integrated.

21.8 PATHWAYS TO GENDER EQUALITY IN ENERGY

Despite the fact that gender equality and energy access are crucial means to enhance development effectiveness and reduce the gaps, both ideological and operational, they are situated far apart from each other. To help these two domains respond to each other, suitable measures have to be worked out, focusing on the national institutional frameworks and their limitations. In this respect, the following factors, among other things, are crucial:

(1) Expanded policy opportunities for gender inclusion in the energy mainstream;
(2) Changing ideological barriers and barriers to gender inclusion;
(3) Rights-based approach to energy;
(4) Support services and access to services for enhancing women's capabilities, skills, financing, and entrepreneurship;
(5) Investing in women for economic advancement.

21.9 GENDER INCLUSION IN THE FORMAL ENERGY SYSTEM

The formal energy systems in the countries in the region are managed through established policies and institutional mechanisms, while the informal sector is unorganized and remains in the hands of producers, suppliers, and users operating at different scales, more for their well-being than for profit or business. Gender inclusion in the energy mainstream is justified by the synergy between women and energy, which exists along several strings; the first is formed through their engagement in the primary energy supply domain and usage; the second is in commercial energy supply and usage; the third is the social domain, conditioned by the conventional consumption practices and ideologies influencing women to be in the biomass energy chain performing their roles and responsibilities under the relationship between women and men; the fourth is the energy governance domain, where exclusions, constraints, or opportunities for women exist; and the fifth is the energy policies and practices that are in place and that respond to pressing issues.

The energy sector is driven by the ideology of supplying a public utility, energy technology, and the formally operated commercial types. Seeking an energy environment conducive to gender equality is beyond the interests or the mandate of the energy practitioners and the energy professionals responsible to the state agencies in their mandate to provide modern energy carriers. The structure of the energy sector in many countries is designed without equality concerns but allows conditions to reinforce conventional gender divisions through the formal structures. These features – and the divisions between 'formal' and 'informal', 'commercial' and 'subsistence' sources, 'modern' energy carriers and 'conventional' sources, and 'modern technology' and 'traditional' – provide enabling conditions for men to occupy the formal stream and women to be in the informal and subsistence stream.

An analysis of the energy sector in Sri Lanka shows that the formal structure is dominated by the large-scale commercial suppliers, which are differentiated from the informal domain (see Figure 21.2). The formal stream is a vested responsibility of the energy sector of the country, while the informal stream is the domain of the local people and is heavily occupied by women. The informal sector, with renewable sources, contributes a

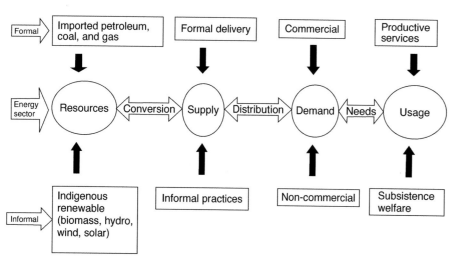

Figure 21.2. Flowchart of dual tracks separating women from the formal energy supply system.

massive share. But it is isolated from the formal sector, with its imported sources, which is under organized institutional management. Under this structure, renewable resources, subsistence uses, and non-commercial energy account for a huge share. More than 70% of this is absorbed into the domestic sector in many countries in the region. From the perspective of gender and women's inclusion, the roles played by women are crucial to the biomass-based primary energy supply and to demand management. Biomass in the primary energy supply comes to around 47% and is around 49% of the energy consumption by domestic, commercial, and other small consumers. Women's roles in the informal renewable sector and their contribution to the energy supply and managing the demand are firmly instated in connection with the household sphere. Therefore, the lack of institutional frameworks for this whole stream raises questions pertaining to the essential role of government in supply security and the willingness to engage women in decision-making, thus contributing to energy efficiency management.

The four nodes are in the mainstream – resources, supply, demand, and usage – and are connected with operational loops associated with conversion, distribution, and needs. The social contexts are stronger throughout, regarding renewable energy resources, but in regard to the formally delivered commercial types, the social aspects are connected through the demand and the usage. This suggests that technological aspects situated in these nodes and the operational loops differentiate the formally operated commercial systems from the informal, renewable resource-based system. The demand for a gender-inclusive operational system is driven by the roles played by women in maintaining sustainable production, demand, and local practices. A regional gender assessment of energy policies and programmes in South Asia shows that gender equality issues in energy have to deal with the gaps that exist between the energy paradigm and the local contextual base (ENERGIA, 2015a). In all the countries in South Asia, women play a leading role in household energy management and home-based enterprises, as well as energy-inclusive livelihood activities and managing the land-based energy resources.

21.10 AGENCY FOR SUSTAINABLE ENERGY MANAGEMENT

Energy management has been expanded, moving beyond supply to the inclusion of end users. The contextual conditions of South Asia favour this simply because the bulk of the energy used in the region has to be sustainably produced and supplied, to satisfy the demand. The wide range of ecosystems with energy potentials are affected by environmental and energy resource degradation, biodiversity depletion, and pollution resulting from over-exploitation of the conventional energy sources. The vulnerability of men and women in subsistence economies and the

issue of energy security among those with a low income but depending on biomass have been deepened. The gender-specific differences in entitlement to resources also contribute to this situation. Resource entitlement has been an instrument in getting access to financing, markets, and technology, and in this way the entitlement differences obstruct women's equal participation in developing renewable energy and integrating local experiences and knowledge into energy management. Women require better access to financing, institutional mechanisms, capital, social organizations, and representation in decision-making in order to engage in renewable energy resource development. Household management as handled by women is a raw model to replicate the efficient and effective management of energy. It is a strong agency that ought to be harnessed by the development practitioners. For instance, in biomass energy systems, their roles extend beyond gathering and portaging fuelwood. They rejuvenate the systems by integrating and managing perennial species with fuelwood, producing greater potential for the land where they work. In the rural landscape, the mosaics providing biomass for cooking fuel are managed by women. Nearly 60–70% of the work related to enrichment, integration, and periodic harvesting is handled by women. They maintain home gardens as green energy mosaics or energy supply mosaics.

The energy-related issues in many countries in South Asia are created by positioning men and women at the tail end of supply lines as beneficiaries or as the users of energy, without recognizing and including them as managers of energy demand who are responsible for energy efficiency and for transferring power into services and production. The representation of them as suppliers, energy service generators, and end users is a right as well as a condition essential for sharing responsibility for energy and its efficiency. Evidence from various countries reveals that there is little consultation between the energy sector policy makers and the end users, nor the civil society organizations. The technology- and supply-driven policy objectives are not equipped with gender-specific development targets and so concentrate on supplying energy for limited areas like lighting, transportation, and industry. Measurable objectives in regard to gender, production, and income are the missing loops in the energy sector. The evidence gathered through gender-inclusive energy development in Sri Lanka, Bhutan, and Nepal demonstrates that women in rural areas undertake energy-based business ventures. For example, in Sri Lanka, where adequate training, together with access to knowledge, markets, financing, and technology, is provided and their social capital has been established (ENERGIA, 2015b). Several transitions have been made in regard to gender relations, household income and women's share of earning, household and community-based economic development, energy efficiency, technology adoption and applications, and the ideology on women in energy enterprises.

Gender inclusion is a challenge to the development process, the energy sector in particular. It is important to note that it is not included in the technical mandate of energy or the existing institutional settings, so it is placed upon the agencies responsible for social, human, and gender development or the ministries of women's affairs. The role of women in energy is evident from the information related to energy use, such as household energy management for generating multiple services like cooking, lighting, and for appliances. In Sri Lanka, in 2014, the total energy demand derived from the household and commercial sector was 171.1 PJ, and almost 76% was for biomass, 8% for petroleum, and 16% for electricity. A noteworthy transition has occurred with the household electrification policy, by which almost 100% of the households have been provided with electricity. The perceived benefits of having electricity are quite high among women. Their increased labour efficiency, intra-household mobility, clean indoor atmosphere, reduced risks, extended hours of work, leisure, and access to information and sources of knowledge reveal the effectiveness of having a source with shared benefits (Wickramasinghe, 2005). Household lighting enables women to accomplish many tasks and responsibilities more easily and efficiently, turning energy access into an effective way to facilitate development. It has increased their agency in deciding consumption of electricity and monitoring the unit costs of all the household appliances (ADB, 2015). Changing energy-related behaviour within individual households and replicating lessons through women's networks proved extremely effective in Sri Lanka. In rural areas, where mechanization takes place in connection with agricultural commercialization, changes have occurred in relation to mechanized water pumping, irrigation, milling, and grinding, which allowed women to reduce their workload related to subsistence and invest that time in income-generating activities.

Considerations have heightened as to how energy decisions impact men and women differently and how energy has to be designed to meet practical, productive, and strategic needs. Models for engendering energy sector policy for the direct inclusion of women through participation and women representatives, civil society groups, women activists, researchers, and NGOs are being considered. However, in South Asia, even though it is at the forefront of ensuring sustainable energy for all, multiple deprivations have occurred, violating women's equal rights, participation, and entitlements; these deprivations stem from the socially established norms and the cultural practices. The conventional operational practices and the social perceptions of energy obstruct the elimination of social barriers preventing women's participation in energy. A socially inclusive process, responding to the social and economic dynamics, ought to be accommodated into the energy sector, into its operational paradigm. This requires favourable conditions, including a comprehensive, gender-disaggregated database for the energy sector, human skills in gender-inclusive development, consultative and mobilization skills, gender-responsive policies, programmes and projects with institutional capacities, budgetary provisions, monitoring, and an evaluation framework with gender-specific indicators, not only regarding the number of men and women who participate but also considering the output and impact of energy. The energy sector should be reflective of gender-equality concerns, which insist on equal rights, opportunities, entitlement to resources, and benefits for men and women. These in one way rationalize the grounds on which men and women are able to participate in energy; in another way, they are grounded in the concept of the equal right to be benefited by energy.

21.11 RIGHTS-BASED APPROACH TO GENDER INCLUSION

The potential for modern energy access to resolve gender inequalities while expanding economic options for women who occupy a low position on the development ladder is greater than before. Many aspects are connected with women's rights, which are nurtured by human rights discussions, and to various dimensions pertaining to the right to services, property, employment, and freedom to make decisions. The Convention on the Elimination of all forms of Discrimination Against Women (CEDAW) has enabled policy makers to prioritize the issues affecting women and the circumstances obstructing equality. Their rights have been recognized as a prerequisite for the advancement of women. The underlying argument insisting on a rights-based approach to energy is that unequal distribution of power in Asian society prevents women from having equal opportunities to participate and benefit from energy and the energy services. The perspective of women's rights also extends beyond access to energy carriers and merges with a wide range of issues related to land rights, which are important in determining women's participation in bioenergy and hydro-energy development, in particular. As it has been discussed by Agarwal (1994), in Asia the circumstances affecting women's land rights are highly diverse, culturally sensitive but institutionally ignored. There are significant variations in asset ownership, especially ownership over land and access to loans, which are crucial for resolving issues of inequality and deprivations. Assets are critical because they can be leveraged to acquire other assets, sustain enterprises, or diversify livelihoods. Women in the region are more vulnerable to poverty than men, not simply because they have lower incomes, but also because their ability to access economic opportunities is constrained by discriminatory attitudes that restrict their mobility, limit employment choices, and hinder control over assets (ENERGIA,

2015a). The men's legal ownership to land formalizes their contracts and control over land. This allows wider opportunities for men to lead modern bioenergy development, including technologies and deciding on capital investments. The injustice here is that women, who provide more than 60% of labour, varying within and between countries, do not have autonomy over land and energy crops.

The global move during the recent past in developing biofuel to supplement fossil fuel consumption has initiated serious discussions about women's rights. Their rights to productive resources, to land and their livelihood security, and women's rights to engage in decision-making have serious development implications. Much pressure has been created recently in connection with land-grabbing for energy-crop plantations. Countries like Brazil, Indonesia, Malaysia, and many others in the biofuel business stimulate discussion demanding gender-sensitive policy frameworks for such development. A synthesis of research presented by the World Rainforest Movement (WRM) (2012), referring to the work carried out by the Sawit Foundation and others, has made it clear that the large-scale palm oil plantation industry has forced women to lose their livelihood sources, so they have to adjust either as wives of the workers in the new plantation-based economy or as an exploited source of labour. The WRM stated that in Asia, working in the industrial oil palm sector has not improved women's lives, and gender inequality has persisted or even worsened, while women also suffer exploitation in the workplace, both on industrial plantations and in the nurseries. It is important to recognize that prospects for utilizing these new opportunities cannot be generalized, and the applications vary in terms of scales and levels. The lessons learned in Sri Lanka have shown that there are entrepreneurial and environmental opportunities with the capacity for empowering women in rural areas (Wickramasinghe, 2009, 2010), but effectiveness relies on the willingness of state agencies to follow gender-inclusive processes and the readiness of the institutions to include gender as a key factor.

The rights-based approach to energy may lead to a paradigm shift, changing the direction of the intervention flow, making it more sensitive to the rights of people. It is important to note that the initiative towards modern energy access for all is driven by the recognition that all persons have the right to access to modern energy carriers, which would solve deprivations that exist in energy access and the unequal distribution of energy services and benefits. The detrimental effects of gender inequalities that have been neglected so far need to be resolved, enhancing women's contribution and responsible participation required for economic growth. Participation of the deprived sectors in energy is a challenge, especially with regard to women. Women are active energy practitioners with a stake in endorsing end-use efficiency.

21.12 PARTICIPATION MECHANISM FOR EQUALITY

Participation and equality are situated on the two sides of the same coin, strengthening each other. Participation requires well-planned social engineering, followed by an effective social mobilization process. Within the context of the family-based operation system in most of the countries in Asia, women are in the centre, managing the households for the well-being of their families. Women's income, education, health, employment, social status, knowledge, and skills contribute to the total process, in which equality and energy play vital roles helping to make the process effective. The grassroots experience indicates that various strategies like diagnosis of cultural and social barriers and issues are effective for internalizing the initiatives and stimulating women to participate in energy projects. The benefits of women's participation move up the social ladder from individuals to families and then to communities, while promoting gender equality, rights, opportunities, and entitlements.

Equal participation and its contribution to gender equality are influenced by the local contexts, including household dynamics, livelihood and the ecological settings, and resources. In renewable energy, interventions in three communities in Poyangala, Rambukoluwa, and Dawatagala in Sri Lanka show that women initially participated to represent their families in planning micro-hydro projects. Then they developed a self-interest and integrated their energy needs to implement a project. Gender inclusion was achieved by women while gaining technical skills and making decisions on electricity distribution, applications, and getting credit to broaden their productive use of electricity. They established a local fund to operate revolving funds, thus financing grinding mills and water pumps for irrigating crops. Decisions over the application of electricity generated during the day time were made by women, enhancing the application for productive purposes. This evidence suggests that technical knowledge and skills gained by women through their participation in energy can be translated into gender-responsive action. Tangible benefits are the increased income, production, and time savings, which illustrate the effectiveness, while psychological well-being, leisure, social engagements, collective spirit, sharing, convenience, and many others point out the effectiveness of women's participation on the well-being of women, children, their families, and the community.

21.13 ENERGY EFFICIENCY AND EFFECTIVE APPLICATION

Energy efficiency and application is an effective tool for the end users for enhancing productivity and economic development. During the recent past, various measures have been taken to increase energy efficiency, extending the matters beyond energy generation and supply, touching the technology and end users. It is important to revisit the arguments concerning the contribution of enhanced energy efficiency to gender-specific development interests of the countries and vice versa. It is also a means to enhance social resilience to crisis situations, reducing vulnerability to energy shocks like periodic scarcities and climate change. In reality, at the grassroots level, efficiency implies reduced consumption and lower cost per unit of energy.

Efficiency measures have been used with specific support extended by the nations with the commitment of the people, particularly in residential energy efficiency. Such measures have enabled users to reduce electricity consumption by 30–40% and reduce the cost of energy. Energy efficiency measures introduced by the energy sector in Sri Lanka motivated women to undertake management roles in their households. More than 80% of the households involved in the project adopted efficiency and conservation measures by structuring energy use, making behavioural changes, replacing items like ceiling fans and rice cookers with appliances that consume less energy, and by using CFL bulbs. Energy efficiency and lowering energy intensity have been instrumentalized largely in the household sector, where women lead household management. Efficiency and conservation are the two interrelated aspects achieved through behavioural and attitudinal changes in end users. Equal opportunities enable women to select devices that help them to increase productivity and labour efficiency. Women in rural areas have developed various technologies using local materials. One example is the change-over from exclusively high fuelwood-consuming three-stone open hearths to semi-circular mud hearths made by them. The consumption has been brought down by at least 30–40% by rural women themselves.

In India and Nepal, some women are in the stove industry. Women in Bangladesh, who make straw sticks by wrapping straw in cowdung, enhance the efficiency and the convenience of using straw as a source of energy. Women reduce the pressure on wood resources by expanding the variability of the material that goes into kitchens in biomass bundles. The efficiency of the improved cookstoves, for instance, has been accepted as an effective measure by the end users, useful for saving time and human energy spent in work related to wood-fuel supply, cooking, and cleaning. India and Nepal have made several transitions in regard to enhancing energy efficiency during the last decade. For instance, in 2009, the government of India launched the National Biomass Cookstoves Initiatives for deploying cleaner biomass cookstoves for household cooking. The micro-financing programme of Grameen Shakthi in Bangladesh and the Alternative Energy Promotion Centre in Nepal have been focused on improving energy efficiency, effective application of improved technology for reducing the drudgery of work handled by women, and empowering women to lead rural energy technologies. South Asia offers favourable conditions for the implementation of the programmes initiated by the Global Alliance for Clean Cookstoves launched in 2010, with the '100 by 20' goal of having 100 million homes adopt clean and efficient fuels by 2020. Women are the change agents capable of adopting technology and their management in household and communities. Similarly, the Biogas Support Programme in Nepal, launched in 1992, has disseminated more than 250,000 biogas plants and over the years has made progressive change by mainstreaming gender equity and social inclusion, targeting the poorer sectors of the population (ENERGIA, 2015a). Several elements – such as access to micro-financing, technical training, and capacity-building, credit, and saving schemes, as well as partnership with the private sector, women's organizations, and NGOs – have been able to make a progressive change in reducing gender gaps, ideological barriers, and expanding access to clean energy.

In the household sector, efficiency covers a wide spectrum, including gender-specific gains and benefits that inspire the end users to reduce consumption by gaining maximum returns per unit of energy or raw material resources. The ultimate contributions are in favour of the energy sector as a whole and the resources which help the contribution of energy to expand services to underserved areas and social sectors without overexploiting the sources or the resources. Evidence available from these countries reveals that the lower the productive use of energy and the adoption of modern technology, the greater the poverty, gender inequality, and backwardness. It is crucial to measure the impacts of clean energy, whether cooking energy or electricity, in terms of productivity enhancement, income, and employment generation. Field assessment of the application of modern technology for poverty eradication carried out in Sri Lanka showed that water pumping directly contributed to women's economic empowerment. When it was combined with drip irrigation systems, women increased their income by more than 40% throughout the year. It is not only the biomass-based cooking and bioenergy resource management that place women in the forefront of conservation, but also accommodating practices and energy behaviour with conservation implications. The reduction of electricity consumption during the peak period in the evening has become of practical interest to women in the households. Overloading of supply lines has been controlled by avoiding clothes ironing, water boiling, leaving the light bulbs on in the areas that do not require illumination, grinding, and excessive use of refrigerators during the peak periods. The household-based conservation practices become effective means to reach the goals of sustainable energy for all. The participation of millions of households where women's agency is important is a prerequisite to achieving effective results. These are to be recognized and capitalized upon as instruments in energy sector development. The equality aspects, stressing how a unit of energy saved by some consumers becomes a greater input for improving the lives of those who do not enjoy equal opportunities, should be taken into consideration in energy development.

A gender-inclusive approach with strategies for gender mainstreaming should be formulated, analysing the effectiveness of measures included by women as pathways for enhancing energy efficiency. Along with this, men and women should be provided with opportunities with the ability to assess their contribution to efficiency, conservation, and green energy development, convincing the energy sector of the implications, by using experience-based knowledge.

21.14 INVESTING IN WOMEN FOR EFFECTIVENESS

The social, economic, and environmental contexts of the SAARC countries provide ground conditions through which inequalities have been entrenched, placing a greater weight of poverty and deprivations on women. The existing gaps in employment, workforce participation, education, income, employment, property, the use of electricity, appliances, and technology locate entry points for working out energy strategies and targets. Investing in women is aimed at building capabilities and capacities to move forward, reducing gender-based differentiation of work and remunerations, as well as support services.

The most crucial concerns are the creation of conditions for women to engage in paid work, enhancing women's labour force participation. These are deeply discussed by UN Women (2015), which reviews the progress of the world's women. Accordingly, 'paid work can be a foundation for substantive equality for women, but only when it is compatible with women's and men's shared responsibility for unpaid care and domestic work; when it gives women enough time for leisure and learning; and when it provides earnings that are sufficient to maintain an adequate standard of living' (p. 66). This implies that paid work for women means a huge transition, more than simply a matter concerning equal opportunities. Build on this the crucial necessity for getting access to electricity, appliances, leisure items, and time-saving household utensils (which heavily rely on increased income), and then access to financing can be stressed. Women spending more than 15 to 16 hours a day on domestic chores have no choice, unless adjustments are made with their spouse or children for sharing and bearing the work load. Responsibility for domestic work, unpaid care, and work for subsistence are the areas marked by huge labour concentration.

Empirical evidence suggests that over the years, women's labour force participation stagnated, and globally only half of the women are in the labour force, compared to more than three quarters of men (UN Women, 2015). This demonstrates that globally there is a 26% gap between women's and men's labour force participation, and in developing regions, the proportion of women's employment that is informal and unprotected is 76%. The variations within and between countries in South Asia in the labour force participation of men and women are rather significant. Pakistan shows a huge gap between men and women (ILO, 2015); it is 82.9% for men and 24.6% for women, indicating social and cultural constraints to women entering the labour market and the strength of the social expectations demanding that they take the burden of household chores. The means or pathways to reduce the gaps are specific to contextual conditions; where there are persistent barriers to education it is an equalizer, whereas in Sri Lanka the reduced education inequality has not made a huge reduction in the gap in the labour force participation. Multiple pathways, such as economic opportunities, technology, vocational skills, and financing, are needed to deal with this situation. Access to energy and devices and capacity to pay back the recurrent cost of electricity are crucial for making a change. The main concern here, on the one hand, is to make use of energy or invest in providing energy solutions to save their time spent on fetching water, collecting fuelwood, and lengthy hours of cooking for remunerative work, and the concern on the other is to make them capable through capacity-building to enter the labour market.

21.15 GENDER CONSIDERATIONS AND EMPOWERING WOMEN

The basic premise for working on energy access to improve gender equality, and improving gender equality for efficient management of energy for development effectiveness, is structured by reviewing the lessons learned in the field and through the literature. Why should women have a stake in energy? What changes should be expected by promoting women in the energy sector as stakeholders or by mainstreaming gender into energy? How does gender equality become a practical reality in the energy sector for assuring development effectiveness? The main reason is the potential contribution of women to managing energy and economic advancement. The countries in the SAARC region offer examples of practices used by women. In all these countries, women commit their time and energy and engage themselves in catering for household energy, which is central to the well-being of the people. The opportunity cost of their labour is rather high. In some cases, health burdens borne by women have multiple development implications. With regard to renewable energy resources, particularly in biomass and hydro-energy resources, women's agency is central for the conservation of the resources. The deepening crisis of the availability of alternative sources and increasing prices place pressure on local resources that are managed by women. Women have become a repository of knowledge gained through their engagement in growing and providing biomass of different qualities and quantities from various sources. A gender-inclusive policy is a requisite to capture these potentials.

WHO, in evaluating the costs and the benefits of household energy, has looked into several combinations of approaches with models/options enabling the policymakers to make decisions responding to the local context (see WHO, 2007). Women have to decide fuel options and the best combination of fuel and improved technologies and devices for efficient adaptation and effective applications. The areas that women and men contribute to energy and gain effective results in development differ. A general overview produced through analysis suggests that inclusion of gender considerations into energy decision-making is a way to share the responsibility and ownership over the management with users (Table 21.6).

Functioning households and communities are the operational models for making a transitional move. Empowering women can be ensured through recognition and inclusion, providing equal opportunities and by engaging them in decision-making processes. The underlying purpose is to enable women to make decisions and to become capable partners to work with state agencies and other stakeholders like financing, the private sector, donors, NGOs, and others. Civil society organizations in many countries, especially in India, Bangladesh, and Nepal, illustrate the power of collective action and authority to express their concerns, with some control over decisions. In this regard, civil society organizations are to be strengthened as mechanisms for responding to the context and for developing coherent and coordinated policies linking all the areas concerning development, to make effective improvements. Women's organizations are crucial because women are the activists in their own household energy systems, individually handling 60–80% of the household energy. They activate the 'green energy chain' – the biomass energy chain and resource flow from various sources to the end-use units; they also organize the supply and manage the

Table 21.6. Areas in Sri Lanka with gender-specific considerations.

Means contributing to energy	Strategies for inclusion of women	Strategies for inclusion of men
Management of sources and resources	Responding to women's work in farm-based occupations and specific energy resource development options	Response to men's concerns over land use, energy crops, and task-specific work
Integrating, labour, lessons, and experience	Integrating time and labour and local practices; preferred species with special energy capacities; harvesting and processing methods for energy resource development	Integrating energy crops compatible with agricultural crops
Knowledge of energy trends	Energy as a code for getting access, recognizing customary rights in developing commercial options	Energy-based enterprise options
Energy efficiency	Investing in empowering women through training, information, and knowledge to make decisions, to apply efficiency measures in household and agriculture	Sharing knowledge and inputs to secure efficient appliances
Conservation technologies	Household and farm-based energy conservation, combined with household management and conservation farming	Selecting best practices, short rotation coppicing with regeneration potentials
Enhanced returns on investments	Establish producer and supplier groups/sub-contracting that create income and commercial opportunities	Increase multiple market options through sustainable production
Forming energy mosaics or landscapes rich in 'bioenergy hot spots' and mosaics	Strengthen social networks, knitting family-based systems through dense hedges	Energy-producing mosaics connecting plots
Energy efficiency	Energy into household management, knowledge, and information of efficiency measures, and management improvements	Adopting of energy-efficient technologies and practices
Conservation beyond farm boundaries	Working through groups in catchments providing water for pico-hydro and micro-hydro and in riparian areas for species and spring restoration	Conservation combined with land management
Social capital for resources and conservation	Action groups formed by bringing villagers together in self-help work. Exchange of planting materials and establishing species banks for sharing	Extending support for conservation-related work

Source: Author's field work and research in Sri Lanka

demand using various technologies. Economically, the commodity value of the energy that they supply to household energy systems ought to be taken into account in national systems. Research covering such analysis is essential to make decisions based on an understanding of the women's contribution to energy systems of the households, nations, and the region. The expanding demand for renewable energy in the commercial sector is an opportunity for the land-based economies of the region.

21.16 POLICY FOR ADVOCATING GENDER EQUALITY

The energy policies of the countries in the region are focused on several areas. Providing basic energy needs to the people of the respective countries, efficiency of energy supply and demand, conservation and energy security (particularly of the commercial sources) and promotion of renewable and indigenous sources are quite visible. Gender sensitivity of policies indicates the preparedness of the energy sector to deal with dynamic social, economic, and environmental changes. In their task of supplying energy, nations have defined basic energy needs by focusing heavily on electricity supply used for illumination, for small appliances, and for communication and information. The gender goals of the overall policy or of the sub-sectors and the energy strategies are considered outside the mandate. The sensitivity of the energy policies is crucial to indicate the areas of specific attention, preparedness, and the ability of energy to respond to gender considerations. Conscious efforts are being made by international agencies like ADB and ENERGIA to carry out gender analysis or gender audits to assess the sensitivity of the existing policies. Such efforts have synthesized the situation of many countries in the region, such as India, Bhutan, Nepal, and Pakistan. There is increasing evidence to suggest that what is needed for energy development is to recognize gender-based differences and create opportunities for men and women to benefit from energy while enhancing their agency. The basic thesis behind this argument is that energy affects men and women differently, since the roles, responsibilities, needs, and constraints faced by women differ from those of men. It has also been recognized that the lack of data reflecting these differences is a significant obstacle to introducing gender-sensitive policies. Countries like Sri Lanka, which concentrate on commercial sources like fossil fuel and electricity, are less concerned about the specific issues connected with gender.

The present systems are designed predominantly for centralized structures, providing a less supportive environment for small-scale operations and the sectors. Under these circumstances, the decentralized institutional structures of SAARC countries need to define gender-inclusive energy development. The decentralized options and mechanisms play a crucial role in developing the local systems, such as small hydro projects, including pico-hydro and micro-hydro, dendro energy plants, wind energy farms, and solar power systems based on the locally available resources. The existing policy framework insists on providing basic energy needs of the people, with the aim of enhancing their living standards and providing gainful economic opportunities. This is driven by the responsibility of the energy sector for supplying energy for the end users or the people, without getting into gender-specific considerations. The gaps in policy are to be filled with knowledge and understanding of gender roles, responsibilities, and skills to bridge them with energy and energy services. Lack of data on gender-specific parameters is a barrier to gender-inclusive policy formulation.

Approaches like participatory planning, social inclusion, decentralized planning, capacity-building (at all levels, from the stage of data collection to monitoring and evaluation) can be used to engender the policy process – if the approaches are enriched with gender planning instruments. All these are interdependent and effective, but effectiveness depends on the efficiency and the capacity of the agencies to apply them in various situations. The participatory approaches have been widely applied in development planning as tools for engaging people, integrating their concerns and interests, and responding to them. In turn, it is also assumed that energy policies planned through participatory processes, be they national or decentralized, would benefit by producing effective results. The policy environments hardly advocate participatory planning or applying gender analytic tools for integrating gender interests into energy. Setting gender goals for the energy sector and setting energy-related strategies to achieve gender goals are complementary.

Countries in Asia have national policies on gender equality and mainstreaming to work out strategies and action plans for advancing women in energy and through energy inputs and services. This indicates that the agencies working on gender have to work with multiple sectors – such as education, health, enterprise development, technology, and information – to structure gender-specific energy demand in order to reduce the existing gaps and resolve the impediments. For instance, in securing rights to biomass energy enterprises, women have to secure means of access to land services to sustain production. The voice of women has been less effective in energy enterprise development because of their lack of land rights and capital investments. In South Asia, the conditions permitting women to have rights to land and crops vary, but many models would be useful for empowering women. However, if women lack strong social capital and energy entrepreneurial skills, it will be difficult to convince the energy industry of the potential contributions of women. This forces us to turn back to the discussion on women's participation, which is not defined in terms of their collective strength and the possible application of land-based occupations for prospective undertakings. When women's organizations focus on energy or include energy into their agendas, it helps them to facilitate policy dialogue, undertake contract farming for energy, and to represent their concerns and issues relevant to energy.

Strong points of contact or organized demands can support and facilitate the integration of gender equality into national and regional policies. Policies are the instruments to instate rights, safeguard against exploitation, affirm workplace security, and stimulate rules or laws enabling women to be part of the monetary economy. Policy instruments are needed to facilitate various energy development models to overcome the impediments to capital gains and to give women their due recognition. The national policy for gender equality should be applied in all circumstances, irrespective of the size of the operation. The gender-inclusive mandate of the institutions, budgetary provisions, human capacities, energy portfolios, information and materials, skills and experience, research, and extension services must be more sensitive to equality issues. The circumstances prevailing in most of the countries are responsive to technical aspects and crises in energy supply, so adding another dimension of sensitivity has to be planned with expertise. The capacities and the roles of various stakeholders – including state agencies, the private sector, donors, projects, NGOs, communities, civil society organizations, and women's organizations in particular – should be enhanced and tapped so that they may effectively address and reconcile the issues of gender, equality, rights, and entitlements.

21.17 CONCLUSION AND RECOMMENDATIONS

The analysis presented in this paper could be strengthened through the evidence-based lessons that are available from the countries in the region. It is quite clear that the mixture of multiple sources supplying energy is under different management, authority, and governance; none of them is guided by the principles of equality or the wish to ensure equal participation of men and women or equal access to benefits. Such a change requires, as suggested by Guruswamy (2016), underlying policies that are situated in an integrated framework. The variations between countries captured to some extent in this paper strongly suggest the importance of national commitments to look into the wide variations that exist within each country, both in energy-related parameters and also regarding gender equality aspects. Women need opportunities to participate in the centralized and commercial systems. In the decentralized and informal systems, at least some opportunities are there for customary practices. How to facilitate a gender-inclusive process in energy, dealing with a judicious mix of energy supply, is the question in hand, because

the measures of equality entail different implications for men's and women's energy needs. The energy service requirements are multiple and diverse, and so while expanding such opportunities to enhance and ensure effectiveness, it is essential to establish enabling conditions for women to secure equal opportunities in science education, technology, training, and financing. The concerns expressed in this paper lead to the following suggestions for realizing development effectiveness through gender equality and energy access in South Asia.

(1) Women's social capital

Establishing women's social organizations and linking them with interrelated development sectors and formulation of suitable policies should be a priority. The notion of 'universal access to energy' or 'sustainable energy for all' has different implications for men and women. The state machineries should introduce supportive policies and mechanisms for gender mainstreaming to strengthen accountability. Equal opportunities help ensure the end users' contributions to and responsibility for energy. To address the gender inequalities that persist in the countries of the region, each country requires a well-designed package for gender inclusion and empowerment. Capacity-building, awareness-raising, and training will help women to work towards equality, securing opportunities that will enable them to participate in energy sector activities and realize the goals of energy with gender targets in an effective manner.

(2) Networking

Networking within and between countries is a strong instrument for building solidarity, linkages, and synergies. The energy sector and women's civil society organizations are to work in partnership. The evidence-based knowledge from across the region is to be shared, drawing attention to persisting gaps and good lessons on gender equality, participation, representation, and effectiveness of partnerships in transforming the situations. Networking can bring together a wide range of stakeholders and thus establish trans-boundary cooperation and collaboration towards gender equality goals.

(3) Grassroots representation

The requirement here is to have representation by grassroots men and women as energy managers in their own operational units and at the level of policymaking. It is an effective means of moving towards a transition by shrinking and even erasing the gaps between men and women created by hierarchical tiers. Such representation, however, is not entertained in the conventional energy supply-based models. Therefore, as a first step, other models, such as community-based energy development, enterprise models, cluster- or niche-based models of energy resource management, and many others, ought to be reviewed to learn the pros and cons and their effectiveness for development. In this regard, it is important to ensure a policy commitment to empowering women, gender equality, and building women's social capital.

(4) Exchange and sharing

This refers to a wide range of aspects, including human skills, knowledge, information, technologies, and funding. Intertwining of expertise has been a successful tool for enhancing cooperation and replication. A comprehensive analysis of energy sector policies and gender situations, along with the existing materials and evidence, would provide a good starting point for integrating gender equality into energy. The limitations caused by a lack of civil society organizations engaged in lobbying and advocating for gender equality would also be overcome by facilitating linkages.

(5) National and regional multi-stakeholder forums

This is a means to discuss issues impeding development that are to be treated as urgent and to deal with the targets for the future. It is important to review the experience of the energy experts, researchers, activists, NGOs, CBOs, women's organizations, and the policy makers, and engage them in discussions and strategic planning. Even if civil society organizations representing women are available, it is unwise to expect that the linkages will naturally function smoothly. The technology, targets, resources, and the language of negotiation must be agreeable to the parties with a stake in the matter.

(6) Favourable policy environment

The desire would not be 'women's organizations or activists fighting for gender equality' but should be 'working with energy for gender equality for development effectiveness' at various levels, through national policies supported by a regional machinery. It is essential to bring about a gender-inclusive policy environment and an institutional framework conducive to such a state of affairs to address gender inequality issues. It is also important to realize at this juncture that the effectiveness of various interventions in changing the local situation is still low or has been rather slow. This is partly owing to the fact that the policies in the countries in the SAARC region have been relatively unresponsive to gender equality, women's participation and representation, and engagement in policy advocacy. This also could be considered as a reflection of the inadequacy of the pro-poor or pro-women interventions to deal with the gravity of

the situation. How to begin a more effective process is a question that may be asked by the energy experts, as they look for answers from gender experts and women activists.

ACKNOWLEDGEMENT

The author wishes to acknowledge the collaboration and support extended by Professor Pak Sum Low from the stage of drafting of this paper to reviewing and finalizing for publication.

REFERENCES

ADB (2015) *Gender Equality Results Case Study: Sri Lanka, Improving Connectivity to Support Livelihoods and Gender Equality*. Manila, Philippines, ADB.

ADB (2018) *Gender Equality and Social Inclusion Assessment of the Energy Sector: Enhancing Social Sustainability of Energy Development in Nepal*. Manila, Philippines, ADB.

Agarwal, Bina. (1994) *A Field of One's Own: Gender and Land Rights in South Asia*. Cambridge, Cambridge University Press.

ENERGIA (2015a) *A Regional Gender Assessment of Energy Policies and Programmes in South Asia*. The Hague, The Netherlands, International Network on Gender and Sustainable Energy.

ENERGIA (2015b) *Sri Lanka Women Come Together in Producer Groups to Assemble LED Bulbs*. The Hague, The Netherlands, International Network on Gender and Sustainable Energy.

FAO (1999) Gender aspect of woodfuel flows in Sri Lanka: A case study in Kandy District. Regional Wood Energy Development Project (RWEDP), Field Document No. 55, FAO Regional Office, Bangkok, Thailand. http://www.fao.org/3/X5668E/x5668e00.htm

Guruswamy, L. (2016) *International Energy and Poverty: The Emerging Contours*. London and New York, Routledge.

IEA (2010) *Energy Poverty: How to Make Modern Energy Access Universal? Special Early Report on the World Energy Outlook 2010 for the UN General Assembly on the Millennium Development Goals*. Paris, France, International Energy Agency.

(2011) *World Energy Outlook: Energy for All, Financing Access for the Poor*. Paris, France, International Energy Agency.

(2017) *Energy Access Outlook 2017: From Poverty to Prosperity*. https://www.iea.org/topics/energy-access

ILO (2015) Key Indicators of the Labour Market (KILM) database. January 2015. https://www.ilo.org/global/statistics-and-databases/research-and-databases/kilm/lang--en/index.htm

Masse, R. and Samaranayaka, M. R. (2002) EnPoGen study in Sri Lanka. *ENERGIA NEWS*, 5(3), 14–16.

Trace, S. (2016) Measuring access for different needs. In L. Guruswamy (ed.), *International Energy and Poverty: The*

Emerging Contours, pp. 160–178. London and New York, Routledge.

UN Women (2015) *Progress of the World's Women 2015–2016: Transforming Economies, Realizing Rights.* New York, UN Women.

UNDP (2010a) *Power, Voice and Rights: A Turning Point for Gender Equality in Asia and the Pacific.* Asia-Pacific Human Development Report. Colombo, Sri Lanka, UNDP, Regional Centre for Asia and the Pacific.

(2010b) *Human Development Report, 2010.* New York, UNDP.

(2016) *Human Development Report, 2016.* New York, UNDP.

United Nations (2005) *The Energy Challenges for Achieving the Millennium Development Goals.* New York, United Nations.

WHO (2007) *Evaluation of the Costs and Benefits of Household Energy and Health Interventions at Global and Regional Levels.* Geneva, Switzerland, World Health Organization.

(2016) *Population using solid fuels (estimates) data by country.* Global Health Observatory data repository. Available from http://apps.who.int/gho/data/node.main.135?lang=en.

Wickramasinghe, A. (2005) Gender, modern biomass energy technology and poverty. ENERGIA News Letter, Vol. 8, No. 2, December 2005, pp. 9–10. The Hague, The Netherlands, ENERGIA Secretariat. https://www.energia.org/cm2/wp-content/uploads/2019/01/en-2005-12.pdf

(2009) Integrating biofuels into small farm operations for income and economic development. In G. Karlsson and K. Banda (eds.), *Biofuels for Sustainable Rural Development and Empowerment of Women: Case Studies from Africa and Asia*, pp. 34–38. The Hague, The Netherlands, ENERGIA Secretariat.

(2010) Biofuel: A green energy option for mitigating humanitarian crises of climate change. IUFRO World Series Volume 27, 11–13. Vienna, Austria, IUFRO Headquarters Secretariat.

(2011) Energy access and transition to cleaner cooking fuels and technologies in Sri Lanka: issues and policy limitations. *International Journal of Energy Policy*, **39**(12), 7,567–7,574.

World Bank (2011) *Engendering Development: Through Gender Equality in Rights, Resources and Voice.* Washington, DC, World Bank.

(2012) *World Development Report: Gender Equality and Development.* Washington, DC, World Bank.

(2015) *Progress towards Sustainable Energy, 2015. Global Tracking Framework Report.* Washington, DC, World Bank.

World Economic Forum (2016) *Global Gender Gap Report.* Geneva, Switzerland.

World Rainforest Movement (2012) Monoculture tree plantations, jobs and work. Monthly bulletin, Issue 178, May 2012. https://wrm.org.uy/bulletins/issue-178

22 The biosphere and the interactions between stratospheric ozone depletion and climate change

JAN C. VAN DER LEUN[1] AND JANET F. BORNMAN[2]

[1]Ecofys, Utrecht, The Netherlands

[2]Food Futures Institute, Murdoch University, Western Australia

Editor's note: This chapter was first drafted by Professor Jan C. van der Leun, who unfortunately passed away on 6 July 2016. In order to make this chapter publishable in this book, I invited Professor Janet F. Bornman, who had worked closely with Professor van der Leun in UNEP's Environmental Effects Assessment Panel (EEAP) established in 1988 under the Montreal Protocol on Substances that Deplete the Ozone Layer, to revise and update the chapter as a co-author. I am most grateful that Professor Bornman kindly accepted the invitation. Professor van der Leun was founding Co-Chair of EEAP until his retirement in 2010. Within this role and also through his research, he made significant contributions to the assessment of environmental effects of stratospheric ozone depletion, and is internationally well known and recognized. The UNEP Environmental Effects Assessment Panel continues to build on the legacy left by Professor van der Leun. The publication of this chapter is a tribute to him. There is also a commemorative issue of 13 papers in the journal, *Photochemical & Photobiological Sciences*, published in 2018. Please see: https://pubs.rsc.org/en/journals/articlecollectionlanding?sercode=pp&themeid=77d56c80-8548-4fe4-bbe6-eddea6e5d5b9.

Keywords
Biosphere; stratosphere; troposphere; ozone layer; climate change; greenhouse gases; greenhouse effect; ozone depletion

Abstract
Two global environmental problems are occurring in the atmosphere: changing dynamics of the stratospheric ozone layer and rapid climate change. The two problems and their interactions are discussed, especially from the viewpoint of the consequences for living organisms and the involvement of living organisms in the interactions.

22.1 INTRODUCTION

Two global environmental problems have presented themselves in the atmosphere in recent decades: changing dynamics of the stratospheric ozone layer and rapid climate change. The Montreal Protocol and its Amendments have successfully controlled the ozone depleting substances (ODSs). However, many of these ODSs are also potent greenhouse gases. While ODSs have decreased significantly under the Montreal Protocol, emissions of several forms of hydrofluorocarbons (HFCs) have increased. HFCs, while not a threat to the stratospheric ozone layer, nevertheless have a high global warming potential (GWP), thus contributing to the greenhouse effect. Consequently, in 2016, the Kigali Amendment to the Montreal Protocol was adopted in Kigali, Rwanda, aimed at all countries gradually phasing out HFCs by more than 80% over the next three decades. These measures are projected to decrease drastically the warming effects of HFCs.

The way in which stratospheric ozone is affecting climate, and vice versa, will be discussed in the light of what this means for living organisms on the one hand, and on the other hand, what living organisms mean for these interactions.

It is not surprising that the atmosphere is first to reach the stage of global pollution, because worldwide transportation of pollutants usually moves faster in air than in water, and because the mass of the atmosphere is much smaller than that of the oceans. Ultimately, the water may well catch up, since many of the pollutants end up there.

The layers of the atmosphere involved in the problems to be discussed are the troposphere and the stratosphere. The troposphere is the lowest layer, where the weather occurs. It is roughly 15 km above the Earth's surface, and characterized by vertical movements of the air, in which the clouds and rain are formed. Climate change has its core in this layer. Higher up is the stratosphere, roughly between 15 and 50 km above the Earth's surface. Vertical air movements are practically absent there, but horizontal winds can blow freely. The stratosphere is where about 90% of the ozone is found, the so-called ozone layer. It is also where the ozone is being depleted over the Antarctic areas in spring, and recently also unexpectedly over the Arctic. The two environmental problems, climate change and stratospheric ozone depletion, therefore occur in different layers of the atmosphere. In spite of this spatial separation, it is becoming increasingly clear that the two problems influence each other in several ways.

22.2 CLIMATE CHANGE

It would be much colder on Earth, and in the lower layers of the atmosphere, if there were no 'greenhouse effect'. The sunlight warms the Earth's surface, and as a consequence, the surface emits infrared (heat) radiation. Some of the gases in the air absorb that radiation and so increase the temperature of the air. This works like a warm blanket over the surface. The important absorbing gases (greenhouse gases) are water vapour, carbon dioxide (CO_2), and methane (CH_4). Without this greenhouse effect, the temperatures at the surface would be lower by 25 to 30 degrees Celsius. It is not an exaggeration to say that the greenhouse effect is a necessary condition for life as we know it.

This important process has become increasingly subject to rapid change by human activities. For a long time, it was thought that human influences were too small to have noticeable impact on systems as large as the global atmosphere. However, during the past decades, it has become convincingly clear that our activities do increase the concentrations of greenhouse gases in the atmosphere. The burning of oil, coal, and natural gas, as well as deforestation, have significantly added to the concentration of carbon dioxide in the atmosphere. The global growth of the human population leads to more agriculture and cattle-breeding, which are causing increasing emissions of methane. These changes reinforce the greenhouse effect, leading to rising temperatures (IPCC, 2018), which in turn increase the evaporation of water, bringing more water vapour into the air, so again amplifying the greenhouse effect.

Effects of higher temperatures include more extremes in weather and climate, melting of snow and ice and rising sea levels. Consequences for living organisms are already evident in many places. Insurance companies, for instance, have noticed the increasing claims for damage from storms, floods, and wild fires. These consequences will become worse if mankind does not succeed in stopping this development.

22.3 STRATOSPHERIC OZONE DEPLETION

Protection for living organisms is provided by the ozone layer in the stratosphere; it absorbs most of the damaging ultraviolet (UV) radiation in sunlight. This protection is provided by a relatively small quantity of matter; the mass of stratospheric ozone is less than one-millionth of the mass of the atmosphere. The amount of stratospheric ozone is the result of a dynamic equilibrium between the formation of ozone by sunlight and a gradual chemical breakdown. Sunlight splits

oxygen into oxygen atoms (O), which can recombine to form oxygen (O_2), or the oxygen atoms can combine with the oxygen molecules to create ozone (O_3). The rate of ozone breakdown has been amplified by human-made chemicals such as chlorofluorocarbons (CFCs) and hydrochlorofluorocarbons (HCFCs), used primarily in refrigeration and cleaning, and methyl bromide, used for soil disinfection. As a consequence, the stratospheric ozone layer has become 'thinner', and more of the solar UV radiation reaches the Earth's surface, particularly over the Antarctic.

This has many consequences for life on Earth. In the present context, we will deal with effects on living organisms. Even an unchanged solar UV radiation may cause damage to plants, animals, and humans (see Assessment Report, 2003; Bornman et al., 2015; Bais et al., 2018). In some plants, increased UV radiation may lead to decreased plant height and leaf area. Aquatic organisms, especially the small ones, are negatively affected. In humans and other animals, the skin and eyes are the main target areas. Exposure of the skin to intense UV radiation not only can cause skin damage and skin cancer, but can also modulate the immune system. The human eye is a vulnerable target. UV radiation is one of the main causes of cataracts, a clouding of the eye lens, which leads to poor vision and may end in blindness. In areas where medical treatment is not available, it is a leading cause of blindness. Other eye diseases include loss of central vision and increased blurred vision (age-related macular degeneration, although the role of UV radiation here is not clear) and invasive growths of the cornea (pterygium), among others. However, UV radiation is also beneficial to life on Earth, depending on the intensity and amount of exposure. The most widely recognized benefit is the production of vitamin D in the skin, which supports bone health and may also decrease the risk of some internal body cancers, autoimmune (such as multiple sclerosis) and infectious diseases, and cardiovascular disease (Bais et al., 2018; Lucas et al., 2019).

22.4 PROTECTION OF THE STRATOSPHERIC OZONE LAYER

The only realistic way to counter environmental problems is to take away the causes or at least reduce them. Individual and national activities are certainly useful, but for a real solution to these global problems, worldwide cooperation is necessary. In this respect, we have the Vienna Convention for the Protection of the Ozone Layer (1985), which has its specifications in the Montreal Protocol on Substances that Deplete the Ozone Layer (1987). International actions are coordinated by the United Nations Environment Programme. The Montreal Protocol was the first multilateral environmental treaty to be universally ratified by 198 countries.

About 100 human-made chemicals have been listed as ODSs. Implementation plans have been made to eliminate production and use of these chemicals, first in the developed countries, and after a 'grace period' also in the developing countries. Via a Multilateral Fund, rich countries help poor countries with the costs involved in the transition to alternatives to the ODSs. The Vienna Convention really works: 98% of the ODSs are already out of use, and the remaining substances are scheduled to follow, with limited exceptions for essential and other exempted use. However, continual monitoring of the effects of the ODS replacements is necessary, since many of these are powerful greenhouse gases, contributing to a warming Earth.

The recovery of the stratospheric ozone layer is expected, and there are indications of this recovery over the Antarctic, although the ozone 'hole' continues to occur in early spring each year before closing up. While upper stratospheric ozone outside the polar regions has increased since 2000, no significant trend of recovery has yet been detected globally (WMO, 2018). Recovery is a slow process, because several of the ODSs already in the atmosphere will stay there for 100 years or more. During the period of the annual Antarctic ozone 'hole', the loss of ozone is more than 50%. In mid-latitudes, the ozone loss is on average 5%, and in the tropics, there has been no measurable loss. Without the early and active protective action of the Montreal Protocol and its Amendments, these losses would have been much higher, and would have continued to increase in the present century, with annual global losses in stratospheric ozone exceeding 60% (Newman et al., 2009), accompanied by large increases in UV irradiance (McKenzie et al., 2011; Bais et al., 2019). These events would have had serious implications for human health and the environment.

22.5 PROTECTION AGAINST CLIMATE CHANGE

There is also international cooperation to counter climate change by the United Nations Framework Convention on Climate Change (UNFCCC, 2019a). Measures to be taken to reduce global warming gases are specified in the Kyoto Protocol, which entered into force in February 2005. Currently 192 countries have ratified the Kyoto Protocol (UNFCCC, 2019b). The initial goal for the signatory countries was to reduce the emission of greenhouse gases by, on average, 5%, in 2012 against the levels of 1990. For several of these countries, it has been difficult to achieve this goal. However, in 2010, the decrease in annual ODS emissions under the Montreal Protocol was estimated to provide about five times the climate benefit compared with the annual emissions reduction target for the first commitment period (2008–2012) of the Kyoto Protocol (Ajavon et al., 2015).

Taking into account that a reduction of the emissions by 5% is not enough by far to solve the problem, the development is not encouraging. The solution is more difficult than in the case of stratospheric ozone depletion, because much heavier economic interests are involved, especially in the use of oil, coal, and gas. It appears that solving this problem will take more time, as noted by the Copenhagen Accord in December 2009, and will require continuing efforts towards constraining increases in average global temperature by the Doha Amendment to the Kyoto Protocol (2012). However, the number of countries required to accept the Amendment for it to come into effect has not yet been achieved, as of January 2019. The Paris Agreement in 2015 has had a more positive impact, with ratification by 184 countries as of January 2019. In November 2020, the USA officially withdrew from the Paris Agreement, even though it is the second largest emitter of carbon dioxide, after China. After a change in the presidency, the USA rejoined this Agreement in February 2021. Of concern is the so-called emissions gap between the targets of the Paris Agreement and the inadequate actions taken by the participating countries (IPCC, 2018). The slow progress towards climate change mitigation and adaptation is partly due to a lack of strong political will and the fact that climate change is an even slower process than ozone depletion. This implies that what goes wrong will be wrong for an even longer time. The slowness is caused by the large heat capacity of the oceans; this enormous mass of water warms slowly, but once warmed, it also cools down slowly (Hansen et al., 2004; Wijffels et al., 2016). We are facing a serious problem of unsustainability, with the world's oceans having already absorbed 93% of the Earth's additional heat load since 1970 (Wijffels et al., 2016).

22.6 INTERACTIONS OF CLIMATE CHANGE AND STRATOSPHERIC OZONE DEPLETION

Climate change and stratospheric ozone depletion influence each other (Arblaster et al., 2011; Thompson et al., 2011; Bornman et al., 2015; Robinson and Erickson, 2015; Chipperfield et al., 2017). Greenhouse gases, including carbon dioxide and ODSs with large global warming potentials, have been implicated in causing increases in temperature and changes in stratospheric circulation, which affect the stratospheric ozone layer, and could delay recovery of the ozone layer (Shindell et al., 1998; Ajavon et al., 2015), but with large variations according to season, latitude, and altitude (Rosenfield et al., 2002).

Apart from the direct effects of ozone depletion on the penetration of UV radiation to the Earth's surface, aerosols, and climate change factors such as changing cloudiness, will also influence the penetration of solar UV radiation to the surface. Decreases in cloudiness and aerosols have been reported at some mid-latitude sites, resulting in increased UV-B radiation, while the UV-B radiation is projected to decrease over high latitudes in the northern hemisphere (Bais *et al.*, 2015).

In and around Antarctica, stratospheric ozone depletion causes the ozone 'hole' each year when the sunlight returns after the polar night. That 'hole' persists for a few months and then disappears. Stratospheric ozone depletion can also influence climate, particularly in the southern hemisphere. These ozone-driven changes in climate have been implicated in temperature and precipitation changes in Antarctica (Gillet and Thompson, 2003; Bandoro *et al.*, 2014). While the 'hole' exists, the westerly winds around Antarctica are reinforced, and the temperature is higher over large parts of the southern hemisphere (Thompson and Solomon, 2002; Polvani *et al.*, 2011; Robinson and Erickson, 2015; Bais *et al.*, 2018, 2019). This amplifies the temperature rise from the increasing greenhouse effect. Also, changes in rainfall in the southern hemisphere and parts of Asia have occurred (Lim *et al.*, 2016a, 2016b; Duc *et al.*, 2017; Bais *et al.*, 2018).

22.7 WHAT DO THESE INTERACTIONS MEAN FOR LIVING ORGANISMS?

In some cases, the combination of climate change and stratospheric ozone depletion works in a compensating way. For plants, UV radiation can have negative effects on plant growth as well as beneficial outcomes, and these are often modulated by ambient environmental conditions such as temperature, water availability, carbon dioxide concentration, and presence of plant pests. For instance, plant defence mechanisms against pests can be activated by UV radiation through biochemical pathways (increased polyphenolic compounds that deter pests) (Mazza *et al.*, 1999; Zavala *et al.*, 2015; Dillon *et al.*, 2017; Bornman *et al.*, 2019). These evolving environmental conditions also modify food quality (Wargent and Jordan, 2013; Williamson *et al.*, 2014; Bornman *et al.*, 2019), which has implications for human health (Dykes and Rooney, 2007; Umeno *et al.*, 2016; Wu *et al.*, 2017a).

Organisms living under snow and ice will be subjected to the increased UV radiation caused by stratospheric ozone depletion as rising temperatures accompanying climate change melt the snow and ice. Many aquatic organisms are sensitive to UV radiation and may incur damage; in particular, this has been observed in some algae and small plankton (e.g., zooplankton, phytoplankton, and protozoa) (Harrison and Smith, 2009; Peng *et al.*, 2017; Williamson *et al.*, 2019), which are a source of food for much of aquatic life. The melting of snow and ice on land may also result in earlier seasonal damage by UV radiation and last longer.

Effects from higher temperatures can interact with those of UV radiation; for example, in aquatic and terrestrial organisms, these interactions may modify organism response beneficially, negatively, or have no apparent effect (Xiao *et al.*, 2015; Wu *et al.*, 2017b; Williamson *et al.*, 2019; Bornman *et al.*, 2015, 2019).

The induction of skin cancer in mice by UV radiation was found to proceed faster at higher environmental temperature (Bain *et al.*, 1943; Freeman and Knox, 1964). This temperature effect may also apply to skin cancer in human populations, but there is still uncertainty in the results reported so far (van der Leun and de Gruijl, 2002; van der Leun *et al.*, 2008; Lucas *et al.*, 2019). Climate change and related temperatures are modifying human behavioural patterns in relation to time spent outdoors, contributing to increases in skin cancer and eye diseases such as cataract in some cases, and insufficient exposure to the beneficial effects of UV radiation (e.g. production of vitamin D in the skin) in other cases (Lucas *et al.*, 2019).

Temperature and UV radiation are widely known to markedly contribute to the degradation of plastics and wood materials (Adelhafidi *et al.*, 2015; Tolvaj *et al.*, 2015; Živković *et al.*, 2016; Greco *et al.*, 2017; Andrady *et al.*, 2019), and sophisticated technology is being developed to extend the life-time of these materials, especially those used outdoors and in the building industry (Andrady *et al.*, 2019).

22.8 WHAT DO LIVING ORGANISMS MEAN FOR THE INTERACTIONS?

The oceans are a 'sink' for carbon dioxide in the atmosphere and so reduce the greenhouse effect. The uptake of carbon dioxide in the water is largely stimulated by the life processes of the phytoplankton. Increased exposure to UV radiation reduces the productivity of phytoplankton (Smith *et al.*, 1992; Lubin *et al.*, 2004; Bancroft *et al.*, 2007; Llabrés *et al.*, 2013; Williamson *et al.*, 2019). This reduces the uptake of carbon dioxide from the atmosphere, which increases the greenhouse effect. It is not clear how large this effect is on a world scale under the current conditions of the stratospheric ozone layer.

That living organisms, especially small ones, could have an important influence on the large global systems is still difficult to imagine. But there are long-term interactions between the atmosphere and life on Earth. While the quantity of oxygen in the atmosphere is continuously reduced by oxidative reactions, and by the breathing of animals and humans, it is replenished by the photosynthesis of plants. In this way, plant life maintains the oxygen, and so the ozone layer that is formed from the oxygen. And in its turn, the ozone layer protects life on Earth.

A less admirable influence on the atmosphere by living organisms is the disturbance now caused by humans in the two great protective systems there, the stratospheric ozone layer and the greenhouse effect. This justifies every effort to work for a recovery of both systems.

22.9 WHAT ABOUT THE FUTURE?

With continued efforts to eliminate the production and emissions of ODSs, and if rapid climate change can be kept more under control, the stratospheric ozone layer is expected to recover; however, a complete solution will take a long time, in the order of half a century.

Climate change is more worrying. In spite of the efforts started in many countries to limit the emission of greenhouse gases, the worldwide emissions of carbon dioxide from the use of fossil fuels and the emissions of other greenhouse gases (HFCs, PFCs, SF_6, and CH_4) are still growing. It will be necessary to take more drastic actions to reduce the emissions of all greenhouse gases. For carbon dioxide, the only good long-term solution is in renewable energy, from sunlight, wind, biomass, and water movements, which are clean and do not increase the greenhouse effect. Solar radiation has more than enough energy for all the needs of the world's population. Part of the renewable energy gained may be used to produce hydrogen, an energy carrier that makes it possible to use the energy at different times and locations. This may even become an important source of income for poor but sunny countries, which could become producers and exporters of the energy of the future.

ACKNOWLEDGEMENTS

The authors thank Dr Stephen O. Andersen and an anonymous reviewer for their helpful suggestions for the manuscript.

REFERENCES

Adelhafidi, A., Babaghayou, I. M., Chabira, S. F. and Sebaa, M. (2015) Impact of solar radiation effects on the physicochemical properties of polyethylene (PE) plastic film. *Procedia-Social and Behavioral Sciences*, **195**, 2,210–2,217.

Ajavon, A. L., Bornman, J. F., Maranion, B. A., Paul, N. D., Pizano, M., Newman, P. A., Pyle, J. A., Ravishankara, A. R. and Woodcock, A. A. (2015) Synthesis of the 2014 Reports of the Scientific, Environmental Effects, and Technology and Economic Assessment Panels of the Montreal Protocol. United Nations Environment Programme (UNEP), Nairobi, pp. 1–27. ISBN 978–9966-076–16-8.

Andrady, A. L., Pandey, K. K., Heikkilä, A. M., Redhwi, H. H. and Torikai, A. (2019) Interactive effects of solar UV radiation and climate change on material damage. *Photochemical and Photobiological Sciences* (In Press). DOI: 10.1039/C8PP90065E.

Arblaster, J. M., Meehl, G. A. and Karoly, D. J. (2011) Future climate change in the Southern Hemisphere: competing effects of ozone and greenhouse gases. *Geophysical Research Letters*, **38**(2), L02701, DOI: 10.1029/2010GL045384.

Assessment Report (2003) Environmental effects of ozone depletion and its interactions with climate change: 2002 assessment. *Photochemical and Photobiological Sciences*, **2**, 1–72.

Bain, J. A., Rusch, P. and Kline, B. E. (1943) The effect of temperature upon ultraviolet carcinogenesis with wave lengths 2,800–3,400 Å. *Cancer Research*, **3**, 610–612.

Bais, A. F., McKenzie, R. L., Bernhard, G., Aucamp, P. J., Ilyas, M., Madronich, S. and Tourpali, K. (2015) Ozone depletion and climate change: impacts on UV radiation. *Photochemical and Photobiological Sciences*, **14**(1), 19–52.

Bais, A. F., Lucas, R. M., Bornman, J. F., Williamson, C. E., Sulzberger, B., Austin, A. T., Wilson, S. R., Andrady, A. L., Bernhard, G., McKenzie, R. L., Aucamp, P. J., Madronich, S., Neale, R. E., Yazar, S., Young, A. R., de Gruijl, F. R., Norval, M., Takizawa, Y., Barnes, P. W., Robson, T. M., Robinson, S. A., Ballaré, C. L., Flint, S. D., Neale, P. J., Hylander, S., Rose, K. C., Wängberg, S. Å., Häder, D.-P., Worrest, R. C., Zepp, R. G., Paul, N. D., Cory, R. M., Solomon, K. R., Longstreth, J., Pandey, K. K., Redhwi, H. H., Torikai, A. and Heikkila, A. M. (2018) Environmental effects of ozone depletion, UV radiation and interactions with climate change: update 2017, UNEP Environmental Effects Assessment Panel. *Photochemical and Photobiological Sciences*, **17**(2), 127–179.

Bais, A. F., Bernhard, G., McKenzie, R. L., Aucamp, P. J., Young, P. J., Ilyas, M., Jöckel, P. and Deushi, M. (2019) Ozone-climate interactions and effects on solar ultraviolet radiation. *Photochemical and Photobiological Sciences* (In Press). DOI: 10.1039/c8pp90059 k.

Bancroft, B. A., Baker, N. J. and Blaustein, A. R. (2007) Effects of UVB radiation on marine and freshwater organisms: a synthesis through meta-analysis. *Ecology Letters*, **10**(4), 332–345.

Bandoro, J., Solomon, S., Donohoe, A., Thompson, D. W. and Santer, B. D. (2014) Influences of the Antarctic ozone hole on Southern Hemispheric summer climate change. *Journal of Climate*, **27**(16), 6,245–6,264.

Bornman, J. F., Barnes, P. W., Robinson, S. A., Ballaré, C. L., Flint, S. D. and Caldwell, M. M. (2015) Solar ultraviolet radiation and ozone depletion-driven climate change: effects on terrestrial ecosystems. *Photochemical and Photobiological Sciences*, **14**(1), 88–107.

Bornman, J. F., Barnes, P. W., Robson, T. M., Robinson, S. A., Jansen, M. A. K., Ballaré, C. L. and Flint, S. D. (2019) Linkages between stratospheric ozone, UV radiation and climate change and their implications for terrestrial ecosystems. *Photochemical and Photobiological Sciences*, **18**(3), 681–716. DOI: 10.1039/C8PP90061b.

Chipperfield, M. P., Bekki, S., Dhomse, S., Harris, N. R., Hassler, B., Hossaini, R., Steinbrecht, W., Thiéblemont, R. and Weber, M. (2017) Detecting recovery of the stratospheric ozone layer. *Nature*, **549**, 211–218.

Dillon, F. M., Chludil, H. D. and Zavala, J. A. (2017) Solar UV-B radiation modulates chemical defenses against *Anticarsia gemmatalis* larvae in leaves of field-grown soybean. *Phytochemistry*, **141**, 27–36.

Duc, H. N., Rivett, K., MacSween, K. and Le-Anh, L. (2017) Association of climate drivers with rainfall in New South Wales, Australia, using Bayesian model averaging. *Theoretical and Applied Climatology*, **127**(1–2), 169–185.

Dykes, L. and Rooney, L. W. (2007) Phenolic compounds in cereal grains and their health benefits. *Cereal Foods World*, **52**(3), 105–111.

Freeman, R. G. and Knox, J. M. (1964) Influence of temperature on ultraviolet injury. *Archives of Dermatology*, **89**, 858–864.

Gillet, N. P. and Thompson, D. J. W. (2003) Simulation of recent southern hemisphere climate change. *Science*, **302**, 273–275.

Greco, A., Ferrari, F. and Maffezzoli, A. (2017) UV and thermal stability of soft PVC plasticized with cardanol derivatives. *Journal of Cleaner Production*, **164**, 757–764.

Hansen, J., Nazarenko, L., Ruedy, R., Sato, M., Willis, J., Del Genio, A., Koch, D., Lacis, A., Lo, K., Menon, S., Novakov, T., Perlwitz, J., Russell, G., Schmidt, G. A. and Tausnev, N. (2004) Earth's energy imbalance: Confirmation and implications. *Science*, **308**(5,727), 1,431–1,435.

Harrison, J. W. and Smith, R. E. (2009) Effects of ultraviolet radiation on the productivity and composition of freshwater phytoplankton communities. *Photochemical and Photobiological Sciences*, **8**(9), 1,218–1,232.

IPCC (2018) Summary for policymakers. In V. Masson-Delmotte, P. Zhai, H. O. Pörtner, D. Roberts, J. Skea, P. R. Shukla, A. Pirani, W. Moufouma-Okia, C. Péan, R. Pidcock, S. Connors, J. B. R. Matthews, Y. Chen, X. Zhou, M. I. Gomis, E. Lonnoy, T. Maycock, M. Tignor and T. Waterfield (eds.), *Global Warming of 1.5°C. An IPCC Special Report on the Impacts of Global Warming of 1.5°C above Pre-Industrial Levels and Related Global Greenhouse Gas Emission Pathways, in the Context of Strengthening the Global Response to the Threat of Climate Change, Sustainable Development, and Efforts to Eradicate Poverty*. World Meteorological Organization, Geneva, Switzerland.

Lim, E. P., Hendon, H. H., Arblaster, J. M., Delage, F., Nguyen, H., Min, S. K. and Wheeler, M. C. (2016a) The impact of the Southern Annular Mode on future changes in Southern Hemisphere rainfall. *Geophysical Research Letters.*, **43**(13), 7,160–7,167.

Lim, E. P., Hendon, H. H., Arblaster, J. M., Chung, C., Moise, A. F., Hope, P., Young, G. and Zhao, M. (2016b) Interaction of the recent 50 year SST trend and La Niña 2010: amplification of the Southern Annular Mode and Australian springtime rainfall. *Climate Dynamics*, **47**(7–8), 2,273–2,291.

Llabrés, M., Agustí, S., Fernández, M., Canepa, A., Maurin, F., Vidal, F. and Duarte, C. M. (2013) Impact of elevated UVB radiation on marine biota: a meta-analysis. *Global Ecology and Biogeography*, **22**(1), 131–144.

Lubin, D., Arrigo, K. R. and van Dijken, G. L. (2004) Increased exposure of Southern Ocean phytoplankton to ultraviolet radiation. *Geophysical Research Letters*, **31**, LO9304, DOI: 10.1029/2004GLO19633.

Lucas, R. M., Yazar, S., Young, A. R., Norval, M., de Gruijl, F. R., Takizawa, Y., Rhodes, L. E., Sinclair, C. A. and Neale, R. E. (2019) Human health in relation to exposure to solar ultraviolet radiation under changing stratospheric ozone and climate. *Photochemical and Photobiological Sciences*, **18**(3), 641–680. DOI: 10.1039/C8PP90060D.

Mazza, C. A., Zavala, J., Scopel, A. L. and Ballaré, C. L. (1999) Perception of solar UVB radiation by phytophagous insects: behavioral responses and ecosystem implications. *Proceedings of the National Academy of Sciences of the United States of America*, **96**, 980–985.

McKenzie, R. L., Aucamp, P. J., Bais, A. F., Björn, L. O., Ilyas, M. and Madronich, S. (2011) Ozone depletion and climate change: impacts on UV radiation. *Photochemical and Photobiological Sciences*, **10**, 182–198.

Newman, P. A., Oman, L. D., Douglass, A. R., Fleming, E. L., Frith, S. M., Hurwitz, M. M., Kawa, S. R., Jackman, C. H., Krotkov, N. A., Nash, E. R. and Nielsen, J. E. (2009) What would have happened to the ozone layer if chlorofluorocarbons (CFCs) had not been regulated? *Atmospheric Chemistry and Physics*, **9**(6), 2,113–2,128.

Peng, S., Liao, H., Zhou, T. and Peng, S. (2017) Effects of UVB radiation on freshwater biota: a meta-analysis. *Global Ecology and Biogeography*, **26**(4), 500–510.

Polvani, L. M., Waugh, D. W., Correa, G. J. and Son, S.-W. (2011) Stratospheric ozone depletion: the main driver of twentieth-century atmospheric circulation changes in the Southern Hemisphere. *Journal of Climate*, **24**(3), 795–812.

Robinson, S. A. and Erickson, D. J. (2015) Not just about sunburn: the ozone hole's profound effect on climate has significant implications for Southern Hemisphere ecosystems. *Global Change Biology*, **21**(2), 515–527.

Rosenfield, J. E., Douglass, A. R. and Considine, D. B. (2002) The impact of increasing carbon dioxide on ozone recovery. *Journal of Geophysical Research: Atmospheres*, **107**(D6), 4049. DOI: 10.1029/2001JD000824.

Shindell, D. T., Rind, D. and Lonergan, P. (1998) Increased polar stratospheric ozone losses and delayed eventual recovery owing to increased greenhouse-gas concentrations. *Nature*, **392**, 589–592.

Smith, R. C., Prézelin, B. B., Baker, K. S., Bidigare, R. R., Boucher, N. P., Coley, T., Karentz, D., MacIntyre, S., Matlick, H. A., Menzies, D., Ondrusek, M., Wan, Z. and Waters, K. J. (1992) Ozone depletion: ultraviolet radiation and phytoplankton biology in Antarctic waters. *Science*, **255**, 952–959.

Thompson, D. W. and Solomon, S. (2002) Interpretation of recent Southern Hemisphere climate change. *Science*, **296**(5,569), 895–899.

Thompson, D. W., Solomon, S., Kushner, P. J., England, M. H., Grise, K. M. and Karoly, D. J. (2011) Signatures of the Antarctic ozone hole in Southern Hemisphere surface climate change. *Nature Geoscience*, **4**(11), 741–749.

Tolvaj, L., Popescu, C. M., Molnar, Z. and Preklet, E. (2015) Effects of air relative humidity and temperature on photodegradation processes in beech and spruce wood. *BioResources*, **11**(1), 296–305.

Umeno, A., Horie, M., Murotomi, K., Nakajima, Y. and Yoshida, Y. (2016) Antioxidative and antidiabetic effects of natural polyphenols and isoflavones. *Molecules*, **21**(6), 708. DOI:10.3390/molecules21060708.

UNFCCC (2019a) UNFCCC Process. https://unfccc.int/process#:2cf7f3b8-5c04-4d8a-95e2-f91ee4e4e85d

UNFCCC (2019b) The Kyoto Protocol – Status of Ratification. https://unfccc.int/process/the-kyoto-protocol/status-of-ratification

van der Leun, J. C. and de Gruijl, F. R. (2002) Climate change and skin cancer. *Photochemical and Photobiological Sciences*, **1**, 324–326.

van der Leun, J. C., Piacentini, R. D. and de Gruijl, F. R. (2008) Climate change and human skin cancer. *Photochemical and Photobiological Sciences*, **7**(6), 730–733.

Wargent, J. J. and Jordan, B. R. (2013) From ozone depletion to agriculture: understanding the role of UV radiation in sustainable crop production. *New Phytologist*, **197**, 1,058–1,076.

Wijffels, S., Roemmich, D., Monselesan, D., Church, J. and Gilson, J. (2016) Ocean temperatures chronicle the ongoing warming of Earth. *Nature Climate Change*, **6**(2), 116–118.

Williamson, C., Zepp, R., Lucas, R., Madronich, S., Austin, A. R., Ballaré, C. L., Norval, M., Sulzberger, B., Bais, A., McKenzie, R., Robinson, S., Häder, D-P. , Paul, N. D. and Bornman, J. F. (2014) Solar ultraviolet radiation in a changing climate. *Nature Climate Change*, **4**, 434–441.

Williamson, C. E., Neale, P. J., Hylander, S. Rose, K. C., Figuero, F. L., Robinson, S. A., Häder, D.-P., Wängberg, S.-Å. and Worrest, R. C. (2019) The interactive effects of stratospheric ozone depletion, UV radiation, and climate change on aquatic ecosystems. *Photochemical and Photobiological Sciences* (In Press). DOI: 10.1039/c8pp90062 k.

WMO (World Meteorological Organization) (2018) Executive Summary: Scientific Assessment of Ozone Depletion: 2018, World Meteorological Organization, Global Ozone Research and Monitoring Project – Report No. 58. Geneva, Switzerland.

Wu, G., Bornman, J. F., Bennett, S. J., Clarke, M. W., Fang, Z. and Johnson, S. K. (2017a) Individual polyphenolic profiles and antioxidant activity in sorghum grains are influenced by very low and high solar UV radiation and genotype. *Journal of Cereal Science*, **77**, 17–23.

Wu, Y., Yue, F., Xu, J. and Beardall, J. (2017b) Differential photosynthetic responses of marine planktonic and benthic diatoms to ultraviolet radiation under various temperature regimes. *Biogeosciences*, **14**(22), 5,029–5,037.

Xiao, X., De Bettignies, T., Olsen, Y. S., Agusti, S., Duarte, C. M. and Wernberg, T. (2015) Sensitivity and acclimation of three canopy-forming seaweeds to UVB radiation and warming. *PloS One*, **10**(12), e0143031.

Zavala, J. A., Mazza, C. A., Dillon, F. M., Chludil, H. D. and Ballaré, C. L. (2015) Soybean resistance to stink bugs (*Nezara viridula* and *Piezodorus guildinii*) increases with exposure to solar UV-B radiation and correlates with isoflavonoid content in pods under field conditions. *Plant Cell Environment*, **38**(5), 920–928.

Živković, V., Arnold, M., Pandey, K. K., Richter, K. and Turkulin, H. (2016) Spectral sensitivity in the photodegradation of fir wood (*Abies alba* Mill.) surfaces: correspondence of physical and chemical changes in natural weathering. *Wood Science and Technology*, **50**(5), 989–1,002.

23 The political challenge of linking climate change and sustainable development policies: Risks and prospects

R. JAMES FERGUSON

Faculty of Society and Design, Bond University, Queensland 4229, Australia

Keywords

Climate change; Sustainable Development Goals; Paris Agreement; UNFCCC; mitigation; adaptation; climate change impact; environmental pluralism; environmental diplomacy; climate risk and damage

Abstract

The need to link climate change mitigation and adaptation with environmental, social, and developmental sustainability is well entrenched in the parallel political negotiations on climate change, following on from the Paris Agreement (2015) and the Sustainable Development Goals (as they have evolved after the Millennium Development Goals). The outcomes of the Paris climate change talks suggest a strong shift towards politically realistic targets for ongoing emissions cuts, even if these voluntary targets are structured via national action plans and intended nationally determined contributions (INDCs). A major review of progress towards these targets was set for 2018 and 2023, and thereafter every five years. Likewise, widespread support for the Sustainable Development Goals (SDGs) suggests a balanced vision that may help developing states transition towards 'green', low-emission economies and still adapt to the loss and damage that will still be incurred due to climate change impacts down through 2050. With the hope of capping temperature rises to within or less than 1.5–2.0°C above pre-industrial levels, and emissions targeted to peak by 2030, climate change conferences through 2015–2018 provide a robust framework for further implementation of the Paris Agreement. However, the past track of environmental diplomacy suggests that serious problems lurk beneath the current consensus, and risk derailing both global emissions reductions and a truly global push towards sustainability. A successful diplomatic process may still fail to adequately reduce emissions for a less than 2°C rise, and uncertainty as to climate impact risks could result in hedging towards adaptation rather than mitigation strategies. Uneven implementation of sustainable development goals and climate adaptation frameworks could slow down both agendas. In the worst-case scenario, these goals could undercut each other, with developing countries switching to belated national development and adaptation efforts if collective action on emission targets and related funding wavers. A pluralist, multi-actor approach will continue to evolve, refining both climate change and sustainable development mechanisms over the next decade, but it still needs strong leadership from major states within the European Union and the 'BASIC' (Brazil, South Africa, India, China) coalition. Such approaches must reassure developing states of the benefits of sustaining emissions cuts alongside balanced implementation of the SDGs and continued use of resilient, 'low-emission' adaptation strategies.

23.1 INTRODUCTION: PARALLEL TRACKS AND INTERACTING POLICIES

Climate change and its social impacts have emerged as crucial challenges for 21st-century international relations (Busby, 2018), with the United Nations having a leading role in seeking cooperative approaches via inter-state, multilevel, and multi-actor diplomacy over the last five decades. The diplomatic interaction of environmental protection and developmental sustainability was well-established in the 1972 UN Conference on the Human Environment (the Stockholm Conference), with its Declaration listing 26 principles and 109 recommendations for protecting the environment and the prudent use of natural resources, including the idea for the creation of the United Nations Environmental Programme as an organization (UN, 1972; Keong, 2018). Sustainable development as a global issue came into further focus with the *Report of the World Commission on Environment and Development: Our Common Future*, developed through 1982–1987 after a process of extensive consultation (Brundtland, 1987). It identified globally shared environmental risks that required a shift towards sustainable development across resource and energy use, food security, eco-systems, industrial and economic structures, as well as population and urban challenges. These concerns were taken further in the United Nations Conference on Environment and Development (UNCED, the 'Earth Summit'), held in 1992 in Rio de Janeiro. Its vision of global action for sustainable development was outlined in the 27 principles of the *Rio Declaration on Environment and Development*, including precautionary approaches to environmental risk, responsibilities to other states, and the need to manage shared resources for future generations (UNGA, 1992).

The related Agenda 21 outlined a more detailed programme for sustainable development:

Agenda 21 is a large and detailed action plan, which is not legally binding, for global sustainable development in the twenty-first century. It is a consensus document, with its 40 chapters and 500 pages reflecting the competing interests and perspectives in the political process which created it. In seeking to integrate environment and development, it has a strong emphasis on community participation in decision-making, and recognizes the complementary roles of regulatory and market approaches to implementation. Agenda 21 called for the creation of a Commission on Sustainable Development as the major, high level institution to ensure effective follow-up of UNCED. The Commission was established by the UN General Assembly shortly after the Conference. (Diesendorf and Hamilton, 1997, p. 69)

This process helped shape the core agendas of fundamental environmental conventions and from 1992 led on to the UN Framework Convention on Climate Change (UNFCCC) and the Convention on Biological Diversity (Keong, 2018). In turn, major conferences in the 1990s on poverty, international development goals, population, and education helped frame a new commitment to the shared global partnership that would emerge at the UN Millennium Summit of September 2000 (Hulme, 2009). The Millennium Development Goals had evolved through the convergence of thinking in several organizations (the UNGA, the G8, UNDP, UNEP, WHO, UNESCO, UNICEF, the CSD, the OECD), including eventual support from 22 international agencies which 'spun onto' the MDGs or helped fund them, including the World Bank, the Asian Development Bank, and the African Development Bank (Fehling *et al.*, 2013). Alongside the wider development targets, the UN Millennium Declaration focused on environmental sustainability and protecting 'our common environment', which emerged as the Seventh Millennium Development Goal, with the MDGs running as a monitored global programme through 2000–2015 (UNGA, 2000, Section IV; UN, 2015a). Targets within the Seventh Goal included integrating sustainable development principles into country policies, the reversal of environmental resource losses, reduction of biodiversity losses, improving

access to safe water and sanitation, and improving slum dwellers' lives (UN, 2015a, pp. 52–61). After the 2012 Rio + 20 Summit (the United Nations Conference on Sustainable Development), these goals were expanded in the subsequent Sustainable Development Goals, negotiated in detail through 2012–2015. Several of these SDGs related directly to environmental issues, and as a whole they require strong ecological protection and sustainable use of the environmental resources and services to achieve resilient human societies (UNGA, 2015; see further Section 23.3).

On a parallel track, climate change debates were driven by the need to address human-generated atmospheric changes that were increasingly acknowledged in the 1980s. A major 1988 Conference in Toronto (the World Conference on the Changing Atmosphere) brought together scientists and policy makers across 13 working groups on a range of global atmospheric problems. The conference came to a number of recommendations, including the need to reduce carbon dioxide emissions by circa 20% by 2005 over 1988 levels, regardless of whether this reduction was 'efficient or sufficient'; that is, it was a pragmatic estimation designed to act as a political trigger for further action (Usher, 1989, p. 26). The need for reliable, verifiable but accessible scientific estimates of climate change risks and impacts became increasingly clear as the costs, differentiated responsibilities, and need for early climate change action began to emerge, with the World Climate Programme (WCP) initially providing an early international framework for research cooperation (Keong, 2018).

Through 1988–1989, the Intergovernmental Panel on Climate Change (IPCC) was set up (by the UNEP and the World Meteorological Organization) to provide detailed assessments, based on existing scientific research, including analysis of possible responses for both adaptation and mitigation. This process included work by hundreds of scientists, supported by several working groups, task forces, and leading authors, as well as national and expert review processes. The first IPCC assessment report in 1990 outlined the need for serious cuts in emissions, laying the foundation for the signing of the Climate Convention in Rio in 1992 and for subsequent meetings of parties to implement this process, with the first Conference of Parties (COP) held in 1995 (Jordan and Brown, 1997, p. 279; COP, 2007). The United Nations Framework Convention on Climate Change remained the fundamental basis for subsequent negotiations, with issues such as developing countries taking the lead, differentiated responsibilities and capacities, financing and technology transfer to developing countries, and adaptation costs outlined but not resolved in detail (UN, 1992, Articles 3 and 4; Low, 2018).

Regular meetings of the UNFCCC parties thereafter tracked towards the differentiated emissions targets for industrialized states in the Kyoto Protocol of 1997, followed by further rounds of negotiations leading to the Paris Agreement of 2015. The IPCC provided essential scientific and technical data supporting this process, including major assessment reports looking at adaptation, mitigation, and a synthesis of climate change issues (see IPCC, 2014a, 2014b, 2014c; the sixth assessment reports are underway). Its Working Group II, in particular, addresses the impact of climate change on socio-economic systems, and the interactions of adaptation and sustainable development across different sectors and countries (IPCC, 2014a). It also produces a number of special reports to help policy makers, for example, the reports on *Managing Risks of Extreme Events and Disaster to Advance Climate Change Adaptation*, the report on *Renewable Energy Source and Climate Change Mitigation*, and the Special Report, *Global Warming of 1.5°C* (IPCC, 2011, 2012, 2016, 2019). Likewise, the Subsidiary Body for Scientific and Technological Advice (SBSTA) and the Subsidiary Body for Implementation (SBI) were set up to create bridges between scientific information and the policy needs of the COPs and to help with the implementation and operationalization of the Convention, the Kyoto Protocol, and the Paris Agreement.

After 2015, intensive rounds of negotiations were required to cope with the withdrawal of the United States from the Paris Agreement, to balance and expand the funding of mitigation and adaptation capacities, and to ensure functional work programmes that would allow implementation of the Paris Agreement, including the Paris Agreement Work Programme and the Paris Agreement Implementation Guidelines (see further Section 4 of this Chapter). At the same time, sustainable development diplomacy (supporting the SDGs) was extremely active through 2012–2018, with ongoing reviews of progress on these goals both at the national level and exploring their inter-linkages. For example, the High-Level Political Forum of July 2018 studied the theme of 'Transformation towards Sustainable and Resilient Societies', addressing a subset of resource, societal, and environmental goals (SDGs 6, 7, 11, 12, 15, and 17) which are interrelated and need a multidimensional rather than a sectorial approach to secure net gains (OECD, 2018, pp. 22–23).

The aim of this chapter is to provide an exploratory narrative of the way that climate change and sustainable development policies have evolved and interacted in the diplomatic and public spheres. Although generally convergent agenda, there are real risks of divergent national priorities and break-away policies emerging if the Paris Agreement is not effectively implemented, or if emission and adaptation funding is not sufficiently mobilized within the context of sustainable development down through 2030. The chapter hopes to inform public debate and provide some reflective insights for policy makers, activists, and

diplomats deeply engaged in the assessment of complex scientific data while balancing conflicting societal interests.

23.2 LINKING ENVIRONMENTAL AND DEVELOPMENTAL SUSTAINABILITY

The need to link environmental, social, and developmental sustainability seems well entrenched in international political negotiations on climate change via the Paris Conference (COP 21, 2015), the following climate change conferences through 2016–2018, and in the Sustainable Development Goals (SDGs) as they have evolved since 2012, extending the agenda set up in the earlier Millennium Development Goals. The outcome of the Paris Agreement (2015) suggested a strong shift towards realistic targets for ongoing emissions cuts, even if these targets are structured via national action plans and monitored by intended nationally determined contributions (INDCs). A major review of progress towards these targets was set for late 2018 and 2023, and thereafter every five years. A balanced, funded, and implemented vision of 'green' development may help developing states make further emission reductions and adapt to the loss and damage that will still be incurred owing to climate change impacts down through 2050.

With the hope of capping temperature rises above pre-industrial levels to within the 1.5–2.0°C range, and emissions targeted to peak circa 2030–2050, the Paris Agreement is a robust agenda, using joint mitigation and adaptation approaches to achieve long-term goals (Ingalls and Dwyer, 2016; Oberthur and Groen, 2017). Substantial progress has been made by the 197 parties involved in the UNFCCC, with 195 countries signing on to the Paris Agreement itself, and 184 countries ratifying it by January 2019. By 16 April 2016, some 190 Parties had submitted an INDC. Thereafter, Nationally Determined Contributions (NDCs) were to be submitted every five years, with 181 parties listed in the Interim NDC registry by January 2019, and a round of NDCs (new or updated) to be provided by 2020 (UNFCCC, 2019; Climate Analytics, 2018). Combined with progress on the SDGs and the Sendai Framework for Disaster Risk Reduction (SFDRR, a 2015–2030 framework), there seems to be a serious focus on building global resilience in the context of sustainable development, poverty eradication, and the capacity to cope with climate change and related-disaster impacts (UNISDR, 2015; Szabo et al., 2016).

However, the past track of environmental diplomacy suggests that serious problems lurk beneath the current consensus, and they risk derailing implementation of emissions reduction targets and a truly global push towards sustainability as outlined in the SDG frameworks (UN, 2013, 2015a, 2015b). The concept of sustainability has moved well beyond its initial definition from the 1980s Brundtland Commission as 'sustainable development is a process of change in which the exploitation of resources, the direction of investments, the orientation of technological development; and institutional change are all in harmony and enhance both current and future potential to meet human needs and aspirations' (Brundtland, 1987, chapter 2, section 1). The parameters of environmental and societal sustainability have come to include the key resources and services that the natural environment provides to maintain qualitatively high human living conditions: clean water and air, stable climate, maintenance of usable soil, sufficient biodiversity to sustain ecosystems, and the renewable resources needed for modern societies. Although no overarching agreement has been made on the exact borders to these parameters, one approach outlines a sustainability transition for the 21st century in which 'a stabilizing world population meets its needs and reduces hunger and poverty while maintaining the planet's life-support systems and living resources' (Kates and Parris, 2003, p. 8,062). The Yale University Environmental Sustainability project (running in different forms from 2005 to 2018) has outlined the complex linkages between environmental and societal sustainability, resulting in 20 indicators used in assessing national-level outcomes:

> Environmental sustainability is a fundamentally multidimensional concept. Some environmental challenges arise from development and industrialization – natural resource depletion (especially of nonrenewable resources), pollution, and ecosystem destruction. Other challenges are a function of underdevelopment and poverty-induced short-term thinking – resource depletion (especially of potentially renewable resources such as forests and water) and lack of investment in capacity and infrastructure committed to pollution control and ecosystem protection. (ESI, 2005, p. 1; see further EPI, 2016, 2018, 2020)

Sustainability thus emerges out of the needs of human societies and an estimation of the functional boundaries of ecosystems at local, national, regional, and global levels. These factors interact with human value-choices as to how far natural resources should be converted into human capital, how much environmental risk should be entertained even if scientific uncertainty exists as to the exact limits of such planetary boundaries, and how far human societies can adapt to biodiversity loss, climate change impacts, and destabilization of nitrogen cycles (Millennium Ecosystem Assessment, 2005; Schmidt, 2008; Eastwood, 2011; Keong, 2018).

Numerous estimates of climate change onset and likely damage to human societies and states have been developed (Morton, 2011; Viola *et al.*, 2012; Bowyer *et al.*, 2014; IPCC, 2014a), with an emerging sense that urgent preventive measures are needed to avoid wholescale and irreversible ecological damage. In one perhaps alarmist view:

> Research now demonstrates that the continued functioning of the Earth system as it has supported the well-being of human

civilization in recent centuries is at risk. Without urgent action, we could face threats to water, food, biodiversity and other critical resources: these threats risk intensifying economic, ecological and social crises, creating the potential for a humanitarian emergency on a global scale. (Brito and Stafford-Smith, 2012, p. 5)

This sense of urgency helped push forward the intense bargaining from 2009, leading to the Doha Amendment of 2012 to allow continuation of emissions cuts, including the Clean Development Mechanism and the International Emission Trading schemes, and looking towards a second global commitment period. In turn, the 2015 Paris Agreement included both developed and developing states in a collectively binding agreement that demonstrated a hybrid approach to achieving consensus across diverse state interests. The approach combined 'bottom up flexibility' to get broad participation and top-down rules to generate accountability and higher targets, using a non-adversarial and non-punitive approach to compliance and implementation (C2ES, 2015). In spite of this diplomatic success, concerns have been raised about the implementation of the Paris Agreement within an effective time frame, and the risk of trade-offs and hedging among complex interest groups and lobbies, operating at different global, national, and local levels (Ingalls and Dwyer, 2016). Furthermore, even full implementation of the current deal still seems to be 'insufficient for avoiding dangerous climate change', intensifying related debates as to how to manage climate risk and how to fund remediation and adaptation measures (Oberthur and Groen, 2017, p. 1; see further UNEP, 2016b). From this point of view, the Paris Agreement is a starting point for stronger collective action embracing a wider pattern of actors than the states that are the legal parties in the accord, as explored in the next section.

23.3 DIPLOMATIC SUCCESS, ENVIRONMENTAL FAILURE?

Behind the current climate change agreements stand decades of difficult and complex negotiations between the involved states, with extensive engagement by the IPCC, UN agencies, including the UNEP, UNDP, the United Nations Commission on Sustainable Development, the Economic and Social Commission for Asia and the Pacific (ESCAP), and the UNGA, along with numerous NGOs, scientific agencies, corporate lobby groups, and diverse civil society organizations (see e.g., UNESCAP, 2017a; UNDP, 2018). Dialogue behind the scenes helped lay down the perception that a renewed, inclusive climate change deal was possible, following on from the Kyoto Protocol, even if all was not smooth sailing. The Copenhagen meeting in 2009, for example, suffered from some overly high expectations of an early binding agreement, especially by

Australian Prime Minister Kevin Rudd, with sovereignty issues, national development priorities, and burden-sharing concerns limiting outcomes at that stage (Curran, 2011; IISS, 2010). Though the Copenhagen meeting did not adopt a new, legally binding accord, it did lay the basis for future important developments. The meeting generated some political consensus among major parties, including the United States, China, India, Brazil, and South Africa, but a formal adoption of the Accord was rejected. Sudan, Bolivia, Nicaragua, Cuba, and Venezuela were vigorously opposed to it, in part because of the closed nature of the great power diplomacy at play in some of the informal negotiations (Bodansky, 2010; UN, 2009). However, it made progress in accepting the principle of keeping target temperatures below a 2°C rise, with a preferred target of 1.5°C, supported the foundation of an expanded Green Climate Fund, and tried to balance mitigation and adaptation issues, including funding and technology factors (Massai 2010; Keong, 2018).[1]

Beyond the foundational scientific assessments and reporting of the Intergovernmental Panel on Climate Change, several political coalitions have had a major impact on recent climate change negotiations. Key coalitions, alongside the pivotal roles of Japan and the European Union, have shaped negotiations for two decades. These include the G77 group of developing countries (now with 134 members), the Least Developed Country Group (48 states), the Alliance of Small Island States (AOSIS), the Small Island Developing States group (SIDS),[2] the Independent Association of Latin America and the Caribbean (AILAC), plus the BASIC 'coalition' of Brazil, South Africa, India, and China (IISS, 2010; Eastwood, 2011; Baptiste and Rhiney, 2016; Edwards *et al.*, 2017). Further groupings include the 'Africa group', keen to keep the 2°C limit intact and support adaptation capacities; the Like Minded Developing Countries (LMDC) group, which supported differentiation between developed and developing countries; and the mixed 'Umbrella group', arguing that post-Kyoto emission targets should be 'fairly' distributed in relation to actual emission levels (Audet, 2013). The small island states focused on the need to push ambitious targets to below the 1.5°C rise, enhancing the transfer of technology to aid resilience, and the effort to create a third pillar of climate action to address loss and damage beyond mitigation and adaptation frameworks (Calliari, 2018). Fiji also provided strong leadership for the cooperative 'Pacific Way', developed through 2017–2018 as the Talanoa Dialogue (see further Section 4), as well as supporting the Ocean Pathway

Partnership and new health initiatives for Small Island Developing States (UNFCCC, 2017; Winkler and Depledge, 2018). Developing countries focused on differentiated responsibilities and climate finance for adaptation, while the BASIC group wanted self-monitored national reduction plans that were compatible with existing national development strategies, combined with funding and technological support for developing nations (Gupta and Chaudhary, 2014; Jarju, 2016; Oberthur and Groen, 2017). In the long term, AOSIS, the G77 and China, including a number of African and Latin American states (the ALBA group and the Bolivarian Alliance for the People of Our America), strategically focused on compensation mechanisms, based on the advantages and responsibilities that had accrued to earlier industrialized states as major polluters. Though specific liabilities were rejected by developed states, including the EU as a whole, Norway, and the United States, this 'ecological justice' argument may have helped the push for the more ambitious target of less than a 1.5°C rise (Calliari, 2018).

Thereafter, debates within the EU itself (including the European Council, the European Commission, and the European External Action Service and its Green Diplomacy Network), the G7, the G20, the Major Economies Forum on Energy and Climate, and thematic sessions of the United Nation General Assembly in 2014 and 2015 provided the ground work for a successful round in Paris through late 2015 (Oberthur and Groen, 2017). Likewise, bilateral dialogues through 2015 between China and the United States, France and China, Germany and Brazil, plus investments in solar energy offered to India by Germany and France, helped smooth the way for the Paris negotiations (Oberthur and Groen, 2017). The EU overall helped facilitate a grand coalition of advanced and developing economies:

> A crucial part of the EU's efforts focused on coalition-building, especially with progressive developing countries. These efforts had important roots in the Cartagena Dialogue for Progressive Action set up under the lead of the United Kingdom (UK) and Australia in 2010 as a nucleus of a broader coalition with ambitious developing countries, including progressive Latin American and Caribbean countries, small island states and least developed countries. The Cartagena Dialogue helped pave the way to the Durban coalition that, under the lead of the EU, secured the mandate for the Paris Agreement. ... It was essentially revived in the course of 2015: Spearheaded by the Marshall Islands and the EU, intensifying efforts throughout 2015 culminated in the creation of the 'high ambition coalition' during the second week of the Paris conference. This coalition between the EU and many smaller developing countries quickly grew to include the US, other developed countries and eventually also Brazil. (Oberthur and Groen, 2017, p. 13)

Beyond these actors, a large number of environmental NGOs, CSOs (civil society organizations), information portals, and

---

[1] I am grateful for the advice of the reviewers for a more balanced approach towards the Copenhagen climate negotiations of 2009.

[2] SIDS and AOSIS have overlapping memberships, with SIDS comprising the bulk of the AOSIS, a slightly larger group of small island and low-lying coastal countries that has been active in climate change negotiations (GIZ, 2017).

action and lobby groups have been involved in providing scientific studies and technical support, developing position papers and submissions, enhancing public awareness and, to some degree, monitoring compliance, and endorsing forward-thinking positions (Raustiala, 1997; Kanie *et al.*, 2013; Calliari, 2018). Groups such as the Natural Resource Defence Council (NRDC), the Climate Action Network, Greenpeace, Global Witness, and others have published extensive documents monitoring these issues, alongside the information networks created by OneWorld Net, the International Institute for Sustainable Development, SustainAbility, the Global Development Network, ActionAid, Care, the WWF, Oxfam, and hundreds of smaller organizations. These groups, along with media representatives, though non-voting observers at the UNFCCC Conference of Parties, still have important consultative roles and have been mobilized as part of the multi-stakeholder pathway towards a low-emissions future (Bäckstrand *et al.*, 2017). This input, though not always rigorous, was very important for developing and small island states, giving them greater credibility and weight during informal sessions and in the public arena.

Indeed, although there were some closed sessions at the Paris talks, the EU and France were keen to build inclusive trust via numerous open and break-out sessions to cope with the huge range of issues that were canvassed (Oberthur and Groen, 2017). In general, the non-state actors provided essential functions in providing the shared, deep, and open information networks required for a sustainable international regime, shaping opinion and policy consensus alongside the scientific input from the IPCC and other agencies (Haas, 2014). At the 2015 Paris meeting, of the 28,000 accredited participants, some 8,000 were non-state observers, who have been increasingly shaping a 'hybrid' multilateralism, and engaging in 'monitoring of national action and experimentation with local, regional and transnational mitigation and adaptation strategies' (Bäckstrand *et al.*, 2017, p. 562). Rational convergence of policies by the main state stakeholders required a receptive public and informed media, creating a persuasive public diplomacy that provided state leaders room for give-and-take on sensitive areas that impacted on domestic energy policies, economic growth, jobs, and trade.

Nonetheless, the Paris Agreement left many areas framed rather generally, including issues of adaptation and climate change damage funding, while seeking to draw in private sector and other non-state actors (Oberthur and Groen, 2017). The UNFCCC envisioned numerous actors engaging in emission and adaptation strategies, including cities and city networks (such as the C40 Cities Climate Leadership Group), subnational states, companies, and investors in clean technologies (UNFCCC, 2015c). Likewise, recent climate change diplomacy seeks to engage different societal and institutional agencies, including 7,000 cities (generating 32% of global GDP),

subnational states and regions (GDP of circa US$12.5 trillion), more than 5,000 companies from 90 countries (revenue of US$38 trillion) and 500 investors with assets worth more than US$25 trillion (UNFCCC, 2015c). Therefore, public-private coalitions are seen as major drivers of clean technologies and urban reform that make national targets achievable, as well as providing investment and strategies that make a global 'sustainability shift' possible (C2ES, 2015). The C40 Cities Climate Leadership group from 2005, which has been active in reducing their own emissions via efficient technologies and transfer of 'best practices', has been reporting and lobbying at the UNFCCC from 2009 onwards, and has sought to work ahead of national emissions targets (Steffen, 2012; Muggah, 2013; Curtis, 2015). Indeed, in the view of the C40 group, cities (among other 'non-party stakeholders') are now leading actors in the delivery of the post-Paris agenda and will be crucial in preparing a 'decarbonization' path from 2018 onwards, with its frameworks providing opportunities for energy sector and emission reform (C40, 2016; Li *et al.*, 2017). Indeed, individual US states, cities, businesses, and citizens have created their own action networks (We Are Still In and the US Climate Action Centre) through 2017–2020 to generate bottom-up carbon emission pledges regardless of Trump administration policies.

On a parallel track, the Rio + 20 Conference set the stage for a new round of negotiations on sustainability from 2012 onwards, drawing in governments, IGOs, NGOs, local groups, businesses, and policy networks, with 50,000 representatives attending the conference (Chivers, 2012). This interacted with the phase of intense negotiations for new goals to follow on from the Millennium Development Goals that had been run through 2000–2015. The SDGs themselves were negotiated through a high-level 27-member panel consulting with 5,000 civil society groups, followed by an extended consultation process with 83 national groups. The major report was debated from 2013 and evolved through extensive deliberations of the Open Working Group, leading to the synthesis report of 2014, with the SDGs being formally adopted from September 2015 via the UN General Assembly (UN Secretary-General, 2014; UNGA, 2015). Data collection, monitoring, and implementation require large-scale input from a wide range of stakeholders, including NGOs, CSOs, the private sector, and regional commissions, alongside national reporting (Leadership Group, 2015). The sustainable development goals explicitly seek to protect and promote sustainable use of both the oceans and terrestrial ecosystems (Goals 14 and 15) and acknowledge the crucial need to 'combat climate change and its impacts' in SDG Goal 13, but they do not explicitly prioritize these goals, viewing them as 'integrated and indivisible' for achieving economic, social, and environmental sustainability (UNGA, 2015, pp. 1, 3, 23–25, 32; see also UNEP, 2016a). Climate change itself is to be defined by the UNFCCC track, while practical implementation will be run in conjunction with national priorities and policies (UN Secretary-General, 2014; Szabo *et al.*, 2016; UNEP, 2016a).

The UN mobilization of these goals has begun to address their cross-impact under conditions of competitive financing, with path-dependent outcomes across different sub-targets being explored in annual reports. Indeed, one of the concerns of the UN Synthesis Report of 2014 was the emphasis on optimizing all finance streams towards sustainable development, with an emphasis on positive outcomes for the 'poorest and most vulnerable', followed by the need 'for coherence and alignment with climate finance' (UN Secretary General 2014, paragraphs 87 and 90). Though laudable in providing a comprehensive and inclusive set of development goals, tensions remain across the different aspects of what is being 'sustained'. Indeed, a 'deep ecology' approach might view the SDGs as a compromise framework subsuming environmental goals within a human-needs approach that parallels the national development plans of the BASIC group (Brazil, South Africa, India, and China) and poorer developing states (Ferguson and Dellios, 2018). From this point of view, the SDGs would represent a development-based policy-capture of environmental goals. However, the likely answer to this is to ensure that 'environmental sustainability is fully integrated within global, regional and national SDG implementation', which remained a pressing task for the 2018 and 2019 UN High Levels Political Forums (Kettunen *et al.*, 2018, p. 12).

Indeed, the alignment of sustainable development goals, climate change targets, and disaster risk reduction efforts has become a complex multilevel scientific and diplomatic problem (Szabo *et al.*, 2016). This alignment is necessary but remains a work in progress, as has been recognized by the UNEP:

> [S]elected SDGs and associated targets are aligned, while others potentially conflict with the climate change mitigation objectives of the Paris Agreement. For SDGs that are path-contingent, there is often general or even specific knowledge of the 'dos' and 'don'ts' of particular policies and practices that can help to minimize trade-offs and maximize synergies between different interests. Previous United Nations Environment (UNEP) Emissions Gap Reports have discussed such best practices for a number of key sectors and issues including agriculture, buildings, energy, forestry, and transport.
>
> The need for an integrated approach to the sustainable development and the realization of the SDGs is nowhere more relevant than in the context of climate change. The potential to meet the long-term temperature objective of the Paris Agreement rests within the framework that the SDGs provide. Equally, the potential to achieve the SDGs rests with our ability to address the climate change mitigation challenge. (UNEP, 2016a, p. 47)

Several crucial decision points need to be traversed before these positive trends can be viewed as irreversible. One major 'crossing point' has been the achievement of the threshold ratification level for the Paris Agreement to come into force, requiring 55 countries accounting for 55% of global emissions. This was achieved on 5 October 2016, though ratifications were at first slow to accumulate, with the Paris Agreement coming into legal force 30 days thereafter on 4 November 2016, with a stronger pattern of ratifications through 2017 (UN, 2019). However, through 2016–2017, the received national pledges remained insufficient to reach the main environmental outcomes: temperatures rises might still rise towards a 3.2°C global increase by 2100 with a likely overshoot above even the least-costly 2°C scenario based on UNFCCC and UNEP reports (UNFCCC, 2016; UNEP, 2017a, 2017b). The 2017 UNEP *Emissions Gap Report* noted that urgent action by states and non-state actors is needed to close the emission gap before 2030, or else it will be unlikely that the goal of keeping global warming well below 2°C can be achieved (UNEP, 2017b).

In turn, continued climate change impacts may undermine the ability to meet many SDGs by 2030, with up to an extra 100 million people living in extreme poverty because of ongoing climate impact on natural and human systems (UNEP, 2016a). Furthermore, even the existing targets have been viewed as still allowing for sufficient temperature rise to harm vulnerable environments (Oberthur and Groen, 2017, p. 15). These factors mean that sustaining and implementing the Paris Agreement and the SDGs rests on a continuing political consensus that has limited resilience in terms of political good-will and 'reserves' in terms of the precautionary principle. The actual impact of even a 1.5–2.0°C rise for vulnerable communities could still be considerable, with these targets chosen as acceptable policy compromises, rather than comprehensive scientific certainty that they would avoid all dangerous outcomes.[3] These agreements rely on complex bargaining and sustained political commitment over the next decade. We can see this by briefly addressing lessons from the historical track of environmental diplomacy.

The logic of necessary consensus, ongoing negotiation, differentiation of targets, and moral responsibility creates a climate of collective bargaining and hedging in which the decision of certain states or groups can become decisive in ways that lead to unexpected or irrational outcomes. This means that individual states and even small coalitions can have a big impact on the negotiation process. For the Kyoto Protocol of 1997, Japan was one of the key states which pushed the agreement forward, in spite of last-minute wrangling over emission targets by countries such as Australia. For the period 2011–2015 the EU, including France and Germany, performed as a forward-thinking

---

[3] I am grateful to Professor Pak Sum Low's reminder of the need for caution on erroneous scientific 'assumptions' surrounding the 2°C figure (Low, 2018).

collective, operating very much in the role of a climate change middle power, acting as a flexible promoter of an acceptable set of targets, being both a leader and negotiator on contentious issues (Oberthur and Groen, 2017). Likewise, as we have seen, the input of small island states as the 'first affected, least responsible' helped create a wider coalition of interests with the G77 and the BASIC group, shaping dialogue on temperature-rise targets and the way consensus national commitments would be augmented, a trend continuing with Fiji's support of the 2018 Talanoa Dialogue.

The other reality of negotiations is that they are highly asymmetric across several domains, for example, the relative impact and vulnerability to climate change across different states, the ability to fund mitigation and adaptation strategies, and differing political influence on regional and global-level policies (Calliari, 2018). Indeed, some states might be viewed as 'climate change superpowers' because of their high emissions, economic and technological ability to reduce these levels, and related diplomatic influence. They are therefore de facto veto holders that could undermine strong emission targets globally in their own right, as well as potential leaders for defections by other states (Schreurs, 2012; Viola *et al.*, 2012). China, the United States, and to a lesser degree India, Russia, and the EU (which has already seriously reduced emissions) could currently be viewed as climate change superpowers, though not necessarily 'veto-holders'. Therefore, the US failure to ratify the Kyoto Protocol led to a slowing of implementation, necessitating Ukrainian and Russian ratification for the treaty to come into effect. Likewise, major developing states, including China, Brazil, and India, became essential ingredients in any shaping of a realistic climate change deal through 2009–2015. In this sense, climate change politics is very much a multipolar affair, with China and the United States emerging as divergent geopolitical hubs, alongside the wider collections listed earlier (Oberthur and Groen, 2017).

Through 2016–2018, with the election of Donald Trump as president, the United States withdrew from the Paris Agreement, meanwhile drawing up its own agenda embracing shale oil, coal, and 'environmental stewardship' under rubrics such as the 'America First' energy plan. Initial fears had been that the US absence would undermine the Paris Agreement as a whole. In reality, the United States was unlikely to meet its prior 2025 target of a 26–28% emissions reduction (compared to 2005), whether inside or outside the agreement, with a more likely reduction of only 11–13% given current policies, though there had been some increased use of renewable power sources through 2017 (IEA, 2018). Moreover, the United States may suffer considerable loss of prestige and reduced gains in the renewable energy sector, with an estimated US$8 trillion in these markets over the next 25 years (Bodnar, 2017). However,

the US withdrawal has not legally ended the Paris Agreement and will not destroy its environmental practicality. With circa 15% of global emissions in 2012, and 15.99% in 2016, the United States was an important but not an essential contributor to legal ratification of the Paris Agreement (Oberthur and Groen, 2017). Lack of US engagement, however, could lead to a rethink on national targets among other major emitters, especially developing states with an emphasis on climate justice issues, or lessen the resolve of states with high levels of domestic cynicism or resistance to climate change requirements, for example, Russia or Australia. Therefore, it has been suggested that the Paris Agreement will need to be made 'drop-out-proof' or find ways to deal with a reluctant United States (Kemp, 2017). In reality, reinforcement of commitments by many parties to make the agreement work has kept the negotiations alive, with strong leadership being shown by China, the BASIC group, the EU, and island states over the last five years. The BASIC group Ministerial Meeting in May 2018 stressed that the global effort against climate change was an 'irreversible process' and promised support for the Work Programme to operationalize all provisions of the Paris Agreement in a balanced manner, as reported by the Ministry of Ecology and Environment, People's Republic of China (MEE, 2018).

Implementation of the emission cuts mandated via the Paris Agreement poses real economic and technical challenges for many states. Even Japan, as one of the main supporters for early action on environmental and climate change issues, will find transition to a lower emission economy a challenge. As part of its commitments at the Paris talks, Japan would seek to reduce emissions by 26% over 2013 levels (Timperley, 2018), thereby requiring an increase in renewable power generation, but also needing to have a baseline electrical grid using safe nuclear power plants (a controversial issue given the Fukushima disaster on 11 March 2011). Therefore, the targeted reduction of coal usage, as outlined in its Energy Mix 2030 goals, became increasingly problematic for the period 2015–2023, since the addition of new coal-fired plants was not stopped until March 2019 (Koppenborg, 2017; Nicholas and Buckley, 2019). Likewise, reforms under the Trump administration have reversed much of Obama's Clean Power Plan and re-opened public lands for potential coal leasing, while countries such as Indonesia, India, and Australia remain heavily reliant on coal plants for much of their energy mix (Bodnar, 2017). Australia, for example, plans to expand coal exports to India, with new coal mines in central Queensland being considered in spite of environmental concerns (Rosewarne, 2016). These factors mean that non-state contributions to emission cuts, the adoption of clean and resilient technologies, effective carbon markets, and 'green accounting' will be increasingly important for achieving global climate change and the Sustainable Development Goals.

23.4 ADAPTATION STRATEGIES IN THE CONTEXT OF PERCEIVED RISK

Current estimates already suggest a direct overshoot above the suggested 1.5°C target, and serious problems in even meeting the higher 2.0°C limit within existing frameworks (see Section 23.3). The 2017 *Emissions Gap Report* suggests that, even if fully implemented, current Nationally Determined Contributions could still lead to an increase of temperatures by 3.0–3.2°C through 2100 (UNEP, 2017b). This would be viewed as disastrous by key groups, including AOSIS, SIDS, and members of the G77. Even a moderate onset of climate change effects might involve serious challenges for developing states and small islands because of sea-level rises, increased storms, hurricanes, cyclones, extended droughts or floods, and damage to existing infrastructure (see IPCC, 2014a and UNESCAP, 2017b, which list such problems and related adaptation strategies). Beyond this, a number of poorer, developing states would have increased social risk and state vulnerability, suffering much greater environmental damage than they can adapt to or manage nationally. Countries as diverse as Bangladesh, Bolivia, Ghana, Gambia, and the Philippines see expected climate change as passing their capacity to adapt, thereby undermining national development gains, reducing Human Development Index (HDI) indicators, increasing poverty, and creating serious problems in human security (Mead, 2015; Calliari, 2018).

Beyond this, 'climate change hotspots' have been identified as areas likely to be highly impacted by climate change and having vulnerable communities, often compounded by cross-border and transnational challenges, for example, river deltas, basins, and arid regions in Africa and Asia, as well as river systems dependent on Himalayan glaciers (ICA, 2012; Szabo *et al.*, 2016). Here regional responses by groups such as the South Asian Association for Regional Cooperation (SAARC), the Association of Southeast Asian Nations (ASEAN), the Mekong River Commission, and the Caribbean Community (CARICOM) are useful, alongside national and global-level monitoring (Szabo *et al.*, 2016; Sembiring, 2018). The need for regional monitoring and cooperation can be seen in the Caribbean, where any significant rise of sea level, for example, of one metre, would increase storm damage and risk coastal infrastructure, requiring many islands to spend significa-tion portions of their GDP to adapt (ECLAC, 2018; Pulwarty *et al.*, 2010). The rationale of a regional response led to the creation of the Caribbean Community Climate Change Centre, which since 2005 has been a central clearing house on these issues, cooperating with both the UNFCCC process as well as the UNEP (UNEP, 2010).

These trends indicate that vulnerable and poorer countries need to seriously increase appropriate adaptation strategies,

however these are financed.[4] Developing countries are seen as most vulnerable, because of cross impacts on food security, clean water, infrastructure, and provision of services that are already underfunded. The Water-Food-Energy nexus is crucial for sustaining development but also highly vulnerable via flow-on effects of drought on food costs, reduction in hydro-power resources, and costs to already strained national budgets (Mazo, 2010; WEF, 2014). Annual adaptation costs for developing countries are now estimated to be higher than thought in earlier years, with the UNEP suggesting that global annual adaptation costs could be 'between US$280 billion and US$500 billion by 2050' (UNEP, 2017a, p. 18). In general terms, there are increasing gaps in estimated adaptation funding for 2016, 2030, and 2050. Likewise, the increased investment needed to sustain the SDGs in less developed countries could become a political hurdle in coming years. Investment costs to meet the SDGs in developing countries could be in the range of US$3.3–4.5 trillion annually, with on average a shortfall of US$2.5 trillion estimated through 2015–2030 (UNCTAD, 2017, p. 12; UNDP, 2017, p. 57). Other estimates are even higher, with the IEA suggesting that the energy sector alone might require US$3.5 trillion invested annually down to 2050, about twice current levels, to meet the climate change target of less than 2°C rise (IEA, 2017).

The SDGs contain a logic pretexted on a linked environmental and developmental sustainability; that is, they mobilize notions of inter-generational and intra-generational justice. Therefore, alongside preservation of ecosystem sustainability, there is an emphasis on ending poverty, maintaining multiscale agriculture systems and food security, improving the health of the entire population, having inclusive economic growth with reduced inequality, and creating sustainable cities. Several of the SDGs do focus primarily on environmental issues, including management of water and sanitation (no. 6), taking urgent action on climate change (no. 13), conservation and sustainable use of oceans and maritime resources (no. 14), plus protecting and restoring ecosystems (no. 15). Overall, however, the conservation of the environment is linked to sustainable human use of these ecosystems, ensuring their availability 'for all' and their sustainable management. This is a realistic political outcome, making environmental targets align with developmental agendas (UNEP, 2016a). Such linkages make the current gaps in mandatory compensation and damage-funding more palatable for developing countries, while not imposing forced fund transfers from developed states. In environmental sustainability terms, this might be viewed as a 'low sustainability agenda' focused

---

[4] For the dangers of maladaptation based on poor planning responses to climate change, see Magnan *et al.* (2016).

on ecologically minimal boundaries, rather than maximizing protection of habitats and ecosystems globally. As such, transition into a low-emission global economy remains largely voluntary, thereby increasing the level of adaptation needed by developing states in the medium term. Another problem with this human-centred agenda is that future failures in funding and implementing emission strategies could again defer emission cuts and extend the period of rising temperatures, dropping environmental outcomes from low-sustainability towards severe ecological damage in more vulnerable local and regional cases. This is particularly problematic for low-lying island communities in the Pacific, the Indian Ocean, and the Caribbean, for at least five major river basins in Africa and Asia, and for the African Sahel as a whole, leading to a potential failure of related human sociopolitical systems and adding millions of 'climate refugees' to existing UN burdens (ICA, 2012; for critical debates on this terminology, see Berchin *et al.*, 2017; Hingley, 2017; for New Zealand's adoption of a humanitarian visa for climate refugees, see Hall, 2017).

Regional risk mechanisms have begun to fill this gap but still need extensive external support: for example, the Caribbean Catastrophe Risk Insurance Facility received some initial funding from the World Bank, EU, UK, and France, as well as annual premiums from member states and general support from the African, Caribbean and Pacific Group of States Natural Disaster Risk Reduction Programme (Pulwarty *et al.*, 2010). ASEAN, after a long history of environmental diplomacy and monitoring, through 2015–2018 begun to implement the early stages of its Southeast Asia Disaster Risk Insurance Facility (SEADRIF), working with the ASEAN + 3 group (Japan, China, and South Korea) to provide resilience against natural disasters, which are likely to be exacerbated by climate change (World Bank, 2017; see further Thirawat *et al.*, 2016).

However, loss and damage (L&D) issues beyond adaptation frameworks have only been partly integrated into current agreements, with ongoing development of a five-year plan based on the Warsaw International Mechanism (WIM). This was created in 2013 with the aim of information-gathering to facilitate early warning mechanisms, risk assessments, and insurance systems. Ongoing submissions have been made on this process from 2017 by groups such as CARE and the United Nations University's Institute for Environment and Human Security, with protracted debate continuing in the G77. The limited place for this agenda can be seen in the cautious phrasing of Decision 2 of COP 19 in 2013, where a formulation was added 'acknowledging that loss and damage associated with the adverse effects of climate change includes, and in some cases involves more than, that which can be reduced by adaptation' (Calliari, 2018, p. 736; see further UNFCCC, 2014). The Paris Agreement provided direct mention of 'the importance of averting, minimizing

and addressing loss and damage associated with the adverse effects of climate change' (UN, 2015b, Article 8), but also noted that 'Article 8 of the Agreement does not involve or provide a basis for any liability or compensation' (UN, 2015b, paragraph 52). This was probably part of a wider diplomatic bargain:

> In this perspective, the compromise reached on Article 8 of the Paris Agreement might be more fragile than it seems. Paragraph 52 of the accompanying decision states that the article should not 'involve or provide a basis for any liability or compensation' claims. This formulation was the result of the diplomatic work carried out behind the scenes by the US and the small island representatives, in which the latter probably gave up the possibility of a legal remedy in order to have the 1.5°C temperature goal placed in the text. President Obama's pledge of a contribution of USD 30 million to climate risk insurance schemes in the Pacific, Central America and Africa might also have contributed to paving the way for a compromise. The solution, however, was not supported by developing countries as a whole and indeed marked a division among them with respect to the way L&D should be advanced in climate talks. (Calliari, 2018, pp. 740–741, discussing UN, 2015b)

An initial Work Plan on the WIM has explored several action areas, with the Executive Committee then creating a five-year work plan, but did not lead to strong agreement on how to fund these issues. Indeed, this process has been criticized since it 'focuses on voluntary contributions to insurance schemes … lacks attention to instruments which would apply to slow-onset events and/or non-economic loss and damage' and does not provide a 'dedicated and adequate flow of finance to address loss and damage' (Gewirtzman *et al.*, 2018, p. 1,078).

We can see then that trends since 2013 certainly indicate the intensified global awareness of the need to collectively manage climate change impacts and related sustainable development issues. Ongoing meetings through 2017–2018 indicate the rapidly evolving efforts to effectively publicize, monitor, and implement the Paris Agreement. The climate change talks (COP 23) held at Bonn in November 2017 (but hosted under the presidency of Fiji) reiterated the urgent need to get on track both in implementing the Paris Agreement and in achieving the 2030 Agenda for SDGs, including coordinated actions from many actors including government, investment groups, cities, business groups, and civil society (UNFCCC, 2017). At that meeting, Fiji introduced the idea of shared stories as a means of finding constructive common solutions, leading to the Talanoa Dialogue, which will feed into the political processes of COP 24, including improved input on gender and indigenous issues (Winkler and Depledge, 2018; UNFCCC, 2018). The April–May 2018 inter-sessional climate talks in Bonn discussed ways to carry forward the Paris Agreement Work Programme, including work on sustainable agriculture and food security in the context of climate change and adaptation needs, supporting the hoped-for roadmap on these issues (the Koronivia Joint Work on Agriculture). The 2018 Bonn Conference also hoped to boost education and public awareness on these issues via the Action Plan for Climate Empowerment (UNFCCC, 2018).

However, serious problems remain in implementing these complex and technical 'grand bargains' and in avoiding possible trade-offs in their overlapping agendas. This was seen in the Bonn COP 23, where once again disputes between developed and developing countries emerged over the limited level of climate of finance and low levels of actual Adaptation Fund expenditure, along with the debate on differentiated emissions targets:

> The issue of differentiation continued to be raised strongly, with the Like-Minded Developing Countries (including China) and the Arab Group arguing for a two-part structuring of commitments – between developed and developing countries – that others considered unacceptably 'bifurcated'. With a strong push for bifurcation in mitigation, virtually no technical work was possible. Finding a more nuanced approach to differentiation had been central in the run up to Paris and shaped both the overall framing of the Agreement, and specific provisions. It seems, however, that simply moving beyond the Annex I and non-Annex I categories has not resolved all the underlying tensions over the differentiation of commitments between countries and groups. (Winkler and Depledge, 2018, p. 141)

These tensions have also returned in the debate over providing a total of US$100 billion per annum for climate funds by 2020, with concerns over how these funds may be managed and accessed. As noted by the BASIC group of ministers in May 2018:

> Ministers reiterated their deepest concern over attempts by some developed countries to unilaterally apply new eligibility criteria for developing countries' access to funding under the Global Environment Facility (GEF) and the Green Climate Fund (GCF). They recalled that such criteria are not compatible with guidance from the Conference of the Parties and are a departure from the letter and the spirit of the Convention and its Paris Agreement. Furthermore, they indicated that such attempts violate the terms of the Instrument for the Establishment of the Restructured Global Environment Facility, as well as the Governing Instrument of the Green Climate Fund, falling outside the mandate of the GEF Council and of the GCF Board on eligibility criteria. They stressed the view that such attempts are tantamount to renegotiating the Paris Agreement and potentially undermine the level of ambition of developing countries in the global effort against climate change. Furthermore, Ministers noted with concern the lack of adequacy of financial resources provided by developed countries to the GCF and GEF to assist developing countries in their climate actions. (MEE, 2018, Section 17)

The UNFCCC process and the 2030 Agenda for Sustainable Development have been led by the UN and the continued dialogue between state parties, but have increasingly drawn on a wide range of actors and interest groups to gain the momentum for a shift in global thinking that has made these agreements possible, given domestic economic pressures and divergent political interests. This constructive pluralism, however, still needs strong leadership to ensure effective funding and implementation, a crucial process on the road down to 2030.

23.5 PROSPECTS: EVOLVING BEYOND ENVIRONMENTAL PLURALISM

This analysis may seem pessimistic in that it suggests a diplomatic process easily derailed by the interests of a number of climate 'superpowers' and bargaining coalitions, with the agreements aimed at consensus diplomatic targets rather than ecologically crucial boundaries, and thereby subject to complex trade-offs between mitigation, adaptation, and national developmental strategies. However, several sets of overlapping interests may help drive these initiatives forward.

Complex interdependence between states in the global economy suggests that it is extremely difficult for developed states to insulate themselves from disasters in the developing world, which provides new export markets, sources for energy and mineral resources, and destinations for investment. Furthermore, climate change effects are transboundary, transnational, and differential in impact, generating non-traditional security concerns, including environmental refugees, disruption of global food security, damage to transport and infrastructure networks, and intensified natural disasters. As such, the dangers of withdrawal from mitigation and adaptation strategies are high for all parties, and few states would be certain to gain by complete withdrawal from current agreements (Oberthur and Groen, 2017). Even Russia, among the most climate-sceptic of states, saw benefits in joining the Kyoto Protocol though it did not submit a quantitative emission limitation for the second commitment period of 2008–2012 (UNFCCC, 2012). Russia may find it relatively easy to meet its planned domestic emissions target of a reduction of 25–30% by 2030 (below the high Soviet-era 1990 levels), given recent slowing of national GDP growth, though the country delayed actual ratification of the Paris Agreement until October 2019 (Korppoo and Kokorin, 2017; CAIT, 2018). Indeed, growing awareness of the 'new climate economy' has begun to change the Russian obsession with nuclear power and hydrocarbons, leading to the first modest targets for renewable energy sources, especially wind-power options (Oberthur and Groen, 2017; IRENA, 2017).

The growing investment in renewable energy, most notable in China over the last decade, has been increasingly followed by India and Southeast Asian countries. At the global level, public and private investment in renewables of US$2.9 trillion through 2004–2017 has outstripped investment in fossil fuels in recent years, partly offset by lower costs for solar and wind power units (FS-UNEP, 2018, p. 11). In spite of extended dependence on coal for several countries, the shift towards 'green' technologies and related profits offers a focus for commercial development that has helped shape progressive government policies in the European Union, Southeast Asia, China (the largest investor in renewable energy from 2012), India, Chile, the Pacific Islands, the Caribbean islands, and California, easing transition towards more sustainable energy policies (CCCCC, 2012; Vidaurri, 2015; Henderson and Joffe, 2016). Indeed, 'widespread adoption of renewables' has been seen as one of the main low-cost pathways towards capping temperature rises at 1.5°C through the 2030–2100 period (UNEP, 2016a).

Beyond state-actors as the main parties to these international accords, there has been a sustained momentum by other communities of interest, including corporations, investors, cities, sub-state governments, and a wide range of NGOs and CSOs, with public-private collaborations as a major transition strategy (see Section 23.3). Therefore, local government financing and ready commercial bank loans for emerging energy 'majors' such as Suntech and the China Longyuan Power have been important, alongside widespread public demands for a cleaner environment in China (Zeng *et al.*, 2014). Globally, public-private coalitions, along with the C40 Cities, the Compact of Mayors, CDP (the Carbon Disclosure Project) and its 'We Mean Business' campaign, are also active in this area. The Non-State Actor Zone for Climate Action (NAZCA) by 2015 had already mobilized '11,000 commitments from 2,250 cities, 150 regions, 2,025 companies, 424 investors, and 235 civil society organizations' (C2ES, 2015). Although the future emission-reduction contributions by such groups are hard to assess, the UNEP suggests that they will make a major contribution to meeting global targets, given current trends (UNEP, 2016a). This was strengthened at the COP 23 meeting in Bonn (November 2017), with the Bonn-Fiji Commitment of Local and Regional Leaders to Deliver the Paris Agreement at All Levels, engaging 1,019 local and regional governments from some 86 countries. They committed themselves to raising climate action initiatives, with emission reduction targets being added to the carbon Climate Registry, as well as urging their states to conclude the Paris Implementation Guidelines by 2018 (CARO, 2017).

This 'environmental pluralism' is part of the wider shift towards ecological and developmental sustainability in the 21st century (see Kanie *et al.*, 2013; Rooji *et al.*, 2016). If a full understanding of the interactive components of this sustainability transition has yet to be modelled, it is not surprising that a truly comprehensive implementation agenda is still evolving. Current trends suggest that a pluralist, multi-actor approach, operating diplomatically as 'hybrid multilateralism', will continue to emerge, refining both climate change knowledge sets

and sustainable development mechanisms over the next decade (Bäckstrand *et al.*, 2017). This requires continued expansion of climate adaptation, risk and damage assessments, and related funding mechanisms beyond existing agreements. The details of the Paris Agreement Work Programme and the Paris Agreement Implementation Guidelines, as well as questions over funding mechanisms for developing countries, mean that further negotiations will be needed on these issues. Divisions remain between states such as China and India, who had supported differentiation in the NDC rules and guidance for developing states, versus the earlier positions of EU and Japan, arguing for a single approach with clearly quantifiable commitments (Evan and Timperley, 2018). Here it can only be hoped that a convergent framework can be hammered out, possibly by revived cooperation among leading European states and China. Signs of this began to emerge in mid-July 2018 at the China-EU Summit in Beijing, where both sides confirmed a strong commitment to the Paris Agreement, to moving forward with the Paris Agreement Work Programme, to supporting clean energy transitions, and to implementing the 2030 Agenda for Sustainable Development (EC, 2018). The leaders' statement after this meeting contained strong support for the US$100 billion annual fund, providing assistance to developing countries for mitigation and adaptation (EC, 2018, section 10). Depending on the economic impact of the COVID-19 pandemic, this may yet form a new round of inter-state leadership, shaping the more diffuse multi-actor support for the fundamental principles of the Paris Agreement and the wider 2030 Agenda for Sustainable Development.

ACKNOWLEDGEMENTS

I would like to thank the three reviewers (Dr Rezaul Karim, Professor Shelley Burgin, and 'anonymous') for their critical and constructive advice, which has greatly improved this chapter from its original form.

REFERENCES

Audet, R. (2013) Climate justice and bargaining coalitions: a discourse analysis. *International Environmental Agreements: Politics, Law and Economics*, **13**, 369–396. DOI: 10.1007/s10784-012-9195-9.

Bäckstrand, K., Kuyper, J., Linnér, B. and Lövbrand, E. (2017) Non-state actors in global climate governance: from Copenhagen to Paris and beyond. *Environmental Politics*, **26**(4), 561–579. https://doi.org/10.1080/09644016.2017.1327485

Baptiste, A. and Rhiney, K. (2016) Climate justice and the Caribbean: an introduction. *Geoform*, **73**, 17–21.

Berchin, I, Valduga, I., Garcia, J. and de Andrade Guerra, J. (2017) Climate change and forced migrations: an effort towards recognizing climate refugees. *Geoforum*, **84**, 147–150. DOI: 10.1016/j.geoforum.2017.06.022. https://www.asil.org/insights/volume/14/issue/3/copenhagen-climate-change-accord

Bodansky, D. (2010) The Copenhagen Climate Change Accord. *Insights* (American Society of International Law), 16 February 2010.

Bodnar, P. (2017) Is the Paris Climate Agreement dead? *Foreign Policy*. https://foreignpolicy.com/2017/03/28/is-the-paris-climate-agreement-dead-trump-energy-coal-clean-power-obama/

Bowyer, P., Bender, S., Rechid, D. and Shaller, M. (2014) *Adapting to Climate Change: Methods and Tools for Climate Risk Management.* Climate Service Centre Report no. 17. http://www.climate-service-center.de/about/news_and_events/news/063446/index.php.en

Brito, L. and Stafford-Smith, M. (2012) *State of the Planet Declaration.* Planet Under Pressure: New Knowledge towards Solutions conference, London, 26–29 March 2012. http://www.igbp.net/download/18.6b007aff13cb59eff6411bbc/1376383161076/SotP_declaration-A5-for_web.pdf

Brundtland, G. H., Chairman (1987) *Report of the World Commission on Environment and Development: Our Common Future.* United Nations Documents, 1987. Reproduced in http://www.un-documents.net/wced-ocf.htm.

Busby, J. (2018) Warming world: why climate change matters more than anything else. *Foreign Affairs*, July/August 2018. https://www.foreignaffairs.com/articles/2018–06-14/warming-world

C2ES (2015) Outcomes of the U.N. Climate Change Conference in Paris. Centre for Climate and Energy Solutions, December 2015. https://www.c2es.org/site/assets/uploads/2015/12/outcomes-of-the-u-n-climate-change-conference-in-paris.pdf

C40 (2016) Roadmap for the Global Climate Action Agenda: View by the C40 Cities Climate Leadership Group. C40 Cities Climate Leadership Group, July 2016. https://unfccc.int/files/parties_observers/submissions_from_observers/application/pdf/626.pdf

CAIT (2018) CAIT Climate Data Explorer: Russian Federation. World Resources Institute, online database, 3 December 2018. https://climateactiontracker.org/countries/russian-federation/

Calliari, E. (2018) Loss and damage: A critical discourse analysis of parties' positions in climate change negotiations. *Journal of Risk Research*, **21**(6), 725–747. https://www.tandfonline.com/doi/full/10.1080/13669877.2016.1240706

CARO (2017) The Bonn-Fiji Commitment. Climate of local and regional leaders to deliver the Paris Agreement at all levels. COP 23, Bonn, 12 November 2017. https://www.uclg.org/sites/default/files/bonn-fiji-commitment-of-local-and-regional-leaders.pdf

CCCCC (2012) Small Island Developing States (SIDS) Sustainable Energy Initiative. Caribbean Community Climate Change Centre. http://www.caribbeanclimate.bz/ongoing-projects/2001–2012-sids-dock.html

Chivers, D. (2012) Sustainability for sale? The unofficial guide to Rio + 20. *New Internationalist*, **453**, June 2012, 16–19.

Climate Analytics (2018) Paris Agreement Ratification Tracker. Climate Analytics. Access via https://climateanalytics.org/ (accessed 13 July 2018).

COP (2007) *Report of the Conference of the Parties on its Twelfth Session, Held at Nairobi from 6 to 17 November 2006.* UN, Conference of the Parties, January 2007. Access via http://unfccc.int/

Curran, G. (2011) Modernising climate policy in Australia: climate narratives and the undoing of a Prime Minister. *Environment and Planning C: Government and Policy*, **29**(6), 1,004–1,117.

Curtis, S. (2015) Commentary – A foreign policy for cities? *Global Insight.* The Chicago Council on Global Affairs, 1 December 2015. https://www.thechicagocouncil.org/blog/global-insight/foreign-policy-global-cities

Diesendorf, M. and Hamilton, C. (1997) *Human Ecology, Human Economy: Ideas for an Ecologically Sustainable Future.* Sydney, Allen and Unwin.

Eastwood, L. (2011) Climate change negotiations and civil society participation: shifting and contested terrain. *Theory in Action*, **4**(1), 8–37.

EC (2018) *EU-China Leaders' Statement on Climate Change and Clean Energy.* European Commission. Beijing, 16 July 2018. https://ec.europa.eu/clima/sites/clima/files/news/20180713_statement_en.pdf

ECLAC (2018) *The Caribbean Outlook 2018* (LC/SES.37/14/Rev.1). Santiago: Economic Commission for Latin America and the Caribbean. https://repositorio.cepal.org/bitstream/handle/11362/43581/4/S1800607_en.pdf

Edwards, G., Cavelier Adarve, I., Bustos, M. and Roberts, J. (2017) Small group, big impact: how AILAC helped shape the Paris Agreement. *Climate Policy*, **17**(1), 71–85. DOI: 10.1080/14693062.2016.1240655.

EPI (2016) *2016 Report: Key Findings. Environmental Performance Index.* Yale Centre for Environmental Law and Policy (Yale University) and Centre for International Earth Science Information Network (Columbia University). http://epi.yale.edu/chapter/key-findings

—— (2018) *2018 Environmental Performance Index: Executive Summary.* Yale Centre for Environmental Law and Policy (Yale University) and Centre for International Earth Science Information Network (Columbia University). https://epi.envirocenter.yale.edu/downloads/epi2018policymakerssummaryv01.pdf

—— (2020) Results Overview. In *Environmental Performance Index.* Yale Centre for Environmental Law and Policy (Yale University) and Centre for International Earth Science Information Network (Columbia University), 2020. https://epi.yale.edu/epi-results/2020/component/epi

ESI (2005) *2005 Environmental Sustainability Index: Benchmarking National Environmental Stewardship.* New Haven, CT. Yale Centre for Environmental Law and Policy (Yale University) and Centre for International Earth Science Information

Network (Columbia University). http://sedac.ciesin.columbia
.edu/es/esi/ESI2005_Main_Report.pdf

Evan, S. and Timperley, J. (2018) Bonn climate talks: Key outcomes
from the May 2018 climate conference. *Carbon Brief*, 11 May
2018. https://www.carbonbrief.org/bonn-climate-talks-key-
outcomes-from-the-may-2018-un-climate-conference

Fehling, M., Nelson, B. and Venkatapuram, S. (2013) Limitations
of the Millennium Development Goals: a literature review.
Global Public Health, **8**(10), 1,109–1,122. http://dx.doi.org/10
.1080/17441692.2013.845676

Ferguson, R. J. and Dellios, R. (2018) Between development and
sustainability: adaptation strategies for China and Indonesia.
In K. Roy and S. Kar (eds.), *Developmental State and
Millennium Development Goals*, pp. 257–284. New Jersey,
World Scientific.

FS-UNEP (2018) *Global Trends in Renewable Energy Investment
2018*. Frankfurt am Main, Frankfurt School, UNEP Centre/
BNEF. http://www.iberglobal.com/files/2018/renewable_
trends.pdf

Gewirtzman, J., Natson, S., Richards, J., Hoffmeister, V., Durand,
A., Weikmans, R., Huq, S. and Roberts, J. (2018) Financing
loss and damage: reviewing options under the Warsaw
International Mechanism. *Climate Policy*, **18**(8), 1,076–1,086.
https://doi.org/10.1080/14693062.2018.1450724

GIZ (2017) Climate change realities in Small Island Developing
States in the Caribbean. Bonn, Deutsche Gessellschaft für
Internationale Zusammenarbeit (GIZ) GmbH. https://www
.adaptationcommunity.net/wp-content/uploads/2017/05/
Grenada-Study.pdf

Gupta, J. and Chaudhary, J. (2014) Walk the talk on climate,
BASIC Group tells developed countries. *India Climate
Dialogue*, 8 August 2014. http://indiaclimatedialogue
.net/2014/08/08/walk-talk-climate-basic-group-tells-devel-
oped-countries/

Haas, P. M. (2014) The enduring relevance of international regimes.
E-International Relations, 22 January 2014. https://www.e-ir
.info/2013/01/22/the-enduring-relevance-of-international-
regimes/

Hall, N. (2017) Six things New Zealand's new government needs to
do to make climate refugee visas work. *The Conversation*, 30
November 2017. https://theconversation.com/six-things-new-
zealands-new-government-needs-to-do-to-make-climate-refugee-
visas-work-87740

Henderson, G. and Joffe, P. (2016) China's climate action: looking
back, and looking ahead to the 13th five-year plan. *China
FAQs*, 3 March 2016. https://www.wri.org/blog/2016/03/
chinas-climate-action-looking-back-and-looking-ahead-13th-
five-year-plan

Hingley, R. (2017) 'Climate refugees': an Oceanic perspective.
Asia and the Pacific Policy Studies, **4**(1), 158–165. DOI:
10.1002/app5.163.

Hulme, D. (2009) *The Millennium Development Goals (MDGs): A
Short History of the World's Biggest Promise*. BWPI Working
Paper 100. Brooks World Poverty Institute, University of

Manchester, September 2009. http://hummedia.manchester
.ac.uk/institutes/gdi/publications/workingpapers/bwpi/
bwpi-wp-10009.pdf

ICA (2012) *Global Water Security*. Intelligence Community
Assessment. Office of the Director of National Intelligence
(USA), 2 February 2012. https://www.dni.gov/files/documents/
Special%20Report_ICA%20Global%20Water%20Security.pdf

IEA (2017) *Perspectives for the Energy Transition: Investment
Needs for a Low-Carbon Energy System*. Paris, International
Energy Agency. https://www.irena.org/-/media/Files/IRENA/
Agency/Publication/2017/Mar/Perspectives_for_the_Energy_
Transition_2017.pdf?la=en&hash=56436956B74DBD
22A9C6309ED76E3924A879D0C7

(2018) *Global Energy and CO² Status Report 2017*. Paris,
International Energy Agency, March 2018. https://www.iea
.org/publications/freepublications/publication/GECO2017.pdf

IISS (International Institute for Strategic Studies) (2010)
Copenhagen Accord faces first test. *Strategic Comments*,
16(1), 1–4. https://doi.org/10.1080/13567881003718500

Ingalls, M. L. and Dwyer, M. B. (2016) Missing the forest for the
trees? Navigating the trade-offs between mitigation and adaptation under REDD. *Climatic Change*, **136**, 353–366.

IPCC (2011) *Renewable Energy Sources and Climate Change
Mitigation*. Cambridge, Cambridge University Press. https://
www.ipcc.ch/site/assets/uploads/2018/03/SRREN_Full_
Report-1.pdf

(2012) *Managing the Risks of Extreme Events and Disaster to
Advance Climate Change Adaptation*. Cambridge, Cambridge
University Press. https://www.ipcc.ch/site/assets/
uploads/2018/03/SREX_Full_Report-1.pdf

(2014a) *Climate Change 2014: Synthesis Report. Contribution of
Working Groups I, II and III to the Fifth Assessment Report of
the Intergovernmental Panel on Climate Change*. Geneva,
Switzerland, IPCC. https://www.ipcc.ch/site/assets/
uploads/2018/02/SYR_AR5_FINAL_full.pdf

(2014b) *Climate Change 2014: Mitigation of Climate Change.
Contribution of Working Group III to the Fifth Assessment Report
of the Intergovernmental Panel on Climate Change*. Cambridge,
Cambridge University Press. Access via https://www.cambridge
.org/core/books/climate-change-2014-mitigation-of-
climate-change/81F2F8D8D234727D153EC10D428A2E6D

(2014c) *Climate Change 2014: Impacts, Adaptation, and
Vulnerability. Part A: Global and Sectoral Aspects.
Contribution of Working Group II to the Fifth Assessment
Report of the Intergovernmental Panel on Climate Change*.
Cambridge, Cambridge University Press. https://www.ipcc.ch/
site/assets/uploads/2018/02/WGIIAR5-PartA_FINAL.pdf

(2016) *Decision IPCC/XLIV-4. Sixth Assessment Report (AR6)
Products, Outline of the Special Report on 1.5°C*. https://www
.ipcc.ch/site/assets/uploads/2018/11/Decision_Outline_SR_
Oceans.pdf

(2019) *Global Warming of 1.5°C: An IPCC Special Report on
the Impacts of Global Warming of 1.5°C Above Pre-industrial
Levels and Related Global Greenhouse Gas Emission*

Pathways, in the Context of Strengthening the Global Response to the Threat of Climate Change, Sustainable Development, and Efforts to Eradicate Poverty, ed. Masson-Delmotte, V., et al. https://www.ipcc.ch/site/assets/uploads/sites/2/2019/06/SR15_Full_Report_High_Res.pdf

IRENA (2017), *REmap 2030 Renewable Energy Prospects for Russian Federation*, Working paper, IRENA, Abu Dhabi. https://www.irena.org/-/media/Files/IRENA/Agency/Publication/2017/Apr/IRENA_REmap_Russia_paper_2017.pdf

Jarju, P. O. (2016) Climate diplomacy delivered Paris: Now it's time to up the stakes. *Climate Home*, 25 February 2016. http://www.climatechangenews.com/2016/02/25/climate-diplomacy-delivered-paris-now-its-time-to-up-the-stakes/

Jordan, A. and Brown, K. (1997) The international dimensions of sustainable development. In R. M. Auty and K. Brown (eds.), *Approaches to Sustainable Development*, pp. 370–295. London, Pinter.

Kanie, N., Hass, P., Andresen, S., Auld, G., Cashore, B., Chesek, P., de Oliveira, J., Renckens, S., Stokke, O., Stevens, C., Van Deveer, S. and Iguchi, M. (2013) Green pluralism: lessons for improved environmental governance in the 21st century. *Environment*, **55**(5), 14–30.

Kates, R. W. and Parris, T. M. (2003) Long-term trends and a sustainability transition. *Proceedings of the National Academy of Science*, **100**(14), 8062-8067. https://www.pnas.org/content/100/14/8062

Kemp, L. (2017) US-proofing the Paris Climate Agreement. *Climate Policy*, **17**(1), 86–101.

Kettunen, M., Charveriat, C., Farmer, A., Gionfra, S., Schweitzer, J. P. and Stainforth, T. (2018) *Sustainable Development Goals (SDGs) at the UN High Level Political Forum (HLPF)*, New York, 16–18 July 2018. European Parliament Briefing. https://ieep.eu/uploads/articles/attachments/4080637c-161f-4926-b73e-335846fd066d/ENVI%202018-13%20SDG%20Briefing%20PE%20619.026%20(Publication).pdf?v=63698104097

Keong, C. Y. (2018) From Stockholm Declaration to Millennium Development Goals: the United Nation's journey to environmental sustainability. In K. Roy and S. Kar (eds.), *Developmental State and the Millennium Development Goals: Country Experiences*, pp. 209–256. Singapore, World Scientific.

Koppenborg, F. (2017) Will the silent comeback of coal threaten Japan's climate goals? *East Asia Forum*, 6 April 2017. http://www.eastasiaforum.org/2017/04/06/will-the-silent-comeback-of-coal-threaten-japans-climate-goals/

Korppoo, A. and Kokorin, A. (2017) Russia's 2020 GHG emissions target: emission trends and implementation. *Climate Policy*, **17**(2), 113–130. https://doi.org/10.1080/14693062.2015.1075373

Leadership Group (2015) *Indicators and a Monitoring Framework for Sustainable Development Goals: Launching a Data Revolution for the SDGs. A Report by the Leadership Council of the Sustainable Development Solutions Network*. Sustainable Development Solutions Network, 16 January 2015. https://sustainabledevelopment.un.org/content/documents/2013150612-FINAL-SDSN-Indicator-Report1.pdf

Li, Anthony H. F. (2016) Hopes of limiting global warming? China and the Paris Agreement on climate change. *China Perspectives*, No. 1, 2016: 49–54.

Li, Z., Galeano Galván, M., Ravesteijn, W. and Qi, Z. (2017) Towards low carbon based economic development: Shanghai as a C40 city. *Science of the Total Environment*, **576**, 538–548. https://doi.org/10.1016/j.scitotenv.2016.10.034

Low, P. S. (2018) Climate change: International negotiations and politics. Research seminar, Faculty of Science and Design, Bond University, Robina, Queensland, Australia, 27 July 2018.

Magnan, A., Schipper, E., Burkett, M., Bharwani, S., Burton, I., Eriksen, S., Gemenne, F., Schaar, J. and Ziervogel, G. (2016) Addressing the risk of maladaptation to climate change. *Wiley Interdisciplinary Reviews: Climate Change*, **7**(5), 646–665. https://doi.org/10.1002/wcc.409

Massai, L. (2010) The long way to the Copenhagen Accord: the climate change negotiations in 2009. *Review of European Community and International Environmental Law*, **19**(1), 104–121.

Mazo, J. (2010) *Climate Conflict: How Global Warming Threatens Security and What To Do About It*. Adelphi Paper, No. 409. London, International Institute for Strategic Studies.

Mead, L. (2015) Human security and climate change. *SDG Knowledge Hub*, 27 January 2015. http://sdg.iisd.org/commentary/policy-briefs/human-security-and-climate-change/

MEE (2018) Joint Statement Issued at the Conclusion of the 26th BASIC Ministerial Meeting on Climate Change, Durban, South Africa. Department of Environmental Affairs, Republic of South Africa and Ministry of Ecology and Environment, People's Republic of China, 20 May 2018. https://www.environment.gov.za/mediarelease/jointstatement_conclusionof26thbasicministerialmeeting

Millennium Ecosystem Assessment (2005) *Ecosystems and Human Well-being: Synthesis*. Washington, DC, Island Press. https://www.millenniumassessment.org/documents/document.356.aspx.pdf

Morton, K. (2011) Climate change and security at the third pole. *Survival*, **53**(1), 121–132.

Muggah, R. (2013) The fragile city arrives. *E-International Relations*, 23 November 2013. https://www.e-ir.info/2013/11/23/the-fragile-city-arrives/

Nicholas, S. and Buckley, T. (2017) Japanese thermal coal consumption approaching long term decline. Institute for Energy Economic and Financial Analysis Report. July 2019. http://ieefa.org/wp-content/uploads/2019/07/Japan_Coal_July-2019.pdf

Oberthur, S. and Groen, L. (2017) Explaining goal achievement in international relations: the EU and the Paris Agreement on climate change. *Journal of European Public Policy*, **24**, 1–20. DOI: 10.1080/13501763.2017.1291708.

OECD (2018) *Policy Coherence for Sustainable Development 2018: Towards Sustainable and Resilient Societies*. Paris, OECD Publishing.

Pulwarty, R., Nurse, L. and Trotz, U. (2010) Caribbean islands in a changing climate. *Environment*, **52**(6), 16–27.

Raustiala, K. (1997) States, NGOs, and international environmental institutions. *International Studies Quarterly*, **4**(41), 719–740.

Rooji, B., Stern, R. E. and Furst, K. (2016) The authoritarian logic of regulatory pluralism: understanding China's new environmental actors. *Regulation and Governance*, **10**(1), 3–13.

Rosewarne, S. (2016) The transnationalization of the Indian coal economy and Australian political economy: the fusion of regimes of accumulation? *Energy Policy*, **99**, 214–223. http://dx.doi.org/10.1016/j.enpol.2016.05.022

Schmidt, J. R. (2008) Why Europe leads on climate change. *Survival*, **50**(4), 83–96.

Schreurs, M. (2012) Rio + 20: Assessing progress to date and future challenges. *Journal of Environment and Development*, **21**(1), 19–23.

Sembiring, M. (2018) The case for a dedicated regional mechanism for climate change: a comparative assessment. *NTS Insight*, IN18-04. http://www.rsis.edu.sg/wp-content/uploads/2018/07/NTS-insight-Climate-Change.pdf

Steffen, A. (2012) How to save the global economy: Build green cities. *Foreign Policy*, January-February 2012. https://foreignpolicy.com/2012/01/03/how-to-save-the-global-economy-build-green-cities/

Szabo, S., Nicholls, R., Neumann, B., Renaud, F., Matthews, Z., Sebesvari, Z., Kouchak, A., Bales, R., Ruktanonchai, C., Kloos, J., Foufoula-Georgiou, E., Wester, P., New, M., Rhyner, J. and Hutton, C. (2016) Making SDGs work for climate change hotspots. *Environment: Science and Policy for Sustainable Development*, **58**(6), 24–33.

Thirawat, N., Udompol, S. and Ponjan, P. (2016) Disaster risk reduction and International catastrophe risk insurance facility. *Mitigation and Adaptation Strategies for Global Change*, **22**(7), 1,021–1,039. https://doi.org/10.1007/s11027-016-9711-2

Timperley, J. (2018) The carbon brief profile: Japan. *Carbon Brief*, 25 June 2018. https://www.carbonbrief.org/carbon-brief-profile-japan

UN (1972) *Report of the United Nations Conference on the Human Environment*. Stockholm, 5–16 June 1972. http://www.un-documents.net/aconf48-14r1.pdf

(1992) *United Nations Framework Convention on Climate Change*. https://unfccc.int/resource/docs/convkp/conveng.pdf

(2009) *Report of the Conference of the Parties on Its Fifteenth Session, Held in Copenhagen from 7 to 19 December 2009–Addendum Part Two: Action Taken by the Conference of the Parties at Its Fifteenth Session.* UNFCCC, 30 March 2009. https://unfccc.int/resource/docs/2009/cop15/eng/11a01.pdf

(2013) *A New Global Partnership: Eradicate Poverty and Transform Economies Through Sustainable Development.* New York, United Nations Publications. https://sustainabledevelopment.un.org/content/documents/8932013–05%20-%20HLP%20Report%20-%20A%20New%20Global%20Partnership.pdf

(2015a) Resolution Adopted by the General Assembly on 25th of September 2015, 70/1. *Transforming Our World: The 2030 Agenda for Sustainable Development.* A/RES/70/1. New York, United Nations General Assembly. https://www.un.org/en/development/desa/population/migration/generalassembly/docs/globalcompact/A_RES_70_1_E.pdf

(2015b) *Adoption of the Paris Agreement.* Paris, United Nations, Conference of Parties, Twenty-First Session, 30 November to 11 December 2015. https://unfccc.int/resource/docs/2015/cop21/eng/l09r01.pdf

(2019) What is the Paris Agreement. United Nations Climate Change: Process and Meetings, 2019. https://unfccc.int/process/the-paris-agreement/what-is-the-paris-agreement-0

UN Secretary-General (2014) *The Road to Dignity by 2030: Ending Poverty, Transforming All Lives and Protecting the Planet. Synthesis Report of the Secretary-General on the Post-2015 Agenda.* New York. http://www.un.org/disabilities/documents/reports/SG_Synthesis_Report_Road_to_Dignity_by_2030.pdf

UNCTAD (2017) *World Investment Report 2017.* Geneva, United Nations Conference on Trade and Development. http://unctad.org/en/PublicationsLibrary/wir2017_en.pdf?user=46

UNDP (2017) *Global Trends: Challenges and Opportunities in the Implementation of the Sustainable Development Goals.* United Nations Development Programme and United Nations Research Institute for Social Development. http://www.undp.org/content/dam/undp/library/SDGs/English/Global%20Trends_UNDP%20and%20UNRISD_FINAL.pdf

(2018) *A Climate Resilient, Zero-Carbon Future: The UNDP's Vision for Sustainable Development through the Paris Agreement.* United Nations Development Programme, 2018. http://www.undp.org/content/undp/en/home/librarypage/climate-and-disaster-resilience-/Climatecommitment.html

UNEP (2010) *Latin America and the Caribbean: Atlas of Our Changing Environment.* United Nations Environment Programme. Access via https://na.unep.net/atlas/lac/book.php.

(2016a) *The Emissions Gap Report* 2016. Nairobi, United Nations Environment Programme. https://www.unenvironment.org/resources/emissions-gap-report-2016

(2016b) *The Adaptation Finance Gap Report 2016.* Nairobi, United Nations Environment Programme. http://www.unep.org/climatechange/adaptation/gapreport2016/

(2017a) *The Adaptation Gap Report: Towards Global Assessment.* Nairobi, United National Environment Programme. https://wedocs.unep.org/bitstream/handle/20.500.11822/22172/adaptation_gap_2017.pdf?sequence=1&isAllowed=y

(2017b) *The Emissions Gap Report: A UN Environment Synthesis Report.* Nairobi, United National Environment Programme. http://wedocs.unep.org/bitstream/handle/20.500.11822/22070/EGR_2017.pdf?sequence=1&isAllowed=y

UNESCAP (2017a) *Responding to Climate Change Challenge in Asia and the Pacific: Achieving the Nationally Determined Contributions (NDCs).* Bangkok, United Nations Economic and Social Commission for Asia and the Pacific. https://www.unescap.org/sites/default/files/Download.pdf

(2017b) *Integrating Disaster Risk Reduction and Climate Change Adaptation into the Agriculture Sector in Small Island*

Developing States in the Pacific: A Policy Note. Bangkok, United Nations Economic and Social Commission for Asia and the Pacific. https://www.unescap.org/sites/default/files/publication_WEBdrr01_Agri.pdf

UNFCCC (2012) Doha Amendment to the Kyoto Protocol. UNFCCC Files, 2012. https://unfccc.int/files/kyoto_protocol/application/pdf/kp_doha_amendment_english.pdf

(2014) *Report of the Conference of the Parties on Its Nineteenth Session.* Warsaw, 11–23 November 2013, distributed 31 January 2014. http://unfccc.int/resource/docs/2013/cop19/eng/10a01.pdf#page=6

(2015a) INDCs as communicated by parties: Submissions. http://www4.unfccc.int/submissions/indc/Submission%20Pages/submissions.aspx

(2015b) Historical Paris Agreement on climate change: 195 nations set path to keep temperature rise well below 2 degrees Celsius. UN Climate Change Newsroom, 13 December 2015. https://unfccc.int/news/finale-cop21

(2015c) Cities and regions across the world unite to launch major five-year vision to take action on Climate Change. UN Climate Change News, 8 December 2015. https://unfccc.int/news/lpaa-focus-cities-regions-across-the-world-unite-to-launch-major-five-year-vision-to-take-action-on-climate-change

(2016) *Aggregate Effect of the Intended Nationally Determined Contributions: An Update.* United Nations, 2 May 2016. http://unfccc.int/resource/docs/2016/cop22/eng/02.pdf

(2017) Concrete climate action commitments at COP 23. United Nations Climate Change. https://unfccc.int/news/concrete-climate-action-commitments-at-cop23

(2018) Urgency underlined as Bonn climate talks close. United Nations Climate Change. https://unfccc.int/news/urgency-underlined-as-bonn-climate-talks-close

(2019) National Determined Contributions (NDCs). United Nations Climate Change. https://unfccc.int/process/the-paris-agreement/nationally-determined-contributions/ndc-registry#eq-2

UNGA (1992) *Rio Declaration on Environment and Development.* UN General Assembly, Report on the United Nations Conference on Environment and Development, Rio de Janeiro, 3–14 June 1992. https://www.un.org/en/development/desa/population/migration/generalassembly/docs/globalcompact/A_CONF.151_26_Vol.I_Declaration.pdf

(2000) 55/2. United Nations Millennium Declaration. New York, United Nations General Assembly. https://www.ohchr.org/EN/ProfessionalInterest/Pages/Millennium.aspx

(2015) *Transforming Our World: The 2030 Agenda for Sustainable Development.* Resolution adopted by the General Assembly on 25 September 2015. http://www.un.org/ga/search/view_doc.asp?symbol=A/RES/70/1&Lang=E

UNISDR (2015) *Sendai Framework for Disaster Risk Reduction 2015–2030.* Geneva, United Nations Office for Disaster Risk Reduction. http://www.preventionweb.net/files/43291_sendaiframeworkfordrren.pdf

Usher, P. (1989) World conference on the changing atmosphere: Implications for global security – The conference statement. February 1989. *Environment: Science and Policy for Sustainable Development,* **31**(1), 25–27.

Vidaurri, F. (2015) Renewable energy and investment in ASEAN. *ASEAN Briefing,* 4 November 2015. http://www.aseanbriefing.com/news/2015/11/04/renewable-energy-and-investment-in-asean.html

Viola, E., Franchini, M. and Ribeiro, T. (2012) Climate governance in an international system under conservative hegemony: the role of major powers. *Revista Brasileira de Política Internaciona,* **55**, 9–29.

WEF (2014) *Climate Adaptation: Seizing the Challenge.* Geneva, World Economic Forum. http://www3.weforum.org/docs/GAC/2014/WEF_GAC_ClimateChange_AdaptationSeizingChallenge_Report_2014.pdf

Winkler, H. and Depledge, J. (2018) Fiji-in-Bonn: will the 'Talanoa Spirit' prevail? *Climate Policy,* **18**(2), 141–145. https://doi.org/10.1080/14693062.2018.1417001

World Bank (2017) Southeast Asian countries reach milestone agreement to strengthen resilience. https://www.worldbank.org/en/events/2017/05/05/southeast-asian-countries-reach-milestone-agreement

Zeng, M., Liu, X., Li, Y. and Peng, L. (2014) Review of renewable energy investment and financing in China: Status, mode, issues and countermeasures. *Renewable and Sustainable Energy Reviews,* **31**, 23–37. http://dx.doi.org/10.1016/j.rser.2013.11.026

24 Social vulnerability to climate change in Cambodia, Lao PDR, and Vietnam

NGUYEN HUU NINH[1], LUONG QUANG HUY[2,‡], PHILIP MICHAEL KELLY[2,*], AND PHAN TOAN[3,+]

[1]Centre for Environment Research, Education and Development, Hanoi, Vietnam
[2]Climatic Research Unit, School of Environmental Sciences, University of East Anglia, Norwich, United Kingdom
[3]Northwestern University, Evanston, IL, USA

Keywords

Global environmental change; climate change; vulnerability; resilience; adaptation; poverty; inequality; social capital; Cambodia; Lao PDR; Vietnam

Abstract

Reducing vulnerability to environmental change must be a key component of any strategy for sustainable development. We consider the situation of the nations of the Lower Mekong, namely Cambodia, Lao PDR, and Vietnam, focusing on the threat of climate change. We distinguish between physical vulnerability, characterized in terms of spatial exposure to hazardous events, and social vulnerability, which is a function of the social conditions and historical circumstances that put people at risk. As vulnerability is a dynamic condition, we frame the assessment in terms of the processes and trends that are shaping current patterns of vulnerability and resilience. The nations of the Lower Mekong face a range of potential trends in climate, with changes in the incidence of flooding, variability in water availability, the occurrence of drought and heat stress, the frequency and/or intensity of tropical cyclones, and, in coastal areas, sea-level rise posing the major risks. A baseline assessment of the social, economic, and political trends that are influencing present-day levels of social vulnerability highlights the fact that poverty is the largest barrier to developing the capacity to cope and adapt effectively with change. The situation of the poorest members of society is being adversely affected by trends in inequality, disparities in property rights, dismantling of agricultural cooperatives, unions, and various forms of financial support and changes in social structure and institutions. We identify an important tension that can exist between efforts aimed at improving the general economic situation and what is needed to improve resilience to climate stress, particularly among the rural poor. As far as adaptation is concerned, there are lessons for other regions in the traditional approaches developed within the Lower Mekong, as these nations have a rich history of managing their dynamic natural environment.

24.1 INTRODUCTION

The Intergovernmental Panel on Climate Change (IPCC) warns that 'climate change is projected to impinge on sustainable development of most developing countries of Asia, as it compounds the pressures on natural resources and the environment associated with rapid urbanization, industrialization, and economic development' (IPCC, 2007). Alongside remedial action to limit emissions, levels of vulnerability, virtually synonymous with the capacity to adapt, will determine the ultimate impact of global climate change. Reducing vulnerability should, therefore, be a key component of any strategy for sustainable development, and this necessitates vulnerability assessment.

In assessing vulnerability, it is useful to distinguish between physical vulnerability, generally characterized in terms of spatial exposure to hazardous events (such as droughts and floods), and social vulnerability, which is a function of the social conditions and historical circumstances that put people at risk when confronted by a diverse range of climatic, political, or economic stresses (Adger and Kelly, 1999, 2001; Kelly and Adger, 2000). Both physical vulnerability and social vulnerability are aspects of the general concept of vulnerability but provide different perspectives on options for intervention. An approach based solely on physical vulnerability focuses attention on places at risk. Methods aimed at reducing physical risk may, however, increase the vulnerability of populations to extreme events (Hewitt, 1997; Comfort et al., 1999; Shrubsole, 2000).

‡ Current address: Department of Climate Change, Ministry of Natural Resources and Environment, Hanoi, Vietnam.
* Current address: Tanelorn Associates, PO Box 4260, Kamo, Whangarei 0141, New Zealand.
+ Current address: Research Department, Federal Reserve Bank of Richmond, VA 23219–4528, USA.

For example, a structural coping solution, such as flood protection in some coastal areas in Vietnam, will not necessarily discourage people from living in such high-risk areas but may encourage development and, consequently, increase vulnerability. Social vulnerability emphasizes the inequitable distribution of damages and risks among groups of people (Wu *et al.*, 2002). Here, vulnerability is a result of social processes and structures that constrain access to the resources (e.g. wealth and real income, formal and informal social security) that enable people to cope with impacts (Blaikie *et al.*, 1994). Thus, Hewitt (1997) argues that protection from the social forces that create inequitable exposure to risk is as, or even more, important than structural protection from natural hazards. An approach based on social vulnerability focuses attention on the societal factors that determine the capacity to cope, respond, and adapt to stress, rather than the potential hazard itself. Kelly and Adger (2000) argue that this makes an approach to climate impacts based on assessing social vulnerability in the present day more robust than approaches based on scenarios and speculative forecasts of physical impacts, which are inevitably shrouded in uncertainty.

The chapter is concerned with the social vulnerability of the nations of the Lower Mekong region (formerly French Indochina), that is, Cambodia, Lao PDR, and Vietnam, lying under the influence of the summer-time southwest and winter-time northeast monsoon systems of Southeast Asia. Following Kelly and Adger (2000), in this review, we define social vulnerability, broadly, as the ability of an individual, group, or society to cope with, respond to, and, in the long run, adapt to a range of external stresses, including both environmental and societal change. In the context of global environmental change research, the study of social vulnerability in this region is at a relatively early stage. We therefore assess the current situation through a baseline assessment of the social, economic, and political trends that are shaping present-day levels of vulnerability to global environmental change in the Lower Mekong region, focusing on the threat of climate change. We consider differential levels of vulnerability within the region and, particularly, within each nation. The chapter begins with a consideration of the social, economic, geographical, and political background of the three nations of the Lower Mekong, which provides a context for the discussion of social vulnerability.

24.2 GEOGRAPHICAL AND SOCIO-ECONOMIC CONTEXT

During the late 19th century and early 20th century, Indochina was known to the world as one of the richest in natural resources and most culturally diverse colonies of the French. With a history of conflict and managing the impact of natural hazards, such as drought, flood, and cyclone impacts, often associated with the variable monsoon system of the region, the nations of this region have developed robust coping systems, which are still evident in traditional farming practices (Appa Rao *et al.*, 2002) and sophisticated social systems, such as Vietnam's cyclone protection system (Kelly *et al.*, 2001). It is important that the strengths of these nations are not forgotten. Nevertheless, the region is now considered one of the poorest in the world, despite its location alongside the so-called Asian tigers, and it must also be considered among the most vulnerable. The social vulnerability of the nations of the Lower Mekong is a function of their specific social, economic, geographical, and political characteristics. The brief contextual account of the key features of each nation that follows draws on country reports (Kingdom of Cambodia, 2002a, 2003; Socialist Republic of Vietnam, 2003a; Lao People's Democratic Republic, 2004; World Bank, 2009, 2010) and the data sources cited in Tables 24.1 and 24.2, which detail key societal, economic, and human development statistics. Statistics in the tables are for the years noted.

Vietnam is dominated by the two major deltas, the Red River delta in the north and the Mekong delta to the south. These are fertile agricultural areas, home to the majority of the population. Vietnam is now the world's second-largest exporter of rice. Alongside fisheries, aquaculture is a focus of coastal development, and mineral extraction is significant in the seas off Vietnam. In 2016, agriculture accounted for 16% of Gross Domestic Product (GDP), its role decreasing as industrialization develops (Table 24.1).

Lao PDR occupies the northwest portion of the Indochinese peninsula. It is a mountainous country, especially in the north, where peaks rise above 2,800 m. Dense forests cover the northern and eastern areas. The Mekong River, which forms the boundary with Myanmar and Thailand, flows through the country for more than 1,500 km of its course. Agriculture employs most of the Laotian workforce. In 2016, this economic sector accounted for 17.23% of the national GDP (Table 24.1). Rice cultivation is the most profitable agricultural activity. Forests cover over half of the country. Though rich in mineral resources, the mining industry is largely undeveloped. Lao PDR also has massive hydroelectric potential and, despite a relative lack of development, electricity is a prime export. Most manufactured items have to be imported and there is a continuing foreign trade deficit.

Cambodia is situated at the centre of the Indochinese peninsula. It consists of a large alluvial plain ringed by mountains, with the Mekong River on the east. The plain is centred round Lake Tonle Sap, which is a natural storage basin of the Mekong. Rice is the country's prime crop; livestock raising and extensive fishing are also important supplements. Agriculture accounted for 24.74% of GDP in 2016 (Table 24.1), falling from 33.49% in 2009 (World Bank, 2021).

Table 24.1. Basic national statistics (data for the year(s) indicated).

	Vietnam	Lao PDR	Cambodia
Land area (square kilometres)	331,114	236,800	181,035
Population (millions) (2016)	94.57	6.76	15.76
Urban population (%) (2016)	34.51	33.74	22.58
Annual population growth (%) (2016)	1.03	1.54	1.57
Population below national poverty line (%)	9.8 (2016)	18.3 (2018)	17.7 (2012)
Poverty headcount ratio at $1.90 ($ 2011 PPP) (% of population) (2012)	2.7 (2012)/ 2.6 (2014)	14.5% (2012)	n/a
Poverty headcount ratio at $3.20 ($ 2011 PPP) (% of population) (2012)	13% (2012)/ 11.0 (2014)	46.6 (2012)	n/a
Gross National Income *per capita*, Atlas Method (US$) (2016)	2,080	2,120	1,140
Growth in Gross Domestic Product (GDP) (%) (2015/16)	6.68/6.21	7.27/7.02	7.04/7.03
Role of agriculture (value added, % of GDP) (2016)	16.32	17.23	24.74
Role of industry (value added, % of GDP) (2016)	32.72	28.76	29.45

Source: World Bank data at https://data.worldbank.org/ (accessed 22 May 2021)

Table 24.2. Key development indicators of the Lower Mekong nations and other selected nations in Southeast Asia.

Indicator	Cambodia	Lao PDR	Vietnam	Thailand	Myanmar
Human Development Index Rank (2015)	143	138	115	87	145
Human Development Index value (2015)	0.563	0.586	0.683	0.740	0.556
Gender Inequality Index Rank (2015)	112	106	71	79	80
Gender Inequality Index Value (2015)	0.479	0.468	0.337	0.366	0.374
Palma ratio: Ratio of the richest 10% of the population's share of gross national income (GNI) divided by the poorest 40 percent's share (2010–2015)	1.2	1.7	1.6	1.7	n/a
Education index* (2015)	0.459	0.474	0.617	0.641	0.410
Education index rank (2013)	136	139	121	89	150
Life expectancy at birth (years) (2016)**	68.98	66.92	75.17	76.40	66.21
Population using an improved drinking water source (%) (2012)***	71	72	95	96	86
Prevalence of HIV, total (% population ages 15–49) (2016)**	0.6	0.3	0.3	1.2	0.8

Key: n/a: not available

Sources: United Nations Development Programme, *Human Development Report 2016* (http://www.hdr.undp.org/en/data)

*Calculated using data of Mean Years of Schooling and Expected Years of Schooling in the *Human Development Report 2016*;

**World Bank data at https://data.worldbank.org/ (accessed 24 May 2021);

***UN data at http://data.un.org/Data.aspx?d=WHO&f=MEASURE_CODE%3aWHS5_122 (accessed 24 May 2021).

Vietnam, covering 45% of the region, is home to more than 80% of the population of the Lower Mekong. With a population of 94.6 million in 2016, Vietnam's human resources are considered a significant asset and source of resilience. Lao PDR and Cambodia, though covering 31% and 24% of the region, respectively, had populations of 6.8 million and 15.8 million in 2016, which add up to only 19.3% of the regional total. In 2016, 10% of the population of Vietnam lived below the national poverty line, compared to 18.3%

in 2018 in Lao PDR and 17.7% in 2012 in Cambodia (Table 24.1). https://data.worldbank.org/indicator/SI.POV.NAHC?locations=LA https://data.worldbank.org/indicator/SI.POV.NAHC?locations=KH

All three nations are undergoing rapid socio-economic change. In Vietnam, the policy of *doimoi*, literally renovation or new changes, since the mid-1980s and the end of the United States-led trade embargo in 1994, has brought stability, significant progress in reducing inflation and poverty levels, and

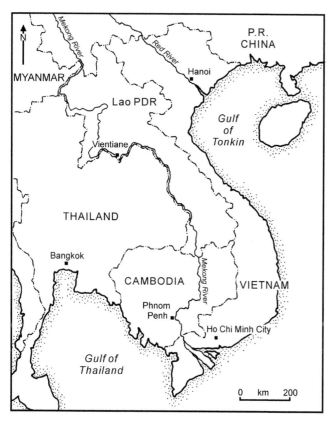

Figure 24.1. Geographical location map, region of the Lower Mekong.

strong economic growth at a rate averaging close to 7% per annum in the early years of the 21st century. The policy of *doi-moi* brought about a major programme of economic reform, with industrialization, rural development and poverty reduction major priorities. *Doimoi* has been described as a development process by the people and for the people. Vietnam is increasingly attracting foreign direct investment.

In Lao PDR, during the 1990s, under the 'New Economic Mechanism' reform process, price controls were removed; farmers were allowed to work on their plots; the exchange rate system was unified; the government's monopoly on trade was removed; the number of state enterprises was reduced; commercial banks were established; and private companies were permitted. A comparatively open foreign investment law was adopted. In the years immediately following these reforms, GDP growth rates averaged 6.5%.

In Cambodia, the genocidal Khmer Rouge regime (1975–1979) had a devastating impact on the country's institutions and human capacity. The nation is still suffering from the conflict that racked Cambodia during the latter part of the 20th century, as the Pol Pot regime was followed by a long period of political tension. During the early 21st century, close to 60% of Cambodia's domestic budget was financed by donors, primarily through loans. Cambodia's economic growth strategy is based

on the private sector. The trade regime has opened up, with tariff areas reduced and tariff rates lowered. Accession to the World Trade Organization (WTO) in September 2004 accelerated economic development, but in the global recession, the country experienced a sharp decline in its GDP growth rate, from 6.69% in 2008 to 0.09% in 2009 (World Bank, 2019).

Three key characteristics of the Lower Mekong nations, relevant to this discussion of social vulnerability, emerge from this review. First, a sizeable proportion of each population is poor. Second, despite increasing levels of industrialization and urban growth, much of each nation's population remains dependent on agriculture (both irrigated and rain-fed) and, as such, is particularly susceptible to the impact of natural hazards and environmental change. Finally, all three nations are undergoing rapid social and economic change as a result of a political commitment to reform or renovation. In all cases, the economies are more open to international pressures, stresses, and assistance than previously.

24.3 PHYSICAL EXPOSURE AND SOCIETAL CONSEQUENCES

Before considering the social vulnerability of the region, it is necessary to define the physical risks associated with climate change and to consider how society might be affected in the absence of an adaptive response (Kelly and Adger, 2000; Kelly *et al.*, 2001). We synthesize the major conclusions of assessments conducted by the IPCC (McLean *et al.*, 1998; Lal *et al.*, 2001; Cruz *et al.*, 2007) and present the findings of reviews undertaken by the national governments of Cambodia and Vietnam in preparing their National Communications under the United Nations Framework Convention on Climate Change (Kingdom of Cambodia, 2002b; Socialist Republic of Vietnam, 2003b, 2010). (The Initial National Communication from the Government of Lao PDR does not cover impacts and adaptation.) It is noteworthy that most work on regional climate trends and potential impacts has been conducted for Vietnam, with pioneering work undertaken in Cambodia, but relatively little research on the situation of Lao PDR. Given the difficulties inherent in projecting future climate under global warming conditions, it is advisable to consider these impact estimates as illustrative rather than predictive. In the context of an analysis of social vulnerability, they serve to define the domain of the assessment, highlighting specific areas as priorities for investigation (Kelly and Adger, 2000).

The potential impacts of global warming on the Lower Mekong region have been assessed by McLean *et al.* (1998), Lal *et al.* (2001), and Cruz *et al.* (2007). We briefly summarize the main conclusions. The latest projections of surface air temperatures suggest a warming of the region during the course of the 21st century at about the same rate as the global average. By the end of the 21st century, rainfall levels are forecast to increase, particularly during the first half of the year. The monsoon circulation is likely to strengthen. As far as the great rivers of the region, such as the Mekong, are concerned, flow rates will be dependent on conditions integrated over a wide area (cf. Kite, 2001). The synthesis by the IPCC (2007) highlights the risk that, overall, freshwater availability may decrease over Southeast Asia. It is considered, though, that crop yields could increase by up to 20%. The IPCC projects that endemic morbidity and mortality due to diarrheal disease, mostly associated with floods and droughts, may rise. Of great concern along the coastal margin of the region is the possibility of an adverse trend in tropical cyclone frequency and intensity. Model projections of changes in cyclone characteristics are not reliable, and it is extremely difficult to provide estimates of likely future trends for the region (Kelly and Adger, 2000). Similarly, trends in the El Niño Southern Oscillation (ENSO), which have a notable impact on year-to-year climate variability over parts of the Lower Mekong region (Kelly et al., 2001), are difficult to predict. The potential for increased climate variability must be considered one of the major threats to agrarian economies. Finally, sea-level rise could have substantial impacts in the coastal zones of Cambodia and Vietnam. In a survey of low-lying areas in 84 coastal developing countries undertaken by Dasgupta et al. (2009), Vietnam ranks first in terms of GDP, urban area, and wetlands at risk in the event of a one-metre rise in sea level.

As far as the societal consequences of these potential trends are concerned, Cambodia's Initial National Communication (Kingdom of Cambodia, 2002b) identifies the following threats. Rice production may become more variable owing to the increase in flood frequency and intensity, in particular, in the rice-growing areas surrounding the Tonle Sap Lake and the Mekong River. A decrease in the area of wet forest may occur, accompanied by an increase in the area of moist forest; the dry forest extent would remain the same. Forest productivity and biodiversity might also change. Historically, malaria incidence is strongly correlated with wet season rainfall, so any increase in rainfall levels could increase this threat. If sea level rises by one metre, about 0.4% of the total area of Koh Kong province would be permanently under water.

Vietnam's Initial and Second National Communications (Socialist Republic of Vietnam, 2003b, 2010) identify the following potential threats. Climate change could have profound impacts on surface water resources and water resource management (including hydropower production), with annual run-off projections varying from a slight increase to a substantial decrease and peak discharge and evapotranspiration increasing. The length of the agricultural growing period would increase. Crop yield and productivity would be affected. Climate change would have serious impacts on vegetation coverage and the forest. Changes in the boundary distribution of primary forest as

well as secondary forest may occur. Extinction of some animals and plants may lead to the loss of precious biogenetic resources. Any increase of temperature and drought would lead to increased risk of forest fires and the spread of pests and diseases. Sea-level rise and the changes in the storm climate would severely affect the coastal zone. Sectors considered vulnerable to sea-level rise include agriculture and food security, aquaculture, sea and coastal ecological systems, water resources (surface and ground water), energy, tourism, residential space, infrastructure, and industrial zones, with poor farmers and fishermen, senior citizens, children, and women particularly at risk. Finally, there would be direct negative impacts on human health.

With these considerations in mind, the following physical risks warrant particular attention in the nations of the Lower Mekong:

- Flooding and increased variability in water availability (related to rainfall trends and increased temperature and evapotranspiration);
- Drought;
- Heat stress;
- A change in the frequency and/or intensity of tropical cyclones; and
- Sea-level rise.

As far as societal impacts are concerned, focal areas include agriculture, fisheries, ecosystems, human health, water resource management, urban areas, and the coastal zone. Irrigated agriculture may be less susceptible to drought, though flooding and heat stress pose a threat to both irrigated and rain-fed agriculture.

Vulnerability analysis must concern itself with the emergence of unexpected extreme events during the early stages of global warming, as the boundaries of the previous 'normal' climate are crossed, and then the possibility of increased inter-annual variability and longer-term trends in climate as the impact develops. Assessing vulnerability is, therefore, a matter of considering the capacity to respond to and cope with short-term climate extremes, as well as the ability to adapt to long-term trends. In resource-constrained countries such as Cambodia, Lao PDR, and Vietnam, the immediate emphasis should be on coping with extreme events as the most immediate manifestation of anthropogenic warming.

24.4 SOCIAL VULNERABILITY IN THE LOWER MEKONG REGION

24.4.1 Studying vulnerability

Having set the context and identified focal areas, we now consider social vulnerability to climate change. Levels of social vulnerability constantly change, reflecting their dependence on the constant interaction of a range of political, economic, and social processes (Leichenko and O'Brien, 2002; Eriksen *et al.*, 2005). The dynamic nature of vulnerability renders quantitative analysis difficult (Brooks *et al.*, 2005; Eriksen and Kelly, 2007), and many analysts favour assessment based on study of the processes that determine levels of vulnerability rather than vulnerability per se (Kelly and Adger, 2000; Eriksen *et al.*, 2005). Given that study of social vulnerability remains at the exploratory stage, it would be unwise to advocate any single approach or perspective; all can contribute to the development of understanding. Following Sen (1981, 1990), the concept of entitlements, in the sense of access to resources, has provided a fruitful basis for vulnerability analysis (see, e.g., Adger and Kelly, 1999, 2001). This approach resonates with the Vietnamese concept of *chu dong*, to be able to control things oneself and not depend on outside forces (Beckman *et al.*, 2002). Beckman *et al.* (2002) show that, in central Vietnam, households that have the resources to clear the land, control access to water, and have access to inputs can recover quickly from flood impacts. Analysis of social capital, an important resource, provides another significant perspective (Pelling, 1998). Degrees of marginality, susceptibility, adaptability, fragility, and risk also play a part in shaping vulnerability (Liverman, 1994). Adger *et al.* (2001a) illustrate the range of approaches that can be taken in assessing social vulnerability, collecting a series of case studies relevant to Vietnam and other nations of Southeast Asia.

To date, most research into social vulnerability in the region of the Lower Mekong, as elsewhere, has been based on analysis of current conditions, rather than future projections, identifying the key processes that shape vulnerability to current hazards and trends as an analogue for the future. Three critical factors that determine levels of social vulnerability emerge from this body of work: poverty and inequality; property rights, especially changes in land allocation and ownership; and changes in the institutional environment. Baseline information used in this assessment is taken from the governmental and intergovernmental reports cited earlier.

24.4.2 Poverty and inequality

Poverty determines individual access to resources and underpins the process of marginalization (Adger and Kelly, 1999). The poor have access to a narrower range of coping strategies, have fewer and less diverse entitlements, and lack empowerment. Inequality shapes the differential access to resources across the community. A high level of inequality is frequently associated with a reduced commitment to collective responsibility and action. As resources are concentrated into the hands of a smaller proportion of the population, collective entitlements are lost and individual entitlements reside with fewer people. Though other factors are important, assessing levels of poverty and inequality is fundamental to the definition of patterns of vulnerability.

Box 24.1. Characteristics of the poor in the nations of the Lower Mekong.

- The household head of the poor is most likely to be a farmer: in 2003, almost 80% of the poor worked in agriculture;
- Most of the poor live in rural, isolated, or disaster-prone areas, where the physical and social infrastructure is relatively undeveloped;
- Most of the poor have small landholdings or are landless;
- The poor have limited access to credit and financial support from both government and the private sector;
- Poor households are more than likely to have many children and/or few labourers;
- Ethnic minorities include a disproportionate number of poor people; and
- The poor have limited education.

Common characteristics of the poor across the Lower Mekong region (Box 24.1) provide insight into patterns of social vulnerability. Throughout the region, most of the poor live in rural areas, where the physical and social infrastructure is relatively undeveloped. The household head is most likely to be a farmer. Many of the poor of the region have small landholdings or are landless. Dependence on agriculture, in this setting, brings with it exposure to natural disasters. Thus, lacking the resources to cope, a key aspect of the lives of the poor in the region is vulnerability to natural shocks, such as extreme weather events. Beckman *et al.* (2002) and Lindskog *et al.* (2005) demonstrate this point in recent studies at the village level in Vietnam.

Across the region as a whole, more than 80% of the population is dependent on rain-fed or irrigated agriculture and lives alongside waterways prone to seasonal flooding, along rivers, in low-lying deltaic regions or in the coastal zone. At the macro-level, disaster management is cited as a priority issue in reducing vulnerability and ensuring environmental sustainability in Cambodia (Kingdom of Cambodia, 2002a). Patterns of inequality determine the distribution of vulnerability. In Cambodia, for example, a survey by the National Institute of Statistics has shown that 82% of the poorest villages experienced some form of natural disaster, compared with only 26% of the richest (National Institute of Statistics, 1999). Not only are the poorer areas more likely to experience natural disasters, they are also less able to cope when disaster strikes. Within Xuan Thuy District in Vietnam, Adger (1999) has shown that the poor have limited access to credit sources. Dismantling of agricultural cooperatives and unions and governmental subsidies in all three countries means bank loans and credits are granted on a case by case basis, creating more difficulties for the disadvantaged.

The poverty differential between urban and rural areas is widening. The Cambodian population living under the poverty line is concentrated in rural areas. Cambodia has limited formal support systems for the poor. In Lao PDR, there has been significant progress in poverty reduction since the early 1990s, with poverty levels improving from 46% of the population under the poverty line in 1992/93 to 23.4% in 2016; the rural-urban difference in poverty incidence is again notable, with poverty levels in rural areas twice those in urban areas (data for late 1990s). In Vietnam, the poverty rate is greatest in the remote, rural areas of the northeast and northwest, the upland areas of the north central coast, and the northern part of the central highlands. In contrast, the lowest poverty rates are found in the main cities, Hanoi and Ho Chi Minh City, and in the southeast, one of the popular tourism areas in Vietnam.

24.4.3 Property rights

Economic reform is contributing to the overall wealth of communities, but this may be at the expense of equality. For example, the destruction of the mangrove ecosystem and its replacement by commercial aquaculture has been a common trend across Southeast Asia (cf. Dierberg and Kiattisimkul, 1996). In Vietnam, it has amounted to the privatization of what was previously a communally managed resource, which provided a range of income sources to the local people. This process can lead to conflict among users of the remaining mangrove areas, eroding social capital and reducing social cohesion and resilience (Adger et al., 2001b). The poor, who made use of the mangrove as a diverse source of income, are now denied this means of livelihood diversification (Nguyen Hoang Tri et al., 2001). Labour opportunities within aquaculture, a capital-intensive activity, are limited, and the net effect of aquaculture development is to heighten levels of inequality. There are benefits to the community as a whole as the local economy develops, but these favour the rich. In this instance, the effects on social vulnerability are reinforced as the physical exposure of the coastline is exacerbated by the removal of the natural protection afforded by the mangrove (Nguyen Hoang Tri et al., 2001).

Access to resources is a critical determinant of vulnerability (Adger and Kelly, 1999); in a region such as the Lower Mekong, access is frequently mediated by the allocation of agricultural land. Leef (2001) identifies constraints in land-use rights, lack of access to market and extension services, and limited credit as seriously disadvantaging the minority peoples of upland Vietnam; the poor are disproportionately likely to be from an ethnic minority. According to Schenk et al. (1999), the Hmong minority, the poorest community in Yen Chau District in Vietnam, have no access at all to formal credit. This is because of their geographical isolation, language difficulties, and the lack of collateral. Women in mountainous areas tend also to lack access to credit (Tran Thi Que, 1998). Ethnic minorities are, in general, restricted in their access to resources and are marginalized from decision-making (Rambo et al., 1995).

Changing property rights represents one of the major reform processes affecting the poor. In recent decades, both Vietnam and Lao PDR have experienced dramatic productivity increases following moves to decollectivize agriculture and restore production responsibilities to households. In Vietnam, national legislation adopted in 1993 validated the rights of farmers with respect to the land that they cultivate. While all land belongs to the state, agricultural land is allocated to farmers for long-term use (Luttrell, 2001). In addition, with possession of a legal title, farmers are permitted to exchange, transfer, lease, inherit, and mortgage their land-use rights. Similarly, the Lao 1991 Constitution protects state, collective, and private forms of ownership. During the 1990s, legislation underpinned the development of market-based rules and institutions to support private-sector development. All agricultural production and most of manufacturing production are now privately owned. Different from Vietnam and Lao PDR, the Cambodian government has liberalized the economic system in favour of a free-market economy. As part of the process, the government reformed the existing land management system by reintroducing private property rights. Ownership, possession rights, and concession rights are being granted to individuals, and the local government system is reallocating land to private households. Under the 1992 land law, those who have been in legally valid possession of land for five years could be registered as the owner. These trends in land ownership are having complex effects on patterns of vulnerability.

In Vietnam, changes in agricultural practices, including mechanization, and limited land availability have increased the excess labour force in rural areas. As well as stimulating rural-rural migration (e.g. to the central highlands, where coffee has become a major crop), this has created a large number of rural-urban migrants, seeking available employment opportunities. Research by Winkels (2004, 2005) has demonstrated the importance of social networks in the migration process. The increased vulnerability of migrants, divorced from local support networks, is a concern. The income from migrants is, however, an important means of income diversification and, hence, decreasing vulnerability back home (Adger et al., 2002; Zhang et al., 2006).

There is concern that the trade in property rights may lead to increased differentiation in opportunities and outcomes between the poor and the rich, heightening levels of inequality. Landlessness among the rural poor is increasing in both Vietnam and Lao PDR (Oxfam GB, 2002). Adger (1999) argues that the salt-makers, the poorest section of a coastal community in the Red River delta of northern Vietnam, have been marginalized in the process of land allocation. A feedback process is at work, as the initial effect of inequality, a limited voice in the community, is reinforced by the denial of land rights. Subversion can provide an opportunity to regain historic rights and resources (Luttrell, 2005). In August 2001, a new land law was enacted in Cambodia and, with the removal of a previous area limit on private land ownership, the concentration of land in the hands of a small number of private owners is now possible. Moreover, issuing land-use rights certificates or contracts has proceeded slowly in rural areas, contributing to a very slow rate of land market development. In contrast, the market in urban areas is developing rapidly, resulting in increasing urban-rural inequality.

24.4.4 Institutional change

Institutions and their roles are evolving in response to the reform processes taking place in all three countries, and these changes are influencing levels of poverty, inequality, and access to resources in diverse ways. The term *institutions* refers, in this context, to both the formal institutions of the state, their structure and behaviour, and the informal 'rules of the game' that societies follow (Adger and Kelly, 1999; Adger, 2000). At the macro-level, World Bank reports have focused on issues of governance (Vietnam) and accountability (Cambodia) in the context of poverty alleviation and other social goals (World Bank, 2004a, 2004b). At the local level, Lindskog *et al.* (2005) argue that Vietnam's transition from a state-led planned economy to a more market-oriented economy has created more opportunities for improving livelihoods at the household level, but has also resulted in a significant evolution of local institutions, which are now less able to influence the processes affecting local markets and resource management as the scale of these processes expands, thereby weakening traditional coping mechanisms. As Pelling (1998) has argued, social capital, the value created by social networks, is an important resource in traditional communities, underpinning coping strategies. Adger (2000) has shown that, in Vietnam, institutional development can undermine

Figure 24.2. Ha Nam Island in northern Vietnam is home to more than 55,000 people, growing rice and vegetables irrigated by water from a canal that comes from a reservoir 15 km distant. Much of the island is below sea level, as much as 3 m below in some places, and it is only made habitable by the 40 km of dike, up to 5.5 m high, encircling it. It is known as the 'floating boat'. Fishing boats, docked for protection and maintenance inside the dike, have to be winched over the sea wall. A complex set of social arrangements, including the social capital manifest in the community's commitment to collective action, reduces the extreme physical exposure of the inhabitants (Kelly *et al.*, 2001). The critical question is whether or not these arrangements can withstand the combined impact of socio-economic trends, sea-level rise, and climate change.
Photo © Mick Kelly

traditional forms of social capital; in some cases, the removal of formal modes of social security in the course of modernization may result in the re-emergence of historic coping mechanisms, such as informal credit (Adger, 2000) and, as access to resources is undermined, the creation of 'invisible institutions' (Luttrell, 2005). Adger *et al.* (2002) discuss the potential impact of migration trends in Vietnam on social capital.

Vietnam's storm and flood protection system is a complex amalgam of formal and informal institutions. It plays a critical role in minimizing the impact of the regular landfall of storms on the 3,000-km coastline of Vietnam and other natural hazards (Kelly *et al.*, 2001). The system retains characteristics that have developed over the course of centuries: pragmatic evolution in the light of experience; a multi-sectoral approach reaching into all levels of society; a sense of anticipation and forward planning; neighbourhood responsibility; and moral justice. It is now responding to the social and economic changes affecting Vietnam. Some trends, such as the loss of forms of social capital, such as collective action, and the withdrawal of state support, are eroding the effectiveness of the storm and flood protection system. For example, at the local level, there has long been an obligation to provide labour each year as part of the communal system of dike maintenance and repair. The traditional, earthen method of dike construction is based on low-cost materials but requires plentiful and, hence, cheap labour. Now, it is possible to pay a substitute tax and avoid the labour obligation. With some of this new income diverted into supporting activities unrelated to dike maintenance (Adger, 1999), and the costs of buying in the necessary labour high, the net result has been major problems in ensuring the integrity of the dike system and a return to the collective obligation in some areas (Kelly *et al.*, 2001). Capital investment is not available to upgrade the construction methods and avoid the need for a considerable labour input. Despite difficulties, though, the increase in financial resources resulting from recent rates of economic growth and greater international assistance are undoubtedly strengthening the system. Moreover, the resurgence of informal institutions, such as credit unions, is offsetting the loss of formal collective institutions.

It would be unwise to attempt to define whether the overall effect of recent trends on the effectiveness of Vietnam's hazard protection system, and, hence, levels of vulnerability, has been positive or negative. In fact, because of the complex mesh of influences on levels of vulnerability, assessing overall effects on an individual, a community, or a nation at any point in time is frequently problematic, if not impossible. One of the key lessons emerging from recent studies of social vulnerability, in the nations of the Lower Mekong and elsewhere, is that taking a process-based approach can lead to the identification of those factors and trends that increase or decrease vulnerability,

particularly in the case of the weaker members of the community. This outcome, as a basis for policy development and intervention, is, arguably, more valuable than any attempt to 'measure' vulnerability for, say, comparative purposes.

24.5 CONCLUSIONS

Social vulnerability is not a static characteristic. It is the result of a complex set of dynamic processes. This strongly manifests in the nations of the Lower Mekong, where the rapid rate of social and economic change provides a graphic context for vulnerability analysis. Fast-paced changes in society are already demanding a long-term adaptive response from the people of the Lower Mekong and we see trends in equality and societal structure and support mechanisms significantly affecting levels of social vulnerability to global environmental change. Policies implemented to promote economic development are having positive and negative effects. At the broadest level, in improving the health of the national economy, the effect on social vulnerability should be positive. But at the community level, the effects are mixed with a tendency for the impact on the poorer, more vulnerable members of society to be negative, reinforcing their existing situation.

Though rich in natural resources and with much potential in economic development, for most of their population, the nations of the Lower Mekong remain agrarian societies, still heavily dependent on the environment. As such, the people of Cambodia, Lao PDR, and Vietnam are deeply susceptible to natural catastrophes and, in the longer term, to environmental change. Poverty is the largest barrier to developing the capacity to adapt and cope effectively with change, whether environmental or socio-economic in origin. And for the poorer members of society, a web of processes exacerbates their situation, adversely affecting levels of social vulnerability to climate change by distorting access to resources and/or limiting social capital:

- An increase in income inequality, across the local community and between urban and rural areas;
- Disparities in property rights between the poor and the well-off in both urban and rural areas;
- Dismantling of agricultural cooperatives, unions, governmental subsidies, and financial support and a lack of credit and bank loan access; and
- Changes in social structure due, for example, to changes in agricultural practices, including mechanization, and limited employment and land availability, and the erosion of certain local institutions.

We have identified an important tension that can exist between governmental and intergovernmental efforts aimed at improving the general economic situation and what is needed to improve resilience to environmental stress, particularly among the rural poor. It should also be noted, in passing, that measures intended to mitigate the climate problem, such as the development of biofuel crops (oil palm and jatropha) and large-scale hydropower systems, could increase vulnerability to climate impacts by taking land away from the poor.

While the broad picture can be discerned, much work needs to be done to define and understand the vulnerability of the societies of the region. To date, most social vulnerability studies have focused on the agricultural sector of the three nations, or on the coastal zone of Vietnam and, to a lesser extent, Cambodia, but, as these economies are developing rapidly, urban areas (cf. Drakakis-Smith and Kilgour, 2001) and the industrial and the service sectors also warrant attention. We have noted deficiencies in the scenarios for the future defining of potential changes in the regional environment; specifically, in the case of Lao PDR, there has been a regrettable lack of research on climate impacts, largely a reflection of limited international support and a lack of local capacity, which should be addressed as a matter of some urgency. It is notable that most research into social vulnerability has been based on case studies, usually local in nature, and it is difficult to assess the extent to which their conclusions are of general relevance. Moreover, studies have tended to be restricted to a single nation, neglecting the improvement in understanding that could result from comparison across nations. As illustrated earlier, differences in the reform processes between the three countries are resulting in differential impacts on levels of vulnerability, for example, due to consequent trends in land ownership.

We suggest that the most effective manner in which to improve understanding of social vulnerability within each nation and across the region would be through effective cooperation between analysts in Cambodia, Lao PDR, and Vietnam. Focusing, first of all, on vulnerability to short-term hazards, which is a pressing concern in all three nations, it is recommended that this network of analysts link with stakeholders, including, above all, the marginalized members of society, to undertake participatory research. This will ensure not only full cooperation with decision-makers at all levels, but will also guarantee the integration of indigenous knowledge. In all three nations, it is critical that the process of social and economic reform and its impact on the disadvantaged and marginalized should be monitored and analysed. This will provide invaluable guidance with respect to the factors and processes shaping vulnerability to climate change, could provide insight into ways of responding to other manifestations of global environmental change, and will enable timely intervention to offset adverse trends and make the most of emerging opportunities.

Finally, we note that, as far as reducing vulnerability is concerned, there are lessons for other regions in the traditional approaches developed within the Lower Mekong, as these nations have a rich history of managing their dynamic natural environment. Traditional approaches extend from farming practices at the local level, through informal institutions, including the self-reliance inherent in the Vietnamese concept of *chu dong* (Beckman *et al.*, 2002), to institutions on a national scale, such as the storm and flood protection system that weaves its way through all levels of Vietnamese society.

ACKNOWLEDGEMENTS

The authors acknowledge the invaluable contribution of members of the Indochina Global Change Network to this assessment. They thank Hoang Thi Bich Hop for her assistance in preparing the data tables and Dr Peter King, Dr Marco Roncarati, and an anonymous referee for their perceptive comments on an earlier draft of the text. This chapter is an expanded version of a report prepared for the Monsoon Asia Integrated Regional Study (MAIRS).

REFERENCES

Adger, W. N. (1999) Exploring income inequality in rural, coastal Vietnam. *Journal of Development Studies*, **35**, 96–119.

Adger, W. N. (2000) Institutional adaptation to environmental risk under the transition in Vietnam. *Annals of the Association of American Geographers*, **90**(4), 738–758.

Adger, W. N. and Kelly, P. M. (1999) Social vulnerability to climate change and the architecture of entitlements. *Mitigation and Adaptation Strategies for Global Change*, **4**, 253–266.

Adger, W. N. and Kelly, P. M. (2001) Social vulnerability and resilience. In W. N. Adger, P. M. Kelly and Nguyen Huu Ninh (eds.), *Living with Environmental Change: Social Vulnerability, Adaptation and Resilience in Vietnam*, pp. 19–34. London, Routledge.

Adger, W. N., Kelly, P. M. and Nguyen Huu Ninh (eds.) (2001a) *Living with Environmental Change: Social Vulnerability, Adaptation and Resilience in Vietnam*. London, Routledge.

Adger, W. N., Kelly, P. M., Nguyen Huu Ninh and Ngo Cam Thanh (2001b) Property rights, institutions and resource management: coastal resources under doi moi. In W. N. Adger, P. M. Kelly and Nguyen Huu Ninh (eds.), *Living with Environmental Change: Social Vulnerability, Adaptation and Resilience in Vietnam*, pp. 79–92. London, Routledge.

Adger, W. N., Kelly, P. M., Winkels, A., Luong Quang Huy and Locke, C. (2002) Migration, remittances, livelihood trajectories and social resilience. *Ambio*, **31**(4), 358–366.

Appa Rao, S., Bounphanousay, C., Schiller, J. M., Alcantara, A. P. and Jackson, M. T. (2002) Naming of traditional rice varieties by farmers in the Lao PDR. *Genetic Resources and Crop Evolution*, **49**, 83–88.

Beckman, M., Le Van An and Le Quang Bao (2002) *Living with Floods. Coping and Adaptation Strategies of Households and Local Institutions in Central Vietnam. SEI REPSI Report Series No. 5*. Stockholm, Stockholm Environment Institute.

Blaikie, P., Cannon, T., Davis, I. and Wisner, B. (1994) *At Risk: Natural Hazards, People's Vulnerability and Disasters*. London, Routledge.

Brooks, N., Adger, W. N. and Kelly, P. M. (2005) The determinants of vulnerability and adaptive capacity at the national level and the implications for adaptation. *Global Environmental Change*, **15**(2), 151–163.

Comfort, L., Wisner, B., Cutter, S., Pulwarty, R., Hewitt, K., Oliver-Smith, A., Wiener, J., Fordham, M., Peacock, W. and Krimgold, F. (1999) Reframing disaster policy: the global evolution of vulnerable communities. *Environmental Hazards*, **1**(1), 39–44.

Cruz, R. V., Harasawa, H., Lal, M., Wu, S., Anokhin, Y., Punsalmaa, B., Honda, Y., Jafari, M., Li, C. and Nguyen Huu Ninh (2007) Asia. In M. L. Parry, O. F. Canziani, J. P. Palutikof, P. J. van der Linden and C. E. Hanson (eds.), *Climate Change 2007: Impacts, Adaptation and Vulnerability*, pp. 469–506. Cambridge, Cambridge University Press. https://www.ipcc.ch/site/assets/uploads/2018/02/ar4-wg2-chapter10-2.pdf

Dasgupta, S., Laplante, B., Meisner, C., Wheeler, D. and Yan, J. (2009) The impact of sea level rise on developing countries: a comparative analysis. *Climatic Change*, **93**(3), 379–388.

Dierberg, F. E. and Kiattisimkul, W. (1996) Issues, impacts and implications of shrimp aquaculture in Thailand. *Environmental Management*, **20**, 649–666.

Drakakis-Smith, D. and Kilgour, A. (2001) Sustainable urbanisation and environmental issues in Vietnam. In W. N. Adger, P. M. Kelly and Nguyen Huu Ninh (eds.), *Living with Environmental Change: Social Vulnerability, Adaptation and Resilience in Vietnam*, pp. 213–233. London, Routledge.

Eriksen, S. and Kelly, P. M. (2007) Developing credible vulnerability indicators for policy assessment. *Mitigation and Adaptation Strategies for Global Change*, **12**(4), 495–524.

Eriksen, S., Brown, K. and Kelly, P. M. (2005) The dynamics of vulnerability: locating coping strategies in Kenya and Tanzania. *Geographical Journal*, **171**(4), 287–305.

Hewitt, K. (1997) *Regions of Risk: A Geographical Introduction to Disaster*. Harlow, UK, Longman.

Intergovernmental Panel on Climate Change (IPCC) (2007) *Climate Change 2007: Impacts, Adaptation and Vulnerability, Summary for Policymakers*. Geneva, IPCC. https://www.ipcc.ch/site/assets/uploads/2018/02/ar4-wg2-spm-1.pdf

Kelly, P. M. and Adger, N. W. (2000) Theory and practice in assessing vulnerability to climate change and facilitating adaptation. *Climatic Change*, **47**(4), 325–352.

Kelly, P. M., Hoang Minh Hien and Tran Viet Lien (2001) Responding to El Niño and La Niña: averting tropical cyclone impacts. In W. N. Adger, P. M. Kelly and Nguyen Huu Ninh (eds.), *Living with Environmental Change: Social Vulnerability, Adaptation and Resilience in Vietnam*, pp. 154–181. London, Routledge.

Kingdom of Cambodia (2002a) *National Poverty Reduction Strategy 2003–2005*. Phnom Penh, Council for Social Development.

Kingdom of Cambodia (2002b) *Initial National Communication under the United Nations Framework Convention on Climate Change*. Phnom Penh, Ministry of Environment.

Kingdom of Cambodia (2003) *Cambodia Millennium Development Goals Report 2003*. Phnom Penh, Ministry of Planning.

Kite, G. (2001) Modelling the Mekong: Hydrological simulation for environmental impact studies. *Journal of Hydrology*, **253**(1–4), 1–13.

Lal, M., Harasawa, H. and Murdiyarso, D. (2001) Asia. In J. J. McCarthy, O. F. Canziani, N. A. Leary, D. J. Dokken and K. S. White (eds.), *Climate Change 2001: Impacts, Adaptation and Vulnerability*, pp. 533–590. Cambridge, Cambridge University Press.

Lao People's Democratic Republic (2004) *National Growth and Poverty Eradication Strategy (NGPES)*. Vientiane, Lao People's Democratic Republic.

Leef, A. (2001) Sustainable agriculture in the northern uplands: attitudes, constraints and priorities of ethnic minorities. In W. N. Adger, P. M. Kelly and Nguyen Huu Ninh (eds.), *Living with Environmental Change: Social Vulnerability, Adaptation and Resilience in Vietnam*, pp. 109–121. London, Routledge.

Leichenko, R. and O'Brien, K. (2002) The dynamics of rural vulnerability to global change: the case of Southern Africa. *Mitigation and Adaptation Strategies for Global Change*, **7**(1), 1–18.

Lindskog, E., Dow, K., Nilsson Axberg, G., Miller, F. and Hancock, A. (2005) *When Rapid Changes in Environmental, Social and Economic Conditions Converge: Challenges to Sustainable Livelihoods in Dak Lak, Vietnam*. Stockholm, Stockholm Environment Institute.

Liverman, D. M. (1994) Vulnerability to global environmental change. In S. L. Cutter (ed.), *Environmental Risks and Hazards*, pp. 326–342. Englewood Cliffs, NJ, Prentice Hall.

Luttrell, C. (2001) Historical perspectives on environment and development. In W. N. Adger, P. M. Kelly and Nguyen Huu Ninh (eds.), *Living with Environmental Change: Social Vulnerability, Adaptation and Resilience in Vietnam*, pp. 59–75. London, Routledge.

Luttrell, C. (2005) Invisible institutions: informal means of gaining access to natural resources in coastal Vietnam. In G. Mutz and R. Klump (eds.), *Modernisation and Social Transformation in Vietnam: Social Capital Formation and Institution Building*. Hamburg, Institute for Asian Studies.

McLean, R. F., Sinha, S. K., Mirza, M. Q. and Lal, M. (1998) Tropical Asia. In R. T. Watson, M. C. Zinyowera and R. H. Moss (eds.), *The Regional Impacts of Climate Change: An*

Assessment of Vulnerability, pp. 381–407. Cambridge, Cambridge University Press.

National Institute of Statistics (1999) *Cambodia Socio-Economic Survey*. Phnom Penh, Ministry of Planning.

Nguyen Hoang Tri, Phan Nguyen Hong, Adger, W. N. and Kelly, P. M. (2001) Mangrove conservation and restoration for enhanced resilience. In W. N. Adger, P. M. Kelly and Nguyen Huu Ninh (eds.), *Living with Environmental Change: Social Vulnerability, Adaptation and Resilience in Vietnam*, pp. 136–153. London, Routledge.

Oxfam GB (2002) *Landless and Near-Landless Farmers in the Provinces of Tra Vinh and Dong Thap: Problems and Solutions*. Oxford, Oxfam.

Pelling, M. (1998) Participation, social capital and vulnerability to urban flooding in Guyana. *Journal of International Development*, **10**(4), 469–486.

Rambo, A. T., Reed, R. R., Cuc, L. T. and DiGregorio, M. R. (eds.) (1995) *The Challenges of Highland Development in Vietnam*. Honolulu, Hawaii, East-West Centre.

Schenk, R., Neef, A. and Heidhues, F. (1999) Factors influencing access to credit of smallholders in Northern Vietnam. *Vietnam's Socio-Economic Development: A Social Science Review*, **18**, 56–65.

Sen, A. K. (1981) *Poverty and Famines: An Essay on Entitlement and Deprivation*. Oxford, Clarendon.

Sen, A. K. (1990) Food, economics and entitlements. In J. Drèze and A. K. Sen (eds.), *The Political Economy of Hunger. Volume 1*, pp. 34–50. Oxford, Clarendon.

Shrubsole, D. (2000) Flood management in Canada at a crossroads. *Environmental Hazards*, **2**(2), 63–75.

Socialist Republic of Vietnam (2003a) *The Comprehensive Poverty Reduction and Growth Strategy (CPRGS)*. Hanoi, Socialist Republic of Vietnam.

Socialist Republic of Vietnam (2003b) *Initial National Communication under the United Nations Framework Convention on Climate Change*. Hanoi, Ministry of Natural Resources and Environment.

Socialist Republic of Vietnam (2010) *Second National Communication under the United Nations Framework Convention on Climate Change*. Hanoi, Ministry of Natural Resources and Environment.

Tran Thi Que (1998) Microfinance market in mountainous areas: a case study. *Vietnam's Socio-Economic Development: A Social Science Review*, **14**, 45–61.

Winkels, A. (2004) *Migratory Livelihoods in Vietnam: Vulnerability and the Role of Migrant Networks*. PhD thesis. Norwich, University of East Anglia, UK.

Winkels, A. (2005) Frontier migration and social capital in Vietnam. In G. Mutz and R. Klump (eds.), *Modernisation and Social Transformation in Vietnam*, pp. 94–115. Hamburg, Institut für Asienkunde.

World Bank (2004a) *Cambodia at the Crossroads. Strengthening Accountability to Reduce Poverty, Report No. 30636-KH*. Washington, DC, World Bank.

World Bank (2004b) *Vietnam Development Report 2005, Report No. 30462-VN*. Washington, DC, World Bank.

World Bank (2009) *Poverty Profile and Trend in Cambodia: Findings from the 2007 Cambodia Socio-Economic Survey (CSES), Report No. 48618-KH*. Washington, DC, World Bank. http://documents1.worldbank.org/curated/en/504061468237543422/pdf/486180WP0P11191ofile120071withCover.pdf

World Bank (2010) *Vietnam Development Report 2011: Natural Resources Management*. Washington, DC, World Bank. http://documents.worldbank.org/curated/en/509191468320109685/Vietnam-development-report-2011-natural-resources-management

World Bank (2019) *GDP growth (annual %) – Cambodia*. Washington, DC, World Bank. https://data.worldbank.org/indicator/NY.GDP.MKTP.KD.ZG?locations=KH (accessed 15 October 2019)

World Bank (2021) Agriculture, forestry, and fishing, value added (% of GDP) – Cambodia. Washington, DC, World Bank. https://data.worldbank.org/indicator/NV.AGR.TOTL.ZS?locations=KH (accessed 24 May 2021)

Wu, S. Y., Yarnal, B. and Fisher, A. (2002) Vulnerability of coastal communities to sea-level rise: A case study of Cape May County, New Jersey, USA. *Climate Research*, **22**(3), 255–270.

Zhang, H. X., Kelly, P. M., Locke, C., Winkels, A. and Adger, W. N. (2006) Migration in a transitional economy: beyond the planned and spontaneous dichotomy in Vietnam. *Geoforum*, **37**(6), 1,066–1,081.

25 Sustainable development in Bangladesh: Bridging the SDGs and climate action

SHABABA HAQUE[1,*], NAZNIN NASIR[2,*], M. FEISAL RAHMAN[1,2,*], AND SALEEMUL HUQ[1,3]

[1]International Centre for Climate Change and Development (ICCCAD), Independent University, Dhaka, Bangladesh
[2]Department of Environmental Science, School of Environmental Science and Management, Independent University, Dhaka, Bangladesh
[3]International Institute for Environment and Development (IIED), London, United Kingdom

Keywords

Sustainable Development Goals; climate change; climate resilience; national policy framework; good governance; climate finance and ODA; financing gap

Abstract

The United Nations Sustainable Development Goals (SDGs), or the 2030 Agenda, is the successor of the Millennium Development Goals (MDGs) and has a timeline ranging from the year 2015 to 2030. Consisting of 17 goals and 169 targets, the SDGs aim to address the root causes of some of the most pressing environmental, social, and economic problems being faced by the world.

For Bangladesh, a country that performed particularly well on the MDGs, the SDGs present a great opportunity to build on the progress made with the MDGs and make transformational changes that can help boost the country's overall development. The highly ambitious SDGs have 17 goals touching all sectors, from education and health to building sustainable infrastructure. Although the wide scope of the agenda has the potential to see greater change, it also faces substantial barriers. For Bangladesh, some of the main barriers include the effects of climate change, which can potentially offset the achievements of many of these SDG targets, and another is the lack of funding mechanisms for implementing necessary actions.

The impacts of climate change will be of concern for a country like Bangladesh, which is already vulnerable to environmental effects. Given the influence the Climate Agenda and the 2030 Agenda have on each other, they play a significant role in the success of one another. As such, while addressing the SDGs it is of key importance to implement national plans and policies that incorporate SDG targets as well as climate action.

Financing the SDGs is also a critical issue for Bangladesh, as most of the funding needs to be from domestic resources. It is estimated that implementation of the SDGs will cost Bangladesh on average about US\$66.32 billion annually between 2017 and 2030. For the implementation to be successful, it needs a variety of financial resources: public and private, national and international, concessional and non-concessional. It is also important to establish a framework that can ensure that climate finance is new and additional to official development assistance (ODA) pledges and addresses issues of financial accountability and good governance.

For Bangladesh to be as successful in achieving the Sustainability Development Goals, as it was the Millennium Development Goals, the county will need to treat climate change as a cross-cutting issue that will affect the ability to attain any of the other goals. Only through developing national plans of action that are focused on climate resilience and implementing effective financial mechanisms will it be possible for Bangladesh to fulfil these transformational goals.

25.1 BACKGROUND

A lot happened in the year 2015. It was the year the international community came together and agreed to the Paris Agreement on climate change, the Sendai Framework for Disaster Risk Reduction, and the Sustainable Development Goals (SDGs), also known as the 2030 Agenda. Although the three frameworks are housed in various institutions, the overarching theme of these agreements is sustainability and climate resilience (Huq, 2016a). If addressed cohesively, these initiatives can potentially support the efforts of Least Developed Countries (LDCs) like Bangladesh to socially and economically develop in a way that renders them resilient against climate change. While the goals under the SDGs, both individually and collectively, aim to create a sustainable future, it is important to note that failure to address climate change, whether through

* Current address: Department of Geography, Durham University, Durham, United Kingdom

mitigation or adaptation, will ultimately obstruct the ability to achieve almost any of the other goals. Therefore, it is crucial to prioritize the issue of climate change when implementing national actions for the achievement of the SDGs.

The SDGs were preceded by the Millennium Development Goals (MDGs), which were established in the year 2000. While the relatively simple and straightforward MDGs led to many success stories around the world, some important global issues were left out. A 2015 UN assessment of the MDGs noted that 'progress towards the MDGs has repeatedly shown that the poorest and those disadvantaged because of gender, age, disability or ethnicity are often bypassed' (Thompson, 2015). Learning from the mistakes of the MDGs, the SDGs consist of 17 all-encompassing development goals, which are broken into 169 targets, with an attempt to resolve the structural causes of issues instead of addressing only surface problems. In order to ensure that no one is left behind, the High-Level Political Forum (HLPF) discussed the need for addressing this in a twin-track approach: integrating SDGs within universal social policy frameworks while also developing targeted policies and programmes that specifically cater to the needs of those who are more vulnerable (Sustainable Development Knowledge Forum, 2018).

In terms of achieving the MDGs, Bangladesh is seen as a success story by many. The MDGs played a substantial role towards the country's development. Bangladesh made remarkable progress in the areas of poverty reduction, food security, enrolment in primary education, infant mortality and maternal care, immunization coverage and incidence of communicable diseases, and safe water and sanitation access (El Arifeen *et al.*, 2014; GED, 2016a). Although Bangladesh was on track for most of the MDGs, there were certain areas that were not fully addressed and under the current climate crisis these areas need immediate attention. For instance, Bangladesh's performance on the environmental sustainability goal under the MDGs was not satisfactory. While the MDGs targeted 5% of terrestrial and marine areas to be protected, Bangladesh managed to protect only 1.81% and 1.34%, respectively. The target also demanded that more of the country's land area be covered with trees and pointed out the need to provide safe and sustainable sources of water for all (GED, 2016a).

The SDGs in this regard, with their comprehensive set of targets, have the potential to meet the development gaps of the MDGs while also building on the successes of the MDGs. In terms of protecting the environment, the SDGs have dissected the broad goal of environmental sustainability to give equal importance to climate change (goal 13), life under water (goal 14), clean water and sanitation (goal 6), and life on land (goal 15) (United Nations, 2016). By doing so, it ensures that all these agenda items are given individual priority. Under the SDGs,

Bangladesh can address more targets within these separate goals, which will help resolve many intricate environmental problems the country faces, including those associated with climate change.

However, at the same time, in many ways the elaborate priorities of the SDGs can also make it a difficult task to successfully achieve them. One of the key obstacles to achieving the SDGs in Bangladesh is the amount of funding required for implementing actions under these goals. Given Bangladesh's climate vulnerability, another significant barrier to the achievement of the SDGs will be the long-term and short-term impacts of climate change, which will not only impact goal 13 of the SDGs but will directly and indirectly affect almost all other sectors in the country.

The primary focus of this chapter is to discuss the need for bridging SDGs and climate action in order to promote climate-resilient development in Bangladesh. In doing so, the chapter will depict ways in which climate change may impact the successful achievement of the SDGs, as well as discussing how the implementation of SDGs may facilitate climate-resilient development. In addition to this, the chapter will also elaborate on the means for addressing some of the key challenges associated with financing the SDGs and highlight aspects of aligning SDGs and climate change within the national regulatory framework.

25.2 SDGS AND THE CLIMATE CHANGE CONNECTION: THE BANGLADESH PERSPECTIVE

According to the fifth IPCC report, the impacts of climate change will burden countries that are already poverty-stricken; this includes most of the Least Developed Countries (LDCs) (IPCC, 2014). Bangladesh, owing to its geographic location, is susceptible to climate disasters, and its high population density and incidence of poverty make it highly vulnerable to the impacts of such calamities. It has been estimated that more than 70 million people could be affected by climate change in Bangladesh (Alam and Laurel, 2005). It is also noted that, although most parts of the country are prone to climate impacts, it is the population residing in the coastal areas that is more at risk (Alam and Laurel, 2005).

Therefore, given the multifaceted nature of the goals and targets, there are many instances of overlaps and trade-offs, of which the tie between climate change and the achievement of SDGs in Bangladesh is undeniable. The two issues are highly interlinked with each other; on one hand, climate change impacts in Bangladesh can prevent key SDG targets from being met, while on the other hand, addressing the SDG targets will help build the framework for a more climate-resilient nation.

25.2.1 The inevitable interlink of SDGs and climate change

SDG 13 declares the need for taking urgent action to reduce the impacts of climate change; the three main targets under SDG 13 precisely outline some of the key movements required for building climate resilience on a global scale. The three targets include:

1. Strengthening resilience and adaptive capacity to climate-related hazards and natural disasters in all countries;
2. Integrating climate change measures into national policies, strategies, and planning;
3. Improving education, awareness-raising, and human and institutional capacity on climate change mitigation, adaptation, impact reduction, and early warning.

Although climate action is a standalone goal under the SDGs, the effects of climate change in Bangladesh will likely impact almost all the components of the SDGs; from poverty eradication to water resources, and from sustainable cities to economic growth, climate change manages to affect all aspects of sustainability.

Through making the disadvantaged population more deprived, climate change will not only enhance pre-existing inequalities (goal 10) within Bangladesh but, as the country becomes increasingly affected by a changing climate, implementing effective climate action (goal 13) will also become more difficult (Wright *et al.*, 2015). This will result in making the country more susceptible to the impacts of climate change and less able to achieve the SDGs.

25.2.2 Climate change effects on poverty, hunger, and health

In Bangladesh, climate change will impact the country's agriculture and food production. According to Wassmann *et al.* (2009), the rising temperature is already reaching critical levels during the susceptible stages of the rice plants, which could potentially affect rice production. The increase in temperature also leads to a rise in sea levels, which affects coastal and deltaic rice production in Bangladesh. According to a World Bank report (Yu *et al.*, 2010), climate change will result in loss of long-term rice production by an average of 7.4% each year for the period of 2005–2050, which translates to about US$26 billion in lost agricultural GDP over that period. The report further noted that Bangladesh will lose in total about US$121 billion, or 5% of the national GDP, during the period 2005–2050. Similar to the findings of Yu *et al.* (2010), a study by the International Food Policy Research Institute (Thomas *et al.* 2013) also indicated increased loss of agricultural yield due to climate change. The study noted that the impact of climate change on wheat in particular will be severe, with the total yield nearly 20% lower in 2050. Climate change will also likely have an adverse impact on open-water fisheries. Increased salinity can lead to scarcity of various breeds of fishes that are unable to breed in saline water (Allison *et al.*, 2009). It has also been suggested that a loss of small fish species will have significant impacts on the animal protein intake of poor women and children (Dasgupta *et al.*, 2017).

The issues of poverty and hunger have a knock-on effect on each other. According to a brief paper by IIED (Wright *et al.*, 2015), if Bangladesh has lower crop yields because of climate change, there could be at least a 15% net increase in poverty. Climate change in Bangladesh is therefore detrimental to existing poverty situations by affecting the livelihood of the groups that are already vulnerable. Those living in climate vulnerable zones, such as the coastal areas of the country, are often forced to migrate under unfavourable circumstances, leaving them in far worse socio-economic conditions. It will also have an impact on the urban poor living in climate vulnerable conditions (Alam and Rabbani, 2007).

The effects of climate change are detrimental to human health. The aftermath of climate-induced natural disasters, such as floods and cyclones, contaminates water sources and spreads diseases like diarrhoea, cholera, and other water-borne illnesses. It is also seen that salinity intrusion in coastal areas can have negative effects on pregnant women. The impact of climate variability on three childhood diseases (diarrhoea, fever, and acute respiratory infections) in Bangladesh has been reported to be significant (Mani and Wang, 2014). Persons displaced because of climate change-induced impacts and natural disasters are often susceptible to malnutrition and vector-borne diseases from living in poor environmental conditions (GED, 2009).

For these reasons and more, unless the threats of climate change are dealt with, it will not be possible to eradicate poverty (SDG 1), ensure food security (SDG 2), or promote health and well-being (SDG 3) in Bangladesh.

25.2.3 Climate change impacting water security and marine resources

Climate change has a significant impact on water and marine resources in Bangladesh. The country is prone to extreme climate events, such as cyclones and storm surges, which have an intense effect on the water supply and existing sanitation infrastructures (GED, 2009). Owing to Bangladesh's high population density, climate change-induced changes to the country's hydrology and water resources will have severe impacts on the country's economy, particularly where people are reliant on surface water for irrigation and fisheries. As the country's river salinity increases because of climate change, there will be a shortage of freshwater, which eventually will have detrimental effects on the aquatic ecosystems in the Southwest coastal areas of Bangladesh (Dasgupta *et al.*, 2014a, 2014b, 2017). Increased salinity in drinking water may adversely affect women, in particular pregnant mothers living in southwestern coastal Bangladesh, as was documented by Khan *et al.* (2014), who observed that pregnant women in that region had much higher rates of pre-eclampsia and gestational hypertension than pregnant women living in non-coastal areas, thought to be because of high levels of sodium intake.

Furthermore, women and adolescent girls are at higher risk from sea-level rise and associated impacts. During the dry season, as freshwater sources become scarce, they must walk further, sometime up to several kilometres every day, to collect water for their families. These journeys are not always pleasant and safe, as they must endure long distances on foot and risk instances of sexual harassment. Also, women and adolescent girls in the area suffer gynaecological problems due to using saline water during menstruation (VoSB, 2015). Therefore, climate change and associated impacts will render the achievement of both goal 5 (gender equality) and goal 6 (clean water and sanitation) of the SDGs more difficult.

The barriers set by water-related issues in Bangladesh are not just limited to goal 6; they will also have an impact on the achievement of goal 14 of the SDGs, which is focused on minimizing ocean acidification and protecting marine ecosystems. A recent World Bank study (Jekobsen *et al.*, 2002) noted that an increase in sea levels will have a profound impact on the lives of the coastal population, making it crucial to address goal 14 with regard to the ongoing and impending effects of climate change. Some of the main impacts of climate change on Bangladesh's coastal regions include sea-level rise, salinity intrusion, an increase in the frequency and intensity of cyclones and the reduction of freshwater sources. It is also noted that as the sea-level rises, there is a consequent increase in water salinity across the coastal regions (Faisal and Parveen, 2004). In this way, salinity intrusion threatening freshwater ecosystems can potentially impact both freshwater and marine fisheries (Allison *et al.*, 2009), which will directly impact goal 14 and indirectly impact goal 2 (hunger).

25.2.4 Climate change hinders safe and inclusive settlement

According to the IPCC's fourth assessment report (Cruz *et al.*, 2007), climate change exposes the Bay of Bengal to intense extreme weather events, such as storms, tidal flooding, and cyclones, which disrupts the livelihood of the coastal population and damages infrastructure along the coastal belts. Although Bangladesh has made substantial improvements in reducing

cyclone-related fatalities, cyclones still pose a severe threat to coastal areas. The worst-affected sectors are housing and agriculture (GED, 2009). A World Bank study (2010) reported that, during an average cyclone, the housing sector suffers damages and losses equal to US$900 million. Building of climate-resilient infrastructure, road networks, and emergency shelters can be useful in saving lives as well as minimizing the other losses.

Natural calamities due to climate change tend to be one of the key underlying reasons for internal migration, which adds to the problem of unplanned urbanization (Black, 2010). Approximately 55% of the urban population in Bangladesh resides in unplanned slums in major cities, which are already vulnerable to environmental calamities (Uddin, 2018). As climate migrants add to this process of rapid urbanization, there are concerns regarding human security and environmental degradation within the inhabited area (Huq, 2001). Lack of necessary infrastructure, proper employment opportunities, and suitable environmental and health facilities make the urban poor increasingly vulnerable to climate-induced disasters (Denissen, 2012). Although it primarily affects goal 11, which aims to ensure safe, resilient, and sustainable human settlements, it also has an indirect effect on the achievement of goal 8 (job opportunities for all), as most migrants remain unemployed for a long period of time after their displacement.

The impacts of climate change also act against the targets set by goal 5 (empowering women), as women in Bangladesh are disproportionately vulnerable to the effects of climate change. Studies show that when there is a shortage of water, it is the women and children who are usually sent to fetch water from further away, which not only adds an additional burden of responsibility but also risks their health and safety (GED, 2009).

25.2.5 SDGs with climate resilience

Climate change is an ongoing phenomenon that is likely to have both short-term and long-term impacts. However, the SDGs are time-bound and goal-oriented, with a vision to transform the world by 2030. Many of the goals of the SDGs are coherent with the actions taken for combating climate change. In fact, the Paris Agreement has set the stage to address climatic challenges through various adaptation and mitigation efforts that also pave the pathway for SDG success. Sindico (2016), assessing the 2030 Agenda and the Paris Agreement, noted that the latter contained both direct and indirect references to the SDGs and sustainable development and argued that such a close relationship between the two documents underscores the need to integrate the SDGS into the implementation of the Paris Agreement. The discussion in this section will briefly point out how addressing climate change and working towards SDGs may be mutually beneficial.

Goal 7 of the SDGs is focused on ensuring clean energy for all, which will contribute to minimizing greenhouse gas emission. The Bangladesh government aims to provide access to electricity for all by the year 2021 (GED, 2015), and using clean sources for doing so will eventually lower emissions as well as helping the off-grid vulnerable communities build resilience against the warming climate. Rapid and unplanned urbanization remains a key concern in Bangladesh, as it leaves cities highly vulnerable to the impacts of climate change. Goal 9 of the SDGs, which promotes sustainable industrialization, will help Bangladesh innovate and build infrastructure works in a responsible and environmentally friendly manner. In addition, goal 11 will lead to building safe and sustainable cities and human settlements. Therefore, addressing these goals will consequently lead to enhancing urban climate resilience in Bangladesh.

Similarly, efforts and policies for combating climate change such as the Kyoto Protocol also enforce the need for clean energy options to reduce greenhouse gas emissions in the atmosphere, which not only contributes to goal 7 (energy for all) but also helps goal 8 (employment). For example, the renewable energy industry in 2017 created more than 500,000 new jobs globally, and the industry now employs more than 10 million people (IRENA, 2018). Therefore, investing in industries focused on sustainable low-carbon development will also produce more job opportunities for Bangladesh.

Lastly, goal 16 aims to build effective, inclusive, and accountable institutions at all levels; by doing so, it will be possible to establish good governance within various institutions in Bangladesh. A study conducted by Bhuiyan (2015) noted the lack of good governance in terms of addressing climate change as one of the key barriers to climate adaptation that will undermine adaptation capacity in the near future.

25.3 ALIGNING IMPLEMENTATION OF SDGS AND CLIMATE GOALS WITH THE NATIONAL POLICY FRAMEWORK

Agenda 2030 sets ambitious goals for the global community, in an effort to achieve development in an inclusive and environmentally sustainable manner. Institutional structures in many countries around the world are often unable to integrate economic development with environmental protection. Furthermore, as discussed, climate change, being related to many of the SDGs, is anticipated to further delay the progress towards achieving Agenda 2030. The Paris Agreement offers an aspiring, long-term goal, global commitments, and a range of necessary tools, including commitment to finance from developed countries to address climate change (Maxwell, 2015). In addition, Bangladesh is also a signatory of the Sendai

Framework on Disaster Risk Reduction, which was also agreed upon in 2015. All three global agreements will have to be implemented from 2016 to 2030.

Huq (2016a) argued that climatic goals can be categorized as mitigation and adaptation goals and, therefore, collectively across the three agreements there are 20 goals – 17 goals for the 2030 Agenda, two goals for the Paris agreement, and the DRR goal for the Sendai Framework. Although the 20 goals originated from different constituencies and ran through separate negotiation tracks to reach consensus, there is considerable overlap and opportunities for synergies with regard to implementation (as discussed in Section 25.2), which should be considered for effective and successful implementation of the three agreements (Huq, 2016b). For successful implementation of the agreements, Bangladesh needs to include the key goals in national and sectorial policies.

The government of Bangladesh has already started acting towards that aim, with the Planning Commission at the Ministry of Planning taking the lead in ensuring synergies among all 17 goals (Huq, 2016b). The Planning Commission has mapped the SDGs under different ministries, identifying lead ministries that will be in charge of implementing actions for specific goals. The overlap between the goals and ministries is also determined through this plan, so that the ministries are better able to collaborate when planning actions (GED, 2016b).

The Planning Commission is responsible for the long-term, medium-term, and annual development plan in Bangladesh. The seventh five-year plan (FYP) prepared by the Commission coincides with the final year of MDGs and the launch of the United Nations' post-2015 Sustainable Development Goals (SDGs), providing the country with an opportunity for integration. The seventh FYP has dedicated a chapter on environment and climate change, so even though the Paris Agreement was formulated later, climate change adaptation and mitigation in a broader context were already taken into consideration in the seventh FYP. The development approach of the plan is in line with the global 2030 Agenda for higher growth with appropriate measures for environmental sustainability (GED, 2015). The plan intends to ensure growth and acceleration in a broad-based inclusive fashion and provide benefits to all citizens. As such, eradication of extreme poverty remains one of the central principles of the strategies of the seventh FYP. The sustainable development strategy of the plan revolves around three key themes: (1) Climate Change Management and Resilience (comprising adaptation and mitigation); (2) Environmental Management; and (3) Disaster Management (GED, 2015).

The Perspective Plan of Bangladesh 2010–2021 has set a goal to make the country a middle-income country by 2021. The plan will pursue 'a development scenario where citizens will have a higher standard of living, will be better educated, will face better social justice, will have a more equitable socio-economic environment, and the sustainability of development will be ensured through better protection from climate change and natural disasters' (IMF, 2013).

With regard to addressing climate change, the Bangladesh Climate Change Strategy and Action Plan (BCCSAP) (2009) remains the key strategy document till 2018, and includes both adaptation and mitigation actions. The document lists 44 actions under six pillars to build capacity and climate resilience. For implementation of the actions, the government set up two separate funds: domestic revenue funds the Bangladesh Climate Change Trust Fund (BCCTF), and the Bangladesh Climate Change Resilience Fund (BCCRF) is donor-funded. Collectively, these two funds have invested more than a billion dollars over the past six years.

Bangladesh, despite being a nation with some of the lowest emissions, has shown its commitment and solidarity with the global community in developing clean energy and reducing emissions to fight climate change. Bangladesh's Nationally Determined Contributions (NDC) (formerly INDC), submitted to the United Nations Framework Convention on Climate Change (UNFCCC) in 2015, sets out a plan to reduce an unconditional 5% and a conditional 15% of greenhouse gas (GHG) emissions from business-as-usual levels by 2030 from the power, industry, and transportation sectors (MoEF, 2015). According to the Renewable Energy Policy (2008), Bangladesh intends to increase the usage of renewable energy and targets to meet 10% of the total power demand from renewable energy sources by 2020 (MoPMR, 2008). However, it should also be mentioned that, as the sources of natural gas will be depleted, over time the use of coal is projected to rise substantially from a meagre 3% in 2015 to 50% by 2030 (GED, 2015). Such a striking increase in the usage of coal is in contrast with the government's commitment to the Paris Agreement and the SDG 2030 agenda.

Although the country, as indicated earlier, has a regulatory framework, which will play a supporting role, implementation of the SDGs and addressing climate change would still face many challenges owing to inefficient governance systems in place (in addition to financing challenges to be discussed in Section 25.4). Lack of coordination between government agencies, little access to information, lack of capacity and resources, low participation of the civil society and common citizens, and political influences and vested interests – all these contribute to transparency and accountability issues and inefficient governance systems.

In conjunction with transparent, accountable, and efficient governance systems, appropriate institutional mechanisms should also be in place for successful implementation, in order to mainstream climate change and environmental sustainability.

In this regard, Bangladesh's experience with two parallel climate funds, BCCTF and BCCRF, can be cited. Although the two funds were innovative and forward-thinking when they were created, corruption allegations, poor management, and conflict between associated entities ultimately led to considerable misallocation of the funds. One of the key lessons the country has learned out of this experience is that climate financing should be mainstreamed into the national planning and budgeting systems and that, in addition to the Ministries of Environment and Forest for Bangladesh, other key ministries, such as Planning and Finance, need to be involved for appropriate utilization funds (Bjornestad *et al.*, 2016; Huq, 2016b, 2016c).

25.4 FINANCING NEEDS AND CHALLENGES

Finance remains one of the key determinants towards successful achievement of SDGs and addressing climate change, especially for countries with limited financial capacity. Despite political uncertainty, global economic slow-down, and a growing infrastructure deficit, Bangladesh has made commendable advancements in the socio-economic sphere in recent years. The country has made admirable success in terms of attaining MDGs, the experience of which will help the country in attaining the SDGs. However, as the actions for achieving SDGs will have to be done largely through domestic resources and finances, addressing the financing gap will be one of the key hurdles for Bangladesh. Bangladesh already has some experience of funding climate actions from its own revenue, which might be useful in planning for financing the implementation of SDGs. The subsequent discussion in this section will highlight the financing needs as well as challenges that the country will have to consider.

25.4.1 Estimated financing gap for implementing SDGs

Achieving the SDGs in all countries will require additional global investments in the range of US$5 trillion to US$7 trillion per year up to 2030 (UNCTAD, 2014). According to UNCTAD, developing countries will require between US$3.3 trillion and US$4.5 trillion a year for financing basic infrastructure (roads, rail and ports; power stations; water and sanitation), food security (agriculture and rural development), climate change mitigation and adaptation, health, and education. However, considering the current rate of public and private investment, developing countries will face an annual financing gap of US$2.5 trillion for the aforementioned areas (about 3.2% of world GDP) (UNCTAD, 2014).

In Bangladesh, the General Economic Division (GED) of the Planning Commission estimates that the total unsynchronized additional (not considering the overlaps among the SDGs) cost for implementing the SDGs will amount to up to US$1,162.76 billion, assuming that the prices during the period of FY 2017–2030 are constant with the 2015/2016 prices (GED, 2017). According to the GED report, the total additional synchronized cost of implementing SDGs after removing overlaps amounts to US$928.48 billion (for FY 2017–2030) (average US$66.32 billion per annum). Figure 25.1 presents the year-wise additional synchronized cost for achieving SDGs in Bangladesh, which indicates that the additional cost of implementing the SDGs would increase from US$26.28 billion in FY 2017–2018 to US$119.65 billion in 2030.

Further analysis by GED on goal-wise synchronized additional costs indicates that a total sum of US$535.64 billion additional costs will be required for achieving SDGs 7, 8, and 9, which is followed by the cost for implementing goal 13 – US$121.58 billion (GED, 2017).

25.4.2 Key challenges towards addressing the financing gap

Implementation of the SDGs and climate actions will need resources: public and private, national and international, concessional and non-concessional. Five sources have been suggested by GED for the additional funds required for implementing the SDG: public financing, private sector financing, public-private partnership (PPP), external sources such as foreign direct investment (FDI) and foreign aid and grants, and finally, non-government organizations (NGOs). It has been estimated that for FY 2017–2030, the private sector would account for 42% of the financing requirement, followed by 34% from the public sector and 15% from external sources (GED, 2017). Implementation will also require resolving some critical issues related to financing, for example, how domestic revenue can be increased, how the orders

of magnitude of financing – public and private – can be mobilized, and how the distinction between 'development finance' and 'climate finance' can be overcome, while also addressing the issue of good governance.

25.4.2.1 Limited domestic revenue

Domestic resource mobilization is perceived as one of the main challenges for Bangladesh in attaining the SDGs. Currently, Bangladesh has one of the lowest revenue-to-GDP ratios in the world (10.21% in 2016) (World Bank, 2018) and borrowing remains one of the biggest sources of financing (18% of GDP in 2015) for the government (Bjornestad et al., 2016). In 2015, revenue as a share of GDP was around 10%, and official development assistance (ODA) was about 2% (Bjornestad et al., 2016). Outside of the public sector, the most important development finance flows were private investment, worth US$23.3 billion in 2014 (Bjornestad et al., 2016). Remittances in Bangladesh averaged US$1.21 billion from 2012 until 2016 (Trading Economics, 2016). As the country transitions to a middle-income country status, access to International Development Association grants and non-concessional borrowing will be reduced, which will further strain domestic resource mobilization.

The narrow tax base and monetary losses from exemptions and tax holidays have contributed to a low tax revenue to GDP ratio which needs to be increased considerably if SDGs are to be achieved (Bjornestad et al., 2016). The tax administration is planning to increase tax collection by increasing capacity of the relevant departments and by modernizing the tax collection system, so that it can ultimately provide support for spot checks, automatic tax report generation, and enforcement of tax compliance in the future (Bjornestad et al., 2016). Net loss from illicit financial outflow is another major challenge, for example: the country lost between US$6 billion and US$9 billion in 2014 alone to illicit outflows (Salomon and Spangers, 2017). It has

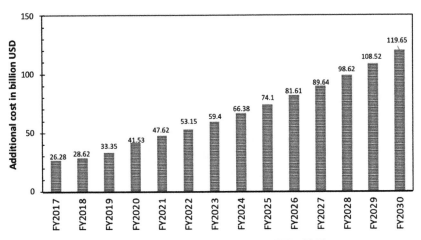

Figure 25.1. Year-wise additional synchronized cost (from GED, 2017).

been suggested that the country can meet part of its financing needs by curbing the illegal outflow of funds.

25.4.2.2 Stagnant private investment

It has been argued that the role of the private sector is critical, as many of the goals outlined in the SDGs are directly linked to the private sector. Private investment, including national and international sources, has been stuck at a certain percentage of the gross domestic product in Bangladesh for the last several years for many reasons. The government's seventh five-year plan recognizes that about 77–80% of investment needs to come from the private sector, as public sector investment alone cannot bring about the increase in gross investment needed (Bjornestad *et al.*, 2016).

The seventh FYP has set a target to increase foreign direct investment (FDI) inflows from approximately US$1.7 to US$9.6 billion in 2020 (Bjornestad *et al.*, 2016). The investment climate for Bangladesh appears to be quite unattractive, according to different international measurements. The performance of Bangladesh in attracting FDI inflows has been unsatisfactory. The Global Competitiveness Report, produced by the World Economic Forum (2016), ranks Bangladesh 107th among 140 economies. The top five challenging factors for doing business in Bangladesh, as identified by the report, are inadequate supply of infrastructure, corruption, inefficient government bureaucracy, government instability, and limited access to financing. These measurements indicate many areas where the country would need to make significant improvements and reforms to attract more investment.

In regard to involvement of the private sector in climate-resilient development, engaging the private sector in adaptation interventions, as opposed to mitigation, has various challenges. As adaptation typically addresses loss of value due to climate change, characteristically adaptation activities appear to be less appealing for private sector investment. However, the private sector can make unique contributions to adaptation in Bangladesh through innovative technologies, design of resilient infrastructure, development and implementation of improved information systems, involvement in adaptation finance planning, and the management of major projects (*The Daily Star*, 2015b). Therefore, more involvement of the private sector in planning adaptation activities and initiatives is crucial to enable Bangladesh to effectively address climate change impacts. For the reasons mentioned earlier, government agencies and institutions should facilitate dialogue and create an environment with the private sector in order to induce private financing.

25.4.2.3 ODA and climate finance

As climate change and development are intricately connected, it is hard to separate climate adaptation finance from development finance in climate-vulnerable countries like Bangladesh (Steele, 2015). While it is necessary to spend on basic SDG provisions such as food security, health, education, and water/sanitation, it should be ensured that the spending is climate resilient as well (Steele, 2015). Although developed countries, under the UNFCCC, agreed that climate finance will be 'new and additional' to development assistance, in practice, almost every developed country has mixed development finance with climate finance. This particular action is the reason a certain percentage of their contribution towards their ODA pledges is also counted as their UNFCCC pledge (Huq, 2016a). Therefore, a framework is required to ensure that climate finance is new and additional to ODA pledges. This is highly relevant for Bangladesh, since 50% of the additional synchronized costs for implementing goal 13 are expected to be sourced from external sources (GED, 2017).

As international public climate finance increases, there is a growing concern that investment in climate change mitigation is crowding out poverty reduction (Steele, 2015). There is evidence that, as support to climate finance (especially to mitigation activities) in middle-income countries increases, funds to meet SDGs in LDCs are falling. It has been reported that average climate mitigation finance for middle-income countries was nearly 25% of the total ODA to LDCs in 2011, which led to the negotiators' argument that international public climate finance for mitigation in middle-income countries should be additional to ODA, in order to protect financial support for the SDGs, which will limit the risk that ODA money is diverted from funding poverty reduction (Steele, 2015). With regard to Bangladesh, the flow of external climate change finance to support local initiatives has been slower than expected, and it has been suggested that the country might have to focus more on mobilizing climate finance from bilateral donors or domestic sources (Bjornestad *et al.*, 2016).

25.4.3 Good governance for financing SDGs

While identifying financial gaps and sources of funding is an essential first step, it is also necessary to ensure that the available funds are managed and disbursed in a transparent, efficient, accountable, and ethical manner. Managing funds in such a manner is important for demonstrating commitment and capacity for ensuring good governance. In the absence of good governance, integrity, and effectiveness, the level of confidence required for the continued flow and availability of funds among national and international sources will diminish (Iftekharuzzaman, 2013).

Bangladesh, as it continues its economic growth, is about to set a bad precedent with regard to utilizing foreign aid. It has been reported that nearly US$20 billion foreign aid remained unused in 2014–2015, as the government failed to utilize the existing aid in the pipeline (Rahman, 2015). The government has taken steps to improve the situation, such as formation of an online portal for tracking aid data (AIMS platform at the Economic Relations Division), formation of a joint committee comprising officials from the government and development partners, and electronic tendering for procurement. However, there is still a need for substantial improvements to be made (Rahman, 2015).

As Bangladesh graduates out of LDC status, access to grant and concessional loans will become limited. However, Bangladesh, being a climate-vulnerable nation, will still remain eligible for climate finance. In fact, the Green Climate Fund (GCF), which will become the major climate fund and will mobilize US$100 billion by 2020, is expected to substantially increase access to climate finance for Bangladesh and other vulnerable countries. Currently, the Economic Relations Division (ERD) of Bangladesh, under the Finance Ministry of the GoB, has been assigned as the Designated National Authority for direct access to the GCF, along with two institutions that have been identified as national implementing entity (NIE) or direct access entity (DAE). The two recently accredited NIEs for GCF are Infrastructure Development Company, Ltd. (IDCOL) and Palli Karma-Sahayak Foundation (PKSF) (GCF, 2018). Up to September 2018, three projects from Bangladesh, which were all submitted by multilateral implementing entities (MIE) (KfW, UNDP, and World Bank), have been approved by the GCF board (GCF, 2018). While Bangladesh's performance in securing GCF projects, in comparison with many developing countries, is better, there is also a substantial need for capacity improvement, especially considering the fact that by 2020, GCF is going to be a major source of global climate finance.

The experience of Bangladesh with vertical funds (as mentioned in Section 25.3) indicates that for appropriate utilization, climate funds need to be integrated within the overall national development strategy, with significant engagement of the Planning Commission and the Ministry of Finance, alongside other line ministries. The government of Bangladesh and other stakeholders must recognize that being climate vulnerable will not secure Bangladesh's place in the global climate finance pool. Therefore, there is no alternative to establishing transparent and robust governance systems at the national level to track the funds, as well as to ensure that they indeed reach and help the most vulnerable communities at the local level.

25.5 CONCLUSION AND WAY FORWARD

Bangladesh is rapidly moving ahead on the development trajectory and is racing towards the title of a middle-income country. While Bangladesh has performed particularly well on the MDGs, without building on the progress made by MDGs, Bangladesh's growth will not be sustainable. In this context, the

Sustainable Development Goals (SDGs) provided the country with an excellent opportunity. The ambitious targets set by these goals go beyond the scope of the MDGs and address key environmental issues that are of great significance in a climate-vulnerable country like Bangladesh.

In order to successfully implement the SDGs in Bangladesh, it is important to understand the role of climate change and the significance of mobilizing the country's limited financial resources with regard to its impacts. It is important to institutionalize climate change and SDGs in a way that ensures that both agendas mutually benefit each other.

The Paris Agreement for Climate Change and the SDGs go hand in hand. The Paris Agreement aims to address climate change in the context of both sustainable development and eradicating poverty. A key trade-off in Bangladesh's future development plans is between energy and climate mitigation actions. It is therefore important to ensure total energy security in the country, while reducing emissions as much as possible. Investing in the country's Nationally Determined Contributions (which targets the power, transport, and industry sectors primarily) and submitting a more ambitious NDC after five years will help achieve low-carbon and climate-resilient development. Implementing the NDCs with extensive focus on priority sectors, such as energy, land use, transportation, waste, agriculture, and water, will also help achieve a broad range of SDGs.

Considering the complex interlinkages between the two agendas, the government ministries and agencies alone will not be able to implement the SDGs and the Paris Agreement. Successful implementation will require the inclusion of many other stakeholders, especially the private sector. The private sector has a major role to play, starting from the investment sector of banks and insurance companies making green investments.

The government of Bangladesh and the civil society are already working towards achieving the SDGs by 2030. The country has put in place planning mechanisms for taking action, as well as monitoring progress. However, developing countries like Bangladesh have limited resources in terms of institutional capacity, knowledge, technical skills, and, most importantly, finance. Therefore, increasing South-South cooperation will certainly help countries learn from other countries' experiences and provide a platform for knowledge-sharing and capacity-building to help Bangladesh grow in a sustainable and environmentally responsible manner.

ACKNOWLEDGEMENTS

The authors would like to express their utmost gratitude to Dr Rezaul Karim for taking the time to review the chapter and giving us valuable feedback. The authors would also like to thank all the anonymous reviewers for their feedback and comments, which certainly helped improve the chapter overall. A special thanks goes to Dr Pak Sum Low for giving us the opportunity to write this chapter.

REFERENCES

Alam, M. and Laurel, A. M. (2005) Facing up to climate change in South Asia. The Gatekeeper Series. **118**, 1–23. http://pubs.iied .org/pdfs/9545IIED.pdf (accessed 5 August 2018)

Alam, M. and Rabbani, M. D. G. (2007) Vulnerabilities and responses to climate change for Dhaka. *Environment and Urbanization*, **19**(1), 81–97.

Allison, E. H., Perry, A. L., Badjeck, M. C., Neil Adger, W., Brown, K., Conway, D., Halls, A. S., Pilling, G. M., Reynolds, J. D., Andrew, N. L. and Dulvy, N. K. (2009) Vulnerability of national economies to the impacts of climate change on fisheries. *Fish and Fisheries*, **10**(2), 173–196.

Bhuiyan, S. (2015) Adapting to climate change in Bangladesh. *South Asia Research*, **35**(3), 349–367.

Bjornestad, L., Hossain, J., Sinha, J. and Stratta, N. (2016) Strengthening Finance for the Seventh Five-Year Plan and SDGs in Bangladesh. Government of the People's Republic of Bangladesh. http://www.bd.undp.org/content/bangladesh/en/ home/library/Sustainable_Development_Goals/strengthening-finance-for-the-7th-five-year-plan-and-sdgs-in-ban.html (accessed 19 August 2018)

Black, R. (2010) Environmental refugees: Myth or reality? New Issues in Refugee Research. Geneva: UNHCR Evaluation and Policy Analysis Unit. Working Paper No. 34. http://www .unhcr.org/research/RESEARCH/3ae6a0d00.pdf (accessed 10 August 2018)

Cruz, R. V., Harasawa, H., Lal, M., Wu, S., Anokhin, Y., Punsalmaa, B., Honda, Y., Jafari, M., Li, C. and Nguyen Huu Ninh, N. (2007) Asia. In M. L. Parry, O. F Canziani, J. P. Palutikof, P. J. van der Linden and C. E. Hanson (eds.), *Climate Change 2007: Impacts, Adaptation and Vulnerability.* Contribution of Working Group II to the Fourth Assessment Report of the Intergovernmental Panel on Climate Change. Cambridge, Cambridge University Press, 469–506.

Dasgupta, S., Hossain, M. M., Huq, M. and Wheeler, D. (2014a) Facing the hungry tide: Climate change, livelihood threats, and household responses in coastal Bangladesh (English). Policy Research working paper, No. WPS 7148. Paper is funded by the Knowledge for Change Program (KCP). Washington, DC, World Bank Group. http://documents.worldbank.org/curated/ en/558921468006267567/Facing-the-hungry-tide-climate-change-livelihood-threats-and-household-responses-in-coastal-Bangladesh (accessed 19 August 2018)

Dasgupta, S., Kamal, F. A., Khan, Z. H., Choudhury, S. and Nishat, A. (2014b) River salinity and climate change: evidence from coastal Bangladesh (English). Policy Research working paper,

No. WPS 6817. Washington, DC, World Bank Group. http:// documents.worldbank.org/curated/en/522091468209055387/ River-salinity-and-climate-change-evidence-from-coastal-Bangladesh (accessed 19 August 2018)

Dasgupta, S., Huq, M., Mustafa, M. G., Sobhan, M. I. and Wheeler, D. (2017) The impact of aquatic salinization on fish habitats and poor communities in a changing climate: evidence from southwest coastal Bangladesh. *Ecological Economics*, **139**, 128–139.

Denissen, A. (2012) Climate change and its impacts on Bangladesh. NCDO. http://www.ncdonl/artikel/climate-change-its-impacts-bangladesh (accessed 19 August 2018)

El Arifeen, S., Hill, K., Ahsan, K. Z., Jamil, K., Nahar, Q. and Streatfield, P. K. (2014) Maternal mortality in Bangladesh: a countdown to 2015 country case study. *The Lancet*, **384**(9,951), 1,366–1,374.

Faisal, I. M. and Parveen, S. (2004) Food security in the face of climate change, population growth and resource constraints: implications for Bangladesh. *Environmental Management*, **34**(4), 487–498.

Green Climate Fund (2018) Country Directory: Bangladesh. http:// www.greenclimate.fund/how-we-work/tools/country-directory (accessed 18 August 2018)

GED (General Economics Division) (2009) Policy Study on the Probable Impacts of Climate Change on Poverty and Economic Growth and the Options of Coping with Adverse Effect of Climate Change in Bangladesh. Dhaka: Support to Monitoring PRS and MDGs in Bangladesh, GED, Planning Commission, Government of the People's Republic of Bangladesh and UNDP Bangladesh. http://www.climatechange .gov.bd/sites/default/files/GED_policy_report.pdf (accessed 9 August 2018)

(2015) Seventh Five-Year Plan FY2016-FY2021: accelerating Growth Empowering Citizens. Planning Commission, Government of Bangladesh. https://www.unicef.org/bangladesh/ sites/unicef.org.bangladesh/files/2018-10/7th_FYP_18_02 _2016.pdf (accessed 6 October 2020)

(2016a) Millennium development goals: end-period stocktaking and final evaluation report (2000–2015). Dhaka: GED. http:// www.sdg.gov.bd/uploads/pages/58f8d8e69b131_1_MDG-Report-Final-Layout.pdf (accessed 19 August 2018)

(2016b) A handbook mapping of ministries by targets in the implementation of SDGs aligning with Seventh Five-Year Plan Plan (2016–2020). http://www.plancomm.gov.bd/wp-content/ uploads/2016/03/A-Handbook-Mapping-of-Ministries_-targets_-SDG_-7-FYP_2016.pdf (accessed 19 August 2018)

(2017) SDGs financing strategy: Bangladesh perspective. Planning Commission, Government of Bangladesh. www .plancomm.gov.bd/wp-content/uploads/2017/11/SDGs%20 Financing%20Strategy_Final.pdf (accessed 15 August 2018)

Huq, S. (2001) Climate change and Bangladesh. *Science*, **294** (5,547), 1617.

(2016a) Political economy of climate finance. *The Daily Star*, 4 February. http://www.thedailystar.net/supplements/25th-anniversary-special-part-4/political-economy-climate-finance-211957 (accessed 12 August 2018)

(2016b) 2016: A new beginning for the world and Bangladesh. *The Daily Star*, 24 January. http://www.thedailystar.net/op-ed/2016-new-beginning-the-world-and-bangladesh-206140 (accessed 12 August 2018)

(2016c) Fifteen years of climate change adaptation planning. *The Daily Star*, 17 July. http://www.thedailystar.net/op-ed/fifteen-years-climate-change-adaptation-planning-1254658 (accessed 12 August 2018)

Iftekharuzzaman (2013) Preface. In *Report: an assessment of Climate Finance Governance in Bangladesh*. Transparency International Bangladesh (TIB). https://www.ti-bangladesh.org/beta3/images/max_file/pub_cfg_asses_13_en.pdf (accessed 17 August 2018)

IMF (2013) *Bangladesh: Poverty Reduction Strategy Paper*. Washington, DC, International Monetary Fund. https://www.imf.org/external/pubs/ft/scr/2013/cr1363.pdf

IPCC (2014) Climate Change 2014: Synthesis Report. Contribution of Working Groups I, II and III to the Fifth Assessment Report of the Intergovernmental Panel on Climate Change [Core Writing Team, R. K. Pachauri and L. A. Meyer (eds.)]. IPCC, Geneva, Switzerland.

IRENA (2018) *Renewable Energy and Jobs: Annual Review 2018*. International Renewable Energy Agency, Abu Dhabi. http://irena.org/publications/2018/May/Renewable-Energy-and-Jobs-Annual-Review-2018 (accessed 19 August 2018)

Jekobsen, F., Azam, M. H. and Kabir, M. M. U. (2002) Residual flow on the Meghna estuary on the coast line of Bangladesh estuarine. *Coastal and Shelf Science*, 55(4), 587–597.

Khan, A. E., Scheelbeek, P. F. D., Shilpi, A. B., Chan, Q., Mojumder, S. K., Rahman, A., Haines, A. and Vineis, P. (2014) Salinity in drinking water and the risk of (pre-) eclampsia and gestational hypertension in coastal Bangladesh: a case-control study. *PLoS One*, 9(9), e108715.

Mani, M. and Wang, L. (2014) Climate change and health impacts: how vulnerable is Bangladesh and what needs to be done? Washington, DC, World Bank. https://openknowledge.worldbank.org/handle/10986/21820 (accessed 17 August 2018)

Maxwell, S. (2015) Climate compatible development pathway or pipedream? CPD Anniversary Lecture. http://cpd.org.bd/wp-content/uploads/2016/01/CPD-Anniversary-Lecture-2015-Climate-Compatible-Development-Pathway-or-Pipedream-Simon-Maxwell.pdf (accessed 17 August 2018)

MoEF (Ministry of Environment and Forests) (2015) *Intended Nationally Determined Contributions (INDC)*. Submitted to the UNFCC by the Government of Bangladesh. http://www4.unfccc.int/submissions/INDC/Published%20Documents/Bangladesh/1/INDC_2015_of_Bangladesh.pdf (accessed 17 August 2018)

MoPMR (Ministry of Power, Energy and Mineral Resources) (2008) Renewable Policy of Bangladesh. http://www.sreda.gov.bd/index.php/acts-policies-rules/20–1-repenglish (accessed 10 August 2015)

Rahman, S. (2015) Bangladesh moves into crisis of aid utilisation. http://www.thedailystar.net/business/bangladesh-moves-crisis-aid-utilisation-172582 (accessed 18 August 2018)

Salomon, M. and Spanjers, J. (2017). *Illicit Financial Flows to and from Developing Countries: 2005–2014*. Washington, DC, Global Financial Integrity.

Sindico, F. (2016) Paris, climate change, and sustainable development. *Climate Law*, 6, 130–141.

Steele, P. (2015) Development finance and climate finance: achieving zero poverty and zero emissions. IIED Policy and Planning. http://www.iied.org/development-finance-climate-finance-achieving-zero-poverty-zero-emissions (accessed 12 August 2016)

Sustainable Development Knowledge Forum (2018) High-level political forum: sustainable development knowledge platform. https://sustainabledevelopment.un.org/hlpf (accessed 20 August 2018)

Thomas, T. S., Mainuddin, K., Chiang, C., Rahman, A., Haque, A., Islam, N., Quasem, S. and Sun, Y. (2013) Agriculture and adaptation in Bangladesh: current and projected impacts of climate change. Vol. 1,281. International Food Policy Research Institute.

Thompson, S. (2015) What are the Sustainable Development Goals? World Economic Forum. https://www.weforum.org/agenda/2015/09/what-are-the-sustainable-development-goals/ (accessed 4 August 2016)

Trading Economics (2016) Bangladesh remittances. http://www.tradingeconomics.com/bangladesh/remittances?embed (accessed 10 August 2016)

Uddin, N. (2018) Assessing urban sustainability of slum settlements in Bangladesh: evidence from Chittagong city. *Journal of Urban Management*, 7(1), 32–42.

United Nations (2015) Bangladeshi Prime Minister wins UN environment prize for leadership on climate change. https://news.un.org/en/story/2015/09/508702 (accessed 18 August 2018)

(2016) Sustainable Development Goals. http://www.un.org/sustainabledevelopment/sustainable-development-goals/ (accessed 12 August 2018)

UNCTAD (United Nations Conference on Trade and Development) (2014) World investment report – Investing in the SDGs: An action plan. New York, United Nations. http://unctad.org/en/PublicationsLibrary/wir2014_en.pdf (accessed 18 August 2018)

VoSB (Voice of South Bangladesh) (2015) *Gender and Water Poverty: Salinity in Rampal and Saronkhola, Bagerhat*. Study funded by the Embassy of the Kingdom of the Netherlands, through the Gender and Water Alliance. http://genderandwater.org/en/bangladesh/gwapb-products/knowledge-development/research-report/gender-and-water-poverty-salinity-in-rampal-and-saronkhola-bagerhat (accessed 19 August 2018)

Wassmann, R., Jagadish, S. V. K., Sumfleth, K., Pathak, H., Howell, G., Ismail, A., Serraj, R., Redona, E., Singh, R. K. and Heuer, S. (2009) Regional vulnerability of climate change impacts on Asian rice production and scope for adaptation. In D. L. Sparks (ed.), *Advances in Agronomy*. Burlington, MA, Academic Press. 102, 91–133.

Wright, H., Huq, S. and Reeves, J. (2015) Impact of climate change on Least Developed Countries: are the SDGs possible? IIED Briefing. May 2015. http://pubs.iied.org/pdfs/17298IIED.pdf (accessed 10 August 2018)

World Bank (2010) Bangladesh – Economics of adaptation to climate change: Main report (English). Washington, DC, World Bank. http://documents.worldbank.org/curated/en/841911468331803769/Main-report (accessed 19 August 2018)

World Bank (2018) Revenue, excluding grants (% GDP) https://data.worldbank.org/indicator/GC.REV.XGRT.GD.ZS?locations=BD-8S-1W-XO&view=chart (accessed 10 December 2018)

World Economic Forum (2016) The Global Competitiveness Report 2015–2016. Weforum. http://reports.weforum.org/global-competitiveness-report-2015–2016/ (accessed 10 August 2018)

Yu, W. M., Alam, M., Hassan, A., Khan, A. S., Ruane, A. C., Rosenzweig, C., Major, D. and Thurlow, J. (2010) Climate change risks and food security in Bangladesh. London, Washington, DC, World Bank. http://documents.worldbank.org/curated/en/419531467998254867/pdf/690860ESW0P-1050Climate0Change0Risks.pdf (accessed 7 August 2018)

26 Sustainable development in Pakistan: Vulnerabilities and opportunities

SAFDAR ULLAH KHAN[1], ZAFAR MANZOOR[2], GULASEKARAN RAJAGURU[1], AND SHABIB HAIDER SYED[3]

[1]*Bond Business School, Bond University, Queensland, Australia*
[2]*Forman Christian College (A Chartered University), Lahore, Pakistan*
[3]*Minhaj University, Lahore, Pakistan*

Keywords

Pakistan; Millennium Development Goals; Sustainable Development Goals; interconnectedness of sustainable development indicators; vector autoregressive (VAR); Granger causality; climate change

Abstract

Pakistan, like many other developing countries, has not been able to meet the United Nations Millennium Development Goals of 2015, largely because of weak institutions and a lack of policy enforcement. Pakistan has been a front-line state in the war against terrorism and is currently facing serious challenges owing to its new geopolitical settings. In this chapter, we present current trends of many development indicators directly or indirectly related to the United Nations Sustainable Development Goals 2030 and attempt to establish causal linkages among key indicators. The findings reveal important insights into the interconnectedness of various indicators, which may be useful in guiding appropriate policy actions to successfully achieve the objectives of sustainable development in Pakistan.

26.1 INTRODUCTION

'We don't have plan B because there is no planet B'.

(Ban Ki-moon, 2016)

Sustainability, as we know it today, emerged in the 1970s as a remedy for social and environmental destruction, and it is relevant because of its impact on economic growth. Sustainable development has been attracting a significant amount of attention throughout the world as it ties together social, environmental, and economic challenges facing humanity. The concept of sustainable development has been defined by the World Commission on Environment and Development as meeting 'the needs of the present without compromising the ability of future generations to meet their own needs' (WCED, 1987). Economists consider development to be sustainable only if the capital assets in the economy either do not deplete or do not surge over time (Khan *et al.*, 2011).

For Pakistan, the pattern of development has remained fragmented because of many political and environmental factors. Pakistan was considered to be a country rich in agriculture and natural resources at the time of its independence (Spielman *et al.*, 2016). However, since then, Pakistan has faced multidimensional development challenges, including depletion of natural resources, deforestation, damaged terrestrial ecosystems, desertification, erosion of soil and land, water shortages, and pollution, along with a long list of geopolitical issues. All these challenges are further compounded by the nation's war against terrorism for the last one and a half decades. In order to meet these challenges, some important steps have been taken. The National Conservation Strategy and the use of Environmental Accounting at a national level are examples of these steps. However, only limited success has been observed because of the lack of resources and effective policy enforcements. Consequently, large sections of society have remained economically deprived or are on the verge of social marginalization. The sustainable development path in Pakistan has become even trickier owing to an exploding population. Constant population growth has been working as a catalyst in bringing about environmental degradation, climate change, social deprivation, deforestation, poverty, energy crises, and water shortages in Pakistan (Ahmed and Long, 2012).

Because of the issues highlighted earlier, a scientific assessment of development goals, in terms of their complex interconnectedness, is required in order to achieve the development milestones. In the past, Pakistan could not meet its Millennium Development Goals (MDGs) during the period 2000 to 2015. This is partially because of the lack of any scientific guidelines to enable policy makers to understand the dynamic relationship between development goals. This chapter aims to address this gap by presenting a state-of-the-art empirical investigation, which may result in a very useful guide for appropriate policy actions to meet the new goals of the United Nations, known as the Sustainable Development Goals (SDGs).

The rest of the chapter is organized as follows: Section 26.2 discusses current trends of major development indicators, including the environment, water resources, and agriculture, along with the issues of corruption, terrorism, and crime. These indicators are crucial in attaining all types of development goals in a country. This is followed by a discussion on the Millennium Development Goals of Pakistan in Section 26.3. In Section 26.4, we investigate the interconnectedness of Sustainable Development Goals, also known as the 2030 agenda, set by the United Nations in 2015. Section 26.5 concludes the chapter.

26.2 COMMON DEVELOPMENT INDICATORS

There is a long list of development indicators in many national and international documents. We present common indicators that provide a basis for assessing the Millennium Development Goals and/or Sustainable Development Goals. These are rapid climate change, deforestation, glacial melting, rising sea level, water shortages, energy shortages, pollution, greenhouse gas emissions, agriculture (in particular, livestock and agroforestry) impacts, and the issues of corruption, terrorism, and crime.

26.2.1 Climate change

Being situated in one of the most vulnerable spots in the world's geographic landscape, Pakistan is susceptible to chaotic climate change (as observed in Faisal, 2017). Global warming has already pushed Pakistan into Earth's heat surplus zone. Coupled with late monsoons, erratic and intensive rain patterns, and long dry spells in winter, Pakistan is set to witness severe climatic disasters, including droughts and floods.

The major climate-related concerns of Pakistan include increased deforestation, monsoon variability, recession of the Karakorum and Himalayan glaciers, heat waves, high intrusion of saline water, escalated risks of extreme climatic disasters, and severe heat-stressed environments in semi-arid and arid areas, affecting agricultural productivity (Asian Development Bank, 2017).

Pakistan's susceptibility to the effects of climate change is well acknowledged and widely recognized. The country has witnessed frequent episodes of extreme weather conditions in the last decade. Glacial lake outbursts, scorching heat waves, recurrent floods, melting glaciers, and prolonged droughts have drastically contributed to loss of life, property, and economic prosperity. For instance, the disastrous floods of 2010 resulted in a loss of US\$10 billion, took 1,600 human lives and, to top it off, inundated 38,600 square kilometres of land. Likewise, the heatwave that struck Karachi in June 2015 killed more than 1,200 people. There has been a significant increase in the occurrence of extreme events in Pakistan in the past two decades, including its worst drought in history in 1998–2001; intense heatwaves in Karachi during 2003, 2005, 2007, 2010, and 2017; massive urban flooding in Lahore in 2007 and 2010; and severe cyclones in 2007 and 2010 (Asian Development Bank, 2017).

The country is particularly vulnerable to the challenges of climate change, as it lies in the region of the world where the temperature increase is expected to be much higher than the global average. A significant warming climatic trend was observed in Pakistan from 1961 to 2007, with a mean annual temperature increase of 0.47°C. The land area of Pakistan is mostly arid and semi-arid, where more than 60% of the area receives rainfall of 250 mm or less (Asian Development Bank, 2017). Figure 26.1 shows historical trends of precipitation and temperature.

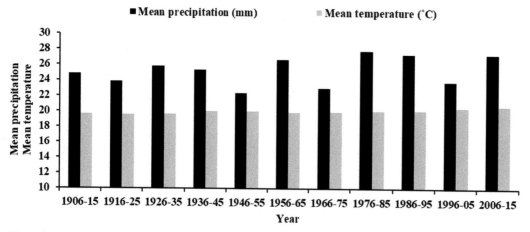

Figure 26.1. Decade-wise trends of mean temperatures and precipitation (*Source*: World Bank, 2017).

The Asian Development Bank (2017) further indicated an increase in the heatwave days per year by 31 days since 1980, whereas a decrease in periods of cold weather was also experienced in northeastern and southern parts of Pakistan. Over the past few years, warming trends have been observed in Pakistan; the higher average minimum temperatures have caused a prolonged negative impact on animal and agricultural productivity (Janjua et al., 2010). Correspondingly, water requirements have significantly increased.

26.2.2 Deforestation

The country has been facing rapid deforestation at an unprecedented rate, rising from 0.75% in 2009 to 2.9% in 2015 (Ministry of Climate Change, 2015). A loss of 42,000 hectares (2.1%) of forests in Pakistan has been observed per year (Food and Agriculture Organization of the United Nations (FAO), 2016). Deforestation on such a scale is extremely harmful for society and the environment. The 'timber mafia' in Pakistan, especially in Khyber Pakhtunkhwa (KPK), has treated the forest wood as 'booty' (Ministry of Climate Change, 2015). This alarming deforestation rate has further raised concerns for the country's climate. Massive forest destruction is causing disruptions in water supplies, with reduced agricultural productivity, soil erosion, environmental degradation, increases in landslides, and loss of biomass in Pakistan. The formation of a glacial lake (Atta Abad Lake) is one of the major disasters caused by the landslides. It caused the village of Ayeenabad to be completely submerged, and the major areas of Shishkat, Gulmit, and Gojal were also affected. Furthermore, this has affected 25,000 human lives in that region (Khan et al., 2011).

26.2.3 Agriculture, livestock, and forestry

Changes in the climate have significantly impacted various sectors, including agriculture, livestock, forestry, water, energy, and coastal areas. The agricultural sector contributes almost 21% to the gross domestic product of Pakistan (Hanif et al., 2010). The unstable climate has affected water availability in cultivation areas, resulting in a 6% reduction in wheat yield. Consequently, basmati rice yield decreased approximately 15% to 18% in the year of 2016 (Asian Development Bank, 2017).

Similarly, the livestock sector of Pakistan has also been hit hard by the climatic shifts, which have further degraded the grazing system across the country. The grazing lands and pastures are depleting because of floods, with rising temperature and erratic precipitation. According to a report by Naheed et al. (2015), livestock production is likely to decrease by 20% to 30% in coming years because of rising temperatures. This is followed by decreasing trends in growing cattle and other important livestock, which are the leading sources of earnings in most of rural Pakistan.

26.2.4 Melting glaciers and rises in sea levels

All the rivers of the country, fed by the Himalayan, Hindu Kush, and Karakoram glaciers, are reportedly receding because of global warming. The western part of the Himalayan glacier is expected to recede within the next 50 years, causing the Indus to rise, draining reservoirs. In contrast to the above, the surveys conducted during 1997 to 2007 suggest that the Karakoram glaciers, ranging from 40 to 70 km in length, are exhibiting a thickening of 5 to 15 metres (Asian Development Bank, 2017). In all circumstances, however, the impact of climate change on the western Himalayas is noteworthy.

26.2.5 Energy crises

Along with limited water resources, Pakistan is facing an energy crisis, which may cause delays in meeting developmental goals. Pakistan is primarily dependent upon three major energy resources, including oil, coal, and natural gas, for generating electricity. The crisis in the energy sector can be traced back to 2009, when a sharp increase in oil prices was experienced across the world, including Pakistan (Rehman et al., 2017). Therefore, in 2009–2010, Pakistan observed an increase in oil prices, and, correspondingly, electricity and gas supplies dropped substantially. Furthermore, the lower stock of water reserves in Tarbela and Mangla hydro dams contributed to the energy shortage (Ansari and Unar, 2011). As a result, Pakistan observed a drop of 2.0% in GDP during 2009–2010 (Javed et al., 2016). In addition to the energy crisis, a lower share (2%) of renewable energy in electricity generation may make the overall energy requirements for sustainable growth and development still more severe (Figure 26.2).

Fashina et al. (2018) commented on the slow development of indigenous energy resources and considered this a major bottleneck in Pakistan's sustainable energy development. Abbasi et al. (2017) observed that, because the natural gas reserves are being depleted in Pakistan, the gas deficit is expected to grow at an unprecedented rate. Furthermore, the gas reserves are expected to stand at 242.96 million cubic metres by 2022, while the anticipated domestic gas supply will remain at 59.75 million cubic metres, indicating an expected shortfall of 183.21 million cubic metres.

Electricity consumption at the household level has increased because of many competing factors, such as rising population and domestic consumption. The government of Pakistan has recently prioritized the industrial sector and vowed to provide uninterrupted power to the manufacturing and processing industries (Abbasi et al., 2017).

Pakistan currently has low crude oil reserves,[1] with no future prospects of reaching oil self-sufficiency. According to Valasai

---

[1] 256 million barrels (about 35 million tonnes) as at 31 December 2017 (*Source*: Eni, 2018).

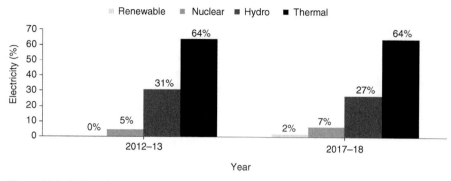

Figure 26.2. Pakistan's energy mix (electricity) (*Source*: Ministry of Finance, 2018).

et al. (2017), the ongoing energy crisis in Pakistan can be easily traced back to energy policies adopted in the 1990s. These policies worked as a doorway for enabling private sector investors to produce thermal electricity from imports of oil and natural gas. Because of this, the energy import bills of Pakistan rose substantially. Scant indigenous oil resources to cater for the energy demands of a growing economy forced Pakistan to rely on imported oil. For example, during the months of July to March in the 2017 fiscal year, crude oil imports were 5.9 million tonnes, with a value of US$1.84 billion (Ministry of Finance, 2017).

26.2.6 Pollution

Environmental pollution can easily destabilize the development process of any developing or transitional economy dependent on natural resources (Alam *et al.*, 2012). Environmental constraints, such as air pollution, water pollution, freshwater scarcity, and degradation of fisheries and forests, are putting hurdles in the way of sustainable development in Pakistan. The current development patterns in Pakistan are not considered to be sustainable. Alam *et al.* (2012) described rapid industrial growth and urbanization as the major causes of environmental degradation across the country. Geomorphological and ecological disruptions arising from excessive energy extraction and processing plants result in both air and noise pollution (Asian Development Bank, 2017).

26.2.7 Greenhouse gas (GHG) emissions

It has been reported that the total greenhouse gas emissions in Pakistan in 2017 were 369 million tonnes of carbon dioxide (CO_2) equivalent (Asian Development Bank, 2017). Indications are that deforestation, increasing use of coal, oil, and natural gas, and the growing population may further increase GHG emissions in the coming decade. The resulting carbon dioxide emitted into the environment is considered to be the largest source of Pakistan's GHG emissions (Asian Development Bank, 2017).

Alam *et al.* (2012) estimated that a 1% increase in the economic growth rate would contribute to growth in carbon dioxide emissions by 0.84% per annum by 2020. Despite being one of the countries with the lowest per capita GHG emissions, Pakistan is still on the list of the 10 most climate-affected countries. Figure 26.3 shows the trend of CO_2 emissions per capita (from fuel combustion only) of Pakistan from 1990 to 2016, together with the trends for Bangladesh, India, and the world. The rate of CO_2 emissions per capita in Pakistan remains low, ranging from 0.52 tonne in 1990 to 0.85 tonne in 2007, after which it declined to 0.73 tonne in 2013 before rising to 0.80 tonne in 2016. The declining trend of CO_2 emissions per capita for Pakistan from 2007 to 2013 was caused by lower energy consumption coupled with the slowdown of economic growth in Pakistan during that period (PBS, 2019).

Of the three South Asian countries, India's CO_2 emissions per capita are highest (0.61 tonne in 1990 to 1.57 tonnes in 2016), followed by Pakistan (0.52 tonne in 1990 to 0.80 tonne in 2016), while Bangladesh (0.11 tonne in 1990 to 0.45 tonne in 2016) is the lowest. Although the trends reveal that the CO_2 emissions per capita for Pakistan, India, and Bangladesh are rising, they are still well below the world average, which ranges from 3.89 tonnes in 1990 to 4.35 tonnes in 2016.

The major source of GHG emissions in Pakistan has been in the electricity sector, followed by the manufacturing, transport, and residential sectors. The energy sector includes the consumption of fossil fuels used for electricity generation. Oil combustion for generating electricity contributes 62% to the GHG emissions of the energy sector, while natural gas contributes 38%, as estimated during 2016. Manufacturing industries involved in combustion activities related to the production of cement, fertilizer, and bricks contributed 23% of total GHG emissions in Pakistan in 2016 (Mir *et al.*, 2017). For example, in the case of the production of bricks, there are high GHG emissions from lignite oil, agricultural residues, rubber tyres, and plastics burnt in kilns. Figure 26.4 shows the

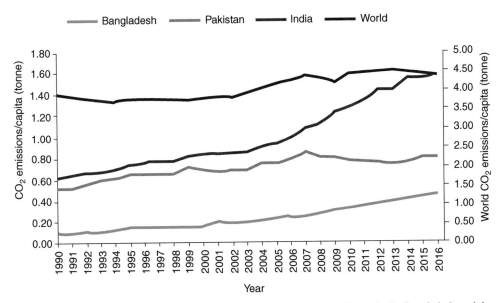

Figure 26.3. CO_2 emissions per capita (from fuel combustion only) for Pakistan, India, Bangladesh, and the world (*Source*: IEA Statistics, 1990–2016).

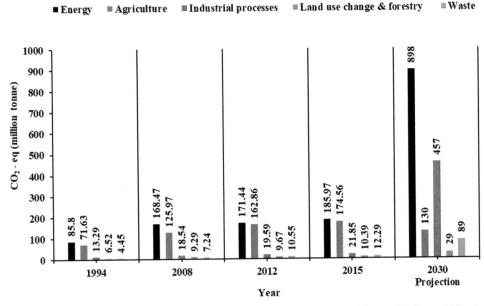

Figure 26.4. Inventory of GHG emissions (in Mt CO_2 equivalent) for Pakistan (*Source*: Ministry of Climate Change, 2016).

GHG emissions for the six major socio-economic sectors for the years 1994, 2008, 2012, and 2015, and the projected emissions through to 2030, as provided in the Intended Nationally Determined Contribution of Pakistan (Ministry of Climate Change, 2016).

In order to find a sustainable path, Pakistan needs to reduce its GHG emissions by utilizing domestic resources in combination with international financial assistance. Since the major GHG contributor in Pakistan is the energy sector, finding

clean energy alternatives will help in reducing the GHG emissions per annum. The agriculture sector is also seen as contributing 175 Mt CO_2 equivalent in the overall GHG emissions, so finding new ways to produce crops and fodder can also reduce GHG emissions in Pakistan (Ministry of Climate Change, 2016).

It is noted that the GHG-projected emissions for 2030 are 4.8 times and 20.8 times higher for the energy and industrial processes, respectively, than those in 2015.

26.2.8 Water crises

Pakistan, being a semi-arid country and an agrarian economy, depends heavily on the Indus River and its tributaries[2] to meet its water needs. In order to lock in sustained economic growth for a long time, water availability and its efficient utilization are extremely pertinent (State Bank of Pakistan, 2017). Neighbouring regional countries are either dependent on multiple basins or are receiving sufficient amounts of rainfall, as compared with Pakistan. India, Bangladesh, and Nepal derive most of their water from the tropical monsoon climate and rainfall, which exceeds 1,000 mm per annum; however, Pakistan records less than 500 mm per annum (Arshad *et al.*, 2017). In addition, Pakistan's water conservation strategies are also facing challenges owing to evaporation losses and extensive pumping of underground water. Limited storage of water and weak irrigation infrastructure have also contributed to the water crises in Pakistan (Arshad *et al.*, 2017).

Per capita surface water availability in Pakistan has decreased significantly over the past 65 years, from 5,260 m³ per capita per year in 1951 to about 1,000 m³ per capita per year in 2016 (Ministry of Water Resources, 2018). In addition, groundwater supplies are also rapidly depleting, with no future strategy to save the groundwater. Figure 26.5 shows the surface water availability per capita per year for Pakistan from 1951 to 2013, with a projection for 2025, with three thresholds also indicated: water stress (<1,700 m³ per capita per year), water scarcity (<1,000 m³ per capita per year), and absolute water scarcity (<500 m³ per capita per year) (State Bank of Pakistan, 2017). The figure indicates that Pakistan had reached the water stress threshold (<1,700 m³ per capita) in 1990, and it reached the water scarcity threshold (<1,000 m³ per capita) in 2013. Pakistan is projected to be approaching the threshold for absolute water scarcity (<500 m³ per capita) by 2025 (Figure 26.5). Luo *et al.* (2015) of the World Resources Institute have projected that by 2040 under the business-as-usual scenario, Pakistan would become one of the top 33 countries under extremely high water stress (i.e., >80% of ratio of withdrawals to available water). Water scarcity affects health, food security, and energy security. The National Water Policy 2018 highlights the concern for growing conflicts and social unrest in the country due to water scarcity (Ministry of Water Resources, 2018). The over-pumping in the regions of Kohat, Bannu, and Dera Ismail Khan has contributed largely to distressing and lowering water tables, with the deep saline groundwater entering freshwater reserves. There is a need for regulations to curb over-extraction of groundwater and promote aquifer recharge (Ministry of Water Resources, 2018).

Water scarcity in Pakistan is caused by several major issues, including water politics, climate change, population growth, and

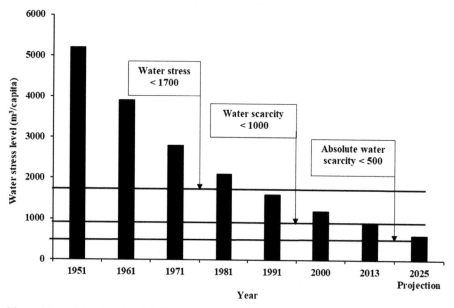

Figure 26.5. Water stress levels in Pakistan (observed from 1951 to 2013, and projected for 2025). This figure is adapted from State Bank of Pakistan (2017). The three thresholds (i.e. water stress (<1,700 m³/capita/year), water scarcity (<1,000 m³/capita/year), and absolute water scarcity (<500 m³/capita/year) were proposed by Falkenmark (1986).

---

[2] Kabul, Jhelum, Chenab, Ravi, and Sutlej rivers.

urbanization. Poor water management and lack of policy enforcement have negatively impacted water availability. Rising temperatures are also contributing towards the water crisis in Pakistan (Bano and Arshad, 2018). Erratic monsoon seasons and droughts have played their part in worsening the water situation. On top of these, Pakistan is unable to save floodwater owing to a scarcity of dams and rapid deforestation.

Water storage capacity in Pakistan is inadequate (State Bank of Pakistan, 2017; Ministry of Water Resources, 2018). Pakistan's reservoirs are using about 8% storage capacity of their surface flows, compared with more than 40% storage capacity in India (Pakistan Economic Forum, 2015).The three major reservoirs, Mangla (1967), Chashma (1971), and Tarbela (1978), have a total designed capacity of 19,427.31 million cubic metres (15.75 million acre feet), which has reduced to 16,158.59 million cubic metres (13.1 million acre feet) because of sedimentation. They can save water for only 30 days. More recently, the water levels at the above reservoirs have reached minimum levels (State Bank of Pakistan, 2017).

Apart from storage issues, water wastage rates are also escalating in Pakistan. The unsustainable methods of pumping waste water have led to the intrusion of brackish water into the freshwater resources. This has caused the overall quality of water to drop – more than 50 million people living in Pakistan are at risk of arsenic poisoning because of groundwater extraction in areas where arsenic naturally occurs (Nadeem and McArthur, 2018). The underground water is estimated to have arsenic levels of more than 200 micrograms per litre, which is much higher than the WHO recommendation of 10 micrograms per litre. The water pollution stems from the fact that 90% of untreated industrial and household water is directly discharged into drains,

ponds, rivers, and streams. The waste water contains chemicals, fertilizers, and pesticides that not only contaminate freshwater bodies, but also seep into the groundwater aquifers, affecting the quality of drinking water and giving rise to serious health concerns.

Apart from the aforementioned challenges and development indicators, the most recent debate includes corruption, terrorism, and crime as major hurdles in achieving sustainable development in Pakistan.

26.2.9 Corruption

Pakistan has observed serious political instability – many governments have been dismissed because of their involvement in corruption. Therefore, the military claimed it would be able to replace the corrupt politicians (Ali, 2017). However, despite numerous efforts, Pakistan was unable to improve governance and eliminate corruption under all three military rules, that is, General Ayub's period (1958–1968), Zia's regime (1977–1988), and Musharraf's rule (1999–2008). The country still remains in the very bottom ranks of the Corruption Perceptions Index (see Figure 26.6). Transparency International (2017) observed that the country has unaccountable government regimes, high-profile corruption scandals and a lack of public trust in the public systems. Khan (2011) identified corruption as a bigger hurdle than terrorism in hindering sustainable development in Pakistan. This is also observed by the barometer of Transparency International, which indicates that people in Pakistan believe police, judiciary, and government officials to be highly corrupt. In order to address the issue of corruption and a weak law and order system, the Pakistani government pledged in 2013 to create

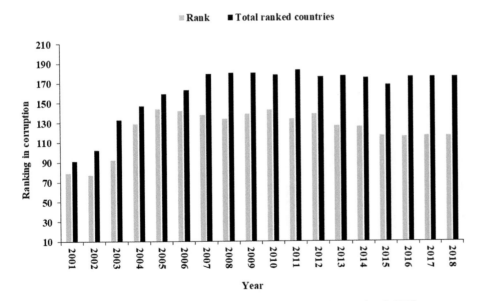

Figure 26.6. Pakistan's ranking in corruption (*Source*: Transparency International, 2018).

conditions that would enable strict enforcement of rule of law by strengthening the judicial system and revamping the criminal justice system (Government of Pakistan, 2018).

26.2.10 Terrorism

Pakistan is facing the great challenges of extremism and terrorism, making it very difficult to achieve developmental goals. The country has suffered the loss of many civilian lives and observed huge collateral damage against the backdrop of its continuing war against terrorism for the last one and a half decades. Terrorism and the war on terror have temporarily displaced individuals, the elderly, women and children and resulted in many refugees. This has also led to a huge erosion of heritage, culture, and civic values. The country paid a cost estimated at more than US$126.79 billion, as well as losses of more than

61,000 civilian lives between 2002 and 2017 (Ali, 2017). During this period, Pakistan received considerable aid and foreign investment to maintain law and order. However, with the intensification of conflicts and terrorism attacks and the worsening situation for law and order, the economic growth rate plummeted.

Researchers have analysed the causal linkages between economic growth and terrorism at the subnational level in Pakistan. The results reveal that the economy of Sindh, KPK, and Baluchistan has been more affected by the negative shocks of terrorism than Punjab has. Terrorism also adversely affected foreign investment and the tourism industry (Ali, 2017). Figures 26.7 and 26.8 show the cost of terrorism in terms of monetary value and fatalities. It can be seen that the highest cost of terrorism was experienced in 2011, while it declined afterwards and reached US$2.07 billion in 2018.

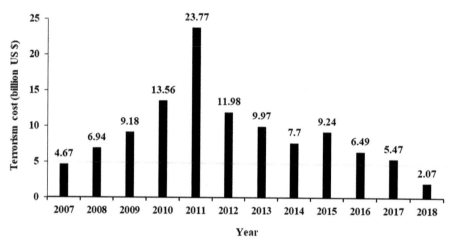

Figure 26.7. Monetary cost of terrorism (*Source*: Ministry of Finance, 2018).

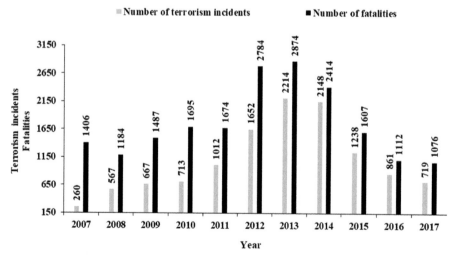

Figure 26.8. Terrorism incidents and fatalities in Pakistan, 2007–2017 (*Source*: Global Terrorism Database, 2017).

26.2.11 Crime

An increasing crime rate and an inefficient judicial system are additional impediments in meeting the sustainable development challenges in the country. In particular, criminal acts, such as burglary, robbery, kidnapping, murder, and attempted murder, are some of the major challenges faced by many developing nations, including Pakistan (Vorrath and Beisheim, 2015). A large number of studies have identified the negative relationship between crime and economic growth of a country (Northup and Klaer, 2002; Mulok *et al.*, 2016; Rios, 2016; Kathena and Sheefini, 2017).

In the case of Pakistan, the criminal justice system has failed to ensure the protection of life and property rights (Syed and Ahmad, 2013). In the year 2015 alone, more than 230,000 appeals and petitions were pending in the High Court and Supreme Court (see Figures 26.9 and 26.10).

It is observed that, to attain the Sustainable Development Goals, including social sustainability, countries must focus on reducing violence and diversion of financial resources towards crime control initiatives (UNODC, 2015). This is because, with increased criminal activities, including homicide, theft, burglary, dacoity (banditry), rioting, rape, and robbery, developing nations like Pakistan and similar countries are unlikely to achieve the development goals (Panda *et al.*, 2016).

26.3 MILLENNIUM DEVELOPMENT GOALS OF PAKISTAN

The Millennium Development Goals (MDGs) were established at the United Nations Millennium Summit in September 2000, as a vision to fight illiteracy, poverty, and hunger, and to ensure environmental sustainability. As a part of the UN objectives, the

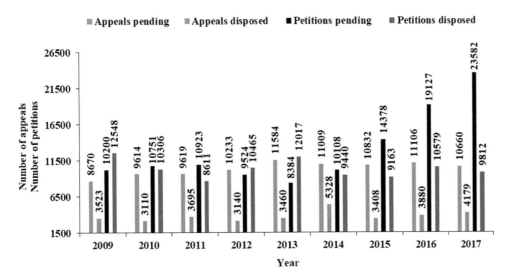

Figure 26.9. Pending and disposed appeals and petitions in the Supreme Court (*Source*: Pakistan Statistical Year Book, 2017).

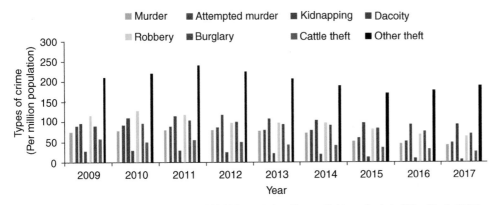

Figure 26.10. Crimes reported by type per 1,000,000 population (*Source*: Pakistan Statistical Year Book, 2017).

MDGs provided a yardstick to measure the speed of development in UN member countries. They also helped to assess the role of non-governmental organizations (NGOs) in contributing towards development in a given country (Pakistan Institute for Parliamentary Services, 2014). The MDGs included measurable targets particularly related to reducing poverty, hunger, inequality, unemployment, illiteracy, diseases, and child mortality. These were set to be achieved by 2015; however, the acceleration framework of MDGs continues until the end of 2018.

Pakistan has spent around US$30.371 billion in efforts to achieve MDGs, in the areas of social welfare, education, health, and employment (Haq, 2017). The country has achieved only partial success in eradicating poverty, controlling child mortality rates, achieving environmental sustainability, and promoting gender equality. Pakistan lagged behind and stayed off-track on 24 of its indicators, while achieving only nine of the indicators under eight MDGs (UNDP, 2015). It has been observed that approximately 38% of the population is still living below the poverty line. MDGs required 13% of the population to have a

minimum level of dietary energy consumption; however, 58% of the population in Pakistan was below the benchmark set by the MDGs in 2011. In 2015, 60% of the population was below the minimum threshold of dietary energy. Regarding educational attainments, the nation targeted an 88% literacy rate by 2015 but ended up with only 58% (Pakistan Institute for Parliamentary Services, 2014).

Pakistan also could not achieve the goal of gender equality, despite major efforts being made by the government to make gender equality applicable in Pakistan. However, Pakistan was able to root out discrimination from the National Assembly, resulting in 22% of the seats being held by women (Pakistan Institute for Parliamentary Services, 2014).

Among many other reasons, lack of public policy enforcement, poor institutional capacity, flawed policies, financial constraints at provincial and federal levels, and improper planning remain key impediments in meeting the MDGs. This is further discussed in the next section. Table 26.1 presents target value of MDGs for Pakistan along with their current level of achievement.

Table 26.1. Millennium Development Goals and indicators for Pakistan.

Goals and indicators	National value	Target value
Eradication of extreme poverty and hunger		
Proportion of population below the calorie-based food plus non-food poverty line	12.40	13.00
Underweight children under the age of five years	31.50	19.00
Proportion of population below the minimum level of dietary energy consumption	30.00	13.00
Achieve universal primary achievement		
Net primary enrolment ratio (%)	57.00	100.00
Completion/survival rate grade 1 to 5 (%)	50.00	100.00
Literacy rate (%)	58.00	88.00
Promote gender equality and women empowerment		
GPI primary education	0.90	1.00
GPI secondary education	0.81	1.00
GPI youth literacy	0.81	1.00
Reduce child mortality		
Mortality rate under 5 (deaths per 1,000 live births)	89.00	52.00
Infant mortality rate (deaths per 1,000 live births)	74.00	40.00
Ratio of fully immunized children (12–23 months)	80.00	90.00
Ratio of children under 1 year old immunized against measles	81.00	90.00
Ratio of children under 5 suffering from diarrhoea in the last 30 days (%)	8.00	10.00
Female health workers coverage (% of target population)	83.00	100.00
Improve maternal health		
Maternal mortality ratio	276.00	140.00
Ratio of births attended by birth attendants (skilled)	52.10	90.00
Contraceptive prevalence rate	35.40	55.00
Total fertility rate	3.80	2.10
Ratio of women (age cohort 15–49) who had given birth during the last 3 years and made at least one antenatal consultation	68.00	100.00
Combat HIV AIDS, malaria, and other diseases		
HIV prevalence among 15–49-year-old pregnant women per 10,000 population	0.41	0.50
HIV prevalence among 15–49-year-old pregnant women per 10,000 population	48.60	50.00

Table 26.1. (cont.)

Goals and indicators	National value	Target value
Ratio of population in malaria-risk areas using effective prevention and treatment measures	40.00	75.00
Incidence of TB/10,000	230.00	45.00
TB cases detected and cured under DOTS/10,000	91.00	85.00
Ensuring environmental sustainability (ratio w.r.t target)		
Forest cover (%)	0.87	1.00
Land area protected for conservation of wildlife (%)	0.97	1.00
GDP (1980–1981 base year) per ton of oil equivalent (energy efficiency)	0.94	1.00
Sulphur content in high-speed diesel	1.20	1.00
Ratio of population with access to water sources	0.96	1.00
Ratio of population with access to sanitation	0.80	1.00
Ratio of regularized Katchi Abadies*	NA	1.00

Note: * Katchi Abadies are slum areas.

(*Source:* Extracted from Pakistan Institute for Parliamentary Services, 2014)

26.4 SUSTAINABLE DEVELOPMENT GOALS (2030 AGENDA)

Sustainable Development Goals (SDGs), also known as global goals or the 2030 Agenda, aim to end poverty, protect the environment and ensure peace and prosperity across the world. The SDGs were set by the United Nations along with member countries in 2015 to succeed the MDGs. However, unlike the MDGs, the SDGs have a broader scope for all developing and developed countries.

Millennium Development Goals have not been achieved by many developing countries, including Pakistan. This has led many critics to challenge the applicability of MDGs. For example, Deneulin and Shahani (2009) analysed the weak justification behind the chosen objectives of MDGs. In the same vein, Kabeer (2010) found MDGs to have unrealistic objectives in the presence of significant heterogeneities within developing countries. Similarly, many have criticized the inadequate attention towards environmental sustainability and the agricultural sector in the MDGs. Others noted that MDGs focused primarily on donors' success instead of the achievements of the goals (UNDP, 2003).

Because of the failure to achieve MDGs and the present state of development in Pakistan, it requires great attention to assess the nature and potential for achievement of the recent SDGs. To achieve this, we present a baseline analysis of SDGs and then estimate the interconnectedness among goals. This should help policy makers in various ways to design appropriate policy actions to achieve some success in meeting the SDGs.

Table 26.2 presents baseline information regarding the current state of selected SDGs in Pakistan. As can be seen, the country reached the lowest value in the Human Development Index of 0.55, as compared with its neighbouring South Asian countries (Lead, 2016). Pakistan's National Assembly Secretariat, in its 34th session, reported that 29.5% of the people (55 million) live below the poverty line (Pakistan Institute for Parliamentary Services, 2014). In per capita terms, 21.04% of the population stand below the poverty line (an income of US$1.25 per adult per day) (Pakistan Institute for Parliamentary Services, 2014).

Furthermore, the Global Food Security Index has ranked Pakistan at 79th out of 109 countries in terms of achieving the first SDG goal of 'no hunger'. Moreover, the country has not achieved the desired outcome of children's health and well-being. Almost 45% of deaths in children under the age of five are caused by poor nutrition. The Food and Agriculture Organization of the United Nations found that 37.5 million people in Pakistan are undernourished, and the World Food Programme (WFP) noted that about 50% of women and children are malnourished (Lead, 2016). In relation to good health and well-being, Pakistan is currently confronting many challenges with health-related services. This is witnessed by infant mortality and poor maternal health, which is broadly linked with low levels of women's empowerment. Likewise, the goals of gender equality and quality education are closely related to each other.

26.4.1 Estimating interconnectedness of SDGs

Sustainable Development Goals are a mix of social, economic, and environmental goals that require careful analysis. To achieve a comprehensive view, the interconnectedness is investigated among SDGs through a time series analysis. The summary statistics of the selected indicators from SDGs reveal great parallels in vulnerability for many indicators during the sample period (see Appendix Table A2).[3] In particular, the indicators of infant mortality rate, safe drinking water availability, access to electricity, life below water, assistance required to reduce inequality, and

Table 26.2. Sustainable Development Goals and Pakistan's baseline.

Sustainable Development Goals	
1. No poverty	21.04% population was estimated to be under poverty line of US$1.25. 60.19% population was estimated to be below poverty line of US$2.
2. Zero hunger	58.10% food insecure households. 169 kcal/person/day intensity of food deprivation.
3. Good health and well-being	Mortality rate of 88 per 1,000 live births of age less than five years. Children maternal mortality ratio of 170 per 100 k live births.
4. Quality education	58% of overall literacy rate. 25.02 million children aged 5–16 are still out of school.
5. Gender equality	Ranked at 142 out of 144 in terms of women's economic participation. Ranked at 132 out of 144 in women's education.
6. Clean water and sanitation	35% of population have access to safe drinking water. 52% have access to improved sanitation.
7. Affordable and clean energy	91.4% of population have access to electricity. Renewable energy has less than 1% share in total energy mix.
8. Decent work and economic growth	6.2% unemployment rate. 53.1% labour force participation rate.
9. Industry, innovation, and infrastructure	10.9% of population use of internet. 20.3% of industry contribution in total GDP.
10. Reduced inequalities	Gini coefficient of 30. 1.55 Palma Index top 10% to bottom 40% consumption ratio.
11. Sustainable cities and communities	5.0% growth rate of cities population. Urban population of 47.0% lives in nine cities only.
12. Responsible consumption and production	25% energy loss in all sectors. 68.3% of electricity is generated from fossil fuels.
13. Climate action	Total GHG emissions of 310 Mt of CO_2 eq. 6.0% of the total budget is allocated to climate financing.
14. Life below water	350 million gallons/day raw sewage and industrial waste flows into Arabian Sea. Rank 222 on Global Ocean Health Index.
15. Life on land	68 million hectares of land is affected by desertification and degradation. Only 2.1% of national forest cover.
16. Peace, justice, and strong institutions	Three million cases are pending in judiciary. On average, 9,000 deaths annually are due to terrorist activities.
17. Partnerships for the goals	

(*Sources:* Adapted from UNDP (2017); retrieved from SDG Indicators, at https://unstats.un.org/sdgs/indicators/database/; and Lead (2016) at http://www.lead.org.pk/lead/attachments/SDGFlyer_english.pdf.)

official development assistance show high fluctuations. Therefore, it is difficult to predict the progress made in the above indicators of those particular goals. Furthermore, the correlation analysis reveals important information regarding the strength of the linear association between selected indicators (see Appendix Table A3). For example, we find very strong correlation between goals of 'zero poverty', 'no hunger', 'good health and well-being', 'clean water and sanitation', 'affordable and clean energy', and 'life and

land'. The remaining goals are also highly correlated with one another. The above correlation analysis confirms interconnectedness and provides a basis to understand the development process in the country. Although correlation analysis explores the relationship between SDGs, it does not provide a causal direction between them. The dynamic causal relationships between various SDGs are examined through the vector autoregressive (VAR) model. Appendix B explains unit root tests, vector autoregressive models, and their application to Granger causality tests to examine the interconnectedness between SDGs in greater detail.

[3] The selected indicators from SDGs and definitions are presented in Appendix Table A1.

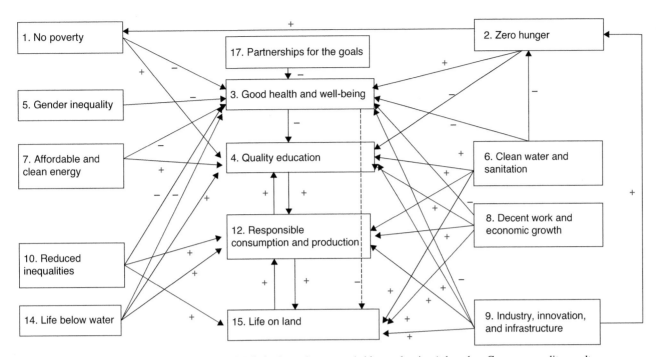

Figure 26.11. The direction of causality among SDGs is shown by arrows (with + and – signs), based on Granger causality results.

The interconnectedness between selected SDGs is summarized in Figure 26.11.[4] SDGs 11, 13, and 16 are excluded because not enough data are available for dynamic analysis. The results show that direct public spending reduces poverty (SDG1) and the infant mortality rate as a measure of good health and well-being (SDG3), and it improves the quality of education (SDG4). Reduction in infant mortality rates is also achieved by improving gender equality (SDG5), affordable clean energy (SDG7), clean water and sanitation (SDG6), decent work and economic growth (SDG8), and industry, innovation, and infrastructure (SDG9). It is further diminished by lowering hunger and the prevalence of undernourishment (SDG2) and reducing gender inequality (SDG10).

The quality of education is found to be influenced by nine other sustainable development goals. Affordable clean energy, lowering poverty and hunger, clean water and sanitation, improved industrial output, economic growth and consumption, and increases in marine key biodiversity areas have a direct effect on quality education. Moreover, the sustainable goals of decent work, economic growth, industry innovation, and infrastructure show very high effects on other SDGs. In particular, both of these SDGs have a positive effect on quality education, and responsible consumption and production goals. It also appears that they help to lower the infant mortality rates by the means of improving good health and well-being. The policy

measures targeted towards these two SDGs (SDG8 and SDG9) will have the most significant spillover effects on other SDGs. In addition, reduced inequalities (SDG10), clean water sanitation (SDG6), and life below water (SDG14) have significant impacts on the other SDGs, with spillover effects on three other SDGs. The policy measures targeted towards these three SDGs will also be beneficial in achieving the remaining three SDGs (i.e., SDGs 11, 13, and 16) which are not included in the analysis.

26.5 CONCLUSION

Overall, we find a mixed picture of Pakistan's development in terms of achieving the SDGs set by the United Nations. The country has suffered a diverse range of problems that have further hindered the process of sustainable development over the last few decades. These include direct challenges to sustainable development, such as environmental degradation, climate change, energy crises, shortage of water, poverty, and inequality, while at the same time, indirect challenges like corruption, crime, terrorism, and extremism are taxing its resources and shrinking the capacity to address these important issues. This study helps to advance our knowledge by finding directions of causality between various sustainable development indicators. This may further provide useful insights to applied researchers and policy makers by identifying the best courses of action necessary to overcome the economic and social challenges.

[4] See Appendix Table B2 for the statistical significance of the Granger causality test results.

ACKNOWLEDGEMENTS

This chapter is based on many studies for Pakistan conducted by national and international researchers over the long period of time. Editorial assistance from Chamkaur Gill in preparation of earlier version of this chapter is gratefully acknowledged. Very helpful suggestions and comments were received from Dr Muhammad Idrees, Dr Ros Taplin, Dr Goh Yong Kheng (specially on statistical analysis), two anonymous reviewers, and Dr Pak Sum Low.

REFERENCES

Abbasi, A., Mehmood, F., Wasti, A., Kamal, M. and Fatima, Z. (2017) Rethinking Pakistan's energy equation: Iran-Pakistan gas pipeline. *Sustainable Development Policy*, **5**(2), 1–12.

Ahmed, K. and Long, W. (2012) Environmental Kuznets curve and Pakistan: An empirical analysis. *Procedia Economics and Finance*, **1**, 4–13.

Alam, S., Fatima, A. and Bhatti, M. S. (2012) Sustainable development in Pakistan in the context of energy consumption demand and environmental degradation. *Journal of Asian Economics*, **18**(5), 825–837.

Ali, M. (2017) Implementing the 2030 Agenda in Pakistan: the critical role of enabling environment in the mobilization of domestic and external resources. Discussion Paper 14/2017, German Development Institute. Bonn. https://www.die-gdi.de/uploads/media/DP_14.2017.pdf

Ansari, A. K. and Unar, I. N. (2011) Sustainable development indicators for energy in Pakistan. *Energy, Environment and Sustainable Development*, **2**(6), 25–38.

Arshad, M., Kachele, H. and Krupnik, T. J. (2017) Climate variability, farmland value and farmers' perception of climate change: implications for adaptation in rural Pakistan. *International Journal of Sustainable Development and World Energy*, **24**(6), 532–544.

Asian Development Bank (2017) Climate Change Profile of Pakistan. https://www.adb.org/sites/default/files/publication/357876/climate-change-profile-pakistan.pdf

Ban Ki-moon (2016) Secretary General's remarks to the press at COP22. https://www.un.org/sustainabledevelopment/blog/2016/11/secretary-generals-remarks-to-the-press-at-cop22/

Bano, I. and Arshad, M. (2018) Climatic changes impact on water availability. In M. Arshad (ed.), *Perspectives on Water Usage for Biofuels Production: Aquatic Contamination and Climate Change*, pp. 39–54. Springer, Cham. https://link.springer.com/chapter/10.1007/978-3-319-66408-8_2

Deneulin, S. and Shahani, L. (2009) *An Introduction to the Human Development and Capability Approach: Freedom and Agency*. London, Earthscan, IDRC (International Development Research Centre).

Dickey, D. A. and Fuller, W. A. (1979) Distribution of the estimators for autoregressive time series with a unit root. *Journal of the American Statistical Association*, **74**(366a), 427–431.

Eni (2018) *World Oil Review 2018, Volume 1*. Rome, Italy, Ente Nazionale Idrocarburi (ENI). https://www.eni.com/assets/documents/documents-en/WORLD-OIL-REVIEW-2018-Volume-1.pdf

Faisal, F. (2017) Sustainability: an imperative for improving governance and management in Pakistan. *Pakistan Social and Economic Review*, **55**(1), 53–78.

Falkenmark, M. (1986) Freshwater – time for a modified approach. *Ambio*, **15**, 192–200.

Fashina, A., Mundu, M., Akiyode, O., Abdullah, L., Sanni, D. and Ounyesiga, L. (2018) The drivers and barriers of renewable energy applications and development: a review. *Clean Technologies*, **1**(1), 3.

Food and Agriculture Organization of the United Nations (FAO) (2016) *Global Forest Resources Assessment. How Are the World's Forests Changing? (Second edition)*. Rome, FAO. http://www.fao.org/3/a-i4793e.pdf

Global Terrorism Database (2017) *Terrorism*. Our World in Data website: https://ourworldindata.org/terrorism#global-terrorism-database-gtd-and-bruce-hoffman.

Hanif, U., Syed, S. H., Ahmad, R. and Malik, K. A. (2010) Economic impact of climate change on the agricultural sector of Punjab. *Pakistan Development Review*, **49**(4), 771–798. http://www.pide.org.pk/pdf/PDR/2010/Volume4/771–798.pdf

Haq, R. (2017) Pakistan Way Off Track on Millennium Development Goals. https://tribune.com.pk/story/1391752/depressed-data-pakistan-way-off-track-mdgs

IEA (International Energy Agency) Statistics (1990–2016) CO_2 emissions per capita. CO_2 emissions from fuel combustion only. Emissions are calculated using IEA's energy balances and the 2006 IPCC Guidelines. https://www.iea.org/statistics/index.html?country=WORLD&year=2016&category=Emissions&indicator=CO2ByPop&mode=chart&dataTable=INDICATORS

Janjua, P. Z., Samad, G., Khan, N. U. and Nasir, M. (2010) Impact of climate change on wheat production: a case study of Pakistan. *The Pakistan Development Review*, **49**(4), 799–822.

Javed, M. S., Raza, R., Hassan, I., Saeed, R., Shaheen, N., Iqbal, J. and Shaukat, S. F. (2016) The energy crisis in Pakistan: a possible solution via biomass-based waste. *Journal of Renewable and Sustainable Energy*, **8**(4), 043102. https://aip.scitation.org/doi/10.1063/1.4959974

Kabeer, N. (2010) Can the MDGs provide a pathway to social justice? The challenges of intersecting inequalities. Institute of Development Studies, University of Sussex, Brighton UK and UN MDG Achievement Fund, NY, USA 10017. https://www.ids.ac.uk/files/dmfile/MDGreportwebsiteu2WC.pdf

Kathena, I. N. and Sheefni, J. P. (2017) The relationship between economic growth and crime rates in Namibia. *European Journal of Basic and Applied Sciences*, **4**(1), 2,059–3,058.

Khan, I. (2011) Corruption bigger hurdle than terror for Pakistan progress: EU. *The Pakistan Development Review*, **27**, 959–985.

Khan, K., Ashraf, C.M. and Faridi, R. (2011) Climate Change Effect on the Hunza Lake and Geomorphologic Status of the Hunza River Basin, Gilgit-Baltistan, Pakistan. Retrieved 2 July 2018. https://www.pref.ibaraki.jp/soshiki/seikatsukankyo/

kasumigauraesc/04_kenkyu/kaigi/docments/kosyou/14/2011wlc_Khalidakhan.pdf

Lead (2016) Sustainable Development Goals: 2015–2030. http://www.lead.org.pk/lead/attachments/sdgflyer_english.pdf

Luo, T., Young, R. and Reig, P. (2015) *Aqueduct Projected Water Stress Country Rankings. Technical Note.* Washington, DC, World Resources Institute. www.wri.org/publication/aqueduct-projected-water-stresscountry-rankings

Ministry of Climate Change (2015) Achievements of the Ministry of Climate Change. http://mocc.gov.pk/moclc/userfiles1/file/Final%20Report%20MOCC%20-2%20years-%2005_10_2015%20(1)

Ministry of Climate Change. (2016) Pakistan's Intended Nationally Determined Contribution (PAK-INDC), Government of Pakistan. http://www.mocc.gov.pk/frmDetails.aspx https://www4.unfccc.int/sites/submissions/INDC/Published%20Documents/Pakistan/1/Pak-INDC.pdf

Ministry of Finance (2017) *Pakistan Economic Survey 2016–17.* Government of Pakistan. http://finance.gov.pk/survey_1617.html http://www.finance.gov.pk/survey/chapters_17/Pakistan_ES_2016_17_pdf.pdf

Ministry of Finance (2018) *Pakistan Economic Survey 2017–18.* Government of Pakistan. http://www.finance.gov.pk/survey/chapters_18/Economic_Survey_2017_18.pdf

Ministry of Water Resources (2018) National Water Policy 2018. Ministry of Water Resources. http://waterbeyondborders.net/wp-content/uploads/2018/07/Pakistan-National-Water-Policy-2018.pdf

Government of Pakistan. April 2018. https://www.mowr.gov.pk/wp-content/uploads/2018/06/National-Water-policy-2018–2.pdf

Mir, K. A., Purohit, P. and Mehmood, S. (2017) Sectoral assessment of greenhouse gas emissions in Pakistan. *Environmental Science and Pollution Research*, **24**(35), 27,345–27,355.

Mulok, D., Kogid, M., Lily, J. and Asid, R. (2016) The relationship between crime and economic growth in Malaysia: re-examine using bound test approach. *Malaysian Journal of Business and Economics*, **3**(1), 15–26.

Nadeem, S. and McArthur, J. M. (2018) Arsenic and other water-quality issues affecting groundwater, Indus Plain. *Hydrological Processes*, **32**(9), 1,235–1,253.

Naheed, S., Raza, I., Hassan, T., Muhammad, Z. and Fatima, A. (2015) Impact of climate change on livestock composition in Pakistan. *Science, Technology and Development*, **34**(4), 270–273.

Northrup, B. and Klaer, J. (2002) Effects of GDP on violent crime. *The Journal of Law and Economics*, **45**(1), 1–39.

PBS (Pakistan Bureau of Statistics) (2019) Macroeconomic indicators. http://www.pbs.gov.pk/sites/default/files/tables/Table-1_0.pdf

Pakistan Economic Forum (2015) Water Panel Draft Report 2015. https://www.wrdc.com.pk/Documents/WaterReport2015.pdf

Pakistan Institute for Parliamentary Services (2014) National MDGs orientation for parliamentary task forces. Retrieved 2 July 2018. http://www.na.gov.pk/mdgs/MDGs-BOOKLET.PDF

Pakistan Statistical Year Book (2017) Social & Culture. Retrieved from Pakistan Bureau of Statistics. http://www.pbs.gov.pk/sites/default/files//other/Pakistan_Statistical_yearbook_2017.pdf.

Panda, S., Chakraborty, M. and Misra, S. K. (2016) Assessment of social sustainable development in urban India by a composite index. *International Journal of Sustainable Built Environment*, **5**(2), 435–450.

Phillips, P. C. and Perron, P. (1988) Testing for a unit root in time series regression. *Biometrika*, **75**(2), 335–346.

Rehman, S. A., Cai, Y., Mirjat, N. H., Walasai, G. D., Shah, I. A. and Ali, S. (2017) The future of sustainable energy production in Pakistan: a system dynamics-based approach for estimating Hubbert Peaks. *Energies*, **10**(1,858), 1–24.

Rios, V. (2016) *The Impact of Crime and Violence on Economic Sector Diversity.* Washington, DC, The Wilson Center. Unpublished.

Spielman, D. J., Richard, J., Clay, R. and Soy, R. (2016) *Agriculture and the Rural Economy in Pakistan: Issues, Outlooks, and Policy Priorities.* Philadelphia, PA, University of Pennsylvania Press.

State Bank of Pakistan (2017) Annual Report 2016–2017 (State of the Economy). Chapter 7, Water sustainability in Pakistan: Key issues and challenges. http://www.sbp.org.pk/reports/annual/arFY17/Chapter-07.pdf

Syed, S H. and Ahmad, E. (2013) Poverty, inequality, political instability and property crimes in Pakistan: a time series analysis. *Asian Journal of Law and Economics*, **4**(1–2), 1–28.

Transparency International (2018) Pakistan. https://www.transparency.org/country/PAK

UNDP (2003) Human Development Report 2003: *Millennium Development Goals: A Compact among Nations to End Human Poverty.* New York, UNDP.

UNDP (2015) Millennium Development Goals. http://www.un.org/millenniumgoals/2015_MDG_Report/pdf/MDG%202015%20rev%20(July%201).pdf

UNDP (2017) The Sustainable Development Goals Report. https://unstats.un.org/sdgs/report/2017/

UNODC (2015) Accounting for Security and Justice in the Post-2015 Development Agenda. http://www.unodc.org/documents/about-unodc/Post-2015-Development-Agenda/UNODC_-_Accounting_for_Security_and_Justice_in_the_Post-2015_Development_Agenda.pdf

Valasai, G. D., Uqaili, M. A., Memon, H. R., Samoo, S. R., Mirjat, N. H. and Harijan, K. (2017) Overcoming electricity crisis in Pakistan: a review of sustainable electricity options. *Renewable and Sustainable Energy Reviews*, **72**, 734–745.

Vorrath, J. and Beisheim, M. (2015) Organized crime in the 2030 Agenda for Sustainable Development. https://www.swp-berlin.org/fileadmin/contents/products/comments/2015C45_vrr_bsh.pdf

WCED (World Commission on Environment and Development) (1987) *Our Common Future*, Brundtland, G. H. (ed.), Oxford, UK, Oxford University Press.

World Bank (2017) World Development Report. http://www.world-bank.org/content/dam/Worldbank/Publications/WDR/WDR%202016/WDR2016_overview_presentation.pdf

Appendix A

Table A1. Variable descriptions for UN SDGs.

Sustainable Development Goals		Indicator
Goal 1	No poverty	Proportion of total government spending on essential services (%)
Goal 2	Zero hunger	Prevalence of undernourishment (%)
Goal 3	Good health and well-being	Infant mortality rate (deaths per 1,000 live births)
Goal 4	Quality education	Gender parity index of trained teachers, by education level (ratio)
Goal 5	Gender equality	Proportion of seats held by women in national parliaments (% of total number of seats)
Goal 6	Clean water and sanitation	Proportion of population using safely managed drinking water services (%)
Goal 7	Affordable and clean energy	Proportion of population with access to electricity (%)
Goal 8	Decent work and economic growth	Annual growth rate of real GDP per capita (%)
Goal 9	Industry, innovation, and infrastructure	Manufacturing value added as a proportion of GDP (%)
Goal 10	Reduced inequality	Total assistance for development (millions of current US dollars)
Goal 12	Responsible consumption and production	Domestic material consumption per unit of GDP, by type of raw material (kilograms per constant 2011 US dollars)
Goal 14	Life below water	Average proportion of Marine Key Biodiversity Areas covered by protected areas (%)
Goal 15	Life and land	Red list index
Goal 17	Partnerships to achieve the goals	Total official development assistance (gross disbursement) for technical cooperation (millions of 2016 US dollars)

Notes: Goals and corresponding indicators are selected from United Nations Global Database, retrieved from https://unstats.un.org/sdgs/indicators/database/. We have selected the indicators based on the data availability for relatively longer periods of time.

Table A2. Descriptive statistics: 2000–2017.

Goals	Mean	Median	Standard Deviation	Kurtosis	Skewness	Range	Minimum	Maximum
Goal 1	12.31	12.22	1.65	1.06	0.06	6.96	8.49	15.45
Goal 2	22.06	21.20	2.02	−0.83	0.58	6.40	19.30	25.70
Goal 3	75.58	75.65	7.52	−1.18	0.05	23.90	64.20	88.10
Goal 4	0.80	0.81	0.04	1.65	−1.33	0.14	0.70	0.84
Goal 5	21.54	21.57	0.65	−1.01	0.11	1.93	20.59	22.51
Goal 6	37.09	37.19	0.95	−1.61	−0.22	2.55	35.64	38.19
Goal 7	87.70	89.51	7.22	−1.15	−0.25	23.89	75.26	99.15
Goal 8	2.14	2.36	1.76	−0.50	0.25	5.96	−0.48	5.48
Goal 9	12.43	12.86	1.06	0.21	−0.97	4.01	10.05	14.06
Goal 10	2,761.19	3,212.02	1,449.56	−0.37	−0.47	5,164.40	173.63	5,338.03
Goal 12	4.10	4.03	0.23	0.89	1.00	0.87	3.80	4.67
Goal 14	36.73	39.28	7.44	6.04	−2.71	23.82	15.46	39.28
Goal 15	0.88	0.88	0.03	−1.11	−0.32	0.10	0.82	0.92
Goal 17	635.38	426.25	482.99	0.04	1.22	1,539.20	72.23	1,611.44

Source: Authors' calculations.

Table A3. Correlation between Sustainable Development Goals for Pakistan.

Goals	Goal 1	Goal 2	Goal 3	Goal 4	Goal 5	Goal 6	Goal 7	Goal 8	Goal 9	Goal 10	Goal 12	Goal 14	Goal 15	Goal 17
Goal 1	1.00													
Goal 2	0.37	1.00												
Goal 3	0.02	0.91	1.00											
Goal 4	-0.34	-0.69	-0.56	1.00										
Goal 5	-0.01	0.19	0.24	0.09	1.00									
Goal 6	0.16	0.91	0.97	-0.51	0.21	1.00								
Goal 7	-0.06	-0.92	-0.98	0.63	-0.17	-0.94	1.00							
Goal 8	0.52	0.06	-0.05	-0.26	-0.38	0.07	0.03	1.00						
Goal 9	-0.05	-0.72	-0.67	0.77	-0.03	-0.54	0.73	-0.03	1.00					
Goal 10	-0.26	-0.70	-0.62	0.74	-0.23	-0.55	0.70	-0.12	0.76	1.00				
Goal 12	0.24	0.80	0.79	-0.84	0.01	0.78	-0.80	0.25	-0.64	-0.68	1.00			
Goal 14	0.55	-0.36	-0.56	0.44	-0.03	-0.39	0.57	0.26	0.70	0.45	-0.42	1.00		
Goal 15	0.05	0.90	0.99	-0.50	0.28	0.98	-0.96	-0.05	-0.58	-0.58	0.77	-0.48	1.00	
Goal 17	-0.17	-0.66	-0.72	0.13	-0.66	-0.77	0.68	0.16	0.20	0.45	-0.43	0.13	-0.78	1.00

Source: Authors' calculations.

Appendix B

Vector autoregression

We considered the following vector autoregressive (VAR) model to analyse the interconnectedness between the sustainability goals:

$$y_t = \mu + \sum_{i=1}^{p} \Phi_i y_{t-i} + \varepsilon_t, \qquad (1)$$

where y_t is a 14x1 vector of sustainability goals. The stationary variables are used in levels and the non-stationary variables are used in first differences. The stationary/non-stationary properties of all variables (SDGs) are examined by conducting three popular unit root tests in the following part.

UNIT ROOT TEST

The time series property of the data is examined by conducting the Augmented Dickey-Fuller (ADF), Phillips-Perron (PP), and Kwiatkowski–Phillips–Schmidt–Shin (KPSS) unit root tests. The test for integration is based on the ADF test, which involves formulating the ADF regression (Dickey and Fuller, 1979):

$$\Delta z_t = \mu + \gamma t + \rho z_{t-1} + \sum_{i=1}^{p} \delta_i \Delta z_{t-i} + \varepsilon, \qquad (2)$$

where t is the time trend. The lag length p is selected to ensure that the residuals are white noise. In essence, the test of whether the variable z_t is non-stationary is equivalent to the test of the significance of ρ, that is, H_0: $\rho=0$, in equation (2). Alternatively, Phillips and Perron (1988) proposed a nonparametric method of controlling for higher-order serial correlation in the series. The test regression for the PP (Phillips and Perron) test is the AR(1) process:

$$\Delta z_t = \mu + \rho z_{t-1} + \varepsilon_t.$$

While the ADF test corrects for higher-order serial correlation by adding lagged differenced terms on the right-hand side of equation (2), the PP test makes the correction to the t-statistic of the ρ coefficient from the AR(1) regression to account for the serial correlation. We used the Newey-West heteroskedasticity autocorrelation consistent estimate for this purpose. The asymptotic distribution of the PP t-statistic is the same as the ADF t-statistic. In addition to the tests based on non-stationary null hypothesis, we also conducted the KPSS test, which assumes the null hypothesis to be stationary. It is essential to examine the unit root properties for each time series (sustainability goals) using both types of tests to ensure that the results are not influenced by the weak power of these tests, especially in a small sample. The unit root test results are reported in Appendix Table B1. The results show that all SDGs are stationary except Goal 2, Goal 4, Goal 7, Goal 10, Goal 12, and Goal 17. All variables other than these six SDGs are used in levels in the VAR model represented by equation (1). The subsequent unit root test on these six SDGs indicates that they are stationary in first difference and incorporated in difference form in the subsequent analysis.

Therefore, from equation (1), y_t takes the following form:

$$y_t = (G1_t, \Delta G2_t, G3_t, \Delta G4_t, G5_t, G6_t, \Delta G7_t, G8_t, G9_t, \Delta G10_t, \\ \Delta G12_t, G14_t, G15_t, \Delta G17_t)$$

The optimal lag length of $p = 1$ is justified through Schwarz criteria, and therefore we estimate the following VAR (1) model:

$$y_t = \mu + \Phi_1 y_{t-1} + \varepsilon_t$$

Φ_1 is a 14x14 coefficient matrix representing the interconnectedness between the sustainability goals, and ε_t is a vector of residuals. The i-th row and j-th column of the matrix Φ_1 is represented by φ_{ij}. The interconnectedness between the sustainability goals is examined through the Granger causality test. The Granger non-causality from the sustainability goal j to i is examined by testing the null hypothesis that H_0 : $\varphi_{ij} = 0$ against the alternative, which is H_0 : $\varphi_{ij} \neq 0$. The statistical significance of the interconnectedness (Granger causality) between the sustainability goals is presented in Appendix Table B2. Rows and columns of Table A3 are the cause and effect variables, respectively.

Table B1. Results of unit root test.

Goals	Levels			First difference		
	ADF	PP	KPSS	ADF	PP	KPSS
Goal 1	−4.29***	−3.15**	0.08	−	−	−
Goal 2	−1.92	−0.43	0.49**	−3.80***	−3.13**	0.12
Goal 3	−5.12***	−4.78***	0.26	−	−	−
Goal 4	−2.36	−2.36	0.48**	−6.25***	−6.79***	0.30
Goal 5	−4.39***	−4.38***	0.15	−	−	−
Goal 6	−3.75***	−2.96***	0.23	−	−	−
Goal 7	−1.19	−1.51	0.55**	−13.46***	−14.63***	0.29
Goal 8	−3.59**	−3.98***	0.08	−	−	−
Goal 9	−2.78*	−2.78*	0.33	−	−	−
Goal 10	−2.29	−2.29	0.49**	−4.07***	−4.60***	0.24
Goal 12	−2.22	−2.14	0.62**	−5.03***	−10.13***	0.32
Goal 14	−12.43***	−10.41***	0.08	−	−	−
Goal 15	−11.69***	−9.15***	0.26	−	−	−
Goal 17	−1.01	−0.85	0.50**	−3.96***	−6.25***	0.05

Notes: ADF, PP: *, **, and *** represent rejection of unit root hypothesis at the 10%, 5%, and 1% level of significance, respectively. KPSS: *, **, and *** represent rejection of stationarity at the 10%, 5%, and 1% level of significance, respectively.

Table B2. Results of Granger causality test for Pakistan.

-Effects-

Causes↓	Goal 1	Goal 2	Goal 3	Goal 4	Goal 5	Goal 6	Goal 7	Goal 8	Goal 9	Goal 10	Goal 12	Goal 14	Goal 15	Goal 17
Goal 1	–	0.00	5.95**	2.77*	0.03	0.43	0.57	0.14	0.30	1.99	0.32	0.00	0.11	1.02
Goal 2	4.87**	–	79.08***	13.73***	0.12	0.05	0.22	0.56	1.06	0.03	0.96	1.56	0.80	0.37
Goal 3	2.68	0.08	–	3.47*	0.00	1.03	0.44	0.78	0.15	0.00	0.23	1.45	16.27***	0.00
Goal 4	0.00	0.04	0.58	–	0.04	0.01	0.24	0.18	0.12	0.19	11.82***	0.94	2.10	0.02
Goal 5	0.14	2.91	53.65***	0.00	–	0.00	0.03	0.01	0.03	0.07	0.36	0.00	0.39	0.02
Goal 6	0.13	9.81***	195.5***	23.44***	0.00	–	0.06	0.14	1.86	1.74	11.32***	0.01	25.18***	0.21
Goal 7	0.07	0.69	8.59***	3.86**	0.03	0.10	–	0.81	0.01	0.42	1.66	0.15	0.62	0.00
Goal 8	0.10	0.14	329.92***	10.79***	0.42	0.15	0.10	–	0.01	1.77	2.79*	0.16	6.87***	0.34
Goal 9	0.20	3.28*	138.65***	12.85***	0.04	0.15	0.01	0.00	–	0.23	4.62***	0.34	1.13	0.00
Goal 10	0.26	0.13	15.84***	1.40	0.01	0.05	0.56	0.05	2.44	–	9.09***	0.00	8.92***	0.06
Goal 12	0.35	0.28	0.78	52.27***	0.03	0.05	0.00	0.13	0.63	0.61	–	1.63	2.99*	0.01
Goal 14	0.01	0.69	3.18*	34.47***	0.08	0.01	0.16	0.67	0.04	0.33	4.34*	–	0.25	0.11
Goal 15	0.83	2.05	1.93	7.52***	0.01	1.17	0.04	0.00	0.97	0.70	8.31***	0.78	–	0.18
Goal 17	0.03	1.40	13.35***	0.23	0.04	0.13	0.79	0.00	0.32	0.05	2.26	0.00	0.23	–

Notes: *, **, and *** represent rejection of Granger non-causality at the 10%, 5%, and 1% level of significance, respectively.

27 Beyond protected areas: Biodiversity conservation and global change in Asia and the Pacific

GERNOT BRODNIG[1]

The World Bank, Washington, DC

Keywords

Protected areas; biodiversity conservation; climate change; invasive alien species; global change

Abstract

Protected areas have been the cornerstones of biodiversity conservation in the recent past. Many of them are under threat from local pressures, such as resource extraction and habitat encroachment. In addition, conservation managers are increasingly faced with global change and its drivers. These include climate change, globalization of trade and investment patterns, violent conflict, and migration, as well as HIV/AIDS and other pandemics. This chapter will explore a couple of these drivers of change in the Asia-Pacific context and assess their respective impacts on ecosystems and biodiversity. It will highlight the importance of adopting perspectives over a longer time and at larger spatial scales, and the need to look beyond the boundaries of conservation areas to address these challenges.

27.1 INTRODUCTION

Asia represents one of the most ecologically diverse regions in the world, with numerous endangered and endemic species of fauna and flora. Five countries in the region – China, India, Indonesia, Malaysia, and Philippines – are recognized as mega-diverse countries. Asia encompasses 13 of the 35 globally recognized biodiversity hotspots (CEPF, 2015), and the region has 555 mammal species, 659 bird species, and 3,979 plant species listed as threatened (critically endangered, endangered, vulnerable) in the IUCN Red List (IUCN, 2017).

The establishment and management of protected areas is an important tool for the conservation of this biodiversity. In Asia and the Pacific, more than 17% of the land area has been set aside for national parks, reserves, etc., and in some countries

such as Bhutan (48%) or Cambodia (26%), levels are much higher (UNEP-WCMC, 2018).

Despite their shortcomings – lack of funding and staff, encroachments – these conservation areas represent the main tool in stemming biodiversity loss and ecosystem degradation.

The experiences with protected areas in Asia and elsewhere have highlighted the importance of maintaining relatively undisturbed ecosystems and the various goods and services derived from them. Conservation planners and protected area managers have developed ever more refined tools and methods in designing and managing them. Protected areas have become more and more sophisticated through the development of corridors, transboundary areas, and ecological networks (Mittermeier *et al.*, 2005; Hansen and deFries, 2007). As a result, park managers are increasingly tasked with a host of diverse issues that highlight the ever-growing complexity of stakeholders, ranging from local communities to international travellers, whose interests and values need to be taken into account. Given this widening circle, policy choices and management interventions often occur outside protected areas and are aimed at mainstreaming conservation issues into production landscapes and other forms of economic activity.

Despite all these efforts, evidence is mounting that biodiversity conservation and protected area management might need to be even more flexible to adapt to major transformations in our socio-economic, institutional, and biophysical environments, usually captured by terms such as 'globalization' or 'global change'.

The World Parks Congress in Durban (Phillips, 2004) had identified global change – defined as 'a transformation, which occurs on a worldwide scale or exhibits sufficient cumulative effects to have worldwide impacts' – as one of the major challenges for the protected area system. The literature (e.g. Barber *et al.*, 2004) on this challenge distinguishes three broad categories of inter-related factors:

- Socio-economic changes: Human population growth and dynamics, economic growth, trade and consumption, and poverty and inequality;

---

[1] Formerly with the UNDP Regional Centre in Bangkok, Thailand.

- Biophysical changes: Climate change, conversion and fragmentation of natural habitats, hydrological change, invasive alien species, and biodiversity loss; and
- Institutional changes: Changing global norms, global trends in governance and institutions, and globalization of communications, knowledge, and culture.

This is not an exhaustive list of global drivers with significant impacts on the biological sustainability of the global protected area network and its constituent components, nor is it meant to be a set of threats that will inevitably overwhelm local and national efforts to conserve and sustainably use biodiversity. Global change also brings opportunities such as new financial tools, the generation and exchange of new forms of knowledge, or a growing awareness about the economic value of protected areas.

This chapter examines the challenges emerging from two distinct but related global threats: climate change and invasive alien species (IAS). These two phenomena were chosen to illustrate impacts at various scales (ecosystem, species, and genetic) of biodiversity, as well as in relation to different protected area management approaches. Climate change, including global warming, has the potential to significantly alter biomes and ecosystems and will require conservation managers to reorient their planning and monitoring systems. Invasive alien species are particularly notable for crowding out other species and often elude national and local controls owing to the proliferation of trade and travel. Using examples from Asia and the Pacific, the chapter identifies the impacts of these drivers, as well as some of the responses at the policy and management level. We conclude with some general observations on the future of biodiversity conservation and protected areas in Asia and the Pacific.

27.2 CLIMATE CHANGE: SOME LIKE IT HOT

Climate change is the quintessential global environmental phenomenon that increasingly permeates every aspect of our livelihoods. While there is still significant uncertainty about the scope and impacts of climate change and its concomitant phenomena (global warming, climate variability, extreme weather events), there is widespread consensus that a major part of these transformations is the result of human activities. Whether it is our increasingly energy-hungry industries, our ever-growing transportation needs, or simply the imperative to feed our growing population, emissions of greenhouse gases are still on the rise. The nature of climate change and its repercussions for our ecosystems and economies have been well documented (IPCC, 2013, 2014) and are beyond the scope of this chapter, which focuses on the impacts on biodiversity and the integrity of protected areas.

A high level of uncertainty still surrounds the impacts of climate change on biodiversity and its individual components; non-linear relationships, multi-scale interactions, and long timeframes make accurate prognoses difficult. There are, however, distinct patterns emerging that illustrate the interactions between climate change and biological resources.

At the ecosystem level, impacts of climate change tend to be most pronounced in transition zones that separate ecosystems. Changes in precipitation and temperature can cause these boundaries to move, allowing some ecosystems to expand into new areas, while others diminish in size as the climate becomes inhospitable to the species they contain. The IPCC (2014) and other studies (Bellard et al., 2012; Garcia et al., 2014; Scheffers et al., 2016) have highlighted the effects on various ecosystems.

At the species level, and as a result of changes in ecosystem composition and functionality, some authors have postulated sharp increases in extinction rates (Parmesan and Yohe, 2003; Root et al., 2003). In an influential paper, Thomas et al. (2004) include samples from five regions of the world and suggest that 24% of species in these regions will be on their way to extinction by 2050 because of climate change. Urban (2015) revisited this analysis, highlighting the uncertainties of these estimates, particularly for Asia, where the number of studies is still very limited. Other observed impacts of climate change include shifts in the timing of reproduction in certain species, abundance variations, and increased frequencies of pest and disease outbreaks.

Last but not least, climate change also affects species at the level of cells and genes. Changes in the genetic makeup of species are expected as organisms adapt to new climatic conditions. One early study on fruit flies in Australia (Umina et al., 2005) has shown the subtle impacts of global warming (Box 27.1).

> **Box 27.1. Genetic drift**
>
> The researchers sampled the genes of the vinegar fly, *Drosophila melanogaster*, in 20 locations in Australia. They tested the frequency of particular genes, including the gene for alcohol dehydrogenase (Adh), an enzyme that breaks down compounds the flies use for energy. The study replicated an older one done 20 years ago, when scientists found that vinegar flies in Australia had two different forms of the Adh gene: one adapted to tropical climates and one to cool climates. Back then, the researchers found the frequency of the tropical Adh genes slowly decreased as they went south, while the frequency of temperate Adh genes increased. Twenty years on, Umina et al. (2005) have discovered the frequency of the tropical version of the Adh gene has increased across the board.

Many of the impacts tend to be aggravated where species have no alternative habitats. Species restricted to small areas, or in small populations, are also particularly vulnerable. A catastrophic event such as disease or drought, for example, can kill off a small population. And populations in small, isolated habitats are unlikely to be replenished once decimated by outbreaks of fire or other catastrophes. All these circumstances are often the very reasons why and where conservation priorities and protected areas have been established, that is, to protect endangered ecosystems and endemic species in often isolated patches. Biodiversity hotspots are areas with exceptional concentrations of endemic species facing extraordinary threats of habitat destruction. With warming temperatures, many species are expected to move poleward or upwards in altitude (Thomas et al., 2012). This implies that the locations of hotspot reserves may need to allow for such movement, which may require a somewhat larger region to be conserved.

Therefore, conservation planners and park managers face a dilemma: The existing system of protected areas might not be appropriate in the light of shifting ecosystem boundaries and species migration. At the same time, however, these areas play a vital role in protecting biodiversity against other threats, such as land conversion, resource extraction, and others. Abandoning protected areas because of the uncertainties of climate change would be akin to throwing out the baby with the bathwater.

Instead, planners and managers need to adapt and incorporate climate change considerations in ecosystem planning and park management. For existing areas, this calls for assessments of likely changes in habitat and species ranges over time, and under different climate change scenarios. Conservation targets, for example, can be adjusted for range and population variations predicted to take place owing to climate change. Increasing redundancy may be necessary to achieve representation when climate change impacts are taken into account (Lawler, 2009), and requirements for persistence are likely to change when expected range shifts and migration needs are reflected.

Resilience to climate change needs to be adopted as an explicit goal. Consideration of shifts in species and habitat ranges, for example, may alter the balance of priority given to expanding the size of existing sites versus establishing new sites. In virtually all cases, the importance of connectivity (buffer zones, corridors, habitat mosaics) to allow movement of species and habitats is expected to grow.

Any adaptation strategy will be fraught with serious uncertainties, given the nature of climate change and our embryonic knowledge about it. Nevertheless, there is room for the development of a set of robust indicators to monitor the potential impacts of climate change. It is along these lines that one of the most sensitive and vulnerable ecosystems in the world, the Great Barrier Reef Marine Park in Australia, is approaching the challenge.

One of the most pervasive impacts of climate change and global warming on marine ecosystems is coral bleaching. Reef corals turn white as they lose their symbiotic algae (zooxanthellae), whose photosynthetic pigments give coral reefs their colour. Loss of the zooxanthellae removes a source of energy for the corals. Although bleached corals can survive for some time, they can die if conditions do not return to normal. In 1997–1998, a massive worldwide bleaching event triggered by elevated sea surface temperatures resulted in widespread coral mortality. The Great Barrier Reef Marine Park in Australia escaped the worst of that event but has faced the challenge of bleaching in ensuing years, including massive bleaching events in 2016 and 2017.

In response to these threats, the Great Barrier Reef Marine Park Authority (GBRMPA) developed annual Coral Bleaching Risk and Impact Assessment Plans, which adopt a three-pronged strategic approach for monitoring bleaching risk and assessing coral bleaching impacts when events occur. The three primary components of the plan consist of an early warning system, incident response activities, and a communications strategy (GBRMPA, 2013). These plans allowed the GBRMPA to have an up-to-date understanding of the vulnerability of the marine park.

In recent years, the magnitude, diversity, and uncertainty of impacts led the Marine Park Authority to complement the urgent and short-term management responses with a longer-term vision and the adoption of resilience-based management approaches. The latter aim to enhance the ability of the reef system to cope with local and global pressures through recovery and reorganization between disturbances (Anthony et al., 2015). For example, the Great Barrier Reef blueprint for resilience (GBRMPA, 2017) proposes to build a resilience network, which identifies coral reefs that are disproportionately important to the reef's resilience and to evaluate these areas to determine the best resilience-building activities to reduce impacts.

Climate change considerations also affect the selection of new protected areas. Conservation planning needs to incorporate the potential for shifts in species ranges, precipitation and fire regimes, and so forth, into decision-making processes for new sites. Science-based principles are needed to guide the design and management of conservation areas to enable them to maximize survival and recovery, and to mitigate the adverse impacts of climate-related threats to biodiversity. One study (Hannah et al., 2007) highlights the need for additional protected areas, based on modelling the climate impacts, such as species dispersal patterns. It also notes, though, that many of these efforts will be overwhelmed by the size and persistence of climate effects, if not coupled with robust mitigation measures. In a comprehensive review of recommendations for climate-smart biodiversity conservation, Heller and Zavaleta

(2009) point to the need for incorporating social science approaches and insights to achieve more holistic and actionable strategies, as many of the planning and management options will take place in human-dominated landscapes and their complex governance regimes.

The preceding examples illustrate the fact that climate change is adding a new dimension of complexity to biodiversity conservation and protected areas management. Conservation paradigms need to be reassessed in light of the existing and potential changes in ecosystem and species dynamics. Climate change indicators must become part and parcel of conservation planning and management, and the selection of new sites has to incorporate adaptation criteria to make those areas more resilient.

27.3 INVASIVE ALIEN SPECIES: UNINVITED COMPANY

Another phenomenon of major impact on the planet's biodiversity that has grown exponentially in the recent past is invasive alien species (IAS). Also known as non-natives or exotic species, they can pose major threats to ecosystems by invading new habitats to the detriment of native communities. Invasives are not a new phenomenon. There is, however, mounting evidence of a rapid recent growth in the number and impact of IAS (Mooney and Hobbs, 2000; McGeoch *et al.*, 2010) as a result of an increasingly global economy. Countries that are more effectively tied into the global trading system tend to have more IAS, being positively linked to the development of terrestrial and maritime transport networks, migration rates, number of tourists visiting the country, and trade in commodities (Hulme, 2009). The routes by which invasive alien species enter new habitats are known as *pathways*, while the means by which they travel to new destinations are known as *vectors*.

Based on a framework developed by Hulme *et al.* (2008), alien species may arrive and enter a new region through three broad mechanisms: importation of a commodity, arrival of a transport vector (stowaways), or spread from a neighbouring region. The commodity route includes the intentional release of organisms, for example, for landscaping, their inadvertent escape from zoos, aquaria, and the like, and transport as a contaminant such as pests.

A review of the frequencies of pathways of more than 500 invasive alien species profiled in the Global Invasive Species Database (GISD) shows that the most prolific routes are the escapes from horticulture, the pet/aquarium trade, and agriculture. This is closely followed by releases for landscape improvement, ballast water, and the transportation of soil and vegetation (CBD, 2014).

In Asia, invasive alien plants such as water hyacinth, salvinia, giant mimosa, and lantana have established themselves in freshwater and terrestrial ecosystems throughout Asia (Bambaradeniya, 2004). Among invasive alien animals, mollusc species such as the giant African snail and the golden apple snail have spread in many parts of the region, causing immense economic damage. While many IAS have been introduced deliberately for economic and aesthetic purposes, several others have entered accidentally. At present, the major pathways for introduction of IAS in the Asia and Pacific region include aquaculture development, and the horticultural and ornamental fish trade (Box 27.2). The spread of IAS in the region has been aggravated by rapid development activities, such as modification of inland water systems for irrigation projects, urbanization, agricultural expansion, and transport infrastructure.

Impacts of invasive alien species vary greatly in type, scale, and severity. As with climate change, we can distinguish impacts at the three levels of biodiversity: the genetic, species, and ecosystem levels. Their impact on ecosystem processes includes disturbance of nutrient cycling, pollination, regeneration of soils, and energy flows. Invasive alien species can also alter the frequency, spread, and the intensity of fire and obstruct water flows. By increasing surface run-off and soil erosion, the structure, stability, and functions of communities are disturbed, and their habitat negatively affected. At the species and community levels, invasive alien species often displace native biota through competition, predation, or the transmission of diseases, thereby reducing growth and survival rates and – in some cases – leading to the extinction of local populations. Invasive alien species can decrease genetic diversity through the loss of genetically distinct populations, erosion of genes and gene

> ### Box 27.2. Flowerhorn: Good luck or not?
>
> Linked to the global marketplace, the world is becoming increasingly urban, with cities often the entry points for many alien species. Many urban dwellers seek ornamentals from a wide range of sources, and these may become invasive. Unfortunately, few urbanites are aware of the problems of invasive species, as they are quite removed from their natural environments (McNeely, 2001).
>
> For example, in Kuala Lumpur and other cities of Southeast Asia, large numbers of unwanted flowerhorn cichlids, a popular aquarium fish, have been released in the wild, where they potentially represent a serious threat to native species. The fish are being released, as their owners fear that killing this fish will bring bad luck, or people buy them with the express purpose of setting them free, thinking that this will get rid of their *suey* or bad luck. Unfortunately, it is mainly bad luck for the native ecosystems.

complexes, and hybridization of introduced species with native ones (Vilà et al., 2011; Simberloff et al., 2013).

Invasives might also be helped by the effects of climate change. For instance, as many invasive plant species spread very rapidly and are tolerant and resilient, temperature and other climatic variations might give them an additional edge. For example, Song et al. (2010) showed that a heatwave led to a decrease in biomass of a native herbaceous Wedelia species, whereas its invasive relative flourished.

The same holds true for invasive fauna. As species shift ranges and habitat compositions change in response to climate change, animals that are generalists may have greater competitive success than specialists. Invasive animal species tend to be generalists, which may increase their success and threaten some native species (Green et al., 2003; Hellman et al., 2008).

It is a moot point that these impacts are particularly felt in protected areas and other sensitive ecosystems. Therefore, the Convention on Biological Diversity (Article 8(h)) urges Parties 'as far as possible and as appropriate, to prevent the introduction of, control or eradicate those alien species which threaten ecosystems, habitats or species'. And Aichi Target 9 postulates that 'by 2020, invasive alien species and pathways are identified and prioritized, priority species are controlled or eradicated and measures are in place to manage pathways to prevent their introduction and establishment'. In addition, the Global Invasive Species Programme (GISP) launched a Global Strategy on IAS, and IUCN published Guidelines for the Prevention of Biodiversity Loss Caused by IAS. All these instruments recognize that preventing new IAS is a global challenge that must be addressed at both the international and national levels, and is therefore largely beyond the scope and powers of protected area managers.

This holds particularly true with regard to the first pillar of the fight against invasives: prevention. In light of the numerous pathways mentioned earlier, protected area managers need to operate at a scale that exceeds the conservation area itself, which often requires extensive collaboration with other stakeholders, such as custom officials, agricultural extension services, and others. Quarantine controls, for example, though originally designed to protect human health and agricultural commerce, can play a critical role as a country's first line of defence in containing the spread of invasive alien species. The international quarantine regime is well placed to spearhead the fight against invasive alien species, but there are considerable problems with current structures. An analysis of how international trade law, and in particular the 1994 Agreement on Sanitary and Phytosanitary Measures, may conflict with international and national quarantine measures shows that the World Trade Organization, in its enthusiasm to prevent quarantine laws being used as a disguised restriction on trade, has discouraged members from using such laws to stem the spread of invasive alien species (SCBD, 2001).

Even further removed from the reach of protected area managers are pathways and vectors linked to transoceanic transport. The most serious problem for biodiversity here is ballast water. About 80% of commodities are carried by ships, which provide many vectors (anchor chains, sediments, ballast water) to transport alien organisms on a transoceanic scale. Some 10 million tons of ballast water are shipped annually, carrying diverse marine species with a planktonic life cycle and human pathogens. Ballast water is thus instrumental in the global distribution of potentially invasive species and waterborne diseases.

The International Maritime Organization (IMO) oversees the International Convention for the Control and Management of Ships' Ballast Water and Sediments, which entered into force in 2017. Under the Convention, all ships in international traffic are required to manage their ballast water and sediments to a certain standard, according to a ship-specific ballast water management plan. All ships will also have to carry a ballast water record book and an international ballast water management certificate. More specifically, all ships using ballast water exchange should, whenever possible, conduct ballast water exchange at least 200 nautical miles from the nearest land and in water at least 200 meters in depth, taking into account guidelines developed by IMO.

Where prevention fails to stop the introduction of an alien species, an eradication programme, that is, the elimination of the entire population of an alien species, in the managed area, is the preferred method of action and often the key to a successful and cost-effective solution. Where this is not feasible owing to costs or other factors, control (long-term reduction in density and abundance to below an acceptable threshold) and containment (restriction of an alien species to a defined geographical range) may be acceptable fallback options.

Various control strategies exist, each with their own strengths and weaknesses. Biological control is the intentional use of natural enemies or naturally synthesized substances against invasives. While this is often the most comprehensive mode of control, it can lead to unintended consequences, as the case of the cane toad in Australia demonstrates. Originally introduced from Hawaii to combat another pest, cane beetles, they have become a major scourge themselves.

Where biological control is not feasible, mechanical control is often an alternative. It can, however, be very costly and labour-intensive, as the various efforts around the globe to rid inland freshwater ecosystems of the water hyacinth have shown. One positive benefit from mechanical control of certain invasive species is the potential to make harvesting a source of alternative income generation. In Southeast Asia, water hyacinth furniture and handicrafts have helped many local communities around protected areas to improve their livelihoods (Shaanker *et al.*, 2010).

Given the unintended consequences of biological control and the costs of mechanical control, many countries rely on chemical control, which usually involves the application of pesticides. While often highly effective, this approach is not always feasible in fragile ecological systems, as the agents used can have deleterious effects on habitats and species.

In sum, in our globalized world, invasive alien species have emerged as a serious threat to the resilience of ecosystems and the integrity of protected areas. As with climate change, conservation planners and managers need to take a much more outward-looking approach to stem the tide of invasion. This entails close collaboration with stakeholders across borders and disciplines to prevent the introduction of IAS, as well as decisive action on the ground, using a whole gamut of measures to fight those threats at the doorsteps of protected areas.

27.4 CONCLUSIONS

In the past, prevailing conservation paradigms stipulated that protected areas are islands in an ocean of development that preserve the last few pristine ecosystems and endangered species. This 'fortress conservation' approach was difficult to sustain in light of increasing population pressures, and a more inclusive approach to biodiversity conservation and protected area management has taken root. It emphasizes sustainable use of biological resources and the sharing of benefits with local stakeholders.

This chapter has argued that conservation planners and managers are facing another generation of challenges that emanate primarily outside protected areas and their vicinities, in many cases far away from the sites. These factors of global change have led to transformations that have shattered our existing understanding and concepts of conservation areas. Climate change could make many of the existing parks and reserves obsolete if and when ecosystem boundaries and species ranges shift, and genetic adaptations lead to new population configurations. With the spiralling growth in trade and travel, invasive alien species might become an overwhelming force for native biota.

All this calls for a major reorientation towards an approach to biodiversity conservation and protected areas management, which incorporates dimensions of uncertainty and complexity to ensure greater resilience for species and ecosystems. As always, the first step is awareness-raising and the development of the necessary capacities and tools to assess the scope and magnitude of changes. This will include the willingness and ability to work under significant levels of uncertainty, favouring the precautionary approach. Assessments of global change need to be complemented by appropriate management interventions, from early detection to mitigation and adaptation, through the building of broad-based alliances at multiple scales.

While the previous pages might have left a somewhat pessimistic picture of biodiversity conservation and protected areas in the face of global change, the latter has also opened up many opportunities, such as exponential scientific knowledge, new sources of financing and more inclusive governance, all of which will be necessary in adapting our stewardship to current and future global transformations.

ACKNOWLEDGMENTS

I am grateful to the United Nations Development Programme (UNDP) for its encouragement and support to write this chapter during my time at the Regional Centre in Bangkok. I would also like to thank the two reviewers, Dr A. N. Gillison and Professor D. Schmidt-Vogt, for their helpful comments.

REFERENCES

Anthony, K. R. N., Marshall, P. M., Abdullah, A. and Beeden, R. (2015) Operationalizing resilience for the adaptive management of coral reefs. *Global Change Biology*, **21**, 48–61.

Bambaradeniya, C. N. B. (2004) Management of Invasive Alien Species: An Asian perspective on the way forward. Proceedings of a Global Synthesis Workshop on 'Biodiversity Loss and Species Extinctions: Managing Risk in a Changing World', Sub-theme: Invasive Alien Species – Coping with Aliens.

Barber, C. V., Miller, K. R. and Boness, M. (eds.) (2004) *Securing Protected Areas in the Face of Global Change: Issues and Strategies*. Gland, Switzerland and Cambridge, UK, IUCN.

Bellard, C., Bertelsmeier, C., Leadley, P., Thuiller, W. and Courchamp, F. (2012) Impacts of climate change on the future of biodiversity. *Ecology Letters*, **15**(4), 365–377.

CBD (Convention on Biological Diversity) (2014) UNEP/CBD/SBSTTA/18/9/Add.1. Pathways of introduction of invasive species, their prioritization and management. https://www.cbd.int/doc/meetings/sbstta/sbstta-18/official/sbstta-18-09-add1-en.pdf

CEPF (2015). The biodiversity hotspots maps. Critical Ecosystem Partnership Fund. http://www.cepf.net/resources/hotspots/Pages/default.aspx

Garcia, R. A., Cabeza, M., Rahbek, C. and Araújo, M. B. (2014) Multiple dimensions of climate change and their implications for biodiversity. *Science*, **344**(6,183), 1247579.

GBRMPA (Great Barrier Reef Marine Park Authority) (2013) *Coral Bleaching Risk and Impact Assessment Plan* (2nd ed.). Townsville, Australia, GBRMPA.

(2017) *Great Barrier Reef Blueprint for Resilience*. Townsville, Australia, GBRMPA.

Green, R. E., Harley, M., Miles, L., Scharlemann, J., Watkinson, A. and Watts, O. (eds.) (2003) *Global Climate Change and Biodiversity*. Sandy, Bedfordshire, UK, Royal Society for the Protection of Birds (RSPB).

Hannah, L., Midgley, G., Andelman, S., Araújo, M., Hughes, G., Martinez-Meyer, E., Pearson, R. and Williams, P. (2007) Protected area needs in a changing climate. *Frontiers in Ecology and the Environment*, **5**(3), 131–138.

Hansen, A. J. and DeFries, R. (2007) Ecological mechanisms linking protected areas to surrounding lands. *Ecological Applications*, **17**(4), 974–988.

Heller, N. E. and Zavaleta, E. S. (2009) Biodiversity management in the face of climate change: A review of 22 years of recommendations. *Biological Conservation*, **142**(1), 14–32.

Hellmann, J. J., Byers, J. E., Bierwagen, B. G. and Dukes, J. S. (2008) Five potential consequences of climate change for invasive species. *Conservation Biology*, **22**(3), 534–543.

Hulme, P. E., Bacher, S., Kenis, M., Klotz, S., Kuhn, I., Minchin, D., Nentwig, W., Olenin, S., Panov, V., Pergl, J., Pyšek, P., Roques, A., Sol, D., Solarz, W. and Vilà, M. (2008) Grasping at the routes of biological invasions: A framework for integrating pathways into policy. *Journal of Applied Ecology*, **45**, 403–414.

Hulme, P. E. (2009) Trade, transport and trouble: Managing invasive species pathways in an era of globalization. *Journal of Applied Ecology*, **46**(1), 10–18.

IPCC (Intergovernmental Panel on Climate Change) (2013) *Climate Change 2013. The Physical Science Basis. Contribution of Working Group I to the Fifth Assessment Report of the Intergovernmental Panel on Climate Change*. Cambridge, New York, Cambridge University Press.

(2014) *Climate Change 2014. Impacts, Adaptation, and Vulnerability. Part A: Global and Sectoral Aspects. Contribution of Working Group II to the Fifth Assessment Report of the Intergovernmental Panel on Climate Change*. Cambridge, New York, Cambridge University Press.

IUCN (International Union for Conservation of Nature) (2017) The IUCN Red List of Threatened Species. Version 2017–3. www.iucnredlist.org (accessed 3 March 2018)

Lawler, J. (2009) Climate change adaptation strategies for resource management and conservation planning. *Annals of the New York Academy of Sciences*, **1,162**, 79–98.

McGeoch, M. A., Butchart, S. H., Spear, D., Marais, E., Kleynhans, E. J., Symes, A., … and Hoffmann, M. (2010) Global indicators of biological invasion: Species numbers, biodiversity impact and policy responses. *Diversity and Distributions*, **16**, 95–108.

McNeely, J. A. (2001) *The Great Reshuffling: Human Dimensions of Invasive Alien Species*. Gland, Switzerland and Cambridge, UK, IUCN.

Mittermeier, R. A., Kormos, C. F., Goetsch Mittermeier, C. and Gil, P. R. (2005) *Transboundary Conservation: A New Vision for Protected Areas*. No. 333.782 T772 t. México, MX, CEMEX.

Mooney, H. A. and Hobbs, R. J. (eds.) (2000) *Invasive Species in a Changing World*. Washington, DC, Island Press.

Parmesan, C. and Yohe, G. (2003) A globally coherent fingerprint of climate change impacts across natural systems. *Nature*, **421**, 37–42.

Phillips, A. (2004) *The Durban Action Plan* (revised version, March 2004). Gland, Switzerland and Cambridge, UK, IUCN.

Root, T. L., Price, J. T., Hall, K. R., Schneider, S. H., Rosenzweig, C. and Pounds, J. A. (2003) Fingerprints of global warming on wild animals and plants. *Nature*, **421**, 57–60.

SCBD (Secretariat of the Convention on Biological Diversity) (2001) Review of the efficiency and efficacy of existing legal instruments applicable to invasive alien species. Montréal, SCBD (CBD Technical Series no. 2). https://www.cbd.int/doc/publications/cbd-ts-02.pdf

Scheffers, B. R., De Meester, L., Bridge, T. C., Hoffmann, A. A., Pandolfi, J. M., Corlett, R. T., Butchart, S. H., Pearce-Kelly, P., Kovacs, K. M., Dudgeon, D., Pacifici, M., Rondinini, C., Foden, W. B., Martin, T. G., Mora, C., Bickford, D. and Watson, J. E. (2016) The broad footprint of climate change from genes to biomes to people. *Science*, **354**(6,313), aaf7671.

Shaanker, U. R., Joseph, G., Aravind, N. A., Kannan, R. and Ganeshaiah, K. N. (2010) Invasive plants in tropical human dominated landscapes: Need for an inclusive management strategy. In C. Perrings, H. Mooney and M. Williamson (eds.), *Bioinvasions and Globalization: Ecology, Economics, Management, and Policy*, pp. 202–219. Oxford, UK, Oxford University Press.

Simberloff, D., Martin, J. L., Genovesi, P., Maris, V., Wardle, D. A., Aronson, J., Courchamp, F., Galil, B., García-Berthou, E., Pascal, M., Pyšek, P., Sousa, R., Tabacchi, E. and Vilà, M. (2013) Impacts of biological invasions: What's what and the way forward. *Trends in Ecology & Evolution*, **28**(1), 58–66.

Song, L., Chow, W. S., Sun, L., Li, C. and Peng, C. (2010) Acclimation of photosystem II to high temperature in two Wedelia species from different geographical origins: Implications for biological invasions upon global warming. *Journal of Experimental Botany*, **61**, 4,087–4,096.

Thomas, C. D., Cameron, A., Green, R. E., Bakkenes, M., Beaumont, L. J., Collingham, Y. C., Erasmus, B. F., De Siqueira, M. F., Grainger, A., Hannah, L., Hughes, L., Huntley, B., Van Jaarsveld, A. S., Midgley, G. F., Miles, L., Ortega-Huerta, M. A., Peterson, A. T., Phillips, O. L. and Williams, S. E. (2004) Extinction risk from climate change. *Nature*, **427**, 145–148.

Thomas, C. D., Gillingham, P. K., Bradbury, R. B., Roy, D. B., Anderson, B. J., Baxter, J. M., Bourn, N. A. D., Crick, H. Q. P., Findon, R. A., Fox, R., Hodgson, J. A., Holt, A. R., Morecroft, M. D., O'Hanlon, N. J., Oliver, T. H., Pearce-Higgins, J. W., Procter, D. A., Thomas, J. A., Walker, K. J., Walmsley, C. A., Wilson, R. J. and Hill, J. K. (2012) Protected areas facilitate species' range expansions. *Proceedings of the National Academy of Sciences*, **109**(35), 14,063–14,068.

Umina, P. A., Weeks, A. R., Kearney, M. R., McKechnie, S. W. and Hoffmann, A. A. (2005) A rapid shift in a classic clinal pattern in Drosophila reflecting climate change. *Science*, **308**(5,722), 691–693.

UNEP-WCMC (2018) Protected Area Profile for Asia and Pacific from the World Database of Protected Areas, March 2018. www.protectedplanet.net

Urban, M. C. (2015) Accelerating extinction risk from climate change. *Science*, **348**(6,234), 571–573.

Vilà, M., Espinar, J. L., Hejda, M., Hulme, P. E., Jarošík, V., Maron, J. L., Pergl, J., Schaffner, U., Sun, Y. and Pyšek, P. (2011) Ecological impacts of invasive alien plants: A meta-analysis of their effects on species, communities and ecosystems. *Ecology Letters*, **14**(7), 702–708.

28 Causes of land-use change and biodiversity loss in Monsoon Asia

DIETRICH SCHMIDT-VOGT

Chair of Silviculture, Faculty of Environment and Natural Resources, Freiburg University, Freiburg, Germany

Keywords

Land-use change; biodiversity; agrobiodiversity; swidden cultivation; intensification; South Asia; Southeast Asia

Abstract

Monsoon Asia comprises those parts of tropical Asia that are under the influence of a seasonally dry monsoonal climate. Monsoon Asia includes South Asia and Southeast Asia, as well as the southern and eastern periphery of East Asia. Owing to favourable climatic conditions, as well as other biogeographic factors, these parts of Asia are particularly rich in biodiversity and harbour most of Asia's biodiversity hotspots. Biodiversity is strongly linked to habitat conditions and thus also to land use as one of the factors affecting habitat quality. Land use, however, is changing from historic agricultural systems to modern commercial systems. Land-use change has accelerated all over Monsoon Asia since the 1960s, mainly as a result of economic growth, infrastructure development, emerging trade networks, development programmes, and policies governing resource exploitation and conservation. Land-use change is generally understood to have a negative effect on biodiversity, mainly through habitat destruction, habitat fragmentation, introduction of exotic species, pollution, and other processes. Deforestation and forest degradation are in this respect considered to be the most detrimental processes of land-use and land-cover change in Monsoon Asia. Our understanding of deforestation processes and their effects on biodiversity is, however, hampered by the low quality or poor interpretation of land-cover data, insufficient knowledge of drivers and underlying causes of deforestation, and the rapidity with which economic and political transitions are happening in this part of the world. Another aspect of land-use change causing biodiversity losses is the decline of agrobiodiversity in South and Southeast Asia as a result of agricultural intensification promoted by government policies.

28.1 A PROFILE OF MONSOON ASIA

Monsoon Asia comprises those parts of tropical and subtropical Asia that are under the influence of a monsoonal climate. Monsoon Asia includes South Asia, Southeast Asia, and the southern and eastern periphery of East Asia. It is a region of generally favourable conditions that has been described as 'the golden fringe to a beggar's mantle' or 'the golden crescent' (Dobby, 1962). It is also a region of great diversity, including biodiversity. The case studies in this chapter are mostly from Southeast Asia because of the outstanding importance of this region with respect to biodiversity (Sodhi *et al.*, 2004; Corlett, 2014).

Monsoon Asia adjoins the plateaus and ranges of High Asia, which are the sources of most of its large rivers, for example, the Ganges, Brahmaputra, Salween, and Mekong. Mainland Monsoon Asia is divided into peninsulas by bays and gulfs which, together with the large archipelagos in the south and to the east, account for the predominantly maritime character of this region. The region is highly diverse in terms of geology and topography, and owes its shape mainly to tectonic activities along the boundaries of the Eurasian, Indian, and Philippine plates. The collision of the Indian Subcontinent has pushed up the Himalayas and the Tibetan Highland and has also strongly affected Mainland Southeast Asia by forming new mountain ranges and breaking up old ones. The large archipelagos of Monsoon Asia, that is, the Malay Archipelago, the Philippines, and Japan, are affected by subduction processes, causing intensive volcanic activity. Volcanic soils, as well as the alluvial soils of the plains and basins, are generally fertile, while upland soils, especially those that have developed on old rocks, such as the Precambrian rocks of the Deccan plateau on the Indian Subcontinent, are low in nutrient content.

The defining feature of this region is its climate. Monsoonal climates are characterized by a seasonal reversal of the dominant wind direction. The southwesterly winds that prevail during the summer months over those parts of Monsoon Asia, which will be the focus of this chapter, are replaced in winter by north-easterly winds. The effect of this reversal depends on the configuration of land and sea and on the local topography. Over the peninsular parts of Monsoon Asia, that is, over the Indian Subcontinent and Mainland Southeast Asia, the reversal results in alternating influxes of maritime and continental air, and thus in alternate wet and dry seasons. The 'Southwest Monsoon', which blows inland from June to September, brings forth the rainy season, while the 'Northeast Monsoon', which blows overland from October to April, causes the dry season. Over islands and over the narrow southern parts of the peninsulas, where winds from both directions carry maritime air, the seasonal change is less distinct, and rainfall is possible throughout the year. Temperatures are generally high and vary only slightly over the year with the exception of continental locations in the northern parts of Mainland Southeast Asia, where seasonal temperature changes are more distinct. The season of higher temperatures coincides with the rainy season in most locations, which is one of the main reasons for the generally high biological productivity. Seasonality has created some of the most distinctive ecosystems of Southeast Asia, such as the *dipterocarp* forests with their periodic mass fruiting (Sodhi and Brook, 2006).

Forest is the dominant land cover under the prevailing conditions of a warm and predominantly moist climate. Exceptions are riverine grasslands as well as the savannas and deserts that can be found in some places, such as the Ayeyarwady basin, the Deccan plateau, Punjab and Rajasthan in India, and Sind and Baluchistan in Pakistan. The most widespread forest type is monsoon forest, which is composed of evergreen and deciduous trees in varying proportions, depending on soil moisture and length of the dry season. In regions where total annual rainfall is more than 1,800 mm, and where there is no distinct dry season, monsoon forest is replaced by tropical rain forest (Richards, 1996). The most complex conditions are found in the mountain ranges along the northern rim of Monsoon Asia, that is, in the Himalaya-Karakoram-Hindukush ranges, where tropical and subtropical vegetation types are replaced by temperate and alpine vegetation types along an altitudinal gradient.

The generally favourable biophysical conditions described earlier contribute to the fact that Monsoon Asia is a region with many large areas of high population density. Despite a rapid surge in the rate of urbanization throughout Monsoon Asia, there are still extensive areas where rural conditions prevail, even though rural economies are in many cases no longer based on agriculture alone (Rigg, 2003, 2013).

Agriculture and modern forestry are activities which affect land cover more directly and extensively than other land uses. Throughout Monsoon Asia, rice is the most important agricultural crop. It is grown as wet rice on irrigated fields or as dry rice on rain-fed upland fields, often by the practice of shifting or swidden cultivation. Pastoralism, especially with ruminants, is more prevalent in South Asia than in Southeast Asia, where the emphasis of livestock keeping is on pigs, poultry, and water buffalo. Smallholder farming predominates, but agribusinesses are on the increase. In the course of agrarian change, smallholders adopt commercial crops and often plant them in monocultures. Important plantation crops for agribusiness and commercial smallholder farming are rubber, various tree species for pulp and paper production, coffee, tea, cassava, and maize. Oil palm, which is the commercially most valuable plantation crop in the southern parts of Mainland Southeast Asia and in the Malay Archipelago, is grown mainly by agribusiness. The current interest in biofuels may provide additional momentum for the expansion of such plantations. Commercial trade in tropical timbers started in the 19th century under colonial rule with the exploitation of teak forests in British India and the Dutch East Indies, but became more intense in the 20th century with the emergence of Japan and China as economic powers and consumers of wood and wood products, and owing to the interest of the newly independent states in resource exploitation.

28.2 BIODIVERSITY IN MONSOON ASIA

The term 'biodiversity' is defined as variety and variability in nature, which manifests itself at three different levels: genetic level, species level, and ecosystem level. It is used in this sense also in this chapter. The terms 'biological diversity' and 'biodiversity' are essentially synonyms and were first coined in 1980 and 1985. They have become very common and are now used extensively in the literature. However, as a consequence of this proliferation, 'biodiversity' is often no longer used in the original sense of referring to diversity as a quality of natural phenomena, but increasingly as a synonym for broader and sometimes rather vague entities such as 'nature' and 'biological resources' (Schmidt-Vogt, 2006). This is in contradiction to the dictum of Otto Solbrig, one of the patrons of biodiversity, that 'diversity is a property, not an entity in itself' (Solbrig, 2000, p. 107).

Monsoon Asia is exceedingly rich in biodiversity, and Southeast Asia ranks as one of the foremost regions in the world in terms of species richness and endemism (Sodhi *et al.*, 2004; Corlett, 2014). Myers *et al.* (2000) identified 25 'biodiversity hotspots' in the world, that is, areas characterized by outstanding species richness, high concentrations of endemic species, and high risk of habitat loss or degradation. Four of these hotspots – Indo-Burma, Sundaland, Wallacea, and the Philippines – are located in Southeast Asia, and one – Western Ghats and Sri Lanka – in South Asia. Conservation International has adopted and modified the hotspot concept of Myers and currently lists 35 hotspots. On maps showing the location of biodiversity hotspots, Southeast Asia, where the individual hotspots lie closely adjacent to each other, appears as one solid block of rich and endangered biodiversity.

The rich biodiversity of Monsoon Asia is caused to a large extent by its position, topography, and geological history. Monsoon Asia is located at the boundary of three biogeographical realms: the Palearctic realm, the Indomalayan realm, and the Australasian realm. Migration of species across the boundaries of these realms has contributed to the overall species richness of this region. This has been reinforced by geographical conditions along these boundaries, that is, complex mountain topography along the boundary between the Palearctic realm and the Indomalayan realm, and extensive archipelagos along the boundary between the Indomalayan realm and the Australasian realm, both providing a complex set of habitats for the intermingling of species. Climate changes of the past have helped to further augment biodiversity. During the Pleistocene glacial periods, declining temperatures caused temperate species from northern Asia to extend their ranges southward. Fluctuating sea levels, as a consequence of the alteration of glacials and interglacials, provided favourable conditions for speciation when rising sea levels turned mountains into islands or permitted migrations when subsiding sea levels created connections between islands (Sodhi *et al.*, 2004). In contrast to the temperate regions of the northern hemisphere, where ice ages were cataclysmic events causing major disruptions, climatic conditions over Monsoon Asian have remained comparatively stable for long geological periods. Location, geological history, landscape diversity, global and regional climate histories, and proximity of marine bodies are thus the most important biophysical factors underlying the rich biodiversity of this region.

Human influence, which is normally thought to have a negative effect on biodiversity, may also have contributed to biodiversity in this region through land-use systems that are characterized by high levels of agrobiodiversity or agrodiversity. Agrobiodiversity has been defined as 'the variety and variability of animals, plants and microorganisms used directly and indirectly for agriculture' (FAO, 1999) and is thus very similar to the earlier term 'biodiversity'. Agrodiversity, on the other hand, is an expanded concept which has been defined as 'the dynamic variation in cropping systems, output and management practice that occurs within and between agroecosystems [which] arises from biophysical differences, and from the many and changing ways in which farmers manage diverse genetic resources and natural variability, and organize their management in dynamic social and economic contexts' (Brookfield 2001, p. 46).

Biodiversity in Monsoon Asia is threatened by various activities and circumstances. Sodhi *et al.* (2004) argue that Southeast Asia could lose 42% of its biodiversity by the year 2100. The main driver of biodiversity loss in Monsoon Asia is the destruction or degradation of forests as the main habitat of this region, mainly due to agricultural expansion and logging. Southeast Asia is around 44% forested, that is, more than half of the original forest cover has gone (Corlett, 2014). With respect to agro-biodiversity, the most important factor is the replacement of historic and autochthonous land-use systems by more intensive land-use systems involving mono-cropping, as a result of foreign or domestic agribusiness and national policies. Other factors causing biodiversity loss are hunting and wildlife trade, mining, forest fires (often associated with plantation establishment), invasive species, urbanization, pollution, and climate change (Sodhi *et al.*, 2004; Corlett, 2014).

28.3 LAND-USE CHANGE IN MONSOON ASIA

According to Houghton (1994), land-use change can occur in basically two forms:

– A change in the area of an existing land use, that is, the conversion from one land-cover category to another; and
– A change in the intensity of an existing land use, for example, by introduction of genetically enhanced species, and intensification of farming practices, such as mono-cropping, mechanization, and use of agrochemicals.

As mentioned earlier, the most critical change processes with respect to biodiversity in Monsoon Asia are deforestation and forest degradation processes, which belong to the first category of land-use changes according to Houghton. Deforestation is here defined as the conversion of forest to non-forest land-cover categories, such as grassland or farmland, forest degradation as a process of change in the condition of forests, for example, from closed forest to open forest or from tall forest to more stunted forest types. Another important distinction is that between primary forests and secondary forests. Primary forests are defined as largely undisturbed natural or original forests, whereas secondary forests are 'forests regenerating largely through natural processes after significant human disturbance of the original forest vegetation' (de Jong and Chokkalingam, 2001, p. 568).

Southeast Asia is particularly threatened by deforestation. Sodhi *et al.* (2004) argue that Southeast Asia could lose three-quarters of its original forest by 2100. Myanmar is a case in point. With 63% of forest cover, making it still the most-forested country of Southeast Asia, Myanmar has sustained huge losses of forest, 20,000 sq km alone in the period from 2002–2014 (Bhagwat *et al.*, 2017). Drivers of deforestation in Myanmar, as well as the emerging threats to forests in the period of political transition that Myanmar is currently going through, have been studied by Lim *et al.* (2017) and Prescott *et al.* (2017). Significant exceptions to this negative trend are Vietnam and China, where forest cover has increased. Xu (2011) has, however, pointed out the dubious value for biodiversity of this newly acquired forest cover, much of which consists of tree plantations, for example, eucalyptus and rubber, which, according to terminology used in China, are classified as forest (Zhai *et al.*, 2017).

Assessments of land-cover changes over such large areas are fraught with problems and uncertainties. Common problems are the low quality of the data set, non-matching land-use categories, reclassification of land-cover types, lack of interpretative skills, and the dynamic nature of some land cover, such as in swidden landscapes.

In a thorough analysis of land-cover changes in the Lower Mekong Basin (LMB), using the land-cover data sets of MRC/ GTZ for 1993 and 1997 (MRC and GTZ, 1998), Heinimann (2006) and Heinimann *et al.* (2007) have looked more closely into the dynamics of land-use and land-cover changes in this region. The Lower Mekong Basin comprises parts of Laos, Thailand, Cambodia, and Vietnam, and covers 620,000 sq km of mainland Southeast Asia. Around 70% of the forest cover of the LMB consists of forests of medium to low cover densities and of forest mosaics, which Heinimann *et al.* (2007) summarily referred to as secondary forests. Relatively undisturbed dense forests constituted only 13% of the entire forest area in the basin. It was found that the largest share of deforestation and degradation processes affects secondary forests. The deforestation rates for secondary forests are three times higher than the deforestation rates for other forest categories and account for two-thirds of all deforestation. Conversion from secondary forest to non-forest is in most cases a two-step process, whereby conversion of secondary forest to shrub land and to a mosaic of cropping and shrub land is followed by intensification processes leading to permanent agricultural lands. In some cases, however, as for instance in Thailand, deforestation can be a one-step process of direct conversion of secondary forests to permanent agriculture. A relatively new phenomenon is the conversion of secondary forest to rubber, eucalyptus, and coffee plantations that is happening on a large scale in southwest China, Vietnam, and Laos (Thongmanivong and Fujita, 2006; Xu, 2006; Zhai *et al.*, 2017). Dense forest, on the other hand, was a relatively stable category with an overall net decrease of 1.7% from 1993 to 1997. Most losses of dense forests are due to forest degradation processes that lead to an increase in secondary forests (Heinimann *et al.*, 2007).

The second category of land-use change according to Houghton (1994) is intensification of land-use practices such as agricultural intensification. Agricultural intensification is here understood as a set of activities that are intended to increase either the productivity or the profitability of a tract of land

(Rasmussen *et al.*, 2018). It can include the introduction of new species or genetic strains of crops or animals, monocultures, mechanization, irrigation, and the use of agrochemicals. A frequently cited example from Monsoon Asia is the Green Revolution, which essentially was based on the introduction of high-yielding varieties of rice and other grains, but which also included accompanying technology packages. The Green Revolution began in the mid-1960s and was driven in Asia by seeds developed by the International Rice Research Institute (IRRI) in the Philippines. It was initially greeted with praise, but critics soon began to point out negative effects, such as increasing socio-economic disparities and environmental degradation due to intensive irrigation and heavy use of agrochemicals. From a biodiversity-concerned point of view, the main negative effect of the Green Revolution was the degradation of agrobiodiversity or agrodiversity. The main effect of the Green Revolution on agrobiodiversity was to replace the great number of genetic varieties of *Oryza sativa* that had been developed and used by farmers over a very long time with only a few genetically enhanced strains. Subsidiary effects of the introduction of these strains were environmental degradation, such as salinization of soils due to inappropriate irrigation practices, as well as destruction of biodiversity in the soil and in other supporting ecosystems due to the application of herbicides and pesticides (Pingali, 2012). Other examples of intensification of existing land-use practices include the large-scale introduction of cash crops in Monsoon Asia, such as cassava, cabbage, maize, and rubber.

28.4 EFFECTS OF LAND-USE CHANGE ON BIODIVERSITY

Land-use change, especially when it leads to land-cover changes such as deforestation and forest degradation, is understood to have a predominantly negative effect on biodiversity. Loss of primary forest is considered to be particularly detrimental to biodiversity. The area of primary forests is therefore used in the FAO Global Forest Resources Assessment Reports as an indicator of biological diversity.

Going back to the regional example of the LMB, a careful examination of the dynamics underlying net forest loss has shown that deforestation mainly affects secondary forests. This observation is confirmed by a recent survey of forest-cover change trends in southern and southwestern China, which has shown that an overall increase of forest cover due to the expansion of tree crop plantations is paralleled by a decrease in natural forests, which in this study is synonymous with mature secondary forest (Zhai *et al.*, 2017).

Secondary forests are commonly regarded as forests of inferior quality with respect to ecological and economic parameters.

Box 28.1. Swidden cultivation.

Swidden or shifting cultivation is an agricultural system, predominantly of the tropics, in which land under natural vegetation is cleared and cultivated and then left fallow for a period that is generally longer than the cultivation period. Fallows are managed or left untended. In rotational swidden farming, the same plot of land is cleared again after a fallow period of ideally more than 10 years to allow the regeneration of woody vegetation.

Research, however, has shown that at least some types of secondary forests are characterized by species richness and structural complexity, and that secondary forests can play a significant role in rural livelihoods (Schmidt-Vogt, 2001; Sovu et al., 2009; Wangpakapattanawong et al., 2010; Thanichanon et al., 2013), for example, through the provision of wild food plants (Delang, 2006). There are many different types of secondary forests in the tropics (Chokkalingam et al., 2001), which differ from each other with respect to their origin and condition. The majority of secondary forests in the LMB, for instance, have originated from logging and from swidden cultivation. According to Mittelman (2001), logging is the predominant cause of secondary forest formation in the lowlands, while swidden farming is predominant – or was predominant until recently – in the uplands (Box 28.1).

Swidden cultivation is still practised over some parts of upland Southeast Asia, but also in peripheral areas of South Asia and East Asia (Fox and Vogler, 2005; Schmidt-Vogt et al., 2009). However, compared with other parts of the tropics, swidden cultivation in Southeast Asia is on the decline (Padoch et al., 2007;

van Vliet et al., 2012; Heinimann et al., 2017). The effect of swidden farming on biodiversity and forest cover is a controversial issue. It is vilified as the main cause of forest destruction by some and romanticized as an indigenous and therefore ecologically benign land use by others. For a thorough discussion of the effects of swidden and swidden transitions on biodiversity, see Forsyth and Walker (2008), Rerkasem et al. (2009), Delang and Li (2012), Sajise (2015) and Schmidt-Vogt (2015). The effect of swidden farming on biodiversity depends on the type of swidden farming practised as well as on changes in the practice of swiddening due to population and policy pressures, such as shortening of the fallow period and increasing the frequency of fire. There is, however, evidence that rotational swiddening in its original form with short cultivation periods, and a fallow period of more than 10 years, which periodically regenerates a cover of secondary forests, is capable of sustaining a relatively high level of plant diversity (Schmidt-Vogt, 1998, 1999; de Jong and Chokkalingam, 2001; Sovu et al., 2009; Wangpakapattanawong et al., 2010). Its chief contributions, however, are seen in maintaining a diversity of shifting landscape mosaics, which are capable of providing ecosystem services better than a more homogeneous landscape (Swift et al., 2004), as well as by maintaining intermediate-scale ecological disturbances that benefit light-demanding pioneer as well as grazing and browsing species (Siebert and Belsky, 2014). A serious problem with respect to understanding and even quantifying the provision of ecosystem services and biodiversity benefits by swidden landscapes was for a long time the difficulty of putting these landscapes on a map (Schmidt-Vogt et al., 2009). Because of the rotational nature of swiddening, swidden landscapes are dynamic and landscape mosaics in a constant state of flux (Figure 28.1). Messerli et al. (2009) and Hett et al. (2012) have now proposed a methodology

Figure 28.1. Swidden field with relict emergents (trees left standing when the swidden is cleared) in northern Chin State, Myanmar, near Falam. Photo taken by Dietrich Schmidt-Vogt on 7 May 2015.

of quantifying such landscape mosaics and for distinguishing the inherent dynamics of a swidden landscape from degradation and deforestation trends.

When permanent agriculture, which is often based on only a few cash crops, replaces rotational swidden cultivation, the overall result is biodiversity loss as well as a loss of overall landscape diversity (Rerkasem et al., 2009). It is for this reason, among others, that a reassessment of swidden cultivation is currently taking place, which emphasizes the ability of swidden farmers to maintain diversity and adapt their land-use systems to changing conditions (Kerkhoff and Sharma, 2006; Xu et al., 2009; Cairns, 2007, 2015, 2017; Siebert and Belsky, 2017). The conservation value of swiddening landscapes has been discussed in more detail in Finegan and Nasi (2004), Rerkasem et al. (2009), and Schmidt-Vogt (2015). Improved management of fallows is in this context seen as a way to achieve multiple benefits, including maintenance or enhancement of biodiversity on various levels – the individual fallow plots, the farm, and on the landscape level (Rambo, 2007). While there is reason to describe the process of secondary forest formation through swiddening as forest degradation (Schmidt-Vogt, 1998), this is a process, at least in areas where rotational swiddening with a sufficient fallow period still prevails, that is from a biodiversity point of view preferable to the conversion of secondary forests to permanent agriculture or to commercial tree plantations.

The transition from swidden to commercial tree plantations, common in southwest China, Laos, and Vietnam (van Vliet et al., 2012), is promoted by policies that pursue a variety of goals: economic growth, poverty eradication, environmental conservation, and the suppression of opium (Lu, 2017). In Laos, tree plantations are promoted for environmental considerations but also as a means to eradicate swidden cultivation. The government of Laos has an overall strategy to attain a 70% forest cover by the year 2020 and pursues this goal mainly through plantation forestry, which includes tree planting on private farmland, but also the issuing of leases to private enterprises for the establishment of rubber and eucalypt plantations (Inthavong and Schmidt-Vogt, 2005).

Another famous example is the Sloping Land Conversion Programme (SLCP) of China, which was launched in 1999 in response to the 1998 floods in the Yangtze River watershed (Delang and Yuan, 2015). The programme aimed at restoring natural ecosystems and redressing environmental degradation caused by cropland expansion and deforestation, by encouraging farmers to convert croplands on steep slopes to forest and grassland by providing grain and cash subsidies. In tropical China, farmers utilized these subsidies to plant rubber trees (Chen et al., 2016; Zhai et al., 2017). However, because of the

programme's focus on planting ecological trees, they were permitted to use programme subsidies for planting economic trees such as rubber on only 20% of their land (Delang and Yuan, 2015). The expansion of rubber cultivation and its implications for biodiversity (Ahrends et al., 2015) will be described using the example of Xishuangbanna Prefecture of Yunnan Province in southwest China.

The rapidly growing car industry, especially in China, is driving the expansion of rubber plantations in Southeast Asia. The traditional rubber-growing areas in the peninsular and insular parts of Southeast Asia, notably Indonesia, Malaysia, and southern Thailand, are converted to oil palm, which is even more lucrative than rubber. Expansion of rubber is therefore taking place further to the north in the continental parts of Southeast Asia (Fox and Castella, 2013). In Xishuangbanna, the area of rubber plantations has expanded between 1988 and 2010 from 4.5% to 22.2%. While the majority of plantations were initially located below 900 m, which constitutes the upper limit of suitability for rubber tree growth, rubber plantations are increasingly established at higher altitudes, where rubber growth is still possible due to newly developed clones, but where productivity is lower (Chen et al., 2016). The expansion of rubber plantations poses a serious threat to biodiversity when it is associated with deforestation and expansion into natural reserves. A study of forest-cover change trends in Xishuangbanna and Hainan Island, where rubber cultivation is important, has shown that an overall increase in plantation forest cover runs parallel to a decrease in the cover of natural or mature secondary forests, which indicates that rubber plantations expand into forest areas (Zhai et al., 2017). The expansion of rubber into higher altitudes, where most of the remaining forest cover of Xishuangbanna is located, poses a serious threat of deforestation. This process runs parallel to an expansion of rubber plantations into nature reserves. The area covered by rubber plantations inside nature reserves has increased in Xishuangbanna from 0.1% in 1988 to 9.8% in 2010 (Chen et al., 2016). A decrease of area under rubber that followed upon a sharp decline in the price of rubber in 2011 has, however, not yet had any measurable positive effect on biodiversity (Zhang et al., 2019)

Another example of policies leading to an increase in forest cover is the introduction and implementation of community forestry in South Asia, particularly in Nepal, where community forestry can now look back on a history of more than 40 years. Community forestry is a strategy, first propagated by FAO (1978), to devolve control over forest resources to local communities with the aim of improving the condition of resources, as well as local livelihoods. One of the main objectives of introducing community forestry to Nepal was to counter the threat of deforestation, especially in upland Nepal, which at that time was perceived as a major environmental calamity. Early community forestry projects were therefore mainly aimed at enlisting community support for reforestation activities. Research using GIS has provided evidence that in some locations the implementation of community forestry has resulted in an increase of forest cover (Gautam *et al.*, 2003). An increase in forest cover does not, however, as in the case of Laos noted earlier, necessarily imply an improvement in environmental quality or biodiversity conservation value. A ground survey carried out by two members of the same research team that measured these forest-cover changes demonstrated, however, that local user groups acting under community forestry were capable of restoring forest from a highly degraded state, and to manage them for useful products, while maintaining a high level of plant diversity (Webb and Gautam, 2001). The effects of the Nepal community forestry programme on biodiversity have been studied comprehensively by Luintel *et al.*, 2018. While community forestry has been successful in greening denuded landscapes and providing the basis for an improvement of biodiversity, biodiversity conservation per se has never been the top priority of community forestry policy (Khadka and Schmidt-Vogt, 2008).

Land-use change as change in the intensity of land-use practices can have variable effects on biodiversity. In Monsoon Asia, the aim of intensification is to increase the yield of important food crops and to increase the monetary returns from cash crops. Examples are the Green Revolution in South Asia and Southeast Asia, already mentioned earlier, and the expansion of maize cultivation in Laos and Vietnam for markets in Thailand. Agrobiodiversity has been greatly reduced by these developments. There have been, however, recent instances of a shift from intensification towards diversification as a strategy to achieve not only productivity increases, but also livelihood and environmental sustainability (Conway and Barbier, 1991; Brookfield, 2001; Minang *et al.*, 2015). Thailand is a particularly instructive example in this respect because of the great importance of agricultural production in the national economy, the strong push towards commercialized cropping in the 1970s and 1980s, and the change in policies and practices that followed the economic crisis of 1997. In Northeast Thailand, where intensification has caused severe soil degradation, farmers have organized themselves into groups, some of which have adopted integrated farming in order to regain productivity through species diversification and resource integration (Tipraqsa *et al.*, 2007). In Thailand, this policy change is promoted not only by farmers associations at the grassroots level, but also at the government level through the late King's Policy of Self-Sufficiency (Suwanraks, 2000). A resurgence of intensification in the form of mono-cropping for biofuels such as sugar cane and oil palm caused by concern over climate change, however, seems to be already under way.

28.5 SUMMARY AND CONCLUSIONS

Land-use change in Monsoon Asia, especially land-use change in the form of deforestation, is commonly regarded as a threat to biodiversity. An examination of land-use change in Monsoon Asia, focusing on Southeast Asia as the most outstanding part of Monsoon Asia in terms of biodiversity endowment, has shown that the situation is more complex than appears on the surface. While the focus of the deforestation and biodiversity loss debate is on the loss of primary forest, the regional example of the LMB has shown that, in some regions, secondary forests can be more strongly affected by deforestation than primary forests. Secondary forests have for a long time been regarded as degraded and of low value for biodiversity conservation. Recent research on secondary forests, especially research on swidden fallow secondary forests, has shown that such forests can be diverse, at least with respect to plant diversity, and that they can contribute to diversity on a landscape level as constituent parts of a mosaic of other land uses. Loss of secondary forests is therefore a concern from the perspective of biodiversity conservation. Conversely, increase in forest cover, which is often thought to improve biodiversity, can be due to an increase in the area of commercial tree plantations with limited value for biodiversity conservation.

Agricultural intensification, which is regarded as a major agent of decline in agrobiodiversity, has varied over the course of time. A period of accelerated intensification, which started in the 1960s, and which was mainly based on technology innovations and the emergence of a world market, has by no means come to an end, but has, at least locally, been supplemented by policy attempts to promote integrated land-use systems to enhance ecosystem services and local livelihoods. Promotion of commercial crops such as rubber, oil palm, coffee, and maize in monocultures is, however, still the predominant trend, posing a serious threat to biodiversity. This trend is augmented by market-based conservation interventions such as Payments for Ecosystem Services (PES), as in the case of REDD+ policies (Roth and Dressler, 2012). Agricultural intensification to replace extensive farming systems, such as swiddening, and to motivate land sparing has become central to REDD+ policy formulation in many tropical countries. However, by increasing productivity and future agricultural land rents, agricultural intensification can create incentives for more agricultural expansion and deforestation with negative implications for biodiversity (Phelps *et al.*, 2013).

To address the problem of biodiversity loss caused by land-use changes requires the closing or at least the narrowing of several knowledge gaps. These include an insufficient understanding of land-use change processes and their proximate and underlying drivers. Many land-cover change assessments are based on insufficient methodology or skills. The wide divergence of forest cover assessment by different authors and organizations is a case in point. This also raises the need for uniformly collected baseline data. Improvement of land cover assessment on a regional scale is therefore an important requirement for the future. Also important is more knowledge about biodiversity of land-cover types, such as secondary forests, on which not much research has been done so far. Another important field of inquiry is drivers of land-use change. Despite a great deal of work that has been done in this area, there are still many methodological problems of linking land-cover changes detected by remote sensing technology to land-use decisions made at various levels.

Important tasks, beyond closing knowledge gaps, are to create in the countries of Monsoon Asia, through education, awareness of the value of biodiversity, and to help generate the political will to promote and support land use that is compatible with the aims of biodiversity conservation.

ACKNOWLEDGEMENTS

I am grateful to Dr Pak Sum Low for inviting me to contribute this chapter, and to Dr Andrew Gillison, Dr Jill Belsky, and Dr Claudio Delang for their valuable comments on earlier drafts.

REFERENCES

Ahrends, A., Hollingsworth, P. M., Ziegler, A. D., Fox, J. M., Chen, H., Su, Y. and Xu, J. (2015) Current trends of rubber plantation expansion may threaten biodiversity and livelihoods. *Global Environmental Change*, **34**, 48–58.

Bhagwat, T., Hess, A., Horning, N., Khaing, T., Thein, Z. M, Aung, K. M., Aung, K. H., Phyo, P., Tun, Y. L., Oo, A. H., Neil, A., Thu, W. N., Songer, M., Connette, L. K., Bernd, A., Huang, Q., Connette, G. and Leimgruber, P. (2017) Losing a jewel: rapid declines in Myanmar's intact forest from 2002–2014. *PLOS ONE*, **12**(5), 1–22. https://doi.org/10.1371/journal.pone.0176364

Brookfield, H. (2001) *Exploring Agrodiversity*. New York, Columbia University Press.

Cairns, M. (ed.) (2007) *Voices from the Forest: Integrating Indigenous Knowledge into Sustainable Upland Farming*. Washington, DC, RFF Press.

Cairns, M. (ed.) (2015) *Shifting Cultivation and Environmental Change: Indigenous People, Agriculture and Forest Conservation*. London and New York, Earthscan from Routledge.

Cairns, M. (ed.) (2017) *Shifting Cultivation Policies: Balancing Environmental and Social Sustainability*. Wallingford, MA, and Boston, CAB International.

Chen, H., Yi, Z., Schmidt-Vogt, D., Ahrends, A., Beckschaefer, P., Kleinn, C., Ranjitkar, S. and Xu., J. (2016) Pushing the limits: the pattern and dynamics of rubber monoculture expansion in Xishuangbanna, SW China. *PLOS ONE*, **11**(2), 1–15. DOI: 10.1371/journal.pone.0150062.

Chokkalingam, U., Smith, J., de Jong, W. and Sabogal, C. (2001) A conceptual framework for the assessment of tropical secondary forest dynamics and sustainable development potential in Asia. *Journal of Tropical Forest Science*, **13**(4), 577–600.

Conway, G. R. and Barbier, E. W. (1991) *After the Green Revolution: Sustainable Agriculture for Development*. London, Earthscan Publications.

Corlett, R. T. (2014) *The Ecology of Tropical East Asia*. Oxford, Oxford University Press.

de Jong, W. and Chokkalingam, U. (2001) The evolution of swidden fallow secondary forests in Asia. *Journal of Tropical Forest Science*, **13**(4), 800–815.

Delang, C. O. (2006) Not just minor forest products: the economic rationale for the consumption of wild food plants by subsistence farmers. *Ecological Economics*, **59**, 64–73.

Delang, C. O. and Li, W. M. (2012) *Ecological Succession on Fallowed Shifting Cultivation Fields*. Heidelberg, Springer.

Delang, C. O. and Yuan, Z. (2015) *China's Grain for Green Program: A Review of the Largest Ecological Restoration and Rural Development Program in the World*. Heidelberg, Springer.

Dobby, E. H. G. (1962) *Monsoon Asia*. London, University of London Press.

FAO (1978) Forestry for local community development. Food and Agriculture Organization of the United Nations, Rome.

FAO (1999) Agricultural biodiversity. FAO/Netherlands conference on the multifunctional character of agriculture and land. Background Paper 1. Maastricht.

Finegan, B. and Nasi, R. (2004) The biodiversity and conservation potential of shifting cultivation landscapes. In G. Schroth, G. A. B. da Fonseca, C. A. Harvey, C. Gascon, H. L. Vasconcelos and A.-M. N. Izac (eds.), *Agroforestry and Biodiversity Conservation in Tropical Landscapes*, pp. 153–197. Washington, DC, Covelo, CA, and London, Island Press.

Forsyth, T. and Walker, A. (2008) *Forest Guardians, Forest Destroyers: The Politics of Environmental Knowledge in Northern Thailand*. Seattle, WA, University of Washington Press.

Fox, J. and Castella, J.-C. (2013) Expansion of rubber (*Hevea brasiliensis*) in Mainland Southeast Asia: what are the prospects for smallholders? *The Journal of Peasant Studies*, **40**(1), 155–170.

Fox, J. and Vogler, J. B. (2005) Land-use and land-cover change in Montane Mainland Southeast Asia. *Environmental Management*, **36**(3), 394–403.

Gautam, A. E., Webb, E. L., Shivakoti, G. and Zoebisch, M. (2003) Land use dynamics and landscape change pattern in a mountain watershed in Nepal. *Agriculture, Ecosystems and Environment*, **99**, 83–96.

Heinimann, A. (2006) Patterns of land cover change in the Lower Mekong Basin: the relevance of meso-scale approaches PhD thesis. Berne, Switzerland, University of Berne.

Heinimann, A., Mertz, O., Frolking, S., Christanzen, A. E., Hurni, K., Sedano, F., Chini, L. P., Sahajpal, R., Hansen, M. and Hurtt, G. (2017) A global view of shifting cultivation: Recent, current, and future extent. *PLOS ONE*, **12**(9), 1–21. https://doi .org/10.1371/journal.pone.0184479.

Heinimann, A., Messerli, P., Schmidt-Vogt, D. and Wiesmann, U. (2007) The dynamics of secondary forest landscapes in the Lower Mekong Basin. *Mountain Research and Development*, **27**(3), 232–241.

Hett, C., Castella, J.-C., Heinimann, A., Messerli, P. and Pfund, J.-L. (2012) A landscape mosaics approach for characterizing swidden systems from a REDD+ perspective. *Applied Geography*, **32**(2), 608–618. DOI:10.1016/j.apgeog.2011.07.011.

Houghton, R. A. (1994) The worldwide extent of land use change. *BioScience*, **44**(5), 305–313.

Inthavong, C. and Schmidt-Vogt, D. (2005) On-farm tree planting in the uplands of Lao PDR: experiences, challenges, policy implications. *Asian Profile*, **33**(1), 37–52.

Kerkhoff, E. and Sharma, E. (eds.), (2006) *Debating shifting cultivation in the Eastern Himalayas: Farmers' innovations as lessons for policy*. Kathmandu, ICIMOD.

Khadka, S. and Schmidt-Vogt, D. (2008). Integrating biodiversity conservation and addressing economic needs: an experience with Nepal's community forestry. *Local Environment*, **13**(1), 1–13.

Lim, C. L., Prescott, G. W., De Alban, J. D. T., Ziegler, A. D. and Webb, E. L. (2017) Untangling the proximate causes and underlying drivers of deforestation and forest degradation in Myanmar. *Conservation Biology*, **31**(6), 1–11. DOI:10.1111/ cobi.12984.

Lu, J. N. (2017) Tapping into rubber: China's opium replacement program and rubber production in Laos. *The Journal of Peasant Studies*, **44**(4), 726–747.

Luintel, H., Bluffstone, R. A. and Scheller, R. M. (2018) The effects of the Nepal community forestry program on biodiversity conservation and carbon storage. *PLOS ONE*, **13**(6), 1–19. https://doi.org/10.1371/journal.pone.0199526

Messerli, P., Heinimann, A. and Epprecht, M. (2009) Finding homogeneity in heterogeneity: a new approach for quantifying landscape mosaics developed for the Lao PDR. *Human Ecology*, **37**(3), 291–304.

Minang, P., van Noordwijk, M., Freeman, O. E., Mbow, C., de Leeuw, J. and Catacutan, D. (eds.) (2015) *Climate-smart Landscapes: Multifunctionality in Practice*. Nairobi, Kenya, World Agroforestry Centre (ICRAF).

Mittelman, A. (2001) Secondary forests in the lower Mekong subregion: an overview of their extent, roles and importance. *Journal of Tropical Forest Science*, **13**(4), 671–690.

MRC (Mekong River Commission) and GTZ (Gesellschaft für Technische Zusammenarbeit) (1998) Forest cover data set for the Lower Mekong Basin. 1998. Forest Cover Monitoring Project, Mekong River Commission and Deutsche Gesellschaft für Technische Zusammenarbeit, Phnom Penh, Cambodia.

Myers, N., Mittermaier, R. A., Mittermaier, C. G., da Fonseca, G. A. B. and Kent, J. (2000) Biodiversity hotspots for conservation priorities. *Nature*, **403**, 853–858.

Padoch, C., Coffey, K., Mertz, O., Leisz, S., Fox, J. and Wadley, R. L. (2007) The demise of swidden in Southeast Asia? Local realities and regional ambiguities. *Geografisk Tidskrift, Danish Journal of Geography*, **107**(1), 29–41.

Phelps, J., Carrasco, L. R., Webb, E. L., Koh, L. P. and Pascual, U. (2013) Agricultural intensification escalates future conservation costs. *Proceedings of the National Academy of Sciences of the United States of America*, **110**, 7,601–7,606.

Pingali, P. L. (2012) Green Revolution: impacts, limits, and the path ahead. *Proceedings of the National Academy of Sciences of the United States of America*, **109**, 12,302–12,308.

Prescott, G. W., Sutherland, W. J., Aguirre, D., Baird, M., Bowman, V., Brunner, J. G., Cosier, M., Dapcie, M., De Alban, J. D. T., Diment, A., Fogerite, J., Fox, J., Hurd, J., Kyaw Min Thein, LaJeunesse Connett, K., Lasmana, F., Lim, C. L., Lynam, A., Than, M. M., McCarron, B., McCarthy, J. F., McShea, W., Momberg, F., Mon, M. S., Oberndorf, R., Rhelps, J., Rao, M., Thawng, S. C. L., Htun, S., Schmidt-Vogt, D., Thein, S., Speechly, S., Springate-Baginski, O., Steinmetz, R., Talbott, K., Myint, T., Oo, T. N., Thaung, T. L., Tizard, R., Whitten, T., Williamson, G., Wilson, T., Win, H., Woods, K., Ziegler, A. D., Zrust, M. and Webb, E. L. (2017) Political transition and emerging forest conservation issues in Myanmar. *Conservation Biology*, **31**, 1–14. DOI: 10.1111/cobi.13021.

Rambo, T. (2007) Observations on the role of improved fallow management in swidden agricultural systems. In M. Cairns (ed.), *Voices from the Forest: Integrating Indigenous Knowledge into Sustainable Farming*, pp. 780–801. Washington, DC, RFF Press.

Rasmussen, L. V., Coolsaet, B., Martin, A., Mertz, O., Pascual, U., Corbera, E., Dawson, N., Fisher, J. A., Franks, P. and Ryan, C. M. (2018) Social-ecological outcomes of agricultural intensification. *Nature Sustainability*, **1**(1), 275–282. https://doi .org/10.1038/s41893-018–0070-8

Rerkasem, K., Lawrence, D., Padoch, C., Schmidt-Vogt, D., Ziegler, A. D. and Brun, T. B. (2009) Consequences of swidden transitions for crop and fallow biodiversity in Southeast Asia. *Human Ecology*, **37**(3), 281–289.

Richards, P. W. (1996) *The Tropical Rain Forest: An Ecological Study*. Cambridge, Cambridge University Press.

Rigg, J. (2003) *Southeast Asia: The Human Landscape of Modernization and Development*. New York, Routledge.

Rigg, J. (2013) From rural to urban: A geography of boundary crossing in Southeast Asia. *TRaNS: Transnational and National Studies of Southeast Asia*, **1**(1), 5–26.

Roth, R. J. and Dressler, W. (2012) Market-oriented conservation governance: The particularities of place. *Geoforum*, **43**, 363–366.

Sajise, P. E. (2015) Biodiversity and swidden agroecosystems: An analysis and some implications. In M. Cairns (ed.), *Shifting Cultivation and Environmental Change: Indigenous People, Agriculture and Forest Conservation*, pp. 401–419. London and New York, Earthscan from Routledge.

Schmidt-Vogt, D. (1998) Defining degradation: the impacts of swidden on forests in northern Thailand. *Mountain Research and Development*, **18**(2), 135–149.

Schmidt-Vogt, D. (1999) Swidden farming and fallow vegetation in northern Thailand. *Geoecological Research*, **8**. Stuttgart, Franz Steiner.

Schmidt-Vogt, D. (2001) Secondary forests in swidden agriculture in the highlands of Thailand. *Journal of Tropical Forest Science*, **13**(4), 748–767.

Schmidt-Vogt, D. (2006) Comment on 'Gernot Brodnig: biodiversity conservation and the Millennium Development Goals'. *Regional Development Dialogue*, **27**(1), 9–11.

Schmidt-Vogt, D. (2015) Second thoughts on secondary forests: Can swidden cultivation be compatible with conservation? In M. Cairns (ed.), *Shifting Cultivation and Environmental Change: Indigenous People, Agriculture and Forest Conservation*, pp. 388–400. London and New York, Earthscan from Routledge.

Schmidt-Vogt, D., Leisz, S., Mertz, O., Heinimann, A., Thiha, Messerli, P., Epprecht, M., Cu, P. V., Chi, V. K., Hardiono, M. and Truong, D. M. (2009) An assessment of trends in the extent of swidden in Southeast Asia. *Human Ecology*, **37**(3), 269–280.

Siebert, F. and Belsky, J. M. (2014) Historic livelihoods and land uses as ecological disturbances and their role in enhancing biodiversity: an example from Bhutan. *Biological Conservation*, **177**, 82–89.

Siebert, F. and Belsky, J. M. (2017) Keeping ecological disturbance on the land: Recreating swidden effects in Bhutan. In M. Cairns (ed.), *Shifting Cultivation Policies: Balancing Environment and Social Sustainability*, pp. 460–469. Wallingford and Boston, CAB International.

Sodhi, N. S. and Brook, B. W. (2006) *Southeast Asian Biodiversity in Crisis*. Cambridge, Cambridge University Press.

Sodhi, N., Koh, L. P., Brook, B. W. and Ng, P. K. L. (2004) Southeast Asian biodiversity: an impending disaster. *Trends in Ecology and Evolution*, **19**(12), 654–660.

Solbrig, O. T. (2000) The theory and practice of the science of biodiversity: a personal assessment. In M. Kato (ed.), *The Biology of Biodiversity*, pp. 107–117. Tokyo, Springer.

Sovu, Tigabu, M., Savadogu, P., Oden, P. C. and Xayvongsa, L. (2009) Recovery of secondary forest on swidden cultivation fallows in Laos. *Forest Ecology and Management*, **258**, 2,666–2,675.

Suwanraks, R. (2000) Sufficiency economy. *TDRI Quarterly Review*, **15**(1), 6–17.

Swift, M. J., Izac, A.-M. N. and van Nordwijk, M. (2004) Biodiversity and ecosystem services in agricultural landscapes: are we asking the right questions? *Agriculture, Ecosystems and Environment*, **104**, 113–134.

Thanichanon, P., Schmidt-Vogt, D., Messerli, P., Heinimann, A. and Epprecht, M. (2013) Secondary forests and local livelihood along a gradient of accessibility: a case study in Luang Prabang. *Society and Natural Resources*, **26**(11), 1,283–1,299.

Thongmanivong, S. and Fujita, Y. (2006) Recent land use and livelihood transition in northern Laos. *Mountain Research and Development*, **26**(3), 237–244.

Tipraqsa, P., Craswell, E. T., Noble, A. D. and Schmidt-Vogt, D. (2007) Resource integration for multiple benefits: multifunctionality of integrated farming systems in Northeast Thailand. *Agricultural Systems*, **94**, 694–703.

van Vliet, N., Mertz, O., Heinimann, A., Langake, T., Pascual, U., Schmook, B., Adams, C., Schmidt-Vogt, D., Messerli, P., Leisz, S., Castella, J.-C., Joergensen, L., Birch-Thomsen, T., Hett, C., Bech-Bruun, T., Ickowitz, A., Vu, K. C., Yasuyuki, K. C., Fox, J., Padoch, C., Dressler, W. and Ziegler, A. D. (2012) Trends, drivers and impacts of changes in swidden cultivation in tropical forest-agriculture frontiers: a global assessment. *Global Environmental Change*, **22**, 418–429.

Wangpakapattanawong, P., Kavinchan, N., Vaidhayakarn, C., Schmidt-Vogt, D. and Elliott, S. (2010) Fallow to forest: applying indigenous and scientific knowledge to tropical forest restoration. *Forest Ecology and Management*, **260**, 1,399–1,406.

Webb, E. L. and Gautam, A. (2001) Effects of community forest management on the structure and diversity of a successional broadleaf forest in Nepal. *International Forestry Review*, **3**(2), 146–157.

Xu, J. (2006) The political, social, and ecological transformation of a landscape: the case of rubber in Xishuangbanna, China. *Mountain Research and Development*, **26**(3), 254–262.

Xu, J. (2011) China's new forests aren't as green as they seem. *Nature*, **477**, 371.

Xu, J., Lebel, L. and Sturgeon, J. (2009) Functional links between biodiversity, livelihoods, and culture in a Hani swidden landscape in southwest China. *Ecology and Society*, **14**(2), 20.

Zhai, D., Xu, J., Dai, C.-Z. and Schmidt-Vogt, D. (2017) Lost in transition: natural forest loss in the forest transition of tropical China. *Plant Diversity*, **39**(3), 149–153. DOI:10.1016/j.pld.2017.05.005

Zhang, J.-Q., Corlett, R. T., Zhai, D. (2019) After the rubber boom: good news and bad news for biodiversity in Xishuangbanna, Yunnan, China. Regional Environmental Change. https://doi.org/10.1007/s10113-019-01509-4

29 Assessing linkages between land use and biodiversity: A case study from the Eastern Himalayas using low-cost, high-return survey technology

ANDREW N. GILLISON[1], AMIRTHARAJ C. WILLIAMS[2], GOPALA AREENDRAN[3], AND RAJEEV SEMWAL[4,*]

[1]Center for Biodiversity Management, Yungaburra, Queensland 4884, Australia
[2]WWF-Myanmar
[3]WWF-India
[4]School of Environmental Sciences, Jawaharlal Nehru University, New Delhi, India

Keywords

Conservation management; biodiversity hotspot; eastern Himalayas; gradsects; plant functional types; rapid biodiversity assessment; spatial modelling; habitat indicators; transboundary conservation; global change impact

Abstract

To assess the impacts of global change and to sustainably manage biodiversity requires access to baseline data that can be used effectively by planners and resource managers. Too often, the high cost and severe logistical constraints associated with traditional methods of natural resource surveys limit the availability of such data. To address this problem, we present an alternative, low-cost, high-return, and readily transferable methodology that utilizes both ground-based and remotely sensed data. We illustrate this approach using results from an initial biodiversity baseline study of a proposed strategic conservation 'hotspot': the North Bank Landscape (NBL) of the Brahmaputra River in the eastern Himalayan foothills, which includes parts of Assam, Arunachal Pradesh, North Bengal, and Bhutan. The NBL contains significant populations of Asian elephants, tigers, clouded leopards, golden langurs, and other rare and endangered fauna. Following a brief training course in survey methodology, 14 trainees conducted a gradient-based (gradsect) survey of vascular plant species, plant functional types (PFTs), vegetation structure, site physical features, and mammalian habitat along a georeferenced land-use intensity gradient within the NBL. We found that plant species and PFT diversity were highly correlated with vegetation structure, which was, in turn, closely associated with mammalian habitat. This correlation provided a set of indicators for assessing and forecasting the impact of land use on both plant and animal biodiversity. The value of these indicators was further reinforced though their highly significant correlation with satellite imagery, which enhanced their potential for mapping habitat on a regional as well as local scale. Spatial modelling of the gradient-based survey locations revealed a high level of regional environmental representativeness. Our results from the field survey in India show that, compared with similarly sampled forested landscapes recorded so far in 20 countries, the NBL is second to the world's richest hotspot (Sumatra) in plant species diversity and comparable in PFT diversity and Plant Functional Complexity (PFC). While the results satisfy key criteria for listing the NBL as a global hotspot, the generic, low-cost methodology has wider implications for assessing the impact of global change on biodiversity.

29.1 INTRODUCTION

Bioregional planning for sustainable management requires adequate baseline information that can be readily accessed and updated by both planners and managers. Although problematic in terms of research and implementation, the absence of such information can readily lead to management failure (cf. Sayer and Campbell, 2004, p. 226; Sayer et al., 2013). Land management models developed under relatively stable environmental and socio-economic conditions will succeed only where the ecosystem drivers are well understood (Sala et al., 2000; FAO, 2013; SDSN, 2013). Where ecosystem stability is threatened by global climate change, the need for additional baseline information becomes even more critical for adaptive management. Under such conditions, the cost of acquiring data using traditional resource survey methodologies is likely to exceed the capacity of most management agencies. Alternative, cost-effective methods are few and far between.

Biodiversity baseline data are but one element of the resource management matrix, whose elements are too often considered stand-alone data. The reasons for this lie in the nature of the data, which are often highly subjective or else are restricted to species lists that, by themselves, are of little value to economists and planning agencies. Nonetheless, species inventories remain the primary focus of most biodiversity studies. Biodiversity

* Current status: Independent researcher, New Delhi, India

without value is biodiversity without a sustainable future. The challenge therefore is to attach value by seeking linkages that attach value between biodiversity baseline data and other related elements of the biophysical resource. Once obtained, cross-linked information of this kind can feed more readily into planning for adaptive management, thus enhancing both the value of biodiversity and the possibilities for its sustainable management. Traditional methods for designing and implementing biodiversity baseline studies can be extremely costly and time-demanding, especially methods that embrace sample designs based on purely systematic (e.g. grid) or randomized plot design, as these are highly impractical in complex and logistically difficult environments. For most purposes, especially where there is a need to know the nature and distribution of biodiversity patterns in a study region, standardized, rapid appraisal protocols involving gradient-based, georeferenced data using gradsects[1] are likely to be far more cost-effective. Partly because the sampling protocol aims at maximizing environmental coverage, gradsects are becoming more widely used, as they also provide a more representative basis for

extrapolating and testing results than surveys involving purely random or systematic sample design. The purpose of this chapter is to illustrate, by means of a case study, how this technology can be combined with a rapid on-site sampling protocol and readily transferred and applied in the field by persons with relatively little previous training. Finally, by comparing results with similar studies elsewhere, we explore its potential for wider application in biophysical and socio-economic environments throughout the Asia-Pacific region.

29.2 STUDY AREA

The North Bank Landscape (NBL) that comprised the focus of this study within India covers an area of about 85,000 km^2 within the Himalayan foothills (Figure 29.1). The NBL lies between the northern bank of the Brahmaputra River in the south to the foothills of the eastern Himalayas in the north, and the Manas River in the west to the Dibang River in the east. It forms a highly significant, strategic conservation zone containing an estimated 10% of the entire Indian population of Asian

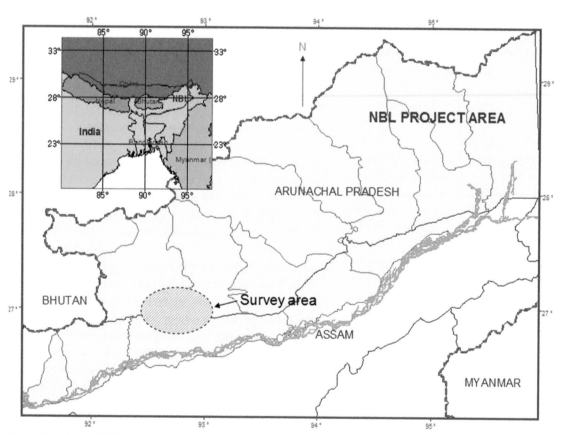

Figure 29.1. Map of NBL project area showing survey location within India.

[1] Gradsects are purposively located, gradient-oriented transects, usually located within a nested, hierarchical series of environmentally significant gradients (Gillison and Brewer, 1985).

elephants (*Elephas maximus*), as well as significant populations of tigers (*Panthera tigris*), pygmy hogs (*Sus salvanius*), hispid hares (*Caprolagus hispidus*), golden langurs (*Trachypithecus geei*), and clouded leopards (*Pardofelis nebulosa*), among other endangered species. Many of these species are under increasing threat from illegal poaching from both within and beyond the NBL borders. The zone includes a subsidiary reserve system (KaSoPaNa) of 6,440 km² comprising the Kameng-Sonitpur, Pakke, and Nameri Reserves in Assam-Arunachal in India. It is an important part of a proposed wider conservation strategy – the Eastern Himalayas Conservation Alliance (EHCA), which includes the upper Chindwin watershed, Hukaung Valley, Naga Hills, and northern Kachin region of Burma (Williams, 2002). The proposed EHCA is consistent with other regional conservation proposals to link reserves, for example, one between India and Bhutan (Sherpa and Norbu, 1999). According to Rawat and Wikramanayake (2001), plans to use ecoregions as basic units for conserving biodiversity are supported by similar proposals to establish linkages through conservation landscapes in other areas of the eastern Himalayas (WWF and ICIMOD, 2001). A similar initiative (Basnet, 2003) for establishing a framework for transboundary biodiversity conservation for Nepal, China, and India is consistent with the transfrontier, ecosystem-based approach proposed by the World Bank (2000).

Within the eastern Himalayas, the NBL forms part of the much broader 'Indo-Burma' global biodiversity 'hotspot' (Myers *et al.*, 2000; Gillison, 2004). It contains elements of several terrestrial ecoregions identified by Olson *et al.* (2001), namely the eastern Himalayan broadleaf forests (IM0401), the Himalayan subtropical broadleaf forests, the Brahmaputra Valley semi-evergreen forests (IM0105), and minor fragments of the Terai and Duar grasslands (IM0701). The NBL also falls within the Tropical and Subtropical Moist Broadleaf Forest biome identified as vulnerable within the Global 200 set of terrestrial ecoregions defined by Olson and Dinerstein (2002). High regional biodiversity is due in part to the evolutionary history of the Himalayas, which formed as a result of the upward movement of the Deccan Plateau into the Eurasian continent during the early Tertiary period. This has left a rich legacy of floristic and faunal elements from both Indian and Malesian sources (Rodgers and Panwar, 1988). The eastern Himalayas contain elements of the Indo-Malayan, Indo-Chinese, Sino-Malayan, and East Asiatic floras, as well as several Gondwanan relics (Rawat and Wikramanayake, 2001). Apart from the overlapping ecoregions of Olson *et al.* (2001), this complexity is mirrored in a variety of biogeographic classifications that tend to overlap in the NBL, notably the Himalayan highlands and Burma monsoon forest provinces of Udvardy (1975), the biounits of MacKinnon (1997) and BirdLife International's EBA, eastern Himalayas (Statersfield *et al.*, 1998).

Under a seasonal monsoonal climate with high annual rainfall (1,500–3,000 mm), deep alluvial deposits formed from rivers draining the southern slopes of the eastern Himalayas once supported extensive, species-rich forests that have been progressively converted to agriculture (Rawat *et al.*, 2001). Relatively recent and largely uncontrolled human settlement in forested areas on the alluvial plains and lower foothills to the north of the Brahmaputra River has further impacted remaining forests. Since 1972, approximately 14% of natural forest within NBL has been lost together with 65% of semi-evergreen forest in the lowland Brahmaputra valley. Many important faunal and floristic habitats have also disappeared, and the remainder are under increasing threat. Other than a limited periodic census of key fauna in some restricted areas, there have been no systematic surveys of plant or animal biota in the eastern Himalayas or the NBL. Yet baseline information of this kind is essential for identifying habitat indicators and for conservation planning. Apart from highlighting the conservation potential of NBL within a regional context, an important aim of this investigation was to help lay the foundation for an improved conservation knowledge base by using the results of an initial survey to provide a logical and cost-efficient sampling framework for further baseline studies.

29.3 IN-COUNTRY TRAINING

Under the sponsorship of WWF-India, 14 trainees from a wide range of conservation management agencies (including three co-authors in this chapter) attended an intensive six-day course, during which they received instruction in basic survey methods (see Section 29.4). As a 'hands-on' application of these methods, the trainees subsequently undertook a partially supervised field survey that was completed in six days, the results of which form the core of this chapter. While the data analyses have been performed by ANG, detailed remote-sensing analysis was carried out by a team member (GA) at WWF-India HQ.

29.4 MATERIALS AND METHODS

29.4.1 Survey design and sample plot location

Sustainable conservation management requires an understanding of the spatial and temporal ranges of key taxa and the principal environmental factors governing their distribution and survival. Overly restrictive sampling can lead to serious misinterpretation of species' response to environmental change and incorrect assumptions about the surrogacy of indicators for biodiversity conservation management (Gillison and Liswanti, 2004). If the initial purpose of a survey is to maximize information about the distribution of species and related functional types within an area, then purposive selection of transects within a hierarchy of environmental gradients (gradsects) is likely to be more cost-effective than random or purely systematic sampling (Gillison and Brewer, 1985). Evidence for improved efficiency of the gradsect approach over other, more logistically demanding traditional, statistical survey designs is supported by independent field evaluations at different management scales, including mountainous regions similar to the eastern Himalayas (Wessels *et al.*, 1998; Sandmann and Lertzman, 2003). This sampling strategy is now coming into increasing favour (UNEP-CBD, 1996, 2001; WCMC, 1996; USGS-NPS, 2003; FAO, 2005; Parker *et al.*, 2011; Ferrer-Paris *et al.*, 2012; NPS, 2012).

As with overall survey design, the selection of sample plot size and plot location should be purpose and scale-driven. Vegetation surveys completed in more than 1,600 locations worldwide indicate that a 40 x 5 m (200 m²) transect is adequate for most survey purposes and is less prone to observer fatigue than larger transects, especially in complex, humid tropical forests, where all vascular plants species (as distinct from only trees) are to be recorded (Gillison, 2004). In constructing preliminary gradsects, we combined field reconnaissance with local information from park rangers and WWF personnel, together with recent satellite imagery (Landsat Thematic Mapper (TM) and Enhanced Thematic Mapper (ETM+) and a Landsat false colour composite with a 4,3,2,1 band sequence) (Figure 29.2). The primary environmental gradient was assumed to be thermal, as indicated by elevation, with secondary and tertiary gradients following key drainage systems. Finally, we superimposed a subjectively assessed land-use 'intensity' gradient, as indicated by varying degrees of forest removal, slash and burn (jhum), forest plantations, and intensive, sedentary agriculture. Altogether 14 transects were positioned to represent the key characteristics of these overlapping gradients. Sample sites (Table 29.1) ranged from relatively intact to highly disturbed,

Figure 29.2. Landsat false colour composite satellite image within NBL showing sample transect locations within the Bhareli drainage system; scale 1:420,000.

upland and lowland forest, Sal (*Shorea assamica* Dyer) timber plantation, annually fired shrub savanna, degraded cow pasture, and rice fields, including fields under active cultivation and others abandoned because of repeated damage by elephants.

29.4.2 Data collection

At each transect, we recorded georeferenced (handheld GPS) biophysical data according to an established protocol using the VegClass system (Gillison, 2002). A subsequent analysis of satellite imagery suggested transect number 8 may have been incorrectly georeferenced, and for this reason it was dropped from the analysis. For this preliminary survey, soils were characterized according to field estimates of soil texture. Digital photographs of vegetation were recorded at each site, together with informal observations of animal signs. Other variables included vegetation structure, all vascular plant species, and plant functional types (PFTs) (Table 29.2). For the present study and as described elsewhere (Gillison and Carpenter, 1997), Plant Functional Types (PFTs) are combinations of adaptive morphological or functional elements or traits such as leaf size class, leaf inclination class, leaf form, and type (distribution of chlorophyll tissue) coupled with a modified life form classification and type of above-ground rooting system.[2] VegClass uses an internal rule set to estimate functional 'distance' within and between PFTs to summarize and quantify similarities and differences within and between transects, as well as generating distance matrices that can be used directly in multivariate analysis.

Although, in practice, PFTs and species tend to be closely correlated, they are theoretically independent, as more than one species can occur in one PFT and vice versa. Nowhere is this more evident than in humid tropical closed forests, where many canopy tree species frequently collapse into one PFT. Functional types permit the recording of adaptive responses of plant individuals, which can reveal within and between species responses to the environment in a way that is not achievable with a species taxonomic diagnosis. Unlike species, and because the PFT classification system is finite and generic, PFTs can be readily used to compare data sets derived from geographically remote regions where, for example, plant adaptive responses and environments may be similar but where species differ. The combination of taxonomic and functional traits therefore adds a more useful quantitative dimension to biodiversity than if species alone are used. Multidisciplinary, baseline surveys in Sumatra, Thailand, and the

---

[2] In VegClass, PFTs are constructed according to a specific rule set from a minimum set of 35 functional attributes (Gillison and Carpenter, 1997). A PFT for an individual of *Shorea assamica* with **me**sophyll-sized, **co**mposite inclination, **do**rsiventral and **de**ciduous leaves supported by a **ph**anerophytic life form would be **me-co-do-de-ph**. An algorithm is used to calculate a metric distance between PFTs and between transects.

Table 29.1. Site localities and vegetation types for all transects*.

Transect ID	Latitude	Longitude	Elev (m)	Vegetation type	Location
NBL01	27° 0' 48" N	92° 38' 49" E	100	Degraded pasture grazed by cattle	Bhalukpong, Sonitpur, Assam
NBL02	26° 59' 58" N	92° 53' 7" E	126	Highly disturbed riverine forest with dominant *Dillenia indica* and Urticaceae Elephant damage	Nameri Tiger Reserve, near Bhareli River
NBL03	26° 57' 28" N	92° 51' 15" E	92	Selectively logged forest in Tiger Reserve Elephant, gaur	Nameri Tiger Reserve near river Khari
NBL04	26° 56' 58" N	92° 51' 17" E	109	Selectively logged forest in Tiger Reserve Elephant, gaur, deer	Nameri Tiger Reserve near river Khari
NBL05	26° 56 33" N	92° 51' 5" E	86	Annually fired shrub savanna, dominated by *Leea crispa, Saccharum spontaneum* Elephant, gaur, deer	Nameri Tiger Reserve, Potasali Camp
NBL06	27° 2' 3" N	92° 36' 58" E	88	Degraded forest with signs of Samba deer	Tipi – inside Pakke sanctuary
NBL07	27° 2' 5" N	92° 40' 2" E	165	Disturbed forest, signs of elephants	Mithun Nala, Nameri Tiger Reserve
NBL08*	27° 2' 10" N	92° 39' 58" E?	165	Rainforest disturbed by humans and animals Elephant	Nameri NP, on the bank of Mithun Nala River along the ridge
NBL09	27° 5' 59" N	92° 31' 52" E	1040	Riverine forest moderately disturbed on boulder field	1 km south of Sissa, on the eastern bank of the river Sissa
NBL10	26° 56' 0" N	92° 48' 6" E	93	Four-year-old rice plot abandoned due to elephant damage	Gamani Forestry Village, Balipara RF
NBL11	26° 55' 57" N	92° 48' 6" E	90	Annual padi rice, damaged by elephants	Gamani Village (Forestry Village), Balipara RF
NBL12	27° 2' 0" N	92° 6' 0" E	156	Highly disturbed riverine forest, elephant resting place	Nameri Tiger Reserve near Bhareli River
NBL13	27° 5' 31" N	92° 35' 8" E	470	Two years abandoned jhum plot	Elephant Flat Village
NBL14	26° 55' 24" N	92° 48' 39" E	85	Sal (*Shorea assamica*) plantation 30 years old, after clearing natural forest with natural Sal	Salari, Balipara RF

*Site removed from analysis due to possible GPS error.

western Amazon basin show strong statistical support for the use of PFTs in combination with vascular plant species as overall biodiversity indicators (Watt and Zborowski, 2000; Jones *et al.*, 2002; Gillison *et al.*, 2013).

29.4.3 Data analysis

Species:area and PFT:area curves were examined for sample representativeness where failure to asymptote indicated a need for additional samples. Transect data were compiled using the VegClass software package, which was also used to calculate plant functional complexity (PFC – the minimum spanning tree distance between all PFTs in a transect) (Gillison, 2002). A complete linear (Pearson) correlation matrix was generated for all biophysical variables including PFT diversity indices and PFC. In order to

identify readily observable 'best bet' variables as biodiversity indicators, both single and multiple combinations of vegetation structural variables were examined first for their correlation with species and PFT diversity or richness (number per sample) and PFC and second for their practicability. While individual or 'best subsets' of variables were assessed for indicator value, additional information was acquired through multi-dimensional scaling (MDS) of the raw data.[3] In the present case, for the 13 transects we undertook a single axis score in an MDS of raw Landsat imagery (bands 2,3) of the NBL region and a separate, single axis

---

[3] We used the Gower Metric combined with a semi-strong hybrid scaling option with a single-vector solution available in the PATN (version 3.11) multivariate analysis package developed by L. Belbin and A. Collins (Blatant Fabrications), 2006.

Table 29.2. Plant diversity and vegetation structural values for all transects.

Plot ID	Spp	PFTs	Spp: PFT	PFC	Ht	CcTot	Cc Wdy	Cc Nwdy	Wdy Plt	Bryo	Litt	BA	MFI	FCIV
NBL01	46	25	1.84	112	0.3	95	0	95	1	1	4	0.01	100.00	0.00
NBL02	72	47	1.53	232	12	95	70	25	8	4	2	13.33	44.75	78.88
NBL03	94	59	1.59	262	15	90	70	20	10	5	1	19.67	45.75	36.03
NBL04	73	46	1.59	230	14	80	70	10	8	4	0	30.00	39.50	42.06
NBL05	34	27	1.26	158	1.8	100	30	70	8	1	1	0.10	54.25	50.86
NBL06	107	74	1.45	314	16	95	85	10	9	4	2.5	22.67	49.25	52.52
NBL07	91	56	1.63	288	10	98	80	18	8	4	1.5	11.33	48.50	78.52
NBL09	83	60	1.38	314	16	95	80	15	8	6	2.5	22.33	27.25	98.27
NBL10	41	29	1.41	168	0.04	70	0	70	1	1	0.3	0.01	0.00	0.00
NBL11	18	14	1.29	116	0.1	60	5	55	1	1	0.3	0.01	0.00	0.00
NBL12	59	38	1.55	214	18	60	70	10	9	4	3	22.67	34.25	80.97
NBL13	84	59	1.42	294	1.5	90	2	88	4	1	2	1.00	51.43	74.19
NBL14	30	22	1.36	140	20	60	55	5	9	2	0.3	11.00	14.50	112.93

Spp = species; PFTs = Plant Functional Types; PFC = Plant Functional Complexity; Ht = Mean canopy height (m); CcTot = Total crown cover %; CcWdy = crown cover % woody plants; CcNwdy = crown cover % Non-woody plants; Wdy Plt = cover abundance of woody plants < 2 m tall; Bryo = cover abundance of bryophytes; Litt = litter depth (cm); BA = basal area woody plants (m^2 ha^{-1}); MFI = Mean furcation index canopy trees; FICV = coefficient of variation % of furcation index (Gillison, 2002).

score in an MDS of five plant-based variables (plant species richness, PFT richness, PFC, mean canopy height, and basal area of all woody plants) that are already known to exhibit high indicator value for fauna in other tropical countries, such as Brazil and Sumatra (Gillison *et al.*, 2013). We then regressed the axis scores of the satellite data against the vegetation data using both linear and second-order polynomial regressions. The purpose of this exercise was to determine whether certain plant-based variables known from field experience to be useful faunal habitat indicators might be sufficiently well correlated with satellite imagery for extrapolative mapping and testing purposes. Landsat bands 2,3,4, together with a digital elevation model of the NBL, were selected for analysis using DOMAIN potential mapping software

(Carpenter *et al.*, 1993). Whereas many predictive modelling procedures require both presence and absence data, DOMAIN produces similarity values based on presence alone and can operate effectively with relatively few georeferenced points. This is a distinct advantage where species distributional data are few and where the cost of intensive surveys is high. As such, DOMAIN has the capacity to generate low-cost, readily testable, distribution maps of species, functional types, and habitat. In order to assess the level of regional representativeness of all sites investigated, the distribution points for all thirteen transects were used via DOMAIN to generate a grid-based classification map based on the similarity value of each pixel or grid to the original environmental domain envelope constructed for all transect sites (Figure 29.3).

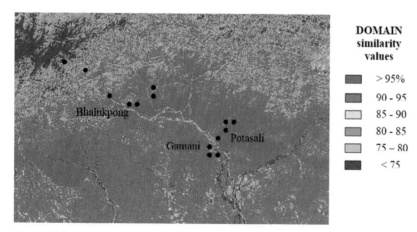

DOMAIN similarity values

- > 95%
- 90 - 95
- 85 - 90
- 80 - 85
- 75 – 80
- < 75

Figure 29.3. DOMAIN comparison for all NBL sites, based on Landsat satellite imagery and elevation. High similarity values (>90%) indicate areas of similar 'habitat'.

We compared the NBL species and PFT diversity data with the highest values recorded for a transect in an analogous series of similarly forested, ecoregional gradsects in 20 other countries where the data were collected using the same sampling protocol. Graphs of linear regressions of species diversity against PFT diversity were also used to illustrate differences between NBL and other gradsects across a range of humid, tropical forested landscapes in Sumatra, Thailand, Cameroon, Brazil, the Perúvian Amazon basin, Fiji, and northeastern Australia.

29.5 RESULTS

Plant diversity, PFC, and vegetation structural values are listed in Table 29.2. We recorded 601 unique plant species and 245 unique PFTs for all transects.[4] Plant species are highly correlated with PFTs and PFC (Figure 29.4a, b), while species and PFT diversity and PFC are closely correlated with vegetation structure, in particular mean canopy height, basal area of all woody plants, crown cover percentage of non-woody plants (important

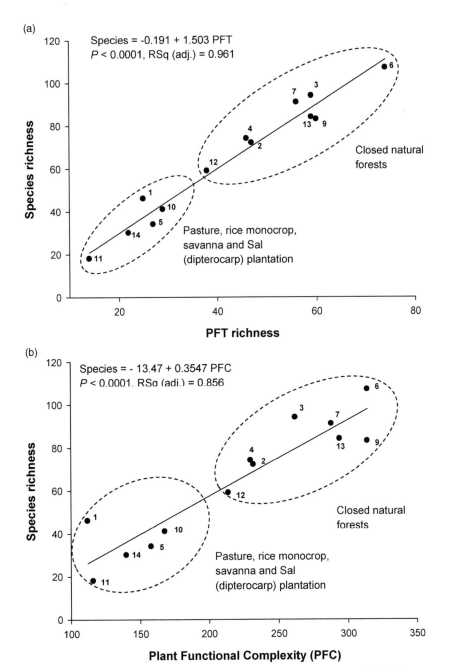

Figure 29.4. Plant species richness regressed against (a) PFT richness; and (b) PFC for NBL gradsect.

[4] Complete data summaries are available on request from the contact author.

Table 29.3. Correlation matrix between plant-based variables and Landsat imagery*.

Plant variable	Raw 2	Raw 3	MDSSat	MDSVeg	Spp	PFT	PFC	Ht
MDSveg	0.806	0.807	0.807					
	0.001	0.001	0.001					
Spp	−0.679	−0.710	−0.709	−				
	0.011	0.007	0.007					
PFT	−0.673	−0.685	−0.705	−	0.982			
	0.012	0.010	0.007		0.000			
PFC	−0.667	−0.693	−0.719	−	−	0.968		
	0.013	0.009	0.006			0.000		
Ht	−0.771	−0.741	−0.770	−0.967	0.932	−	−	
	0.002	0.004	0.002	0.000	0.000			
CcTotal	−	−	−	−	0.586	0.578	−	−
					0.035	0.038		
CcWdy	−0.732	−0.694	−0.730	−0.821	0.631	0.917	0.630	0.881
	0.004	0.009	0.005	0.001	0.021	0.025	0.021	0.000
CcNwdy	0.581	0.556	0.579	0.891	−	−	−	−0.929
	0.037	0.048	0.038	0.000				0.000
WdyPlt	−0.778	−0.711	−0.747	−0.891	−	−	−	0.849
	0.002	0.006	0.003	0.001				0.000
Bryo	−0.670	−0.702	−0.727	−0.740	0.706	0.685	0.707	0.783
	0.012	0.007	0.005	0.004	0.007	0.010	0.007	0.002
BA	−0.727	−0.692	−0.690	−0.844	0.607	0.583	0.578	0.858
	0.005	0.009	0.009	0.000	0.028	0.037	0.039	0.000
FICV	−0.758	−0.740	−0.796	−0.736	−	−	−	0.698
	0.003	0.004	0.001	0.004				0.008

* Spp = species richness; PFT = Plant Functional Type richness; PFC = Plant Functional Complexity; Ht = mean canopy height (m); CcTotal = total crown cover %'; CcWdy = crown cover % woody plants; CcNwdy = crown cover % non-woody plants; WdyPlt = cover-abundance of woody plants < 2 m tall; Bryo = bryophyte cover-abundance; BA = basal area all woody plants (m² ha⁻¹); FICV = coefficient of variation % of furcation index; Raw 2,3 = raw data values from Landsat bands 2,3; MDSSat = multidimensional scaling (eigenvector values from single vector solution) of combined Landsat Raw 2,3 data; MDSVeg = MDS of combined Spp, PFT, PFC, Ht, BA (variables known to be good indicators of faunal habitat). Upper cell = *r* value, lower cell = *P* value. Only correlations with *P* < 0.05 included.

for certain herbivores and browsers), cover-abundance of bryophytes (liverworts and mosses), and variation in furcation index[5] of woody plants (Table 29.3). No significant correlates were recorded between Landsat band 4 values and plant-based variables. However, bands 2 and 3 were highly correlated with vegetation structure and to a slightly lesser extent with richness in species and PFTs as well as PFC. Multidimensional scaling of the raw data from Landsat bands 2 and 3 correlated strongly with

an MDS based on five plant variables known from other studies (Gillison *et al.*, 2016; Jones *et al.*, 2004) to be good indicators of vertebrate and invertebrate habitat (Table 29.3, Figure 29.5).

The DOMAIN potential mapping analysis based on the 13 transects and Landsat bands 2,3 and a digital elevation model (DEM) indicates a very high level of representativeness within the NBL study region for areas <1,200 m a.s.l. (Figure 29.5). When compared with similarly sampled forested sites in 20 other countries recorded so far (Table 29.4, Figure 29.6), the NBL is second only to the world's richest (Sumatra) in overall plant species. However, the NBL study shows comparable values with Sumatra with respect to plant functional type *alpha* (within plot) diversity and plant functional complexity (PFC).

---

[5] Furcation index (FI) is the distance from the apex of a woody plant to the first break in the linear axis of the main stem, expressed as a percentage of total height (Gillison, 2002). High variation (cv%) in FI usually indicates a history of continuing disturbance, whereas low cv% indicates a more stable environment.

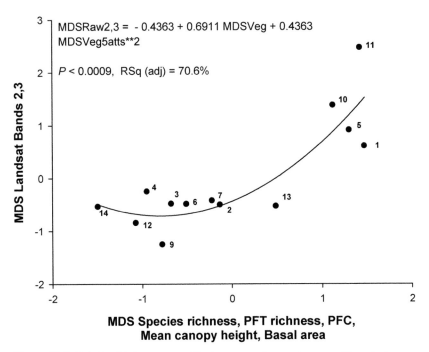

Figure 29.5. Relationship between satellite imagery and ground survey of key plant-based, animal habitat indicators.

Table 29.4. Comparative diversity in plant species, PFTs and PFC values in humid lowland tropical and subtropical forests in 21 countries*.

No.	Country	Location	Georeference	Transect ID	Forest type	Species diversity	PFT diversity	PFC value
1	Indonesia (Sumatra)	Tesso Nilo, Riau Province	0° 14' 51" S 101° 58' 16" E	TN02	Primary forest, partially logged 1997	217	73	370
2	Indonesia (Sumatra)	Pancuran Gading, Jambi Province	1° 10' 12" S 102° 06' 50" E	BS10	Primary forest interplanted with 'jungle' rubber (*Hevea brasiliensis*)	112	47	236
3	India	Arunachal Pradesh, Tipi – Pakke Sanctuary.	27° 2' 3" N 92° 36' 58" E	NBL06	Primary forest, selectively logged	107	74	314
4	Indonesia (Borneo)	Gunung Banalang, Long Puak, Pujungan, East Kalimantan	2° 43' 32" N 115° 39' 46"E	BUL02	Disturbed complex forest along ridge	104	44	232
5	Cameroon	Awae Village	3° 36' 05" N 11° 36' 15" E	CAM 01	Late secondary forest Previously logged	103	43	232
6	Papua New Guinea	Kuludagi/West New Britain Province	5° 38' 46" S 150° 06' 14" E	KIMBE2	Primary forest	99	52	234
7	Costa Rica	Braulio Carillo, Parque Nacional	10° 09' 42" N 83° 56' 18" W	CR001	Partially disturbed forest, palm dominated. Many epiphytes	94	71	336
8	Brazil	Pedro Peixoto, Acré (West Amazon basin)	10° 01' 13" S 67° 09' 39" W	BRA19	ICRAF ASB Site, secondary forest (Capoeira) 3–4 years after abandonment	82	43	230

Table 29.4 (cont.)

No.	Country	Location	Georeference	Transect ID	Forest type	Species diversity	PFT diversity	PFC value
9	Indonesia (West Papua)	Biak Island, Marauw	01° 09' 02" S 136° 16' 28" E	BIAK01	Disturbed coastal primary forest on limestone	75	62	358
10	Brazil	Alcalinas Canamá, NW Mato Grosso (West Amazon basin)	10° 04' 06" S 58° 46' 00" W	PN24	Primary forest on shallow granitic soils	75	54	298
11	Perú	Jenaro Herrera, Ucayali River (West Amazon basin)	4° 58' 00" S 73° 45' 00" W	PE02	'High terrace' primary forest – selective logging	72	39	208
12	Vietnam	Cuc Phuong National Park, Ninh Binh Province	20° 48' 33" N 105 42' 44" E	FSIV02	Partly disturbed primary forest on limestone	69	46	252
13	Perú	Von Humboldt forest reserve, Pucallpa (W. Amazon basin)	8° 48' 01" S 75° 03' 54" W	PUC01	Primary forest selectively logged, 1960	63	31	258
14	Fiji	Bua, Vanua Levu	16° 47' 36" S 178° 36' 45" E	FJ55	Disturbed lowland forest on ridge	60	37	258
15	Thailand	Ban Huay Bong, Mae Chaem watershed	18° 30' 42" N 98° 24' 13" E	MC18	Humid-seasonal, deciduous dipterocarp forest, fallow system	59	44	200
16	Malaysia (Borneo)	Danum Valley, Sabah	4° 53' 03" N 117° 57' 48" E	DANUM3	Primary forest subject to reduced impact logging, Nov. 1993	56	39	208
17	Kenya	Shimba Hills near Mombasa	4° 11' 33" S 39° 25 34" E	K01	Semi-deciduous forest in game park area. Previously logged	56	33	214
18	Guyana	Iwokrama forest reserve	4° 35' 02" N 58° 44' 51" W	IWOK01	Primary swamp forest in blackwater system	52	34	192
19	Philippines	Mt. Makiling, Luzon	14° 08' 46" N 131° 13' 50" E	PCLASS1	Regenerating forest planted in 1968 with *Swietenia macrophylla*, *Parashorea*, and *Pterocarpus indicus*	52	26	194
20	Indonesia (Borneo)	Batu Ampar, Central Kalimantan	0° 47' 48" N 117° 06' 23" E	BA02	Primary forest, heavily logged 1991/92	46	33	188
21	Australia	Atherton tableland, North Queensland	17° 18' 28" S 145° 25' 20" E	DPI06	Upland humid forest managed for sustainable timber extraction	46	25	160
22	Panama	Barro Colorado island	9° 09' 43" N 79° 50' 46" W	BARRO1	Primary forest, ground layer grazed by native animals	43	30	196
23	Bolivia	Las Trancas (Santa Cruz)	16° 31' 40" N 61° 50' 48" W	BOL02	Primary forest. Logged 1996	42	31	198

Table 29.4 (cont.)

No.	Country	Location	Georeference	Transect ID	Forest type	Species diversity	PFT diversity	PFC value
24	Brazil	Reserva Biologica da Campina, km 50 near Manaus (East Amazon basin)	2° 35' 21" S 60° 01' 55" W	BRA24	Moderately disturbed forest on siliceous sands	42	27	166
25	Vanuatu	Yamet, near Umetch, Aneityum Island	20° 12' 32" S 169° 52' 33" E	VAN11	Coastal primary forest, partially logged, with *Agathis macrophylla* (Kauri) overstorey	38	22	180
26	Mexico	Zona Maya, Yucatan peninsula	19° 02' 26" N 88° 03' 20" E	YUC02	Logged secondary lowland forest	37	26	148
27	West Indies (France)	Near Mont Pelée, Martinique	0° 47' 48" N 117° 06' 23" E	MQUE1	Humid, lowland forest on volcanic slopes, locally disturbed	32	24	286
28	Argentina	Iguazú Parque Nacional de las Cataratas	25° 39' 00" S 54° 35' 00" W	IGUAZU01	Lowland forest, disturbed	28	24	208
29	French Guyana	B.E.C., 16 km from Kourou	14° 49' 23" N 61° 7' 37" W	FRG05	*Terra firme* forest on siliceous sand	28	18	110
30	Indonesia (Borneo)	Mandor Nature Reserve, north of Pontianak	0° 17' 12" N 109° 33' 00" E	PA02	Primary forest in blackwater system on siliceous sand	25	21	180

*Data summary from transects with highest records of vascular plant species and Plant Functional Type (PFT) and Plant Functional Complexity (PFC) values extracted from a series of global, ecoregional surveys and restricted to 'lowland' (0–900 m elevation) humid, closed forests. All data collected using a standard 'VegClass' sampling protocol (Gillison, 2002). Forest conditions range from relatively pristine to secondary. *Source:* International Centre for Research in Agroforestry, Alternatives to Slash and Burn Programme (ICRAF/ASB); Center for International Forestry Research (CIFOR); WWF AREAS project, India, PróNatura (Brazil), UNDP/GEF and Center for Biodiversity Management (CBM) (www.cbmglobe.org).

29.6 DISCUSSION

Plant species identification at the scale recorded in each transect for all vascular plant species is likely to be problematic in complex, humid tropical, and sub-tropical forests. Our baseline study indicates that, in the absence of a field botanist or lack of access to readily identifiable taxa, plant species diversity in the study area can be estimated by using PFT values in the linear regression equation with a high degree of confidence (Figure 29.4). With the exception of Sumatra, the diversity patterns observed in the NBL transects are consistent with those obtained from surveys along similar land-use intensity gradients in other tropical and subtropical ecoregions (Gillison, 2001). The species:PFT regression slope for NBL (Figures 29.5, 29.6) is a close match with humid, west tropical Africa (Cameroon), mid-montane Southeast Asia (northern Thailand), and the Brazilian western Amazon basin. However, the NBL species

and PFT diversity and PFC values far exceed those of the richest humid, tropical, old-growth forests recorded to date in northeastern Australia, which contain refugia for some of the world's most ancient angiosperm families.

Despite evident overlaps between Sundanese (Sumatran) and lowland Himalayan plant families and genera, the regions are clearly demarcated at species level. The inclusion of the eastern Himalayas within the broader context of an 'Indo-Burma' hotspot (Conservation International, 2005) may need revision, given an increasingly pragmatic focus on conservation priorities worldwide. In this respect, additional data and further examination of the status of biodiversity within the broad 'Indo-Burma–Sundaland' megazone are needed to better differentiate regional conservation priorities (Rastogi and Chettri, 2001). Within the 'Indo-Burma' hotspot, for example, best-management guidelines developed for specific socio-economic environments and

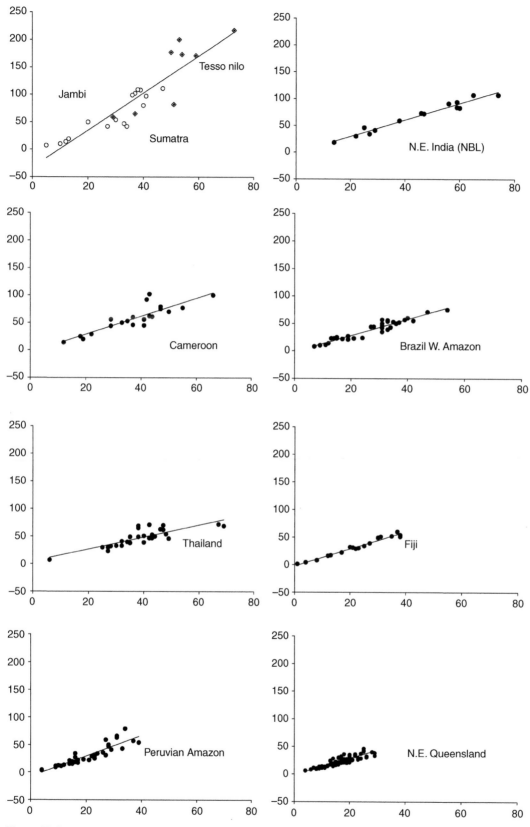

Figure 29.6. Linear regressions between diversity (richness) in plant species and PFTs, comparing NBL with other global ecoregional gradsects (each point represents a single 40 x 5 m transect) (ref. **Table 29.4**).

ecosystems in lowland, seasonal Cambodia and Laos may not apply to the NBL. On the other hand, the high global ranking in plant diversity detected for the NBL coupled with the currently high degree of environmental threat supports its recognition as a biodiversity 'hotspot' in its own right (cf. Myers *et al.*, 2000; Hobohm, 2003).

Our results indicate that, despite the relatively few sample points, the gradsect approach captured the major environmental gradients for the region under study including animal habitats (Figure 29.5). Based on satellite imagery and elevation, the DOMAIN surface generated for all sites suggests that, with some clear exceptions at higher elevations, points sampled along the gradsect account for most of the physical environmental variability within the study area. Further sampling of vegetation and fauna will establish a basis for improved mapping of species and their habitats. In the current study, areas with DOMAIN similarity values less than 80% suggest priority areas for additional surveys. For ground-truthing satellite imagery, readily measureable canopy-based variables that are typically correlated with plant diversity include mean canopy height, percentage of crown cover, and basal area. These can be used for rapid assessment and monitoring following the establishment of plant functional and vegetation structural baselines.

An examination of species:area and PFT:area curves indicates that further sampling is required for all forest sites, but that sampling frequency for other vegetation types is adequate. The biophysical heterogeneity of the NBL and the steepness of key environmental gradients indicate gradient-based surveys or gradsects using small (e.g. 200 m²) plots are likely to be far more cost-efficient in assessing and monitoring biodiversity than traditional techniques involving randomly positioned, large plots of 1 ha or more. Once regional baselines have been established for species, then PFT composition and vegetation structure may ultimately provide the most practical units for rapidly assessing and monitoring change in biodiversity and for conservation planning.

Within the NBL, vegetation impact from large mammals, particularly elephants, is increasing with uncontrolled reduction of natural forest habitats by recent settlers. In the lowlands, we observed intensive impacts from elephants on agricultural land that in some cases caused farmers to abandon rice fields. This type of impact is intensifying conflict between elephants and humans in the NBL. Contrary to a common perception that elephants may be naturally restricted to the lowland plains, we recorded elephant damage to upland forests on slopes exceeding 60%. While elephant impact on vegetation is generally conspicuous, a less visible but significant impact is browsing by smaller, more numerous ungulates, in particular Samba deer (*Cervus unicolor*). In all forested sites in the Nameri Tiger Reserve, we found widespread evidence of browsing in the

herbaceous and shrub layer, where deer target a wide range of species, among them semi-succulent Commelinaceae (*Forrestia hookeri*) and Piperaceae (*Piper longum*), as well as Chloranthaceae (*Chloranthus elatior*), and Acanthaceae (*Strobilanthes* sp.). In each forest transect, but especially NBL 3 and 4, browsing was associated with increased coppicing and ground cover – habitat features readily detected by the survey protocol (especially cover-abundance of woody plants <2 m tall). Although clearly important, the extent to which browsing is a natural component of forest ecosystem dynamics is unknown in the NBL. A comparison with forests in other countries, where intermediate disturbance leads to higher biodiversity (Sheil and Burslem, 2003), suggests the high plant diversity and PFC values in NBL forests may be associated in part with browsing pressure from large mammals.

Conservation management of large, environmentally heterogeneous areas with complex habitats will rely heavily on cost-effective indicators for assessing and monitoring biotic assemblages. This can become particularly critical for forested habitats occupied by large ungulates. Previous studies (Lawton *et al.*, 1998; Azevedo *et al.*, 2002) provide little scientific support for the use of species to predict the occurrence of other species. Supporting evidence for the use of species and other taxon-based and vegetation structural indicators is emerging with more recent in-depth, gradient-based studies at landscape level in India and elsewhere (Negi and Gadgil, 2002; MacNally and Fleishman, 2004; Sauberer *et al.*, 2004). In this preliminary survey, while we did not aim to identify specific indicators for monitoring large mammal habitats, we did identify readily observable vegetation structural indicators of plant species diversity, PFT diversity, and PFC that are known to be useful faunal habitat indicators in other tropical forests (Watt and Zborowski, 2000; Gillison *et al.*, 2013). Of especial interest in this study is the apparent failure of crown cover percentage as an indicator of biodiversity. Crown cover (usually estimated as projective foliage cover percentage (Specht, 1970)) is one of the most widely used descriptors of vegetation structure at both local and formation level. When applied in homogeneous vegetation types such as forest or grassland, crown cover can play a useful role as an ecological descriptor. However, if both vegetation types are combined in analysis, the values may become meaningless (100% crown cover in grassland cannot be readily compared in ecological terms with the same value in forests). For this reason, the VegClass method distinguishes between woody and non-woody components of crown cover. Thus, a transect with 95% crown cover may decompose into 45% woody and 50% non-woody components. Our results show that when disaggregated in this way, crown cover can become more ecologically meaningful, with associated improvement as a biodiversity indicator (Table 29.3).

Most agencies concerned with the conservation management of the eastern Himalayas recognize the need to establish transnational corridors to help sustain broad-ranging habitats for larger mammals such as elephants. Efficient GIS-based, design-selection procedures are available that can facilitate interactive selection of the most appropriate zones for a specific conservation target (Walker and Faith, 1998; Pressey and Cowling, 2001). However, the success of such procedures will depend largely on the quality of the baseline data. A major impediment to conservation management is a widespread conviction that acquiring large scale baseline data is beyond the capacity of most conservation agencies. As we have indicated in the present study, this mindset may change where it can be demonstrated that generic, low-input, high-return methods are available for rapid, comparative biodiversity assessment within and between regions. Using such a methodology, we have acquired new and significant regional data that provide a readily testable baseline model of vegetation response to land-use impact and a logical framework for a more detailed investigation of related impacts on faunal habitat. Comparison with results of similar plant-based biodiversity assessment in other tropical and subtropical ecoregional gradients (Table 29.4) supports characterization of NBL as a global biodiversity 'hotspot'. This, together with increasing vulnerability of regional biodiversity to uncontrolled, cross-border exploitation, supports the argument for transnational conservation management in the eastern Himalayas.

The results from the case study have implications beyond the NBL. The successful application of the methodology by persons with relatively little training confirms that the system is readily transferable, and this is consistent with results in other countries. The generic nature of the gradient-based survey method that also incorporates the rapid, quantitative recording of functional, taxonomic, and structural characteristics of plants significantly extends the solely species-based approach to measuring and quantifying biodiversity. As shown in other studies (Diaz *et al.*, 2016; Gillison, 2013, 2019a, b; Gillison *et al.*, 2016), the quantitative baseline data have the potential for attaching value to biodiversity through links with agricultural and possibly ecosystem productivity. As such, it may provide an improved means of forecasting the impact of global change on biodiversity in a way that facilitates planning for adaptive, sustainable management within and beyond the Asia-Pacific region.

ACKNOWLEDGEMENTS

The training programme and survey were sponsored by WWF-India in association with WWF-USA and the Asian Rhino and Elephant Action Strategy (AREAS) programme, with financial assistance from the Conservation Research Centre (CRC) Zoological Park of the Smithsonian Institution and the MacArthur Foundation. Participants in the field survey (in alphabetical order) included T. Aziz, A, M. M. Babu, A. Baig, S. Bairagi, H. Kr. Baishya, P. J. Bora, P. K. Dutta, C. Loma, A. Sharma, P. Sharma, P. A. Sharma, and P. K. Sharma. The Assamese Forest Department kindly provided logistical support. We are indebted to J. Sayer, T. H. Booth, D. Schmidt-Vogt, and an anonymous referee for constructive comments. We also thank the editor, P. S. Low, for his assistance and guidance in the preparation of this chapter.

REFERENCES

Azevedo-Ramos, C., de Carvalho Jr., O. and Nasi, R. (2002) *Animal Indicators: A Tool to Assess Biotic Integrity after Logging Tropical Forests?* CIFOR Report. Bogor, Indonesia, Centre for International Forestry Research.

Basnet, K. (2003) Transboundary biodiversity conservation initiative: An example from Nepal. *Journal of Sustainable Forestry*, **17**, 205–226.

Carpenter, G., Gillison, A. N. and Winter, J. (1993) DOMAIN: A flexible modelling procedure for mapping potential distributions of plants and animals. *Biodiversity and Conservation*, **2**, 667–680.

Conservation International (2005) Biodiversity hotspots, Indo-Burma. http://www.biodiversityhotspots.org/xp/Hotspots/indo_burma/ (accessed 28 April 2005)

Díaz, S., Kattge, J., Cornelissen, J. H. C., Wright, I. J., Lavorel, S., Dray, S., Reu, B., Kleyer, M., Wirth, C., Prentice, I. C., Garnier, E., Bönisch, G., Westoby, M., Poorter, H., Reich, P. B., Moles, A. T., Dickie, J., Gillison, A. N., Zanne, A. E., Chave, J., Wright, S. J., Sheremet'ev, S. N., Jactel, H., Baraloto, C., Cerabolini, B., Pierce, S., Shipley, B., Kirkup, D., Casanoves, F., Joswig, J. S., Günther, A., Falczuk, V., Rüger, N., Mahecha, M. D. and Gorné, L. D. (2016) The global spectrum of plant form and function. *Nature*, **529**, 167–171. DOI: 10.1038/nature16489

FAO (2005) Food and Agriculture Organization of the United Nations, Statistical Databases. http://apps.fao.org/page/form?collection=Production.Crops.Primary&Domain=Production&servlet=1&language=EN&hostname=apps.fao.org&version=default (accessed April 2005).

FAO (2013) *Climate-Smart Agriculture: Sourcebook*. Rome, FAO. http://www.fao.org/docrep/018/i3325e/i3325e.pdf (accessed 6 October 2020)

Ferrer-Paris, J. R., Sanchez-Mercado, A., Rodríguez, J. P. and Rodríguez, G. A (2012) Detection histories for eight species of Amazona parrots in Venezuela during the NeoMaps bird surveys in 2010. DOI:10.1594/PANGAEA.803430.

Gillison, A. N. (2001) Vegetation Survey and Habitat Assessment of the Tesso Nilo Forest Complex; Pekanbaru, Riau Province, Sumatra, Indonesia. Report prepared for WWF-US. October-November. https://www.cbmglobe.org/pdf/TessoNiloReport.pdf (accessed 6 October 2020)

Gillison, A. N. (2002) A generic, computer-assisted method for rapid vegetation classification and survey: Tropical and temperate case studies. *Conservation and Ecology*, **6**, 3. http://www.ecologyandsociety.org/vol6/iss2/art3/print.pdf

Gillison, A. N. (2004) Biodiversity assessment in the North Bank landscape, north east India. WWF-India, New Delhi.

Gillison, A.N. (2013) Plant functional types and traits at the community, ecosystem and world level. In E. van der Maarel and J. Franklin (eds.), *Vegetation Ecology* (2nd ed.), pp. 347–386. Oxford, UK, John Wiley & Sons, Ltd. DOI:10.1002/9781118452592.ch12.

Gillison, A. N. (2019a) Plant functional indicators of vegetation response to climate change, past present and future: I. Trends, emerging hypotheses and plant functional modality. *Flora*, **254**, 12–30.

Gillison, A. N. (2019b) Plant functional indicators of vegetation response to climate change, past present and future: II. Modal plant functional types as response indicators for present and future climates. *Flora*, **254**, 31–58.

Gillison, A. N. and Brewer, K. R. W. (1985) The use of gradient directed transects or gradsects in natural resource surveys. *Journal of Environmental Management*, **20**, 103–127.

Gillison, A. N. and Carpenter, G. (1997). A plant functional attribute set and grammar for dynamic vegetation description and analysis. *Functional Ecology*, **11**, 775–783.

Gillison, A. N. and Liswanti, N. (2004) Assessing biodiversity at landscape level: The importance of environmental context. In T. P. Tomich, M. van Noordwijk and D. E. Thomas (eds.), *Environmental Services and Land Use Change: Bridging the Gap between Policy and Research in Southeast Asia*. Special issue of *Agriculture, Ecosystems and Environment*, **104**, 75–86.

Gillison, A. N., Asner. G. P., Mafalacusser, J., Banze, A., Izidine, S., da Fonseca, A. R. and Pacate, H. (2016) Biodiversity and agriculture in dynamic landscapes: Integrating ground and remotely-sensed baseline surveys. *Journal of Environmental Management.*, **177**, 9–19. https://pubmed.ncbi.nlm.nih.gov/27064732/

Gillison, A. N., Bignell, D. E., Brewer, K. R. W., Fernandes, E. C. M., Jones, D. T., Sheil, D., May, P. H., Watt, A. D., Constantino, R., Couto, E. G. and Hairiah, K. (2013) Plant functional types and traits as biodiversity indicators for tropical forests: Two biogeographically separated case studies including birds, mammals and termites. *Biodiversity and Conservation*, **22**, 1,909–1,930.

Hobohm, C. (2003) Characterization and ranking of biodiversity hotspots: Centres of species richness and endemism. *Biodiversity and Conservation*, **12**, 279–287.

Jones, D. T., Susilo, F.-X., Bignell, D. E., Hardiwinoto, S., Gillison, A. N. and Eggleton, P. (2002) Termite assemblage collapse along a land-use intensification gradient in lowland central Sumatra, Indonesia. *Journal of Applied Ecology*, **40**, 380–391.

Lawton, J. H., Bignell, D. E., Bolton, B., Bloemers, G. F., Eggleton, P., Hammond, P. M., Hodda, M., Holt, R. D., Larsen, T. B., Mawdsley, N. A., Stork, N. E., Srivastava, D. S. and Watt, A. D. (1998) Biodiversity inventories, indicator taxa and effects of habitat modification in tropical forest. *Nature*, **391**, 72–76. https://doi.org/10.1038/34166

MacKinnon, J. (ed.) (1997) *Protected Areas Systems Review of the Indo-Malayan Realm*. Asian Bureau for Conservation, Ltd., Hong Kong, China, and World Conservation Monitoring Centre, Cambridge, United Kingdom.

MacNally, R. and Fleishman, E. (2004) A successful predictive model of species richness based on indicator species. *Conservation Biology*, **18**, 646–654.

Myers, M., Mittermeier, R. A., Mittermeier, C. G., da Fonseca, G. A. B. and Kent, J. (2000) Biodiversity hotspots for conservation priorities. *Nature*, **403**, 853–858.

Negi, H. R. and Gadgil, M. (2002) Cross-taxon surrogacy of biodiversity in the Indian Garhwal Himalaya. *Biological Conservation*, **105**, 143–155.

NPS (National Park Service, USA) (2012) Gradsect and Field Sampling Plan for Big Bend National Park/ Rio Grande National Wild and Scenic River. National Park Service. BiblioGov. 13 September.

Olson, D. M. and Dinerstein, E. (2002) The Global 200: Priority ecoregions for global conservation. *Annals of the Missouri Botanical Garden*, **89**, 199–224.

Olson, D. M., Dinerstein, E., Wikramanayake, E. D., Burgess, N. D., Powell, G. V. N., Underwood, E. C., D'Amico, J. A., Itoua, I., Strand, H. E., Morrison, J. C. and Loucks, C. J. (2001) Terrestrial ecoregions of the world: a new map of life on Earth. *BioScience*, **51**, 933–938.

Parker, V. T., Schile, L. M., Vasey, M. C. and Callaway, J. C. (2011) Efficiency in assessment and monitoring methods: scaling down gradient-directed transects. *Ecosphere*, **2**, 99.

Pressey, R. L. and Cowling, R. M. (2001) Reserve selection algorithms and the real world. *Conservation Biology*, **15**, 275–277.

Rastogi, A. and Chettri, N. (2001) Extended biodiversity 'hotspot' analysis: a case of eastern Himalayan region, India. International Conference on Tropical Ecosystems: Structure, Diversity and Human Welfare, Bangalore, India, pp. 622–628. 15–18 July.

Rawat, G. S., Desai, A., Somanathan, H. and Wikramanayake, E. D. (2001) Brahmaputra Valley semi-evergreen forests (IM0105) (see Olson *et al.*, 2001). http://www.worldwildlife.org/wildworld/profiles/terrestrial_im.html (accessed 6 October 2020)

Rawat, G. S. and Wikramanayake, E. D. (2001) Eastern Himalayan broadleaf forests (IM0401) (see Olson *et al.*, 2001). http://www.worldwildlife.org/wildworld/profiles/terrestrial/im/im0401_full.html (accessed 6 October 2020)

Rodgers, W. A. and Panwar, H. S. (1988) Planning a wildlife protected areas network in India. Dept. of Environment, Forests, and Wildlife/ Wildlife Institute of India Report, Vols. 1 and 2. Wildlife Institute of India.

Sala, O. E., Chapin III, F. S., Armesto, J. J., Berlow, E., Bloomfield, J., Dirzo, R., Huber-Sanwald, E., Huenneke, L. F., Jackson, R. B., Kinzig, A. and Leemans, R. (2000) Global biodiversity scenarios for the year 2100. *Science*, **287**, 1,770–1,774.

Sandmann, H. and Lertzman, K. P. (2003) Combining high-resolution aerial photography with gradient-directed transects to guide field sampling and forest mapping in mountainous terrain. *Forest Science*, **49**, 429–443.

Sauberer, N., Zulka, K. P., Abensperg-Traun, M., Berg, H.-M., Bieringer, G., Milasowszky, N., Moser, D., Plutzar, C., Pollheimer, M., Storch, C. and Tröstl, R. (2004) Surrogate taxa for biodiversity in agricultural landscapes of eastern Austria. *Biological Conservation*, **117**, 181–190.

Sayer, J. and Campbell, B. (2004) *The Science of Sustainable Development: Local Livelihoods and the Global Development.* Cambridge, Cambridge University Press.

Sayer, J., Sunderland, T., Ghazoul, J., Pfund, J.-L., Sheil, D., Meijard, E., Venter, M., Boedihartono, A. K., Day, M., Garcia, C., van Oosten, C. and Buck, L. E. (2013) Ten principles for a landscape approach to reconciling agriculture, conservation, and other competing land uses. *Proceedings of the National Academy of Sciences of the United States of America*, **110**, 8,349-8,356. http://www.pnas.org/content/early/2013/05/14/1210595110 (Accessed 6 Oct. 2020)

SDSN (Sustainable Development Solutions Network) (2013) Solutions for Sustainable Agriculture and Food Systems. Technical Report for the Post-2015 Development Agenda 18 September. Prepared by the Thematic Group on Sustainable Agriculture and Food Systems. http://unsdsn.org/wp-content/uploads/2014/02/130919-TG07-Agriculture-Report-WEB.pdf (accessed 22 August 2016).

Sheil, D. and Burslem, D. F. R. P. (2003) Disturbing hypotheses in tropical forests. *Trends in Ecology & Evolution*, **18**, 18–26.

Sherpa, M. N. and Norbu, U. P. (1999) Linking protected areas for ecosystem conservation: a case study from Bhutan. *PARKS*, **9**, 35–45.

Specht, R. L. (1970) Vegetation. In G. W. Leeper (ed.), *The Australian Environment*, (4th ed.) pp. 44–67. Commonwealth Scientific and Industrial Organisation (CSIRO), Melbourne, Melbourne University Press.

Statersfield, A. J., Corsby, M. J., Long, A. J. and Wege, D. C. (1998) *Global Directory of Endemic Bird Areas.* Cambridge, Birdlife International.

Udvardy, M. D. F. (1975) A Classification of the Biogeographical Provinces of the World. IUCN Occasional Paper No. 18.

UNEP-CBD (1996) United Nations Environment Programme, Convention on Biological Diversity. Assessment of Biological Diversity and Methodologies for Future Assessments.

UNEP-CBD (2001) United Nations Environment Programme, Convention on Biological Diversity. Review of the Impact of Climate Change on Forest Biological Diversity, UNEP/CBD/AHTEG-BDCC/1/2.

USGS-NPS (2003) United States Geological Survey – National Park Service, Vegetation Mapping Program 5.0: Field methods. http://biology.usgs.gov/npsveg/fieldmethods/sect5.html (accessed 6 October 2020)

Walker, P. A. and Faith, D. P. (1998) *TARGET Software Priority Area Setting.* Commonwealth Scientific and Industrial Research Organization, Canberra.

Watt, A. W. and Zborowski, P. (2000) Canopy insects: Canopy arthropods and butterfly survey: Preliminary report. In A. N. Gillison (ed.), *Above-Ground Biodiversity Assessment Working Group Summary Report 1996–99: Impact of Different Land Uses on Biodiversity*, pp. 69–90. Nairobi, Kenya, Alternatives to Slash and Burn project. ICRAF.

WCMC (1996) Assessing biodiversity status and sustainability. B. Groombridge and M. D. Jenkins (eds.). *World Conservation Monitoring Centre, Biodiversity Series No 5*. Cambridge, World Conservation Press.

Wessels, K. J., Van Jaarsveld, A. S., Grimbeek, J. D. and Van der Linde, M. J. (1998) An evaluation of the gradsect biological survey method. *Biological Conservation*, **7**, 1,093–1,121.

Williams, A. C. (2002) Eastern Himalayas Conservation Alliance: setting the stage for on-the-ground conservation networks. World Wide Fund for Nature (WWF) and Asian Rhino and Elephant Action Strategy (AREAS) proposal (unpublished).

World Bank (2000) Transboundary Reserves: World Bank Implementation of the Ecosystem Approach. Report No. 20892. K. MacKinnon (compiler). Working paper. Washington, DC, World Bank.

WWF and ICIMOD (2001) Ecoregion-based conservation in the Eastern Himalaya: identifying important areas for biodiversity conservation. In E. D. Wikramanayake, C. Carpenter, H. Strand and M. McKnight (eds). *World Wildlife Fund (WWF) and Centre for Integrated Mountain Development (ICIMOD)*, Kathmandu, Nepal Programme.

30 Where to invade next: Inaction on biological invasions threatens sustainability in a small island developing state of the tropical South Pacific

MARIE-ISABELL LENZ[1,2,7], STEPHEN GALVIN[2], GUNNAR KEPPEL[3],
SUNIL GOPAUL[2,4], MATTHIAS KOWASCH[5], MICHAEL J. DYER[3,2],
DICK WATLING[6], SHERRI Y. F. LODHAR[2], GEON C. HANSON[2],
STEFAN ERASMI[7], AND HANS JUERGEN BOEHMER[2,8,9*]

[1]United Nations University (UNU-EHS), Bonn
[2]School of Geography, Earth Science, and Environment, University of the South Pacific (USP), Suva
[3]UniSA STEM and Future Industries Institute, University of South Australia, Adelaide
[4]Forest Monitoring Division, Guyana Forestry Commission
[5]University College of Teacher Education Styria, Graz
[6]NatureFiji-Mareqeti Fiji
[7]Department of Geography, University of Goettingen
[8]Institute for Applied Ecological Studies (IFANOS), Nuremberg
[9]Institute of Geography, University of Jena
*Corresponding author: jboehmer@wzw.tum.de; http://orcid.org/0000–0002-9176–4836

Keywords

Biodiversity conservation; CBD; Convention on Biological Diversity; Fiji; forest reserve; *Iguana iguana*; island biogeography; invasive alien species; mahogany plantation; nature conservation; *Pinanga coronata*; SIDS; sustainable development; terrestrial biodiversity; tropical rainforest

Abstract

Oceanic island ecosystems contain a disproportionate number of Earth's terrestrial species, many of them endemic or indigenous to only one or a few islands. Consequently, the importance of islands in the quest to protect terrestrial biodiversity has been increasingly recognized and included in global environmental agreements. Nevertheless, oceanic island ecosystems remain extremely vulnerable to anthropogenic disturbance and its impacts, particularly in terms of the uncontrolled spread of introduced species, so-called biological invasions, leading to substantial biodiversity loss and fundamental changes in ecosystem functioning and structure. The South Pacific region is a hotspot of biodiversity but also has the world's highest concentration of invasive alien plant species. Although the issue of biological invasions has been increasingly acknowledged by local governments and international agreements, invasive alien species are often not monitored properly on Pacific islands. Furthermore, knowledge of the potential impact of invasive alien species regularly does not result in on-the-ground action, adding to the growing extinction threat. This inaction persists despite international and national efforts for sustainable use and nature conservation of terrestrial biodiversity in the region's Small Island Developing States. We illustrate this problem with two relatively recent biological invaders in Fiji: the ivory cane palm (*Pinanga coronata*) and the green iguana (*Iguana iguana*). We use these examples to examine the potential consequences of continuing inaction, despite awareness in relevant government departments, for native forest biodiversity and human livelihoods. Through an examination of the institutional background, we discuss steps towards good governance and sustainable development of terrestrial biodiversity in the Small Island Developing States of the tropical South Pacific, where on-the-ground action to control, eradicate, and prevent invasive alien species is desperately needed.

30.1 SUSTAINABLE DEVELOPMENT, ISLAND BIODIVERSITY, AND BIOLOGICAL INVASIONS

In late 2017, global attention was focused on the South Pacific region and its Small Island Developing States (SIDS) during the 23rd Conference of Parties (COP 23), jointly hosted by Fiji and Germany, at the World Climate Conference in Bonn, Germany. As did previous events of this kind, this Conference highlighted the position of South Pacific islands at the forefront of climate change with wide-ranging discussions on climate change mitigation and adaptation. However, the South Pacific region is also at the forefront of biodiversity loss due to the inherent vulnerability of island ecosystems (Keppel *et al.*, 2014) and the ineffectiveness of conservation actions (Keppel *et al.*, 2012; Brodie *et al.*, 2013). In this chapter we will highlight how insufficient management of invasive alien species is threatening native biodiversity and human livelihoods in the Pacific and will illustrate this with the case studies of two emerging invasive alien species that are having devastating impacts on native rainforest ecosystems in Fiji.

The need to halt the alarming rate of global biodiversity loss is addressed by the United Nations' Sustainable Development Goals (SDGs) to be accomplished by 2030 (IAEG-SDGs, 2016). Target 15.5 highlights the need to reduce the degradation of natural habitats, to halt the loss of biodiversity, and to protect and prevent the extinction of threatened species. Tropical oceanic islands have high, often endemic biodiversity (Kier *et al.*, 2009; Keppel *et al.*, 2016), and therefore play a key role in the protection of Earth's terrestrial biodiversity (e.g. Genovesi, 2011; Kueffer *et al.*, 2014). In the tropical South Pacific, the French territory of New Caledonia, the East Melanesian Islands, and Polynesia/Micronesia are recognized global biodiversity hotspots (Mittermeier *et al.*, 2005). Islands therefore provide opportunities for formulating new strategies for sustainable use of marine, freshwater, and terrestrial ecosystems, with disproportionate benefits for biodiversity conservation (SCBD, 2005; Clout and Williams, 2009). Furthermore, islands remain essential testing grounds for the development of theoretical and practical methods in the fields of evolution, invasion biology, ecology, biogeography, and conservation (e.g. MacArthur and Wilson, 1967; Vitousek, 2004; Pungetti, 2012; Kueffer *et al.*, 2014; Fernández-Palacios *et al.*, 2015).

Oceanic island ecosystems are highly vulnerable to human disturbances and their impacts, particularly biological invasions (e.g. Kier *et al.*, 2009; Kueffer *et al.*, 2010; Keitt *et al.*, 2011; Clout and Veitch, 2011; Genovesi, 2011; Meyer, 2014; Van Kleunen *et al.*, 2015). In New Caledonia, 83% of the endemic plant species are considered threatened (Pouteau and Birnbaum, 2016). Invasion by non-indigenous species is one of the most pressing issues in applied ecology, second only to habitat destruction as a primary cause of biodiversity loss (Enserink, 1999; Boehmer, 2011a). Management of invasive alien species (IAS) is mandated for all signatories in Article 8 (h) of the Convention on Biological Diversity, which declares that parties shall 'prevent the introduction of, or control or eradicate, those alien species which threaten ecosystems, habitats or species' (SCBD, 2005, p. 133). This multilateral environmental agreement is 'the only globally applicable, legally binding instrument to address generally alien species introduction, control and eradication across all biological taxa and ecosystems' (Shine *et al.*, 2000, p. 14).

The Pacific islands have experienced great biodiversity losses since human colonization, with invasive alien species contributing

considerably (e.g. Smith, 1985; Denslow *et al.*, 2009; Keppel *et al.*, 2014). Some alien species can cause fundamental changes in indigenous ecosystems, including the extirpation of native species (Nishida and Evenhuis, 2000; SCBD, 2001; Mueller-Dombois, 2006). Oceanic islands harbour more naturalized alien plants than similarly sized mainland regions, and Pacific islands show the steepest increase in the cumulative number of naturalized species per unit area on Earth (Van Kleunen *et al.*, 2015). Several introduced plant species are now dominant elements of Pacific forests (see, e.g. Meyer *et al.*, 2008; Boehmer and Niemand, 2009; Minden *et al.*, 2010a, 2010b; Mueller-Dombois *et al.*, 2013).

Plants, at 89%, are the most frequently introduced species in the Pacific region (UNEP-WCMC, 2016). The Pacific Islands Ecosystems at Risk (PIER) database lists, as of February 2021, 1,979 invasive alien plant species (Denslow *et al.*, 2009; PIER, 2020a), a notable increase in the 1,132 identified six years prior (Meyer, 2014). Of those 1,979 species, 612 have been recorded in Fiji (PIER, 2020b). Only 12 of the species identified in the PIER database have been comprehensively examined, predominantly through studies in Hawaii and the Galapagos Islands (Meyer, 2014). This illustrates the dearth of knowledge about IAS on Pacific islands and suggests that many invasive alien species on South Pacific islands remain undocumented.

The ecological impacts of invasive alien plants have severe consequences for the more than 65 million people who live in SIDS (Reaser *et al.*, 2007; IPCC, 2019). This is particularly relevant where forests provide significant livelihood opportunities for people in rural areas (FAO, 2014), as is the case in the South Pacific (Mohamed and Clark, 1996). The livelihoods of these biodiversity-dependent people are under increasing pressure, as invasive alien plants are a major factor in the loss of ecosystem goods and services (Kueffer *et al.*, 2010). Safeguarding island forests from invasive alien plants is, therefore, critical in order to ensure the lasting protection of natural resources and that future generations have access to these goods and ecosystem services.

Management of invasive alien species in Pacific SIDS is hampered by their geographic and economic circumstances, which place constraints on suitable options for the monitoring, documentation, and risk assessment of invasive species taxa (SCBD, 2005). The vast geographic dispersion complicates close collaboration among Pacific island countries and territories (Meyer, 2014), and funding for conservation remains limited and mostly tied to short funding cycles (Keppel *et al.*, 2012). These limitations also restrict the ability to determine the species that have the greatest actual and potential impact in the region and therefore require immediate action (Tye, 2009). Furthermore, most land is under indigenous tenure (e.g. Jupiter *et al.*, 2014; SPREP, 2016a; DoE, 2020), making the nationwide implementation of action plans more challenging (DoE, 2007; SPREP,

2016a). For example, in Fiji, more than 87% of the land, and 90% of the forest, is under customary (*iTaukei*) ownership.

30.1.1 The transdisciplinary nature of managing biological invasions: International agreements

Economic development, anthropogenic disturbance, and habitat diversity influence invasive alien plant species richness on oceanic islands (Daehler, 2008; Tye, 2009; Kueffer *et al.*, 2010). Denslow *et al.* (2009) illustrate that economic and transportation development can increase the number of invasive alien species, suggesting that, on average, the presence of an airport with a paved runway adds 108 PIER-listed invasive alien species to an island. Accordingly, invasion biology cuts across several academic disciplines and is an integrative interdisciplinary and transdisciplinary research field (Boehmer, 2011a).

The ninth CBD Conference prioritized IAS, highlighting that 'the significant adverse ecological and economic effects of certain alien species on biological diversity and human health' should be addressed (SCBD, 2005, p. 504). In this context, 'alien species' include alien invasive species and pathogens that carry vector-borne diseases spreading across biogeographic boundaries. The impacts of these 'alien species' are forecast to be exacerbated by climate change (Settele *et al.*, 2014). The conference further emphasized the transdisciplinary nature of the field, highlighting the need for a comprehensive and interdisciplinary approach instead of a sectoral approach (Perrings *et al.*, 2010).

To address remaining gaps and inconsistencies in this international framework (Clout and Williams, 2009), relevant issues for managing IAS were included in the 2010 Biodiversity Targets (CBD, 2013) and the Aichi Biodiversity Target 9, as part of the CBD's Strategic Plan for Biodiversity 2011–2020 (Butchart *et al.*, 2010; CBD, 2013). For the Aichi Targets to be met, contracting parties of the CBD are urged to work together in a coordinated manner and with collective action (SCBD, 2005) to enhance the 'detailed knowledge of native biodiversity and of potential interactions between invading non-native species and native species' (Baur and Schmidlin, 2007, p. 257).

Despite these efforts, implementation of many objectives remains problematic. This is due to the diversity of CBD members, the broadness and non-binding character of the policies, a lack of concrete enforcement mechanisms, and the lack of concrete penalties or sanctions (Perrings *et al.*, 2010; Genovesi, 2011; Andresen *et al.*, 2012). Only a few objectives have binding value; for example, the aforementioned Article 8 (h) is, in reality, merely a 'broadly phrased obligation' to manage IAS (Shine *et al.*, 2000, p. 14). Instead, contracting parties are called upon to formulate their own action plans and to choose appropriate measures to preserve and protect biodiversity. Implementations

of the broad and highly interpretable goals remain under the contracting parties' own evaluation and responsibility (Shine *et al.*, 2000). While protocols potentially offer more binding regulations (Andresen *et al.*, 2012), only two have been adopted: the Cartagena Protocol on Biosafety (Perrings *et al.*, 2010) and the Nagoya Protocol (Andresen and Rosendal, 2014), neither of which has been ratified by many countries.

IAS have also been incorporated into Target 15.8 of the Sustainable Development Goals (IAEG-SDGs, 2016). However, the SDGs do not explicitly acknowledge that invasive alien species management requires a transdisciplinary approach to prevent negative social, economic, and environmental impacts. Those impacts, in turn, would reduce the success of sustainable development, economic growth, biodiversity conservation, the provision of ecosystem services, food and water security, poverty alleviation, and health (Jupiter *et al.*, 2014; GEF, 2016).

30.1.2 Regional biodiversity policies in the South Pacific

Reaser *et al.* (2007) and Meyer (2014) emphasize that globalization is a central factor in the spread of invasive alien plants. This makes close international cooperation essential for successful invasive alien species management in the South Pacific. The CBD supports this notion. It acknowledges, in its Guiding Principles for the Implementation of Article 8 (h), the extraordinary situation that SIDS are facing in dealing with invasive alien species. The CBD also highlights that the situation requires further support and allocation of resources (SCBD, 2005).

Although ecosystem functioning and biodiversity sustain human well-being, health, culture, and the economy in Pacific island communities (Jupiter *et al.*, 2014), the 'coverage of the land and seas of Oceania by protected areas is low' (SPREP, 2016a, p. 44). UNEP (2016) also noted that in the Pacific islands, more than anywhere in the Asia-Pacific region, control of invasive alien species is very poor and considerable efforts are needed to make progress towards Aichi Target 9. Invasive alien species constitute a tremendous and increasing threat to ecosystem functioning and biodiversity in the Pacific (Daigneault and Brown, 2013; Meyer, 2014). Despite these strong ecological impacts that degrade livelihoods, research and policies have primarily focused on species that affect national economic interests – including plant pests – and/or human health (DoE, 2007, 2014).

The CBD advises that, for the successful abatement of invasive alien species, the legal framework for biodiversity conservation and mitigation of the threat of invasive alien species needs to be internationally constituted. Regional organizations can function as connectors and coordinators, defining and utilizing national priorities, such as capacity-building, guidance, specific implementation, and management strategies (Sherley *et al.*, 2000; Perrings *et al.*, 2010; Andresen *et al.*, 2012). The development of mechanisms for transboundary, regional, and multilateral cooperation (Reaser *et al.*, 2003) has allowed particular gaps in the international regulatory framework to be filled (Clout and Williams, 2009). Joint collaboration of regional networks and national policies may help countries by formulating mutual standards in research, management measures, and key policy tools, each of which is essential for successful and cost-effective alien species management (Shine, 2006). Furthermore, the promotion of structure-building facilitates the exchange of information, and technical expertise gained from experience, early warning systems, and the identification of common priorities and threats are crucial (Perrings *et al.*, 2010).

Several of the South Pacific's regional projects, organizations, and networks have addressed the conservation of biodiversity and non-native contaminants with a range of policies and legislative measures on various spatial scales (Jupiter *et al.*, 2014). The South Pacific Regional Environment Programme (SPREP), the Secretariat of the Pacific Community (SPC), the Pacific Invasive Initiative (PII), and the Pacific Invasive Learning Network (PILN) are the main regional agencies tackling the issue of invasive alien species (Tye, 2009). A set of regional guidelines for invasive species management in the Pacific was endorsed in 2009 by the 26 member countries and territories of SPREP. The objectives and strategic plans are to provide information, awareness, infrastructure, protocols, legislation, funding, and linkages (Sherley *et al.*, 2000; Tye, 2009) necessary for protecting the ecosystems of Pacific island countries and territories from invasive alien species (Tye, 2009; Perrings *et al.*, 2010; Jupiter *et al.*, 2014). 'An ideal future scenario for invasive species management will include ecosystem-based adaptation at island and national scales, involve local communities, build capacity, use a multi-partner approach, and communicate successful strategies and tools' (SPREP, 2016b, p. 12).

Another SPREP initiative is the Framework for Nature Conservation and Protected Areas in the Pacific Islands Region (2014–2020). The framework offers guidance to help accomplish the CBD Aichi Targets through the implementation of National Biodiversity Strategy and Action Plans (NBSAPs). Each signatory of the CBD is required to implement the NBSAP goals on a national and supra-national level, in addition to various other international, regional, and local conservation initiatives (SCBD, 2005; Jupiter *et al.*, 2014; SPREP, 2014, 2016a; DoE, 2020). Of the region covered by SPREP, 14 countries are signatory parties to the CBD, and 13 of these have a National Biodiversity Strategy and Action Plan (SPREP, 2016a). SPREP further coordinates the Regional Invasive Species

Programme, which was created to produce a regional invasive alien species strategy for the Pacific islands and was formalized in 2005 (Tutangata, 2000; Reaser *et al.*, 2003).

30.1.3 Challenges for regional cooperation

The situation of SIDS in the Pacific is particularly complex. The Pacific Ocean encompasses one-third of the globe, as much as the Indian, Atlantic, and Arctic oceans combined, and is the planet's largest single geographical feature (GEF, 1993). The extensive dispersion of islands within nations and territories, as well as the vast oceanic distances between them, make many islands relatively inaccessible (Meyer *et al.*, 2008), thus complicating management of IAS and adding to the extinction problem faced by the region. This situation creates issues for regional cooperation (Tye, 2009) owing to a general lack, and uneven distribution, of regional biological information and data relating to native and non-native species and groups (Ash and Vodonivalu, 1989, in DoE, 2007).

Amid a multitude of frameworks, agreements, stakeholder networks, financial mechanisms, and databases, the region has implemented a number of regional projects. One example is the GEF (Global Environment Facility)-IAS Project (2011–2016), which produced guiding publications on key invasive species issues and a Battler Resource Base, with up-to-date information on invasive alien species, aiming to improve the capacities of Pacific islands (SPREP, 2017; Moverley, 2019). A current regional project, building on previous successes, is continuing to strengthen regional and national capacities to effectively address IAS through the establishment of a Pacific Regional Invasive Species Management Support Service (PRISMSS), a regional mechanism that provides technical assistance to Pacific SIDS on demand. Another example is the Pacific Invasive Species Guidelines Reporting Database, initiated in 2016, containing national, territorial, and regional progress. This was established to help implement the 2009 Guidelines for Invasive Species Management in the Pacific (SPREP, 2017). Significant implementation (addressing eradication but also control, biosecurity, and associated capacity-building) has been delivered by BirdLife International and Island Conservation.

However, to effectively manage invasive alien species, Pacific islands must improve central governance capacity for implementing laws, regulations, and management measures (Jupiter *et al.*, 2014). Shine (2006) mentions that trained personnel, adequate quarantine measures, risk assessment facilities, necessary funding, and political will are still lacking. Existing legislation and policies are often weak and do not comprehensively address the impact of invasive alien species on biodiversity (Sherley *et al.*, 2000). In addition, legislation and policies are inadequately implemented, monitored, and enforced, with the focus often being on the economic impact rather than biodiversity conservation (SBSTTA, 2005, in Shine, 2006; Jupiter *et al.*, 2014).

Even though the majority of Pacific SIDS have national policies addressing IAS, only nine have adopted laws concerned with IAS (SPREP, 2014). Furthermore, effective invasive alien species management requires monitoring of potential or known invaders, early warning systems to prevent the spread of certain species, and the identification of common priorities and threats (Perrings *et al.*, 2010). However, only the Federal State of Micronesia, Vanuatu, and the Solomon Islands used their 'National Biodiversity Strategy and Action Plan' or 'National Invasive Species Strategy and Action Plan' to highlight the need to monitor the spread of IAS (PII, 2010; DEPC, 2018).

30.2 MANAGEMENT OF INVASIVE ALIEN SPECIES IN FIJI

In Fiji, the Department of Environment (DoE) is the chair of the Biodiversity Steering Committee (BSC). This board is responsible for the coordination and implementation of the National Biodiversity Strategy and Action Plan (DoE, 2007). IAS are defined as one of seven thematic fields for the implementation of biodiversity conservation through the plan (DoE, 2014, 2020). In 2009, a meeting of the Species Management Committee, along with other groups and stakeholders, in Suva assessed major threats to native biodiversity caused by IAS and investigated necessary measures for the mitigation of these threats by creating an implementation framework for species conservation (DoE, 2014). This meeting resulted in current efforts for the prevention of new introductions, management of established species in key biodiversity areas, and the eradication of specific species on small islands (DoE, 2014).

Unlike five other Pacific SIDS (PII, 2010), Fiji does not, to date, have a National Invasive Species Strategy and Action Plan in place. However, within its current NBSAP (2020–2025), objectives have been formulated for action to improve national legislation, policies, and strategies regarding the management of IAS (DoE, 2020). Those objectives include plans for a legislative review and gap analysis, the development of a National Invasive Species Strategy and Action Plan (NISSAP), and the support and strengthening of its previously established Fijian Invasive Species Task Force (DoE, 2020), which manages invasive alien species as part of Fiji's National Biodiversity Strategy and Action Plan (DoE, 2014). In a policy document for the CBD, the government further announced the creation of an Emergency Response Plan. The aim of this plan is to alleviate and manage the risks posed by IAS and pest outbreaks, with the intention of incorporating it into Fiji's National Disaster Management Programme (CBD, 2008).

However, it is questionable whether the government authorities in Fiji have the capacity and resources to conserve biodiversity or monitor and manage invasive alien species (Keppel *et al.*, 2012; Jupiter *et al.*, 2014), although the CBD requires signatories to carry out risk assessments as an empirical tool to estimate possible risks posed by invasive alien species (Daehler *et al.*, 2004; SCBD, 2005). This activity would support and expand the effects of environmental impact assessments (EIAs), which are legally obligatory and mandate government authorities to undertake a biosecurity risk assessment of incoming regulated articles and products (Jupiter *et al.*, 2014). However, undertaking such risk assessments is often difficult to implement, given that relevant government departments are generally under-staffed and under-funded, and are focused on resource exploitation rather than environmental conservation (Keppel *et al.*, 2012; Jupiter *et al.*, 2014).

In recent years, emphasis has been placed on capacity-building (UNEP-WCMC, 2016) and better control over the import of IAS at national borders of South Pacific countries, which is a difficult task without additional human and financial resources (King, 2007). As is the case with the conservation sector in the Pacific (Keppel *et al.*, 2012), the focus has been on developing management concepts, policy guidelines, and data-sharing initiatives in meetings and workshops. 'However, this strategy may underemphasize the importance of enhancing internal biosecurity measures. The major challenge now is not only to prevent new introductions ... but also to control populations of existing invasive species' (Aalbersberg *et al.*, 2012, p. 123). Controlling IAS, therefore, will require on-the-ground implementation, starting with applied research, on-the-job training, enforcement, and well-directed action.

The following two case studies of IAS in Fiji, the ivory cane palm (*Pinanga coronata*) and the green (or 'American') iguana (*Iguana iguana*), highlight the urgency of on-the-ground action to control existing populations. Both species are recent, emerging IAS, with potentially devastating consequences for native biodiversity and sustainable livelihoods. Each biological invasion is a unique process and has to be assessed in detail, in particular when it comes to predictions of the potential impact on native biodiversity and ecosystems, and the development of appropriate management strategies (Boehmer *et al.*, 2001; Fischer *et al.*, 2009; Kowarik *et al.*, 2011).

30.2.1 Case study 1: The rapid spread of ivory cane palm in Fiji's forests

About 50% of Fiji's land area is composed of tropical lowland rainforest (Mueller-Dombois and Fosberg, 1998). Biodiversity in these forests is extremely high and more than half of the species are endemic to the archipelago (Keppel *et al.*, 2010). Within the Southwest Pacific, the number of endemic species in Fijian rainforests is surpassed only by New Caledonia and the Australian wet tropics (Ibanez *et al.*, 2018). Fiji's rainforests are the nation's most diverse terrestrial ecosystems (Keppel, 2014) and contain over 99% of the national endemic flora and fauna (Olson *et al.*, 2010; DoE, 2014). The DoE (2014) describes native forests as being of essential importance for Fiji's biodiversity conservation, and they provide important genetic resources, as well as cultural and economic value, supporting the livelihoods of many Fijians (DoE, 2007; SPREP, 2016a). Yet primary forest coverage decreased by 21% between 1991 and 2007 (DoE, 2014).

The ivory cane palm is native to Java and Sumatra (Kimura and Simbolon, 2002; Witono *et al.*, 2002; Witono, 2003; Witono and Rondo, 2006; Keppel and Watling, 2011). In Indonesia, it is one of the dominant species in rainforests, extending from sea level to 1,800 m a.s.l. (Witono *et al.*, 2002; Witono, 2003). The natural tendency to form mono-dominant stands implies that *P. coronata* can outcompete and displace other understorey species (Watling, 2005; Daehler and Baker, 2006). The palm was brought to Fiji for ornamental purposes in the 1970s and started spreading from gardens close to the Colo-i-Suva forest reserve on Fiji's main island of Viti Levu (Keppel and Watling, 2011). Its invasive potential was first recognized in the early 1990s (Watling and Chape, 1992). Today, it is rapidly spreading, forming dense stands in the mahogany plantations of Colo-i-Suva (CIS) and neighbouring native forests, where it is displacing native species (Dyer, 2017; Dyer *et al.*, 2018, 2019), potentially forming a novel ecosystem (Boehmer *et al.*, 2016; see Fehr *et al.*, 2020).

We used an assessment questionnaire, the Alberta Risk Assessment Tool, which ranks the potential invasiveness (i.e., potential to invade) of a species via 58 questions in three categories (environmental, economic, and social) (IASWG, 2008), to carefully examine the potential risk to native biodiversity in Fiji's rainforests (Lenz, 2016). The risk assessment tool highlighted the rapid growth and regional dispersal abilities of *P. coronata* as a particular concern. The species has the potential to disperse up to several kilometres in a single event, in addition to possibly doubling its population in less than 10 years (Hanson, 2017). *Pinanga coronata* is already abundant in the Colo-i-Suva forest reserve, utilizing anthropogenic and natural pathways, which facilitate continuous reintroduction of the species into the area (Dyer *et al.*, 2018, 2019). In addition, the entire forest reserve provides suitable habitat and climate for the spread of *P. coronata*. Other indicators of its ability to rapidly invade are its adaptability and tolerance to a broad range of environmental conditions and its efficient reproduction (Hanson, 2017).

There is a clear research deficit regarding the environmental impacts of ivory cane palm. It has been demonstrated that *P. coronata* has significant negative relationships with native tree fern species (*Cyathea* spp.) and herbs (Mathieu, 2015; Dyer *et al.*, 2018), and the palm is therefore likely displacing these species of the forest understorey. Overall, *P. coronata* invasion leads to a significant decrease of taxonomic diversity in native plants and the soil fauna of invaded rainforest (Forey *et al.*, 2021). However, little is known about how the cane palm outcompetes native species, its potential as a vector or host of diseases, or its ability to hybridize with native palm species. It also impacts aspects of the ecosystem, such as light availability, nutrient cycling, and the ability of indigenous plant species, to regenerate (Gopaul, 2018). Many of these documented effects of *P. coronata* are similar to those associated with kahili ginger (*Hedychium gardnerianum*) in Hawaii (Minden *et al.*, 2010a, 2010b). Environmental effects received the highest result of the three categories evaluated using the risk assessment tool.

The economic impacts of *P. coronata* on agriculture and livestock are also largely unknown. To date, industries such as aquaculture, tourism, and energy do not appear to be impacted. Due to the palm's re-sprouting ability, it may increase the efforts required by rural farmers to prepare forested land for planting in shifting agriculture systems (where an area is cleared, cultivated for a few years, and then abandoned for a new area until fertility has been naturally restored). Within forestry, the predicted losses are 3–4% because it is assumed that dense ivory cane palm populations bind nutrients and reduce tree growth in the vicinity (IASWG, 2008). This impact is yet to be quantified, and more severe long-term consequences could exist. For example, dense cane palm cover may prevent the regeneration of timber species (Dyer *et al.*, 2018), reducing the density and hence yield of timber species. Research on tree growth and regeneration in areas affected by *P. coronata* is therefore urgently required.

The social effects of the invasive alien species are diverse and ambiguous. In addition, some aspects, such as the potential loss of food supplies, particularly important for the subsistence lifestyle in Fiji, remain unknown. However, there appears to be no effect on human health and well-being, recreational activities, and the urban environment, with perhaps only a mild effect in terms of aesthetic or traditional/cultural values. In contrast, the species influence on the perception of natural values has been categorized as severe because of its potential impact on biodiversity. The social effects have the lowest assessed score, which is insignificant when compared with the sum of the economic effects (Lenz, 2016). These impacts increase as the species aggressively spreads and expands throughout the area and into adjacent areas. In 2016, the palm's populations in CIS and the nearby Savura forest reserves already covered more than 1,500 hectares (Dyer *et al.*, 2019).

In summary, the ivory cane palm has considerable potential to reduce native biodiversity (Lodhar *et al.*, submitted), to change the structure and dynamics of forests (Morley *et al.*, submitted), and to affect the overall ecosystem functioning. In addition, a general negative impact upon Fiji's forestry can be expected. Despite these obvious threats, nothing has been done to contain the species. This invasion may have been prevented entirely if action had been taken when the ivory cane palm was first identified as invasive with serious ecological threats in 1992 (Watling and Chape, 1992) or when it was reported to be forming dense populations and dominating parts of the forest understory of southeast Viti Levu in 2005 (Watling, 2005). Furthermore, Keppel and Watling (2011) recommended immediate eradication of the palm ten years ago, when the species was first observed in a native forest reserve.

In spite of this, remedial actions of eradication or control have not been implemented and apparently have not even been discussed. The only two invasive alien plant species that have been formally acknowledged as a major threat to the genetic resources of Fiji's forests are the African tulip tree (*Spathodea campanulata*) and mission grass (*Pennisetum polystachion*) (FAO, 2010; Brown and Daigneault, 2014), and even the ecological impacts of these species have not been researched. Despite repeated efforts by local experts over the last 25 years, there remains a need for the political authorities to address the growing *P. coronata* invasion problem. Worse still, the Pacific Island Ecosystems at Risk project database does not include *P. coronata* among the list of the region's high-risk invasive alien palms (Meyer *et al.*, 2008; PIER, 2020a).

30.2.2 Case study 2: Green iguanas eating local livelihoods

The green iguana is an invasive alien animal species with well-known economic and ecological impacts. It is native to parts of Central and South America but has established feral populations on several islands (e.g. Puerto Rico and Hawaii) and parts of continental mainland United States (e.g. Florida), where its populations reach high densities (Falcón *et al.*, 2013). The species poses considerable threats to native biodiversity and is displacing the critically endangered, congeneric *Iguana delicatissima* in some of the Lesser Antilles (van den Burg *et al.*, 2018). As a predominantly herbivorous, but potentially opportunistically omnivorous, species, the iguana poses threats to the native flora and fauna (Falcón *et al.*, 2013). In addition, the green iguana has been shown to eat important food and commercial plants (Falcón *et al.*, 2013; CI-Pacific, 2013). Furthermore, the species is impacting air and car traffic due to very high population densities on Puerto Rico (Falcón *et al.*, 2013).

In Fiji, the green iguana was illegally introduced and released on a single property on the island of Qamea in the year 2000 (CI-Pacific, 2013) and was positively identified and reported on the same island in 2008. It has since also been observed on the islands of Koro, Laucala, Matagi, and Taveuni (Thomas *et al.*, 2011; DoE, 2020). The initial response to this potentially harmful invasive alien species was swift and driven by the local non-profit organization NatureFiji-MareqetiViti and the Fijian government. An initial risk assessment, which included scientific research and creating community awareness, was undertaken (CI-Pacific, 2013). The government introduced legislation that made moving green iguanas between islands illegal and punishable by high fines through the Biosecurity Authority Fiji (at the time named the Fiji Department of Biosecurity Services) in March 2010 and funded an eradication plan through the Fiji Ministry of Primary Industries (Thomas *et al.*, 2011).

Although strongly supported by the government, these initial management actions were mainly carried out and implemented by NatureFiji-MareqetiViti. However, after producing a preliminary environmental management plan together with the Biosecurity Authority of Fiji (BAF), NatureFiji-MareqetiViti withdrew from leading Fiji's response to enable BAF to take the lead in 2011. Since then, there have been only a few management efforts. As of February 2021, BAF has trained 41 police officers as Temporary Biosecurity Officers to provide a much-needed capacity to monitor the invasive iguana (BAF, 2014). While efforts continue to be constrained by limited funding (DoE, 2020), the only on-the-ground action was in early 2015, when the Republic of Fiji Military Forces dispatched more than 100 soldiers to affected islands and killed 40 iguanas (Radio New Zealand, 2015). This, of course, is insufficient to control an agile, quickly spreading invasive animal which, in the meantime, has reached Fiji's second largest island, Vanua Levu (Fiji Broadcasting Commission, 2017; see also Falcón *et al.*, 2013).

Therefore, despite the well-established threat that this invasive alien species poses to native biodiversity and local livelihoods, little has been done on the ground to prevent increasing population sizes and the continuing spread of the green iguana. The results of this inaction could be catastrophic. Fiji has several endemic iguana species in the genus *Brachylophus* (Fisher *et al.*, 2017), which could potentially be displaced by the invasive alien iguana, while the subsequent impacts on native plant species through potential grazing of seedlings by adults remain unstudied. More importantly, livelihoods could be affected as the green iguana has been reported feeding on the commercial food crops taro (*Colocasia esculenta*) and Pacific spinach (*Abelmoschus manihot*) (CI-Pacific, 2013).

30.3 REASONS FOR INACTION ON INVASIVE ALIEN SPECIES

Like many other Pacific island countries and territories, Fiji has ratified the CBD (1993/2) and has been a member of the Convention since 1993/12. However, there is currently no framework in place to target the management of invasive alien species to meet Fiji's obligations under Article 8 (h) of the CBD. Fiji's Forest Decree No. 31 of 1992 (GoF, 1992) fails to provide a plan or requirement for invasive alien species management. It simply enables the Department of Forests to undertake management, such as silviculture in the country's reserves. Since 2008, the Biosecurity Authority of Fiji has been the country's entity that intercepts exotic pests, plants, diseases, and animals assessed to be dangerous to agriculture, forestry, and livestock industries.

A review of the most important IAS in Fiji shows a list dominated by pests, animal diseases, and animals, with only two invasive alien plant species included (Wainqolo and Timote, 2005; FAO, 2010). Clearly invasive alien plants and, in particular, invasive alien palms are not prioritized for management even though their threats have been brought to the attention of national and local authorities. There seems to be some disconnect between highly active international agencies who rely on information provided by national agencies for developing appropriate strategies and the reality on the ground. It is safe to say that, considering the volatile nature of invasive alien plants, Fiji's strategy to combat their spread is insufficient. Given the lack of legislative procedure and institutional structures, there is a need for Fiji to support existing regional frameworks for invasive alien species management.

The Guidelines for Invasive Species Management in the Pacific have been in place since the 2000s. These guidelines were developed in partnership with SPREP and the Secretariat of the Pacific Community (SPC). The SPREP strategy presents a logical framework for managing the threat of IAS by generating support and building capacity among concerned stakeholders. This should be achieved through baseline risk assessments as well as the implementation of strategies such as eradication, border control, containment, chemical control, and, finally, restoration programmes (Tye, 2009). So far, however, implementation has been minimal.

The number of invasive alien species in Fiji and, indeed, the South Pacific is steadily rising. Fiji's tropical setting and ease of accessibility from throughout the Pacific make it a favoured travel destination. The country continuously harbours cruise and cargo ships and has a particularly notable number of important economic and political international organizations. Therefore, IAS continue to be introduced and establish themselves, with some of them going on to spread through the island network (DoE, 2014). Furthermore, the lack of adequate legislation, the inefficiency of current strategies, and the apparent reluctance to implement on-the-ground eradication efforts are preventing successful management of IAS in Fiji.

30.4 CONCLUSION

Sharing of knowledge regarding successful management measures and research efforts for IAS on Pacific islands needs to be strengthened as it constitutes an important showcase for future conservation strategies and the mitigation of the impacts of invasive alien species. Furthermore, climate change will intensify irreversible ecological changes in ecosystems (Wardell-Johnson *et al.*, 2011) and facilitate the establishment and spread of alien species (e.g. Taylor and Kumar, 2016). Collaboration and effective knowledge exchange among Pacific SIDS are particularly important as responses of IAS on islands to climate change are difficult to predict (e.g. Boehmer and Niemand, 2009; Boehmer, 2011b, 2011c; Mueller-Dombois *et al.*, 2013) and likely to differ with geographical context (Bellard *et al.*, 2014; Malcolm *et al.*, 2006).

Increasing awareness and understanding in the Pacific cultural context (e.g. Raynor and Kostka, 2003; Weeks and Adams, 2018) and capacity-building (Keppel *et al.*, 2012) are important components for successful IAS mitigation (Sherley, 2000). Given the importance of customary land tenure in Fiji and other SIDS of the South Pacific, it is vital to increase public awareness of the issue of IAS, particularly among *iTaukei* villagers and forestry staff (e.g. Keppel *et al.*, 2012). The task of making people at all levels aware of biodiversity loss and the risks presented by IAS could be addressed with education for sustainable development (ESD), which stresses 'the significance of all forms of education in teaching and learning for a more sustainable future' (Bagoly-Simó, 2013, p. 57).

However, capacity-building and the development of policy guidelines and eradication plans, while important, will not contain an IAS. Effective management also requires on-the-ground action, which has been neglected in our two case studies. As a result, the invasions of the ivory cane palm and the green iguana are now impending ecological, and possibly economic disasters that become increasingly difficult to avert as both species continue to spread. An apparent lack of legislation and impetus to control potentially harmful IAS in Fiji is further compounding the escalating situation. On-the-ground action to control, eradicate, and prevent IAS is desperately needed; awareness and education are not enough as they will not stop these threats spreading through Fiji's islands, nor will they reverse the biodiversity loss where intervention is needed now.

The case studies show that IAS are posing a serious threat to forest biodiversity and sustainability in Fiji. While successful management (i.e. control and eradication) of these silent invaders would have been entirely feasible at the early stages of their invasions, it is becoming increasingly difficult as the two species are continuing to spread. Without national support through legislative measures, funding, and cross-sectoral integration, combating the spread of IAS in Fiji will remain an insurmountable challenge. Mandated government agencies and interested non-government organizations are needed to establish and implement interventions on the ground. These should be supported by the facilitation of upskilling and applied research as well as monitoring (including up-to-date methods such as the use of high-resolution aerial imagery; Mertelmeyer *et al.*, 2018), evaluation, legislation, enforcement, awareness, and education.

Given the limited resources and geographic dispersion, Pacific SIDS must focus on the most harmful invaders, target the most vulnerable regions, and increase potential and quick reaction capabilities for dealing with biological invasions (Genovesi, 2007; Denslow *et al.*, 2009; Lowry *et al.*, 2020). These planning activities must be supported by on-the-ground management actions, owing to the fact that species can efficiently spread within an island state network (Wittenberg and Cock, 2001), as illustrated by the examples of the ivory cane palm and the green iguana in Fiji. Continuing inaction on IAS will therefore produce an unprecedented ecological and economic crisis in many SIDS of the South Pacific by undermining terrestrial biodiversity, ecosystem services, and sustainability.

ACKNOWLEDGEMENTS

The authors would like to thank the Research Office of the University of the South Pacific (USP), the European Commission (Education, Audiovisual, and Culture Executive Agency, EACEA), the Australian Government (Department of Foreign Affairs and Trade), and the German Academic Exchange Service (DAAD) for financial support. Marika Tuiwawa, Alifereti Naikatini, Isaac Rounds, Sainivalati Vido, Jean-Benoit Mathieu, Kevin Sese, and Joshua Kera assisted in fieldwork and identification of species. Comments by Russell Sinclair (School of Biological Sciences, Department of Ecology and Environmental Science, University of Adelaide), Stephen E. Williams (College of Science and Engineering, James Cook University, Townsville), Steve Cranwell (BirdLife International), and an anonymous reviewer helped to significantly improve the manuscript.

REFERENCES

Aalbersberg, B., Avosa, M., James, R., Kaluwin, C., Lokani, P., Opu, J., Siwatibau, S., Tuiwawa, M., Waqa-Sakiti, H. and Tordoff, A. W. (2012) *East Melanesian Islands Biodiversity Hotspot: Suva, Fiji*. University of the South Pacific, on behalf of Critical Ecosystem Partnership Fund.

Andresen, S., Boasson, E. L. and Hønneland, G. (2012) *International Environmental Agreements: An Introduction*. London, Routledge.

Andresen, S. and Rosendal, K. (2014) Complexity in international regimes: Implications for biodiversity and climate change. Paper presented at Earth System Governance Norwich Conference, 3 July. http://norwich2014.earthsystemgovernance .org/wp-content/uploads/2014/06/Institutionalcomplex ABSsa22062014.pdf

BAF (Biosecurity Authority Fiji) (2014) BAF joins forces with the Fiji Police Force to address Biosecurity Risks. http://www.baf .com.fj/employment/press-releases/125-baf-joins-forces-with-the-fiji-police-force-to-address-biosecurity-risks

Bagoly-Simó, P. (2013) Tracing sustainability: an international comparison of ESD implementation into lower secondary education. *Journal of Education for Sustainable Development*, **7**(1), 91–108.

Baur, B. and Schmidlin, S. (2007) Effects of invasive non-native species on the native biodiversity in the River Rhine. In W. Nentwig (ed.), *Biological Invasions (Ecological Studies, vol. 193)*, pp. 257–274. Berlin, Heidelberg, and New York, Springer-Verlag.

Bellard, C., Leclerc, C., Leroy, B., Bakkenes, M., Veloz, S., Thuiller, W. and Courchamp, F. (2014) Vulnerability of biodiversity hotspots to global change. *Global Ecology and Biogeography*, **23**, 31–38.

Boehmer, H. J. (2011a) Biologische Invasionen: Muster, Prozesse und Mechanismen der Bioglobalisierung (Biological invasions: Patterns, processes and mechanisms of bioglobalization). *Geographische Rundschau*, **3**, 4–10.

(2011b) Vulnerability of tropical montane rainforests to climate change. In H. G. Brauch, Ú. O. Spring, C. Mesjasz, J. Grin, P. Kameri-Mbote, B. Chourou, P. Dunay and J. Birkmann (eds.), *Coping with Global Environmental Change, Disasters and Security: Threats, Challenges, Vulnerabilities and Risks*. Hexagon Series on Human Environmental Security and Peace, vol. 5, pp. 789–802. Berlin, Heidelberg, and New York, Springer-Verlag. https://doi.org/10.1007/978-3-642-17776-7_46

(2011c) Störungsregime, Kohortendynamik und Invasibilität: Zur Komplexität der Vegetationsdynamik im Regenwald Hawaiis (Disturbance regimes, cohort dynamics, and invasibility: On the complexity of vegetation dynamics in Hawaii's rainforests). *Laufener Spezialbeitraege*, 2011, 111–117. https://www .anl.bayern.de/publikationen/spezialbeitraege/doc/ lsb2011_018_boehmer_vegetationsdynamik_regenwald.pdf

Boehmer H. J., Hanson, G. C., Lodhar, S. Y. F., Mathieu, J.-B., Lenz, M.-I., Galvin, S. and Lowry, J. H. (2016) Rapid emergence of a novel ecosystem in a Pacific island forest reserve. *Proceedings of the 49th Annual Meeting of the Ecological Society of Germany, Austria and Switzerland*, pp. 276–277.

Boehmer, H. J., Heger, T. and Trepl, L. (2001) *Case Studies on Alien Species in Germany. Robinia pseudoacacia, Reynoutria japonica, Senecio inaequidens, Dreissena polymorpha, Ondatra zibethicus, Mustela vison.* Berlin, Umweltbundesamt UBA-Texte 13/01.

Boehmer, H. J. and Niemand, C. (2009) Die neue Dynamik pazifischer Wälder. Wie Klimaextreme und biologische Invasionen Inselökosysteme verändern (The new dynamics of Pacific forests: How climatic anomalies and biological invasions change island ecosystems). *Geographische Rundschau*, **61**, 32–37.

Brodie, G., Pikacha, P. and Tuiwawa, M. (2013) Biodiversity and conservation in the Pacific islands: why are we not succeeding? In N. S. Sodhi, L. Gibson and P. H. Raven (eds.), *Conservation Biology: Voices from the Tropics*, pp. 181–187. Oxford, Wiley.

Brown, P. and Daigneault, A. (2014) Cost-benefit analysis of managing the invasive African tulip tree (*Spathodea campanulata*) in the Pacific. *Environmental Science and Policy*, **39**, 65–76.

Butchart, S. H., Walpole, M., Collen, B., van Strien, A., Scharlemann, J. P., Almond, R. E., Baillie, J. E., Bomhard, B., Brown, C., Bruno, J., Carpenter, K. E., Carr, G. M., Chanson, J., Chenery, A. M., Csirke, J., Davidson, N. C., Dentener, F., Foster, M., Galli, A., Galloway, J. N., Genovesi, P., Gregory, R. D., Hockings, M., Kapos, V., Lamarque, J. F., Leverington, F., Loh, J., McGeoch, M. A., McRae, L., Minasyan, A., Hernández Morcillo, M., Oldfield, T. E., Pauly, D., Quader, S., Revenga, C., Sauer, J. R., Skolnik, B., Spear, D., Stanwell-Smith, D., Stuart, S. N., Symes, A., Tierney, M., Tyrrell, T. D., Vié, J. C. and Watson, R. (2010) Global biodiversity: indicators of recent declines. *Science*, **328**(5,982), 1,164–1,168.

CBD (Convention on Biological Diversity) (2008) Bioinvasion and global environmental governance: the transnational policy network on invasive alien species: Fiji's actions on IAS. https:// www.cbd.int/invasive/doc/legislation/Fiji.pdf

—— (2013) Quick guides to the Aichi Biodiversity Targets, 2nd version. Montreal, Canada, CBD.

CI-Pacific (Conservation International Pacific Islands Programme) (2013) *Biodiversity Conservation Lessons Learned. Technical Series 12: Emergency Response to Introduced Green Iguanas in Fiji.* Apia, Samoa, CEPF and CI-Pacific.

Clout, M. N. and Veitch, C. R. (2011) Turning the tide of biological invasion: the potential for eradicating invasive species. In C. R. Veitch, M. N. Clout and D. R. Towns (eds.), *Island Invasives: Eradication and Management*. Proceedings of the International Conference on Island Invasives (Preface), pp. 1–3. Gland, Switzerland, IUCN, and Auckland, New Zealand, CBB.

Clout, M. N. and Williams, P. A. (2009) *Invasive Species Management: A Handbook of Principles and Techniques.* Oxford, Oxford University Press.

Daehler, C. C. (2008) Invasive plant problems in the Hawaiian Islands and beyond: insights from history and psychology. In B. Tokarska-Guzik, J. H. Brock, G. Brundu, L. Child, C. C. Daehler and P. Pyšek (eds.), *Plant Invasions: Human Perception, Ecological Impacts and Management*, pp. 3–20. Leiden, Netherlands, Backhuys Publishing.

Daehler, C. C. and Baker, R. F. (2006) New records of naturalized and naturalizing plants around Lyon Arboretum, Mānoa Valley, O'ahu. In N. L. Evenhuis and L. G. Eldredge (eds.), *Records of the Hawaii Biological Survey for 2004–2005*. Bishop Museum Occasional Papers 87, 3–18. Honolulu, Hawaii, Bishop Museum Press.

Daehler, C. C., Denslow, J. S., Ansari, S. and Kuo, H.-C. (2004) A risk-assessment system for screening out invasive pest plants from Hawaii and other Pacific islands. *Conservation Biology*, **18**(2), 361–368.

Daigneault, A. and Brown, P. (2013) Invasive species management in the Pacific using survey data and benefit-cost analysis. Paper presented at the 57th AARES annual conference, 5–8 February, Sydney, Australia. https://www.landcareresearch .co.nz/uploads/public/researchpubs/paper-AARES-invasive -species-management.pdf

Denslow, J. S., Space, J. C. and Thomas, P. A. (2009) Invasive exotic plants in the tropical Pacific islands: patterns of diversity. *Biotropica*, **41**(2), 162–170.

DEPC (Department of Environmental Protection and Conservation) (2018) *Vanuatu National Biodiversity Strategy and Action Plan (NBSAP) 2018–2030.* Port Vila, Vanuatu, Government of Vanuatu.

DoE (Department of Environment) (2007) *Implementation Framework 2010–2014. For the National Biodiversity Strategy and Action Plan 2007.* Suva, Fiji, CBD.

—— (2014) *Fiji's Fifth National Report to the United Nations.* Suva, Fiji, CBD.

—— (2020) *National Biodiversity Strategy and Action Plan 2020– 2025.* Suva, Fiji, Government of Fiji.

Dyer, M. J. B. (2017) Distribution of the invasive palm *Pinanga coronata* and its effects on native tree ferns in the Colo-i-Suva area, Viti Levu, Fiji. University of the South Pacific, Faculty of Science, Technology and Environment, and University of South Australia.

Dyer, M. J. B., Keppel, G., Watling, D., Tuiwawa, M., Vido, S. and Boehmer, H. J. (2019) Using expert knowledge and field surveys to guide management of an invasive alien palm in a Pacific Island lowland rainforest. In C. R. Veitch, M. N. Clout, A. R. Martin, J. C. Russell and C. J. West (eds.), *Island Invasives: Scaling Up to Meet the Challenge. Occasional Paper of the IUCN Species Survival Commission N° 62*, 417–423. Gland, Switzerland, IUCN, and Dundee, Scotland.

Dyer, M. J., Keppel, G., Tuiwawa, M., Vido, S. and Boehmer, H. J. (2018) Invasive alien palm *Pinanga coronata* threatens native tree ferns in an oceanic island rainforest. *Australian Journal of Botany*, **66**(8), 647–656.

Enserink, M. (1999) Biological invaders sweep in. *Science*, **285**(5,435), 1,834–1,836.

Falcón, W., Ackerman, J. D., Recart, W. and Daehler, C. C. (2013) Biology and impacts of Pacific island invasive species. 10. *Iguana*, the green iguana (Squamata: Iguanidae). *Pacific Science*, **67**(2), 157–186.

FAO (Food and Agriculture Organization of the United Nations) (2010) *The State of the World's Forest Genetic Resources: Republic of Fiji Country Report*. Suva, Fiji, Secretariat of Pacific Communities (SPC). http://www.fao.org/3/i3825e/i3825e24.pdf

(2014) *The State of the World's Forest Genetic Resources*. Rome, FAO. http://www.fao.org/3/i3825e/i3825e.pdf?utm_source=publication&utm_medium=qrcode&utm_campaign=sofgr14

Fehr, V., Buitenwerf, R. and Svenning, J.-C. (2020) Non-native palms (Arecaceae) as generators of novel ecosystems: a global assessment. *Diversity and Distributions*, **26**, 1,523–1,538.

Fernández-Palacios, J. M., Kueffer, C. and Drake, D. R. (2015) A new golden era in island biogeography. *Frontiers of Biogeography*, **7**(1), 14–20.

Fiji Broadcasting Commission (2017) BAF officers create awareness. http://www.fbc.com.fj/fiji/50130/baf-officers-create-awareness

Fischer, L. K., von der Lippe, M. and Kowarik, I. (2009) Tree invasion in managed tropical forests facilitates endemic species. *Journal of Biogeography*, **36**, 2,251–2,263.

Fisher, R. N., Niukula, J., Watling, D. and Harlow, P. S. (2017) A new species of iguana *Brachylophus* Cuvier 1829 (Sauria: Iguania: Iguanidae) from Gau Island, Fiji Islands. *Zootaxa*, **4,273**(3), 407–422.

Forey, E., Lodhar, S. Y. F., Gopaul, S., Boehmer, H. J. and Chauvat, M. (2021) A functional trait-based approach to underline the impact of an alien palm invasion on plant and soil communities in a South Pacific island. *Austral Ecology*. https://doi.org/10.1111/aec.12995

GEF (Global Environment Facility) (1993) *Regional: South Pacific Biodiversity Conservation Programme*. Apia, Samoa, SPREP.

(2016) *GEF-6 Project Identification Form. Strengthening National and Regional Capacities to Reduce the Impact of Invasive Alien Species on Globally Significant Biodiversity in the Pacific*. UNEP.

Genovesi, P. (2007) Limits and potentialities of eradication as a tool for addressing biological invasions. In W. Nentwig (ed.), *Biological Invasions (Ecological Studies, vol. 193)*, 385–402. Berlin, Heidelberg, and New York, Springer-Verlag.

(2011) Are we turning the tide? Eradications in times of crisis: how the global community is responding to biological invasions. In C. R. Veitch, M. N. Clout and D. R. Towns (eds.), *Island Invasives: Eradication and Management. Proceedings of the International Conference on Island Invasives*, pp. 5–8. Gland, Switzerland, IUCN, and Auckland, New Zealand, CBB. https://portals.iucn.org/library/sites/library/files/documents/SSC-OP-042.pdf, pp. 5–8.

GoF (Government of Fiji) (1992) *Forest Decree 1992/No. 31*.

Gopaul, S. (2018) Abiotic effects of the invasive alien palm *Pinanga coronata* in the Colo-i-Suva Forest Reserve, Fiji. Suva, Fiji, University of the South Pacific, Faculty of Science, Technology and Environment.

Hanson, G. (2017) Population structure, allometry, and spread of alien ivory cane palm, *Pinanga coronata*, in a protected forest landscape on Viti Levu, Fiji. Suva, Fiji, University of the South Pacific, Faculty of Science, Technology and Environment.

IAEG-SDGs (Inter-Agency and Expert Group on SDG Indicators) (2016) Final List of Proposed Sustainable Development Goal Indicators. United Nations Statistical Commission/United Nations Economic and Social Council.

IASWG (Invasive Alien Species Working Group) (2008) Alberta Invasive Alien Species Risk Assessment Tool, Version 3. Edmonton, Canada, Alberta Ministry of Agriculture and Forestry. https://www1.agric.gov.ab.ca/$department/deptdocs.nsf/all/prm13262/$FILE/background.pdf

Ibanez, T., Blanchard, E., Hequet, V., Keppel, G., Laidlaw, M., Pouteau, R., Vandrot, H. and Birnbaum, P. (2018) High endemism and stem density distinguish New Caledonian from other high-diversity rainforests in the Southwest Pacific. *Annals of Botany*, **121**, 25–35.

IPCC (Intergovernmental Panel on Climate Change) (2019) Summary for policymakers. In H.-O. Pörtner, D. C. Roberts, V. Masson-Delmotte, P. Zhai, M. Tignor, E. Poloczanska, K. Mintenbeck, A. Alegría, M. Nicolai, A. Okem, J. Petzold, B. Rama and N. M. Weyer (eds.), *IPCC Special Report on the Ocean and Cryosphere in a Changing Climate*. In press.

Jupiter, S., Mangubhai, S. and Kingsford, R. T. (2014) Conservation of biodiversity in the Pacific islands of Oceania: Challenges and opportunities. *Pacific Conservation Biology*, **20**(2), 206–220.

Keitt, B., Campbell, K., Saunders, A., Wang, Y., Heinz, R., Newton, K. and Tershy, B. (2011) The global invasive vertebrate eradication database: a tool to improve and facilitate restoration of island ecosystems. In C. R. Veitch, M. N. Clout and D. R. Towns (eds.), *Island Invasives: Eradication and Management. Proceedings of the International Conference on Island Invasives*, pp. 74–77. Gland, Switzerland, IUCN, and Auckland, New Zealand, CBB.

Keppel, G. (2014) The importance of expert knowledge in conservation planning: comment to an article by C. J. Klein *et al. Marine Policy*, **48**, 202–203.

Keppel, G. Buckley, Y. M. and Possingham, H. P. (2010) Drivers of lowland rain forest community composition, diversity and structure on the islands of the tropical South Pacific. *Journal of Ecology*, **98**, 87–95.

Keppel, G., Morrison, C., Watling, D., Tuiwawa, M. V. and Rounds, I. A. (2012) Conservation in tropical Pacific island countries: why most current approaches are failing. *Conservation Letters*, **5**, 256–265.

Keppel, G. and Watling, D. (2011) Ticking time bombs: current and potential future impacts of four invasive plant species on the biodiversity of lowland tropical rainforests in south-east Viti Levu, Fiji. *South Pacific Journal of Natural and Applied Sciences*, **29**(1), 43–45.

Keppel, G., Morrison, C., Meyer, J.-Y. and Boehmer, H. J. (2014) Isolated and vulnerable: the history and future of Pacific island terrestrial biodiversity. *Pacific Conservation Biology*, **20**(2), 136–145.

Keppel, G. Gillespie, T. W., Ormerod, P. and Fricker, G. A. (2016) Habitat diversity predicts orchid diversity in the tropical Southwest Pacific. *Journal of Biogeography*, **43**(12), 1–11.

Kier, G. Kreft, H., Lee, T. M., Jetz, W., Ibisch, P. L., Nowicki, C., Mutke, J. and Barthlott, W. (2009) A global assessment of endemism and species richness across island and mainland regions. *Proceedings of the National Academy of Science of the United States of America*, **106**(23), 9,322–9,327.

Kimura, M. and Simbolon, H. (2002) Allometry and life history of a forest understory palm *Pinanga coronata* (Arecaceae) on Mount Halimun, West Java. *Ecological Research*, **17**, 323–338.

King, P. (2007) *Regional: Mainstreaming Environmental Consideration in Economic and Development Planning Processed in Selected Pacific Developing Member Countries. Technical Assistance Consultant's Report for the Asian Development Bank – Country Environmental Analysis: Vanuatu.* Manila, Philippines, Asian Development Bank.

Kowarik, I., Jaeger, H., Fischer, L. and Von der Lippe, M. (2011) Auf den Einzelfall kommt es an! Unterschiedliche Auswirkungen derselben invasiven Art auf ozeanische Inseln. (The individual case matters! Different impacts of the same invasive plants on oceanic islands). *Geographische Rundschau*, **3**, 48–53.

Kueffer, C., Daehler, C. C., Torres-Santana, C. W., Lavergne, C., Meyer, J.-Y., Otto, R. and Silva, L. (2010) A global comparison of plant invasions on oceanic islands. *Perspectives in Plant Ecology, Evolution and Systematics*, **12**(2), 145–161.

Kueffer, C., Drake, D. R. and Fernández-Palacios, J. M. (2014) Island biology: Looking towards the future. *Biology Letters*, **10**, 1–4.

Lenz, M.-I. (2016) *Risk Assessment of the Invasive Alien Ivory Cane Palm* (Pinanga coronata) *in the Forests of Colo-i-Suva Forest Reserve, Viti Levu, Fiji.* Göttingen, Germany, Georg-August-University-Göttingen.

Lodhar, S. Y. F., Forey, E., Galvin, S., Lowry, J. H., Gopaul, S., Hanson, G. C., Chauvat, M. and Boehmer, H. J. (subm.) An invasive alien palm threatens functional and taxonomic diversity of a tropical island rainforest.

Lowry, B. J., Lowry, J. H., Keppel, G., Thaman, R. R. and Boehmer, H. J. (2020) Spatial patterns of presence, abundance, and richness of invasive woody plants in relation to urbanization in a tropical island setting. *Urban Forestry and Urban Greening*, 48, Article 126516.

MacArthur, R. H. and Wilson, E. O. (1967) *The Theory of Island Biogeography.* Princeton, NJ, Princeton University Press.

Malcolm, J. R., Liu, C.-R., Neilson, R. P., Hansen, L. and Hannah, L. (2006) Global warming and extinctions of endemic species from biodiversity hotspots. *Conservation Biology*, **20**, 538–548.

Mathieu, J.-B. (2015) Diversity of understory vegetation in a submontane tropical rainforest under impact of an invasive alien palm species. Suva, Fiji, University of the South Pacific, Faculty of Science, Technology and Environment, and Quebec, Canada, University of Laval.

Mertelmeyer, L., Jacobi, J. D., Boehmer, H. J. and Mueller-Dombois, D. (2018) High-resolution aerial imagery for assessing changes in canopy status in Hawaii's 'Ōhi'a (*Metrosideros polymorpha*) rainforest. In K. Fujiwara, A. Greller and F. Pedrotti (eds.), *Geographical Changes in Vegetation and Plant Functional Types,* Chapter 13, pp. 291–301. Berlin, Heidelberg, New York, Springer.

Meyer, J.-Y. (2014) Critical issues and new challenges for research and management of invasive plants in the Pacific islands. *Pacific Conservation Biology*, **20**(2), 146–164.

Meyer, J.-Y., Lavergne, C. and Hodel, D. R. (2008) Time bombs in gardens: invasive ornamental palms in tropical islands, with emphasis on French Polynesia (Pacific Ocean) and the Mascarenes (Indian Ocean). *Palms*, **52**(2), 71–83.

Minden, V., Hennenberg, K. J., Porembski, S. and Boehmer, H. J. (2010a) Invasion and management of alien *Hedychium gardnerianum* (kahili ginger, Zingiberaceae) alter plant species composition of a montane rainforest on the island of Hawai'i. *Plant Ecology*, **206**, 321–333.

Minden, V., Jacobi, J. D., Porembski, S. and Boehmer, H. J. (2010b) Effects of invasive alien kahili ginger (*Hedychium gardnerianum*) on native plant species regeneration in a Hawaiian rainforest. *Applied Vegetation Science*, **13**, 5–14.

Mittermeier, R. A., Gil, P. R., Hoffman, M., Pilgrim, J., Brooks, T., Mittermeier, C. G., Lamoreux, J. and da Fonseca, G. A. B. (2005) *Hotspots Revisited: Earth's Biologically Richest and Most Threatened Terrestrial Ecoregions.* Chicago, IL, University of Chicago Press.

Mohamed, N. and Clark, K. (1996) *Forestry on Customary-owned Land: Some Experiences from the South Pacific.* Rural Development Forestry Network (RDFN), Network Paper 19a. Overseas Development Institute, Regent's College, London.

Morley, J., Annighoefer, P., Seidel, D., Lodhar, S. Y. F., Gopaul, S., Galvin, S., Lowry, J. H. and Boehmer, H. J. (subm.) Effects of an invasive alien palm on forest structure in a tropical island forest reserve.

Moverley, D. (2019) Battling invasive species in the Pacific. In C. R. Veitch, M. N. Clout, A. R. Martin, J. C. Russell and C. J. West (eds.), *Island Invasives: Scaling up to Meet the Challenge.* Occasional Paper of the IUCN Species Survival Commission Nº 62, pp 417--423. Gland, Switzerland, IUCN, and Dundee, Scotland.

Mueller-Dombois, D. (2006) Pacific island forests: successionally impoverished and now threatened to be overgrown by aliens? *Pacific Science*, **62**(3), 303–308. http://www.issg.org/pdf/publications/2019_Island_Invasives/PrintFiles/Moverley.pdf

Mueller-Dombois, D. and Fosberg, F. R. (1998) *Vegetation of the Tropical Pacific Islands. (Ecological Studies, vol. 132).* New York, Springer-Verlag.

Mueller-Dombois, D., Jacobi, J. D., Boehmer, H. J. and Price, J. P. (2013) *'Ōhi'a Lehua Rainforest. The Story of a Dynamic Ecosystem with Relevance to Forests Worldwide.* Honolulu, HI, Friends of the Joseph Rock Herbarium.

Nishida, G. M. and Evenhuis, N. L. (2000) Arthropod pests of significance in the Pacific: a preliminary assessment of selected groups. In G. Sherley (ed.) *Invasive Species of the Pacific: A Technical Review and Draft Strategy*, pp. 115–129. Apia, Samoa, SPREP.

Olson, D., Farley, L., Patrick, A., Watling, D., Tuiwawa, M., Masibalavu, V., Lenoa, L., Bogiva, A., Qauqau, I., Atherton, J., Caginitoba, A., Tokota'a, M., Prasad, S., Naisilisili, W., Raikabula, A., Mailautoka, K., Morley, C. and Allnutt, T. (2010) Priority forests for conservation in Fiji: landscapes, hotspots, processes. *Oryx*, **44**, 57–70.

Perrings, C., Mooney, H. and Williamson, M. (eds.) (2010) *Bioinvasion and Globalization: Ecology, Economics, Management, and Policy*. Oxford, Oxford University Press.

PIER (Pacific Island Ecosystems at Risk) (2020a) All PIER species listed by scientific name. http://www.hear.org/pier/scientificnames/

(2020b) PIER plant species present in Fiji listed by scientific name. http://www.hear.org/pier/locations/pacific/fiji/specieslist.htm

PII (Pacific Invasives Initiative) (2010) *Invasive Species Management in the Pacific: A Review of National Plans and Current Activities*. Auckland, New Zealand, PII. http://www.pacificinvasivesinitiative.org/site/pii/files/resources/publications/PII/pii_ism_in_the_pacific_a_review_of_national_plans_and_current_activities.pdf

Pouteau, R. and Birnbaum, P. (2016) Island biodiversity hotspots are getting hotter: vulnerability of tree species to climate change in New Caledonia. *Biological Conversation*, **201**, 111–119.

Pungetti, G. (2012) Islands, culture, landscape and seascape. *Journal of Marine and Island Cultures*, **1**, 51–54.

Radio New Zealand (2015) Fiji military in major iguana-culling operation. https://www.radionz.co.nz/international/pacific-news/267169/fiji-military-in-major-iguana-culling-operation

Raynor, B. and Kostka, M. (2003) Back to the future: using traditional knowledge to strengthen biodiversity conservation in Pohnpei, Federated States of Micronesia. *Ethnobotany Research and Applications*, **1**, 55–63.

Reaser, J. K., Meyerson, L. A., Cronk, Q., De Poorter, M., Eldrege, L. G., Green, E., Kairo, M., Latasi, P., Mack, R. N., Mauremootoo, J., O'Dowd, D., Orapa, W., Sastroutomo, S., Saunders, A., Shine, C., Thrainsson, S. and Vaiutu, L. (2007) Ecological and socioeconomic impacts of invasive alien species in island ecosystems. *Environmental Conservation*, **34**(2), 98–111.

Reaser, J. K., Yeager, B. B., Phifer, P. R., Hancock, A. K. and Gutierrez, A. T. (2003) Environmental diplomacy and the global movement of invasive alien species: A U.S. perspective. In G. M. Ruiz and J. T. Carlton (eds.), *Invasive Species. Vectors and Management Strategies*, pp. 362–381. Washington, DC, Island Press.

SCBD (2001) Assessment and management of alien species that threaten ecosystems, habitats and species (CBD Technical Paper 1). Montreal, SCBD.

(2005) *Handbook of the Convention on Biological Diversity* (3rd ed.). Montreal, CBD.

Settele, J., Scholes, R., Betts, R., Bunn, S., Leadley, P., Nepstad, D., Overpeck, J. T. and Taboada, M. A. (2014) *Climate Change 2014: Impacts, Adaptation, and Vulnerability. Part A: Global and Sectoral Aspects*. Contribution of Working Group II to the Fifth Assessment Report of the Intergovernmental Panel on Climate Change. C. B. Field, V. R. Barros, D. J. Dokken, K. J. Mach, M. D. Mastrandrea, T. E. Bilir, M. Chatterjee, K. L. Ebi, Y. O. Estrada, R. C. Genova, B. Girma, E. S. Kissel, A. N. Levy, S. MacCracken, P. R. Mastrandrea and L. L. White (eds.). Cambridge and New York, Cambridge University Press.

Sherley, G. (ed.) (2000) *Invasive Species in the Pacific: A Technical Review and Draft Regional Strategy*. Apia, Samoa, SPREP.

Sherley, G., Timmins, S. and Lowe, S. (2000) Draft invasive species strategy for the Pacific islands region. Nadi: regional invasive species workshop. In G. Sherley (ed.), *Invasive Species in the Pacific: A Technical Review and Draft Regional Strategy*, pp. 1–6. Apia, Samoa, SPREP.

Shine, C. (2006) *Overview of Existing International/Regional Mechanisms to Ban or Restrict Trade in Potentially Invasive Alien Species*. Strasbourg, Council of Europe.

Shine, C., Williams, N. and Guendling, L. (2000) *A Guide to Designing Legal and Institutional Frameworks on Alien Invasive Species*. Gland, Switzerland; Cambridge, UK; and Bonn, Germany, IUCN.

Smith, C. P. (1985) Impact of alien plants on Hawaii's native biota. In C. P. Stone and J. M. Scott (eds.), *Hawaii's Terrestrial Ecosystems: Preservation and Management*, pp. 180–250. Honolulu, HI, Cooperative National Park Resources Unit, University of Hawaii.

SPREP (Secretariat of the Pacific Regional Environment Programme) (2014) *Framework for Nature Conservation and Protected Areas in the Pacific Islands Region 2014–2020*. Apia, Samoa, SPREP.

(2016a) *State of Conservation in Fiji: Country Report 2013*. Apia, Samoa, SPREP.

(2016b) *Battling Invasive Species in the Pacific: Outcomes of the Regional GEF-PAS IAS Project: Prevention, Control and Management of Invasive Species in the Pacific Islands*. Apia, Samoa, SPREP.

(2017) *SPREP Annual Report: 2016*. Apia, Samoa, SPREP.

Taylor, S. and Kumar, L. (2016) Will climate change impact the potential distribution of a native vine (*Merremia peltata*) which is behaving invasively in the Pacific region? *Ecology and Evolution*, **6**(3), 742–754.

Thomas, N., Surumi, J., Macedru, K., Mataitoga, W., Qeteqete, S., Naikatini, A., Niukula, J., Heffernan, A., Fisher, R. N. and Harlow, P. S. (2011) *Iguana*: a feral population in Fiji. *Oryx*, **45**, 321–323.

Tutangata, T. I. (2000) Sinking islands, vanishing worlds. *Earth Island Journal*, **15**(2), 44.

Tye, A. (2009) *Guidelines for Invasive Species Management in the Pacific: A Pacific Strategy for Managing Pests, Weeds and Other Invasive Species.* Apia, Samoa, SPREP.

UNEP-WCMC (United Nations Environment Programme – World Conservation Monitoring Centre) (2016) *The State of Biodiversity in Asia and the Pacific: A Mid-term Review of Progress towards the Aichi Biodiversity Targets.* Cambridge, UNEP-WCMC and IUCN.

van den Burg, M., Breuil, M. and Knapp, C. (2018) *Iguana delicatissima.* The IUCN Red List of Threatened Species 2018. e.T10800A122936983. https://www.iucnredlist.org/species/10800/122936983

Van Kleunen, M., Dawson, W., Essl, F., Pergl, J., Winter, M., Weber, E., Kreft, H., Weigelt, P., Kartesz, J., Nishino, M., Antonova, L. A., Barcelona, J. F., Cabezas, F. J., Cárdenas, D., Cárdenas-Toro, J., Castaño, N., Chacón, C., Chatelain, C., Ebel, A. L., Figueiredo, D., Fuentes, N., Groom, Q. J., Henderson, L., Inderjit, Kupriyanov, A., Masciadri, S., Meerman, J., Morozova, O., Moser, D., Nickrent, D., Patzelt, A., Pelser, P. B., Baptiste, M. P., Poopath, M., Schulze, M., Seebens, H., Shu, W., Thomas, J., Velayos, M., Wieringa, J. J. and Pyšek, P. (2015) Global exchange and accumulation of non-native plants. *Nature,* **525,** 100–103.

Vitousek, P. M. (2004) *Nutrient Cycling and Limitation: Hawai'i as a Model System.* Oxford, UK, and Princeton, NJ, Princeton University Press.

Wainqolo, I. and Timote, V. (Fijian Forestry Department and Fiji Quarantine Inspection Service) (2005) Forest invasive species: Country report: Fiji. In P. McKenzie, C. Brown, S. Jianghua and W. Jian (eds.), *The Unwelcome Guests. Proceedings of the Asia-Pacific Forest Invasive Species Conference,* 17–23 August, Kunming, China. http://www.fao.org/docrep/008/ae944e/ae944e00.htm

Wardell-Johnson, G. W., Keppel, G. and Sander, J. (2011) Climate change impacts on the terrestrial biodiversity and carbon stocks of Oceania. *Pacific Conservation Biology,* **17,** 220–240.

Watling, D. (2005) *Palms of the Fiji Islands.* Suva, Fiji, Environmental Consultants Fiji.

Watling, D. and Chape, S. (1992) *Fiji: State of the Environment Report.* Gland, Switzerland, IUCN.

Weeks, R. and Adams, V. M. (2018) Research priorities for conservation and natural resource management in Oceania's small-island developing states. *Conservation Biology,* **32,** 72–83.

Witono, J. R. (2003) Phenetic study on clustered *Pinanga* of Java and Bali. *Biodiversitas,* **4**(1), 38–42.

Witono, J. R., Mogea, J. P. and Somadikarta, S. (2002) *Pinanga* in Java and Bali. *Palms,* **46**(4), 193–202.

Witono, J. R. and Rondo, K. (2006) Genetic analysis of some species of *Pinanga* (Palmae) by using ISSR markers. *Berita Biologi,* **8**(1), 19–26.

Wittenberg, R. and Cock, M. J. W. (eds.) (2001) *Invasive Alien Species: A Toolkit of Best Prevention and Management Practices.* Wallingford, UK, CAB International. https://www.cabi.org/cabebooks/ebook/20013135502

31 Did the Indian Ocean tsunami trigger a shift towards disaster risk reduction?[1]

SÁLVANO BRICEÑO[*]

*Member, Steering Committee for Disaster Risk Reduction (SC/DRR), International Science Council, Regional Office for Latin America and the Caribbean (ISC/ROLAC)

Keywords

Indian Ocean tsunami; disaster risk reduction; early warning, natural hazards; vulnerability; Hyogo Framework; sustainable development; Sendai Framework

Abstract

The earthquake and tsunami disaster of 26 December 2004 presents many extremes: the devastation was without precedent for a disaster of this type, covering a large geographical area. The level of the response was also without precedent. Another unusual development was the rapid recognition that many lives could have been saved had disaster risk reduction been more aggressively carried out in the region prior to the disaster. This chapter argues that this recognition provided a key opportunity to build more systematically on existing humanitarian, environment, and development commitments and helped develop more systematic disaster risk reduction capabilities in the region and the rest of the world.

31.1 INTRODUCTION

The response to the Indian Ocean tsunami has been without precedent. Local and international commitment to provide support for the immediate needs of the affected communities, as well as, to a certain extent, to support reconstruction efforts, has highlighted the continued strong sense of solidarity towards victims of large disasters triggered by natural hazards.

The response also provided us with new insights on what works, what does not, and how best to improve our preparedness, response, and recovery capabilities. This article reviews the approach to the response to the tsunami, which included early warning, and a review of what we learned on attempts to integrate disaster risk reduction into reconstruction.

Finally, it looks at how these lessons have been adopted by a broad range of stakeholders, from the global to the local levels, to improve preparedness and reduce risks of future disasters.

31.2 A NEW TYPE OF RESPONSE WITH THE UN FLASH APPEAL: INCLUDING EARLY WARNING OF TSUNAMIS

UN Flash Appeals are tools used in cases of breaking emergencies to attract attention to the most urgent needs, as well as to structure a coordinated response and outline financial requirements of various international agencies. The United Nations Office for the Coordination of Humanitarian Affairs (OCHA) usually takes 72 hours to issue a Flash Appeal and it typically covers the humanitarian needs for the first six months. In this case, considering the scale of this response, the UN Flash Appeal for the tsunami totalled more than US$1.2 billion and lasted more than two years.

In the context of the Flash Appeal for the tsunami, the rapid recognition that many lives and assets would have been saved had an effective early warning system been in place in the Indian Ocean led to an unusual development. Probably for the first time, an element of disaster risk reduction – in this case early warning systems – was integrated in a UN Flash Appeal to be coordinated by the International Strategy for Disaster Reduction (ISDR) secretariat, currently known as the United Nations Office for Disaster Risk Reduction (UNDRR). The innovative nature of this inclusion requires some reflection on the process and its implications and longer-term impact, as it could become an opportunity to increase our common commitment to the subject as well as greater effectiveness.

The ISDR secretariat, through its Platform for the Promotion of Early Warning (PPEW)[2] based in Bonn, identified within days the immediate need for the evaluation and strengthening of early

---

[1] A magnitude 9 earthquake followed by a tsunami, fires, and nuclear accidents, struck Japan on 11 March 2011; the reflections in this chapter are fully applicable to this new tragedy, showing that managing multiple risks in an increasingly vulnerable planet, which requires the strengthening of a common ethical perspective, the essence of sustainable development, is possibly the greatest challenge to humanity in history.

[2] As an ISDR platform, this programme ceased to exist; however, most of its activities continue as part of the UNISDR work programme.

warning systems in countries affected by the tsunami and informed OCHA. It also rapidly contacted relevant partners, in particular the Intergovernmental Oceanographic Commission (IOC) of United Nations Educational, Scientific and Cultural Organization (UNESCO/IOC) and the World Meteorological Organization (WMO), who play an important role in monitoring and disseminating information on natural hazards. In the context of tsunami warnings, UNESCO/IOC has built up solid experience in the Pacific region and has been advocating for a long time for the need for a system in other regions of the world, including the Indian Ocean. The ISDR secretariat also consulted and involved a broader range of development- and environment-focused organizations, facilitating a team effort among international organizations that proved to be effective and productive.

31.3 AN EFFECTIVE EARLY WARNING SYSTEM: THE SUM OF MANY PARTS

To guarantee its effectiveness, all the elements of an early warning system must be functional and inter linked. The massive loss of life caused by the Indian Ocean tsunami disaster inevitably focused attention on the value of early warning systems for rapid-onset disasters. However, after the tsunami, many actors pointed out that it is only when an early warning is acted upon that makes it useful. In this case, in addition to official will, the transmission, acceptance, and use of information to those who are vulnerable is a critical step, often called the 'last mile', and unfortunately such information transfer often breaks down (UK, 2006).

Another issue is enabling these technical early warning mechanisms to become sustainable, as there is a risk that they may not be well maintained once the tsunami becomes a distant memory in the communities affected. To this end, there have been calls for both the integration of these systems into multi-hazard frameworks and the creation of 'end-to-end' early warning systems (UNDP, 2005). This latter reference places more emphasis on community participation, awareness-raising, and institutional risk reduction mechanisms – especially community preparedness measures (TEC, 2006).

An important lesson learned from the 2004 Indian Ocean tsunami is that disaster risk reduction evolved gradually in developing countries, with interests and resources waning as new crises occur and other priorities demand the public's attention. This meant that many countries had not formed capacities in the fundamentals of risk reduction,[3] although some countries

manifest good practices in some aspects. At the country level, there are limited incentives, resources, enabling policy environment and limited stakeholder support for disaster risk management in general, often limiting meaningful achievements. To this end, the ISDR secretariat, working in consortium with other ISDR system partners,[4] is jointly implementing a European Commission (EC) funded project on building the resilience of communities and nations to natural hazards through aiming at increased capacities of countries affected by the Indian Ocean tsunami in post-disaster recovery and disaster risk reduction.

31.4 LINKING HUMANITARIAN RESOURCES TO DISASTER RISK REDUCTION

Often, in the weeks following large catastrophic events, leading experts in the field call for a shift in the collective approach to dealing with natural hazards and to focus more efforts on reducing risk and vulnerability. The attention by decision makers on the issue of disasters is commonly called the 'window of opportunity'.

In the case of the tsunami, this window of opportunity coincided with the second World Conference on Disaster Reduction (WCDR). Three weeks after the tsunami disaster, governments, heads of international and regional organizations, non-governmental organizations (NGOs), experts, and the media gathered at Kobe, Hyogo, Japan, from 18 to 22 January 2005, for the largest such event on the subject. At Kobe, the recognition by participants of the need to shift our mindset was palpable.

At the WCDR, governments set out an ambitious plan of action for the coming 10 years: the *Hyogo Framework for Action 2005–2015: Building the Resilience of Nations and Communities to Disasters*, or simply the Hyogo Framework, as it is now commonly called. The WCDR also confirmed the commitment of governments to build on disaster events in order to promote and strengthen disaster risk reduction. For one, the importance of strengthening early warning systems, as an integral part of disaster risk reduction and within the relief and recovery efforts following the tsunami, was reiterated. And two, in support of this concept, a number of governments and institutions[5] announced significant commitments through the ISDR as part of the UN Flash Appeal segment on early warning.

---

[3] ISDR Framework fundamentals include the following: policy priority, risk assessment, early warning, awareness, education, knowledge development, public or community participation, reducing underlying risk factors, recovery planning, building safety, insurance, and preparedness for response, all in the context of sustainable development.

[4] The Indian Ocean Tsunami Consortium included the International Federation of Red Cross/Red Crescent Societies (IFRC), UNDP, UNEP, UNESCO/IOC, UN/OCHA, the World Bank, the World Meteorological Organization (WMO), and UNISDR.

[5] The contributions were from Japan (US$4,000,000), the European Commission (US$2,007,000), Sweden (US$1,400,000), Norway (US$1,400,000), Finland (US$1,293,000), Germany (US$386,000), and the Netherlands (US$367,000) – amounting to a total of about US$10,500,000, or just less than 1% of the total UN Flash Appeal.

Related to this, a proposed voluntary target to provide up to 10% of funds spent in response to disasters on risk reduction was openly discussed. These resources would help trigger longer-term development investments on the subject. It is worth noting that several countries, such as Germany, Japan, Norway, and Sweden, either have already reached this target or are in the process of doing so. The United Kingdom is another example: the Department for International Development (DFID) now allocates 10% of its budget for responding to any specific disaster, to mitigate the likelihood and effects of future disasters in that location. Furthermore, the British House of Commons has asked DFID to persuade other donors to follow the lead they have begun to take and devote at least 10% of their total humanitarian budget to disaster risk reduction (UK, 2006).

Switzerland also recognized the need to focus more attention on disaster risk reduction in its development and humanitarian aid. For example, the Swiss Agency for Development and Cooperation (SDC) recognizes the complementary role of development cooperation and humanitarian aid in addressing the risks and impact of natural hazards. After the 2004 tsunami, the Humanitarian Aid Department of SDC further developed an advanced approach towards integrating risk reduction (prevention, mitigation, and preparedness) in sustainable development programming. This approach focuses on disaster risk reduction and recognizes how vulnerability, identified in human, social, as well as economic and environmental terms, is a major reason for the massive increase in victims and economic losses, caused by vulnerability to natural hazards (OECD, 2006). Similarly, an assessment of the Norwegian Agency for Development Cooperation (NORAD) assistance after the tsunami found the need to link relief, rehabilitation/recovery, and development. It also remains as a significant lesson from evaluations of humanitarian response to disasters triggered by natural hazards, recommending that it becomes a key principle of Good Humanitarian Donorship and therefore an important evaluation criterion for humanitarian organizations (NORAD, 2007).

Furthermore, in 2006, the World Bank initiated the Global Facility for Disaster Reduction and Recovery (GFDRR), a long-term partnership under the ISDR system to support integration of disaster risk reduction in development. This is particularly focused on country strategies and processes, towards the fulfilment of principal goals of the Hyogo Framework. With initial contribution of US$5 million a year from World Bank's Development Grant Facility for global and regional partnerships under Track I, and the UK's support of US$8 million in 2007–2009 for country programmes under Track II, the GFDRR has developed substantive engagement with partners at all levels to make a stronger case for disaster reduction as a core dimension of sustainable development.

As the key partner under Track I, the UNISDR is making significant progress to engage with regional and sub-regional organizations in Africa, the Americas, the Middle East and North Africa, East Asia, South Asia, West Asia, Southeastern Europe, and the Pacific to strengthen regional cooperation in risk mitigation, catastrophic risk financing, and adaptation to climate change. Track I support is also helping to widen global dialogue on risk reduction with different stakeholders, particularly the private sector, media networks, and academic, training, and research organizations. It seeks to standardize approaches and tools for risk identification, risk mitigation, and risk financing in partnership with members of the ISDR system.[6]

The World Bank report, *Hazards of Nature, Risks to Development*, also emphasizes the close links between the so-called natural disasters and development. Humanitarian response and development cooperation have often been organized and perceived as separate spheres. This divide has been institutionalized in the division of labour between humanitarian agencies and development organizations within the international system of humanitarian activity and development cooperation (Suhrke and Ofstad, 2005).[7]

In this regard, lesson learned from the 2004 Indian Ocean tsunami for the International Disaster Response Laws, Rules and Principles programme (IDRL) by the International Federation of Red Cross and Red Crescent Societies (IFRC) is a good step towards responding to these issues (IFRC, 2006).[8] The IDRL, which focuses on legal preparedness, can be used as a means of 'clarifying and strengthening respective responsibilities, accountabilities and authority of affected states and international agencies' (Telford *et al.*, 2006).

Substantial progress has been made in recognizing the importance of risk reduction in relief and reconstruction efforts. Numerous lessons and good practices have also accumulated in the years after the 2004 Indian Ocean tsunami. The question now is not whether or not we are seeing a shift towards risk reduction in the aftermath of the 2004 tsunami; rather, it is how we can positively engage this ongoing shift so that good intentions are converted to concrete practice with real impacts on the

---

[6] http://www.unisdr.org/eng/partner-netw/wb-isdr/wb-isdr.htm and http://www.gfdrr.org/gfdrr/

[7] In 2010, the World Bank, in collaboration with UNISDR, issued a new report, *Natural Hazards, Unnatural Disasters*, which analyses with greater detail the economic aspects of disaster risk reduction, available at https://www.gfdrr.org/index.php/en/publication/natural-hazards-unnatural-disasters-economics-effective-prevention

[8] http://www.ifrc.org/what-we-do/disaster-law/about-disaster-law/international-disaster-response-laws-rules-and-principles/idrl-guidelines/

ground, by mobilizing in an organized and effective manner relevant sectors and stakeholders.[9]

31.5 MOBILIZING POLITICAL WILL TOWARDS DISASTER RISK REDUCTION

The effect of the 2004 tsunami on the political landscape was larger than the mobilization of resources alone. It drew attention towards more inclusion of disaster risk reduction as an important aspect of preparedness, response, and recovery. It also cemented consensus at global and regional fora on the importance of this issue and for the steps necessary to enable integration.

For example, in April 2007, a decision of the UN Secretary-General Ban Ki-Moon, through the UN Policy Committee, declared that 'the Secretary-General and other senior UN Officials, including the Deputy Secretary-General, the Under Secretary-General for Humanitarian Affairs and the UNDP Administrator will systematically seek commitments of key actors, particularly governments, international financial institutions, donors, civil society and private sector. These efforts are crucial to (i) incorporate disaster risk reduction into their policies and (ii) make specific identifiable investments to reduce disaster risks of vulnerable communities and countries'.[10] In addition, former UN Secretary-General Kofi Annan recommended in his report, *Delivering as One*, to the UN General Assembly in November 2006 on UN Reform that the UN must solve its multidimensional fragmentation problems in order to be able to develop adequate response capacity and effectively fulfil its obligations in the humanitarian sector. There is the additional recommendation that the UN's role as coordinator should be further developed by focusing on six specific areas, including a call for more investment in risk reduction, early warning and innovative disaster assistance strategies and mechanisms (United Nations, 2006).

Finally, while disaster reduction is an issue to be pursued annually in the UN General Assembly, since the 2004 Indian Ocean tsunami, the United Nations Economic and Social Council (ECOSOC) has been able to reinforce risk reduction policy messages by asking the General Assembly to give

priority to integrating disaster risk reduction strategies into relevant legal, policy, and planning instruments. This has been done mainly through the implementation of the International Strategy for Disaster Reduction, reinforced by the Hyogo Framework (United Nations, 2005b).[11]

At the regional level, similar directives have been created. For example, in Asia, at the Association of Southeast Asian Nations (ASEAN) Leaders' Meeting on Aftermath of Earthquake and Tsunami held on 6 January 2005, leaders adopted the Declaration on Action to Strengthen Emergency Relief, Rehabilitation, Reconstruction and Prevention. This declaration distinguishes three phases: emergency relief, rehabilitation and reconstruction, and prevention and mitigation. This also led to the further development of the ASEAN Agreement on Disaster Management and Emergency Response. The agreement is expected to provide a framework for the development of operational procedures to respond collectively and expeditiously to disasters.

Similarly, in the backdrop of the 2004 Indian Ocean tsunami and the Kashmir earthquake of October 2005, at the 13th Summit of the South Asian Association for Regional Cooperation (SAARC), heads of states and governments considered issues of regional cooperation for preparedness and mitigation of national disasters and approved a proposal of India to set up a SAARC Disaster Management Centre, based at the National Institute of Disaster Management in New Delhi.

31.6 RECOVERY: AN OPPORTUNITY FOR MORE EFFECTIVE NATIONAL AND LOCAL ACTION

It was often mentioned after the Indian Ocean tsunami that if reconstruction were to be developmental, it would do well to be anchored in local civil society and government organizations. In many events, however, these organizations and their staff may have been lost. In Aceh, 20% of government officials are reckoned to have been killed in the Indian Ocean tsunami, so the remaining staff, who needed to rebuild their own lives, were poached by incoming international humanitarian and reconstruction agencies or were overwhelmed by work (ProVentionConsortium, 2006). In reconstruction surrounding the tsunami, it has been particularly clear that it is difficult to build developmental approaches and goals into the rebuilding of shelter and livelihoods. This highlights the need to invest in disaster risk reduction before a disaster event.

---

[9] At the World Humanitarian Summit (Istanbul, 23–24 May 2016), 'Member States committed to improve practices around data collection, analysis and early warning, including the establishment of a global risk platform. The Secretary-General committed to making all United Nations plans and programmes risk informed. These efforts would not only greatly assist in responding better to crises, but would also lead to more predictable finance to allow early action, such as through risk finance and insurance.'

[10] Decision of the Secretary-General – 10 April 2007 Policy Committee Meeting (United Nations, 2005a).

[11] In 2015, the Third World Conference on Disaster Risk Reduction adopted the Sendai Framework for Disaster Risk Reduction 2015–2030 as a follow-up to the Hyogo Framework, providing renewed policy guidance on the topic.

It is worthwhile bearing in mind that the importance of disaster risk reduction has been stressed on many occasions,[12] and the cost-benefit of reducing the vulnerability of communities to disasters has been demonstrated, albeit not systematically nor strongly enough.

Despite this, opportunities for risk reduction during reconstruction have only been supported to a limited extent. In Sri Lanka, the government originally imposed a 'buffer zone' in which no buildings were to be allowed within 200 metres from the sea. From the perspective of fishermen who need to live close to the sea for their livelihood, the risks of future tsunamis on the scale of the recent one are far less than the risks they face if fishing is interrupted and they go into debt (TEC, 2006).

Humanitarian aid has been growing in volume and as a share of Official Development Assistance (ODA). Funds made available for humanitarian assistance have more than doubled from US$2 billion in 1990 to US$5.5 billion by 2000. From 1999–2001, total humanitarian assistance averaged US$5.5 billion a year and represented about 10% of Official Development Assistance.[13] However, this increase has not led to greater investments in reducing risk despite its being recognized as a top humanitarian priority. This highlights the gap of general understanding and practice of these integration principles. For example, while the World Bank's Poverty Reduction Strategy Papers (PRSPs) could offer a framework for integrating risk reduction and development, after the 2004 tsunami, few of the main actors took the PRSPs or the Millennium Development Goals (MDGs) into account – so much so that the Tsunami Evaluation Committee found only 13 mentions of the MDGs and a single mention of the PRSPs in a review of 24,000 documents.[14]

More worrying, institutions in countries and in organizations that have a stake in the subject, including the United Nations, are not yet structured to adequately support all aspects of disaster risk reduction. A scoping study on links between disaster risk reduction, poverty, and development conducted by the United Kingdom's Department for International Development (UK/DFID, 2004 b) has pointed to the unwise separation of emergency and development activities of large bilateral and multilateral agencies, including the separation of funding arrangements. This is one of the explanations why a systematic and holistic approach to assessing and addressing disaster risk is still lacking.

Experience demonstrates that this integration will require time and continued commitment to the subject before sectoral development policy and programming can sufficiently integrate disaster risk issues. The reasons are varied and include the lack of sufficient awareness among leaders and the public, the lack of incentives, inappropriate institutional and funding structures, and competing interests of different programme sectors for development assistance in the context of diminishing resources.

Therefore, in the short and medium term, there remains a need to find ways to raise awareness to overcome some of the existing barriers and provide the knowledge and resources necessary to justify investments for disaster risk reduction.

One opportunity is to build on existing humanitarian commitments to initiate disaster risk reduction activities, even if this may apply predominantly in the case of large disasters for which the emergency needs are mostly covered and the attention on the underlying causes is very high. Such an approach also would help address shortcomings in humanitarian assistance following disasters. These could include engaging more local authorities and supporting governance and technical capabilities that are needed for long-term resilience.

The types of activities involved would vary in nature from one type of disaster, and from one region to another. Careful consideration has to be given to the most appropriate way to provide continuity and to incorporate activities into existing or new sectoral development programmes.

---

[12] The Johannesburg Plan of Implementation (JPoI) of the World Summit on Sustainable Development (WSSD) reconfirms the goals of the International Strategy for Disaster Reduction (A/56/195), to engage in an integrated, multi-hazard, inclusive approach to address vulnerability, risk assessment, and disaster management, with the objective of reducing human, social, economic, and environmental losses due to natural hazards and related technological and environmental disasters, as an essential element of a safer world in the 21st century.

- The United Nations General Assembly regularly commits to the ISDR and disaster reduction, encouraging governments to invest in disaster risk reduction. The most recent resolutions are A/RES/59/231, A/RES/59/232, A/RES/60/195, A/RES/60/196, A/RES/61/198, A/RES/61/199, A/RES/61/200, A/RES/62/192, A/RES/63/216, A/RES/63/217, A/RES/64/200, and A/RES/65/157. For more info see http://www.unisdr.org/eng/about_isdr/bd-ga-resolution-eng.htm.
- The Mauritius Strategy for the Further Implementation of the Programme of Action for the Sustainable Development of Small Island Developing States, adopted at the Mauritius Summit, January 2005, calls for the strengthening of the International Strategy for Disaster Reduction (ISDR).
- The second World Conference on Disaster Reduction, 18–22 January 2005, adopted the Hyogo Framework for Action 2005–2015: Building the Resilience of Nations and Communities to Disasters.
- IFRC 28th International Conference, December 2003.

For a more comprehensive listing of relevant frameworks and declarations, see the Annex of the Hyogo Framework for Action and information document: Extracts Relevant to Disaster Risk Reduction from International Policy Initiatives 1994–2003, Inter-Agency Task Force on Disaster Reduction, ninth meeting, 4–5 May 2004, at http://www.unisdr.org/eng/task%20force/tf-meetigns/9th%20TF%20mtg/Info-doc-Extracts-int-policy-agendas.doc.

[13] Data collated by the Development Assistance Committee (DAC) of the Organization for Economic Cooperation and Development (OECD) and the Financial Tracking System of the Office for the Coordination of Humanitarian Affairs (OCHA).

[14] http://proventionconsortium.net/

This approach would require both commitment and flexibility on the part of humanitarian players, including the need to assume a longer-term view of resourcing requirements for risk reduction. For example, the nature of disaster risk reduction activities makes it more difficult for partners to spend funds and show tangible results within short timeframes as required for humanitarian frameworks, hence the need for humanitarian actors to focus on awareness-raising activities, promoting and facilitating DRR without aiming at implementing risk reduction technical measures that are part of development plans and programmes.

It would also require a coordinated approach for the multilateral and bilateral partners involved. Firstly, it would be necessary to demonstrate to humanitarian partners the added value of the process and to ensure that resources are effectively used to address aspects related to disaster risk reduction that would help trigger longer-term sustainable efforts, as mentioned earlier. These priorities would need to be based on the available agreed principles of Good Humanitarian Donorship and follow the guidance contained in the Hyogo Framework.[15] It is noteworthy that in the case of the tsunami UN Flash Appeal, considerable resistance to the use of the ISDR Trust Fund as a mechanism through which to channel these resources came from the organizations that would ultimately benefit from such a system.

It appears, therefore, that if this shift were to take place, institutional mechanisms, such as the Global Platform for Disaster Risk Reduction, the ISDR Inter-agency Group (key international organizations), the ISDR Support Group (governments), and the governance of the UN Trust Fund for Disaster Reduction, would need to be strengthened to build the necessary confidence and overcome these obstacles.[16]

31.7 CAN WE TAKE THIS EXPERIENCE ONE STEP FURTHER?

The ISDR system has streamlined its focus and prioritized its activities to support the implementation of the Hyogo Framework. The broad range of actors involved in these activities have a unique opportunity. The United Nations system for disaster reduction is in better shape than ever before, and current efforts to further strengthen its mode of operation allow it to respond to these challenges.

In the meantime, it is important that disaster risk reduction is not wrongly perceived as taking away essential humanitarian resources from where they are needed. To the contrary, including disaster risk reduction into the humanitarian process creates mutually beneficial situations, benefiting considerably the most vulnerable communities in the longer term by making them more resilient. Most affected developing countries continually insist on their preference for sustainable risk reduction support rather than just short-term relief assistance.

ACKNOWLEDGEMENTS

The comments from the reviewers Dr Michael J. Ernst and Dr Ilan Kelman have improved the quality of the earlier version of this chapter. Support has been provided by ISDR colleagues Mr Terry Jeggle, Mr Jerry Velasquez, and Ms Yuki Matsuoka in producing this article.

REFERENCES

IFRC (2006) *Legal Issues from the International Response to the Tsunami in Indonesia, An International Disaster Response Laws, Rules and Principles (IDRL) Programme Case Study.* July 2006. Jakarta.

NORAD (2007) *Humanitarian Response to Natural Disasters: A Synthesis of Evaluation Findings, Synthesis Report 1/2007.* Oslo, January 2007.

OECD (2006) *Humanitarian Aid in DAC Peer Reviews: A Compilation of Coverage 2004–05.* Paris, 17 January 2006.

ProVention Consortium (2006) *Incentives for Reducing Risk: A Reflection on Key Themes, Issues and Ideas on Risk Reduction Raised at the 2006 ProVention Forum,* March 2006. ProVention Consortium.

Suhrke, A. and Ofstad, A. (2005). *Filling 'the Gap': Lessons Well Learnt by the Multilateral Aid Agencies.* Christian Michelsen Institutt, Bergen, Norway.

TEC (Tsunami Evaluation Coalition) (2006) *Links between Relief, Rehabilitation and Development in the Tsunami Response.* March 2006.

Telford, J., Cosgrave, J. and Houghton, R. (2006) *Joint Evaluation of the International Response to the Indian Ocean Tsunami: Synthesis Report.* Tsunami Evaluation Coalition.

UK (2006) *Minutes of the Hearings of the House of Commons International Development Committee, Humanitarian Response to Natural Disasters.* Seventh Report of Session 2005–06, Volume I, 2006, United Kingdom.

UK/DFID (2004) *Disaster Risk Reduction: A Development Concern: A Scoping Study on Links between Disaster Risk Reduction, Poverty and Development.* Conflict and Humanitarian Affairs Department, London.

UNDP (2005) *2005 Report on the UNDP Thematic Trust Fund for Crisis Prevention and Recovery.* New York.

---

[15] Now succeeded by the 2015 Sendai Framework and the recommendations of the 2016 World Humanitarian Summit.

[16] See UN GA Resolution A/RES/61/198. The current ISDR system has replaced the Inter-agency Task force for Disaster Reduction (IATF/DR) with the Global Platform for Disaster Risk Reduction, which has held sessions in Geneva on June 2007, June 2009, May 2011, and May 2015 (the next one planned for 2017 in Cancun, Mexico), and includes governments, international, regional, and civil society organizations. The UN Trust Fund for Disaster Reduction is also being strengthened to provide the financial mechanism to the wider ISDR system partners.

United Nations (2005a) *Strengthening of the Coordination of Emergency Humanitarian Assistance of the United Nations.* Report of the Secretary-General, June 2005 (A/60/87–E/2005/78).

(2005b) Hyogo Framework for Action 2005-2015: Building the Resilience of Nations and Communities to Disasters (A/CONF.206/6). http://www.un-documents.net/hfa.htm

(2006) Report of the Secretary-General's Highlevel Panel on System-wide Coherence: 'Delivering as One' (A/61/5wz83). New York.

(2006) *Report of the Secretary-General's High-Level Panel on System-wide Coherence: 'Delivering as One'* (A/61/583). New York.

RECOMMENDED READING

Benson, C. and Clay, E. J. (2004) *Understanding the Economic and Financial Impacts of Natural Disasters. Disaster Risk Management Series Paper #4.* Washington, DC, World Bank.

DKKV/ISDR (2002) *Early Warning and Sustainable Development.* Input Paper prepared in the context of the WSSD and on-going work on early warning.

Handmer, J. (2002) *Preparing for a European Approach to Flood Warning.* Paper presented at the second MITCH Workshop 'Advances in Flood Forecasting, Flood Warning and Emergency Management'. Barcelona, July 2002.

IFRC (2002) *World Disasters Report 2002: Focus on Reducing Risk.* International Federation of the Red Cross and Red Crescent Societies, Geneva.

India, National Centre for Disaster Management (2002) *The Report of the High-Powered Committee on Disaster Management.* New Delhi, Department of Agriculture and Cooperation, Government of India.

Kent, R., Dalton, M., von Hippel, K. and Maurer, R. (2003) *Changes in Humanitarian Financing: Implications for the United Nations.* 11 October 2003. King's College London, Humanitarian Futures Programme.

Omachi, T. and Le-Huu, T. (2003b) *Overview of the Natural Disaster and Flood Forecasting and Warning Systems in the Region.* Paper presented at the Regional Consultation on Early Warning Systems in Asia and the Pacific, Bandung, Indonesia, 26–28 May 2003.

Omachi, T., Le-Huu, T. and Ono, Y. (2003a) *Consultation Workshop on Early Warning Systems: Effectiveness of Early Warning Systems in Asia/Pacific.* Bandung, Indonesia, 26–28 May 2003, Workshop Report. UNESCAP, UN/ ISDR, BGR, DGGMR. 17 July 2003.

Plate, J. E. (2003) *Regional Consultation Europe Report for EWC II,* Potsdam, 4 August 2003. UNISDR, Geneva.

Tearfund (2003) *Natural Disaster Risk Reduction: The Policy and Practice of Selected Institutional Donors.* Tearfund Research Report.

UK/DFID (2004[a]) *Disaster Risk Reduction: A Development Concern: Action to Reduce Risks from Natural Disasters Must Be at the Centre of Development Policy.* London, Conflict and Humanitarian Affairs Department.

UNISDR (2003) *Background Paper. Overview of the Preparatory Process, Major Themes and Expected Outputs of the Second International Conference on Early Warning (EWC-II).* Prepared by the UNISDR secretariat, Geneva, Switzerland.

UNISDR (2003) *Synthesis of the Findings of the Early Warning Regional Consultations in Africa, Asia, the American Hemisphere and Europe.* UNI/ISDR secretariat.

UNISDR (2004) *Living with Risk: A Global Review of Disaster Reduction Initiatives. International Strategy for Disaster Reduction.* Geneva, UNISDR.

UNISDR (2006) *Global Survey of Early Warning Systems.* Geneva, UNISDR.

UNISDR (2009 and 2011) *Global Assessment Report on Disaster Risk Reduction.* Geneva, UNISDR. https://www.undrr.org/publication/global-assessment-report-disaster-risk-reduction-2019

United Nations (1995) *Secretary-General's Report on Early Warning Capacities of the United Nations Systems with Regard to Natural and Similar Disasters.* Presented to the Fiftieth Session of the United Nations General Assembly, October 1995. A/50/526. New York.

United Nations (1997) *Secretary-General's Report on Improved Effectiveness of Early Warning Systems with Regard to Natural and Similar Disasters.* Report presented to the Fifty-Second Session of the United Nations General Assembly, October 1997. A/52/561. New York.

USA National Science and Technology Council (2000) *Effective Disaster Warnings. Report by the Working Group on Natural Disaster Information Systems, Subcommittee on Natural Disaster Reduction.* Washington, DC, National Science and Technology Council, Committee on Environment and Natural Resources of the Executive Office of the President of the United States, November 2000.

Villagran de Leon, J. C., Scott. J., Cardenas, C. and Thompson, S. (2003) *Early Warning Systems in the American Hemisphere: Context, Current Status and Future Trends.* Hemispheric Consultation on Early Warning, Antigua Guatemala, 3–5 June 2003.

Vordzorgbe, S. (2003) *Regional Report on Early Warning of Natural Disaster in Africa.* Report prepared for the Second International Conference on Early Warning, 16–18 October, UN/ISDR, Nairobi. July 2003. https://www.unisdr.org/2006/ppew/info-resources/ewc2/upload/downloads/Africa.pdf

Walker, P., Wisner, B., Leaning, J. and Minear, L. (2005) *Smoke and Mirrors: Deficiencies in Disaster Funding. BMJ,* 330, 247–250, 29 January 2005.

Wigmore, L. (2003) *50 Years Back and 100 Years Forward: Remembering the Works Flooding in Living Memory and Looking to the Future. UK Environment Agency News,* 23 January 2003.

Wisner, B., Blaikie, P., Cannon, T. and Davis, I. (2004) *At Risk: Natural Hazards, People's Vulnerability and Disasters* (2nd ed.). London and New York, Routledge.

32 Cyclone Nargis and disaster risk management in Myanmar

TUN LWIN[1] AND SWAN YEE TUN LWIN

Myanmar Climate Change Watch, Yangon, Myanmar

Keywords

Cyclone Nargis; disaster; risk; early warning; climate change; lessons learned; Myanmar

Abstract

The devastating cyclone 'Nargis' struck the Myanmar coast on the evening of 2 May 2008. Prior to Nargis, no cyclone making landfall in Myanmar had ever been on the list of 'deadliest tropical cyclones' in the whole tropical region. Official figures reported that 84,500 people were killed and 53,800 went missing (IFRC, 2011). Nargis became the eighth-deadliest tropical cyclone in the world, in addition to leaving a huge impact on the social and economic sectors of the country, with an estimated cost of more than 11 trillion kyat (US$8,317,580) in damages.

The effect of climate change is evident when one looks at the case of Nargis, especially upon studying its track. Tun Lwin (2008) found that the latitude of recurvature of Bay of Bengal storms in the pre-monsoon season had shifted southwards from the latitude of Bangladesh (>20° North) to the latitude of the Myanmar delta area (around 16° North). This latitudinal shift is clearly seen after the 1980s in the decadal average of 850 hPa winds. In addition, the decadal mean sea surface temperature anomalies (SSTA) in the Bay of Bengal for the pre-monsoonal periods clearly show that they have changed from negative to positive, starting from 1980. Furthermore, a maximum positive SSTA centre is observed in the vicinity of Preparis Island, one of the Andaman Islands, from which most storms with a landfall on the Myanmar coast originate. These changes have had a significant impact on the region, as a result.

The high loss of human lives and property during Nargis was due to the high vulnerability of the delta areas associated with both climatic and non-climatic factors. This chapter discusses those factors so as to learn lessons, with a view to reducing the risks in similar disasters in the future. Disaster risk reduction and management will have significant implications for sustainable development in Myanmar.

32.1 INTRODUCTION

Myanmar is situated in the western-most part of Southeast Asia, between latitude 10°–29.5° North and longitude 92°–100.5° East. It is the second largest country in Southeast Asia, with a total land area of 676,578 square kilometres and a population of 54.2 million (Department of Population, 2019). Its coastline covers almost the whole east coast of the Bay of Bengal.

Although Myanmar suffers less from the impacts of natural disasters than neighbouring countries like Bangladesh, India, and Thailand, climate change has caused the risk of climate-related disasters to increase, especially during the last three decades, when Myanmar was identified as the third most-affected country suffering from extreme weather events during the period of 1997–2016, by the Climate Risk Index 2018 (Eckstein *et al.*, 2018). Therefore, the need to study these changes and the resulting impacts has never been greater than it is now, in order to reduce Myanmar's vulnerability to the adverse effects of climate-related disasters, given that their propensity to strike has become greater.

This chapter first discusses the historical events of cyclones in Myanmar and then focuses on the havoc wreaked by Cyclone Nargis in May 2008 and its underlying causes. This case study is critical for improving disaster management policies within the nation.

32.2 STORMS AND CYCLONES IN MYANMAR

Myanmar borders the Bay of Bengal and the Andaman Sea. Its 2,400-km-long coastline on the east of the Bay of Bengal is threatened by storms, cyclones, storm and wave surges, and

---

[1] Former Director-General (2004–2009), Department of Meteorology and Hydrology, Yangon, Myanmar. Unfortunately, Dr Tun Lwin passed away on 4 November 2019.

other associated weather phenomena that could evolve into natural disasters. Overall, storms and cyclones are among the most devastating natural disasters in Myanmar, accounting for 11% of all disasters. Historically, cyclones made landfall on the coast of Myanmar about once every three years. From 2000 onwards, the average number of cyclones making landfall became two every three years. Since 2006, however, the frequency of cyclones making landfall in Myanmar has increased further to almost every year.

The Bay of Bengal, in the North Indian Ocean, stretches northwards from the equator to the river mouths of the Brahmaputra, Ganges, and Magna, and eastwards from the coast of Chennai, India, to Myanmar. Although the area is not geographically vast, it is a central area for tropical cyclone generation. Cyclones generally move west towards India once generated; if there is a slight recurvature, they tend to move towards Bangladesh; if the recurvature is sudden and more extreme, they move towards Myanmar, crossing its coast at lower latitudes.

Annually, from April to December, there are about 10 tropical storms in the Bay of Bengal. Severe cyclones occur during the pre-monsoon period of mid-April to mid-May and the post-monsoon period of October to December. Conversely, the tropical storms that form during the monsoon period of June to September are weak and short-lived, making landfall mainly over the Indian coast. In the post-monsoon periods, remnants of typhoons in the South China Sea regenerate as they enter the Bay of Bengal and the Andaman Sea, turning into storms in the Bay of Bengal. A statistical analysis of 100 years of historical records of Bay of Bengal storms found that every storm originating near Preparis Island in the Andaman Sea later made landfall over the coast of Myanmar.

During the period of 1877–2009 (Table 32.1), 1,303 tropical storms formed in the Bay of Bengal. Eighty-three of them (6.3% of the total Bay storms) made landfall on the Myanmar coast. Among them, 27 (33.0%) were in May; 15 (18%) were in April; 14 (17%) were in October and November; and 9 (11%) were in December.

32.3 STORM SURGES IN MYANMAR

The majority of storms and cyclones are accompanied by three destructive forces: strong winds as high as 190–225 km/h, heavy rain of 120–255 mm in 24 hours, and storm surges with waves higher than 3–3.6 metres. Depending on the vulnerability of the place of landfall, the greatest damage is mainly due to the storm surge.

Climatologically, there exists two clear storm seasons for Myanmar: the pre- and post-monsoon periods. The pre-monsoon period (combination of April and May) accounts for

Table 32.1. Historical record of Bay of Bengal storms and storms that crossed the Myanmar coast for the period 1877–2009.

Month	No. of storms formed in the Bay of Bengal	No. of storms that crossed Myanmar coast
JAN	16 (1%)	2 (2%)
FEB	3 (0%)	1 (1%)
MAR	8 (1%)	–
APR	33 (3%)	15 (18%)
MAY	96 (7%)	27 (33%)
JUN	121 (9%)	1 (1%)
JUL	185 (14%)	–
AUG	201 (15%)	–
SEP	216 (17%)	–
OCT	201 (15%)	14 (17%)
NOV	146 (11%)	14 (17%)
DEC	77 (6%)	9 (11%)
Total	1,303 (100%)	83 (100%)
Annual	9.79	0.62
% of Bay storms		0.63

Source: Tun Lwin (2015)

42 storms (51.0%), and the post-monsoon period (combination of October and November) and the early winter month of December accounts for 37 storms (45%).

In the six decades from 1947 to 2009, a total of 36 cyclones crossed Myanmar's coast (Table 32.2). Extensive storm surge was associated with 11 of these cyclones and caused the most fatalities. The deadliest during this period was the May 2008 cyclone, Cyclone Nargis, with a death toll of 138,373, the highest ever recorded in Myanmar's history. The previous records were 1,037 in the May 1968 Sittwe cyclone, 304 during the May 1975 Pathein cyclone, and 37 lives during the May 2006 Mala cyclone. Therefore, based on historical precedence, we can surmise that the deadliest storms occur in May.

Storms with maximum wind speed exceeding 160 km/h usually generate storm surges upon entering coastal areas. In May 2006, Cyclone Mala, with maximum sustained winds of 225 km/h, struck Myanmar's Rakhine coast. It produced a maximum storm surge height of 4.57 meters. Cyclone Nargis's sustained wind speed of 225 km/h generated a maximum surge height of 7.02 meters on the deltaic shoreline. The difference in surge height in the associated storms between the two events is a function of both wind speed and the topography of the shoreline. As a result, the vulnerability of the coastal population to storms and cyclones is much higher in the deltaic coastal area than on the Rakhine coast.

Table 32.2. List of killer storms in the Bay of Bengal that crossed the Myanmar coast.

Dates of TRS in the Bay of Bengal	Place of landfall	Loss of human lives and property
6–8 OCT 1948	Sittwe	**Sittwe**: A few people dead; estimated damage 10 million kyat
22–24 OCT 1952	Sittwe	**Yangon**: 4 dead
1–4 MAY 1962	Gwa	**Sittwe and Pathein**: Estimated damage 10 million kyat 27 dead; 90% of houses destroyed; estimated damage 82.4 million kyat
15–18 MAY 1967	Kyaukphyu	**Pathein District**: Estimated damage 10 million kyat **Kyaukphyu**: Estimated damage 20 million kyat
20–24 OCT 1967	Sittwe	**Sittwe**: 2 dead; 90% of houses damaged; >10 million kyat in damages **Kyauktaw**: 90% of houses damaged **Ratheytaung**: 90% of houses damaged **Monywa** district: >100 people dead; >1,000 cattle lost; estimated damage 5 million kyat Water level of **Upper Chindwin River** rose 3 metres overnight
7–10 MAY 1968	Sittwe	**Sittwe**: 1,037 dead; 17,537 cattle lost; 57,663 houses destroyed; estimated damage 10 million kyat
5–7 MAY 1975	Pathein-Gwa	303 dead; 10,191 cattle lost; 246,700 houses destroyed; estimated loss 446.5 million kyat
12–17 MAY 1978	Kyaukphyu	90% destroyed; estimated damage 200 million kyat
16–19 MAY 1992	Thandwe	**Manaung, Rambre, Kyaukphyu, Thandwe, and Taungote**: 27 dead; >150 million kyat in damages
29 APR–2 MAY 1994	Maungdaw	26 dead; estimated damage 59 million kyat
25–29 APR 2006 (Mala)	Near Gwa	1 dead; estimated damage 428.56 million kyat
28 APR–3 MAY 2008 (Nargis)	Heingyi Island	138,373 dead (including missing); 300,000 household animals killed; 75,000 houses, 4,000 schools, 600 villages damaged; estimated cost 11.6 trillion kyat

Source: Tun Lwin (1981, 2015)

32.4 LOCATIONS IN MYANMAR VULNERABLE TO STORM SURGES

Myanmar's 2,400-km-long coastline can be broken up into three segments: the Rakhine, the Ayeyarwaddy (also romanized as Irrawaddy) Deltaic, and the Mon-Tanintharyi coasts, as seen in Figure 32.1, all of which have experienced storm surge devastation (Table 32.3). The Rakhine coast consists of the Rakhine State; the Ayeyarwaddy Deltaic coast, the Ayeyarwaddy Division and the Yangon Division; and the Tanintharyi coast, the Mon State and the Tanintharyi Division.

The northern Rakhine coast, adjacent to the area most vulnerable to storm surges along the Bangladesh coast, consists of large offshore islands with intervening, partially covered areas of marshy and mangrove forests. This setting does provide partial protection from surge waves. However, the very

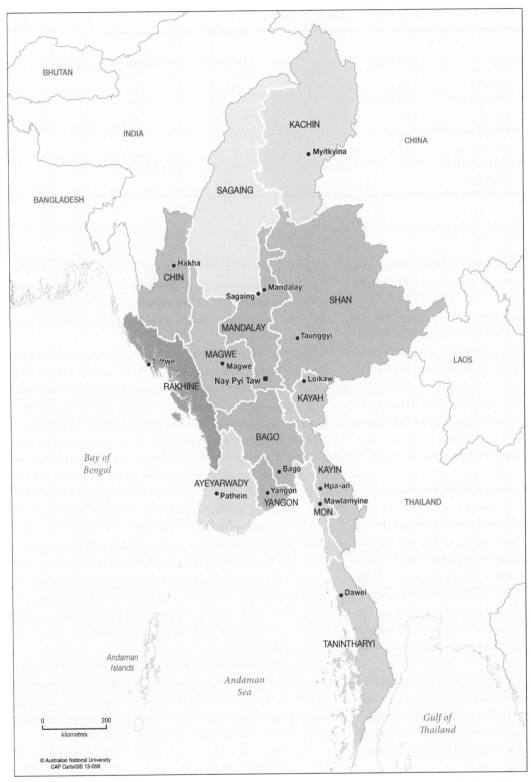

Figure 32.1. Myanmar states and regions, with capital cities. (*Source*: CartoGIS Services, College of Asia and the Pacific, Australian National University, 2012)

Table 32.3. List of storm surge devastation in association with cyclones in Myanmar.

No.	Name	Date	Peak surge	Landfall point	Death toll	Damage (mil kyat)
1	Sittwe Cyclone	07–05-1968	4.25 m	Near Sittwe	1,037	800
2	Pathein Cyclone	07–05-1975	3.00 m	Near Pathein	304	776
3	Gwa Cyclone	04–05-1982	3.70 m	Near Gwa	31	38
4	Maungdaw Cyclone	02–05-1994	3.66 m	Near Maungdaw	10	78
5	Mala Cyclone	29–04-2006	4.57 m	Near Gwa	1	429
6	Nargis Cyclone	02–05-2008 to 03–05-2008	7.02 m	Near Heingyi	138,373	11.6×10^6

Source: Tun Lwin (1981, 2015)

gentle slope and flat nature of the northern Rakhine coast, with numerous streamlets, increase the vulnerability of the region to storm surges.

The southern Rakhine coast is overall less protected, as it is primarily rocky and sandy, with limited marshy and mangrove areas. Therefore, with its three popular resort areas, this part is comparatively more vulnerable to the storm surge hazard than the other two.

The Ayeyarwaddy Delta is a large delta with wetlands and mangrove forests that provide partial protection from storm waves. The delta front is wide, with shoals in some places, serving to slow down the speed and force of incoming waves (e.g. tsunami waves). However, most parts of the Ayeyarwaddy and Yangon Divisions of the Ayeyarwaddy Delta are susceptible to storm surges, especially as more and more natural forest cover and coastal vegetation has been lost to deforestation (TCG, 2008). Immediately to the east lies the river mouth of Sittaung, a wide estuary that widens southwards to form the Gulf of Mottama. Owing to the low elevations of this area, the high water volume due to numerous tributaries, several open or bell-shaped river mouths, very shallow surface slope, and dense population, the Ayeyarwaddy Delta has the highest vulnerability in Myanmar to storm surges (Tun Lwin, 2015).

The Tanintharyi coast consists of more than 800 islands that are sparsely populated, with most of the settlements on the eastern coasts. Compared to the Rakhine and the Ayeyarwaddy Deltaic coasts, the Tanintharyi coast, being at a lower latitude, has a lower possibility of severe storms and cyclones and thus a lower possibility of tsunamis and storm surges.

32.5 THE KILLER CYCLONE NARGIS OF 2008

Geographically, Myanmar is exposed to the threat of cyclones and the associated severe weather phenomena and sea waves.

As previously noted, the frequency, location, and patterns of recurvature have changed dramatically over the last three decades. In particular, the latitude of recurvature has become progressively lower, and changes in direction have become more drastic and abrupt.

Cyclone Nargis reached its strongest intensity before crossing the deltaic coast on 2 May 2018, as seen in Figure 32.2, and there was clear evidence of these changes when it struck. The Category 3 cyclone abnormally intensified into a Category 5 storm within a few hours (Figure 32.3) prior to crossing Myanmar's Ayeyarwaddy Delta coast. Its track was peculiar in that it deviated from the usual storm track, even though the seasonality and locality of its formation did not (Figure 32.4). It struck the nation on 2 May and 3 May 2008, making landfall in the Ayeyarwaddy Division, approximately 250 km southwest of Yangon, the country's largest city. More than 50 townships, mainly in the Yangon and Ayeyarwaddy Divisions, were affected (Figure 32.5), and it is estimated that about 95% of the damage and fatalities that occurred in the past two decades were due to this event (Eckstein *et al.*, 2018). As a result, Nargis was the worst natural disaster in the history of Myanmar and the most devastating cyclone to strike Asia since 1991.

With wind speeds of up to 200 km/h accompanied by heavy rain, the damage was most severe in the Delta region, where the effects of the extreme winds were accompanied by a storm surge of 3.6 metres. According to field survey reports, at places the peak surge was measured as high as 7.02 metres.

32.5.1 Prediction of Nargis

The Department of Meteorology and Hydrology (DMH) had monitored Cyclone Nargis since its birth on 24 April 2008 and was able to make forecasts and issue warnings starting from 28 April, when the disturbance attained cyclonic intensity. The Regional Integrated Multi-hazard Early Warning System

Figure 32.2. Cyclone NARGIS at its peak intensity just before making landfall at Myanmar. (*Source*: Kitamoto Asanobu, National Institute of Informatics, 2008)

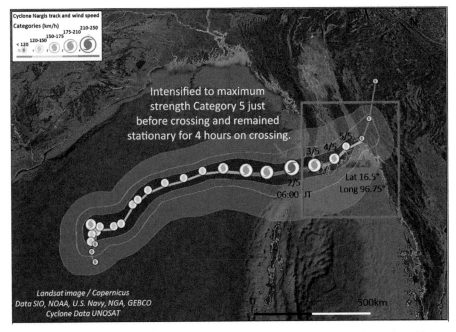

Figure 32.3. Trajectory of Tropical Cyclone Nargis in May 2008 on a 6-h time lapse, from 18 April to 4 May 2008. (*Source*: Shida, 2008)

(RIMES) Centre was an integral part of this process for the DMH. Given that the then-Director-General of DMH was the Chairman of RIMES, DMH was a profound member of RIMES and received animation forecasts prepared by the RIMES Centre regularly.

Figure 32.6 shows the Storm Animation Forecast made by the RIMES Centre at the Asian Institute of Technology (AIT), Bangkok. The figure shows the storm's forecast development from the early stage on 27 April 2008 up to its landfall on 2 May. The landfall point on entering the coast was forecast at Heingyi Island,

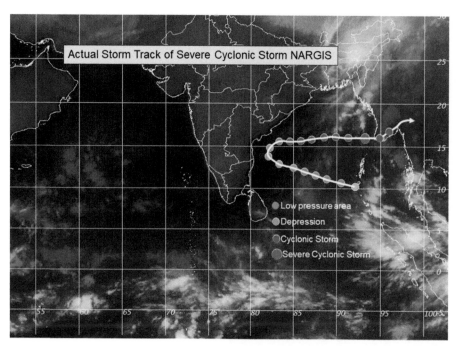

Figure 32.4. Actual storm track of Nargis for the period 22 April–4 May 2008 by Tun Lwin. Formation in seasonality and locality were normal, but the track was not.

in the Delta region, at 84 hours elapsed time (12 UTC on 2 May 2008). After crossing the coast, the storm was forecast to move eastward until 120 hours (00 UTC on 3 May 2008).

The RIMES Centre made a perfect forecast for 120 hours (five days in advance) that the storm would cross the Myanmar coast near Heingyi Island. As a result, DMH was able to issue cyclone early warnings almost every 2–3 hours for the entire five days. According to the survey done afterwards by DMH and other organizations, the local people responded that almost everyone knew of the warnings at least 48 hours in advance. It is therefore believed that the early warnings for Cyclone Nargis were more than satisfactory (RIMES Centre, 2008).

32.6 SHIFTING RISKS IN MYANMAR

Myanmar – and in particular the high-risk areas of the Rakhine, the Ayeyarwaddy Delta, and the Mon-Tanintharyi areas – is exposed and vulnerable to a range of natural disasters, and continuously experiences strong storm surge devastation. Cyclone Nargis tragically demonstrated that these disasters are not only increasing in intensity but can have a devastating impact on the people and economy of Myanmar. These disasters and their impacts are ever-changing as a result of climatic and non-climatic factors and require the government of Myanmar, and specifically its disaster management community, to become more proactive in terms of understanding the increasing threats of

climatological disasters and the need to strengthen its disaster management capacity more effectively.

In particular, the lack of disaster preparedness education, public awareness, and an overall weakness in disaster management capability substantially increase the risk of even more devastating disasters. The following section presents a short overview of the increasing impacts of climate change on Myanmar as a background for an assessment of the needs, in order to improve disaster management. Suggested strategies for the nation will be discussed in detail following the overview.

32.6.1 Increasing risks from climatic change

Climate change is a growing threat to the physical security and the natural resources upon which the people of Myanmar depend for their livelihoods. Specifically, the region is increasingly vulnerable to the greater incidence and scale of hazardous events, such as cyclones and prolonged droughts, as a result of climate change. The potential impacts of climatic changes are already evident in the region. For example, prior to Nargis, incremental changes to the local environment in terms of the salinization of soils due to seawater rise had already been observed. As a result, villagers converted areas that were no longer viable for rice production into salt farms, which had direct implications for household food production and security.

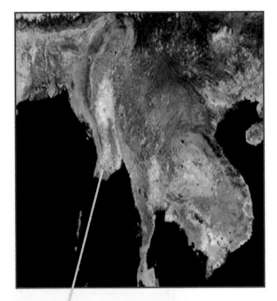

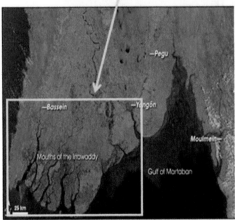

Figure 32.5. Areas seriously affected by Nargis, captured by NASA's Terra Satellite on 15 April 2008. (*Source*: NASA/MODIS Rapid Response Team, 2008)

A similar problem has been the salinization and contamination of groundwater sources (e.g. ponds and wells) during the dry season. Limited access to drinking water is now a common problem in many of the coastal villages of Labutta and Bogalay townships, especially during the dry season (from November to May). As a result, villages in the Delta have increasingly resorted to importing fresh water from other villages. Given limited household incomes for purchasing potable water, this has created added pressure to generate cash, which can be sourced only by further eroding the natural resource base (Ahmed *et al.*, 2008).

Beyond the above observed impacts of climatic change with respect to water and food security issues, three additional issues are of great significance in terms of future climatic

disasters: sea surface temperature anomalies (SSTAs), storm recurving, and the shifting time of monsoon seasons (Ahmed *et al*, 2008).

32.6.2 Sea surface temperature anomalies

As previously summarized in the discussion of Cyclone Nargis, there are indications of changing patterns of storm paths and the intensity of storms as a result of climate change impacting SSTAs over the Bay of Bengal. Changes in SSTAs are critical to formation of cyclones. A minimum threshold temperature of 26.5 C for sea surface temperature is necessary for tropical depressions to form and the consequent generation of storms and cyclones.

A study of decadal SSTAs over the Bay of Bengal, from the first storm season of Myanmar (first day of April to last day of May) over the periods of 1960–1969, 1970–1979, 1980–1989, 1990–1999, and 2000–2008, was carried out by Tun Lwin (2009) (see also DMH, 1950–2000 and 1970–2000). The results show that negative SSTAs were observed for the decades of 1960–1969 and 1970–1979, which meant that the potential for storm formation in the Bay of Bengal was significantly lower prior to 1980 (see Figures 32.7a and 32.7b). However, from 1980–1989 (Figure 32.7c), the SSTAs became positive, with a maximum positive SSTA centre near the Andaman Islands of the Andaman Sea. This trend persisted throughout the decades of 1990–1999 (Figure 32.7d) and 2000–2008 (Figure 32.7e), indicating that the potential for storm formation in the Bay of Bengal had increased during those three decades.

32.6.3 Storm recurvature in the Bay of Bengal

A shift in the mean synoptic systems means changes in the synoptic situations controlling the movement of storms. The 10-year average of 850 hPa-level winds for the first storm season of Myanmar (the first day of April to the last day of May) for each of the five decades 1961–1970, 1971–1980, 1981–1990, 1991–2000, and 2001–2008, is analysed separately (Tun Lwin, 2002). The 850 hPa- and 500 hPa-level troughs in the westerlies are clearly seen to shift from their normal position from north of 20°N to low latitudes of between 10°N and 15°N latitudes, starting from 1980 onwards. The 500 hPa trough is the mechanism responsible for the recurving of storms to the northeast as the Bay storms from the south Bay encounter this trough. A storm recurving to the northeast by the trough at its position north of 20°N means that the storm will most likely move to Bangladesh. However, if the 500 hPa-level trough moves down south

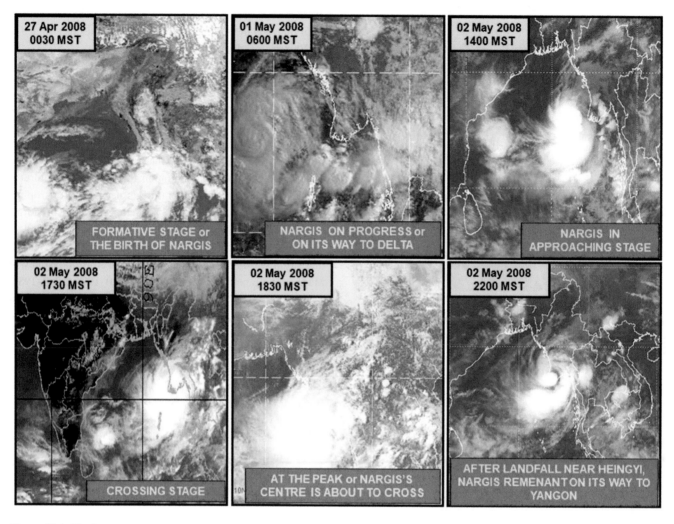

Figure 32.6. The forecast positions of Nargis show the development of the storm from 27 April 2008 to landfall on 2 May 2008. (*Source*: RIMES Centre, 2008) (*Note*: MST (Myanmar Standard Time) is 6 hours and 30 minutes ahead of UTC.)

towards 15°N latitude, and if the Bay storm encounters this trough at that latitude, the recurving storm will then move to Myanmar. This may be the reason why Myanmar was struck by three consecutive storms in each and every year of the last three-year period, 2006–2008.

Starting from 1978, the number of total storms forming in the Bay of Bengal has decreased sharply from an annual frequency of 10.4 before 1978 to 6.0 after 1978. That accounts for a 40% reduction in Bay storm formation. A recent study made on the relationship between storm frequency and intensity revealed that these two are more or less inversely proportional (Coastal Protection and Restoration Authority, 2017). That is, the lower the frequency, the higher the intensity. It is therefore deducible that more intense cyclones are forming after 1978 owing to the decrease in the number of storms.

32.6.4 Shifting pre- and post-monsoon periods

Tun Lwin (2002) investigated the changing climate over Myanmar from the period of 1950 to 2000. He has shown that since 1978 the onset of the monsoon season has been later, and the end of the monsoon season has been earlier. The fact that the periods of pre- and post-monsoon seasons grew longer after 1978 (Figure 32.8) clearly indicates that the threat of storms for Myanmar's coast increased after 1978 (Tun Lwin, 2002).

Moreover, pre- and post-monsoon periods are periods when unstable weather conditions prevail. During these periods, series of thunderstorm clouds – namely cumulonimbus, abbreviated Cb – form extensively and have associated extreme local weather, such as tornadoes, thunderstorms, torrential rain, hail, and downbursts. Flash floods and land erosion occasionally accompany heavy rains, especially in hilly areas.

(a)

1960–1969 Mean SSTAs

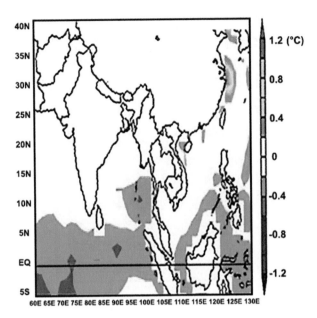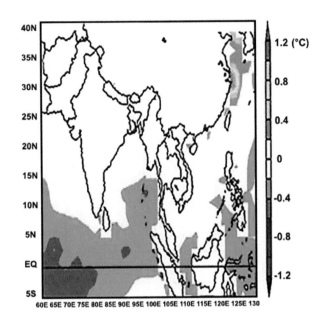

APRIL THIRD DEKAD   **MAY FIRST DEKAD**

1960–1969

(b)

1970–1979 Mean SSTAs

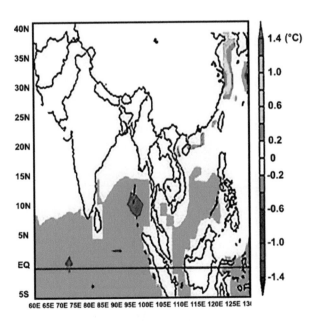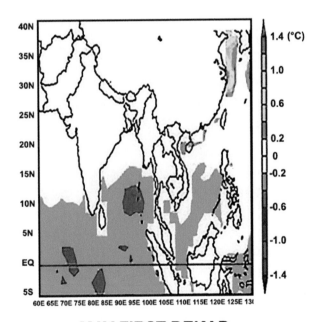

APRIL THIRD DEKAD   **MAY FIRST DEKAD**

1970–1979

(c)
1980–1989 Mean SSTAs

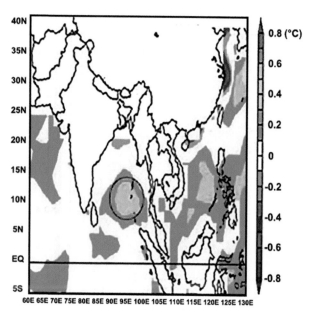

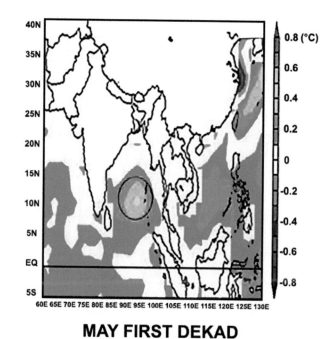

APRIL THIRD DEKAD

MAY FIRST DEKAD

1980–1989

(d)
1990–1999 Mean SSTAs

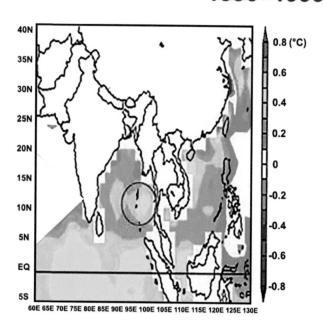

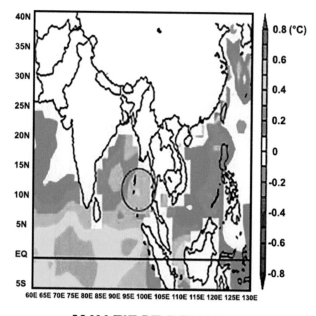

APRIL THIRD DEKAD

MAY FIRST DEKAD

1990–1999

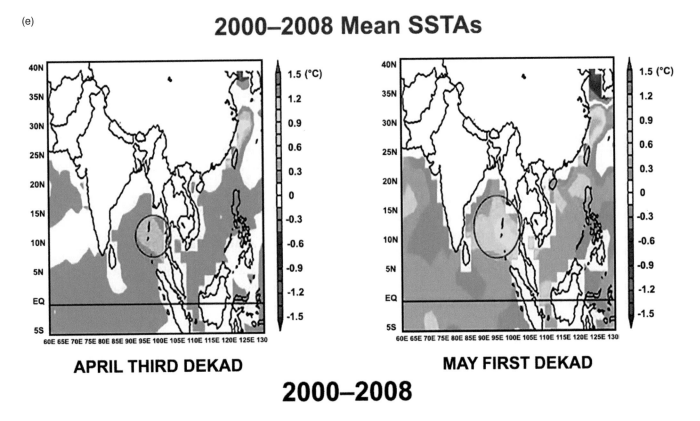

Figure 32.7. Decadal mean sea surface temperature anomalies for the periods (a) 1960–1969; (b) 1970–1979; (c) 1980–1989; (d) 1990–1999; and (e) 2000–2008. (*Data source*: DMH; figures by Tun Lwin) (*Note*: Dekad refers to a period of 10 days, and every month has three dekads. First two dekads have 10 days each (i.e., 1–10, 11–20), and the third varies from 8–11 days depending on the month.)

Extension of Pre- and Post-Monsoon Seasons After 1978

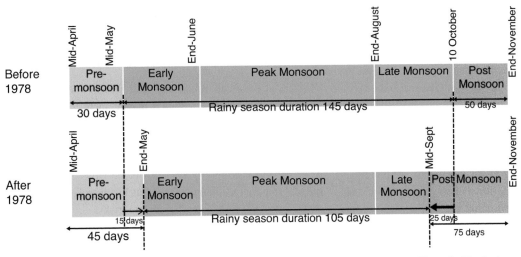

Figure 32.8. Expansion of pre- and post-monsoon periods after 1978 due to climate change. Figure by Tun Lwin.

The impact of this monsoonal rain shift was analysed by the DMH, which showed that after 2001, monsoon rainfall increased in intensity, resulting in increased runoff, which in turn dramatically impacted on agriculture by increasing soil degradation and land erosion and resulting in increased flash floods.

32.7 ASSESSMENT OF DISASTER MANAGEMENT IN MYANMAR

The impact of Cyclone Nargis had a profound international and national impact with respect to two major issues: (a) the impact of climate change on extreme hydro-meteorological events and (b) issues of national disaster management capacity to respond to and mitigate the impacts of increasingly intense natural disasters. The authors have addressed earlier the shifting risks from climate change impacts on SSTAs, the shifting and recurving of extreme events, and the shifting timing and intensity of monsoonal seasons.

Following Cyclone Nargis, a post-survey team, composed of scientists from DMH and the Asian Disaster Preparedness Centre (ADPC), were sent to the Nargis-affected areas in the Yangon and Ayeyarwaddy Divisions within a week after the storm passed over the Delta. The team made an assessment of the Myanmar disaster management system by interviewing and surveying government authorities, local communities, and officials and United Nations agencies within the area. The results of this survey (Ahmed *et al.*, 2008) showed that there were many underlying causes of the high vulnerability and high loss of life from Cyclone Nargis:

- Though 84,500 people lost their lives and 53,800 went missing because of high storm surge waves, the majority of the people did not know what a storm surge was;
- The cyclone warnings were given to local people at least three days ahead. However, because of the lack of past experiences, that is, they had never experienced such an intense storm in the past, the majority of people did not take the authority's warnings seriously enough;
- Although the authority tried to evacuate the residents, they did not cooperate with the authority because of their disbelief of the impacts of storm surges;
- When the storm came to their places where they were hiding, there were no emergency plans for shelters, plans for moving out from the area, plans for finding places like life-saving ground, and the like;
- Most communities had a low level of preparedness; as a result, more than 200 small villages located along the coast were totally wiped out by the large surge waves of Nargis (ADPC and DMH, 2008);

- There were more underlying causes that had made the vulnerability even higher. The risk analysis and hazard mapping were not carried out for the deltaic area. Therefore, people were lacking in knowledge as to their extent of risk and how vulnerable their area was;
- Even though early warning in Nargis was more than acceptable and was considered timely and accurate, the disaster management plan was not sufficient, according to the scores on resilience in the eight components of the survey. Serious efforts should be made to improve all components.

Critical components of these issues are discussed in more detail in the following sections.

32.7.1 Lack of awareness and knowledge

Communities lack awareness and knowledge about the importance of sound natural resource management practices, essential for ensuring the sustainability of their livelihoods. Prior to Cyclone Nargis, most communities in the Ayeyarwaddy Delta had little or no access to training or awareness-raising activities on sustainable resource management. Government extension services in forestry, agriculture, and fisheries were insufficient, as there was a serious lack of human and financial resources. The shortage of civil society organizations also meant that very few non-governmental organizations (NGOs) were available to fill the gap in capacity-building needs.

Limited community awareness is compounded by poverty and the lack of alternative livelihoods, which are driving causes of the over-exploitation of forest resources, fisheries, and agricultural land. One positive outcome of Cyclone Nargis is that NGOs now have access to donor funding and technical assistance that will enable them to provide capacity-building activities to improve resource management practices (Tun Lwin, 2008).

32.7.2 Extent of environmental degradation

Poverty, unsustainable land use, and lack of knowledge and awareness of improved resource management techniques, as well as land tenure insecurity, have all contributed to widespread environmental degradation, which prevailed even before the impact of Nargis. The serious deterioration of natural resources in the Ayeyarwaddy and Yangon Divisions has subsequently imposed a limitation on local livelihoods and development, contributing to increasing disaster risks.

The fragility of ecosystems in Nargis-affected areas means that communities lost a significant portion of their remaining natural capital as a result of the cyclone, thus further compromising people's capacities to effectively recover from this major disaster. The high level of poverty in the area is evidence that most households had little or no economic capital in reserve to cope with the cyclone's aftermath (Khin Lay Swe, 2009).

32.7.3 Deforestation and over-exploitation of forest resources

The destruction of mangrove forests is an illustrative example of how the loss of this valuable resource has deprived communities of the chance to maximize their potential in terms of environmental, social, economic, and risk reduction benefits. Over the last 80 years, nearly 75% of mangroves in the Ayeyarwaddy Delta have been lost, mainly as the result of human activities. The data show that from a peak of about 260,000 ha (625,222 acres) in 1924, mangrove forests had declined to 67,000 ha (160,930 acres) by 2007. Nearly half of the decrease in mangroves has taken place over the last 15 years, especially after 2001. Cyclone Nargis in itself directly affected 16,800 ha (41,514 acres) of natural forest and 21,000 ha (51,892 acres) of forest plantations, and there was a significant difference in the percentage of uprooted trees in the direct path of the storm at 56.7%, compared with 4.2% in other areas (U Ohn, 2009).

The main reason for mangrove deforestation is the harvesting of timber for firewood and charcoal for home consumption, as well as income generation. Other driving factors include conversion to paddy fields, salt farms, shrimp ponds, and settlement areas.

Mangrove deforestation has taken place in communal lands and land leased by individuals from the government, as well as in reserved and protected forests. The loss of mangroves means that these natural habitats, which serve as breeding grounds for a number of fish species, can no longer provide communities with a sustainable source of income. Moreover, the reduction in fish catches has also impaired food security.

In addition to their socio-economic benefits, mangroves play an essential role in coastal protection. Their loss has not only undermined livelihood sustainability in the Delta but also aggravated the catastrophic impact caused by Cyclone Nargis.

Despite these critical benefits, deforestation of forest resources other than mangroves has become a common practice in Nargis-affected areas. Trees are cleared for other income-generating activities such as farming or for direct use (i.e., firewood/charcoal, building materials, fence posts, boats, and thatching for houses). For example, nipa palms (*Nypa fruticans*) along riversides are over-harvested for thatching, while *Palmyra spp.* on riverbanks and around paddy fields are utilized for both thatching and timber. Moreover, households with access to land generally encroach on adjoining forested lands (including mangroves) in order to raise production yields by expanding paddy fields. Forest cover loss in this region has consequently reduced natural protection against high winds and tidal surges, as well as the availability of forest products (U Ohn, 2009).

32.7.4 Response to natural disasters

Cyclone Nargis caused heavy loss of lives and property damage and had a huge impact on the society and economy of the country that will persist for years to come, particularly with respect to the livelihoods and food security of the people in the Delta area. Overall, the performance of Myanmar's disaster management community, both government officials and disaster managers, has been respectable in terms of dealing with natural disasters (Khin Lay Swe, 2009). For instance, Myanmar has been hit by 83 storms in the past 130 years and no storm prior to Nargis has had loss of life exceeding 1,500 people. In May 2006, during Cyclone Mala in Rakhine State, not a single human life was lost when the storm hit the town of Gwa and its neighbouring areas.

But it is important to note that during the period of 1997–2016, out of the 10 countries most affected by extreme weather events, Myanmar had the lowest number of total events in 1997–2016; however, it had the highest death toll and deaths per 100,000 inhabitants (Eckstein *et al.*, 2018). This shows that, whereas Myanmar is relatively low in vulnerability to extreme weather events, it lacks preparedness, readiness, and response capability.

The country recognizes that many improvements need to be made and challenges met in order to modernize disaster management to acceptable standards (Tun Lwin, 2015).

32.7.5 Pursuing development priorities over environmental sustainability

In the past, the economic efforts focused on development priorities rather than on natural resource sustainability. Attention was directed towards increasing production by harnessing more land area and building infrastructure, such as embankments (e.g. the Paddy I and Paddy II projects in the 1980s), without fully considering environmental impacts. Established in 1990, the National Commission for Environmental Affairs (NCEA) deals mainly with policies related to multilateral environmental agreements. Agenda 21 was then developed as a way to reflect the political commitments of the government by having a framework for incorporating environmental considerations into future national and sectoral development programs (NCEA, 1997). However, NCEA has neither sufficient staff nor resources to provide technical advice and coordinate environmental management across all line agencies. Moreover, it has a limited capacity to play a significant role in environmental management at the local level.

Although the NCEA has drafted an environment law, it has not yet been enacted. As a result, there are few legislative provisions to ensure that the environment is taken into account in formulating and implementing policies and plans that impact on natural resources. In the aftermath of Cyclone Nargis, the government has committed to developing and implementing a national disaster preparedness plan. This provides opportunities for ensuring that long-term planning addresses both resource management issues as well as other prevailing risk factors in an integrated manner.

32.7.6 Weak implementation and enforcement of laws and policies

Although there are laws, regulations, and policies that exist at the national level in support of environmental sustainability, such as the 1995 Forestry Instructions and the Fisheries Legislation, those responsible for their implementation do not fully comprehend the purpose of promoting sustainability or understand how to apply these instruments in practice. As a result, these directives are often implemented in a rigid manner that does not support the spirit of the law.

In addition, there is variable interpretation of these laws, which means that their full implementation remains largely ad hoc and differs from district to district. Similarly, many laws, particularly those affecting biodiversity and the management of natural resources such as forests, fisheries, and land, are poorly enforced.

The lack of understanding of these laws and regulations by regional and local officials, as well as by communities, is made worse by inadequate human and financial resources for law enforcement (Wegerdt and Mark, 2008).

32.7.7 Inadequate coordination

Another key factor contributing to environmental degradation is weak coordination between sectoral government agencies at the national and sub-national levels (horizontal coordination). Each sectoral agency develops and implements its own sector-specific policies, with insufficient consultation or regard for their impacts on other sectors. This compartmentalization is aggravated by the lack of vertical coordination between different layers of government at national, divisional, district, and village levels. National policies tend to apply a blueprint approach, which makes it difficult for local authorities to implement the laws and policies effectively in their localities, especially as they strive to meet national targets for rice or timber production (Tun Lwin, 2008; ADPC and DMH, 2008).

32.7.8 Need for improvement in technical capacity

Government staff across national agencies spanning different sectors need technical capacity-building to adequately integrate environmental considerations into their sectoral policies,

programmes, and plans. This is also applicable to sub-national levels. Local authorities in general have little awareness of how to promote sustainable natural resource management. As a result, local civil servants of various agencies (i.e. agriculture, forestry, etc.) who are charged with implementing their department's sectoral policies are unable to address the environmental aspects of their work adequately. They may have technical knowledge within their own discipline, but with limited understanding of the environmental impacts and implications of their advice to vulnerable groups like farmers and fishers (Tun Lwin, 2008).

32.7.9 Need for upgraded land-use planning

The National Land Use Commission was established in 1995, with its subordinate regional and community-level land-use supervision committees. The Commission is responsible for reviewing and developing policies on land management. In addition, the 1995 Forest Policy highlighted the importance of land-use planning and set out policy measures to determine programme strategies and action plans.

Although the Forest Department has initiated a number of land-use planning activities in the Ayeyarwaddy Delta, there has been little or no coordination between key stakeholders, especially between relevant government agencies. This has resulted in ineffective land-use planning processes in the Delta. Consequently, land-use practices remain geared towards income generation, regardless of their sustainability and long-term environmental consequences. Instead, decisions are made based on the basis of short-term financial gain. For example, as discussed previously, mangrove forest areas are converted to paddy land, which then experiences creeping salinization and thus limited rice cropping to just a few harvesting seasons. As rice yields decline, farmers have to switch to salt farming. Financial gains are therefore short-lived, resulting in the permanent loss of a valuable resource with its multiple benefits, including ecological, socio-economic, and risk-reduction values.

The lack of land-use planning also constrains the ability of local areas to respond effectively to national government targets in the production of agricultural (paddy rice), forestry (timber), and fish products. For example, local authorities presently address national government directives for increased production of rice or timber in their area by expanding areas under paddy cultivation or through deforestation, respectively, without any consideration of their environmental impacts. However, if local authorities are able to devise coastal zone management plans or land-use plans, they could then pursue national production targets through a more rational allocation of their land and water resources, which would take into account the environmental consequences of their decisions.

32.7.10 Inadequate information on natural resources

As environmental monitoring and surveillance systems are lacking in areas affected by Nargis, there is limited or no reliable information to inform policy development or decision-making, at both national and local levels. Recovery efforts to address the impacts of Cyclone Nargis have highlighted the information vacuum on environmental conditions in the Ayeyarwaddy Delta. There is not enough data on forest, land, and fishing resources, or biodiversity (ecosystems, flora, and fauna), as well as water sources, including drinking water. Hence, policy development and planning remain seriously hampered from the start, which undermines their effective implementation (Tun Lwin, 2008).

32.7.11 Need for more investment

There is a need for investment in human resources, extension services, agricultural research, and information management, as well as in improved farming technology, which could sustainably raise production yields. Local authorities are therefore forced to meet their production quotas by encouraging farmers to extend paddy cultivation on marginal or fragile lands unsuitable for farming. In addition, the lack of investment has resulted in the deterioration of tangible assets. For instance, the erosion of embankments has not only placed agricultural lands under threat of seawater incursion but also increased vulnerability to natural hazards, such as floods and storm surges (Wegerdt and Mark, 2008).

32.8 CONCLUSION

Just after the landfall of Nargis, a WMO fact-finding mission visited DMH on 10–15 May 2008. They discussed the situation with DMH officials, UN organizations, governmental organizations, and the general public during the course of their mission. On 22 May, the WMO issued a press release titled 'Cyclone warnings were sufficient: Deaths inevitable'.

Still, a key question remains: If the warnings were sufficient, why, then, did 140,000 people lose their lives? The short answer to this is that disaster management is a social science issue. Science alone could not accomplish the goals of disaster prevention. There are many areas where the social sectors – such as public participation, public education, public awareness, multi-agency cooperation, good management, rules and regulations, public drills, public information, and more – play vital roles in combating the impacts of natural disasters. These are the areas that were lacking and have much room for improvement. As Mami Mizutori, the UN Special Representative for Disaster Risk Reduction and head of UNISDR, and Achim Steiner, the Administrator of the UNDP, write in their article in commemoration of the 10-year anniversary of Cyclone Nargis, 'When we forget about catastrophic events like Cyclone Nargis, it is at our peril' (Mizutori and Steiner, 2018).

Unless all of the eight basic components of disaster management are developed proportionately, particularly in developing and under-developed nations, people from underserving countries will continue to suffer tragically from the impacts of natural disasters.

The work presented in this chapter may be considered as preliminary, and further work, especially in the context of climate change and risk assessment, is needed.

ACKNOWLEDGEMENTS

We thank the Department of Meteorology and Hydrology (DMH), CARE Myanmar, and Action Aid for providing assistance in making the assessment of the impacts of Cyclone Nargis in the Yangon and deltaic areas, and the members of the Climate Change Vulnerability and Adaptation Assessment Team, DMH, for undertaking analysis as an important component of the Initial National Communication to UNFCCC. Several NGOs, such as the Forest Resource Environment Development and Conservation Association (FREDA), Ecodev, Global Green, and Myanmar Egress, have shared their experiences and their respective roles in activities related to climate change, as well as Nargis Field Assessments.

We acknowledge the use of Rapid Response imagery from the Land, Atmosphere Near real-time Capability for EOS (LANCE) system operated by NASA's Earth Science Data and Information System (ESDIS), with funding provided by NASA Headquarters.

Dr Allen Clark of the East-West Center, Hawaii, and an anonymous reviewer have provided very comprehensive and useful comments on the draft of this chapter.

REFERENCES

Ahmed, A. K., Subbiah, A. R. and Tun Lwin (2008) *Joint Rapid Situation Assessment Report: Status and Context of Coastal Townships of Yangon and Ayeyarwady Divisions during Tropical Cyclone Nargis in Myanmar*. Thailand, Jointly prepared by the Myanmar Department of Meteorology and Hydrology (DMH) and the Asian Disaster Preparedness Centre (ADPC).

ASEAN Secretariat (2008) *Cyclone Nargis, Myanmar: ASEAN Emergency Rapid Assessment Team Mission Report, 9–18 May 2008*. Jakarta, Indonesia, ASEAN Secretariat.

Coastal Protection and Restoration Authority (2017) 2017 Coastal Master Plan: C2-4: Tropical Storm Intensity and Frequency. Version Final (p. 24). Baton Rouge, Louisiana, Coastal

Protection and Restoration Authority. http://coastal.la.gov/wp-content/uploads/2017/04/Attachment-C2-4_FINAL_5.15.2017.pdf

Department of Population (2019) Myanmar Population. Department of Population, Ministry of Labour, Immigration and Population, Republic of the Union of Myanmar. http://www.dop.gov.mm/en (accessed on 22 June 2019).

DMH (Department of Meteorology and Hydrology) (1950–2000) *The Myanmar Daily Weather Reports (MDWR)*. Yangon, Myanmar, Department of Meteorology and Hydrology.

(1970–2000) *The Climatic Atlas for 1960–1969, 1970–1979, 1980–1989, 1990–2000*. Yangon, Myanmar, Department of Meteorology and Hydrology.

Eckstein, D., Kunzel, V. and Schafer, L. (2018) *Global Climate Risk Index 2018: Who Suffers Most from Extreme Weather Events? Weather-Related Loss Events in 2016 and 1997 to 2016*. Briefing paper. Berlin, Germany. Germanwatch Think Tank and Research.

IFRC (International Federation of Red Cross and Red Crescent Societies) (2011) Myanmar: Cyclone Nargis 2008 Facts and Figures. Published 3 May 2011, 12:16 CET. https://www.ifrc.org/en/news-and-media/news-stories/asia-pacific/myanmar/myanmar-cyclone-nargis-2008-facts-and-figures/

Khin Lay Swe (2009) *The Policy Implications of Agriculture, Livelihoods and Disaster Risk Reduction*. Yangon, Myanmar, Pro-rector, Yezin Agricultural University, Ministry of Agriculture and Irrigation.

Mizutori, M. and Steiner, A. (2018) Lessons of cyclone Nargis still need to be applied. Opinion piece. Retrieved from https://www.unisdr.org/archive/58129.

NASA/MODIS Rapid Response Team (2008) *NASA Satellite Captures Image of Cyclone Nargis Flooding in Burma*. Retrieved from https://www.nasa.gov/topics/earth/features/nargis_floods.html.

NCEA (National Commission for Environmental Affairs) (1997) *Myanmar Agenda 21*. Myanmar.

RIMES Centre (2008) *120 Hours Storm Animation Forecast of Cyclone Nargis Issued on 28th April 2008*. Bangkok, Asian Institute of Technology.

Shida, Kuniyuki (2008) Tropical Cyclone Nargis: Warnings and information issued by the Department of Meteorology and Hydrology (DMH) of Myanmar, with WMO Assistance. https://www.wmo.int/pages/prog/dra/rap/documents/Shida2.pdf

TCG (Tripartite Core Group) (2008) Annex 12: Coastal Environment and Natural Resources Management. In *Post-Nargis Joint Assessment (PONJA) Report*, p. 124. Presented in Singapore; released concurrently in Yangon. https://reliefweb.int/report/myanmar/myanmar-post-nargis-joint-assessment

Tun Lwin (1981) A preliminary study to develop storm surge prediction techniques in Myanmar. Paper read at WMO Workshop on Storm Surge Prediction, 1981, Yangon, Myanmar.

(2002) Climate change over Myanmar during the last five decades. *Water Resources Journal*, ST/ESCAP/SER.C/212 (pp. 95–106). United Nations Economic and Social Commission for Asia and the Pacific (UNESCAP).

(2008) *Nargis: The Killer from the Sea*. Presentation made at World Meteorological Organization Headquarters, Geneva, and at international workshops, seminars, and talks.

(2009) *The Recent Climate Changes in Myanmar*. Kuala Lumpur, Malaysia. Paper presented at the UNEP/UNDP Workshop on Coastal Community Resilience and Disaster Risk Reduction (CCR and DRR).

(2015) *Nargis and I*. Yangon, Myanmar, Aung Publishing House.

U Ohn (2009) *Policy Framework for Protecting and Restoring of Mangroves and Other Natural Resources in the Delta for Sustainable Livelihoods*. Yangon, Myanmar, Forest Resource Environment Development and Conservation Association (FREDA).

Wegerdt, J. and Mark, S. S. (2008) *Post-Nargis Needs Assessment and Monitoring: ASEAN's Pioneering Response*. Jakarta, Indonesia, ASEAN Secretariat.

Index